A SHORT HISTORY

OF THE

ENGLISH PEOPLE

ENGLAND IN THE NINETEENTH CENTURY.

A SHORT HISTORY

OF THE

ENGLISH PEOPLE

BY

JOHN RICHARD GREEN

HONORARY FELLOW OF JESUS COLLEGE, OXFORD

REVISED AND ENLARGED, WITH EPILOGUE BY

ALICE STOPFORD GREEN

WITH MAPS AND TABLES

AMERICAN BOOK COMPANY

NEW YORK   CINCINNATI   CHICAGO

10112

INTRODUCTION.

THE story of how the Short History of the English People came to be written would be the story of Mr. Green's life, from the time when his boyish interest was first awakened by the world beyond himself until his work was done. So closely are the work and the worker bound together that unless the biography be fully written no real account of the growth of the book can indeed be given. But in issuing a Revised Edition of the History, a slight sketch of the historical progress of the writer's mind, and of the gradual way in which the plan of his work grew up, may not seem out of place.

John Richard Green, who was born at Oxford in December 1837, was sent at eight years old to Magdalen Grammar School, then held in a small room within the precincts of the College. The Oxford world about him was full of suggestions of a past which very early startled his curiosity and fired his imagination. The gossiping tales of an old dame who had seen George the Third drive through the town in a coach and six were his first lessons in history. Year after year he took part with excited fancy in the procession of the Magdalen choir boys to the College tower on May Day, to sing at the sunrising a Hymn to the Trinity which had replaced the Mass chanted in pre-Reformation days, and to "jangle" the bells in recognition of an immemorial festival. St. Giles' Fair, the "beating of the bounds," even the name of "Pennyfarthing Street," were no less records of a mysterious past than Chapel or College or the very trees of Magdalen Walk; and he once received, breathless and awe-struck, a prize from the hands of the centenarian President of the College, Dr. Routh, the last man who ever wore a wig in Oxford, a man who had himself seen Dr. Johnson stand in the High Street with one foot on either side of the kennel that ran down the middle of the way, the street boys standing round, "none daring to interrupt the meditations of the great lexicographer." "You are a clever boy," said the old man as he gave the prize and shook him by the hand.

His curiosity soon carried him beyond Oxford ; and in very early days he learned to wander on Saints' days and holidays to the churches of neighbouring villages, and there shut himself in to rub brasses and study architectural mouldings. Other interests followed on his ecclesiastical training. He remembered the excitement which was produced in Oxford by Layard's discovery of the Nestorians in the Euphrates valley. One day Mr. Ramsay gathered round him the boys who were at play in Magdalen Walk and told them of his journey to see these people ; and one at least of his hearers plunged eagerly into problems then much discussed of the relations of orthodox believers to Monophysites, and the distinctions between heresy and schism, questions which occupied him many years. Knowledge of this kind, he said long afterwards, had been a real gain to him. "The study of what the Monophysites did in Syria, and the Monothelites in Egypt, has taught me what few historians know —the intimate part religion plays in a nation's history, and how closely it joins itself to a people's life."

Living in a strictly Conservative atmosphere, he had been very diligently brought up as a Tory and a High Churchman. But when he was about fourteen, orthodox Conservatism and school life came to a close which then seemed to him very tragic. A school essay was set on Charles the First ; and as the boy read earnestly every book he could find on the subject, it suddenly burst on him that Charles was wrong. The essay, written with a great deal of feeling under this new and strong conviction, gained the prize over the heads of boys older and till then reputed abler ; but it drew down on him unmeasured disapproval. Canon Mozley, who examined, remonstrated in his grave way : "Your essay is very good, but remember I do not agree with your conclusions, and you will in all probability see reason to change them as you grow older." The head-master took a yet more severe view of such a change of political creed. But the impulse to Liberalism had been definitely given ; and had indeed brought with it many other grave questionings. When at the next examination he shot up to the head of the school, his master advised that he should be withdrawn from Magdalen, to the dismay both of himself and of the uncle with whom he lived. The uncle indeed had his own grounds of alarm. John had one day stood at a tailor's window in Oxford where Lord John Russell's Durham Letter was spread out to view, and, as he read it, had come to his own conclusions as to its wisdom. He even declared the Ecclesiastical Titles Act to be absurd. His uncle, horrified at so extreme a heresy, with angry decision ordered him to find at once another home ; and when after a time the agitation had died away and he was allowed to come back, it was on the condition of never again alluding to so painful a subject. The new-found errors clung to him, however, when he went shortly afterwards to live in the country with a tutor. " I wandered about the fields thinking," he said, " but I never went back from the opinions I had begun to form."

It was when he was about sixteen that Gibbon fell into his hands; and from that moment the enthusiasm of history took hold of him. " Man and man's history " became henceforth the dominant interest of his life. When he returned to Oxford with a scholarship to Jesus College, an instinct of chivalrous devotion inspired his resolve that the study of history should never become with him "a matter of classes or fellowships," nor should be touched by the rivalries, the conventional methods, the artificial limitations, and the utilitarian aims of the Schools. College work and history work went on apart, with much mental friction and difficulty of adjustment and sorrow of heart. Without any advisers, almost without friends, he groped his way, seeking in very solitary fashion after his own particular vocation. His first historical efforts were spent on that which lay immediately about him ; and the series of papers which he sent at this time to the *Oxford Chronicle* on " Oxford in the last Century " are instinct with all the vivid imagination of his later work, and tell their tale after a method and in a style which was already perfectly natural to him. He read enormously, but history was never to him wholly a matter of books. The Town was still his

teacher. There was then little help to be had for the history of
Oxford or any other town. " So wholly had the story of the towns,"
he wrote later, "passed out of the minds of men that there is still
not a history of our country which devotes a single page to it, and
there is hardly an antiquary who has cared to disentomb the tragic
records of fights fought for freedom in this narrow theatre from
the archives which still contain them. The treatise of Brady written
from a political, that of Madox from a narrow antiquarian, point of
view ; the summaries of charters given by the Commissioners under
the Municipal Reform Act ; the volumes of Stephens and Merewether ; and here and there a little treatise on isolated towns are the
only printed materials for the study of the subject." Other materials
were abundant. St. Giles' Fair was full of lessons for him. He
has left an amusing account of how, on a solemn day which came
about once in eight years, he marched with Mayor and Corporation
round the city boundaries. He lingered over the memory of St.
Martin's Church, the centre of the town life, the folk-mote within
its walls, the low shed outside where mayor and bailiff administered
justice, the bell above which rang out its answer to the tocsin of
the gownsmen in St. Mary's, the butchery and spicery and vintnery
which clustered round in the narrow streets. " In a walk through
Oxford one may find illustrations of every period of our annals.
The cathedral still preserves the memory of the Mercian St. Frideswide ; the tower of the Norman Earls frowns down on the waters
of the Mill ; around Merton hang the memories of the birth of our
Constitution ; the New Learning and the Reformation mingle in
Christ Church ; a 'grind' along the Marston Road follows the track
of the army of Fairfax ; the groves of Magdalen preserve the living
traditions of the last of the Stewarts."

Two years, however, of solitary effort to work out problems of
education, of life, of history, left him somewhat disheartened and
bankrupt in energy. A mere accident at last brought the first counsel
and encouragement he had ever known. Some chance led him one
day to the lecture-room where Stanley, then Canon of Christ Church,
was speaking on the history of Dissent. Startled out of the indifference with which he had entered the room, he suddenly found

himself listening with an interest and wonder which nothing in Oxford had awakened, till the lecturer closed with the words, "'*Magna est veritas, et prævalebit*,' words so great that I could almost prefer them to the motto of our own University, '*Dominus illuminatio mea.*'" In his excitement he exclaimed, as Stanley, on leaving the hall, passed close by him, "Do you know, sir, that the words you quoted, '*Magna est veritas, et prævalebit*,' are the motto of the Town?" "Is it possible? How interesting! When will you come and see me and talk about it?" cried Stanley; and from that moment a warm friendship sprang up. "Then and after," Mr. Green wrote, "I heard you speak of work, not as a thing of classes and fellowships, but as something worthy for its own sake, worthy because it made us like the great Worker. 'If you cannot or will not work at the work which Oxford gives you, at any rate work at something.' I took up my old boy-dreams of history again. I think I have been a steady worker ever since."

It was during these years at Oxford that his first large historical schemes were laid. His plan took the shape of a History of the Archbishops of Canterbury; and seeking in Augustine and his followers a clue through the maze of fifteen centuries, he proposed under this title to write in fact the whole story of Christian civilization in England. "No existing historians help me," he declared in his early days of planning; "rather I have been struck by the utter blindness of one and all to the subject which they profess to treat—the national growth and developement of our country." When in 1860 he left Oxford for the work he had chosen as curate in one of the poorest parishes of East London, he carried with him thoughts of history. Letters full of ardent discussion of the theological and social problems about him still tell of hours saved here and there for the British Museum, of work done on Cuthbert, on Columba, on Irish Church History—of a scheme for a history of Somerset, which bid fair to extend far, and which led direct to Glastonbury, Dunstan, and Early English matters. Out of his poverty, too, he had gathered books about him, books won at a cost which made them the objects of a singular affection; and he never opened a volume of his "Acta Sanctorum" without a lingering memory of the painful efforts by which he had brought together the volumes one by one, and how many days he had gone without dinner when there was no other way of buying them.

But books were not his only sources of knowledge. To the last he looked on his London life as having given him his best lessons in history. It was with his churchwardens, his schoolmasters, in vestry meetings, in police courts, at boards of guardians, in service in chapel or church, in the daily life of the dock-labourer, the tradesman, the costermonger, in the summer visitation of cholera, in the winter misery that followed economic changes, that he learnt what the life of the people meant as perhaps no historian had ever learnt it before. Constantly struck down as he was by illness, even the days of sickness were turned to use. Every drive, every railway journey, every town he passed through in brief excursions for health's sake, added something to his knowledge ; if he was driven to recover strength to a seaside lodging he could still note a description of Ebbsfleet or Richborough or Minster, so that there is scarcely a picture of scenery or of geographical conditions in his book which is not the record of a victory over the overwhelming languor of disease.

After two years of observation, of reading, and of thought, the Archbishops no longer seemed very certain guides through the centuries of England's growth. They filled the place, it would appear, no better than the Kings. If some of them were great leaders among the people, others were of little account ; and after the sixteenth century the upgrowth of the Nonconformists broke the history of the people, taken from the merely ecclesiastical point of view, into two irreconcilable fractions, and utterly destroyed any possibility of artistic treatment of the story as a whole. In a new plan he looked far behind Augustine and Canterbury, and threw himself into geology, the physical geography of our island in pre-historic times, and the study of the cave-men and the successive races that peopled Britain, as introductory to the later history of England. But his first and dominating idea quickly thrust all others aside. It was of the English People itself that he must write if he would write after his own heart. The nine years spent in the monotonous reaches of dreary streets that make up Hoxton and Stepney, the close contact with sides of life little known to students, had only deepened the impressions with which the idea of a people's life had in Oxford struck on his imagination. "A State," he would say, "is accidental; it can be made or unmade, and is no real thing to me. But a nation is very real to me. That you can neither make nor destroy." All his writings, the historical articles which he sent to the *Saturday Review* and letters to his much-honoured friend, Mr. Freeman, alike tended in the same direction, and show how persistently he was working out his philosophy of history. The lessons which years before he had found written in the streets and lanes of his native town were not forgotten. "History," he wrote in 1869, "we are told by publishers, is the most unpopular of all branches of literature at the present day, but it is only unpopular because it seems more and more to sever itself from all that can touch the heart of a people. In mediæval history, above all, the narrow ecclesiastical character of the annals which serve as its base, instead of being corrected by a wider research into the memorials which surround us, has been actually intensified by the partial method of their study, till the story of a great people seems likely to be lost in the mere squabbles of priests. Now there is hardly a better corrective for all this to be found than to set a man frankly in the streets of a simple English town, and to bid him work out the history of the men who had lived and died there. The mill by the stream, the tolls in the market place, the brasses of its burghers in the church, the names of its streets, the lingering memory of its guilds, the mace of its mayor, tell us more of the past of England than the spire of Sarum or the martyrdom of Canterbury. We say designedly of the past of England, rather than of the past of English towns. . . . In England the history of the town and of the country are one. The privilege of the burgher has speedily widened into the liberty of the people at large. The municipal charter has merged into the great charter of the realm. All the little struggles over toll and tax, all the little claims of 'custom' and franchise, have told on the general advance of liberty and law. The townmotes of the Norman reigns tided free discussion and self-government over from the Witanagemot of the old England to the Parliament of the new. The husting court, with its resolute assertion of justice by one's peers, gave us the whole fabric of our judicial legislation. The Continental town lost its individuality by sinking to the servile level of the land from which it had isolated itself. The English town lost its individuality by lifting the country at large to its own level of freedom and law."

The earnestness, however, with which he had thrown himself into his parish work left no time for any thought of working out his cherished plans. His own needs were few, and during nearly three years he spent on the necessities of schools and of the poor more than the whole of the income he drew from the Church, while he provided for his own support by writing at night, after his day's work was done, articles for the *Saturday Review*. At last, in 1869, the disease which had again and again attacked him fell with renewed violence on a frame exhausted with labours and anxieties. All active work was for ever at an end—the doctors told him there was little hope of prolonging his life six months. It was at this moment, the first moment of leisure he had ever known, that he proposed "to set down a few notions which I have conceived concerning history," which "might serve as an introduction to better things if I lived, and might stand for some work done if I did not." The "Short History" was thus begun. When the six months had passed he had resisted the first severity of the attack, but he remained with scarcely a hold on life; and incessantly vexed by the suffering and exhaustion of constant illness, perplexed by questions as to the mere means of livelihood, thwarted and hindered by difficulties about books in the long winters abroad, he still toiled on at his task. "I wonder," he said once in answer to some critic, "how in those years of physical pain and despondency I could ever have written the book at all." Nearly five years were given to the work. The sheets were written and re-written, corrected and cancelled and begun again till it seemed as though revision would never have an end. "The book is full of faults," he declared sorrowfully, "which make me almost hopeless of ever learning to write well." As the work went on his friends often remonstrated with much energy. Dean Stanley could not forgive its missing so dramatic an opening as Cæsar's landing would have afforded. Others judged severely his style, his method, his view of history, his selection and rejection of facts.

Their judgement left him "lonely," he said; and with the sensitive-ness of the artistic nature, its quick apprehension of unseen danger, its craving for sympathy, he saw with perhaps needless clearness of vision the perils to his chance of winning a hearing which were pro-phesied. He agreed that the "faults" with which he was charged might cause the ruin of his hopes of being accepted either by historians or by the public; and yet these very "faults," he insisted, were bound up with his faith. The book was in fact, if not in name, the same as that which he had planned at Oxford; to correct its "faults" he must change his whole conception of history; he must renounce his belief that it was the great impulses of national feeling, and not the policy of statesmen, that formed the ground-work and basis of the history of nations, and his certainty that political history could only be made intelligible and just by basing it on social history in its largest sense.

"I may be wrong in my theories," he wrote, "but it is better for me to hold to what I think true, and to work it out as I best can, even if I work it out badly, than to win the good word of some people I respect and others I love" by giving up a real conviction. Amid all his fears as to the failings of his work he still clung to the belief that it went on the old traditional lines of English historians. However Gibbon might err in massing together his social facts in chapters apart, however inadequate Hume's attempts at social history might be, however Macaulay might look at social facts merely as bits of external ornament, they all, he maintained, professed the faith he held. He used to protest that even those English historians who desired to be merely "external and pragmatic" could not altogether reach their aim as though they had been "High Dutchmen." The free current of national life in England was too strong to allow them to become ever wholly lost in State-papers; and because he believed that Englishmen could therefore best combine the love of accuracy and the appreciation of the outer aspects of national or political life with a perception of the spiritual forces from which these mere outer phenomena proceed, he never doubted that "the English ideal of history would in the long run be what Gibbon made it in his day—the first in the world."

When at last, by a miracle of resolution and endurance, the

"Short History" was finished, "I felt," he wrote later, "as if I were some young knight challenging the world with my new method, and something of the trumpet ring is in passage after passage." But with discouraging reports of critics his despondency deepened. "You mayn't succeed this time," said a friend, "but you are sure to succeed some day." He never forgot that Mr. Stopford Brooke and his publisher were unwavering in their belief in his work.

The book was published in 1874, when he was little more than 36 years of age. Before a month was over, in the generous welcome given it by scholars and by the English people, he found the reward of his long endurance. Mr. Green in fact was the first English historian who had either conceived or written of English history from the side of the principles which his book asserted ; and in so doing he had given to his fellow-citizens such a story of their Commonwealth as to this day no other country in the world possesses. The opposition and criticism which he met with were in part a measure of the originality of his conception. Success, however, and criticism alike came to him as they come to the true scholar. "I know," he said in this first moment of unexpected recognition, "what men will say of me, 'He died learning.'"

I know of no excuse which I could give for attempting any revision of the "Short History," save that this was my husband's last charge to me. Nor can I give any other safeguard for the way in which I have performed the work than the sincere and laborious effort I have made to carry out that charge faithfully. I have been very careful not to interfere in any way with the plan or structure of the book, and save in a few exceptional cases, in which I knew Mr. Green's wishes, or where a change of chronology made some slight change in arrangement necessary, I have not altered its order. My work has been rather that of correcting mistakes of detail which must of a certainty occur in a story which covers so vast a field ; and in this I have been mainly guided throughout by the work of revision done by Mr. Green himself in his larger "History." In this History he had at first proposed merely to prepare a library edition of the "Short History" revised and corrected. In his hands, however, it became a wholly different book, the chief part of it having been re-written at much greater length and on an altered plan. I have therefore only used its corrections so far as they could be adapted to a book of different scope and arrangement. In his own judgment (and he judged himself severely), the errors of detail in the " Short History " were not the mistakes that lead to a false interpretation of the period, or betray an unhistoric mode of regarding the general course of events. In some passages, even where I knew that Mr. Green's own criticism went far beyond that of any of his critics, I have not felt justified in making any attempt to expand or re-write what could only have been re-written by himself. In other matters which have been the subject of comments of some severity, the grounds of his own decision remained unshaken ; as for example, the scanty part played by Literature after 1660, which Mr. Green regretted he had not explained in his first preface. It was necessary that the book should be brought to an end in about eight hundred pages. Something must needs be left out, and he deliberately chose Literature, because it seemed to him that after 1660 Literature ceased to stand in the fore-front of national characteristics, and that Science, Industry, and the like, played a much greater part. So " for truth's sake " he set aside a strong personal wish to say much that was in his mind on the great writers of later times, and turned away to cotton-spinning and Pitt's finance. "It cost me much trouble," he said, "and I knew the book would not be so bright, but I think I did rightly."

It was in this temper that all his work was done. The sincerity, the patient self-denial, the earnestness of purpose, that underlay all his vivid activity were recognized by one who was ever to him a master in English History. " Mr. Green," wrote Dr. Stubbs, " possessed in no scanty measure all the gifts that contribute to the making of a great historian. He combined, so far as the history of England is concerned, a complete and firm grasp of the subject in its unity and integrity with a wonderful command of details, and a thorough sense of perspective and proportion. All his work was real and original work ; few people besides those who knew him well would see under the charming ease and vivacity of his style the deep research and sustained industry of the laborious student. But it was so; there was no department of our national records that he had not studied and, I think I may say, mastered. Hence, I think, the unity of his dramatic scenes and the cogency of his historical arguments. Like other people he made mistakes sometimes ; but scarcely ever does the correction of his mistakes affect either the essence of the picture or the force of the argument. And in him the desire of stating and pointing the truth of history was as strong as the wish to make both his pictures and his arguments telling and forcible. He never treated an opposing view with intolerance or contumely ; his handling of controversial matter was exemplary. And then, to add still more to the debt we owe him, there is the wonderful simplicity and beauty of the way in which he tells his tale, which more than anything else has served to make English history a popular, and as it ought to be, if not the first, at least the second study of all Englishmen."

I have to thank those friends of Mr. Green, Dr. Stubbs, Dr. Creighton, Professor Bryce, and Mr. Lecky, who, out of their regard for his memory, have made it a pleasure to me to ask their aid and counsel. I owe a special gratitude to Professor Gardiner for a ready help which spared no trouble and counted no cost, and for the rare generosity which placed at my disposal the results of his own latest and unpublished researches into such matters as the pressing of recruits for the New Model, and the origin of the term Ironside as a personal epithet of Cromwell. Mr. Osmund Airy has very kindly given me valuable suggestions for the Restoration period ; and throughout the whole work Miss Norgate has rendered services which the most faithful and affectionate loyalty could alone have prompted.

1888.

In this later edition some further corrections have been made in matters relating to Ireland, in consequence of the researches of later scholars and new material discovered in the last thirty-five years since the " Short History " was published. I give my sincere thanks to Dr. Norman Moore for his valuable advice and help in this matter.

1911.

In the Epilogue, I gratefully acknowledge special assistance given me by Mr. F. R. Harris in the survey of continental problems throughout the middle of the nineteenth century.

1916.   ALICE STOPFORD GREEN.

PREFACE TO THE FIRST EDITION.

THE aim of the following work is defined by its title; it is a history, not of English Kings or English Conquests, but of the English People. At the risk of sacrificing much that was interesting and attractive in itself, and which the constant usage of our historians has made familiar to English readers, I have preferred to pass lightly and briefly over the details of foreign wars and diplomacies, the personal adventures of kings and nobles, the pomp of courts, or the intrigues of favourites, and to dwell at length on the incidents of that constitutional, intellectual, and social advance in which we read the history of the nation itself. It is with this purpose that I have devoted more space to Chaucer than to Cressy, to Caxton than to the petty strife of Yorkist and Lancastrian, to the Poor Law of Elizabeth than to her victory at Cadiz, to the Methodist revival than to the escape of the Young Pretender.

Whatever the worth of the present work may be, I have striven throughout that it should never sink into a "drum and trumpet history." It is the reproach of historians that they have too often turned history into a mere record of the butchery of men by their fellow-men. But war plays a small part in the real story of European nations, and in that of England its part is smaller than in any. The only war which has profoundly affected English society and English government is the Hundred Years' War with France, and of that war the results were simply evil. If I have said little of the glories of Cressy, it is because I have dwelt much on the wrong and misery which prompted the verse of Longland and the preaching of Ball. But on the other hand, I have never shrunk from telling at length the triumphs of peace. I have restored to their place among the achievements of Englishmen the "Faerie Queen" and the "Novum Organum." I have set Shakspere among the heroes of the Elizabethan age, and placed the scientific inquiries of the Royal Society side by side with the victories of the New Model. If some of the conventional figures of military and political history occupy in my pages less than the space usually given them, it is because I have had to find a place for figures little heeded in common history —the figures of the missionary, the poet, the printer, the merchant, or the philosopher.

In England, more than elsewhere, constitutional progress has been the result of social development. In a brief summary of our history such as the present, it was impossible to dwell as I could have wished to dwell on every phase of this development; but I have endeavoured to point out, at great crises, such as those of the Peasant Revolt or the Rise of the New Monarchy, how much of our political history is the outcome of social changes; and throughout I have drawn greater attention to the religious, intellectual, and industrial progress of the nation itself than has, so far as I remember, ever been done in any previous history of the same extent.

The scale of the present work has hindered me from giving in detail the authorities for every statement. But I have prefixed to each section a short critical account of the chief contemporary authorities for the period it represents as well as of the most useful modern works in which it can be studied. As I am writing for English readers of a general class I have thought it better to restrict myself in the latter case to English books, or to English translations of foreign works where they exist. This is a rule which I have only broken in the occasional mention of French books, such as those of Guizot or Mignet, well known and within reach of ordinary students. I greatly regret that the publication of the first volume of the invaluable Constitutional History of Professor Stubbs came too late for me to use it in my account of those early periods on which it has thrown so great a light.

I am only too conscious of the faults and oversights in a work, much of which has been written in hours of weakness and ill health. That its imperfections are not greater than they are, I owe to the kindness of those who have from time to time aided me with suggestions and corrections; and especially to my dear friend Mr. E. A. Freeman, who has never tired of helping me with counsel and criticism. Thanks for like friendly help are due to Professor Stubbs and Professor Bryce, and in literary matters to the Rev. Stopford Brooke, whose wide knowledge and refined taste have been of the greatest service to me. I am indebted to the kindness of Miss Thompson for permission to use the Genealogical Tables prefixed to my work, and to Mr. Freeman for a like permission to use some of the maps in his "Old English History."

The Chronological Annals which precede the text will, I trust, be useful in the study of those periods where the course of my story has compelled me to neglect the strict chronological order of succession. In using this book as a school book, both teacher and scholar would do well to study them side by side with the text.

CONTENTS.

		PAGE
CHRONOLOGICAL ANNALS		xxv–xl
GENEALOGICAL TABLES		xli–lv

CHAPTER I.

THE ENGLISH KINGDOMS, 607—1013.

Sect. 1.—Britain and the English **1**

  ,,   2.—The English Conquest, 449—577 . . . .   **7**

  ,,   3.—The Northumbrian Kingdom, 588—685 . . . .   **16**

  ,,   4.—The Three Kingdoms, 685—828 . . . .   **36**

  ,,   5.—Wessex and the Danes, 802—880 . . . .   **44**

  ,,   6.—The West-Saxon Realm, 893—1013 . . . .   **53**

CHAPTER II.

ENGLAND UNDER FOREIGN KINGS, 1013—1204.

Sect. 1.—The Danish Kings, 1013—1042 . . . .   **63**

  ,,   2.—The English Restoration, 1042—1066 . . . .   **67**

  ,,   3.—Normandy and the Normans, 912—1066 . . . .   **71**

  ,,   4.—The Conqueror, 1042—1066 . . . .   **74**

  ,,   5.—The Norman Conquest, 1068—1071 . . . .   **81**

  ,,   6.—The English Revival, 1071—1127 . . . .   **87**

  ,,   7.—England and Anjou, 870—1154 . . . .   **98**

  ,,   8.—Henry the Second, 1154—1189 . . . . **104**

  ,,   9.—The fall of the Angevins, 1189—1204 . . . . **112**

CHAPTER III.

THE GREAT CHARTER, 1204—1265.

                                                                    PAGE
Sect. 1.—English Literature under the Norman and Angevin Kings 117
  „   2.—John, 1204—1215 122
  „   3.—The Great Charter, 1215—1217 128
  „   4.—The Universities 132
  „   5.—Henry the Third, 1216—1257 141
  „   6.—The Friars 147
  „   7.—The Barons' War, 1258—1265 152

CHAPTER IV.

THE THREE EDWARDS, 1265—1360.

Sect. 1.—The Conquest of Wales, 1265—1284 161
  „   2.—The English Parliament, 1283—1295 169
  „   3.—The Conquest of Scotland, 1290—1305 181
  „   4.—The English Towns 193
  „   5.—The King and the Baronage, 1290—1327 201
  „   6.—The Scotch War of Independence, 1306—1342 211

CHAPTER V.

THE HUNDRED YEARS' WAR, 1336—1431.

Sect. 1.—Edward the Third, 1336—1360 217
  „   2.—The Good Parliament, 1360—1377 231
  „   3.—John Wyclif 235
  „   4 —The Peasant Revolt, 1377—1381 244
  „   5.—Richard the Second, 1381—1399 255
  „   6.—The House of Lancaster, 1399—1422 264

CHAPTER VI.

THE NEW MONARCHY, 1422—1540.

		PAGE
Sect. 1.—Joan of Arc, 1422—1451		271
„ 2.—The Wars of the Roses, 1450—1471		281
„ 3.—The New Monarchy, 1471—1509		288
„ 4.—The New Learning, 1509—1520		303
„ 5.—Wolsey, 1515—1531		320
„ 6.—Thomas Cromwell, 1530—1540		331

CHAPTER VII.

THE REFORMATION.

Sect. 1.—The Protestants, 1540—1553		349
„ 2.—The Martyrs, 1553—1558		361
„ 3.—Elizabeth, 1558—1560		369
„ 4.—England and Mary Stuart, 1560—1572		382
„ 5.—The England of Elizabeth		392
„ 6.—The Armada, 1572—1588		405
„ 7.—The Elizabethan Poets		420
„ 8.—The Conquest of Ireland, 1588—1610		442

CHAPTER VIII.

PURITAN ENGLAND.

Sect. 1.—The Puritans, 1583—1603		460
„ 2.—The First of the Stuarts, 1604—1623		474
„ 3.—The King and the Parliament, 1623—1629		493
„ 4.—New England		505
„ 5.—The Personal Government, 1629—1640		514
„ 6.—The Long Parliament, 1640—1644		534
„ 7.—The Civil War, July 1642—August 1646		547
„ 8.—The Army and the Parliament, 1646—1649		559
„ 9.—The Commonwealth, 1649—1653		572
„ 10.—The Fall of Puritanism, 1653—1660		582

CHAPTER IX.

THE REVOLUTION.

PAGE

Sect. 1.—England and the Revolution 605
 ,, 2.—The Restoration, 1660—1667 616
 ,, 3.—Charles the Second, 1667—1673 629
 ,, 4.—Danby, 1673—1678 642
 ,, 5.—Shaftesbury, 1679—1682 652
 ,, 6.—The Second Stuart Tyranny, 1682—1688 661
 ,, 7.—William of Orange 672
 ,, 8.—The Grand Alliance, 1689—1697 684
 ,, 9.—Marlborough, 1698—1712 701
 ,, 10.—Walpole, 1712—1742 720

CHAPTER X.

MODERN ENGLAND.

Sect. 1.—William Pitt, 1742—1762 735
 ,, 2.—The Independence of America, 1761—1782 757
 ,, 3.—The Second Pitt, 1783—1793 786
 ,, 4.—The War with France, 1793—1815 806

EPILOGUE.

Sect. 1.—The Social Revolution, 1815—1914 837
 " 2.—Foreign and Colonial Policy, 1815—1914 906

INDEX 1009

LIST OF MAPS.

1. England . . . . *Front.*
2. Britain in the midst of the English Conquest 12
3. England in the Ninth Century 44
4. Empire of the Angevins 104
5. France at the Treaty of Bretigny 217
6. The American Colonies in 1640 507

CHRONOLOGICAL ANNALS

OF

ENGLISH HISTORY.

CHRONOLOGICAL ANNALS

OF

ENGLISH HISTORY

THE ENGLISH KINGDOMS.

449—1016.

449	**English land in Britain.**
457	Kent conquered by English.
477	Landing of South Saxons.
491	Siege of Anderida.
495	Landing of West Saxons.
519	**Cerdic** and **Cynric,** Kings of West Saxons.
520	British victory at Mount Badon.
547	Ida founds kingdom of Bernicia.
552	West Saxons take Old Sarum.
560	**Æthelberht,** King of Kent, died 616.
568	—— driven back by West Saxons.
571	West Saxons march into Mid-Britain.
577	—— conquer at Deorham.
584	—— defeated at Faddiley.
588	**Æthelric** creates Kingdom of Northumbria.
593	**Æthelfrith,** King of Northumbria, died 617.
597	*Augustine converts Kent.*
603	Battle of Dægsastan.
613	Battle of Chester.
617	**Eadwine,** King of Northumbria, died 633.
626	—— overlord of Britain.
	Penda, King of the Mercians, died 655.
627	Eadwine becomes Christian.
633	—— slain at Hatfield.
635	**Oswald,** King of Bernicia, died 642.
	—— defeats Welsh at Hevenfeld.
	Aidan settles at Holy Island.
	Conversion of Wessex.

642	Oswald slain at Maserfeld.
651	**Oswiu,** King of Northumbria, died 670.
655	—— Victory at Winwæd.
658	West Saxons conquer as far as the Parret.
659	**Wulfhere** King in Mercia.
661	—— drives West Saxons over Thames.
664	Council of Whitby.
	Cædmon at Whitby.
668	*Theodore made Archbishop of Canterbury.*
670	**Ecgfrith,** King of Northumbria, died 685.
675	**Æthelred,** King of Mercia, died 704.
681	*Wilfrid converts South Saxons.*
682	Centwine of Wessex conquers Mid-Somerset.
685	Ecgfrith defeated and slain at Nectansmere.
688	**Ine,** King of West Saxons, died 726.
715	—— defeats Ceolred of Mercia at Wanborough.
716	**Æthelbald,** King of Mercia, died 757.
733	Mercian conquest of Wessex.
735	*Death of Bæda.*
753	*Death of Boniface.*
754	Wessex recovers freedom in Battle of Burford.
756	Eadberht of Northumbria takes Alcluyd.
758	**Offa,** King of Mercia, died 796.
775	—— subdues Kentish men at Otford.
779	—— defeats West Saxons at Bensington.
786	—— places Beorhtric on throne of Wessex.
787	—— creates Archbishopric at Lichfield.
	First landing of Danes in England.

796 **Cenwulf,** King of Mercia, died 821.
802 **Ecgberht** becomes King in Wessex, died 839.
803 Cenwulf suppresses Archbishopric of Lichfield.
808 Charles the Great restores Eardwulf in Northumbria.
815 Ecgberht subdues the West Welsh to the Tamar.
821 Civil war in Mercia.
825 Ecgberht defeats Mercians at Ellandun.
—— overlord of England south of Thames.
Revolt of East Anglia against Mercia.
827 Defeat of Mercians by East Anglians.
828 Mercia and Northumbria submit to Ecgberht.
Ecgberht overlord of all English kingdoms.
—— invades Wales.
837 —— defeats Danes at Hengestesdun.
839 **Æthelwulf,** King of Wessex, died 858.
849 Ælfred born.
851 Danes defeated at Aclea.
853 Ælfred sent to Rome.
855 Æthelwulf goes to Rome.
857 **Æthelbald,** King of Wessex, died 860.
860 **Æthelberht,** King of Wessex, died 866.
866 **Æthelred,** King of Wessex, died 871.
867 Danes conquer Northumbria.
868 Peace of Nottingham with Danes.
870 Danes conquer and settle in East Anglia.
871 Danes invade Wessex.
Ælfred, King of Wessex, died 901.
874 Danes conquer Mercia.
876 Danes settle in Northumbria.
877 Ælfred defeats Danes at Exeter.
878 Danes overrun Wessex.
Ælfred victor at Edington.
Peace of Wedmore.
883 Ælfred sends envoys to Rome and India.

886 Ælfred takes and refortifies London.
893 Danes reappear in Thames and Kent.
894 Ælfred drives Hasting from Wessex.
895 Hasting invades Mercia.
896 Ælfred drives Danes from Essex.
897 Hasting quits England.
Ælfred creates a fleet.
901 **Eadward the Elder,** died 925.
912 Northmen settle in Normandy.
913
918 } Æthelflæd conquers Danish Mercia.
921 Eadward subdues East Anglia and Essex.
924 —— owned as overlord by Northumbria, Scots, and Strathclyde.
925 **Æthelstan,** died 940.
926 —— drives Welsh from Exeter.
934 —— invades Scotland.
937 Victory of Brunanburh.
940 **Eadmund,** died 946.
943 Dunstan made Abbot of Glastonbury.
945 Cumberland granted to Malcolm, King of Scots.
946 **Eadred,** died 955.
954 —— makes Northumbria an Earldom.
955 **Eadwig,** died 959.
956 Banishment of Dunstan.
957 Revolt of Mercia under Eadgar.
958 **Eadgar,** died 975.
959 *Dunstan Archbishop of Canterbury.*
975 **Eadward the Martyr,** died 978.
978 **Æthelred the Unready,** died 1016.
987
1040 } Fulk the Black, Count of Anjou.
994 Invasion of Swein.
1002 Massacre of Danes.
1003 Swein harries Wessex.
1012 Murder of Archbishop Ælfheah.
1013 All England submits to Swein.
Flight of Æthelred to Normandy.
1016 **Eadmund Ironside,** King, and dies.

ENGLAND UNDER FOREIGN KINGS.
1016—1204.

1016 **Cnut,** King, died 1035.
1020 Godwine made Earl of Wessex.
1027 Cnut goes to Rome.
Birth of William of Normandy.
1035 Harald and Harthacnut divide England.
1037 **Harald,** King, died 1040.
1040 **Harthacnut,** King, died 1042.
1040
1060 } Geoffry Martel, Count of Anjou.
1042 **Eadward the Confessor,** died 1066.
1045 *Lanfranc at Bec.*

1047 Victory of William at Val-ès-dunes.
1051 Banishment of Godwine.
William of Normandy visits England.
1052 Return of Godwine.
1053 Death of Godwine.
Harold made Earl of West Saxons.
1054 William's victory at Mortemer.
1055 Harold's first campaign in Wales.
1054
1060 } Norman conquest of Southern Italy.
1058 William's victory at the Dive.

1060	Normans invade Sicily.	**1138**	Revolt of Earl Robert.
1063	Harold conquers Wales.		Battle of the Standard.
1066	**Harold,** King.	**1139**	Seizure of the Bishops.
	—— conquers at Stamford Bridge.		Landing of Matilda.
	—— defeated at Senlac or Hastings.	**1141**	Battle of Lincoln.
	William of Normandy, King, died 1087.	**1147**	*Birth of Gerald of Wales.*
1068 **1071** }	Norman Conquest of England.	**1148**	Matilda withdraws to Normandy.
			Archbishop Theobald driven into exile.
1070	Reorganization of the Church.	**1149**	Henry of Anjou in England.
	Lanfranc Archbishop of Canterbury.	**1151**	Henry becomes Duke of Normandy.
1075	Rising of Roger Fitz-Osbern.	**1152**	Henry marries Eleanor of Guienne.
1081	William invades Wales.	**1153**	Henry in England. Treaty of Wallingford.
1085	Failure of Danish invasion.	**1154**	**Henry the Second,** died 1189.
1086	Completion of Domesday Book.	**1159**	Expedition against Toulouse.
1087	**William the Red,** died 1100.		The Great Scutage.
1093	*Anselm, Archbishop.*	**1162**	Thomas made Archbishop of Canterbury.
1094	Revolt of Wales against the Norman Marchers.	**1164**	Constitutions of Clarendon.
			Council of Northampton.
1095	Revolt of Robert de Mowbray.		Flight of Archbishop Thomas.
1096	Normandy left in pledge to William.	**1166**	Assize of Clarendon.
1097	William invades Wales.	**1170**	Strongbow's invasion of Ireland.
	Anselm leaves England.		Inquest of Sheriffs.
1098	War with France.		Death of Archbishop Thomas.
1100	**Henry the First,** died 1135.	**1172**	Henry's Conquest of Ireland.
	Henry's Charter.	**1173** **1174** }	Rebellion of Henry's sons.
1101	Robert of Normandy invades England.		
1106	Settlement of question of investitures.	**1176**	Assize of Northampton.
	English Conquest of Normandy.	**1178**	Reorganization of Curia Regis.
1109 **1129** }	Fulk of Jerusalem, Count of Anjou.	**1181**	Assize of Arms.
		1189	Revolt of Richard.
1110	War with France.		**Richard the First,** died 1199.
1111	War with Anjou.	**1190** **1194** }	Richard's Crusade.
1113	Peace of Gisors.		
1114	Marriage of Matilda with Henry V.	**1194** **1196** }	War with Philip Augustus.
1120	Wreck of White Ship.		
1121	Henry's campaign in Wales.	**1194** **1246** }	Llewelyn ap-Jorwerth in North Wales.
1123	Revolt of Norman baronage.		
1124	France and Anjou support William Clito.	**1197**	Richard builds Château Gaillard.
1128	Matilda married to Geoffry of Anjou.	**1199**	**John,** dies 1216.
	Death of the Clito in Flanders.	**1200**	—— recovers Anjou and Maine.
1134	Revolt of Wales.		*Layamon writes the Brut.*
1135	**Stephen** of Blois, died 1154.	**1203**	Murder of Arthur.
1138	Normandy repulses the Angevins.	**1204**	French conquest of Anjou and Normandy

THE GREAT CHARTER.

1204—1295.

1205	Barons refuse to fight for recovery of Normandy.	**1211**	John reduces Llewelyn - ap - Jorwerth to submission.
1206	*Stephen Langton Archbishop of Canterbury.*	**1213**	John becomes the Pope's vassal.
		1214	Battle of Bouvines.
1208	Innocent III. puts England under Interdict.		*Birth of Roger Bacon.*
		1215	The Great Charter.
1210	John divides Irish Pale into counties.	**1216**	Lewis of France called in by the Barons.

1216	**Henry the Third,** died 1272.
	Confirmation of the Charter.
1217	Lewis returns to France.
	Charter again confirmed.
1219	Hubert de Burgh, Justiciar.
1221	*Friars land in England.*
1223	Charter again confirmed at London.
1224	Revolt of Faukes de Breauté.
1225	Fresh confirmation of Charter.
1228	Stephen Langton's death.
1229	Papal exactions.
1230	Failure of Henry's campaign in Poitou.
1231	Conspiracy against the Italian clergy.
1232	Fall of Hubert de Burgh.
1237	Charter again confirmed.
1238	Earl Simon of Leicester marries Henry's sister.
1242	Defeat of Henry at Taillebourg.
	Barons refuse subsidies.
1246 **1283**	Llewelyn-ap-Gruffydd, Prince in North Wales.
1248	Irish refusal of subsidies.
	Earl Simon in Gascony.
1253	Earl Simon returns to England.
1258	Provisions of Oxford.
1264	Mise of Amiens.

1264	Battle of Lewes.
1265	Commons summoned to Parliament.
	Battle of Evesham.
1267	*Roger Bacon writes his "Opus Majus."*
	Llewelyn-ap-Gruffydd owned as Prince of Wales.
1270	Edward goes on Crusade.
1272	**Edward the First,** died 1307.
1277	Edward reduces Llewelyn-ap-Gruffydd to submission.
1279	Statute of Mortmain.
1282	Conquest of Wales.
1283	Statute of Merchants.
1285	Statute of Winchester.
1290	Statute "Quia Emptores."
	Expulsion of the Jews.
	Marriage Treaty of Brigham.
1291	Parliament at Norham concerning Scotch succession.
1292	Edward claims appeals from Scotland.
	Death of Roger Bacon.
1294	Seizure of Guienne by Philip of France.
1295	French fleet attacks Dover.
	Final organization of the English Parliament.

THE WAR WITH SCOTLAND AND FRANCE.

1296—1485.

1296	Edward conquers Scotland.
1297	Victory of Wallace at Stirling.
	Outlawry of the Clergy.
	Barons refuse to serve in Guienne.
1298	Edward conquers Scots at Falkirk.
	Truce with France.
1301	Barons demand nomination of Ministers by Parliament.
	Barons exact fresh Confirmation of the Charters.
1304	Submission of Scotland.
1305	Parliament of Perth.
1306	Rising of Robert Bruce.
1307	Parliament of Carlisle.
	Edward the Second, died 1327.
1308	Gaveston exiled.
1310	The Lords Ordainers draw up Articles of Reform.
1312	Death of Gaveston.
1314	Battle of Bannockburn.
1316	Battle of Athenree.
1318	Edward accepts the Ordinances.
1322	Death of Earl of Lancaster. Ordinances annulled.
1328	Truce with the Scots.

1324	French attack Aquitaine.
1325	The Queen and Prince Edward in France.
1326	Queen lands in England.
1327	Deposition of Edward II.
	Edward the Third, died 1377.
1328	Treaty of Northampton recognizes independence of Scotland.
1329	Death of Robert Bruce.
1330	Death of Roger Mortimer.
1332	Edward Balliol invades Scotland.
1333	Battle of Halidon Hill.
	Balliol does homage to Edward.
1335 **1336**	Edward invades Scotland.
1336	France again declares war.
1337 **1338**	War with France and Scotland.
	Edward claims crown of France.
1339	Balliol driven from Scotland.
	Edward attacks France from Brabant.
1340	Battle of Sluys.
1341 **1342**	War in Britanny and Guienne.
1346	Battles of Crécy and Neville's Cross.

1347	Capture of Calais.
	Truce with France.
1348	First appearance of the Black Death.
1349 } 1351 }	Statutes of Labourers.
1351	First Statute of Provisors.
1353	First Statute of Præmunire.
1355	Renewal of French War.
1356	Battle of Poitiers.
1366	Statute of Kilkenny.
1367	The Black Prince victorious at Navarete.
1368	*Wyclif's treatise " De Dominio."*
1370	Storm of Limoges.
1372	Victory of Spanish fleet off Rochelle.
1374	Revolt of Aquitaine.
1376	The Good Parliament.
1377	Its work undone by the Duke of Lancaster.
	Wyclif before the Bishop of London.
	Richard the Second, died 1399.
1378	Gregory XI. denounces Wyclif's heresy.
1380	*Longland's " Piers the Ploughman."*
1381	Wyclif's declaration against Transubstantiation.
	The Peasant Revolt.
1382	Condemnation of Wyclif at Blackfriars.
	Suppression of the Poor Preachers.
1384	Death of Wyclif.
1386	Barons force Richard to dismiss the Earl of Suffolk.
1389	Truce with France.
1394	Richard in Ireland.
1396	Richard marries Isabella of France.
	Truce with France prolonged.
1397	Murder of the Duke of Gloucester.
1398	Richard's plans of tyranny.
1399	Deposition of Richard.
	Henry the Fourth, died 1413.
1400	Revolt of Owen Glyndwr in Wales.
1401	Statute of Heresy.
1402	Battle of Homildon Hill.
1403	Revolt of the Percies.
1403 } 1405 }	French descents on England.
1405	Revolt of Archbishop Scrope.
1407	French attack Gascony.

1411	English force sent to aid Duke of Burgundy in France.
1413	**Henry the Fifth,** died 1422.
1414	Lollard Conspiracy.
1415	Battle of Agincourt.
1417	Henry invades Normandy.
1419	Alliance with Duke of Burgundy.
1420	Treaty of Troyes.
1422	**Henry the Sixth,** died 1471.
1424	Battle of Verneuil.
1428 } 1429 }	Siege of Orleans.
1430	County Suffrage restricted.
1431	Death of Joan of Arc.
1435	Congress of Arras.
1445	Marriage of Margaret of Anjou.
1447	Death of Duke of Gloucester.
1450	Impeachment and death of Duke of Suffolk.
	Cade's Insurrection.
	Loss of Normandy.
1451	Loss of Guienne.
1454	Duke of York named Protector.
1455	First Battle of St. Albans.
1456	End of York's Protectorate.
1459	Failure of Yorkist revolt.
1460	Battle of Northampton.
	York acknowledged as successor.
	Battle of Wakefield.
1461	Second Battle of St. Albans.
	Battle of Mortimer's Cross.
	Edward the Fourth, died 1483.
	Battle of Towton.
1461 } 1471 }	Warwick the King-maker.
1464	Edward marries Lady Grey.
1470	Warwick driven to France.
	Flight of Edward to Flanders.
1471	Battles of Barnet and Tewkesbury.
1475	Edward invades France.
1476	*Caxton settles in England.*
1483	Murder of **Edward the Fifth.**
	Richard the Third, died 1485.
	Buckingham's Insurrection.
1485	Battle of Bosworth.

THE TUDORS.

1485—1603.

1485	**Henry the Seventh,** died 1509.
1487	Conspiracy of Lambert Simnel.
1490	Treaty with Ferdinand and Isabella.
1492	Henry invades France.
1497	Cornish rebellion.
	Perkin Warbeck captured.

1497	Sebastian Cabot lands in America.
1499	*Colet and Erasmus at Oxford.*
1501	Arthur Tudor marries Catharine of Aragon.
1502	Margaret Tudor marries James the Fourth.
1505	*Colet Dean of S. Paul's.*
1509	**Henry the Eighth,** died 1547.

1509 *Erasmus writes the "Praise of Folly."*
1512 War with France.
1513 Battles of the Spurs and of Flodden.
Wolsey becomes chief Minister.
1515 *More's "Utopia."*
1517 Luther denounces Indulgences.
1520 Field of Cloth of Gold.
Luther burns the Pope's Bull.
1521 Quarrel of Luther with Henry the Eighth.
1522 Renewal of French war.
1523 Wolsey quarrels with the Commons.
1525 Exaction of Benevolences defeated.
Peace with France.
Tyndale translates the New Testament.
1526 Henry resolves on a Divorce. Persecution of Protestants.
1529 Fall of Wolsey. Ministry of Norfolk and More.
1531 King acknowledged as "Supreme Head of the Church of England."
1532 Statute of Appeals.
1534 Acts of Supremacy and Succession.
1535 Cromwell Vicar-General.
Death of More.
Overthrow of the Geraldines in Ireland.
1536 Dissolution of lesser Monasteries.
1537 Pilgrimage of Grace.
1538 English Bible issued.
1539 Execution of Lord Exeter.
Law of Six Articles.
Suppression of greater Abbeys.
1542 Completion of the Tudor Conquest of Ireland.
1544 War with France.
1547 Execution of Earl of Surrey.
Edward the Sixth, died 1553.
Battle of Pinkie Cleugh.
Suppression of Chantries.
1548 English Book of Common Prayer.
1549 Western Rebellion. End of Somerset's Protectorate.
1551 Death of Somerset.
1553 **Mary,** died 1558.
Chancellor discovers Archangel.
1554 Mary marries Philip of Spain.
England absolved by Cardinal Pole.
1555 Persecution of Protestants begins.
1556 Burning of Archbishop Cranmer.
1557 War with France.
1558 Loss of Calais.
Elizabeth, died 1603.
1559 —— restores Royal Supremacy and English Prayer Book.
1560 War in Scotland.
1561 Mary Stuart lands in Scotland.
1562 Rebellion of Shane O'Neill in Ulster.

1562 Elizabeth supports French Huguenots.
Hawkins begins Slave Trade with Africa.
1563 First penal statute against Catholics.
English driven out of Havre.
Thirty-nine Articles imposed on clergy.
1565 Mary marries Darnley.
1566 Darnley murders Rizzio.
Royal Exchange built.
1567 Murder of Darnley.
Defeat and death of Shane O'Neill.
1568 Mary flies to England.
1569 Revolt of the northern Earls.
1570 Bull of Deposition published.
1571 Conspiracy and death of Norfolk.
1572 Rising of the Low Countries against Alva.
Cartwright's "Admonition to the Parliament."
1575 Queen refuses Netherlands.
1576 *First public Theatre in Blackfriars.*
Landing of the Seminary Priests.
1577 Drake sets sail for the Pacific.
1579 *Lyly's "Euphues."*
Spenser publishes "Shepherd's Calendar."
1580 Campian and Parsons in England.
Revolt of the Desmonds.
Massacre of Smerwick.
1583 Plots to assassinate Elizabeth.
New powers given to Ecclesiastical Commission.
1584 Murder of Prince of Orange.
Armada gathers in the Tagus.
Colonization of Virginia.
1585 English Army sent to Netherlands.
Drake on the Spanish Coast.
1586 Battle of Zutphen.
Babington's Plot.
1587 *Shakspere in London.*
Death of Mary Stuart.
Drake burns Spanish fleet at Cadiz.
Marlowe's "Tamburlaine."
1588 Defeat of the Armada.
Martin Marprelate Tracts.
1589 Drake plunders Corunna.
1590 *Publication of the "Faerie Queen."*
1593 *Shakspere's "Venus and Adonis."*
1594 Hooker's "Ecclesiastical Polity."
1596 *Jonson's "Every Man in his Humour."*
Descent upon Cadiz.
1597 Ruin of the Second Armada.
Bacon's "Essays."
1598 Revolt of Hugh O'Neill.
1599 Expedition of Earl of Essex in Ireland.
1601 Execution of Essex.
1603 Mountjoy completes the conquest of Ireland.
Death of Elizabeth.

THE STUARTS.

1603—1688.

1603 James the First, died 1625.
Millenary Petition.

1604 Parliament claims to deal with both Church and State.
Hampton Court Conference.

1605 Gunpowder Plot.
Bacon's "Advancement of Learning."

1610 Parliament's Petition of Grievances.
Plantation of Ulster.

1613 Marriage of the Elector Palatine.

1614 First quarrels with the Parliament.

1616 Trial of the Earl and Countess of Somerset.
Dismissal of Chief Justice Coke.
Death of Shakspere.

1617 Bacon Lord Keeper.
Proposals for the Spanish Marriage.
The Declaration of Sports.

1617
1618 } Expedition and death of Ralegh.

1618 Beginning of Thirty Years' War.

1620 Invasion of the Palatinate.
Landing of the Pilgrim-Fathers in New England.

1621 *Bacon's "Novum Organum."*
Impeachment of Bacon.
James tears out the Protestation of the Commons.

1623 Journey of Prince Charles to Madrid.

1624 Resolve of War against Spain.

1625 Charles the First, died 1649.
First Parliament dissolved.
Failure of expedition against Cadiz.

1626 Buckingham impeached.
Second Parliament dissolved.

1627 Levy of Benevolence and Forced Loan.
Failure of expedition to Rochelle.

1628 The Petition of Right.
Murder of Buckingham.
Laud Bishop of London.

1629 Dissolution of Third Parliament.
Charter granted to Massachusetts.
Wentworth Lord President of the North.

1630 Puritan Emigration to New England.

1633 Wentworth Lord Deputy in Ireland.
Laud Archbishop of Canterbury.
Milton's "Allegro" and "Penseroso."
Prynne's "Histrio-mastix."

1634 *Milton's "Comus."*

1636 Juxon Lord Treasurer.
Book of Canons and Common Prayer issued for Scotland.
Hampden refuses to pay Ship-money.

1637 Revolt of Edinburgh.
Trial of Hampden.

1638 *Milton's "Lycidas."*
The Scotch Covenant.

1639 Leslie at Dunse Law.
Pacification of Berwick.

1640 The Short Parliament.
The Bishops' War.
Great Council of Peers at York.
Long Parliament meets, *Nov.*
Pym leader of the Commons.

1641 Execution of Strafford, *May.*
Charles visits Scotland.
Hyde organizes royalist party.
The Irish Massacre, *Oct.*
The Grand Remonstrance, *Nov.*

1642 Impeachment of Five Members, *Jan.*
Charles before Hull, *April.*
Royalists withdraw from Parliament.
Charles raises Standard at Nottingham, *August 22.*
Battle of Edgehill, *Oct. 23.*
Hobbes writes the "De Cive."

1643 Assembly of Divines at Westminster.
Rising of the Cornishmen, *May.*
Death of Hampden, *June.*
Battle of Roundway Down, *July.*
Siege of Gloucester, *Aug.*
Death of Falkland, *Sept.*
Charles negotiates with Irish Catholics.
Taking of the Covenant, *Sept. 25.*

1644 Fight at Cropredy Bridge, *June.*
Battle of Marston Moor, *July 2.*
Surrender of Parliamentary Army in Cornwall, *Sept. 2.*
Battle of Tippermuir, *Sept. 2.*
Battle of Newbury, *Oct.*
Milton's "Areopagitica."

1645 Self-denying Ordinance, *April.*
New Model raised.
Battle of Naseby, *June 14.*
Battle of Philiphaugh, *Sept.*

1646 Charles surrenders to the Scots, *May.*

1647 Scots surrender Charles to the Houses, *Jan. 30.*
Army elects Agitators, *April.*
The King seized at Holmby House, *June.*
"Humble Representation" of the Army, *June.*
Expulsion of the Eleven Members.
Army occupies London, *Aug.*
Flight of the King, *Nov.*

1647 Secret Treaty of Charles with the Scots, *Dec.*

1648 Outbreak of the Royalist Revolt, *Feb.*
Revolt of the Fleet, and of Kent, *May.*
Fairfax and Cromwell in Essex and Wales, *June—July.*
Battle of Preston, *Aug.* 17.
Surrender of Colchester, *Aug.* 27
Pride's Purge, *Dec.*
Royal Society begins at Oxford.

1649 Execution of Charles I , *Jan.* 30.
Scotland proclaims Charles II. King.
England proclaims itself a Commonwealth.
Cromwell storms Drogheda, *Sept.* 11.

1650 Cromwell enters Scotland.
Battle of Dunbar, *Sept.* 3.

1651 Battle of Worcester, *Sept.* 3.
Hobbes's " Leviathan."

1652 Union with Scotland.
Outbreak of Dutch War, *May.*
Victory of Tromp, *Nov.*

1653 Victory of Blake, *Feb.*
Cromwell drives out the Parliament, *April* 20.
Constituent Convention (Barebones Parliament), *July.*
Convention dissolves, *Dec.*
The Instrument of Government.
Oliver Cromwell, Lord Protector, died 1658.

1654 Peace concluded with Holland.
First Protectorate Parliament, *Sept.*

1655 Dissolution of the Parliament, *Jan.*
The Major-Generals.
Settlement of Scotland and Ireland.
Settlement of the Church.
Blake in the Mediterranean.
War with Spain and Conquest of Jamaica.

1656 Second Protectorate Parliament, *Sept.*

1657 Blake's victory at Santa Cruz.
Cromwell refuses title of King.
Act of Government.

1658 Parliament dissolved, *Feb.*
Battle of the Dunes.
Capture of Dunkirk.
Death of Cromwell, *Sept.* 3.
Richard Cromwell, Lord Protector, died 1712.

1659 Third Protectorate Parliament.
Parliament dissolved.
Long Parliament recalled.
Long Parliament again driven out.

1660 Monk enters London.
The "Convention" Parliament.
Charles the Second, lands at Dover, *May,* died 1685.

1660 Union of Scotland and Ireland undone.

1661 Cavalier Parliament begins.

1662 Act of Uniformity re-enacted.
Puritan clergy driven out.
Royal Society at London.

1663 Dispensing Bill fails.

1664 Conventicle Act.

1665 Dutch War begins.
Five Mile Act.
Plague of London.
Newton's Theory of Fluxions.

1666 Fire of London.

1667 The Dutch in the Medway.
Dismissal of Clarendon.
Peace of Breda.
Lewis attacks Flanders.
Milton's " Paradise Lost."

1668 The Triple Alliance.
Peace of Aix-la-Chapelle.
Ashley shrinks back from toleration to Catholics.

1670 Treaty of Dover.
Bunyan's "Pilgrim's Progress" written.

1671 *Milton's " Paradise Regained " and " Samson Agonistes."*
Newton's Theory of Light.

1672 Closing of the Exchequer.
Declaration of Indulgence.
War begins with Holland.
Ashley made Chancellor.

1673 Declaration of Indulgence withdrawn.
The Test Act.
Shaftesbury dismissed.
Shaftesbury takes the lead of the Country Party.

1674 Bill of Protestant Securities fails.
Charles makes Peace with Holland.
Danby Lord Treasurer.

1675 Treaty of mutual aid between Charles and Lewis.

1677 Shaftesbury sent to the Tower.
Bill for Security of the Church fails.
Address of the Houses for War with France.
Prince of Orange marries Mary.

1678 Peace of Nimeguen.
Oates invents the Popish Plot.

1679 New Parliament meets.
Fall of Danby.
New Ministry with Shaftesbury at its head.
Temple's plan for a new Council.
Habeas Corpus Act passed.
Exclusion Bill introduced.
Parliament dissolved.
Shaftesbury dismissed.

1680 Committee for agitation formed.

1680 Monmouth pretends to the throne.
Petitioners and Abhorrers.
Exclusion Bill thrown out by the Lords.
Trial of Lord Stafford.

1681 Parliament at Oxford.
Treaty with France.
Limitation Bill rejected.
Shaftesbury and Monmouth arrested.

1682 Conspiracy and flight of Shaftesbury.
Penn founds Pennsylvania.

1683 Death of Shaftesbury.
Rye-house Plot.
Execution of Lord Russell and Algernon Sidney.

1684 Town charters quashed.
Army increased.

1685 **James the Second,** died 1701.
Insurrection of Argyll and Monmouth.
Battle of Sedgemoor, *July* 6.
The Bloody Circuit.
Army raised to 20,000 men.

1635 Revocation of Edict of Nantes.

1686 Test Act dispensed with by royal authority.
Ecclesiastical Commission set up.

1687 *Newton's "Principia."*
Expulsion of the Fellows of Magdalen.
Dismissal of Lords Rochester and Clarendon.
Declaration of Indulgence.
The Boroughs regulated.
William of Orange protests against the Declaration.
Tyrconnell made Lord Deputy in Ireland.

1688 Clergy refuse to read the new Declaration of Indulgence.
Birth of James's son.
Invitation to William.
Trial of the Seven Bishops.
Irish troops brought over to England.
Lewis attacks Germany.
William of Orange lands at Torbay.
Flight of James.

MODERN ENGLAND.
1689—1914.

1689 Convention Parliament.
Declaration of Rights.
William and Mary made King and Queen.
William forms the Grand Alliance against Lewis.
Battle of Killiecrankie, *July* 27.
Siege of Londonderry.
Mutiny Bill.
Toleration Bill.
Bill of Rights.
Secession of the Non-jurors.

1690 Abjuration Bill and Act of Grace.
Battle of Beachy Head, *June* 30.
Battle of the Boyne, *July* 1.
William repulsed from Limerick.

1691 Battle of Aughrim, *July.*
Capitulation and Treaty of Limerick.

1692 Massacre of Glencoe.
Battle of La Hogue, *May* 19.

1693 Sunderland's plan of a Ministry.

1694 Bank of England set up.
Death of Mary.

1696 Currency restored.

1697 Peace of Ryswick.

1698 First Partition Treaty.

1700 Second Partition Treaty.

1701 Duke of Anjou becomes King of Spain.
Act of Settlement passed.

1701 Death of James II.

1702 **Anne,** died 1714.

1704 Battle of Blenheim, *August* 13.
Harley and St. John take office.

1705 Victories of Peterborough in Spain.

1706 Battle of Ramillies, *May* 23.

1707 Act of Union with Scotland.

1708 Dismissal of Harley and St. John.
Battle of Oudenarde.

1709 Battle of Malplaquet.

1710 Trial of Sacheverell.
Tory Ministry of Harley and St. John.

1712 Dismissal of Marlborough.

1713 Treaty of Utrecht.

1714 **George the First,** died 1727.
Ministry of Townshend and Walpole.

1715 Jacobite Revolt under Lord Mar.

1716 The Septennial Bill.

1717 The Triple Alliance.
Ministry of Lord Stanhope.

1718 The Quadruple Alliance.

1720 Failure of the Peerage Bill.
The South Sea Company.

1721 Ministry of Sir Robert Walpole.

1723 Exile of Bishop Atterbury.

1727 War with Austria and Spain.
George the Second, died 1760.

1729 Treaty of Seville.

1730 Free exportation of American rice allowed.

1731 Treaty of Vienna.
1733 Walpole's Excise Bill.
War of the Polish Succession.
Family compact between France and Spain.
1737 Death of Queen Caroline.
1738 *The Methodists appear in London.*
1739 War declared with Spain.
1740 War of the Austrian Succession.
1742 Resignation of Walpole.
1743 Battle of Dettingen, *June* 27.
1745 Ministry of Henry Pelham.
Battle of Fontenoy, *May* 31.
Charles Edward lands in Scotland.
Battle of Prestonpans, *Sept.* 21.
Charles Edward reaches Derby, *Dec.* 4.
1746 Battle of Falkirk, *Jan.* 23.
Battle of Culloden, *April* 16.
1748 Peace of Aix-la-Chapelle.
1751 Clive's surprise of Arcot.
1754 Death of Henry Pelham.
Ministry of Duke of Newcastle.
1755 The Seven Years' War.
Defeat of General Braddock.
1756 Loss of Port Mahon.
Retreat of Admiral Byng.
1757 Convention of Closter-Seven.
Ministry of William Pitt.
Battle of Plassey, *June* 23.
1758 Capture of Louisburg and Cape Breton.
Capture of Fort Duquesne.
1759 Battle of Minden, *August* 1.
Capture of Fort Niagara and Ticonderoga.
Wolfe's victory on Heights of Abraham.
Battle of Quiberon Bay, *Nov.* 20.
1760 **George the Third** died 1820.
Battle of Wandewash.
1761 Pitt resigns office.
Ministry of Lord Bute.
Brindley's Canal over the Irwell.
1763 Peace of Paris.
Ministry of George Grenville.
Wedgwood establishes potteries.
1764 First expulsion of Wilkes from House of Commons.
Hargreaves invents Spinning Jenny.
1765 Stamp Act passed.
Ministry of Lord Rockingham.
Meeting and Protest of American Congress.
Watt invents Steam Engine.
1766 Repeal of the Stamp Act.
Ministry of Lord Chatham.
1768 Ministry of the Duke of Grafton.
Second expulsion of Wilkes.
Arkwright invents Spinning Machine.

1769 Wilkes three times elected for Middlesex.
House of Commons seats Col. Luttrell.
Occupation of Boston by British troops.
Letters of Junius.
1770 Chatham's proposal of Parliamentary Reform.
Ministry of Lord North.
1771 Last attempt to prevent Parliamentary reporting.
Beginning of the great English Journals.
1773 Hastings appointed Governor-General.
Boston tea-riots.
1774 Military occupation of Boston.
Its port closed.
Massachusetts Charter altered.
Congress assembles at Philadelphia.
1775 Rejection of Chatham's plan of conciliation.
Skirmish at Lexington.
Americans, under Washington, besiege Boston.
Battle of Bunker's Hill.
Southern Colonies expel their Governors.
1776 *Crompton invents the Mule.*
Arnold invades Canada.
Evacuation of Boston.
Declaration of Independence, *July* 4.
Battles of Brooklyn and Trenton.
Adam Smith's "Wealth of Nations."
1777 Battle of Brandywine.
Surrender of Saratoga, *Oct.* 17.
Chatham proposes Federal Union.
Washington at Valley Forge.
1778 Alliance of France and Spain with United States.
Death of Chatham.
1779 Siege of Gibraltar.
Armed Neutrality of Northern Powers.
The Irish Volunteers.
1780 Capture of Charlestown.
Descent of Hyder Ali on the Carnatic.
1781 Defeat of Hyder at Porto Novo.
Surrender of Cornwallis at Yorktown.
1782 Ministry of Lord Rockingham.
Victories of Rodney.
Repeal of Poynings' Act.
Pitt's Bill for Parliamentary Reform.
Burke's Bill of Economical Reform.
Shelburne Ministry.
Repulse of Allies from Gibraltar.
1783 Treaties of Paris and Versailles.
Coalition Ministry of Fox and North.
Fox's India Bill.
Ministry of Pitt.
1784 Pitt's India Bill.
Financial Reforms.

1785	Parliamentary Reform Bill.
	Free Trade Bill between England and Ireland.
1786	Trial of Warren Hastings.
1787	Treaty of Commerce with France
1788	The Regency Bill.
1789	Meeting of States-General at Versailles.
	New French Constitution.
	Triple Alliance for defence of Turkey.
1790	Quarrel over Nootka Sound.
	Pitt defends Poland.
	Burke's " Reflections on the French Revolution."
1791	Representative Government set up in Canada.
	Fox's Libel Act.
	Burke's " Appeal from the New to the Old Whigs."
1792	Pitt hinders Holland from joining the Coalition.
	France opens the Scheldt.
	Pitt's efforts for peace.
	The United Irishmen.
1793	France declares War on England.
	Part of Whigs join Pitt.
	English army lands in Flanders.
	English driven from Toulon.
1794	English driven from Holland.
	Suspension of Habeas Corpus Act.
	Victory of Lord Howe, June 1.
1796	Burke's " Letters on a Regicide Peace."
1797	England alone in the War with France.
	Battle of Camperdown.
	Battle of Cape St. Vincent.
1798	Irish revolt crushed at Vinegar Hill.
	Battle of the Nile.
1799	Pitt revives the Coalition against France.
	Conquest of Mysore.
1800	Surrender of Malta to English Fleet.
	Armed Neutrality of Northern Powers.
	Act of Union with Ireland.
1801	George the Third rejects Pitt's Plan of Catholic Emancipation.
	Administration of Mr. Addington.
	Surrender of French army in Egypt.
	Battle of Copenhagen.
1802	Peace of Amiens.
	Publication of " Edinburgh Review."
1803	War declared against Buonaparte.
	Battle of Assaye.
1804	Second Ministry of Pitt.
1805	Battle of Trafalgar, Oct. 21.
1806	Death of Pitt, Jan. 23.
	Ministry of Lord Grenville.
	Death of Fox.
1807	Orders in Council.

1807	Abolition of Slave Trade.
	Ministry of Duke of Portland.
	Seizure of Danish Fleet.
1808	Battle of Vimiera, and Convention of Cintra.
1809	America passes Non-Intercourse Act.
	Battle of Corunna, Jan. 16.
	Wellesley drives Soult from Oporto.
	Battle of Talavera, July 28.
	Expedition against Walcheren.
	Ministry of Spencer Perceval.
	Revival of Parliamentary Reform.
1810	Battle of Busaco.
	Lines of Torres Vedras.
1811	Prince of Wales becomes Regent.
	Battle of Fuentes d'Onore, May 5.
	Luddite Riots.
1812	Assassination of Spencer Perceval.
	Ministry of Lord Liverpool.
	Storm of Ciudad Rodrigo and Badajoz.
	America declares War against England.
	Battle of Salamanca, July 22.
	Wellington retreats from Burgos.
	Victories of American Frigates.
1813	Battle of Vitoria, June 21.
	Battles of the Pyrenees.
	Wellington enters France, Oct.
	Americans attack Canada.
1814	Battle of Orthes.
	Battle of Toulouse, April 10.
	Battle of Chippewa, July.
	Raid upon Washington.
	British repulses at Plattsburg and New Orleans.
1815	Battle of Quatre Bras, June 16.
	Battle of Waterloo, June 18.
	Treaty of Vienna.
1817	Colonization in Australia.
	Bentham's doctrine of utility.
1818	Congress of Aix-la-Chapelle.
1819	The Six Acts carried.
	Singapore annexed.
1820	**George the Fourth,** died 1830.
	Cato Street Conspiracy.
	Bill for the Queen's Divorce.
	Reform of Criminal Law by Mackintosh.
1821	Catholic Relief Bill thrown out by the Lords.
1822	Congress of Verona.
	Canning Foreign Minister.
1823	Freedom of South American Republics recognized.
	The Monroe Doctrine.
1824	Repeal of Combination Laws.
	Emigration to South Africa.
1826	Annexation of Assam.

1826	Riots to destroy power looms.
1827	Ministry of Mr. Canning.
	Ministry of Lord Goderich.
	Battle of Navarino.
1828	Ministry of Duke of Wellington.
	First Co-operative Society.
	First Free Colony in Australia.
	Repeal of Test and Corporation Acts.
1829	Settlement in Western Australia.
	First Trades Union.
	Catholic Emancipation Bill.
1830	**William the Fourth,** died 1837.
	Ministry of Lord Grey.
	Opening of Liverpool and Manchester Railway.
	Belgian independence assured.
1831	Reform Bill introduced, *March* 1.
1832	Parliamentary Reform Bill passed, *June 7.*
1833	Coercion Act for Ireland.
	Factory Act.
	State grant for education.
	Suppression of Colonial Slavery.
	East Indian Trade thrown open.
1834	New Poor Law.
	Ministry of Lord Melbourne.
	Trades Union demonstrations.
	Central Criminal Court established.
	Ministry of Sir Robert Peel.
1835	Ministry of Lord Melbourne replaced.
	Municipal Corporation Act.
	Kaffir War.
1836	Newspaper stamp duty reduced.
	The Great Trek in South Africa.
	South Australia colonized.
	Civil Marriages Act.
1837	**Victoria,** died 1901.
	Natal founded by the Dutch.
1838	Formation of Anti-Corn-Law League.
	Lord Durham in Canada.
	The People's Charter adopted.
	Afghan War.
1839	Committee of Privy Council for Education.
	New postage scheme.
	Annexation of Aden.
	New Zealand permanently colonized.
	War with China.
1840	Constitution granted to Canada.
	Irish Municipal Act.
	Quadruple Alliance with France, Portugal, and Spain.
1841	Conference of London.
	Ministry of Sir Robert Peel.
	Hong-Kong ceded to England.
	New Zealand a separate Colony.
1842	Income-tax revived.
	Treaty of Washington.

1842	Treaty of Nanking.
	Massacre of English in Afghanistan.
1843	Annexation of Scinde.
1844	Trial of O'Connell.
	Natal declared British Colony.
	The Rochdale Pioneers.
1845	Sikh War.
	Irish potato crop fails.
	Manchester Anti-Corn-Law Meeting.
1846	Repeal of the Corn Laws.
	Ministry of Lord John Russell.
1847	Famine in Ireland.
	Coercion Bill for Ireland.
	Cape Colony refuses to admit convicts.
1848	Suppression of the Chartists.
	Treason Felony Act for Ireland.
	Habeas Corpus Act suspended in Ireland.
	First Public Health Act.
1849	Irish Encumbered Estates Act.
	Piræus blockaded by British Fleet.
	Annexation of the Punjab.
	Gold discoveries in Australia and California.
1850	Don Pacifico Debate.
	Australian Colonies Bill passed.
1851	Lord Palmerston's dismissal.
1852	Militia Bill in alarm of Napoleon III.
	Ministry of Lord Derby, *Feb.*
	Death of the Duke of Wellington.
	Ministry of Lord Aberdeen, *Dec.*
	Sand River Convention.
	Constitutions for New Zealand Colonies.
1853	Gladstone's first Budget.
	British Kaffraria annexed.
1854	First Cape Parliament.
	Ultimatum to Russia, *Feb.*
	Siege of Sebastopol begins, *Oct.* 17.
	Corrupt Practices Act carried.
1855	Ministry of Lord Palmerston.
	Capture of Sebastopol, *Sept.* 8.
	Surrender of Kars, *Nov.*
1856	Peace of Paris, *March* 30.
	Annexation of Oudh.
	Second Chinese War.
1857	Indian Mutiny.
	Capture of Canton.
1858	Second Ministry of Lord Derby, *Feb.*
	Atlantic Cable laid.
	War with China resumed.
	Treaty of Tientsin.
	Property qualification for Parliament abolished.
	Queen proclaimed Sovereign of India.
1859	Second Ministry of Lord Palmerston.
	Support of Italian independence.
	Volunteer Movement.
	Queensland a separate Colony.

1860 Commercial Treaty of France and England.
Paper Duty Bill rejected by the Lords.
Burning of Peking Palace.

1861 Post Office Savings Banks.
Commissioners seized on the *Trent*.
Death of the Prince Consort, *Dec.*

1862 The *Alabama* leaves the Mersey.
Committee of Public Accounts.

1863 Ionian Islands ceded to Greece.

1864 Intervention refused in Schleswig-Holstein.

1865 Ministry of Lord John Russell.
Gladstone's Reform Bill.

1866 Habeas Corpus Act suspended in Ireland.
Third Ministry of Lord Derby, *June.*
Reform Demonstrations; Hyde Park Riots.

1867 Second Reform Act.
British North America Act creates Dominion of Canada.

1868 Ministry of Disraeli, *Feb.*
Abyssinian Expedition; Magdala taken.
Election Petitions transferred to the Judges.
Irish Reform Bill passed.
Scotch Reform Bill.
Ministry of Gladstone, *Dec.*

1869 Disestablishment of Church of Ireland.
Opening of the Suez Canal.

1870 Irish Land Act, *Feb.*
Elementary Education Bill, *Feb.*
Peace Preservation Act, Ireland.
Civil Service open to Competition.
Army Reforms.
Treaty with France and Germany for neutrality of Belgium.
Home Rule League founded in Ireland.

1871 Conference of London.
Abolition of Religious Tests in Universities.
Treaty of Washington.
Army Purchase abolished.
Local Government Board established.

1872 Ballot Bill passed.
Geneva Arbitration on *Alabama.*
Self-government in Cape Colony.
Unions of agricultural labourers.

1873 British Residents appointed to Malay States.
Supreme Court of Judicature Act.
Religious Tests for Dublin University abolished.

1874 Second Ministry of Disraeli, *Feb.*
War with Ashanti.
First labour member elected.

1875 Marquis of Hartington Liberal Leader.

1875 Artisans' Dwellings Act.
Peace Preservation Act in Ireland.
Trade Union legislation.
Purchase of Shares in Suez Canal.
Indian Tour of Prince of Wales, *Oct.*
Andrássy Note submitted to the Powers.
Central Government established for New Zealand.
Fiji Islands annexed.

1876 The Berlin Note refused by England.
British Fleet in Besika Bay, *May.*
Gladstone's campaign on Bulgarian Atrocities.
Disraeli created Earl of Beaconsfield.
The new imperialism.
Conference at Constantinople.

1877 The Queen proclaimed Empress of India.
Gordon Governor-General of the Sudan.
The Protocol of London.
Permissive Federation Act for South Africa.
Transvaal annexed, *April.*
Chamberlain and the caucus.
Parnell opens obstruction in Parliament.

1878 Fleet ordered to Constantinople, *Jan.*
Treaty of San Stefano, *March.*
Indian troops ordered to Malta.
Beaconsfield's secret Treaty with Russia, *May* 30.
Beaconsfield's secret Treaty with Turkey, *June* 6.
Congress of Berlin, *June* 13.

1879 Zulu War; Isandhlwana and Rorke's Drift, *Jan.*
Invasion of Afghanistan.
Irish Land League formed by Davitt.
The Midlothian campaign.

1880 Ministry of Gladstone, *April.*
Bill to allow arrest on Suspicion in Ireland.
Bradlaugh refused leave to affirm allegiance.
Burials Bill granting relief to Nonconformists.
Ground Game Act to protect farmers.
Employers' Liability Act.
Prosecution of Parnell.
Afghan War.
Boer Revolt in the Transvaal, *Dec.*

1881 New Rules of Procedure.
Death of Lord Beaconsfield.
Second Irish Land Bill.
Parnell imprisoned.
Boer War.

1882 Murder of Lord F. Cavendish and Mr. Burke.
Prevention of Crimes Bill.

1882 British Fleet at Alexandria, *June.*
Battle of Tel-el-Kebir, *Aug.*
Afrikander Bond in Cape Colony.
Gladstone's Rules of Procedure.
Triple Alliance formed.

1883 Corrupt Practices Bill.
Agricultural Holdings Bill.
Defeat of Hicks Pasha in the Sudan.

1884 General Gordon sent to Khartum, *Jan.*
Third Reform Bill carried.
Convention of London with the Transvaal.
Conference of Berlin.
Great Boer treks in South Africa.
German and British annexations in New Guinea.

1885 Fall of Khartum; Sudan evacuated.
Russian forces occupy Pendjeh.
Redistribution Bill.
Ministry of Lord Salisbury, *June.*
Upper Burmah annexed, *Nov.*
Canadian Pacific Railway completed.
Annexation of South Bechuanaland.

1886 Bradlaugh admitted to Parliament, *Jan.*
Third Ministry of Gladstone, *Feb.*
Home Rule Bill lost, *June.*
Ministry of Lord Salisbury, *July.*
Gold rush to the Transvaal.

1887 New Rules of Procedure.
Crimes Act, Ireland.
Land Act, Ireland, *Aug.*
First Colonial Conference.
Great Britain and France in New Hebrides.

1888 New Rules of Procedure in the House of Commons.
Local Government Act.
Irish Land Purchase Bill.
Part of New Guinea annexed.

1889 End of Parnell Commission.

1890 Death of Parnell.
Congested Districts Board, Ireland.
Heligoland ceded to Germany.
Protectorate of Zanzibar.

1891 Royal Commission on labour conditions.
Balfour's Land Purchase Act.
Factory and Workshops Act.
Free elementary education.

1892 Fourth Ministry of Gladstone, *Aug.*

1893 Second Home Rule Bill rejected by Lords.
Matabele War.
Responsible government in Natal.

1894 Parish Councils Bill.
Ministry of Lord Rosebery, *March.*
Protectorate of Uganda.
Election expenses paid.

1894 Treaty with Japan.
Harcourt's Death Duties Budget.

1895 Ministry of Lord Salisbury, *June.*
Jameson Raid, *Dec.*
Chitral occupied.

1896 Franco-British Treaty on Siam.
Dongola occupied.
The five admirals occupy Crete.
Employers' Liability Act.
New Rules of Procedure.
Gladstone's campaign on Armenian Massacres.

1897 Second Colonial Conference.
Workmen's Compensation Bill, *July.*

1898 Lease of Wei-hai-wei, *April.*
Occupation of Omdurman and the Sudan.
The Fashoda dispute.

1899 Irish Local Government Act.
Peace Conference at the Hague.
Second Boer War.
Khartum taken by Kitchener.

1900 Boer Republics annexed.
Australian Commonwealth Act.
Protectorate of Lagos and Nigeria.
European forces in Peking, *Aug.*

1901 **Edward the Seventh,** died 1910.

1902 Anglo-Japanese Alliance.
Ministry of Mr. Balfour.
Peace of Vereeniging.

1903 Chamberlain's resignation.
Irish Land Purchase Act.

1904 Treaty of London with France.

1905 Premier given official status.
Tariff reform agitation.
March to Lhassa.
Ministry of Campbell-Bannerman.

1906 Self-government given to the Transvaal.
Trades Disputes Act.
Algeciras Conference.

1907 Dominion of New Zealand established.
South African Customs Union.
Second Hague Conference.
Resolution limiting veto of Lords.

1908 Ministry of Mr. Asquith.

1909 Old-Age Pensions Act.
Budget rejected by the Lords.
South African Constitution, *Sept.*

1910 **George the Fifth.**

1911 Parliament Act.
Renewal of Japanese Alliance.
Declaration of London.
The *Panther* at Agadir.
National Insurance Act.

1912 Legal Minimum Wage for Coal-miners.

1913 Welsh Disestablishment Act.

1914 Declaration of War, *Aug.* 4.
Home Rule Act.

GENEALOGICAL TABLES.

KINGS OF THE HOUSE OF CERDIC, FROM ECGBERHT.

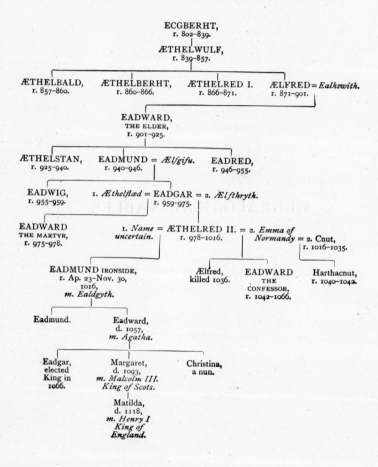

ECGBERHT,
r. 802–839.

ÆTHELWULF,
r. 839–857.

ÆTHELBALD,   ÆTHELBERHT,   ÆTHELRED I.   ÆLFRED = *Ealhswith.*
r. 857–860.   r. 860–866.   r. 866–871.   r. 871–901.

EADWARD,
THE ELDER,
r. 901–925.

ÆTHELSTAN,   EADMUND = *Ælfgifu.*   EADRED,
r. 925–940.   r. 940–946.   r. 946–955.

EADWIG,   1. *Æthelflæd* = EADGAR = 2. *Ælfthryth.*
r. 955–959.   r. 959–975.

EADWARD   1. *Name* = ÆTHELRED II. = 2. *Emma of*
THE MARTYR,   *uncertain.*   r. 978–1016.   *Normandy* = 2. Cnut,
r. 975–978.   r. 1016–1035.

EADMUND IRONSIDE,   Ælfred,   EADWARD   Harthacnut,
r. Ap. 23–Nov. 30,   killed 1036.   THE   r. 1040–1042.
1016,   CONFESSOR,
m. Ealdgyth.   r. 1042–1066.

Eadmund.   Eadward,
d. 1057,
m. Agatha.

Eadgar,   Margaret,   Christina,
elected   d. 1093,   a nun.
King in   *m. Malcolm III.*
1066.   *King of Scots.*

Matilda,
d. 1118,
m. Henry I
King of
England.

THE DANISH KINGS.

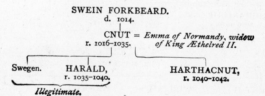

SWEIN FORKBEARD.
d. 1014.

CNUT = *Emma of Normandy, widow*
r. 1016–1035.   *of King Æthelred II.*

Swegen.   HARALD,   HARTHACNUT,
r. 1035–1040.   r. 1040–1042.

Illegitimate.

DUKES OF THE NORMANS.

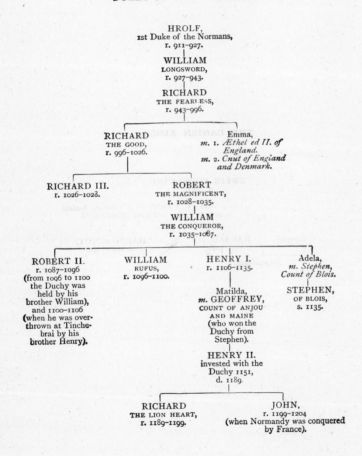

HROLF,
1st Duke of the Normans,
r. 911–927.

WILLIAM
LONGSWORD,
r. 927–943.

RICHARD
THE FEARLESS,
r. 943–996.

RICHARD
THE GOOD,
r. 996–1026.

Emma,
m. 1. *Æthel ed II. of
England.*
m. 2. *Cnut of England
and Denmark.*

RICHARD III.
r. 1026–1028.

ROBERT
THE MAGNIFICENT,
r. 1028–1035.

WILLIAM
THE CONQUEROR,
r. 1035–1087.

ROBERT II.
r. 1087–1096
(from 1096 to 1100
the Duchy was
held by his
brother William),
and 1100–1106
(when he was over-
thrown at Tinche-
brai by his
brother Henry).

WILLIAM
RUFUS,
r. 1096–1100.

HENRY I.
r. 1106–1135.

Adela,
*m. Stephen,
Count of Blois.*

Matilda,
m. GEOFFREY,
COUNT OF ANJOU
AND MAINE
(who won the
Duchy from
Stephen).

STEPHEN,
OF BLOIS,
s. 1135.

HENRY II.
invested with the
Duchy 1151,
d. 1189.

RICHARD
THE LION HEART,
r. 1189–1199.

JOHN,
r. 1199–1204
(when Normandy was conquered
by France).

Claim of EDWARD III. to the French Crown.

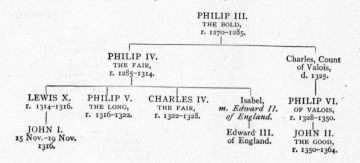

Descent of HENRY IV.

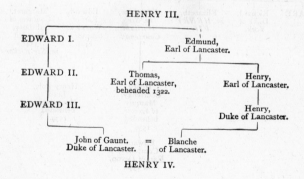

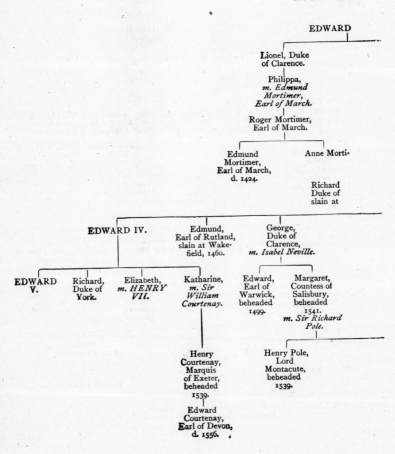

HOUSE OF

EDWARD

Lionel, Duke
of Clarence.

Philippa,
*m. Edmund
Mortimer,
Earl of March.*

Roger Mortimer,
Earl of March.

Edmund   Anne Morti-
Mortimer,
Earl of March,
d. 1424.

Richard
Duke of
slain at

EDWARD IV.   Edmund,   George,
                  Earl of Rutland,   Duke of
                  slain at Wake-   Clarence,
                  field, 1460.   *m. Isabel Neville.*

EDWARD   Richard,   Elizabeth,   Katharine,   Edward,   Margaret,
V.   Duke of   *m. HENRY*   *m. Sir*   Earl of   Countess of
          York.   *VII.*   *William*   Warwick,   Salisbury,
                                   Courtenay. beheaded   beheaded
                                                 1499.   1541.
                                                              *m. Sir Richard
                                                              Pole.*

                                   Henry   Henry Pole,
                                   Courtenay,   Lord
                                   Marquis   Montacute,
                                   of Exeter,   beheaded
                                   beheaded   1539.
                                   1539.

                                   Edward
                                   Courtenay,
                                   Earl of Devon,
                                   d. 1556.

YORK

III.

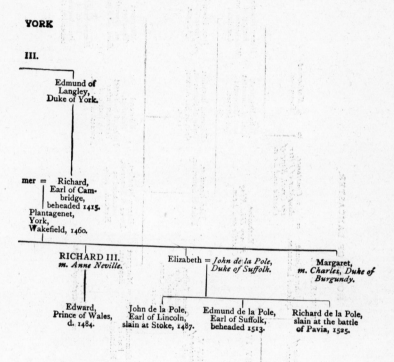

Edmund of
Langley,
Duke of York.

mer = Richard,
Earl of Cam-
bridge,
beheaded 1415.

Plantagenet,
York,
Wakefield, 1460.

RICHARD III.
m. Anne Neville.

Elizabeth = *John de la Pole,*
Duke of Suffolk.

Margaret,
m. Charles, Duke of
Burgundy.

Edward,
Prince of Wales,
d. 1484.

John de la Pole,
Earl of Lincoln,
slain at Stoke, 1487.

Edmund de la Pole,
Earl of Suffolk,
beheaded 1513.

Richard de la Pole,
slain at the battle
of Pavia, 1525.

Reginald Pole,
Archbishop of
Canterbury,
and Cardinal,
d. 1558.

HOUSE OF LANCASTER.

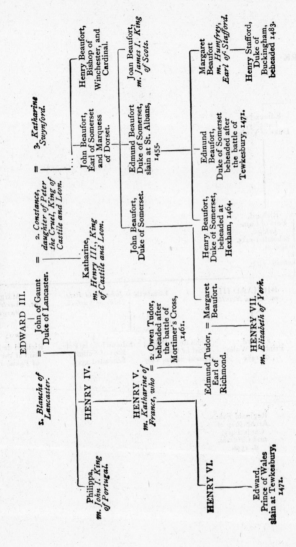

DESCENDANTS OF THE DAUGHTERS OF HENRY VII.

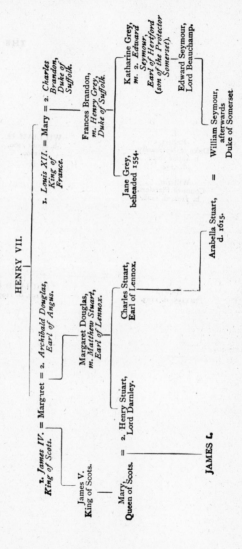

HENRY VII.

1. *James IV.* = Margaret = 2. *Archibald Douglas,*
King of Scots.   *Earl of Angus.*

1. *Louis XII.* = Mary = 2. *Charles*
King of   *Brandon,*
France.   *Duke of*
                             Suffolk.

James V.
King of Scots.

Margaret Douglas,
m. Matthew Stuart,
Earl of Lennox.

Frances Brandon,
m. Henry Grey,
Duke of Suffolk.

Mary, = 2. Henry Stuart,
Queen of Scots.   Lord Darnley.

Charles Stuart,
Earl of Lennox.

Jane Grey,
beheaded 1554.

Katharine Grey,
m. 2. *Edward*
Seymour,
Earl of Hertford
(son of the Protector
Somerset).

Edward Seymour,
Lord Beauchamp.

JAMES I.

Arabella Stuart,
d. 1615.

=   William Seymour,
     afterwards
     Duke of Somerset.

THE SOVEREIGNS

Since the

WILLIAM I.
m. Matilda

|

Robert,   WILLIAM II.
Duke of Normandy,   b. about 1060,
b. about 1056,   d. 1100.
d. 1134.

William,
Count of Flanders,
b. 1101, d. 1128.

|

Henry,   RICHARD I.
b. 1155, d. 1183.   b. 1157, d. 1199.

OF ENGLAND.

Norman Conquest.

b. about 1027, d. 1087.
of Flanders.

HENRY I. b. 1068, d. 1135. *m.* 1. *Matilda of* *Scotland.*	**Adela,** d. 1137. *m. Stephen,* *Count of* *Blois.*
Matilda, d. 1167, *m.* 2. *Geoffrey,* *Count of* *Anjou.*	**STEPHEN,** d. 1154. *m. Matilda* *of Boulogne.*

HENRY II.
b. 1133, d. 1189.
m. Eleanor of
Aquitaine.

Eustace, Count of Boulogne, d. 1153.	William, Count of Boulogne, d. 1160.

Geoffrey, b. 1158, d. 1186. *m. Constance,* *heiress of* *Brittany.*	**JOHN,** b. 1166, d. 1216. *m.* 2. *Isabel of* *Angoulême.*
Arthur, Duke of Brittany, b. 1187.	**HENRY III.** b. 1206, d. 1272. *m. Eleanor of* *Provence.*
	EDWARD I. b. 1239, d. 1307. *m.* 1. *Eleanor* *of Castile.*
	EDWARD II. b. 1284. murdered 1327. *m. Isabel of* *France.*
	EDWARD III. b. 1312, d. 1377. *m. Philippa of* *Hainault.*

[See next page.]

THE SOVEREIGNS

EDWARD

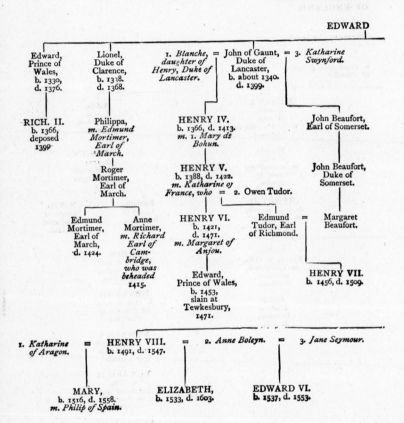

| Edward, Prince of Wales, b. 1330, d. 1376. | Lionel, Duke of Clarence, b. 1338. d. 1368. | *1. Blanche, daughter of Henry, Duke of Lancaster.* = | John of Gaunt, Duke of Lancaster, b. about 1340. d. 1399. | = *3. Katharine Swynford.* |

RICH. II.
b. 1366,
deposed
1399

Philippa,
*m. Edmund
Mortimer,
Earl of
March.*

HENRY IV.
b. 1366, d. 1413.
*m. 1. Mary de
Bohun.*

John Beaufort,
Earl of Somerset.

Roger
Mortimer,
Earl of
March.

HENRY V.
b. 1388, d. 1422.
*m. Katharine of
France, who* = 2. Owen Tudor.

John Beaufort,
Duke of
Somerset.

Edmund
Mortimer,
Earl of
March,
d. 1424.

Anne
Mortimer,
*m. Richard
Earl of
Cam-
bridge,
who was
beheaded
1415.*

HENRY VI.
b. 1421,
d. 1471.
*m. Margaret of
Anjou.*

Edmund
Tudor, Earl
of Richmond.

=

Margaret
Beaufort.

Edward,
Prince of Wales,
b. 1453,
slain at
Tewkesbury,
1471.

HENRY VII.
b. 1456, d. 1509.

| *1. Katharine of Aragon.* = | HENRY VIII. b. 1491, d. 1547. | = *2. Anne Boleyn.* = | *3. Jane Seymour.* |

MARY,
b. 1516, d. 1558.
m. Philip of Spain.

ELIZABETH,
b. 1533, d. 1603.

EDWARD VI.
b. 1537, d. 1553.

OF ENGLAND—continued.

III.

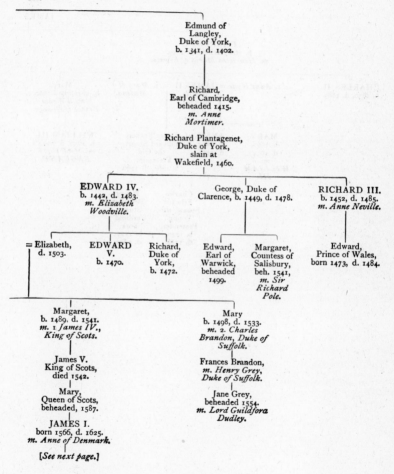

Edmund of
Langley,
Duke of York,
b. 1341, d. 1402.

Richard,
Earl of Cambridge,
beheaded 1415.
*m. Anne
Mortimer.*

Richard Plantagenet,
Duke of York,
slain at
Wakefield, 1460.

EDWARD IV.
b. 1442, d. 1483.
*m. Elizabeth
Woodville.*

George, Duke of
Clarence, b. 1449, d. 1478.

RICHARD III.
b. 1452, d. 1485.
m. Anne Neville.

= Elizabeth,
d. 1503.

EDWARD
V.
b. 1470.

Richard,
Duke of
York,
b. 1472.

Edward,
Earl of
Warwick,
beheaded
1499.

Margaret,
Countess of
Salisbury,
beh. 1541,
*m. Sir
Richard
Pole.*

Edward,
Prince of Wales,
born 1473, d. 1484.

Margaret,
b. 1489, d. 1541.
*m. 1 James IV.,
King of Scots.*

James V.
King of Scots,
died 1542.

Mary,
Queen of Scots,
beheaded, 1587.

JAMES I.
born 1566, d. 1625.
m. Anne of Denmark.

[See next page.]

Mary
b. 1498, d. 1533.
*m. 2. Charles
Brandon, Duke of
Suffolk.*

Frances Brandon,
*m. Henry Grey,
Duke of Suffolk.*

Jane Grey,
beheaded 1554.
*m. Lord Guildford
Dudley.*

THE SOVEREIGNS

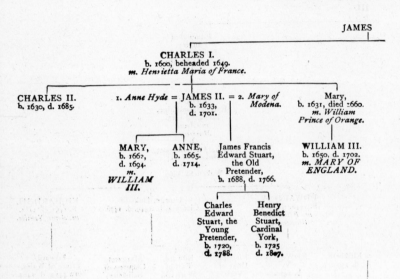

JAMES

CHARLES I.
b. 1600, beheaded 1649.
m. Henrietta Maria of France.

CHARLES II.
b. 1630, d. 1685.

1. *Anne Hyde* = JAMES II. = 2. *Mary of Modena.*
b. 1633,
d. 1701.

Mary,
b. 1631, died 1660.
*m. William
Prince of Orange.*

MARY,
b. 166?,
d. 1694.
*m.
WILLIAM
III.*

ANNE,
b. 1665.
d. 1714.

James Francis
Edward Stuart,
the Old
Pretender,
b. 1688, d. 1766.

WILLIAM III.
b. 1650, d. 1702.
*m. MARY OF
ENGLAND.*

Charles
Edward
Stuart, the
Young
Pretender,
b. 1720,
d. 1788.

Henry
Benedict
Stuart,
Cardinal
York,
b. 1725
d. 1807.

OF ENGLAND—continued.

I.

Elizabeth,
b. 1596, d. 1662.
*m. Frederick,
Elector Palatine.*

Sophia,
d. 1714.
*m. Ernest Augustus,
Elector of Hanover.*

GEORGE I.
b. 1660, d. 1727.
*m. Sophia Dorothea
of Zell.*

GEORGE II.
b. 1683, d. 1760.
*m. Caroline of
Brandenburg-
Anspach.*

Frederick,
Prince of Wales,
b. 1707, d. 1751.

GEORGE III.
b. 1738, d. 1820.
*m. Charlotte of
Mecklenburg-
Strelitz.*

| GEORGE IV.
b. 1762, d. 1830.
*m. Caroline of
Brunswick-
Wolfenbüttel.*] | WILLIAM IV.
b. 1765, d. 1837. | Edward,
Duke of Kent,
b. 1767, d. 1820. | Ernest Augustus,
King of Hanover.
b. 1771, d. 1851. |

Charlotte,
b. 1796, d. 1817.

VICTORIA,
b. 1819, d. 1901.
*m. Prince Albert of
Saxe-Coburg and Gotha.*

EDWARD VII.
b. 1841, d. 1910.
*m. Alexandra Caroline
of Denmark.*

GEORGE V.
b. 1865.
*m. Victoria Mary
of Teck.*

A SHORT HISTORY

OF

THE ENGLISH PEOPLE.

CHAPTER I.

THE ENGLISH KINGDOMS, 607—1013.

Section I.—Britain and the English.

[*Authorities.*—For the constitution and settlement of the English, see Kemble's "Saxons in England" and especially the "Constitutional History of England" by Dr. Stubbs. Sir Francis Palgrave's History of the English Commonwealth is valuable, but to be used with care. A vigorous and accurate sketch of the early constitution may be found in Mr. Freeman's History of the Norman Conquest, vol. i. See also "The Making of England" and "The Conquest of England" by J. R. Green.]

FOR the fatherland of the English race we must look far away from England itself. In the fifth century after the birth of Christ, the one country which we know to have borne the name of Angeln or the Engleland lay in the district which we now call Sleswick, a district in the heart of the peninsula which parts the Baltic from the northern seas. Its pleasant pastures, its black-timbered homesteads, its prim little townships looking down on inlets of purple water, were then but a wild waste of heather and sand, girt along the coast with sunless woodland, broken here and there by meadows which crept down to the marshes and the sea. The dwellers in this district, however, seem to have been merely an outlying fragment of what was called the Engle or English folk, the bulk of whom lay probably along the middle Elbe and on the Weser. To the north of the English in their Sleswick home lay another kindred tribe, the Jutes, whose name is still preserved in their district of Jutland. To the south of them

Old England

B

a number of German tribes had drawn together in their home-land between the Elbe and the Ems, and in a wide tract across the Ems to the Rhine, into the people of the Saxons. Engle, Saxon, and Jute all belonged to the same Low German branch of the Teutonic family; and at the moment when history discovers them, they were being drawn together by the ties of a common blood, common speech, common social and political institutions. Each of them was destined to share in the conquest of the land in which we live; and it is from the union of all of them when its conquest was complete that the English people has sprung.

The
English
People

Of the temper and life of the folk in this older England we know little. But, from the glimpses which we catch of them when conquest had brought them to the shores of Britain, their political and social organization must have been that of the German race to which they belonged. The basis of their society was the free man. He alone was known as "the man," or "the churl;" and two phrases set his freedom vividly before us. He was "the free-necked man," whose long hair floated over a neck that had never bent to a lord. He was "the weaponed man," who alone bore spear and sword, for he alone possessed the right which in such a state of society formed the main check upon lawless outrage, the right of private war. Among the English, as among all the races of mankind, justice had originally sprung from each man's personal action. There had been a time when every freeman was his own avenger. But even in the earliest forms of English society of which we catch traces this right of self-defence was being modified and restricted by a growing sense of public justice. The "blood-wite," or compensation in money for personal wrong, was the first effort of the tribe as a whole to regulate private revenge. The freeman's life and the freeman's limb had each on this system its legal price. "Eye for eye," ran the rough customary code, and "limb for limb," or for each fair damages. We see a further step towards the recognition of a wrong as done not to the individual man, but to the people at large, in another custom of early date. The price of life or limb was paid, not by the wrong-doer to the man he wronged, but by the family or house of the wrong-doer to the family or house of the wronged. Order and law were thus made to rest in each little group of English people upon the blood-bond which knit its families together; every outrage was held to have been done by all who were linked by blood to the doer of it, every crime to have been done against all who were linked by blood to the sufferer from it. From this sense of the value of the family bond, as a means of restraining the wrong-doer by forces which the tribe as a whole did not as yet possess, sprang the first rude forms of English justice. Each kinsman was his kinsman's keeper, bound to protect him from wrong, to hinder him from wrong-doing, and to suffer with and pay for him, if wrong

Sec. I.

Britain
and the
English

The
English
Society

were done. So fully was this principle recognized that, even if any man was charged before his fellow-tribesmen with crime, his kinsfolk still remained in fact his sole judges; for it was by their solemn oath of his innocence or his guilt that he had to stand or fall.

The blood-bond gave both its military and social form to Old English society. Kinsmen fought side by side in the hour of battle, and the feelings of honour and discipline which held the host together were drawn from the common duty of every man in each little group of warriors to his house. And as they fought side by side on the field, so they dwelled side by side on the soil. Harling abode by Harling, and Billing by Billing; and each "wick" or "ham" or "stead" or "tun" took its name from the kinsmen who dwelt together in it. The home or "ham" of the Billings would be Billingham, and the "tun" or township of the Harlings would be Harlington. But in such settlements, the tie of blood was widened into the larger tie of land. Land with the German race seems at a very early time to have become the accompaniment of full freedom. The freeman was strictly the freeholder, and the exercise of his full rights as a free member of the community to which he belonged was inseparable from the possession of his "holding." The landless man ceased for all practical purposes to be free, though he was no man's slave. In the very earliest glimpse we get of the German race we see them a race of land-holders and land-tillers. Tacitus, the first Roman who sought to know these destined conquerors of Rome, describes them as pasturing on the forest glades around their villages, and ploughing their village fields. A feature which at once struck him as parting them from the civilized world to which he himself belonged, was their hatred of cities, and their love even within their little settlements of a jealous independence. "They live apart," he says, "each by himself, as woodside, plain, or fresh spring attracts him." And as each dweller within the settlement was jealous of his own isolation and independence among his fellow settlers, so each settlement was jealous of its independence among its fellow settlements. Of the character of their life in this early world, however, we know little save what may be gathered from the indications of a later time. Each little farmer commonwealth was girt in by its own border or "mark," a belt of forest or waste or fen which parted it from its fellow villages, a ring of common ground which none of its settlers might take for his own, but which sometimes served as a death-ground where criminals met their doom, and was held to be the special dwelling-place of the nixie and the will-o'-the-wisp. If a stranger came through this wood, or over this waste, custom bade him blow his horn as he came, for if he stole through secretly he was taken for a foe, and any man might lawfully slay him. Inside this boundary the "township," as the village was then called from the "tun" or rough fence and trench that served as its simple fortification, formed a ready-made fortress in war, while in peace its entrenchments were serviceable in the feuds of village with village, or house with house. Within the village we find from the first a marked social difference between two orders of its indwellers. The bulk of its homesteads were those of its freemen or "ceorls;" but amongst these were the larger homes of "eorls," or men distinguished among their fellows by noble blood, who were held in an hereditary reverence, and from whom the leaders of the village were chosen in war time, or rulers in time of peace. But the choice was a purely voluntary one, and the man of noble blood enjoyed no legal privilege among his fellows. The holdings of the freemen clustered round a moot-hill or sacred tree where the community met from time to time to order its own industry and to frame its own laws. Here plough-land and meadow-land were shared in due lot among the villagers, and field and homestead passed from man to man. Here strife of farmer with farmer was settled according to the "customs" of the township as its "elder men" stated them, and the wrong-doer was judged and his fine assessed by the kinsfolk; and here men were chosen to follow headman or ealdorman to hundred court or war. It is with a reverence such as is stirred by the sight of the head-waters of some mighty river that one looks back to these tiny moots, where the men of the village met to order the village life and the village industry, as their descendants, the men of a later England, meet in Parliament at Westminster, to frame laws and do justice for the great empire which has sprung from this little body of farmer-commonwealths in Sleswick.

The religion of the English was the same as that of the whole German family. Christianity, which had by this time brought about the conversion of the Roman Empire, had not penetrated as yet among the forests of the North. Our own names for the days of the week still recall to us the gods whom our fathers worshipped. Wednesday is the day of Woden, the war-god, the guardian of ways and boundaries, the inventor of letters, the common god of the whole conquering people, whom every tribe held to be the first ancestor of its kings. Thursday is the day of Thunder, or, as the Northmen called him, Thor, the god of air and storm and rain; as Friday is Frea's-day, the god of peace and joy and fruitfulness, whose emblems, borne aloft by dancing maidens, brought increase to every field and stall they visited. Saturday may commemorate an obscure god Sætere; Tuesday the dark god, Tiw, to meet whom was death. Behind these floated dim shapes of an older mythology; Eostre, the goddess of the dawn, or of the spring, who lends her name to the Christian festival of the Resurrection; "Wyrd," the death-goddess, whose memory lingered long in the "weird" of northern superstition; or the Shield-Maidens, the "mighty women" who, an old rime tells us, "wrought on the battle-field their toil, and hurled the thrilling javelins." Nearer to the popular fancy lay deities of wood and fell, or the hero-gods of legend and song; "Nicor," the water-sprite, who gave us our water-nixies and "Old Nick"; "Weland," the forger of mighty shields and sharp-biting swords, whose memory lingers in the stories of "Weyland's Smithy" in Berkshire; while the name of Ailesbury may preserve the last trace of the legend of Weland's brother, the sun-archer Ægil. But it is only in broken fragments that this mass of early faith and early poetry still lives for us, in a name, in the grey stones of a cairn, or in snatches of our older song: and the faint traces of worship or of priesthood which we find in later history show how lightly it clung to the national life.

Britain

From Sleswick and the shores of the Northern Sea we must pass, before opening our story, to a land which, dear as it is now to Englishmen, had not as yet been trodden by English feet. The island of Britain had for nearly four hundred years been a province of the Empire. A descent of Julius Cæsar revealed it (B.C. 55) to the Roman world, but nearly a century elapsed before the Emperor Claudius attempted its definite conquest. The victories of Julius Agricola (A.D. 78—84) carried the Roman frontier to the Firths of Forth and of Clyde, and the work of Roman civilization followed hard upon the Roman sword. Population was grouped in cities such as York or Lincoln, cities governed by their own municipal officers, guarded by massive walls, and linked together by a network of roads, which extended from one end of the island to the other. Commerce sprang up in ports like that of London; agriculture flourished till Britain was able at need to supply the necessities of Gaul; its mineral resources were explored in the tin mines of Cornwall, the lead mines of Somerset and Northumberland, and the iron mines of the Forest of Dean. The wealth of the island grew fast during centuries of unbroken peace, but the evils which were slowly sapping the strength of the Roman Empire at large must have told heavily on the real wealth of the province of Britain. Here, as in Italy or Gaul, the population probably declined as the estates of the landed proprietors grew larger, and the cultivators sank into serfs whose cabins clustered round the luxurious villas of their lords. The mines, if worked by forced labour, must have been a source of endless oppression. Town and country were alike crushed by heavy taxation, while industry was fettered by laws that turned every trade into an hereditary caste. Above all, the purely despotic system of the Roman Government, by crushing all local independence, crushed all local vigour. Men forgot how to fight for their country when they forgot how to govern it.

Such causes of decay were common to every province of the Empire; but there were others that sprang from the peculiar circumstances of Britain itself. The island was weakened by a disunion within, which arose from the partial character of its civilization. It was only in the towns that the conquered Britons became entirely Romanized. Over large tracts of country the rural Britons seemed to have remained apart, speaking their own tongue, owning some traditional allegiance to their native chiefs, and even retaining their native laws. The use of the Roman language may be taken as marking the progress of Roman civilization, and though Latin had wholly superseded the language of the conquered peoples in Spain or Gaul, its use seems to have been confined in Britain to the townsfolk and the wealthier landowners without the towns. The dangers that sprang from such a severance between the two elements of the population must have been stirred into active life by the danger which threatened Britain from the North. The Picts who had been sheltered from Roman conquest by the fastnesses of the Highlands were roused in their turn to attack by the weakness of the province and the hope of plunder. Their invasions penetrated to the heart of the island. Raids so extensive could hardly have been effected without help from within, and the dim history of the time allows us to see not merely an increase of disunion between the Romanized and un-Romanized population of Britain, but even an alliance between the last and their free kinsfolk, the Picts. The struggles of Britain, however, lingered on till dangers nearer home forced the Empire to recall its legions and leave the province to itself. Ever since the birth of Christ the countries which lay round the Mediterranean Sea, and which then comprehended the whole of the civilized world, had rested in peace beneath the rule of Rome. During four hundred years its frontier had held at bay the barbarian world without—the Parthian of the Euphrates, the Numidian of the African desert, the German of the Danube or the Rhine. It was this mass of savage barbarism that at last broke in on the Empire as it sank into decay. In the western dominions of Rome the triumph of the invaders was complete. The Franks conquered and colonized Gaul. The West-Goths conquered and colonized Spain. The Vandals founded a kingdom in Africa. The Burgundians encamped in the border-land between Italy and the Rhone. The East-Goths ruled at last in Italy itself. And now that the fated hour was come, the Saxon and the Engle too closed upon their prey.

It was to defend Italy against the Goths that Rome in 410 recalled her legions from Britain. The province, thus left unaided, seems to have fought bravely against its assailants, and once at least to have driven back the Picts to their mountains in a rising of despair. But the threat of fresh inroads found Britain torn with civil quarrels which made a united resistance impossible, while its Pictish enemies strengthened themselves by a league with marauders from Ireland, (Scots as they were then called), whose pirate-boats were harrying the western coast of the island, and with a yet more formidable race of pirates who had long been pillaging along the British Channel. These were the English. We do not know whether it was the pressure of other tribes or the example of their German brethren who were now moving in a general attack on the Empire from their forest homes, or simply the barrenness of their coast, which drove the hunters, farmers, fishermen, of the English tribes to sea. But the daring spirit of their race already broke out in the secrecy and suddenness of their swoop, in the fierceness of their onset, in the careless glee with which they seized either sword or oar. "Foes are they," sang a Roman poet of the time, "fierce beyond other foes, and cunning as they are fierce ; the sea is their school of war, and the storm their friend ; they are sea-wolves that live on the pillage of the world." To meet the league of Pict, Scot, and Saxon by the forces of the province itself became impossible ; and the one course left was to imitate the fatal policy by which the Empire had invited its own doom while striving to avert it, the policy of matching barbarian against barbarian. The rulers of Britain resolved to break the league by detaching from it the free-booters who were harrying her eastern coast, and to use their new allies against the Pict. By the usual promises of land and pay, a band of warriors from Jutland were drawn for this purpose in 449 to the shores of Britain, with their chiefs, Hengest and Horsa, at their head.

Section II.—The English Conquest. 449—577.

[*Authorities for the Conquest of Britain.*—The only extant British account is that of the monk *Gildas*, diffuse and inflated, but valuable as the one authority for the state of the island at the time, and as giving, in the conclusion of his work, the native story of the conquest of Kent. I have examined his general character, and the objections to his authenticity, &c., in two papers in the *Saturday Review* for April 24 and May 8, 1869. The conquest of Kent is the only one of which we have any record from the side of the conquered. The English conquerors have left brief jottings of the conquest of Kent, Sussex, and Wessex, in the curious annals which form the opening of the compilation now known as the "English Chronicle." They are undoubtedly historic, though with a slight mythical intermixture. We possess no materials for the history of the English in their invasion of Mid-Britain or Mercia, and a fragment of the annals of Northumbria embodied in the later compilation which bears the name of Nennius alone throws light upon their actions in the North. Dr. Guest's papers in the "Origines Celticæ" are the best modern narratives of the conquest. The story has since been told by Mr. Green in "The Making of England.]

It is with the landing of Hengest and his war-band at Ebbsfleet on the shores of the Isle of Thanet that English history begins. No spot in Britain can be so sacred to Englishmen as that which first felt the tread of English feet. There is little indeed to catch the eye in Ebbsfleet itself, a mere lift of higher ground, with a few grey cottages dotted over it, cut off nowadays from the sea by a reclaimed meadow

SEC. II.

THE
ENGLISH
CONQUEST
449
TO
577

and a sea-wall. But taken as a whole, the scene has a wild beauty of its own. To the right the white curve of Ramsgate cliffs looks down on the crescent of Pegwell Bay ; far away to the left, across grey marsh-levels, where smoke-wreaths mark the sites of Richborough and Sandwich, the coast-line bends dimly to the fresh rise of cliffs beyond Deal. Everything in the character of the ground confirms the national tradition which fixed here the first landing-place of our English fathers, for great as the physical changes of the country have been since the fifth century, they have told little on its main features. It is easy to discover in the misty level of the present Minster marsh what was once a broad inlet of sea parting Thanet from the mainland of Britain, through which the pirate-boats of the first Englishmen came sailing with a fair wind to the little gravel-spit of Ebbsfleet ; and Richborough; a fortress whose broken ramparts still rise above the grey flats which have taken the place of this older sea-channel, was the common landing-place of travellers from Gaul. If the war-ships of the pirates therefore were cruising off the coast at the moment when the bargain with the Britons was concluded, their disembarkation at Ebbsfleet almost beneath the walls of Richborough would be natural enough. But the after-current of events serves to show that the choice of this landing-place was the result of a settled design. Between the Briton and his hireling soldiers there could be little trust. Quarters in Thanet would satisfy the followers of Hengest, who still lay in sight of their fellow-pirates in the Channel, and who felt themselves secured against the treachery which had so often proved fatal to the barbarian by the broad inlet which parted their camp from the mainland. Nor was the choice less satisfactory to the provincial, trembling—and, as the event proved, justly trembling—lest in his zeal against the Pict he had introduced an even fiercer foe into Britain. His dangerous allies were cooped up in a corner of the land, and parted from it by a sea-channel which was guarded by the strongest fortresses of the coast.

The need of such precautions was seen in the disputes which arose as soon as the work for which the mercenaries had been hired was done. The Picts were hardly scattered to the winds in a great battle when danger came from the Jutes themselves. Their numbers probably grew fast as the news of the settlement spread among the pirates in the Channel, and with the increase of their number must have grown the difficulty of supplying rations and pay. The dispute which rose over these questions was at last closed by Hengest's men with a threat of war. The threat, however, as we have seen, was no easy one to carry out. Right across their path in any attack upon Britain stretched the inlet of sea that parted Thanet from the mainland, a strait which was then traversable only at low water by a long and dangerous ford, and guarded at either mouth by the fortresses of Richborough and

Sec. II.

The
English
Conquest
449
to
577

Reculver. The channel of the Medway, with the forest of the Weald bending round it from the south, furnished another line of defence in the rear, while strongholds on the sites of our Canterbury and Rochester guarded the road to London ; and all around lay the soldiers placed at the command of the Count of the Saxon Shore, to hold the coast against the barbarian. Great however as these difficulties were, they failed to check the sudden onset of the Jutes. The inlet seems to have been crossed, the coast-road to London seized, before any force could be collected to oppose the English advance ; and it was only when they passed the Swale and looked to their right over the potteries whose refuse still strews the mudbanks of Upchurch, that their march seems to have swerved abruptly to the south. The guarded walls of Rochester probably forced them to turn southwards along the ridge of low hills which forms the eastern boundary of the Medway valley. Their way led them through a district full of memories of a past which had even then faded from the minds of men ; for the hill-slopes which they traversed were the grave-ground of a vanished race, and scattered among the boulders that strewed the ground rose the cromlechs and huge barrows of the dead. One mighty relic survives in the monument now called Kit's Coty House, which had been linked in old days by an avenue of huge stones to a burial-ground near Addington. It was from a steep knoll on which the grey weather-beaten stones of this monument are reared that the view of their first battle-field would break on the English warriors ; and a lane which still leads down from it through peaceful homesteads would guide them across the ford which has left its name in the little village of Aylesford. The Chronicle of the conquering people tells nothing of the rush that may have carried the ford, or of the fight that went struggling up through the village. It only tells that Horsa fell in the moment of victory ; and the flint-heap of Horsted, which has long preserved his name, and was held in after-time to mark his grave, is thus the earliest of those monuments of English valour of which Westminster is the last and noblest shrine.

The victory of Aylesford did more than give East Kent to the English ; it struck the key-note of the whole English conquest of Britain. The massacre which followed the battle indicated at once the merciless nature of the struggle which had begun. While the wealthier Kentish landowners fled in panic over sea, the poorer Britons took refuge in hill and forest till hunger drove them from their lurking-places to be cut down or enslaved by their conquerors. It was in vain that some sought shelter within the walls of their churches ; for the rage of the English seems to have burned fiercest against the clergy. The priests were slain at the altar, the churches fired, the peasants driven by the flames to fling themselves on a ring of pitiless steel. It is a picture such as this which distinguishes the conquest of Britain from that of

SEC. II.

THE
ENGLISH
CONQUEST
449
TO
577

the other provinces of Rome.   The conquest of Gaul by the Frank, or of Italy by the Lombard, proved little more than a forcible settlement of the one or the other among tributary subjects who were destined in a long course of ages to absorb their conquerors.   French is the tongue, not of the Frank, but of the Gaul whom he overcame ; and the fair hair of the Lombard is now all but unknown in Lombardy.   But the English conquest for a hundred and fifty years was a sheer dispossession and driving back of the people whom the English conquered.   In the world-wide struggle between Rome and the German invaders no land was so stubbornly fought for or so hardly won.   The conquest of Britain was indeed only partly wrought out after two centuries of bitter warfare.   But it was just through the long and merciless nature of the struggle that of all the German conquests this proved the most thorough and complete.   So far as the English sword in these earlier days reached, Britain became England, a land, that is, not of Britons, but of Englishmen.   It is possible that a few of the vanquished people may have lingered as slaves round the homesteads of their English conquerors, and a few of their household words (if these were not brought in at a later time) mingled oddly with the English tongue. But doubtful exceptions such as these leave the main facts untouched. When the steady progress of English conquest was stayed for a while by civil wars a century and a half after Aylesford, the Briton had disappeared from half of the land which had been his own, and the tongue, the religion, the laws of his English conqueror reigned without a rival from Essex to the Peak of Derbyshire and the mouth of the Severn, and from the British Channel to the Firth of Forth.

Aylesford, however, was but the first step in this career of conquest. How stubborn the contest was may be seen from the fact that it took sixty years to complete the conquest of Southern Britain alone.   It was twenty years before Kent itself was won.   After a second defeat at the passage of the Cray, the Britons "forsook Kent-land and fled with much fear to London ;" but the ground was soon won back again, and it was not until 465 that a series of petty conflicts made way for a decisive struggle at Wippedsfleet.   Here however the overthrow was so terrible that all hope of saving the bulk of Kent seems to have been abandoned, and it was only on its southern shore that the Britons held

their ground.   Eight years later the long contest was over, and with the fall of Lymne, whose broken walls look from the slope to which they cling over the great flat of Romney Marsh, the work of the first conqueror was done.   But the greed of plunder drew fresh war-bands from the German coast.   New invaders, drawn from among the Saxon tribes that lay between the Elbe and the Rhine, were seen in 477, only four years later, pushing slowly along the strip of land which lay westward of Kent between the Weald and the sea.   Nowhere has the physical aspect of the country been more utterly changed.   The vast

SEC. II.

THE
ENGLISH
CONQUEST
449
TO
577

sheet of scrub, woodland, and waste which then bore the name of the Andredsweald stretched for more than a hundred miles from the borders of Kent to the Hampshire Downs, extending northward almost to the Thames, and leaving only a thin strip of coast along its southern edge. This coast was guarded by a great fortress which occupied the spot now called Pevensey, the future landing-place of the Norman Conqueror. The fall of this fortress of Anderida in 491 established the kingdom of the South-Saxons; "Ælle and Cissa," ran the pitiless record of the conquerors, "beset Anderida, and slew all that were therein, nor was there afterwards one Briton left." Another tribe of Saxons was at the same time conquering on the other side of Kent, to the north of the estuary of the Thames, and had founded the settlement of the East-Saxons, as these warriors came to be called, in the valleys of the Colne and the Stour. To the northward of the Stour, the work of conquest was taken up by the third of the tribes whom we have seen dwelling in their German homeland, whose name was destined to absorb that of Saxon or Jute, and to stamp itself on the land they won. These were the Engle, or Englishmen. Their first descents seem to have fallen on the great district which was cut off from the rest of Britain by the Wash and the Fens and long reaches of forest, the later East Anglia, where the conquerors settled as the North-folk and the South-folk, names still preserved to us in the modern counties. With this settlement the first stage in the conquest was complete. By the close of the fifth century the whole coast of Britain, from the Wash to Southampton Water, was in the hands of the invaders. As yet, however, the enemy had touched little more than the coast; great masses of woodland or of fen still prisoned the Engle, the Saxon, and the Jute alike within narrow limits. But the sixth century can hardly have been long begun when each of the two peoples who had done the main work of conquest opened a fresh attack on the flanks of the tract they had won. On its northern flank the Engle appeared in the estuaries of the Forth and of the Humber. On its western flank, the Saxons appeared in the Southampton Water.

The true conquest of Southern Britain was reserved for a fresh band of Saxons, a tribe whose older name was that of the Gewissas, but who were to be more widely known as the West-Saxons. Landing westward of the strip of coast which had been won by the war-bands of Ælle, they struggled under Cerdic and Cynric up from Southampton Water in 495 to the great downs where Winchester offered so rich a prize. Five thousand Britons fell in a fight which opened the country to these invaders, and a fresh victory at Charford in 519 set the crown of the West-Saxons on the head of Cerdic. We know little of the incidents of these conquests; nor do we know why at this juncture they seem to have been suddenly interrupted. But it is certain that a

SEC. II.

THE
ENGLISH
CONQUEST
449
TO
577

552

568

583

victory of the Britons at Mount Badon in the year 520 checked the progress of the West-Saxons, and was followed by a long pause in their advance; for thirty years the great belt of woodland which then curved round from Dorset to the valley of the Thames seems to have barred the way of the assailants. What finally broke their inaction we cannot tell. We only know that Cynric, whom Cerdic's death left king of the West-Saxons, again took up the work of invasion by a new advance in 552. The capture of the hill-fort of Old Sarum threw open the reaches of the Wiltshire Downs ; and pushing northward to a new battle at Barbury Hill, they completed the conquest of the Marlborough Downs. From the bare uplands the invaders turned eastward to the richer valleys of our Berkshire, and after a battle with the Kentish men at Wimbledon, the land south of the Thames which now forms our Surrey was added to their dominions. The road along the Thames was however barred to them, for the district round London seems to have been already won and colonized by the East-Saxons. But a march of their King Cuthwulf made them masters in 571 of the districts which now form Oxfordshire and Buckinghamshire ; and a few years later they swooped from the Wiltshire uplands on the rich prey that lay along the Severn. Gloucester, Cirencester, and Bath, cities which had leagued under their British kings to resist this onset, became the spoil of a Saxon victory at Deorham in 577, and the line of the great western river lay open to the arms of the conquerors. Under a new king, Ceawlin, the West-Saxons penetrated to the borders of Chester, and Uriconium, a town beside the Wrekin, recently again brought to light, went up in flames. A British poet sings piteously the death-song of Uriconium, " the white town in the valley," the town of white stone gleaming among the green woodland, the hall of its chieftain left " without fire, without light, without songs," the silence broken only by the eagle's scream, " the eagle who has swallowed fresh drink, heart's blood of Kyndylan the fair." The raid, however, was repulsed, and the blow proved fatal to the power of Wessex. Though the West-Saxons were destined in the end to win the overlordship over every English people, their time had not come yet, and the leadership of the English race was to fall, for nearly a century to come, to the tribe of invaders whose fortunes we have now to follow.

Rivers were the natural inlets by which the northern pirates everywhere made their way into the heart of Europe. In Britain the fortress of London barred their way along the Thames from its mouth, and drove them, as we have seen, to an advance along the southern coast and over the downs of Wiltshire, before reaching its upper waters. But the rivers which united in the estuary of the Humber led like open highways into the heart of Britain, and it was by this inlet that the great mass of the invaders penetrated into the interior of the island. Like the invaders of East Anglia, they were

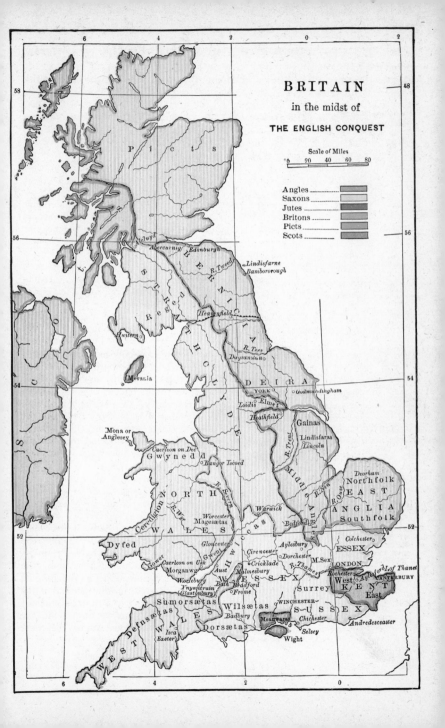

BRITAIN

in the midst of

THE ENGLISH CONQUEST

Scale of Miles

Angles
Saxons
Jutes
Britons
Picts
Scots

of the English tribe from Sleswick. As the storm fell in the opening of the sixth century on the Wolds of Lincolnshire that stretch southward from the Humber, the conquerors who settled in the deserted country were known as the "Lindiswara," or "dwellers about Lindum." A part of the warriors who had entered the Humber, turned southward by the forest of Elmet which covered the district around Leeds, followed the course of the Trent. Those who occupied the wooded country between the Trent and the Humber took from their position the name of Southumbrians. A second division, advancing along the curve of the former river and creeping down the line of its tributary, the Soar, till they reached Leicester, became known as the Middle-English. The marshes of the Fen country were settled by tribes known as the Gyrwas. The head waters of the Trent were the seat of those invaders who penetrated furthest to the west, and camped round Lichfield and Repton. This country became the borderland between Englishmen and Britons, and the settlers bore the name of "Mercians," men, that is, of the March or border. We know hardly anything of this conquest of Mid-Britain, and little more of the conquest of the North. Under the Romans, political power had centred in the vast district between the Humber and the Forth. York had been the capital of Britain and the seat of the Roman prefect; and the bulk of the garrison maintained in the island lay cantoned along the Roman wall. Signs of wealth and prosperity appeared everywhere; cities rose beneath the shelter of the Roman camps; villas of British landowners studded the vale of the Ouse and the far-off uplands of the Tweed, where the shepherd trusted for security against Pictish marauders to the terror of the Roman name. This district was assailed at once from the north and from the south. A part of the invading force which entered the Humber marched over the Yorkshire wolds to found a kingdom, which was known as that of the Deiri, in the fens of Holderness and on the chalk downs eastward of York. But they were soon drawn onwards, and after a struggle of which we know nothing, York, like its neighbour cities, lay a desolate ruin, while the conquerors spread northward, slaying and burning along the valley of the Ouse. Meanwhile the pirates had appeared in the Forth, and won their way along the Tweed; Ida and the men of fifty keels which followed him reared the capital of the northernmost kingdom of the English, that of Bernicia, on the rock of Bamborough, and won their way slowly along the coast against a stubborn resistance which formed the theme of British songs. The strife between the kingdoms of Deira and Bernicia for supremacy in the North was closed by their being united under King Æthelric of Bernicia; and from this union was formed a new kingdom, the kingdom of Northumbria.

It was this century of conquest by the English race which really

Sec. II.

The
English
Conquest

449
to
577

c. 550

500–520

588

Gildas
c. 516–570

SEC. II.

THE
ENGLISH
CONQUEST
449
TO
577

made Britain England. In our anxiety to know more of our fathers, we listen to the monotonous plaint of Gildas, the one writer whom Britain has left us, with a strange disappointment. Gildas had seen the invasion of the pirate hosts, and it is to him we owe our knowledge of the conquest of Kent. But we look in vain to his book for any account of the life or settlement of the English conquerors. Across the border of the new England that was growing up along the southern shores of Britain, Gildas gives us but a glimpse—doubtless he had but a glimpse himself—of forsaken walls, of shrines polluted by heathen impiety. His silence and his ignorance mark the character of the struggle. No British neck had as yet bowed before the English invader, no British pen was to record his conquest. A century after their landing the English are still known to their British foes only as " barbarians," " wolves," " dogs," " whelps from the kennel of barbarism," " hateful to God and man." Their victories seemed victories of the powers of evil, chastisements of a divine justice for national sin. Their ravage, terrible as it had been, was held to be almost at an end : in another century—so ran old prophecies—their last hold on the land would be shaken off. But of submission to, or even of intercourse with the strangers there is not a word. Gildas tells us nothing of their fortunes, or of their leaders.

The
English
Settle-
ment

In spite of his silence, however, we may still know something of the way in which the new English society grew up in the conquered country, for the driving back of the Briton was but the prelude to the settlement of his conqueror. What strikes us at once in the new England is, that it was the one purely German nation that rose upon the wreck of Rome. In other lands, in Spain, or Gaul, or Italy, though they were equally conquered by German peoples, religion, social life, administrative order, still remained Roman. In Britain alone Rome died into a vague tradition of the past. The whole organization of government and society disappeared with the people who used it. The villas, the mosaics, the coins which we dig up in our fields are no relics of our English fathers, but of a Roman world which our fathers' sword swept utterly away. Its law, its literature, its manners, its faith, went with it. The new England was a heathen country. The religion of Woden and Thunder triumphed over the religion of Christ. Alone among the German assailants of Rome the English rejected the faith of the Empire they helped to overthrow. Elsewhere the Christian priesthood served as mediators between the barbarian and the conquered, but in the conquered part of Britain Christianity wholly disappeared. River and homestead and boundary, the very days of the week, bore the names of the new gods who displaced Christ. But if England seemed for the moment a waste from which all the civilization of the world had fled away, it contained within itself the germs of a nobler life than that which had been destroyed. The base of the new English society was the freeman whom we have seen tilling, judging, or sacrificing for himself in his far-off fatherland by the Northern Sea. However roughly he dealt while the struggle went on with the material civilization of Britain, it was impossible that such a man could be a mere destroyer. War was no sooner over than the warrior settled down into a farmer, and the home of the peasant churl rose beside the heap of goblin-haunted stones that marked the site of the villa he had burnt. Little knots of kinsfolk drew together in "tun" and "ham" beside the Thames and the Trent as they had settled beside the Elbe or the Weser, not as kinsfolk only, but as dwellers in the same plot, knit together by their common holding within the same bounds. Each little village-commonwealth lived the same life in Britain as its farmers had lived at home. Each had its moot hill or sacred tree as a centre, its "mark" as a border ; each judged by witness of the kinsfolk and made laws in the assembly of its freemen, and chose the leaders for its own governance, and the men who were to follow headman or ealdorman to hundred-court or war.

SEC. II.

THE
ENGLISH
CONQUEST
449
TO
577

In more ways than one, indeed, the primitive organization of English society was affected by its transfer to the soil of Britain. Conquest begat the King. It is probable that the English had hitherto known nothing of kings in their own fatherland, where each tribe lived under the rule of its own customary Ealdorman. But in a war such as that which they waged against the Britons it was necessary to find a common leader whom the various tribes engaged in conquests such as those of Kent or Wessex might follow ; and such a leader soon rose into a higher position than that of a temporary chief. The sons of Hengest became kings in Kent ; those of Ælle in Sussex ; the West-Saxons chose Cerdic for their king. Such a choice at once drew the various villages and tribes of each community closer together than of old, while the new ruler surrounded himself with a chosen war-band of companions, servants, or "thegns" as they were called, who were rewarded for their service by gifts from the public land. Their distinction rested, not on hereditary rank, but on service done to the King, and they at last became a nobility which superseded the "eorls" of the original English constitution. And as war begat the King and the military noble, so it all but begat the slave. There had always been a slave class, a class of the unfree, among the English as among all German peoples ; but the numbers of this class, if unaffected by the conquest of Britain, were swelled by the wars which soon sprang up among the English conquerors. No rank saved the prisoner taken in battle from the doom of slavery, and slavery itself was often welcomed as saving the prisoner from death. We see this in the story of a noble warrior who had fallen wounded in a fight between two English tribes, and was carried as a bond-slave to the house of a thegn hard by. He declared himself a

England and the Conquest

SEC. II.

THE
ENGLISH
CONQUEST
449
TO
557

peasant, but his master penetrated the disguise. "You deserve death," he said, "since all my brothers and kinsfolk fell in the fight;" but for his oath's sake he spared his life and sold him to a Frisian at London, probably a merchant such as those who were carrying English captives at that time to the market-place of Rome. But war was not the only cause of the increase of this slave class. The number of the "unfree" were swelled by debt and crime. Famine drove men to "bend their heads in the evil days for meat;" the debtor unable to discharge his debt flung on the ground the freeman's sword and spear, took up the labourer's mattock, and placed his head as a slave within a master's hands. The criminal whose kinsfolk would not make up his fine became a crime-serf of the plaintiff or the king. Sometimes a father, pressed by need, sold children and wife into bondage. The slave became part of the live-stock of the estate, to be willed away at death with horse or ox whose pedigree was kept as carefully as his own. His children were bondsmen like himself; even the freeman's children by a slave-mother inherited the mother's taint. "Mine is the calf that is born of my cow," ran the English proverb. The cabins of the un-free clustered round the home of the rich landowner as they had clustered round the villa of the Roman gentleman; ploughman, shep-herd, goatherd, swineherd, oxherd and cowherd, dairymaid, barnman, sower, hayward and woodward, were often slaves. It was not such a slavery as that we have known in modern times, for stripes and bonds were rare; if the slave were slain, it was by an angry blow, not by the lash. But his lord could slay him if he would; it was but a chattel the less. The slave had no place in the justice-court, no kinsman to claim vengeance for his wrong. If a stranger slew him, his lord claimed the damages; if guilty of wrong-doing, "his skin paid for him" under the lash. If he fled he might be chased like a strayed beast, and flogged to death for his crime, or burned to death if the slave were a woman.

Section III.—The Northumbrian Kingdom, 588—685.

[*Authorities.*—Bæda's "Historia Ecclesiastica Gentis Anglorum" is the one primary authority for this period. I have spoken fully of it and its writer in the text. The meagre regnal and episcopal annals of the West-Saxons have been brought by numerous insertions from Bæda to the shape in which they at present appear in the "English Chronicle." The Poem of Cædmon has been published by Mr. Thorpe, and copious summaries of it are given by Sharon Turner ("Hist. of Anglo-Saxons," vol. iii. cap. 3) and Mr. Morley ("English Writers," vol. i.) The life of Wilfrid by Eddi, and those of Cuthbert by Bæda and an earlier contemporary biographer, which are appended to Mr. Stevenson's edition of the "Historia Ecclesiastica," throw great light on the religious condition of the North. For Guthlac of Crowland, see the "Acta

Sanctorum" for April xi.　For Theodore, and the English Church which he organized, see Kemble ("Saxons in England." vol. ii. cap. 8—10), and above all the invaluable remarks of Dr. Stubbs in his "Constitutional History."

588 to 685

Æthelberht

The conquest of the bulk of Britain was now complete.　Eastward of a line which may be roughly drawn along the moorlands of Northumberland and Yorkshire, through Derbyshire and skirting the Forest of Arden, to the mouth of the Severn, and thence by Mendip to the sea, the island had passed into English hands.　From this time the character of the English conquest of Britain was wholly changed.　The older wars of extermination came to an end, and as the invasion pushed westward in later times the Britons were no longer wholly driven from the soil, but mingled with their conquerors.　A far more important change was that which was seen in the attitude of the English conquerors from this time towards each other.　Freed to a great extent from the common pressure of the war against the Britons, their energies turned to combats with one another, to a long struggle for overlordship which was to end in bringing about a real national unity. The West-Saxons, beaten back from their advance along the Severn valley, and overthrown in a terrible defeat at Faddiley, were torn by internal dissensions, even while they were battling for life against the Britons.　Strife between the two rival kingdoms of Bernicia and Deira in the north absorbed the power of the Engle in that quarter, till in 588 the strength of Deira suddenly broke down, and the Bernician king, Æthelric, gathered the two peoples into a realm which was to form the later kingdom of Northumbria.　Amid the confusion of north and south, the primacy among the conquerors was seized by Kent, where the kingdom of the Jutes rose suddenly into greatness under a king called Æthelberht, who before 597 established his supremacy over the Saxons of Middlesex and Essex, as well as over the English of East Anglia and of Mercia as far north as the Humber and the Trent.

584

The overlordship of Æthelberht was marked by a renewal of that intercourse of Britain with the Continent which had been broken off by the conquests of the English.　His marriage with Bertha, the daughter of the Frankish King Charibert of Paris, created a fresh tie between Kent and Gaul.　But the union had far more important results than those of which Æthelberht may have dreamed.　Bertha, like her Frankish kinsfolk, was a Christian.　A Christian bishop accompanied her from Gaul to Canterbury, the royal city of the kingdom of Kent ; and a ruined Christian church, the church of St. Martin, was given them for their worship.　The marriage of Bertha was an opportunity which was at once seized by the bishop who at this time occupied the Roman See, and who is justly known as Gregory the Great.　A memorable story tells us how, when but a young Roman deacon,

Landing of Augustine

c. 589

SEC. III.

THE
NORTH-
UMBRIAN
KINGDOM

588
TO
685

Gregory had noted the white bodies, the fair faces, the golden hair of some youths who stood bound in the market-place of Rome. "From what country do these slaves come?" he asked the traders who brought them. "They are English, Angles!" the slave-dealers answered. The deacon's pity veiled itself in poetic humour. "Not Angles but Angels," he said, "with faces so angel-like! From what country come they?" "They come," said the merchants, "from Deira." "De ira!" was the untranslateable reply; "aye, plucked from God's ire, and called to Christ's mercy! And what is the name of their king?" "Ælla," they told him; and Gregory seized on the words as of good omen. "Alleluia shall be sung in Ælla's land!" he cried, and passed on, musing how the angel-faces should be brought to sing it. Only three or four years had gone by, when the deacon had become Bishop of Rome, and Bertha's marriage gave him the opening he sought. After cautious negotiations with the rulers of Gaul, he sent a Roman abbot, Augustine, at the head of a band of monks, to preach the gospel to the English people. The missionaries landed in 597 on the very spot where Hengest had landed more than a century before in the Isle of Thanet; and the king received them sitting in the open air on the chalk-down above Minster, where the eye nowadays catches miles away over the marshes the dim tower of Canterbury. He listened to the long sermon as the interpreters whom Augustine had brought with him from Gaul translated it. "Your words are fair," Æthelberht replied at last with English good sense, "but they are new and of doubtful meaning;" for himself, he said, he refused to forsake the gods of his fathers, but he promised shelter and protection to the strangers. The band of monks entered Canterbury bearing before them a silver cross with a picture of Christ, and singing in concert the strains of the litany of their church. "Turn from this city, Lord," they sang, "Thine anger and wrath, and turn it from Thy holy house, for we have sinned." And then in strange contrast came the jubilant cry of the older Hebrew worship, the cry which Gregory had wrested in prophetic earnestness from the name of the Yorkshire king in the Roman market-place, "Alleluia!"

Reunion
of Eng-
land
and the
Western
World

It is strange that the spot which witnessed the landing of Hengest should be yet better known as the landing-place of Augustine. But the second landing at Ebbsfleet was in no small measure the reversal and undoing of the first. "Strangers from Rome" was the title with which the missionaries first fronted the English king. The march of the monks as they chanted their solemn litany was, in one sense, the return of the Roman legions who had retired at the trumpet-call of Alaric. It was to the tongue and the thought not of Gregory only but of such men as his own Jutish fathers had slaughtered and driven over sea that Æthelberht listened in the preaching of Augustine. Canterbury, the earliest royal city of the new England, became the

SEC. III.

THE
NORTH-
UMBRIAN
KINGDOM
588
TO
685

centre of Latin influence. The Roman tongue became again one of
the tongues of Britain, the language of its worship, its correspondence,
its literature.   But more than the tongue of Rome returned with
Augustine.   Practically his landing renewed the union with the
western world which the landing of Hengest had all but destroyed.
The new England was admitted into the older commonwealth of
nations.   The civilization, arts, letters, which had fled before the sword
of the English conquest, returned with the Christian faith.   The fabric
of the Roman law indeed never took root in England, but it is impossible not to recognize the result of the influence of the Roman
missionaries in the fact that the codes of customary English law began
to be put into writing soon after their arrival.

As yet these great results were still distant ; a year passed before
Æthelberht yielded, and though after his conversion thousands of the
Kentish men crowded to baptism, it was years before he ventured to
urge the under-kings of Essex and East Anglia to receive the creed of
their overlord.   This effort of Æthelberht however only heralded a
revolution which broke the power of Kent for ever.   The tribes of
Mid-Britain revolted against his supremacy, and gathered under the
overlordship of Rædwald of East Anglia.   The revolution clearly
marked the change which had passed over Britain.   Instead of a chaos
of isolated peoples, the conquerors were now in fact gathered into three
great groups.   The Engle kingdom of the north reached from the
Humber to the Forth.   The southern kingdom of the West-Saxons
stretched from Watling Street to the Channel.   And between these
was roughly sketched out the great kingdom of Mid-Britain, which,
however its limits might vary, retained a substantial identity from the
time of Æthelberht till the final fall of the Mercian kings.   For the
next two hundred years the history of England lies in the struggle of
Northumbrian, Mercian, and West-Saxon kings to establish their
supremacy over the general mass of Englishmen, and unite them in a
single England.

In this struggle the lead was at once taken by Northumbria, which
was rising into a power that set all rivalry at defiance.   Under Æthelfrith, who had followed Æthelric in 593, the work of conquest went on
rapidly.   In 603 the forces of the northern Britons were annihilated in
a great battle at Dægsastan, and the rule of Northumbria was established from the Humber to the Forth.   Along the west of Britain
there stretched the unconquered kingdoms of Strathclyde and Cumbria,
which extended from the river Clyde to the Dee, and the smaller British
states which occupied what we now call Wales.   Chester formed the
link between these two bodies ; and it was Chester that Æthelfrith
chose in 613 for his next point of attack.   Some miles from the city
two thousand monks were gathered in the monastery of Bangor, and
after imploring in a three days' fast the help of Heaven for their

SEC. III.

THE
NORTH-
UMBRIAN
KINGDOM
588
TO
685

country, a crowd of these ascetics followed the British army to the field. Æthelfrith watched the wild gestures and outstretched arms of the strange company as it stood apart, intent upon prayer, and took the monks for enchanters. "Bear they arms or no," said the king, "they war against us when they cry against us to their God," and in the surprise and rout which followed the monks were the first to fall.

The British kingdoms were now utterly parted from one another. By their victory at Deorham the West-Saxons had cut off the Britons of Devon and Cornwall from the general body of their race. By his victory at Chester Æthelfrith broke this body again into two several parts, by parting the Britons of Wales from those of Cumbria and Strathclyde. From this time the warfare of Briton and Englishman died down into a warfare of separate English kingdoms against separate British kingdoms, of Northumbria against Cumbria and Strathclyde, of Mercia against modern Wales, of Wessex against the tract of British country from Mendip to the Land's End. Nor was the victory of Chester of less importance to England itself. With it Æthelfrith was at once drawn to new dreams of ambition as he looked across his southern border, where Rædwald of East Anglia was drawing the peoples of Mid-Britain under his overlordship.

**Eadwine
617-633**

The inevitable struggle between East Anglia and Northumbria seemed for a time averted by the sudden death of Æthelfrith. Marching in 617 against Rædwald, who had sheltered Eadwine, an exile from the Northumbrian kingdom, he perished in a defeat at the river Idle. Eadwine mounted the Northumbrian throne on the fall of his enemy, and carried on the work of government with an energy as ceaseless as that of Æthelfrith himself. His victories over Pict and Briton were followed by the winning of lordship over the English of Mid-Britain; Kent was bound to him in close political alliance; and the English conquerors of the south, the people of the West-Saxons, alone remained independent. But revolt and slaughter had fatally broken the power of the West-Saxons when the Northumbrians

626

attacked them. A story preserved by Bæda tells something of the fierceness of the struggle which ended in the subjection of the south to the overlordship of Northumbria. Eadwine gave audience in an Easter court which he held in a king's town near the river Derwent to Eumer, an envoy of Wessex, who brought a message from its king. In the midst of the conference the envoy started to his feet, drew a dagger from his robe, and rushed madly on the Northumbrian sovereign. Lilla, one of the king's war-band, threw himself between Eadwine and his assassin; but so furious was the stroke that even through Lilla's body the dagger still reached its aim. The king however recovered from his wound to march on the West-Saxons; he slew and subdued all who had conspired against him, and returned victorious to his

SEC. III.

THE
NORTH-
UMBRIAN
KINGDOM

588
TO
685

own country. The greatness of Northumbria now reached its height. Within his own dominions Eadwine displayed a genius for civil government which shows how completely the mere age of conquest had passed away. With him began the English proverb so often applied to after kings, " A woman with her babe might walk scatheless from sea to sea in Eadwine's day." Peaceful communication revived along the deserted highways ; the springs by the roadside were marked with stakes, and a cup of brass set beside each for the traveller's refreshment. Some faint traditions of the Roman past may have flung their glory round this new " Empire of the English ;" some of its majesty had at any rate come back with its long-lost peace. A royal standard of purple and gold floated before Eadwine as he rode through the villages ; a feather-tuft attached to a spear, the Roman tufa, preceded him as he walked through the streets. The Northumbrian king was in fact supreme over Britain as no king of English blood had been before. Northward his frontier reached the Forth, and was guarded by a city which bore his name, Edinburgh, Eadwine's burgh, the city of Eadwine. Westward, he was master of Chester, and the fleet he equipped there subdued the isles of Anglesey and Man. South of the Humber he was owned as overlord by the whole English race, save Kent ; and even Kent was bound to him by his marriage with its king's sister.

With the Kentish queen came Paulinus, one of Augustine's followers, whose tall stooping form, slender aquiline nose, and black hair falling round a thin worn face, were long remembered in the north ; and the Wise Men of Northumbria gathered to deliberate on the new faith to which Paulinus and his queen soon converted Eadwine. To finer minds its charm lay in the light it threw on the darkness which encompassed men's lives, the darkness of the future as of the past. " So seems the life of man, O king," burst forth an aged Ealdorman, " as a sparrow's flight through the hall when you are sitting at meat in winter-tide, with the warm fire lighted on the hearth, but the icy rain-storm without. The sparrow flies in at one door and tarries for a moment in the light and heat of the hearth-fire, and then flying forth from the other vanishes into the wintry darkness whence it came. So tarries for a moment the life of man in our sight, but what is before it, what after it, we know not. If this new teaching tells us aught certainly of these, let us follow it." Coarser argument told on the crowd. " None of your people, Eadwine, have worshipped the gods more busily than I," said Coifi the priest, " yet there are many more favoured and more fortunate. Were these gods good for anything they would help their worshippers." Then leaping on horseback, he hurled his spear into the sacred temple at Godmanham, and with the rest of the Witan embraced the religion of the king.

But the faith of Woden and Thunder was not to fall without a

SEC. III.

THE
NORTH-
UMBRIAN
KINGDOM
588
TO
685
The
Heathen
Struggle

struggle. Even in Kent a reaction against the new creed began with the death of Æthelberht. Rædwald of East Anglia resolved to serve Christ and the older gods together; and a pagan and Christian altar fronted one another in the same royal temple. The young kings of the East-Saxons burst into the church where Mellitus, the Bishop of London, was administering the Eucharist to the people, crying, "Give us that white bread you gave to our father Saba," and on the bishop's refusal drove him from their realm. The tide of reaction was checked for a time by Eadwine's conversion, until Mercia sprang into a sudden greatness as the champion of the heathen gods. Under Eadwine Mercia had submitted to the lordship of Northumbria; but its king, Penda, saw in the rally of the old religion a chance of winning back its independence. Penda had not only united under his own rule the Mercians of the Upper Trent, the Middle-English of Leicester, the Southumbrians, and the Lindiswaras, but he had even been strong enough to tear from the West-Saxons their possessions along the Severn. So thoroughly indeed was the union of these provinces effected, that though some were detached for a time after Penda's death, the name of Mercia from this moment must be generally taken as covering the whole of them. Alone, however, he was as yet no match for Northumbria. But the old severance between the English people and the Britons was fast dying down, and Penda boldly broke through the barrier which parted the two races, and allied himself with the Welsh king, Cadwallon, in an attack on Eadwine. The armies met in 633 at Hatfield, and in the fight which followed Eadwine was defeated and slain. The victory was turned to profit by the ambition of Penda, while Northumbria was torn with the strife which followed Eadwine's fall. To complete his dominion over Mid-Britain, Penda marched against East Anglia. The East Engle had returned to heathendom from the oddly mingled religion of their first Christian king, Rædwald; but the new faith was brought back by the present king, Sigeberht. Before the threat of Penda's attack Sigeberht left his throne for a monastery, but his people dragged him again from his cell on the news of Penda's invasion in 634, in faith that his presence would bring them the favour of Heaven. The monk-king was set in the forefront of the battle, but he would bear no weapon save a wand, and his fall was followed by the rout of his army and the submission of his kingdom. Meanwhile Cadwallon remained harrying in the heart of Deira, and made himself master even of York. But the triumph of the Britons was as brief as it was strange. Oswald, a second son of Æthelfrith, placed himself at the head of his race, and a small Northumbrian force gathered in 635 under their new king near the Roman Wall. Oswald set up a cross of wood as his standard, holding it with his own hands till the hollow in which it was fixed was filled in by his soldiers; then throwing himself on his knees, he cried to his host to pray to the living God. Cadwallon, the last great hero of the British race, fell fighting on the "Heaven's Field," as after times called the field of battle, and for seven years the power of Oswald equalled that of Æthelfrith and Eadwine.

It was not the Church of Paulinus which nerved Oswald to this struggle for the Cross. Paulinus had fled from Northumbria at Eadwine's fall; and the Roman Church in Kent shrank into inactivity before the heathen reaction. Its place in the conversion of England was taken by missionaries from Ireland. To understand, however, the true meaning of the change, we must remember that before the landing of the English in Britain, the Christian Church comprised every country, save Germany, in Western Europe, as far as Ireland itself. The conquest of Britain by the pagan English thrust a wedge of heathendom into the heart of this great communion and broke it into two unequal parts. On the one side lay Italy, Spain, and Gaul, whose Churches owned obedience to the See of Rome, on the other the Church of Ireland. But the condition of the two portions of Western Christendom was very different. While the vigour of Christianity in Italy and Gaul and Spain was exhausted in a bare struggle for life, Ireland, which remained unscourged by invaders, drew from its conversion an energy such as it has never known since. Christianity had been received there with a burst of popular enthusiasm, and letters and arts sprang up rapidly in its train. The science and Biblical knowledge which fled from the Continent took refuge in famous schools which made Durrow and Armagh the universities of the West. The new Christian life soon beat too strongly to brook confinement within the bounds of Ireland itself. Patrick, the first missionary of the island, had not been half a century dead when Irish Christianity flung itself with a fiery zeal into battle with the mass of heathenism which was rolling in upon the Christian world. Irish missionaries laboured among the Picts of the Highlands and among the Frisians of the northern seas. An Irish missionary, Columban, founded monasteries in Burgundy and the Apennines. The canton of St. Gall still commemorates in its name another Irish missionary before whom the spirits of flood and fell fled wailing over the waters of the Lake of Constance. For a time it seemed as if the course of the world's history was to be changed, as if the older Celtic race that Roman and German had swept before them had turned to the moral conquest of their conquerors, as if Celtic and not Latin Christianity was to mould the destinies of the Churches of the West.

On a low island of barren gneiss-rock off the west coast of Scotland an Irish refugee, Columba, had raised the famous monastery of Iona. Oswald in youth found refuge within its walls, and on his accession to the throne of Northumbria he called for missionaries from among its monks. The first despatched in answer to his call obtained little

SEC. III.

THE
NORTH-
UMBRIAN
KINGDOM

588
TO
685

success. He declared on his return that among a people so stubborn and barbarous success was impossible. "Was it their stubbornness or your severity?" asked Aidan, a brother sitting by; "did you forget God's word to give them the milk first and then the meat?" All eyes turned on the speaker as fittest to undertake the abandoned mission, and Aidan sailing at their bidding fixed his bishop's stool or see in the island-peninsula of Lindisfarne. Thence, from a monastery which gave to the spot its after name of Holy Island, preachers poured forth over the heathen realms. Boisil guided a little troop of missionaries to the valley of the Tweed. Aidan himself wandered on foot preaching among the peasants of Bernicia. The new religion served as a prelude to the Northumbrian advance. If Oswald was a saint, he was none the less resolved to build up again the realm of Eadwine. Having extended his supremacy over the Britons of Strath-clyde and won the submission of the Lindiswaras, he turned to reassert his supremacy over Wessex. The reception of the new faith became the mark of submission to his overlordship. A preacher, Birinus, had already penetrated from Gaul into Wessex; in Oswald's presence its king received baptism, and established with his assent a see for his people in the royal city of Dorchester on the Thames. Oswald ruled as wide a realm as his predecessor; but for after times the memory of his greatness was lost in the legends of his piety. A new conception of kingship began to blend itself with that of the warlike glory of Æthel-frith or the wise administration of Eadwine. The moral power which was to reach its height in Ælfred first dawns in the story of Oswald. In his own court the king acted as interpreter to the Irish missionaries in their efforts to convert his thegns. " By reason of his constant habit of praying or giving thanks to the Lord he was wont wherever he sat to hold his hands upturned on his knees." As he feasted with Bishop Aidan by his side, the thegn, or noble of his war-band, whom he had set to give alms to the poor at his gate, told him of a multitude that still waited fasting without. The king at once bade the untasted meat before him be carried to the poor and his silver dish be divided piecemeal among them. Aidan seized the royal hand and blessed it. " May this hand," he cried, "never grow old."

Prisoned, however, as it was by the conversion of Wessex to the central districts of England, heathendom fought desperately for life. Penda was still its rallying-point; but if his long reign was one continuous battle with the new religion, it was in fact rather a struggle against the supremacy of Northumbria than against the supremacy of the Cross. East Anglia became at last the field of contest between the two powers. In 642 Oswald marched to deliver it from Penda; but in a battle called the battle of the Maserfeld he was overthrown and slain. His body was mutilated and his limbs set on stakes by the brutal con-queror; but legend told that when all else of Oswald had perished, the

SEC. III.

THE
NORTH-
UMBRIAN
KINGDOM
588
TO
685

"white hand" that Aidan had blessed still remained white and un-corrupted. For a few years after his victory at the Maserfeld Penda stood supreme in Britain. Wessex owned his overlordship as it had owned that of Oswald, and its king threw off the Christian faith and married Penda's sister. Even Deira seems to have bowed to him, and Bernicia alone refused to yield. Year by year Penda carried his ravages over the north; once he reached even the royal city, the im-pregnable rock-fortress of Bamborough. Despairing of success in an assault, he pulled down the cottages around, and, piling their wood against its walls, fired the mass in a fair wind that drove the flames on the town. "See, Lord, what ill Penda is doing," cried Aidan from his hermit cell in the islet of Farne, as he saw the smoke drifting over the city; and a change of wind—so ran the legend of Northumbria's agony—drove back at the words the flames on those who kindled them. But in spite of Penda's victories, the faith which he had so often struck down revived everywhere around him. Burnt and harried as it was, Bernicia still clung to the Cross. The East-Saxons again became Christian. Penda's own son, whom he had set over the Middle-Eng-lish, received baptism and teachers from Lindisfarne. The mission-aries of the new faith appeared fearlessly among the Mercians them-selves, and Penda gave no hindrance. Heathen to the last, he stood by unheeding if any were willing to hear; hating and scorning with a certain grand sincerity of nature "those whom he saw not doing the works of the faith they had received." But the track of Northumbrian missionaries along the eastern coast marked the growth of Northum-brian overlordship, and the old man roused himself for a last stroke at his foes. On the death of Oswald Oswiu had been called to fill his throne, and in 655 he met the pagan host near the river Winwæd. It was in vain that the Northumbrians had sought to avert Penda's attack by offers of ornaments and costly gifts. "Since the pagans will not take our gifts," Oswiu cried at last, "let us offer them to One that will;" and he vowed that if successful he would dedicate his daughter to God and endow twelve monasteries in his realm. Victory at last declared for the faith of Christ. The river over which the Mercians fled was swollen with a great rain; it swept away the frag-ments of the heathen host, Penda himself was slain, and the cause of the older gods was lost for ever.

The terrible struggle was followed by a season of peace. For four years after the battle of Winwæd Mercia was subject to Oswiu's overlordship. But in 659 a general rising of the people threw off the Northumbrian yoke. The heathendom of Mercia however was dead with Penda. "Being thus freed," Bæda tells us, "the Mercians with their king rejoiced to serve the true King, Christ." Its three provinces, the earlier Mercia, the Middle-English, and the Lindiswaras, were united in the bishopric of Ceadda, the St. Chad to whom the Mercian

SEC. III.

THE
NORTH-
UMBRIAN
KINGDOM
588
TO
685

see of Lichfield still looks as its founder. Ceadda was a monk of
Lindisfarne, so simple and lowly in temper that he travelled on foot
on his long mission journeys, till Archbishop Theodore in later days
with his own hands lifted him on horseback. The poetry of Christian
enthusiasm breaks out in his death-legend, as it tells us how voices of
singers singing sweetly descended from Heaven to the little cell beside
St. Mary's church where the bishop lay dying. Then "the same song
ascended from the roof again, and returned heavenward by the way
that it came." It was the soul of his brother, the missionary Cedd,
come with a choir of angels to solace the last hours of Ceadda. In
Northumbria the work of his fellow missionaries has almost been lost
in the glory of Cuthbert. No story better lights up for us the new
religious life of the time than the story of this apostle of the Lowlands.
It carries us at its outset into the northernmost part of Northumbria,
the country of the Teviot and the Tweed. Born on the southern edge
of the Lammermoor, Cuthbert found shelter at eight years old in a
widow's house in the little village of Wrangholm. Already in youth
there was a poetic sensibility beneath the robust frame of the boy
which caught even in the chance word of a game a call to higher
things. Later on, a traveller coming in his white mantle over the hill-
side and stopping his horse to tend Cuthbert's injured knee seemed to
him an angel. The boy's shepherd life carried him to the bleak
upland, still famous as a sheep-walk, though the scant herbage scarce
veils the whinstone rock, and there meteors plunging into the night
became to him a company of angelic spirits, carrying the soul of
Bishop Aidan heavenward. Slowly Cuthbert's longings settled into a
resolute will towards a religious life, and he made his way at last to a
group of log-shanties in the midst of an untilled solitude where a few

651

Irish monks from Lindisfarne had settled in the mission-station of
Melrose. To-day the land is a land of poetry and romance. Cheviot
and Lammermoor, Ettrick and Teviotdale, Yarrow and Annan-water,
are musical with old ballads and border minstrelsy. Agriculture has
chosen its valleys for her favourite seat, and drainage and steam-power
have turned sedgy marshes into farm and meadow. But to see the
Lowlands as they were in Cuthbert's day we must sweep meadow and
farm away again, and replace them by vast solitudes, dotted here and
there with clusters of wooden hovels, and crossed by boggy tracks over
which travellers rode spear in hand and eye kept cautiously about
them. The Northumbrian peasantry among whom he journeyed were
for the most part Christians only in name. With Teutonic indifference they had yielded to their thegns in nominally accepting the new
Christianity, as these had yielded to the king. But they retained their
old superstitions side by side with the new worship; plague or mishap
drove them back to a reliance on their heathen charms and amulets;
and if trouble befell the Christian preachers who came settling among

Sec. III.

The
North-
umbrian
Kingdom
588
to
685

them they took it as proof of the wrath of the older gods. When some log-rafts which were floating down the Tyne for the construction of an abbey at its mouth drifted with the monks who were at work on them out to sea, the rustic bystanders shouted, "Let nobody pray for them ; let nobody pity these men, who have taken away from us our old worship ; and how their new-fangled customs are to be kept nobody knows." On foot, on horseback, Cuthbert wandered among listeners such as these, choosing above all the remoter mountain villages from whose roughness and poverty other teachers turned aside. Unlike his Irish comrades, he needed no interpreter as he passed from village to village ; the frugal, long-headed Northumbrians listened willingly to one who was himself a peasant of the Lowlands, and who had caught the rough Northumbrian burr along the banks of the Tweed. His patience, his humorous good sense, the sweetness of his look, told for him, and not less the stout vigorous frame which fitted the peasant-preacher for the hard life he had chosen. "Never did man die of hunger who served God faithfully," he would say, when nightfall found them supperless in the waste. "Look at the eagle overhead ! God can feed us through him if He will"—and once at least he owed his meal to a fish that the scared bird let fall. A snow-storm drove his boat on the coast of Fife. "The snow closes the road along the shore," mourned his comrades ; "the storm bars our way over sea." "There is still the way of Heaven that lies open," said Cuthbert.

While missionaries were thus labouring among its peasantry, Northumbria saw the rise of a number of monasteries, not bound indeed by the strict ties of the Benedictine rule, but gathered on the loose Celtic model of the family or the clan round some noble and wealthy person who sought devotional retirement. The most notable and wealthy of these houses was that of Streoneshealh, where Hild, a woman of royal race, reared her abbey on the summit of the dark cliffs of Whitby, looking out over the Northern Sea. Her counsel was sought even by nobles and kings ; and the double monastery over which she ruled became a seminary of bishops and priests. The sainted John of Beverley was among her scholars. But the name which really throws glory over Whitby is the name of a lay-brother from whose lips flowed the first great English song. Though well advanced in years, Cædmon had learnt nothing of the art of verse, the alliterative jingle so common among his fellows, "wherefore being sometimes at feasts, when all agreed for glee's sake to sing in turn, he no sooner saw the harp come towards him than he rose from the board and turned homewards. Once when he had done thus, and gone from the feast to the stable where he had that night charge of the cattle, there appeared to him in his sleep One who said, greeting him by name, ' Sing, Cædmon, some song to Me.' ' I cannot sing,' he answered ; ' for this cause left I the feast and came hither.' He who talked with him answered, ' However

SEC. III.

THE
NORTH-
UMBRIAN
KINGDOM
588
TO
685

that be, you shall sing to Me.' 'What shall I sing?' rejoined Cædmon. 'The beginning of created things,' replied He. In the morning the cowherd stood before Hild and told his dream. Abbess and brethren alike concluded 'that heavenly grace had been conferred on him by the Lord.' They translated for Cædmon a passage in Holy Writ, 'bidding him, if he could, put the same into verse.' The next morning he gave it them composed in excellent verse, whereon the abbess, understanding the divine grace in the man, bade him quit the secular habit and take on him the monastic life." Piece by piece the sacred story was thus thrown into Cædmon's poem. " He sang of the creation of the world, of the origin of man, and of all the history of Israel ; of their departure from Egypt and entering into the Promised Land ; of the incarnation, passion, and resurrection of Christ, and of his ascension ; of the terror of future judgment, the horror of hell-pangs, and the joys of heaven."

English Song

To men of that day this sudden burst of song seemed a thing necessarily divine. " Others after him strove to compose religious poems, but none could vie with him, for he learned the art of poetry not from men nor of men, but from God." It was not indeed that any change had been wrought by Cædmon in the outer form of English song. The collection of poems which is connected with his name has come down to us in a later West-Saxon version, and though modern criticism is still in doubt as to their authorship, they are certainly the work of various hands. The verse, whether of Cædmon or of other singers, is accented and alliterative, without conscious art or development or the delight that springs from reflection, a verse swift and direct, but leaving behind it a sense of strength rather than of beauty, obscured too by harsh metaphors and involved construction. But it is eminently the verse of warriors, the brief passionate expression of brief passionate emotions. Image after image, phrase after phrase, in these early poems, start out vivid, harsh and emphatic. The very metre is rough with a sort of self-violence and repression ; the verses fall like sword-strokes in the thick of battle. The love of natural description, the background of melancholy which gives its pathos to English verse, the poet only shared with earlier singers. But the faith of Christ brought in, as we have seen, new realms of fancy. The legends of the heavenly light, Bæda's story of "The Sparrow," show the side of English temperament to which Christianity appealed—its sense of the vague, vast mystery of the world and of man, its dreamy revolt against the narrow bounds of experience and life. It was this new poetic world which combined with the old in the so-called epic of Cædmon. In its various poems the vagueness and daring of the Teutonic imagination pass beyond the limits of the Hebrew story to a " swart hell without light and full of flame," swept only at dawn by the icy east wind, on whose floor lie

SEC. III.

THE
NORTH-
UMBRIAN
KINGDOM

588
TO
685

bound the apostate angels. The human energy of the German race, its sense of the might of individual manhood, transformed in English verse the Hebrew Tempter into a rebel Satan, disdainful of vassalage to God. "I may be a God as He," Satan cries amidst his torments. "Evil it seems to me to cringe to Him for any good." Even in this terrible outburst of the fallen spirit, we catch the new pathetic note which the Northern melancholy was to give to our poetry. "This is to me the chief of sorrow, that Adam, wrought of earth, should hold my strong seat—should dwell in joy while we endure this torment. Oh, that for one winter hour I had power with my hands, then with this host would I—but around me lie the iron bonds, and this chain galls me." On the other hand the enthusiasm for the Christian God, faith in whom had been bought so dearly by years of desperate struggle, breaks out in long rolls of sonorous epithets of praise and adoration. The temper of the poets brings them near to the earlier fire and passion of the Hebrew, as the events of their time brought them near to the old Bible history with its fights and wanderings. "The wolves sing their dread evensong ; the fowls of war, greedy of battle, dewy-feathered, scream around the host of Pharaoh," as wolf howled and eagle screamed round the host of Penda. Everywhere we mark the new grandeur, depth, and fervour of tone which the German race was to give to the religion of the East.

But even before Cædmon had begun to sing, the Christian Church of Northumbria was torn in two by a strife whose issue was decided in the same abbey of Whitby where Cædmon dwelt. The labours of Aidan, the victories of Oswald and Oswiu, seemed to have annexed England to the Irish Church. The monks of Lindisfarne, or of the new religious houses whose foundation followed that of Lindisfarne, looked for their ecclesiastical tradition, not to Rome but to Ireland ; and quoted for their guidance the instructions, not of Gregory, but of Columba. Whatever claims of supremacy over the whole English Church might be pressed by the see of Canterbury, the real metropolitan of the Church as it existed in the north of England was the Abbot of Iona. But Oswiu's queen brought with her from Kent the loyalty of the Kentish church to the Roman see, and a Roman party at once formed about her. Her efforts were seconded by those of two young thegns whose love of Rome mounted to a passionate fanaticism. The life of Wilfrid of York was a series of flights to Rome and returns to England, of wonderful successes in pleading the right of Rome to the obedience of the Church of Northumbria, and of as wonderful defeats. Benedict Biscop worked towards the same end in a quieter fashion, coming backwards and forwards across the sea with books and relics and cunning masons and painters to rear a great church and monastery at Wearmouth, whose brethren owned obedience to the Roman See. In 652 they first set out for a visit to the imperial city ; and the elder,

SEC. III.

THE
NORTH-
UMBRIAN
KINGDOM

588
TO
685

Benedict Biscop, soon returned to preach ceaselessly against the Irish usages. He was followed by Wilfrid, whose energy soon brought the quarrel to a head. The strife between the two parties rose so high at last that Oswiu was prevailed upon to summon in 664 a great council at Whitby, where the future ecclesiastical allegiance of England should be decided. The points actually contested were trivial enough. Colman, Aidan's successor at Holy Island, pleaded for the Irish fashion of the tonsure, and for the Irish time of keeping Easter; Wilfrid pleaded for the Roman. The one disputant appealed to the authority of Columba, the other to that of St. Peter. "You own," cried the king at last to Colman, "that Christ gave to Peter the keys of the kingdom of heaven—has He given such power to Columba?" The bishop could but answer "No." "Then will I rather obey the porter of Heaven," said Oswiu, "lest when I reach its gates he who has the keys in his keeping turn his back on me, and there be none to open." The importance of Oswiu's judgment was never doubted at Lindisfarne, where Colman, followed by the whole of the Irish-born brethren and thirty of their English fellows, forsook the see of Aidan and sailed away to Iona. Trivial in fact as were the actual points of difference which severed the Roman Church from the Irish, the question to which communion Northumbria should belong was of immense moment to the after fortunes of England. Had the Church of Aidan finally won, the later ecclesiastical history of England would probably have resembled that of Ireland. Devoid of that power of organization which was the strength of the Roman Church, the Celtic Church in its own Irish home took the clan system of the country as the basis of Church government. Tribal quarrels and ecclesiastical controversies became inextricably confounded; and the clergy, robbed of all really spiritual influence, contributed no element save that of disorder to the state. Hundreds of wandering bishops, a vast religious authority wielded by hereditary chieftains, the dissociation of piety from morality, the absence of those larger and more humanizing influences which contact with a wider world alone can give, this is the picture which the Irish Church of later times presents to us. It was from such a chaos as this that England was saved by the victory of Rome in the Synod of Whitby.

Theodore
669–690

The Church of England, as we know it to-day, is the work, so far as its outer form is concerned, of a Greek monk, Theodore of Tarsus, whom Rome, after her victory at Whitby, despatched in 669 as Archbishop of Canterbury, to secure England to her sway. Theodore's work was determined in its main outlines by the previous history of the English people. The conquest of the Continent had been wrought either by races such as the Goths, who were already Christian, or by heathens like the Franks, who bowed to the Christian faith of the nations they conquered. To this oneness of religion between the

SEC. III.

THE
NORTH-
UMBRIAN
KINGDOM

588
TO
685

German invaders of the Empire and their Roman subjects was owing
the preservation of all that survived of the Roman world.   The Church
everywhere remained untouched.   The Christian bishop became the
defender of the conquered Italian or Gaul against his Gothic and
Lombard conqueror, the mediator between the German and his subjects, the one bulwark against barbaric violence and oppression.   To
the barbarian on the other hand he was the representative of all that
was venerable in the past, the living record of law, of letters, and
of art.   But in Britain priesthood and people had been exterminated together.   When Theodore came to organize the Church of
England, the very memory of the older Christian Church which existed
in Roman Britain had passed away.   The first Christian missionaries,
strangers in a heathen land, attached themselves necessarily to the
courts of the kings, who were their first converts, and whose conversion
was generally followed by that of their people.   The English bishops
were thus at first royal chaplains, and their diocese was naturally
nothing but the kingdom.   The kingdom of Kent became the diocese
of Canterbury, and the kingdom of Northumbria the diocese of York.
In this way too realms which are all but forgotten are commemorated
in the limits of existing sees.   That of Rochester represented till of
late an obscure kingdom of West Kent, and the frontier of the original
kingdom of Mercia might be recovered by following the map of the
ancient bishopric of Lichfield.   Theodore's first work was to order
the dioceses ; his second was to add many new sees to the old ones,
and to group all of them round the one centre of Canterbury.   All ties
between England and the Irish Church were roughly broken.   Lindisfarne sank into obscurity with the flight of Colman and his monks.
The new prelates, gathered in synod after synod, acknowledged the
authority of their one primate.   The organization of the episcopate
was followed during the next hundred years by the development of the
parish system.   The loose system of the mission-station, the monastery
from which priest and bishop went forth on journey after journey to
preach and baptize, as Aidan went forth from Lindisfarne or Cuthbert
from Melrose, naturally disappeared as the land became Christian.
The missionaries became settled clergy.   The holding of the English
noble or landowner became the parish, and his chaplain the parish
priest, as the king's chaplain had become the bishop, and the kingdom
his diocese.   A source of permanent endowment for the clergy was
found at a later time in the revival of the Jewish system of tithes, and
in the annual gift to Church purposes of a tenth of the produce of the
soil ; while discipline within the Church itself was provided for by an
elaborate code of sin and penance in which the principle of compensation which lay at the root of Teutonic legislation, crept into the
relations between God and the soul.

In his work of organization, in his increase of bishoprics, in his

SEC. III.

THE
NORTH-
UMBRIAN
KINGDOM

588
TO
685

Mercia
under
Wulfhere

659-675

arrangement of dioceses, and the way in which he grouped them round the see of Canterbury, in his national synods and ecclesiastical canons, Theodore was unconsciously doing a political work. The old divisions of kingdoms and tribes about him, divisions which had sprung for the most part from mere accidents of the conquest, were fast breaking down. The smaller states were by this time practically absorbed by the three larger ones, and of these three Mercia and Wessex had for a time bowed to the overlordship of Northumbria. The tendency to national unity which was to characterize the new England had thus already declared itself; but the policy of Theodore clothed with a sacred form and surrounded with divine sanctions a unity which as yet rested on no basis but the sword. The single throne of the one primate at Canterbury accustomed men's minds to the thought of a single throne for their one temporal overlord at York, or, as in later days, at Lichfield or at Winchester. The regular subordination of priest to bishop, of bishop to primate, in the administration of the Church, supplied a mould on which the civil organization of the state quietly shaped itself. Above all, the councils gathered by Theodore were the first of all national gatherings for general legislation. It was at a much later time that the Wise Men of Wessex, or Northumbria, or Mercia, learned to come together in the Witenagemot of all England. It was the ecclesiastical synods which by their example led the way to our national parliament, as it was the canons enacted in such synods which led the way to a national system of law. But if the movement towards national unity was furthered by the centralizing tendencies of the Church, it was as yet hindered by the upgrowth of a great rival power to contest the supremacy with Northumbria. Mercia, as we have seen, had recovered from the absolute subjection in which it was left after Penda's fall by shaking off the supremacy of Oswiu, and by choosing Wulfhere for its king. Wulfhere was a vigorous and active ruler, and the peaceful reign of Oswiu left him free to build up again during the sixteen years of his rule the power which had been lost at Penda's death. Penda's realm in Central Britain was quickly restored, and Wulfhere's dominion extended even over the Severn and embraced the lower valley of the Wye. He had even more than his father's success. After a great victory in 661 over the West-Saxons, his ravages were carried into the heart of Wessex, and the valley of the Thames opened to his army. To the eastward, the East-Saxons and London came to own his supremacy; while southward he pushed across the river over Surrey. In the same year, 661, Sussex, perhaps in dread of the West-Saxons, found protection in accepting Wulfhere's overlordship, and its king was rewarded by a gift of two outlying settlements of the Jutes, the Isle of Wight and the lands of the Meon-wara along the Southampton Water, which we must suppose had been reduced by Mercian arms. The Mercian supremacy which thus

SEC. III.

THE
NORTH-
UMBRIAN
KINGDOM
588
TO
685
Progress
of
Mercia

reached from the Humber to the Channel and stretched westward to
the Wye was the main political fact in Britain when Theodore landed
on its shores.   In fact, with the death of Oswiu in 670 all effort was
finally abandoned by Northumbria to crush the rival states in Central
or Southern Britain.

The industrial progress of the Mercian kingdom went hand in hand
with its military advance.   The forests of its western border, the
marshes of its eastern coast, were being cleared and drained by
monastic colonies, whose success shows the hold which Christianity
had now gained over its people.   Heathenism indeed still held its
own in the western woodlands ; we may perhaps see Woden-worship-
ping miners at Alcester in the dæmons of the legend of Bishop Ecgwine
of Worcester, who drowned the preacher's voice with the din of their
hammers.   But in spite of their hammers Ecgwine's preaching left
one lasting mark behind it.   The bishop heard how a swineherd,
coming out from the forest depths on a sunny glade, saw forms which
were possibly those of the Three Fair Women of the old German mythology, seated round a mystic bush, and singing their unearthly song.
In his fancy the fair women transformed themselves into a vision of
the Mother of Christ ; and the silent glade soon became the site
of an abbey dedicated to her, and of a town which sprang up under
its shelter—the Evesham which was to be hallowed in after time
by the fall of Earl Simon of Leicester.   Wilder even than the western
woodland was the desolate fen-country on the eastern border of the
kingdom, stretching from the " Holland," the sunk, hollow land of
Lincolnshire, to the channel of the Ouse, a wilderness of shallow waters
and reedy islets wrapped in its own dark mist-veil and tenanted only
by flocks of screaming wild-fowl.   Here through the liberality of King
Wulfhere rose the abbey of Medeshamstead, our later Peterborough.
On its northern border a hermit, Botulf, founded a little house which
as ages went by became our Botulf's town or Boston.   The abbey
of Ely was founded in the same wild fen-country by the Lady Æthelthryth, the wife of King Ecgfrith, who in the year 670 succeeded Oswiu
on the throne of Northumbria.   Here, too, Guthlac, a youth of the
royal race of Mercia, sought a refuge from the world in the solitude
of Crowland, and so great was the reverence he won, that only two
years had passed since his death when the stately abbey of Crowland
rose over his tomb.   Earth was brought in boats to form a site ; the
buildings rested on oaken piles driven into the marsh, a stone church
replaced the hermit's cell, and the toil of the new brotherhood changed
the pools around them into fertile meadow-land.

But while Mercia was building up its dominion in Mid-Britain,
Northumbria was far from having sunk from its old renown either in
government or war.   Ecgfrith had succeeded his father Oswiu in 670,
and made no effort to reverse his policy, or attempt to build up again

D

Sec. III.
THE
NORTH-
UMBRIAN
KINGDOM
588
TO
685

a supremacy over the states of southern Britain. His ambition turned rather to conquests over the Briton than to victories over his fellow Englishmen. The war between Briton and Englishman, which had languished since the battle of Chester, had been revived some twenty years before by an advance of the West-Saxons to the south-west. Unable to save the possessions of Wessex in the Severn valley and on the Cotswolds from the grasp of Penda, the West-Saxon king, Cenwealh, seized the moment when Mercia was absorbed in the last struggle of Penda against Northumbria to seek for compensation in an attack on his Welsh neighbours. A victory at Bradford on the

655

Avon enabled him to overrun the country north of Mendip which had till then been held by the Britons; and a second campaign in 658, which ended in a victory on the skirts of the great forest that covered Somerset to the east, settled the West-Saxons as conquerors round the sources of the Parret. It may have been the example of the West-Saxons which spurred Ecgfrith to enlarge the bounds of his kingdom by a series of attacks upon his British neighbours in the west. His armies chased the Britons from southern Cumbria and made the districts of Carlisle, the Lake country, and our Lancashire English ground. His success in this quarter was quickly followed by fresh gain in the north, where he pushed his conquests over the Scots beyond Clydesdale, and subdued the Picts over the Firth of Forth, so that their territory on the northern bank of the Forth was from this time reckoned as Northumbrian ground. The monastery of Abercorn

670-675

on the shore of the Firth of Forth, in which a few years later a Northumbrian bishop, Trumwine, fixed the seat of a new bishopric, was a sign of the subjection of the Picts to the Northumbrian over-lordship. Even when recalled from the wars to his southern border by an attack of Wulfhere's in 675, the vigorous and warlike Ecgfrith proved a different foe from the West-Saxon or the Jute, and the defeat of the king of Mercia was so complete that he was glad to purchase peace by giving up to his conqueror the province of the Lindiswaras or Lincolnshire. A large part of the conquered country of the Lake district was bestowed upon the see of Lindisfarne, which was at this time filled by one whom we have seen before labouring as the Apostle of the Lowlands. After years of mission labour at Melrose, Cuthbert had quitted it for Holy Island, and preached among the moors of Northumberland as he had preached beside the banks of the Tweed. He remained there through the great secession which followed on the Synod of Whitby, and became prior of the dwindled company of brethren, now torn with endless disputes, against which his patience and good humour struggled in vain. Worn out at last he fled to a little island of basaltic rock, one of a group not far from Ida's fortress of Bamborough, strewn for the most part with kelp and seaweed, the home of the gull and the seal. In the midst of it rose his hut of rough stones and turf, dug deep into the rock and roofed with logs and straw.

The reverence for his sanctity dragged Cuthbert back in old age to fill the vacant see of Lindisfarne. He entered Carlisle, which the king had bestowed upon the bishopric, at a moment when all Northumbria was waiting for news of a fresh campaign of Ecgfrith's against the Britons in the north. The power of Northumbria was already however fatally shaken. In the south, Mercia had in 679 renewed the attempt which had been checked by Wulfhere's defeat. His successor, the Mercian king Æthelred, again seized the province of the Lindiswaras, and the war he thus began with Northumbria was only ended by a peace negotiated through Archbishop Theodore, which left him master of Middle England. Old troubles too revived on Ecgfrith's northern frontier, where a rising of the Picts forced him once more to cross the Firth of Forth, and march in the year 685 into their land A sense of coming ill weighed on Northumbria, and its dread was quickened by a memory of the curses which had been pronounced by the bishops of Ireland on the king, when his navy, setting out a year before from the newly-conquered western coast, swept the Irish shores in a raid which seemed like sacrilege to those who loved the home of Aidan and Columba. As Cuthbert bent over a Roman fountain which still stood unharmed amongst the ruins of Carlisle, the anxious bystanders thought they caught words of ill-omen falling from the old man's lips. "Perhaps," he seemed to murmur, "at this very hour the peril of the fight is over and done." "Watch and pray," he said, when they questioned him on the morrow; "watch and pray." In a few days more a solitary fugitive escaped from the slaughter told that the Picts had turned desperately to bay as the English army entered Fife; and that Ecgfrith and the flower of his nobles lay, a ghastly ring of corpses, on the far-off moorland of Nectansmere.

To Cuthbert the tidings were tidings of death. His bishopric was soon laid aside, and two months after his return to his island-hermitage the old man lay dying, murmuring to the last words of concord and peace. A signal of his death had been agreed upon, and one of those who stood by ran with a candle in each hand to a place whence the light might be seen by a monk who was looking out from the watch-tower of Lindisfarne. As the tiny gleam flashed over the dark reach of sea, and the watchman hurried with his news into the church, the brethren of Holy Island were singing, as it chanced, the words of the Psalmist : "Thou hast cast us out and scattered us abroad ; Thou hast also been displeased ; Thou hast shown thy people heavy things ; Thou hast given us a drink of deadly wine." The chant was the dirge, not of Cuthbert only, but of his Church and his people. Over both hung the gloom of a seeming failure. Strangers who knew not Iona and Columba entered into the heritage of Aidan and Cuthbert. As the

Roman communion folded England again beneath her wing, men forgot that a Church which passed utterly away had battled with Rome for the spiritual headship of Western Christendom, and that throughout the great struggle with the heathen reaction of Mid-Britain the new religion had its centre not at Canterbury, but at Lindisfarne. Nor were men long to remember that from the days of Æthelfrith to the days of Ecgfrith English politics had found their centre at York. But forgotten or no, Northumbria had done its work. By its missionaries and by its sword it had won England from heathendom to the Christian Church. It had given her a new poetic literature. Its monasteries were already the seat of whatever intellectual life the country possessed. Above all it had first gathered together into a loose political unity the various tribes of the English people, and by standing at their head for half a century had accustomed them to a national life, out of which England, as we have it now, was to spring.

Section IV.—The Three Kingdoms, 685–828.

[*Authorities.*—A few incidents of Mercian history are preserved among the meagre annals of Wessex, which form, during this period, "The English Chronicle." But for the most part we are thrown upon later writers, especially Henry of Huntingdon and William of Malmesbury, both authors of the twelfth century, but having access to older materials now lost. The letters of Boniface and those of Alcuin, which form the most valuable contemporary materials for this period, are given by Dr. Giles in his "Patres Ecclesiæ Anglicanæ   They have also been carefully edited by Jaffé in his series of "Monumer a Germanica."]

The supremacy of Northumbria over the English people had fallen for ever with the death of Oswiu, and its power over the tribes of the north was as completely broken by the death of Ecgfrith and the defeat of Nectansmere. To the north, the flight of Bishop Trumwine from Abercorn announced the revolt of the Picts from her rule. In the south, Mercia proved a formidable rival under Æthelred, who had succeeded Wulfhere in 675. Already his kingdom reached from the Humber to the Channel; and Æthelred in the first years of his reign had finally reduced Kent beneath his overlordship. All hope of national union seemed indeed at an end, for the revival of the West-Saxon power at this moment completed the parting of the land into three states of nearly equal power out of which it seemed impossible that unity could come. Since their overthrow at Faddiley, a hundred years before, the West-Saxons had been weakened by anarchy and civil war, and had been at the mercy alike of the rival English states and of the Britons. We have seen however that in 652 a revival of power had enabled them to drive back the Britons to the Parret. A second interval of order in 682 strengthened King Centwine again to take up war with the Britons, and push his frontier as far as the Quantocks. A third rally of the West-Saxons in 685 under Ceadwalla enabled them to turn on their English enemies and conquer Sussex. Ine, the greatest of their early kings, whose reign covered the long period from 688 to 726, carried on during the whole of it the war for supremacy. Eastward, he forced Kent, Essex and London to own his rule. On the west, he pushed his way southward round the marshes of the Parret to a more fertile territory, and guarded the frontier of his new conquests by a fortress on the banks of the Tone, which has grown into the present Taunton. The West-Saxons thus became masters of the whole district which now bears the name of Somerset, the land of the Somersætas, where the Tor rose like an island out of a waste of flood-drowned fen that stretched westward to the Channel. At the base of this hill Ine established on the site of an older British foundation his famous monastery of Glastonbury. The little hamlet in which it stood took its English name from one of the English families, the Glæstings, who chose the spot for their settlement; but it had long been a religious shrine of the Britons, and the tradition that a second Patrick rested there drew thither the wandering scholars of Ireland. The first inhabitants of Ine's abbey found, as they alleged, "an ancient church, built by no art of man ;" and beside this relic of its older Welsh owners, Ine founded his own abbey-church of stone. The spiritual charge of his conquests he committed to his kinsman Ealdhelm, the most famous scholar of his day, who became the first bishop of the new see of Sherborne, which the king formed out of the districts west of Selwood and the Frome, to meet the needs of the new parts of his kingdom. Ine's code, the earliest collection of West-Saxon laws which remains to us, shows a wise solicitude to provide for the civil as well as the ecclesiastical needs of the mixed population over which he now ruled. His repulse of the Mercians, when they at last attacked Wessex, proved how well he could provide for its defence. Æthelred's reign of thirty years was one of almost unbroken peace, and his activity mainly showed itself in the planting and endowment of monasteries, which gradually changed the face of the realm. Ceolred however, who in 709 became king of Mercia, took up the strife with Wessex for the overlordship of the south, and in 715 he marched into the very heart of Wessex ; but he was repulsed in a bloody encounter at Wanborough. Able however as Ine was to hold Mercia at bay, he was unable to hush the civil strife that was the curse of Wessex, and a wild legend tells the story of the disgust which drove him from the world. He had feasted royally at one of his country houses, and on the morrow, as he rode from it, his queen bade him turn back thither. The king returned to find his house stripped of curtains and vessels, and foul with refuse and the dung of cattle, while in the royal bed where he had

SEC. IV.

THE THREE
KINGDOMS
685
TO
828
Æthel-
bald of
Mercia
716–757

slept with Æthelburh rested a sow with her farrow of pigs. The scene had no need of the queen's comment: " See, my lord, how the fashion of this world passeth away ! " In 726 Ine laid down his crown, and sought peace and death in a pilgrimage to Rome.

The anarchy that had driven Ine from the throne broke out on his departure in civil strife which left Wessex an easy prey to the successor of Ceolred. Among those who sought Guthlac's retirement at Crowland came Æthelbald, a son of Penda's brother, flying from Ceolred's hate. Driven off again and again by the king's pursuit, Æthelbald still returned to the little hut he had built beside the hermitage, and comforted himself in hours of despair with his companion's words. " Know how to wait," said Guthlac, " and the kingdom will come to thee ; not by violence or rapine, but by the hand of God." In 716 Ceolred fell frenzy-smitten at his board, and Mercia chose Æthelbald for its king. For the first ten years of his reign he shrank from a conflict with the victor of Wanborough; but with Ine's withdrawal he took up again the fierce struggle with Wessex for the complete supremacy of the south. He penetrated into the very heart of the West-Saxon kingdom, and his siege and capture of the royal town of Somerton in 733 ended the war. For twenty years the overlordship of Mercia was recognized by all Britain south of the Humber. It was at the head of the forces, not of Mercia only, but of East Anglia and Kent, as well as of the West-Saxons, that Æthelbald marched against the Welsh ; and he styled himself " King not of the Mercians only, but of all the neighbouring peoples who are called by the common name of Southern English." But the aim of Æthelbald was destined to the same failure as that of his predecessors. For twenty years indeed he met the constant outbreaks of his new subjects with success ; and it was not till 754 that a general rising forced him to call his whole strength to the field. At the head of his own Mercians and of the subject hosts of Kent, Essex and East Anglia, Æthelbald marched to the field of Burford, where the West-Saxons were again marshalled under the golden dragon of their race : but after hours of desperate fighting in the forefront of the battle, a sudden panic seized the Mercian king, and the supremacy of Mid-Britain passed away for ever as he fled first of his army from the field. Three years later he was surprised and slain in a night attack by his ealdormen ; and in the anarchy that followed, Kent, Essex, and East Anglia threw off the yoke of Mercia.

While the two southern kingdoms were wasting their energies in this desperate struggle, Northumbria had set aside its efforts at conquest for the pursuits of peace. Under the reigns of Ecgfrith's successors, Aldfrith the Learned and the four kings who followed him, the kingdom became in the middle of the eighth century the literary centre of Western Europe. No schools were more famous than those of Jarrow and York. The whole learning of the age seemed to be summed up in a Northumbrian scholar. Bæda—the Venerable Bede, as later times styled him—was born in 673, nine years after the Synod of Whitby, on ground which passed a year later to Benedict Biscop as the site of the great abbey which he reared by the mouth of the Wear. His youth was trained and his long tranquil life was wholly spent in an off-shoot of Benedict's house which was founded by his friend Ceolfrid. Bæda never stirred from Jarrow. "I have spent my whole life in the same monastery," he says, "and while attentive to the rule of my order and the service of the Church my constant pleasure lay in learning, or teaching, or writing." The words sketch for us a scholar's life, the more touching in its simplicity that it is the life of the first great English scholar. The quiet grandeur of a life consecrated to knowledge, the tranquil pleasure that lies in learning and teaching and writing, dawned for Englishmen in the story of Bæda. While still young, he became teacher ; and six hundred monks, besides strangers that flocked thither for instruction, formed his school of Jarrow. It is hard to imagine how among the toils of the schoolmaster and the duties of the monk Bæda could have found time for the composition of the numerous works that made his name famous in the west. But materials for study had accumulated in Northumbria through the journeys of Wilfrid and Benedict Biscop and the libraries which were forming at Wearmouth and York. The tradition of the older Irish teachers still lingered to direct the young scholar into that path of Scriptural interpretation to which he chiefly owed his fame. Greek, a rare accomplishment in the west, came to him from the school which the Greek Archbishop Theodore founded beneath the walls of Canterbury. His skill in the ecclesiastical chant was derived from a Roman cantor whom Pope Vitalian sent in the train of Benedict Biscop. Little by little the young scholar thus made himself master of the whole range of the science of his time ; he became, as Burke rightly styled him, "the father of English learning." The tradition of the older classic culture was first revived for England in his quotations of Plato and Aristotle, of Seneca and Cicero, of Lucretius and Ovid. Virgil cast over him the same spell that he cast over Dante ; verses from the Æneid break his narratives of martyrdoms, and the disciple ventures on the track of the great master in a little eclogue descriptive of the approach of spring. His work was done with small aid from others. "I am my own secretary," he writes ; "I make my own notes. I am my own librarian." But forty-five works remained after his death to attest his prodigious industry. In his own eyes and those of his contemporaries the most important among these were the commentaries and homilies upon various books of the Bible which he had drawn from the writings of the Fathers. But he was far from confining himself to theology. In treatises compiled as text-books for his scholars Bæda threw together all that the world had then accumulated in astronomy

**Death of
Bæda**

and meteorology, in physics and music, in philosophy, grammar, rhetoric, arithmetic, medicine. But the encyclopædic character of his researches left him in heart a simple Englishman. He loved his own English tongue; he was skilled in English song; his last work was a translation into English of the Gospel of St. John, and almost the last words that broke from his lips were some English rimes upon death.

But the noblest proof of his love of England lies in the work which immortalizes his name. In his "Ecclesiastical History of the English Nation" Bæda became the first English historian. All that we really know of the century and a half that follows the landing of Augustine we know from him. Wherever his own personal observation extended the story is told with admirable detail and force. He is hardly less full or accurate in the portions which he owed to his Kentish friends, Albinus and Nothelm. What he owed to no informant was his own exquisite faculty of story-telling, and yet no story of his own telling is so touching as the story of his death. Two weeks before the Easter of 735 the old man was seized with an extreme weakness and loss of breath. He still preserved, however, his usual pleasantness and good humour, and in spite of prolonged sleeplessness continued his lectures to the pupils about him. Verses of his own English tongue broke from time to time from the master's lips—rude rimes that told how before the "need-fare," Death's stern "must-go," none can enough bethink him what is to be his doom for good or ill. The tears of Bæda's scholars mingled with his song. "We never read without weeping," writes one of them. So the days rolled on to Ascension-tide, and still master and pupils toiled at their work, for Bæda longed to bring to an end his version of St. John's Gospel into the English tongue, and his extracts from Bishop Isidore. "I don't want my boys to read a lie," he answered those who would have had him rest, "or to work to no purpose after I am gone." A few days before Ascension-tide his sickness grew upon him, but he spent the whole day in teaching, only saying cheerfully to his scholars, "Learn with what speed you may; I know not how long I may last." The dawn broke on another sleepless night, and again the old man called his scholars round him and bade them write. "There is still a chapter wanting," said the scribe, as the morning drew on, "and it is hard for thee to question thyself any longer." "It is easily done," said Bæda; "take thy pen and write quickly." Amid tears and farewells the day wore away to eventide. "There is yet one sentence unwritten, dear master," said the boy. "Write it quickly," bade the dying man. "It is finished now," said the little scribe at last. "You speak truth," said the master; "all is finished now." Placed upon the pavement, his head supported in his scholars' arms, his face turned to the spot where he was wont to pray, Bæda chanted the solemn "Glory to

God." As his voice reached the close of his song he passed quietly away.

First among English scholars, first among English theologians, first among English historians, it is in the monk of Jarrow that English literature strikes its roots. In the six hundred scholars who gathered round him for instruction he is the father of our national education. In his physical treatises he is the first figure to which our science looks back. Bæda was a statesman as well as a scholar, and the letter which in the last year of his life he addressed to Ecgberht of York shows how vigorously he proposed to battle against the growing anarchy of Northumbria. But his plans of reform came too late, though a king like Eadberht, with his brother Ecgberht, the first Archbishop of York, might for a time revive the fading glories of his kingdom. Eadberht repelled an attack of Æthelbald on his southern border ; while at the same time he carried on a successful war against the Picts. Ten years later he penetrated into Ayrshire, and finally made an alliance with the Picts, which enabled him in 756 to conquer Strathclyde and take its capital Alcluyd, or Dumbarton. But at the moment when his triumph seemed complete, his army was utterly destroyed as it withdrew homewards, and so crushing was the calamity that even Eadberht could only fling down his sceptre and withdraw with his brother the Archbishop to a monastery. From this time the history of Northumbria is only a wild story of lawlessness and bloodshed. King after king was swept away by treason and revolt, the country fell into the hands of its turbulent nobles, the very fields lay waste, and the land was scourged by famine and plague. Isolated from the rest of the country during fifty years of anarchy, the northern realm hardly seemed to form part of the English people.

The work in fact of national consolidation among the English seemed to be fatally arrested. The battle of Burford had finally settled the division of Britain into three equal powers. Wessex was now as firmly planted south of the Thames as Northumbria north of the Humber. But this crushing defeat was far from having broken the Mercian power; and under Offa, whose reign from 758 to 796 covers with that of Æthelbald nearly the whole of the eighth century, it rose to a height unknown since the days of Wulfhere. Years however had to pass before the new king could set about the recovery of Kent ; and it was only after a war of three years that in 775 a victory at Otford gave it back to the Mercian realm. With Kent Offa doubtless recovered Sussex and Surrey, as well as Essex and London ; and four years later a victory at Bensington completed the conquest of the district that now forms the shires of Oxford and Buckingham. For the nine years that followed however Mercia ventured on no further attempt to extend her power over her English neighbours. Like her rivals, she turned on the Welsh. Pushing after 779 over the Severn, whose upper course had served till now as the frontier between Briton and Englishman, Offa drove the King of Powys from his capital, which changed its old name of Pengwyrn for the significant English title of the Town in the Scrub or bush, Scrobsbyryg, or Shrewsbury. The border-line he drew after his inroad is marked by a huge earthwork which runs from the mouth of Wye to that of Dee, and is still called Offa's Dyke. A settlement of Englishmen on the land between this dyke and the Severn served as a military frontier for the Mercian realm. Here, as in the later conquests of the Northumbrians and the West-Saxons, the older plan of driving off the conquered from the soil was definitely abandoned. The Welsh who chose to remain dwelt undisturbed among their English conquerors ; and it was probably to regulate the mutual relations of the two races that Offa drew up the code of laws which bore his name. In Mercia as in Northumbria attacks on the Britons marked the close of all dreams of supremacy over the English themselves. Under Offa Mercia sank into virtual isolation. The anarchy into which Northumbria sank after Eadberht's death never tempted him to cross the Humber ; nor was he shaken from his inaction by as tempting an opportunity which presented itself across the Thames. It must have been in the years that followed the battle of Burford that the West-Saxons made themselves masters of the shrunken realm of Dyvnaint, which still retains its old name in the form of Devon, and pushed their frontier westward to the Tamar. But in 786 their progress was stayed by a fresh outbreak of anarchy. The strife between the rivals that disputed the throne was ended by the defeat of Ecgberht, the heir of Ceawlin's line, and his flight to Offa's court. The Mercian king however used his presence not so much for schemes of aggrandizement as to bring about a peaceful alliance ; and in 789 Ecgberht was driven from Mercia, while Offa wedded his daughter to the West-Saxon king Beorhtric. The true aim of Offa indeed was to unite firmly the whole of Mid-Britain, with Kent as its outlet towards Europe, under the Mercian crown, and to mark its ecclesiastical as well as its political independence by the formation in 787 of an archbishopric of Lichfield, as a check to the see of Canterbury in the south, and a rival to the see of York in the north.

But while Offa was hampered in his projects by the dread of the West-Saxons at home, he was forced to watch jealously a power which had risen to dangerous greatness over sea, the power of the Franks. Till now, the interests of the English people had lain wholly within the bounds of the Britain they had won. But at this moment our national horizon suddenly widened, and the fortunes of England became linked to the general fortunes of Western Christendom. It was by the work of English missionaries that Britain was first drawn into political relations with the Frankish court. The Northumbrian Willibrord, and the more famous West-Saxon Boniface or Winfrith, followed in the track of earlier preachers, both Irish and English, who had been labouring among the heathens of Germany, and especially among those who had now become subject to the Franks. The Frank king Pippin's connexion with the English preachers led to constant intercourse with England; a Northumbrian scholar, Alcuin, was the centre of the literary revival at his court. Pippin's son Charles, known in after days as Charles the Great, maintained the same interest in English affairs. His friendship with Alcuin drew him into close relations with Northern Britain. Ecgberht, the claimant of the West-Saxon throne, had found a refuge with him since Offa's league with Beorhtric in 787. With Offa too his relations seem to have been generally friendly. But the Mercian king shrank cautiously from any connexion which might imply a recognition of Frankish supremacy. He had indeed good grounds for caution. The costly gifts sent by Charles to the monasteries of England as of Ireland showed his will to obtain an influence in both countries; he maintained relations with Northumbria, with Kent, with the whole English Church. Above all, he harboured at his court exiles from every English realm, exiled kings from Northumbria, East-Anglian thegns, fugitives from Mercia itself; and Ecgberht probably marched in his train when the shouts of the people and priesthood of Rome hailed him as Roman Emperor. When the death of Beorhtric in 802 opened a way for the exile's return to Wessex, the relations of Charles with the English were still guided by the dream that Britain, lost to the Empire at the hour when the rest of the western provinces were lost, should return to the Empire now that Rome had risen again to more than its old greatness in the west; and the revolutions which were distracting the English kingdoms told steadily in his favour.

The years since Ecgberht's flight had made little change in the state of Britain. Offa's completion of his kingdom by the seizure of East Anglia had been followed by his death in 796; and under his successor Cenwulf the Mercian archbishopric was suppressed, and there was no attempt to carry further the supremacy of the Midland kingdom. Cenwulf stood silently by when Ecgberht mounted the West-Saxon throne, and maintained peace with the new ruler of Wessex throughout his reign. The first enterprise of Ecgberht indeed was not directed against his English but his Welsh neighbours. In 815 he marched into the heart of Cornwall, and after eight years of fighting, the last fragment of British dominion in the west came to an end. As a nation Britain had passed away with the victories of Deorham and Chester; of the separate British peoples who had still carried on the struggle with the three English kingdoms, the Britons of Cumbria and of Strathclyde had already bowed to Northumbrian rule; the

SEC. IV.

THE THREE KINGDOMS

685
TO
828

800

The Fall of Mercia

802

Britons of Wales had owned by tribute to Offa the supremacy of
Mercia ; the last unconquered British state of West Wales as far as
the Land's End now passed under the mastery of Wessex.

While Wessex was regaining the strength it had so long lost, its
rival in Mid-Britain was sinking into helpless anarchy. Within, Mercia
was torn by a civil war which broke out on Cenwulf's death in 821 ;
and the weakness which this left behind was seen when the old strife
with Wessex was renewed by his successor Beornwulf, who in 825
penetrated into Wiltshire, and was defeated in a bloody battle at
Ellandun. All England south of the Thames at once submitted to
Ecgberht of Wessex, and East Anglia rose in a desperate revolt which
proved fatal to its Mercian rulers. Two of its kings in succession fell
fighting on East-Anglian soil ; and a third, Wiglaf, had hardly mounted
the Mercian throne when his exhausted kingdom was called on again
to encounter the West-Saxon. Ecgberht saw that the hour had come
for a decisive onset. In 828 his army marched northward without a
struggle ; Wiglaf fled helplessly before it ; and Mercia bowed to the
West-Saxon overlordship. From Mercia Ecgberht marched on Northumbria ; but half a century of anarchy had robbed that kingdom of all
vigour, and pirates were already harrying its coast ; its nobles met him
at Dore in Derbyshire, and owned him as their overlord. The work
that Oswiu and Æthelbald had failed to do was done, and the whole
English race in Britain was for the first time knit together under a
single ruler. Long and bitter as the struggle for independence was
still to be in Mercia and in the north, yet from the moment that
Northumbria bowed to its West-Saxon overlord, England was made
in fact if not as yet in name.

Section V.—Wessex and the Danes, 802—880.

[*Authorities.*—Our history here rests mainly on the English (or Anglo-Saxon)
Chronicle. The earlier part of this is a compilation, and consists of (1) Annals
of the conquest of South Britain, (2) Short notices of the kings and bishops of
Wessex, expanded into larger form by copious insertions from Bæda, and after
his death by briefer additions from some northern sources. (3) It is probable
that these materials were thrown together, and perhaps translated from Latin
into English, in Ælfred's time, as a preface to the far fuller annals which begin
with the reign of Æthelwulf, and widen into a great contemporary history when
they reach that of Ælfred himself. Of their character and import as a part of
English literature, I have spoken in the text. The " Life of Ælfred " which
bears the name of Asser is probably contemporary, or at any rate founded on
contemporary authority. There is an admirable modern life of the king by
Dr. Pauli. For the Danish wars, see "The Conquest of England " by J R.
Green.]

The effort after a national sovereignty had hardly been begun, when
the Dane struck down the short-lived greatness of Wessex. While
Britain was passing through her ages of conquest and settlement, the

ENGLAND
in the
NINTH CENTURY

Scale of Miles
0   20   40   60   80

Wessex and its immediate
Dependencies

Sites of Battles marked thus ____ +

Picts

Alclyd

Edinburgh

STRATHCLYDE

Jedburgh

NORTHUMBRIA

Man

DEIRA

YORK

Manchester

Thelwall

Peakland

Gainas

Lindesey

Chester

Nottingham

Repton

R. Trent

Holland

Crowland

Northfolk

Norwich

Shrewsbury Lichfield

Buttington Wednesfield

Bridgenorth

NORTH WALES

Tamworth

Medeshamstead
(Peterborough)

EAST

Tettenhall

Warwick R. Nen

ANGLIA

Magesætas

Worcester

Hereford

R. Ouse

Southfolk

Brecknock

Bedford

Dyfed

Severn

Burford

Kirtlington

Hertford

Essex

Gwent

Cirencester

Bensington

St. Albans

Caerleon

Malmesbury Cricklade Wallingford

Oakley

Morganwg

Pucklechurch

Kempsford

M. Sex LONDON

Gloucester

Chippenham

Wantage

Aescesdun

R. Thames

Bristol

Bath

Wanborough

Reading

Merton

I. Sheppey

Calne

Watchet

Wedmore

Frome

Edandun

Easing

Surrey

CANTERBURY

Athelney

Wells

(Wilton) WINCHESTER

Kent

Appledore

Aller

Somerton

Salisbury

Andrédesweald

Appledore

Taunton

Shaftesbury

SUSSEX

Axminster

Sherborne

Wimborne

Gafulford

WEST WALES

Hengestesdun

Dorchester

Wareham

Corfesgate

Swanwick

Exeter

2 W.Gr.

SEC. V.

WESSEX
AND THE
DANES
802
TO
880

dwellers in the Scandinavian peninsula and the isles of the Baltic had lain hidden from Christendom, waging their battle for existence with a stern climate, a barren soil, and stormy seas. Forays and plunder-raids over sea eked out their scanty livelihood, and as the eighth century closed, these raids found a wider sphere than the waters of the north. Ecgberht had not yet brought all Britain under his sway when the Wi-kings or "creek-men," as the adventurers were called, were seen hovering off the English coast, and growing in numbers and hardihood as they crept southward to the Thames. The first sight of the northmen is as if the hand on the dial of history had gone back three hundred years. The Norwegian fiords, the Frisian sandbanks, poured forth pirate fleets such as had swept the seas in the days of Hengest and Cerdic. There was the same wild panic as the black boats of the invaders struck inland along the river-reaches, or moored around the river islets, the same sights of horror, firing of homesteads, slaughter of men, women driven off to slavery or shame, children tossed on pikes or sold in the market-place, as when the English invaders attacked Britain. Christian priests were again slain at the altar by worshippers of Woden; letters, arts, religion, government disappeared before these northmen as before the northmen of old. But when the wild burst of the storm was over, land, people, government reappeared unchanged. England still remained England; the conquerors sank quietly into the mass of those around them; and Woden yielded without a struggle to Christ. The secret of this difference between the two invasions was that the battle was no longer between men of different races. It was no longer a fight between Briton and German, between Englishman and Welshman. The life of these northern folk was in the main the life of the earlier Englishmen. Their customs, their religion, their social order were the same; they were in fact kinsmen bringing back to an England that had forgotten its origins the barbaric England of its pirate forefathers. Nowhere over Europe was the fight so fierce, because nowhere else were the combatants men of one blood and one speech. But just for this reason the fusion of the northmen with their foes was nowhere so peaceful and so complete.

Britain had to meet a double attack from its new assailants. The northmen of Norway had struck westward to the Shetlands and Orkneys, and passed thence by the Hebrides to Ireland; while their kinsmen who now dwelt in the old Engle-land steered along the coasts of Frisia and Gaul. Shut in between the two lines of their advance, Britain lay in the very centre of their field of operations; and at the close of Ecgberht's reign, when the decisive struggle first began, their attacks were directed to the two extremities of the West-Saxon realm. After having harried East Anglia and slain in Kent, they swept up the Thames to the plunder of London; while the pirates in the Irish

SEC. V.

WESSEX
AND THE
DANES

802
TO
880

851

853

866

870

Channel roused all Cornwall to revolt. It was in the alliance of the northmen with the Britons that the danger of these earlier inroads lay. Ecgberht indeed defeated the united forces of these two enemies in a victory at Hengest-dun, but an unequal struggle was carried on for years to come in the Wessex west of Selwood. King Æthelwulf, who followed Ecgberht in 839, fought strenuously in the defence of his realm; in the defeat of Charmouth, as in the victory at Aclea, he led his troops in person against the sea-robbers; and he drove back the Welsh of North Wales, who were encouraged by the invaders to rise in arms. Northmen and Welshmen were beaten again and again, and yet the peril grew greater year by year. The dangers to the Christian faith from these heathen assailants roused the clergy to his aid. Swithun, Bishop of Winchester, became Æthelwulf's minister; Ealhstan, Bishop of Sherborne, was among the soldiers of the Cross, and with the ealdormen led the fyrds of Somerset and Dorset to drive the invaders from the mouth of the Parret. At last hard fighting gained the realm a little respite; in 858 Æthelwulf died in peace, and for eight years the Northmen left the land in quiet. But these earlier forays had been mere preludes to the real burst of the storm. When it broke in its full force upon the island, it was no longer a series of plunder-raids, but the invasion of Britain by a host of conquerors who settled as they conquered. The work was now taken up by another people of Scandinavian blood, the Danes. At the accession of Æthelred, the third of Æthelwulf's sons, who had mounted the throne after the short reigns of his brothers, these new assailants fell on Britain. As they came to the front, the character of the attack wholly changed. The petty squadrons which had till now harassed the coast of Britain made way for larger hosts than had as yet fallen on any country in the west; while raid and foray were replaced by the regular campaign of armies who marched to conquer, and whose aim was to settle on the land they won. In 866 the Danes landed in East Anglia, and marched in the next spring across the Humber upon York. Civil strife as usual distracted the energies of Northumbria. Its subject-crown was disputed by two claimants, and when they united to meet this common danger both fell in the same defeat before the walls of their capital. Northumbria at once submitted to the Danes, and Mercia was only saved by a hasty march of King Æthelred to its aid. But the Peace of Nottingham, by which Æthelred rescued Mercia in 868, left the Danes free to turn to the rich spoil of the great abbeys of the Fen. Peterborough, Crowland, Ely, went up in flames, and their monks fled or were slain among the ruins. From thence they struck suddenly for East Anglia itself, whose king, Eadmund, brought prisoner before the Danish leaders, was bound to a tree and shot to death with arrows. His martyrdom by the heathen made him the St. Sebastian of English legend; in later days his figure gleamed from the pictured windows of church after

Sec. V.

Wessex
and the
Danes

802
to
880

church along the eastern coast, and the stately abbey of St. Edmundsbury rose over his relics. With Eadmund ended the line of East
Anglian under-kings, for his kingdom was not only conquered, but ten
years later it was divided among the soldiers of a Danish host, whose
leader, Guthrum, assumed its crown. How great was the terror stirred
by these successive victories was shown in the action of Mercia, which,
though it was as yet still spared from actual conquest, crouched in
terror before the Danes, acknowledged them in 870 as its overlords,
and paid them tribute.

In four years the work of Ecgberht had been undone, and England
north of the Thames had been torn from the overlordship of Wessex.
So rapid a conquest as the Danish conquests of Northumbria, Mercia,
and East Anglia, had only been made possible by the temper of these
kingdoms themselves. To them the conquest was simply their transfer
from one overlord to another, and it would seem as if they preferred
the lordship of the Dane to the overlordship of the West-Saxon. It
was another sign of the enormous difficulty of welding these kingdoms
together into a single people. The time had now come for Wessex to
fight, not for supremacy, but for life. As yet it seemed paralyzed by
terror. With the exception of his one march on Nottingham, King
Æthelred had done nothing to save his under-kingdoms from the
wreck. But the Danes no sooner pushed up Thames to Reading than
the West-Saxons, attacked on their own soil, turned fiercely at bay. The
enemy penetrated indeed into the heart of Wessex as far as the
heights that overlook the Vale of White Horse. A desperate battle
drove them back from Ashdown ; but their camp in the tongue of
land between the Kennet and Thames proved impregnable, and fresh
forces pushed up the Thames to join their fellows. In the midst of
the struggle Æthelred died, and left his youngest brother Ælfred to
meet a fresh advance of the foe. They had already encamped at
Wilton before the young king could meet them, and a series of defeats
forced him to buy the withdrawal of the pirates and win a few years'
breathing-space for his realm. It was easy for the quick eye of Ælfred
to see that the Danes had withdrawn simply with the view of gaining
firmer footing for a new attack ; indeed, three years had hardly passed
before Mercia was invaded, and its under-king driven over sea to
make place for a tributary of the Danes. From Repton half their
host marched northwards to the Tyne, dividing a land where there
was little left to plunder, colonizing and tilling it, while Guthrum
led the rest into East Anglia to prepare for their next year's attack on
Wessex. The greatness of the contest had now drawn to Britain the
whole strength of the northmen ; and it was with a host swollen by
reinforcements from every quarter that Guthrum at last set sail for the
south. In 876 the Danish fleet appeared before Wareham, and when
a treaty with Ælfred won their withdrawal, they threw themselves

SEC. V.

WESSEX
AND THE
DANES

802
TO
880

into Exeter and allied themselves with the Welsh.   Through the winter Ælfred girded himself for this new peril.   At break of spring his army closed round the town, while a hired fleet cruised off the coast to guard against rescue.   The peril of their brethren in Exeter forced a part of the Danish host which had remained at Wareham to put to sea with the view of aiding them, but they were driven by a storm on the rocks of Swanage, and Exeter was at last starved into surrender, while the Danes again swore to leave Wessex.

Peace of Wedmore

They withdrew in fact to Gloucester, but Ælfred had hardly disbanded his troops when his enemies, roused by the arrival of fresh hordes eager for plunder, reappeared at Chippenham, and at the opening of 878 marched ravaging over the land.   The surprise was complete, and for a month or two a general panic left no hope of resistance.   Ælfred, with his small band of followers, could only throw himself into a fort raised hastily in the isle of Athelney, among the marshes of the Parret.   It was a position from which he could watch closely the movements of his foes, and with the first burst of spring he called the thegns of Somerset to his standard, and still gathering his troops as he moved, marched through Wiltshire on the Danes.   He found their host at Edington, defeated it in a great battle, and after a siege of fourteen days forced them to surrender.   Their leader, Guthrum, was baptized as a Christian and bound by a solemn peace or "frith" at Wedmore in Somerset.   In form the Peace of Wedmore seemed indeed a surrender of the bulk of Britain to its invaders.   All Northumbria, all East Anglia, the half of Central England was left subject to the northmen.   Throughout this Dane-law, as it was called, the conquerors settled down among the conquered population as lords of the soil, thickly in the north and east, more thinly in the central districts, but everywhere guarding jealously their old isolation, and gathering in separate "heres" or armies round towns which were only linked in loose confederacies.   The peace had in fact saved little more than Wessex itself.   But in saving Wessex it saved England.   The spell of terror was broken.   The tide of invasion was turned.   Only one short struggle broke a peace of fifteen years.

Ælfred

871-901

With the Peace of Wedmore in 878 began a work even more noble than this deliverance of Wessex from the Dane.   "So long as I have lived," wrote Ælfred in later days, "I have striven to live worthily." He longed when death overtook him "to leave to the men that come after a remembrance of him in good works."   The aim has been more than fulfilled.   The memory of the life and doings of the noblest of English rulers has come down to us living and distinct through the mist of exaggeration and legend that gathered round it.   Politically or intellectually, the sphere of Ælfred's action may seem too small to justify a comparison of him with the few whom the world claims as its greatest men.   What really lifts him to their level is the moral grandeur of his life. He lived solely for the good of his people. He is the first instance in the history of Christendom of a ruler who put aside every personal aim or ambition to devote himself wholly to the welfare of those whom he ruled. In his mouth "to live worthily" meant a life of justice, temperance, self-sacrifice. The Peace of Wedmore at once marked the temper of the man. Warrior and conqueror as he was, with a disorganized England before him, he set aside at thirty the dream of conquest to leave behind him the memory not of victories but of "good works," of daily toils by which he secured peace, good government, education for his people. His policy was one of peace. He abandoned all thought of the recovery of the West-Saxon over-lordship. With England across the Watling Street, a Roman road which ran from Chester to London, in other words with Northumbria, East-Anglia, and the half of Mercia, Ælfred had nothing to do. All that he retained was his own Wessex, with the upper part of the valley of the Thames, the whole valley of the Severn, and the rich plains of the Mersey and the Dee. Over these latter districts, to which the name of Mercia was now confined, while the rest of the Mercian kingdom became known as the Five Boroughs of the Danes, Ælfred set the ealdorman Æthelred, the husband of his daughter Æthelflæd, a ruler well fitted by his courage and activity to guard Wessex against inroads from the north. Against invasion from the sea, he provided by the better organization of military service, and by the creation of a fleet. The country was divided into military districts, each five hides sending an armed man at the king's summons and providing him with food and pay. The duty of every freeman to join the host remained binding as before ; but the host or fyrd was divided into two halves, each of which took by turns its service in the field, while the other half guarded its own burhs and townships. To win the sea was a harder task than to win the land, and Ælfred had not to organize, but to create a fleet. He steadily developed however his new naval force, and in the reign of his son a fleet of a hundred English ships held the mastery of the Channel.

Sec. V.

Wessex
and the
Danes

802
to
880

The defence of his realm thus provided for, he devoted himself to its good government. In Wessex itself, spent by years of deadly struggle, with law, order, the machinery of justice and government weakened by the pirate storm, material and moral civilization had alike to be revived. His work was of a simple and practical order. In politics as in war, or in his after dealings with letters, he took what was closest at hand and made the best of it. In the reorganization of public justice his main work was to enforce submission to the justice of hundred-moot and shire-moot alike on noble and ceorl, " who were constantly at obstinate variance with one another in the folk-moots, so that hardly any one of them would grant that to be true doom that had been judged for doom by the ealdorman and reeves." "All the law

E

SEC. V.

WESSEX
AND THE
DANES

802
TO
880

dooms of his land that were given in his absence he used to keenly question, of what sort they were, just or unjust; and if he found any wrongdoing in them he would call the judges themselves before him." "Day and night," says his biographer, he was busied in the correction of local injustice : "for in that whole kingdom the poor had no helpers, or few, save the king himself." Of a new legislation the king had no thought. "Those things which I met with," he tells us, "either of the days of Ine, my kinsman, or of Offa, king of the Mercians, or of Æthelberht, who first among the English race received baptism, those which seemed to me rightest, those I have gathered, and rejected the others." But unpretending as the work might seem, its importance was great. With it began the conception of a national law. The notion of separate systems of tribal customs for the separate peoples passed away ; and the codes of Wessex, Mercia, and Kent blended in the doom-book of a common England.

The new strength which had been won for Ælfred's kingdom in six years of peace was shown when the next pirate onset fell on the land. A host from Gaul pushed up the Thames and thence to Rochester, while the Danes of Guthrum's kingdom set aside the Peace of Wedmore and gave help to their brethren. The war however was short, and ended in victory so complete on Ælfred's side that in 886 a new peace was made which pushed the West-Saxon frontier forward into the realm of Guthrum, and tore from the Danish hold London and half of the old East-Saxon kingdom. From this moment the Danes were thrown on an attitude of defence, and the change made itself at once felt among the English. The foundation of a new national monarchy was laid. "All the Angel-cyn turned to Ælfred," says the chronicle, "save those that were under bondage to Danish men." Hardly had this second breathing-space been won than the king turned again to his work of restoration. The spirit of adventure that made him to the last a mighty hunter, the reckless daring of his early manhood, took graver form in an activity that found time amidst the cares of state for the daily duties of religion, for converse with strangers, for study and translation, for learning poems by heart, for planning buildings and instructing craftsmen in gold-work, for teaching even falconers and dog-keepers their business. But his mind was far from being prisoned within his own island. He listened with keen attention to tales of far-off lands, to the Norwegian Othere's account of his journey round the North Cape to explore the White Sea, and Wulfstan's cruise along the coast of Esthonia ; envoys bore his presents to the churches of India and Jerusalem, and an annual mission carried Peter's-pence to Rome. Restless as he was, his activity was the activity of a mind strictly practical. Ælfred was pre-eminently a man of business, careful of detail, laborious and methodical. He carried in his bosom a little hand-book in which he jotted down things as they

SEC. V.

WESSEX
AND THE
DANES

802
TO
880

struck him, now a bit of family genealogy, now a prayer, now a story such as that of Bishop Ealdhelm singing sacred songs on the bridge. Each hour of the king's day had its peculiar task ; there was the same order in the division of his revenue and in the arrangement of his court. But active and busy as he was, his temper remained simple and kindly. We have few stories of his life that are more than mere legends, but even legend itself never ventured to depart from the outlines of a character which men knew so well. During his months of waiting at Athelney, while the country was overrun by the Danes, he was said to have entered a peasant's hut, and to have been bidden by the house-wife, who did not recognize him, to turn the cakes which were baking on the hearth. The young king did as he was bidden, but in the sad thoughts which came over him he forgot his task, and bore in amused silence the scolding of the good wife, who found her cakes spoilt on her return. This tale, if nothing more than a tale, could never have been told of a man without humour. Tradition told of his genial good-nature, of his chattiness over the adventures of his life, and above all of his love for song. In his busiest days Ælfred found time to learn the old songs of his race by heart, and bade them be taught in the palace-school. As he translated the tales of the heathen mytho-logy he lingered fondly over and expanded them, and in moments of gloom he found comfort in the music of the Psalms.

Neither the wars nor the legislation of Ælfred were destined to leave such lasting traces upon England as the impulse he gave to its litera-ture. His end indeed even in this was practical rather than literary. What he aimed at was simply the education of his people. Letters and civilization had almost vanished in Great Britain. In Wessex itself learning had disappeared. "When I began to reign," said Ælfred, " I cannot remember one south of Thames who could explain his service-book in English." The ruin the Danes had wrought had been no mere material ruin. In Northumbria the Danish sword had left but few survivors of the school of Ecgberht or Bæda. To remedy this ignorance Ælfred desired that at least every free-born youth who possessed the means should "abide at his book till he can well under-stand English writing." He himself superintended a school which he had established for the young nobles of his court. At home he found none to help him in his educational efforts but a few prelates and priests who remained in the fragment of Mercia which had been saved from the invaders, and a Welsh bishop, Asser. "Formerly," the king writes bitterly, " men came hither from foreign lands to seek for instruction, and now when we desire it we can only obtain it from abroad." He sought it among the West-Franks and the East-Franks. A scholar named Grimbald came from St. Omer to preside over the abbey he founded at Winchester ; and John the Old-Saxon was fetched, it may be from the Westphalian abbey of Corbey, to rule a

SEC. V.

WESSEX
AND THE
DANES
802
TO
880
**Ælfred's
Transla-
tions**

monastery that Ælfred's gratitude for his deliverance from the Danes raised in the marshes of Athelney.

The work, however, which most told on English culture was done not by these scholars but by the king himself. Ælfred resolved to throw open to his people in their own tongue the knowledge which had till then been limited to the clergy. He took his books as he found them ; they were the popular manuals of his age ; the compilation of Orosius, then the one accessible book of universal history, the history of his own people by Bæda, the Consolation of Boethius, the Pastoral of Pope Gregory. He translated these works into English, but he was far more than a translator, he was an editor for the people. Here he omitted, there he expanded. He enriched Orosius by a sketch of the new geographical discoveries in the north. He gave a West-Saxon form to his selections from Bæda. In one place he stops to explain his theory of government, his wish for a thicker population, his conception of national welfare as consisting in a due balance of the priest, the soldier, and the churl. The mention of Nero spurs him to an outbreak on the abuses of power. The cold Providence of Boethius gives way to an enthusiastic acknowledgement of the goodness of God. As Ælfred writes, his large-hearted nature flings off its royal mantle, and he talks as a man to men. " Do not blame me," he prays with a charming simplicity, " if any know Latin better than I, for every man must say what he says and do what he does according to his ability." But simple as was his aim, Ælfred created English literature. Before him, England possessed noble poems in the work of Cædmon, and his fellow-singers, and a train of ballads and battle-songs. Prose she had none. The mighty roll of the books that fill her libraries begins with the translations of Ælfred, and above all with the chronicle of his reign. It seems likely that the king's rendering of Bæda's history gave the first impulse towards the compilation of what is known as the English or Anglo-Saxon Chronicle, which was certainly thrown into its present form during his reign. The meagre lists of the kings of Wessex and of the bishops of Winchester, which had been preserved from older times, were roughly expanded into a national history by insertions from Bæda ; but it is when it reaches the reign of Ælfred that the Chronicle suddenly widens into the vigorous narrative, full of life and originality, that marks the gift of a new power to the English tongue. Varying as it does from age to age in historic value, it remains the first vernacular history of any Teutonic people, the earliest and most venerable monument of Teutonic prose. The writer of English history may be pardoned if he lingers too fondly over the figure of the king in whose court, at whose impulse, it may be in whose very words, English history begins.

Section VI.—The West-Saxon Realm, 893—1013.

[*Authorities.*—Mainly the English Chronicle, which varies much during this period.　Through the reign of Eadward it is copious, and a Mercian chronicle is embedded in it ; its entries then become scanty, and are broken with grand English songs till the reign of Æthelred, when its fulness returns.　" Florence of Worcester" is probably a translation of a copy of the Chronicle now lost. The " Laws " form the basis of our constitutional knowledge of the time, and fall into two classes.　Those of Eadward, Æthelstan, Eadmund, and Eadgar are, like the earlier laws of Æthelberht and Ine, "mainly of the nature of amendments of custom."　Those of Ælfred, Æthelred, Cnut, with those that bear the name of Eadward the Confessor, "aspire to the character of codes." All are printed in Mr. Thorpe's " Ancient Laws and Institutes of the Anglo-Saxons ;" but the extracts given by Dr. Stubbs ("Select Charters," pp. 59—74) contain all that directly bears on our constitution.　Mr. Kemble's "Codex Diplomaticus Ævi Saxonici" contains a vast mass of charters, &c., belonging to this period.　The lives of Dunstan are collected by Dr. Stubbs in one of the Rolls volumes.　For this period see also Mr. Green's "Conquest of England."]

Ælfred's work of peace was however to be once more interrupted by a new invasion which in 893 broke under the Danish leader Hasting upon England.　After a year's fruitless struggle to force the strong position in which Ælfred covered Wessex, the Danish forces left their fastnesses in the Andredsweald and crossed the Thames, while a rising of the Danelaw in their aid revealed the secret of this movement.　Followed by the Londoners, the king's son Eadward and the Mercian Ealdorman Æthelred stormed the Danish camp in Essex, followed the host as it rode along Thames to rouse new revolts in Wales, caught it on the Severn, and defeating it with a great slaughter, drove it back to its old quarters in Essex.　Ælfred himself held Exeter against attack from a pirate fleet and their West-Welsh allies ; and when Hasting once more repeated his dash upon the west and occupied Chester, Æthelred drove him from his hold and forced him to fall back to his camp on the Lea.　Here Ælfred came to his lieutenant's aid, and the capture of the Danish ships by the two forts with which the king barred the river virtually ended the war.　The Danes streamed back from Wales, whither they had retreated, to their old quarters in Frankland, and the new English fleet drove the freebooters from the Channel.

The last years of Ælfred's life seem to have been busied in providing a new defence for his realm by the formation of alliances with states whom a common interest drew together against the pirates.　But four years had hardly passed since the victory over Hasting when his death left the kingdom to his son Eadward.　Eadward, though a vigorous and active ruler, clung to his father's policy of rest.　It was not till 910 that a rising of the Danes on his northern frontier, and an attack

SEC. VI.

THE WEST-
SAXON
REALM
893
TO
1013

of a pirate fleet on the southern coast, forced him to re-open the war. With his sister Æthelflæd, who was in 912 left sole ruler of Mercia by the death of the Ealdorman Æthelred, he undertook the systematic reduction of the Danelaw. While he bridled East Anglia by the seizure of southern Essex, and the erection of the forts of Hertford and Witham, the fame of Mercia was safe in the hands of its " Lady." Æthelflæd girded her strength for the conquest of the "Five Boroughs," the rude Danish confederacy which had taken the place of the eastern half of the older Mercian kingdom. Derby represented the original Mercia on the upper Trent, Lincoln the Lindiswaras, Leicester the Middle-English, Stamford the province of the Gyrwas—the marshmen of the Fens—Nottingham probably that of the Southumbrians. Each of the " Five Boroughs " seems to have been ruled by its earl with his separate " host ; " within each twelve "lawmen" administered Danish law, while a common justice-court existed for the whole confederacy.

In her attack upon this powerful league Æthelflæd abandoned the older strategy of battle and raid for that of siege and fortress-building. Advancing along the line of Trent, she fortified Tamworth and Stafford on its head-waters, then turning southward secured the valley of the Avon by a fort at Warwick. With the lines of the great rivers alike secure, and the approaches to Wales on either side of Arden in her hands, she in 917 closed on Derby. The raids of the Danes of Middle-England failed to draw the Lady of Mercia from her prey ; and Derby was hardly her own when, turning southward, she forced the surrender of Leicester.

Æthelflæd died in the midst of her triumphs, and Eadward at once annexed Mercia to Wessex. The brilliancy of her exploits had already been matched by his own successes as he closed in on the district of the Five Boroughs from the south. South of the Middle-

English and the Fens lay a tract watered by the Ouse and the Nen— originally the district of a tribe known as the South-English, and now, like the Five Boroughs of the north, grouped round the towns of Bedford, Huntingdon, and Northampton. The reduction of these was followed by that of East Anglia ; the Danes of the Fens submitted

with Stamford, the Southumbrians with Nottingham. Lincoln, the last of the Five Boroughs as yet unconquered, no doubt submitted at the same time. From Mid-Britain the king advanced cautiously to an attack on Northumbria. He had already seized Manchester, and was preparing to complete his conquests, when the whole of the North suddenly laid itself at his feet. Not merely Northumbria but the Scots

and the Britons of Strathclyde " chose him to father and lord." The submission had probably been brought about, like that of the North-Welsh to Ælfred, by the pressure of mutual feuds, and it was as valueless as theirs. Within a year after Eadward's death the north was again on fire. Æthelstan, Ælfred's golden-haired grandson whom the

King had girded as a child with a sword set in a golden scabbard and a gem-studded belt, incorporated Northumbria with his dominions ; then turning westward broke a league which had been formed between the North-Welsh and the Scots, forced them to pay annual tribute, to march in his armies, and to attend his councils. The West-Welsh of Cornwall were reduced to a like vassalage, and the Britons driven from Exeter, which they had shared till then with its English inhabitants. A league of the Scot King, Constantine with the Irish Ostmen was punished by an army which wasted his kingdom, while a fleet ravaged its coasts. But the revolt only heralded the formidable confederacy in which Scotland, Cumberland, and the British and Danish chiefs of the west and east rose at the appearance of the fleet of Olaf in the Humber. The king's victory at Brunanburh, sung in noblest warsong, seemed the wreck of Danish hopes, but the work of conquest was still to be done. On Æthelstan's death and the accession of his young brother Eadmund, the Danelaw rose again in revolt ; the men of the Five Boroughs joined their kinsmen in Northumbria, and a peace which was negotiated by the two archbishops, Odo and Wulfstan, practically restored the old balance of Ælfred's day, and re-established Watling Street as the boundary between Wessex and the Danes. Eadmund however possessed the political and military ability of his house. The Danelaw was once more reduced to submission ; he seized on an alliance with the Scots as a balance to the Danes, and secured the aid of their king by investing him with the fief of Cumberland. But his triumphs were suddenly cut short by his death. As the king feasted at Pucklechurch a robber, Leofa, whom he had banished, seated himself at the royal board, and drew his sword on the cupbearer who bade him retire. Eadmund, springing to his thegn's aid, seized the robber by his hair and flung him to the ground, but Leofa had stabbed the king ere rescue could arrive.

The completion of the West-Saxon realm was in fact reserved for the hands, not of a king or warrior, but of a priest. With the death of Eadmund a new figure comes to the front in English affairs. Dunstan stands first in the line of ecclesiastical statesmen who counted among them Lanfranc and Wolsey, and ended in Laud. He is still more remarkable in himself, in his own vivid personality after nine centuries of revolution and change. He was born in the little hamlet of Glastonbury, beside Ine's church ; his father, Heorstan, was a man of wealth and kinsman of three bishops of the time and of many thegns of the court. It must have been in his father's hall that the fair diminutive boy, with his scant but beautiful hair, caught his love for "the vain songs of ancient heathendom, the trifling legends, the funeral chants," which afterwards roused against him the charge of sorcery. Thence too he may have derived his passionate love of music, and his custom of carrying his harp in hand on journey or visit. The

SEC. VI.

THE WEST-SAXON REALM

893 TO **1013**

Æthelstan 925–940

Brunanburh 937

Eadmund 940–946

Dunstan

SEC. VI.

THE WEST-
SAXON
REALM

893
TO
1016

wandering scholars of Ireland left their books in the monastery of Glastonbury, as they left them along the Rhine and the Danube ; and Dunstan plunged into the study of sacred and profane letters till his brain broke down in delirium.   His knowledge became famous in the neighbourhood and reached the court of Æthelstan, but his appearance there was the signal for a burst of ill-will among the courtiers, though many of them were kinsmen of his own, and he was forced to withdraw.   Even when Eadmund recalled him to the court, his rivals drove him from the king's train, threw him from his horse as he passed through the marshes, and with the wild passion of their age trampled him underfoot in the mire.   The outrage ended in fever, and in the bitterness of his disappointment and shame Dunstan rose from his

c. 940   sick bed a monk.   But in England at this time the monastic profession seems to have been little more than a vow of celibacy, and his devotion took no ascetic turn.   His nature was sunny, versatile, artistic, full of strong affections and capable of inspiring others with affections as strong.   Quick-witted, of tenacious memory, a ready and fluent speaker, gay and genial in address, an artist, a musician, he was at the same time an indefatigable worker, busy at books, at building, at handicraft.   Throughout his life he won the love of women ; he now became the spiritual guide of a woman of high rank, who lived only for charity and the entertainment of pilgrims.   " He ever clave to her, and loved her in wondrous fashion."   His sphere of activity widened as the wealth of his devotee was placed unreservedly at his command ; we see him followed by a train of pupils, busy with literature, writing, harping, painting, designing.   One morning a lady summons him to her house to design a robe which she is embroidering.   As he bends with her maidens over their toil, his harp hung upon the wall sounds without mortal touch tones which the startled ears around frame into a joyous antiphon.   The tie which bound him to this scholar-life was broken by the death of his patroness ; and towards the close of Eadmund's reign Dunstan was again called to the court.   But the old jealousies revived, and counting the game lost he prepared again to withdraw.   The King had spent the day in the chase ; the red deer which he was pursuing dashed over Cheddar cliffs, and his horse only checked itself on the brink of the ravine while Eadmund in the bitterness of death was repenting of his injustice to Dunstan.   He was at once summoned on the King's return.   "Saddle your horse," said Eadmund, "and ride with me !"   The royal train swept over the marshes to Dunstan's home ; and greeting him with the kiss of peace, the king seated him in the priestly chair as Abbot of Glastonbury.

**Dunstan's
adminis-
tration**

From that moment Dunstan may have exercised influence on public affairs ; but it was not till the accession of Eadred, Eadmund's brother, that his influence became supreme as leading counsellor of the crown. We may trace his hand in the solemn proclamation of the king's

SEC. VI.

THE WEST-
SAXON
REALM
893
TO
1013

crowning. Eadred's election was the first national election where
Briton, Dane, and Englishman were alike represented ; his coronation
was the first national coronation, the first union of the primate of the
north and the primate of the south in setting the crown on the
head of one who was to rule from the Forth to the Channel. A
revolt of the north two years later was subdued ; at the outbreak of a
fresh rising the Archbishop of York, Wulfstan, was thrown into prison ;
and with the submission of the Danelaw in 954 the long work of
Ælfred's house was done. Dogged as his fight had been, the Dane at
last owned himself beaten. From the moment of Eadred's final
triumph all resistance came to an end. The north was finally
brought into the general organization of the English realm, and the
Northumbrian under-kingdom sank into an earldom under Oswulf.
The new might of the royal power was expressed in the lofty titles
assumed by Eadred ; he was not only " King of the Anglo-Saxons,"
but " Cæsar of the whole of Britain."

The death of Eadred however was a signal for the outbreak of
political strife. The boy-king Eadwig was swayed by a woman of
high lineage, Æthelgifu ; and the quarrel between her and the older
counsellors of Eadred broke into open strife at the coronation feast.
On the young king's insolent withdrawal to her chamber Dunstan, at
the bidding of the Witan, drew him roughly back to the hall. But
before the year was over the wrath of the boy-king drove the abbot
over sea, and his whole system went with him. The triumph of
Æthelgifu was crowned in 957 by the marriage of her daughter to the
king. The marriage was uncanonical, and at the opening of 958
Archbishop Odo parted the king from his wife by solemn sentence ;
while the Mercians and Northumbrians rose in revolt, proclaimed
Eadwig's brother Eadgar their king, and recalled Dunstan, who
received successively the sees of Worcester and of London. The
death of Eadwig restored the unity of the realm. Wessex submitted
to the king who had been already accepted by the north, and Dunstan,
now raised to the see of Canterbury, wielded for sixteen years as the
minister of Eadgar the secular and ecclesiastical powers of the realm.
Never had England seemed so strong or so peaceful. Without, a
fleet cruising round the coast swept the sea of pirates ; the Danes of
Ireland had turned from foes to friends ; eight vassal kings rowed
Eadgar (so ran the legend) in his boat on the Dee. The settlement of
the north indicated the large and statesmanlike course which Dunstan
was to pursue in the general administration of the realm. He seems
to have adopted from the beginning a national rather than a West-
Saxon policy. The later charge against his rule, that he gave too
much power to the Dane and too much love to strangers, is the best
proof of the unprovincial temper of his administration. He employed
Danes in the royal service and promoted them to high posts in Church

SEC. VI.

THE WEST-
SAXON
REALM

893
TO
1013

and State. In the code which he promulgated he expressly reserved
to the north its old Danish rights, "with as good laws as they best
might choose." His stern hand restored justice and order, while his
care for commerce was shown in the laws which regulated the coinage
and the enactments of common weights and measures for the realm.
Thanet was ravaged when the wreckers of its coast plundered a trading
ship from York. Commerce sprang into a wider life. "Men of the
Empire," traders of Lower Lorraine and the Rhine-land, "men of
Rouen," were seen in the streets of London, and it was by the foreign
trade which sprang up in Dunstan's time that London rose to the
commercial greatness it has held ever since. But the aims of the
primate-minister reached beyond this outer revival of prosperity and
good government. The Danish wars had dealt rudely with Ælfred's
hopes ; his educational movement had ceased with his death, the
clergy had sunk back into worldliness and ignorance, not a single
book or translation had been added to those which the king had left.
Dunstan resumed the task, if not in the larger spirit of Ælfred, at
least in the spirit of a great administrator. The reform of monasticism
which had begun in the abbey of Cluny was stirring the zeal of
English churchmen, and Eadgar showed himself zealous in the cause
of introducing it into England. With his support, Æthelwold, Bishop
of Winchester, carried the new Benedictinism into his diocese, and
a few years later Oswald, Bishop of Worcester, brought monks into
his own cathedral city. Tradition ascribed to Eadgar the formation
of forty monasteries, and it was to his time that English monasticism
looked back in later days as the beginning of its continuous life.
But after all his efforts, monasteries were in fact only firmly planted
in Wessex and East Anglia, and the system took no hold in Northumbria or in the bulk of Mercia. Dunstan himself took little part
in it, though his influence was strongly felt in the literary revival
which accompanied the revival of religious activity. He himself while
abbot was famous as a teacher. His great assistant Æthelwold raised
Abingdon into a school second only to Glastonbury. His other great
helper, Oswald, laid the first foundations of the historic school of
Worcester. Abbo, the most notable scholar in Gaul, came from
Fleury at the primate's invitation.

**Decline
of
Slavery**

After times looked back fondly to "Eadgar's Law," as it was called,
in other words to the English Constitution as it shaped itself in the
hands of Eadgar's minister. A number of influences had greatly
modified the older order which had followed on the English conquest. Slavery was gradually disappearing before the efforts of the
Church. Theodore had denied Christian burial to the kidnapper, and
prohibited the sale of children by their parents, after the age of seven.
Ecgberht of York punished any sale of child or kinsfolk with excommunication. The murder of a slave by lord or mistress, though no

Sec. VI.

The West-
Saxon
Realm
893
to
1013

crime in the eye of the State, became a sin for which penance was due to the Church.   The slave was exempted from toil on Sundays and holydays ; here and there he became attached to the soil and could only be sold with it ; sometimes he acquired a plot of ground, and was suffered to purchase his own release.   Æthelstan gave the slave-class a new rank in the realm by extending to it the same principles of mutual responsibility for crime which were the basis of order among the free.   The Church was far from contenting herself with this gradual elevation ; Wilfrid led the way in the work of emancipation by freeing two hundred and fifty serfs whom he found attached to his estate at Selsey.   Manumission became frequent in wills, as the clergy taught that such a gift was a boon to the soul of the dead.   At the Synod of Chelsea the bishops bound themselves to free at their decease all serfs on their estates who had been reduced to serfdom by want or crime. Usually the slave was set free before the altar or in the church-porch, and the Gospel-book bore written on its margins the record of his emancipation.   Sometimes his lord placed him at the spot where four roads met, and bade him go whither he would   In the more solemn form of the law his master took him by the hand in full shire-meeting, showed him open road and door, and gave him the lance and sword of the freeman.   The slave-trade from English ports was prohibited by law, but the prohibition long remained ineffective.   A hundred years later than Dunstan the wealth of English nobles was said sometimes to spring from breeding slaves for the market.   It was not till the reign of the first Norman king that the preaching of Wulfstan and the in- fluence of Lanfranc suppressed the trade in its last stronghold, the port of Bristol.

But the decrease of slavery went on side by side with an increasing degradation of the bulk of the people.   Political and social changes had long been modifying the whole structure of society : and the very foundations of the old order were broken up in the degradation of the freeman, and the upgrowth of the lord with his dependent villeins. The political changes which were annihilating the older English liberty were in great measure due to a change in the character of English kingship.   As the lesser English kingdoms had drawn together, the wider dominion of the King had removed him further and further from his people, and clothed him with a mysterious dignity.   Every reign raised him higher in the social scale.   The bishop, once ranked his equal in value of life, sank to the level of the ealdorman.   The ealdor- man himself, once the hereditary ruler of a smaller state, became a mere delegate of the king, with an authority curtailed in every shire by that of the royal reeves—officers despatched to levy the royal revenues and administer the royal justice.   Religion deepened the sense of awe.   The king, if he was no longer sacred as the son of Woden, was yet more sacred as "the Lord's Anointed"; and treason

SEC. VI.

THE WEST-
SAXON
REALM
893
TO
1013

against him became the worst of crimes. The older nobility of blood died out before the new nobility of the court. From the oldest times of Germanic history each chief or king had his war-band, his comrades, warriors bound personally to him by their free choice, sworn to fight for him to the death, and avenge his cause as their own. When Cynewulf of Wessex was foully slain at Merton his comrades "ran at once to the spot, each as he was ready and as fast as he could," and despising all offers of life, fell fighting over the corpse of their lord. The fidelity of the war-band was rewarded with grants from the royal domain ; the king became their lord or hlaford, " the dispenser of gifts ;" the comrade became his " servant " or thegn. Personal service at his court was held not to degrade but to ennoble. " Cup-thegn," and "horse-thegn," and "hordere," or treasurer, became great officers of state. The thegn advanced with the advance of the king. He absorbed every post of honour ; he became ealdorman, reeve, bishop, judge ; while his wealth increased as the common folkland passed into the hands of the king, and was carved out by him into estates for his dependents.

**Decline
of the
English
Freeman**

The principle of personal allegiance embodied in the new nobility tended to widen into a theory of general dependence. From Ælfred's day it was assumed that no man could exist without a lord. The ravages and the long insecurity of the Danish wars aided to drive the free farmer to seek protection from the thegn. His freehold was surrendered to be received back as a fief, laden with service to its lord. Gradually the "lordless man " became a sort of outlaw in the realm. The free churl sank into the villein, and changed from the freeholder who knew no superior but God and the law, to the tenant bound to do service to his lord, to follow him to the field, to look to his court for justice, and render days of service in his demesne. While he lost his older freedom he gradually lost, too, his share in the government of the state. The life of the earlier English state was gathered up in its folk-moot. There, through its representatives chosen in every hundred-moot, the folk had exercised its own sovereignty in matters of justice as of peace and war ; while beside the folk-moot, and acting with it, had stood the Witenagemot, the group of " wise men " gathered to give rede to the king and through him to propose a course of action to the folk. The preliminary discussion rested with the nobler sort, the final decision with all. The clash of arms, the " Yea" or " Nay " of the crowd, were its vote. But when by the union of the lesser realms the folk sank into a portion of a wider state, the folk-moot sank with it ; political supremacy passed to the court of the far-off lord, and the influence of the people on government came to an end. Nobles indeed could still gather round the king ; and while the folk-moot passes out of political notice, the Witenagemot is heard of more and more as a royal council. It shared in the higher justice, the imposition of taxes, the making of laws, the conclusion of treaties, the control of war, the disposal of public lands, the appointment of great officers of state. There were times when it even claimed to elect or depose the king. But with these powers the bulk of the nobles had really less and less to do. The larger the kingdom the greater grew the distance from their homes ; and their share in the general deliberations of the realm dwindled to nothing. Practically the national council shrank into a gathering of the great officers of Church and State with the royal thegns, and the old English democracy passed into an oligarchy of the closest kind. The only relic of the popular character of English government lay at last in the ring of citizens who at London or Winchester gathered round the wise men and shouted their " Ay " or " Nay " at the election of a king.

It is in the degradation of the class in which its true strength lay that we must look for the cause of the ruin which already hung over the West-Saxon realm. Eadgar was but thirty-two when he died in 975 ; and the children he left were mere boys. His death opened the way for bitter political strife among the nobles of his court, whose quarrel took the form of a dispute over the succession. Civil war was, in fact, only averted by the energy of the primate ; seizing his cross, he settled the question of Eadgar's successor by the coronation of his son Eadward, and confronted his enemies successfully in two assemblies of the Wise Men. In that of Calne the floor of the room gave way, and according to monkish tradition Dunstan and his friends alone remained unhurt. But not even the fame of a miracle sufficed to turn the tide. The assassination of Eadward was followed by the triumph of Dunstan's opponents, who broke out in " great joy " at the coronation of Eadward's brother Æthelred, a child of ten years old. The government of the realm passed into the hands of the great nobles who upheld Æthelred, and Dunstan withdrew powerless to Canterbury, where he died nine years later.

During the eleven years from 979 to 990, when the young king reached manhood, there is scarcely any internal history to record. New danger however threatened from abroad. The North was girding itself for a fresh onset on England. The Scandinavian peoples had drawn together into their kingdoms of Denmark, Sweden, and Norway ; and it was no longer in isolated bands but in national hosts that they were about to seek conquests in the South. The seas were again thronged with northern freebooters, and pirate fleets, as of old, appeared on the English coast. In 991 came the first burst of the storm, when a body of Norwegian Wikings landed, and utterly defeated the host of East Anglia on the field of Maldon. In the next year Æthelred was forced to buy a truce from the invaders and to suffer them to settle in the land ; while he strengthened himself by a treaty of alliance with Normandy, which was now growing into a great power over sea. A fresh attempt to expel the invaders only proved the signal for the

Sec. VI.

The West-
Saxon
Realm

893
to
1013

Fall of
the West
Saxon
Kingdom

*Eadward
the Martyr*

975-978

*Æthelred
the
Unready*

979-1016

SEC. VI.

THE WEST-
SAXON
REALM
893
TO
1013

gathering of pirate-hosts such as England had never seen before, under Swein and Olaf, claimants to the Danish and Norwegian thrones. Their withdrawal in 995 was followed by fresh attacks in 997 ; danger threatened from Normans and from Ost-men, with wikings from Man, and northmen from Cumberland ; while the utter weakness of the realm was shown by Æthelred's taking into his service Danish mercenaries, who seem to have been quartered through Wessex as a defence against their brethren.   Threatened with a new attack by Swein, who was now king, not only of Denmark, but by the defeat and death of Olaf, of Norway itself, Æthelred bound Normandy to his side by a marriage with its duke's sister Emma.   But a sudden panic betrayed him into an act of basest treachery which ruined his plans of defence at home.

Massacre of Danes

1002

Urged by secret orders from the king, the West-Saxons rose on St. Brice's day and pitilessly massacred the Danes scattered among them. Gunhild, the sister of their king Swein, a Christian convert, and one of the hostages for the peace, saw husband and child butchered before her eyes ere she fell threatening vengeance on her murderers.   Swein swore at the news to wrest England from Æthelred.   For four years

1003–1007

he marched through the length and breadth of southern and eastern England, " lighting his war-beacons as he went " in blazing homestead and town.   Then for a heavy bribe he withdrew, to prepare for a later and more terrible onset.   But there was no rest for the realm.   The fiercest of the Norwegian jarls took his place, and from Wessex the war extended over East Anglia and Mercia.   Canterbury was taken and sacked, Ælfheah the Archbishop dragged to Greenwich, and there in default of ransom brutally slain.   The Danes set him in the midst of their husting, pelting him with stones and ox-horns, till one more pitiful than the rest clave his skull with an axe.

But a yet more terrible attack was preparing under Swein in the North, and in 1013 his fleet entered the Humber, and called on the Danelaw to rise in his aid.   Northumbria, East Anglia, the Five Boroughs, all England north of Watling Street, submitted to him at Gainsborough.   Æthelred shrank into a King of Wessex, and of a Wessex helpless before the foe.   Resistance was impossible.   The war was terrible but short.   Everywhere the country was pitilessly harried, churches plundered, men slaughtered.   But with the one exception of London, there was no attempt at defence.   Oxford and Winchester flung open their gates.   The thegns of Wessex submitted to the northmen at Bath.   Even London was forced at last to give way, and Æthelred fled over sea to a refuge in Normandy.   With the flight of the king ended the long struggle of Wessex for supremacy over Britain.   The task which had baffled the energies of Eadwine and Offa, and had proved too hard for the valour of Eadward and the statesmanship of Dunstan, the task of uniting England finally into a single nation, was now to pass to other hands.

CHAPTER II.

ENGLAND UNDER FOREIGN KINGS.

1013—1204.

Section I.—The Danish Kings.

[*Authorities.*—We are still aided by the collections of royal laws and charters. The English Chronicle is here of great importance ; its various copies
differ much in tone, &c., from one another, and may to some extent be regarded as distinct works. Florence of Worcester is probably the translator
of a valuable copy of the Chronicle which has disappeared. For the reign of
Cnut see Green's "Conquest of England." The authority of the contemporary biographer of Eadward (in Luard's "Lives of Eadward the Confessor,"
published by the Master of the Rolls) is "primary," says Mr. Freeman, "for
all matters strictly personal to the King and the whole family of Godwine.
He is, however, very distinctly not an historian, but a biographer, sometimes
a laureate." All modern accounts of this reign have been superseded by the
elaborate history of Mr. Freeman ("Norman Conquest," vol. ii.) For the
Danish kings and the House of Godwine, see the "Conquest of England,"
by Mr. Green.]

BRITAIN had become England in the five hundred years that followed
the landing of Hengest, and its conquest had ended in the settlement
of its conquerors, in their conversion to Christianity, in the birth of a
national literature, of an imperfect civilization, of a rough political
order. But through the whole of this earlier age every attempt to fuse
the various tribes of conquerors into a single nation had failed. The
effort of Northumbria to extend her rule over all England had been
foiled by the resistance of Mercia ; that of Mercia by the resistance of
Wessex. Wessex herself, even under the guidance of great kings and
statesmen, had no sooner reduced the country to a seeming unity than
local independence rose again at the call of the Danes. The tide of
supremacy rolled in fact backwards and forwards ; now the South won
lordship over the North, now the North won lordship over the South.
But whatever titles kings might assume, or however imposing their
rule might appear, Northumbrian remained apart from West-Saxon,
Dane from Englishman. A common national sympathy held the
country roughly together, but a real national union had yet to come.

Through the two hundred years that lie between the flight of
Æthelred from England to Normandy and that of John from Normandy to England our story is a story of foreign rule. Kings from
Denmark were succeeded by kings from Normandy, and these by
kings from Anjou. Under Dane, Norman, or Angevin, Englishmen

**The
foreign
rule**

Sec. I.

The
Danish
Kings
1013
to
1042

were a subject race, conquered and ruled by foreign masters ; and yet it was in these years of subjection that England first became really England. Provincial differences were crushed into national unity by the pressure of the stranger. The same pressure redressed the wrong which had been done to the fabric of national society by the degradation of the free landowner at the close of the preceding age into a feudal dependent on his lord. The English lords themselves sank into a middle class as they were pushed from their place by the foreign baronage who settled on English soil ; and this change was accompanied by a gradual elevation of the class of servile and semi-servile cultivators which gradually lifted them into almost complete freedom. The middle-class which was thus created was reinforced by the upgrowth of a corresponding class in our towns. Commerce and trade were promoted by the justice and policy of the foreign kings ; and with their advance rose the political importance of the trader. The boroughs of England, which at the opening of this period were for the most part mere villages, were rich enough at its close to buy liberty from the Crown. Rights of self-government, of free speech, of common deliberation, which had passed from the people at large into the hands of its nobles, revived in the charters and councils of the towns. A moral revival followed hard on this political developement. The occupation of every see and abbacy by strangers who could only speak to their flocks in an unknown tongue had severed the higher clergy from the lower priesthood and the people ; but religion became a living thing as it passed to the people themselves, and hermit and friar carried spiritual life home to the heart of the nation at large. At the same time the close connexion with the Continent which foreign conquest brought about secured for England a new communion with the artistic and intellectual life of the world without her. The old mental stagnation was broken up, and art and literature covered England with great buildings and busy schools. Time for this varied progress was gained by the long peace which England owed to the firm government of her Kings, while their political ability gave her administrative order, and their judicial reforms built up the fabric of her law. In a word, it is to the stern discipline of these two hundred years that we owe not merely English wealth and English freedom, but England itself.

The first of our foreign masters was the Dane. The countries of Scandinavia which had so long been the mere starting-points of the pirate-bands who had ravaged England and Ireland had now settled down into comparative order. It was the aim of Swein to unite them in a great Scandinavian Empire, of which England should be the head ; and this project, interrupted for a time by his death, was resumed with yet greater vigour by his son Cnut. Fear of the Dane was still great in the land, and Cnut had no sooner appeared off the English coast than Wessex, Mercia, and Northumberland joined in owning him for their

SEC. I.

THE
DANISH
KINGS
1013
TO
1042
Cnut

lord, and in discarding again the rule of Æthelred, who had returned on the death of Swein. When Æthelred's death in 1016 raised his son Eadmund Ironside to the throne, the loyalty of London enabled him to struggle bravely for a few months against the Danes ; but a decisive victory at Assandun and the death of his rival left Cnut master of the realm. Conqueror as he was, the Dane was no foreigner in the sense that the Norman was a foreigner after him. His language differed little from the English tongue. He brought in no new system of tenure or government. Cnut ruled, in fact, not as a foreign conqueror but as a native king. The goodwill and tranquillity of England were necessary for the success of his larger schemes in the north, where the arms of his English subjects aided him in later years in uniting Denmark and Norway beneath his sway. Dismissing therefore his Danish "host," and retaining only a trained body of household troops or hus-carls to serve in sudden emergencies, Cnut boldly relied for support within his realm on the justice and good government he secured it. His aim during twenty years seems to have been to obliterate from men's minds the foreign character of his rule, and the bloodshed in which it had begun. The change in himself was as startling as the change in his policy. When he first appears in England, it is as the mere northman, passionate, revengeful, uniting the guile of the savage with his thirst for blood. His first acts of government were a series of murders. Eadric of Mercia, whose aid had given him the crown, was felled by an axe-blow at the King's signal ; a murder removed Eadwig, the brother of Eadmund Ironside, while the children of Eadmund were hunted even into Hungary by his ruthless hate. But from a savage such as this Cnut rose suddenly into a wise and temperate king. Stranger as he was, he fell back on "Eadgar's law," on the old constitution of the realm, and owned no difference between conqueror and conquered, between Dane and Englishman. By the creation of four earldoms, those of Mercia, Northumberland, Wessex, and East Anglia, he recognized provincial independence, but he drew closer than of old the ties which bound the rulers of these great dependencies to the Crown. He even identified himself with the patriotism which had withstood the stranger. The Church had been the centre of national resistance to the Dane, but Cnut sought above all its friendship. He paid homage to the cause for which Ælfheah had died, by his translation of the Archbishop's body to Canterbury. He atoned for his father's ravages by costly gifts to the religious houses. He protected English pilgrims against the robber-lords of the Alps. His love for monks broke out in the song which he composed as he listened to their chant at Ely : "Merrily sang the monks in Ely when Cnut King rowed by" across the vast fen-waters that surrounded their abbey. "Row, boatmen, near the land, and hear we these monks sing."

F

SEC. I.

THE
DANISH
KINGS
1013
TO
1042

Cnut's letter from Rome to his English subjects marks the grandeur of his character and the noble conception he had formed of kingship. " I have vowed to God to lead a right life in all things," wrote the King, " to rule justly and piously my realms and subjects, and to administer just judgement to all. If heretofore I have done aught beyond what was just, through headiness or negligence of youth, I am ready with God's help to amend it utterly." No royal officer, either for fear of the King or for favour of any, is to consent to injustice, none is to do wrong to rich or poor " as they would value my friendship and their own well-being." He especially denounces unfair exactions : " I have no need that money be heaped together for me by unjust demands." " I have sent this letter before me," Cnut ends, " that all the people of my realm may rejoice in my well-doing ; for as you your-selves know, never have I spared nor will I spare to spend myself and my toil in what is needful and good for my people."

**England
at peace**

Cnut's greatest gift to his people was that of peace. With him began the long internal tranquillity which was from this time to be the special note of our national history. During two hundred years, with the one terrible interval of the Norman Conquest, and the disturbance under Stephen, England alone among the kingdoms of Europe enjoyed unbroken repose. The wars of her Kings lay far from her shores, in France or Normandy, or, as with Cnut, in the more distant lands of the North. The stern justice of their government secured order within. The absence of internal discontent under Cnut, perhaps too the exhaustion of the kingdom after the terrible Danish inroads, is proved by its quiet during his periods of absence. Every-thing witnesses to the growing wealth and prosperity of the country. A great part of English soil was indeed still utterly uncultivated. Wide reaches of land were covered with wood, thicket, and scrub ; or consisted of heaths and moor. In both the east and the west there were vast tracts of marsh land ; fens nearly one hundred miles long severed East Anglia from the midland counties ; sites like that of Glastonbury or Athelney were almost inaccessible. The beaver still haunted marshy hollows such as those which lay about Beverley, the London craftsmen chased the wild boar and the wild ox in the woods of Hampstead, while wolves prowled round the homesteads of the North. But peace and the industry it encouraged were telling on this waste ; stag and wolf were retreating before the face of man, the farmer's axe was ringing in the forest, and villages were springing up in the clearings. The growth of commerce was seen in the rich trading-ports of the eastern coast. The main trade lay probably in skins and ropes and ship masts ; and above all in the iron and steel that the Scandinavian lands so long supplied to Britain. But Dane and Norwegian were traders over a yet wider field than the northern seas ; their barks entered the Mediterranean, while the overland route through Russia brought the wares of Constantinople and the East. "What do you bring to us?" the merchant is asked in an old English dialogue. "I bring skins, silks, costly gems, and gold," he answers, "besides various garments, pigment, wine, oil, and ivory, with brass, and copper, and tin, silver and gold, and such like." Men from the Rhineland and from Normandy, too, moored their vessels along the Thames, on whose rude wharves were piled a strange medley of goods: pepper and spices from the far East, crates of gloves and gray cloths, it may be from the Lombard looms, sacks of wool, iron-work from Liége, butts of French wine and vinegar, and with them the rural products of the country itself—cheese, butter, lard, and eggs, with live swine and fowls.

Cnut's one aim was to win the love of his people, and all tradition shows how wonderful was his success. But the greatness of his rule hung solely on the greatness of his temper, and at his death the empire he had built up at once fell to pieces. Denmark and England, parted for a few years by the accession of his son Harald to the throne of the last, were re-united under a second son, Harthacnut; but the love which Cnut's justice had won turned to hatred before the lawlessness of his successors. The long peace sickened men of this fresh outburst of bloodshed and violence. "Never was a bloodier deed done in the land since the Danes came," ran the popular song, when Harald's men seized Ælfred, a brother of Eadmund Ironside, who had returned to England from Normandy. Every tenth man was killed, the rest sold for slaves, and Ælfred himself blinded and left to die at Ely. Harthacnut, more savage even than his predecessor, dug up his brother's body and flung it into a marsh; while a rising at Worcester against his hus-carls was punished by the burning of the town and the pillage of the shire. His death was no less brutal than his life; "he died as he stood at his drink in the house of Osgod Clapa at Lambeth." England wearied of kings like these: but their crimes helped her to free herself from the impossible dream of Cnut. The North, still more barbarous than herself, could give her no new element of progress or civilization. It was the consciousness of this and the hatred of such rulers as Harald and Harthacnut which co-operated with the old feeling of reverence for the past in calling back the line of Ælfred to the throne.

Section II.—The English Restoration, 1042—1066.

It is in such transitional moments of a nation's history that it needs the cool prudence, the sensitive selfishness, the quick perception of what is possible, which distinguished the adroit politician whom the death of Cnut left supreme in England. Godwine is memorable in our

SEC. I.

THE DANISH KINGS

1013
TO
1042

Fall of the Danish rule

Harald 1035–1039
Harthacnut 1040–1042

Godwine

Sec. II.

The
English
Restora-
tion
1042
to
1066

history as the first English statesman who was neither king nor priest. Originally of obscure origin, his ability had raised him high in the royal favour; he was allied to Cnut by marriage, entrusted by him with the earldom of Wessex, and at last made Viceroy or justiciar in the government of the realm. In the wars of Scandinavia he had shown courage and skill at the head of a body of English troops who supported Cnut, but his true field of action lay at home. Shrewd, eloquent, an active administrator, Godwine united vigilance, industry, and caution with a singular dexterity in the management of men. During the troubled years that followed the death of Cnut he had done his best to continue his master's policy in securing the internal union of England under a Danish sovereign and in preserving her connexion with the North. But at the death of Harthacnut Cnut's policy had become impossible, and abandoning the Danish cause Godwine drifted with the tide of popular feeling which called Eadward, the son of Æthelred, to the throne.

Eadward had lived from his youth in exile at the court of Normandy. A halo of tenderness spread in after-time round this last King of the old English stock; legends told of his pious simplicity, his blitheness and gentleness of mood, the holiness that gained him his name of "Confessor" and enshrined him as a saint in his abbey-church at Westminster. Gleemen sang in manlier tones of the long peace and glories of his reign, how warriors and wise counsellors stood round his throne, and Welsh and Scot and Briton obeyed him. His was the one figure that stood out bright against the darkness when England lay trodden under foot by Norman conquerors; and so dear became his memory that liberty and independence itself seemed incarnate in his name. Instead of freedom, the subjects of William or Henry called for the "good laws of Eadward the Confessor." But it was as a mere shadow of the past that the exile really returned to the throne of Ælfred; there was something shadow-like in the thin form, the delicate complexion, the transparent womanly hands that contrasted with the blue eyes and golden hair of his race; and it is almost as a shadow that he glides over the political stage. The work of government was done by sterner hands. The King's weakness left Godwine master of the realm, and he ruled firmly and wisely. Abandoning with reluctance all interference in Scandinavian politics, he guarded England with a fleet which cruised along the coast. Within, though the earldoms still remained jealously independent, there were signs that a real political unity was being slowly brought about. It was rather within than without that Godwine's work had to be done, and that it was well done was proved by the peace of the land.

Throughout Eadward's earlier reign England lay in the hands of its three earls, Siward of Northumbria, Leofric of Mercia, and Godwine of Wessex, and it seemed as if the old tendency to provincial separation was to triumph with the death of Cnut. What hindered this severance was the ambition of Godwine. His whole mind seemed set on the aggrandizement of his family. He had given his daughter to the king as wife. His own earldom embraced all England south of Thames. His son Harold was Earl of East Anglia ; his son Swein secured an earldom in the west ; and his nephew Beorn was established in central England. But the first blow to Godwine's power came from the lawlessness of Swein. He seduced the abbess of Leominster, sent her home again with a yet more outrageous demand of her hand in marriage, and on the King's refusal to grant it fled from the realm. Godwine's influence secured his pardon, but on his very return to seek it Swein murdered his cousin Beorn, who had opposed the reconciliation. He again fled to Flanders, and a storm of national indignation followed him over sea. The meeting of the Wise Men branded him as "nithing," the "utterly worthless," yet in a year his father wrested a new pardon from the King and restored him to his earldom. The scandalous inlawing of such a criminal left Godwine alone in a struggle which soon arose with Eadward himself. The King was a stranger in his realm, and his sympathies lay naturally with the home and friends of his youth and exile. He spoke the Norman tongue. He used in Norman fashion a seal for his charters. He set Norman favourites in the highest posts of Church and State. Strangers such as these, though hostile to the minister, were powerless against Godwine's influence and ability, and when at a later time they ventured to stand alone against him they fell without a blow. But the general ill-will at Swein's inlawing enabled them to stir Eadward to attack the Earl. A trivial quarrel brought the opportunity. On his return from a visit to the court Eustace Count of Boulogne, the husband of the King's sister, demanded quarters for his train in Dover. Strife arose, and many both of the burghers and foreigners were slain. All Godwine's better nature withstood Eadward when the King angrily bade him exact vengeance from the town for the affront to his kinsman ; and he claimed a fair trial for the townsmen. Eadward looked on his refusal as an outrage, and the quarrel widened into open strife. Godwine at once gathered his forces and marched upon Gloucester, demanding the expulsion of the foreign favourites ; but even in a just quarrel the country was cold in his support. The Earls of Mercia and Northumberland united their forces to those of Eadward ; and in a gathering of the Wise Men at London Swein's outlawry was renewed, while Godwine, declining with his usual prudence a useless struggle, withdrew over-sea to Flanders.

But the wrath of the nation was appeased by his fall. Great as were Godwine's faults, he was the one man who now stood between England and the rule of the strangers who flocked to the Court ; and

SEC. II.

THE
ENGLISH
RESTORA-
TION
1042
TO
1066

Exile of Godwine
1051

SEC. II.

THE
ENGLISH
RESTORA-
TION

1042
TO
1066

1052

**Earl
Harold**

1053–1065

a year had hardly passed when at the appearance of his fleet in the Thames Eadward was once more forced to yield. The foreign prelates and bishops fled over-sea, outlawed by the same meeting of the Wise Men which restored Godwine to his home. He returned only to die, and the direction of affairs passed quietly to his son.

Harold came to power unfettered by the obstacles which had beset his father, and for twelve years he was the actual governor of the realm. The courage, the ability, the genius for administration, the ambition and subtlety of Godwine were found again in his son. In the internal government of England he followed out his father's policy while avoiding its excesses. Peace was preserved, justice administered, and the realm increased in wealth and prosperity. Its gold work and embroidery became famous in the markets of Flanders and France. Disturbances from without were crushed sternly and rapidly ; Harold's military talents displayed themselves in a campaign against Wales, and in the boldness and rapidity with which, arming his troops with weapons adapted for mountain conflict, he penetrated to the heart of its fastnesses and reduced the country to complete submission. But it was a prosperity poor in the nobler elements of national activity, and dead to the more vivid influences of spiritual life. Literature, which on the Continent was kindling into a new activity, died down in England into a few psalters and homilies. The few minsters raised by king or earls contrasted strangely with the religious enthusiasm which was covering Normandy and the Rhineland with stately buildings. The Church sank into lethargy. Stigand, the Archbishop of Canterbury, was the adherent of an antipope, and the highest dignity of the English Church was kept in a state of suspension. No important ecclesiastical synod, no Church reform, broke the slumbers of its clergy. Abroad Europe was waking to a new revival of literature, of art, of religion, but England was all but severed from the Continent. Like Godwine, Harold's energy seemed to devote itself wholly to self-aggrandizement. With the gift of the Northumbrian earldom on Siward's death to Harold's brother Tostig, all England, save a small part of the older Mercia, lay in the hands of the house of Godwine. As the childless Eadward drew to the grave his minister drew closer and closer to the throne. One obstacle after another was swept from his path. A revolt of the Northumbrians drove Tostig, his most dangerous opponent, to Flanders, and the Earl was able to win over the Mercian house of Leofric to his cause by owning Morkere, the brother of the Mercian Earl Eadwine, as Tostig's successor. His aim was in fact attained without a struggle, and the nobles and bishops who were gathered round the death-bed of the Confessor passed quietly at once from it to the election and coronation of Harold.

SEC. III.

NORMANDY
AND THE
NORMANS

912
TO
1066

Section III.—Normandy and the Normans, 912–1066.

[*Authorities.*—Dudo of S. Quentin, a verbose and confused writer, has preserved the earliest Norman traditions. His work is abridged and continued by William of Jumièges, a contemporary of the Conqueror, whose work forms the base of the "Roman de Rou," composed by Wace in the time of Henry the Second. The religious movement is best told by Ordericus Vitalis, a Norman writer of the twelfth century, gossiping and confused, but full of valuable information. For Lanfranc see "Lanfranci Opera, ed. Giles," and the life in Hook's "Archbishops of Canterbury." For Anselm see the admirable biography by Dean Church. The general history of Normandy is told diffusely but picturesquely by Sir F. Palgrave, "Normandy and England," more accurately and succinctly by Mr. Freeman, "History of Norman Conquest," vols. i. and ii.]

The quiet of Harold's accession was at once broken by news of danger from a land which, strange as it seemed then, was soon to become almost a part of England itself. A walk through Normandy teaches one more of the age of our history which we are about to traverse than all the books in the world. The story of the Conquest stands written in the stately vault of the minster at Caen which still covers the tomb of the Conqueror. The name of each hamlet by the roadside has its memories for English ears ; a fragment of castle wall marks the home of the Bruce, a tiny little village preserves the name of the Percy. The very look of the country and its people seem familiar to us ; the peasant in his cap and blouse recalls the build and features of the small English farmer ; the fields about Caen, with their dense hedgerows, their elms, their apple-orchards, are the very picture of an English country-side. On the windy heights around rise the square grey keeps which Normandy handed on to the cliffs of Richmond or the banks of Thames, while huge cathedrals lift themselves over the red-tiled roofs of little market towns, the models of the stately fabrics which superseded the lowlier churches of Ælfred or Dunstan.

Hrolf the Ganger, or Walker, a Norwegian and a pirate leader like Guthrum or Hasting, had wrested the land on either side the mouth of Seine from the French king, Charles the Simple, at the moment when Ælfred's children were beginning their conquest of the English Danelaw. The treaty in which France purchased peace by this cession of the coast was a close imitation of the peace of Wedmore. Hrolf, like Guthrum, was baptized, received the king's daughter in marriage. and became his vassal for the territory which now took the name of "the Northman's land" or Normandy. But vassalage and the new faith sat alike lightly on the pirate. No such ties of blood and speech tended to unite the northman with the French among whom he settled along the Seine as united him to the Englishmen among

The
Norman
settlement

*Peace of
Clair-sur-
Epte*

912

SEC. III.

NORMANDY
AND THE
NORMANS
912
TO
1066

whom he settled along the Humber.   William Longsword, the son of Hrolf, though wavering towards France and Christianity, remained a northman in heart ; he called in a Danish colony to occupy his conquest of the Cotentin, the peninsula which runs out from St. Michael's Mount to the cliffs of Cherbourg, and reared his boy among the northmen of Bayeux, where the Danish tongue and fashions most stubbornly held their own.   A heathen reaction followed his death, and the bulk of the Normans, with the child Duke Richard, fell away for the time from Christianity, while new pirate-fleets came swarming up the Seine.   To the close of the century the whole people are still " Pirates " to the French around them, their land the " Pirates' land," their Duke the " Pirates' Duke."

Yet in the end the same forces which merged the Dane in the Englishman told even more powerfully on the Dane in France.   No race has ever shown a greater power of absorbing all the nobler characteristics of the peoples with whom they came in contact, or of infusing their own energy into them.   During the long reign of Duke Richard the Fearless, the son of William Longsword, heathen Norman pirates became French Christians, and feudal at heart.   The old Norse language lived only at Bayeux, and in a few local names. As the old northern freedom died silently away, the descendants of the pirates became feudal nobles, and the " Pirates' land " sank into the most loyal of the fiefs of France.   The change of manners was accompanied by a change of faith, a change which bound the land where heathendom had fought stubbornly for life to the cause of Christianity and the Church.   The Dukes were the first to be touched by the new faith, but as the religious movement spread to the people it was welcomed with an almost passionate fanaticism.   Every road was crowded with pilgrims.   Monasteries rose in every forest glade.   Herlouin, a knight of Brionne, sought shelter from the world in a little valley edged in with woods of ash and elm, through which a beck or rivulet (to which his house owed its after-name) runs down to the Risle.   He was one day busy building an oven with his own hands when a stranger greeted him with " God save you ! "   " Are you a Lombard ? " asked the knight-abbot, struck with the foreign look of the man.   " I am," he replied : and praying to be made a monk, the stranger fell down at the mouth of the oven and kissed Herlouin's feet.   The Lombard was Lanfranc of Pavia, a scholar especially skilled in the traditions of the Roman law, who had wandered across the Alps to found a school at Avranches, and was now drawn to a religious life by the fame of Herlouin's sanctity. The religious impulse was a real one, but Lanfranc was destined to be known rather as a great administrator and statesman than as a saint. His teaching raised Bec in a few years into the most famous school of Christendom : it was in fact the first wave of the intellectual movement which was spreading from Italy to the ruder

Sec. III.

NORMANDY
AND THE
NORMANS

912
TO
1066

Anselm

countries of the West. The whole mental activity of the time seemed concentrated in the group of scholars who gathered round him ; the fabric of the canon law and of mediæval scholasticism, with the philosophical scepticism which first awoke under its influence, all trace their origin to Bec.

The most famous of these scholars was Anselm of Aosta, an Italian like Lanfranc himself, and who was soon to succeed him as Prior and teacher at Bec. Friends as they were, no two men could be more strangely unlike. Anselm had grown to manhood in the quiet solitude of his mountain-valley, a tender-hearted poet-dreamer, with a soul pure as the Alpine snows above him, and an intelligence keen and clear as the mountain air. The whole temper of the man was painted in a dream of his youth. It seemed to him as though heaven lay, a stately palace, amid the gleaming hill-peaks, while the women reaping in the corn-fields of the valley became harvest-maidens of its heavenly King. They reaped idly, and Anselm, grieved at their sloth, hastily climbed the mountain-side to accuse them to their lord. As he reached the palace the King's voice called him to his feet, and he poured forth his tale ; then at the royal bidding bread of an unearthly whiteness was set before him, and he ate and was refreshed. The dream passed with the morning ; but the sense of heaven's nearness to earth, the fervid loyalty to the service of his Lord, the tender restfulness and peace in the Divine presence which it reflected became the life of Anselm. Wandering like other Italian scholars to Normandy, he became a monk under Lanfranc, and on his teacher's removal to higher duties succeeded him in the direction of the Abbey of Bec. No teacher has ever thrown a greater spirit of love into his toil. " Force your scholars to improve ! " he burst out to another teacher who relied on blows and compulsion. " Did you ever see a craftsman fashion a fair image out of a golden plate by blows alone ? Does he not now gently press it and strike it with his tools, now with wise art yet more gently raise and shape it ? What do your scholars turn into under this ceaseless beating ? " " They turn only brutal," was the reply. " You have bad luck," was the keen answer, " in a training that only turns men into beasts." The worst natures softened before this tenderness and patience. Even the Conqueror, so harsh and terrible to others, became another man, gracious and easy of speech, with Anselm.

But amidst his absorbing cares as a teacher, the Prior of Bec found time for philosophical speculations, to which we owe the great scientific inquiries which built up the theology of the middle ages. His famous works were the first attempts of any Christian thinker to elicit the idea of God from the very nature of the human reason. His passion for abstruse thought robbed him of food and sleep. Sometimes he could hardly pray. Often the night was a long watch till he could seize his conception and write it on the wax tablets which lay beside him. But not even a fever of intense thought such as this could draw Anselm's heart from its passionate tenderness and love. Sick monks in the infirmary could relish no drink save the juice which his hand had squeezed for them from the grape-bunch. In the later days of his archbishoprick a hare chased by the hounds took refuge under his horse, and his voice grew loud as he forbade a huntsman to stir in the chase while the creature darted off again to the woods. Even the greed of lands for the Church to which so many religious men yielded found its characteristic rebuke, as the battling lawyers saw Anselm quietly close his eyes in court and go peacefully to sleep.

Section IV.—The Conqueror, 1042—1066.

[*Authorities.*—Primarily the "Gesta Willelmi" of his chaplain, William of Poitiers, a violent partizan of the Duke. William of Jumièges is here a contemporary, and of great value. Orderic and Wace, with the other riming chronicle of Benoît de Sainte-More, come in the second place. For the invasion and Senlac we have, in addition, the contemporary "Carmen de Bello Hastingensi," by Guy, Bishop of Amiens, and the invaluable pictures of the Bayeux Tapestry. The English accounts are most meagre. The invasion and battle of Senlac are the subject of Mr. Freeman's third volume ("Hist. of Norman Conquest").]

It was not this new fervour of faith only which drove Norman pilgrims in flocks to the shrines of Italy and the Holy Land. The old northern spirit of adventure turned the pilgrims into Crusaders, and the flower of Norman knighthood, impatient of the stern rule of their Dukes, followed Roger de Toesny against the Moslem of Spain, or enlisted under the banner of the Greeks in their war with the Arabs who had conquered Sicily. The Normans became conquerors under Robert Guiscard, a knight who had left his home in the Cotentin with a single follower, but whose valour and wisdom soon placed him at the head of his fellow-soldiers in Italy. Attacking the Greeks, whom they had hitherto served, the Norman knights wrested Apulia from them in

an overthrow at Cannæ, Guiscard himself led them to the conquest of Calabria and the great trading cities of the coast, while thirty years of

warfare gave Sicily to the followers of his brother Roger. The two conquests were united under a line of princes to whose munificence art owes the splendour of Palermo and Monreale, and literature the first outburst of Italian song. Normandy, still seething with vigorous life, was stirred to greed and enterprize by this plunder of the South, and the rumour of Guiscard's exploits roused into more ardent life the daring ambition of its Duke.

William the Great, as men of his own day styled him, William the Conqueror, as by one event he stamped himself on our history was now Duke of Normandy. The full grandeur of his indomitable will, his large and patient statesmanship, the loftiness of aim which lifts him out of the petty incidents of his age, were as yet only partly disclosed. But there never was a moment from his boyhood when he was not among the greatest of men. His life was one long mastering of difficulty after difficulty. The shame of his birth remained in his name of "the Bastard." His father, Duke Robert, had seen Arlotta, the daughter of a tanner of the town, washing her linen in the little brook by Falaise, and loving her had made her the mother of his boy. Robert's departure on a pilgrimage from which he never returned left William a child-ruler among the most turbulent baronage in Christendom, and treason and anarchy surrounded him as he grew to manhood. Disorder broke at last into open revolt. Surprised in his hunting-seat at Valognes by the rising of the Bessin and Cotentin districts, in which the pirate temper and lawlessness lingered longest, William had only time to dash through the fords of Vire with the rebels on his track. A fierce combat of horse on the slopes of Val-ès-dunes, to the south-eastward of Caen, left him master of the duchy, and the old Scandinavian Normandy yielded for ever to the new civilization which streamed in with French alliances and the French tongue. William was himself a type of the transition. In the young duke's character the old world mingled strangely with the new, the pirate jostled roughly with the statesman. William was the most terrible, as he was the last outcome of the northern race. The very spirit of the "sea-wolves" who had so long "lived on the pillage of the world" seemed embodied in his gigantic form, his enormous strength, his savage countenance, his desperate bravery, the fury of his wrath, the ruthlessness of his revenge. "No knight under heaven," his enemies confessed, "was William's peer." Boy as he was, horse and man went down before his lance at Val-ès-dunes. All the fierce gaiety of his nature broke out in the chivalrous adventures of his youth, in his rout of fifteen Angevins with but five soldiers at his back, in his defiant ride over the ground which Geoffry Martel claimed from him, a ride with hawk on fist as though war and the chase were one. No man could bend his bow. His mace crashed its way through a ring of English warriors to the foot of the Standard. He rose to his greatest heights in moments when other men despaired. His voice rang out like a trumpet to rally his soldiers as they fled before the English charge at Senlac. In his winter march on Chester he strode afoot at the head of his fainting troops, and helped with his own hands to clear a road through the snowdrifts. With the northman's daring broke out the northman's pitilessness. When the townsmen of Alençon hung raw hides along their walls in scorn of the baseness of his birth, with cries of "Work for the Tanner!" William tore out his prisoners' eyes, cut off their hands and feet, and flung them into the town. At the close of his greatest victory he refused Harold's body a grave. Hundreds of Hampshire men were driven from their

Sec. IV.

THE
CONQUEROR

1042
TO
1066

1027

1035

1047

homes to make him a hunting-ground, and his harrying of Northumbria left the north of England a desolate waste. There is a grim, ruthless ring about his very jests. In his old age Philip of France mocked at the Conqueror's unwieldy bulk and at the sickness which confined him to his bed at Rouen. "King William has as long a lying-in," laughed his enemy, "as a woman behind her curtains!" "When I get up," swore William, "I will go to mass in Philip's land, and bring a rich offering for my churching. I will offer a thousand candles for my fee. Flaming brands shall they be, and steel shall glitter over the fire they make." At harvest-tide town and hamlet flaring into ashes along the French border fulfilled the Conqueror's vow. There is the same savage temper in the loneliness of his life. He recked little of men's love or hate. His grim look, his pride, his silence, his wild outbursts of passion, spread terror through his court. "So stark and fierce was he," says the English Chronicler, "that none dared resist his will." His graciousness to Anselm only brought out into stronger relief the general harshness of his tone. His very wrath was solitary. "To no man spake he, and no man dared speak to him," when the news reached him of Harold's accession to the throne. It was only when he passed from the palace to the loneliness of the woods that the King's temper unbent. "He loved the wild deer as though he had been their father. Whosoever should slay hart or hind man should blind him." Death itself took its colour from the savage solitude of his life. Priests and nobles fled as the last breath left him, and the Conqueror's body lay naked and lonely on the floor.

It was the genius of William which lifted him out of this mere northman into a great general and a great statesman. The growth of the Norman power was jealously watched by Geoffry Martel, the Count of Anjou, and his influence succeeded in converting France from friend to foe. The danger changed William at once from the chivalrous knight-errant of Val-ès-dunes into a wary strategist. As the French army crossed the border he hung cautiously on its flanks, till a division which had encamped in the little town of Mortemer had been surprised

and cut to pieces by his soldiers. A second division was still held at bay by the duke himself, when Ralph de Toesny, climbing up into a tree, shouted to them the news of their comrades' fall. "Up, up, Frenchmen! you sleep too long: go bury your friends that lie slain at Mortemer." A second and more formidable invasion four years later was met with the same cautious strategy. William hung on the Frenchmen's flank, looking coolly on while town and abbey were plundered, the Bessin ravaged, Caen sacked, and the invaders prepared to cross the Dive at Varaville and carry fire and sword into the rich land of Lisieux. But only half the army was over the river when the Duke fell suddenly upon its rear. The fight raged till the rising of the tide cut the French forces, as William had foreseen, hopelessly in

two.   Huddled together on a narrow causeway, swept by the Norman
arrows, knights, footmen, and baggage train were involved in the
same ruin.   Not a man escaped, and the French king, who had
been forced to look on helplessly from the opposite bank, fled home
to die.   The death of Geoffry Martel left William without a rival
among the princes of France.   Maine, the border land between
Norman and Angevin, and which had for the last ten years been
held by Anjou, submitted without a struggle to his rule.   Britanny,
which had joined the league of his foes, was reduced to submission by
a single march.

SEC. IV.

THE
CONQUEROR
1042
TO
1066
1060

All this activity abroad was far from distracting the Duke's attention
from Normandy itself.   It was hard to secure peace and order in a
land filled with turbulent robber-lords.   " The Normans must be trodden
down and kept under foot," said one of their poets, "for he only who
bridles them may use them at his need."   William "could never love
a robber."   His stern protection of trader and peasant roused the
baronage through his first ten years to incessant revolt.   His very
kinsfolk headed the discontent, and summoned the French king to
their aid.   But the victories of Mortemer and Varaville left the rebels
at his mercy.   Some rotted in his dungeons, some were driven into
exile, and joined the conquerors of Apulia and Sicily.   The land
settled down into peace and order, and William turned to the reform
of the Church.   Malger, the Archbishop of Rouen, a mere hunting and
feasting prelate, was summarily deposed, and his place filled by
Maurilius, a French ecclesiastic of piety and learning.   Frequent
councils under the Duke's guidance amended the morals of the clergy.
The school of Bec, as we have seen, had become a centre of education ; and William, with the keen insight into men which formed so
marked a feature in his genius, selected its prior as his chief adviser.
In a strife with the Papacy which the Duke had provoked by his
marriage with Matilda of Flanders, Lanfranc took the side of Rome,
and his opposition had been punished by a sentence of banishment.
The Prior set out on a lame horse, the only one his house could afford,
and was overtaken by the Duke, impatient that he should quit Normandy.   "Give me a better horse and I shall go the quicker," replied
the imperturbable Lombard, and the Duke's wrath passed into laughter
and good-will.   From that hour Lanfranc became his minister and
counsellor, whether for affairs in the duchy itself or for the more
daring schemes of ambition which were opened up to him by the
position of England.

For half a century the two countries had been drawing nearer
together.   At the close of the reign of Richard the Fearless the
Danish descents upon the English coast had found support in Normandy, and their fleet had wintered in her ports.   It was to revenge
these attacks that Æthelred had despatched a fleet across the Channel

Sec. IV.
THE
CONQUEROR
1042
TO
1066

1051

1066

The eve
of the
struggle

to ravage the Cotentin, but the fleet was repulsed, and the strife appeased by Æthelred's marriage with Emma, a sister of Richard the Good. Æthelred with his children found shelter in Normandy from the Danish kings, and, if Norman accounts are to be trusted, contrary winds alone prevented a Norman fleet from undertaking their restoration. The peaceful recall of Eadward to the throne seemed to open England to Norman ambition, and Godwine was no sooner banished than Duke William appeared at the English court, and received, as he afterwards asserted, a promise of succession to its throne from the King. Such a promise, unconfirmed by the national assembly of the Wise Men, was utterly valueless, and for the moment Godwine's recall put an end to William's hopes. They are said to have been revived by a storm which threw Harold, while cruising in the Channel, on the French coast, and William forced him to swear on the relics of saints to support the Duke's claim as the price of his own return to England: but the news of the King's death was at once followed by that of Harold's accession, and after a burst of furious passion the Duke prepared to enforce his claim by arms. William did not claim the Crown. He claimed simply the right which he afterwards used when his sword had won it, of presenting himself for election by the nation, and he believed himself entitled so to present himself by the direct commendation of the Confessor. The actual election of Harold which stood in his way, hurried as it was, he did not recognize as valid. But with this constitutional claim was inextricably mingled his resentment at the private wrong which Harold had done him, and a resolve to exact vengeance on the man whom he regarded as untrue to his oath.

The difficulties in the way of his enterprise were indeed enormous. He could reckon on no support within England itself. At home he had to extort the consent of his own reluctant baronage ; to gather a motley host from every quarter of France, and to keep it together for months ; to create a fleet, to cut down the very trees, to build, to launch, to man the vessels ; and to find time amidst all this for the common business of government, for negotiations with Denmark and the Empire, with France, Britanny, and Anjou, with Flanders and with Rome. His rival's difficulties were hardly less than his own. Harold was threatened with invasion not only by William but by his brother Tostig, who had taken refuge in Norway and secured the aid of its king, Harald Hardrada. The fleet and army he had gathered lay watching for months along the coast. His one standing force was his body of hus-carls, but their numbers only enabled them to act as the nucleus of an army. On the other hand the Land-fyrd, or general levy of fighting-men, was a body easy to raise for any single encounter, but hard to keep together. To assemble such a force was to bring labour to a standstill. The men gathered under the King's standard were the farmers and ploughmen of their fields.   The ships were the fishing-vessels of the coast.   In September the task of holding them together became impossible, but their dispersion had hardly taken place when the two clouds which had so long been gathering burst at once upon the realm.   A change of wind released the landlocked armament of William ; but before changing, the wind which prisoned the Duke had flung the host of Harald Hardrada on the coast of Yorkshire.   The King hastened with his household troops to the north, and repulsed the invaders in a decisive overthrow at Stamford Bridge, in the neighbourhood of York ; but ere he could hurry back to London the Norman host had crossed the sea, and William, who had anchored on the 28th off Pevensey, was ravaging the coast to bring his rival to an engagement.   His merciless ravages succeeded, as they were intended, in drawing Harold from London to the south ; but the King wisely refused to attack with the forces he had hastily summoned to his banner.   If he was forced to give battle, he resolved to give it on ground he had himself chosen, and advancing near enough to the coast to check William's ravages, he entrenched himself on a hill known afterwards as that of Senlac, a low spur of the Sussex Downs near Hastings. His position covered London, and drove William to concentrate his forces.   With a host subsisting by pillage, to concentrate is to starve ; and no alternative was left to William but a decisive victory or ruin.

Along the higher ground that leads from Hastings the Duke led his men in the dim dawn of an October morning to the mound of Telham. It was from this point that the Normans saw the host of the English gathered thickly behind a rough trench and a stockade on the height of Senlac.   Marshy ground covered their right ; on the left, the most exposed part of the position, the hus-carls or body-guard of Harold, men in full armour and wielding huge axes, were grouped round the Golden Dragon of Wessex and the Standard of the King.   The rest of the ground was covered by thick masses of half-armed rustics who had flocked at Harold's summons to the fight with the stranger.   It was against the centre of this formidable position that William arrayed his Norman knighthood, while the mercenary forces he had gathered in France and Britanny were ordered to attack its flanks.   A general charge of the Norman foot opened the battle ; in front rode the minstrel Taillefer, tossing his sword in the air and catching it again while he chaunted the song of Roland.   He was the first of the host who struck a blow, and he was the first to fall.   The charge broke vainly on the stout stockade behind which the English warriors plied axe and javelin with fierce cries of " Out, out," and the repulse of the Norman footmen was followed by a repulse of the Norman horse.   Again and again the Duke rallied and led them to the fatal stockade.   All the fury of fight that glowed in his Norseman's blood, all the headlong valour

SEC. IV.

THE
CONQUEROR

1042
TO
1066

1066

Sep. 28
1066

The
Battle of
Senlac
Oct. 14

that had spurred him over the slopes of Val-ès-dunes, mingled that day with the coolness of head, the dogged perseverance, the inexhaustible faculty of resource which had shone at Mortemer and Varaville. His Breton troops, entangled in the marshy ground on his left, broke in disorder, and as panic spread through the army a cry arose that the Duke was slain. " I live," shouted William, as he tore off his helmet, " and by God's help will conquer yet." Maddened by repulse, the Duke spurred right at the Standard ; unhorsed, his terrible mace struck down Gyrth, the King's brother; again dismounted, a blow from his hand hurled to the ground an unmannerly rider who would not lend him his steed. Amidst the roar and tumult of the battle he turned the flight he had arrested into the means of victory. Broken as the stockade was by his desperate onset, the shield-wall of the warriors behind it still held the Normans at bay till William by a feint of flight drew a part of the English force from their post of vantage. Turning on his disorderly pursuers, the Duke cut them to pieces, broke through the abandoned line, and made himself master of the central ground. Meanwhile the French and Bretons made good their ascent on either flank. At three the hill seemed won, at six the fight still raged around the Standard, where Harold's hus-carls stood stubbornly at bay on a spot marked afterwards by the high altar of Battle Abbey. An order from the Duke at last brought his archers to the front, and their arrow-flight told heavily on the dense masses crowded around the King. As the sun went down a shaft pierced Harold's right eye ; he fell between the royal ensigns, and the battle closed with a desperate melly over his corpse. While night covered the flight of the English, the Conqueror pitched his tent on the very spot where his rival had fallen, and " sate down to eat and drink among the dead."

Securing Romney and Dover, the Duke marched by Canterbury upon London. Faction and intrigue were doing his work for him as he advanced. Harold's brothers had fallen with the King on the field of Senlac, and there was none of the house of Godwine to contest the crown ; while of the old royal line there remained but a single boy, Eadgar the Ætheling, son of the eldest of Eadmund Ironside's children, who had fled before Cnut's persecution as far as Hungary for shelter. Boy as he was, he was chosen king ; but the choice gave little strength to the national cause. The widow of the Confessor surrendered Winchester to the Duke. The bishops gathered at London inclined to submission. The citizens themselves faltered as William, passing by their walls, gave Southwark to the flames. The throne of the boy-king really rested for support on the Earls of Mercia and Northumbria, Eadwine and Morkere ; and William, crossing the Thames at Wallingford and marching into Hertfordshire, threatened to cut them off from their earldoms. The masterly movement brought about an instant submission. Eadwine and Morkere retreated hastily home from London, and the city gave way at once. Eadgar himself was at the head of the deputation who came to offer the crown to the Norman Duke. "They bowed to him," says the English annalist pathetically, "for need." They bowed to the Norman as they had bowed to the Dane, and William accepted the crown in the spirit of Cnut. London indeed was secured by the erection of a fortress which afterwards grew into the Tower, but William desired to reign not as a conqueror but as a lawful king. He received the crown at Westminster from the hands of Archbishop Ealdred, amidst shouts of " Yea, Yea," from his new English subjects. Fines from the greater landowners atoned for a resistance which was now counted as rebellion ; but with this exception every measure of the new sovereign indicated his desire of ruling as a successor of Eadward or Ælfred. As yet indeed the greater part of England remained quietly aloof from him, and he can hardly be said to have been recognized as king by Northumberland or the greater part of Mercia. But to the east of a line which stretched from Norwich to Dorsetshire his rule was unquestioned, and over this portion he ruled as an English king. His soldiers were kept in strict order. No change was made in law or custom. The privileges of London were recognized by a royal writ which still remains, the most venerable of its muniments, among the city's archives. Peace and order were restored. William even attempted, though in vain, to learn the English tongue that he might personally administer justice to the suitors in his court. The kingdom seemed so tranquil that only a few months had passed after the battle of Senlac when William, leaving England in charge of his brother, Odo Bishop of Bayeux, and his minister, William Fitz-Osbern, returned for a while to Normandy.

Section V.--The Norman Conquest, 1068—1071.

[*Authorities.*—The Norman writers as before, Orderic being particularly valuable and detailed. The Chronicle and Florence of Worcester are the primary English authorities (for the so-called " Ingulf of Croyland " is a forgery of the 14th century). Domesday Book is of course indispensable for the Norman settlement ; the introduction to it by Sir Henry Ellis gives a brief account of its chief results. Among secondary authorities Simeon of Durham is useful for northern matters, and William of Malmesbury valuable from his remarkable combination of Norman and English feeling. The Norman Constitution is described at length by Lingard, but best studied in the Constitutional History and Select Charters of Dr. Stubbs. The " Anglia Judaica " of Toovey gives some account of the Jewish colonies. For the history as a whole, see Mr. Freeman's " Norman Conquest," vol. iv.]

It is not to his victory at Senlac, but to the struggle which followed his return from Normandy, that William owes his title of the " Conqueror." During his absence Bishop Odo's tyranny had forced the

Sec. V.

The
Norman
Conquest
1068
to
1071

Kentishmen to seek aid from Count Eustace of Boulogne ; while the
Welsh princes supported a similar rising against Norman oppression
in the west.   But as yet the bulk of the land held fairly to the new
king.   Dover was saved from Eustace ; and the discontented fled over
sea to seek refuge in lands as far off as Constantinople, where Englishmen from this time formed great part of the body-guard or Varangians
of the Eastern Emperors.   William returned to take his place again
as an English King.   It was with an English force that he subdued
a rising in the south-west led by Exeter, and it was at the head
of an English army that he completed his work by marching to the
North.   His march brought Eadwine and Morkere again to submission ;
a fresh rising ended in the occupation of York, and England as far as
the Tees lay quietly at William's feet.

It was in fact only the national revolt of 1068 that transformed the
King into a Conqueror.   The signal for this revolt came from without.
Swein, the king of Denmark, had for two years been preparing
to dispute England with the Norman, and on the appearance of his
fleet in the Humber all northern, all western and south-western England
rose as one man.   Eadgar the Ætheling with a band of exiles who
had taken refuge in Scotland took the head of the Northumbrian
revolt ; in the south-west the men of Devon, Somerset, and Dorset

gathered to the sieges of Exeter and Montacute ; while a new Norman
castle at Shrewsbury alone bridled a rising in the west.   So ably had
the revolt been planned that even William was taken by surprise.
The news of the loss of York and of the slaughter of three thousand
Normans who formed its garrison reached him as he was hunting in
the Forest of Dean ; and in a wild outburst of wrath the king swore
" by the splendour of God " to avenge himself on the North.   But wrath
went hand in hand with the coolest statesmanship.   William saw clearly
that the centre of resistance lay in the Danish fleet, and pushing
rapidly to the Humber with a handful of horsemen, he purchased by a
heavy bribe its inactivity and withdrawal.   Then leaving York to the
last, William turned rapidly westward with the troops which gathered
round him, and swept the Welsh border as far as Shrewsbury, while
William Fitz-Osbern broke the rising round Exeter.   His success set
the king free to fulfil his oath of vengeance on the North.   After a long
delay before the flooded waters of the Aire he entered York, and
ravaged the whole country as far as the Tees with fire and sword.
Town and village were harried and burnt, their inhabitants slain or
driven over the Scotch border.   The coast was especially wasted that
no hold might remain for any future invasion of the Danes.   Harvest,
cattle, the very implements of husbandry were so mercilessly destroyed
that the famine which followed is said to have swept off more than a
hundred thousand victims, and half a century later the land still lay
bare of culture and deserted of men for sixty miles northward of York.

The work of vengeance was no sooner over than William led his army back from the Tees to York, and thence to Chester and the West. Never had he shown the grandeur of his character so memorably as in this terrible march. The winter was severe, the roads choked with snowdrifts or broken by torrents ; provisions failed, and the army, drenched with rain and forced to consume its horses for food, broke out into open mutiny at the order to advance across the bleak moorlands that part Yorkshire from the West. The mercenaries from Anjou and Britanny demanded their release from service, and William granted their prayer with scorn. On foot, at the head of the troops which remained faithful, the King forced his way by paths inaccessible to horses, often aiding his men with his own hands to clear the road. The last hopes of the English ceased on his arrival at Chester ; the King remained undisputed master of the conquered country, and busied himself in the erection of numerous castles which were henceforth to hold it in subjection. Two years passed quietly ere the last act of the conquest was reached. By the withdrawal of the Dane the hopes of England rested wholly on the aid it looked for from Scotland, where Eadgar the Ætheling had taken refuge, and where his sister Margaret had become the wife of King Malcolm. It was probably some assurance of Malcolm's aid which roused Eadwine and Morkere to a new revolt, which was at once foiled by the vigilance of the Conqueror. Eadwine fell in an obscure skirmish, while Morkere found refuge for a time in the marshes of the eastern counties, where a desperate band of patriots gathered round an outlawed leader, Hereward. Nowhere had William found so stubborn a resistance ; but a causeway two miles long was at last driven across the fens, and the last hopes of English freedom died in the surrender of Ely. Malcolm alone held out till the Conqueror summoned the whole host of the crown, and crossing the Lowlands and the Forth penetrated into the heart of Scotland. He had reached the Tay when the king's resistance gave way, and Malcolm appeared in the English camp and swore fealty at William's feet.

The struggle which ended in the fens of Ely had wholly changed William's position. He no longer held the land merely as elected king, he added to his elective right the right of conquest. The system of government which he originated was, in fact, the result of the double character of his power. It represented neither the purely feudal system of the Continent nor the system of the older English royalty. More truly perhaps it may be said to have represented both. As the successor of Eadward, William retained the judicial and administrative organization of the older English realm. As the conqueror of England he introduced the military organization of feudalism so far as was necessary for the secure possession of his conquests. The ground was already prepared for such an organization ; we have seen the

Sec. V.

The
Norman
Conquest
1068
to
1071

SEC. V.

THE
NORMAN
CONQUEST
1068
TO
1071

beginnings of English feudalism in the warriors, the "companions" or "thegns" who were personally attached to the king's war-band, and received estates from the folk-land in reward for their personal services. In later times this feudal distribution of estates had greatly increased, as the bulk of the nobles followed the king's example and bound their tenants to themselves by a similar process of subinfeudation. On the other hand, the pure freeholders, the class which formed the basis of the original English society, had been gradually reduced in number, partly through imitation of the class above them, but still more through the incessant wars and invasions which drove them to seek protectors among the thegns at the cost of their independence. Feudalism, in fact, was superseding the older freedom in England even before the reign of William, as it had already superseded it in Germany or France. But the tendency was quickened and intensified by the Conquest ; the desperate and universal resistance of his English subjects forced William to hold by the sword what the sword had won, and an army strong enough to crush at any moment a national revolt was necessary for the preservation of his throne. Such an army could only be maintained by a vast confiscation of the soil. The failure of the English risings cleared the way for its establishment ; the greater part of the higher nobility fell in battle or fled into exile, while the lower thegnhood either forfeited the whole of their lands or redeemed a portion of them by the surrender of the rest. We see the completeness of the confiscation in the vast estates which William was enabled to grant to his more powerful followers. Two hundred manors in Kent, with an equal number elsewhere, rewarded the services of his brother Odo, and grants almost as large fell to William's counsellors, Fitz-Osbern and Montgomery, or to barons like the Mowbrays and the Clares. But the poorest soldier of fortune found his part in the spoil. The meanest Norman rose to wealth and power in the new dominion of his lord. Great or small, however, each estate thus granted was granted on condition of its holder's service at the king's call ; and when the larger holdings were divided by their owners into smaller sub-tenancies, the under-tenants were bound by the same conditions of service to their lord. "Hear, my lord," swore the feudal dependant, as kneeling without arms and bareheaded he placed his hands within those of his superior : "I become liege man of yours for life and limb and earthly regard, and I will keep faith and loyalty to you for life and death, God help me." The kiss of his lord invested him with land or "fief" to descend to him and his heirs for ever. A whole army was by this means encamped upon the soil, and William's summons could at any moment gather an overwhelming force around his standard.

Such a force however, effective as it was against the conquered, was hardly less formidable to the Crown itself. William found himself fronted in his new realm by the feudal baronage whom he had so hardly subdued to his will in Normandy, nobles impatient of law, as jealous of the royal power, and as eager for unbridled military and judicial independence within their own manors here as there. The genius of the Conqueror was shown in his quick discernment of this danger, and in the skill with which he met it. He availed himself of the old legal constitution of the country to hold justice firmly in his own hands. He retained the local courts of the hundred and the shire, where every freeman had a place, while he subjected all to the jurisdiction of the King's Court, which towards the close of the earlier English monarchy had assumed the right of hearing appeals and of calling up cases from any quarter to its bar. The authority of the crown was maintained by the abolition of the great earldoms which had overshadowed it, those of Wessex, Mercia, and Northumberland, and by the royal nomination of sheriffs for the government of the shires. Large as the estates he granted were, they were scattered over the country in a way which made union between the landowners, or the hereditary attachment of great masses of vassals to a separate lord, equally impossible. In other countries a vassal owed fealty to his lord against all foes, be they king or no. By a usage however which William enacted, and which was peculiar to England, each sub-tenant, in addition to his oath of fealty to his lord, swore fealty directly to the Crown, and loyalty to the King was thus established as the supreme and universal duty of all Englishmen. The feudal obligations, too, the rights and dues owing from each estate to the King, were enforced with remarkable strictness. Each tenant was bound to appear if needful thrice a year at the royal court, to pay a heavy fine or rent on succession to his estate, to contribute an "aid" in money in case of the King's capture in war, or the knighthood of the King's eldest son, or the marriage of his eldest daughter. An heir who was still a minor passed into the crown's wardship, and all profit from his estate went for the time to the King. If the estate devolved upon an heiress, her hand was at the King's disposal, and was generally sold to the highest bidder. Over the whole face of the land most manors were burthened with their own "customs," or special dues to the Crown : and it was for the purpose of ascertaining and recording these that William sent into each county the commissioners whose inquiries are preserved in Domesday Book. A jury empanelled in each hundred declared on oath the extent and nature of each estate, the names, number, condition of its inhabitants, its value before and after the Conquest, and the sums due from it to the Crown.

William found another check on the aggressive spirit of the feudal baronage in his organisation of the Church. One of his earliest acts was to summon Lanfranc from Normandy to aid him in its reform; and the deposition of Stigand, which raised Lanfranc to the see of Canter-

SEC. V.

THE
NORMAN
CONQUEST

1068
TO
1071

The
English
baronage

The
Church
of the
Normans

SEC. V.

THE
NORMAN
CONQUEST

1068
TO
1071

bury, was followed by the removal of most of the English prelates and abbots, and by the appointment of Norman ecclesiastics in their place. The new archbishop did much to restore discipline, and William's own efforts were no doubt partly directed by a real desire for the religious improvement of his realm. "In choosing abbots and bishops," says a contemporary, "he considered not so much men's riches or power as their holiness and wisdom. He called together bishops and abbots and other wise counsellors in any vacancy, and by their advice inquired very carefully who was the best and wisest man, as well in divine things as in worldly, to rule the Church of God." But honest as they were, the King's reforms tended directly to the increase of the royal power. The new bishops and abbots were cut off by their foreign origin from the flocks they ruled, while their popular influence was lessened by the removal of ecclesiastical cases from shire or hundred-court, where the bishop had sat side by side with the civil magistrate, to the separate court of the bishop himself. The change was pregnant with future trouble to the Crown ; but for the moment it told mainly in removing the bishop from his traditional contact with the popular assembly, and in effacing the memory of the original equality of the religious with the civil power. The dependence of the Church on the royal power was strictly enforced. Homage was exacted from bishop as from baron. No royal tenant could be excommunicated without the King's leave. No synod could legislate without his previous assent and subsequent confirmation of its decrees. No papal letters could be received within the realm save by his permission. William firmly repudiated the claims which were now beginning to be put forward by the court of Rome. When Gregory VII. called on him to do fealty for his realm, the King sternly refused to admit the claim. "Fealty I have never willed to do, nor do I will to do it now. I have never promised it, nor do I find that my predecessors did it to yours."

But the greatest safeguard of the crown lay in the wealth and personal power of the kings. Extensive as had been his grants to noble and soldier, William remained the greatest landowner in his realm. His rigid exaction of feudal dues added wealth to the great Hoard at Winchester, which had been begun by the spoil of the conquered. But William found a more ready source of revenue in the settlement of the Jewish traders, who followed him from Normandy, and who were enabled by the royal protection to establish themselves in separate quarters or "Jewries" of the chief towns of England. The Jew had no right or citizenship in the land ; the Jewry in which he lived was, like the King's forest, exempt from the common law. He was simply the King's chattel, and his life and goods were absolutely at the King's mercy. But he was too valuable a possession to be lightly thrown away. A royal justiciary secured law to the Jewish merchant, who had no standing-ground in the local courts ; his bonds were deposited for safety in a chamber of the royal palace at Westminster ; he was protected against the popular hatred in the free exercise of his religion, and allowed to build synagogues and to direct his own ecclesiastical affairs by means of a chief Rabbi. That the presence of the Jew was, at least in the earlier years of his settlement, beneficial to the kingdom at large there can be little doubt. His arrival was the arrival of a capitalist ; and heavy as was the usury he necessarily exacted in the general insecurity of the time, his loans gave an impulse to industry such as England had never felt before. The century which followed the Conquest witnessed an outburst of architectural energy which covered the land with castles and cathedrals ; but castle and cathedral alike owed their existence to the loans of the Jew. His own example gave a new direction to domestic architecture. The buildings which, as at Lincoln and S. Edmundsbury, still retain their title of "Jews' Houses" were almost the first houses of stone which superseded the mere hovels of the English burghers. Nor was the influence of the Jews simply industrial. Through their connection with the Jewish schools in Spain and the East they opened a way for the revival of physical science. A Jewish medical school seems to have existed at Oxford ; Roger Bacon himself studied under English Rabbis. But to the kings the Jew was simply an engine of finance. The wealth which his industry accumulated was wrung from him whenever the Crown had need, and torture and imprisonment were resorted to if milder entreaties failed. It was the gold of the Jew that filled the royal exchequer at the outbreak of war or of revolt. It was in the Hebrew coffers that the Norman kings found strength to hold their baronage at bay.

Sec. V.

The Norman Conquest

1068
to
1071

Section VI.—The English Revival, 1071–1127.

[*Authorities.*—Orderic and the English chroniclers, as before. Eadmer, a monk of Canterbury, in his "Historia Novorum" and his "Life of Anselm," is the chief source of information for the reign of William the Second. William of Malmesbury and Henry of Huntingdon are both contemporary authorities during that of Henry the First : the latter remains a brief but accurate annalist ; the former is the leader of a new historic school, who treat English events as part of the history of the world, and emulate classic models by a more philosophical arrangement of their materials. See for them the opening section of the next chapter. On the early history of our towns the reader may gain something from Mr. Thompson's "English Municipal History" (London, 1857) ; more from the "Charter Rolls" (published by the Record Commissioners); for S. Edmundsbury see "Chronicle of Jocelyn de Brakelond" (Camden Society). The records of the Cistercian Abbeys of Yorkshire in "Dugdale's Monasticon," illustrate the religious revival. Henry's administration is admirably explained for the first time by Dr. Stubbs in his "Constitutional History."]

The Conquest was hardly over when the struggle between the baronage and the Crown began. The wisdom of William's policy in

William and the Barons

SEC. VI.

THE
ENGLISH
REVIVAL

1071
TO
1127

1075

the destruction of the great earldoms which had overshadowed the throne was shown in an attempt at their restoration made by Roger, the son of his minister William Fitz-Osbern, and by the Breton, Ralf de Guader, whom the King had rewarded for his services at Senlac with the earldom of Norfolk. The rising was quickly suppressed, Roger thrown into prison, and Ralf driven over sea; but the intrigues of the baronage soon found another leader in William's half-brother, the Bishop of Bayeux. Under pretence of aspiring by arms to the papacy, Bishop Odo collected money and men, but the treasure was at once seized by the royal officers, and the Bishop arrested in the midst of the court. Even at the King's bidding no officer would venture to seize on a prelate of the Church; it was with his own hands that William was forced to effect his arrest. "I arrest not the Bishop, but the Earl of Kent," laughed the Conqueror, and Odo remained a prisoner till William's death. It was in fact this vigorous personality of William which proved the chief safeguard of his throne. "Stark he was," says the English chronicler, "to men that withstood him. Earls that did aught against his bidding he cast into bonds; bishops he stripped of their bishoprics, abbots of their abbacies. He spared not his own brother: first he was in the land, but the King cast him into bondage. If a man would live and hold his lands, need it were that he followed the King's will." But stern as his rule was, it gave peace to the land. Even amidst the sufferings which necessarily sprang from the circumstances of the Conquest itself, from the erection of castles, or the enclosure of forests, or the exactions which built up the great hoard at Winchester, Englishmen were unable to forget "the good peace he made in the land, so that a man might fare over his realm with a bosom full of gold." Strange touches of a humanity far in advance of his age contrasted with the general temper of his government. One of the strongest traits in his character was his aversion to shed blood by process of law; he formally abolished the punishment of death, and only a single execution stains the annals of his reign. An edict yet more honourable to him put an end to the slave-trade which had till then been carried on at the port of Bristol. The pitiless warrior, the stern and aweful king was a tender and faithful husband, an affectionate father. The lonely silence of his bearing broke into gracious converse with pure and sacred souls like Anselm. If William was "stark" to rebel and baron, men noted that he was "mild to those that loved God."

The
English
and their
Kings

1085

In power as in renown the Conqueror towered high above his predecessors on the throne. The fear of the Danes, which had so long hung like a thunder-cloud over England, passed away before the host which William gathered to meet a great armament assembled by King Cnut. A mutiny dispersed the Danish fleet, and the murder of its King removed all peril from the North. Scotland, already humbled by

William's invasion, was bridled by the erection of a strong fortress at Newcastle-upon-Tyne ; and after penetrating with his army to the heart of Wales, the King commenced its systematic reduction by settling barons along its frontier. It was not till his closing years that his unvarying success was disturbed by a rebellion of his son Robert and a quarrel with France ; as he rode down the steep street of Mantes, which he had given to the flames, his horse stumbled among the embers, and William, flung heavily against his saddle, was borne home to Rouen to die. The sound of the minster bell woke him at dawn as he lay in the convent of St. Gervais, overlooking the city— it was the hour of prime—and stretching out his hands in prayer the Conqueror passed quietly away. With him passed the terror which had held the baronage in awe, while the severance of his dominions roused their hopes of successful resistance to the stern rule beneath which they had bowed. William bequeathed Normandy to his eldest son Robert ; William, his second son, hastened with his father's ring to England, where the influence of Lanfranc at once secured him the crown. The baronage seized the opportunity to rise in arms under pretext of supporting the claims of Robert, whose weakness of character gave full scope for the growth of feudal independence, and Bishop Odo placed himself at the head of the revolt. The new King was thrown almost wholly on the loyalty of his English subjects. But the national stamp which William had given to his kingship told at once. Bishop Wulfstan of Worcester, the one surviving bishop of English blood, defeated the insurgents in the West ; while the king, summoning the freemen of country and town to his host under pain of being branded as "nithing" or worthless, advanced with a large force against Rochester, where the barons were concentrated. A plague which broke out among the garrison forced them to capitulate, and as the prisoners passed through the royal army, cries of "gallows and cord" burst from the English ranks. At a later period of his reign a conspiracy was organized to place Stephen of Albemarle, a near cousin of the royal house, upon the throne ; but the capture of Robert Mowbray, the Earl of Northumberland, who had placed himself at its head, and the imprisonment and exile of his fellow-conspirators, again crushed the hopes of the baronage.

While the spirit of national patriotism rose to life again in this struggle of the crown against the baronage, the boldness of a single ecclesiastic revived a national opposition to the mere administrative despotism which now pressed heavily on the land. If William the Red inherited much of his father's energy as well as his policy towards the conquered English, he inherited none of his moral grandeur. His profligacy and extravagance soon exhausted the royal hoard, and the death of Lanfranc left him free to fill it at the expense of the Church. During the vacancy of a see or abbey its revenues went to the royal

Sec. VI.

The
English
Revival
1071
to
1127

Death of
the
Conqueror
1087

The Red
King and
the
Church

SEC. VI.

THE
ENGLISH
REVIVAL

1071
TO
1127

*Anselm
Archbishop*
1093

treasury, and so steadily did William refuse to appoint successors to the prelates whom death removed, that at the close of his reign one archbishoprick, four bishopricks, and eleven abbeys were found to be without pastors. The see of Canterbury itself remained vacant till a dangerous illness frightened the king into the promotion of Anselm, who happened at the time to be in England on the business of his house. The Abbot of Bec was dragged to the royal couch and the cross forced into his hands, but William had no sooner recovered from his sickness than he found himself face to face with an opponent whose meek and loving temper rose into firmness and grandeur when it fronted the tyranny of the King. The Conquest, as we have seen, had robbed the Church of all moral power as the representative of the higher national interests against a brutal despotism by placing it in a position of mere dependence on the crown ; and though the struggle between William and the archbishop turned for the most part on points which have no direct bearing on our history, the boldness of Anselm's attitude not only broke the tradition of ecclesiastical servitude, but infused through the nation at large a new spirit of independence. The real character of the contest appears in the Primate's answer, when his remonstrances against the lawless exactions from the Church were met by a demand for a present on his own promotion, and his first offer of five hundred pounds was contemptuously refused. " Treat me as a free man," Anselm replied, " and I devote myself and all that I have to your service, but if you treat me as a slave you shall have neither me nor mine." A burst of the Red King's fury drove the Archbishop from court, and he finally decided to quit the country, but his example had not been lost, and the close of William's reign found a new spirit of freedom in England with which the greatest of the Conqueror's sons was glad to make terms.

As a soldier the Red King was little inferior to his father. Normandy had been pledged to him by his brother Robert in exchange for a sum which enabled the Duke to march in the first Crusade for the delivery of the Holy Land, and a rebellion at Le Mans was subdued by the fierce energy with which William flung himself at the news of it into the first boat he found, and crossed the Channel in face of a storm. " Kings never drown," he replied contemptuously to the remonstrances of his followers. Homage was again wrested from Malcolm by a march to the Firth of Forth, and the subsequent death of that king threw Scotland into a disorder which enabled an army under Eadgar Ætheling to establish Eadgar, the son of Margaret, as an English feudatory on the throne. In Wales William was less triumphant, and the terrible losses inflicted on the heavy Norman cavalry in the fastnesses of Snowdon forced him to fall back on the slower but wiser policy of the Conqueror. Triumph and defeat alike ended in a strange and tragical close ; the Red King was found dead by peasants in a glade of the New Forest, with the arrow either of a hunter or an assassin in his breast. Robert was still on his return from the Holy Land, where his bravery had redeemed much of his earlier ill-fame, and the English crown was at once seized by his younger brother Henry, in spite of the opposition of the baronage, who clung to the Duke of Normandy and the union of their estates on both sides the Channel under a single ruler. Their attitude threw Henry, as it had thrown Rufus, on the support of the English, and the two great measures which followed his coronation, his grant of a charter, and his marriage with Matilda, mark the new relation which was thus brought about between the people and their King. Henry's Charter is important, not merely as a direct precedent for the Great Charter of John, but as the first limitation which had been imposed on the despotism established by the Conquest. The "evil customs" by which the Red King had enslaved and plundered the Church were explicitly renounced in it, the unlimited demands made by both the Conqueror and his son on the baronage exchanged for customary fees, while the rights of the people itself, though recognized more vaguely, were not forgotten. The barons were held to do justice to their under-tenants and to renounce tyrannical exactions from them, the King promising to restore order and the "law of Eadward," the old constitution of the realm, with the changes which his father had introduced. His marriage gave a significance to these promises which the meanest English peasant could understand. Edith, or Matilda, was the daughter of King Malcolm of Scotland and of Margaret, the sister of Eadgar Ætheling. She had been brought up in the nunnery of Romsey by its abbess, her aunt Christina, and the veil which she had taken there formed an obstacle to her union with the King which was only removed by the wisdom of Anselm. The Archbishop's recall had been one of Henry's first acts after his accession, and Matilda appeared before his court to tell her tale in words of passionate earnestness. She had been veiled in her childhood, she asserted, only to save her from the insults of the rude soldiery who infested the land, had flung the veil from her again and again, and had yielded at last to the unwomanly taunts, the actual blows of her aunt. "As often as I stood in her presence," the girl pleaded, "I wore the veil, trembling as I wore it with indignation and grief. But as soon as I could get out of her sight I used to snatch it from my head, fling it on the ground, and trample it under foot. That was the way, and none other, in which I was veiled." Anselm at once declared her free from conventual bonds, and the shout of the English multitude when he set the crown on Matilda's brow drowned the murmur of Churchman or of baron. The taunts of the Norman nobles, who nicknamed the King and his spouse "Godric and Godgifu," were lost in the joy of the people at large. For the first time since the Conquest an English sovereign sat on the English throne. The blood of Cerdic

SEC. VI.

THE
ENGLISH
REVIVAL
1071
TO
1127

*Henry's
Charter*

*Henry's
marriage*

SEC. VI.

THE
ENGLISH
REVIVAL

1071
TO
1127

The
English
towns

and Ælfred was to blend itself with that of Hrolf and the Conqueror. Henceforth it was impossible that the two peoples should remain parted from each other ; so quick indeed was their union that the very name of Norman had passed away in half a century, and at the accession of Henry's grandson it was impossible to distinguish between the descendants of the conquerors and those of the conquered at Senlac.

We can dimly trace the progress of this blending of the two races together in the case of the burgher population in the towns.

One immediate result of the Conquest had been a great immigration into England from the Continent. A peaceful invasion of the industrial and trading classes of Normandy followed quick on the conquest of the Norman soldiery. Every Norman noble as he quartered himself upon English lands, every Norman abbot as he entered his English cloister, gathered French artists or French domestics around his new castle or his new church. Around the Abbey of Battle, for instance, which William had founded on the site of his great victory, " Gilbert the Foreigner, Gilbert the Weaver, Benet the Steward, Hugh the Secretary, Baldwin the Tailor," mixed with the English tenantry. More especially was this the case with the capital. Long before the landing of William, the Normans had had mercantile establishments in London. Such settlements however naturally formed nothing more than a trading colony ; but London had no sooner submitted to the Conqueror than "many of the citizens of Rouen and Caen passed over thither, preferring to be dwellers in this city, inasmuch as it was fitter for their trading and better stored with the merchandize in which they were wont to traffic." In some cases, as at Norwich, the French colony isolated itself in a separate French town, side by side with the English borough. But in London it seems to have taken at once the position of a governing class. Gilbert Beket, the father of the famous archbishop, was believed in later days to have been one of the portreeves of London, the predecessors of its mayors ; he held in Stephen's time a large property in houses within the walls, and a proof of his civic importance was preserved in the annual visit of each newly-elected chief magistrate to his tomb in the little chapel which he had founded in the churchyard of S. Paul's. Yet Gilbert was one of the Norman strangers who followed in the wake of the Conqueror ; he was by birth a burgher of Rouen, as his wife was of a burgher family from Caen.

It was partly to this infusion of foreign blood, partly no doubt to the long internal peace and order secured by the Norman rule, that the English towns owed the wealth and importance to which they attained during the reign of Henry the First. In the silent growth and elevation of the English people the boroughs led the way : unnoticed and despised by prelate and noble they had alone preserved or won back again the full tradition of Teutonic liberty. The rights of self-govern-

SEC. VI.

THE
ENGLISH
REVIVAL
1071
TO
1127

ment, of free speech in free meeting, of equal justice by one's equals, were brought safely across the ages of tyranny by the burghers and shopkeepers of the towns. In the quiet, quaintly-named streets, in town-mead and market-place, in the lord's mill beside the stream, in the bell that swung out its summons to the crowded borough-mote, in merchant-gild and church-gild and craft-gild, lay the life of Englishmen who were doing more than knight and baron to make England what she is, the life of their home and their trade, of their sturdy battle with oppression, their steady, ceaseless struggle for right and freedom. It is difficult to trace the steps by which borough after borough won its freedom. The bulk of them were situated in the royal demesne, and, like other tenants, their customary rents were collected and justice administered by a royal officer. Amongst our towns London stood chief, and the charter which Henry granted it became the model for the rest. The King yielded the citizens the right of justice : every townsman could claim to be tried by his fellow-townsmen in the town-court or hustings, whose sessions took place every week. They were subject only to the old English trial by oath, and exempt from the trial by battle which the Normans had introduced. Their trade was protected from toll or exaction over the length and breadth of the land. The King however still nominated in London as elsewhere the portreeve, or magistrate of the town, nor were the citizens as yet united together in a commune or corporation ; but an imperfect civic organization existed in the "wards" or quarters of the town, each governed by its own alderman, and in the "gilds" or voluntary associations of merchants or traders which ensured order and mutual protection for their members. Loose too as these bonds may seem, they were drawn firmly together by the older English traditions of freedom which the towns preserved. In London, for instance, the burgesses gathered in town-mote when the bell swung out from S. Paul's to deliberate freely on their own affairs under the presidency of their aldermen. Here too they mustered in arms if danger threatened the city, and delivered the city-banner to their captain, the Norman baron Fitz-Walter, to lead them against the enemy. Few boroughs had as yet attained to power such as this, but charter after charter during Henry's reign raised the townsmen of boroughs from mere traders, wholly at the mercy of their lord, into customary tenants, who had purchased their freedom by a fixed rent, regulated their own trade, and enjoyed exemption from all but their own justice.

The advance of towns which had grown up not on the royal domain but around abbey or castle was slower and more difficult. The story of S. Edmundsbury shows how gradual was the transition from pure serfage to an imperfect freedom. Much that had been plough-land in the time of the Confessor was covered with houses under the Norman rule. The building of the great abbey-church drew its craftsmen and

SEC. VI.

THE
ENGLISH
REVIVAL

1071
TO
1127

masons to mingle with the ploughmen and reapers of the Abbot's domain. The troubles of the time helped here as elsewhere the progress of the town ; serfs, fugitives from justice or their lord, the trader, the Jew, naturally sought shelter under the strong hand of S. Edmund. But the settlers were wholly at the Abbot's mercy. Not a settler but was bound to pay his pence to the Abbot's treasury, to plough a rood of his land, to reap in his harvest-field, to fold his sheep in the Abbey folds, to help bring the annual catch of eels from the Abbey waters. Within the four crosses that bounded the Abbot's domain land and water were his ; the cattle of the townsmen paid for their pasture on the common ; if the fullers refused the loan of their cloth, the cellarer would refuse the use of the stream, and seize their cloths wherever he found them. No toll might be levied from tenants of the Abbey farms, and customers had to wait before shop and stall till the buyers of the Abbot had had the pick of the market. There was little chance of redress, for if burghers complained in folk-mote, it was before the Abbot's officers that its meeting was held ; if they appealed to the alderman, he was the Abbot's nominee, and received the horn, the symbol of his office, at the Abbot's hands.

Like all the greater revolutions of society, the advance from this mere serfage was a silent one ; indeed its more galling instances of oppression seem to have slipped unconsciously away. Some, like the eel-fishing, were commuted for an easy rent ; others, like the slavery of the fullers and the toll of flax, simply disappeared. By usage, by omission, by downright forgetfulness, here by a little struggle, there by a present to a needy abbot, the town won freedom. But progress was not always unconscious, and one incident in the history of S. Edmundsbury is remarkable, not merely as indicating the advance of law, but yet more as marking the part which a new moral sense of man's right to equal justice was to play in the general advance of the realm. Rude as the borough was, it had preserved its right of meeting in full assembly of the townsmen for government and law. Justice was administered in presence of the burgesses, and the accused acquitted or condemned by the oath of his neighbours. Without the borough bounds however the system of the Norman judicature prevailed ; and the rural tenants who did suit and service at the Cellerar's court were subject to the decision of the trial by battle. The execution of a farmer named Ketel, who was subject to this feudal jurisdiction, brought the two systems into vivid contrast. He seems to have been guiltless of the crime laid to his charge, but the duel went against him, and he was hanged just without the gates. The taunts of the townsmen woke his fellow-farmers to a sense of wrong. " Had Ketel been a dweller within the borough," said the burgesses, " he would have got his acquittal from the oaths of his neighbours, as our liberty is ; " and even the monks were moved to a decision that their tenants should enjoy equal liberty and justice with the townsmen. The franchise of the town was extended to the rural possessions of the Abbey without it ; the farmers "came to the toll-house, were written in the alderman's roll, and paid the town-penny."

Sec. VI.

The
English
Revival

1071
to
1127

The
religious
revival

The moral revolution which events like this indicate was backed by a religious revival which forms a marked feature in the reign of Henry the First. Pious, learned, and energetic as the bishops of William's appointment had been, they were not Englishmen. Till the reign of Henry the First no Englishman occupied an English see. In language, in manner, in sympathy, the higher clergy were completely severed from the lower priesthood and the people, and the severance went far to paralyze the constitutional influence of the Church. Anselm stood alone against Rufus, and when Anselm was gone no voice of ecclesiastical freedom broke the silence of the reign of Henry the First. But at the close of Henry's reign and throughout that of Stephen, England was stirred by the first of those great religious movements which it was afterwards to experience in the preaching of the Friars, the Lollardism of Wyclif, the Reformation, the Puritan enthusiasm, and the mission work of the Wesleys. Everywhere in town and country men banded themselves together for prayer ; hermits flocked to the woods ; noble and churl welcomed the austere Cistercians, a reformed outshoot of the Benedictine order, as they spread over the moors and forests of the North. A new spirit of devotion woke the slumber of the religious houses, and penetrated alike to the home of the noble Walter de l'Espec at Rievaulx, or of the trader Gilbert Beket in Cheapside. London took its full share in the revival. The city was proud of its religion, its thirteen conventual and more than a hundred parochial churches. The new impulse changed its very aspect. In the midst of the city Bishop Richard busied himself with the vast cathedral church of S. Paul which Bishop Maurice had begun ; barges came up the river with stone from Caen for the great arches that moved the popular wonder, while street and lane were being levelled to make space for its famous churchyard. Rahere, once a canon of S. Paul's, raised the Priory of S. Bartholomew in Smithfield. Queen Maud founded S. Giles's in Holborn. The old English Cnichtenagild surrendered their soke of Aldgate as a site for the new priory of Holy Trinity. The tale of this house paints admirably the temper of the citizens at the time. Its founder, Prior Norman, had built church and cloister and bought books and vestments in so liberal a fashion that at last no money remained to buy bread. The canons were at their last gasp when many of the city folk, looking into the refectory as they paced round the cloister in their usual Sunday procession, saw the tables laid but not a single loaf on them. "Here is a fine set-out," cried the citizens, "but where is the bread to come from ?" The women present vowed to bring a loaf every Sunday, and there was

HISTORY OF THE ENGLISH PEOPLE. [CHAP.

SEC. VI.

THE
ENGLISH
REVIVAL

1071
TO
1127

soon bread enough and to spare for the priory and its priests. We see the strength of the new movement in the new class of ecclesiastics that it forced on the stage ; men like Anselm or John of Salisbury, or the two great prelates who followed one another after Henry's death in the see of Canterbury, Theobald and Thomas, drew whatever influence they wielded from a belief in their holiness of life and unselfishness of aim. The paralysis of the Church ceased as the new impulse bound the prelacy and people together, and its action, when at the end of Henry's reign it started into a power strong enough to save England from anarchy, has been felt in our history ever since.

Henry's administration

From this revival of English feeling Henry himself stood jealously aloof ; but the enthusiasm which his marriage had excited enabled him to defy the claims of his brother and the disaffection of his nobles. Robert landed at Portsmouth to find himself face to face with an English army which Anselm's summons had gathered round the King ; and his retreat left Henry free to deal sternly with the rebel barons. Robert of Belesme, the son of Roger of Montgomery, was now their chief ; but 60,000 English footmen followed the king through the rough passes which led to Shrewsbury, and an early surrender alone saved Robert's life. Master of his own realm and en-

1105

riched by the confiscated lands of the revolted baronage, Henry crossed into Normandy, where the misgovernment of Robert had alienated the clergy and trades, and where the outrages of the Norman nobles forced the more peaceful classes to call the King to their aid. On the field of Tenchebray his forces met those of the Duke, and a decisive English victory on Norman soil avenged the shame of Hastings. The conquered duchy became a dependency of the English crown, and Henry's energies were frittered away through a quarter of a century in crushing its revolts, the hostility of the French, and the efforts of his nephew, William the son of Robert, to regain the crown which his father had lost at Tenchebray. In England, however, all was peace. The vigorous administration of Henry the First completed in fullest detail the system of government which the Conqueror had sketched. The vast estates which had fallen to the crown through revolt and forfeiture were granted out to new men dependent on royal favour. On the ruins of the great feudatories whom he had crushed the King built up a class of lesser nobles, whom the older barons of the Conquest looked down on in scorn, but who formed a counterbalancing force and furnished a class of useful administrators whom Henry employed as his sheriffs and judges. A new organization of justice and finance bound the kingdom together under the royal administration. The clerks of the Royal Chapel were formed into a body of secretaries or royal ministers, whose head bore the title of Chancellor. Above them stood the Justiciar, or lieutenant-general of the king-

Sec. VI.

The
English
Revival

1071
to
1127

dom, who in the frequent absence of the King acted as Regent, and whose staff, selected from the barons connected with the royal household, were formed into a Supreme Court of the realm. The King's Court, as this was called, permanently represented the whole court of royal vassals, which had hitherto been summoned thrice in the year. As the royal council, it revised and registered laws, and its "counsel and consent," though merely formal, preserved the principle of the older popular legislation. As a court of justice it formed the highest court of appeal: it could call up any suit from a lower tribunal on the application of a suitor, while the union of several sheriffdoms under some of its members connected it closely with the local courts. As a financial body, its chief work lay in the assessment and collection of the revenue. In this capacity it took the name of the Court of Exchequer from the chequered table, much like a chess-board, at which it sat, and on which accounts were rendered. In their financial capacity its justices became "barons of the Exchequer." Twice every year the sheriff of each county appeared before these barons and rendered the sum of the fixed rent from royal domains, the Danegeld or land tax, the fines of the local courts, the feudal aids from the baronial estates, which formed the chief part of the royal revenue. Local disputes respecting these payments or the assessment of the town-rents were settled by a detachment of barons from the court who made the circuit of the shires, and whose fiscal visitations led to the judicial visitations, the "judges' circuits," which still form so marked a feature in our legal system.

From this work of internal reform Henry's attention was called suddenly by one terrible loss to the question of the succession to the throne. His son William " the Ætheling," as the English fondly styled the child of their own Matilda, had with a crowd of nobles accompanied the King on his return from Normandy ; but the White Ship in which he had embarked lingered behind the rest of the royal fleet while the young nobles, excited with wine, hung over the ship's side and chased away with taunts the priest who came to give the customary benediction. At last the guards of the King's treasure pressed the vessel's departure, and, driven by the arms of fifty rowers, it swept swiftly out to sea. All at once the ship's side struck on a rock at the mouth of the harbour, and in an instant it sank beneath the waves. One terrible cry, ringing through the stillness of the night, was heard by the royal fleet ; but it was not till the morning that the fatal news reached the King. He fell unconscious to the ground, and rose never to smile again. Henry had no other son, and the whole circle of his foreign foes closed round him the more fiercely that the son of Robert was now his natural heir. The king hated William, while he loved Matilda, the daughter who still remained to him, who had been married to the Emperor Henry the Fifth, and whose husband's death

SEC. VII.

ENGLAND
AND
ANJOU

870
TO
1154

now restored her to her father. He recognized her as his heir, though the succession of a woman seemed strange to the feudal baronage ; nobles and priests were forced to swear allegiance to her as their future mistress, and Henry affianced her to the son of the one foe he really feared, Count Fulk of Anjou.

Section VII.—England and Anjou, 870—1154.

[*Authorities*.—The chief documents for Angevin history have been collected in the " Chroniques d'Anjou," published by the Historical Society of France (Paris, 1856–1871). The best known of these is the " Gesta Consulum," a compilation of the twelfth century (given also by D'Achery, " Spicilegium," 4to. vol. x. p. 534), in which the earlier romantic traditions are simply dressed up into historical shape by copious quotations from the French historians. Save for the reigns of Geoffry Martel, and Fulk of Jerusalem, it is nearly valueless. The short autobiography of Fulk Rechin is the most authentic memorial of the earlier Angevin history ; and much can be gleaned from the verbose life of Geoffry the Handsome by John of Marmoutier. For England, Orderic and the Chronicle die out in the midst of Stephen's reign ; here, too, end William of Malmesbury, Huntingdon, the " Gesta Stephani," a record in great detail by one of Stephen's clerks, and the Hexham Chroniclers, who are most valuable for its opening (published by Mr. Raine for the Surtees Society). The blank in our historical literature extends over the first years of Henry the Second. The lives and letters of Beket have been industriously collected and published by Canon Robertson in the Rolls Series.]

To understand the history of England under its Angevin rulers, we must first know something of the Angevins themselves. The character and the policy of Henry the Second and his sons were as much a heritage of their race as the broad lands of Anjou. The fortunes of England were being slowly wrought out in every incident of the history of the Counts, as the descendants of a Breton woodman became masters not of Anjou only, but of Touraine, Maine, and Poitou, of Gascony and Auvergne, of Aquitaine and Normandy, and sovereigns at last of the great realm which Normandy had won. The legend of the father of their race carries us back to the times of our own Ælfred, when the Danes were ravaging along Loire as they ravaged along Thames. In the heart of the Breton border, in the debateable land between France and Britanny, dwelt Tortulf the Forester, half-brigand, half-hunter as the gloomy days went, living in free outlaw-fashion in the woods about Rennes. Tortulf had learned in his rough forest school " how to strike the foe, to sleep on the bare ground, to bear hunger and toil, summer's heat and winter's frost, how to fear nothing save ill-fame." Following King Charles the Bald in his struggle with the Danes, the woodman won broad lands along Loire, and his son Ingelger, who had swept the northmen from Touraine and the land to the west, which they had burned and wasted into a vast

SEC. VII.

ENGLAND
AND
ANJOU
870
TO
1154

solitude, became the first Count of Anjou. But the tale of Tortulf and Ingelger is a mere creation of some twelfth century *jongleur*, and the earliest Count whom history recognizes is Fulk the Red. Fulk attached himself to the Dukes of France who were now drawing nearer to the throne, and received from them in guerdon the county of Anjou. The story of his son is a story of peace, breaking like a quiet idyll the war-storms of his house. Alone of his race Fulk the Good waged no wars : his delight was to sit in the choir of Tours and to be called " Canon." One Martinmas eve Fulk was singing there in clerkly guise when the king, Lewis d'Outremer, entered the church. " He sings like a priest," laughed the King, as his nobles pointed mockingly to the figure of the Count-Canon ; but Fulk was ready with his reply. " Know, my lord," wrote the Count of Anjou, " that a king unlearned is a crowned ass." Fulk was in fact no priest, but a busy ruler, governing, enforcing peace, and carrying justice to every corner of the wasted land. To him alone of his race men gave the title of " the Good."

Himself in character little more than a bold dashing soldier, Fulk's son, Geoffry Grey-gown, sank almost into a vassal of his powerful neighbours, the Counts of Blois and Champagne. The vassalage was roughly shaken off by his successor. Fulk Nerra, Fulk the Black, is the greatest of the Angevins, the first in whom we can trace that marked type of character which their house was to preserve with a fatal constancy through two hundred years. He was without natural affection. In his youth he burnt a wife at the stake, and legend told how he led her to her doom decked out in his gayest attire. In his old age he waged his bitterest war against his son, and exacted from him when vanquished a humiliation which men reserved for the deadliest of their foes. " You are conquered, you are conquered ! " shouted the old man in fierce exultation, as Geoffry, bridled and saddled like a beast of burden, crawled for pardon to his father's feet. In Fulk first appeared the low type of superstition which startled even superstitious ages in the early Plantagenets. Robber as he was of Church lands, and contemptuous of ecclesiastical censures, the fear of the judgement drove Fulk to the Holy Sepulchre. Barefoot and with the strokes of the scourge falling heavily on his shoulders, the Count had himself dragged by a halter through the streets of Jerusalem, and courted the doom of martyrdom by his wild outcries of penitence. He rewarded the fidelity of Herbert of Le Mans, whose aid saved him from utter ruin, by entrapping him into captivity and robbing him of his lands. He secured the terrified friendship of the French king by despatching twelve assassins to cut down before his eyes the minister who had troubled it. Familiar as the age was with treason and rapine and blood, it recoiled from the cool cynicism of his crimes, and believed the wrath of Heaven to have been revealed against the union of the worst forms of evil in Fulk the Black. But neither the wrath of

Sec. VII.

England
and
Anjou
870
to
1154
The
great-
ness of
Anjou

Heaven nor the curses of men broke with a single mishap the fifty years of his success.

At his accession Anjou was the least important of the greater provinces of France. At his death in 1040 it stood, if not in extent, at least in real power, first among them all. Cool-headed, clear-sighted, quick to resolve, quicker to strike, Fulk's career was one long series of victories over all his rivals. He was a consummate general, and he had the gift of personal bravery, which was denied to some of his greatest descendants. There was a moment in the first of his battles when the day seemed lost for Anjou; a feigned retreat of the Bretons had drawn the Angevin horsemen into a line of hidden pitfalls, and the Count himself was flung heavily to the ground. Dragged from the medley of men and horses, he swept down almost singly on the foe "as a storm-wind" (so rang the pæan of the Angevins) "sweeps down on the thick corn-rows," and the field was won. To these qualities of the warrior he added a power of political organization, a capacity for far-reaching combinations, a faculty of statesmanship, which became the heritage of the Angevins, and lifted them as high above the intellectual level of the rulers of their time as their shameless wickedness degraded them below the level of man. His overthrow of Britanny on the field of Conquereux was followed by the gradual absorption of Southern Touraine, while his restless activity covered the land with castles and abbeys. The very spirit of the Black Count seems still to frown from the dark tower of Durtal on the sunny valley of the Loire. A victory at Pontlevoi crushed the rival house of Blois; the seizure of Saumur completed his conquests in the south, while Northern Touraine was won bit by bit till only Tours resisted the Angevin. The treacherous seizure of its count, Herbert Wake-dog, left Maine at his mercy ere the old man bequeathed his unfinished work to his son. As a warrior Geoffry Martel was hardly inferior to his father. A decisive victory left Poitou at his mercy, a second wrested Tours from the Count of Blois; and the seizure of Le Mans brought him to the Norman border. Here however his advance was checked by the genius of William the Conqueror, and with his death the greatness of Anjou seemed for the time to have come to an end.

995

1016

1044–1060

The
Angevin
marriage

1109–1129

Stripped of Maine by the Normans and weakened by internal dissensions, the weak administration of the next count, Fulk Rechin, left Anjou powerless against its rivals. It woke to fresh energy with the accession of his son, Fulk of Jerusalem. Now urging the turbulent Norman nobles to revolt, now supporting Robert's son William against his uncle, offering himself throughout as the loyal supporter of France, which was now hemmed in on all sides by the forces of the English king and of his allies the Counts of Blois and Champagne, Fulk was the one enemy whom Henry the First really feared. It was to disarm his restless hostility that the king gave to his son, Geoffry the Handsome, the hand of his daughter Matilda. No marriage could have been more unpopular, and the secrecy with which it was effected was held by the barons as freeing them from the oath which they had sworn ; for no baron, if he was without sons, could give a husband to his daughter save by his lord's consent, and by a strained analogy the nobles contended that their own assent was necessary to the marriage of Matilda. A more pressing danger lay in the greed of her husband Geoffry, who from his habit of wearing the common broom of Anjou (the *planta genista*) in his helmet had acquired, in addition to his surname of "the Handsome," the more famous title of "Plantagenet." His claims ended at last in intrigues with the Norman nobles, and Henry hurried to the border to meet an expected invasion ; but the plot broke down at his presence, the Angevins retired, and the old man withdrew to the forest of Lions to die.

Sec. VII.

England
and
Anjou
870
to
1154

"God give him," wrote the Archbishop of Rouen from Henry's death-bed, "the peace he loved." With him indeed closed the long peace of the Norman rule. An outburst of anarchy followed on the news of his departure, and in the midst of the turmoil Earl Stephen, his nephew, appeared at the gates of London. Stephen was a son of the Conqueror's daughter, Adela, who had married a Count of Blois ; he had been brought up at the English court, and his claim as nearest male heir, save his brother, of the Conqueror's blood (for his cousin, the son of Robert, had fallen in Flanders) was supported by his personal popularity. Mere swordsman as he was, his good-humour, his generosity, his very prodigality made him a favourite with all. No noble however had as yet ventured to join him, nor had any town opened its gates when London poured out to meet him with uproarious welcome. Neither barons nor prelates were present to constitute a National Council, but the great city did not hesitate to take their place. The voice of her citizens had long been accepted as representative of the popular assent in the election of a king ; but it marks the progress of English independence under Henry that London now claimed of itself the right of election. Undismayed by the absence of the hereditary counsellors of the crown, its "Aldermen and wise folk gathered together the folkmoot, and these providing at their own will for the good of the realm, unanimously resolved to choose a king." The solemn deliberation ended in the choice of Stephen ; the citizens swore to defend the King with money and blood, Stephen swore to apply his whole strength to the pacification and good government of the realm.

If London was true to her oath, Stephen was false to his. The nineteen years of his reign are years of a misrule and disorder unknown in our history. Stephen had been acknowledged even by the partizans of Matilda, but his weakness and prodigality soon gave room to feudal revolt. In 1138 a rising of the barons, planned by Earl Robert of

SEC. VII.

ENGLAND
AND
ANJOU
870
TO
1154

*Battle of the
Standard*
1138

Gloucester, in southern and western England was aided by the King of Scots, who poured his forces over the northern border. Stephen himself marched on the western rebels, and left them few strongholds save Bristol. The pillage and cruelties of the wild tribes of Galloway and the Highlands roused the spirit of the north; baron and freeman gathered at York round Archbishop Thurstan, and marched to the field of Northallerton to await the foe. The sacred banners of S. Cuthbert of Durham, S. Peter of York, S. John of Beverley, and S. Wilfrid of Ripon hung from a pole fixed in a four-wheeled car which stood in the centre of the host. "I who wear no armour," shouted the chief of the Galwegians, "will go as far this day as any one with breastplate of mail;" his men charged with wild shouts of "Albin, Albin," and were followed by the Norman knighthood of the Lowlands. The rout, however, was complete; the fierce hordes dashed in vain against the close English ranks around the Standard, and the whole army fled in confusion to Carlisle.

But Stephen had few kingly qualities save that of a soldier's bravery, and the realm soon began to slip from his grasp. Released from the stern hand of Henry, the barons fortified their castles, and their example was necessarily followed, in self-defence, by the great prelates and nobles who had acted as ministers to the late King. Roger, Bishop of Salisbury, the justiciar, and his son Roger the Chancellor, were carried away by the panic. They fortified their castles, and appeared at court followed by a strong force at their back. The weak violence of the king's temper suddenly broke out. He seized Roger with his son the Chancellor and his nephew the Bishop of Lincoln at Oxford, and forced them to surrender their strongholds. Shame broke the justiciar's heart; he died at the close of the year, and his nephew Nigel of Ely, the Treasurer, was driven from the realm. The fall of Roger's house shattered the whole system of government. The King's violence, while it cost him the support of the clergy, opened the way for Matilda's landing in England; and the country was soon divided between the adherents of the two rivals, the West supporting Matilda, London and the East Stephen. A defeat at Lincoln left the latter a captive in the hands of his enemies, while Matilda was received throughout the land as its "Lady." But the disdain with which she repulsed the claim of London to the enjoyment of its older privileges called its burghers to arms, and her resolve to hold Stephen a prisoner roused his party again to life. Flying to Oxford, she was besieged there by Stephen, who had obtained his release; but she escaped in white robes by a postern, and crossing the river unobserved on the ice, made her way to Abingdon. Six years later she returned to Normandy. The war had in fact become a mere chaos of pillage and bloodshed. The outrages of the feudal baronage showed from what horrors the rule of the Norman kings had saved England. No more ghastly picture of a nation's misery has

Sec. VII.

England
and
Anjou

870
to
1154

ever been painted than that which closes the English Chronicle, whose last accents falter out amidst the horrors of the time. "They hanged up men by their feet and smoked them with foul smoke. Some were hanged up by their thumbs, others by the head, and burning things were hung on to their feet. They put knotted strings about men's heads and writhed them till they went into the brain. They put men into prisons where adders and snakes and toads were crawling, and so they tormented them. Some they put into a chest short and narrow and not deep, and that had harp stones within, and forced men therein so that they broke all their limbs. In many of the castles were hateful and grim things called rachenteges, which two or three men had enough to do to carry. It was thus made: it was fastened to a beam and had a sharp iron to go about a man's neck and throat, so that he might noways sit, or lie, or sleep, but he bore all the iron. Many thousands they starved with hunger."

England was rescued from this feudal anarchy by the efforts of the Church. In the early part of Stephen's reign his brother Henry, the Bishop of Winchester, acting as Papal Legate for the realm, had striven to supply the absence of any royal or national authority by convening synods of bishops, and by asserting the moral right of the Church to declare sovereigns unworthy of the throne. The compact between king and people which became a part of constitutional law in the Charter of Henry had gathered new force in the Charter of Stephen, but its legitimate consequence in the responsibility of the crown for the execution of the compact was first drawn out by these ecclesiastical councils. From their alternate depositions of Stephen and Matilda flowed the after depositions of Edward and Richard, and the solemn act by which the succession was changed in the case of James. Extravagant and unauthorized as their expression of it may appear, they expressed the right of a nation to good government. Henry of Winchester, however, "half monk, half soldier," as he was called, possessed too little religious influence to wield a really spiritual power; it was only at the close of Stephen's reign that the nation really found a moral leader in Theobald, the Archbishop of Canterbury. "To the Church," Thomas justly said afterwards, with the proud consciousness of having been Theobald's right hand, "Henry owed his crown and England her deliverance." Thomas was the son of Gilbert Beket, the portreeve of London, the site of whose house is still marked by the Mercers' chapel in Cheapside. His mother Rohese was a type of the devout woman of her day; she weighed her boy each year on his birthday against money, clothes, and provisions which she gave to the poor. Thomas grew up amidst the Norman barons and clerks who frequented his father's house with a genial freedom of character tempered by the Norman refinement; he passed from the school of Merton to the University of Paris, and returned to fling

SEC. VII.

ENGLAND
AND
ANJOU
870
TO
1154

1152

1153

himself into the life of the young nobles of the time. Tall, handsome, bright-eyed, ready of wit and speech, his firmness of temper showed itself in his very sports; to rescue his hawk which had fallen into the water he once plunged into a millrace, and was all but crushed by the wheel. The loss of his father's wealth drove him to the court of Archbishop Theobald, and he soon became the Primate's confidant in his plans for the rescue of England. Henry, the son of Matilda and Geoffry, had now by the death of his father become master of Normandy and Anjou, while by his marriage with its duchess, Eleanor of Poitou, he had added Aquitaine to his dominions. Thomas, as Theobald's agent, invited Henry to appear in England, and on the Duke's landing the Archbishop interposed between the rival claimants to the crown. The Treaty of Wallingford abolished the evils of the long anarchy; the castles were to be razed, the crown lands resumed, the foreign mercenaries banished from the country. Stephen was recognized as King, and in turn acknowledged Henry as his heir. But a year had hardly passed when Stephen's death gave his rival the crown.

Section VIII.—Henry the Second, 1154—1189.

[*Authorities.*—Up to the death of Archbishop Thomas we have only the letters of Beket himself, Foliot, and John of Salisbury, collected by Canon Robertson and Dr. Giles; but this dearth is followed by a vast outburst of historical industry. From 1169 till 1192 our primary authority is the Chronicle known as that of Benedict of Peterborough, whose authorship Dr. Stubbs has shown to be more probably due to the royal treasurer, Bishop Richard Fitz-Neal. It is continued to 1201 by Roger of Howden. Both are works of the highest value, and have been edited for the Rolls series by Dr. Stubbs, whose prefaces have thrown a new light on the constitutional history of Henry's reign. The history by William of Newburgh (which ends in 1198) is a work of the classical school, like William of Malmesbury, but distinguished by its fairness and good sense. To these may be added the chronicles of Ralf Niger, with the additions of Ralf of Coggeshall, that of Gervase of Canterbury, and the Life of S. Hugh of Lincoln. A mass of general literature lies behind these distinctively historical sources, in the treatises of John of Salisbury, the voluminous works of Giraldus Cambrensis, the "trifles" and satires of Walter Map, Glanvill's treatise on Law, Fitz-Neal's "Dialogue on the Exchequer," the romances of Gaimar and Wace, the poem of the San Graal. Lord Lyttelton's "Life of Henry the Second" is a full and sober account of the time; Canon Robertson's Biography of Beket is accurate, but hostile in tone. In his "Select Charters" Dr. Stubbs has printed the various "Assizes," and the Dialogus de Scaccario, which explains the financial administration of the Curia Regis.]

Young as he was, Henry mounted the throne with a resolute purpose of government which his reign carried steadily out. His practical, serviceable frame suited the hardest worker of his time. There was something in his build and look, in the square stout frame, the fiery face, the close-cropped hair, the prominent eyes, the bull neck, the

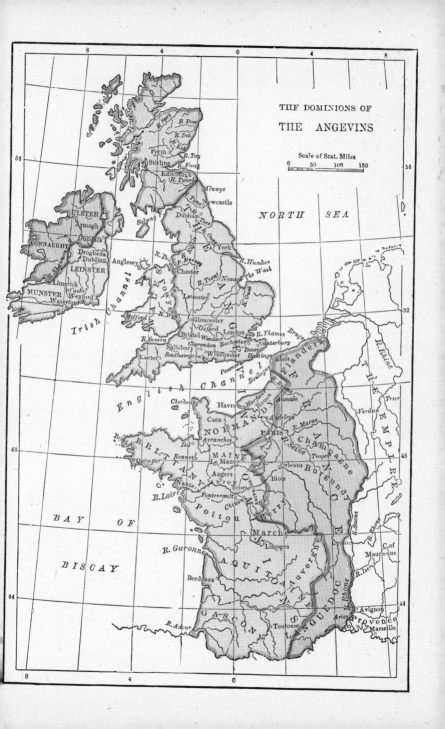

THE DOMINIONS OF

THE ANGEVINS

Scale of Stat. Miles
0   50   100   150

coarse strong hands, the bowed legs, that marked out the keen, stirring, coarse-fibred man of business. " He never sits down," said one who observed him closely ; "he is always on his legs from morning till night." Orderly in business, careless in appearance, sparing in diet, never resting or giving his servants rest, chatty, inquisitive, endowed with a singular charm of address and strength of memory, obstinate in love or hatred, a fair scholar, a great hunter, his general air that of a rough, passionate, busy man, Henry's personal character told directly on the character of his reign. His accession marks the period of amalgamation, when neighbourhood and traffic and intermarriage drew Englishmen and Normans rapidly into a single people. A national feeling was thus springing up before which the barriers of the older feudalism were to be swept away. Henry had even less reverence for the feudal past than the men of his day ; he was indeed utterly without the imagination and reverence which enable men to sympathize with any past at all. He had a practical man's impatience of the obstacles thrown in the way of his reforms by the older constitution of the realm, nor could he understand other men's reluctance to purchase undoubted improvements by the sacrifice of customs and traditions of bygone days. Without any theoretical hostility to the co-ordinate powers of the state, it seemed to him a perfectly reasonable and natural course to trample either baronage or Church under foot to gain his end of good government. He saw clearly that the remedy for such anarchy as England had endured under Stephen lay in the establishment of a kingly government unembarrassed by any privileges of order or class, administered by royal servants, and in whose public administration the nobles acted simply as delegates of the sovereign. His work was to lie in the organization of judicial and administrative reforms which realized this idea. But of the great currents of thought and feeling which were tending in the same direction he knew nothing. What he did for the moral and social impulses which were telling on men about him was simply to let them alone. Religion grew more and more identified with patriotism under the eyes of a King who whispered, and scribbled, and looked at picture-books during mass, who never confessed, and cursed God in wild frenzies of blasphemy. Great peoples formed themselves on both sides of the sea round a sovereign who bent the whole force of his mind to hold together an Empire which the growth of nationality must inevitably destroy. There is throughout a tragic grandeur in the irony of Henry's position, that of a Sforza of the fifteenth century set in the midst of the twelfth, building up by patience and policy and craft a dominion alien to the deepest sympathies of his age, and fated to be swept away in the end by popular forces to whose existence his very cleverness and activity blinded him. But indirectly and unconsciously, his policy did more than that of all his predecessors to pre-

Sec. VIII.

Henry the Second

1154
to
1189

Sec. VIII.

Henry the
Second

1154
to
1189

Henry
and the
Church

pare England for the unity and freedom which the fall of his house was to reveal.

He had been placed on the throne, as we have seen, by the Church. His first work was to repair the evils which England had endured till his accession by the restoration of the system of Henry the First ; and it was with the aid and counsel of Theobald that the foreign marauders were driven from the realm, the castles demolished in spite of the opposition of the baronage, the King's Court and Exchequer restored. Age and infirmity however warned the Primate to retire from the post of minister, and his power fell into the younger and more vigorous hands of Thomas Beket, who had long acted as his confidential adviser and was now made Chancellor. Thomas won the personal favour of the King. The two young men had, in Theobald's words, " but one heart and mind ; " Henry jested in the Chancellor's hall, or tore his cloak from his shoulders in rough horse-play as they rode through the streets. He loaded his favourite with riches and honours, but there is no ground for thinking that Thomas in any degree influenced his system of rule. Henry's policy seems for good or evil to have been throughout his own. His work of reorganization went steadily on amidst troubles at home and abroad. Welsh outbreaks forced him in 1157 to lead an army across the border. The next year saw him drawn across the Channel, where he was already master of a third of the present France. He had inherited Anjou, Maine, and Touraine from his father, Normandy from his mother, and the seven provinces of the South, Poitou, Saintonge, the Angoumois, La Marche, the Limousin, Périgord, and Gascony belonged to his wife. As Duchess of Aquitaine Eleanor had claims on Toulouse, and these Henry prepared in 1159 to enforce by arms. He was however luckless in the war. King Lewis of France threw himself into Toulouse. Conscious of the ill-compacted nature of his wide dominions, Henry shrank from an open contest with his suzerain ; he withdrew his forces, and the quarrel ended in 1160 by a formal alliance and the betrothal of his eldest son to the daughter of Lewis. Thomas had fought bravely throughout the campaign, at the head of the 700 knights who formed his household. But the King had other work for him than war. On Theobald's death he at once forced on the monks of Canterbury, and on Thomas himself, his election as Archbishop. His purpose in

this appointment was soon revealed. Henry proposed to the bishops that a clerk convicted of a crime should be deprived of his orders, and handed over to the King's tribunals. The local courts of the feudal baronage had been roughly shorn of their power by the judicial reforms of Henry the First ; and the Church courts, as the Conqueror had created them, with their exclusive right of justice over the clerical order, in other words over the whole body of educated men throughout the realm, formed the one great exception to the system which was concentrating all jurisdiction in the hands of the king. The bishops yielded, but opposition came from the very prelate whom Henry had created to enforce his will. From the moment of his appointment Thomas had flung himself with the whole energy of his nature into the part he had to play. At the first intimation of Henry's purpose he had pointed with a laugh to his gay attire—" You are choosing a fine dress to figure at the head of your Canterbury monks ; " but once monk and primate, he passed with a fevered earnestness from luxury to asceticism. Even as minister he had opposed the King's designs, and foretold their future opposition : " You will soon hate me as much as you love me now," he said, " for you assume an authority in the affairs of the Church to which I shall never assent." A prudent man might have doubted the wisdom of destroying the only shelter which protected piety or learning against a despot like the Red King, and in the mind of Thomas the ecclesiastical immunities were parts of the sacred heritage of the Church. He stood without support ; the Pope advised concession, the bishops forsook him, and Thomas bent at last to agree to the Constitutions drawn up at the Council of Clarendon. The King had appealed to the ancient " customs " of the realm, and it was to state these " customs " that a court was held at Clarendon near Salisbury. The report presented by bishops and barons formed the " Constitutions of Clarendon," a code which in the bulk of its provisions simply re-enacted the system of the Conqueror. Every election of bishop or abbot was to take place before royal officers, in the King's chapel, and with the King's assent. The prelate elect was bound to do homage to the King for his lands before consecration, and to hold his lands as a barony from the king, subject to all feudal burthens of taxation and attendance in the King's court. No bishop might leave the realm without the royal permission. No tenant in chief or royal servant might be excommunicated, or their land placed under interdict, but by the King's assent. What was new was the legislation respecting ecclesiastical jurisdiction. The King's court was to decide whether a suit between clerk and layman, whose nature was disputed, belonged to the Church courts or the King's. A royal officer was to be present at all ecclesiastical proceedings, in order to confine the Bishop's court within its own due limits, and a clerk once convicted there passed at once under the civil jurisdiction. An appeal was left from the Archbishop's court to the King's court for defect of justice, but none might appeal to the Papal court save with the King's consent. The privilege of sanctuary in churches or churchyards was repealed, so far as property and not persons was concerned. After a passionate refusal the Primate at last gave his assent to the Constitutions ; but this assent was soon retracted, and the King's savage resentment threw the moral advantage of the position into the Archbishop's hands. Vexatious charges were brought against him ; in the Council

*Flight of
Archbishop
Thomas*
1164

of Northampton a few months later his life was said to be in danger, and all urged him to submit. But in the presence of danger the courage of the man rose to its full height. Grasping his archiepiscopal cross he entered the royal court, forbade the nobles to condemn him, and appealed to the Papal See. Shouts of "Traitor! traitor!" followed him as he retired. The Primate turned fiercely at the word: "Were I a knight," he retorted, "my sword should answer that foul taunt!" At nightfall he fled in disguise, and reached France through Flanders. For six years the contest raged bitterly; at Rome, at Paris, the agents of the two powers intrigued against each other. Henry stooped to acts of the meanest persecution in driving the Primate's kinsmen from England, and in threats to confiscate the lands of the Cistercians that he might force the monks of Pontigny to refuse Thomas a home; while Beket himself exhausted the patience of his friends by his violence and excommunications, as well as by the stubbornness with which he clung to the offensive clause "Saving the honour of my order," the addition of which would have practically neutralized the King's reforms. The Pope counselled mildness, the French king for a time withdrew his support, his own clerks gave way at last. "Come up," said one of them bitterly when his horse stumbled on the road, "saving the honour of the Church and my order." But neither warning nor desertion moved the resolution of the Primate. Henry, in dread of papal excommunication, resolved at last on the coronation of his son, in defiance of the privileges of Canterbury, by the Archbishop of York. But the Pope's hands were now freed by his successes in Italy, and his threat of an interdict forced the king to a show of submission. The Archbishop was allowed to return after a reconciliation with Henry at Fréteval, and the Kentishmen flocked around him with uproarious welcome as he entered Canterbury. "This is England," said his clerks, as they saw the white headlands of the coast. "You will wish yourself elsewhere before fifty days are gone," said Thomas sadly, and his foreboding showed his appreciation of Henry's character. He was now in the royal power, and orders had already been issued in the younger Henry's name for his arrest, when four knights from the King's court, spurred to outrage by a passionate outburst of their master's wrath, crossed the sea and forced their way into the Archbishop's palace. After a stormy parley with him in his chamber they withdrew to arm. Thomas was hurried by his clerks into the cathedral, but as he reached the steps leading from the transept to the choir his pursuers burst in from the cloisters. "Where," cried Reginald Fitzurse in the dusk of the dimly-lighted minster, "where is the traitor, Thomas Beket?" The Primate turned resolutely back: "Here am I, no traitor, but a priest of God," he replied, and again descending the steps he placed himself with his back against a pillar and fronted his foes. All the bravery, the violence of his old knightly life seemed to revive in Thomas as he tossed back the

*Beket's
return*
1170

threats and demands of his assailants. "You are our prisoner," shouted Fitzurse, and the four knights seized him to drag him from the church. "Do not touch me, Reginald," shouted the Primate, "pander that you are, you owe me fealty ; " and availing himself of his personal strength he shook him roughly off. "Strike, strike," retorted Fitzurse, and blow after blow struck Thomas to the ground. A retainer of Ranulf de Broc with the point of his sword scattered the Primate's brains on the ground. "Let us be off," he cried triumphantly, "this traitor will never rise again."

The brutal murder was received with a thrill of horror throughout Christendom ; miracles were wrought at the martyr's tomb ; he was canonized, and became the most popular of English saints ; but Henry's show of submission to the Papacy averted the excommunication which at first threatened to avenge the deed of blood. The judicial provisions of the Constitutions of Clarendon were in form annulled, and liberty of election was restored to bishopricks and abbacies. In reality however the victory rested with the King. Throughout his reign ecclesiastical appointments were practically in his hands, while the King's Court asserted its power over the spiritual jurisdiction of the bishops. The close of the struggle left Henry free to complete his great work of legal reform. He had already availed himself of the expedition against Toulouse to deliver a blow at the baronage by allowing the lower tenants to commute their personal service in the field for a money payment under the name of "scutage," or shield-money. The King thus became master of resources which enabled him to dispense with the military support of his tenants, and to maintain a force of mercenary soldiers in their place. The diminution of the military power of the nobles was accompanied by measures which robbed them of their legal jurisdiction. The circuits of the judges were restored, and instructions were given them to enter the manors of the barons and make inquiry into their privileges ; while the office of sheriff was withdrawn from the great nobles of the shire and entrusted to the lawyers and courtiers who already furnished the staff of justices. The resentment of the barons found an opportunity of displaying itself when the King's eldest son, whose coronation had given him the title of King, demanded to be put in possession of his English realm, and on his father's refusal took refuge with Lewis of France. France, Flanders, and Scotland joined the league against Henry ; his younger sons, Richard and Geoffry, took up arms in Aquitaine. In England a descent of Flemish mercenaries under the Earl of Leicester was repulsed by the loyal justiciars near S. Edmundsbury ; but Lewis had no sooner entered Normandy and invested Rouen than the whole extent of the danger was revealed. The Scots crossed the border, Roger Mowbray rose in revolt in Yorkshire, Ferrars, Earl of Derby, in the midland shires, Hugh Bigod in the eastern counties, while a

Henry
and the
baronage

The great
scutage

Inquest of
sheriffs
1170

Sec. VIII.

Henry the
Second
1154
TO
1189

1174

*Assize of
Arms*
1181

**Henry
and the
law**

*Assize of
Clarendon*
1166

*Trial by
jury*

Flemish fleet prepared to support the insurrection by a descent upon the coast. The murder of Archbishop Thomas still hung around Henry's neck, and his first act in hurrying to England to meet these perils was to prostrate himself before the shrine of the new martyr, and to submit to a public scourging in expiation of his sin. But the penance was hardly wrought when all danger was dispelled by a series of triumphs. The King of Scotland, William the Lion, surprised by the English under cover of a mist, fell into the hands of his minister, Ranulf de Glanvill, and at the retreat of the Scots the English rebels hastened to lay down their arms. With the army of mercenaries which he had brought over sea Henry was able to return to Normandy, to raise the siege of Rouen, and to reduce his sons to submission. The revolt of the baronage was followed by fresh blows at their power. A further step was taken a few years later in the military organization of the realm by the Assize of Arms, which restored the national militia to the place which it had lost at the Conquest. The substitution of scutage for military service had freed the crown from its dependence on the baronage and its feudal retainers ; the Assize of Arms replaced this feudal organization by the older obligation of every freeman to serve in the defence of the realm. Every knight was bound to appear at the King's call in coat of mail and with shield and lance, every freeholder with lance and hauberk, every burgess and poorer freeman with lance and helmet. The levy of an armed nation was thus placed wholly at the disposal of the King for purposes of defence.

The measures we have named were only part of Henry's legislation. His reign, it has been truly said, "initiated the rule of law" as distinct from the despotism, whether personal or tempered by routine, of the Norman kings. It was in successive "Assizes" or codes issued with the sanction of great councils of barons and prelates, that he perfected by a system of reforms the administrative measures which Henry the First had begun. The fabric of our judicial legislation commences with the Assize of Clarendon, the first object of which was to provide for the order of the realm by reviving the old English system of mutual security or frankpledge. No stranger might abide in any place save a borough, and there but for a single night, unless sureties were given for his good behaviour; and the list of such strangers was to be submitted to the itinerant justices. In the provisions of this assize for the repression of crime we find the origin of trial by jury, so often attributed to earlier times. Twelve lawful men of each hundred, with four from each township, were sworn to present those who were known or reputed as criminals within their district for trial by ordeal. The jurors were thus not merely witnesses, but sworn to act as judges also in determining the value of the charge, and it is this double character of Henry's jurors that has descended to our "grand jury," who still remain charged with the duty of presenting criminals for trial after examination of the witnesses against them. Two later steps brought the jury to its modern condition. Under Edward the First witnesses acquainted with the particular fact in question were added in each case to the general jury, and by the separation of these two classes of jurors at a later time the last became simply "witnesses" without any judicial power, while the first ceased to be witnesses at all, and became our modern jurors, who are only judges of the testimony given. With this assize, too, the practice which had prevailed from the earliest English times of "compurgation" passed away. Under this system the accused could be acquitted of the charge by the voluntary oath of his neighbours and kinsmen; but this was abolished by the Assize of Clarendon, and for the next fifty years his trial, after the investigation of the grand jury, was found solely in the ordeal or "judgement of God," where innocence was proved by the power of holding hot iron in the hand, or by sinking when flung into the water, for swimming was a proof of guilt. It was the abolition of the whole system of ordeal by the Council of Lateran which led the way to the establishment of what is called a "petty jury" for the final trial of prisoners. The Assize of Clarendon was expanded in that of Northampton, which was drawn up immediately after the rebellion of the Barons. Henry, as we have seen, had restored the King's Court and the occasional circuits of its justices: by the Assize of Northampton he rendered this institution permanent and regular by dividing the kingdom into six districts, to each of which he assigned three itinerant justices. The circuits thus defined correspond roughly with those that still exist. The primary object of these circuits was financial, but the rendering of the King's justice went on side by side with the exaction of the King's dues, and this carrying of justice to every corner of the realm was made still more effective by the abolition of all feudal exemptions from the royal jurisdiction. The chief danger of the new system lay in the opportunities it afforded to judicial corruption; and so great were its abuses that Henry was soon forced to restrict for a time the number of justices to five, and to reserve appeals from their court to himself in council. The Court of Appeal which he thus created, that of the King in Council, gave birth as time went on to tribunal after tribunal. It is from it that the judicial powers now exercised by the Privy Council are derived, as well as the equitable jurisdiction of the Chancellor. In the next century it becomes the Great Council of the realm, from which the Privy Council drew its legislative, and the House of Lords its judicial character. The Court of Star Chamber and the Judicial Committee of the Privy Council are later offshoots of Henry's Court of Appeal. The King's Court, which became inferior to this higher jurisdiction, was divided after the Great Charter into the three distinct

Sec. VIII.

Henry the Second

1154
TO
1189

1216

Assize of North-ampton
1176

1178

SEC. VIII.

HENRY THE
SECOND
1154
TO
1189
Death of
Henry
the
Second
1183–1186

1189

courts of the King's Bench, the Exchequer, and the Common Pleas, which by the time of Edward the First received distinct judges, and became for all purposes separate.

For the ten years which followed the revolt of the barons Henry's power was at its height ; and an invasion, which we shall tell hereafter, had annexed Ireland to his English crown. But the course of triumph and legislative reform was rudely broken by the quarrels and revolts of his sons. The successive deaths of Henry and Geoffry were followed by intrigues between Richard, now his father's heir, who had been entrusted with Aquitaine, and Philip, who had succeeded Lewis on the throne of France. The plot broke out at last in actual conflict ; Richard did homage to Philip, and their allied forces suddenly appeared before Le Mans, from which Henry was driven in headlong flight towards Normandy. From a height where he halted to look back on the burning city, so dear to him as his birthplace, the King hurled his curse against God : " Since Thou hast taken from me the town I loved best, where I was born and bred, and where my father lies buried, I will have my revenge on Thee too—I will rob Thee of that thing Thou lovest most in me." Death was upon him, and the longing of a dying man drew him to the home of his race, but Tours fell as he lay at Saumur, and the hunted King was driven to beg mercy from his foes. They gave him the list of the conspirators against him : at the head of them was his youngest and best-loved son, John. " Now," he said, as he turned his face to the wall, " let things go as they will—I care no more for myself or for the world." He was borne to Chinon by the silvery waters of Vienne, and muttering, " Shame, shame on a conquered King," passed sullenly away.

Section IX.—The Fall of the Angevins, 1189—1204.

[*Authorities.*—In addition to those mentioned in the last Section, the Chronicle of Richard of Devizes, and the " Itinerarium Regis Ricardi," edited by Dr. Stubbs, are useful for Richard's reign. Rigord's " Gesta Philippi," and the " Philippis Willelmi Britonis," the chief authorities on the French side, are given in Duchesne, " Hist. Franc. Scriptores," vol. v.]

We need not follow Richard in the Crusade which occupied the beginning of his reign, and which left England for four years without a ruler,—in his quarrels in Sicily, his conquest of Cyprus, his victory at Jaffa, his fruitless march upon Jerusalem, the truce he concluded with Saladin, his shipwreck as he returned, or his two imprisonments in Germany. Freed at last from his captivity, he returned to face new perils. During his absence, the kingdom had been entrusted to William of Longchamp, Bishop of Ely, head of Church and State, as at once Justiciar and Papal Legate. Longchamp was loyal to the King but his exactions and scorn of Englishmen roused a fierce hatred among the baronage, and this hatred found a head in John, traitor to his brother as to his father. John's intrigues with the baronage and the French king ended at last in open revolt, which was, however, checked by the ability of the new Primate, Hubert Walter; and Richard's landing in 1194 was followed by his brother's complete submission. But if Hubert Walter had secured order in England, oversea Richard found himself face to face with dangers which he was too clear-sighted to undervalue. Destitute of his father's administrative genius, less ingenious in his political conceptions than John, Richard was far from being a mere soldier. A love of adventure, a pride in sheer physical strength, here and there a romantic generosity, jostled roughly with the craft, the unscrupulousness, the violence of his race ; but he was at heart a statesman, cool and patient in the execution of his plans as he was bold in their conception. "The devil is loose ; take care of yourself," Philip had written to John at the news of the king's release. In the French king's case a restless ambition was spurred to action by insults which he had borne during the Crusade, and he had availed himself of Richard's imprisonment to invade Normandy, while the lords of Aquitaine rose in revolt under the troubadour Bertrand de Born. Jealousy of the rule of strangers, weariness of the turbulence of the mercenary soldiers of the Angevins or of the greed and oppression of their financial administration, combined with an impatience of their firm government and vigorous justice to alienate the nobles of their provinces on the Continent. Loyalty among the people there was none ; even Anjou, the home of their race, drifted towards Philip as steadily as Poitou. But in warlike ability Richard was more than Philip's peer. He held him in check on the Norman frontier and surprised his treasure at Fréteval, while he reduced to submission the rebels of Aquitaine. England, drained by the tax for Richard's ransom, groaned under its burdens as Hubert Walter raised vast sums to support the army of mercenaries which Richard led against his foes

Crushing taxation had wrung from England wealth which again filled the royal treasury, and during a short truce Richard's bribes detached Flanders from the French alliance, and united the Counts of Chartres, Champagne, and Boulogne with the Bretons in a revolt against Philip. He won a valuable aid by the election of his nephew Otto to the German throne, and his envoy, William Longchamp, knitted an alliance which would bring the German lances to bear on the King of Paris. But the security of Normandy was requisite to the success of these wider plans, and Richard saw that its defence could no longer rest on the loyalty of the Norman people. His father might trace his descent through Matilda from the line of Hrolf, but the Angevin ruler was in fact a stranger to the Norman. It was impossible for a Norman to recognize his Duke with any real sympathy in the Angevin prince whom he saw moving along the border at the

Château Gaillard

SEC. IX.

THE FALL
OF THE
ANGEVINS
1189
TO
1204

head of Brabançon mercenaries, in whose camp the old names of the Norman baronage were missing, and Merchadé, a Provençal ruffian, held supreme command. The purely military site which Richard selected for the new fortress with which he guarded the border showed his realization of the fact that Normandy could now only be held by force of arms. As a monument of warlike skill his " Saucy Castle," Château-Gaillard, stands first among the fortresses of the middle ages. Richard fixed its site where the Seine bends suddenly at Gaillon in a great semicircle to the north, and where the valley of Les Andelys breaks the line of the chalk cliffs along its banks. Blue masses of woodland crown the distant hills ; within the river curve lies a dull reach of flat meadow, round which the Seine, broken with green islets, and dappled with the grey and blue of the sky, flashes like a silver bow on its way to Rouen. The castle formed a part of an entrenched camp which Richard designed to cover his Norman capital. Approach by the river was blocked by a stockade and a bridge of boats, by a fort on the islet in mid stream, and by the fortified town which the King built in the valley of the Gambon, then an impassable marsh. In the angle between this valley and the Seine, on a spur of the chalk hills which only a narrow neck of land connects with the general plateau, rose at the height of 300 feet above the river the crowning fortress of the whole. Its outworks and the walls which connected it with the town and stockade have for the most part gone, but time and the hand of man have done little to destroy the fortifications themselves—the fosse, hewn deep into the solid rock, with casemates hollowed out along its sides, the fluted walls of the citadel, the huge donjon looking down on the brown roofs and huddled gables of Les Andelys. Even now in its ruin we can under-stand the triumphant outburst of its royal builder as he saw it rising against the sky : " How pretty a child is mine, this child of but one year old ! "

Richard's death

The easy reduction of Normandy on the fall of Château-Gaillard at a later time proved Richard's foresight ; but foresight and sagacity were mingled in him with a brutal violence and a callous indifference to honour. " I would take it, were its walls of iron," Philip exclaimed in wrath as he saw the fortress rise. " I would hold it, were its walls of butter," was the defiant answer of his foe. It was Church land, and the Archbishop of Rouen laid Normandy under interdict at its seizure, but the King met the interdict with mockery, and intrigued with Rome till the censure was withdrawn. He was just as defiant of a "rain of blood," whose fall scared his courtiers. " Had an angel from heaven bid him abandon his work," says a cool observer, " he would have answered with a curse." The twelvemonth's hard work, in fact, by securing the Norman frontier, set Richard free to deal his long-planned blow at Philip. Money only was wanting, and the king

SEC. IX.

THE FALL
OF THE
ANGEVINS

1189
TO
1204

listened with more than the greed of his race to the rumour that a treasure had been found in the fields of the Limousin. Twelve knights of gold seated round a golden table were the find, it was said, of the Lord of Châlus. Treasure-trove at any rate there was, and Richard prowled around the walls, but the castle held stubbornly out till the King's greed passed into savage menace ; he would hang all, he swore —man, woman, the very child at the breast. In the midst of his threats an arrow from the walls struck him down. He died as he had lived, owning the wild passion which for seven years past had kept him from confession lest he should be forced to pardon Philip, forgiving with kingly generosity the archer who had shot him.

The Angevin dominion broke to pieces at his death. John was acknowledged as king in England and Normandy, Aquitaine was secured for him by its Duchess, his mother ; but Anjou, Maine, and Touraine did homage to Arthur, the son of his elder brother Geoffry, the late Duke of Britanny. The ambition of Philip, who protected his cause, turned the day against Arthur ; the Angevins rose against the French garrisons with which the French king practically annexed the country, and John was at last owned as master of the whole dominion of his house. A fresh outbreak of war in Poitou was fatal to his rival ; surprised at the siege of Mirebeau by a rapid march of the King, Arthur was taken prisoner to Rouen, and murdered there, as men believed, by his uncle's hand. The brutal outrage at once roused the French provinces in revolt, while the French king marched straight on Normandy. The ease with which its conquest was effected can only be explained by the utter absence of any popular resistance on the part of the Normans themselves. Half a century before the sight of a Frenchman in the land would have roused every peasant to arms from Avranches to Dieppe, but town after town surrendered at the mere summons of Philip, and the conquest was hardly over before Normandy settled down into the most loyal of the provinces of France. Much of this was due to the wise liberality with which Philip met the claims of the towns to independence and self-government, as well as to the overpowering force and military ability with which the conquest was effected. But the utter absence of all opposition sprang from a deeper cause. To the Norman his transfer from John to Philip was a mere passing from one foreign master to another, and foreigner for foreigner Philip was the less alien of the two. Between France and Normandy there had been as many years of friendship as of strife ; between Norman and Angevin lay a century of bitterest hate. Moreover, the subjection to France was the realization in fact of a dependence which had always existed in theory ; Philip entered Rouen as the over-lord of its Dukes ; while the submission to the house of Anjou had been the most humiliating of all submissions, the submission to an equal.

It was the consciousness of this temper in the Norman people that

SEC. IX.

THE FALL
OF THE
ANGEVINS
1189
TO
1204

forced John to abandon all hope of resistance on the failure of his attempt to relieve Château-Gaillard, by the siege of which Philip commenced his invasion. The skill with which the combined movements for its relief were planned proved the King's military ability. The besiegers were parted into two masses by the Seine ; the bulk of their forces were camped in the level space within the bend of the river, while one division was thrown across it to occupy the valley of the Gambon, and sweep the country around of its provisions. John proposed to cut the French army in two by destroying the bridge of boats which formed the only communication between the two bodies, while the whole of his own forces flung themselves on the rear of the French division encamped in the *cul-de-sac* formed by the river-bend, and without any exit save the bridge. Had the attack been carried out as ably as it was planned, it must have ended in Philip's ruin ; but the two assaults were not made simultaneously, and were successively repulsed. The repulse was followed by the utter collapse of the military system by which the Angevins had held Normandy ; John's treasury was exhausted, and his mercenaries passed over to the foe. The King's despairing appeal to the Duchy itself came too late ; its nobles were already treating with Philip, and the towns were incapable of resisting the siege train of the French. It was despair of any aid from Normandy that drove John over sea to seek it as fruitlessly from England, but with the fall of Château-Gaillard, after a gallant struggle, the province passed without a struggle into the French King's hands. In 1204 Philip turned on the south with as startling a success. Maine, Anjou, and Touraine passed with little resistance into his hands, and the death of Eleanor was followed by the submission of the bulk of Aquitaine. Little was left save the country south of the Garonne ; and from the lordship of a vast empire that stretched from the Tyne to the Pyrenees John saw himself reduced at a blow to the realm of England. On the loss of Château-Gaillard in fact hung the destinies of England, and the interest that attaches one to the grand ruin on the heights of Les Andelys is, that it represents the ruin of a system as well as of a camp. From its dark donjon and broken walls we see not merely the pleasant vale of Seine, but the sedgy flats of our own Runnymede.

CHAPTER III.

THE GREAT CHARTER.

1204—1265.

Section I.—English Literature under the Norman and Angevin Kings.

[*Authorities.*—For the general literature of this period, see Mr. Morley's "English Writers from the Conquest to Chaucer," vol. i. part ii. The prefaces of Mr. Brewer and Mr. Dimock to his collected works in the Rolls Series give all that can be known of Gerald de Barri. The Poems of Walter Map have been edited by Mr. Wright for the Camden Society ; Layamon, by Sir F. Madden.]

IT is in a review of the literature of England during the period that we have just traversed that we shall best understand the new English people with which John, when driven from Normandy, found himself face to face.

In his contest with Beket, Henry the Second had been powerfully aided by the silent revolution which now began to part the purely literary class from the purely clerical. During the earlier ages of our history we have seen literature springing up in ecclesiastical schools, and protecting itself against the ignorance and violence of the time under ecclesiastical privileges. Almost all our writers from Bæda to the days of the Angevins are clergy or monks. The revival of letters which followed the Conquest was a purely ecclesiastical revival ; the intellectual impulse which Bec had given to Normandy travelled across the Channel with the new Norman abbots who were established in the greater English monasteries ; and writing-rooms or scriptoria, where the chief works of Latin literature, patristic or classical, were copied and illuminated, the lives of saints compiled, and entries noted in the monastic chronicle, formed from this time a part of every religious house of any importance. But the literature which found this religious shelter was not so much ecclesiastical as secular. Even the philosophical and devotional impulse given by Anselm produced no English work of theology or metaphysics. The literary revival which followed the Conquest took mainly the old historical form. At Durham, Turgot and Simeon threw into Latin shape the national annals to the time of

The literary revival

SEC. I.

ENGLISH
LITERATURE
UNDER THE
NORMAN
AND ANGE-
VIN KINGS

Henry the First with an especial regard to northern affairs, while the earlier events of Stephen's reign were noted down by two Priors of Hexham in the wild border-land between England and the Scots. These however were the colourless jottings of mere annalists ; it was in the Scriptorium of Canterbury, in Osbern's lives of the English saints, or in Eadmer's record of the struggle of Anselm against the Red King and his successor, that we see the first indications of a distinctively English feeling telling on the new literature. The national impulse is yet more conspicuous in the two historians that followed. The war-songs of the English conquerors of Britain were preserved by Henry, an Archdeacon of Huntingdon, who wove them into annals compiled from Bæda and the Chronicle ; while William, the librarian of Malmesbury, as industriously collected the lighter ballads which embodied the popular traditions of the English Kings.

Litera-
ture and
the Court

William of
Malmesbury

It is in William above all others that we see the new tendency of English literature.   In himself, as in his work, he marks the fusion of the conquerors and the conquered, for he was of both English and Norman parentage, and his sympathies were as divided as his blood. The form and style of his writings show the influence of those classical studies which were now reviving throughout Christendom.   Monk as he is, he discards the older ecclesiastical models and the annalistic form.   Events are grouped together with no strict reference to time, while the lively narrative flows rapidly and loosely along, with constant breaks of digression over the general history of Europe and the Church.   It is in this change of historic spirit that William takes his place as first of the more statesmanlike and philosophic school of

The Court
historians

historians who began soon to arise in direct connection with the Court, and amongst whom the author of the chronicle which commonly bears the name of " Benedict of Peterborough," with his continuator Roger of Howden, are the most conspicuous.   Both held judicial offices under Henry the Second, and it is to their position at Court that they owe the fulness and accuracy of their information as to affairs at home and abroad, their copious supply of official documents, and the purely political temper with which they regard the conflict of Church and State in their time.   The same freedom from ecclesiastical bias, com- bined with remarkable critical ability, is found in the history of William, the Canon of Newburgh, who wrote far away in his Yorkshire monastery. The English court, however, had become the centre of a distinctly secular literature. The treatise of Ranulf de Glanvill, the justiciar of Henry the Second, is the earliest work on English law, as that of the royal treasurer, Richard Fitz-Neal, on the Exchequer is the earliest on English government.

Gerald of
Wales

Still more distinctly secular than these, though the work of a priest who claimed to be a bishop, are the writings of Gerald de Barri. Gerald is the father of our popular literature, as he is the originator of

Sec. I.

English
Literature
under the
Norman
and Ange-
vin Kings

the political and ecclesiastical pamphlet. Welsh blood (as his usual name of Giraldus Cambrensis implies) mixed with Norman in his veins, and something of the restless Celtic fire runs alike through his writings and his life. A busy scholar at Paris, a reforming archdeacon in Wales, the wittiest of Court chaplains, the most troublesome of bishops, Gerald became the gayest and most amusing of all the authors of his time. In his hands the stately Latin tongue took the vivacity and picturesqueness of the jongleur's verse. Reared as he had been in classical studies, he threw pedantry contemptuously aside. "It is better to be dumb than not to be understood," is his characteristic apology for the novelty of his style: "new times require new fashions, and so I have thrown utterly aside the old and dry method of some authors, and aimed at adopting the fashion of speech which is actually in vogue to-day." His tract on the conquest of Ireland and his account of Wales, which are in fact reports of two journeys undertaken in those countries with John and Archbishop Baldwin, illustrate his rapid faculty of careless observation, his audacity, and his good sense. They are just the sort of lively, dashing letters that we find in the correspondence of a modern journal. There is the same modern tone in his political pamphlets; his profusion of jests, his fund of anecdote, the aptness of his quotations, his natural shrewdness and critical acumen, the clearness and vivacity of his style, are backed by a fearlessness and impetuosity that made him a dangerous assailant even to such a ruler as Henry the Second. The invectives in which Gerald poured out his resentment against the Angevins are the cause of half the scandal about Henry and his sons which has found its way into history. His life was wasted in an ineffectual struggle to secure the see of St. David's, but his pungent pen played its part in rousing the spirit of the nation to its struggle with the Crown.

A tone of distinct hostility to the Church developed itself almost from the first among the singers of romance. Romance had long before taken root in the court of Henry the First, where under the patronage of Queen Maud the dreams of Arthur, so long cherished by the Celts of Britanny, and which had travelled to Wales in the train of the exile Rhys ap Tewdor, took shape in the History of the Britons by Geoffry of Monmouth. Myth, legend, tradition, the classical pedantry of the day, Welsh hopes of future triumph over the Saxon, the memories of the Crusades and of the world-wide dominion of Charles the Great, were mingled together by this daring fabulist in a work whose popularity became at once immense. Alfred of Beverley transferred Geoffry's inventions into the region of sober history, while two Norman *trouvères*, Gaimar and Wace, translated them into French verse. So complete was the credence they obtained, that Arthur's tomb at Glastonbury was visited by Henry the Second, while the child of his son Geoffry and of Constance of Britanny bore the name of the

SEC. I.

ENGLISH
LITERATURE
UNDER THE
NORMAN
AND ANGE-
VIN KINGS

Celtic hero. Out of Geoffry's creation grew little by little the poem of the Table Round. Britanny, which had mingled with the story of Arthur the older and more mysterious legend of the Enchanter Merlin, lent that of Lancelot to the wandering minstrels of the day, who moulded it, as they wandered from hall to hall, into the familiar tale of knighthood wrested from its loyalty by the love of woman. The stories of Tristram and Gawayne, at first as independent as that of Lancelot, were drawn with it into the whirlpool of Arthurian romance.; and when the Church, jealous of the popularity of the legends of chivalry, invented as a counteracting influence the poem of the Sacred Dish, the San Graal which held the blood of the Cross invisible to all eyes but those of the pure in heart, the genius of a court poet, Walter de Map, wove the rival legends together, sent Arthur and his knights wandering over sea and land in the quest of the San Graal, and crowned the work by the figure of Sir Galahad, the type of ideal knighthood, without fear and without reproach.

Walter de Map

　　Walter stands before us as the representative of a sudden outburst of literary, social, and religious criticism which followed the growth of romance and the appearance of a freer historical tone in the court of the two Henries. Born on the Welsh border, a student at Paris, a favourite with the King, a royal chaplain, justiciar, and ambassador, the genius of Walter de Map was as various as it was prolific. He is as much at his ease in sweeping together the chit-chat of the time in his "Courtly Trifles" as in creating the character of Sir Galahad. But he only rose to his fullest strength when he turned from the fields of romance to that of Church reform, and embodied the ecclesiastical abuses of his day in the figure of his "Bishop Goliath." The whole spirit of Henry and his court in their struggle with Beket is reflected and illustrated in the apocalypse and confession of this imaginary prelate. Picture after picture strips the veil from the corruption of the mediæval Church, its indolence, its thirst for gain, its secret immorality. The whole body of the clergy, from Pope to hedge-priest, is painted as busy in the chase for gain ; what escapes the bishop is snapped up by the archdeacon, what escapes the archdeacon is nosed and hunted down by the dean, while a host of minor officials prowl hungrily around these greater marauders. Out of the crowd of figures which fills the canvas of the satirist, pluralist vicars, abbots "purple as their wines," monks feeding and chattering together like parrots in the refectory, rises the Philistine Bishop, light of purpose, void of conscience, lost in sensuality, drunken, unchaste, the Goliath who sums up the enormities of all, and against whose forehead this new David slings his sharp pebble of the brook.

Revival of the English tongue

　　It is only, however, as the writings of Englishmen that Latin or French works like these can be claimed as part of English literature. The spoken tongue of the nation at large remained of course English as before; William himself had tried to learn it that he might administer justice to his subjects; and for a century after the Conquest only a few new words crept in from the language of the conquerors. Even English literature, banished as it was from the court of the stranger and exposed to the fashionable rivalry of Latin scholars, survived not only in religious works, in poetic paraphrases of gospels and psalms, but in the great monument of our prose, the English Chronicle. It was not till the miserable reign of Stephen that the Chronicle died out in the Abbey of Peterborough. But the "Sayings of Ælfred," which embodied the ideal of an English king and gathered a legendary worship round the great name of the English past, show a native literature going on through the reign of Henry the Second. The appearance of a great work of English verse coincides in point of time with the loss of Normandy, and the return of John to his island realm. "There was a priest in the land whose name was Layamon; he was son of Leovenath: may the Lord be gracious to him! He dwelt at Earnley, a noble church on the bank of Severn (good it seemed to him!) near Radstone, where he read books. It came in mind to him and in his chiefest thought that he would tell the noble deeds of England, what the men were named, and whence they came, who first had English land." Journeying far and wide over the land, the priest of Earnley found Bæda and Wace, the books too of S. Albin and S. Austin. "Layamon laid down these books and turned the leaves; he beheld them lovingly: may the Lord be gracious to him! Pen he took with fingers and wrote a book-skin, and the true words set together, and compressed the three books into one." Layamon's church is now Areley, near Bewdley, in Worcestershire. His poem was in fact an expansion of Wace's "Brut," with insertions from Bæda. Historically it is worthless, but as a monument of our language it is beyond all price. After Norman and Angevin English remained unchanged. In more than thirty thousand lines not more than fifty Norman words are to be found. Even the old poetic tradition remains the same; the alliterative metre of the earlier verse is only slightly affected by riming terminations, the similes are the few natural similes of Cædmon, the battles are painted with the same rough, simple joy. It is by no mere accident that the English tongue thus wakes again into written life on the eve of the great struggle between the nation and its King. The artificial forms imposed by the Conquest were falling away from the people as from its literature, and a new England, quickened by the Celtic vivacity of de Map and the Norman daring of Gerald, stood forth to its conflict with John.

Layamon

Section II.—John. 1204—1215.

[*Authorities.*— Our chief sources of information are the Chronicle embodied in the "Memoriale" of Walter of Coventry ; and the "Chronicle of Roger of Wendover," the first of the published annalists of S. Alban's, whose work was subsequently revised and continued in a more patriotic tone by another monk of the same abbey, Matthew Paris. The Annals of Waverley, Dunstable, and Burton are important for the period. The great series of the Royal Rolls begin now to be of the highest value. The French authorities as before. For Langton, see Hook's biography in the "Lives of the Archbishops." The best modern account of this reign is in Mr. Pearson's "History of England," vol. ii.]

John

"Foul as it is, hell itself is defiled by the fouler presence of John." The terrible verdict of the King's contemporaries has passed into the sober judgement of history. Externally John possessed all the quickness, the vivacity, the cleverness, the good-humour, the social charm which distinguished his house. His worst enemies owned that he toiled steadily and closely at the work of administration. He was fond of learned men like Gerald of Wales. He had a strange gift of attracting friends and of winning the love of women. But in his inner soul John was the worst outcome of the Angevins. He united into one mass of wickedness their insolence, their selfishness, their unbridled lust, their cruelty and tyranny, their shamelessness, their superstition, their cynical indifference to honour or truth. In mere boyhood he had torn with brutal levity the beards of the Irish chieftains who came to own him as their lord. His ingratitude and perfidy had brought down his father with sorrow to the grave. To his brother he had been the worst of traitors. All Christendom believed him to be the murderer of his nephew, Arthur of Britanny. He abandoned one wife and was faithless to another. His punishments were refinements of cruelty—the starvation of children, the crushing old men under copes of lead. His court was a brothel where no woman was safe from the royal lust, and where his cynicism loved to publish the news of his victims' shame. He was as craven in his superstition as he was daring in his impiety. He scoffed at priests and turned his back on the mass even amidst the solemnities of his coronation, but he never stirred on a journey without hanging relics round his neck. But with the supreme wickedness of his race he inherited its profound ability. His plan for the relief of Château-Gaillard, the rapid march by which he shattered Arthur's hopes at Mirebeau, showed an inborn genius for war. In the rapidity and breadth of his political combinations he far surpassed the statesmen of his time. Throughout his reign we see him quick to discern the difficulties of his position, and inexhaustible in the resources with which he met them. The overthrow of his continental power only spurred him to the formation of a great league which all but brought Philip to the ground; and the sudden revolt of all England was parried by a shameless alliance with the Papacy. The closer study of John's history clears away the charges of sloth and incapacity with which men tried to explain the greatness of his fall. The awful lesson of his life rests on the fact that it was no weak and indolent voluptuary, but the ablest and most ruthless of the Angevins who lost Normandy, became the vassal of the Pope, and perished in a struggle of despair against English freedom.

The whole energies of the King were bent on the recovery of his lost dominions on the Continent. He impatiently collected money and men for the support of the adherents of the House of Anjou who were still struggling against the arms of France in Poitou and Guienne, and had assembled an army at Portsmouth in the summer of 1205, when his project was suddenly thwarted by the resolute opposition of the Primate and the Earl of Pembroke, William Marshal. So completely had both the baronage and the Church been humbled by his father, that the attitude of their representatives indicated the new spirit of national freedom which was rising around the King. John at once braced himself to a struggle with it. The death of Hubert Walter, a few weeks after his protest, enabled him, as it seemed, to neutralize the opposition of the Church by placing a creature of his own at its head. John de Grey, Bishop of Norwich, was elected by the monks of Canterbury at his bidding and enthroned as Primate. In a previous though informal gathering, however, the convent had already chosen its sub-prior, Reginald, as Archbishop, and the rival claimants hastened to appeal to Rome; but the result of their appeal was a startling one both for themselves and for the King. Innocent the Third, who now occupied the Papal throne, had pushed its claims of supremacy over Christendom further than any of his predecessors: after a careful examination he quashed both the contested elections. The decision was probably a just one; but Innocent did not stop there; whether from love of power, or, as may fairly be supposed, in despair of a free election within English bounds, he commanded the monks who appeared before him to elect in his presence Stephen Langton to the archiepiscopal see. Personally a better choice could not have been made, for Stephen was a man who by sheer weight of learning and holiness of life had risen to the dignity of Cardinal, and whose after career placed him in the front rank of English patriots. But in itself the step was an usurpation of the rights both of the Church and of the Crown. The King at once met it with resistance, and replied to the Papal threats of interdict if Langton were any longer excluded from his see, by a counter threat that the interdict should be followed by the banishment of the clergy and the mutilation of every Italian he could seize in the realm. Innocent, however, was not a man to draw back from his purpose, and the interdict fell at last upon the land. All worship save that of a few privileged orders, all administration of the Sacraments save that of private baptism, ceased over the length and breadth of the country : the church-bells were silent, the dead lay unburied on the ground. The King replied by confiscating the lands of the clergy who observed the interdict, by subjecting them in spite of their privileges to the royal courts, and often by leaving outrages on them unpunished. " Let him go," said John, when a Welshman was brought before him for the murder of a priest, "he has killed my enemy !" A year passed before the Pope proceeded to the further sentence of excommunication. John was now formally cut off from the pale of the Church ; but the new sentence was met with the same defiance as the old. Five of the bishops fled over sea, and secret disaffection was spreading widely, but there was no public avoidance of the excommunicated King. An Archdeacon of Norwich who withdrew from his service was crushed to death under a cope of lead, and the hint was sufficient to prevent either prelate or noble from following his example. Though the King stood alone, with nobles estranged from him and the Church against him, his strength seemed utterly unbroken. From the first moment of his rule John had defied the baronage. The promise to satisfy their demand for redress of wrongs in the past reign, a promise made at his election, remained unfulfilled ; when the demand was repeated he answered it by seizing their castles and taking their children as hostages for their loyalty. The cost of his fruitless threats of war had been met by heavy and repeated taxation. The quarrel with the Church and fear of their revolt only deepened his oppression of the nobles. He drove De Braose, one of the most powerful of the Lords Marchers, to die in exile, while his wife and grandchildren were believed to have been starved to death in the royal prisons. On the nobles who still clung panic-stricken to the court of the excommunicate king John heaped outrages worse than death. Illegal exactions, the seizure of their castles, the preference shown to foreigners, were small provocations compared with his attacks on the honour of their wives and daughters. But the baronage still submitted ; and the King's vigour was seen by the rapidity with which he crushed a rising of the nobles in Ireland, and foiled an outbreak of the Welsh. Hated as he was the land remained still. Only one weapon now remained in Innocent's hands. An excommunicate king had ceased to be a Christian, or to have claims on the obedience of Christian subjects. As spiritual heads of Christendom, the Popes had ere now asserted their right to remove such a ruler from his throne and to give it to a worthier than he ; and

this right Innocent at last felt himself driven to exercise. He issued a bull of deposition against John, proclaimed a crusade against him, and committed the execution of his sentence to Philip of France.

John met it with the same scorn as before. His insolent disdain suffered the Roman legate, Cardinal Pandulf, to proclaim his deposition to his face at Northampton. An enormous army gathered at his call on Barham Down ; and the English fleet dispelled all danger of invasion by crossing the Channel, by capturing a number of French ships, and by burning Dieppe.

But it was not in England only that the King showed his strength and activity. Vile as he was, John possessed in a high degree the political ability of his race, and in the diplomatic efforts with which he met the danger from France he showed himself his father's equal. The barons of Poitou were roused to attack Philip from the south. John bought the aid of the Count of Flanders on his northern border. The German King, Otto, pledged himself to bring the knighthood of Germany to support an invasion of France. But at the moment of his success in diplomacy John suddenly gave way. It was in fact the revelation of a danger at home which shook him from his attitude of contemptuous defiance. The bull of deposition gave fresh energy to every enemy. The Scotch King was in correspondence with Innocent. The Welsh princes who had just been forced to submission broke out again in war. John hanged their hostages, and called his host to muster for a fresh inroad into Wales, but the army met only to become a fresh source of danger. Powerless to resist openly, the baronage had plunged almost to a man into secret conspiracies ; many promised aid to Philip on his landing. John, in the midst of hidden enemies, was only saved by the haste with which he disbanded his army and took refuge in Nottingham Castle. His daring self-confidence, the skill of his diplomacy, could no longer hide from him the utter loneliness of his position. At war with Rome, with France, with Scotland, Ireland and Wales, at war with the Church, he saw himself disarmed by this sudden revelation of treason in the one force left at his disposal. With characteristic suddenness he gave way. He endeavoured by remission of fines to win back his people. He negotiated eagerly with the Pope, consented to receive the Archbishop, and promised to repay the money he had extorted from the Church. The shameless ingenuity of the King's temper was seen in his immediate resolve to make Rome his ally, to turn its spiritual thunder against his foes, to use it in breaking up the confederacy it had formed against him. His quick versatile temper saw the momentary gain to be won. On the 15th of May 1213 he knelt before the legate Pandulf, surrendered his kingdom to the Roman See, took it back again as a tributary vassal, swore fealty and did liege homage to the Pope.

In after times men believed that England thrilled at the news with a sense of national shame such as she had never felt before. "He has become the Pope's man," the whole country was said to have murmured ; "he has forfeited the very name of King ; from a free man he

SEC. II.

JOHN
1204
TO
1215

The
Pope's
vassal

The
Battle of
Bouvines

has degraded himself into a serf." But we see little trace of such a feeling in the contemporary accounts of the time. As a political measure indeed the success of John's submission was complete. The French army at once broke up in impotent rage, and when Philip turned against the enemy whom John had raised up for him in Flanders, five hundred English ships under the Earl of Salisbury fell upon the fleet which accompanied his army along the coast and utterly destroyed it. The league which John had so long matured at last disclosed itself. The King himself landed in Poitou, rallied its nobles round him, crossed the Loire in triumph, and won back Angers, the home of his race. At the same time Otto, reinforcing his German army by the knighthood of Flanders and Boulogne as well as by a body of English troops, threatened France from the north. For the moment Philip seemed lost, and yet on the fortunes of Philip hung the fortunes of English freedom. But in this crisis of her fate France was true to herself and her King; the townsmen marched from every borough to Philip's rescue, priests led their flocks to battle with the Church banners flying at their head. The two armies met near the

bridge of Bouvines, between Lille and Tournay, and from the first the day went against the allies. The Flemish were the first to fly; then the Germans in the centre were overwhelmed by the numbers of the French; last of all the English on the right were broken by a fierce onset of the Bishop of Beauvais, who charged mace in hand and struck the Earl of Salisbury to the ground. The news of this complete overthrow reached John in the midst of his triumphs in the South, and scattered his hopes to the winds. He was at once deserted by the Poitevin nobles, and a hasty retreat alone enabled him to return, baffled and humiliated, to his island kingdom.

It is to the victory of Bouvines that England owes her Great Charter. From the hour of his submission to the Papacy, John's vengeance on the barons had only been delayed till he should return a conqueror from the fields of France. A sense of their danger nerved the baronage to resistance; they refused to follow the King on his foreign campaign till the excommunication were removed, and when it was removed they still refused, on the plea that they were not bound to serve in wars without the realm. Furious as he was at this new attitude of resistance, the time had not yet come for vengeance, and John sailed for Poitou with the dream of a great victory which should lay Philip and the barons alike at his feet. He returned from his defeat to find the nobles no longer banded together in secret conspiracies, but openly united in a definite claim of liberty and law. The leader in this great change was the new Archbishop whom Innocent had set on the throne of Canterbury. From the moment of his landing in England, Stephen Langton had assumed the constitutional position of the Primate as champion of the old English customs and law against the

personal despotism of the kings. As Anselm had withstood William
the Red, as Theobald had rescued England from the lawlessness of
Stephen, so Langton prepared to withstand and rescue his country
from the tyranny of John. He had already forced him to swear to
observe the laws of the Confessor, a phrase in which the whole of the
national liberties were summed up. When the baronage refused to
sail to Poitou, he compelled the King to deal with them not by arms
but by process of law. Far however from being satisfied with resistance such as this to isolated acts of tyranny, it was the Archbishop's
aim to restore on a formal basis the older freedom of the realm. The
pledges of Henry the First had long been forgotten when the Justiciar,
Geoffrey Fitz-Peter, brought them to light at a Council held at S.
Albans. There in the King's name the Justiciar promised good
government for the time to come, and forbade all royal officers to
practise extortion as they prized life and limb. The King's peace was
pledged to those who had opposed him in the past ; and observance
of the laws of Henry the First was enjoined upon all within the realm.
Langton saw the vast importance of such a precedent. In a fresh
meeting of the barons at S. Paul's he produced the Charter of Henry
the First, and it was at once welcomed as a base for the needed
reforms. All hope however hung on the fortunes of the French campaign ; the victory at Bouvines gave strength to John's opponents, and
after the King's landing the barons secretly met at S. Edmundsbury,
and swore to demand from him, if needful by force of arms, the restoration of their liberties by Charter under the King's seal. Early in
January in the year 1215 they presented themselves in arms before
the King, and preferred their claim. The few months that followed
showed John the uselessness of resistance ; nobles and Churchmen
were alike arrayed against him, and the commissioners whom he sent
to plead his cause at the shire-courts brought back the news that no
man would help him against the Charter. At Easter the barons again
gathered in arms at Brackley, and renewed their claim. "Why do
they not ask for my kingdom ?" cried John in a burst of passion ; but
the whole country rose as one man at his refusal. London threw open
her gates to the forces of the barons, now organised under Robert
Fitz-Walter as "Marshal of the Army of God and Holy Church." The
example of the capital was followed by Exeter and Lincoln ; promises
of aid came from Scotland and Wales ; the northern barons marched
hastily to join their comrades in London. There was a moment when
John found himself with seven knights at his back, and before him a
nation in arms. He had summoned mercenaries and appealed to his
liege lord, the Pope ; but summons and appeal were alike too late.
Nursing wrath in his heart the tyrant bowed to necessity, and called
the barons to a conference at Runnymede.

Sec. III.

The Great
Charter

1215
TO
1217

1215
June 15

Section III.—The Great Charter, 1215—1217.

[*Authorities.*—The text of the Charter is given by Dr. Stubbs, with valuable comments, in his "Select Charters." Mr. Pearson gives a useful analysis of it.]

An island in the Thames between Staines and Windsor had been chosen as the place of conference : the King encamped on one bank, while the barons covered the marshy flat, still known by the name of Runnymede, on the other. Their delegates met in the island between them, but the negotiations were a mere cloak to cover John's purpose of unconditional submission. The Great Charter was discussed, agreed to, and signed in a single day.

One copy of it still remains in the British Museum, injured by age and fire, but with the royal seal still hanging from the brown, shrivelled parchment. It is impossible to gaze without reverence on the earliest monument of English freedom which we can see with our own eyes and touch with our own hands, the great Charter to which from age to age patriots have looked back as the basis of English liberty. But in itself the Charter was no novelty, nor did it claim to establish any new constitutional principles. The Charter of Henry the First formed the basis of the whole, and the additions to it are for the most part formal recognitions of the judicial and administrative changes introduced by Henry the Second. But the vague expressions of the older charter were now exchanged for precise and elaborate provisions. The bonds of unwritten custom which the older grant did little more than recognize had proved too weak to hold the Angevins ; and the baronage now threw them aside for the restraints of written law. It is in this way that the Great Charter marks the transition from the age of traditional rights, preserved in the nation's memory and officially declared by the Primate, to the age of written legislation, of Parliaments and Statutes, which was soon to come. The Church had shown its power of self-defence in the struggle over the interdict, and the clause which recognized its rights alone retained the older and general form. But all vagueness ceases when the Charter passes on to deal with the rights of Englishmen at large, their right to justice, to security of person and property, to good government. " No freeman," ran the memorable article that lies at the base of our whole judicial system, " shall be seized or imprisoned, or dispossessed, or outlawed, or in any way brought to ruin : we will not go against any man nor send against him, save by legal judgement of his peers or by the law of the land." " To no man will we sell," runs another, " or deny, or delay, right or justice." The great reforms of the past reigns were now formally recognized ; judges of assize were to hold their circuits four times in the year, and the King's Court was no longer to follow the King in his wanderings over the realm, but to sit in a fixed place. But the denial of justice under John was a small danger compared with the lawless exactions both of himself and his predecessor. Richard had increased the amount of the scutage which Henry the Second had introduced, and applied it to raise funds for his ransom. He had restored the Dane-geld, or land-tax, so often abolished, under the new name of "carucage," had seized the wool of the Cistercians and the plate of the churches, and rated moveables as well as land. John had again raised the rate of scutage, and imposed aids, fines, and ransoms at his pleasure without counsel of the baronage. The Great Charter met this abuse by the provision on which our constitutional system rests. With the exception of the three customary feudal aids which still remained to the Crown, "no scutage or aid shall be imposed in our realm save by the common council of the realm ; " and to this Great Council it was provided that prelates and the greater barons should be summoned by special writ, and all tenants in chief through the sheriffs and bailiffs, at least forty days before. The provision defined what had probably been the common usage of the realm ; but the definition turned it into a national right, a right so momentous that on it rests our whole Parliamentary life.

The rights which the barons claimed for themselves they claimed for the nation at large. The boon of free and unbought justice was a boon for all, but a special provision protected the poor. The forfeiture of the freeman on conviction of felony was never to include his tenement, or that of the merchant his wares, or that of the countryman his wain. The means of actual livelihood were to be left even to the worst. The under-tenants or farmers were protected against all lawless exactions of their lords in precisely the same terms as these were protected against the lawless exactions of the Crown. The towns were secured in the enjoyment of their municipal privileges, their freedom from arbitrary taxation, their rights of justice, of common deliberation, of regulation of trade. "Let the city of London have all its old liberties and its free customs, as well by land as by water. Besides this, we will and grant that all other cities, and boroughs, and towns, and ports, have all their liberties and free customs." The influence of the trading class is seen in two other enactments, by which freedom of journeying and trade was secured to foreign merchants, and an uniformity of weights and measures was ordered to be enforced throughout the realm. There remained only one question, and that the most difficult of all ; the question how to secure this order which the Charter had established in the actual government of the realm. The immediate abuses were easily swept away, the hostages restored to their homes, the foreigners banished from the country. But it was less easy to provide means for the control of a King whom no man could trust,

K

SEC. III.

THE GREAT
CHARTER

1215
TO
1217

**John
and the
Charter**

and a council of twenty-five barons were chosen from the general body of their order to enforce on John the observance of the Charter, with the right of declaring war on the King should its provisions be infringed. Finally, the Charter was published throughout the whole country, and sworn to at every hundred-mote and town-mote by order from the King.

"They have given me five-and-twenty over-kings," cried John in a burst of fury, flinging himself on the floor and gnawing sticks and straw in his impotent rage. But the rage soon passed into the subtle policy of which he was a master. Some days after he left Windsor, and lingered for months along the southern shore, waiting for news of the aid he had solicited from Rome and from the Continent. It was not without definite purpose that he had become the vassal of Rome. While Innocent was dreaming of a vast Christian Empire with the Pope at its head to enforce justice and religion on his under-kings, John believed that the Papal protection would enable him to rule as tyrannically as he would. The thunders of the Papacy were to be ever at hand for his protection, as the armies of England are at hand to protect the vileness and oppression of a Turkish Sultan or a Nizam of Hyderabad. His envoys were already at Rome, and Innocent, indignant that a matter which might have been brought before his court of appeal as overlord should have been dealt with by armed revolt, annulled the Great Charter and suspended Stephen Langton from the exercise of his office as Primate. Autumn brought a host of foreign soldiers from over sea to the King's standard, and advancing against the disorganized forces of the barons, John starved Rochester into submission and marched ravaging through the midland counties to the North, while his mercenaries spread like locusts over the whole face of the land. From Berwick the King turned back triumphant to coop up his enemies in London, while fresh Papal excommunications fell on the barons and the city. But the burghers set Innocent at defiance. "The ordering of secular matters appertaineth not to the Pope," they said, in words that seem like mutterings of the coming Lollardry ; and at the advice of Simon Langton, the Archbishop's brother, bells swung out and mass was celebrated as before. With the undisciplined militia of the country and the towns, however, success was impossible against the trained forces of the King, and despair drove the barons to seek aid from France. Philip had long been waiting the opportunity for his revenge upon John, and his son Lewis at once accepted the crown in spite of Innocent's excommunications, and landed in Kent with a considerable force. As the barons had foreseen, the French mercenaries who constituted John's host refused to fight against the French sovereign. The whole aspect of affairs was suddenly reversed. Deserted by the bulk of his troops, the King was forced to fall rapidly back on the Welsh Marches, while his rival entered London and received the submission of the larger part of England. Only Dover held out obstinately against Lewis. By a series of rapid marches John succeeded in distracting the plans of the barons and in relieving Lincoln ; then after a short stay at Lynn he crossed the Wash in a fresh movement to the north. In crossing, however, his army was surprised by the tide, and his baggage with the royal treasures washed away.

The fever which seized the baffled tyrant in the abbey of Swineshead was inflamed by a gluttonous debauch, and John entered Newark only to die. His death changed the whole face of affairs, for his son Henry was but a child of nine years old, and the royal authority passed into the hands of one who stands high among English patriots, William Marshal. The boy-king was hardly crowned when the Earl and the Papal Legate issued in his name the very Charter against which his father had died fighting ; only the clauses which regulated taxation and the summoning of Parliament were as yet declared to be suspended. The nobles soon streamed away from the French camp ; for national jealousy and suspicions of treason told heavily against Lewis, while the pity which was excited by the youth and helplessness of Henry was aided by a sense of injustice in burthening the child with the iniquity of his father. One bold stroke of William Marshal decided the struggle. A joint army of French and English barons under the Count of Perche and Robert Fitz-Walter was besieging Lincoln, when the Earl, rapidly gathering forces from the royal castles, marched to its relief. Cooped up in the steep narrow streets, and attacked at once by the Earl and the garrison, the barons fled in hopeless rout ; the Count of Perche fell on the field ; Robert Fitz-Walter was taken prisoner. Lewis, who was investing Dover, retreated to London, and called for aid from France. But a more terrible defeat crushed his remaining hopes. A small English fleet, which had set sail from Dover under Hubert de Burgh, fell boldly on the reinforcements which were crossing under the escort of Eustace the Monk, a well-known freebooter of the Channel. The fight admirably illustrates the naval warfare of the time. From the decks of the English vessels bowmen poured their arrows into the crowded transports, others hurled quicklime into their enemies' faces, while the more active vessels crashed with their armed prows into the sides of the French ships. The skill of the mariners of the Cinque Ports decided the day against the larger forces of their opponents, and the fleet of Eustace was utterly destroyed. The royal army at once closed in upon London, but resistance was really at an end. By the treaty of Lambeth Lewis promised to withdraw from England on payment of a sum which he claimed as debt ; his adherents were restored to their possessions, the liberties of London and other towns confirmed, and the prisoners on either side set at liberty. The expulsion of the stranger

left English statesmen free to take up again the work of reform ; and
a fresh issue of the Charter, though in its modified form, proclaimed
clearly the temper and policy of the Earl Marshal.

Section IV.—The Universities.

[*Authorities.*—For the Universities we have the collection of materials
edited by Mr. Anstey under the name of "Munimenta Academica."
I have borrowed much from two papers of my own in "Macmillan's
Magazine," on "The Early History of Oxford." For Bacon, see his
"Opera Inedita," in the Rolls Series, with Mr. Brewer's admirable intro-
duction, and Dr. Whewell's estimate of him in his "History of the Inductive
Sciences."]

From the turmoil of civil politics we turn to the more silent but
hardly less important revolution from which we may date our national
education. It is in the reign of Henry the Third that the English
universities begin to exercise a definite influence on the intellectual life
of Englishmen. Of the early history of Cambridge we know little or
nothing, but enough remains to enable us to trace the early steps by
which Oxford attained to its intellectual eminence. The establishment
of the great schools which bore the name of Universities was everywhere throughout Europe a special mark of the new impulse that
Christendom had gained from the Crusades. A new fervour of study
sprang up in the West from its contact with the more cultured East.
Travellers like Adelard of Bath brought back the first rudiments of
physical and mathematical science from the schools of Cordova or
Bagdad. In the twelfth century a classical revival restored Cæsar and
Vergil to the list of monastic studies, and left its stamp on the pedantic
style, the profuse classical quotations of writers like William of Malmesbury or John of Salisbury. The scholastic philosophy sprang up in the
schools of Paris. The Roman law was revived by the imperialist
doctors of Bologna. The long mental inactivity of feudal Europe
broke up like ice before a summer's sun. Wandering teachers such as
Lanfranc or Anselm crossed sea and land to spread the new power of
knowledge. The same spirit of restlessness, of inquiry, of impatience
with the older traditions of mankind, either local or intellectual, that
had hurried half Christendom to the tomb of its Lord, crowded the
roads with thousands of young scholars hurrying to the chosen seats
where teachers were gathered together. A new power had sprung up
in the midst of a world as yet under the rule of sheer brute force.
Poor as they were, sometimes even of servile race, the wandering
scholars who lectured in every cloister were hailed as "masters" by the
crowds at their feet. Abelard was a foe worthy of the menaces of

councils, of the thunders of the Church. The teaching of a single Lombard was of note enough in England to draw down the prohibition of a King. When Vacarius, probably a guest in the court of Archbishop Theobald, where Beket and John of Salisbury were already busy with the study of the Civil Law, opened lectures on it at Oxford, he was at once silenced by Stephen, who was then at war with the Church, and jealous of the power which the wreck of the royal authority was throwing into Theobald's hands.

At the time of the arrival of Vacarius Oxford stood in the first rank among English towns. Its town church of S. Martin rose from the midst of a huddled group of houses, girt in with massive walls, that lay along the dry upper ground of a low peninsula between the streams of Cherwell and the upper Thames. The ground fell gently on either side, eastward and westward, to these rivers, while on the south a sharper descent led down across swampy meadows to the city bridge. Around lay a wild forest country, the moors of Cowley and Bullingdon fringing the course of Thames, the great woods of Shotover and Bagley closing the horizon to the south and east. Though the two huge towers of its Norman castle marked the strategic importance of Oxford as commanding the river valley along which the commerce of Southern England mainly flowed, its walls formed, perhaps, the least element in its military strength, for on every side but the north the town was guarded by the swampy meadows along Cherwell, or by the intricate network of streams into which the Thames breaks among the meadows of Osney. From the midst of these meadows rose a mitred abbey of Austin Canons, which, with the older priory of S. Frideswide, gave the town some ecclesiastical dignity. The residence of the Norman house of the D'Oillis within its castle, the frequent visits of English kings to a palace without its walls, the presence again and again of important councils, marked its political weight within the realm. The settlement of one of the wealthiest among the English Jewries in the very heart of the town indicated, while it promoted, the activity of its trade. No place better illustrates the transformation of the land in the hands of its Norman masters, the sudden outburst of industrial effort, the sudden expansion of commerce and accumulation of wealth which followed the Conquest. To the west of the town rose one of the stateliest of English castles, and in the meadows beneath the hardly less stately abbey of Osney. In the fields to the north the last of the Norman kings raised his palace of Beaumont. The canons of S. Frideswide reared the church which still exists as the diocesan cathedral, while the piety of the Norman Castellans rebuilt almost all the parish churches of the city, and founded within their new castle walls the church of the Canons of S. George. We know nothing of the causes which drew students and teachers within the walls of Oxford. It is possible that here as elsewhere a new teacher had quickened older educational foundations, and that the cloisters of Osney and S. Frideswide already possessed schools which burst into a larger life under the impulse of Vacarius. As yet, however, the fortunes of the University were obscured by the glories of Paris. English scholars gathered in thousands round the chairs of William of Champeaux or Abelard. The English took their place as one of the "nations" of the French University. John of Salisbury became famous as one of the Parisian teachers. Beket wandered to Paris from his school at Merton. But through the peaceful reign of Henry the Second Oxford was quietly increasing in numbers and repute. Forty years after the visit of Vacarius its educational position was fully established. When Gerald of Wales read his amusing Topography of Ireland to its students, the most learned and famous of the English clergy were, he tells us, to be found within its walls. At the opening of the thirteenth century Oxford was without a rival in its own country, while in European celebrity it took rank with the greatest schools of the Western world. But to realize this Oxford of the past we must dismiss from our minds all recollections of the Oxford of the present. In the outer aspect of the new University there was nothing of the pomp that overawes the freshman as he first paces the "High," or looks down from the gallery of S. Mary's. In the stead of long fronts of venerable colleges, of stately walks beneath immemorial elms, history plunges us into the mean and filthy lanes of a mediæval town. Thousands of boys, huddled in bare lodging-houses, clustering round teachers as poor as themselves in church porch and house porch, drinking, quarrelling, dicing, begging at the corners of the streets, take the place of the brightly-coloured train of doctors and Heads. Mayor and Chancellor struggled in vain to enforce order or peace on this seething mass of turbulent life. The retainers who followed their young lords to the University fought out the feuds of their houses in the streets. Scholars from Kent and scholars from Scotland waged the bitter struggle of North and South. At nightfall roysterer and reveller roamed with torches through the narrow lanes, defying bailiffs, and cutting down burghers at their doors. Now a mob of clerks plunged into the Jewry, and wiped off the memory of bills and bonds by sacking a Hebrew house or two. Now a tavern row between scholar and townsman widened into a general broil, and the academical bell of S. Mary's vied with the town bell of S. Martin's in clanging to arms. Every phase of ecclesiastical controversy or political strife was preluded by some fierce outbreak in this turbulent, surging mob. When England growled at the exactions of the Papacy, the students besieged a legate in the abbot's house at Osney. A murderous town and gown row preceded the opening of the Barons' War. "When Oxford draws knife," ran the old rime, "England's soon at strife."

But the turbulence and stir was a stir and turbulence of life. A keen

Sec. IV.

The
Univer-
sities

Edmund
Rich

thirst for knowledge, a passionate poetry of devotion, gathered thousands round the poorest scholar, and welcomed the barefoot friar. Edmund Rich—Archbishop of Canterbury and saint in later days— came to Oxford, a boy of twelve years old, from the little lane at Abingdon that still bears his name. He found his school in an inn that belonged to the abbey of Eynsham, where his father had taken refuge from the world. His mother was a pious woman of the day, too poor to give her boy much outfit besides the hair shirt that he promised to wear every Wednesday ; but Edmund was no poorer than his neighbours. He plunged at once into the nobler life of the place, its ardour for knowledge, its mystical piety. "Secretly," perhaps at eventide when the shadows were gathering in the church of S. Mary's, and the crowd of teachers and students had left its aisles, the boy stood before an image of the Virgin, and placing a ring of gold upon its finger took Mary for his bride. Years of study, broken by a fever that raged among the crowded, noisome streets, brought the time for completing his education at Paris ; and Edmund, hand in hand with a brother Robert of his, begged his way, as poor scholars were wont, to the great school of Western Christendom. Here a damsel, heedless of his tonsure, wooed him so pertinaciously that Edmund consented at last to an assignation ; but when he appeared it was in company of grave academical officials, who, as the maiden declared in the hour of penitence which followed, "straightway whipped the offending Eve out of her." Still true to his Virgin bridal, Edmund, on his return from Paris, became the most popular of Oxford teachers. It is to him that Oxford owes her first introduction to the Logic of Aristotle. We see him in the little room which he hired, with the Virgin's chapel hard by, his grey gown reaching to his feet, ascetic in his devotion, falling asleep in lecture time after a sleepless night of prayer, with a grace and cheerfulness of manner which told of his French training, and a chivalrous love of knowledge that let his pupils pay what they would. "Ashes to ashes, dust to dust," the young tutor would say, a touch of scholarly pride perhaps mingling with his contempt of worldly things, as he threw down the fee on the dusty window-ledge, whence a thievish student would sometimes run off with it. But even knowledge brought its troubles ; the Old Testament, which with a copy of the Decretals long formed his sole library, frowned down upon a love of secular learning from which Edmund found it hard to wean himself. At last, in some hour of dream, the form of his dead mother floated into the room where the teacher stood among his mathematical diagrams. "What are these?" she seemed to say ; and seizing Edmund's right hand, she drew on the palm three circles interlaced, each of which bore the name of one of the Persons of the Christian Trinity. "Be these," she cried, as her figure faded away, "thy diagrams henceforth, my son."

SEC. IV.

THE
UNIVER-
SITIES

**The Uni-
versities
and Feu-
dalism**

The story admirably illustrates the real character of the new training, and the latent opposition between the spirit of the Universities
and the spirit of the Church.   The feudal and ecclesiastical order of
the old mediæval world were both alike threatened by the power that
had so strangely sprung up in the midst of them.   Feudalism rested
on local isolation, on the severance of kingdom from kingdom and
barony from barony, on the distinction of blood and race, on the
supremacy of material or brute force, on an allegiance determined by
accidents of place and social position.   The University, on the other
hand, was a protest against this isolation of man from man.   The
smallest school was European and not local.   Not merely every province of France, but every people of Christendom, had its place among
the "nations" of Paris or Padua.   A common language, the Latin
tongue, superseded within academical bounds the warring tongues of
Europe.   A common intellectual kinship and rivalry took the place of
the petty strifes which parted province from province or realm from
realm.   What the Church and Empire had both aimed at and both
failed in, the knitting of Christian nations together into a vast commonwealth, the Universities for a time actually did.   Dante felt himself as
little a stranger in the "Latin" quarter around Mont Ste. Geneviève as
under the arches of Bologna.   Wandering Oxford scholars carried the
writings of Wyclif to the libraries of Prague.   In England the work of
provincial fusion was less difficult or important than elsewhere, but
even in England work had to be done.   The feuds of Northerner and
Southerner which so long disturbed the discipline of Oxford witnessed
at any rate to the fact that Northerner and Southerner had at last been
brought face to face in its streets.   And here as elsewhere the spirit of
national isolation was held in check by the larger comprehensiveness
of the University.   After the dissensions that threatened the prosperity
of Paris in the thirteenth century, Norman and Gascon mingled with
Englishmen in Oxford lecture-halls.   At a later time the rebellion of
Owen Glyndwr found hundreds of Welshmen gathered round its
teachers.   And within this strangely mingled mass, society and
government rested on a purely democratic basis.   Among Oxford
scholars the son of the noble stood on precisely the same footing with
the poorest mendicant.   Wealth, physical strength, skill in arms,
pride of ancestry and blood, the very grounds on which feudal society
rested, went for nothing in the lecture-room.   The University was
a state absolutely self-governed, and whose citizens were admitted by
a purely intellectual franchise.   Knowledge made the "master."   To
know more than one's fellows was a man's sole claim to be a "ruler"
in the schools : and within this intellectual aristocracy all were equal.
When the free commonwealth of the masters gathered in the aisles of
S. Mary's all had an equal right to counsel, all had an equal vote in
the final decision.   Treasury and library were at their complete dis-

SEC. IV.

THE
UNIVER-
SITIES

The Uni-
versities
and the
Church

posal. It was their voice that named every officer, that proposed and sanctioned every statute. Even the Chancellor, their head, who had at first been an officer of the Bishop, became an elected officer of their own.

If the democratic spirit of the Universities threatened feudalism, their spirit of intellectual inquiry threatened the Church. To all outer seeming they were purely ecclesiastical bodies. The wide extension which mediæval usage gave to the word "orders" gathered the whole educated world within the pale of the clergy. Whatever might be their age or proficiency, scholar and teacher were alike clerks, free from lay responsibilities or the control of civil tribunals, and amenable only to the rule of the Bishop and the sentence of his spiritual courts This ecclesiastical character of the University appeared in that of its head. The Chancellor, as we have seen, was at first no officer of the University, but of the ecclesiastical body under whose shadow it had sprung into life. At Oxford he was simply the local officer of the Bishop of Lincoln, within whose immense diocese the University was then situated. But this identification in outer form with the Church only rendered more conspicuous the difference of its spirit. The sudden expansion of the field of education diminished the importance of those purely ecclesiastical and theological studies which had hitherto absorbed the whole intellectual energies of mankind. The revival of classical literature, the rediscovery as it were of an older and a greater world, the contact with a larger, freer life, whether in mind, in society, or in politics, introduced a spirit of scepticism, of doubt, of denial into the realms of unquestioning belief. Abelard claimed for reason the supremacy over faith. Florentine poets discussed with a smile the immortality of the soul. Even to Dante, while he censures these, Vergil is as sacred as Jeremiah. The imperial ruler in whom the new culture took its most notable form, Frederic the Second, the "World's Wonder" of his time, was regarded by half Europe as no better than an infidel. A faint revival of physical science, so long crushed as magic by the dominant ecclesiasticism, brought Christians into perilous contact with the Moslem and the Jew. The books of the Rabbis were no longer a mere accursed thing to Roger Bacon. The scholars of Cordova were no mere Paynim swine to Abelard of Bath. How slowly indeed and against what obstacles science won its way we know from the witness of Roger Bacon. "Slowly," he tells us, "has any portion of the philosophy of Aristotle come into use among the Latins. His Natural Philosophy and his Metaphysics, with the Commentaries of Averroes and others, were translated in my time, and interdicted at Paris up to the year of grace 1237 because of their assertion of the eternity of the world and of time, and because of the book of the divinations by dreams (which is the third book, De Somniis et Vigiliis), and because of many passages erroneously translated. Even his Logic was slowly received and lectured on. For St. Edmund, the Archbishop of Canterbury, was the first in my time who read the Elements at Oxford. And I have seen Master Hugo, who first read the book of Posterior Analytics, and I have seen his writing. So there were but few, considering the multitude of the Latins, who were of any account in the philosophy of Aristotle ; nay, very few indeed, and scarcely any up to this year of grace 1292."

We shall see in a later page how fiercely the Church fought against this tide of opposition, and how it won back the allegiance of the Universities through the begging Friars. But it was in the ranks of the Friars themselves that the intellectual progress of the Universities found its highest representative. The life of Roger Bacon almost covers the thirteenth century ; he was the child of royalist parents, who had been driven into exile and reduced to poverty by the civil wars. From Oxford, where he studied under Edmund of Abingdon, to whom he owed his introduction to the works of Aristotle, he passed to the University of Paris, where his whole heritage was spent in costly studies and experiments. " From my youth up," he writes, " I have laboured at the sciences and tongues. I have sought the friend-ship of all men among the Latins who had any reputation for know-ledge. I have caused youths to be instructed in languages, geometry, arithmetic, the construction of tables and instruments, and many needful things besides." The difficulties in the way of such studies as he had resolved to pursue were immense. He was without instru-ments or means of experiment. " Without mathematical instruments no science can be mastered," he complains afterwards, "and these instruments are not to be found among the Latins, nor could they be made for two or three hundred pounds. Besides, better tables are indispensably necessary, tables on which the motions of the heavens are certified from the beginning to the end of the world without daily labour, but these tables are worth a king's ransom, and could not be made without a vast expense. I have often attempted the composi-tion of such tables, but could not finish them through failure of means and the folly of those whom I had to employ." Books were difficult and sometimes even impossible to procure. " The philosophical works of Aristotle, of Avicenna, of Seneca, of Cicero, and other ancients cannot be had without great cost ; their principal works have not been translated into Latin, and copies of others are not to be found in ordinary libraries or elsewhere. The admirable books of Cicero de Republica are not to be found anywhere, so far as I can hear, though I have made anxious inquiry for them in different parts of the world, and by various messengers. I could never find the works of Seneca, though I made diligent search for them during twenty years and more. And so it is with many more most useful books connected with the science of morals." It is only words like these of his own that bring home to us the keen thirst for knowledge, the patience, the energy of Roger Bacon. He returned as a teacher to Oxford, and a touching record of his devotion to those whom he taught remains in the story of John of London, a boy of fifteen, whose ability raised him above the general level of his pupils. "When he came to me as a poor boy," says Bacon, in recommending him to the Pope, "I caused him to be nurtured and instructed for the love of God, especially since for aptitude and innocence I have never found so towardly a youth. Five or six years ago I caused him to be taught in languages, mathematics, and optics, and I have gratuitously instructed him with my own lips since the time that I received your mandate. There is no one at Paris who knows so much of the root of philosophy, though he has not produced the branches, flowers, and fruit because of his youth, and because he has had no experience in teaching. But he has the means of surpassing all the Latins if he live to grow old and goes on as he has begun."

The pride with which he refers to his system of instruction was justified by the wide extension which he gave to scientific teaching in Oxford. It is probably of himself that he speaks when he tells us that "the science of optics has not hitherto been lectured on at Paris or elsewhere among the Latins, save twice at Oxford." It was a science on which he had laboured for ten years. But his teaching seems to have fallen on a barren soil. From the moment when the friars settled in the Universities scholasticism absorbed the whole mental energy of the student world. The temper of the age was against scientific or philosophical studies. The older enthusiasm for knowledge was dying down ; the study of law was the one source of promotion, whether in Church or state ; philosophy was discredited, literature in its purer forms became almost extinct. After forty years of incessant study, Bacon found himself in his own words "unheard, forgotten, buried." He seems at one time to have been wealthy, but his wealth was gone. "During the twenty years that I have specially laboured in the attainment of wisdom, abandoning the path of common men, I have spent on these pursuits more than two thousand pounds, on account of the cost of books, experiments, instruments, tables, the acquisition of languages, and the like. Add to all this the sacrifices I have made to procure the friendship of the wise, and to obtain well-instructed assistants." Ruined and baffled in his hopes, Bacon listened to the counsels of his friend Grosseteste and renounced the world. He became a friar of the order of S. Francis, an order where books and study were looked upon as hindrances to the work which it had specially undertaken, that of preaching among the masses of the poor. He had written hardly anything. So far was he from attempting to write, that his new superiors had prohibited him from publishing anything under pain of forfeiture of the book and penance of bread and water. But we can see the craving of his mind, the passionate instinct of creation which marks the man of genius, in the joy with which he seized the strange opportunity which suddenly opened before him. "Some few chapters on different subjects, written at the entreaty of friends," seem to have got abroad, and were brought by one of his chaplains under the notice of Clement the Fourth. The Pope at once invited him to write. Again difficulties stood in his way. Materials, transcription, and other expenses for such a work as he projected would cost at least £60, and the Pope had not sent a penny. He begged help from his family, but they were ruined like himself. No one would lend to a mendicant friar, and when his friends raised the money it was by pawning their goods in the hope of repayment from Clement. Nor was this all; the work itself, abstruse and scientific as was its subject, had to be treated in a clear and popular form to gain the Papal ear. But difficulties which would have crushed another man only roused Roger Bacon to an almost superhuman energy. In little more than a year the work was done. The "greater work," itself in modern form a closely printed folio, with its successive summaries and appendices in the "lesser" and the "third" works (which make a good octavo more) were produced and forwarded to the Pope within fifteen months.

The Opus Majus

No trace of this fiery haste remains in the book itself. The "Opus Majus" is alike wonderful in plan and detail. Bacon's main plan, in the words of Dr. Whewell, is "to urge the necessity of a reform in the mode of philosophizing, to set forth the reasons why knowledge had not made a greater progress, to draw back attention to sources of knowledge which had been unwisely neglected, to discover other sources which were yet wholly unknown, and to animate men to the undertaking by a prospect of the vast advantages which it offered." The developement of his scheme is on the largest scale; he gathers together the whole knowledge of his time on every branch of science which it possessed, and as he passes them in review he suggests improvements in nearly all. His labours, both here and in his after works, in the field of grammar and philology, his perseverance in insisting on the necessity of correct texts, of an accurate knowledge of languages, of an exact interpretation, are hardly less remarkable than his scientific investigations. But from grammar he passes to mathematics, from mathematics to experimental philosophy. Under the name of mathematics was included all the physical science of the time. "The neglect of it for nearly thirty or forty years," pleads Bacon passionately, "hath nearly destroyed the entire studies of Latin Christendom. For he who knows not mathematics cannot know any other sciences: and what is more, he cannot discover his own ignorance or find its proper remedies." Geography, chronology, arithmetic, music, are brought into something of scientific form, and the same rapid examination is devoted to the question of climate, to hydrography, geography, and astrology. The subject of optics, his own especial study, is treated with greater fulness ; he enters into the question of the anatomy of the eye, besides discussing the problems which lie more strictly within the province of optical science. In a word, the "Greater Work," to borrow the phrase of Dr. Whewell, is "at once the Encyclopædia and the Novum Organum of the thirteenth century." The whole of the after works of Roger Bacon—and treatise after treatise has of late been disentombed from our libraries—are but developements in detail of the magnificent conception he had laid before Clement. Such a work was its own great reward. From the world around Roger Bacon could look for and found small recognition. No word of acknowledgement seems to have reached its author from the Pope. If we may credit a more recent story, his writings only gained him a prison from his order. "Unheard, forgotten, buried," the old man died as he had lived, and it has been reserved for later ages to roll away the obscurity that had gathered round his memory, and to place first in the great roll of modern science the name of Roger Bacon.

Section V.—Henry the Third, 1216—1257.

[*Authorities.*—The two great authorities for this period are the historiographers of St. Albans, Roger of Wendover, whose work ends in 1235, and his editor and continuator Matthew Paris. The first is full but inaccurate, and with strong royal and ecclesiastical sympathies : of the character of Matthew, I have spoken at the close of the present section. The Chronicles of Dunstable, Waverley, and Burton (published in Mr. Luard's "Annales Monastici") supply many details. The "Royal Letters," edited by Dr. Shirley, with an admirable preface, are, like the Patent and Close Rolls, of the highest value. For opposition to Rome, see "Grosseteste's Letters," edited by Mr. Luard.]

The death of the Earl Marshal in 1219 left the direction of affairs in the hands of a new legate, Pandulf, of Stephen Langton who had just returned forgiven from Rome, and of the Justiciar, Hubert de Burgh. It was an age of transition, and the temper of the Justiciar was eminently transitional. Bred in the school of Henry the Second, he had little sympathy with national freedom ; his conception of good government, like that of his master, lay in a wise personal administration, in the preservation of order and law. But he combined with this a thoroughly English desire for national independence, a hatred of foreigners, and a reluctance to waste English blood and treasure in Continental struggles. Able as he proved himself, his task was one of no common difficulty. He was hampered by the constant interference of Rome. A Papal legate resided at the English court, and claimed a share in the administration of the realm as the representative of its over-lord, and as guardian of the young sovereign. A foreign party, too, had still a footing in the kingdom, for William Marshal had been unable to rid himself of men like Peter des Roches or Faukes de Breauté, who had fought on the royal side in the struggle against Lewis. Hubert had to deal too with the anarchy which that struggle left behind it. From the time of the Conquest the centre of England had been covered with the domains of great nobles, whose longings were for feudal independence, and whose spirit of revolt had been held in check, partly by the stern rule of the Kings, and partly by their creation of a baronage sprung from the Court and settled for the most part in the North. The oppression of John united both the older and these newer houses in the struggle for the Charter. But the character of each remained unchanged, and the close of the struggle saw the feudal party break out in their old lawlessness and defiance of the Crown. For a time the anarchy of Stephen's days seemed revived. But the Justiciar was resolute to crush it, and he was backed by the strenuous efforts of Stephen Langton. The Earl of Chester, the head of the feudal baronage, though he rose in armed rebellion, quailed before the march of Hubert and the Primate's threats of excommunication. A more formidable foe remained in the Frenchman, Faukes de Breauté, the sheriff of six counties, with six royal castles in his hands, and allied both with the rebel barons and Llewelyn of Wales. His castle of

1224

Bedford was besieged for two months before its surrender, and the stern justice of Hubert hanged the twenty-four knights and their retainers who formed the garrison before its walls. The blow was effectual ; the royal castles were surrendered by the barons, and the land was once more at peace. Freed from foreign soldiery, the country was freed also from the presence of the foreign legate. Langton wrested a promise from Rome that so long as he lived no future legate should be sent to England, and with Pandulf's resignation in 1221 the direct interference of the Papacy in the government of the realm came to an

*Langton
and the
Charter
1216*

end. But even these services of the Primate were small compared with his services to English freedom. Throughout his life the Charter was the first object of his care. The omission of the articles which restricted the royal power over taxation in the Charter which was published at Henry's accession was doubtless due to the Archbishop's absence and disgrace at Rome. The suppression of disorder seems to have revived the older spirit of resistance among the royal ministers ; when Langton demanded a fresh confirmation of the Charter in Parlia-

1223

ment at London, William Brewer, one of the King's councillors, protested that it had been extorted by force, and was without legal validity. " If you loved the King, William," the Primate burst out in anger, " you would not throw a stumbling-block in the way of the peace of the realm." The King was cowed by the Archbishop's wrath, and at once promised observance of the Charter. Two years after, its solemn promulgation was demanded by the Archbishop and the barons as the price of a subsidy, and Henry's assent established the principle, so fruitful of constitutional results, that redress of wrongs precedes a grant to the Crown.

The death of Stephen Langton in 1228 proved a heavy blow to English freedom. In 1227 Henry had declared himself of age; and though Hubert still remained Justiciar, every year saw him more powerless in his struggle with Rome and with the tendencies of the King. In the mediæval theory of the Papacy, the constitution of Christendom as a spiritual realm took the feudal form of the secular kingdoms within its pale, with the Pope for sovereign, bishops for his barons, the clergy for his under vassals. As the King demanded aids and subsidies in case of need from his liegemen, so it was believed might the head of the Church from the priesthood. At this moment the Papacy, exhausted by its long struggle with Frederick the Second, grew more and more extortionate in its demands. It regarded England as a vassal kingdom, and as bound to aid its overlord. The baronage, however, rejected the demand of aid from the laity, and the Pope fell back on the clergy. He demanded a tithe of all the moveables of the priesthood, and a threat of excommunication silenced their murmurs. Exaction followed exaction, the very rights of the lay patrons were set aside, and under the name of "reserves" presentations to English benefices were sold in the Papal market, while Italian clergy were quartered on the best livings of the Church. The general indignation found vent at last in a wide conspiracy; letters from "the whole body of those who prefer to die rather than be ruined by the Romans" were scattered over the kingdom by armed men; tithes gathered for the Pope and foreign clergy were seized and given to the poor, the Papal commissioners beaten, and their bulls trodden under foot. The remonstrances of Rome only revealed the national character of the movement; but as inquiry proceeded the hand of the Justiciar himself was seen to have been at work. Sheriffs had stood idly by while the violence was done; royal letters had been shown by the rioters as approving their acts; and the Pope openly laid the charge of the outbreak on the secret connivance of Hubert de Burgh. The charge came at a time when Henry was in full collision with his minister, to whom he attributed the failure of his attempts to regain the foreign dominions of his house. An invitation from the barons of Normandy had been rejected through Hubert's remonstrances, and when a great armament gathered at Portsmouth for a campaign in Poitou, it was dispersed for want of transport and supplies. The young King drew his sword and rushed madly on the Justiciar, whom he charged with treason and corruption by the gold of France; but the quarrel was appeased, and the expedition deferred for the year. The failure of the

SEC. V.

HENRY THE
THIRD

1216
TO
1257

Hubert's
fall

*Langton's
death*
1228

1229

143C

campaign in the following year, when Henry took the field in Britanny and Poitou, was again laid at the door of Hubert, whose opposition was said to have prevented an engagement. The Papal accusation filled up the measure of Henry's wrath. Hubert was dragged from a chapel at Brentwood where he had taken refuge, and a smith was ordered to shackle him. "I will die any death," replied the smith, "before I put iron on the man who freed England from the stranger and saved Dover from France." On the remonstrances of the Bishop of London Hubert was replaced in sanctuary, but hunger compelled him to surrender; he was thrown a prisoner into the Tower, and though soon released he remained powerless in the realm. His fall left England without a check to the rule of Henry himself.

There was a certain refinement in Henry's temper which won him affection even in the worst days of his rule. The Abbey-church of Westminster, with which he replaced the ruder minster of the Confessor, remains a monument of his artistic taste. He was a patron and friend of artists and men of letters, and himself skilled in the "gay science" of the troubadour. From the cruelty, the lust, the impiety of his father he was absolutely free. But of the political capacity which had been the characteristic of his house he had little or none. Profuse, changeable, impulsive alike in good and ill, unbridled in temper and tongue, reckless in insult and wit, Henry's delight was in the display of an empty and prodigal magnificence, his one notion of government a dream of arbitrary power. But frivolous as the King's mood was, he clung with a weak man's obstinacy to a distinct line of policy. He cherished the hope of recovering his heritage across the sea. He believed in the absolute power of the Crown; and looked on the pledges of the Great Charter as promises which force had wrested from the King and which force could wrest back again. The claim which the French kings were advancing to a divine and absolute power gave a sanction in Henry's mind to the claim of absolute authority which was still maintained by his favourite advisers in the royal council. The death of Langton, the fall of Hubert de Burgh, left him free to surround himself with dependent ministers, mere agents of the royal will. Hosts of hungry Poitevins and Bretons were at once summoned over to occupy the royal castles and fill the judicial and administrative posts about the Court. His marriage with

Eleanor of Provence was followed by the arrival in England of the Queen's uncles. The "Savoy," as his house in the Strand was named, still recalls Peter of Savoy, who arrived five years later to take for a while the chief place at Henry's council-board; another brother, Boniface, was on Archbishop Edmund's death consecrated to the highest post in the realm save the Crown itself, the Archbishoprick of Canterbury. The young Primate, like his brother, brought with him foreign fashions strange enough to English folk. His armed retainers pillaged the markets. His own archiepiscopal fist felled to the ground the prior of St. Bartholomew-by-Smithfield, who opposed his visitation. London was roused by the outrage ; on the King's refusal to do justice a noisy crowd of citizens surrounded the Primate's house at Lambeth with cries of vengeance, and the "handsome archbishop," as his followers styled him, was glad to escape over sea. This brood of Provençals was followed in 1243 by the arrival of the Poitevin relatives of John's queen, Isabella of Angoulême. Aymer was made Bishop of Winchester ; William of Valence received the earldom of Pembroke. Even the King's jester was a Poitevin. Hundreds of their dependants followed these great lords to find a fortune in the English realm. The Poitevin lords brought in their train a bevy of ladies in search of husbands, and three English earls who were in royal wardship were wedded by the King to foreigners. The whole machinery of administration passed into the hands of men ignorant and contemptuous of the principles of English government or English law. Their rule was a mere anarchy ; the very retainers of the royal household turned robbers, and pillaged foreign merchants in the precincts of the Court ; corruption invaded the judicature ; Henry de Bath, a justiciar, was proved to have openly taken bribes and to have adjudged to himself disputed estates.

That misgovernment of this kind should have gone on unchecked, in defiance of the provisions of the Charter, was owing to the disunion and sluggishness of the English baronage. On the first arrival of the foreigners, Richard, the Earl Marshal, a son of the great Regent, stood forth as their leader to demand the expulsion of the strangers from the royal Council, and though deserted by the bulk of the nobles, he defeated the foreign forces sent against him, and forced the King to treat for peace. But at this moment the Earl was drawn by an intrigue of Peter des Roches to Ireland ; he fell in a petty skirmish, and the barons were left without a head. Edmund Rich, whom we have seen as an Oxford teacher and who had risen to the Archbishoprick of Canterbury, forced the King to dismiss Peter from court ; but there was no real change of system, and the remonstrances of the Archbishop and of Robert Grosseteste, Bishop of Lincoln, remained fruitless. In the long interval of misrule which followed, the financial straits of the King forced him to heap exaction on exaction. The Forest Laws were used as a means of extortion, sees and abbeys were kept vacant, loans were wrested from lords and prelates, the Court itself lived at free quarters wherever it moved. Supplies of this kind however were utterly insufficient to defray the cost of the King's prodigality. A sixth of the royal revenue was wasted in pensions to foreign favourites. The debts of the Crown mounted to four times its annual income. Henry was forced to appeal to the Great Council of the realm, and aid was granted on condition that the King confirmed the Charter. The

L

SEC. V.

HENRY THE
THIRD

1216
TO
1257

1242

Charter was confirmed and steadily disregarded ; and the resentment of the barons expressed itself in a determined protest and a refusal of further subsidies. In spite of their refusal however Henry gathered money enough for a costly expedition for the recovery of Poitou. The attempt ended in failure and shame. At Taillebourg the forces under Henry fled in disgraceful rout before the French as far as Saintes, and only the sudden illness of Lewis the Ninth and a disease which scattered his army saved Bordeaux from the conquerors. The treasury was drained, and Henry was driven to make a fresh appeal to the baronage. The growing resolution of the nobles to enforce good government was seen in their demand that the confirmation of the Charter was to be followed by the election of Justiciar, Chancellor, and Treasurer in the Great Council, and that a perpetual Council was to attend the King and devise further reforms. The plan broke against Henry's resistance and a Papal prohibition. The scourge of Papal taxation fell heavily on the clergy. After vain appeals to Rome and to the King, Archbishop Edmund retired to an exile of despair at Pontigny, and tax-gatherer after tax-gatherer with powers of excommunication, suspension from orders, and presentation to benefices, descended on the unhappy priesthood. The wholesale pillage kindled a wide spirit of resistance. Oxford gave the signal by hunting a Papal legate out of the city, amid cries of " usurer " and " simoniac " from the mob of students. Fulk Fitz-Warenne in the name of the barons bade a Papal collector begone out of England. " If you tarry three days longer," he added, "you and your company shall be cut to pieces." For a time Henry himself was swept away by the tide of national

indignation. Letters from the King, the nobles and the prelates protested against the Papal exactions, and orders were given that no money should be exported from the realm. But the threat of interdict soon drove Henry back on a policy of spoliation, in which he went hand in hand with Rome.

The story of this period of misrule has been preserved for us by an annalist whose pages glow with the new outburst of patriotic feeling which this common oppression of the people and the clergy had produced. Matthew Paris is the greatest, as he is in reality the last, of our monastic historians. The school of S. Alban's survived indeed till a far later time, but the writers dwindle into mere annalists whose view is bounded by the abbey precincts, and whose work is as colourless as it is jejune. In Matthew the breadth and precision of the narrative, the copiousness of his information on topics whether national or European, the general fairness and justice of his comments, are only surpassed by the patriotic fire and enthusiasm of the whole. He had succeeded Roger of Wendover as chronicler at S. Alban's ; and the Greater Chronicle with an abridgement of it which has long passed under the name of Matthew of

III.] THE GREAT CHARTER. 147

Sec. V.

Henry the
Third

1216
TO
1257

Westminster, a "History of the English," and the "Lives of the Earlier Abbots," were only a few among the voluminous works which attest his prodigious industry. He was an artist as well as an historian, and many of the manuscripts which are preserved are illustrated by his own hand. A large circle of correspondents—bishops like Grosseteste, ministers like Hubert de Burgh, officials like Alexander de Swereford—furnished him with minute accounts of political and ecclesiastical proceedings. Pilgrims from the East and Papal agents brought news of foreign events to his scriptorium at S. Alban's. He had access to and quotes largely from state documents, charters, and exchequer rolls. The frequency of the royal visits to the abbey brought him a store of political intelligence, and Henry himself contributed to the great chronicle which has preserved with so terrible a faithfulness the memory of his weakness and misgovernment. On one solemn feast-day the King recognized Matthew, and bidding him sit on the middle step between the floor and the throne, begged him to write the story of the day's proceedings. While on a visit to S. Alban's he invited him to his table and chamber, and enumerated by name two hundred and fifty of the English baronies for his information. But all this royal patronage has left little mark on his work. "The case," as he says, "of historical writers is hard, for if they tell the truth they provoke men, and if they write what is false they offend God." With all the fulness of the school of court historians, such as Benedict or Hoveden, Matthew Paris combines an independence and patriotism which is strange to their pages. He denounces with the same unsparing energy the oppression of the Papacy and the King. His point of view is neither that of a courtier nor of a churchman, but of an Englishman, and the new national tone of his chronicle is but an echo of the national sentiment which at last bound nobles and yeomen and churchmen together into a people resolute to wrest freedom from the Crown.

Section VI.—The Friars.

[*Authorities.*—Eccleston's Tract on their arrival in England and Adam Marsh's Letters, with Mr. Brewer's admirable Preface, in the "Monumenta Franciscana" of the Rolls series. Grosseteste's Letters in the same series, edited by Mr. Luard. For a general account of the whole movement, see Milman's "Latin Christianity," vol. iv. caps. 9 and 10.]

From the tedious record of misgovernment and political weakness which stretches over the forty years we have passed through, we turn with relief to the story of the Friars.

Never, as we have seen, had the priesthood wielded such boundless

England
and the
Church

power over Christendom as in the days of Innocent the Third and his immediate successors. But its religious hold on the people was loosening day by day. The old reverence for the Papacy was fading away before the universal resentment at its political ambition, its lavish use of interdict and excommunication for purely secular ends, its degradation of the most sacred sentences into means of financial extortion. In Italy the struggle that was opening between Rome and Frederick the Second disclosed a spirit of scepticism which among the Epicurean poets of Florence denied the immortality of the soul, and attacked the very foundations of the faith itself. In Southern Gaul, Languedoc and Provence had embraced the heresy of the Albigenses, and thrown off all allegiance to the Papacy. Even in England, though there were no signs as yet of religious revolt, and though the political action of Rome had been in the main on the side of freedom, there was a spirit of resistance to its interference with national concerns which broke out in the struggle against John. " The Pope has no part in secular matters," had been the reply of London to the interdict of Innocent. And within the English Church itself there was much to call for reform. Its attitude in the strife for the Charter as well as the after work of the Primate had made it more popular than ever ; but its spiritual energy was less than its political. The disuse of preaching, the decline of the monastic orders into rich landowners, the non-residence and ignorance of the parish priests, robbed the clergy of spiritual influence. The abuses of the time foiled even the energy of such men as Bishop Grosseteste of Lincoln. His constitutions forbid the clergy to haunt taverns, to gamble, to share in drinking bouts, to mix in the riot and debauchery of the life of the baronage. But such prohibitions only witness to the prevalence of the evils they denounce. Bishops and deans were withdrawn from their ecclesiastical duties to act as ministers, judges, or ambassadors. Benefices were heaped in hundreds at a time on royal favourites like John Mansel. Abbeys absorbed the tithes of parishes, and then served them by half-starved vicars, while exemptions purchased from Rome shielded the scandalous lives of canons and monks from all episcopal discipline. And behind all this was a group of secular statesmen and scholars, waging indeed no open warfare with the Church, but noting with bitter sarcasm its abuses and its faults.

To bring the world back again within the pale of the Church was the aim of two religious orders which sprang suddenly to life at the opening of the thirteenth century. The zeal of the Spaniard Dominic was roused at the sight of the lordly prelates who sought by fire and sword to win the Albigensian heretics to the faith. " Zeal," he cried, " must be met by zeal, lowliness by lowliness, false sanctity by real sanctity, preaching lies by preaching truth." His fiery ardour and rigid orthodoxy were seconded by the mystical piety, the imaginative enthusiasm of Francis of Assisi. The life of Francis falls like a stream of tender light across the darkness of the time. In the frescoes of Giotto or the verse of Dante we see him take Poverty for his bride. He strips himself of all, he flings his very clothes at his father's feet, that he may be one with Nature and God. His passionate verse claims the Moon for his sister and the Sun for his brother, he calls on his brother the Wind, and his sister the Water. His last faint cry was a "Welcome, Sister Death!" Strangely as the two men differed from each other, their aim was the same—to convert the heathen, to extirpate heresy, to reconcile knowledge with orthodoxy, to carry the Gospel to the poor. The work was to be done by the entire reversal of the older monasticism, by seeking personal salvation in effort for the salvation of their fellow-men, by exchanging the solitary of the cloister for the preacher, the monk for the friar. To force the new "brethren" into entire dependence on those among whom they laboured their vow of Poverty was turned into a stern reality ; the "Begging Friars" were to subsist on the alms of the poor, they might possess neither money nor lands, the very houses in which they lived were to be held in trust for them by others. The tide of popular enthusiasm which welcomed their appearance swept before it the reluctance of Rome, the jealousy of the older orders, the opposition of the parochial priesthood. Thousands of brethren gathered in a few years round Francis and Dominic; and the begging preachers, clad in their coarse frock of serge, with a girdle of rope round their waist, wandered barefooted as missionaries over Asia, battled with heresy in Italy and Gaul, lectured in the Universities, and preached and toiled among the poor.

To the towns especially the coming of the Friars was a religious revolution. They had been left for the most part to the worst and most ignorant of the clergy, the mass-priest, whose sole subsistence lay in his fees. Burgher and artisan were left to spell out what religious instruction they might from the gorgeous ceremonies of the Church's ritual, or the scriptural pictures and sculptures which were graven on the walls of its minsters. We can hardly wonder at the burst of enthusiasm which welcomed the itinerant preacher, whose fervid appeal, coarse wit, and familiar story brought religion into the fair and the market-place. The Black Friars of Dominic, the Grey Friars of Francis, were received with the same delight. As the older orders had chosen the country, the Friars chose the town. They had hardly landed at Dover before they made straight for London and Oxford. In their ignorance of the road the two first Grey Brothers lost their way in the woods between Oxford and Baldon, and fearful of night and of the floods, turned aside to a grange of the monks of Abingdon. Their ragged clothes and foreign gestures, as they prayed for hospitality, led the porter to take them for jongleurs, the jesters and jugglers of the day, and the news of this break in the monotony of their lives brought prior, sacrist, and cellarer to the door to welcome them and witness their tricks. The disappointment was too much for the temper of the monks, and the brothers were kicked roughly from the gate to find their night's lodging under a tree. But the welcome of the townsmen made up everywhere for the ill-will and opposition of both clergy and monks. The work of the Friars was physical as well as moral. The rapid progress of population within the boroughs had outstripped the sanitary regulations of the Middle Ages, and fever or plague or the more terrible scourge of leprosy festered in the wretched hovels of the suburbs. It was to haunts such as these that Francis had pointed his disciples, and the Grey Brethren at once fixed themselves in the meanest and poorest quarters of each town. Their first work lay in the noisome lazar-houses; it was amongst the lepers that they commonly chose the site of their homes. At London they settled in the shambles of Newgate; at Oxford they made their way to the swampy ground between its walls and the streams of Thames. Huts of mud and timber, as mean as the huts around them, rose within the rough fence and ditch that bounded the Friary. The order of Francis made a hard fight against the taste for sumptuous buildings and for greater personal comfort which characterized the time. "I did not enter into religion to build walls," protested an English provincial when the brethren pressed for a larger house; and Albert of Pisa ordered a stone cloister, which the burgesses of Southampton had built for them, to be razed to the ground. "You need no little mountains to lift your heads to heaven," was his scornful reply to a claim for pillows. None but the sick went shod. An Oxford Friar found a pair of shoes one morning, and wore them at matins. At night he dreamt that robbers leapt on him in a dangerous pass between Gloucester and Oxford with shouts of "Kill, kill!" "I am a friar," shrieked the terror-stricken brother. "You lie," was the instant answer, "for you go shod." The Friar lifted up his foot in disproof, but the shoe was there. In an agony of repentance he woke and flung the pair out of window.

The
Friars
and the
Univer-
sities
It was with less success that the order struggled against the passion for knowledge. Their vow of poverty, rigidly interpreted as it was by their founders, would have denied them the possession of books or materials for study. "I am your breviary, I am your breviary," Francis cried passionately to a novice who asked for a psalter. When the news of a great doctor's reception was brought to him at Paris, his countenance fell. "I am afraid, my son," he replied, "that such doctors will be the destruction of my vineyard. They are the true doctors who with the meekness of wisdom show forth good works for the edification of their neighbours." At a later time Roger Bacon, as we have seen, was suffered to possess neither ink, parchment, nor books; and only the Pope's injunctions could dispense with the

stringent observance of the rule. But one kind of knowledge indeed their work almost forced on them. The popularity of their preaching soon led them to the deeper study of theology. Within a short time after their establishment in England we find as many as thirty readers or lecturers appointed at Hereford, Leicester, Bristol, and other places, and a regular succession of teachers provided at each University. The Oxford Dominicans lectured on theology in the nave of their new church, while philosophy was taught in the cloister. The first provincial of the Grey Friars built a school in their Oxford house, and persuaded Grosseteste to lecture there. His influence after his promotion to the see of Lincoln was steadily exerted to secure study among the Friars, and their establishment in the University. He was ably seconded by his scholar, Adam Marsh, or de Marisco, under whom the Franciscan school at Oxford attained a reputation throughout Christendom. Lyons, Paris, and Köln borrowed from it their professors : it was owing, indeed, to its influence that Oxford now rose to a position hardly inferior to that of Paris itself as a centre of scholasticism. The three most profound and original of the schoolmen—Roger Bacon, Duns Scotus, and Ockham—were among its scholars ; and they were followed by a crowd of teachers hardly less illustrious in their day.

But the result of this powerful impulse was soon seen to be fatal to the wider intellectual activity which had till now characterized the Universities. Theology in its scholastic form, which now found its only efficient rivals in practical studies such as medicine and law, resumed its supremacy in the schools ; while Aristotle, who had been so long held at bay as the most dangerous foe of mediæval faith, was now turned by the adoption of his logical method in the discussion and definition of theological dogma into its unexpected ally. It was this very method that led to "that unprofitable subtlety and curiosity" which Lord Bacon notes as the vice of the scholastic philosophy. But "certain it is "—to continue the same great thinker's comment on the Friars—"that if these schoolmen to their great thirst of truth and unwearied travel of wit had joined variety of reading and contemplation, they had proved excellent lights to the great advancement of all learning and knowledge." What, amidst all their errors, they undoubtedly did was to insist on the necessity of rigid demonstration and a more exact use of words, to introduce a clear and methodical treatment of all subjects into discussion, and above all to substitute an appeal to reason for unquestioning obedience to authority. It was by this critical tendency, by the new clearness and precision which scholasticism gave to enquiry, that in spite of the trivial questions with which it often concerned itself, it trained the human mind through the next two centuries to a temper which fitted it to profit by the great disclosure of knowledge that brought about the

SEC. VII.

THE
BARONS'
WAR

1258
TO
1265

Renascence. And it is to the same spirit of fearless enquiry as well as to the strong popular sympathies which their very constitution necessitated that we must attribute the influence which the Friars undoubtedly exerted in the coming struggle between the people and the Crown. Their position is clearly and strongly marked throughout the whole contest. The University of Oxford, which had now fallen under the direction of their teaching, stood first in its resistance to Papal exactions and its claim of English liberty. The classes in the towns on whom the influence of the Friars told most directly were the steady supporters of freedom throughout the Barons' war. Adam Marsh was the closest friend and confidant both of Grosseteste and Earl Simon of Montfort.

Section VII.—The Barons' War, 1258—1265.

[*Authorities.*—At the very outset of this important period we lose the price-less aid of Matthew Paris. He is the last of the great chroniclers; the Chronicles of his successor at S. Alban's, Rishanger (published by the Master of the Rolls), are scant and lifeless jottings, somewhat enlarged for this period by his fragment on the Barons' War (published by Camden Society). Something may be gleaned from the annals of Burton, Melrose, Dunstable, Waverley, Osney, and Lanercost, the Royal Letters, the (royalist) Chronicle of Wykes, and (for London) the "Liber de Antiquis Legibus." Mr. Blaauw has given a useful summary of the period in his "Barons' War."]

When a thunderstorm once forced the King, as he was rowing on the Thames, to take refuge at the palace of the Bishop of Durham, Earl Simon of Montfort, who was a guest of the prelate, met the royal barge with assurances that the storm was drifting away, and that there was nothing to fear. Henry's petulant wit broke out in his reply. "If I fear the thunder," said the King, "I fear you, Sir Earl, more than all the thunder in the world."

The man whom Henry dreaded as the champion of English freedom was himself a foreigner, the son of a Simon de Montfort whose name had become memorable for his ruthless crusade against the Albigensian heretics in Southern Gaul. Though fourth son of this crusader, Simon became possessor of the English earldom of Leicester, which he inherited through his mother, and a secret match with Eleanor, the King's sister and widow of the second William Marshal, linked him to the royal house. The baronage, indignant at this sudden alliance with a stranger, rose in a revolt which failed only through the deser-tion of their head, Earl Richard of Cornwall; while the censures of the Church on Eleanor's breach of a vow of chastity, which she had

made at her first husband's death, were hardly averted by a journey

to Rome. Simon returned to find the changeable King quickly
alienated from him and to be driven by a burst of royal passion from
the realm. He was, however, soon restored to favour, and before long
took his stand in the front rank of the patriot leaders. In 1248 he
was appointed Governor of Gascony, where the stern justice of his
rule, and the heavy taxation which his enforcement of order made
necessary, earned the hatred of the disorderly nobles. The complaints
of the Gascons brought about an open breach with the King. To
Earl Simon's offer of the surrender of his post if the money he had
spent in the royal service were, as Henry had promised, repaid him,
the King hotly retorted that he was bound by no promise to a false
traitor. Simon at once gave Henry the lie; "and but that thou
bearest the name of King it had been a bad hour for thee when thou
utteredst such a word!" A formal reconciliation was brought about,
and the Earl once more returned to Gascony, but before winter had
come he was forced to withdraw to France. The greatness of his
reputation was shown in an offer which its nobles made him of the
regency of their realm during the absence of King Lewis on the crusade.
But the offer was refused; and Henry, who had himself undertaken the pacification of Gascony, was glad before the close of 1253
to recall its old ruler to do the work he had failed to do. Simon's
character had now thoroughly developed. He had inherited the strict
and severe piety of his father; he was assiduous in his attendance on
religious services whether by night or day; he was the friend of
Grosseteste and the patron of the Friars. In his correspondence with
Adam Marsh we see him finding patience under his Gascon troubles
in the perusal of the Book of Job. His life was pure and singularly
temperate; he was noted for his scant indulgence in meat, drink, or
sleep. Socially he was cheerful and pleasant in talk; but his natural
temper was quick and ardent, his sense of honour keen, his speech
rapid and trenchant. His impatience of contradiction, his fiery temper,
were in fact the great stumbling-blocks in his after career. But the
one characteristic which overmastered all was what men at that time
called his "constancy," the firm immoveable resolve which trampled
even death under foot in its loyalty to the right. The motto which
Edward the First chose as his device, "Keep troth," was far truer as
the device of Earl Simon. We see in his correspondence with what
a clear discernment of its difficulties both at home and abroad he
"thought it unbecoming to decline the danger of so great an exploit"
as the reduction of Gascony to peace and order; but once undertaken,
he persevered in spite of the opposition he met with, the failure of all
support or funds from England, and the King's desertion of his cause,
till the work was done. There is the same steadiness of will and
purpose in his patriotism. The letters of Grosseteste show how early
he had learned to sympathize with the bishop in his resistance to Rome,

SEC. VII.

THE
BARONS'
WAR

1258
TO
1265

1248

SEC. VII.

THE
BARONS'
WAR
1258
TO
1265

and at the crisis of the contest he offers him his own support and that of his associates. He sends to Adam Marsh a tract of Grosseteste's on "the rule of a kingdom and of a tyranny," sealed with his own seal. He listens patiently to the advice of his friends on the subject of his household or his temper. "Better is a patient man," writes honest Friar Adam, "than a strong man, and he who can rule his own temper than he who storms a city." "What use is it to provide for the peace of your fellow-citizens and not guard the peace of your own household?" It was to secure "the peace of his fellow-citizens" that the Earl silently trained himself as the tide of misgovernment mounted higher and higher, and the fruit of his discipline was seen when the crisis came. While other men wavered and faltered and fell away, the enthusiastic love of the people gathered itself round the stern, grave soldier who "stood like a pillar," unshaken by promise or threat or fear of death, by the oath he had sworn.

In England affairs were going from bad to worse. The Pope still weighed heavily on the Church. Two solemn confirmations of the Charter failed to bring about any compliance with its provisions. In 1248, in 1249, and again in 1255, the Great Council fruitlessly renewed its demand for a regular ministry, and the growing resolve of the nobles to enforce good government was seen in their offer of a grant on condition that the chief officers of the Crown were appointed by the Council. Henry indignantly refused the offer, and sold his plate to the citizens of London to find payment for his household. The barons were mutinous and defiant. "I will send reapers and reap your fields for you," Henry had threatened Earl Bigod of Norfolk when he refused him aid. "And I will send you back the heads of your reapers," retorted the Earl. Hampered by the profusion of the court and by the refusal of supplies, the Crown was penniless, yet new expenses were

incurred by Henry's acceptance of a Papal offer of the kingdom of Sicily in favour of his second son Edmund. Shame had fallen on the English arms, and the King's eldest son, Edward, had been disastrously defeated on the Marches by Llewelyn of Wales. The tide of discontent, which was heightened by a grievous famine, burst its bounds in the irritation excited by the new demands from both Henry and Rome with which the year 1258 opened, and the barons repaired in arms to a Great Council summoned at London. The past half-century had shown both the strength and weakness of the Charter : its strength as a rallying-point for the baronage, and a definite assertion of rights which the King could be made to acknowledge ; its weakness in providing no means for the enforcement of its own stipulations. Henry had sworn again and again to observe the Charter, and his oath was no sooner taken than it was unscrupulously broken. The barons had secured the freedom of the realm ; the secret of their long patience during the reign of Henry lay in the difficulty of securing its right administration. It was this difficulty which Earl Simon was prepared to solve. With the Earl of Gloucester he now appeared at the head of the baronage in arms, and demanded the appointment of a committee of twenty-four to draw up terms for the reform of the state. Although half the committee consisted of royal ministers and favourites, it was impossible to resist the tide of popular feeling. By the "Provisions of Oxford" it was agreed that the Great Council should assemble thrice in the year, whether summoned by the King or no ; and on each occasion "the Commonalty shall elect twelve honest men who shall come to the Parliaments, and at other times when occasion shall be when the King and his Council shall send for them, to treat of the wants of the King and of his kingdom. And the Commonalty shall hold as established that which these Twelve shall do." Three permanent committees were named—one to reform the Church, one to negotiate financial aids, and a Permanent Council of Fifteen to advise the King in the ordinary work of government. The Justiciar, Chancellor, and the guardians of the King's castles swore to act only with the advice and assent of the Permanent Council, and the first two great officers, with the Treasurer, were to give account of their proceedings to it at the end of the year. Annual sheriffs were to be appointed from among the chief tenants of the county, and no undue fees were to be exacted for the administration of justice in their court.

A royal proclamation in the English tongue, the first in that tongue since the Conquest which has reached us, ordered the observance of these Provisions. Resistance came only from the foreign favourites, and an armed demonstration drove them in flight over sea. The whole royal power was now in fact in the hands of the committees appointed by the Great Council ; and the policy of the administration was seen in the prohibitions against any further payments, secular or ecclesiastical, to Rome, in the formal withdrawal from the Sicilian enterprise, in the negotiations conducted by Earl Simon with France, which finally ended in the absolute renunciation of Henry's title to his lost provinces, and in the peace which put an end to the incursions of the Welsh. Within, however, the measures of the barons were feeble and selfish. The Provisions of Westminster, published by them under popular pressure in the following year, for the protection of tenants and furtherance of justice, brought little fruit ; and a tendency to mere feudal privilege showed itself in an exemption of all nobles and prelates from attendance at the sheriff's courts. It was in vain that Earl Simon returned from his negotiations in France to press for more earnest measures of reform, or that the King's son Edward remained faithful to his oath to observe the Provisions, and openly supported him. Gloucester and Hugh Bigod, faithless to the cause of reform, drew with the feudal party to the side of the King ; and Henry, procuring from the Pope a bull which annulled the Provisions and freed him from his oath

Sec. VII.

The
Barons'
War

1258
to
1265

*Provisions
of Oxford*
July 1258

SEC. VII.

THE
BARONS'
WAR

1258
TO
1265

**The
struggle
with the
Crown**

1263

to observe them, regained possession of the Tower and the other castles, appointed a new Justiciar, and restored the old authority of the Crown.

Deserted as he was, the Earl of Leicester was forced to withdraw for eighteen months to France, while Henry ruled in open defiance of the Provisions. The confusion of the realm renewed the disgust at his government; and the death of Gloucester removed the one barrier to action. In 1263 Simon landed again as the unquestioned head of the baronial party. The march of Edward with a royal army against Llewelyn of Wales was viewed by the barons as a prelude to hostilities against themselves; and Earl Simon at once swept the Welsh border, marched on Dover, and finally appeared before London. His power was strengthened by the attitude of the towns. The new democratic spirit which we have witnessed in the Friars was now stirring the purely industrial classes to assert a share in the municipal administration, which had hitherto been confined to the wealthier members of the merchant gilds, and at London and elsewhere a revolution, which will be described at greater length hereafter, had thrown the government of the city into the hands of the lower citizens. The "Communes," as the new city governments were called, showed an enthusiastic devotion to Earl Simon and his cause. The Queen was stopped in her attempt to escape from the Tower by an angry mob, who drove her back with stones and foul words. When Henry attempted to surprise Leicester in his quarters in Southwark, the Londoners burst the gates which had been locked by the richer burghers against him, and rescued him by a welcome into the city. The clergy and Universities went in sympathy with the towns, and in spite of the taunts of the royalists, who accused him of seeking allies against the nobility in the common people, the popular enthusiasm gave a strength to Earl Simon which enabled him to withstand the severest blow which had yet been dealt to his cause. The nobles drew to the King. The dread of civil war gave strength to the cry for compromise, and it was agreed that the strife should be left to the arbitration of Lewis the Ninth of France. In the Mise of Amiens Lewis gave his verdict wholly in favour of the King. The Provisions of Oxford were annulled. Only the charters granted before the Provisions were to be observed. The appointment and removal of all officers of state was to be wholly with the King, and he was suffered to call aliens to his councils. The blow was a hard one, and the decision of Lewis was at once confirmed by the Pope. The barons felt themselves bound by the award; only the exclusion of aliens—a point which they had not purposed to submit to arbitration—they refused to concede. Simon at once resolved on resistance. Luckily, the French award had reserved the rights of Englishmen to the liberties they had enjoyed before the Provisions of Oxford, and it was easy for Simon to prove that the arbitrary power it gave to the Crown was as contrary to the Charter as to the Provisions themselves.   London was the first to reject the decision ; its citizens mustered at the call of the town-bell at Saint Paul's, seized the royal officials, and plundered the royal parks.   But an army had already mustered in great force at the King's summons, and Leicester found himself deserted by baron after baron.   Every day brought news of ill.   A detachment from Scotland joined Henry's forces.   The younger De Montfort was taken prisoner.   Northampton was captured, the King raised the siege of Rochester, and a rapid march of Earl Simon's only saved London itself from a surprise by Edward.   Betrayed as he was, the Earl remained firm to the cause.   He would fight to the end, he said, even were he and his sons left to fight alone.   With an army reinforced by 15,000 Londoners, he marched to the relief of the Cinque Ports, which were now threatened by the King.   Even on the march he was forsaken by many of the nobles who followed him. Halting at Fletching in Sussex, a few miles from Lewes, where the royal army was encamped, Earl Simon with the young Earl of Gloucester offered the King compensation for all damage if he would observe the Provisions.   Henry's answer was one of defiance, and though numbers were against him the Earl resolved on battle.   His skill as a soldier reversed the advantages of the ground ; marching at dawn he seized the heights eastward of the town, and moved down these slopes to an attack.   His men, with white crosses on back and breast, knelt in prayer before the battle opened.   Edward was the first to open the fight ; his furious charge broke the Londoners on Leicester's left, and in the bitterness of his hatred he pursued them for four miles, slaughtering three thousand men.   He returned to find the battle lost.   Crowded in the narrow space with a river in their rear, the royalist centre and left were crushed by Earl Simon ; the Earl of Cornwall, now King of the Romans, who, as the mocking song of the victors ran, " makede him a castel of a mulne post " (" he weened that the mill-sails were mangonels" goes on the sarcastic verse), was made prisoner, and Henry himself captured.   Edward cut his way into the Priory only to join in his father's surrender.

The victory of Lewes placed Earl Simon at the head of the state. " Now England breathes in the hope of liberty," sang a poet of the time ; " the English were despised like dogs, but now they have lifted up their head and their foes are vanquished."   The song announces with almost legal precision the theory of the patriots.   " He who would be in truth a king, he is a ' free king ' indeed if he rightly rule himself and his realm.   All things are lawful to him for the government of his kingdom, but nothing for its destruction.   It is one thing to rule according to a king's duty, another to destroy a kingdom by resisting the law."   " Let the community of the realm advise, and let it be

SEC. VII.

THE
BARONS'
WAR

1258
TO
1265

*Battle of
Lewes
May* 14*t*
1264

**Simon's
rule**

SEC. VII.

THE
BARONS'
WAR

1258
TO
1265

known what the generality, to whom their own laws are best known, think on the matter. They who are ruled by the laws know those laws best, they who make daily trial of them are best acquainted with them ; and since it is their own affairs which are at stake, they will take more care, and will act with an eye to their own peace." "It concerns the community to see what sort of men ought justly to be chosen for the weal of the realm." The constitutional restrictions on the royal authority, the right of the whole nation to deliberate and decide on its own affairs, and to have a voice in the selection of the administrators of government, had never been so clearly stated before. But the moderation of the terms agreed upon in the Mise of Lewes, a convention between the King and his captors, shows Simon's sense of the difficulties of his position. The question of the Provisions was again to be submitted to arbitration ; and a parliament in June, to which four knights were summoned from every county, placed the administration till this arbitration was complete in the hands of a new council of nine, to be nominated by the Earls of Leicester and Gloucester and the patriotic Bishop of Chichester. Responsibility to the community was provided for by the declaration of a right in the body of barons and prelates to remove either of the Three Electors, who in turn could displace or appoint the members of the Council. Such a constitution was of a different order from the cumbrous and oligarchical Committees of 1258. But the plans for arbitration broke down, Lewis refused to review his decision, and the Pope formally condemned the barons' cause. The Earl's difficulties thickened every day. The Queen gathered an army in France for an invasion, and the barons on the Welsh border were still in arms. It was impossible to make binding terms with an imprisoned King, yet to release Henry without terms was to renew the war. A new parliament was summoned in January, 1265, to Westminster, but the weakness of the patriotic party among the baronage was shown in the fact that only twenty-three earls and barons could be found to sit beside the hundred and twenty ecclesiastics. But it was just this sense of his weakness that drove Earl Simon to a constitutional change of mighty issue in our history. As before, he summoned two knights from every county. But he created a new force in English politics when he summoned to sit beside them two citizens from every borough. The attendance of delegates from the towns had long been usual in the county courts when any matter respecting their interests was in question ; but it was the writ issued by Earl Simon that first summoned the merchant and the trader to sit beside the knight of the shire, the baron, and the bishop in the parliament of the realm.

It is only this great event however which enables us to understand the large and prescient nature of Earl Simon's designs. Hardly a few months had passed since the victory of Lewes, and already, when the burghers took their seats at Westminster, his government was tottering to its fall. Dangers from without the Earl had met with complete success; a general muster of the national forces on Barham Down put an end to the projects of invasion entertained by the mercenaries whom the Queen had collected in Flanders; the threats of France died away into negotiations; the Papal Legate was forbidden to cross the Channel, and his bulls of excommunication were flung into the sea. But the difficulties at home grew more formidable every day. The restraint upon Henry and Edward jarred against the national feeling of loyalty, and estranged the mass of Englishmen who always side with the weak. Small as the patriotic party among the barons had always been, it grew smaller as dissensions broke out over the spoils of victory. The Earl's justice and resolve to secure the public peace told heavily against him. John Giffard left him because he refused to allow him to exact ransom from a prisoner contrary to the agreement made after Lewes. The young Earl Gilbert of Gloucester, though enriched with the estates of the foreigners, resented Leicester's prohibition of a tournament, his naming the wardens of the royal castles by his own authority, and his holding Edward's fortresses on the Welsh marches by his own garrisons. Gloucester's later conduct proves the wisdom of Leicester's precautions. In the spring Parliament of 1265 he openly charged the Earl with violating the Mise of Lewes, with tyranny, and with aiming at the crown. Before its close he withdrew to his own lands in the west, and secretly allied himself with Roger Mortimer and the Marcher barons. Earl Simon soon followed him to the west, taking with him the King and Edward. He moved along the Severn, securing its towns, advanced westward to Hereford, and was marching at the end of June along bad roads into the heart of South Wales to attack the fortresses of Earl Gilbert in Glamorgan when Edward suddenly made his escape from Hereford and joined Gloucester at Ludlow. The moment had been skilfully chosen, and Edward showed a rare ability in the movements by which he took advantage of the Earl's position. Moving rapidly along the Severn he seized Gloucester and the bridges across the river, destroyed the ships by which Leicester strove to escape across the Channel to Bristol, and cut him off altogether from England. By this movement too he placed himself between the Earl and his son Simon, who was advancing from the east to his father's relief. Turning rapidly on this second force Edward surprised it at Kenilworth and drove it with heavy loss within the walls of the castle. But the success was more than compensated by the opportunity which his absence gave to the Earl of breaking the line of the Severn. Taken by surprise and isolated as he was, Simon had been forced to seek for aid and troops in an avowed alliance with Llewelyn, and it was with Welsh reinforcements that he turned to the east. But the seizure of his ships and of the bridges of

Sec. VII.

The
Barons'
War

1258
to
1265

1264

SEC. VII.

THE
BARONS'
WAR

1258
TO
1265

the Severn held him a prisoner in Edward's grasp, and a fierce attack drove him back, with broken and starving forces, into the Welsh hills. In utter despair he struck northward to Hereford ; but the absence of Edward now enabled him on the 2nd of August to throw his troops in boats across the Severn below Worcester. The news drew Edward quickly back in a fruitless counter-march to the river, for the Earl had already reached Evesham by a long night march on the morning of the 4th, while his son, relieved in turn by Edward's counter-march, had pushed in the same night to the little town of Alcester. The two armies were now but some ten miles apart, and their junction seemed secured. But both were spent with long marching, and while the Earl, listening reluctantly to the request of the King, who accompanied him, halted at Evesham for mass and dinner, the army of the younger Simon halted for the same purpose at Alcester.

Battle of Evesham
1265

"Those two dinners doleful were, alas !" sings Robert of Gloucester; for through the same memorable night Edward was hurrying back from the Severn by country cross-lanes to seize the fatal gap that lay between them. As morning broke his army lay across the road that led northward from Evesham to Alcester. Evesham lies in a loop of the river Avon where it bends to the south ; and a height on which Edward ranged his troops closed the one outlet from it save across the river. But a force had been thrown over the river under Mortimer to seize the bridges, and all retreat was thus finally cut off. The approach of Edward's army called Simon to the front, and for the moment he took it for his son's. Though the hope soon died away a touch of soldierly pride moved him as he recognized in the orderly advance of his enemies a proof of his own training. "By the arm of St. James," he cried, "they come on in wise fashion, but it was from me that they learnt it." A glance however satisfied him of the hopelessness of a struggle ; it was impossible for a handful of horsemen with a mob of half-armed Welshmen to resist the disciplined knighthood of the royal army. "Let us commend our souls to God," Simon said to the little group around him, "for our bodies are the foe's." He bade Hugh Despenser and the rest of his comrades fly from the field. "If he died," was the noble answer, "they had no will to live." In three hours the butchery was over. The Welsh fled at the first onset like sheep, and were cut ruthlessly down in the cornfields and gardens where they sought refuge. The little group of knights around Simon fought desperately, falling one by one till the Earl was left alone. So terrible were his sword-strokes that he had all but gained the hill-top when a lance-thrust brought his horse to the ground, but Simon still rejected the summons to yield, till a blow from behind felled him, mortally wounded, to the ground. Then with a last cry of "It is God's grace" the soul of the great patriot passed away.

CHAPTER IV.

THE THREE EDWARDS.

1265—1360.

Section I.—The Conquest of Wales, 1265—1284.

[*Authorities.*—For the general state of Wales, see the "Itinerarium Cambriæ" of Giraldus Cambrensis : for its general history, the "Brut-y-Tywysogion," and "Annales Cambriæ," published by the Master of the Rolls ; the Chronicle of Caradoc of Lancarvan, as given in the tran lation by Powel ; and Warrington's "History of Wales." Stephen's "Literature of the Cymry" affords a general view of Welsh poetry ; the "Mabinogion" have been published by Lady Charlotte Guest. In his essays on "The Study of Celtic Literature," Mr. Matthew Arnold has admirably illustrated the characteristics of the Welsh Poetry. For English affairs the monastic annals we have before mentioned are supplemented by the jejune entries of Trivet and Murimuth.]

WHILE literature and science after a brief outburst were crushed in England by the turmoil of the Barons' War, a poetic revival had brought into sharp contrast the social and intellectual condition of Wales.

The
Welsh
Litera-
ture

To all outer seeming Wales had in the thirteenth century become utterly barbarous. Stripped of every vestige of the older Roman civilization by ages of bitter warfare, of civil strife, of estrangement from the general culture of Christendom, the unconquered Britons had sunk into a mass of savage herdsmen, clad in the skins and fed by the milk of the cattle they tended, faithless, greedy, and revengeful, retaining no higher political organization than that of the clan, broken by ruthless feuds, united only in battle or in raid against the stranger. But in the heart of the wild people there still lingered a spark of the poetic fire which had nerved it four hundred years before, through Aneurin and Llywarch Hen, to its struggle with the Saxon. At the hour of its lowest degradation the silence of Wales was suddenly broken by a crowd of singers. The song of the twelfth century burst forth, not from one bard or another, but from the nation at large. "In every house," says the shrewd Gerald de Barri, "strangers who arrived in the morning were entertained till eventide with the talk of maidens and the music of the harp." The romantic literature of the race found an admirable means of utterance in its tongue, as real a developement of the old Celtic language heard by Cæsar as the Romance tongues are developements of Cæsar's Latin, but which at

M

SEC. I.

THE CON-
QUEST OF
WALES

1265
TO
1284

a far earlier date than any other language of modern Europe had attained to definite structure and to settled literary form. No other mediæval literature shows at its outset the same elaborate and completed organization as that of the Welsh. But within these settled forms the Celtic fancy plays with a startling freedom. In one of the later poems Gwion the Little transforms himself into a hare, a fish, a bird, a grain of wheat ; but he is only the symbol of the strange shapes in which the Celtic fancy embodies itself in the tales or "Mabinogion" which reached their highest perfection in the legends of Arthur. Its gay extravagance flings defiance to all fact, tradition, probability, and revels in the impossible and unreal. When Arthur sails into the unknown world, it is in a ship of glass. The "descent into hell," as a Celtic poet paints it, shakes off the mediæval horror with the mediæval reverence, and the knight who achieves the quest spends his years of infernal durance in hunting and minstrelsy, and in converse with fair women. The world of the Mabinogion is a world of pure phantasy, a new earth of marvels and enchantments, of dark forests whose silence is broken by the hermit's bell, and sunny glades where the light plays on the hero's armour. Each figure as it moves across the poet's canvas is bright with glancing colour. "The maiden was clothed in a robe of flame-coloured silk, and about her neck was a collar of ruddy gold in which were precious emeralds and rubies. Her head was of brighter gold than the flower of the broom, her skin was whiter than the foam of the wave, and fairer were her hands and her fingers than the blossoms of the wood-anemone amidst the spray of the meadow fountain. The eye of the trained hawk, the glance of the falcon, was not brighter than hers. Her bosom was more snowy than the breast of the white swan, her cheek was redder than the reddest roses." Everywhere there is an Oriental profusion of gorgeous imagery, but the gorgeousness is seldom oppressive. The sensibility of the Celtic temper, so quick to perceive beauty, so eager in its thirst for life, its emotions, its adventures, its sorrows, its joys, is tempered by a passionate melancholy that expresses its revolt against the impossible, by an instinct of what is noble, by a sentiment that discovers the weird charm of nature. Some graceful play of pure fancy, some tender note of feeling, some magical touch of beauty, relieves its wildest extravagance. As Kalweh's greyhounds bound from side to side of their master's steed, they "sport round him like two sea-swallows." His spear is "swifter than the fall of the dewdrop from the blade of reed-grass upon the earth when the dew of June is at the heaviest." A subtle, observant love of nature and natural beauty takes fresh colour from the passionate human sentiment with which it is imbued, sentiment which breaks out in Gwalchmai's cry of nature-love, "I love the birds and their sweet voices in the lulling songs of the wood," in his watches at night beside the fords "among the

Sec. I.

The Con-
quest of
Wales

1265
to
1284

untrodden grass" to hear the nightingale and watch the play of the sea-mew. Even patriotism takes the same picturesque form ; the Welsh poet hates the flat and sluggish land of the Saxon ; as he dwells on his own, he tells of " its sea-coast and its mountains, its towns on the forest border, its fair landscape, its dales, its waters, and its valleys, its white sea-mews, its beauteous women." But the song passes swiftly and subtly into a world of romantic sentiment : " I love its fields clothed with tender trefoil, I love the marches of Merioneth where my head was pillowed on a snow-white arm." In the Celtic love of woman there is little of the Teutonic depth and earnestness, but in its stead a childlike spirit of delicate enjoyment, a faint distant flush of passion like the rose-light of dawn on a snowy mountain peak, a playful delight in beauty. " White is my love as the apple blossom, as the ocean's spray ; her face shines like the pearly dew on Eryri ; the glow of her cheeks is like the light of sunset." The buoyant and elastic temper of the French *trouvère* was spiritualized in the Welsh singers by a more refined poetic feeling. " Whoso beheld her was filled with her love. Four white trefoils sprang up wherever she trod." The touch of pure fancy removes its object out of the sphere of passion into one of delight and reverence.

It is strange, as we have said, to pass from the world of actual Welsh history into such a world as this. But side by side with this wayward, fanciful stream of poesy and romance ran a torrent of intenser song. The old spirit of the earlier bards, their joy in battle, their love for freedom, their hatred of the Saxon, broke out in ode after ode, in songs extravagant, monotonous, often prosaic, but fused into poetry by the intense fire of patriotism which glowed within them. The rise of the new poetic feeling indeed marked the appearance of a new energy in the long struggle with the English conqueror.

Of the three Welsh states into which all that remained unconquered of Britain had been broken by the victories of Deorham and Chester, two had long ceased to exist. The country between the Clyde and the Dee had been gradually absorbed by the conquests of Northumbria and the growth of the Scot monarchy. West Wales, between the British Channel and the estuary of the Severn, had yielded to the sword of Ecgberht. But a fiercer resistance prolonged the independence of the great central portion which alone in modern language preserves the name of Wales. In itself the largest and most powerful of the British states, it was aided in its struggle against Mercia by the weakness of its assailant, the youngest and least powerful of the English states, as well as by the internal warfare which distracted the energies of the invaders. But Mercia had no sooner risen to supremacy among the English kingdoms than it took the work of conquest vigorously in hand. Offa tore from Wales the border land between the Severn and the Wye ; the raids of his successors carried

SEC. I.

THE CON-
QUEST OF
WALES

1265
TO
1284

fire and sword into the heart of the country ; and an acknowledgement of the Mercian over-lordship was wrested from the Welsh princes. On the fall of Mercia this passed to the West-Saxon kings. The Laws of Howel Dda own the payment of a yearly tribute by " the prince of Aberffraw " to " the King of London." The weakness of England during her long struggle with the Danes revived the hopes of British independence. But with the fall of the Danelaw the Welsh princes were again brought to submission, and when in the midst of the Confessor's reign the Welsh seized on a quarrel between the houses of Leofric and Godwine to cross the border and carry their attacks into

1063

England itself, the victories of Harold re-asserted the English supremacy. His light-armed troops disembarking on the coast penetrated to the heart of the mountains, and the successors of the Welsh prince Gruffydd, whose head was the trophy of the campaign, swore to observe the old fealty and render the old tribute to the English Crown.

**The
Conquest
of South
Wales**

A far more desperate struggle began when the wave of Norman conquest broke on the Welsh frontier. A chain of great earldoms, settled by William along the border-land, at once bridled the old marauding forays. From his county palatine of Chester, Hugh the Wolf harried Flintshire into a desert ; Robert of Belesme, in his earldom of Shrewsbury, " slew the Welsh," says a chronicler, " like sheep, conquered them, enslaved them, and flayed them with nails of iron." Backed by these greater baronies a horde of lesser adventurers obtained the royal " licence to make conquest on the Welsh." Monmouth and Abergavenny were seized and guarded by Norman castellans ; Bernard of Neufmarché won the lordship of Brecknock ; Roger of Montgomery raised the town and fortress in Powysland

1094

which still preserves his name. A great rising of the whole people in the days of the second William at last recovered some of this Norman spoil. The new castle of Montgomery was burned, Brecknock and Cardigan were cleared of the invaders, and the Welsh poured ravaging over the English border. Twice the Red King carried his arms fruitlessly among the mountains, against enemies who took refuge in their fastnesses till famine and hardship had driven his broken host into retreat. The wiser policy of Henry the First fell back on his father's system of gradual conquest, and a new tide of invasion flowed along the coast, where the land was level and open and accessible from the sea. The attack was aided by internal strife. Robert Fitz-Hamo, the lord of Gloucester, was summoned to his aid by a Welsh chieftain ; and the defeat of Rhys ap Tewdor, the last prince under whom Southern Wales was united, produced an anarchy which enabled Robert to land safely on the coast of Glamorgan, to conquer the country round, and to divide it among his soldiers. A force of Flemings and Englishmen followed the Earl of Clare as he landed

SEC. I.

THE CON-
QUEST OF
WALES

1265
TO
1284

**The
Welsh
revival**

near Milford Haven, and pushing back the British inhabitants settled a " Little England " in the present Pembrokeshire. A few daring adventurers accompanied the Norman Lord of Kemeys into Cardigan, where land might be had for the winning by any one who would " wage war on the Welsh."

It was at this moment, when the utter subjugation of the British race seemed at hand, that a new outburst of energy rolled back the tide of invasion and changed the fitful resistance of the separate Welsh provinces into a national effort to regain independence. A new poetic fire, as we have seen, sprang into life. Every fight, every hero, had suddenly its verse. The names of the older bards were revived in bold forgeries to animate the national resistance and to prophesy victory. It was in North Wales that the new spirit of patriotism received its strongest inspiration from this burst of song. Again and again Henry the Second was driven to retreat from the impregnable fastnesses where the " Lords of Snowdon," the princes of the house of Gruffydd ap Conan, claimed supremacy over Wales. Once a cry arose that the King was slain, Henry of Essex flung down the royal standard, and the King's desperate efforts could hardly save his army from utter rout. In a later campaign the invaders were met by storms of rain, and forced to abandon their baggage in a headlong flight to Chester. The greatest of the Welsh odes, that known to English readers in Gray's translation as " The Triumph of Owen," is Gwalchmai's song of victory over the repulse of an English fleet from Abermenai. The long reigns of the two Llewelyns, the sons of Jorwerth and of Gruffydd, which all but cover the last century of Welsh independence, seemed destined to realize the hopes of their country-men. The homage which the first succeeded in extorting from the whole of the Welsh chieftains placed him openly at the head of his race, and gave a new character to his struggle with the English King. In consolidating his authority within his own domains, and in the assertion of his lordship over the princes of the south, Llewelyn ap Jorwerth aimed steadily at securing the means of striking off the yoke of the Saxon. It was in vain that John strove to buy his friendship by the hand of his daughter Johanna. Fresh raids on the Marches forced the King to enter Wales ; but though his army reached Snowdon it fell back like its predecessors, starved and broken before an enemy it could never reach. A second attack had better success. The chieftains of South Wales were drawn from their new allegiance to join the English forces, and Llewelyn, prisoned in his fastnesses, was at last driven to submit. But the ink of the treaty was hardly dry before Wales was again on fire ; the common fear of the English once more united its chieftains, and the war between John and his barons removed all dread of a new invasion. Absolved from his allegiance to an excommunicated King, and allied with the barons under Fitz-

1157

1194–1283

*Llewelyn ap
Jorwerth*
1194–1246

1211

SEC. I.

THE CON-
QUEST OF
WALES

1265
TO
1284

Llewelyn
ap Jor-
werth
and the
Bards

Walter—too glad to enlist in their cause a prince who could hold in check the nobles of the border country, where the royalist cause was strongest—Llewelyn seized his opportunity to reduce Shrewsbury, to annex Powys, where the English influence had always been powerful, to clear the royal garrisons from Caermarthen and Cardigan, and to force even the Flemings of Pembroke to do him homage.

The hopes of Wales rose higher and higher with each triumph of the Lord of Snowdon. The court of Llewelyn was crowded with bardic singers. "He pours," sings one of them, "his gold into the lap of the bard as the ripe fruit falls from the trees." But gold was hardly needed to wake their enthusiasm. Poet after poet sang of "the Devastator of England," the "Eagle of men that loves not to lie nor sleep," "towering above the rest of men with his long red lance," his "red helmet of battle crested with a fierce wolf." "The sound of his coming is like the roar of the wave as it rushes to the shore, that can neither be stayed nor appeased." Lesser bards strung together his victories in rough jingle of rime and hounded him on to the slaughter. "Be of good courage in the slaughter," sings Elidir, "cling to thy work, destroy England, and plunder its multitudes." A fierce thirst for blood runs through the abrupt, passionate verses of the court singers. "Swansea, that tranquil town, was broken in heaps," bursts out a triumphant poet; "St. Clears, with its bright white lands, it is not Saxons who hold it now!" "In Swansea, the key of Lloegria, we made widows of all the wives." "The dread Eagle is wont to lay corpses in rows, and to feast with the leader of wolves and with hovering ravens glutted with flesh, butchers with keen scent of carcases." "Better," closes the song, "is the grave than the life of man who sighs when the horns call him forth to the squares of battle." But even in bardic verse Llewelyn rises high out of the mere mob of chieftains who live by rapine, and boast as the Hirlas-horn passes from hand to hand through the hall that "they take and give no quarter." "Tender-hearted, wise, witty, ingenious," he was "the great Cæsar" who was to gather beneath his sway the broken fragments of the Celtic race. Mysterious prophecies, the prophecies of Merlin the Wise, floated from lip to lip, to nerve Wales to its last struggle with the invaders. Medrawd and Arthur would appear once more on earth to fight over again the fatal battle of Camlan. The last conqueror of the Celtic race, Cadwallon, still lived to combat for his people. The supposed verses of Taliesin expressed the undying hope of a restoration of the Cymry. "In their hands shall be all the land from Britanny to Man: . . . a rumour shall arise that the Germans are moving out of Britain back again to their fatherland" Gathered up in the strange work of Geoffry of Monmouth, these predictions made a deep impression, not on Wales only, but on its conquerors. It was to meet indeed the dreams of a yet living Arthur that the grave of the legendary hero-king at Glastonbury was found and visited by Henry the Second. But neither trick nor conquest could shake the firm faith of the Celt in the ultimate victory of his race. "Think you," said Henry to a Welsh chieftain who had joined his host, "that your people of rebels can withstand my army?" "My people," replied the chieftain, "may be weakened by your might, and even in great part destroyed, but unless the wrath of God be on the side of its foe it will not perish utterly. Nor deem I that other race or other tongue will answer for this corner of the world before the Judge of all at the last day save this people and tongue of Wales." So ran the popular rime, "Their Lord they will praise, their speech they shall keep, their land they shall lose—except wild Wales." Faith and prophecy seemed justified by the growing strength of the British people. The weakness and dissensions which characterized the reign of Henry the Third enabled Llewelyn ap Jorwerth to preserve a practical independence till the close of his life, when a fresh acknowledgement of the English supremacy was wrested from him by Archbishop Edmund. But the triumphs of his arms were renewed by Llewelyn the son of Gruffydd, whose ravages swept the border to the very gates of Chester, while his conquest of Glamorgan seemed to bind the whole people together in a power strong enough to meet any attack from the stranger. Throughout the Barons' war Llewelyn remained master of Wales. Even at its close the threat of an attack from the now united kingdom only forced him to submission on a practical acknowledgement of his sovereignty. The chieftain whom the English kings had till then scrupulously designated as "Prince of Aberffraw," was now allowed the title of "Prince of Wales," and his right to receive homage from the other nobles of his principality was allowed.

Near, however, as Llewelyn seemed to the final realization of his aims, he was still a vassal of the English crown, and the accession of a new sovereign to the throne was at once followed by the demand of his homage. The youth of Edward the First had already given promise of the high qualities which distinguished him as an English ruler. The passion for law, the instinct of good government, which were to make his reign so memorable in our history, had declared themselves from the first. He had sided with the barons at the outset of their struggle with Henry; he had striven to keep his father true to the Provisions of Oxford. It was only when the Crown seemed falling into bondage that Edward passed to the royal side; and when the danger he dreaded was over he returned to his older attitude. In the first flush of victory, while the doom of Simon was yet unknown, Edward stood alone in desiring his captivity against the cry of the Marcher lords for his death. When all was over he wept over the corpse of his cousin, Henry de Montfort, and followed the Earl's body to the tomb. It was from Earl Simon, as the Earl owned with a

SEC. I.

THE CONQUEST OF WALES

1265
TO
1284

Llewelyn ap Gruffydd 1246–1283

1267

The Conquest of Wales

Sec. I.

The Con-
quest of
Wales

1265
TO
1284

1267

proud bitterness ere his death, that Edward had learned the skill in warfare which distinguished him among the princes of his time.   But he had learned the far nobler lesson of a self-government which lifted him high above them as a ruler among men.   Severing himself from the brutal triumph of the royalist party, he secured fair terms to the conquered, and after crushing the last traces of resistance, he won the adoption by the Crown of the constitutional system of government for which the barons had fought.   So utterly was the land at rest that he felt free to join a crusade in Palestine.   His father's death recalled

him home to meet at once the difficulty of Wales.   During two years Llewelyn rejected the King's repeated summons to him to perform his homage, till Edward's patience was exhausted, and the royal army marched into North Wales.   The fabric of Welsh greatness fell at a

single blow ; the chieftains of the south and centre who had so lately sworn fealty to Llewelyn deserted him to join his English enemies ; an English fleet reduced Anglesea, and the Prince, cooped up in his fastnesses, was forced to throw himself on the royal mercy.   With characteristic moderation his conqueror contented himself with adding to the English dominions the coast-district as far as Conway, and providing that the title of Prince of Wales should cease at Llewelyn's death.   A heavy fine which he had incurred was remitted, and Eleanor the daughter of Simon of Montfort, who had been arrested on her way to join him as his wife, was wedded to him at the English court. For four years all was quiet, but the persuasions of his brother David, who had deserted him in the previous war, and whose desertion had been rewarded with an English lordship, roused Llewelyn to a fresh revolt.   A prophecy of Merlin had announced that when English money became round the Prince of Wales should be crowned at London ; and a new coinage of copper money, coupled with the prohibition to break the silver penny into halves and quarters, as had been usual, was supposed to have fulfilled the prediction.   In the

campaign which followed the Prince held out in Snowdon with the stubbornness of despair, and the rout of an English detachment which had thrown a bridge across the Menai Straits into Anglesea prolonged the contest into the winter.   Terrible however as were the sufferings of the English army, Edward's firmness remained unbroken, and rejecting all proposals of retreat he issued orders for the formation of a new army at Caermarthen to complete the circle of investment round Llewelyn.   The Prince sallied from his mountain-hold for a raid upon Radnorshire, and fell in a petty skirmish on the banks of the Wye.   With him died the independence of his race.   After six months of flight his brother David was arrested and sentenced in full Parliament to a traitor's death.   The submission of the lesser chieftains was followed by the building of strong castles at Conway and Caernarvon, and the settlement of English barons on the confiscated

SEC. II.

THE
ENGLISH
PARLIA-
MENT

1283
TO
1295

soil. A wiser instinct of government led Edward to introduce by the "Statute of Wales" English law and the English administration of justice into Wales. But little came of the attempt; and it was not till the time of Henry the Eighth that the country was actually incorporated in England. What Edward had really done was to break the Welsh resistance. His policy of justice (for the "massacre of the bards" is a mere fable) accomplished its end, and in spite of two later rebellions Wales ceased to be any serious danger to England for a hundred years.

Section II.—The English Parliament, 1283—1295.

[*Authorities.*—The short treatise on the Constitution of Parliament called "Modus tenendi Parliamenta" may be taken as a fair account of its actual state and powers in the fourteenth century. It has been reprinted by Dr. Stubbs, in the invaluable collection of Documents which serves as the base of the present section. Sir Francis Palgrave has illustrated the remedial side of our parliamentary institutions with much vigour and picturesqueness in his "History of the English Commonwealth," but his conclusions are often hasty and prejudiced. On all constitutional points from the reign of Edward the First we can now rely on the judgment and research of Mr. Hallam ("Middle Ages").]

[The second volume of Dr. Stubbs's "Constitutional History" which deals with this period was published after this History was written and the list of authorities prepared.—ED.]

The conquest of Wales marked the adoption of a new attitude and policy on the part of the crown. From the earliest moment of his reign Edward the First definitely abandoned all dreams of recovering the foreign dominions which his grandfather had lost. He concentrated himself on the consolidation and good government of England itself. We can only fairly judge his annexation of Wales, or his attempt to annex Scotland, if we regard them as parts of the same scheme of national administration to which we owe his final establishment of our judicature, our legislation, our Parliament. The King's English policy, like his English name, was the sign of a new epoch. The long period of national formation had come practically to an end. With the reign of Edward begins modern England, the constitutional England in which we live. It is not that any chasm separates our history before it from our history after it, as the chasm of the Revolution divides the history of France, for we have traced the rudiments of our constitution to the first moment of the English settlement in Britain. But it is with these as with our language. The tongue of Ælfred is the very tongue we speak, but in spite of its identity with modern English it has to be learned like the tongue of a stranger. On the other hand, the English of Chaucer is almost as intelligible as our own. In the first the historian and philologer can study the origin and developement of our national speech, in the last a school-boy can enjoy the story of Troilus and Cressida, or listen to the gay chat of the Canterbury Pilgrims. In

The New England

SEC. II.

THE
ENGLISH
PARLIA-
MENT

1283
TO
1295

precisely the same way a knowledge of our earliest laws is indispensable for the right understanding of later legislation, its origin and its developement, while the principles of our Parliamentary system must necessarily be studied in the Meetings of Wise Men before the Conquest or the Great Council of barons after it. But the Parliaments which Edward gathered at the close of his reign are not merely illustrative of the history of later Parliaments, they are absolutely identical with those which still sit at St. Stephen's; and a statute of Edward, if unrepealed, can be pleaded in our courts as formally as a statute of Victoria. In a word, the long struggle of the constitution for actual existence has come to an end. The contests which follow are not contests which tell, like those which preceded them, on the actual fabric of our political institutions; they are simply stages in the rough discipline by which England has learned, and is still learning, how best to use and how wisely to develope the latent powers of its national life, how to adjust the balance of its social and political forces, and to adapt its constitutional forms to the varying conditions of the time. From the reign of Edward, in fact, we are face to face with modern England. King, Lords, Commons, the Courts of Justice, the forms of public administration, our local divisions and provincial jurisdictions, the relations of Church and State, in great measure the framework of society itself, have all taken the shape which they still essentially retain.

Judicial reforms

Much of this great change is doubtless attributable to the general temper of the age, whose special task and object seemed to be that of reducing to distinct form the great principles which had sprung into a new and vigorous life during the century that preceded it. As the opening of the thirteenth century had been an age of founders, creators, discoverers, so its close was an age of lawyers; the most illustrious men of the time were no longer such as Bacon, or Earl Simon, or Francis of Assisi, but men such as St. Lewis of France or Alfonso the Wise, organizers, administrators, framers of laws and institutions. It was to this class that Edward himself belonged. He had little of creative genius or political originality in his character, but he possessed in a high degree the faculty of organization, and his passionate love of law broke out even in the legal chicanery to which he sometimes stooped. In the judicial reforms to which so much of his attention was directed, he showed himself, if not an " English Justinian," at any rate a clear-sighted man of business, developing, reforming, bringing into a lasting shape the institutions of his predecessors. One of his first cares was to complete the judicial reforms begun by Henry II. The most important court of civil jurisdiction, the Sheriff's or County Court, remained unchanged, both in the extent of its jurisdiction, and the character of the Sheriff as a royal officer. But the superior courts

The three Common Law Courts

into which the King's Court had since the Great Charter divided itself,

SEC. II.

THE
ENGLISH
PARLIA-
MENT

1283
TO
1295

those of the King's Bench, Exchequer, and Common Pleas, now received a distinct staff of judges for each court. Of far greater importance than this change, which was in effect but the completion of a process of severance that had long been going on, was the establishment of an equitable jurisdiction side by side with that of the common law. In his reform of 1178 Henry the Second had broken up the older King's Court, which had till then served as the final Court of Appeal, by the severance of the purely legal judges who had been gradually added to it from the general body of his councillors. The judges thus severed from the Council retained the name and the ordinary jurisdiction of " the King's Court," while all cases in which they failed to do justice were reserved for the special cognizance of the royal Council itself. To this final jurisdiction of the King in Council Edward gave a wide developement. His assembly of the ministers, the higher permanent officials, and the law officers of the Crown, for the first time reserved to itself in its judicial capacity the correction of all breaches of the law which the lower courts had failed to repress, whether from weakness, partiality, or corruption, and especially of those lawless outbreaks of the more powerful baronage which defied the common authority of the judges. Though regarded with jealousy by Parliament, the jurisdiction of the Council seems to have been steadily put in force through the two centuries which followed ; in the reign of Henry the Seventh it took legal and statutory form in the shape of the Court of Star Chamber, and its powers are still exercised in our own day by the Judicial Committee of the Privy Council. But the same duty of the Crown to do justice where its courts fell short of giving due redress for wrong expressed itself in the jurisdiction of the Chancellor. This great officer of State, who had perhaps originally acted only as President of the Council when discharging its judicial functions, acquired at a very early date an independent judicial position of the same nature. It is by remembering the origin of the Court of Chancery that we understand the nature of the powers it gradually acquired. All grievances of the subject, especially those which sprang from the misconduct of government officials or of powerful oppressors, fell within its cognizance, as they fell within that of the Royal Council, and to these were added disputes respecting the wardship of infants, dower, rent-charges, or tithes. Its equitable jurisdiction sprang from the defective nature and the technical and unbending rules of the common law. As the Council had given redress in cases where law became injustice, so the Court of Chancery interfered without regard to the rules of procedure adopted by the common law courts, on the petition of a party for whose grievance the common law provided no adequate remedy. An analogous extension of his powers enabled the Chancellor to afford relief in cases of fraud, accident, or abuse of trust, and this side of his jurisdiction was largely

The King in Council

The Court of Chancery

Sec. II.

The
English
Parlia-
ment
1283
to
1295
Edward's
legisla-
tion

extended at a later time through the results of legislation on the tenure of land by ecclesiastical bodies. The separate powers of the Chancellor, whatever was the original date at which they were first exercised, seem to have been thoroughly established under Edward the First.

In legislation, as in his judicial reforms, Edward renewed and consolidated the principles which had been already brought into practical working by Henry the Second. Significant acts announced his determination to carry out Henry's policy of limiting the independent jurisdiction of the Church. He was resolute to force it to become thoroughly national by bearing its due part of the common national burthens, and to break its growing dependence upon Rome. The defiant resistance of the ecclesiastical body was answered in an emphatic way. By falling into the "dead hand" or "mortmain" of the

1279

Church land ceased to render its feudal services; and the Statute "of Mortmain" now forbade the alienation of land to religious bodies in such wise that it should cease to render its due service to the King. The restriction was probably no beneficial one to the country at large, for Churchmen were the best landlords, and it was soon evaded by the ingenuity of the clerical lawyers; but it marked the growing jealousy of any attempt to set aside what was national from serving the general need and profit of the nation. Its immediate effect was to stir the clergy to a bitter resentment. But Edward remained firm, and when the bishops proposed to restrict the royal courts from dealing with cases of patronage or causes which touched the chattels of Churchmen he met

1283

their proposals by an instant prohibition. His care for the trading classes was seen in the Statute of Merchants, which provided for the registration of the debts of traders, and for their recovery by distraint of the debtor's goods and the imprisonment of his person. The Statute of Winchester, the greatest of Edward's measures for the

1285

enforcement of public order, revived and reorganized the old institutions of national police and national defence. It regulated the action of the hundred, the duty of watch and ward, and the gathering of the fyrd or militia of the realm as Henry the Second had moulded it into form in his Assize of Arms. Every man was bound to hold himself in readiness, duly armed, for the King's service in case of invasion or revolt, or to pursue felons when hue and cry were raised after them. Every district was made responsible for crimes committed within its bounds; the gates of each town were required to be closed at nightfall, and all strangers to give an account of themselves to its magistrates. As a security for travellers against sudden attacks from robbers, all brushwood was to be destroyed for a space of two hundred feet on either side the public highway, a provision which illustrates at once

*Justices of
the Peace*
1285

the social and physical condition of the country at the time. To enforce the observance of this act knights were appointed in every shire under the name of Conservators of the Peace, a name which, as the convenience of these local magistrates was more sensibly felt and their powers more largely extended, was changed for that which they still retain of "Justices of the Peace." The great measure which is commonly known as the Statute "Quia Emptores" is one of those legislative efforts which mark the progress of a wide social revolution in the country at large. The number of the greater barons was diminishing every day, while the number of the country gentry and of the more substantial yeomanry was increasing with the increase of the national wealth. This increase showed itself in the growing desire to become proprietors of land. Tenants of the greater barons received under-tenants on condition of their rendering them similar services to those which they themselves rendered to their lords; and the baronage, while duly receiving the services in compensation for which they had originally granted their lands in fee, saw with jealousy the feudal profits of these new under-tenants, the profits of wardship or of reliefs and the like, in a word the whole increase in the value of the estate consequent on its subdivision and higher cultivation, passing into other hands than their own. The purpose of the statute was to check this process by providing that in any case of alienation the sub-tenant should henceforth hold, not of the tenant, but directly of the superior lord. But its result was to promote instead of hindering the transfer and subdivision of land. The tenant who was before compelled to retain in any case so much of the estate as enabled him to discharge his feudal services to the over-lord of whom he held it, was now enabled by a process analogous to the modern sale of "tenant-right," to transfer both land and services to new holders. However small the estates thus created might be, the bulk were held directly of the Crown; and this class of lesser gentry and freeholders grew steadily from this time in numbers and importance.

It is to the same social revolution as well as to the large statesmanship of Edward the First that we owe our Parliament. Neither the Meeting of the Wise Men before the Conquest, nor the Great Council of the Barons after it, had been in any way representative bodies. The first theoretically included all free holders of land, but it shrank at an early time into a gathering of earls, higher nobles, and bishops, with the officers and thegns of the royal household. Little change was made in the composition of this assembly by the Conquest, for the Great Council of the Norman kings was held to include all tenants who held directly of the Crown, the bishops and greater abbots (whose character as independent spiritual members tended more and more to merge in their position as barons), and the great officers of the Court. But though its composition remained the same, the character of the assembly was essentially altered. From a free gathering of "Wise Men" it sank to a Royal Court of feudal vassals. Its functions seem

Sec. II.

The
English
Parlia-
ment
1283
to
1295

1290

The
Great
Council
of the
Realm

SEC. II.

THE
ENGLISH
PARLIA-
MENT

1283
TO
1295

to have become almost nominal, and its powers to have been restricted to the sanctioning, without debate or possibility of refusal, all grants demanded from it by the Crown. Its "counsel and consent," however, remained necessary for the legal validity of every great fiscal or political measure, and its very existence was an effectual protest against the imperial theories advanced by the lawyers of Henry the Second, theories which declared all legislative power to reside wholly in the sovereign. It was in fact under Henry that these assemblies became more regular, and their functions more important. The reforms which marked his reign were issued in the Great Council, and even financial matters were suffered to be debated there. But it was not till the grant of the Great Charter that its powers over taxation were formally recognized, and the principle established that no burthen beyond the customary feudal aids might be imposed "save by the Common Council of the Realm." The same great document first expressly regulated its form. In theory, as we have seen, the assembly consisted of all who held land directly of the Crown. But the same causes which restricted attendance at the Witenagemot to the greater nobles told on the actual composition of the Council of Barons. While the attendance of the ordinary tenants in chief, the Knights or "Lesser Barons," was burthensome from its expense to themselves, their numbers and their dependence on the higher nobles made their assembly dangerous to the Crown. As early, therefore, as the time of Henry the First we find a distinction recognized between the "Greater Barons," of whom the Council was usually composed, and the "Lesser Barons" who formed the bulk of the tenants of the Crown. But though the attendance of the latter had become rare, their right of attendance remained intact. While enacting that the prelates and greater barons should be summoned by special writs to each gathering of the Council, a remarkable provision of the Great Charter orders a general summons to be issued through the Sheriff to all direct tenants of the Crown. The provision was probably intended to rouse the lesser baronage to the exercise of rights which had practically passed into desuetude, but as the clause is omitted in later issues of the Charter we may doubt whether the principle it embodied ever received more than a very limited application. There are traces of the attendance of a few of the lesser knighthood, gentry perhaps of the neighbourhood where the assembly was held, in some of its meetings under Henry the Third, but till a late period in the reign of his successor the Great Council practically remained a gathering of the greater barons, the prelates, and the officers of the Crown. The change which the Great Charter had failed to accomplish was now, however, brought about by the social circumstances of the time. One of the most remarkable of these was the steady decrease in the number of the greater nobles. The bulk of the earldoms had already lapsed

SEC. II.

THE
ENGLISH
PARLIA-
MENT

1283
TO
1295

to the Crown through the extinction of the families of their possessors ;
of the greater baronies, many had practically ceased to exist by their
division among co-heiresses, many through the constant struggle of
the poorer barons to rid themselves of their rank by a disclaimer, so
as to escape the burthen of higher taxation and attendance in Parliament which it involved. How far this diminution had gone we may
see from the fact that hardly more than a hundred barons sat in the
earlier Councils of Edward's reign. But while the number of those
who actually possessed the privilege of assisting in Parliament was
rapidly diminishing, the numbers and wealth of the " lesser baronage,"
whose right of attendance had become a mere constitutional tradition,
was as rapidly increasing. The long peace and prosperity of the
realm, the extension of its commerce, and the increased export of
wool, were swelling the ranks and incomes of the country gentry as
well as of the freeholders and substantial yeomanry. We have already
noticed the growing passion for the possession of land which makes
this reign so critical a moment in the history of the English freeholder ;
but the same tendency had to some extent existed in the preceding
century, and it was a consciousness of the growing importance of this
class of rural proprietors which induced the barons at the time of the
Charter to make their fruitless attempt to induce them to take part in
the deliberations of the Great Council. But while the barons desired
their presence as an aid against the Crown, the Crown itself desired
it as a means of rendering taxation more efficient. So long as the
Great Council remained a mere assembly of magnates it was necessary
for the King's ministers to treat separately with the other orders of the
state as to the amount and assessment of their contributions. The
grant made in the Great Council was binding only on the barons and
prelates who made it ; but before the aids of the boroughs, the Church,
or the shires could reach the royal treasury, a separate negotiation
had to be conducted by the offices of the Exchequer with the reeves
of each town, the sheriff and shire-court of each county, and the archdeacons of each diocese. Bargains of this sort would be the more
tedious and disappointing as the necessities of the Crown increased
in the later years of Edward, and it became a matter of fiscal expediency
to obtain the sanction of any proposed taxation through the presence
of these classes in the Great Council itself.

The effort, however, to revive the old personal attendance of the
lesser baronage, which had broken down half a century before, could
hardly be renewed at a time when the increase of their numbers made
it more impracticable than ever ; but a means of escape from this
difficulty was fortunately suggested by the very nature of the court
through which alone a summons could be addressed to the landed
knighthood. Amidst the many judicial reforms of Henry or Edward
the Shire Court remained unchanged. The haunted mound or the

**Knights
of the
Shire.**

SEC. II.

THE
ENGLISH
PARLIA-
MENT

1283
TO
1295

immemorial oak round which the assembly gathered (for the court was often held in the open air) were the relics of a time before the free kingdom had sunk into a shire, and its folk-moot into a County Court. But save that the King's reeve had taken the place of the King, and that the Norman legislation had displaced the Bishop and set four Coroners by the Sheriff's side, the gathering of the free-holders remained much as of old. The local knighthood, the yeomanry, the husbandmen of the county, were all represented in the crowd that gathered round the Sheriff, as, guarded by his liveried followers, he published the King's writs, announced his demand of aids, received the presentment of criminals and the inquest of the local jurors, assessed the taxation of each district, or listened solemnly to appeals for justice, civil and criminal, from all who held themselves oppressed in the lesser courts of the hundred or the soke. It was in the County Court alone that the Sheriff could legally summon the lesser baronage to attend the Great Council, and it was in the actual constitution of this assembly that the Crown found a solution of the difficulty which we have already stated. For the principle of repre-sentation by which it was finally solved was coeval with the Shire Court itself. In all cases of civil or criminal justice the twelve sworn assessors of the Sheriff, as members of a class, though not formally deputed for that purpose, practically represented the judicial opinion of the county at large. From every hundred came groups of twelve sworn deputies, the "jurors," through whom the presentments of the district were made to the royal officer, and with whom the assess-ment of its share in the general taxation was arranged. The husband-men on the outskirts of the crowd, clad in the brown smock frock which still lingers in the garb of our carters and ploughmen, were broken up into little knots of five, a reeve and four assistants, who formed the representatives of the rural townships. If, in fact, we regard the Shire Courts as lineally the descendants of our earliest English folk-moots, we may justly claim the principle of parliamentary representation as among the oldest of our institutions. But it was only slowly and tentatively that this principle was applied to the recon-stitution of the Great Council. As early as the close of John's reign there are indications of the approaching change in the summons of "four discreet knights" from every county. Fresh need of local support was felt by both parties in the conflict of the succeeding reign, and Henry and his barons alike summoned knights from each shire "to meet on the common business of the realm." It was no doubt with the same purpose that the writs of Earl Simon ordered the choice of knights in each shire for his famous parliament of 1265. Something like a continuous attendance may be dated from the accession of Edward, but it was long before the knights were regarded as more than local deputies for the assessment of taxation, or admitted to a share in the general business of the Great Council. The statute " Quia Emptores," for instance, was passed in it before the knights who had been summoned could attend. Their participation in the deliberative power of Parliament, as well as their regular and continuous attendance, dates only from the Parliament of 1295. But a far greater constitutional change in their position had already taken place through the extension of electoral rights to the freeholders at large. The one class entitled to a seat in the Great Council was, as we have seen, that of the lesser baronage ; and of the lesser baronage alone the knights were in theory the representatives. But the necessity of holding their election in the County Court rendered any restriction of the electoral body physically impossible. The court was composed of the whole body of freeholders, and no sheriff could distinguish the " aye, aye " of the yeoman from the " aye, aye " of the lesser baron. From the first moment therefore of their attendance we find the knights regarded not as mere representatives of the baronage, but as knights of the shire, and by this silent revolution the whole body of the rural freeholders were admitted to a share in the government of the realm.

The financial difficulties of the Crown led to a far more radical revolution in the admission into the Great Council of representatives from the boroughs. The presence of knights from each shire was, as we have seen, the recognition of an older right, but no right of attendance or share in the national " counsel and consent " could be pleaded for the burgesses of the towns. On the other hand, the rapid developement of their wealth made them every day more important as elements in the national taxation. The towns had long since freed themselves from all payment of the dues or fines exacted by the King, as the original lord of the soil on which they had in most cases grown up, by what was called the purchase of the " farm of the borough " ; in other words, by the commutation of these uncertain dues for a fixed sum paid annually to the Crown, and apportioned by their own magistrates among the general body of the burghers. All that the King legally retained was the right enjoyed by every great proprietor of levying a corresponding taxation on his tenants in demesne under the name of " a free aid," whenever a grant was made for the national necessities by the barons of the Great Council. But the temptation of appropriating the growing wealth of the mercantile class proved stronger than legal restrictions, and we find both Henry the Third and his son assuming a right of imposing taxes at pleasure and without any authority from the Council even over London itself. The burgesses could refuse indeed the invitation to contribute to the " free aid " demanded by the royal officers, but the suspension of their markets or trading privileges brought them in the end to submission. Each of these " free aids," however, had to be extorted after a long wrangle between the

Representation of Boroughs

SEC. II.

THE
ENGLISH
PARLIA-
MENT

1283
TO
1295

borough and the officers of the Exchequer ; and if the towns were driven to comply with what they considered an extortion, they could generally force the Crown by evasions and delays to a compromise and abatement of its original demands.   The same financial reasons, therefore, existed for desiring the presence of their representatives in the Great Council as existed in the case of the shires; but it was the genius of Earl Simon which first broke through the older constitutional tradition, and dared to summon two burgesses from each town to the Parliament of 1265. Time had, indeed, to pass before the large and statesmanlike conception of the great patriot could meet with full acceptance.   Through the earlier part of Edward's reign we find a few instances of the presence of representatives from the towns, but their scanty numbers and the irregularity of their attendance show that they were summoned rather to afford financial information to the Great Council than as representatives in it of an Estate of the Realm.   But every year pleaded stronger and stronger for their inclusion, and in the Parliament of 1295 that of 1265 found itself at last reproduced.   " It was from me that he learnt it," Earl Simon had cried, as he recognized the military skill of Edward's onset at Evesham ; " It was from me that he learnt it," his spirit might have exclaimed, as he saw the King gathering at last two burgesses " from every city, borough, and leading town " within his realm to sit side by side with the knights, nobles, and barons of the Great Council.   To the Crown the change was from the first an advantageous one.   The grants of subsidies by the burgesses in Parliament proved more profitable than the previous extortions of the Exchequer.   The proportion of their grant generally exceeded that of the other estates by a tenth.   Their representatives too proved far more compliant with the royal will than the barons or knights of the shire ; only on one occasion during Edward's reign did the burgesses waver from their general support of the Crown.   It was easy indeed to control them, for the selection of boroughs to be represented remained wholly in the King's hands, and their numbers could be increased or diminished at the King's pleasure.   The determination was left to the sheriff, and at a hint from the royal Council a sheriff of Wilts would cut down the number of represented boroughs in his shire from eleven to three, or a sheriff of Bucks declare he could find but a single borough, that of Wycomb, within the bounds of the county.   Nor was this exercise of the prerogative hampered by any anxiety on the part of the towns to claim representative privileges.   It was difficult to suspect that a power before which the Crown would have to bow lay in the ranks of soberly clad traders, summoned only to assess the contributions of their boroughs, and whose attendance was as difficult to secure as it seemed burthensome to themselves and the towns who sent them.   The mass of citizens took little or no part in their choice, for they were elected in the county court by a few of the principal burghers deputed for the purpose ; but the cost of their maintenance, the two shillings a day paid to the burgess by his town, as four were paid to the knight by his county, was a burthen from which the boroughs made desperate efforts to escape.　Some persisted in making no return to the sheriff.　Some bought charters of exemption from the troublesome privilege.　Of the 165 who were summoned by Edward the First more than a third ceased to send representatives after a single compliance with the royal summons.　During the whole time from the reign of Edward the Third to the reign of Henry the Sixth the sheriff of Lancashire declined to return the names of any boroughs at all within that county, " on account of their poverty." Nor were the representatives themselves more anxious to appear than their boroughs to send them.　The busy country squire and the thrifty trader were equally reluctant to undergo the trouble and expense of a journey to Westminster.　Legal measures were often necessary to ensure their presence.　Writs still exist in abundance such as that by which Walter le Rous is " held to bail in eight oxen and four cart-horses to come before the King on the day specified " for attendance in Parliament.　But in spite of obstacles such as these the presence of representatives from the boroughs may be regarded as continuous from the Parliament of 1295.　As the representation of the lesser barons had widened through a silent change into that of the shire, so that of the boroughs—restricted in theory to those in royal demesne—seems practically from Edward's time to have been extended to all who were in a condition to pay the cost of their representatives' support.　By a change as silent within the Parliament itself the burgess, originally summoned to take part only in matters of taxation, was at last admitted to a full share in the deliberations and authority of the other orders of the State.

The admission of the burgesses and knights of the shire to the assembly of 1295 completed the fabric of our representative constitution.　The Great Council of the Barons had become the Parliament of the Realm, a parliament in which every order of the state found itself represented, and took part in the grant of supplies, the work of legislation, and in the end the control of government.　But though in all essential points the character of Parliament has remained the same from that time to this, there were some remarkable particulars in which this assembly of 1295 differed widely from the present Parliament at St. Stephen's.　Some of these differences, such as those which sprang from the increased powers and changed relations of the different orders among themselves, we shall have occasion to consider at a later time.　But a difference of a far more startling kind than these lay in the presence of the clergy.　If there is any part in the Parliamentary scheme of Edward the First which can be regarded as especially his own, it is his project for the representation of the

Sec. **II.**

The
English
Parlia-
ment

1283
to
1295

The
early
Parlia-
ments

*Representa-
tion of the
Clergy.*

SEC. II.

THE
ENGLISH
PARLIA-
MENT

1283
TO
1295

ecclesiastical order. The King had twice at least summoned its "proctors" to Great Councils before 1295, but it was then only that the complete representation of the Church was definitely organized by the insertion of a clause in the writ which summoned a bishop to Parliament requiring the personal attendance of all archdeacons, deans, or priors of cathedral churches, of a proctor for each cathedral chapter, and two for the clergy within his diocese. The clause is repeated in the writs of the present day, but its practical effect was foiled almost from the first by the resolute opposition of those to whom it was addressed. What the towns failed in doing the clergy actually did. Even when forced to comply with the royal summons, as they seem to have been forced during Edward's reign, they sat jealously by themselves, and their refusal to vote supplies in any but their own provincial assemblies, or convocations, of Canterbury and York left the Crown without a motive for insisting on their continued attendance. Their presence indeed, though still occasionally granted on some solemn occasions, became so pure a formality that by the end of the fifteenth century it had sunk wholly into desuetude. In their anxiety to preserve their existence as an isolated and privileged order the clergy flung away a power which, had they retained it, would have ruinously hampered the healthy developement of the state. To take a single instance, it is difficult to see how the great changes of the Reformation could have been brought about had a good half of the House of Commons consisted purely of churchmen, whose numbers would have been backed by the weight of property as possessors of a third of the landed estates of the realm. A hardly less important

Restriction of Parliament to Westminster

difference may be found in the gradual restriction of the meetings of Parliament to Westminster. The names of the early statutes remind us of its convocation at the most various quarters, at Winchester, Acton Burnell, or Northampton. It was at a later time that Parliament became settled in the straggling village which had grown up in the marshy swamp of the Isle of Thorns, beside the palace whose embattled pile towered over the Thames and the great minster which was still rising in Edward's day on the site of the older church of the Confessor. It is possible that, while contributing greatly to its consti-

Parliament as Court of Appeal

tutional importance, this settlement of the Parliament may have helped to throw into the background its character as a supreme court of appeal. The proclamation by which it was called together invited " all who had any grace to demand of the King in Parliament, or any plaint to make of matters which could not be redressed or determined by ordinary course of law, or who had been in any way aggrieved by any of the King's ministers or justices or sheriffs, or their bailiffs, or any other officer, or have been unduly assessed, rated, charged, or surcharged to aids, subsidies, or taxes," to deliver their petitions to receivers who sat in the Great Hall of the Palace of Westminster.

The petitions were forwarded to the King's Council, and it was probably the extension of the jurisdiction of that body, and the subsequent rise of the Court of Chancery, which reduced this ancient right of the subject to the formal election of " Triers of Petitions " at the opening of every new Parliament by the House of Lords, a usage which is still continued. But it must have been owing to some memory of the older custom that the subject always looked for redress against injuries from the Crown or its ministers to the Parliament of the realm.

Section III.—The Conquest of Scotland, 1290—1305.

[*Authorities.*—Scotland itself has no contemporary chronicles for this period : the jingling rimes of Blind Harry are two hundred years later than the death of his hero Wallace. Those of England are meagre and inaccurate ; the most important are the " Annales Angliæ et Scotiæ " and " Annales Regni Scotiæ," Rishanger's Chronicle, his " Gesta Edwardi Primi," and three fragments of annals (all published in the Rolls Series). The portion of the so-called Walsingham's History which relates to this time is now attributed by its latest editor, Mr. Riley, to Rishanger's hand. But the main source of our information lies in the copious collection of state papers preserved in Rymer's " Fœdera," in the " Rotuli Scotiæ," and in the " Documents and Records illustrative of the History of Scotland," edited by Sir F. Palgrave. Mr. Robertson, in his " Scotland under her Early Kings," has admirably illustrated the ages before the quarrel, and Mr. Burton in his History of Scotland has stated the quarrel itself with great accuracy and fairness. For Edward's side see the preface of Sir F. Palgrave to the work above, and Mr. Freeman's essay on " The Relations between the Crowns of England and Scotland."]

The personal character of Edward the First had borne a large part in the constitutional changes which we have described, but it becomes of the highest moment during the war with Scotland which covers the latter half of his reign.

In his own time, and amongst his own subjects, Edward was the object of almost boundless admiration. He was in the truest sense a national King. At the moment when the last trace of foreign conquest passed away, when the descendants of those who won and those who lost at Senlac blended for ever into an English people, England saw in her ruler no stranger, but an Englishman. The national tradition returned in more than the golden hair or the English name which linked him to our earlier Kings. Edward's very temper was English to the core. In good as in evil he stands out as the typical representative of the race he ruled, like them wilful and imperious, tenacious of his rights, indomitable in his pride, dogged, stubborn, slow of apprehension, narrow in sympathy, but like them, too, just in the main, unselfish, laborious, conscientious, haughtily observant of truth and self-respect, temperate, reverent of duty, religious. He inherited

SEC. III.

THE CON-
QUEST OF
SCOTLAND

1290
TO
1305

indeed from the Angevins their fierce and passionate wrath ; his punishments, when he punished in anger, were without pity ; and a priest who ventured at a moment of storm into his presence with a remonstrance dropped dead from sheer fright at his feet. But for the most part his impulses were generous, trustful, averse from cruelty, prone to forgiveness. " No man ever asked mercy of me," he said in his old age, " and was refused." The rough soldierly nobleness of his nature breaks out at Falkirk, where he lay on the bare ground among his men, or in his refusal during a Welsh campaign to drink of the one cask of wine which had been saved from marauders : " It is I who have brought you into this strait," he said to his thirsty fellow-soldiers, " and I will have no advantage of you in meat or drink." A strange tenderness and sensitiveness to affection lay in fact beneath the stern imperiousness of his outer bearing. Every subject throughout his realm was drawn closer to the King who wept bitterly at the news of his father's death, though it gave him a crown ; whose fiercest burst of vengeance was called out by an insult to his mother ; whose crosses rose as memorials of his love and sorrow at every spot where his wife's bier rested. " I loved her tenderly in her lifetime," wrote Edward to Eleanor's friend, the Abbot of Cluny ; " I do not cease to love her now she is dead." And as it was with mother and wife, so it was with his people at large. All the self-concentrated isolation of the earlier Angevins disappears in Edward. He was the first English king since the Conquest who loved his people with a personal love, and craved for their love back again. To his trust in them we owe our Parliament, to his care for them the great statutes which stand in the forefront of our laws. Even in his struggles with her England understood a temper which was so perfectly her own, and the quarrels between King and people during his reign are quarrels where, doggedly as they fought, neither disputant doubted for a moment the worth or affection of the other. Few scenes in our history are more touching than that which closes the long contest over the Charter, when Edward stood face to face with his people in Westminster Hall, and with a sudden burst of tears owned himself frankly in the wrong.

But it was just this sensitiveness, this openness to outer impressions and outer influences, that led to the strange contradictions which meet us in Edward's career. Under the first king whose temper was distinctly English a foreign influence told most fatally on our manners, our literature, our national spirit. The rise of France into a compact and organized monarchy from the time of Philip Augustus was now making its influence dominant in Western Europe. The " chivalry " so familiar in Froissart, that picturesque mimicry of high sentiment, of heroism, love, and courtesy, before which all depth and reality of nobleness disappeared to make room for the coarsest profligacy, the

SEC. III.

THE CON-
QUEST OF
SCOTLAND

1290
TO
1305

narrowest caste-spirit, and a brutal indifference to human suffering, was specially of French creation. There was a nobleness in Edward's nature from which the baser influences of this chivalry fell away. His life was pure, his piety, save when it stooped to the superstition of the time, manly and sincere, while his high sense of duty saved him from the frivolous self-indulgence of his successors. But he was far from being wholly free from the taint of his age. His passionate desire was to be a model of the fashionable chivalry of his day. He had been famous from his very youth as a consummate general ; Earl Simon had admired the skill of his advance at Evesham, and in his Welsh campaign he had shown a tenacity and force of will which wrested victory out of the midst of defeat. He could head a furious charge of horse at Lewes, or organize a commissariat which enabled him to move army after army across the harried Lowlands. In his old age he was quick to discover the value of the English archery, and to employ it as a means of victory at Falkirk. But his fame as a general seemed a small thing to Edward when compared with his fame as a knight. He shared to the full his people's love of hard fighting. His frame, indeed, was that of a born soldier—tall, deep-chested, long of limb, capable alike of endurance or action. When he encountered Adam Gurdon, a knight of gigantic size and renowned prowess, after Evesham he forced him single-handed to beg for mercy. At the opening of his reign he saved his life by sheer fighting in a tournament at Challon. It was this love of adventure which lent itself to the frivolous unreality of the new chivalry. At his "Round Table of Kenilworth" a hundred lords and ladies, "clad all in silk," renewed the faded glories of Arthur's Court. The false air of romance which was soon to turn the gravest political resolutions into outbursts of sentimental feeling appeared in his "Vow of the Swan," when rising at the royal board he swore on the dish before him to avenge on Scotland the murder of Comyn. Chivalry exerted on him a yet more fatal influence in its narrowing of his sympathy to the noble class, and in its exclusion of the peasant and the craftsman from all claim to pity. "Knight without reproach" as he was, he looked calmly on at the massacre of the burghers of Berwick, and saw in William Wallace nothing but a common robber.

Hardly less powerful than the French notion of chivalry in its influence on Edward's mind was the new French conception of kingship, feudality, and law. The rise of a lawyer class was everywhere hardening customary into written rights, allegiance into subjection, loose ties such as commendation into a definite vassalage. But it was specially through French influence, the influence of St. Lewis and his successors, that the imperial theories of the Roman Law were brought to bear upon this natural tendency of the time. When the "sacred majesty" of the Cæsars was transferred by a legal fiction to the royal head of a feudal

SEC. III.

THE CON-
QUEST OF
SCOTLAND

1290
TO
1305

baronage, every constitutional relation was·changed. The "defiance" by which a vassal renounced service to his lord became treason, his after resistance "sacrilege." That Edward could appreciate what was sound and noble in the legal spirit around him was shown in his reforms of our judicature and our Parliament; but there was something as congenial to his mind in its definiteness, its rigidity, its narrow technicalities. He was never wilfully unjust, but he was too often captious in his justice, fond of legal chicanery, prompt to take advantage of the letter of the law. The high conception of royalty which he had borrowed from St. Lewis united with this legal turn of mind in the worst acts of his reign. Of rights or liberties unregistered in charter or roll Edward would know nothing, while his own good sense was overpowered by the majesty of his crown. It was incredible to him that Scotland should revolt against a legal bargain which made her national independence conditional on the terms extorted from a claimant of her throne; nor could he view in any other light but as treason the resistance of his own baronage to an arbitrary taxation which their fathers had borne. It is in the very anomalies of such a character, in its strange union of justice and wrong-doing, of nobleness and meanness, that we must look for any fair explanation of much that has since been bitterly blamed in Edward's conduct and policy.

Scotland

Fairly to understand his quarrel with the Scots, we must clear our minds of the ideas which we now associate with the words "Scotland," or the "Scotch people." At the opening of the fourteenth century the kingdom of the Scots was composed of four districts, each of which had originally its different people, its different speech, or at least dialect, and its different history. The first of these was the Lowland district, at one time called Saxony, and which now bears the name of Lothian and the Merse (or border land), the space, roughly speaking, between the Forth and Tweed. We have seen that at the close of the English conquest of Britain the kingdom of Northumbria stretched from the Humber to the Firth of Forth, and of this kingdom the Lowlands formed simply the northern portion. The English conquest and the English colonization were as complete here as over the rest of Britain. Rivers and hills indeed retained their Celtic names, but the "tons" and "hams" scattered over the country told the story of its Teutonic settlement. Livings and Dodings left their names to Livingstone and Duddingstone; Elphinstone, Dolphinstone and Edmundstone preserved the memory of English Elphins, Dolphins, and Edmunds, who had raised their homesteads beyond the Teviot and the Tweed. To the northward and westward of this Northumbrian land lay the kingdoms of the conquered. Over the "Waste" or "Desert"—the range of barren moors which stretches from Derbyshire to the Cheviots—the Briton had sought a refuge in the long strip of coast between the

Saxony

Cumbria

SEC. III.

THE CON-
QUEST OF
SCOTLAND

1290
TO
1305

Clyde and the Dee which formed the earlier Cumbria. Against this kingdom the efforts of the Northumbrian rulers had been incessantly directed; the victory of Chester had severed it from the Welsh kingdoms to the south; Lancashire, Westmoreland, and Cumberland were already subdued by the time of Ecgfrith; while the fragment which was suffered to remain unconquered between the Firths of Solway and of Clyde, and to which the name of Cumbria is in its later use confined, owned the English supremacy. At the close of the seventh century it seemed likely that the same supremacy would extend over the Celtic tribes to the north. The district north of the Clyde and Forth was originally inhabited chiefly by the Picts, a Latin name for the people who seem to have called themselves the Cruithne. To these Highlanders the country south of the Forth was a foreign land, and significant entries in their rude chronicles tell us how in their forays "the Picts made a raid upon Saxony." But during the period of Northumbrian greatness they had begun to yield at least on their borders some kind of submission to its kings. Eadwine had built a fort at Dunedin, which became Edinburgh and looked menacingly across the Forth; and at Abercorn beside it was established an English prelate with the title of Bishop of the Picts. Ecgfrith, in whose hands the power of Northumbria reached its highest point, marched across the Forth to change this over-lordship into a direct dominion, and to bring the series of English victories to a close. His host poured burning and ravaging across the Tay, and skirted the base of the Grampians as far as the field of Nectansmere, where King Bruidi awaited them at the head of the Picts. The great battle which followed proved a turning-point in the history of the North; the invaders were cut to pieces, Ecgfrith himself being among the slain, and the power of Northumbria was broken for ever. On the other hand, the kingdom of the Picts started into new life with its great victory, and pushed its way in the hundred years that followed westward, eastward, and southward, till the whole country north of the Forth and the Clyde acknowledged its supremacy. But the hour of Pictish greatness was marked by the sudden extinction of the Pictish name. Centuries before, when the English invaders were beginning to harry the south coast of Britain, a fleet of coracles had borne a tribe of the Scots, as the inhabitants of Ireland were at that time called, from the black cliff-walls of Antrim to the rocky and indented coast of South Argyle. The little kingdom of Scot-land which these Irishmen founded slumbered in obscurity among the lakes and mountains to the south of Loch Linnhe, now submitting to the over-lordship of Northumbria, now to that of the Picts, till the extinction of the direct Pictish line of sovereigns raised the Scot King, Kenneth Mac-Alpin, who chanced to be their nearest kinsman, to the vacant throne. For fifty years these rulers of Scottish blood still call themselves "Kings of the Picts;" but with the opening of the tenth

SEC. III.

THE CON-
QUEST OF
SCOTLAND

1290
TO
1305

century the very name passes away, the tribe which had given its chief to the common throne gives its designation to the common realm, and "Pict-land" vanishes from the page of the chronicler or annalist to make way for the "land of the Scots."

It was even longer before the change made way among the people itself, and the real union of the nation with its kings was only effected by the common suffering of the Danish wars. In the north, as in the south of Britain, the invasion of the Danes brought about political unity. Not only were Picts and Scots thoroughly blended into a single people, but by the annexation of Cumbria and the Lowlands, their monarchs became rulers of the territory which we now call Scotland. The annexation was owing to the new policy of the English Kings. Their aim, after the long struggle of England with the northmen, was no longer to crush the kingdom across the Forth, but to raise it into a bulwark against the northmen who were still settled in Caithness and the Orkneys, and for whose aggressions Scotland was the natural highway. On the other hand, it was only in English aid that the Scot Kings could find a support for their throne against these Norse Jarls of Orkney and Caithness. It was probably this common hostility to a common foe which brought about the "commendation" by which the Scots beyond the Forth, with the Welsh of Strath-clyde, chose the English King, Eadward the Elder, "to father and lord." The choice, whatever weight after events may have given to it, seems to have been little more than the renewal of the loose English supremacy over the tribes of the North which had existed during the times of Northumbrian greatness; it certainly implied at the time nothing save a right on either side to military aid, though the aid then rendered was necessarily placed in the hands of the stronger party to the agreement. Such a connexion naturally ceased in the event of any war between the two contracting parties; it was in fact by no means the feudal vassalage of a later time, but rather a military convention. But loose as was the tie which bound the two countries, a closer tie soon bound the Scot King himself to his English overlord. Strath-clyde, which, after the defeat of Nectansmere, had shaken off the English yoke, and which at a later time had owned the supremacy of the Scots, rose into a temporary independence only to be conquered by the English Eadmund. By him it was granted to Malcolm of Scotland on condition that he should become his "fellow-worker" both by land and sea, and became from that time the appanage of the eldest son of the Scottish king. At a later time, under Eadgar or Cnut, the whole of Northern Northumbria, or what we now call the Lothians, was ceded to the Scottish sovereigns, but whether on the same terms of feudal dependence or on the same loose terms of "commendation" as already existed for lands north of the Forth, we have no means of deciding. The retreat, however, of the bounds of the great

924

*Grant of
Strath-clyde
to the Scot
King*

*Grant of
Northern
Northum-
bria*

SEC. III.

THE CON-
QUEST OF
SCOTLAND

1290
TO
1305

**England
and the
Scot
Kings**

English bishopric of the North, the see of St. Cuthbert, as far southward as the Pentland Hills, would seem to imply a greater change in the political character of the ceded district than the first theory would allow.

Whatever change these cessions may have brought about in the relation of the Scottish to the English Kings, they certainly affected in a very marked way their relation both to England and to their own realm. One result of the acquisition of the Lowlands was the ultimate fixing of the royal residence in their new southern dominion at Edinburgh ; and the English civilization with which they were then surrounded changed the Scot Kings in all but blood into Englishmen. A way soon opened itself to the English crown by the marriage of Malcolm with Margaret, the sister of Eadgar Ætheling. Their children were regarded by a large party within England as representatives of the older royal race and as claimants of the throne, and this danger grew as William's devastation of the North not only drove fresh multitudes of Englishmen to settle in the Lowlands, but filled the Scotch court with English nobles who fled thither for refuge. So formidable, indeed, became the pretensions of the Scot Kings, that they forced the ablest of our Norman sovereigns into a complete change of policy. The Conqueror and William the Red had met the threats of the Scot sovereigns by invasions which ended again and again in an illusory homage ; but the marriage of Henry the First with the Scottish Matilda not only robbed the claims of the Scottish line of much of their force, but enabled him to draw it into far closer relations with the Norman throne. King David not only abandoned the ambitious dreams of his predecessors to place himself later at the head of his niece Matilda's party in her contest with Stephen, but as Henry's brother-in-law he figured as the first noble of the English court, and found English models and English support in the work of organization which he attempted within his own dominions. As the marriage with Margaret had changed Malcolm from a Celtic chieftain into an English King, so that of Matilda converted David into a Norman and feudal sovereign. His court was filled with Norman nobles from the South, such as the Balliols and Bruces who were destined to play so great a part afterwards but who now for the first time obtained fiefs in the Scottish realm ; and a feudal jurisprudence modelled on that of England was introduced into the Lowlands. A fresh connexion between the countries began with the grant of lordships in England to the Scot Kings or their sons. Homage was sometimes rendered, whether for these lordships, for the Lowlands, or for the whole Scottish realm, but it was the capture of William the Lion during the revolt of the English baronage which suggested to Henry the Second the project of a closer dependence of Scotland on the English Crown. To gain his freedom, William consented to hold

SEC. III.

THE CON-
QUEST OF
SCOTLAND

1290
TO
1305

his crown of Henry and his heirs, the prelates and lords of the Scotch kingdom did homage to Henry as to their direct lord, and a right of appeal in all Scotch causes was allowed to the superior court of the English suzerain. From this bondage, however, Scotland was soon freed by the prodigality of Richard, who allowed her to buy back the freedom she had forfeited, and from that time the difficulties of the older claim were evaded by a legal compromise. The Scot Kings repeatedly did homage to the English sovereign but with a reservation of rights which were prudently left unspecified. The English King accepted the homage on the assumption that it was rendered to him as overlord of the Scottish realm, and this assumption was neither granted nor denied. For nearly a hundred years the relations of the two countries were thus kept peaceful and friendly, and the death of

Alexander the Third seemed destined to remove even the necessity of protests by a closer union of the two kingdoms. Alexander had wedded his only daughter to the King of Norway, and after long negotiation the Scotch Parliament proposed the marriage of her child Margaret, "the Maid of Norway," with the son of Edward the First. It was, however, carefully provided in the marriage treaty of Brigham

that Scotland should remain a separate and free kingdom, and that its laws and customs should be preserved inviolate. No military aid was to be claimed by the English King, no Scotch appeal to be carried to an English court. But this project was abruptly frustrated by the child's death on her voyage to Scotland, and with the rise of claimant after claimant of the vacant throne Edward was drawn into far other relations to the Scottish realm.

Of the thirteen pretenders to the throne of Scotland, only three could be regarded as serious claimants. By the extinction of the line of William the Lion the right of succession passed to the daughters of his brother David. The claim of John Balliol, Lord of Galloway, rested on his descent from the eldest of these ; that of Robert Bruce, Lord of Annandale, on his descent from the second ; that of John Hastings, Lord of Abergavenny, on his descent from the third. At this crisis the Norwegian King, the Primate of St. Andrew's, and seven of the Scotch Earls, had already appealed to Edward before Margaret's death ; and the death itself was followed by the consent both of the claimants and the Council of Regency to refer the question of the succession to his decision in a Parliament at Norham. But the

over-lordship which the Scots acknowledged was something far less direct and definite than what Edward claimed at the opening of this conference. His claim was supported by excerpts from English monastic chronicles, and by the slow advance of an English army, while the Scotch lords, taken by surprise, found little help in the delay which was granted them, and at last, in common with nine of the claimants themselves, formally admitted Edward's direct suzerainty.

SEC. III.

THE CON-
QUEST OF
SCOTLAND
1290
TO
1305

To the nobles, in fact, the concession must have seemed a small one, for like the principal claimants they were for the most part Norman in blood, with estates in both countries, and looking for honours and pensions from the English Court. From the Commons who were gathered with the nobles at Norham no admission of Edward's claims could be extorted ; but in Scotland, feudalized as it had been by David, the Commons were as yet of little weight, and their opposition was quietly passed by. All the rights of a feudal suzerain were at once assumed by the English King ; he entered into the possession of the country as into that of a disputed fief to be held by its over-lord till the dispute was settled, his peace was sworn throughout the land, its castles delivered into his charge, while its bishops and nobles swore homage to him directly as their lord superior. Scotland was thus reduced to the subjection which she had experienced under Henry the Second, but the full discussion which followed over the various claims to the throne showed that, while exacting to the full what he believed to be his right, Edward desired to do justice to the country itself. The commissioners whom he named to report on the claims to the throne were mainly Scotch ; a proposal for the partition of the realm among the claimants was rejected as contrary to Scotch law ; and the claim of Balliol as representative of the elder branch was finally preferred to that of his rivals.

The castles were at once delivered to the new monarch, and Balliol did homage to Edward with full acknowledgement of the services due to him from the realm of Scotland. For a time there was peace. Edward in fact seemed to have no desire to push farther the rights of his crown. Even allowing that Scotland was a dependent kingdom, it was far from being an ordinary fief of the English crown. By feudal custom a distinction had always been held to exist between the relations of a dependent king to a superior lord and those of a vassal noble to his sovereign. At Balliol's homage Edward had disclaimed, in strict accordance with the marriage treaty of Brigham, any right to the ordinary incidents of a fief, those of wardship or marriage ; but there were other customs of the realm of Scotland as incontestable as these. The Scot King had never been held bound to attend the council of the English baronage, to do service in English warfare, or to contribute on the part of his Scotch realm to English aids. No express acknowledgement of these rights had been given by Edward, but for a time they were practically observed. The claim of independent justice was more doubtful, as it was of higher import than these. It was certain that no appeal from a Scotch King's court to that of his supposed overlord had been allowed since the days of William the Lion, and the judicial independence of Scotland had been expressly reserved in the marriage treaty. But in feudal jurisprudence the right of ultimate appeal was the test of sovereignty. This right

SEC. III.

THE CON-
QUEST OF
SCOTLAND

1290
TO
1305

of appeal Edward now determined to enforce, and Balliol at first gave way. It was alleged, however, that the resentment of his baronage and people forced him to resist ; and while appearing formally at Westminster he refused to answer an appeal save by advice of his Council. He was in fact looking to France, which, as we shall afterwards see, was jealously watching Edward's proceedings, and ready to force him into war. By a new breach of customary law Edward summoned the Scotch nobles to follow him in arms against this foreign foe. But the summons was disregarded, and a second and formal refusal of aid was followed by a secret alliance with France and by a Papal absolution of Balliol from his oath of fealty.

Edward was still reluctant to begin the war, when all hope of accommodation was ended by the refusal of Balliol to attend his Parliament at Newcastle, the rout of a small body of English troops, and the investment of Carlisle by the Scots. Orders were at once given for an advance upon Berwick. The taunts of its citizens stung the King to the quick. " Kynge Edward, waune thou havest Berwick, pike thee ; waune thou havest geten, dike thee," they shouted from behind the wooden stockade, which formed the only rampart of the town. But the stockade was stormed with the loss of a single knight, and nearly eight thousand of the citizens were mown down in a ruthless carnage, while a handful of Flemish traders who held the townhall stoutly against all assailants were burned alive in it. The massacre only ceased when a procession of priests bore the host to the King's presence, praying for mercy, and Edward with a sudden and characteristic burst of tears called off his troops ; but the town was ruined for ever, and the great merchant city of the North sank from that time into a petty seaport. At Berwick Edward received Balliol's defiance. " Has the fool done this folly ? " the King cried in haughty scorn. " If he will not come to us, we will come to him." The terrible slaughter, however, had done its work, and his march was a triumphal progress. Edinburgh, Stirling, and Perth opened their gates, Bruce joined the English army, and Balliol himself surrendered and passed without a blow from his throne to an English prison. No further punishment, however, was exacted from the prostrate realm. Edward simply treated it as a fief, and declared its forfeiture to be the legal consequence of Balliol's treason. It lapsed in fact to the overlord, and its earls, barons, and gentry swore homage in Parliament at Berwick to Edward as their king. The sacred stone on which its older sovereigns had been installed, an oblong block of sandstone, which legend asserted to have been the pillow of Jacob as angels ascended and descended upon him, was removed from Scone and placed in Westminster by the shrine of the Confessor. It was enclosed by Edward's order in a stately seat, which became from that hour the coronation chair of English kings.

To the King himself the whole business must have seemed another and easier conquest of Wales, and the mercy and just government which had followed his first success followed his second also. The government of the new dependency was entrusted to Warenne, Earl of Surrey, at the head of an English Council of Regency. Pardon was freely extended to all who had resisted the invasion, and order and public peace were rigidly enforced. But both the justice and injustice of the new rule proved fatal to it ; the wrath of the Scots, already kindled by the intrusion of English priests into Scotch livings, and by the grant of lands across the border to English barons, was fanned to fury by the strict administration of law, and the repression of feuds and cattle-lifting. The disbanding, too, of troops, which was caused by the penury of the royal exchequer, united with the licence of the soldiery who remained to quicken the national sense of wrong. The disgraceful submission of their leaders brought the people them-selves to the front. In spite of a hundred years of peace the farmer of the Lowlands and the artisan of the towns remained stout-hearted Northumbrian Englishmen ; they had never consented to Edward's supremacy, and their blood rose against the insolent rule of the stranger. The genius of an outlaw knight, William Wallace, saw in their smouldering discontent a hope of freedom for his country, and his daring raids on outlying parties of the English soldiery roused the country at last into revolt. Of Wallace himself, of his life or temper, we know little or nothing ; the very traditions of his gigantic stature and enormous strength are dim and unhistorical. But the instinct of the Scotch people has guided it aright in choosing Wallace for its national hero. He was the first to assert freedom as a national birth-right, and amidst the despair of nobles and priests to call the people itself to arms. At the head of an army drawn principally from the coast districts north of the Tay, which were inhabited by a population of the same blood as that of the Lowlands, Wallace, in September, 1297, encamped near Stirling, the pass between the north and the south, and awaited the English advance. The offers of John of Warenne were scornfully rejected : " We have come," said the Scottish leader, " not to make peace, but to free our country." The position of Wallace, a rise of hills behind a loop of Forth, was in fact chosen with consummate skill. The one bridge which crossed the river was only broad enough to admit two horsemen abreast ; and though the English army had been passing from daybreak, only half its force was across at noon when Wallace closed on it and cut it after a short combat to pieces in the sight of its comrades. The retreat of the Earl of Surrey over the border left Wallace head of the country he had freed, and for a time he acted as " Guardian of the Realm " in Balliol's name, and headed a wild foray into Northumberland. His reduction of Stirling Castle at last called Edward to the field. The King, who marched

SEC. III.

THE CON-
QUEST OF
SCOTLAND

1290
TO
1305

**The
Second
Conquest**

1297–1305

*Battle of
Stirling
Sept.* **1297**

SEC. III.

THE CON-
QUEST OF
SCOTLAND
1290
TO
1305

northward with a larger host than had ever followed his banner, was enabled by treachery to surprise Wallace, as he fell back to avoid an engagement, and to force him to battle near Falkirk. The Scotch force consisted almost wholly of foot, and Wallace drew up his spearmen in four great hollow circles or squares, the outer ranks kneeling, and the whole supported by bowmen within, while a small force of horse were drawn up as a reserve in the rear. It was the formation of Waterloo, the first appearance in our history since the day of Senlac of " that unconquerable British infantry," before which chivalry was destined to go down. For a moment it had all Waterloo's success. " I have brought you to the ring, hop (dance) if you can," are words of rough humour that reveal the very soul of the patriot leader, and the serried ranks answered well to his appeal. The Bishop of Durham,

Battle of Falkirk July, 1298

who led the English van, shrank wisely from the look of the squares. " Back to your mass, Bishop," shouted the reckless knights behind him, but the body of horse dashed itself vainly on the wall of spears. Terror spread through the English army, and its Welsh auxiliaries drew off in a body from the field. But the generalship of Wallace was met by that of the King. Drawing his bowmen to the front, Edward riddled the Scottish ranks with arrows, and then hurled his cavalry afresh on the wavering line. In a moment all was over, and the maddened knights rode in and out of the broken ranks, slaying without mercy. Thousands fell on the field, and Wallace himself escaped with difficulty, followed by a handful of men. But ruined as the cause of freedom seemed, his work was done. He had roused Scotland into life, and even a defeat like Falkirk left her unconquered. Edward remained master only of the ground he stood on ; want of supplies forced him to retreat ; and in the following year a regency of Scotch nobles under Bruce and Comyn continued the struggle for independence. Troubles at home and dangers from abroad stayed

1300

Edward's hand. The barons were pressing more and more vigorously for redress of their grievances and the heavy taxation brought about by the war. France was still menacing, and a claim advanced by Pope

1303

Boniface the Eighth, at its suggestion, to the feudal superiority over Scotland, arrested a fresh advance of the King. A quarrel, however, which broke out between Philippe le Bel and the Papacy removed all obstacles, and enabled Edward to defy Boniface and to wring from France a treaty in which Scotland was abandoned. In 1304 he resumed the work of invasion, and again the nobles flung down their arms as he marched to the North. Comyn, at the head of the Regency, acknowledged his sovereignty, and the surrender of Stirling completed the conquest of Scotland. The triumph of Edward was but the prelude to the full execution of his designs for knitting the two countries together by a clemency and wisdom which reveal the greatness of his statesmanship. A general amnesty was extended to all who had shared in the revolt. Wallace, who refused to avail himself of Edward's mercy, was captured, and condemned to death at Westminster on charges of treason, sacrilege, and robbery. The head of the great patriot, crowned in mockery with a circlet of laurel, was placed upon London Bridge. But the execution of Wallace was the one blot on Edward's clemency. With a masterly boldness he entrusted the government of the country to a council of Scotch nobles, many of whom were freshly pardoned for their share in the war, and anticipated the policy of Cromwell by allotting ten representatives to Scotland in the Common Parliament of his realm. A Convocation was summoned at Perth for the election of these representatives, and a great judicial scheme which was promulgated in this assembly adopted the amended laws of King David as the base of a new legislation, and divided the country for judicial purposes into four districts, Lothian, Galloway, the Highlands, and the land between the Highlands and the Forth, at the head of each of which were placed two justiciars, the one English and the other Scotch.

Section IV.—The English Towns.

[*Authorities.*—For the general history of London see its "Liber Albus" and "Liber Custumarum," in the series of the Master of the Rolls ; for its communal revolution, the "Liber de Antiquis Legibus," edited by Mr. Stapleton for the Camden Society ; for the rising of William Longbeard, the story in William of Newburgh. In his "Essay on English Municipal History" (1867), Mr. Thompson has given a useful account of the relations of Leicester with its Earls. A great store of documents will be found in the Charter Rolls published by the Record Commission, in Brady's work on English Boroughs, and (though rather for Parliamentary purposes) in Stephen's and Merewether's "History of Boroughs and Corporations." But the only full and scientific examination of our early municipal history, at least on one of its sides, is to be found in the Essay prefixed by Dr. Brentano to the "Ordinances of English Gilds," published by the Early English Text Society.]

From scenes such as we have been describing, from the wrong and bloodshed of foreign conquest, we pass to the peaceful life and progress of England itself.

Through the reign of the three Edwards two revolutions, which have been almost ignored by our historians, were silently changing the whole character of English society. The first of these, the rise of a new class of tenant-farmers, we shall have to notice hereafter in its connection with the great agrarian revolt which bears the name of Wat Tyler. The second, the rise of the craftsmen within our towns, and the struggle by which they won power and privilege from the older burghers, is the most remarkable event in the period of our national history at which we have arrived.

O

Sec. IV.

The
English
Towns

The Early
English
Boroughs

The English borough was originally a mere township or group of townships whose inhabitants happened, either for purposes of trade or protection, to cluster together more thickly than elsewhere. It is this characteristic of our boroughs which separates them at once from the cities of Italy and Provence, which had preserved the municipal institutions of their Roman past, from the German towns founded by Henry the Fowler with the special purpose of sheltering industry from the feudal oppression around them, or from the communes of northern France which sprang into existence in revolt against feudal outrage within their walls. But in England the tradition of Rome had utterly passed away, while feudal oppression was held fairly in check by the Crown. The English town, therefore, was in its beginning simply a piece of the general country, organized and governed precisely in the same manner as the townships around it. The burh or borough was probably a more defensible place than the common village; it may have had a ditch or mound about it instead of the quickset-hedge or "tun" from which the township took its name. But its constitution was simply that of the people at large. The obligations of the dwellers within its bounds were those of the townships round, to keep fence and trench in good repair, to send a contingent to the fyrd, and a reeve and four men to the hundred court and shire court; and the inner rule of the borough lay as in the townships about in the hands of its own freemen, gathered in "borough-moot" or "portmannimote." But the social change brought about by the Danish wars, the legal requirement that each man should have a lord, affected the towns, as it affected the rest of the country. Some passed into the hands of great thegns near to them; the bulk became known as in the demesne of the king. A new officer, the lord's or king's reeve, was a sign of this revolution. It was the reeve who now summoned the borough-moot and administered justice in it; it was he who collected the lord's dues or annual rent of the town, and who exacted the services it owed to its lord. To modern eyes these services would imply almost complete subjection. When Leicester, for instance, passed from the hands of the Conqueror into those of its Earls, its townsmen were bound to reap their lord's corn-crops, to grind at his mill, to redeem their strayed cattle from his pound. The great forest around was the Earl's, and it was only out of his grace that the little borough could drive its swine into the woods or pasture its cattle in the glades. The justice and government of the town lay wholly in its master's hands; he appointed its bailiffs, received the fines and forfeitures of his tenants, and the fees and tolls of their markets and fairs. But when once these dues were paid and these services rendered the English townsman was practically free. His rights were as rigidly defined by custom as those of his lord. Property and person alike were secured against arbitrary seizure. He could demand a fair trial on any charge, and even if justice was administered by his master's reeve it was administered in the presence and with the assent of his fellow-townsmen. The bell which swung out from the town tower gathered the burgesses to a common meeting, where they could exercise rights of free speech and free deliberation on their own affairs. Their merchant-gild over its ale-feast regulated trade, distributed the sums due from the town among the different burgesses, looked to the due repairs of gate and wall, and acted, in fact, pretty much the same part as a town-council of to-day. Not only, too, were these rights secured by custom from the first, but they were constantly widening as time went on. Whenever we get a glimpse of the inner history of an English town, we find the same peaceful revolution in progress, services disappearing through disuse or omission, while privileges and immunities are being purchased in hard cash. The lord of the town, whether he were king, baron, or abbot, was commonly thriftless or poor, and the capture of a noble, or the campaign of a sovereign, or the building of some new minster by a prior, brought about an appeal to the thrifty burghers, who were ready to fill again their master's treasury at the price of the strip of parchment which gave them freedom of trade, of justice, and of government. Sometimes a chance story lights up for us this work of emancipation. At Leicester one of the chief aims of its burgesses was to regain their old English trial by compurgation, the rough predecessor of trial by jury, which had been abolished by the Earls in favour of the foreign trial by battle. " It chanced," says a charter of the place, " that two kinsmen, Nicholas the son of Acon, and Geoffrey the son of Nicholas, waged a duel about a certain piece of land, concerning which a dispute had arisen between them ; and they fought from the first to the ninth hour, each conquering by turns. Then one of them fleeing from the other till he came to a certain little pit, as he stood on the brink of the pit, and was about to fall therein, his kinsman said to him ' Take care of the pit, turn back lest thou shouldest fall into it.' Thereat so much clamour and noise was made by the bystanders and those who were sitting around, that the Earl heard these clamours as far off as the castle, and he inquired of some how it was there was such a clamour, and answer was made to him that two kinsmen were fighting about a certain piece of ground, and that one had fled till he reached a certain little pit, and that as he stood over the pit and was about to fall into it the other warned him. Then the townsmen being moved with pity made a covenant with the Earl that they should give him threepence yearly for each house in the High Street that had a gable, on condition that he should grant to them that the twenty-four jurors who were in Leicester from ancient times should from that time forward discuss and decide all pleas they might have among themselves." For the most part the liberties of our towns were bought in this way, by sheer hard bargaining. The earliest English charters, save that of London, date from the years when the treasury of Henry the First was drained by his Norman wars ; and grants of municipal liberty made professedly by the Angevins are probably the result of their costly employment of mercenary troops. At the close, however, of the thirteenth century, this struggle for emancipation was nearly over. The larger towns had secured the administration of justice in their own borough-courts, the privilege of self-government, and the control of their own trade, and their liberties and charters served as models and incentives to the smaller communities which were struggling into life.

The Frith-Gilds

During the progress of this outer revolution, the inner life of the English town was in the same quiet and hardly conscious way developing itself from the common form of the life around it into a form especially its own. Within as without the ditch or stockade which formed the earliest boundary of the borough, land was from the first the test of freedom, and the possession of land was what constituted the townsman. We may take, perhaps, a foreign instance to illustrate this fundamental point in our municipal history. When Duke Berthold of Zahringen resolved to found Freiburg, his " free town," in the Brisgau, the mode he adopted was to gather a group of traders together, and to give each man a plot of ground for his freehold round what was destined to be the market-place of the new community. In England the landless man who dwelled in a borough had no share in its corporate life ; for purposes of government or property the town was simply an association of the landed proprietors within its bounds ; nor was there anything in this association, as it originally existed, which could be considered peculiar or exceptional. The constitution of the English town, however different its form may have afterwards become, was at first simply that of the people at large. We have seen that among the German races society rested on the basis of the family, that it was the family who fought and settled side by side, and the kinsfolk who were bound together in ties of mutual responsibility to each other and to the law. As society became more complex and less stationary it necessarily outgrew these simple ties of blood, and in England this dissolution of the family bond seems to have taken place at the very time when Danish incursions and the growth of a feudal temper among the nobles rendered an isolated existence most perilous for the freeman. His only resource was to seek protection among his fellow-freemen, and to replace the older brotherhood of the kinsfolk by a voluntary association of his neighbours for the same purposes of order and self-defence. The tendency to unite in such 'frith-gilds' or peace-clubs became general throughout Europe during the ninth and tenth centuries, but on the Continent it was roughly met and repressed. The successors of Charles the Great enacted penalties of scourging, nose-slitting, and banishment against voluntary unions, and even a league of the poor peasants of Gaul against the inroads of the northmen was suppressed by the swords of the Frankish nobles. In England the attitude of the Kings was utterly different. The system known at a later time as 'frank-pledge,' or free engagement of neighbour for neighbour, was accepted after the Danish wars as the base of social order. Ælfred recognized the common responsibility of the members of the 'frith-gild' side by side with that of the kinsfolk, and Æthelstan accepted 'frith-gilds' as a constituent element of borough life in the Dooms of London.

The frith-gild, then, in the earlier English town, was precisely similar to the frith-gilds which formed the basis of social order in the country at large. An oath of mutual fidelity among its members was substituted for the tie of blood, while the gild-feast, held once a month in the common hall, replaced the gathering of the kinsfolk round their family hearth. But within this new family the aim of the frith-gild was to establish a mutual responsibility as close as that of the old. "Let all share the same lot," ran its law; "if any misdo, let all bear it." A member could look for aid from his gild-brothers in atoning for any guilt incurred by mishap. He could call on them for assistance in case of violence or wrong: if falsely accused, they appeared in court as his compurgators; if poor they supported, and when dead they buried him. On the other hand, he was responsible to them, as they were to the State, for order and obedience to the laws. A wrong of brother against brother was also a wrong against the general body of the gild, and was punished by fine, or in the last resort by expulsion, which left the offender a 'lawless' man and an outcast. The one difference between these gilds in country and town was, that in the latter case, from their close local neighbourhood, they tended inevitably to coalesce. Under Æthelstan the London gilds united into one for the purpose of carrying out more effectually their common aims, and at a later time we find the gilds of Berwick enacting "that where many bodies are found side by side in one place they may become one, and have one will, and in the dealings of one with another have a strong and hearty love." The process was probably a long and difficult one, for the brotherhoods naturally differed much in social rank, and even after the union was effected we see traces of the separate existence to a certain extent of some one or more of the wealthier or more aristocratic gilds. In London, for instance, the Cnihten-gild, which seems to have stood at the head of its fellows, retained for a long time its separate property, while its Alderman—as the chief officer of each gild was called— became the Alderman of the united gild of the whole city. In Canterbury we find a similar gild of thegns, from which the chief officers of the town seem commonly to have been selected. Imperfect, however, as the union might be, when once it was effected the town passed from a mere collection of brotherhoods into a powerful and organized com-

munity, whose character was inevitably determined by the circumstances of its origin. In their beginnings our boroughs seem to have
been mainly gatherings of persons engaged in agricultural pursuits ;
the first Dooms of London provide especially for the recovery of cattle
belonging to the citizens. But as the increasing security of the country
invited the farmer or the squire to settle apart in his own fields, and
the growth of estate and trade told on the towns themselves, the
difference between town and country became more sharply defined.
London, of course, took the lead in this new developement of civic life.
Even in Æthelstan's day every London merchant who had made three
long voyages on his own account ranked as a thegn. Its 'lithsmen,'
or shipmen's-gild, were of sufficient importance under Harthacnut to
figure in the election of a king, and its principal street still tells of the
rapid growth of trade, in the name of ' Cheap-side,' or the bargaining
place. But at the Norman Conquest the commercial tendency had
become universal. The name given to the united brotherhood is in
almost every case no longer that of the 'town-gild,' but of the
' merchant-gild.'

This social change in the character of the townsmen produced
important results in the character of their municipal institutions.
In becoming a merchant-gild the body of citizens who formed the
' town' enlarged their powers of civic legislation by applying them to the
control of their internal trade. It became their special business to obtain
from the Crown, or from their lords, wider commercial privileges, rights
of coinage, grants of fairs, and exemption from tolls ; while within the
town itself they framed regulations as to the sale and quality of goods,
the control of markets, and the recovery of debts. A yet more important
result sprang from the increase of population which the growth of
wealth and industry brought with it. The mass of the new settlers, composed as they were of escaped serfs, of traders without landed holdings,
of families who had lost their original lot in the borough, and generally
of the artisans and the poor, had no part in the actual life of the town.
The right of trade and of the regulation of trade, in common with all
other forms of jurisdiction, lay wholly in the hands of the landed
burghers whom we have described. By a natural process, too, their
superiority in wealth produced a fresh division between the ' burghers ' of
the merchant-gild and the unenfranchised mass around them. The same
change which severed at Florence the seven Greater Arts, or trades,
from the fourteen Lesser Arts, and which raised the three occupations
of banking, the manufacture and the dyeing of cloth, to a position of
superiority even within the privileged circle of the seven, told, though
with less force, on the English boroughs. The burghers of the merchant-
gild gradually concentrated themselves on the greater operations of
commerce, on trades which required a larger capital, while the meaner
employments of general traffic were abandoned to their poorer neigh-

bours. This advance in the division of labour is marked by such
severances as we note in the thirteenth century of the cloth merchant
from the tailor, or the leather merchant from the butcher. But the
result of this severance was all-important in its influence on the constitution of our towns. The members of the trades thus abandoned by
the wealthier burghers formed themselves into Craft-gilds, which soon
rose into dangerous rivalry with the original Merchant-gild of the town.
A seven years' apprenticeship formed the necessary prelude to full
membership of any trade-gild. Their regulations were of the minutest
character ; the quality and value of work was rigidly prescribed, the
hours of toil fixed "from day-break to curfew," and strict provision
made against competition in labour. At each meeting of these gilds
their members gathered round the Craft-box, which contained the
rules of their Society, and stood with bared heads as it was opened.
The warden and a quorum of gild-brothers formed a court which
enforced the ordinances of the gild, inspected all work done by its
members, confiscated unlawful tools or unworthy goods ; and disobedience to their orders was punished by fines, or in the last resort
by expulsion, which involved the loss of right to trade. A common
fund was raised by contributions among the members, which not only
provided for the trade objects of the gild, but sufficed to found
chantries and masses, and set up painted windows in the church of
their patron saint. Even at the present day the arms of the craft-gild
may often be seen blazoned in cathedrals side by side with those of
prelates and of kings. But it was only by slow degrees that they rose
to such a height as this. The first steps in their existence were the
most difficult, for to enable a trade-gild to carry out its objects with
any success, it was first necessary that the whole body of craftsmen
belonging to the trade should be compelled to belong to it, and
secondly, that a legal control over the trade itself should be secured
to it. A royal charter was indispensable for these purposes, and over
the grant of these charters took place the first struggle with the
merchant gild, which had till then solely exercised jurisdiction over
trade within the boroughs. The weavers, who were the first trade-
gild to secure royal sanction in the reign of Henry the First, were still
engaged in the contest for existence as late as the reign of John, when
the citizens of London bought for a time the suppression of their
gild. Even under the house of Lancaster, Exeter was engaged in
resisting the establishment of a tailors' gild. From the eleventh
century, however, the spread of these societies went steadily on,
and the control of trade passed from the merchant-gilds to the
craft-gilds.

It is this struggle, to use the technical terms of the time, of the
"greater folk" against the "lesser folk," or of the "commune," the
general mass of the inhabitants, against the "prudhommes," or "wiser"

few, which brought about, as it passed from the regulation of trade to the general government of the town, the great civic revolution of the thirteenth and fourteenth centuries. On the Continent, and especially along the Rhine, the struggle was as fierce as the supremacy of the older burghers had been complete. In Köln the craftsmen had been reduced to all but serfage, and the merchant of Brussels might box at his will the ears of "the man without heart or honour who lives by his toil." Such social tyranny of class over class brought a century of bloodshed to the cities of Germany; but in England the tyranny of class over class had been restrained by the general tenor of the law, and the revolution took for the most part a milder form. The longest and bitterest strife of all was naturally at London. Nowhere had the territorial constitution struck root so deeply, and nowhere had the landed oligarchy risen to such a height of wealth and influence. The city was divided into wards, each of which was governed by an alderman drawn from the ruling class. In some, indeed, the office seems to have become hereditary. The "magnates," or "barons," of the merchant-gild advised alone on all matters of civic government or trade regulation, and distributed or assessed at their will the revenues or burthens of the town. Such a position afforded an opening for corruption and oppression of the most galling kind; and it seems to have been the general impression of the unfair assessment levied on the poor, and the undue burthens which were thrown on the unenfranchised

1196   classes, which provoked the first serious discontent. William of the Long Beard, himself one of tne governing body, placed himself at the head of a conspiracy which numbered, in the terrified fancy of the burghers, fifty thousand of the craftsmen. His eloquence, his bold defiance of the aldermen in the town-mote, gained him at any rate a wide popularity, and the crowds who surrounded him hailed him as "the saviour of the poor." One of his addresses is luckily preserved to us by a hearer of the time. In mediæval fashion he began with a text from the Vulgate, "Ye shall draw water with joy from the fountain of the Saviour." "I," he began, "am the saviour of the poor. Ye poor men who have felt the weight of rich men's hands, draw from my fountain waters of wholesome instruction and that with joy, for the time of your visitation is at hand. For I will divide the waters from the waters. It is the people who are the waters, and I will divide the lowly and faithful folk from the proud and faithless folk; I will part the chosen from the reprobate as light from darkness." But it was in vain that by appeals to the King he strove to win royal favour for the popular cause. The support of the moneyed classes was essential to Richard in the costly wars with Philip of France, and the Justiciar, Archbishop Hubert, after a moment of hesitation, issued orders for his arrest. William felled with an axe the first soldier who advanced to seize him, and taking refuge with a few followers in the tower of St. Mary-le-

Bow, summoned his adherents to rise. Hubert, however, who had already flooded the city with troops, with bold contempt of the right of sanctuary, set fire to the tower and forced William to surrender. A burgher's son, whose father he had slain, stabbed him as he came forth, and with his death the quarrel slumbered for more than fifty years.

No further movement, in fact, took place till the outbreak of the Barons' war, but the city had all through the interval been seething with discontent ; the unenfranchised craftsmen, under pretext of preserving the peace, had united in secret frith-gilds of their own, and mobs rose from time to time to sack the houses of foreigners and the wealthier burghers. But it was not till the civil war began that the open contest recommenced. The craftsmen forced their way into the town-mote, and setting aside the opinion of the magnates, chose Thomas Fitz-Thomas for their mayor. Although dissension still raged during the reign of the second Edward, we may regard this election as marking the final victory of the craft-gilds. Under his successor all contest seems to have ceased : charters had been granted to every trade, their ordinances formally recognized and enrolled in the mayor's court, and distinctive liveries assumed to which they owed the name of "Livery Companies" which they still retain. The wealthier citizens, who found their old power broken, regained influence by enrolling themselves as members of the trade-gilds, and Edward the Third himself humoured the current of civic feeling by becoming a member of the gild of Armourers. This event marks the time when the government of our towns had become more really popular than it ever again became till the Municipal Reform Act of our own days. It had passed from the hands of an oligarchy into those of the middle classes, and there was nothing as yet to foretell the reactionary revolution by which the trade-gilds themselves became an oligarchy as narrow as that which they had deposed.

Section V.—The King and the Baronage, 1290—1327.

[*Authorities.*—For Edward I. as before. For Edward II. we have three important contemporaries : on the King's side, Thomas de la More (in Camden, "Anglica, Brittanica, etc.") ; on that of the Barons, Trokelowe's Annals (published by the Master of the Rolls), and the Life by a monk of Malmesbury, printed by Hearne. The short Chronicle by Murimuth is also contemporary in date. Hallam ("Middle Ages") has illustrated the constitutional aspect of the time.]

If we turn again to the constitutional history of England from the accession of Edward the First we find a progress not less real but chequered with darker vicissitudes than the progress of our towns. A great transfer of power had been brought about by the long struggle

SEC. V.

THE KING
AND THE
BARONAGE
1290
TO
1327

for the Charter, by the reforms of Earl Simon, and by the earlier legislation of Edward himself. His conception of kingship indeed was that of a just and religious Henry the Second, but his England was as different from the England of Henry as the Parliament of the one was different from the Great Council of the other. In the rough rimes of Robert of Gloucester we read the simple political creed of the people at large.

> " When the land through God's grace to good peace was brought
>   For to have the old laws the high men turned their thought :
>   For to have, as we said erst, the good old Law,
>   The King made his charter and granted it with sawe."

But the power which the Charter had wrested from the Crown fell not to the people but to the Baronage. The farmer and the artisan, though they could fight in some great crisis for freedom, had as yet no wish to interfere in the common task of government. The vast industrial change in both town and country, which had begun during the reign of Henry the Third, and which continued with increasing force during that of his son, absorbed the energy and attention of the trading classes. In agriculture, the inclosure of common lands and the intro- duction of the system of leases on the part of the great proprietors, coupled with the subdivision of estates which was facilitated by Edward's legislation, was gradually creating out of the masses of rural bondsmen a new class of tenant farmers, whose whole energy was absorbed in their own great rise to social freedom. The very causes which rendered the growth of municipal liberty so difficult, increased the wealth of the towns. To the trade with Norway and the Hanse towns of North Germany, the wool-trade with Flanders, and the wine trade with Gascony, was now added a fast increasing commerce with Italy and Spain. The great Venetian merchant galleys appeared on the English coast, Florentine traders settled in the southern ports, the bankers of Florence and Lucca followed those of Cahors, who had already dealt a death-blow to the usury of the Jews. But the wealth and industrial energy of the country was shown, not only in the rise of a capitalist class, but in a crowd of civil and ecclesiastical buildings which distinguished this period. Christian architecture reached its highest beauty in the opening of Edward's reign, a period marked by the completion of the abbey church of Westminster and the exquisite cathedral church at Salisbury. An English noble was proud to be styled " an incomparable builder," while some traces of the art which was rising across the Alps perhaps flowed in with the Italian ecclesi- astics whom the Papacy was forcing on the English Church. In the abbey of Westminster the shrine of the Confessor, the mosaic pave- ment, and the paintings on the walls of minster and chapter-house, remind us of the schools which were springing up under Giotto and the Pisans.

But even had this industrial distraction been wanting the trading classes had no mind to claim any direct part in the actual work of government. It was a wor . which, in default of the Crown, fell naturally, according to the ideas of the time, to the Baronage. Constitutionally the position of the English nobles had now become established. A King could no longer make laws or levy taxes or even make war without their assent. And in the Baronage the nation reposed an unwavering trust. The nobles of England were no more the brutal foreigners from whose violence the strong hand of a Norman ruler had been needed to protect his subjects ; they were as English as the peasant or the trader. They had won English liberty by their swords, and the tradition of their order bound them to look on themselves as its natural guardians. At the close of the Barons' war, the problem which had so long troubled the realm, the problem of how to ensure its government in accordance with the Charter, was solved by the transfer of the business of administration into the hands of a standing committee of the greater prelates and barons, acting as chief officers of state in conjunction with specially appointed ministers of the Crown. The body thus composed was known as the Continual Council ; and the quiet government of the kingdom by the Council in the long interval between the death of Henry the Third and his son's return shows how effective this rule of the nobles was. It is significant of the new relation which they were to strive to establish between themselves and the Crown that in the brief which announced Edward's accession the Council asserted that the new monarch mounted his throne " by the will of the peers." The very form indeed of the new Parliament, in which the barons were backed by the knights of the shire, elected for the most part under their influence, and by the representatives of the towns, still true to the traditions of the Barons' war ; the increased frequency of these Parliamentary assemblies which gave opportunity for counsel, for party organization, and a distinct political base of action ; above all, the new financial power which their control over taxation enabled them to exert on the throne, ultimately placed the rule of the nobles on a basis too strong to be shaken by the utmost efforts of even Edward himself.

From the first the King struggled fruitlessly against this overpowering influence ; and his sympathies must have been stirred by the revolution on the other side of the Channel, where the French kings were crushing the power of the feudal baronage, and erecting a royal despotism on its ruins. Edward watched jealously over the ground which the Crown had already gained against the nobles. Following the policy of Henry II., at the very outset of his reign he instituted a commission of enquiry into the judicial franchises still existing, and on its report itinerant justices were sent to discover by what right these franchises were held. The writs of " quo warranto " were

SEC. V.

THE KING
AND THE
BARONAGE

1290
TO
1327

The
Baronage
and its
rule

SEC. V.

THE KING
AND THE
BARONAGE
1290
TO
1327

1278

1286–1289

roughly met here and there. Earl Warenne bared a rusty sword, and flung it on the justices' table. " This, sirs," he said, " is my warrant. By the sword our fathers won their lands when they came over with the Conqueror, and by the sword we will keep them." But the King was far from limiting himself to the plans of Henry II.; he aimed further at neutralizing the power of the nobles by raising the whole body of landowners to the same level ; and a royal writ ordered all freeholders who held land of the value of twenty pounds to receive knighthood at the King's hands. While the political influence of the baronage as a leading element in the nation mounted, in fact, the personal and purely feudal power of each individual on his estates as steadily fell. The hold which the Crown had gained on every noble family by its rights of wardship and marriage, the circuits of the royal judges, the ever narrowing bounds within which baronial justice was circumscribed, the blow dealt by scutage at their military power, the prompt intervention of the Council in their feuds, lowered the nobles more and more to the level of their fellow subjects. Much yet remained to be done. Different as the English baronage, taken as a whole, was from a feudal *noblesse* like that of Germany or France, there is in every military class a natural drift towards violence and lawlessness, which even the stern justice of Edward found it difficult to repress. Throughout his reign his strong hand was needed to enforce order on warring nobles. Great earls, such as those of Gloucester and Hereford, carried on private war ; in Shropshire the Earl of Arundel waged his feud with Fulk Fitz Warine. To the lesser and poorer nobles the wealth of the trader, the long wain of goods as it passed along the highway, was a tempting prey. Once, under cover of a mock tournament of monks against canons, a band of country gentlemen succeeded in introducing themselves into the great merchant fair at Boston ; at nightfall every booth was on fire, the merchants robbed and slaughtered, and the booty carried off to ships which lay ready at the quay. Streams of gold and silver, ran the tale of popular horror, flowed melted down the gutters to the sea ; " all the money in England could hardly make good the loss." Even at the close of Edward's reign lawless bands of " trail-bastons," or club-men, maintained themselves by general outrage, aided the country nobles in their feuds, and wrested money and goods by threats from the great tradesmen. The King was strong enough to fine and imprison the Earls, to hang the chief of the Boston marauders, and to suppress the outlaws by rigorous commissions. During Edward's absence of three years from the realm, the judges, who were themselves drawn from the lesser baronage, were charged with violence and corruption. After a careful investigation the judicial abuses were recognized and amended ; two of the chief justices were banished from the country, and their colleagues imprisoned and fined.

SEC. V.

THE KING
AND THE
BARONAGE

1290
TO
1327

Edward
and the
Jews

The next year saw a step which remains the great blot upon Edward's reign. Under the Angevins the popular hatred of the Jews had grown rapidly in intensity. But the royal protection had never wavered. Henry the Second had granted them the right of burial outside of every city where they dwelt. Richard had punished heavily a massacre of the Jews at York, and organized a mixed court of Jews and Christians for the registration of their contracts. John suffered none to plunder them save himself, though he once wrested from them a sum equal to a year's revenue of his realm. The troubles of the next reign brought in a harvest greater than even the royal greed could reap; the Jews grew wealthy enough to acquire estates, and only a burst of popular feeling prevented a legal decision which would have enabled them to own freeholds. Their pride and contempt of the superstitions around them broke out in the taunts they levelled at processions as they passed their Jewries, sometimes as at Oxford in actual attacks upon them. Wild stories floated about among the people of children carried off to Jewish houses, to be circumcised or crucified, and a boy of Lincoln who was found slain in a Jewish house was canonized by popular reverence as "St. Hugh." The first work of the Friars was to settle in the Hebrew quarters and attempt their conversion, but the tide of popular fury rose too fast for these gentler means of reconciliation. When the Franciscans saved seventy Jews from death by their prayers to Henry the Third the populace angrily refused the brethren alms. The sack of Jewry after Jewry was the sign of popular hatred during the Barons' war. With its close, fell on the Jews the more terrible persecution of the law. Statute after statute hemmed them in. They were forbidden to hold real property, to employ Christian servants, to move through the streets without the two white tablets of wool on their breasts which distinguished their race. They were prohibited from building new synagogues, or eating with Christians, or acting as physicians to them. Their trade, already crippled by the rivalry of the bankers of Cahors, was annihilated by a royal order, which bade them renounce usury under pain of death. At last persecution could do no more, and on the eve of his struggle with Scotland, Edward, eager at the moment to find supplies for his treasury, and himself swayed by the fanaticism of his subjects, bought the grant of a fifteenth from clergy and laity by consenting to drive the Jews from his realm. Of the sixteen thousand who preferred exile to apostasy few reached the shores of France. Many were wrecked, others robbed and flung overboard. One shipmaster turned out a crew of wealthy merchants on to a sandbank, and bade them call a new Moses to save them from the sea. From the time of Edward to that of Cromwell no Jew touched English ground.

No share in the enormities which accompanied the expulsion of the Jews can fall upon Edward, for he not only suffered the fugitives to

SEC. V.

THE KING
AND THE
BARONAGE

1290
TO
1327

take their wealth with them, but punished with the halter those who plundered them at sea. But the expulsion was none the less cruel, and the grant of a fifteenth made by the grateful Parliament proved but a poor substitute for the loss which the royal treasury had sustained. The Scotch war more than exhausted the aids granted by the Parliament. The treasury was utterly drained ; the costly fight with the French in Gascony called for supplies, while the King was planning a yet costlier attack on northern France with the aid of Flanders. It was sheer want which drove Edward to tyrannous extortion. His first

1294   blow fell on the Church ; he had already demanded half their annual income from the clergy, and so terrible was his wrath at their resistance, that the Dean of St. Paul's, who had stood forth to remonstrate, dropped dead of sheer terror at his feet. " If any oppose the King's demand," said a royal envoy, in the midst of the Convocation, " let him stand up that he may be noted as an enemy to the King's peace." The outraged churchmen fell back on an untenable plea that their aid was due solely to Rome, and pleaded a bull of exemption, issued by Pope Boniface VIII., as a ground for refusing to comply with further taxation. Edward met their refusal by a general outlawry of the whole

1297   order. The King's courts were closed, and all justice denied to those who refused the King aid. By their actual plea the clergy had put themselves formally in the wrong, and the outlawry soon forced them to submission, but their aid did little to recruit the exhausted treasury, while the pressure of the war steadily increased. Far wider measures of arbitrary taxation were needful to equip an expedition which Edward prepared to lead in person to Flanders. The country gentlemen were compelled to take up knighthood, or to compound for exemption from the burthensome honour. Forced contributions of cattle and corn were demanded from the counties, and the export duty on wool—now the staple produce of the country—was raised to six times its former amount. Though he infringed no positive charter or statute, the work of the Great Charter and the Barons' war seemed suddenly to have been undone. But the blow had no sooner been struck than Edward found himself powerless within his realm. The baronage roused itself to resistance, and the two greatest of the English nobles,

1297   Bohun, Earl of Hereford, and Bigod, Earl of Norfolk, placed themselves at the head of the opposition. Their protest against the war and the financial measures by which it was carried on, took the practical form of a refusal to lead a force to Gascony as Edward's lieutenants, while he himself sailed for Flanders. They availed themselves of the plea that they were not bound to foreign service save in attendance on the King. " By God, Sir Earl," swore the King to Bigod, " you shall either go or hang ! " " By God, Sir King," was the cool reply, " I will neither go nor hang ! " Ere the Parliament he had convened could meet, Edward had discovered his own powerlessness, and, with one of those sudden revulsions of feeling of which his nature was capable, he stood before his people in Westminster Hall and owned, with a burst of tears, that he had taken their substance without due warrant of law. His passionate appeal to their loyalty wrested a reluctant assent to the prosecution of the war, but the crisis had taught the need of further securities against the royal power. While Edward was still struggling in Flanders, the Primate, Winchelsey, joined the two Earls and the citizens of London in forbidding any further levy of supplies till Edward at Ghent solemnly confirmed the Charter with the new clauses added to it prohibiting the King from raising taxes save by general consent of the realm. At the demand of the barons he renewed the Confirmation in 1299, when his attempt to add an evasive clause saving the rights of the Crown proved the justice of their distrust. Two years later a fresh gathering of the barons in arms wrested from him the full execution of the Charter of Forests. The bitterness of his humiliation preyed on him; he evaded his pledge to levy no new taxes on merchandize by the sale to merchants of certain privileges of trading; and a formal absolution from his promises which he obtained from the Pope showed his intention of re-opening the questions he had yielded. His hand was stayed, however, by the fatal struggle with Scotland which revived in the rising of Robert Bruce, and the King's death bequeathed the contest to his worthless son.

Worthless, however, as Edward the Second morally might be, he was far from being destitute of the intellectual power which seemed hereditary in the Plantagenets. It was his settled purpose to fling off the yoke of the baronage, and the means by which he designed accomplishing his purpose was the choice of a minister wholly dependent on the Crown. We have already noticed the change by which the "clerks of the king's chapel," who had been the ministers of arbitrary government under the Normans and Angevins, had been quietly superseded by the prelates and lords of the Continual Council. At the close of his father's reign, a direct demand on the part of the Barons to nominate the great officers of state had been curtly rejected; but the royal choice had been practically limited in the selection of its ministers to the class of prelates and nobles, and, however closely connected with royalty, such officers always to a great extent shared the feelings and opinions of their order. It seems to have been the aim of the young King to undo the change which had been silently brought about, and to imitate the policy of the contemporary sovereigns of France by choosing as his ministers men of an inferior position, wholly dependent on the Crown for their power, and representatives of nothing but the policy and interests of their master. Piers Gaveston, a foreigner sprung from a family of Guienne, had been his friend and companion during his father's reign, at the close of which he had been banished from the realm for his share in intrigues which had divided

SEC. V.

THE KING
AND THE
BARONAGE

1290
TO
1327

1297

1301

1305

1307

Edward
the
Second
1307–1327

SEC. V.

THE KING
AND THE
BARONAGE
1290
TO
1327
1307

Edward from his son.   At the new King's accession he was at once recalled, created Earl of Cornwall, and placed at the head of the administration.   Gay, genial, thriftless, Gaveston showed in his first acts the quickness and audacity of Southern Gaul; the older ministers were dismissed, all claims of precedence or inheritance set aside in the distribution of offices at the coronation, while taunts and defiances goaded the proud baronage to fury.   The favourite was a fine soldier, and his lance unhorsed his opponents in tourney after tourney.   His reckless wit flung nicknames about the Court ; the Earl of Lancaster was "the Actor," Pembroke "the Jew," Warwick "the Black Dog." But taunt and defiance broke helplessly against the iron mass of the

baronage.   After a few months of power the demand of the Parliament for his dismissal could not be resisted, and he was formally banished from the realm.   In the following year it was only by conceding the rights which his father had sought to establish of imposing import

duties on the merchants by their own assent, that Edward procured a subsidy for the Scotch war.   The firmness of the baronage sprang from their having found a head in the Earl of Lancaster, son of Edmund Crouchback.   His weight proved irresistible.   When Edward at the close of the Parliament recalled Gaveston, Lancaster withdrew from the royal Council, and a Parliament which met in 1310 resolved that the affairs of the realm should be entrusted for a year to a body of twenty-one " Ordainers."

A formidable list of " Ordinances " drawn up by the twenty-one met Edward on his return from a fruitless warfare with the Scots. By this long and important statute Gaveston was banished, other advisers were driven from the Council, and the Florentine bankers whose loans had enabled Edward to hold the baronage at bay sent out of the realm.   The customs duties imposed by Edward the First were declared to be illegal.   Parliaments were to be called every year, and in these assemblies the King's servants were to be brought, if need were, to justice.   The great officers of state were to be appointed with the counsel and consent of the baronage, and to be sworn in Parliament. The same consent of the barons in Parliament was to be needful ere the King could declare war or absent himself from the realm.   As the Ordinances show, the baronage still looked on Parliament rather as a political organization of the nobles than as a gathering of the three Estates of the realm.   The lower clergy pass unnoticed ; the Commons are regarded as mere tax-payers whose part was still confined to the presentation of petitions of grievances and the grant of money.   But even in this imperfect fashion the Parliament was a real representation of the country, and Edward was forced to assent to the Ordinances after a long and obstinate struggle.   The exile of Gaveston was the sign of the barons' triumph ; his recall a few months later renewed a strife which was only ended by his capture in Scarborough.   The

Sec. V.

The King
and the
Baronage
1290
to
1327

"Black Dog" of Warwick had sworn that the favourite should feel his teeth ; and Gaveston, who flung himself in vain at the feet of the Earl of Lancaster, praying for pity "from his gentle lord," was beheaded in defiance of the terms of his capitulation on Blacklow Hill. The King's burst of grief was as fruitless as his threats of vengeance ; a feigned submission of the conquerors completed the royal humiliation, and the barons knelt before Edward in Westminster Hall to receive a pardon which seemed the deathblow of the royal power. But if Edward was powerless to conquer the baronage he could still, by evading the observance of the Ordinances, throw the whole realm into confusion. The six years that follow Gaveston's death are among the darkest in our history. A terrible succession of famines intensified the suffering which sprang from the utter absence of all rule during the dissension between the barons and the King. The overthrow of Bannockburn, and the ravages of the Scots in the North, brought shame on England such as it had never known. At last the capture of Berwick by Robert Bruce forced Edward to give way, the Ordinances were formally accepted, an amnesty granted, and a small number of peers belonging to the Barons' party added to the great officers of state.

The Earl of Lancaster, by the union of the four earldoms of Lincoln, Leicester, Derby, and Lancaster, as well as by his royal blood (for like the King he was a grandson of Henry the Third), stood at the head of the English baronage, and the issue of the long struggle with Edward raised him for the moment to supreme power in the realm. But his character seems to have fallen far beneath the greatness of his position. Incapable of governing, he could do little but regard with jealousy the new advisers on whom the King now leaned, the older and the younger Hugh Le Despenser. The rise of the younger, on whom the King bestowed the county of Glamorgan with the hand of its heiress, was rapid enough to excite general jealousy, and Lancaster found little difficulty in extorting by force of arms his exile from the kingdom. But the tide of popular sympathy, already wavering, was turned to the royal cause by an insult offered to the Queen, against whom Lady Badlesmere had closed the doors of Ledes Castle, and the unexpected energy shown by Edward in avenging the insult gave fresh strength to his cause. He found himself strong enough to recall Despenser, and when Lancaster convoked the baronage to force him again into exile, the weakness of their party was shown by the treasonable negotiations into which the Earl entered with the Scots, and by his precipitate retreat to the north on the advance of the royal army. At Boroughbridge his forces were arrested and dispersed, and the Earl himself, brought captive before Edward at Pontefract, was tried and condemned to death as a traitor. "Have mercy on me, King of Heaven," cried Lancaster, as mounted on a grey pony without a bridle he was hurried to execution, "for my earthly King has

Sec. V.
The King
and the
Baronage
1290
to
1327

forsaken me." His death was followed by that of a number of his adherents and by the captivity of others; while a Parliament at York annulled the proceedings against the Despensers, and repealed the Ordinances. It is to this Parliament however, and perhaps to the victorious confidence of the royalists, that we owe the famous provision which reveals the policy of the Despensers, the provision that all laws concerning " the estate of the Crown, or of the realm and people, shall be treated, accorded, and established in Parliaments by our Lord the King and by the consent of the prelates, earls, barons, and commonalty of the realm, according as hath been hitherto accustomed." It would seem from the tenor of this remarkable enactment that much of the sudden revulsion of popular feeling had been owing to the assumption of all legislative action by the baronage alone. But the arrogance of the Despensers, the utter failure of a fresh campaign against Scotland, and the humiliating truce for thirteen years which Edward was forced to conclude with Robert Bruce, soon robbed the Crown of its temporary popularity, and led the way to the sudden catastrophe which closed this disastrous reign. It had been arranged that the Queen, a sister of the King of France, should re-visit her home to conclude a treaty between the two countries, whose quarrel was again verging upon war; and her son, a boy of twelve years old, followed her to do homage in his father's stead for the duchies of Gascony and Aquitaine. Neither threats nor prayers, however, could induce either wife or child to return to his court; and the Queen's connexion with a secret conspiracy of the baronage was revealed when the primate and nobles hurried to her standard on her landing at Orwell. Deserted by all, and repulsed by the citizens of London whose aid he implored, the King fled hastily to the west and embarked with the Despensers for Lundy Isle; but contrary winds flung the fugitives again on the Welsh coast, where they fell into the hands of the new Earl of Lancaster. The younger Despenser was at once hanged on a gibbet fifty feet high, and the King placed in ward at Kenilworth till his fate could be decided by a Parliament summoned for that purpose at Westminster. The Peers who assembled fearlessly revived the constitutional usage of the earlier English freedom, and asserted their right to depose a king who had proved himself unworthy to rule. Not a voice was raised in Edward's behalf, and only four prelates protested when the young Prince was proclaimed King by acclamation, and presented as their sovereign to the multitudes without. The revolution soon took legal form in a bill which charged the captive monarch with indolence, incapacity, the loss of Scotland, the violation of his coronation oath, and oppression of the Church and baronage; and on the approval of this it was resolved that the reign of Edward of Caernarvon had ceased and that the crown had passed to his son, Edward of Windsor.

A deputation of the Parliament proceeded to Kenilworth to procure the assent of the discrowned King to his own deposition, and Edward, "clad in a plain black gown," submitted quietly to his fate. Sir William Trussel at once addressed him in words which better than any other mark the true nature of the step which the Parliament had taken. "I, William Trussel, proctor of the earls, barons, and others, having for this full and sufficient power, do render and give back to you, Edward, once King of England, the homage and fealty of the persons named in my procuracy; and acquit and discharge them thereof in the best manner that law and custom will give. And I now make protestation in their name that they will no longer be in your fealty and allegiance, nor claim to hold anything of you as king, but will account you hereafter as a private person, without any manner of royal dignity." A significant act followed these emphatic words. Sir Thomas Blount, the steward of the household, broke his staff of office, a ceremony only used at a king's death, and declared that all persons engaged in the royal service were discharged. In the following September the King was murdered in Berkeley Castle.

Section VI.—The Scotch War of Independence, 1306—1342.

[*Authorities.*—Mainly the contemporary English Chroniclers and state documents for the reigns of the three Edwards. John Barbour's "Bruce," the great legendary storehouse for his hero's adventures, is historically worthless. Mr. Burton's is throughout the best modern account of the time.]

To obtain a clear view of the constitutional struggle between the kings and the baronage, we have deferred to its close an account of the great contest which raged throughout the whole period in the north.

With the Convocation of Perth the conquest and settlement of Scotland seemed complete. Edward I., in fact, was preparing for a joint Parliament of the two nations at Carlisle, when the conquered country suddenly sprang again to arms under Robert Bruce, the grandson of one of the original claimants of the crown. The Norman house of Bruce formed a part of the Yorkshire baronage, but it had acquired through intermarriages the Earldom of Carrick and the Lordship of Annandale. Both the claimant and his son had been pretty steadily on the English side in the contest with Balliol and Wallace, and Robert had himself been trained in the English court, and stood high in the King's favour. But the withdrawal of Balliol gave a new force to his claims upon the crown, and the discovery of an intrigue which he had set on foot with the Bishop of St. Andrews so roused Edward's jealousy that Bruce fled for his life across the border. In the church of the Grey Friars at Dumfries he met Comyn, the Lord of Badenoch, to whose treachery he attributed the disclosure of

SEC. VI.

THE SCOTCH WAR OF INDEPENDENCE

1306 TO 1342

The Scotch Revolt

1305

1306

SEC. VI.

THE SCOTCH
WAR OF
INDEPEN-
DENCE
1306
TO
1342

his plans, and after the interchange of a few hot words struck him with his dagger to the ground. It was an outrage that admitted of no forgiveness, and Bruce for very safety was forced to assume the crown six weeks after in the Abbey of Scone. The news roused Scotland again to arms, and summoned Edward to a fresh contest with his unconquerable foe. But the murder of Comyn had changed the King's mood to a terrible pitilessness ; he threatened death against all concerned in the outrage, and exposed the Countess of Buchan, who had set the crown on Bruce's head, in a cage or open chamber built for the purpose in one of the towers of Berwick. At the solemn feast which celebrated his son's knighthood Edward vowed on the swan, which formed the chief dish at the banquet, to devote the rest of his days to exact vengeance from the murderer himself. But even at the moment of the vow, Bruce was already flying for his life to the western islands. " Henceforth," he had said to his wife at their coronation, " thou art queen of Scotland and I king." " I fear," replied Mary Bruce, " we are only playing at royalty, like children in their games." The play was soon turned into bitter earnest. A small English force under Aymer de Valence sufficed to rout the disorderly levies which gathered round the new monarch, and the flight of Bruce left his followers at Edward's mercy. Noble after noble was hurried to the block. The Earl of Athole pleaded kindred with royalty ; " His only privilege," burst forth the King, " shall be that of being hanged on a higher gallows than the rest." Knights and priests were strung up side by side by the English justiciars ; while the wife and daughter of Robert Bruce were flung into prison. Bruce himself had offered to capitulate to Prince Edward, but the offer only roused the old King to fury. " Who is so bold," he cried, " as to treat with our traitors without our knowledge ? " and rising from his sick-bed he led his army northwards to complete the conquest. But the hand of death was upon him, and in the very sight of Scotland the old man breathed his last at Burgh-upon-Sands.

The death of Edward arrested only for a moment the advance of his army to the north. The Earl of Pembroke led it across the border, and found himself master of the country without a blow. Bruce's career became that of a desperate adventurer, for even the Highland chiefs in whose fastnesses he found shelter were bitterly hostile to one who claimed to be King of their foes in the Lowlands. It was this adversity that transformed the murderer of Comyn into the noble leader of a nation's cause. Strong and of commanding presence, brave and genial in temper, Bruce bore the hardships of his career with a courage and hopefulness which never failed. In the legends which clustered round his name we see him listening in Highland glens to the bay of the bloodhounds on his track, or holding single-handed a pass against a crowd of savage clansmen. Sometimes the little band which clung to him were forced to support themselves by hunting or fishing, sometimes to break up for safety as their enemies tracked them to the lair. Bruce himself had more than once to fling off his shirt of mail and scramble barefoot for very life up the crags. Little by little, however, the dark sky cleared. The English pressure relaxed, as the struggle between Edward and his barons grew fiercer. James Douglas, the darling of Scotch story, was the first of the Lowland barons to rally again to the Bruce, and his daring gave heart to the King's cause. Once he surprised his own house, which had been given to an Englishman, ate the dinner which had been prepared for its new owner, slew his captives, and tossed their bodies on to a pile of wood gathered at the castle gate. Then he staved in the wine-vats that the wine might mingle with their blood, and set house and woodpile on fire. A terrible ferocity mingled with heroism in the work of freedom, but the revival of the country went steadily on. Bruce's "harrying of Buchan" after the defeat of its Earl, who had joined the English army, at last fairly turned the tide of success. Edinburgh, Roxburgh, Perth, and most of the Scotch fortresses fell one by one into King Robert's hands. The clergy met in council and owned him as their lawful lord. Gradually the Scotch barons who still held to the English cause were coerced into submission, and Bruce found himself strong enough to invest Stirling, the last and the most important of the Scotch fortresses which held out for Edward.

Stirling was in fact the key of Scotland, and its danger roused England out of its civil strife to a vast effort for the recovery of its prey. Thirty thousand horsemen formed the fighting part of the great army which followed Edward to the north, and a host of wild marauders had been summoned from Ireland and Wales to its support. The army which Bruce had gathered to oppose the inroad was formed almost wholly of footmen, and was stationed to the south of Stirling on a rising ground flanked by a little brook, the Bannock burn which gave its name to the engagement. Again two systems of warfare were brought face to face as they had been brought at Falkirk, for Robert, like Wallace, drew up his force in solid squares or circles of spearmen. The English were dispirited at the very outset by the failure of an attempt to relieve Stirling, and by the issue of a single combat between Bruce and Henry de Bohun, a knight who bore down upon him as he was riding peacefully along the front of his army. Robert was mounted on a small hackney and held only a light battle-axe in his hand, but, warding off his opponent's spear, he cleft his skull with so terrible a blow that the handle of the axe was shattered in his grasp. At the opening of the battle the English archers were thrown forward to rake the Scottish squares, but they were without support and were easily dispersed by a handful of horse whom Bruce had held in reserve for the purpose. The body of men-at-arms next flung themselves on

SEC. VI.

THE SCOTCH
WAR OF
INDEPEN-
DENCE

1306
TO
1342

1313

**Bannock
burn**
June 24,
1314

SEC. VI.

THE SCOTCH
WAR OF
INDEPEN-
DENCE

1306
TO
1342

the Scottish front, but their charge was embarrassed by the narrow
space along which the line was forced to move, and the steady resistance of the squares soon threw the knighthood into disorder. "The
horses that were stickit," says an exulting Scotch writer, "rushed and
reeled right rudely." In the moment of failure the sight of a body of
camp-followers, whom they mistook for reinforcements to the enemy,
spread panic through the English host. It broke in a headlong rout.
Its thousands of brilliant horsemen were soon floundering in pits
which had guarded the level ground to Bruce's left, or riding in wild
haste for the border. Few however were fortunate enough to reach it.
Edward himself, with a body of five hundred knights, succeeded in
escaping to Dunbar and the sea. But the flower of his knighthood fell
into the hands of the victors, while the Irishry and the footmen were
ruthlessly cut down by the country folk as they fled. For centuries
after, the rich plunder of the English camp left its traces on the
treasure and vestment rolls of castle and abbey throughout the
Lowlands.

Terrible as was the blow England could not humble herself to relinquish her claim on the Scottish crown. With equal pertinacity
Bruce refused all negotiation while the royal title was refused to him,
and steadily pushed on the recovery of his southern dominions.
Berwick was at last forced to surrender, and held against a desperate

attempt at its recapture; while barbarous forays of the borderers
under Douglas wasted Northumberland. Again the strife between the
Crown and the baronage was suspended to allow the march of a great

English army to the north; but Bruce declined an engagement till
the wasted Lowlands starved the invaders into a ruinous retreat. The

failure forced England to stoop to a truce for thirteen years, in the
negotiation of which Bruce was suffered to take the royal title. But
the truce ceased legally with Edward's deposition. Troops gathered
on either side, and Edward Balliol, a son of the former king John,
was solemnly received as a vassal-king of Scotland at the English
court. Robert was disabled by leprosy from taking the field in person,
but the insult roused him to hurl his marauders again over the border
under Douglas and Randolph. An eye-witness has painted for us the
Scotch army, as it appeared in this campaign: "It consisted of four
thousand men-at-arms, knights and esquires, well mounted, besides
twenty thousand men bold and hardy, armed after the manner of their
country, and mounted upon little hackneys that are never tied up or
dressed, but turned immediately after the day's march to pasture on
the heath or in the fields. . . . They bring no carriages with them on
account of the mountains they have to pass in Northumberland,
neither do they carry with them any provisions of bread and wine, for
their habits of sobriety are such in time of war that they will live for a
long time on flesh half-sodden without bread, and drink the river

water without wine. They have therefore no occasion for pots or pans, for they dress the flesh of the cattle in their skins after they have flayed them, and being sure to find plenty of them in the country which they invade, they carry none with them. Under the flaps of his saddle each man carries a broad piece of metal, behind him a little bag of oatmeal : when they have eaten too much of the sodden flesh and their stomach appears weak and empty, they set this plate over the fire, knead the meal with water, and when the plate is hot put a little of the paste upon it in a thin cake like a biscuit which they eat to warm their stomachs. It is therefore no wonder that they perform a longer day's march than other soldiers." Against such a foe the English troops who marched under their boy-king to protect the border were utterly helpless. At one time the army lost its way in the vast border waste ; at another all traces of the enemy had disappeared, and an offer of knighthood and a hundred marks was made to any who could tell where the Scots were encamped. But when found their position behind the Wear proved unassailable, and after a bold sally on the English camp Douglas foiled an attempt at intercepting him by a clever retreat. The English levies broke hopelessly up, and a fresh foray on Northumberland forced the English court to submit to peace. By the Treaty of Northampton the independence of Scotland was formally recognized, and Bruce acknowledged as its king.

The pride of England, however, had been too much aroused by the struggle to bear easily its defeat. The first result of the treaty was the overthrow of the government which concluded it, a result hastened by the pride of its head, Roger Mortimer, and by his exclusion of the rest of the nobles from all share in the administration of the realm. The first efforts to shake Roger's power were unsuccessful : a league headed by the Earl of Lancaster broke up without result ; and the King's uncle, the Earl of Kent, was actually brought to the block, before the young King himself interfered in the struggle. Entering the Council chamber in Nottingham Castle, with a force which he had introduced through a secret passage in the rock on which it stands, Edward arrested Mortimer with his own hands, hurried him to execution, and assumed the control of affairs. His first care was to restore good order throughout the country, which under the late government had fallen into ruin, and to free his hands by a peace with France for further enterprises in the North. Fortune indeed, seemed at last to have veered to the English side ; the death of Bruce only a year after the Treaty of Northampton left the Scottish throne to a child of but eight years old, and the internal difficulties of the realm broke out in civil strife. To the great barons on either side the border the late peace involved serious losses, for many of the Scotch houses held large estates in England, as many of the English lords held

SEC. VI.

THE SCOTCH
WAR OF
INDEPEN-
DENCE
1306
TO
1342

1328

Scotland
and
Edward
the Third

1330

SEC. VI.

THE SCOTCH
WAR OF
NDEPEN-
DENCE

1306
TO
1342

1332

large estates in Scotland ; and although the treaty had provided for their claims, they had in each case been practically set aside. It is this discontent of the barons at the new settlement which explains the sudden success of Edward Balliol in his snatch at the Scottish throne. In spite of King Edward's prohibition, he sailed from England at the head of a body of nobles who claimed estates in the north, landed on the shores of Fife, and, after repulsing with immense loss an army which attacked him near Perth, was crowned at Scone, while David Bruce fled helplessly to France. Edward had given no open aid to the enterprise, but the crisis tempted his ambition, and he demanded and obtained from Balliol an acknowledgement of the English suzerainty. The acknowledgement, however, was fatal to Balliol himself. He was at once driven from his realm, and Berwick, which he had agreed to surrender to Edward, was strongly garrisoned against an English attack. The town was soon besieged, but a Scotch army under the

regent Douglas, brother to the famous Sir James, advanced to its relief, and attacked a covering force, which was encamped on the strong position of Halidon Hill. The English bowmen, however, vindicated the fame they had first won at Falkirk, and were soon to crown in the victory of Crécy; and the Scotch only struggled through the marsh which covered the English front to be riddled with a storm of arrows, and to break in utter rout. The battle decided the fate of Berwick, and from that time the town remained the one part of Edward's conquests which was preserved by the English crown. Fragment as it was, it was always viewed legally as representing the realm of which it had once formed a part. As Scotland, it had its chancellor, chamberlain, and other officers of State ; and the peculiar heading of Acts of Parliament enacted for England "and the town of Berwick-upon-Tweed" still preserves the memory of its peculiar position. Balliol was restored to his throne by the conquerors, and his formal cession of the Lowlands to England rewarded their aid. During the next three years Edward persisted in the line of policy he had adopted, retaining his hold over Southern Scotland, and aiding his sub-king Balliol in campaign after campaign against the despairing efforts of the nobles who still adhered to the house of Bruce. His perseverance was all but crowned with success, when the outbreak of

war with France saved Scotland by drawing the strength of England across the Channel. The patriot party drew again together. Balliol

found himself at last without an adherent and withdrew to the Court of Edward, while David returned to his kingdom, and won back the

chief fastnesses of the Lowlands. The freedom of Scotland was, in fact, secured. From a war of conquest and patriotic resistance the struggle died into a petty strife between two angry neighbours, which became a mere episode in the larger contest between England and France.

FRANCE AT THE TREATY OF BRETIGNY

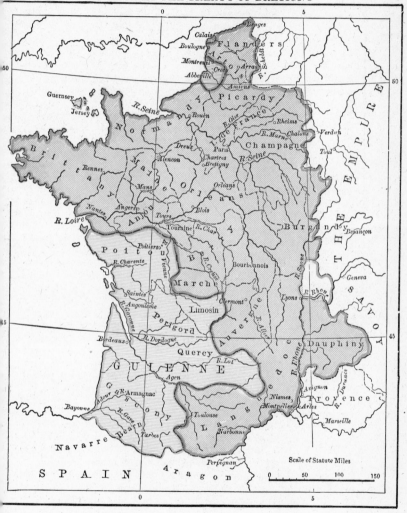

Scale of Statute Miles

CHAPTER V.

THE HUNDRED YEARS' WAR.

1336—1431.

Section I.—Edward the Third, 1336—1360.

[*Authorities.*—The concluding part of the chronicle of Walter of Heming-burgh or Hemingford seems to have been jotted down as news of the passing events reached its author ; it ends at the battle of Crécy. Hearne has pub-lished another contemporary account by Robert of Avesbury, which closes in 1356. A third account by Knyghton, a canon of Leicester, will be found in the collection of Twysden. At the end of this century and the beginning of the next the annals that had been carried on in the Abbey of St. Albans were thrown together by Walsingham in the " Historia Anglicana " which bears his name, a compilation whose history is given in the prefaces to the "Chronica Monasterii S. Albani " (Rolls Series). Rymer's Fœdera is rich in documents for this period, and from this time we have a storehouse of political and social information in the Parliamentary Rolls. For the French war itself our primary authority is the Chronicle of Jehan le Bel, a canon of S. Lambert of Liége, who had himself served in Edward's campaign against the Scots, and spent the rest of his life at the court of John of Hainault. Up to the Treaty of Brétigny, where it closes, Froissart has done little more than copy this work, making however large additions from his own inquiries, especially in the Flemish and Breton campaigns and the account of Crécy. A Hainaulter of Valenciennes, Froissart held a post in Queen Philippa's household from 1361 to 1369 ; and under this influence produced in 1373 the first edition of his well-known Chronicle. A later edition is far less English in tone, and a third ver-sion, begun by him in his old age after long absence from England, is distinctly French in its sympathies. Froissart's vivacity and picturesqueness blind us to the inaccuracy of his details ; as an historical authority he is of little value. The incidental mention of Crécy and the later English expeditions by Villani in his great Florentine Chronicle are important. The best modern account of this period is that by Mr. W. Longman, " History of Edward III." Mr. Morley (" English Writers ") has treated in great detail of Chaucer.]

[Dr. Stubbs' "Constitutional History" (vol. ii.), published since this chapter was written, deals with the whole period.—*Ed.*]

IN the middle of the fourteenth century the great movement towards national unity which had begun under the last of the Norman Kings seemed to have reached its end, and the perfect fusion of conquered and conquerors into an English people was marked by the disuse, even amongst the nobler classes, of the French tongue. In spite of the efforts of the grammar schools, and of the strength of fashion, English was winning its way throughout the reign of Edward the Third to its

England
under
Edward
III.

final triumph in that of his grandson. "Children in school," says a writer of the earlier reign, "against the usage and manner of all other nations, be compelled for to leave their own language, and for to construe their lessons and their things in French, and so they have since Normans first came into England. Also gentlemen's children be taught to speak French from the time that they be rocked in their cradle, and know how to speak and play with a child's toy; and uplandish (or country) men will liken themselves to gentlemen, and strive with great busyness to speak French for to be more told of." "This manner," adds a translator of Richard's time, "was much used before the first murrain (the plague of 1349), and is since somewhat changed; for John Cornwal, a master of grammar, changed the lore in grammar school and construing of French into English; and Richard Pencrych learned this manner of teaching of him, as others did of Pencrych. So that now, the year of our Lord, 1385, and of the second King Richard after the Conquest nine, in all the grammar schools of England children leaveth French, and construeth and learneth in English." A more formal note of the change is found when English was ordered to be used in courts of law in 1362 "because the French tongue is much unknown;" and in the following year it was employed by the Chancellor in opening Parliament. Bishops began to preach in English, and the English tracts of Wyclif made it once more a literary tongue. This drift towards a general use of the national tongue told powerfully on literature. The influence of the French romances everywhere tended to make French the one literary language at the opening of the fourteenth century, and in England this influence had been backed by the French tone of the court of Henry the Third and the three Edwards. But at the close of the reign of Edward the Third the long French romances needed to be translated even for knightly hearers. "Let clerks indite in Latin," says the author of the "Testament of Love," "and let Frenchmen in their French also indite their quaint terms, for it is kindly to their mouths; and let us show our fantasies in such wordes as we learned of our mother's tongue." But the new national life afforded nobler material than "fantasies" now for English literature. With the completion of the work of national unity had come the completion of the work of national freedom. Under the first Edward the Parliament had vindicated its right to the control of taxation, under the second it had advanced from the removal of ministers to the deposition of a King, under the third it gave its voice on questions of peace and war, controlled expenditure, and regulated the course of civil administration. The vigour of English life showed itself socially in the wide extension of commerce, in the rapid growth of the woollen trade, and the increase of manufactures after the settlement of Flemish weavers on the eastern coast; in the progress of the towns, fresh as they were from the victory of the craft-gilds; and in

Sec. I.

Edward
the Third
1336
to
1360

Chaucer
1340–1400

the developement of agriculture through the division of lands, and the rise of the tenant farmer and the freeholder.   It gave nobler signs of its activity in the spirit of national independence and moral earnestness which awoke at the call of Wyclif.   New forces of thought and feeling, which were destined to tell on every age of our later history, broke their way through the crust of feudalism in the socialist revolt of the Lollards, and a sudden burst of military glory threw its glamour over the age of Crécy and Poitiers.

It is this new gladness of a great people which utters itself in the verse of Geoffrey Chaucer.   Chaucer was born about 1340, the son of a London vintner who lived in Thames Street ; and it was in London that the bulk of his life was spent.   His family, though not noble, seems to have been of some importance, for from the opening of his career we find Chaucer in close connexion with the Court.   At sixteen he was made page to the wife of Lionel of Clarence ; at nineteen he first bore arms in the campaign of 1359.   But he was luckless enough to be made prisoner ; and from the time of his release after the treaty of Brétigny he took no further share in the military enterprises of his time.   He seems again to have returned to service about the Court, and it was now that his first poems made their appearance, and from this time John of Gaunt may be looked upon as his patron.   He was employed in seven diplomatic missions which were probably connected with the financial straits of the Crown, and three of these, in 1372, 1374, and 1378, carried him to Italy.   He visited Genoa and the brilliant court of the Visconti at Milan ; at Florence, where the memory of Dante, the "great master" whom he commemorates so reverently in his verse, was still living, he may have met Boccaccio ; at Padua, like his own clerk of Oxenford, he possibly caught the story of Griseldis from the lips of Petrarca.   He was a busy, practical worker ; Comptroller of the Customs in 1374, of the Petty Customs in 1382, a member of the Commons in the Parliament of 1386, and from 1389 to 1391 Clerk of the Royal Works, busy with building at Westminster, Windsor, and the Tower.   A single portrait has preserved for us his forked beard, his dark-coloured dress, the knife and pen-case at his girdle, and we may supplement this portrait by a few vivid touches of his own.   The sly, elvish face, the quick walk, the plump figure and portly waist were those of a genial and humorous man ; but men jested at his silence, his love of study.   "Thou lookest as thou wouldest find an hare," laughs the Host, in the "Canterbury Tales," "and ever on the ground I see thee stare."   He heard little of his neighbours' talk when office work was over.   "Thou goest home to thy own house anon, and also dumb as any stone thou sittest at another book till fully dazed is thy look, and livest thus as an heremite, although," he adds slyly, "thy abstinence is lite" (little).   But of this abstraction from his fellows there is no trace in his verse.   No poetry was ever more human than Chaucer's ; none ever came more frankly and genially home to its readers. The first note of his song is a note of freshness and gladness. " Of ditties and of songes glad, the which he for my sake made, the land fulfilled is over all," Gower makes Love say in his lifetime ; and the impression of gladness remains just as fresh now that four hundred years have passed away. The historical character of Chaucer's work lies on its surface. It stands out in vivid contrast with the poetic literature from the heart of which it sprang. The long French romances were the product of an age of wealth and ease, of indolent curiosity, of a fanciful and self-indulgent sentiment. Of the great passions which gave life to the Middle Ages, that of religious enthusiasm had degenerated into the pretty conceits of Mariolatry, that of war into the extravagances of Chivalry. Love, indeed, remained ; it was the one theme of troubadour and trouvère, but it was a love of refinement, of romantic follies, of scholastic discussions, of sensuous enjoyment—a plaything rather than a passion. Nature had to reflect the pleasant indolence of man ; the song of the minstrel moved through a perpetual May-time ; the grass was ever green ; the music of the lark and the nightingale rang out from field and thicket. There was a gay avoidance of all that is serious, moral, or reflective in man's life : life was too amusing to be serious, too piquant, too sentimental, too full of interest and gaiety and chat. It was an age of talk : " mirth is none," says the Host, " to ride on by the way dumb as a stone ; " and the trouvère aimed simply at being the most agreeable talker of his day. His romances, his rimes of Sir Tristram, his Romance of the Rose, are full of colour and fantasy, endless in detail, but with a sort of gorgeous idleness about their very length, the minuteness of their description of outer things, the vagueness of their touch when it passes to the subtler inner world. It was with this literature that Chaucer had till now been familiar, and it was this which he followed in his earlier work. But from the time of his visits to Milan and Genoa his sympathies drew him not to the dying verse of France, but to the new and mighty upgrowth of poetry in Italy. Dante's eagle looks at him from the sun. " Fraunces

Petrark, the laureat poete," is to him one " whose rethorique sweete enlumyned al Itail of poetrie." The " Troilus " is an enlarged English version of Boccaccio's " Filostrato," the Knight's Tale bears slight traces of his Teseide. It was, indeed, the " Decameron " which suggested the very form of the " Canterbury Tales." But even while changing, as it were, the front of English poetry, Chaucer preserves his own distinct personality. If he quizzes in the rime of Sir Thopaz the wearisome idleness of the French romance, he retains all that was worth retaining of the French temper, its rapidity and agility of movement, its lightness and brilliancy of touch, its airy mockery, its gaiety and good humour, its critical coolness and self-control. The

French wit quickens in him more than in any English writer the
sturdy sense and shrewdness of our national disposition, corrects its
extravagance, and relieves its somewhat ponderous morality.　If, on
the other hand, he echoes the joyous carelessness of the Italian
tale, he tempers it with the English seriousness.　As he follows
Boccaccio, all his changes are on the side of purity; and when the
Troilus of the Florentine ends with the old sneer at the change-
ableness of woman, Chaucer bids us "look Godward," and dwells
on the unchangeableness of Heaven.

　　But the genius of Chaucer was neither French nor Italian, whatever
element it might borrow from either literature, but English to the
core, and from 1384 all trace of foreign influence dies away.　The
great poem on which his fame must rest, the "Canterbury Tales," was
begun after his first visits to Italy, and its best tales were written
between 1384 and 1391.　The last ten years of his life saw a few more
tales added; but his power was lessening, and in 1400 he rested from
his labours in his last home, a house in the garden of St. Mary's Chapel
at Westminster.　The framework—that of a pilgrimage from London
to Canterbury—not only enabled him to string together a number of
tales, composed at different times, but lent itself admirably to the
peculiar characteristics of his poetic temper, his dramatic versatility,
and the universality of his sympathy.　His tales cover the whole field
of mediæval poetry; the legend of the priest, the knightly romance,
the wonder-tale of the traveller, the broad humour of the fabliau,
allegory and apologue are all there.　He finds a yet wider scope for
his genius in the persons who tell these stories, the thirty pilgrims who
start in the May morning from the Tabard in Southwark—thirty
distinct figures, representatives of every class of English society from
the noble to the ploughman.　We see the "verray perfight gentil
knight" in cassock and coat of mail, with his curly-headed squire
beside him, fresh as the May morning, and behind them the brown-
faced yeoman, in his coat and hood of green, with the good bow in
his hand.　A group of ecclesiastics light up for us the mediæval church
—the brawny hunt-loving monk, whose bridle jingles as loud and clear
as the chapel-bell—the wanton friar, first among the beggars and
harpers of the country side—the poor parson, threadbare, learned,
and devout ("Christ's lore and His apostles twelve he taught, and
first he followed it himself")—the summoner with his fiery face—the
pardoner with his wallet "bret-full of pardons, come from Rome all
hot"—the lively prioress with her courtly French lisp, her soft little
red mouth, and "Amor vincit omnia" graven on her brooch.　Learning is there in the portly person of the doctor of physic, rich with the
profits of the pestilence—the busy serjeant-of-law, "that ever seemed
busier than he was"—the hollow-cheeked clerk of Oxford, with his
love of books, and short sharp sentences that disguise a latent tender-

ness which breaks out at last in the story of Griseldis. Around them crowd types of English industry; the merchant; the franklin, in whose house "it snowed of meat and drink;" the sailor fresh from frays in the Channel; the buxom wife of Bath; the broad-shouldered miller; the haberdasher, carpenter, weaver, dyer, tapestry-maker, each in the livery of his craft; and last, the honest ploughman, who would dyke and delve for the poor without hire. It is the first time in English poetry that we are brought face to face not with characters or allegories or reminiscences of the past, but with living and breathing men, men distinct in temper and sentiment as in face or costume or mode of speech; and with this distinctness of each maintained throughout the story by a thousand shades of expression and action. It is the first time too, that we meet with the dramatic power which not only creates each character, but combines it with its fellows, which not only adjusts each tale or jest to the temper of the person who utters it, but fuses all into a poetic unity. It is life in its largeness, its variety, its complexity, which surrounds us in the "Canterbury Tales." In some of the stories, indeed, composed no doubt at an earlier time, there is the tedium of the old romance or the pedantry of the school-man; but taken as a whole the poem is the work not of a man of letters, but of a man of action. Chaucer has received his training from war, courts, business, travel—a training not of books, but of life. And it is life that he loves—the delicacy of its sentiment, the breadth of its farce, its laughter and its tears, the tenderness of its Griseldis or the Smollett-like adventures of the miller and the clerks. It is this largeness of heart, this wide tolerance, which enables him to reflect man for us as none but Shakspere has ever reflected him, and to do this with a pathos, a shrewd sense and kindly humour, a freshness and joyousness of feeling, that even Shakspere has not surpassed.

It is strange that such a voice as this should have awakened no echo in the singers who follow; but the first burst of English song died as suddenly and utterly with Chaucer as the hope and glory of his age. The hundred years which follow the brief sunshine of Crécy and the "Canterbury Tales" are years of the deepest gloom; no age of our history is more sad and sombre than the age which we traverse from the third Edward to Joan of Arc. The throb of hope and glory which pulsed at its outset through every class of English society died at its close into inaction or despair. Material life lingered on indeed, commerce still widened, but its progress was dissociated from all the nobler elements of national well-being. The towns sank again into close oligarchies; the bondsmen struggling forward to freedom fell back into a serfage which still leaves its trace on the soil. Literature reached its lowest ebb. The religious revival of the Lollard was trodden out in blood, while the Church shrivelled into a self-seeking secular priesthood. In the clash of civil strife political freedom was all but extinguished, and the age which began with the Good Parliament ended with the despotism of the Tudors.

The secret of the change is to be found in the fatal war which for more than a hundred years drained the strength and corrupted the temper of the English people. We have followed the attack on Scotland to its disastrous close, but the struggle ere it ended, had involved England in a second contest, to which we must now turn back, a contest yet more ruinous than that which Edward the First had begun. From the war with Scotland sprang the hundred years' struggle with France. From the first France had watched the successes of her rival in the north, partly with a natural jealousy, but still more as likely to afford her an opening for winning the great southern Duchy of Guienne and Gascony—the one fragment of Eleanor's inheritance which remained to her descendants. Scotland had no sooner begun to resent the claims of her over-lord, Edward the First, than a pretext for open quarrel was found by France in the rivalry between the mariners of Normandy and those of the Cinque Ports, which culminated at the moment in a great sea-fight that proved fatal to 8,000 Frenchmen. So eager was Edward to avert a quarrel with France, that his threats roused the English seamen to a characteristic defiance. "Be the King's Council well advised," ran the remonstrance of the mariners, "that if wrong or grievance be done them in any fashion against right, they will sooner forsake wives, children, and all that they have, and go seek through the seas where they shall think to make their profit." In spite, therefore, of Edward's efforts the contest continued, and Philip found an opportunity to cite the King before his court at Paris for wrongs done to him as suzerain. Again Edward endeavoured to avert the conflict by a formal cession of Guienne into Philip's hands during forty days, but the refusal of the French sovereign to restore the province left no choice for him but war. The refusal of the Scotch barons to answer his summons to arms, and the revolt of Balliol, proved that the French outrage was but the first blow in a deliberate and long-planned scheme of attack ; Edward had for a while no force to waste on France, and when the first conquest of Scotland freed his hands, his league with Flanders for the recovery of Guienne was foiled by the strife with his baronage. A truce with Philip set him free to meet new troubles in the north ; but even after the victory of Falkirk Scotch independence was still saved for six years by the threats of France and the intervention of its ally, Boniface the Eighth ; and it was only the quarrel of these two confederates which allowed Edward to complete its subjection. But the rising under Bruce was again backed by French aid and by the renewal of the old quarrel over Guienne—a quarrel which hampered England through the reign of Edward the Second, and which indirectly brought about

Sec. I.

Edward
the Third

1336
TO
1360

**England
and
France**

1293

1294

1296

1304

1305

SEC. 1.

EDWARD
THE THIRD

1336
TO
1360

1332

1335

**The
Opening
of the
War**

1337

1338

1339

his terrible fall. The accession of Edward the Third secured a momentary peace, but the fresh attack on Scotland which marked the opening of his reign kindled hostility anew ; the young King David found refuge in France, and arms, money, and men were despatched from its ports to support his cause. It was this intervention of France which foiled Edward's hopes of the submission of Scotland at the very moment when success seemed in his grasp ; the solemn announcement by Philip of Valois that his treaties bound him to give effective help to his old ally, and the assembly of a French fleet in the Channel drew the King from his struggle in the north to face a storm which his negotiations could no longer avert.

From the first the war took European dimensions. The weakness of the Empire, the captivity of the Papacy at Avignon, left France without a rival among European powers. In numbers, in wealth, the French people far surpassed their neighbours over the Channel. England can hardly have counted four millions of inhabitants, France boasted of twenty. Edward could only bring eight thousand men-at-arms into the field. Philip, while a third of his force was busy elsewhere, could appear at the head of forty thousand. Edward's whole energy was bent on meeting the strength of France by a coalition of powers against her ; and his plans were helped by the dread which the great feudatories of the Empire who lay nearest to him felt of French annexation, as well as by the quarrel of the Empire with the Papacy. Anticipating the later policy of Godolphin and Pitt, Edward became the paymaster of the poorer princes of Germany ; his subsidies purchased the aid of Hainault, Gelders, and Jülich ; sixty thousand crowns went to the Duke of Brabant, while the Emperor himself was induced by a promise of three thousand gold florins to furnish two thousand men-at-arms. Negotiations and profuse expenditure, however, brought the King little fruit save the title of Vicar-General of the Empire on the left of the Rhine ; now the Emperor hung back, now the allies refused to move ; and when the host at last crossed the border, Edward found it impossible to bring the French king to an engagement. But as hope from the Imperial alliance faded away, a fresh hope dawned on the King from another quarter. Flanders was his natural ally. England was the great wool-producing country of the west, but few woollen fabrics were woven in England. The number of weavers' gilds shows that the trade was gradually extending, and at the very outset of his reign Edward had taken steps for its encouragement. He invited Flemish weavers to settle in his country, and took the new immigrants, who chose the eastern counties for the seat of their trade, under his royal protection. But English manufactures were still in their infancy, and nine-tenths of the English wool went to the looms of Bruges or of Ghent. We may see the rapid growth of this export trade in the fact that the King received in a single year more than £30,000 from duties levied on wool alone. A stoppage of this export would throw half the population of the great Flemish towns out of work ; and Flanders was drawn to the English alliance, not only by the interest of trade, but by the democratic spirit of the towns which jostled roughly with the feudalism of France. A treaty was concluded with the Duke of Brabant and the Flemish towns, and preparations were made for a new campaign. Philip gathered a fleet of two hundred vessels at Sluys to prevent his crossing the Channel, but Edward with a far smaller force utterly destroyed the French ships, and marched to invest Tournay. Its siege however proved fruitless ; his vast army broke up, and want of money forced him to a truce for a year. A quarrel of succession to the Duchy of Brittany, which broke out in 1341, and in which of the two rival claimants one was supported by Philip and the other by Edward, dragged on year after year. In Flanders things went ill for the English cause, and the death of the great statesman Van Arteveldt in 1345 proved a heavy blow to Edward's projects. The King's difficulties indeed had at last reached their height. His loans from the great bankers of Florence amounted to half a million of our money ; his overtures for peace were contemptuously rejected ; the claim which he advanced to the French crown found not a single adherent save among the burghers of Ghent. To establish such a claim, indeed, was difficult enough. The three sons of Philip the Fair had died without male issue, and Edward claimed as the son of Philip's daughter Isabella. But though her brothers had left no sons, they had left daughters ; and if female succession were admitted, these daughters of Philip's sons would precede a son of Philip's daughter. Isabella met this difficulty by contending that though females could transmit the right of succession they could not themselves possess it, and that her son, as the nearest living male descendant of Philip, and born in his lifetime, could claim in preference to females who were related to Philip in as near a degree. But the bulk of French jurists asserted that only male succession gave right to the throne. On such a theory the right inheritable from Philip was exhausted ; and the crown passed to the son of his brother Charles of Valois, who in fact peacefully mounted the throne as Philip the Sixth. Edward's claim seems to have been regarded on both sides as a mere formality ; the King, in fact, did full and liege homage to his rival for his Duchy of Guienne ; and it was not till his hopes from Germany had been exhausted, and his claim was found to be useful in securing the loyal aid of the Flemish towns, that it was brought seriously to the front.

The failure of his foreign hopes threw Edward on the resources of England itself, and it was with an army of thirty thousand men that he landed at La Hogue, and commenced a march which was to change the whole face of the war. The French forces were engaged in hold-

SEC. I.

EDWARD
THE THIRD
1336
TO
1360

1340

1330

1331

Crécy

Q

ing in check an English army which had landed in Guienne ; and panic seized the French King as Edward now marched through Normandy, and finding the bridges on the lower Seine broken, pushed straight on Paris, rebuilt the bridge of Poissy and threatened the capital. At this crisis, however, France found an unexpected help in a body of German knights. The Pope having deposed the Emperor Lewis of Bavaria, had crowned as his successor a son of King John of Bohemia, the well-known Charles IV. of the Golden Bull. But against this Papal assumption of a right to bestow the German Crown, Germany rose as one man, and Charles, driven to seek help from Philip, now found himself in France with his father and a troop of five hundred knights. Hurrying to Paris this German force formed the nucleus of an army which assembled at St. Denys ; and which was soon reinforced by 15,000 Genoese cross-bowmen who had been hired from among the soldiers of the Lord of Monaco on the sunny Riviera, and arrived at this hour of need. The French troops too were called from Guienne to the rescue. With this host rapidly gathering in his front Edward abandoned his march on Paris, and threw himself across the Seine to join a Flemish force gathered at Gravelines, and open a campaign in the north. But the rivers in his path were carefully guarded, and it was only by surprising the ford of Blanche-Taque on the Somme, that Edward escaped the necessity of surrendering to the vast host which was now hastening in pursuit. His communications, however, were no sooner secured than he halted at the village of Crécy, in Ponthieu, and resolved to give battle. Half of his army, now greatly reduced in strength by his rapid marches, consisted of the light-armed footmen of Ireland and Wales ; the bulk of the remainder was composed of English bowmen. The King ordered his men-at-arms to dismount, and drew up his forces on a low rise sloping gently to the south-east, with a windmill on its summit from which he could overlook the whole field of battle. Immediately beneath him lay his reserve, while at the base of the slope was placed the main body of the army in two divisions, that to the right commanded by the young Prince of Wales, Edward the Black Prince as he was called, that to the left by the Earl of Northampton. A small ditch protected the English front, and behind it the bowmen were drawn up " in the form of a harrow," with small bombards between them " which, with fire, threw little iron balls to frighten the horses "— the first instance of the use of artillery in field warfare. The halt of the English army took Philip by surprise, and he attempted for a time to check the advance of his army, but the disorderly host rolled on to the English front. The sight of his enemies, indeed, stirred the King's own blood to fury, " for he hated them," and at vespers the fight began. The Genoese crossbowmen were ordered to begin the attack, but the men were weary with the march ; a sudden storm wetted and rendered useless their bowstrings; and the loud shouts with which they leapt forward to the encounter were met with dogged silence in the English ranks. Their first arrow-flight, however, brought a terrible reply. So rapid was the English shot, "that it seemed as if it snowed." "Kill me these scoundrels," shouted Philip, as the Genoese fell back; and his men-at-arms plunged butchering into their broken ranks, while the Counts of Alençon and Flanders, at the head of the French knighthood, fell hotly on the Prince's line. For the instant his small force seemed lost, but Edward refused to send him aid. "Is he dead or unhorsed, or so wounded that he cannot help himself?" he asked the envoy. "No, Sir," was the reply, "but he is in a hard passage of arms, and sorely needs your help." "Return to those that sent you, Sir Thomas," said the King, "and bid them not send to me again so long as my son lives! Let the boy win his spurs; for if God so order it, I will that the day may be his, and that the honour may be with him and them to whom I have given it in charge." Edward could see, in fact, from his higher ground, that all went well. The English bowmen and men-at-arms held their ground stoutly, while the Welshmen stabbed the French horses in the mêlée, and brought knight after knight to the ground. Soon the French host was wavering in a fatal confusion. "You are my vassals, my friends," cried the blind King John of Bohemia, who had joined Philip's army, to the German nobles around him: "I pray and beseech you to lead me so far into the fight that I may strike one good blow with this sword of mine!" Linking their bridles together, the little company plunged into the thick of the combat to fall as their fellows were falling. The battle went steadily against the French: at last Philip himself hurried from the field, and the defeat became a rout: 1,200 knights and 30,000 footmen—a number equal to the whole English force—lay dead upon the ground.

"God has punished us for our sins," cries the chronicler of St. Denys, in a passion of bewildered grief, as he tells the rout of the great host which he had seen mustering beneath his abbey walls. But the fall of France was hardly so sudden or so incomprehensible as the ruin at a single blow of a system of warfare, and of the political and social fabric which rested on it. Feudalism depended on the superiority of the mounted noble to the unmounted churl; its fighting power lay in its knighthood. But the English yeomen and small freeholders who bore the bow in the national fyrd had raised their weapon into a terrible engine of war; in the English archers Edward carried a new class of soldiers to the fields of France. The churl had struck down the noble; the yeoman proved more than a match in sheer hard fighting for the knight. From the day of Crécy feudalism tottered slowly but surely to its grave. To England the day was the beginning of a career of military glory, which, fatal as it

SEC. I.

EDWARD
THE THIRD

1336
TO
1360

*Neville's
Cross*

Oct. 1346

1347

was destined to prove to the higher sentiments and interests of the nation, gave it for the moment an energy such as it had never known before. Victory followed victory. A few months after Crécy a Sçotch army which had burst into the north was routed at Neville's Cross, and its King, David Bruce, taken prisoner ; while the withdrawal of the French from the Garonne enabled the English to recover Poitou. Edward meanwhile turned to strike at the naval superiority of France by securing the mastery of the Channel. Calais was a great pirate-haven ; in one year alone, twenty-two privateers had sailed from its port ; while its capture promised the King an easy base of communication with Flanders, and of operations against France. The siege lasted a year, and it was not till Philip had failed to relieve it that the town was starved into surrender. Mercy was granted to the garrison and the people on condition that six of the citizens gave themselves unconditionally into the King's hands. " On them," said Edward, with a burst of bitter hatred, " I will do my will." At the sound of the town bell, Jehan le Bel tells us, the folk of Calais gathered round the bearer of these terms, " desiring to hear their good news, for they were all mad with hunger. When the said knight told them his news, then began they to weep and cry so loudly that it was great pity. Then stood up the wealthiest burgess of the town, Master Eustache de S. Pierre by name, and spake thus before all : 'My masters, great grief and mishap it were for all to leave such a people as this is to die by famine or otherwise ; and great charity and grace would he win from our Lord who could defend them from dying. For me, I have great hope in the Lord that if I can save this people by my death, I shall have pardon for my faults, wherefore will I be the first of the six, and of my own will put myself barefoot in my shirt and with a halter round my neck in the mercy of King Edward.'" The list of devoted men was soon made up, and the six victims were led before the King. " All the host assembled together ; there was great press, and many bade hang them openly, and many wept for pity. The noble King came with his train of counts and barons to the place, and the Queen followed him, though great with child, to see what there would be. The six citizens knelt down at once before the King, and Master Eustache said thus : 'Gentle King, here be we six who have been of the old bourgeoisie of Calais and great merchants ; we bring you the keys of the town and castle of Calais, and render them to you at your pleasure. We set ourselves in such wise as you see purely at your will, to save the remnant of the people that has suffered much pain. So may you have pity and mercy on us for your high nobleness' sake.' Certes, there was then in that place neither lord nor knight that wept not for pity, nor who could speak for pity ; but the King had his heart so hardened by wrath, that for a long while he could not reply ; then he commanded to cut off their heads. All the knights and lords prayed him with tears, as much as they could, to have pity on them, but he would not hear.   Then spoke the gentle knight, Master Walter de Maunay, and said, ' Ha, gentle sire ! bridle your wrath ; you have the renown and good fame of all gentleness ; do not a thing whereby men can speak any villany of you !   If you have no pity, all men will say that you have a heart full of all cruelty to put these good citizens to death that of their own will are come to render themselves to you to save the remnant of their people.'   At this point the King changed countenance with wrath, and said, ' Hold your peace, Master Walter ! it shall be none otherwise.   Call the headsman !   They of Calais have made so many of my men die, that they must die themselves !'   Then did the noble Queen of England a deed of noble lowliness, seeing she was great with child, and wept so tenderly for pity, that she could no longer stand upright ; therefore she cast herself on her knees before her lord the King, and spake on this wise : ' Ah, gentle sire ! from the day that I passed over sea in great peril, as you know, I have asked for nothing : now pray I and beseech you, with folded hands, for the love of our Lady's Son, to have mercy upon them.'   The gentle King waited for a while before speaking, and looked on the Queen as she knelt before him bitterly weeping.   Then began his heart to soften a little, and he said, ' Lady, I would rather you had been otherwhere ; you pray so tenderly, that I dare not refuse you ; and though I do it against my will, nevertheless take them, I give them to you.'   Then took he the six citizens by the halters and delivered them to the Queen, and released from death all those of Calais for the love of her ; and the good lady bade them clothe the six burgesses and make them good cheer."

Edward now stood at the height of his renown.   He had won the greatest victory of his age.   France, till now the first of European states, was broken and dashed from her pride of place at a single blow.   A naval picture of Froissart sketches Edward for us as he sailed to meet a Spanish fleet which was sweeping the narrow seas.   We see the King sitting on deck in his jacket of black velvet, his head covered by a black beaver hat " which became him well," and calling on Sir John Chandos to troll out the songs he had brought with him from Germany, till the Spanish ships heave in sight and a furious fight begins which ends in a victory that leaves Edward " King of the Seas."   But peace with France was as far off as ever.   Even the truce which for seven years was forced on both countries by sheer exhaustion became at last impossible.   Edward prepared three armies to act at once in Normandy, Brittany, and Guienne, but the plan of the campaign broke down.   The Black Prince, as the hero of Crécy was called, alone won a disgraceful success.   Unable to pay his troops, he staved off their demands by a campaign of sheer pillage.   Northern and central France had by this time fallen into utter ruin ; the royal treasury was empty, the fortresses unoccupied, the troops disbanded for want of pay, the country swept by bandits. Only the south remained at peace, and the young Prince led his army of freebooters up the Garonne into "what was before one of the fat countries of the world, the people good and simple, who did not know what war was; indeed, no war had been waged against them till the Prince came. The English and Gascons found the country full and gay, the rooms adorned with carpets and draperies, the caskets and chests full of fair jewels. But nothing was safe from these robbers. They, and especially the Gascons, who are very greedy, carried off everything." The capture of Narbonne loaded them with booty, and they fell back to Bordeaux, "their horses so laden with spoil that they could hardly move." The next year a march of the Prince's army on the Loire pointed straight upon Paris, and a French army under John, who had succeeded Philip of Valois on the throne, hurried to check his advance. The Prince gave orders for a retreat, but as he approached Poitiers he found the French, who now numbered 60,000 men, in his path. He at once took a strong position in the fields of Maupertuis, his front covered by thick hedges, and approachable only by a deep and narrow lane which ran between vineyards. The Prince lined the vineyards and hedges with bowmen, and drew up his small body of men-at-arms at the point where the lane opened upon the higher plain where he was encamped. His force numbered only 8,000 men, and the danger was great enough to force him to offer the surrender of his prisoners and of the places he had taken, and an oath not to fight against France for seven years, in exchange for a free retreat. The terms were rejected, and three hundred French knights charged up the narrow lane. It was soon choked with men and horses, while the front ranks of the advancing army fell back before a galling fire of arrows from the hedgerows. In the moment of confusion a body of English horsemen, posted on a hill to the right, charged suddenly on the French flank, and the Prince seized the opportunity to fall boldly on their front. The English archery completed the disorder produced by this sudden attack; the French King was taken, desperately fighting; and at noontide, when his army poured back in utter rout to the gates of Poitiers, 8,000 of their number had fallen on the field, 3,000 in the flight, and 2,000 men-at-arms, with a crowd of nobles, were taken prisoners. The royal captive entered London in triumph, and a truce for two years seemed to give healing-time to France. But the miserable country found no rest in itself. The routed soldiery turned into free companies of bandits, while the captive lords procured the sums needed for their ransom by extortion from the peasantry, who were driven by oppression and famine into wild insurrection, butchering their lords, and firing the castles; while Paris, impatient of the weakness and misrule of the Regency, rose in arms against the

SEC. II.

THE GOOD
PARLIA-
MENT
1360
TO
1377

Crown. The "Jacquerie," as the peasant rising was called, had hardly been crushed, when Edward again poured ravaging over the wasted land. Famine, however, proved its best defence. "I could not believe," said Petrarch of this time, "that this was the same France which I had seen so rich and flourishing. Nothing presented itself to my eyes but a fearful solitude, an utter poverty, land uncultivated, houses in ruins. Even the neighbourhood of Paris showed everywhere marks of desolation and conflagration. The streets are deserted, the roads overgrown with weeds, the whole is a vast solitude." The misery of the land at last bent Charles to submission, and in May a treaty was concluded at Brétigny, a small place to the eastward of Chartres. By this treaty the English King waived his claims on the crown of France and on the Duchy of Normandy. On the other hand, his Duchy of Aquitaine, which included Gascony, Poitou, and Saintonge, the Limousin and the Angoumois, Périgord and the counties of Bigorre and Rouergue, was not only restored but freed from its obligations as a French fief, and granted in full sovereignty with Ponthieu, Edward's heritage from the second wife of Edward the First, as well as with Guisnes and his new conquest of Calais.

Section II.—The Good Parliament, 1360—1377.

[*Authorities.*—As in the last period. An anonymous chronicler whose work is printed in the "Archæologia" (vol. 22) gives the story of the Good Parliament ; another account is preserved in the "Chronica Angliæ from 1328 to 1388" (Rolls Series), and fresh light has been recently thrown on the time by the publication of a Chronicle by Adam of Usk from 1377 to 1404.]

If we turn from the stirring but barren annals of foreign warfare to the more fruitful field of constitutional progress, we are at once struck with a marked change which takes place during this period in the composition of Parliament. The division, with which we are so familiar, into a House of Lords and a House of Commons, formed no part of the original plan of Edward the First ; in the earlier Parliaments, each of the four orders of clergy, barons, knights, and burgesses met, deliberated, and made their grants apart from each other. This isolation, however, of the Estates soon showed signs of breaking down. While the clergy, as we have seen, held steadily aloof from any real union with its fellow-orders, the knights of the shire were drawn by the similarity of their social position into a close connexion with the lords. They seem, in fact, to have been soon admitted by the baronage to an almost equal position with themselves, whether as legislators or counsellors of the Crown. The burgesses, on the other hand, took little part at first in Parliamentary proceedings, save in those which related to the taxation of their class. But their position was raised

SEC. II.

THE GOOD
PARLIA-
MENT
1360
TO
1377

1332

by the strifes of the reign of Edward the Second, when their aid was
needed by the baronage in its struggle with the Crown; and their
right to share fully in all legislative action was asserted in the famous
statute of 1322. Gradually too, through causes with which we are
imperfectly acquainted, the knights of the shire drifted from their older
connexion with the baronage into so close and intimate a union with
the representatives of the towns that at the opening of the reign of
Edward the Third the two orders are found grouped formally together,
under the name of "The Commons"; and by 1341 the final decision of
Parliament into two Houses was complete. It is difficult to over-esti-
mate the importance of this change. Had Parliament remained broken
up into its four orders of clergy, barons, knights, and citizens, its power
would have been neutralized at every great crisis by the jealousies and
difficulty of co-operation among its component parts. A permanent
union of the knighthood and the baronage, on the other hand, would
have converted Parliament into a mere representative of an aristocratic caste, and would have robbed it of the strength which it has
drawn from its connexion with the great body of the commercial
classes. The new attitude of the knighthood, their social connexion
as landed gentry with the baronage, their political union with the
burgesses, really welded the three orders into one, and gave that unity
of feeling and action to our Parliament on which its power has ever
since mainly depended. From the moment of this change, indeed, we
see a marked increase of parliamentary activity. The need of continual grants during the war brought about an assembly of Parliament
year by year; and with each supply some step was made to greater
political influence. A crowd of enactments for the regulation of trade,
whether wise or unwise, and for the protection of the subject against
oppression or injustice, as well as the great ecclesiastical provisions of
this reign, show the rapid widening of the sphere of parliamentary
action. The Houses claimed an exclusive right to grant supplies,
and asserted the principle of ministerial responsibility to Parliament. But the Commons long shrank from meddling with purely
administrative matters.

Edward in his anxiety to shift from his
shoulders the responsibility of the war with France, referred to
them for counsel on the subject of one of the numerous propositions of
peace. "Most dreaded lord," they replied, "as to your war and the
equipment necessary for it, we are so ignorant and simple that we
know not how, nor have the power, to devise: wherefore we pray your
Grace to excuse us in this matter, and that it please you, with advice
of the great and wise persons of your Council, to ordain what seems
best to you for the honour and profit of yourself and of your kingdom; and whatsoever shall be thus ordained by assent and agreement on the part of you and your lords we readily assent to, and
will hold it firmly established." But while shrinking from so wide an

extension of their responsibility, the Commons wrested from the Crown a practical reform of the highest value. As yet their petitions, if granted, were often changed or left incomplete in the statute or ordinance which professed to embody them, or were delayed till the session had closed. Thus many provisions made in Parliament had hitherto been evaded or set aside. But the Commons now met this abuse by a demand that on the royal assent being given their petitions should be turned without change into statutes of the realm, and derive force of law from their entry on the rolls of Parliament.

The political responsibility which the Commons evaded was at last forced on them by the misfortunes of the war. In spite of quarrels in Brittany and elsewhere, peace was fairly preserved in the nine years which followed the treaty of Brétigny ; but the shrewd eye of Charles the Fifth, the successor of John, was watching keenly for the moment of renewing the struggle. He had cleared his kingdom of the freebooters by despatching them into Spain, and the Black Prince had plunged into the revolutions of that country only to return from his fruitless victory of Navarete in broken health, and impoverished by the expenses of the campaign. The anger caused by the taxation which this necessitated was fanned by Charles into revolt. He listened, in spite of the treaty, to an appeal from the lords of Aquitaine, and summoned the Black Prince to his Court. "I will come," replied the Prince, "but helmet on head, and with sixty thousand men at my back." War, however, had hardly been declared before the ability with which Charles had laid his plans was seen in his seizure of Ponthieu, and in a rising of the whole country south of the Garonne. The Black Prince, borne on a litter to the walls of Limoges, recovered the town, which had been surrendered to the French, and by a merciless massacre sullied the fame of his earlier exploits ; but sickness recalled him home, and the war, protracted by the caution of Charles, who forbade his armies to engage, did little but exhaust the energy and treasures of England. At last, however, the error of the Prince's policy was seen in the appearance of a Spanish fleet in the Channel, and in a decisive victory which it won over an English convoy off Rochelle. The blow was in fact fatal to the English cause ; it wrested from Edward the mastery of the seas, and cut off his communication with Aquitaine. Charles was roused to new exertions. Poitou, Saintonge, and the Angoumois yielded to his general Du Guesclin, and Rochelle was surrendered by its citizens. A great army under the King's third son, John of Gaunt, Duke of Lancaster, penetrated fruitlessly into the heart of France. Charles had forbidden any fighting. "If a storm rages over the land," said the King, coolly, "it disperses of itself ; and so will it be with the English." Winter, in fact, overtook the Duke in the mountains of Auvergne, and a mere fragment of his host reached Bordeaux. The failure was the signal for a general defection, and ere the summer of

Sec. II.

The Good Parlia- ment
1360 to **1377**

The Loss of Aqui- taine 1360–1396

1366

1367

1369

1372

SEC. II.

THE GOOD
PARLIA-
MENT
1360
TO
1377

1374 had closed the two towns of Bordeaux and Bayonne were all that remained of the English possessions in southern France.

It was a time of shame and suffering such as England had never known. Her conquests were lost, her shores insulted, her fleets annihilated, her commerce swept from the seas; while within she was exhausted by the long and costly war, as well as by the ravages of pestilence. In the hour of distress the eyes of the hard-pressed nobles and knighthood turned greedily on the riches of the Church. Never had her spiritual or moral hold on the nation been less; never had her wealth been greater. Out of a population of some three millions, the ecclesiastics numbered between twenty and thirty thousand. Wild tales of their riches floated about. They were said to own in landed property alone more than a third of the soil, their "spiritualities" in dues and offerings amounting to twice the King's revenue. The throng of bishops round the council-board was still more galling to the feudal baronage, flushed as it was with a new pride by the victories of Crécy and Poitiers. On the renewal of the war the Parliament prayed that the chief offices of state might be placed in lay hands. William of

Wykeham, Bishop of Winchester, resigned the Chancellorship, another prelate the Treasury, to lay dependents of the great nobles; and the panic of the clergy was seen in large grants which they voted in Convocation. The baronage found a leader in John of Gaunt; but even the promise to pillage the Church failed to win for the Duke and his party the goodwill of the lesser gentry and of the burgesses; while the corruption and the utter failure of the new administration and the calamities of the war left it powerless before the Parliament of

1376. The action of this Parliament marks a new stage in the character of the national opposition to the misrule of the Crown. Till now the task of resistance had devolved on the baronage, and had been carried out through risings of its feudal tenantry; but the misgovernment was now that of a main part of the baronage itself in actual conjunction with the Crown. Only in the power of the Commons lay any adequate means of peaceful redress. The old reluctance of the Lower House to meddle with matters of State was roughly swept away therefore by the pressure of the time. The Black Prince, sick as he was to death and anxious to secure his child's succession by the removal of John of Gaunt, the prelates with William of Wykeham at their head, resolute again to take their place in the royal councils and to check the projects of ecclesiastical spoliation, alike found in it a body to oppose to the Duke's administration. Backed by powers such as these, the action of the Commons showed none of their old timidity or self-distrust. The knights of the shire united with the burgesses in a joint attack on the royal council. "Trusting in God, and standing with his followers before the nobles, whereof the chief was John, Duke of Lancaster, whose doings were ever contrary," their speaker, Sir

Sec. II.

The Good
Parlia-
ment

1360
to
1377

Peter de la Mare, denounced the mismanagement of the war, the oppressive taxation, and demanded an account of the expenditure. "What do these base and ignoble knights attempt?" cried John of Gaunt. "Do they think they be kings or princes of the land?" But even the Duke was silenced by the charges brought against the government, and the Parliament proceeded to the impeachment and condemnation of two ministers, Latimer and Lyons. The King himself had sunk into dotage, and was wholly under the influence of a mistress named Alice Perrers; she was banished, and several of the royal servants driven from the Court. One hundred and forty petitions were presented which embodied the grievances of the realm. They demanded the annual assembly of Parliament, and freedom of election for the knights of the shire, whose choice was now often tampered with by the Crown; they protested against arbitrary taxation and Papal inroads on the liberties of the Church; petitioned for the protection of trade, the enforcement of the statute of labourers, and the limitation of the powers of chartered crafts. At the death of the Black Prince his little son Richard was brought into Parliament and acknowledged as heir. But the Houses were no sooner dismissed than Lancaster resumed his power. His haughty will flung aside all restraints of law. He dismissed the new lords and prelates from the Council. He called back Alice Perrers and the disgraced ministers. He declared the Good Parliament no parliament, and did not suffer its petitions to be enrolled as statutes. He imprisoned Peter de la Mare, and confiscated the possessions of William of Wykeham. His attack on this prelate was an attack on the clergy at large. Fresh projects of spoliation were openly canvassed, and it is his support of these plans of confiscation which now brings us across the path of John Wyclif.

Section III.—John Wyclif.

[*Authorities.*—The "Fasciculi Zizaniorum" in the Rolls Series, with the documents appended to it, is a work of primary authority for the history of Wyclif and his followers. A selection from his English tracts has been made by Mr. T. Arnold for the University of Oxford, which has also published his "Trias." The version of the Bible that bears his name has been edited with a valuable preface by Rev. J. Forshall and Sir F. Madden. There are lives of Wyclif by Lewis and Vaughan; and Milman ("Latin Christianity," vol. vi.) has given a brilliant summary of the Lollard movement.]

Nothing is more remarkable than the contrast between the obscurity of Wyclif's earlier life and the fulness and vividness of our knowledge of him during the twenty years which preceded its close. Born in the earlier part of the fourteenth century, he had already passed middle age when he was appointed to the mastership of Balliol College in the University of Oxford, and recognized as first among the schoolmen of his day. Of all the scholastic doctors those of England had been throughout the keenest and the most daring in philosophical speculation; a reckless audacity and love of novelty was the common note of Bacon, Duns Scotus, and Ockham, as against the sober and more disciplined learning of the Parisian schoolmen, Albert and Aquinas. But the decay of the University of Paris during the English wars was transferring her intellectual supremacy to Oxford, and in Oxford Wyclif stood without a rival. From his predecessor, Bradwardine, whose work as a scholastic teacher he carried on in the speculative treatises he published during this period, he inherited the tendency to a predestinarian Augustinianism which formed the groundwork of his later theological revolt. His debt to Ockham revealed itself in his earliest efforts at Church reform. Undismayed by the thunder and excommunications of the Church, Ockham had not shrunk in his enthusiasm for the Empire from attacking the foundations of the Papal supremacy or from asserting the rights of the civil power. The spare, emaciated frame of Wyclif, weakened by study and by asceticism, hardly promised a Reformer who would carry on the stormy work of Ockham; but within this frail form lay a temper quick and restless, an immense energy, an immovable conviction, an unconquerable pride. The personal charm which ever accompanies real greatness only deepened the influence he derived from the spotless purity of his life. As yet indeed even Wyclif himself can hardly have suspected the immense range of his intellectual power. It was only the struggle that lay before him which revealed in the dry and subtle schoolman the founder of our later English prose, a master of popular invective, of irony, of persuasion, a dexterous politician, an audacious partisan, the organizer of a religious order, the unsparing assailant of abuses, the boldest and most indefatigable of controversialists, the first Reformer who dared, when deserted and alone, to question and deny the creed of the Christendom around him, to break through the tradition of the past, and with his last breath to assert the freedom of religious thought against the dogmas of the Papacy.

The attack of Wyclif began precisely at the moment when the Church of the middle ages had sunk to its lowest point of spiritual decay. The transfer of the Papacy to Avignon robbed it of half the awe in which it had been held by Englishmen, for not only had the Popes sunk into creatures of the French King, but their greed and extortion produced almost universal revolt. The claim of first fruits and annates from rectory and bishoprick, the assumption of a right to dispose of all benefices in ecclesiastical patronage, the direct taxation of the clergy, the intrusion of foreign priests into English livings, the opening a mart for the disposal of pardons, dispensations, and indulgences, and the encouragement of appeals to the Papal court produced a widespread national irritation which never slept till the

Reformation. The people scorned a " French Pope," and threatened his legates with stoning when they landed. The wit of Chaucer flouted the wallet of "pardons hot from Rome." Parliament vindicated the right of the State to prohibit any questioning of judgements rendered in the King's courts, or any prosecution of a suit in foreign courts, by the Statute of Præmunire ; and denied the Papal claim to dispose of benefices by that of Provisors. But the effort was practically foiled by the treacherous diplomacy of the Crown. The Pope waived indeed his alleged right to appoint foreigners ; but by a compromise, in which Pope and King combined for the enslaving of the Church, bishopricks, abbacies, and livings in the gift of Churchmen still continued to receive Papal nominees who had been first chosen by the Crown, so that the treasuries of King and Pope profited by the arrangement. The protest of the Good Parliament is a record of the ill-success of its predecessors' attempts. It asserted that the taxes levied by the Pope amounted to five times the amount of those levied by the King, that by reservation during the life of actual holders the Pope disposed of the same bishoprick four or five times over, receiving each time the first fruits. " The brokers of the sinful city of Rome promote for money unlearned and unworthy caitiffs to benefices of the value of a thousand marks, while the poor and learned hardly obtain one of twenty. So decays sound learning. They present aliens who neither see nor care to see their parishioners, despise God's services, convey away the treasure of the realm, and are worse than Jews or Saracens. The Pope's revenue from England alone is larger than that of any prince in Christendom. God gave his sheep to be pastured, not to be shaven and shorn." The grievances were no trifling ones. At this very time the deaneries of Lichfield, Salisbury and York, the archdeaconry of Canterbury, which was reputed the wealthiest English benefice, together with a host of prebends and preferments, were held by Italian cardinals and priests, while the Pope's collector from his office in London sent twenty thousand marks a year to the Papal treasury.

If extortion and tyranny such as this severed the English clergy from the Papacy, their own selfishness severed them from the nation at large. Immense as was their wealth, they bore as little as they could of the common burthens of the realm. They were still resolute to assert their exemption from the common justice of the land, and the mild punishments of the ecclesiastical courts carried little dismay into the mass of disorderly clerks. Privileged as they were against all interference from the lay world without, the clergy penetrated by their control over wills, contracts, divorce, by the dues they exacted, as well as by directly religious offices, into the very heart of the social life around them. No figure was better known or more hated than the summoner who enforced the jurisdiction and levied the dues of their courts. On the other hand, their moral authority was rapidly passing away; the wealthiest churchmen, with curled hair and hanging sleeves, aped the costume of the knightly society to which they really belonged. We have already seen the general impression of their worldliness in Chaucer's picture of the hunting monk and the courtly prioress with her love-motto on her brooch. Over the vice of the higher classes they exerted no influence whatever; the King paraded his mistress as a Queen of Beauty through London, the nobles blazoned their infamy in court and tournament. "In those days," says a chronicler of the time, "arose a great rumour and clamour among the people, that wherever there was a tournament there came a great concourse of ladies of the most costly and beautiful, but not of the best in the kingdom, sometimes forty or fifty in number, as if they were a part of the tournament, in diverse and wonderful male apparel, in parti-coloured tunics, with short caps and bands wound cord-wise round their head, and girdles bound with gold and silver, and daggers in pouches across their body, and then they proceeded on chosen coursers to the place of tourney, and so expended and wasted their goods and vexed their bodies with scurrilous wantonness that the rumour of the people sounded everywhere; and thus they neither feared God nor blushed at the chaste voice of the people." They were not called on to blush at the chaste voice of the Church. The clergy were in fact rent by their own dissensions. The higher prelates were busy with the cares of political office, and severed from the lower priesthood by the scandalous inequality between the revenues of the wealthier ecclesiastics and the "poor parson" of the country. A bitter hatred divided the secular clergy from the regular; and this strife went fiercely on in the Universities. Fitz-Ralf, the Chancellor of Oxford, attributed to the Friars the decline in the number of academical students, and the University checked by statute their admission of mere children into their orders. The older religious orders in fact had sunk into mere landowners, while the enthusiasm of the Friars had in great part died away and left a crowd of impudent mendicants behind it. Wyclif could soon with general applause denounce them as sturdy beggars, and declare that "the man who gives alms to a begging friar is ipso facto excommunicate."

Without the ranks of the clergy stood a world of earnest men who, like "Piers the Ploughman," denounced their worldliness and vice, sceptics like Chaucer laughing at the jingling bells of their hunting abbots, and the brutal and greedy baronage under John of Gaunt, eager to drive the prelates from office and to seize on their wealth. Worthless as the last party seems to us, it was with John of Gaunt that Wyclif allied himself in his effort for the reform of the Church. As yet his quarrel was not with the doctrines of Rome but with its practice, and it was on the principles of Ockham that he defended the Parliament's indignant refusal of the "tribute" which was claimed by the Papacy. But his treatise on "The Kingdom of God" (De Dominio Divino) shows how different his aims really were from the selfish aims of the men with whom he acted. In this, the most famous of his works, Wyclif bases his action on a distinct ideal of society. All authority, to use his own expression, is "founded in grace." Dominion in the highest sense is in God alone ; it is God who, as the suzerain of the universe, deals out His rule in fief to rulers in their various stations on tenure of their obedience to Himself. It was easy to object that in such a case "dominion" could never exist, since mortal sin is a breach of such a tenure, and all men sin. But, as Wyclif urged it, the theory is a purely ideal one. In actual practice he distinguishes between dominion and power, power which the wicked may have by God's permission, and to which the Christian must submit from motives of obedience to God. In his own scholastic phrase, so strangely perverted afterwards, here on earth "God must obey the devil." But whether in the ideal or practical view of the matter, all power or dominion was of God. It was granted by Him not to one person, His Vicar on earth, as the Papacy alleged, but to all. The King was as truly God's Vicar as the Pope. The royal power was as sacred as the ecclesiastical, and as complete over temporal things, even the temporalities of the Church, as that of the Church over spiritual things. On the question of Church and State therefore the distinction between the ideal and practical view of "dominion" was of little account. Wyclif's application of the theory to the individual conscience was of far higher and wider importance. Obedient as each Christian might be to king or priest, he himself, as a possessor of "dominion," held immediately of God. The throne of God Himself was the tribunal of personal appeal. What the Reformers of the sixteenth century attempted to do by their theory of Justification by Faith, Wyclif attempted to do by his theory of "dominion." It was a theory which in establishing a direct relation between man and God swept away the whole basis of a mediating priesthood on which the mediæval Church was built ; but for a time its real drift was hardly perceived. To Wyclif's theory of Church and State, his subjection of their temporalities to the Crown, his contention that like other property they might be seized and employed for national purposes, his wish for their voluntary abandonment and the return of the Church to its original poverty, the clergy were more sensitive. They were bitterly galled when he came forward as the theological bulwark of the Lancastrian party at a time when they were writhing under the attack on Wykeham by the nobles ; and in the prosecution of Wyclif, they resolved to return blow for blow. He was summoned before Bishop Courtenay of London to answer for his heretical propositions concerning the wealth of the Church. The Duke of Lancaster accepted the challenge as really given to himself, and stood by Wyclif's side in the Consistory

Court at St. Paul's. But no trial took place. Fierce words passed between the nobles and the prelate ; the Duke himself was said to have threatened to drag Courtenay out of the church by the hair of his head, and at last the London populace, to whom John of Gaunt was hateful, burst in to their Bishop's rescue, and Wyclif's life was saved with difficulty by the aid of the soldiery. But his courage only grew with the danger. A Papal bull which was procured by the bishops, directing the University to condemn and arrest him, extorted from him a bold defiance. In a defence circulated widely through the kingdom and laid before Parliament, Wyclif broadly asserted that no man could be excommunicated by the Pope " unless he were first excommunicated by himself." He denied the right of the Church to exact or defend temporal privileges by spiritual censures, declared that a Church might justly be deprived by the King or lay lords of its property for defect of duty, and defended the subjection of ecclesiastics to civil tribunals. Bold as the defiance was, it won the support of the people and of the Crown. When he appeared at the close of the year in Lambeth Chapel to answer the Archbishop's summons, a message from the Court forbade the Primate to proceed, and the Londoners broke in and dissolved the session.

Wyclif was still working hand in hand with John of Gaunt in advocating his plans of ecclesiastical reform, when the great insurrection of the peasants, which we shall soon have to describe, broke out under Wat Tyler. In a few months the whole of his work was undone. Not only was the power of the Lancastrian party on which Wyclif had relied for the moment annihilated, but the quarrel between the baronage and the Church, on which his action had hitherto been grounded, was hushed in the presence of a common danger. His " poor preachers " were looked on as missionaries of socialism. The Friars charged him with being a " sower of strife, who by his serpent-like instigation has set the serf against his lord," and though Wyclif tossed back the charge with disdain, he had to bear a suspicion which was justified by the conduct of some of his followers. John Ball, who had figured in the front rank of the revolt, was claimed as one of his adherents, and was alleged to have denounced in his last hour the conspiracy of the " Wyclifites." His most prominent scholar, Nicholas Herford, was said to have openly approved the brutal murder of Archbishop Sudbury. Whatever belief such charges might gain, it is certain that from this moment all plans for the reorganization of the Church were confounded in the general odium which attached to the projects of the peasant leaders, and that any hope of ecclesiastical reform at the hands of the baronage and the Parliament was at an end. But even if the Peasant Revolt had not deprived Wyclif of the support of the aristocratic party with whom he had hitherto co-operated, their alliance must have been dissolved by the new theological position which he had already taken up. Some months before the outbreak of the insurrection, he had by one memorable step passed from the position of a reformer of the discipline and political relations of the Church to that of a protester against its cardinal beliefs. If there was one doctrine upon which the supremacy of the Mediæval Church rested, it was the doctrine of Transubstantiation. It was by his exclusive right to the performance of the miracle which was wrought in the mass that the lowliest priest was raised high above princes. With the formal denial of the doctrine of Transubstantiation which Wyclif issued in the spring of 1381 began that great movement of revolt which ended, more than a century after, in the establishment of religious freedom, by severing the mass of the Teutonic peoples from the general body of the Catholic Church. The act was the bolder that he stood utterly alone. The University, in which his influence had been hitherto all-powerful, at once condemned him. John of Gaunt enjoined him to be silent. Wyclif was presiding as Doctor of Divinity over some disputations in the schools of the Augustinian Canons when his academical condemnation was publicly read, but though startled for the moment he at once challenged Chancellor or doctor to disprove the conclusions at which he had arrived. The prohibition of the Duke of Lancaster he met by an open avowal of his teaching, a confession which closes proudly with the quiet words, " I believe that in the end the truth will conquer." For the moment his courage dispelled the panic around him. The University responded to his appeal, and by displacing his opponents from office tacitly adopted his cause. But Wyclif no longer looked for support to the learned or wealthier classes on whom he had hitherto relied. He appealed, and the appeal is memorable as the first of such a kind in our history, to England at large. With an amazing industry he issued tract after tract in the tongue of the people itself. The dry, syllogistic Latin, the abstruse and involved argument which the great doctor had addressed to his academic hearers, were suddenly flung aside, and by a transition which marks the wonderful genius of the man the schoolman was transformed into the pamphleteer. If Chaucer is the father of our later English poetry, Wyclif is the father of our later English prose. The rough, clear, homely English of his tracts, the speech of the plough-man and the trader of the day, though coloured with the picturesque phraseology of the Bible, is in its literary use as distinctly a creation of his own as the style in which he embodied it, the terse vehement sentences, the stinging sarcasms, the hard antitheses which roused the dullest mind like a whip. Once fairly freed from the trammels of un-questioning belief, Wyclif's mind worked fast in its career of scepticism. Pardons, indulgences, absolutions, pilgrimages to the shrines of the saints, worship of their images, worship of the saints themselves, were successively denied. A formal appeal to the Bible as the one ground

R

of faith, coupled with an assertion of the right of every instructed man to examine the Bible for himself, threatened the very groundwork of the older dogmatism with ruin. Nor were these daring denials confined to the small circle of the scholars who still clung to him ; with the practical ability which is so marked a feature of his character, Wyclif had organized some few years before an order of poor preachers, "the Simple Priests," whose coarse sermons and long russet dress moved the laughter of the clergy, but who now formed a priceless organization for the diffusion of their master's doctrines. How rapid their progress must have been we may see from the panic-struck exaggerations of their opponents. A few years later they complained that the followers of Wyclif abounded everywhere and in all classes, among the baronage, in the cities, among the peasantry of the country-side, even in the monastic cell itself. "Every second man one meets is a Lollard."

"Lollard," a word which probably means "idle babbler," was the nickname of scorn with which the orthodox Churchmen chose to insult their assailants. But this rapid increase changed their scorn into vigorous action. Courtenay, now become Archbishop, summoned a council at Blackfriars, and formally submitted twenty-four propositions drawn from Wyclif's works. An earthquake in the midst

of the proceedings terrified every prelate but the resolute Primate ; the expulsion of ill humours from the earth, he said, was of good omen for the expulsion of ill humours from the Church ; and the condemnation was pronounced. Then the Archbishop turned fiercely upon Oxford as the fount and centre of the new heresies. In an English sermon at St. Frideswide's, Nicholas Herford had asserted the truth of Wyclif's doctrines, and Courtenay ordered the Chancellor to silence him and his adherents on pain of being himself treated as a heretic. The Chancellor fell back on the liberties of the University, and appointed as preacher another Wyclifite, Repyngdon, who did not hesitate to style the Lollards "holy priests," and to affirm that they were protected by John of Gaunt. Party spirit meanwhile ran high among the students ; the bulk of them sided with the Lollard leaders, and a Carmelite, Peter Stokes, who had procured the Archbishop's letters, cowered panic-stricken in his chamber while the Chancellor, protected by an escort of a hundred townsmen, listened approvingly to Repyngdon's defiance. "I dare go no further," wrote the poor Friar to the Archbishop, "for fear of death ; " but he soon mustered courage to descend into the schools where Repyngdon was now maintaining that the clerical order was "better when it was but nine years old than now that it has grown to a thousand years and more." The appearance, however, of scholars in arms again drove Stokes to fly in despair to Lambeth, while a new heretic in open Congregation maintained Wyclif's denial of Transubstantiation. "There is no idolatry," cried William James, "save in the Sacrament of the Altar."

"You speak like a wise man," replied the Chancellor, Robert Rygge. Courtenay however was not the man to bear defiance tamely, and his summons to Lambeth wrested a submission from Rygge which was only accepted on his pledge to suppress the Lollardism of the University. "I dare not publish them, on fear of death," exclaimed the Chancellor when Courtenay handed him his letters of condemnation. "Then is your University an open *fautor* of heretics," retorted the Primate, "if it suffers not the Catholic truth to be proclaimed within its bounds." The royal council supported the Archbishop's injunction, but the publication of the decrees at once set Oxford on fire. The scholars threatened death against the Friars, "crying that they wished to destroy the University." The masters suspended Henry Crump from teaching, as a troubler of the public peace, for calling the Lollards "heretics." The Crown however at last stepped roughly in to Courtenay's aid, and a royal writ ordered the instant banishment of all favourers of Wyclif, with the seizure and destruction of all Lollard books, on pain of forfeiture of the University's privileges. The threat produced its effect. Herford and Repyngdon appealed in vain to John of Gaunt for protection ; the Duke himself denounced them as heretics against the Sacrament of the Altar, and after much evasion they were forced to make a formal submission. Within Oxford itself the suppression of Lollardism was complete, but with the death of religious freedom all trace of intellectual life suddenly disappears. The century which followed the triumphs of Courtenay is the most barren in its annals, nor was the sleep of the University broken till the advent of the New Learning restored to it some of the life and liberty which the Primate had so roughly trodden out.

Nothing marks more strongly the grandeur of Wyclif's position as the last of the great schoolmen, than the reluctance of so bold a man as Courtenay even after his triumph over Oxford to take extreme measures against the head of Lollardry. Wyclif, though summoned, had made no appearance before the "Council of the Earthquake." "Pontius Pilate and Herod are made friends to-day," was his bitter comment on the new union which proved to have sprung up between the prelates and the monastic orders who had so long been at variance with each other ; "since they have made a heretic of Christ, it is an easy inference for them to count simple Christians heretics." He seems indeed to have been sick at the moment, but the announcement of the final sentence roused him to life again. "I shall not die," he is said to have cried at an earlier time when in grievous peril, "but live and declare the works of the Friars." He petitioned the King and Parliament that he might be allowed freely to prove the doctrines he had put forth, and turning with characteristic energy to the attack of his assailants, he asked that all religious vows might be suppressed, that tithes might be diverted to the maintenance of the poor and the clergy maintained by the free alms of their flocks, that the Statutes of

The
death of
Wyclif

Provisors and Præmunire might be enforced against the Papacy, that churchmen might be declared incapable of secular offices, and imprisonment for excommunication cease. Finally, in the teeth of the council's condemnation, he demanded that the doctrine of the Eucharist which he advocated might be freely taught. If he appeared in the following year before the Convocation at Oxford, it was to perplex his opponents by a display of scholastic logic which permitted him to retire without any retractation of his sacramental heresy. For the time his opponents seemed satisfied with his expulsion from the University, but in his retirement at Lutterworth he was forging during these troubled years the great weapon which, wielded by other hands than his own, was to produce so terrible an effect on the triumphant hierarchy. An earlier translation of the Scriptures, in part of which he was aided by his scholar Herford, was being revised and brought to the second form, which is better known as " Wyclif's Bible," when death drew near. The appeal of the prelates to Rome was answered at last by a brief ordering him to appear at the Papal Court. His failing strength exhausted itself in the cold sarcastic reply which explained that his refusal to comply with the summons simply sprang from broken health. " I am always glad," ran the ironical answer, " to explain my faith to any one, and above all to the Bishop of Rome ; for I take it for granted that if it be orthodox he will confirm it, if it be erroneous he will correct it. I assume, too, that as chief Vicar of Christ upon earth the Bishop of Rome is of all mortal men most bound to the law of Christ's Gospel, for among the disciples of Christ a majority is not reckoned by simply counting heads in the fashion of this world, but according to the imitation of Christ on either side. Now Christ during His life upon earth was of all men the poorest, casting from Him all worldly authority. I deduce from these premisses, as a simple counsel of my own, that the Pope should surrender all temporal authority to the civil power and advise his clergy to do the same." The boldness of his words sprang perhaps from a knowledge that his end was near. The terrible strain on energies enfeebled by age and study had at last brought its inevitable result, and a stroke of paralysis while Wyclif was hearing mass in his parish church of Lutterworth was followed on the next day by his death.

Section IV.—The Peasant Revolt, 1377–1381.

[*Authorities.*—For the condition of land and labour at this time see the " History of Prices," by Professor Thorold Rogers, the " Domesday Book of St. Paul's " (Camden Society) with Archdeacon Hale's valuable introduction, and Mr. Seebohm's " Essays on the Black Death " (*Fortnightly Review*, 1865). Among the chroniclers Knyghton and Walsingham are the fullest and most valuable. The great Labour Statutes will be found in the Parliamentary Rolls.]

The religious revolution which we have been describing gave fresh impulse to a revolution of even greater importance, which had for a

Sec. IV.

The
Peasant
Revolt
1377
to
1381

long time been changing the whole face of the country. The manorial system, on which the social organization of every rural part of England rested, had divided the land, for the purposes of cultivation and of internal order, into a number of large estates ; a part of the soil was usually retained by the owner of the manor as his demesne or home-farm, while the remainder was distributed among tenants who were bound to render service to their lord. Under the kings of Ælfred's house, the number of absolute slaves, and the number of freemen, had alike diminished. The slave class, never numerous, had been reduced by the efforts of the Church, perhaps by the general convulsion of the Danish wars. But these wars had often driven the ceorl or freeman to "commend" himself to a thegn who pledged him his protection in consideration of a labour-payment. It is probable that these dependent ceorls are the "villeins" of the Norman epoch, men sunk indeed from pure freedom and bound both to soil and lord, but as yet preserving much of their older rights, retaining their land, free as against all men but their lord, and still sending representatives to hundred-moot and shire-moot. They stood therefore far above the "landless man," the man who had never possessed even under the old constitution political rights, whom the legislation of the English kings had forced to attach himself to a lord on pain of outlawry, and who served as household servant or as hired labourer, or at the best as rent-paying tenant of land which was not his own. The Norman knight or lawyer however saw little distinction between these classes ; and the tendency of legislation under the Angevins was to blend all in a single class of serfs. While the pure "theow" or absolute slave disappeared, therefore, the ceorl or villein sank lower in the social scale. But though the rural population was undoubtedly thrown more together and fused into a more homogeneous class, its actual position corresponded very imperfectly with the view of the lawyers. All indeed were dependents on a lord. The manor-house became the centre of every English village. The manor-court was held in its hall ; it was here that the lord or his steward received homage, recovered fines, held the view of frank-pledge, or enrolled the villagers in their tithing. Here too, if the lord possessed criminal jurisdiction, was held his justice court, and without its doors stood his gallows. Around it lay the demesne or home-farm, and the cultivation of this rested wholly with the "villeins" of the manor. It was by them that the great barn of the lord was filled with sheaves, his sheep shorn, his grain malted, the wood hewn for his hall fire. These services were the labour-rent by which they held their lands, and it was the nature and extent of this labour-rent which parted one class of the population from another. The "villein," in the strict sense of the word, was bound only to gather in his lord's harvest and to aid in the ploughing and sowing of autumn and Lent. The cottar, the bordar,

SEC. IV.

THE
PEASANT
REVOLT
1377
TO
1381

and the labourer were bound to help in the work of the home-farm throughout the year. But these services and the time of rendering them were strictly limited by custom, not only in the case of the ceorl or villein, but in that of the originally meaner "landless man." The possession of his little homestead with the ground around it, the privilege of turning out his cattle on the waste of the manor, passed quietly and insensibly from mere indulgences that could be granted or withdrawn at a lord's caprice into rights that could be pleaded at law. The number of teams, the fines, the reliefs, the services that a lord could claim, at first mere matter of oral tradition, came to be entered on the court-roll of the manor, a copy of which became the title-deed of the villein. It was to this that he owed the name of "copy-holder" which at a later time superseded his older title. Disputes were settled by a reference to this roll or on oral evidence of the custom at issue, but a social arrangement which was eminently characteristic of the English spirit of compromise generally secured a fair adjustment of the claims of villein and lord. It was the duty of the lord's bailiff to exact their due services from the villeins, but his coadjutor in this office, the reeve or foreman of the manor, was chosen by the tenants themselves and acted as representative of their interests and rights.

The first disturbances of the system of tenure which we have described sprang from the introduction of leases. The lord of the manor, instead of cultivating the demesne through his own bailiff, often found it more convenient and profitable to let the manor to a tenant at a given rent, payable either in money or in kind. Thus we find the manor of Sandon leased by the Chapter of St. Paul's at a very early period on a rent which comprised the payment of grain both for bread and ale, of alms to be distributed at the cathedral door, of wood to be used in its bakehouse and brewery, and of money to be spent in wages. It is to this system of leasing, or rather to the usual term for the rent it entailed (feorm, from the Latin *firma*), that we owe the words, "farm" and "farmer," the growing use of which marks the first step in the rural revolution which we are examining. It was a revolution which made little direct change in the manorial system, but its indirect effect in breaking the tie on which the feudal organization of the manor rested, that of the tenant's personal dependence on his lord, and in affording an opportunity by which the wealthier among the tenantry could rise to a position of apparent equality with their older masters and form a new class intermediate between the larger pro-prietors and the customary tenants, was of the highest importance. This earlier step, however, in the modification of the manorial system, by the rise of the Farmer-class, was soon followed by one of a far more serious character in the rise of the Free Labourer. Labour, whatever right it might have attained in other ways, was as yet in the strictest sense bound to the soil. Neither villein nor serf had any choice, either of a master or of a sphere of toil. He was born, in fact, to his holding and to his lord ; he paid head-money for licence to remove from the estate in search of trade or hire, and a refusal to return on recall by his owner would have ended in his pursuit as a fugitive outlaw. But the advance of society and the natural increase of population had for a long time been silently freeing the labourer from this local bondage. The influence of the Church had been exerted in promoting emancipation, as a work of piety, on all estates but its own. The fugitive bondsman found freedom in a flight to chartered towns, where a residence during a year and a day conferred franchise. A fresh step towards freedom was made by the growing tendency to commute labour-services for money-payments. The population was slowly increasing, and as the law of gavel-kind which was applicable to all landed estates not held by military tenure divided the inheritance of the tenantry equally among their sons, the holding of each tenant and the services due from it became divided in a corresponding degree. A labour-rent thus became more difficult to enforce, while the increase of wealth among the tenantry, and the rise of a new spirit of indepen-dence, made it more burthensome to those who rendered it. It was probably from this cause that the commutation of the arrears of labour for a money payment, which had long prevailed on every estate, gradually developed into a general commutation of services. We have already witnessed the silent progress of this remarkable change in the case of St. Edmundsbury, but the practice soon became universal, and "malt-silver," "wood-silver," and "larder-silver," gradually took the place of the older personal services on the court-rolls. The process of commutation was hastened by the necessities of the lords themselves. The luxury of the castle-hall, the splendour and pomp of chivalry, the cost of campaigns, drained the purses of knight and baron, and the sale of freedom to a serf or exemption from services to a villein afforded an easy and tempting mode of refilling them. In this process even kings took part. Edward the Third sent commissioners to royal estates for the especial purpose of selling manumissions to the King's serfs ; and we still possess the names of those who were enfranchised with their families by a payment of hard cash in aid of the exhausted exchequer.

By this entire detachment of the serf from actual dependence on the land, the manorial system was even more radically changed than by the rise of the serf into a copyholder. The whole social condition of the country, in fact, was modified by the appearance of a new class. The rise of the free labourer had followed that of the farmer, labour was no longer bound to one spot or one master : it was free to hire itself to what employer, and to choose what field of employment it would. At the moment we have reached, in fact, the lord of a manor had been reduced over a large part of England to the position of

Sec. IV.

THE
PEASANT
REVOLT

1377
TO
1381

The
Black
Death

Sec. IV.

The
Peasant
Revolt
1377
to
1381

a modern landlord, receiving a rental in money from his tenants, and dependent for the cultivation of his own demesne on paid labourers. But a formidable difficulty now met the landowners who had been driven by the process of enfranchisement to rely on hired labour. Hitherto this supply had been abundant and cheap; but this abundance suddenly disappeared. The most terrible plague which the world ever witnessed advanced at this juncture from the East, and after devastating Europe from the shores of the Mediterranean to the Baltic, swooped at the close of 1348 upon Britain. The traditions of its destructiveness, and the panic-struck words of the statutes which followed it, have been more than justified by modern research. Of the three or four millions who then formed the population of England, more than one-half were swept away in its repeated visitations. Its ravages were fiercest in the greater towns, where filthy and undrained streets afforded a constant haunt

1349 to leprosy and fever. In the burial-ground which the piety of Sir Walter Maunay purchased for the citizens of London, a spot whose site was afterwards marked by the Charter House, more than fifty thousand corpses are said to have been interred. Thousands of people perished at Norwich, while in Bristol the living were hardly able to bury the dead. But the Black Death fell on the villages almost as fiercely as on the towns. More than one-half of the priests of York-shire are known to have perished; in the diocese of Norwich two-thirds of the parishes changed their incumbents. The whole organiza-tion of labour was thrown out of gear. The scarcity of hands made it difficult for the minor tenants to perform the services due for their lands, and only a temporary abandonment of half the rent by the land-owners induced the farmers to refrain from the abandonment of their farms. For a time cultivation became impossible. "The sheep and cattle strayed through the fields and corn," says a contemporary, "and there were none left who could drive them." Even when the first burst of panic was over, the sudden rise of wages consequent on the enormous diminution in the supply of free labour, though accompanied by a corresponding rise in the price of food, rudely disturbed the course of industrial employments; harvests rotted on the ground, and fields were left untilled, not merely from scarcity of hands, but from the strife which now for the first time revealed itself between capital and labour.

While the landowners of the country and the wealthier craftsmen of the town were threatened with ruin by what seemed to their age the extravagant demands of the new labour class, the country itself was torn with riot and disorder. The outbreak of lawless self indulgence which followed everywhere in the wake of the plague told especially upon the "landless men," wandering in search of work, and for the first time masters of the labour market; and the wandering labourer or

Sec. IV.

The
Peasant
Revolt
1377
to
1381

1349

artizan turned easily into the "sturdy beggar," or the bandit of the woods. A summary redress for these evils was at once provided by the Crown in a royal ordinance which was subsequently embodied in the Statute of Labourers. "Every man or woman," runs this famous provision, "of whatsoever condition, free or bond, able in body, and within the age of threescore years, . . . and not having of his own whereof he may live, nor land of his own about the tillage of which he may occupy himself, and not serving any other, shall be bound to serve the employer who shall require him to do so, and shall take only the wages which were accustomed to be taken in the neighbourhood where he is bound to serve" two years before the plague began. A refusal to obey was punished by imprisonment. But sterner measures were soon found to be necessary. Not only was the price of labour fixed by Parliament in the Statute of 1351, but the labour class was once more tied to the soil. The labourer was forbidden to quit the parish where he lived in search of better-paid employment; if he disobeyed he became a "fugitive," and subject to imprisonment at the hands of the justices of the peace. To enforce such a law literally must have been impossible, for corn had risen to so high a price that a day's labour at the old wages would not have purchased wheat enough for a man's support. But the landowners did not flinch from the attempt. The repeated re-enactment of the law shows the difficulty of applying it, and the stubbornness of the struggle which it brought about. The fines and forfeitures which were levied for infractions of its provisions formed a large source of royal revenue, but so ineffectual were the original penalties that the runaway labourer was at last ordered to be branded with a hot iron on the forehead, while the harbouring of serfs in towns was rigorously put down. Nor was it merely the existing class of free labourers which was attacked by this reactionary movement. The increase of their numbers by a commutation of labour services for money payments was suddenly checked, and the ingenuity of the lawyers who were employed as stewards of each manor was exercised in striving to restore to the landowners that customary labour whose loss was now severely felt. Manumissions and exemptions which had passed without question were cancelled on grounds of informality, and labour services from which they held themselves freed by redemption were again demanded from the villeins. The attempt was the more galling that the cause had to be pleaded in the manor-court itself, and to be decided by the very officer whose interest it was to give judgement in favour of his lord. We can see the growth of a fierce spirit of resistance through the statutes which strove in vain to repress it. In the towns, where the system of forced labour was applied with even more rigour than in the country, strikes and combinations became frequent among the lower craftsmen. In the country the free labourers found allies in the villeins whose freedom

SEC. IV.

THE
PEASANT
REVOLT
1377
TO
1381

from manorial service was questioned. These were often men of position and substance, and throughout the eastern counties the gatherings of "fugitive serfs" were supported by an organized resistance and by large contributions of money on the part of the wealthier tenantry. A statute of later date throws light on their resistance. It tells us that "villeins and holders of lands in villeinage withdrew their customs and services from their lords, having attached themselves to other persons who maintained and abetted them; and who, under colour of exemplifications from Domesday of the manors and villages where they dwelt, claimed to be quit of all manner of services, either of their body or of their lands, and would suffer no distress or other course of justice to be taken against them; the villeins aiding their maintainers by threatening the officers of their lords with peril to life and limb, as well by open assemblies as by confederacies to support each other." It would seem not only as if the villein was striving to resist the reactionary tendency of the lords of manors to regain his labour service, but that in the general overturning of social institutions the copyholder was struggling to become a freeholder, and the farmer to be recognized as proprietor of the demesne he held on lease.

A more terrible outcome of the general suffering was seen in a new revolt against the whole system of social inequality which had till then passed unquestioned as the divine order of the world. The cry of the poor found a terrible utterance in the words of "a mad priest of Kent," as the courtly Froissart calls him, who for twenty years found audience for his sermons, in defiance of interdict and imprisonment, in the stout yeomen who gathered in the Kentish churchyards. "Mad" as the landowners called him, it was in the preaching of John Ball that England first listened to a declaration of natural equality and the rights of man. "Good people," cried the preacher, "things will never go well in England so long as goods be not in common, and so long as there be villeins and gentlemen. By what right are they whom we call lords greater folk than we? On what grounds have they deserved it? Why do they hold us in serfage? If we all came of the same father and mother, of Adam and Eve, how can they say or prove that they are better than we, if it be not that they make us gain for them by our toil what they spend in their pride? They are clothed in velvet, and warm in their furs and their ermines, while we are covered with rags. They have wine and spices and fair bread; and we oat-cake and straw, and water to drink. They have leisure and fine houses; we have pain and labour, the rain and the wind in the fields. And yet it is of us and of our toil that these men hold their state." It was the tyranny of property that then as ever roused the defiance of socialism. A spirit fatal to the whole system of the Middle Ages breathed in the popular rime which condensed the levelling doctrine of John

Ball: "When Adam delved and Eve span, who was then the gentleman?"

The rime was running from lip to lip when a fresh instance of public oppression fanned the smouldering discontent into a flame. Edward the Third died in a dishonoured old age, robbed on his death-bed even of his finger-rings by the vile mistress to whom he had clung; and the accession of the child of the Black Prince, Richard the Second, revived the hopes of what in a political sense we must still call the popular party in the Legislature. The Parliament of 1377 took up the work of reform, and boldly assumed the control of a new subsidy by assigning two of their number to regulate its expenditure: that of 1378 demanded and obtained an account of the mode in which the subsidy had been spent. But the real strength of Parliament was directed, as we have seen, to the desperate struggle in which the proprietary classes, whom they exclusively represented, were striving to reduce the labourer into a fresh serfage. Meanwhile the shame of defeat abroad was added to the misery and discord at home. The French war ran its disastrous course: one English fleet was beaten by the Spaniards, a second sunk by a storm; and a campaign in the heart of France ended, like its predecessors, in disappointment and ruin. It was to defray the heavy expenses of the war that the Parliament of 1380 renewed a grant made three years before, to be raised by means of a poll-tax on every person in the realm. The tax brought under contribution a class which had hitherto escaped, men such as the labourer, the village smith, the village tiler; it goaded into action precisely the class which was already seething with discontent, and its exaction set England on fire from sea to sea. As spring went on quaint rimes passed through the country, and served as summons to the revolt which soon extended from the eastern and midland counties over all England south of the Thames. "John Ball," ran one, "greeteth you all, and doth for to understand he hath rung your bell. Now right and might, will and skill, God speed every dele." "Help truth," ran another, "and truth shall help you! Now reigneth pride in price, and covetise is counted wise, and lechery withouten shame, and gluttony withouten blame. Envy reigneth with treason, and sloth is take in great season. God do bote, for now is tyme!" We recognise Ball's hand in the yet more stirring missives of "Jack the Miller" and "Jack the Carter." "Jack Miller asketh help to turn his mill aright. He hath grounden small, small: the King's Son of Heaven he shall pay for all. Look thy mill go aright with the four sailes, and the post stand with steadfastness. With right and with might, with skill and with will; let might help right, and skill go before will, and right before might, so goeth our mill aright." "Jack Carter," ran the companion missive, "prays you all that ye make a good end of that ye have begun, and do

SEC. IV.

THE
PEASANT
REVOLT
1377
TO
1381
The
Peasant
Rising

1379

1381

Sec. IV.

The
Peasant
Revolt
1377
TO
1381

well, and aye better and better: for at the even men heareth the day." " Falseness and guile," sang Jack Trewman, " have reigned too long, and truth hath been set under a lock, and falseness and guile reigneth in every stock.   No man may come truth to, but if he sing ' si dedero.'   True love is away that was so good, and clerks for wealth work them woe.   God do bote, for now is tyme."   In the rude jingle of these lines began for England the literature of political controversy : they are the first predecessors of the pamphlets of Milton and of Burke.   Rough as they are, they express clearly enough the mingled passions which met in the revolt of the peasants : their longing for a right rule, for plain and simple justice ; their scorn of the immorality of the nobles and the infamy of the court ; their resentment at the perversion of the law to the cause of oppression.   The revolt spread like wildfire over the country ; Norfolk and Suffolk, Cambridge and Hertfordshire rose in arms ; from Sussex and Surrey the insurrection extended as far as Devon.   But the actual outbreak began in Kent, where a tiler killed a tax-collector in vengeance for an outrage on his daughter.   The county rose in arms.   Canterbury, where " the whole town was of their mind," threw open its gates to the insurgents, who

plundered the Archbishop's palace and dragged John Ball from its prison, while a hundred thousand Kentish-men gathered round Wat Tyler of Essex and John Hales of Malling.   In the eastern counties the levy of the poll-tax had already gathered crowds of peasants together, armed with clubs, rusty swords, and bows, and the royal commissioners sent to repress the tumult were driven from the field.   While the Essex-men marched upon London on one side of the river, the Kentish-men marched on the other.   Their grievance was mainly political, for villeinage was unknown in Kent ; but as they poured on to Blackheath, every lawyer who fell into their hands was put to death ; " not till all these were killed would the land enjoy its old freedom again," the peasants shouted as they fired the houses of the stewards and flung the records of the manor-courts into the flames.   The whole population joined them as they marched along, while the nobles were paralyzed with fear.   The young King—he was but a boy of fifteen—addressed them from a boat on the river ; but the refusal of his Council under the guidance of Archbishop Sudbury to allow him to land kindled the peasants to fury, and with cries of " Treason "

the great mass rushed on London.   Its gates were flung open by the poorer artizans within the city, and the stately palace of John of Gaunt at the Savoy, the new inn of the lawyers at the Temple, the houses of the foreign merchants, were soon in a blaze.   But the insurgents, as they proudly boasted, were " seekers of truth and justice, not thieves or robbers," and a plunderer found carrying off a silver vessel from the sack of the Savoy was flung with his spoil into the flames.   The general terror was shown ludicrously enough on the following day, when a daring band of peasants, under Tyler himself, forced their way into the Tower, and taking the panic-stricken knights of the royal household in rough horse-play by the beard, promised to be their equals and good comrades in the time to come. But the horse-play changed into dreadful earnest when they found the King had escaped their grasp, and when Archbishop Sudbury and the Prior of St. John were discovered in the chapel ; the primate was dragged from his sanctuary and beheaded, and the same vengeance was wreaked on the Treasurer and the Chief Commissioner for the levy of the hated poll-tax.   Meanwhile the King had ridden from the Tower to meet the mass of the Essex-men, who had encamped without the city at Mile-end, while the men of Hertfordshire and St. Albans occupied Highbury.   " I am your King and Lord, good people," the boy began with a fearlessness which marked his bearing throughout the crisis ; " what will ye ? "   " We will that you free us for ever," shouted the peasants, " us and our lands ; and that we be never named nor held for serfs."   " I grant it," replied Richard ; and he bade them go home, pledging himself at once to issue charters of freedom and amnesty.   A shout of joy welcomed the promise.   Throughout the day more than thirty clerks were busied writing letters of pardon and emancipation, and with these the mass of the Essex and Hertfordshire men withdrew quietly to their homes.   It was with such a charter that William Grindecobbe returned to St. Albans, and breaking at the head of the burghers into the abbey precincts, summoned the abbot to deliver up the charters which bound the town in bondage to his house. But a more striking proof of servitude remained in the millstones, which after a long suit at law had been adjudged to the abbey, and placed within its cloister as a triumphant witness that no townsman might grind corn within the domain of the abbey save at the abbot's will.   Bursting into the cloister the burghers now tore the millstones from the floor, and broke them into small pieces, " like blessed bread in church," so that each might have something to show of the day when their freedom was won again.

Many of the Kentish-men dispersed at the news of the King's pledge to the men of Essex, but thirty thousand men still surrounded Wat Tyler when Richard by a mere chance encountered him the next morning at Smithfield.   Hot words passed between his train and the peasant leader, who advanced to confer with the King ; and a threat from Tyler brought on a brief struggle in which the Mayor of London, William Walworth, struck him with his dagger to the ground.   " Kill, kill," shouted the crowd, " they have slain our captain."   " What need ye, my masters ? " cried the boy-king, as he rode boldly to the front, " I am your Captain and your King !   Follow me."   The hopes of the peasants centred in the young sovereign : one aim of their rising had been to free him from the evil counsellors who, as they believed, abused

Sec. IV.

The
Peasant
Revolt
1377
to
1381

Sec. IV.

The
Peasant
Revolt

1377
to
1381

his youth, and they now followed him with a touching loyalty and trust till he entered the Tower. His mother welcomed him with tears of joy. " Rejoice and praise God," the boy answered, " for I have recovered to-day my heritage which was lost, and the realm of England." But he was compelled to give the same pledge of freedom as at Mile-end, and it was only after receiving his letters of pardon and emancipation that the Kentish-men dispersed to their homes. The revolt, indeed, was far from being at an end. South of the Thames it spread as far as Devonshire ; there were outbreaks in the north ; the eastern counties were in one wild turmoil of revolt. A body of peasants occupied St. Albans. A maddened crowd forced the gates of St. Edmundsbury and wrested from the trembling monks pledges for the confirmation of the liberties of the town. John the Litster, a dyer of Norwich, headed a mass of peasants, under the title of King of the Commons, and compelled the nobles he captured to act as his meat-tasters and to serve him on their knees during his repast. But the withdrawal of the peasant armies with their letters of emancipation gave courage to the nobles. The warlike Bishop of Norwich fell lance in hand on Litster's camp, and scattered the peasants of Norfolk at the first shock : while the King, with an army of 40,000 men, spread terror by the ruthlessness of his executions as he marched in triumph through Kent and Essex. At Waltham he was met by the display of his own recent charters and a protest from the Essex-men that " they were so far as freedom went the peers of their lords." But they were to learn the worth of a king's word. "Villeins you were," answered Richard, "and villeins you are. In bondage you shall abide, and that not your old bondage, but a worse ! " But the stubborn resistance which he met showed the temper of the people. The villagers of Billericay threw themselves into the woods and fought two hard fights before they were reduced to submission. It was only by threats of death that verdicts of guilty could be wrung from the Essex jurors when the leaders of the revolt were brought before them. Grindecobbe was offered his life if he would persuade his followers at St. Albans to restore the charters they had wrung from the monks. He turned bravely to his fellow-townsmen and bade them take no thought for his trouble. " If I die," he said, " I shall die for the cause of the freedom we have won, counting myself happy to end my life by such a martyrdom. Do this to-day as you would have done had I been killed yesterday." But the stubborn will of the conquered was met by as stubborn a will in their conquerors. Through the summer and autumn seven thousand men are said to have perished on the gallows or the field. The royal council indeed showed its sense of the danger of a mere policy of resistance by submitting the question of enfranchisement to the Parliament which assembled on the suppression of the revolt, with words which suggested a compromise. " If you desire to enfranchise and

SEC. V.

RICHARD
THE
SECOND

1381
TO
1399

set at liberty the said serfs," ran the royal message, "by your common assent, as the King has been informed that some of you desire, he will consent to your prayer." But no thoughts of compromise influenced the landowners in their reply. The King's grant and letters, the Parliament answered with perfect truth, were legally null and void: their serfs were their goods, and the King could not take their goods from them but by their own consent. "And this consent," they ended, "we have never given and never will give, were we all to die in one day."

Section V.—Richard the Second, 1381—1399.

[*Authorities.*—The " Annales Ricardi Secundi et Henrici Quarti," published by the Master of the Rolls, are our main authority. They form the basis of the St. Albans compilation which bears the name of Walsingham, and from which the Life of Richard by a monk of Evesham is for the most part derived. The same violent Lancastrian sympathy runs through Walsingham and the fifth book of Knyghton's Chronicle. The French authorities, on the other hand, are vehemently on Richard's side. Froissart, who ends at this time, is supplemented by the metrical history of Creton (" Archæologia," vol. xx.) and the "Chronique de la Traïson et Mort de Richart" (English Historical Society), both the works of French authors, and published in France in the time of Henry the Fourth, probably with the aim of arousing French feeling against the House of Lancaster and the war-policy it had revived. The popular feeling in England may be seen in "Political Songs from Edward III. to Richard III." (Rolls Series). The "Fœdera" and Rolls of Parliament are indispensable for this period: its constitutional importance has been ably illustrated by Mr. Hallam ("Middle Ages "). William Longland's poem, the "Complaint of Piers the Ploughman" (edited by Mr. Skeat for the Early English Text Society), throws a flood of light on the social condition of England at the time ; a poem on "The Deposition of Richard II.," which has been published by the Camden Society, is now ascribed to the same author. The best modern work on Richard II. is that of M. Wallon (" Richard II." Paris, 1864).]

All the darker and sterner aspects of the age which we have been viewing, its social revolt, its moral and religious awakening, the misery of the poor, the protest of the Lollard, are painted with a terrible fidelity in the poem of William Longland. Nothing brings more vividly home to us the social chasm which in the fourteenth century severed the rich from the poor than the contrast between the " Complaint of Piers the Ploughman" and the " Canterbury Tales." The world of wealth and ease and laughter through which the courtly Chaucer moves with eyes downcast as in a pleasant dream is a far-off world of wrong and of ungodliness to the gaunt poet of the poor. Born probably in Shropshire, where he had been put to school and received minor orders as a clerk, " Long Will," as Longland was nicknamed for his tall stature, found his way at an early age to London, and earned a miserable livelihood there by singing "placebos" and "diriges" in the stately funerals of his day. Men took the moody clerk for a

SEC. V.

RICHARD
THE
SECOND

1381
TO
1399

madman; his bitter poverty quickened the defiant pride that made him loth—as he tells us—to bow to the gay lords and dames who rode decked in silver and minivere along the Cheap, or to exchange a " God save you " with the law sergeants as he passed their new house in the Temple. His world is the world of the poor : he dwells on the poor man's life, on his hunger and toil, his rough revelry and his despair, with the narrow intensity of a man who has no outlook beyond it. The narrowness, the misery, the monotony of the life he paints reflect themselves in his verse. It is only here and there that a love of nature or a grim earnestness of wrath quicken his rime into poetry ; there is not a gleam of the bright human sympathy of Chaucer, of his fresh delight in the gaiety, the tenderness, the daring of the world about him, of his picturesque sense of even its coarsest contrasts, of his delicate irony, of his courtly wit. The cumbrous allegory, the tedious platitudes, the rimed texts from Scripture which form the staple of Longland's work, are only broken here and there by phrases of a shrewd common sense, by bitter outbursts, by pictures of a broad Hogarthian humour. What chains one to the poem is its deep under-tone of sadness : the world is out of joint and the gaunt rimer who stalks silently along the Strand has no faith in his power to put it right. His poem covers indeed an age of shame and suffering such as England had never known, for if its first brief sketch appeared two

years after the Peace of Brétigny its completion may be dated at the close of the reign of Edward the Third, and its final issue preceded but by a single year the Peasant Revolt. Londoner as he is, Will's fancy flies far from the sin and suffering of the great city to a May-morning in the Malvern Hills. " I was wery forwandered and went me to rest under a broad bank by a burn side, and as I lay and leaned and looked in the water I slumbered in a sleeping, it sweyved (sounded) so merry." Just as Chaucer gathers the typical figures of the world he saw into his pilgrim train, so the dreamer gathers into a wide field his army of traders and chafferers, of hermits and solitaries, of minstrels, " japers and jinglers," bidders and beggars, ploughmen that " in setting and in sowing swonken (toil) full hard," pilgrims " with their wenches after," weavers and labourers, burgess and bondman, lawyer and scrivener, court-haunting bishops, friars, and pardoners " parting the silver " with the parish priest. Their pilgrimage is not to Canterbury, but to Truth ; their guide to Truth neither clerk nor priest but Peterkin the Ploughman, whom they find ploughing in his field. He it is who bids the knight no more wrest gifts from his tenant nor misdo with the poor. " Though he be thine underling here, well may hap in heaven that he be worthier set and with more bliss than thou. . . . For in charnel at church churles be evil to know, or a knight from a knave there." The gospel of equality is backed by the gospel of labour. The aim of the Ploughman is to

Sec. V.

Richard
the
Second

1381
to
1399

work, and to make the world work with him.   He warns the labourer as he warns the knight.   Hunger is God's instrument in bringing the idlest to toil, and Hunger waits to work her will on the idler and the waster.   On the eve of the great struggle between wealth and labour Longland stands alone in his fairness to both, in his shrewd political and religious common sense.   In the face of the popular hatred which was to gather round John of Gaunt, he paints the Duke in a famous apologue as the cat who, greedy as she might be, at any rate keeps the noble rats from utterly devouring the mice of the people.   Though the poet is loyal to the Church, he proclaims a righteous life to be better than a host of indulgences, and God sends His pardon to Piers when priests dispute it.   But he sings as a man conscious of his loneliness and without hope.   It is only in a dream that he sees Corruption, " Lady Mede," brought to trial, and the world repenting at the preaching of Reason.   In the waking life Reason finds no listeners.   The poet himself is looked upon—he tells us bitterly—as a madman.   There is a terrible despair in the close of his later poem, where the triumph of Christ is only followed by the reign of Antichrist ; where Contrition slumbers amidst the revel of Death and Sin ; and Conscience, hard beset by Pride and Sloth, rouses himself with a last effort, and seizing his pilgrim staff wanders over the world to find Piers Ploughman.

The strife indeed which Longland would have averted raged only the fiercer after the repression of the Peasant Revolt.   The Statutes of Labourers, effective as they proved in sowing hatred between employer and employed, between rich and poor, were powerless for their immediate ends, either in reducing the actual rate of wages or in restricting the mass of floating labour to definite areas of employment.   During the century and a half after the Peasant Revolt villeinage died out so rapidly that it became a rare and antiquated thing.   A hundred years after the Black Death the wages of an English labourer could purchase twice the amount of the necessaries of life which could have been obtained for the wages paid under Edward the Third.   The statement is corroborated by the incidental descriptions of the life of the working classes which we find in Piers Ploughman.   Labourers, Longland tells us, " that have no land to live on but their hands disdained to live on penny ale or bacon, but demanded fresh flesh or fish, fried or baked, and that hot and hotter for chilling of their maw."   The market was still in fact in the labourer's hands, in spite of statutes ; " and but if he be highly hired else will he chide and wail the time that he was made a workman."   The poet saw clearly that as population rose to its normal rate times such as these would pass away.   " Whiles Hunger was their master here would none of them chide or strive against *his* statute, so sternly he looked : and I warn you, workmen, win while ye may, for Hunger hitherward hasteth him fast."   But even

Sec. V.

Richard
the
Second
1381
to
1399

at the time when he wrote there were seasons of the year during which employment for the floating mass of labour was hard to find.   In the long interval between harvest-tide and harvest-tide, work and food were alike scarce in the mediæval homestead.   " I have no penny," says Piers the Ploughman in such a season, in lines which give us the picture of a farm of the day, "pullets for to buy, nor neither geese nor pigs, but two green cheeses, a few curds and cream, and an oaten cake, and two loaves of beans and bran baken for my children.   I have no salt bacon, nor no cooked meat collops for to make, but I have parsley and leeks and many cabbage plants, and eke a cow and a calf, and a cart-mare to draw a-field my dung while the drought lasteth, and by this livelihood we must all live till Lammas-tide (August), and by that I hope to have harvest in my croft."   But it was not till Lammas-tide that high wages and the new corn bade "Hunger go to sleep," and during the long spring and summer the free labourer, and the "waster that will not work but wander about, that will eat no bread but the finest wheat, nor drink but of the best and brownest ale," was a source of social and political danger.   "He grieveth him against God and grudgeth against Reason, and then curseth he the King and all his Council after such law to allow labourers to grieve."   The terror of the landowners expressed itself in legislation which was a fitting sequel to the Statutes of Labourers.   They forbade the child of any tiller of the soil to be apprenticed in a town.   They prayed Richard to ordain "that no bondman or bondwoman shall place their children at school, as has been done, so as to advance their children in the world by their going into the Church."   The new colleges which were being founded at the two Universities at this moment closed their gates upon villeins.   It was the failure of such futile efforts to effect their aim which drove the energy of the great proprietors into a new direction, and in the end revolutionized the whole agricultural system of the country. Sheep-farming required fewer hands than tillage, and the scarcity and high price of labour tended to throw more and more land into sheep-farms.   In the decrease of personal service, as villeinage died away, it became the interest of the lord to diminish the number of tenants on his estate as it had been before his interest to maintain it, and he did this by massing the small allotments together into larger holdings.   By this course of eviction the number of the free-labour class was enormously increased while the area of employment was diminished ; and the social danger from vagabondage and the "sturdy beggar" grew every day greater till it brought about the despotism of the Tudors.

This social danger mingled with the yet more formidable religious peril which sprang from the party violence of the later Lollardry.   The persecution of Courtenay had deprived the religious reform of its more learned adherents and of the support of the Universities, while Sec. V.

Richard
the
Second

1381
to
1399 Wyclif's death had robbed it of its head at a moment when little had been done save a work of destruction. From that moment Lollardry ceased to be in any sense an organized movement, and crumbled into a general spirit of revolt. All the religious and social discontent of the times floated instinctively to this new centre ; the socialist dreams of the peasantry, the new and keener spirit of personal morality, the hatred of the friars, the jealousy of the great lords towards the prelacy, the fanaticism of the reforming zealot, were blended together in a common hostility to the Church and a common resolve to substitute personal religion for its dogmatic and ecclesiastical system. But it was this want of organization, this looseness and fluidity of the new movement, that made it penetrate through every class of society. Women as well as men became the preachers of the new sect. Lollardry had its own schools, its own books ; its pamphlets were passed everywhere from hand to hand ; scurrilous ballads which revived the old attacks of " Golias " in the Angevin times upon the wealth and luxury of the clergy were sung at every corner. Nobles, like the Earl of Salisbury, and at a later time Sir John Oldcastle, placed themselves openly at the head of the cause and threw open their gates as a refuge for its missionaries. London in its hatred of the clergy became fiercely Lollard, and defended a Lollard preacher who had ventured to advocate the new doctrines from the pulpit of St. Paul's. One of its mayors, John of Northampton, showed the influence of the new morality by the Puritan spirit in which he dealt with the morals of the city. Compelled to act, as he said, by the remiss-ness of the clergy, who connived for money at every kind of debauchery, he arrested the loose women, cut off their hair, and carted them through the streets as an object of public scorn. But the moral spirit of the new movement, though infinitely its grander side, was less dan-gerous to the Church than its open repudiation of the older doctrines and systems of Christendom. Out of the floating mass of opinion which bore the name of Lollardry one great faith gradually evolved itself, a faith in the sole authority of the Bible as a source of religious truth. The translation of Wyclif did its work. Scripture, complains a canon of Leicester, " became a vulgar thing, and more open to lay folk and women that knew how to read than it is wont to be to clerks themselves." Consequences which Wyclif had perhaps shrunk from drawing were boldly drawn by his disciples. The Church was declared to have become apostate, its priesthood was denounced as no priesthood, its sacraments as idolatry. It was in vain that the clergy attempted to stifle the new movement by their old weapon of perse-cution. The jealousy entertained by the baronage and gentry of every pretension of the Church to secular power foiled its efforts to make persecution effective. At the moment of the Peasant Revolt, Courtenay procured the enactment of a statute which commissioned the sheriffs to

SEC. V.

RICHARD
THE
SECOND

1381
TO
1399

seize all persons convicted before the bishops of preaching heresy. But the statute was repealed in the next session, and the Commons added to the bitterness of the blow by their protest that they considered it "in nowise their interest to be more under the jurisdiction of the prelates or more bound by them than their ancestors had been in times past." Heresy indeed was still a felony by the common law, and if as yet we meet with no instances of the punishment of heretics by the fire it was because the threat of such a death was commonly followed by the recantation of the Lollard. But the restriction of each bishop's jurisdiction within the limits of his own diocese made it almost impossible to arrest the wandering preachers of the new doctrine, and the civil punishment—even if it had been sanctioned by public opinion —seems to have long fallen into desuetude. Experience proved to the prelates that few sheriffs would arrest on the mere warrant of an ecclesiastical officer, and that no royal court would issue the writ "for the burning of a heretic" on a bishop's requisition. But powerless as the efforts of the Church were for purposes of repression, they were effective in rousing the temper of the Lollards into a bitter fanaticism. The Lollard teachers directed their fiercest invectives against the wealth and secularity of the great Churchmen. In a formal petition to Parliament they mingled denunciations of the riches of the clergy with an open profession of disbelief in transubstantiation, priesthood, pilgrimages, and image worship, and a demand, which illustrates the strange medley of opinions which jostled together in the new movement, that war might be declared unchristian, and that trades such as those of the goldsmith or the armourer, which were contrary to apostolical poverty, might be banished from the realm. They contended (and it is remarkable that a Parliament of the next reign adopted the statement) that from the superfluous revenues of the Church, if once they were applied to purposes of general utility, the King might maintain fifteen earls, fifteen hundred knights, and six thousand squires, besides endowing a hundred hospitals for the relief of the poor.

The distress of the landowners, the general disorganization of the country, in every part of which bands of marauders were openly defying the law, the panic of the Church and of society at large as the projects of the Lollards shaped themselves into more daring and revolutionary forms, added a fresh keenness to the national discontent at the languid and inefficient prosecution of the war. The junction of the French and Spanish fleets had made them masters of the seas; what fragments were left of Guienne lay at their mercy, and the northern frontier of England itself was flung open to France by the alliance of the Scots. The landing of a French force in the Forth roused the whole country to a desperate effort, and a large and well-equipped army of Englishmen penetrated as far as Edinburgh in the vain hope of bringing their enemy to battle. A more terrible blow had been struck in the re-

Sec. V.

Richard
the
Second

1381
to
1399

duction of Ghent by the French troops, and the loss of the one remaining market for English commerce ; while the forces which should have been employed in saving it, and in the protection of the English shores against the threat of invasion, were squandered by John of Gaunt on the Spanish frontier in pursuit of a visionary crown, which he claimed in his wife's right, the daughter of Pedro the Cruel.   The enterprise showed that the Duke had now abandoned the hope of directing affairs at home.   Robert de Vere and Michael de la Pole, the Earl of Suffolk, had stood since the suppression of the revolt at the head of the royal councils, and their steady purpose was to drive the Duke of Lancaster from power.   But the departure of John of Gaunt only called to the front his brother and his son, the Duke of Gloucester and the Earl of Derby ; while the lukewarm prosecution of the war, the profuse expenditure of the Court, and above all the manifest will of the King to free himself from Parliamentary control, estranged the Lower House.   The Parliament impeached Suffolk for corruption, and appointed a commission of regency for a year, of which Gloucester was the leading spirit.   The attempt of the young King at the close of the session to reverse these measures was crushed by the appearance of Gloucester and his friends in arms ; in the Merciless Parliament a charge of high treason hurried into exile or to death Suffolk with his supporters, the five judges who had pronounced the commission to be in itself illegal were banished, and four members of the royal household sent to the block.   But hardly a year had passed when Richard found himself strong enough to break down by a word the government against which he had struggled so vainly.   Entering the Council he suddenly asked his uncle to tell him how old he was.   " Your Highness," replied Gloucester, " is in your twenty-fourth year."   " Then I am old enough to manage my own affairs," said Richard coolly.   " I have been longer under guardianship than any ward in my realm.   I thank you for your past services, my lords, but I need them no longer."

For eight years the King wielded the power which thus passed quietly into his hands with singular wisdom and good fortune.   On the one hand he carried his peace policy into effect by negotiations with France, which brought about a truce renewed year by year till it was prolonged in 1394 for four years, and this period of rest was lengthened for twenty-five years by a subsequent agreement on his marriage with Isabella, the daughter of Charles the Sixth.   On the other he announced his resolve to rule by the advice of his Parliament, submitted to its censure, and consulted it on all matters of importance.   In a short campaign he pacified Ireland ; and the Lollard troubles which had threatened during his absence died away on his return.   But the brilliant abilities which Richard shared with the rest of the Plantagenets were marred by a fitful inconstancy, an insane pride, and a craving for absolute power.   His uncle, the Duke of Gloucester remained at the head of the opposition ;

Sec. V.

Richard
the
Second

1381
to
1399

1397

while the King had secured the friendship of John of Gaunt, and of his son Henry, Earl of Derby. The readiness with which Richard seized on an opportunity of provoking a contest shows the bitterness with which during the long years that had passed since the flight of Suffolk he had brooded over his projects of vengeance. The Duke of Gloucester and the Earls of Arundel and Warwick were arrested on a charge of conspiracy. A Parliament packed with royal partizans was used to crush Richard's opponents. The pardons granted nine years before were recalled; the commission of regency declared to have been illegal, and its promoters guilty of treason. The blow was ruthlessly followed up. The Duke was saved from a trial by a sudden death in his prison at Calais; while his chief supporter, Arundel, the Archbishop of Canterbury, was impeached and banished, and the nobles of his party condemned to death and imprisonment. The measures introduced into the Parliament of the following year showed that besides his projects of revenge Richard's designs had widened into a definite plan of absolute government. It declared null the proceedings of the Parliament of 1388. He was freed from Parliamentary control by the grant to him of a subsidy upon wool and leather for the term of his life. His next step got rid of Parliament itself. A committee of twelve peers and six commoners was appointed in Parliament, with power to continue their sittings after its dissolution and to "examine and determine all matters and subjects which had been moved in the presence of the King, with all the dependences of those not determined." The aim of Richard was to supersede by means of this permanent commission the body from which it originated: he at once employed it to determine causes and carry out his will, and forced from every tenant of the Crown an oath to recognize the validity of its acts and to oppose any attempts to alter or revoke them. With such an engine at his command the King was absolute, and with the appearance of absolutism the temper of his reign suddenly changed. A system of forced loans, the sale of charters of pardon to Gloucester's adherents, the outlawry of seven counties at once on the plea that they had supported his enemies and must purchase pardon, a reckless interference with the course of justice, roused into new life the social and political discontent which was threatening the very existence of the Crown.

By his good government and by his evil government alike, Richard had succeeded in alienating every class of his subjects. He had estranged the nobles by his peace policy, the landowners by his refusal to sanction the insane measures of repression they directed against the labourer, the merchant class by his illegal exactions, and the Church by his want of zeal against the Lollards. Richard himself had no sympathy with the Lollards, and the new sect as a social danger was held firmly at bay. But the royal officers showed little zeal in aiding the bishops to seize or punish the heretical teachers, and

SEC. V.

RICHARD
THE
SECOND
1381
TO
1399

Lollardry found favour in the very precincts of the Court; it was through the patronage of Richard's first queen, Anne of Bohemia, that the tracts and Bible of the Reformer had been introduced into her native land, to give rise to the remarkable movement which found its earliest leaders in John Huss and Jerome of Prague. Richard stood almost alone in fact in his realm, but even this accumulated mass of hatred might have failed to crush him had not an act of jealousy and tyranny placed an able and unscrupulous leader at the head of the national discontent. Henry, Earl of Derby and Duke of Hereford, the eldest son of John of Gaunt, though he had taken part against his royal cousin in the earlier troubles of his reign, had loyally supported him in his recent measures against Gloucester. No sooner, however, were these measures successful than Richard turned his new power against the more dangerous House of Lancaster, and availing himself of a quarrel between the Dukes of Hereford and Norfolk, in which each party bandied accusations of treason against the other, banished both from the realm. Banishment was soon followed by the annulling of leave which had been given to Henry to receive his inheritance on John of Gaunt's death, and the King himself seized the Lancastrian estates. At the moment when he had thus driven his cousin to despair, Richard crossed into Ireland to complete the work of conquest and organization which he had begun there; and Archbishop Arundel, an exile like himself, urged the Duke to take advantage of the King's absence for the recovery of his rights. Eluding the vigilance of the French Court, at which he had taken shelter, Henry landed with a handful of men on the coast of Yorkshire, where he was at once joined by the Earls of Northumberland and Westmoreland, the heads of the great houses of the Percies and the Nevilles; and, with an army which grew as he advanced, entered triumphantly into London. The Duke of York, whom the King had left regent, submitted, and his forces joined those of Henry; and when Richard landed at Milford Haven he found the kingdom lost. His own army dispersed as it landed, and the deserted King fled in disguise to North Wales, to find a second force which the Earl of Salisbury had gathered for his support already disbanded. Invited to a conference with the Duke of Lancaster at Flint, he saw himself surrounded by the rebel forces. "I am betrayed," he cried, as the view of his enemies burst on him from the hill; "there are pennons and banners in the valley." But it was too late for retreat. Richard was seized and brought before his cousin. "I am come before my time," said Lancaster, "but I will show you the reason. Your people, my lord, complain that for the space of twenty years you have ruled them harshly: however, if it please God, I will help you to rule them better." "Fair cousin," replied the King, "since it pleases you, it pleases me well." But Henry's designs went far beyond a share in the government of the realm. The Parliament which assembled in

SEC. V.

RICHARD
THE
SECOND

1381
TO
1399

Westminster Hall received with shouts of applause a formal paper in which Richard resigned the crown as one incapable of reigning and worthy for his great demerits to be deposed. The resignation was confirmed by a solemn Act of Deposition. The coronation oath was read, and a long impeachment, which stated the breach of the promises made in it, was followed by a solemn vote of both Houses which removed Richard from the state and authority of King. According to the strict rules of hereditary descent as construed by the feudal lawyers, by an assumed analogy with the descent of ordinary estates, the crown would now have passed to a house which had at an earlier period played a leading part in the revolutions of the Edwards. The great grandson of the Mortimer who brought about the deposition of Edward the Second had married the daughter and heiress of Lionel of Clarence, the third son of Edward the Third. The childlessness of Richard and the death of Edward's second son without issue placed Edmund, his grandson by this marriage, first among the claimants of the crown ; but he was a child of six years old, the strict rule of hereditary descent had never received any formal recognition in the case of the crown, and precedent had established the right of Parliament to choose in such a case a successor among any other members of the Royal House. Only one such successor was in fact possible. Rising from his seat and crossing himself, Henry of Lancaster solemnly challenged the crown " as that I am descended by right line of blood coming from the good lord King Henry the Third, and through that right that God of His grace hath sent me with help of my kin and of my friends to recover it : the which realm was in point to be undone for default of governance and undoing of good laws." Whatever defects such a claim might present were more than covered by the solemn recognition of Parliament. The two Archbishops, taking the new sovereign by the hand, seated him upon the throne, and Henry in emphatic words ratified the compact between himself and his people. " Sirs," he said to the prelates, lords, knights, and burgesses gathered round him, " I thank God and you, spiritual and temporal, and all estates of the land : and do you to wit it is not my will that any man think that by way of conquest I would disinherit any of his heritage, franchises, or other rights that he ought to have, nor put him out of the good that he has and has had by the good laws and customs of the realm, except those persons that have been against the good purpose and the common profit of the realm."

Section VI.—The House of Lancaster, 1399—1422.

[*Authorities.*—For Henry IV. the " Annales Henrici Quarti " and Walsing-ham, as before. For his successor, the " Acta Henrici Quinti " by Titus Livius, a chaplain in the royal army (English Historical Society) ; a life by Elmham, Prior of Lenton, simpler in style but identical in arrangement and facts with

SEC. VI.

THE
HOUSE OF
LANCASTER

1399
TO
1422

The
Suppres-
sion of
Lollardry

the former work ; a biography by Robert Redman ; a metrical Chronicle by Elmham (published in Rolls Series in "Memorials of Henry V."); and the meagre chronicles of Hardyng and Otterbourne. Monstrelet is the most important French authority for this period ; for the Norman campaigns see M. Puiseux's "Siége de Rouen" (Caen, 1867). Lord Brougham has given a vigorous and, in a constitutional point of view, valuable sketch of this period in his "History of England under the House of Lancaster."]

Raised to the throne by a Parliamentary revolution and resting its claims on a Parliamentary title, the House of Lancaster was precluded by its very position from any resumption of the late struggle for independence on the part of the Crown which had culminated in the bold effort of Richard the Second. During no period of our early history were the powers of the two Houses so frankly recognized. The tone of Henry the Fourth till the very close of his reign is that of humble compliance with the prayers of the Parliament, and even his imperious successor shrank almost with timidity from any conflict with it. But the Crown had been bought by other pledges less noble than that of constitutional rule. The support of the nobles had been partly won by the hope of a renewal of the fatal war with France. The support of the Church had been purchased by the more terrible promise of persecution. The last pledge was speedily redeemed. In the first Convocation of his reign Henry declared himself the protector of the Church and ordered the prelates to take measures for the suppression of heresy and of the wandering preachers. His declaration was but a prelude to the Statute of Heresy which was passed at the opening of 1401. By the provisions of this infamous Act the hindrances which had till now neutralized the efforts of the bishops were taken away. Not only were they permitted to arrest all preachers of heresy, all schoolmasters infected with heretical teaching, all owners and writers of heretical books, and to imprison them, even if they recanted, at the King's pleasure, but a refusal to abjure or a relapse after abjuration enabled them to hand over the heretic to the civil officers, and by these—so ran the first legal enactment of religious bloodshed which defiled our Statute-book—he was to be burned on a high place before the people. The statute was hardly passed when William Sautre, a parish priest at Lynn, became its first victim. Nine years later a layman, John Badby, was committed to the flames in the presence of the Prince of Wales for a denial of transubstantiation. The groans of the sufferer were taken for a recantation, and the Prince ordered the fire to be plucked away ; but the offer of life and of a pension failed to break the spirit of the Lollard, and he was hurled back to his doom. The enmity of France, and the fierce resentment of the Reformers, added danger to the incessant revolts which threatened the throne of Henry. The mere maintenance of his power through the troubled years of his reign is the best proof of the King's ability. A conspiracy of Richard's kinsmen, the Earls of Huntingdon and Kent, was suppressed, and was at once followed by

SEC. VI.

THE
HOUSE OF
LANCASTER
1399
TO
1422

1403

1400

1407

1410

*Death of
Henry IV.*
1413

Richard's death in prison. The Percies broke out in rebellion, and Hotspur, the son of the Earl of Northumberland, leagued himself with the Scots and with the insurgents of Wales. He was defeated and slain in an obstinate battle near Shrewsbury ; but two years later his father rose in a fresh insurrection, and though the seizure and execution of his fellow-conspirator Scrope, the Archbishop of York, drove Northumberland over the border, he remained till his death in a later inroad a peril to the throne. Encouraged meanwhile by the weakness of England, Wales, so long tranquil, shook off the yoke of her conquerors, and the whole country rose at the call of Owen Glyndwr or Glendower, a descendant of its native princes. Owen left the invaders, as of old, to contend with famine and the mountain storms ; but they had no sooner retired than he sallied out from his inaccessible fastnesses to win victories which were followed by the adhesion of all North Wales and great part of the South to his cause, while a force of French auxiliaries was despatched by Charles of France to his aid. It was only the restoration of peace in England which enabled Henry to roll back the tide of Glyndwr's success. By slow and deliberate campaigns continued through four years the Prince of Wales wrested from him the South ; his subjects in the North, discouraged by successive defeats, gradually fell away from his standard ; and the repulse of a bold descent upon Shropshire drove Owen at last to take refuge among the mountains of Snowdon, where he seems to have maintained the contest, single-handed, till his death. With the close of the Welsh rising the Lancastrian throne felt itself secure from without, but the danger from the Lollards remained as great as ever within. The new statute and its terrible penalties were boldly defied. The death of the Earl of Salisbury in the first of the revolts against Henry, though his gory head was welcomed into London by a procession of abbots and bishops who went out singing psalms of thanksgiving to meet it, only transferred the leadership of the party to one of the foremost warriors of the time. Sir John Oldcastle, whose marriage raised him to the title of Lord Cobham, threw open his castle of Cowling to the Lollards as their head-quarters, sheltered their preachers, and set the prohibitions and sentences of the bishops at defiance. When Henry the Fourth died in 1413 worn out with the troubles of his reign, his successor was forced to deal with this formidable question. The bishops demanded that Cobham should be brought to justice, and though the King pleaded for delay in the case of one who was so close a friend, his open defiance at last forced him to act. A body of royal troops arrested Lord Cobham and carried him to the Tower. His escape was the signal for a vast revolt. A secret order summoned the Lollards to assemble in St. Giles's fields outside London. We gather, if not the real aims of the rising, at least the terror that it caused, from Henry's statement that

SEC. VI.

THE
HOUSE OF
LANCASTER
1399
TO
1422

its purpose was "to destroy himself, his brothers, and several of the spiritual and temporal lords;" but the vigilance of the young King prevented the junction of the Lollards of London with their friends in the country, and those who appeared at the place of meeting were dispersed by the royal forces. On the failure of the rising the law was rendered more rigorous. Magistrates were directed to arrest all Lollards and hand them over to the bishops; a conviction of heresy was made to entail forfeiture of blood and of estate; and thirty-nine prominent Lollards were brought to execution. Cobham escaped, and for four years longer strove to rouse revolt after revolt. He was at last captured on the Welsh border and burned as a heretic.

With the death of Oldcastle the political activity of Lollardry came suddenly to an end, while the steady persecution of the bishops, if it failed to extinguish it as a religious movement, succeeded in destroying the vigour and energy which it had shown at the outset of its career. But the House of Lancaster had, as yet, only partially accomplished the aims with which it mounted the throne. In the eyes of the nobles, one of Richard's crimes had been his policy of peace, and the aid which they gave to the revolution sprang partly from their hope of a renewal of the war. The energy of the war-party was seconded by the temper of the nation at large, already forgetful of the sufferings of the past struggle and longing only to wipe out its shame. The internal calamities of France offered at this moment a tempting opportunity for aggression. Its King, Charles the Sixth, was a maniac, while its princes and nobles were divided into two great parties, the one headed by the Duke of Burgundy and bearing his name, the other by the Duke of Orleans and bearing the title of Armagnacs. The struggle had been jealously watched by Henry the Fourth, but his attempt to feed it by pushing an English force into France at once united the combatants. Their strife, however, recommenced more bitterly than ever when the claim of the French crown by Henry the Fifth on his accession declared his purpose of renewing the war. No claim could have been more utterly baseless, for the Parliamentary title by which the House of Lancaster held England could give it no right over France, and the strict law of hereditary succession which Edward asserted could be pleaded, if pleaded at all, only by the House of Mortimer. Not only the claim, indeed, but the very nature of the war itself was wholly different from that of Edward the Third. Edward had been forced into the struggle against his will by the ceaseless attacks of France, and his claim of the crown was a mere afterthought to secure the alliance of Flanders. The war of Henry, on the other hand, though in form a renewal of the earlier struggle on the expiration of the truce made by Richard the Second, was in fact a wanton aggression on the part of a nation tempted by the helplessness of its opponent and galled by the memory of former defeat. Its one excuse

SEC. VI.

THE
HOUSE OF
LANCASTER
1399
TO
1422

indeed lay in the attacks which France for the past fifteen years had directed against the Lancastrian throne, its encouragement of every enemy without and of every traitor within. In the summer of 1415 the King sailed for the Norman coast, and his first exploit was the capture of Harfleur. Dysentery made havoc in his ranks during the siege, and it was with a mere handful of men that he resolved to insult the enemy by a daring march, like that of Edward, upon Calais. The discord, however, on which he probably reckoned for security, vanished before the actual appearance of the invaders in the heart of France; and when his weary and half-starved force succeeded in crossing the Somme, it found sixty thousand Frenchmen encamped on the field of Agincourt right across its line of march. Their position, flanked on either side by woods, but with a front so narrow that the dense masses were drawn up thirty men deep, was strong for purposes of defence but ill suited for attack; and the French leaders, warned by the experience

of Crécy and Poitiers, resolved to await the English advance. Henry, on the other hand, had no choice between attack and unconditional surrender. His troops were starving, and the way to Calais lay across the French army. But the King's courage rose with the peril. A knight in his train wished that the thousands of stout warriors lying idle that night in England had been standing in his ranks. Henry answered with a burst of scorn. "I would not have a single man more," he replied. "If God give us the victory, it will be plain that we owe it to His grace. If not, the fewer we are, the less loss for England." Starving and sick as were the handful of men whom he led, they shared the spirit of their leader. As the chill rainy night passed away, his archers bared their arms and breasts to give fair play to "the crooked stick and the grey goose wing," but for which—as the rime ran—"England were but a fling," and with a great shout sprang forward to the attack. The sight of their advance roused the fiery pride of the French; the wise resolve of their leaders was forgotten, and the dense mass of men-at-arms plunged heavily forward through miry ground on the English front. But at the first sign of movement Henry had halted his line, and fixing in the ground the sharpened stakes with which each man was furnished, his archers poured their fatal arrow flights into the hostile ranks. The carnage was terrible, but the desperate charges of the French knighthood at last drove the English archers to the neighbouring woods, from which they were still able to pour their shot into the enemy's flanks, while Henry, with the men-at-arms around him, flung himself on the French line. In the terrible struggle which followed the King bore off the palm of bravery: he was felled once by a blow from a French mace, and the crown on his helmet was cleft by the sword of the Duke of Alençon; but the enemy was at last broken, and the defeat of the main body of the French was followed at once by the rout of their reserve. The triumph was

Sec. VI.

The
House of
Lancaster
1399
to
1422

The
Conquest
of Nor-
mandy

more complete, as the odds were even greater, than at Crécy. Eleven thousand Frenchmen lay dead on the field, and more than a hundred princes and great lords were among the fallen.

The immediate result of the battle of Agincourt was small, for the English army was too exhausted for pursuit, and it made its way to Calais only to return to England. The war was limited to a contest for the command of the Channel, till the increasing bitterness of the strife between the Burgundians and Armagnacs encouraged Henry to resume his attempt to recover Normandy. Whatever may have been his aim in this enterprise—whether it were, as has been suggested, to provide a refuge for his house, should its power be broken in England, or simply to acquire a command of the seas—the patience and skill with which his object was accomplished raise him high in the rank of military leaders. Disembarking with an army of 40,000 men. near the mouth of the Touque, he stormed Caen, received the surrender of Bayeux, reduced Alençon and Falaise, and detaching his brother the Duke of Gloucester to occupy the Cotentin, made himself master of Avranches and Domfront. With Lower Normandy wholly in his hands, he advanced upon Evreux, captured Louviers, and, seizing Pont-de-l'Arche, threw his troops across the Seine. The end of these masterly movements was now revealed. Rouen was at this time the largest and wealthiest of the towns of France ; its walls were defended by a powerful artillery ; Alan Blanchard, a brave and resolute patriot, infused the fire of his own temper into the vast population ; and the garrison, already strong, was backed by fifteen thousand citizens in arms. But the genius of Henry was more than equal to the difficulties with which he had to deal. He had secured himself from an attack on his rear by the reduction of Lower Normandy, his earlier occupation of Harfleur severed the town from the sea, and his conquest of Pont-de-l'Arche cut it off from relief on the side of Paris. Slowly but steadily the King drew his lines of investment round the doomed city ; a flotilla was brought up from Harfleur, a bridge of boats thrown over the Seine above the town, the deep trenches of the besiegers protected by posts, and the desperate sallies of the garrison stubbornly beaten back. For six months Rouen held resolutely out, but famine told fast on the vast throng of country folk who had taken refuge within its walls. Twelve thousand of these were at last thrust out of the city gates, but the cold policy of the conqueror refused them passage, and they perished between the trenches and the walls. In the hour of their agony women gave birth to infants, but even the new-born babes which were drawn up in baskets to receive baptism were lowered again to die on their mothers' breasts. It was little better within the town itself. As winter drew on one-half of the population wasted away. "War," said the terrible King, " has three handmaidens ever waiting

Sec. VI.

The
House of
Lancaster
1399
to
1422

The
Conquest
of France

1419

1420

1422

on her, Fire, Blood, and Famine, and I have chosen the meekest maid of the three." But his demand of unconditional surrender nerved the citizens to a resolve of despair ; they determined to fire the city and fling themselves in a mass on the English lines ; and Henry, fearful lest his prize should escape him at the last, was driven to offer terms. Those who rejected a foreign yoke were suffered to leave the city, but his vengeance reserved its victim in Alan Blanchard, and the brave patriot was at Henry's orders put to death in cold blood.

A few sieges completed the reduction of Normandy. The King's designs were still limited to the acquisition of that province ; and pausing in his career of conquest, he strove to win its loyalty by a remission of taxation and a redress of grievances, and to seal its possession by a formal peace with the French Crown. The confer- ences, however, which were held for this purpose at Pontoise failed through the temporary reconciliation of the French factions, while the length and expense of the war began to rouse remonstrance and discontent at home. The King's difficulties were at their height when the assassination of the Duke of Burgundy at Montereau, in the very presence of the Dauphin with whom he had come to hold conference, rekindled the fires of civil strife. The whole Burgundian party, with the new Duke, Philip the Good, at its head, flung itself in a wild thirst for revenge into Henry's hands. The mad King, Charles the Sixth, with his Queen and daughters, were in Philip's power ; and in his resolve to exclude the Dauphin from the throne the Duke stooped to buy English aid by giving Catharine, the eldest of the French princesses, in marriage to Henry, by conferring on him the Regency during the life of Charles, and by recognizing his succession to the crown at that sovereign's death. The treaty was solemnly ratified by Charles himself in a conference at Troyes, and Henry, who in his new capacity of Regent had undertaken to conquer in the name of his father-in-law the territory held by the Dauphin, reduced the towns of the Upper Seine and entered Paris in triumph side by side with the King. The States-General of the realm were solemnly convened to the capital ; and strange as the provisions of the Treaty of Troyes must have seemed, they were confirmed without a murmur, and Henry was formally recognized as the future sovereign of France. A defeat of his brother Clarence in Anjou called him back to the war. His reappearance in the field was marked by the capture of Dreux, and a repulse before Orleans was redeemed by his success in the long and obstinate siege of Meaux. At no time had the fortunes of Henry reached a higher pitch than at the moment when he felt the touch of death. But the rapidity of his disease baffled the skill of physicians, and with a strangely characteristic regret that he had not lived to achieve the conquest of Jerusalem, the great conqueror passed away.

CHAPTER VI.

THE NEW MONARCHY.

1422—1540.

Section I.—Joan of Arc, 1422—1451.

[*Authorities.*—The "Wars of the English in France," and Blondel's work "De Reductione Normanniæ," both published by the Master of the Rolls, give ample information on the military side of this period. Monstrelet remains our chief source of knowledge on the French side. The "Procès de Jeanne d'Arc" (published by the Société de l'Histoire de France) is the only real authority for her history. For English affairs we are reduced to the meagre accounts of William of Worcester, of the Continuator of the Crowland Chronicle, and of Fabyan. Fabyan, a London alderman with a strong bias in favour of the House of Lancaster, is useful for London only. The Continuator is one of the best of his class, and though connected with the House of York, the date of his work, which appeared soon after Bosworth Field, makes him fairly impartial; but he is sketchy and deficient in actual facts. The more copious narrative of Polydore Vergil is far superior to these in literary ability, but of later date and strongly Lancastrian in tone. The Rolls of Parliament and Rymer's "Fœdera" are of high value. Among modern writers M. Michelet, in his "History of France" (vol. v.), has given a portrait of the Maid of Orleans at once exact and full of a tender poetry. Lord Brougham ("England under the House of Lancaster") is still useful on constitutional points.]

[Dr. Stubbs' "Constitutional History," vol. iii., published since these pages were written, illustrates this period.—*Ed.*]

AT the moment when death so suddenly stayed his course the greatness of Henry the Fifth had reached its highest point. He had won the Church by his orthodoxy, the nobles by his warlike prowess, the whole people by his revival of the glories of Crécy and Poitiers. In France his cool policy had transformed him from a foreign conqueror into a legal heir to the crown; his title of Regent and of successor to the throne rested on the formal recognition of the estates of the realm; and his progress to the very moment of his death promised a speedy mastery of the whole country.

But the glory of Agincourt and the genius of Henry the Fifth hardly veiled at the close of his reign the weakness and humiliation of the Crown when the succession passed to his infant son. The long minority of Henry the Sixth, who was a boy of nine months old at his father's death, as well as the personal weakness which marked his after-rule, left the House of Lancaster at the mercy of the Parliament. But the Parliament was fast dying down into a mere representation

Disfran- chise- ment of the Com- mons

*Restriction
of Borough
Freedom*

of the baronage and the great landowners. The Commons indeed retained the right of granting and controlling subsidies, of joining in all statutory enactments, and of impeaching ministers. But the Lower House was ceasing to be a real representative of the " Commons " whose name it bore. The borough franchise was suffering from the general tendency to restriction and privilege which in the bulk of towns was soon to reduce it to a mere mockery. Up to this time all freemen settling in a borough and paying their dues to it became by the mere settlement its burgesses ; but from the reign of Henry the Sixth this largeness of borough life was roughly curtailed. The trade companies which vindicated civic freedom from the tyranny of the older merchant gilds themselves tended to become a narrow and exclusive oligarchy. Most of the boroughs had by this time acquired civic property, and it was with the aim of securing their own enjoyment of this against any share of it by "strangers" that the existing burgesses, for the most part, procured charters of incorporation from the Crown, which turned them into a close body, and excluded from their number all who were not burgesses by birth or who failed henceforth to purchase their right of entrance by a long apprenticeship. In addition to this narrowing of the burgess-body, the internal government of the boroughs had almost universally passed, since the failure of the Communal movement in the thirteenth century, from the free gathering of the citizens in borough-mote into the hands of Common Councils, either self-elected or elected by the wealthier burgesses ; and it was to these councils, or to a yet more restricted number of " select men " belonging to them, that clauses in the new charters generally confined the right of choosing their representatives in Parliament. It was with this restriction that the long process of degradation began which ended in reducing the representation of our boroughs to a mere mockery. Great nobles, neighbouring landowners, the Crown itself seized on the boroughs as their prey, and dictated the choice of their representatives. Corruption did whatever force failed to do ; and from the Wars of the Roses to the days of Pitt the voice of the people had to be looked for, not in the members for the towns, but in the knights of the counties. The restriction of the county franchise on the other hand was the direct work of the Parliament itself. Economic changes were fast widening the franchise in the counties. The number of freeholders increased with the subdivision of estates and the social changes which we have already examined, while the increase of independence was marked by the " riots and divisions between the gentlemen and other people," which the statesmen of the day attributed to the excessive number of the voters. In many counties the power of the great lords undoubtedly enabled them to control elections through the number of their retainers. In Cade's revolt the Kentishmen complained that "the people of the shire are

*Restriction
of County
Franchise*

not allowed to have their free elections in the choosing of knights for the shire, but letters have been sent from divers estates to the great nobles of the county, the which enforceth their tenants and other people by force to choose other persons than the common will is." It was primarily to check this abuse that a statute of the reign of Henry the Sixth restricted in 1430 the right of voting in shires to freeholders holding land worth forty shillings (a sum equal in our money to at least twenty pounds) a year, and representing a far higher proportional income at the present time. This "great disfranchising statute," as it has been justly termed, was aimed, in its own words, against voters "of no value, whereof every of them pretended to have a voice equivalent with the more worthy knights and esquires dwelling within the same counties." But in actual working the statute was interpreted in a far more destructive fashion than its words were intended to convey. Up to this time all suitors who found themselves at the Sheriff's Court had voted without question for the Knight of the Shire, but by the new statute the great bulk of the existing voters, every leaseholder and every copyholder, found themselves implicitly deprived of their franchise. A later statute, which seems, however, to have had no practical effect, showed the aristocratic temper, as well as the social changes against which it struggled, in its requirement that every Knight of the Shire should be "a gentleman born."

The death of Henry the Fifth revealed in its bare reality the secret of power. The whole of the royal authority vested without a struggle in a council composed of great lords and Churchmen representing the baronage, at whose head stood Henry Beaufort, Bishop of Winchester, a legitimated son of John of Gaunt by his mistress Catharine Swynford. In the presence of Lollardry and socialism, the Church had at this time ceased to be a great political power and sunk into a mere section of the landed aristocracy. Its one aim was to preserve its enormous wealth, which was threatened at once by the hatred of the heretics and by the greed of the nobles. Lollardry still lived, in spite of the steady persecution, as a spirit of religious and moral revolt; and nine years after the young King's accession we find the Duke of Gloucester traversing England with men-at-arms for the purpose of repressing its risings and hindering the circulation of its invectives against the clergy. The violence and anarchy which had always clung like a taint to the baronage had received a new impulse from the war with France. Long before the struggle was over it had done its fatal work on the mood of the English noble. His aim had become little more than a lust for gold, a longing after plunder, after the pillage of farms, the sack of cities, the ransom of captives. So intense was the greed of gain that only a threat of death could keep the fighting men in their ranks, and the results of victory after victory were lost by the anxiety of the conquerors to deposit their plunder and captives safely

T

at home. The moment the firm hand of great leaders such as Henry the Fifth or Bedford was removed, the war died down into mere massacre and brigandage. " If God had been a captain now-a-days," exclaimed a French general, " He would have turned marauder." The nobles were as lawless and dissolute at home as they were greedy and cruel abroad. The Parliaments, which became mere sittings of their retainers and partizans, were like armed camps to which the great lords came with small armies at their backs. That of 1426 received its name of the " Club Parliament," from the fact that when arms were prohibited the retainers of the barons appeared with clubs on their shoulders. When clubs were forbidden, they hid stones and balls of lead in their clothes. The dissoluteness against which Lollardry had raised its great moral protest reigned now without a check. A gleam of intellectual light was breaking on the darkness of the time, but only to reveal its hideous combination of mental energy with moral worthlessness. The Duke of Gloucester, whose love of letters was shown in the noble library he collected, was the most selfish and profligate prince of his day. The Earl of Worcester, a patron of Caxton, and one of the earliest scholars of the Revival of Letters, earned his title of "butcher" by the cruelty which raised him to a pre-eminence of infamy among the bloodstained leaders of the Wars of the Roses. All spiritual life seemed to have been trodden out in the ruin of the Lollards. Never had English literature fallen so low. A few tedious moralists alone preserved the name of poetry. History died down into the barest and most worthless fragments and annals. Even the religious enthusiasm of the people seemed to have spent itself, or to have been crushed out by the bishops' courts. The one belief of the time was in sorcery and magic. Eleanor Cobham, the wife of the Duke of Gloucester, was convicted of having practised magic against the King's life with a priest, and condemned to do penance in the streets of London. The mist which wrapped the battle-field of Barnet was attributed to the incantations of Friar Bungay. The one pure figure which rises out of the greed, the lust, the selfishness, and unbelief of the time, the figure of Joan of Arc, was regarded by the doctors and priests who judged her as that of a sorceress.

Jeanne d'Arc was the child of a labourer of Domrémy, a little village in the neighbourhood of Vaucouleurs on the borders of Lorraine and Champagne. Just without the cottage where she was born began the great woods of the Vosges, where the children of Domrémy drank in poetry and legend from fairy ring and haunted well, hung their flower garlands on the sacred trees, and sang songs to the "good people" who might not drink of the fountain because of their sins. Jeanne loved the forest ; its birds and beasts came lovingly to her at her childish call. But at home men saw nothing in her but "a good girl, simple and pleasant in her ways," spinning and sewing by her mother's side while the other girls went to the fields, tender to the poor and sick, fond of church, and listening to the church-bell with a dreamy passion of delight which never left her. The quiet life was soon broken by the storm of war as it at last came home to Domrémy. The death of King Charles, which followed hard on that of Henry the Fifth, brought little change. The Dauphin at once proclaimed himself Charles the Seventh of France: but Henry the Sixth was owned as Sovereign over the whole of the territory which Charles had actually ruled; and the incursions which the partizans of Charles, now reinforced by Lombard soldiers from the Milanese and by four thousand Scots under the Earl of Douglas, made with fresh vigour across the Loire were easily repulsed by Duke John of Bedford, the late King's brother, who had been named in his will Regent of France. In genius for war as in political capacity John was hardly inferior to Henry himself. Drawing closer by marriage and patient diplomacy his alliances with the Dukes of Burgundy and Britanny, he completed the conquest of Northern France, secured his communications with Normandy by the capture of Meulan, made himself master of the line of the Yonne by a victory near Auxerre, and pushed forward into the country near Mâcon. It was to arrest his progress that the Constable of Buchan advanced boldly from the Loire to the very borders of Normandy and attacked the English army at Verneuil. But a repulse hardly less disastrous than that of Agincourt left a third of the French knighthood on the field; and the Regent was preparing to cross the Loire when he was hindered by the intrigues of his brother the Duke of Gloucester. The nomination of Gloucester to the Regency in England by the will of the late King had been set aside by the Council, and sick of the powerless Protectorate with which they had invested him, the Duke sought a new opening for his restless ambition in the Netherlands, where he supported the claims of Jacqueline, the Countess in her own right of Holland and Hainault, whom he had married on her divorce from the Duke of Brabant. His enterprise roused the jealousy of the Duke of Burgundy, who regarded himself as heir to the Duke of Brabant, and the efforts of Bedford were paralyzed by the withdrawal of his Burgundian allies as they marched northward to combat his brother. Though Gloucester soon returned to England, the ruinous struggle went on for three years, during which Bedford was forced to remain simply on the defensive, till the cessation of war again restored to him the aid of Burgundy. Strife at home between Gloucester and Beaufort had been even more fatal in diverting the supplies of men and money needed for the war in France, but with temporary quiet in England and peace in Holland Bedford was once more able to push forward to the conquest of the South. The delay, however, brought little help to France, and Charles saw Orleans invested by ten thousand of the allies without power to march to its relief. The war had long

Sec. I.

Joan of
Arc

1422
to
1451

*The Duke of
Bedford*

1424

*The Duke of
Gloucester*

1428

since reached the borders of Lorraine. The north of France, indeed, was being fast reduced to a desert. The husbandmen fled for refuge to the towns, till these in fear of famine shut their gates against them. Then in their despair they threw themselves into the woods and became brigands in their turn. So terrible was the devastation, that two hostile bodies of troops at one time failed even to find one another in the desolate Beauce. The towns were in hardly better case, for misery and disease killed a hundred thousand people in Paris alone. As the outcasts and wounded passed by Domrémy the young peasant girl gave them her bed and nursed them in their sickness. Her whole nature summed itself up in one absorbing passion : she "had pity," to use the phrase for ever on her lip, "on the fair realm of France." As her passion grew she recalled old prophecies that a maid from the Lorraine border should save the land ; she saw visions ; St. Michael appeared to her in a flood of blinding light, and bade her go to the help of the King and restore to him his realm. "Messire," answered the girl, "I am but a poor maiden ; I know not how to ride to the wars, or to lead men-at-arms." The archangel returned to give her courage, and to tell her of "the pity" that there was in heaven for the fair realm of France. The girl wept, and longed that the angels who appeared to her would carry her away, but her mission was clear. It was in vain that her father when he heard her purpose swore to drown her ere she should go to the field with men-at-arms. It was in vain that the priest, the wise people of the village, the captain of Vaucouleurs, doubted and refused to aid her. "I must go to the King," persisted the peasant girl, "even if I wear my limbs to the very knees." "I had far rather rest and spin by my mother's side," she pleaded with a touching pathos, "for this is no work of my choosing, but I must go and do it, for my Lord wills it." "And who," they asked, "is your Lord?" "He is God." Words such as these touched the rough captain at last : he took Jeanne by the hand and swore to lead her to the King. When she reached Chinon she found hesitation and doubt. The theologians proved from their books that they ought not to believe her. "There is more in God's book than in yours," Jeanne answered simply. At last Charles received her in the midst of a throng of nobles and soldiers. "Gentle Dauphin," said the girl, "my name is Jeanne the Maid. The Heavenly King sends me to tell you that you shall be anointed and crowned in the town of Rheims, and you shall be lieutenant of the Heavenly King who is the King of France."

Orleans had already been driven by famine to offers of surrender when Jeanne appeared in the French Court. Charles had done nothing for its aid but shut himself up at Chinon and weep help-lessly. The long series of English victories had in fact so demoralized the French soldiery that a mere detachment of archers under Sir John Fastolfe had repulsed an army, in what was called the "Battle of the Herrings," and conducted the convoy of provisions to which it owed its name in triumph into the camp before Orleans. Only three thousand Englishmen remained there in the trenches after a new withdrawal of their Burgundian allies, but though the town swarmed with men-at-arms not a single sally had been ventured upon during the six months' siege. The success however of the handful of English besiegers depended wholly on the spell of terror which they had cast over France, and the appearance of Jeanne at once broke the spell. The girl was in her eighteenth year, tall, finely formed, with all the vigour and activity of her peasant rearing, able to stay from dawn to nightfall on horseback without meat or drink. As she mounted her charger, clad in white armour from head to foot, with the great white banner studded with fleur-de-lys waving over her head, she seemed "a thing wholly divine, whether to see or hear." The ten thousand men-at-arms who followed her from Blois, rough plunderers whose only prayer was that of La Hire, "Sire Dieu, I pray you to do for La Hire what La Hire would do for you, were you captain-at-arms and he God," left off their oaths and foul living at her word and gathered round the altars on their march. Her shrewd peasant humour helped her to manage the wild soldiery, and her followers laughed over their camp-fires at the old warrior who had been so puzzled by her prohibition of oaths that she suffered him still to swear by his bâton. In the midst of her enthusiasm her good sense never left her. The people crowded round her as she rode along, praying her to work miracles, and bringing crosses and chaplets to be blest by her touch. "Touch them yourself," she said to an old Dame Margaret; "your touch will be just as good as mine." But her faith in her mission remained as firm as ever. "The Maid prays and requires you," she wrote to Bedford, "to work no more distraction in France, but to come in her company to rescue the Holy Sepulchre from the Turk." "I bring you," she told Dunois when he sallied out of Orleans to meet her, "the best aid ever sent to any one, the aid of the King of Heaven." The besiegers looked on overawed as she entered Orleans, and, riding round the walls, bade the people look fearlessly on the dreaded forts which surrounded them. Her enthusiasm drove the hesitating generals to engage the handful of besiegers, and the enormous disproportion of forces at once made itself felt. Fort after fort was taken, till only the strongest remained, and then the council of war resolved to adjourn the attack. "You have taken your counsel," replied Jeanne, "and I take mine." Placing herself at the head of the men-at-arms, she ordered the gates to be thrown open, and led them against the fort. Few as they were, the English fought desperately, and the Maid, who had fallen wounded while endeavouring to scale its walls, was borne into a vineyard, while Dunois sounded the retreat. "Wait a while!" the girl imperiously pleaded, "eat and drink! so soon as my standard touches the wall you shall enter the fort." It touched, and the assailants burst in. On the next day the siege was abandoned, and the force which had conducted it withdrew in good order to the north. In the midst of her triumph Jeanne still remained the pure, tender-hearted peasant girl of the Vosges. Her first visit as she entered Orleans was to the great church, and there, as she knelt at mass, she wept in such a passion of devotion that "all the people wept with her." Her tears burst forth afresh at her first sight of bloodshed and of the corpses strewn over the battle-field. She grew frightened at her first wound, and only threw off the touch of womanly fear when she heard the signal for retreat. Yet more womanly was the purity with which she passed through the brutal warriors of a mediæval camp. It was her care for her honour that had led her to clothe herself in a soldier's dress. She wept hot tears when told of the foul taunts of the English, and called passionately on God to witness her chastity. "Yield thee, yield thee, Glasdale," she cried to the English warrior whose insults had been foulest, as he fell wounded at her feet, "you called me harlot! I have great pity on your soul." But all thought of herself was lost in the thought of her mission. It was in vain that the French generals strove to remain on the Loire. Jeanne was resolute to complete her task, and while the English remained panic-stricken around Paris the army followed her from Gien through Troyes, growing in number as it advanced, till it reached the gates of Rheims. With the coronation of Charles, the Maid felt her errand to be over. "O gentle King, the pleasure of God is done," she cried, as she flung herself at the feet of Charles the Seventh and asked leave to go home. "Would it were His pleasure," she pleaded with the Archbishop as he forced her to remain, "that I might go and keep sheep once more with my sisters and my brothers: they would be so glad to see me again!"

The policy of the French Court detained her while the cities of the north of France opened their gates to the newly-consecrated King. Bedford, however, who had been left without money or men, had now received reinforcements, and Charles, after a repulse before the walls of Paris, fell back behind the Loire; while the towns on the Oise submitted again to the Duke of Burgundy. In this later struggle Jeanne fought with her usual bravery, but with the fatal consciousness that her mission was at an end, and during the defence

of Compiègne she fell into the power of the Bastard of Vendôme, to be sold by her captor into the hands of the Duke of Burgundy and by the Duke into the hands of the English. To the English her triumphs were victories of sorcery, and after a year's imprisonment she was brought to trial on a charge of heresy before an ecclesiastical court with the Bishop of Beauvais at its head. Throughout the long process which followed every art was employed to entangle her in her talk. But the simple shrewdness of the peasant girl foiled the efforts of her judges. "Do you believe," they asked, "that you are in a state of grace?" "If I am not," she replied, "God will put me in it. If I am, God will keep me in it." Her capture, they argued, showed that God had forsaken her. "Since it has pleased God that I should be taken," she answered meekly, "it is for the best." "Will you submit," they demanded at last, "to the judgement of the Church Militant?" "I have come to the King of France," Jeanne replied, "by commission from God and from the Church Triumphant above: to that Church I submit." "I had far rather die," she ended, passionately, "than renounce what I have done by my Lord's command." They deprived her of mass. "Our Lord can make me hear it without your aid," she said, weeping. "Do your voices," asked the judges, "forbid you to submit to the Church and the Pope?" "Ah, no! Our Lord first served." Sick, and deprived of all religious aid, it was no wonder that as the long trial dragged on and question followed question Jeanne's firmness wavered. On the charge of sorcery and diabolical possession she still appealed firmly to God. "I hold to my Judge," she said, as her earthly judges gave sentence against her, "to the King of Heaven and Earth. God has always been my Lord in all that I have done. The devil has never had power over me." It was only with a view to be delivered from the military prison and transferred to the prisons of the Church that she consented to a formal abjuration of heresy. She feared in fact among the English soldiery those outrages to her honour, to guard against which she had from the first assumed the dress of a man. In the eyes of the Church her dress was a crime and she abandoned it ; but a renewed insult forced her to resume the one safeguard left her, and the return to it was treated as a relapse into heresy which doomed her to death. A great pile was raised in the market-place of Rouen where her statue stands now. Even the brutal soldiers who snatched the hated "witch" from the hands of the clergy and hurried her to her doom were hushed as she reached the stake. One indeed passed to her a rough cross he had made from a stick he held, and she clasped it to her bosom. "Oh! Rouen, Rouen," she was heard to murmur, as her eyes ranged over the city from the lofty scaffold, "I have great fear lest you suffer for my death." "Yes! my voices were of God!" she suddenly cried as the last moment came; "they have never deceived me!" Soon the flames reached her, the girl's head sank on her breast, there was one cry of "Jesus!"—"We are lost," an English soldier muttered as the crowd broke up, "we have burned a Saint."

The English cause was indeed irretrievably lost. In spite of a pompous coronation of the boy-king Henry at Paris, Bedford, with the cool wisdom of his temper, seems to have abandoned all hope of permanently retaining France, and to have fallen back on his brother's

SEC. I.

JOAN OF
ARC

1422
TO
1451

1431

original plan of securing Normandy. Henry's Court was established for a year at Rouen, a university founded at Caen, and whatever rapine and disorder might be permitted elsewhere, justice, good government, and security for trade were steadily maintained through the favoured provinces. At home Bedford was resolutely backed by the Bishop of Winchester, who had been raised in 1426 to the rank of Cardinal, and who now again governed England through the Royal Council in spite of the fruitless struggles of the Duke of Gloucester. Even when he had been excluded from the Council by Gloucester's intrigues, Beaufort's immense wealth was poured without stint into the exhausted Treasury till his loans to the Crown amounted to half-a-million ; and he had unscrupulously diverted an army which he had raised at his own cost for the Hussite Crusade in Bohemia to the relief of Bedford after the deliverance of Orleans. The Cardinal's diplomatic ability was seen in the truces he wrung from Scotland, and in his personal efforts to prevent the reconciliation of Burgundy with France. In 1435 however the Duke of Burgundy concluded a formal treaty with Charles ; and his desertion was followed by a yet more fatal blow to the English cause in the death of Bedford. Paris rose suddenly against its English garrison and declared for King Charles. Henry's dominion shrank at once to Normandy and the outlying fortresses of Picardy and Maine. But reduced as they were to a mere handful, and fronted by a whole nation in arms, the English soldiers struggled on with as desperate a bravery as in their days of triumph. Lord Talbot, the most daring of their chiefs, forded the Somme with the waters up to his chin to relieve Crotoy, and threw his men across the Oise in the face of a French army to relieve Pontoise. The Duke of York, who succeeded Bedford as Regent, by his abilities stemmed for a time the tide of ill-fortune, but the jealousy shown to him by the King's counsellors told fatally on the course of the war. A fresh effort for peace was made by the Earl of Suffolk, who swayed the Council after age forced Beaufort to retire to Winchester, and who negotiated for his master a marriage with Margaret, the daughter of Duke René of Anjou. Not only Anjou, of which England possessed nothing, but Maine, the bulwark of Normandy,

1445

were ceded to Duke René as the price of a match which Suffolk regarded as the prelude to peace. But the terms of the treaty and the delays which still averted a final peace gave new strength to the war-party with Gloucester at its head. The danger was roughly met.

1447

Gloucester was arrested as he rode to Parliament on a charge of secret conspiracy ; and a few days later he was found dead in his lodging. But the difficulties he had raised foiled Suffolk in his negotiations ; and though Charles extorted the surrender of Le Mans by a threat of war, the provisions of the treaty remained for the most part unfulfilled. The struggle, however, now became a hopeless one. In two months from

1449

the resumption of the war half Normandy was in the hands of Dunois ;

VI.]   THE NEW MONARCHY.   281

Sec. I.

Joan of
Arc

1422
to
1451

1453

Rouen rose against her feeble garrison and threw open her gates to Charles; and the defeat of an English force at Fourmigny was the signal for revolt throughout the rest of the province. The surrender of Cherbourg in 1450 left Henry not a foot of Norman ground, and the next year the last fragment of the Duchy of Guienne was lost. Gascony indeed once more turned to the English Crown on the landing of an English force under Talbot, Earl of Shrewsbury. But ere the twenty thousand men whose levy was voted by Parliament for his aid could cross the Channel Shrewsbury suddenly found himself face to face with the whole French army. His men were mown down by its guns, and the Earl himself left dead on the field. The surrender of fortress after fortress secured the final expulsion of the English from the soil of France. The Hundred Years' War had ended, not only in the loss of the temporary conquests made since the time of Edward the Third, with the exception of Calais, but in the loss of the great southern province which had remained in English hands ever since the marriage of its Duchess, Eleanor, to Henry the Second, and in the building up of France into a far greater power than it had ever been before.

Section II.—The Wars of the Roses, 1450–1471.

[*Authorities.*—No period, save the last, is scantier in historical authorities. We still possess William of Worcester, Fabyan, and the Crowland Continuator, and for the struggle between Warwick and Edward, the valuable narrative of "The Arrival of Edward IV.," edited for the Camden Society, which may be taken as the official account on the royal side. "The Paston Letters" (edited by Mr. Gairdner) are the first instance in English history of a family correspondence, and throw great light on the social history of the time. Cade's rising has been illustrated in two papers, lately reprinted, by Mr. Durrant Cooper. The Rolls of Parliament are, as before, of the highest value.]

The ruinous issue of the great struggle with France roused England to a burst of fury against the wretched government to whose weakness and credulity it attributed its disasters. Suffolk was impeached, and murdered as he crossed the sea into exile. When the Bishop of Chichester was sent to pay the sailors at Portsmouth, and strove to put them off with less than their due, they fell on him and slew him. In Kent, the great manufacturing district of the day, seething with a busy population, and especially concerned with the French contests through the piracy of the Cinque Ports, where every house showed some spoil from the wars, the discontent broke into open revolt. The rising spread from Kent over Surrey and Sussex. A military levy of the yeomen of the three shires was organized; the insurgents were joined by more than a hundred esquires and gentlemen, and two great landowners of Sussex, the Abbot of Battle and the Prior of Lewes, openly favoured their cause. John Cade, a soldier of some experience in the French wars, took the significant name of Mortimer, and placed

Sec. II.

The Wars
of the
Roses

1450
to
1471

June, 1450

himself at their head; and the army, now twenty thousand men strong, marched on Blackheath. The "Complaint of the Commons of Kent" which they laid before the Royal Council, is of high value in the light which it throws on the condition of the people. Not one of the demands touches on religious reform. The question of villeinage and serfage finds no place in the "Complaint" of 1450. In the seventy years which had intervened since the last peasant rising, villeinage had died naturally away before the progress of social change. The Statutes of Apparel, which from this time encumber the Statute-Book, show in their anxiety to curtail the dress of the labourer and the farmer the progress of these classes in comfort and wealth; and from the language of the statutes themselves, it is plain that as wages rose both farmer and labourer went on clothing themselves better in spite of sumptuary provisions. With the exception of a demand for the repeal of the Statute of Labourers, the programme of the Commons was now not social, but political. The "Complaint" calls for administrative and economical reforms, for a change of ministry, a more careful expenditure of the royal revenue, and for the restoration of freedom of election, which had been broken in upon by the interference both of the Crown and the great landowners. The refusal of the Council to receive the "Complaint" was followed by a victory of the Kentishmen over the royal forces at Sevenoaks; the entry of the insurgents into London, coupled with the execution of Lord Say, the most unpopular of the royal ministers, broke the obstinacy of his colleagues. The "Complaint" was received, pardons were granted to all who had joined in the rising; and the insurgents dispersed to their homes. Cade, who had striven in vain to retain them in arms, sought to form a new force by throwing open the gaols; but his men quarrelled, and Cade himself was slain by the sheriff of Kent as he fled into Sussex. The "Complaint" was quietly laid aside. No attempt was made to redress the grievances which it stated, and the main object of popular hate, the Duke of Somerset, took his place at the head of the Royal Council.

Beaufort, Duke of Somerset, as the grandson of John of Gaunt and his mistress Catharine Swynford, was the representative of a junior branch of the House of Lancaster, whose claims to the throne Henry IV. had barred by a clause in the Act which legitimated their line, but whose hopes of the Crown were roused by the childlessness of Henry VI. He found a rival in the Duke of York, heir of the houses of York, of Clarence, and of Mortimer, who boasted of a double descent from Edward III. In addition to other claims which York as yet refrained from urging, he claimed as descendant of Edmund of Langley, Edward's fifth son, to be regarded as heir presumptive to the throne. Popular favour seems to have been on his side, but in 1453 the birth of the King's son promised to free the Crown from the turmoil of warring factions; Henry, however, at the same time sank into a state of idiotcy which made his rule impossible, and York was appointed Protector of the Realm. But on Henry's recovery the Duke of Somerset, who had been impeached and committed to the Tower by his rival, was restored to power, and supported with singular vigour and audacity by the Queen. York at once took up arms, and backed by the Earls of Salisbury and Warwick, the heads of the great House of Neville, he advanced with 3,000 men upon St. Albans, where Henry was encamped. A successful assault upon the town was crowned by the death of Somerset; and a return of the King's malady brought the renewal of York's Protectorate. Henry's recovery, however, again restored the supremacy of the House of Beaufort, and after a temporary reconciliation between the two parties there was a fresh outbreak of war. Salisbury defeated Lord Audley at Bloreheath, and York with the two Earls raised his standard at Ludlow. The King marched rapidly on the insurgents, and a decisive battle was only averted by the desertion of a part of the Yorkist army and the disbanding of the rest. The Duke himself fled to Ireland, the Earls to Calais, while the Queen, summoning a Parliament at Coventry, pressed on their attainder. But the check, whatever its cause, had been merely a temporary one. In the following Midsummer the Earls again landed in Kent, and backed by a general rising of the county, entered London amidst the acclamations of its citizens. The royal army was defeated in a hard-fought action at Northampton, Margaret fled to Scotland, and Henry was left a prisoner in the hands of the Duke of York.

The position of York as heir presumptive to the crown by descent from Edmund of Langley had ceased with the birth of a son to Henry; but the victory of Northampton no sooner raised him to the supreme control of affairs than he ventured to assert the far more dangerous claims which he had secretly cherished, and to their consciousness of which was owing the bitter hostility of Henry and his Queen. As the descendant of Edmund of Langley he stood only next in succession to the House of Lancaster, but as the descendant of Lionel, the elder brother of John of Gaunt, he stood in strict hereditary right before it. We have already seen how the claims of Lionel had passed to the House of Mortimer: it was through Anne, the heiress of the Mortimers, who had wedded his father, that they passed to the Duke. There was, however, no constitutional ground for any limitation of the right of Parliament to set aside an elder branch in favour of a younger, and in the Parliamentary Act which placed the House of Lancaster on the throne the claim of the House of Mortimer had been deliberately set aside. Possession, too, told against the Yorkist pretensions. To modern minds the best reply to their claim lay in the words used at a later time by Henry himself. " My father was King; his father also was King; I myself have worn the crown forty years from my cradle; you have all sworn fealty to me as your sovereign, and your

Sec. II.

The Wars
of the
Roses

1450
to
1471

1455

1458

Northamp-
ton
1460

The Wars
of the
Roses

SEC. II.

THE WARS
OF THE
ROSES
1450
TO
1471

fathers have done the like to mine.   How then can my right be disputed?"   Long and undisturbed possession, as well as a distinctly legal title by free vote of Parliament, was in favour of the House of Lancaster.   But the persecution of the Lollards, the interference with elections, the odium of the war, the shame of the long misgovernment, told fatally against the weak and imbecile King, whose reign had been a long battle of contending factions.   That the misrule had been serious was shown by the attitude of the commercial class.   It was the rising of Kent, the great manufacturing district of the realm, which brought about the victory of Northampton.   Throughout the struggle which followed, London and the great merchant towns were steady for the House of York.   Zeal for the Lancastrian cause was found only in Wales, in northern England, and in the south-western shires.   It is absurd to suppose that the shrewd traders of Cheapside were moved by an abstract question of hereditary right, or that the wild Welshmen believed themselves to be supporting the right of Parliament to regulate the succession.   But it marks the power which Parliament had now gained that the Duke of York felt himself compelled to convene the two Houses, and to lay his claim before the Lords as a petition of right.   Neither oaths nor the numerous Acts which had settled and confirmed the right to the crown in the House of Lancaster could destroy, he pleaded, his hereditary claim. The baronage received the petition with hardly concealed reluctance, and solved the question, as they hoped, by a compromise.   They refused to dethrone the King, but they had sworn no fealty to his child, and at Henry's death they agreed to receive the Duke as successor to the crown.   But the open display of York's pretensions at once united the partizans of the royal House, and the deadly struggle which received the name of the Wars of the Roses, from the white rose which formed the badge of the House of York and the red rose which was the cognizance of the House of Lancaster, began in the gathering of the North round Lord Clifford, and of the West round the new Duke of Somerset.   York, who had hurried to meet the first with

a far inferior force, was defeated and slain at Wakefield, and the passion of civil war broke fiercely out on the field.   The Earl of Salisbury was hurried to the block, and the head of Duke Richard, crowned in mockery with a diadem of paper, is said to have been impaled on the walls of York.   His second son, Lord Rutland, fell crying for mercy on his knees before Clifford.   But Clifford's father had been the first to fall in the battle of St. Albans which opened the struggle.   "As your father killed mine," cried the savage baron while he plunged his dagger in the young noble's breast, "I will kill you!" The brutal deed was soon to be avenged.   Duke Richard's eldest son, Edward, Earl of March, hurried from the West, and, routing a body of Lancastrians at Mortimer's Cross, struck boldly upon London.   A force of Kentishmen under the Earl of Warwick barred the march of the Lancastrian army on the capital, but after a desperate struggle at St. Albans the Yorkist forces broke under cover of night.   An immediate advance of the conquerors might have decided the contest, but Queen Margaret paused to sully her victory by a series of bloody executions, and the rough northerners who formed the bulk of her army scattered to pillage, while Edward appeared before London.   The citizens rallied at his call, and cries of "Long live King Edward" rang round the handsome young leader as he rode through the streets. A council of Yorkist lords, hastily summoned, resolved that the compromise agreed on in Parliament was at an end and that Henry of Lancaster had forfeited the throne.   The final issue, however, now lay, not with Parliament, but with the sword.   Disappointed of London, the Lancastrian army fell rapidly back on the North, and Edward hurried as rapidly in pursuit.

The two armies encountered one another at Towton Field, near Tadcaster.   In the numbers engaged, as well as in the terrible obstinacy of the struggle, no such battle had been seen in England since the fight of Senlac.   The armies numbered together nearly 120,000 men.   The day had just broken when the Yorkists advanced through a thick snow-fall, and for six hours the battle raged with desperate bravery on either side.   At one critical moment Warwick saw his men falter, and stabbing his horse before them, swore on the cross of his sword to win or die on the field.   The battle was turned by the arrival of Norfolk with a fresh force.   At last the Lancastrians gave way, a river in their rear turned the retreat into a rout, and the flight and carnage, for no quarter was given on either side, went on through the night and the morrow.   Edward's herald counted more than 20,000 Lancastrian corpses on the field, and the losses of the conquerors were hardly less heavy.   But their triumph was complete.   The Earl of Northumberland was slain ; the Earls of Devonshire and Wiltshire were taken and beheaded ; the Duke of Somerset fled into exile.   Henry himself with his Queen was forced to fly over the border and to find a refuge in Scotland.   The cause of the House of Lancaster was lost: and with the victory of Towton the crown of England passed to Edward of York.   A vast bill of attainder wrapped in the same ruin and confiscation the nobles and gentry who still adhered to the House of Lancaster. The struggles of Margaret only served to bring fresh calamities on her adherents.   A new rising in the North was crushed by the Earl of Warwick, and a legend which lights up the gloom of the time with a gleam of poetry told how the fugitive Queen, after escaping with difficulty from a troop of bandits, found a new brigand in the depths of the wood.   With the daring of despair she confided to him her child.   "I trust to your loyalty," she said, "the son of your King." Margaret and her child escaped over the border under the robber's

SEC. II.

THE WARS
OF THE
ROSES

1450
TO
1471

1461

**Towton
Field**

March 29,
1461

1463

SEC. II.

THE WARS
OF THE
ROSES

1450
TO
1471

The
King-
Maker

guidance ; but on the defeat of a new revolt in the battle of Hexham, Henry, after helpless wanderings, was betrayed into the hands of his enemies. His feet were tied to the stirrups, he was led thrice round the pillory, and then conducted as a prisoner to the Tower.

Ruined as feudalism really was by the decline of the baronage, the extinction of the greater houses, and the break-up of the great estates, which had been steadily going on, it had never seemed more powerful than in the years which followed Towton. Out of the wreck of the baronage a family which had always stood high amongst its fellows towered into unrivalled greatness. Lord Warwick was by descent Earl of Salisbury, a son of the great noble whose support had been mainly instrumental in raising the House of York to the throne. He had doubled his wealth and influence by his acquisition of the Earldom of Warwick through a marriage with the heiress of the Beauchamps. His services to the Yorkists were munificently rewarded by the grant of vast estates from the confiscated lands of Lancastrians, and by his elevation to the highest posts in the service of the State. He was captain of Calais, admiral of the fleet in the Channel, and Warden of the Western Marches. This personal power was backed by the power of the House of Neville, of which he was the head. The command of the northern border lay in the hands of his brother, Lord Montagu, who received as his share of the spoil the forfeited Earldom of Northumberland and the estates of his hereditary rivals, the Percies. A younger brother, George Neville, was raised to the See of York and the post of Lord Chancellor. Lesser rewards fell to his uncles, Lords Falconberg, Abergavenny, and Latimer. The vast power which such an accumulation of wealth and honours placed at the Earl's disposal was wielded with consummate ability. In outer seeming Warwick was the very type of the feudal baron. He could raise armies at his call from his own earldoms. Six hundred liveried retainers followed him to Parliament. Thousands of dependants feasted in his courtyard. But few men were really further from the feudal ideal. Active and ruthless warrior as he was, his enemies denied to the Earl the gift of personal daring. In war he was rather general than soldier. His genius in fact was not so much military as diplomatic ; what he excelled in was intrigue, treachery, the contrivance of plots, and sudden desertions. And in the boy-king whom he had raised to the throne he met not merely a consummate general, but a politician whose subtlety and rapidity of conception was destined to leave a deep and enduring mark on the character of the monarchy itself. Edward was but nineteen at his accession, and both his kinship (for he was the King's cousin by blood) and his recent services rendered Warwick during the first three years of his reign all-powerful in the State.

But the final ruin of Henry's cause in the battle of Hexham gave the signal for a silent struggle between the Earl and his young Sovereign. Edward's first step was to avow his union with the widow of a slain

Lancastrian, Dame Elizabeth Grey, at the very moment when Warwick was negotiating for him a French marriage. Her family, the Woodvilles, were raised to greatness as a counterpoise to the Nevilles; her father, Lord Rivers, became treasurer and constable; her son by the first marriage was betrothed to the heiress of the Duke of Exeter, whom Warwick sought for his nephew. Warwick's policy lay in a close connexion with France; foiled in his first project, he now pressed for a marriage of the King's sister, Margaret, with a French prince, but in 1467, while he crossed the sea to treat with Lewis, Edward availed himself of his absence to deprive his brother of the seals, and prepared to wed Margaret to the sworn enemy both of France and of Warwick, Charles the Bold, Duke of Burgundy. Warwick replied to Edward's challenge by a plot to rally the discontented Yorkists round the King's brother, the Duke of Clarence. Secret negotiations ended in the marriage of his daughter to Clarence; and a revolt which instantly broke out threw Edward into the hands of his great subject. But the bold scheme broke down. The Yorkist nobles demanded the King's liberation. Warwick could look for support only to the Lancastrians, but the Lancastrians demanded Henry's restoration as the price of their aid. Such a demand was fatal to the plan for placing Clarence on the throne, and Warwick was thrown back on a formal reconciliation with the King. A new rising broke out in the following spring in Lincolnshire. The King, however, was now ready for the strife. A rapid march to the north ended in the rout of the insurgents, and Edward turned on the instigators of the revolt. But Clarence and the Earl could gather no force to meet him. Yorkist and Lancastrian alike held aloof, and they were driven to flight. Calais, though held by Warwick's deputy, repulsed them from its walls, and the Earl's fleet was forced to take refuge in France, where the Burgundian connexion of Edward secured his enemies the support of Lewis the Eleventh. But the unscrupulous temper of the Earl was seen in the alliance which he at once concluded with the partizans of the House of Lancaster. On the promise of Queen Margaret to wed her son to his daughter Anne, Warwick engaged to restore the crown to the royal captive whom he had flung into the Tower; and choosing a moment when Edward was busy with a revolt in the North, and when a storm had dispersed the Burgundian fleet which defended the Channel, he threw himself boldly on the English shore. His army grew as he pushed northward, and the desertion of Lord Montagu, whom Edward still trusted, drove the King in turn to seek shelter over sea. While Edward fled with a handful of adherents to beg help from Charles the Bold, Henry of Lancaster was again conducted from his prison to the throne, but the bitter hate of the party Warwick had so ruthlessly crushed found no gratitude for the "King Maker." His own conduct, as well as that of his party, when Edward again disembarked in the spring at Ravenspur, showed a weariness of the new alliance, quickened perhaps by their

Sec. II.

The Wars
of the
Roses

1450
to
1471

1469

1470

Fall of
Warwick

SEC. II.

THE WARS
OF THE
ROSES
1450
TO
1471

dread of Margaret, whose return to England was hourly expected. Passing through the Lancastrian districts of the North with a declaration that he waived all right to the crown and sought only his own hereditary dukedom, Edward was left unassailed by a force which Montagu had collected, and was joined on his march by his brother Clarence, who had throughout acted in concert with Warwick. Encamped at Coventry, the Earl himself contemplated a similar treason, but the coming of two Lancastrian leaders put an end to the negotiations. When Montagu joined his brother, Edward marched on London, followed by Warwick's army ; its gates were opened by the perfidy of the Earl's brother, Archbishop Neville ; and Henry of Lancaster passed anew to the Tower. The battle of Barnet, a medley of carnage and treachery which lasted three hours, ended with the fall of Warwick, who was charged with cowardly flight. Margaret had landed too late to bring aid to her great partizan, but the military triumph of Edward was completed by the skilful strategy with which he forced her army to battle at Tewkesbury, and by its complete overthrow. The Queen herself became a captive ; her boy fell on the field, stabbed—as was affirmed—by the Yorkist lords after Edward had met his cry for mercy by a buffet from his gauntlet ; and the death of Henry in the Tower crushed the last hopes of the House of Lancaster.

April 14, 1471

Death of Henry May 4

Section III.—The New Monarchy. 1471–1509.

[*Authorities.*—Edward V. is the subject of a work attributed to Sir Thomas More, and which almost certainly derives much of its information from Archbishop Morton. Whatever its historical worth may be, it is remarkable in its English form as the first historical work of any literary value which we possess written in our modern prose. The "Letters and Papers of Richard III. and Henry VII.," some "Memorials of Henry VII.," including his life by Bernard André of Toulouse, and a volume of "Materials" for a history of his reign have been edited for the Rolls Series. A biography of Henry is among the works of Lord Bacon. Halle's Chronicle extends from Henry IV. to Henry VIII. Miss Halstead, in her "Life of Richard III.," has elaborately illustrated a reign of some constitutional importance. For Caxton, see the biography by Mr. Blades.]

The New Monarchy

There are few periods in our annals from which we turn with such weariness and disgust as from the Wars of the Roses. Their savage battles, their ruthless executions, their shameless treasons, seem all the more terrible from the pure selfishness of the ends for which men fought, the utter want of all nobleness and chivalry in the struggle itself, of all great result in its close. But even while the contest was raging the cool eye of a philosophic statesman could find in it matter for other feelings than those of mere disgust. England presented to Philippe de Commines the rare spectacle of a land where, brutal as was the civil strife, " there are no buildings destroyed or demolished by war, and where the mischief of it falls on those who make the war." The ruin and bloodshed were limited, in fact, to the great lords and their feudal retainers. Once or twice indeed, as at Towton, the towns threw themselves into the struggle, but for the most part the trading and agricultural classes stood wholly apart from it. Slowly but surely the foreign commerce of the country, hitherto conducted by the Italian, the Hanse merchant, or the trader of Catalonia or southern Gaul, was passing into English hands. English merchants were settled at Florence and at Venice. English merchant ships appeared in the Baltic. The first faint upgrowth of manufactures was seen in a crowd of protective statutes which formed a marked feature in the legislation of Edward the Fourth. The general tranquillity of the country at large, while the baronage was dashing itself to pieces in battle after battle, was shown by the remarkable fact that justice remained wholly undisturbed. The law courts sate at Westminster. The judges rode on circuit as of old. The system of jury-trial took more and more its modern form by the separation of the jurors from the witnesses. But if the common view of England during these Wars as a mere chaos of treason and bloodshed is a false one, still more false is the common view of the pettiness of their result. The Wars of the Roses did far more than ruin one royal house or set up another on the throne. If they did not utterly destroy English freedom, they arrested its progress for more than a hundred years. They found England, in the words of Commines, "among all the world's lordships of which I have knowledge, that where the public weal is best ordered, and where least violence reigns over the people." A King of England—the shrewd observer noticed—"can undertake no enterprise of account without assembling his Parliament, which is a thing most wise and holy, and therefore are these Kings stronger and better served" than the despotic sovereigns of the Continent. The English kingship, as a judge, Sir John Fortescue, could boast when writing at this time, was not an absolute but a limited monarchy ; the land was not a land where the will of the prince was itself the law, but where the prince could neither make laws nor impose taxes save by his subjects' consent. At no time had Parliament played so constant and prominent a part in the government of the realm. At no time had the principles of constitutional liberty seemed so thoroughly understood and so dear to the people at large. The long Parliamentary contest between the Crown and the two Houses since the days of Edward the First had firmly established the great securities of national liberty—the right of freedom from arbitrary taxation, from arbitrary legislation, from arbitrary imprisonment, and the responsibility of even the highest servants of the Crown to Parliament and to the law. But with the close of the struggle for the succession this liberty suddenly disappears. We enter on an epoch of constitutional retrogression in which the slow work of the age that went before it was rapidly undone. Parliamentary life was almost suspended, or was turned into a mere form by the overpowering influence of the Crown. The legislative powers of the two Houses were usurped by the royal Council. Arbitrary taxation re-appeared in benevolences and forced loans. Personal liberty was almost extinguished by a formidable spy-system and by the constant practice of arbitrary imprisonment. Justice was degraded by the prodigal use of bills of attainder, by the wide extension of the judicial power of the Royal Council, by the servility of judges, by the coercion of juries. So vast and sweeping was the change that to careless observers of a later day the constitutional monarchy of the Edwards and the Henries seemed suddenly to have transformed itself under the Tudors into a despotism as complete as the despotism of the Turk. Such a view is no doubt exaggerated and unjust. Bend and strain the law as he might, there never was a time when the most wilful of English rulers failed to own the restraints of law ; and the obedience of the most servile among English subjects lay within bounds, at once political and religious, which no theory of King-worship could bring them to overpass. But even if we make these reserves, the character of the Monarchy from the time of Edward the Fourth to the time of Elizabeth remains something strange and isolated in our history. It is hard to connect the kingship of the old English, of the Norman, the Angevin, or the Plantagenet Kings, with the kingship of the House of York or of the House of Tudor.

If we seek a reason for so sudden and complete a revolution, we find it in the disappearance of that organization of society in which our constitutional liberty had till now found its security. Freedom had been won by the sword of the Baronage. Its tradition had been watched over by the jealousy of the Church. The new class of the Commons which had grown from the union of the country squire and the town trader was widening its sphere of political activity as it grew. But at the close of the Wars of the Roses these older checks no longer served as restraints upon the action of the Crown. The baronage had fallen more and more into decay. The Church lingered helpless and perplexed, till it was struck down by Thomas Cromwell. The traders and the smaller proprietors sank into political inactivity. On the other hand, the Crown, which only fifty years before had been the sport of every faction, towered into solitary greatness. The old English kingship, limited by the forces of feudalism or of the religious sanctions wielded by the priesthood, or by the progress of constitutional freedom, faded suddenly away, and in its place we see, all-absorbing and unrestrained, the despotism of the new Monarchy. Revolutionary as the change was, however, we have already seen in their gradual growth the causes which brought it about. The social organization from which our political constitution had hitherto sprung and on which it still rested had been silently sapped by the progress of industry, by the growth of spiritual and intellectual enlightenment, and by changes in the art of war. Its ruin was precipitated by the new attitude of men towards the Church, by the disfranchisement of the Commons, and by the decline of the Baronage. Of the great houses some were extinct, others lingered only in obscure branches which were mere shadows of their former greatness. With the exception of the Poles, the Stanleys, and the Howards, themselves families of recent origin, hardly a fragment of the older baronage interfered from this time in the work of government. Neither the Church nor the smaller proprietors of the country, who with the merchant classes formed the Commons, were ready to take the place of the ruined nobles. Imposing as the great ecclesiastical body still seemed from the memories of its past, its immense wealth, its tradition of statesmanship, it was rendered powerless by a want of spiritual enthusiasm, by a moral inertness, by its antagonism to the deeper religious convictions of the people, and its blind hostility to the intellectual movement which was beginning to stir the world. Somewhat of their old independence lingered indeed among the lower clergy and the monastic orders, but it was through its prelates that the Church exercised a directly political influence, and these showed a different temper from the clergy. Driven by sheer need, by the attack of the barons on their temporal possessions, and of the Lollards on their spiritual authority, into dependence on the Crown, they threw their weight on the side of the King with the simple view of averting by means of the Monarchy the pillage of the Church. But in any wider political sense the influence of the body to which they belonged was insignificant. It is less obvious at first sight why the Commons should share the political ruin of the Church and the Lords, for the smaller county proprietors were growing fast, both in wealth and numbers, while the burgess class, as we have seen, was deriving fresh riches from the developement of trade. But the result of the narrowing of the franchise and of the tampering with elections was now felt in the political insignificance of the Lower House. Reduced by these measures to a virtual dependence on the baronage, it fell with the fall of the class to which it looked for guidance and support. And while its rival forces disappeared, the Monarchy stood ready to take their place. Not only indeed were the churchman, the squire, and the burgess powerless to vindicate liberty against the Crown, but the very interests of self-preservation led them at this moment to lay freedom at its feet. The Church still trembled at the progress of heresy. The close corporations of the towns needed protection for their privileges. The landowner shared with the trader a profound horror of the war and disorder which they had witnessed, and an almost reckless desire to entrust the Crown with any power which would prevent its return. But above all, the landed and monied classes clung passionately to the

Monarchy, as the one great force left which could save them from social revolt. The rising of the Commons of Kent shows that the troubles against which the Statutes of Labourers had been directed still remained as a formidable source of discontent. The great change in the character of agriculture indeed, which we have before described, the throwing together of the smaller holdings, the diminution of tillage, the increase of pasture lands, had tended largely to swell the numbers and turbulence of the floating labour class. The riots against "enclosures," of which ve first hear in the time of Henry the Sixth, and which became a constant feature of the Tudor period, are indications not only of a constant strife going on in every quarter between the landowner and the smaller peasant class, but of a mass of social discontent which was constantly seeking an outlet in violence and revolution. And at this moment the break-up of the military households of the nobles, and the return of wounded and disabled soldiers from the wars, added a new element of violence and disorder to the seething mass. It was in truth this social danger which lay at the root of the Tudor despotism. For the proprietary classes the repression of the poor was a question of life and death. Employer and proprietor were ready to surrender freedom into the hands of the one power which could preserve them from social anarchy. It was to the selfish panic of the landowners that England owed the Statute of Labourers and its terrible heritage of pauperism. It was to the selfish panic of both landowner and merchant that she owed the despotism of the Monarchy.

The founder of the new Monarchy was Edward the Fourth. As a mere boy he showed himself among the ablest and the most pitiless of the warriors of the civil war. In the first flush of manhood he looked on with a cool ruthlessness while grey-haired nobles were hurried to the block. In his later race for power he had shown himself more subtle in his treachery than even Warwick himself. His triumph was no sooner won however than the young King seemed to abandon himself to a voluptuous indolence, to revels with the city-wives of London and the caresses of mistresses like Jane Shore. Tall in stature and of singular beauty, his winning manners and gay carelessness of bearing secured him a popularity which had been denied to nobler kings. But his indolence and gaiety were mere veils beneath which Edward shrouded a profound political ability. No one could contrast more utterly in outward appearance with the subtle sovereigns of his time, with Louis the Eleventh or Ferdinand of Aragon, but his work was the same as theirs, and it was done as completely. While jesting with aldermen, or dallying with his mistresses, or idling over the new pages from the printing-press at Westminster, Edward was silently laying the foundations of an absolute rule. The almost total discontinuance of Parliamentary life was in itself a revolution. Up to this moment the two Houses had played a part which became more and more prominent in the government of the realm. Under the two first Kings of the House of Lancaster Parliament had been summoned almost every year. Not only had the right of self-taxation and initiation of laws been yielded explicitly to the Commons, but they had interfered with the administration of the State, had directed the application of subsidies, and called royal ministers to account by repeated instances of impeachment. Under Henry the Sixth an important step in constitutional progress had been made by abandoning the old form of presenting the requests of the Parliament in the form of petitions which were subsequently moulded into statutes by the Royal Council; the statute itself, in its final form, was now presented for the royal assent, and the Crown was deprived of its former privilege of modifying it. But with the reign of Edward the Fourth not only does this progress cease, but the very action of Parliament itself comes almost to an end. For the first time since the days of John not a single law which promoted freedom or remedied the abuses of power was even proposed. The necessity for summoning the two Houses had, in fact, been removed by the enormous tide of wealth which the confiscations of the civil war poured into the royal treasury. In the single bill of attainder which followed the victory of Towton, twelve great nobles and more than a hundred knights and squires were stripped of their estates to the King's profit. It was said that nearly a fifth of the land had passed into the royal possession at one period or another of the civil war. A grant of the customs was given to the King for life. Edward added to his resources by trading on a vast scale. The royal ships, freighted with tin, wool, and cloth, made the name of the merchant-king famous in the ports of Italy and Greece. The enterprises he planned against France, though frustrated by the refusal of Charles of Burgundy to co-operate with him in them, afforded a fresh financial resource; and the subsidies granted for a war which never took place swelled the royal exchequer. But the pretext of war enabled Edward not only to increase his hoard, but to deal a deadly blow at the liberty which the Commons had won. Setting aside the usage of contracting loans by the authority of Parliament, Edward called before him the merchants of London and requested from each a gift or "benevolence," in proportion to the royal needs. The exaction was bitterly resented even by the classes with whom the King had been most popular, but for the moment resistance was fruitless, and the system of "benevolence" was soon to be developed into the forced loans of Wolsey and of Charles the First. It was to Edward that his Tudor successors owed the introduction of an elaborate spy-system, the use of the rack, and the practice of interference with the purity of justice. In the history of intellectual progress alone his reign takes a brighter colour and the founder of

SEC. III.

THE NEW
MONARCHY

1471
TO
1509

Litera-
ture
after
Chaucer

a new despotism presents a claim to our regard as the patron of Caxton.

Literature indeed seemed at this moment to have died as utterly as freedom itself. The genius of Chaucer, and of the one or more poets whose works have been confounded with Chaucer's, defied for a while the pedantry, the affectation, the barrenness of their age ; but the sudden close of this poetic outburst left England to a crowd of poetasters, compilers, scribblers of interminable moralities, rimers of chronicles, and translators from the worn-out field of French romance. Some faint trace of the liveliness and beauty of older models lingers among the heavy platitudes of Gower, but even this vanished from the didactic puerilities, the prosaic commonplaces, of Occleve and Lydgate. The literature of the Middle Ages was dying out with the Middle Ages themselves ; in letters as in life their thirst for knowledge had spent itself in the barren mazes of the scholastic philosophy, their ideal of warlike nobleness faded away before the gaudy travestie of a spurious chivalry, and the mystic enthusiasm of their devotion shrank at the touch of persecution into a narrow orthodoxy and a flat morality. The clergy, who had concentrated in themselves the intellectual effort of the older time, were ceasing to be an intellectual class at all. The monasteries were no longer seats of learning. " I found in them," said Poggio, an Italian traveller twenty years after Chaucer's death, " men given up to sensuality in abundance, but very few lovers of learning, and those of a barbarous sort, skilled more in quibbles and sophisms than in literature." The erection of colleges, which was beginning, failed to arrest the quick decline of the universities both in the numbers and learning of their students. Those at Oxford amounted to only a fifth of the scholars who had attended its lectures a century before, and " Oxford Latin " became proverbial for a jargon in which the very tradition of grammar had been lost. All literary production was nearly at an end. Historical composition lingered on indeed in compilations of extracts from past writers, such as make up the so-called works of Walsingham, in jejune monastic annals, or worthless popular compendiums. But the only real trace of mental activity is to be found in the numerous treatises on alchemy and magic, on the elixir of life or the philosopher's stone, a fungous growth which most unequivocally witnesses to the progress of intellectual decay. On the other hand, while the older literary class was dying out, a glance beneath the surface shows us the stir of a new interest in knowledge among the masses of the people itself. The correspondence of the Paston family, which has been happily preserved, not only displays a fluency and vivacity as well as a grammatical correctness which would have been impossible in familiar letters a few years before, but shews country squires discussing about books and gathering libraries. The very character of the authorship of the time, its love of compendiums and abridgements of the scientific and historical knowledge of its day, its dramatic performances or mysteries, the commonplace morality of its poets, the popularity of its rimed chronicles, are additional proofs that literature was ceasing to be the possession of a purely intellectual class and was beginning to appeal to the people at large. The increased use of linen paper in place of the costlier parchment helped in the popularization of letters. In no former age had finer copies of books been produced; in none had so many been transcribed. This increased demand for their production caused the processes of copying and illuminating manuscripts to be transferred from the scriptoria of the religious houses into the hands of trade-gilds, like the Gild of St. John at Bruges, or the Brothers of the Pen at Brussels. It was, in fact, this increase of demand for books, pamphlets, or fly-sheets, especially of a grammatical or religious character, in the middle of the fifteenth century that brought about the introduction of printing. We meet with it first in rude sheets simply struck off from wooden blocks, "block-books" as they are now called, and later on in works printed from separate and moveable types. Originating at Maintz with the three famous printers, Gutenberg, Fust, and Schœffer, the new process travelled southward to Strasburg, crossed the Alps to Venice, where it lent itself through the Aldi to the spread of Greek literature in Europe, and then floated down the Rhine to the towns of Flanders. It was probably at the press of Colard Mansion, in a little room over the porch of St. Donat's at Bruges, that Caxton learnt the art which he was the first to introduce into England.

A Kentish boy by birth, but apprenticed to a London mercer, William Caxton had already spent thirty years of his manhood in Flanders, as Governor of the English gild of Merchant Adventurers there, when we find him engaged as copyist in the service of Edward's sister, Duchess Margaret of Burgundy. But the tedious process of copying was soon thrown aside for the new art which Colard Mansion had introduced into Bruges. "For as much as in the writing of the same," Caxton tells us in the preface to his first printed work, the Tales of Troy, "my pen is worn, my hand weary and not steadfast, mine eyes dimmed with over much looking on the white paper, and my courage not so prone and ready to labour as it hath been, and that age creepeth on me daily and feebleth all the body, and also because I have promised to divers gentlemen and to my friends to address to them as hastily as I might the said book, therefore I have practised and learned at my great charge and dispense to ordain this said book in print after the manner and form as ye may see, and is not written with pen and ink as other books be, to the end that every man may have them at once, for all the books of this story here emprynted as ye see were begun in one day and also finished in one day." The printing press

Caxton

1476

was the precious freight he brought back to England, after an absence
of five-and-thirty years. Through the next fifteen, at an age when
other men look for ease and retirement, we see him plunging with
characteristic energy into his new occupation. His "red pale," or
heraldic shield marked with a red bar down the middle, invited buyers
to the press established in the Almonry at Westminster, a little
enclosure containing a chapel and almshouses near the west front of
the church, where the alms of the abbey were distributed to the poor.
"If it please any man, spiritual or temporal," runs his advertisement,
"to buy any pyes of two or three commemorations of Salisbury all
emprynted after the form of the present letter, which be well and truly
correct, let him come to Westminster into the Almonry at the red
pale, and he shall have them good chepe." He was a practical man
of business, as this advertisement shows, no rival of the Venetian
Aldi or of the classical printers of Rome, but resolved to get a living
from his trade, supplying priests with service books, and preachers
with sermons, furnishing the clerk with his "Golden Legend," and
knight and baron with "joyous and pleasant histories of chivalry."
But while careful to win his daily bread, he found time to do much for
what of higher literature lay fairly to hand. He printed all the
English poetry of any moment which was then in existence. His
reverence for "that worshipful man, Geoffry Chaucer," who "ought to
be eternally remembered," is shown not merely by his edition of the
"Canterbury Tales," but by his reprint of them when a purer text of
the poem offered itself. The poems of Lydgate and Gower were added
to those of Chaucer. The Chronicle of Brut and Higden's "Poly-
chronicon" were the only available works of an historical character
then existing in the English tongue, and Caxton not only printed them
but himself continued the latter up to his own time. A translation of
Boethius, a version of the Æneid from the French, and a tract or
two of Cicero, were the stray first-fruits of the classical press in
England.

Busy as was Caxton's printing-press, he was even busier as a translator than as a printer. More than four thousand of his printed pages
are from works of his own rendering. The need of these translations
shows the popular drift of literature at the time ; but keen as the
demand seems to have been, there is nothing mechanical in the temper
with which Caxton prepared to meet it. A natural, simple-hearted
literary taste and enthusiasm, especially for the style and forms of
language, breaks out in his curious prefaces. "Having no work in
hand," he says in the preface to his Eneid, "I sitting in my study
where as lay many divers pamphlets and books, happened that to my
hand came a little book in French, which late was translated out of
Latin by some noble clerk of France—which book is named Eneydos,
and made in Latin by that noble poet and great clerk Vergyl—in

which book I had great pleasure by reason of the fair and honest termes and wordes in French which I never saw to-fore-like, none so pleasant nor so well-ordered, which book as me seemed should be much requisite for noble men to see, as well for the eloquence as the histories; and when I had advised me to this said book I deliberated and concluded to translate it into English, and forthwith took a pen and ink and wrote a leaf or twain." But the work of translation involved a choice of English which made Caxton's work important in the history of our language. He stood between two schools of translation, that of French affectation and English pedantry. It was a moment when the character of our literary tongue was being settled, and it is curious to see in his own words the struggle over it which was going on in Caxton's time. " Some honest and great clerks have been with me and desired me to write the most curious terms that I could find;" on the other hand, "some gentlemen of late blamed me, saying that in my translations I had over many curious terms which could not be understood of common people, and desired me to use old and homely terms in my translations." " Fain would I please every man," comments the good-humoured printer, but his sturdy sense saved him alike from the temptations of the court and the schools. His own taste pointed to English, but " to the common terms that be daily used" rather than to the English of his antiquarian advisers. " I took an old book and read therein, and certainly the English was so rude and broad I could not well understand it," while the Old-English charters which the Abbot of Westminster lent as models from the archives of his house seemed "more like to Dutch than to English." On the other hand, to adopt current phraseology was by no means easy at a time when even the speech of common talk was in a state of rapid flux. " Our language now used varieth far from that which was used and spoken when I was born." Not only so, but the tongue of each shire was still peculiar to itself, and hardly intelligible to men of another county. "Common English that is spoken in one shire varieth from another so much, that in my days happened that certain merchants were in a ship in Thames, for to have sailed over the sea into Zealand, and for lack of wind they tarried at Foreland, and went on land for to refresh them. And one of them, named Sheffield, a mercer, came into a house and asked for meat, and especially he asked them after eggs. And the good wife answered that she could speak no French. And the merchant was angry, for he also could speak no French, but would have had eggs, but she understood him not. And then at last another said he would have eyren, then the good wife said she understood him well. Lo! what should a man in these days now write," adds the puzzled printer, "eggs or eyren? certainly it is hard to please every man by cause of diversity and change of language." His own mother-tongue too was that of " Kent in the Weald, where I doubt not is spoken as broad and rude English as in any place in England ; " and coupling this with his long absence in Flanders, we can hardly wonder at the confession he makes over his first translation, that " when all these things came to fore me, after that I had made and written a five or six quires, I fell in despair of this work, and purposed never to have continued therein, and the quires laid apart, and in two years after laboured no more in this work."

He was still, however, busy translating when he died.   All difficulties, in fact, were lightened by the general interest which his labours aroused.   When the length of the " Golden Legend " makes him " half desperate to have accomplished it " and ready to " lay it apart," the Earl of Arundel solicits him in nowise to leave it and promises a yearly fee of a buck in summer and a doe in winter, once it were done. " Many noble and divers gentle men of this realm came and demanded many and often times wherefore I have not made and imprinted the noble history of the ' San Graal.' "   We see his visitors discussing with the sagacious printer the historic existence of Arthur.   Duchess Margaret of Somerset lent him her " Blanchardine and Eglantine ; " an Archdeacon of Colchester brought him his translation of the work called " Cato ; " a mercer of London pressed him to undertake the " Royal Book " of Philip le Bel.   The Queen's brother, Earl Rivers, chatted with him over his own translation of the " Sayings of the Philosophers." Even kings showed their interest in his work ; his " Tully " was printed under the patronage of Edward the Fourth, his " Order of Chivalry " dedicated to Richard the Third, his " Fayts of Arms " published at the desire of Henry the Seventh.   The fashion of large and gorgeous libraries had passed from the French to the English princes of his day : Henry the Sixth had a valuable collection of books ; that of the Louvre was seized by Duke Humphrey of Gloucester, and formed the basis of the fine library which he presented to the University of Oxford.   Great nobles took an active and personal part of the literary revival.   The warrior, Sir John Fastolf, was a well-known lover of books.   Earl Rivers was himself one of the authors of the day ; he found leisure in the intervals of pilgrimages and politics to translate the " Sayings of the Philosophers " and a couple of religious tracts for Caxton's press. A friend of far greater intellectual distinction, however, than these was found in John Tiptoft, Earl of Worcester.   He had wandered during the reign of Henry the Sixth in search of learning to Italy, had studied at her universities, and become a teacher at Padua, where the elegance of his Latinity drew tears from the most learned of the Popes, Pius the Second, better known as Æneas Sylvius.   Caxton can find no words warm enough to express his admiration of one " which in his time flowered in virtue and cunning, to whom I know none like among the lords of the temporality in science and moral virtue."   But the ruthlessness of the Renascence appeared in Tiptoft side by side with its intellectual vigour, and the fall of one whose cruelty had earned him the surname of "the Butcher" even amidst the horrors of civil war was greeted with sorrow by none but the faithful printer. "What great loss was it," he says in a preface long after his fall, "of that noble, virtuous, and well-disposed lord; when I remember and advertise his life, his science, and his virtue, me thinketh (God not displeased) over great a loss of such a man, considering his estate and cunning."

Among the nobles who encouraged the work of Caxton we have already seen the figure of the King's youngest brother, Richard, Duke of Gloucester. Ruthless and subtle as Edward himself, the Duke at once came to the front with a scheme of daring ambition when the succession of a boy of thirteen woke again the fierce rivalries of the Court. On the King's death Richard hastened to secure the person of his nephew, Edward the Fifth, to overthrow the power of the Queen's family, and to receive from the council the office of Protector of the realm. Little more than a month had passed, when suddenly entering the Council chamber, he charged Lord Hastings, the chief adviser of the late King and loyal adherent of his sons, with sorcery and designs upon his life. As he dashed his hand upon the table the room was filled with soldiers. "I will not dine," said the Duke, addressing Hastings, "till they have brought me your head;" and the powerful minister was hurried to instant execution in the court-yard of the Tower. The Archbishop of York and the Bishop of Ely were thrown into prison, and every check on Richard's designs was removed. Only one step remained to be taken, and two months after his brother's death the Duke consented after some show of reluctance to receive a petition presented by a body of lords and others in the name of the three estates, which, setting aside Edward's children as the fruit of an unlawful marriage and those of Clarence as disabled by his attainder, besought him to take the office and title of King. His young nephews, Edward V. and his brother the Duke of York, were flung into the Tower, and there murdered, as was alleged, by their uncle's order; while the Queen's brother and son, Lord Rivers and Sir Richard Grey, were hurried to execution. Morton, the Bishop of Ely, imprisoned under Buckingham in Wales, took advantage of the disappearance of the two boys to found a scheme which was to unite the discontented Yorkists with what remained of the Lancastrian party, and to link both bodies in a wide conspiracy. All the descendants of Henry IV. had passed away, but the line of John of Gaunt still survived. The Lady Margaret Beaufort, the last representative of the House of Somerset, had married the Earl of Richmond, Edmund Tudor, and become the mother of Henry Tudor. In the act which legitimated the Beauforts an illegal clause had been inserted by Henry IV. which barred their

SEC. III.

THE NEW MONARCHY

1471
TO
1509

Richard the Third

1483

Henry Tudor

1483

succession to the crown ; but as the last remaining scion of the line of Lancaster Henry's claim was acknowledged by the partizans of his House, and he had been driven to seek a refuge in Brittany from the jealous hostility of the Yorkist sovereigns.   Morton's plan was the marriage of Henry Tudor with Elizabeth, the daughter and heiress of Edward IV., and with Buckingham's aid a formidable revolt was organized.   The outbreak was quickly put down.   But daring as was Richard's natural temper, it was not to mere violence that he trusted in his seizure of the throne.   During his brother's reign he had watched keenly the upgrowth of public discontent as the new policy of the monarchy developed itself, and it was as the restorer of its older liberties that he appealed for popular support.   " We be determined," said the citizens of London in a petition to the King, " rather to adventure and to commit us to the peril of our lives and jeopardy of death, than to live in such thraldom and bondage as we have lived long time heretofore, oppressed and injured by extortions and new impositions against the laws of God and man and the liberty and laws of this realm, wherein every Englishman is inherited."   Richard met the appeal by again convoking Parliament, which, as we have seen, had been all but discontinued under Edward, and by sweeping measures of reform.   In the one session of his brief reign the practice of extorting money by " benevolences" was declared illegal, while grants of pardons and remission of forfeitures reversed in some measure the policy of terror by which Edward at once held the country in awe and filled his treasury.   Numerous statutes broke the slumbers of Parliamentary legislation.   A series of mercantile enactments strove to protect the growing interests of English commerce.   The King's love of literature showed itself in the provision that no statutes should act as a hindrance " to any artificer or merchant stranger, of what nation or country he be, for bringing unto this realm or selling by retail or otherwise of any manner of books, written or imprinted."   His prohibition of the iniquitous seizure of goods before conviction of felony, which had prevailed during Edward's reign, his liberation of the bondmen who still remained unenfranchised on the royal domain, and his religious foundations, show Richard's keen anxiety to purchase a popularity in which the bloody opening of his reign might be forgotten. But as the news of the royal children's murder slowly spread, the most pitiless stood aghast at this crowning deed of blood.   The pretence of constitutional rule, too, was soon thrown off, and a levy of benevolences in defiance of the statute which had just been passed woke general indignation.   The King felt himself safe ; he had even won the Queen-mother's consent to his marriage with Elizabeth ; and Henry, alone and in exile, seemed a small danger.   But a wide conspiracy at once revealed itself when Henry landed at Milford Haven, and advanced through Wales.   He no sooner encountered the royal army

1484

*Bosworth
Field*
1485

at Bosworth Field in Leicestershire than treachery decided the day. Abandoned ere the battle began by a division of his forces under Lord Stanley, and as it opened by a second body under the Earl of Northumberland, Richard dashed, with a cry of "Treason, Treason," into the thick of the fight. In the fury of his despair he had already flung the Lancastrian standard to the ground and hewed his way into the very presence of his rival, when he fell overpowered by numbers, and the crown which he had worn, and which was found as the struggle ended lying near a hawthorn bush, was placed on the head of the conqueror.

With the accession of Henry the Seventh ended the long bloodshed of the civil wars. The two warring lines were united by his marriage with Elizabeth: his only dangerous rivals were removed by the successive deaths of the nephews of Edward the Fourth, John de la Pole, Earl of Lincoln, a son of Edward's sister, who had been acknowledged as his successor by Richard the Third; and the Earl of Warwick, a son of Edward's brother the Duke of Clarence, and next male heir of the Yorkist line. Two remarkable impostors succeeded for a time in exciting formidable revolts, Lambert Simnel, under the name of the Earl of Warwick, and Perkin Warbeck, who personated the Duke of York, the second of the children murdered in the Tower. Defeat, however, reduced the first to the post of scullion in the royal kitchen; and the second, after far stranger adventures, and the recognition of his claims by the Kings of Scotland and France, as well as by the Duchess-Dowager of Burgundy, whom he claimed as his aunt, was captured and four years later hanged at Tyburn. Revolt only proved more clearly the strength which had been given to the New Monarchy by the revolution which had taken place in the art of war. The introduction of gunpowder had ruined feudalism. The mounted and heavily-armed knight gave way to the meaner footman. Fortresses which had been impregnable against the attacks of the Middle Ages crumbled before the new artillery. Although gunpowder had been in use as early as Crécy, it was not till the accession of the House of Lancaster that it was really brought into effective employment as a military resource. But the revolution in warfare was immediate. The wars of Henry the Fifth were wars of sieges. The "Last of the Barons," as Warwick has picturesquely been styled, relied mainly on his train of artillery. It was artillery that turned the day at Barnet and Tewkesbury, and that gave Henry the Seventh his victory over the formidable dangers which assailed him. The strength which the change gave to the crown was, in fact, almost irresistible. Throughout the Middle Ages the call of a great baron had been enough to raise a formidable revolt. Yeomen and retainers took down the bow from their chimney corner, knights buckled on their armour, and in a few days an army threatened the throne. But without artillery such an army was now helpless, and the one train of artillery in the kingdom lay at the disposal of the King. It was the consciousness of his strength which enabled the new sovereign to quietly resume the policy of Edward the Fourth. He was forced, indeed, by the circumstances of his descent to base his right to the throne on a Parliamentary title. Without reference either to the claim of blood or conquest, the Houses enacted simply "that the inheritance of the Crown should be, rest, remain, and abide in the most Royal person of their sovereign lord, King Henry the Seventh, and the heirs of his body lawfully ensuing." But the policy of Edward was faithfully followed, and Parliament was but twice convened during the last thirteen years of Henry's reign. The chief aim, indeed, of the King was the accumulation of a treasure which would relieve him from the need of ever appealing for its aid. Subsidies granted for the support of wars which Henry evaded formed the base of a royal treasure, which was swelled by the revival of dormant claims of the crown, by the exaction of fines for the breach of forgotten tenures, and by a host of petty extortions. A dilemma of his favourite minister, which received the name of " Morton's fork," extorted gifts to the exchequer from men who lived handsomely on the ground that their wealth was manifest, and from those who lived plainly on the plea that economy had made them wealthy. Still greater sums were drawn from those who were compromised in the revolts which chequered the King's rule. So successful were these efforts that at the end of his reign Henry bequeathed a hoard of two millions to his successor. The same imitation of Edward's policy was seen in Henry's civil government. Broken as was the strength of the baronage, there still remained lords whom the new monarch watched with a jealous solicitude. Their power lay in the hosts of disorderly retainers who swarmed round their houses, ready to furnish a force in case of revolt, while in peace they became centres of outrage and defiance to the law. Edward had ordered the dissolution of these military households in his Statute of Liveries, and the statute was enforced by Henry with the utmost severity. On a visit to the Earl of Oxford, one of the most devoted adherents of the Lancastrian cause, the King found two long lines of liveried retainers drawn up to receive him. "I thank you for your good cheer, my Lord," said Henry as they parted, "but I may not endure to have my laws broken in my sight. My attorney must speak with you." The Earl was glad to escape with a fine of £10,000. It was with a special view to the suppression of this danger that Henry employed the criminal jurisdiction of the Royal Council. He appointed a committee of his Council as a regular court, to which the place where it usually sat gave the name of the Court of Star Chamber. The King's aim was probably little more than a purpose to enforce order on the land by bringing the great nobles before his own judgment-seat ; but the establishment of the court as a regular and no longer an exceptional tribunal, whose

*Court of
Star
Chamber*

traditional powers were confirmed by Parliamentary statute, and where the absence of a jury cancelled the prisoner's right to be tried by his peers, furnished his son with his readiest instrument of tyranny. But though the drift of Henry's policy was steady in the direction of despotism, his temper seemed to promise the reign of a poetic dreamer rather than of a statesman. The spare form, the sallow face, the quick eye, the shy, solitary humour broken by outbursts of pleasant converse or genial sarcasm, told of an inner concentration and enthusiasm. His tastes were literary and artistic ; he was a patron of the new printing press, a lover of books and of art. But life gave Henry little leisure for dreams or culture. Wrapt in schemes of foreign intrigue, struggling with dangers at home, he could take small part in the one movement which stirred England during his reign, the great intellectual revolution which bears the name of the Revival of Letters.

Section IV.—The New Learning. 1509—1520.

[*Authorities.*—The general literary history of this period is fully and accurately given by Mr. Hallam (" Literature of Europe "), and in a confused but interesting way by Warton ("History of English Poetry"). The most accessible edition of the typical book of the Revival, More's " Utopia," is the Elizabethan translation, published by Mr. Arber ("English Reprints," 1869). The history of Erasmus in England must be followed in his own entertaining Letters, abstracts of some of which will be found in the well-known biography by Jortin. Colet's work and the theological aspect of the Revival has been described by Mr. Seebohm (" The Oxford Reformers of 1498"); for Warham's share, I have ventured to borrow a little from a paper of mine on " Lambeth and the Archbishops," in " Stray Studies."]

Great as were the issues of Henry's policy, it shrinks into littleness if we turn from it to the weighty movements which were now stirring the minds of men. The world was passing through changes more momentous than any it had witnessed since the victory of Christianity and the fall of the Roman Empire. Its physical bounds were suddenly enlarged. The discoveries of Copernicus revealed to man the secret of the universe. Portuguese mariners doubled the Cape of Good Hope and anchored their merchant fleets in the harbours of India. Columbus crossed the untraversed ocean to add a New World to the Old. Sebastian Cabot, starting from the port of Bristol, threaded his way among the icebergs of Labrador. This sudden contact with new lands, new faiths, new races of men quickened the slumbering intelligence of Europe into a strange curiosity. The first book of voyages that told of the Western World, the Travels of Amerigo Vespucci, was soon " in every body's hands." The " Utopia " of More, in its wide range of speculation on every subject of human thought and action, tells us how roughly and utterly the narrowness and limitation of human life had been broken up. The capture of Constantinople by the Turks, and the flight of its Greek scholars to the shores of Italy, opened anew the science and literature of the older world at the very hour when the intellectual energy of the Middle Ages had sunk into exhaustion. The exiled Greek scholars were welcomed in Italy, and Florence, so long the home of freedom and of art, became the home of an intellectual revival. The poetry of Homer, the drama of Sophocles, the philosophy of Aristotle and of Plato woke again to life beneath the shadow of the mighty dome with which Brunelleschi had just crowned the City by the Arno. All the restless energy which Florence had so long thrown into the cause of liberty she flung, now that her liberty was reft from her, into the cause of letters. The galleys of her merchants brought back manuscripts from the East as the most precious portion of their freight. In the palaces of her nobles fragments of classic sculpture ranged themselves beneath the frescoes of Ghirlandajo. The recovery of a treatise of Cicero's or a tract of Sallust's from the dust of a monastic library was welcomed by the group of statesmen and artists who gathered in the Rucellai gardens with a thrill of enthusiasm. Foreign scholars soon flocked over the Alps to learn Greek, the key of the new knowledge, from the Florentine teachers. Grocyn, a fellow of New College, was perhaps the first Englishman who studied under the Greek exile, Chalcondylas ; and the Greek lectures which he delivered in Oxford on his return mark the opening of a new period in our history. Physical as well as literary activity awoke with the re-discovery of the teachers of Greece, and the continuous progress of English science may be dated from the day when Linacre, another Oxford student, returned from the lectures of the Florentine Politian to revive the older tradition of medicine by his translation of Galen.

But from the first it was manifest that the revival of letters would take a tone in England very different from the tone it had taken in Italy, a tone less literary, less largely human, but more moral, more religious, more practical in its bearings both upon society and politics. The awakening of a rational Christianity, whether in England or in the Teutonic world at large, began with the Italian studies of John Colet ; and the vigour and earnestness of Colet were the best proof of the strength with which the new movement was to affect English religion. He came back to Oxford utterly untouched by the Platonic mysticism or the semi-serious infidelity which characterized the group of scholars round Lorenzo the Magnificent. He was hardly more influenced by their literary enthusiasm. The knowledge of Greek seems to have had one almost exclusive end for him, and this was a religious end. Greek was the key by which he could unlock the Gospels and the New Testament, and in these he thought that he could find a new religious standing-ground. It was this resolve of Colet to fling aside the traditional dogmas of his day and to discover a rational and practical religion in the Gospels themselves, which gave its peculiar stamp to the theology of the Renascence. His faith stood simply on a vivid realization of the person of Christ. In the prominence which such a view gave to the moral life, in his free criticism of the earlier Scriptures, in his tendency to simple forms of doctrine and confessions of faith, Colet struck the key-note of a mode of religious thought as strongly in contrast with that of the later Reformation as with that of Catholicism itself. The allegorical and mystical theology on which the Middle Ages had spent their intellectual vigour to such little purpose fell at one blow before his rejection of all but the historical and grammatical sense of the Biblical text. The great fabric of belief built up by the mediæval doctors seemed to him simply "the corruptions of the Schoolmen." In the life and sayings of its Founder he found a simple and rational Christianity, whose fittest expression was the Apostles' creed. "About the rest," he said with characteristic impatience, "let divines dispute as they will." Of his attitude towards the coarser aspects of the current religion his behaviour at a later time before the famous shrine of St. Thomas at Canterbury gives us a rough indication. As the blaze of its jewels, its costly sculptures, its elaborate metal-work burst on Colet's view, he suggested with bitter irony that a saint so lavish to the poor in his lifetime would certainly prefer that they should possess the wealth heaped round him since his death. With petulant disgust he rejected the rags of the martyr which were offered for his adoration, and the shoe which was offered for his kiss. The earnestness, the religious zeal, the very impatience and want of sympathy with the past which we see in every word and act of the man, burst out in the lectures on St. Paul's Epistles which he delivered at Oxford. Even to the most critical among his hearers he seemed "like one inspired, raised in voice, eye, his whole countenance and mien, out of himself." Severe as was the outer life of the new teacher, a severity marked by his plain black robe and the frugal table which he preserved amidst his later dignities, his lively conversation, his frank simplicity, the purity and nobleness of his life, even the keen outbursts of his troublesome temper, endeared him to a group of scholars among whom Erasmus and Thomas More stood in the foremost rank.

"Greece has crossed the Alps," cried the exiled Argyropulos on hearing a translation of Thucydides by the German Reuchlin; but the glory, whether of Reuchlin or of the Teutonic scholars who followed him, was soon eclipsed by that of Erasmus. His enormous industry, the vast store of classical learning which he gradually accumulated, Erasmus shared with others of his day. In patristic reading he may have stood beneath Luther; in originality and profoundness of thought he was certainly inferior to More. His theology, though he made a far greater mark on the world by it than even by

X

his scholarship, he derived almost without change from Colet. But his combination of vast learning with keen observation, of acuteness of remark with a lively fancy, of genial wit with a perfect good sense—his union of as sincere a piety and as profound a zeal for rational religion as Colet's with a dispassionate fairness towards older faiths, a large love of secular culture, and a genial freedom and play of mind—this union was his own, and it was through this that Erasmus embodied for the Teutonic peoples the quickening influence of the New Learning during the long scholar-life which began at Paris and ended amidst darkness and sorrow at Basel. At the time of Colet's return from Italy Erasmus was young and comparatively unknown, but the chivalrous enthusiasm of the new movement breaks out in his letters from Paris, whither he had wandered as a scholar. " I have given up my whole soul to Greek learning," he writes, " and as soon as I get any money I shall buy Greek books—and then I shall buy some clothes." It was in despair of reaching Italy that the young scholar made his way to Oxford, as the one place on this side the Alps where he would be enabled through the teaching of Grocyn to acquire a knowledge of Greek.

But he had no sooner arrived there than all feeling of regret vanished away. " I have found in Oxford," he writes, " so much polish and learning that now I hardly care about going to Italy at all, save for the sake of having been there. When I listen to my friend Colet it seems like listening to Plato himself. Who does not wonder at the wide range of Grocyn's knowledge? What can be more searching, deep, and refined than the judgement of Linacre? When did Nature mould a temper more gentle, endearing, and happy than the temper of Thomas More?"

But the new movement was far from being bounded by the walls of Oxford. The silent influences of time were working, indeed, steadily for its cause. The printing press was making letters the common property of all. In the last thirty years of the fifteenth century ten thousand editions of books and pamphlets are said to have been published throughout Europe, the most important half of them of course in Italy ; and all the Latin authors were accessible to every student before it closed. Almost all the more valuable authors of Greece were published in the first twenty years of the century which followed. The profound influence of this burst of the two great classic literatures upon the world at once made itself felt. " For the first time," to use the picturesque phrase of M. Taine, " men opened their eyes and saw." The human mind seemed to gather new energies at the sight of the vast field which opened before it. It attacked every province of knowledge, and it transformed all. Experimental science, the science of philology, the science of politics, the critical investigation of religious truth, all took their origin from the Renascence—this ' New Birth' of the world. Art, if it lost much in purity and propriety, gained in scope and in the fearlessness of its love of Nature. Literature, if crushed for the moment by the overpowering attraction of the great models of Greece and Rome, revived with a grandeur of form, a large spirit of humanity, such as it had never known since their day. In England the influence of the new movement extended far beyond the little group in which it had a few years before seemed concentrated. The great churchmen became its patrons. Langton, Bishop of Winchester, took delight in examining the young scholars of his episcopal family every evening, and sent all the most promising of them to study across the Alps. Learning found a yet warmer friend in the Archbishop of Canterbury. Immersed as Archbishop Warham was in the business of the state, he was no mere politician. The eulogies which Erasmus lavished on him while he lived, his praises of the Primate's learning, of his ability in business, his pleasant humour, his modesty, his fidelity to friends, may pass for what eulogies of living men are commonly worth. But it is difficult to doubt the sincerity of the glowing picture which he drew of him when death had destroyed all interest in mere adulation. The letters indeed which passed between the great churchman and the wandering scholar, the quiet, simple-hearted grace which amidst constant instances of munificence preserved the perfect equality of literary friendship, the enlightened piety to which Erasmus could address the noble words of his preface to St. Jerome, confirm the judgement of every good man of Warham's day. In the simplicity of his life the Archbishop offered a striking contrast to the luxurious nobles of his time. He cared nothing for the pomp, the sensual pleasures, the hunting and dicing in which they too commonly indulged. An hour's pleasant reading, a quiet chat with some learned new-comer, alone broke the endless round of civil and ecclesiastical business. Few men realized so thoroughly as Warham the new conception of an intellectual and moral equality before which the old social distinctions of the world were to vanish away. His favourite relaxation was to sup among a group of scholarly visitors, enjoying their fun and retorting with fun of his own. But the scholar-world found more than supper or fun at the Primate's board. His purse was ever open to relieve their poverty. " Had I found such a patron in my youth," Erasmus wrote long after, " I too might have been counted among the fortunate ones." It was with Grocyn that Erasmus on a second visit to England rowed up the river to Warham's board at Lambeth, and in spite of an unpromising beginning the acquaintance turned out wonderfully well. The Primate loved him, Erasmus wrote home, as if he were his father or his brother, and his generosity surpassed that of all his friends. He offered him a sinecure, and when he declined it he bestowed on him a pension of a hundred crowns a year. When Erasmus wandered to Paris it was Warham's invitation which recalled him to England. When the rest of his patrons left him to starve on the sour beer of Cambridge it was Warham who sent him fifty angels. " I wish

Sec. IV.
The New Learning
1509
to
1520

Archbishop Warham

1510

SEC. IV.

THE NEW
LEARNING

1509
TO
1520
Henry
the
Eighth

1509

there were thirty legions of them," the Primate puns in his good-humoured way.

Real however as this progress was, the group of scholars who represented the New Learning in England still remained a little one through the reign of Henry the Seventh. But a "New Order," to use their own enthusiastic term, dawned on them with the accession of his son. Henry the Eighth had hardly completed his eighteenth year when he mounted the throne, but the beauty of his person, his vigour and skill in arms, seemed matched by a frank and generous temper and a nobleness of political aims. He gave promise of a more popular system of government by checking at once the extortion which had been practised under colour of enforcing forgotten laws, and by bringing his father's financial ministers, Empson and Dudley, to trial on a charge of treason. No accession ever excited higher expectations among a people than that of Henry the Eighth. Pole, his bitterest enemy, confessed at a later time, that the King was of a temper at the beginning of his reign "from which all excellent things might have been hoped." Already in stature and strength a King among his fellows, taller than any, bigger than any, a mighty wrestler, a mighty hunter, an archer of the best, a knight who bore down rider after rider in the tourney, the young monarch combined with his bodily lordliness a largeness and versatility of mind which was to be the special characteristic of the age that had begun. His sympathies were known to be heartily with the New Learning; for Henry was not only himself a fair scholar, but even in boyhood had roused by his wit and attainments the wonder of Erasmus. The great scholar hurried back to England to pour out his exultation in the "Praise of Folly," a song of triumph over the old world of ignorance and bigotry which was to vanish away before the light and knowledge of the new reign. Folly, in his amusing little book, mounts a pulpit in cap and bells and pelts with her satire the absurdities of the world around her, the superstition of the monk, the pedantry of the grammarian, the dogmatism of the doctors of the schools, the selfishness and tyranny of kings.

**The New
Learning
and
Education**

1510

The irony of Erasmus was backed by the earnest effort of Colet. Four years before he had been called from Oxford to the Deanery of St. Paul's, when he became the great preacher of his day, the predecessor of Latimer in his simplicity, his directness, and his force. He seized the opportunity to commence the work of educational reform by the foundation of his own Grammar School, beside St. Paul's. The bent of its founder's mind was shown by the image of the Child Jesus over the master's chair, with the words "Hear ye Him" graven beneath it. "Lift up your little white hands for me," wrote the Dean to his scholars, in words which show the tenderness that lay beneath the stern outer seeming of the man,—"for me which prayeth for you to God."

All the educational designs of the reformers were carried out in the new foundation. The old methods of instruction were superseded by fresh grammars composed by Erasmus and other scholars for its use. Lilly, an Oxford student who had studied Greek in the East, was placed at its head. The injunctions of the founder aimed at the union of rational religion with sound learning, at the exclusion of the scholastic logic, and at the steady diffusion of the two classical literatures. The more bigoted of the clergy were quick to take alarm. "No wonder," More wrote to the Dean, "your school raises a storm, for it is like the wooden horse in which armed Greeks were hidden for the ruin of barbarous Troy." But the cry of alarm passed helplessly away. Not only did the study of Greek creep gradually into the schools which existed, but the example of Colet was followed by a crowd of imitators. More grammar schools, it has been said, were founded in the latter years of Henry than in the three centuries before. The impulse grew only stronger as the direct influence of the New Learning passed away. The grammar schools of Edward the Sixth and of Elizabeth, in a word the system of middle-class education which by the close of the century had changed the very face of England, were amongst the results of Colet's foundation of St. Paul's. But the "armed Greeks" of More's apologue found a yet wider field in the reform of the higher education of the country. On the Universities the influence of the New Learning was like a passing from death to life. Erasmus gives us a picture of what happened at Cambridge, where he was himself for a time a teacher of Greek. "Scarcely thirty years ago nothing was taught here but the *Parva Logicalia*, Alexander, antiquated exercises from Aristotle, and the *Quæstiones* of Scotus. As time went on better studies were added, mathematics, a new, or at any rate a renovated, Aristotle, and a knowledge of Greek literature. What has been the result? The University is now so flourishing that it can compete with the best universities of the age." Latimer and Croke returned from Italy and carried on the work of Erasmus at Cambridge, where Fisher, Bishop of Rochester, himself one of the foremost scholars of the new movement, lent it his powerful support. At Oxford the Revival met with a fiercer opposition. The contest took the form of boyish frays, in which the young partizans and opponents of the New Learning took sides as Greeks and Trojans. The King himself had to summon one of its fiercest enemies to Woodstock, and to impose silence on the tirades which were delivered from the University pulpit. The preacher alleged that he was carried away by the Spirit. "Yes," retorted the King, "by the spirit, not of wisdom, but of folly." But even at Oxford the contest was soon at an end. Fox, Bishop of Winchester, established the first Greek lecture there in his new college of Corpus Christi, and a Professorship of Greek was at a later time established by the Crown. "The students," wrote an eye-

Sec. IV.

The New
Learning

1509
to
1520

1516

1520

**The New
Learning
and the
Church**

1512

witness, "rush to Greek letters, they endure watching, fasting, toil, and hunger in the pursuit of them." The work was crowned at last by the munificent foundation of Cardinal College, to share in whose teaching Wolsey invited the most eminent of the living scholars of Europe, and for whose library he promised to obtain copies of all the manuscripts in the Vatican.

From the reform of education the New Learning pressed on to the reform of the Church. Warham still flung around the movement his steady protection, and it was by his commission that Colet was enabled to address the Convocation of the Clergy in words which set before them with unsparing severity the religious ideal of the New Learning. "Would that for once," burst forth the fiery preacher, "you would remember your name and profession and take thought for the reformation of the Church! Never was it more necessary, and never did the state of the Church need more vigorous endeavours." "We are troubled with heretics," he went on, "but no heresy of theirs is so fatal to us and to the people at large as the vicious and depraved lives of the clergy. That is the worst heresy of all." It was the reform of the bishops that must precede that of the clergy, the reform of the clergy that would lead to a general revival of religion in the people at large. The accumulation of benefices, the luxury and worldliness of the priesthood, must be abandoned. The prelates ought to be busy preachers, to forsake the Court and labour in their own dioceses. Care should be taken for the ordination and promotion of worthier ministers, residence should be enforced, the low standard of clerical morality should be raised. It is plain that the men of the New Learning looked forward, not to a reform of doctrine, but to a reform of life, not to a revolution which should sweep away the older superstitions which they despised, but to a regeneration of spiritual feeling before which they would inevitably vanish. Colet was soon charged with heresy by the Bishop of London. Warham however protected him, and Henry, to whom the Dean was denounced, bade him go boldly on. "Let every man have his own doctor," said the young King, after a long interview, "and let every man favour his own, but this man is the doctor for me."

**Henry
and
France**

But for the success of the new reform, a reform which could only be wrought out by the tranquil spread of knowledge and the gradual enlightenment of the human conscience, the one thing needful was peace; and the young King to whom the scholar-group looked was already longing for war. Long as peace had been established between the two countries, the designs of England upon the French crown had never been really waived, and Henry's pride dwelt on the older claims of England to Normandy and Guienne. Edward the Fourth and Henry the Seventh had each clung to a system of peace, only broken by the vain efforts to save Britanny from

French invasion. But the growth of the French monarchy in extent and power through the policy of Lewis the Eleventh, his extinction of the great feudatories, and the administrative centralization he introduced, raised his kingdom to a height far above that of its European rivals. The power of France, in fact, was only counterbalanced by that of Spain, which had become a great state through the union of Castile and Aragon, and where the cool and wary Ferdinand of Aragon was building up a vast power by the marriage of his daughter and heiress to the Archduke Philip, son of the Emperor Maximilian. Too weak to meet France single-handed, Henry the Seventh saw in an alliance with Spain a security against his "hereditary enemy," and this alliance had been cemented by the marriage of his eldest son, Arthur, with Ferdinand's daughter, Catharine of Aragon. This match was broken by the death of the young bridegroom; but by the efforts of Spain a Papal dispensation was procured which enabled Catharine to wed the brother of her late husband. Henry, however, anxious to preserve a balanced position between the battling powers of France and Spain, opposed the union; but Henry the Eighth had no sooner succeeded his father on the throne than the marriage was carried out. Throughout the first years of his reign, amidst the tournaments and revelry which seemed to absorb his whole energies, Henry was in fact keenly watching the opening which the ambition of France began to afford for a renewal of the old struggle. Under the successors of Lewis the Eleventh the efforts of the French monarchy had been directed to the conquest of Italy. The passage of the Alps by Charles the Eighth and the mastery which he won over Italy at a single blow lifted France at once above the states around her. Twice repulsed from Naples, she remained under the successor of Charles, Lewis the Twelfth, mistress of Milan and of the bulk of Northern Italy; and the ruin of Venice in the league of Cambray crushed the last Italian state which could oppose her designs on the whole peninsula. A Holy League, as it was called from the accession to it of the Pope, to drive France from the Milanese was formed by the efforts of Ferdinand, aided as he was by the kinship of the Emperor, the support of Venice and Julius the Second, and the warlike temper of Henry the Eighth. "The barbarians," to use the phrase of Julius "were chased beyond the Alps;" but Ferdinand's unscrupulous adroitness only used the English force, which had landed at Fontarabia with the view of attacking Guienne, to cover his own conquest of Navarre. The troop mutinied and sailed home; men scoffed at the English as useless for war. Henry's spirit, however, rose with the need. He landed in person in the north of France, and a sudden rout of the French cavalry in an engagement near Guinegate, which received from its bloodless character the name of the Battle of the

**The
Peace
and the
New
Learning**

Spurs, gave him the fortresses of Térouanne and Tournay. The young conqueror was eagerly pressing on to the recovery of his "heritage of France," when he found himself suddenly left alone by the desertion of Ferdinand and the dissolution of the league. Henry had indeed gained much. The might of France was broken. The Papacy was restored to freedom. England had again figured as a great power in Europe. But the millions left by his father were exhausted, his subjects had been drained by repeated subsidies, and, furious as he was at the treachery of his Spanish ally, Henry was driven to conclude a peace.

To the hopes of the New Learning this sudden outbreak of the spirit of war, this change of the monarch from whom they had looked for a "new order" into a vulgar conqueror, proved a bitter disappointment. Colet thundered from the pulpit of St. Paul's that "an unjust peace is better than the justest war," and protested that "when men out of hatred and ambition fight with and destroy one another, they fight under the banner, not of Christ, but of the Devil." Erasmus quitted Cambridge with a bitter satire against the "madness" around him. "It is the people." he said, in words which must have startled his age,—"it is the people who build cities, while the madness of princes destroys them." The sovereigns of his time appeared to him like ravenous birds pouncing with beak and claw on the hard-won wealth and knowledge of mankind. "Kings who are scarcely men," he exclaimed in bitter irony, "are called 'divine;' they are 'invincible' though they fly from every battle-field; 'serene' though they turn the world upside down in a storm of war; 'illustrious' though they grovel in ignorance of all that is noble; 'Catholic' though they follow anything rather than Christ. Of all birds the Eagle alone has seemed to wise men the type of royalty, a bird neither beautiful nor musical nor good for food, but murderous, greedy, hateful to all, the curse of all, and with its great powers of doing harm only surpassed by its desire to do it." It was the first time in modern history that religion had formally dissociated itself from the ambition of princes and the horrors of war, or that the new spirit of criticism had ventured not only to question but to deny what had till then seemed the primary truths of political order. We shall soon see to what further length the new speculations were pushed by a greater thinker, but for the moment the indignation of the New Learning was diverted to more practical ends by the sudden peace. However he had disappointed its hopes, Henry still remained its friend. Through all the changes of his terrible career his home was a home of letters. His boy, Edward the Sixth, was a fair scholar in both the classical languages. His daughter Mary wrote good Latin letters. Elizabeth began every day with an hour's reading in the Greek Testament, the tragedies of Sophocles, or the orations of Demosthenes. The ladies of the court caught the royal fashion, and were found poring over the pages of Plato. Widely as Henry's ministers differed from each other, they all agreed

in the direction of educational and religious reform, its political and social speculations took a far wider range in the "Utopia" of Thomas More. Even in the household of Cardinal Morton, where he had spent his childhood, More's precocious ability had raised the highest hopes. "Whoever may live to see it," the grey-haired statesman used to say, "this boy now waiting at table will turn out a marvellous man." We have seen the spell which his wonderful learning and the sweetness of his temper threw over Colet and Erasmus at Oxford, and young as he was, More no sooner quitted the University than he was known throughout Europe as one of the foremost figures in the new movement. The keen, irregular face, the grey restless eye, the thin mobile lips, the tumbled brown hair, the careless gait and dress, as they remain stamped on the canvas of Holbein, picture the inner soul of the man, his vivacity, his restless, all-devouring intellect, his keen and even reckless wit, the kindly, half-sad humour that drew its strange veil of laughter and tears over the deep, tender reverence of the soul within. In a higher, because in a sweeter and more loveable form than Colet, More is the representative of the religious tendency of the New Learning in England. The young law-student who laughed at the superstition and asceticism of the monks of his day wore a hair shirt next his skin, and schooled himself by penances for the cell he desired among the Carthusians. It was characteristic of the man that among all the gay, profligate scholars of the Italian Renascence he chose as the object of his admiration the disciple of Savonarola, Pico di Mirandola. Free-thinker as the bigots who listened to his daring speculations termed him, his eye would brighten and his tongue falter as he spoke with friends of heaven and the after-life. When he took office, it was with the open stipulation "first to look to God, and after God to the King." But in his outer bearing there was nothing of the monk or recluse. The brightness and freedom of the New Learning seemed incarnate in the young scholar, with his gay talk, his winsomeness of manner, his reckless epigrams, his passionate love of music, his omnivorous reading, his paradoxical speculations, his gibes at monks, his schoolboy fervour of liberty. But events were soon to prove that beneath this sunny nature lay a stern inflexibility of conscientious resolve. The Florentine scholars who penned declamations against tyrants had covered with their flatteries the tyranny of the house of Medici. More no sooner entered Parliament than his ready argument and keen sense of justice led to the rejection of the Royal demand for a heavy subsidy. "A beardless boy," said the courtiers,— and More was only twenty-six,—"has disappointed the King's purpose;" and during the rest of Henry the Seventh's reign the young lawyer found it prudent to withdraw from public life. But the withdrawal had little effect on his buoyant activity. He rose at once into repute at the bar. He wrote his "Life of Edward the Fifth," the first work in which what we may call modern English prose appears written with purity and clearness of style and a freedom either from antiquated forms of expression or classical pedantry. His ascetic dreams were replaced by the affections of home. It is when we get a glimpse of him in his house at Chelsea that we understand the endearing epithets which Erasmus always lavishes upon More. The delight of the young husband was to train the girl he had chosen for his wife in his own taste for letters and for music. The reserve which the age exacted from parents was thrown to the winds in More's intercourse with his children. He loved teaching them, and lured them to their deeper studies by the coins and curiosities he had gathered in his cabinet. He was as fond of their pets and their games as his children themselves, and would take grave scholars and statesmen into the garden to see his girls' rabbit-hutches or to watch the gambols of their favourite monkey. "I have given you kisses enough," he wrote to his little ones in merry verse when far away on political business, "but stripes hardly ever." The accession of Henry the Eighth dragged him back into the political current. It was at his house that Erasmus penned the "Praise of Folly," and the work, in its Latin title, "Moriæ Encomium," embodied in playful fun his love of the extravagant humour of More. More "tried as hard to keep out of Court," says his descendant, "as most men try to get into it." When the charm of his conversation gave so much pleasure to the young sovereign, "that he could not once in a month get leave to go home to his wife or children, whose company he much desired, . . . he began thereupon to dissemble his nature, and so, little by little, from his former mirth to dissemble himself." More shared to the full the disappointment of his friends at the sudden outbreak of Henry's warlike temper, but the peace again drew him to Henry's side, and he was soon in the King's confidence both as a counsellor and as a diplomatist.

It was on one of his diplomatic missions that More describes himself as hearing news of the Kingdom of "Nowhere." "On a certain day when I had heard mass in Our Lady's Church, which is the fairest, the most gorgeous and curious church of building in all the city of Antwerp, and also most frequented of people, and service being over I was ready to go home to my lodgings, I chanced to espy my friend Peter Gilles talking with a certain stranger, a man well stricken in age, with a black sun-burnt face, a large beard, and a cloke cast trimly about his shoulders, whom by his favour and apparell forthwith I judged to be a mariner." The sailor turned out to have been a companion of Amerigo Vespucci in those voyages to the New World "that be now in print and abroad in every man's hand," and on More's invitation he accompanied him to his house, and "there in my garden upon a bench covered with green turves we sate down, talking together"of the man's marvellous adventures, his desertion in America by Vespucci, his wanderings over the country under the equinoctial line, and at last of his stay in the Kingdom of " Nowhere." It was the story of " Nowhere," or Utopia, which More embodied in the wonderful book which reveals to us the heart of the New Learning. As yet the movement had been one of scholars and divines. Its plans of reform had been almost exclusively intellectual and religious. But in More the same free play of thought which had shaken off the old forms of education and faith turned to question the old forms of society and politics. From a world where fifteen hundred years of Christian teaching had produced social injustice, religious intolerance, and political tyranny, the humourist philosopher turned to a " Nowhere" in which the mere efforts of natural human virtue realized those ends of security, equality, brotherhood, and freedom for which the very institution of society seemed to have been framed. It is as he wanders through this dreamland of the new reason that More touches the great problems which were fast opening before the modern world, problems of labour, of crime, of conscience, of government. Merely to have seen and to have examined questions such as these would prove the keenness of his intellect, but its far-reaching originality is shown in the solutions which he proposes. Amidst much that is the pure play of an exuberant fancy, much that is mere recollection of the dreams of bygone dreamers, we find again and again the most important social and political discoveries of later times anticipated by the genius of Thomas More. In some points, such as his treatment of the question of Labour, he still remains far in advance of current opinion. The whole system of society around him seemed to him "nothing but a conspiracy of the rich against the poor." Its economic legislation was simply the carrying out of such a conspiracy by process of law. " The rich are ever striving to pare away something further from the daily wages of the poor by private fraud and even by public law, so that the wrong already existing (for it is a wrong that those from whom the State derives most benefit should receive least reward) is made yet greater by means of the law of the State." " The rich devise every means by which they may in the first place secure to themselves what they have amassed by wrong, and then take to their own use and profit at the lowest possible price the work and labour of the poor. And so soon as the rich decide on adopting these devices in the name of the public, then they become law." The result was the wretched existence to which the labour-class was doomed, " a life so wretched that even a beast's life seems enviable." No such cry of pity for the poor, of protest against the system of agrarian and manufacturing tyranny which found its expression in the Statute-book, had been heard since the days of Piers Ploughman. But from Christendom More turns with a smile to " Nowhere." In " Nowhere"

the aim of legislation is to secure the welfare, social, industrial, intellectual, religious, of the community at large, and of the labour-class
as the true basis of a well-ordered commonwealth. The end of its
labour-laws was simply the welfare of the labourer. Goods were
possessed indeed in common, but work was compulsory with all. The
period of toil was shortened to the nine hours demanded by modern
artizans, with a view to the intellectual improvement of the worker.
" In the institution of the weal public this end is only and chiefly
pretended and minded that what time may possibly be spared
from the necessary occupations and affairs of the commonwealth, all
that the citizens should withdraw from bodily service to the free
liberty of the mind and garnishing of the same. For herein they
conceive the felicity of this life to consist." A public system of
education enabled the Utopians to avail themselves of their leisure.
While in England half of the population could read no English,
every child was well taught in "Nowhere." The physical aspects of
society were cared for as attentively as its moral. The houses of
Utopia " in the beginning were very low and like homely cottages or
poor shepherd huts made at all adventures of every rude piece of timber
that came first to hand, with mud walls and ridged roofs thatched
over with straw." The picture was really that of the common
English town of More's day, the home of squalor and pestilence.
In Utopia however they had at last come to realize the connexion
between public morality and the health which springs from light,
air, comfort, and cleanliness. " The streets were twenty feet broad;
the houses backed by spacious gardens, and curiously builded after
a gorgeous and gallant sort, with their stories one after another. The
outsides of the walls be made either of hard flint, or of plaster, or else
of brick ; and the inner sides be well strengthened by timber work.
The roofs be plain and flat, covered over with plaster so tempered that
no fire can hurt or perish it, and withstanding the violence of the
weather better than any lead. They keep the wind out of their
windows with glass, for it is there much used, and sometimes also
with fine linen cloth dipped in oil or amber, and that for two commodities, for by this means more light cometh in and the wind is better
kept out."

The same foresight which appears in More's treatment of the questions of Labour and the Public Health is yet more apparent in his
treatment of the question of Crime. He was the first to suggest that
punishment was less effective in suppressing it than prevention. " If
you allow your people to be badly taught, their morals to be corrupted
from childhood, and then when they are men punish them for the very
crimes to which they have been trained in childhood—what is this but
to make thieves, and then to punish them?" He was the first to
plead for proportion between the punishment and the crime, and to

point out the folly of the cruel penalties of his day. " Simple theft is not so great an offence as to be punished with death." If a thief and a murderer are sure of the same penalty, More shows that the law is simply tempting the thief to secure his theft by murder. "While we go about to make thieves afraid, we are really provoking them to kill good men." The end of all punishment he declares to be reformation, "nothing else but the destruction of vice and the saving of men." He advises " so using and ordering criminals that they cannot choose but be good ; and what harm soever they did before, the residue of their lives to make amends for the same." Above all, he urges that to be remedial punishment must be wrought out by labour and hope, so that " none is hopeless or in despair to recover again his former state of freedom by giving good tokens and likelihood of himself that he will ever after that live a true and honest man." It is not too much to say that in the great principles More lays down he anticipated every one of the improvements in our criminal system which have distinguished the last hundred years. His treatment of the religious question was even more in advance of his age. If the houses of Utopia were strangely in contrast with the halls of England, where the bones from every dinner lay rotting in the dirty straw which strewed the floor, where the smoke curled about the rafters, and the wind whistled through the unglazed windows ; if its penal legislation had little likeness to the gallows which stood out so frequently against our English sky ; the religion of " Nowhere" was in yet stronger conflict with the faith of Christendom. It rested simply on nature and reason. It held that God's design was the happiness of man, and that the ascetic rejection of human delights, save for the common good, was thanklessness to the Giver. Christianity, indeed, had already reached Utopia, but it had few priests ; religion found its centre rather in the family than in the congregation : and each household confessed its faults to its own natural head. A yet stranger characteristic was seen in the peaceable way in which it lived side by side with the older religions. More than a century before William of Orange, More discerned and proclaimed the great principle of religious toleration. In " Nowhere" it was lawful to every man to be of what religion he would. Even the disbelievers in a Divine Being or in the immortality of man, who by a single exception to its perfect religious indifference were excluded from public office, were excluded, not on the ground of their religious belief, but because their opinions were deemed to be degrading to mankind, and therefore to incapacitate those who held them from governing in a noble temper. But even these were subject to no punishment, because the people of Utopia were "persuaded that it is not in a man's power to believe what he list." The religion which a man held he might propagate by argument, though not by violence or insult to the religion of others. But while each sect performed its rites in private, all assembled for public worship in a spacious temple, where the vast throng, clad in white, and grouped round a priest clothed in fair raiment wrought marvellously out of birds' plumage, joined in hymns and prayers so framed as to be acceptable to all. The importance of this public devotion lay in the evidence it afforded that liberty of conscience could be combined with religious unity.

Section V.—Wolsey. 1515—1531.

[*Authorities.*—The chronicler Halle, who wrote under Edward the Sixth, has been copied for Henry the Eighth's reign by Grafton, and followed by Holinshed. But for any real knowledge of Wolsey's administration we must turn to the invaluable prefaces which Professor Brewer has prefixed to the Calendars of State Papers for this period, and to the State Papers themselves.]

The New Learning and the Reformation

" There are many things in the commonwealth of Nowhere, which I rather wish than hope to see adopted in our own." It was with these words of characteristic irony that More closed the first work which embodied the dreams of the New Learning. Destined as they were to fulfilment in the course of ages, its schemes of social, religious, and political reform broke helplessly against the temper of the time. At the very moment when More was pleading the cause of justice between rich and poor, social discontent was being fanned by exactions into a fiercer flame. While he aimed sarcasm after sarcasm at king-worship, despotism was being organized into a system. His advocacy of the two principles of religious toleration and Christian comprehension coincides almost to a year with the opening of the strife between the Reformation and the Papacy.

1517

" That Luther has a fine genius," laughed Leo the Tenth, when he heard that a German Professor had nailed some Propositions denouncing the abuse of Indulgences, or of the Papal power to remit certain penalties attached to the commission of sins, against the doors of a church at Wittenberg. But the " Quarrel of Friars," as the controversy was termed contemptuously at Rome, soon took larger proportions. If at the outset Luther flung himself " prostrate at the feet" of the Papacy, and owned its voice as the voice of Christ, the sentence of Leo no sooner confirmed the doctrine of Indulgences than their opponent appealed to a future Council of the Church. Two years

1520

later the rupture was complete. A Papal Bull formally condemned the errors of the Reformer. The condemnation was met with defiance, and Luther publicly consigned the Bull to the flames. A second condemnation expelled him from the bosom of the Church, and the ban of the Empire was soon added to that of the Papacy. " Here stand I ; I can none other," Luther replied to the young Emperor, Charles the Fifth, as he pressed him to recant in the Diet of Worms ; and from

the hiding-place in the Thuringian Forest where he was sheltered by
the Elector of Saxony he denounced not merely, as at first, the abuses
of the Papacy, but the Papacy itself. The heresies of Wyclif were
revived ; the infallibility, the authority of the Roman See, the truth of
its doctrines, the efficacy of its worship, were denied and scoffed at in
vigorous pamphlets which issued from his retreat, and were dispersed
throughout the world by the new printing-press. The old resentment
of Germany against the oppression of Rome, the moral revolt in its
more religious minds against the secularity and corruption of the
Church, the disgust of the New Learning at the superstition which the
Papacy now formally protected, combined to secure for Luther a widespread popularity and the protection of the northern princes of the
Empire. In England however his protest found as yet no echo.
England and Rome were drawn to a close alliance by the difficulties
of their political position. The young King himself, a trained
theologian and proud of his theological knowledge, entered the lists
against Luther with an "Assertion of the Seven Sacraments," for
which he was rewarded by Leo with the title of "Defender of the
Faith." The insolent abuse of the Reformer's answer called More
and Fisher into the field. As yet the New Learning, though scared
by Luther's intemperate language, had steadily backed him in his
struggle. Erasmus pleaded for him with the Emperor ; Ulrich von
Hutten attacked the friars in satires and invectives as violent as his
own. But the temper of the Renascence was even more antagonistic
to the temper of Luther than that of Rome itself. From the golden
dream of a new age, wrought peaceably and purely by the slow progress of intelligence, the growth of letters, the developement of human
virtue, the Reformer of Wittemberg turned away with horror. He had
little or no sympathy with the new culture. He despised reason as
heartily as any Papal dogmatist could despise it. He hated the very
thought of toleration or comprehension. He had been driven by a
moral and intellectual compulsion to declare the Roman system a false
one, but it was only to replace it by another system of doctrine just as
elaborate, and claiming precisely the same infallibility. To degrade
human nature was to attack the very base of the New Learning ;
but Erasmus no sooner advanced to its defence than Luther declared
man to be utterly enslaved by original sin and incapable through any
efforts of his own of discovering truth or of arriving at goodness.
Such a doctrine not only annihilated the piety and wisdom of the
classic past, from which the New Learning had drawn its larger
views of life and of the world ; it trampled in the dust reason itself,
the very instrument by which More and Erasmus hoped to regenerate both knowledge and religion. To More especially, with his
keener perception of its future effect, this sudden revival of a
purely theological and dogmatic spirit, severing Christendom into

warring camps, and annihilating all hopes of union and tolerance, was especially hateful. The temper which hitherto had seemed so "endearing, gentle, and happy," suddenly gave way. His reply to Luther's attack upon the King sank to the level of the work it answered. That of Fisher was calmer and more argumentative; but the divorce of the New Learning from the Reformation was complete.

Wolsey

Nor were the political hopes of the "Utopia" destined to be realized by the minister who at the close of Henry's early war with France mounted rapidly into power. Thomas Wolsey was the son of a wealthy townsman of Ipswich, whose ability had raised him into notice at the close of the preceding reign, and who had been taken by Bishop Fox into the service of the Crown. His extraordinary powers hardly perhaps required the songs, dances, and carouses with his indulgence in which he was taunted by his enemies, to aid him in winning the favour of the young sovereign. From the post of favourite he soon rose to that of minister. Henry's resentment at Ferdinand's perfidy enabled Wolsey to carry out a policy which reversed that of his predecessors. The war had freed England from the fear of French pressure. Wolsey was as resolute to free her from the dictation of Ferdinand, and saw in a French alliance the best security for English independence. In 1514 a treaty was concluded with Lewis. The same friendship was continued to his successor Francis the First, whose march across the Alps for the reconquest of Lombardy was facilitated by Henry and Wolsey, in the hope that while the war lasted England would be free from all fear of attack, and that Francis himself might be brought to inevitable ruin. These hopes were defeated by his great victory at Marignano. But Francis in the moment of triumph saw himself confronted by a new rival. Master of Castile and Aragon, of Naples and the Netherlands, the new Spanish King, Charles the Fifth, rose into a check on the French monarchy such as the policy of Henry or Wolsey had never been able to construct before. The alliance of England was eagerly sought by both sides, and the administration of Wolsey, amid all its ceaseless diplomacy, for seven years kept England out of war. The Peace, as we have seen, restored the hopes of the New Learning; it enabled Colet to reform education, Erasmus to undertake the regeneration of the Church, More to set on foot a new science of politics. But peace as Wolsey used it was fatal to English freedom. In the political hints which lie scattered over the "Utopia" More notes with bitter irony the advance of the new despotism. It was only in "Nowhere" that a sovereign was "removeable on suspicion of a design to enslave his people." In England the work of slavery was being quietly wrought, hints the great lawyer, through the law. "There will never be wanting some pretence for deciding in the King's favour; as that equity is on his side, or the strict letter of the law, or some forced interpretation of it; or if none of these, that the royal prerogative ought with conscientious judges to outweigh all other considerations." We are startled at the precision with which More maps out the expedients by which the law courts were to lend themselves to the advance of tyranny till their crowning judgement in the case of ship-money. But behind these judicial expedients lay great principles of absolutism, which partly from the example of foreign monarchies, partly from the sense of social and political insecurity, and yet more from the isolated position of the Crown, were gradually winning their way in public opinion. " These notions," he goes boldly on, " are fostered by the maxim that the king can do no wrong, however much he may wish to do it ; that not only the property but the persons of his subjects are his own ; and that a man has a right to no more than the king's goodness thinks fit not to take from him." In the hands of Wolsey these maxims were transformed into principles of State. The checks which had been imposed on the action of the sovereign by the presence of great prelates and nobles at his council were practically removed. All authority was concentrated in the hands of a single minister. Henry had munificently rewarded Wolsey's services to the Crown. He had been promoted to the See of Lincoln and thence to the Archbishoprick of York. Henry procured his elevation to the rank of Cardinal, and raised him to the post of Chancellor. The revenues of two sees whose tenants were foreigners fell into his hands ; he held the bishoprick of Winchester and the abbacy of St. Albans ; he was in receipt of pensions from France and Spain, while his official emoluments were enormous. His pomp was almost royal. A train of prelates and nobles followed him wherever he moved; his household was composed of five hundred persons of noble birth, and its chief posts were held by knights and barons of the realm. He spent his vast wealth with princely ostentation. Two of his houses, Hampton Court and York House, the later Whitehall, were splendid enough to serve at his fall as royal palaces. His school at Ipswich was eclipsed by the glories of his foundation at Oxford, whose name of Cardinal College has been lost in its later title of Christ-church. Nor was this magnificence a mere show of power. The whole direction of home and foreign affairs rested with Wolsey alone ; as Chancellor he stood at the head of public justice ; his elevation to the office of Legate rendered him supreme in the Church. Enormous as was the mass of work which he undertook, it was thoroughly done : his administration of the royal treasury was economical ; the number of his despatches is hardly less remarkable than the care bestowed upon each ; even More, an avowed enemy, confesses that as Chancellor he surpassed all men's expectations. The court of Chancery, indeed, became so crowded through the character for expedition and justice which it gained under his rule that subordinate courts had to be created for its relief. It was this concentration of all secular and ecclesiastical power in a single hand which accustomed England to the personal government which began with Henry the Eighth ; and it was, above all, Wolsey's long tenure of the whole Papal authority within the realm, and the consequent suspension of appeals to Rome, that led men to acquiesce at a later time in Henry's claim of religious supremacy. For proud as was Wolsey's bearing and high as were his natural powers he stood before England as the mere creature of the King. Greatness, wealth, authority he held, and owned he held, simply at the royal will. In raising his low-born favourite to the head of Church and State Henry was gathering all religious as well as all civil authority into his personal grasp. The nation which trembled before Wolsey learned to tremble before the King who could destroy Wolsey by a breath.

Wolsey and the Parliament

1519

The rise of Charles of Austria gave a new turn to Wolsey's policy. Possessor of the Netherlands, of Franche Comté, of Spain, the death of his grandfather Maximilian added to his dominions the heritage of the House of Austria in Swabia and on the Danube, and opened the way for his election as Emperor. France saw herself girt in on every side by a power greater than her own ; and to Wolsey and his master the time seemed come for a bolder game. Disappointed in his hopes of obtaining the Imperial crown on the death of Maximilian, Henry turned to the dream of " recovering his French inheritance," which he had never really abandoned, and which was carefully fed by his nephew Charles. Nor was Wolsey forgotten. If Henry coveted France, his minister coveted no less a prize than the Papacy ; and the young Emperor was lavish of promises of support in any coming election. The result of these seductions was quickly seen. In May, 1520, Charles landed at Dover to visit Henry, and King and Emperor rode alone to Canterbury. It was in vain that Francis strove to retain Henry's friendship by an interview near Guisnes, to which the profuse expenditure of both monarchs gave the name of the Field of Cloth of Gold. A second interview between Charles and his uncle as he returned from the meeting with Francis ended in a secret confederacy of the two sovereigns, and the promise of the Emperor to marry Henry's one child, Mary Tudor. Her right to the throne was asserted by a deed which proved how utterly the baronage now lay at the mercy of the King. The Duke of Buckingham stood first in blood as in power among the English nobles ; he was the descendant of Edward the Third's youngest son, and if Mary's succession were denied he stood heir to the throne. His hopes had been fanned by prophets and astrologers, and wild words told his purpose to seize the Crown on Henry's death in defiance of every opponent. But word and act had for two years been watched by the King ; and in 1521 the Duke was arrested, condemned as a traitor by his peers, and beheaded on Tower Hill. The French alliance came to an end,

1520

and at the outbreak of war between France and Spain a secret league was concluded at Calais between the Pope, the Emperor, and Henry. The first result of the new war policy at home was quickly seen. Wolsey's economy had done nothing more than tide the Crown through the past years of peace. But now that Henry had promised to raise forty thousand men for the coming campaign the ordinary resources of the treasury were utterly insufficient. With the instinct of despotism Wolsey shrank from reviving the tradition of the Parliament. Though Henry had thrice called together the Houses to supply the expenses of his earlier struggle with France, Wolsey governed during seven years of peace without once assembling them. War made a Parliament inevitable, but for a while the Cardinal strove to delay its summons by a wide extension of the practice which Edward the Fourth had invented of raising money by forced loans or "Benevolences," to be repaid from the first subsidy of a coming Parliament. Large sums were assessed on every county. Twenty thousand pounds were exacted from London; and its wealthier citizens were summoned before the Cardinal and required to give an account of the value of their estates. Commissioners were despatched into each shire for the purposes of assessment, and precepts were issued on their information, requiring in some cases supplies of soldiers, in others a tenth of a man's income, for the King's service. So poor, however, was the return that in the following year Wolsey was forced to summon Parliament and lay before it the unprecedented demand of a property-tax of twenty per cent. The demand was made by the Cardinal in person, but he was received with obstinate silence. It was in vain that Wolsey called on member after member to answer; and his appeal to More, who had been elected to the chair of the House of Commons, was met by the Speaker's falling on his knees and representing his powerlessness to reply till he had received instructions from the House itself. The effort to overawe the Commons failed, and Wolsey no sooner withdrew than an angry debate began. He again returned to answer the objections which had been raised, and again the Commons foiled the minister's attempt to influence their deliberations by refusing to discuss the matter in his presence. The struggle continued for a fortnight; and though successful in procuring a subsidy, the court party were forced to content themselves with less than half Wolsey's demand. Convocation betrayed as independent a spirit; and when money was again needed two years later, the Cardinal was driven once more to the system of Benevolences. A tenth was demanded from the laity, and a fourth from the clergy in every county by the royal commissioners. There was "sore grudging and murmuring," Warham wrote to the court, "among the people." "If men should give their goods by a commission," said the Kentish squires, "then it would be worse than the taxes of France, and England

1523

1525

should be bond, not free." The political instinct of the nation discerned as of old that in the question of self-taxation was involved that of the very existence of freedom. The clergy put themselves in the forefront of the resistance, and preached from every pulpit that the commission was contrary to the liberties of the realm, and that the King could take no man's goods but by process of law. So stirred was the nation that Wolsey bent to the storm, and offered to rely on the voluntary loans of each subject. But the statute of Richard the Third which declared all exaction of benevolences illegal was recalled to memory ; the demand was evaded by London, and the commissioners were driven out of Kent. A revolt broke out in Suffolk ; the men of Cambridge and Norwich threatened to rise. There was in fact a general strike of the employers. Clothmakers discharged their workers, farmers put away their servants. " They say the King asketh so much that they be not able to do as they have done before this time." Such a peasant insurrection as was raging in Germany was only prevented by the unconditional withdrawal of the royal demand.

Wolsey's defeat saved English freedom for the moment ; but the danger from which he shrank was not merely that of a conflict with the sense of liberty. The murmurs of the Kentish squires only swelled the ever-deepening voice of public discontent. If the condition of the land question in the end gave strength to the Crown by making it the security for public order, it became a terrible peril at every crisis of conflict between the monarchy and the landowners. The steady rise in the price of wool was giving a fresh impulse to the agrarian changes which had now been going on for over a hundred and fifty years, to the throwing together of the smaller holdings, and the introduction of sheep-farming on an enormous scale. The new wealth of the merchant classes helped on the change. They invested largely in land, and these "farming gentlemen and clerking knights," as Latimer bitterly styled them, were restrained by few traditions or associations in their eviction of the smaller tenants. The land indeed had been greatly underlet, and as its value rose the temptation to raise the customary rents became irresistible. " That which went heretofore for twenty or forty pounds a year," we learn from the same source, " now is let for fifty or a hundred." But it had been only by this low scale of rent that the small yeomanry class had been enabled to exist. " My father," says Latimer, " was a yeoman, and had no lands of his own ; only he had a farm of three or four pounds by the year at the uttermost, and hereupon he tilled so much as kept half-a-dozen men. He had walk for a hundred sheep, and my mother milked thirty kine ; he was able and did find the King a harness with himself and his horse while he came to the place that he should receive the King's wages. I can remember that I buckled his harness when he went to Blackheath Field. He kept me to school: he married my sisters with five pounds apiece, so that he brought them up in godliness and fear of God. He kept hospitality for his poor neighbours, and some alms he gave to the poor, and all this he did of the same farm, where he that now hath it payeth sixteen pounds by year or more, and is not able to do anything for his prince, for himself, nor for his children, or give a cup of drink to the poor." Increase of rent ended with such tenants in the relinquishment of their holdings, but the bitterness of ejection was increased by the iniquitous means which were often employed to bring it about. The farmers, if we believe More in 1515, were "got rid of either by fraud or force, or tired out with repeated wrongs into parting with their property." "In this way it comes to pass that these poor wretches, men, women, husbands, orphans, widows, parents with little children, households greater in number than in wealth (for arable farming requires many hands, while one shepherd and herdsman will suffice for a pasture farm), all these emigrate from their native fields without knowing where to go." The sale of their scanty household stuff drove them to wander homeless abroad, to be thrown into prison as vagabonds, to beg and to steal. Yet in the face of such a spectacle as this we still find the old complaint of scarcity of labour, and the old legal remedy for it in a fixed scale of wages. The social disorder, in fact, baffled the sagacity of English statesmen, and they could find no better remedy for it than laws against the further extension of sheep-farms, and a terrible increase of public executions. Both were alike fruitless. Enclosures and evictions went on as before. "If you do not remedy the evils which produce thieves," More urged with bitter truth, "the rigorous execution of justice in punishing thieves will be vain." But even More could only suggest a remedy which, efficacious as it was subsequently to prove, had yet to wait a century for its realization. "Let the woollen manufacture be introduced, so that honest employment may be found for those whom want has made thieves or will make thieves ere long." The mass of social disorder grew steadily greater; while the break up of the great military households of the nobles which was still going on, and the return of wounded and disabled soldiers from the wars, introduced a dangerous leaven of outrage and crime.

This public discontent, as well as the exhaustion of the treasury, added bitterness to the miserable result of the war. To France, indeed, the struggle had been disastrous, for the loss of the Milanese and the capture of Francis the First in the defeat of Pavia laid her at the feet of the Emperor. But Charles had no purpose of carrying out the pledges by which he had lured England into war. Wolsey had seen two partizans of the Emperor successively raised to the Papal chair. The schemes of winning anew "our inheritance of France" had ended in utter failure; England, as before, gained nothing from two useless campaigns, and it was plain that Charles meant it to win nothing. He concluded an armistice with his prisoner; he set aside all projects of a joint invasion; he broke his pledge to wed Mary Tudor, and married a princess of Portugal; he pressed for peace with France which would give him Burgundy. It was time for Henry and his minister to change their course. They resolved to withdraw from all active part in the rivalry of the two powers, and a treaty was secretly concluded with France. But Henry remained on fair terms with the Emperor, and abstained from any part in the fresh war which broke out on the refusal of the French monarch to fulfil the terms by which he had purchased his release. No longer spurred by the interest of great events, the King ceased to take a busy part in foreign politics, and gave himself to hunting and sport. Among the fairest and gayest ladies of his court stood Anne

Anne Boleyn

Boleyn. Her gaiety and wit soon won Henry's favour, and grants of honours to her father marked her influence. In 1524 a new colour was given to this intimacy by a resolve on the King's part to break his marriage with the Queen. The death of every child save Mary may have woke scruples as to the lawfulness of a marriage on which a curse seemed to rest; the need of a male heir may have deepened this impression. But, whatever were the grounds of his action, Henry from this moment pressed the Roman See to grant him a divorce. Clement's consent to his wish, however, would mean a break with the Emperor, Catharine's nephew; and the Pope was now at the Emperor's mercy. While the English envoy was mooting the question

1526

of divorce, the surprise of Rome by an Imperial force brought home to Clement his utter helplessness; the next year the Pope was in fact a prisoner in the Emperor's hands after the storm and sack of Rome. Meanwhile a secret suit which had been brought before Wolsey as legate was suddenly dropped; as Catharine denied the facts on which Henry rested his case her appeal would have carried the matter to the tribunal of the Pope, and Clement's decision could hardly have been a favourable one. The difficulties of the divorce were indeed manifest. One of the most learned of the English bishops, Fisher of Rochester, declared openly against it. The English theologians, who were consulted on the validity of the Papal dispensation which had allowed Henry's marriage to take place, referred the King to the Pope for a decision of the question. The commercial classes shrank from a step which involved an irretrievable breach with the Emperor, who was master of their great market in Flanders. Above all, the iniquity of the proposal jarred against the public conscience. But neither danger nor shame availed against the King's wilfulness and passion. A great party too had gathered to Anne's support. Her uncle the Duke of Norfolk, her father, now Lord Rochford, afterwards Earl of Wiltshire, pushed the divorce resolutely on ; the brilliant group of young courtiers to which her brother belonged saw in her success their own elevation ; and the Duke of Suffolk with the bulk of the nobles hoped through her means to bring about the ruin of the statesman before whom they trembled. It was needful for the Cardinal to find some expedients to carry out the King's will ; but his schemes one by one broke down before the difficulties of the Papal Court. Clement indeed, perplexed at once by his wish to gratify Henry, his own conscientious doubts as to the course proposed, and his terror of the Emperor whose power was now predominant in Italy, even blamed Wolsey for having hindered the King from judging the matter in his own realm, and marrying on the sentence of his own courts. Henry was resolute in demanding the express sanction of the Pope to his divorce, and this Clement steadily evaded. He at last, however, consented to a legatine commission for the trial of the case in England. In this commission Cardinal Campeggio was joined with Wolsey. Months however passed in fruitless negotiations. The Cardinals pressed on Catharine the expediency of her withdrawal to a religious house, while Henry pressed on the Pope that of a settlement of the matter by his formal declaration against the validity of the marriage. At last in 1529 the two Legates opened their court in the great hall of the Blackfriars. Henry briefly announced his resolve to live no longer in mortal sin. The Queen offered an appeal to Clement, and on the refusal of the Legates to admit it she flung herself at Henry's feet. " Sire," said Catharine, " I beseech you to pity me, a woman and a stranger, without an assured friend and without an indifferent counsellor. I take God to witness that I have always been to you a true and loyal wife, that I have made it my constant duty to seek your pleasure, that I have loved all whom you loved, whether I have reason or not, whether they are friends to me or foes. I have been your wife for years, I have brought you many children. God knows that when I came to your bed I was a virgin, and I put it to your own conscience to say whether it was not so. If there be any offence which can be alleged against me I consent to depart with infamy ; if not, then I pray you to do me justice." The piteous appeal was wasted on a King who was already entertaining Anne Boleyn with royal state in his own palace. The trial proceeded, and the court assembled to pronounce sentence. Henry's hopes were at their highest when they were suddenly dashed to the ground. At the opening of the proceedings Campeggio rose to declare the court adjourned. The adjournment was a mere evasion. The pressure of the Imperialists had at last forced Clement to summon the cause to his own tribunal at Rome, and the jurisdiction of the Legates was at an end.

" Now see I," cried the Duke of Suffolk as he dashed his hand on

Sec. V.

WOLSEY

1515
TO
1531
The Fall
of
Wolsey

the table, "that the old saw is true, that there was never Legate or Cardinal that did good to England!" "Of all men living," Wolsey boldly retorted, "you, my lord Duke, have the least reason to dispraise Cardinals, for if I, a poor Cardinal, had not been, you would not now have had a head on your shoulders wherewith to make such a brag in disrepute of us." But both the Cardinal and his enemies knew that the minister's doom was sealed. Through the twenty years of his reign Henry had known nothing of opposition to his will. His imperious temper had chafed at the weary negotiations, the subterfuges and perfidies of the Pope. His wrath fell at once on Wolsey, who had dissuaded him from acting at the first independently, from conducting the cause in his own courts and acting on the sentence of his own judges ; who had counselled him to seek a divorce from Rome and promised him success in his suit. From the close of the Legatine court he would see him no more. If Wolsey still remained minister for a while, it was because the thread of the complex foreign negotiations could not be roughly broken. Here too, however, failure awaited

1529

him as he saw himself deceived and outwitted by the conclusion of peace between France and the Emperor in a new treaty at Cambray. Not only was his French policy no longer possible, but a reconciliation with Charles was absolutely needful, and such a reconciliation could only be brought about by Wolsey's fall. He was at once prosecuted for receiving bulls from Rome in violation of the Statute of Præmunire. A few days later he was deprived of the seals. Wolsey was prostrated by the blow. He offered to give up everything that he possessed if the King would but cease from his displeasure. "His face," wrote the French ambassador, "is dwindled to half its natural size. In truth his misery is such that his enemies, Englishmen as they are, cannot help pitying him." Office and wealth were flung desperately at the King's feet, and for the moment Henry seemed contented with his disgrace. A thousand boats full of Londoners covered the Thames to see the Cardinal's barge pass to the Tower, but he was permitted to retire to Esher. Pardon was granted him on surrender of his vast possessions to the Crown, and he was permitted to withdraw to his diocese of York, the one dignity he had been suffered to retain. But hardly a year had passed before the jealousy of his political rivals was roused by the King's regrets, and on the eve of his installation feast he was arrested on a charge of high treason, and conducted by the Lieutenant of the Tower towards London. Already broken by his enormous labours, by internal disease, and the sense of his fall, Wolsey accepted

the arrest as a sentence of death. An attack of dysentery forced him to rest at the abbey of Leicester, and as he reached the gate he said feebly to the brethren who met him, "I am come to lay my bones among you." On his death-bed his thoughts still clung to the prince whom he had served. "He is a prince," said the dying man to the

Lieutenant of the Tower, "of a most royal courage: sooner than miss any part of his will he will endanger one half of his kingdom : and I do assure you I have often kneeled before him, sometimes for three hours together, to persuade him from his appetite, and could not prevail. And, Master Knyghton, had I but served God as diligently as I have served the king, He would not have given me over in my grey hairs. But this is my due reward for my pains and study, not regarding my service to God, but only my duty to my prince." No words could paint with so terrible a truthfulness the spirit of the new despotism which Wolsey had done more than any of those who went before him to build up. All sense of loyalty to England, to its freedom, to its institutions, had utterly passed away. The one duty which the statesman owned was a duty to his "prince," a prince whose personal will and appetite was overriding the highest interests of the State, trampling under foot the wisest counsels, and crushing with the blind ingratitude of Fate the servants who opposed him. But even Wolsey, while he recoiled from the monstrous form which had revealed itself, could hardly have dreamed of the work of destruction which the royal courage, and yet more royal appetite, of his master was to accomplish in the years to come.

Section VI.—Thomas Cromwell. 1530—1540.

[*Authorities.*—Cromwell's early life as told by Foxe is a mass of fable ; what we really know of it may be seen conveniently put together in Dean Hook's "Life of Archbishop Cranmer." For his ministry, the only real authorities are the State Papers for this period, which are now being calendared for the Master of the Rolls. For Sir Thomas More, we have a touching life by his son-in-law, Roper. The more important documents for the religious history of the time will be found in Mr. Pocock's new edition of Burnet's "History of the Reformation" ; those relating to the dissolution of the Monasteries, in the collection of letters on that subject published by the Camden Society, and in the "Original Letters" of Sir Henry Ellis. A mass of material of very various value has been accumulated by Strype in his collections, which begin at this time. Mr. Froude's narrative ("History of England," vols. i. ii. iii.), though of great literary merit, is disfigured by a love of paradox, by hero-worship, and by a reckless defence of tyranny and crime. It possesses, during this period, little or no historical value.]

The ten years which follow the fall of Wolsey are among the most momentous in our history. The New Monarchy at last realized its power, and the work for which Wolsey had paved the way was carried out with a terrible thoroughness. The one great institution which could still offer resistance to the royal will was struck down. The Church became a mere instrument of the central despotism. The people learned their helplessness in rebellions easily suppressed and avenged with ruthless severity. A reign of terror, organized with consummate and merciless skill, held England panic-stricken at Henry's feet. The noblest heads rolled on the block. Virtue and learning could not save Thomas More : royal descent could not save Lady Salisbury. The putting away of one queen, the execution of another, taught England that nothing was too high for Henry's "courage" or too sacred for his "appetite." Parliament assembled only to sanction acts of unscrupulous tyranny, or to build up by its own statutes the great fabric of absolute rule. All the constitutional safe-guards of English freedom were swept away. Arbitrary taxation, arbitrary legislation, arbitrary imprisonment were powers claimed without dispute and unsparingly exercized by the Crown.

**Thomas
Cromwell**

The history of this great revolution, for it is nothing less, is the history of a single man. In the whole line of English statesmen there is no one of whom we would willingly know so much, no one of whom we really know so little, as Thomas Cromwell. When he meets us in Henry's service he had already passed middle life ; and during his earlier years it is hardly possible to do more than disentangle a few fragmentary facts from the mass of fable which gathered round them. His youth was one of roving adventure. Whether he was the son of a poor blacksmith at Putney or no, he could hardly have been more than a boy when he was engaged in the service of the Marchioness of Dorset. He must still have been young when he took part as a common soldier in the wars of Italy, a "ruffian," as he owned afterwards to Cranmer, in the most unscrupulous school the world contained. But it was a school in which he learned lessons even more dangerous than those of the camp. He not only mastered the Italian language but drank in the manners and tone of the Italy around him, the Italy of the Borgias and the Medici. It was with Italian versatility that he turned from the camp to the counting-house ; he was certainly engaged as a commercial agent to one of the Venetian merchants ; tradition finds him as a clerk at Antwerp ; and in 1512 history at last encounters him as a thriving wool merchant at Middleburg in Zealand. Returning to England, Cromwell continued to amass wealth by adding the trade of scrivener, something between that of a banker and attorney, to his other occupations, as well as by advancing money to the poorer nobles ; and on the outbreak of the second war with France we find him a busy and influential member of the Commons in Parliament. Five years later the aim of his ambition was declared by his entrance into Wolsey's service. The Cardinal needed a man of business for the suppression of some smaller monasteries which he had undertaken, and for the transfer of their revenues to his foundations at Oxford and Ipswich. The task was an unpopular one, and it was carried out with a rough indifference to the feelings it aroused which involved Cromwell in the hate which was gathering round his master. But his wonderful self-reliance and sense of power only broke upon the world at Wolsey's fall. Of the hundreds of dependents who waited on the Cardinal's nod, Cromwell was the only one who clung to him faithfully at the last. In the lonely hours of his disgrace at Esher Wolsey " made his moan unto Master Cromwell, who comforted him the best he could, and desired my lord to give him leave to go to London, where he would make or mar, which was always his common saying." He shewed his consummate craft in a scheme by which Wolsey was persuaded to buy off the hostility of the courtiers by confirming the grants which had been made to them from his revenues, while Cromwell acquired importance as go-between in these transactions. It was by Cromwell's efforts in Parliament that a bill disqualifying Wolsey from all after employment was defeated, and it was by him that the negotiations were conducted which permitted the fallen minister to retire to York. A general esteem seems to have rewarded this rare instance of fidelity to a ruined patron. " For his honest behaviour in his master's cause he was esteemed the most faithfullest servant, and was of all men greatly commended." But Henry's protection rested on other grounds. The ride to London had ended in a private interview with the King, in which Cromwell boldly advised him to cut the knot of the divorce by the simple exercise of his own supremacy. The advice struck the keynote of the later policy by which the daring counseller was to change the whole face of Church and State ; but Henry still clung to the hopes held out by his new ministers, and shrank perhaps as yet from the bare absolutism to which Cromwell called him. The advice at any rate was concealed, and though high in the King's favour, his new servant waited patiently the progress of events.

For success in procuring the divorce, the Duke of Norfolk, who had come to the front on Wolsey's fall, relied not only on the alliance and aid of the Emperor, but on the support which the project was expected to receive from Parliament. The reassembling of the two Houses marked the close of the system of Wolsey. Instead of looking on Parliament as a danger the monarchy now felt itself strong enough to use it as a tool ; and Henry justly counted on warm support in his strife with Rome. Not less significant was the attitude of the men of the New Learning. To them, as to his mere political adversaries, the Cardinal's fall opened a prospect of better things. The dream of More in accepting the office of Chancellor, if we may judge it from the acts of his brief ministry, seems to have been that of carrying out the religious reformation which had been demanded by Colet and Erasmus, while checking the spirit of revolt against the unity of the Church. His severities against the Protestants, exaggerated as they have been by polemic rancour, remain the one stain on a memory that knows no other. But it was only by a rigid severance of the cause of reform from what seemed to him the cause of revolution that More could hope for a successful issue to the projects which the Council laid before Parliament. The Petition of the Commons sounded like an echo of Colet's famous address to the Convocation. It attributed the growth of heresy not more to "frantic and seditious books published in the English tongue contrary to the very true Catholic and Christian faith" than to "the extreme and uncharitable behaviour of divers ordinaries." It remonstrated against the legislation of the clergy in Convocation without the King's assent or that of his subjects, the oppressive procedure of the Church Courts, the abuses of ecclesiastical patronage, and the excessive number of holydays. Henry referred the Petition to the bishops, but they could devise no means of redress, and the ministry persisted in pushing through the Houses their bills for ecclesiastical reform. The questions of Convocation and the bishops' courts were adjourned for further consideration, but the fees of the courts were curtailed, the clergy restricted from lay employments, pluralities restrained, and residence enforced. In spite of a dogged opposition from the bishops the bills received the assent of the House of Lords, "to the great rejoicing of lay people, and the great displeasure of spiritual persons." The importance of the new measures lay really in the action of Parliament. They were an explicit announcement that church-reform was now to be undertaken, not by the clergy, but by the people at large. On the other hand it was clear that it would be carried out, not in a spirit of hostility, but of loyalty to the church. The Commons forced from Bishop Fisher an apology for words which were taken as a doubt thrown on their orthodoxy. Henry forbade the circulation of Tyndale's translation of the Bible as executed in a Protestant spirit, while he promised a more correct version. But the domestic aims of the New Learning were foiled by the failure of the ministry in its negotiations for the divorce. The severance of the French alliance, and the accession of the party to power which clung to alliance with the Emperor, failed to detach Charles from his aunt's cause. The ministers accepted the suggestion of a Cambridge scholar, Thomas Cranmer, that the universities of Europe should be called on for their judgement; but the appeal to the learned opinion of Christendom ended in utter defeat. In France the profuse bribery of the English agents would have failed with the university of Paris but for the interference of Francis himself. As shameless an exercize of Henry's own authority was required to wring an approval of his cause from Oxford and Cambridge. In Germany the very Protestants, in the fervour of their moral revival, were dead against the King. So far as could be seen from Cranmer's test every learned man in Christendom but for bribery and threats would have condemned Henry's cause.

It was at the moment when every expedient had been exhausted by Norfolk and his fellow ministers that Cromwell came again to the front. Despair of other means drove Henry nearer and nearer to the bold plan from which he had shrunk at Wolsey's fall. Cromwell was again ready with his suggestion that the King should disavow the

Papal jurisdiction, declare himself Head of the Church within his realm, and obtain a divorce from his own Ecclesiastical Courts. But with Cromwell the divorce was but the prelude to a series of changes he was bent upon accomplishing. In all the chequered life of the new minister what had left its deepest stamp on him was Italy. Not only in the rapidity and ruthlessness of his designs, but in their larger scope, their clearer purpose, and their admirable combination, the Italian state-craft entered with Cromwell into English politics. He is in fact the first English minister in whom we can trace through the whole period of his rule the steady working out of a great and definite aim. His purpose was to raise the King to absolute authority on the ruins of every rival power within the realm. It was not that Cromwell was a mere slave of tyranny. Whether we may trust the tale that carries him in his youth to Florence or no, his statesmanship was closely modelled on the ideal of the Florentine thinker whose book was constantly in his hand. Even as a servant of Wolsey he startled the future Cardinal, Reginald Pole, by bidding him take for his manual in politics the "Prince" of Machiavelli. Machiavelli hoped to find in Cæsar Borgia or in the later Lorenzo de' Medici a tyrant who after crushing all rival tyrannies might unite and regenerate Italy; and it is possible to see in the policy of Cromwell the aim of securing enlightenment and order for England by the concentration of all authority in the Crown. The last check on royal absolutism which had survived the Wars of the Roses lay in the wealth, the independent synods and jurisdiction, and the religious claims of the Church. To reduce the great ecclesiastical body to a mere department of the State in which all authority should flow from the sovereign alone, and in which his will should be the only law, his decision the only test of truth, was a change hardly to be wrought without a struggle; and it was the opportunity for such a struggle that Cromwell saw in the divorce. His first blow showed how unscrupulously the struggle was to be waged. A year had passed since Wolsey had been convicted of a breach of the Statute of Præmunire. The pedantry of the judges declared the whole nation to have been formally involved in the same charge by its acceptance of his authority. The legal absurdity was now redressed by a general pardon, but from this pardon the clergy found themselves omitted. They were told that forgiveness could be bought at no less a price than the payment of a fine amounting to a million of our present money, and the acknowledgement of the King as "the chief protector, the only and supreme lord, the Head of the Church and Clergy of England." To the first demand they at once submitted; against the second they struggled hard, but their appeals to Henry and to Cromwell met only with demands for instant obedience. A compromise was at last arrived at by the insertion of a qualifying phrase "So far as the law of Christ will allow;" and with this addition the words were again submitted by

SEC. VI.

THOMAS
CROMWELL

1530
TO
1540

**The
Headship
of the
Church**

Warham to the Convocation.   There was a general silence.   "Whoever is silent seems to consent," said the Archbishop.   "Then are we all silent," replied a voice from among the crowd.

There is no ground for thinking that the "Headship of the Church" which Henry claimed in this submission was more than a warning addressed to the independent spirit of the clergy, or that it bore as yet the meaning which was afterwards attached to it.   It certainly implied no independence of Rome ; but it told the Pope plainly that in any strife that might come the clergy were in the King's hand.   The warning was backed by the demand for the settlement of the question addressed to Clement on the part of the Lords and some of the Commons.   "The cause of his Majesty," the Peers were made to say, "is the cause of each of ourselves."   If Clement would not confirm what was described as the judgement of the Universities in favour of the divorce "our condition will not be wholly irremediable.   Extreme remedies are ever harsh of application ; but he that is sick will by all means be rid of his distemper."   The banishment of Catharine from the King's palace gave emphasis to the demand.   The failure of a second embassy to the Pope

left Cromwell free to take more decisive steps in the course on which he had entered.   As his policy developed itself More withdrew from the post of Chancellor ; but the revolution from which he shrank was an inevitable one.   From the reign of the Edwards men had been occupied with the problem of reconciling the spiritual and temporal relations of the realm.   Parliament from the first became the organ of the national jealousy whether of Papal jurisdiction without the kingdom or of the separate jurisdiction of the clergy within it.   The movement, long arrested by religious reaction and civil war, was reviving under the new sense of national greatness and national unity, when it was suddenly stimulated by the question of the divorce, and by the submission of English interests to a foreign Court.   With such a spur it moved forward quickly.   The time had come when England was to claim for herself the fulness of power, ecclesiastical as well as temporal, within her bounds ; and, in the concentration of all authority within the hands of the sovereign which was the political characteristic of the time, to claim this power for the nation was to claim it for the king.   The import of the headship of the Church was brought fully out in one of the propositions laid before the Convocation of 1532.   "The King's Majesty," runs this memorable clause, "hath as well the care of the souls of his subjects as their bodies ; and may by the law of God by his Parliament make laws touching and concerning as well the one as the other."   Under strong pressure Convocation was brought to pray that the power of independent legislation till now exercized by

the Church should come to an end.   Rome was dealt with in the same unsparing fashion. The Parliament forbade by statute any further appeals to the Papal Court; and on a petition from the clergy in Convocation the Houses granted power to the King to suspend the payments of first-fruits, or the year's revenue which each bishop paid to Rome on his election to a see. All judicial, all financial connexion with the Papacy was broken by these two measures. Cromwell fell back on Wolsey's policy. The hope of aid from Charles was abandoned, and by a new league with France he sought to bring pressure on the Papal court. But the pressure was as unsuccessful as before. Clement threatened the King with excommunication if he did not restore Catharine to her place as Queen and abstain from all intercourse with Anne Boleyn till the case was tried. Henry still refused to submit to the judgement of any court outside his realm; and the Pope dared not consent to a trial within it. Henry at last closed the long debate by a secret union with Anne Boleyn. Warham was dead, and Cranmer, an active partizan of the divorce, was named to the see of Canterbury; proceedings were at once commenced in his court; and the marriage of Catharine was formally declared invalid by the new primate at Dunstable. A week later Cranmer set on the brow of Anne Boleyn the crown which she had so long coveted.

As yet the real character of Cromwell's ecclesiastical policy had been disguised by its connexion with the divorce. But though formal negotiations continued between England and Rome, until Clement's final decision in Catharine's favour, they had no longer any influence on the series of measures which in their rapid succession changed the whole character of the English Church. The acknowledgement of Henry's title as its Protector and Head was soon found by the clergy to have been more than a form of words. It was the first step in a policy by which the Church was to be laid prostrate at the foot of the throne. Parliament had shown its accordance with the royal will in the strife with Rome. Step by step the ground had been cleared for the great Statute by which the new character of the Church was defined. The Act of Supremacy ordered that the King "shall be taken, accepted, and reputed the only supreme head on earth of the Church of England, and shall have and enjoy annexed and united to the Imperial Crown of this realm as well the title and state thereof as all the honours, jurisdictions, authorities, immunities, profits and commodities to the said dignity belonging, with full power to visit, repress, redress, reform, and amend all such errors, heresies, abuses, contempts, and enormities, which by any manner of spiritual authority or jurisdiction might or may lawfully be reformed." Authority in all matters ecclesiastical, as well as civil, was vested solely in the Crown. The "courts spiritual" became as thoroughly the King's courts as the temporal courts at Westminster. But the full import of the Act of Supremacy was only seen in the following year, when Henry formally took the title of " on earth Supreme Head of the Church of England," and some months later Cromwell was raised to the post of Vicar-General or Vicegerent of the King in all matters ecclesiastical. His title, like his office, recalled the system of Wolsey ; but the fact that these powers were now united in the hands not of a priest but of a layman, showed the new drift of the royal policy. And this policy Cromwell's position enabled him to carry out with a terrible thoroughness. One great step towards its realization had already been taken in the statute which annihilated the free legislative powers of the convocations of the clergy. Another followed in an Act which under the pretext of restoring the free election of bishops turned every prelate into a nominee of the King. Their election by the chapters of their cathedral churches had long become formal, and their appointment had since the time of the Edwards been practically made by the Papacy on the nomination of the Crown. The privilege of free election was now with bitter irony restored to the chapters, but they were compelled on pain of præmunire to choose the candidate recommended by the King. This strange expedient has lasted till the present time ; but its character has wholly changed with the developement of constitutional rule. The nomination of bishops has ever since the accession of the Georges passed from the King in person to the Minister who represents the will of the people. Practically therefore an English prelate, alone among all the prelates of the world, is now raised to his episcopal throne by the same popular election which raised Ambrose to his episcopal chair at Milan. But at the moment Cromwell's measure reduced the English bishops to absolute dependence on the Crown. Their dependence would have been complete had his policy been thoroughly carried out and the royal power of deposition put in force as well as that of appointment. As it was Henry could warn the Archbishop of Dublin that if he persevered in his " proud folly, we be able to remove you again and to put another man of more virtue and honesty in your place." Even Elizabeth in a burst of ill-humour threatened to " unfrock " the Bishop of Ely. By the more ardent partizans of the Reformation this dependence of the bishops on the Crown was fully recognized. On the death of Henry the Eighth Cranmer took out a new commission from Edward for the exercise of his office. Latimer, when the royal policy clashed with his belief, felt bound to resign the See of Worcester. That the power of deposition was at a later time quietly abandoned was due not so much to any deference for the religious instincts of the nation as to the fact that the steady servility of the bishops rendered its exercise unnecessary.

Master of Convocation, absolute master of the bishops, Henry had become master of the monastic orders through the right of visitation over them which had been transferred by the Act of Supremacy from the Papacy to the Crown. The religious houses had drawn on themselves at once the hatred of the New Learning and of the Monarchy. In the early days of the revival of letters Popes and bishops had joined with princes and scholars in welcoming the diffusion of culture and the hopes of religious reform. But though an abbot or a prior here or there might be found among the supporters of the movement, the monastic orders as a whole repelled it with unswerving obstinacy. The quarrel only became more bitter as years went on. The keen sarcasms of Erasmus, the insolent buffoonery of Hutten, were lavished on the "lovers of darkness" and of the cloister. In England Colet and More echoed with greater reserve the scorn and invective of their friends. As an outlet for religious enthusiasm, indeed, monasticism was practically dead. The friar, now that his fervour of devotion and his intellectual energy had passed away, had sunk into a mere beggar. The monks had become mere landowners. Most of their houses were anxious only to enlarge their revenues and to diminish the number of those who shared them. In the general carelessness which prevailed as to the spiritual objects of their trust, in the wasteful management of their estates, in the indolence and self-indulgence which for the most part characterized them, the monastic houses simply exhibited the faults of all corporate bodies which have outlived the work which they were created to perform. But they were no more unpopular than such corporate bodies generally are. The Lollard cry for their suppression had died away. In the north, where some of the greatest abbeys were situated, the monks were on good terms with the country gentry, and their houses served as schools for their children ; nor is there any sign of a different feeling elsewhere. But in Cromwell's system there was no room for either the virtues or the vices of monasticism, for its indolence and superstition, or for its independence of the throne. Two royal commissioners therefore were despatched on a general visitation of the religious houses, and their reports formed a "Black Book" which was laid before Parliament on their return. It was acknowledged that about a third of the religious houses, including the bulk of the larger abbeys, were fairly and decently conducted. The rest were charged with drunkenness, with simony, and with the foulest and most revolting crimes. The character of the visitors, the sweeping nature of their report, and the long debate which followed on its reception, leaves little doubt that the charges were grossly exaggerated. But the want of any effective discipline which had resulted from their exemption from any but Papal supervision told fatally against monastic morality even in abbeys like St. Alban's : and the acknowledgement of Warham, as well as the partial measures of suppression begun by Wolsey, go far to prove that in the smaller houses at least indolence had passed into crime. But in spite of the cry of "Down with them" which broke from the Commons as the report was read, the country was still far from desiring the utter downfall of the

SEC. VI.

THOMAS
CROMWELL

1530
TO
1540
Enslave-
ment
of the
Clergy

monastic system. A long and bitter debate was followed by a compromise which suppressed all houses whose incomes fell below £200
a year, and granted their revenues to the Crown ; but the great abbeys
were still preserved intact.

The secular clergy alone remained ; and injunction after injunction
from the Vicar-General taught rector and vicar that they must learn to
regard themselves as mere mouthpieces of the royal will. With the
instinct of genius Cromwell discerned the part which the pulpit, as the
one means which then existed of speaking to the people at large, was
to play in the religious and political struggle that was at hand ; and he
resolved to turn it to the profit of the Monarchy. The restriction of
the right of preaching to priests who received licenses from the Crown
silenced every voice of opposition. Even to those who received these
licenses theological controversy was forbidden ; and a high-handed
process of "tuning the pulpits" by directions as to the subject and
tenor of each special discourse made the preachers at every crisis
mere means of diffusing the royal will. As a first step in this process
every bishop, abbot, and parish priest, was required to preach against
the usurpation of the Papacy, and to proclaim the King as the supreme
Head of the Church on earth. The very topics of the sermon were
carefully prescribed ; the bishops were held responsible for the compliance of the clergy with these orders, and the sheriffs were held
responsible for the compliance of the bishops. It was only when all
possibility of resistance was at an end, when the Church was gagged
and its pulpits turned into mere echoes of Henry's will, that Cromwell
ventured on his last and crowning change, that of claiming for the
Crown the right of dictating at its pleasure the form of faith and
doctrine to be held and taught throughout the land. A purified
Catholicism such as Erasmus and Colet had dreamed of was now to
be the religion of England. But the dream of the New Learning was
to be wrought out, not by the progress of education and piety, but by
the brute force of the Monarchy. The Articles of Religion, which
Convocation received and adopted without venturing on a protest,
were drawn up by the hand of Henry himself. The Bible and the
three Creeds were laid down as the sole grounds of faith. The Sacraments were reduced from seven to three, only Penance being allowed
to rank on an equality with Baptism and the Lord's Supper. The
doctrines of Transubstantiation and Confession were maintained, as
they were also in the Lutheran Churches. The spirit of Erasmus was
seen in the acknowledgement of Justification by Faith, a doctrine for
which the friends of the New Learning, such as Pole and Contarini,
were struggling at Rome itself, in the condemnation of purgatory, of
pardons, and of masses for the dead, in the admission of prayers for
the dead, and in the retention of the ceremonies of the Church without
material change. Enormous as was the doctrinal revolution, not a

murmur broke the assent of Convocation, and the Articles were sent by the Vicar-General into every county to be obeyed at men's peril. The policy of reform was carried steadily out by a series of royal injunctions which followed. Pilgrimages were suppressed; the excessive number of holy days diminished; the worship of images and relics discouraged in words which seem almost copied from the protest of Erasmus. His burning appeal for a translation of the Bible which weavers might repeat at their shuttle and ploughmen sing at their plough received at last a reply. At the outset of the ministry of Norfolk and More the King had promised an English version of the scriptures, while prohibiting the circulation of Tyndale's Lutheran translation. The work however lagged in the hands of the bishops; and as a preliminary measure the Creed, the Lord's Prayer, and the Ten Commandments were now rendered into English, and ordered to be taught by every schoolmaster and father of a family to his children and pupils. But the bishops' version still hung on hand; till in despair of its appearance a friend of Archbishop Cranmer, Miles Coverdale, was employed to correct and revise the translation of Tyndale; and the Bible which he edited was published in 1538 under the avowed patronage of Henry himself. The story of the royal supremacy was graven on its very title-page. The new foundation of religious truth was to be regarded throughout England as a gift, not from the Church, but from the King. It is Henry on his throne who gives the sacred volume to Cranmer, ere Cranmer and Cromwell can distribute it to the throng of priests and laymen below.

The debate on the suppression of the monasteries was the first instance of opposition with which Cromwell had met, and for some time longer it was to remain the only one. While the great revolution which struck down the Church was in progress, England looked silently on. In all the earlier ecclesiastical changes, in the contest over the Papal jurisdiction and Papal exactions, in the reform of the Church courts, even in the curtailment of the legislative independence of the clergy, the nation as a whole had gone with the King. But from the enslavement of the clergy, from the gagging of the pulpits, from the suppression of the monasteries, the bulk of the nation stood aloof. It is only through the stray depositions of royal spies that we catch a glimpse of the wrath and hate which lay seething under this silence of a whole people. For the silence was a silence of terror. Before Cromwell's rise and after his fall from power the reign of Henry the Eighth witnessed no more than the common tyranny and bloodshed of the time. But the years of Cromwell's administration form the one period in our history which deserves the name which men have given to the rule of Robespierre. It was the English Terror. It was by terror that Cromwell mastered the King. Cranmer could plead for him at a later time with Henry as "one whose surety was only by your Majesty, who loved your Majesty, as I ever thought, no less than God." But the attitude of Cromwell towards the King was something more than that of absolute dependence and unquestioning devotion. He was "so vigilant to preserve your Majesty from all treasons," adds the Primate, "that few could be so secretly conceived but he detected the same from the beginning." Henry, like every Tudor, was fearless of open danger, but tremulously sensitive to the slightest breath of hidden disloyalty. It was on this inner dread that Cromwell based the fabric of his power. He was hardly secretary before a host of spies were scattered broadcast over the land. Secret denunciations poured into the open ear of the minister. The air was thick with tales of plots and conspiracies, and with the detection and suppression of each Cromwell tightened his hold on the King. And as it was by terror that he mastered the King, so it was by terror that he mastered the people. Men felt in England, to use the figure by which Erasmus paints the time, "as if a scorpion lay sleeping under every stone." The confessional had no secrets for Cromwell. Men's talk with their closest friends found its way to his ear. "Words idly spoken," the murmurs of a petulant abbot, the ravings of a moon-struck nun, were, as the nobles cried passionately at his fall, "tortured into treason." The only chance of safety lay in silence. "Friends who used to write and send me presents," Erasmus tells us, "now send neither letter nor gifts, nor receive any from any one, and this through fear." But even the refuge of silence was closed by a law more infamous than any that has ever blotted the Statute-book of England. Not only was thought made treason, but men were forced to reveal their thoughts on pain of their very silence being punished with the penalties of treason. All trust in the older bulwarks of liberty was destroyed by a policy as daring as it was unscrupulous. The noblest institutions were degraded into instruments of terror. Though Wolsey had strained the law to the utmost he had made no open attack on the freedom of justice. If he had shrunk from assembling Parliaments it was from his sense that they were the bulwarks of liberty. Under Cromwell the coercion of juries and the management of judges rendered the courts mere mouth-pieces of the royal will: and where even this shadow of justice proved an obstacle to bloodshed, Parliament was brought into play to pass bill after bill of attainder. "He shall be judged by the bloody laws he has himself made," was the cry of the Council at the moment of his fall, and by a singular retribution the crowning injustice which he sought to introduce even into the practice of attainder, the condemnation of a man without hearing his defence, was only practised on himself. But ruthless as was the Terror of Cromwell it was of a nobler type than the Terror of France. He never struck uselessly or capriciously, or stooped to the meaner victims of the guillotine. His blows were effective just because he chose his victims from among the noblest and the best. If he struck at the Church, it was through the Carthusians, the holiest and the most renowned of English churchmen. If he struck at the baronage, it was through the Courtenays and the Poles, in whose veins flowed the blood of kings. If he struck at the New Learning it was through the murder of Sir Thomas More. But no personal vindictiveness mingled with his crime. In temper, indeed, so far as we can judge from the few stories which lingered among his friends, he was a generous, kindly-hearted man, with pleasant and winning manners which atoned for a certain awkwardness of person, and with a constancy of friendship which won him a host of devoted adherents. But no touch either of love or hate swayed him from his course. The student of Machiavelli had not studied the "Prince" in vain. He had reduced bloodshed to a system. Fragments of his papers still show us with what a business-like brevity he ticked off human lives among the casual "remembrances" of the day. "Item, the Abbot of Reading to be sent down to be tried and executed at Reading." "Item, to know the King's pleasure touching Master More." "Item, when Master Fisher shall go to his execution, and the other." It is indeed this utter absence of all passion, of all personal feeling, that makes the figure of Cromwell the most terrible in our history. He has an absolute faith in the end he is pursuing, and he simply hews his way to it as a woodman hews his way through the forest, axe in hand.

The choice of his first victim showed the ruthless precision with which Cromwell was to strike. In the general opinion of Europe the foremost Englishman of his time was Sir Thomas More. As the policy of the divorce ended in an open rupture with Rome he had withdrawn silently from the ministry, but his silent disapproval was more telling than the opposition of obscurer foes. To Cromwell there must have been something specially galling in More's attitude of reserve. The religious reforms of the New Learning were being rapidly carried out, but it was plain that the man who represented the very life of the New Learning believed that the sacrifice of liberty and justice was too dear a price to pay even for religious reform. More indeed looked on the divorce and re-marriage as without religious warrant, though his faith in the power of Parliament to regulate the succession made him regard the children of Anne Boleyn as the legal heirs of the Crown. The Act of Succession, however, required an oath to be taken by all persons, which not only recognized the succession, but contained an acknowledgement that the marriage with Catharine was against Scripture and invalid from the beginning. Henry had long known More's belief on this point ; and the summons to take this oath was simply a summons to death. More was at his house at Chelsea when the summons called him to Lambeth, to the house where he had bandied fun with Warham and Erasmus or bent over the easel of Holbein. For a moment there may have been some passing impulse to yield. But it was soon over. " I thank the Lord," More said with a sudden start as the boat dropped silently down the river from his garden steps in the early morning, " I thank the Lord that the field is won." Cranmer and his fellow commissioners tendered to him the new oath of allegiance ; but, as they expected, it was refused. They bade him walk in the garden that he might reconsider his reply. The day was hot and More seated himself in a window from which he could look down into the crowded court. Even in the presence of death, the quick sympathy of his nature could enjoy the humour and life of the throng below. " I saw," he said afterwards, " Master Latimer very merry in the court, for he laughed and took one or twain by the neck so handsomely that if they had been women I should have weened that he waxed wanton." The crowd below was chiefly of priests, rectors and vicars, pressing to take the oath that More found harder than death. He bore them no grudge for it. When he heard the voice of one who was known to have boggled hard at the oath a little while before calling loudly and ostentatiously for drink, he only noted him with his peculiar humour. " He drank," More supposed, " either from dryness or from gladness," or " to show quod ille notus erat Pontifici." He was called in again at last, but only repeated his refusal. It was in vain that Cranmer plied him with distinctions which perplexed even the subtle wit of the ex-chancellor ; he remained unshaken and passed to the Tower. He was followed there by Bishop Fisher of Rochester, charged with countenancing treason by listening to the prophecies of a fanatic called the " Nun of Kent." For the moment even Cromwell shrank from their blood. They remained prisoners while a new and more terrible engine was devised to crush out the silent but widespread opposition to the religious changes. By a statute passed at the close of 1534 a new treason was created in the denial of the King's titles ; and in the opening of 1535 Henry assumed, as we have seen, the title of " on earth supreme Head of the Church of England." In the general relaxation of the religious life the charity and devotion of the brethren of the Charter-house had won the reverence even of those who condemned monasticism. After a stubborn resistance they had acknowledged the royal Supremacy, and taken the oath of submission prescribed by the Act. But by an infamous construction of the statute which made the denial of the Supremacy treason, the refusal of satisfactory answers to official questions as to a conscientious belief in it was held to be equivalent to open denial. The aim of the new measure was well known, and the brethren prepared to die. In the agony of waiting enthusiasm brought its imaginative consolations ; " when the Host was lifted up there came as it were a whisper of air which breathed upon our faces as we knelt ; and there came a sweet soft sound of music." They had not long however to wait. Their refusal to answer was the signal for their doom. Three of the brethren went to the gallows; the rest were flung into Newgate, chained to posts in a noisome dungeon where, "tied and not able to stir," they were left to perish of gaol-fever and starvation. In a fortnight five were dead and the rest at the point of death, "almost despatched," Cromwell's envoy wrote to him, " by the hand of God, of which, considering their behaviour, I am not sorry." The interval of imprisonment had failed to break the resolution of More, and the new statute sufficed to bring him to the block. With Fisher he was convicted of denying the King's title as only supreme head of the Church. The old Bishop approached the block with a book of the New Testament in his hand. He opened it at a venture ere he knelt, and read, "This is life eternal to know Thee, the only true God." Fisher's death was soon followed by that of More. On the eve of the fatal blow he moved his beard carefully from the block. " Pity that should be cut," he was heard to mutter with a touch of the old sad irony, "that has never committed treason."

But it required, as Cromwell well knew, heavier blows even than these to break the stubborn resistance of Englishmen to his projects of change, and he seized his opportunity in the revolt of the North. In the north the monks had been popular; and the outrages with which the dissolution of the monasteries was accompanied gave point to the mutinous feeling that prevailed through the country. The nobles too were writhing beneath the rule of one whom they looked upon as a low-born upstart. "The world will never mend," Lord Hussey was heard to say, "till we fight for it." Agrarian discontent and the love of the old religion united in a revolt which broke out in Lincolnshire. The rising was hardly suppressed when Yorkshire was in arms. From every parish the farmers marched with the parish priest at their head upon York, and the surrender of the city determined the waverers. In a few days Skipton Castle, where the Earl of Cumberland held out with a handful of men, was the only spot north of the Humber which remained true to the King. Durham rose at the call of Lords Latimer and Westmoreland. Though the Earl of Northumberland feigned sickness, the Percies joined the revolt. Lord Dacre, the chief of the Yorkshire nobles, surrendered Pomfret, and was at once acknowledged as their chief by the insurgents. The whole nobility of the north were now in arms, and thirty thousand "tall men and well horsed" moved on the Don, demanding the reversal of the royal policy, a reunion with Rome, the restoration of Catharine's daughter, Mary, to her rights as heiress of the Crown, redress for the wrongs done to the Church, and above all the driving away of base-born counsellors, in other words the fall of Cromwell. Though their advance was checked by negotiation, the organization of the revolt went steadily on throughout the winter, and a Parliament of the North gathered at Pomfret, and formally adopted the demands of the insurgents. Only six

1537

1538

thousand men under Norfolk barred their way southward, and the Midland counties were known to be disaffected. Cromwell, however, remained undaunted by the peril. He suffered Norfolk to negotiate; and allowed Henry under pressure from his Council to promise pardon and a free Parliament at York, a pledge which Norfolk and Dacre alike construed into an acceptance of the demands made by the insurgents. Their leaders at once flung aside the badge of the Five Wounds which they had worn, with a cry "We will wear no badge but that of our Lord the King," and nobles and farmers dispersed to their homes in triumph. But the towns of the North were no sooner garrisoned and Norfolk's army in the heart of Yorkshire than the veil was flung aside. A few isolated outbreaks gave a pretext for the withdrawal of every concession. The arrest of the leaders of the "Pilgrimage of Grace," as the insurrection was styled, was followed by ruthless severities. The country was covered with gibbets. Whole districts were given up to military execution. But it was on the leaders of the rising that Cromwell's hand fell heaviest. He seized his opportunity for dealing at the northern nobles a fatal blow. "Cromwell," one of the chief among them broke fiercely out as he stood at the Council board, "it is thou that art the very special and chief cause of all this rebellion and wickedness, and dost daily travail to bring us to our ends and strike off our heads. I trust that ere thou die, though thou wouldst procure all the noblest heads within the realm to be stricken off, yet there shall one head remain that shall strike off thy head." But the warning was unheeded. Lord Darcy, who stood first among the nobles of Yorkshire, and Lord Hussey, who stood first among the nobles of Lincolnshire, went alike to the block. The Abbot of Barlings, who had ridden into Lincoln with his canons in full armour, swung with his brother Abbots of Whalley, Woburn, and Sawley from the gallows. The Abbots of Fountains and of Jervaulx were hanged at Tyburn side by side with the representative of the great line of Percy. Lady Bulmer was burnt at the stake. Sir Robert Constable was hanged in chains before the gate of Hull. The blow to the north had not long been struck when Cromwell turned to deal with the west. The opposition to his system gathered above all round two houses who represented what yet lingered of Yorkist tradition, the Courtenays and the Poles. Margaret, the Countess of Salisbury, a daughter of the Duke of Clarence by the heiress of the Earl of Warwick, was at once representative of the Nevilles and a niece of Edward the Fourth. Her third son, Reginald Pole, after refusing the highest offers from Henry as the price of his approval of the divorce, had taken refuge in Rome, where he had bitterly attacked the King in a book on "The Unity of the Church." "There may be found ways enough in Italy," Cromwell wrote to him in significant words, "to rid a treacherous subject. When Justice can take no place by process of law at home, sometimes she may be enforced to take new means abroad." But he had left hostages in Henry's hands. " Pity that the folly of one witless fool should be the ruin of so great a family. Let him follow ambition as fast as he can, those that little have offended (saving that he is of their kin), were it not for the great mercy and benignity of the prince, should and might feel what it is to have a traitor as their kinsman." Pole answered by pressing the Emperor to execute a bull of excommunication and deposition which was now launched by the Papacy. Cromwell was quick with his reply. Courtenay, the Marquis of Exeter, was a kinsman of the Poles, and like them of royal blood, a grandson through his mother of Edward the Fourth. He was known to have bitterly denounced the "knaves that ruled about the King;" and his threats to "give them some day a buffet" were formidable in the mouth of one whose influence in the western counties was supreme. He was at once arrested with Lord Montacute, Pole's elder brother, on a charge of treason, and both were beheaded on Tower Hill, while the Countess of Salisbury was attainted and sent to the Tower.

Never indeed had Cromwell shown such greatness as in his last struggle against Fate. "Beknaved" by the King whose confidence in him waned as he discerned the full meaning of the religious changes, met too by a growing opposition in the Council as his favour declined, the temper of the man remained indomitable as ever. He stood absolutely alone. Wolsey, hated as he had been by the nobles, had been supported by the Church; but Churchmen hated Cromwell with an even fiercer hate than the nobles themselves. His only friends were the Protestants, and their friendship was more fatal than the hatred of his foes. But he shewed no signs of fear or of halting in the course he had entered on. His activity was as boundless as ever. Like Wolsey he had concentrated in his hands the whole administration of the state; he was at once foreign minister and home minister and Vicar-General of the Church, the creator of a new fleet, the organizer of armies, the president of the terrible Star Chamber. But his Italian indifference to the mere show of power contrasted strongly with the pomp of the Cardinal. His personal habits were simple and unostentatious. If he clutched at money, it was to feed the vast army of spies whom he maintained at his own expense, and whose work he surveyed with a sleepless vigilance. More than fifty volumes still remain of the gigantic mass of his correspondence. Thousands of letters from " poor bedesmen," from outraged wives and wronged labourers and persecuted heretics, flowed in to the all-powerful minister whose system of personal government had turned him into the universal court of appeal. So long as Henry supported him, however reluctantly, he was more than a match for his foes. He was strong enough to expel his chief opponent, Bishop Gardiner of Winchester, from the

SEC. VI.

THOMAS
CROMWELL

1530
TO
1540

1538

royal Council. He met the hostility of the nobles with a threat which marked his power. "If the lords would handle him so, he would give them such a breakfast as never was made in England, and that the proudest of them should know." His single will forced on a scheme of foreign policy whose aim was to bind England to the cause of the Reformation while it bound Henry helplessly to his minister. The daring boast which his enemies laid afterwards to his charge, whether uttered or not, is but the expression of his system. "In brief time he would bring things to such a pass that the King with all his power should not be able to hinder him." His plans rested, like the plan which proved fatal to Wolsey, on a fresh marriage of his master. The short-lived royalty of Anne Boleyn had ended in charges of adultery and treason, and in her death in May, 1536. Her rival and successor in Henry's affections, Jane Seymour, died next year in child-birth ; and Cromwell replaced her with a German consort, Anne of Cleves, a sister-in-law of the Lutheran elector of Saxony. He dared even to resist Henry's caprice, when the King revolted on their first interview at the coarse features and unwieldy form of his new bride. For the moment Cromwell had brought matters "to such a pass" that it was impossible to recoil from the marriage. The marriage of Anne of Cleves, however, was but the first step in a policy which, had it been carried out as he designed it, would have anticipated the triumphs of Richelieu. Charles and the House of Austria could alone bring about a Catholic reaction strong enough to arrest and roll back the Re-formation ; and Cromwell was no sooner united with the princes of North Germany than he sought to league them with France for the overthrow of the Emperor. Had he succeeded, the whole face of Europe would have been changed, Southern Germany would have been secured for Protestantism, and the Thirty Years War averted. He failed as men fail who stand ahead of their age. The German princes shrank from a contest with the Emperor, France from a struggle which would be fatal to Catholicism ; and Henry, left alone to bear the resentment of the House of Austria and chained to a wife he loathed, turned savagely on Cromwell. The nobles sprang on him with a fierceness that told of their long-hoarded hate. Taunts and execrations burst from the Lords at the Council table, as the Duke of Norfolk, who had been charged with the minister's arrest, tore the ensign of the Garter from his neck. At the charge of treason Cromwell flung his cap on the ground with a passionate cry of despair. "This then," he exclaimed, "is my guerdon for the services I have done ! On your consciences, I ask you, am I a traitor ?" Then with a sudden sense that all was over he bade his foes "make quick work, and not leave me to languish in prison." Quick work was made, and a yet louder burst of popular applause than that which hailed the attainder of Cromwell hailed his execution.

CHAPTER VII.

THE REFORMATION.

Section I.—The Protestants. 1540—1553.

[*Authorities.*—For the close of Henry's reign and for that of Edward, we have a mass of material in Strype's "Memorials," and his lives of Cranmer, Cheke, and Smith, in Mr. Pocock's edition of "Burnet's History of the Reformation," in Hayward's Life of Edward, and Edward's own Journal, in Holinshed's "Chronicle," and Machyn's "Diary" (Camden Society). For the Protectorate see the correspondence published by Mr. Tytler in his "England under Edward VI. and Mary"; much light is thrown on its close by Mr. Nicholls in the "Chronicle of Queen Jane" (Camden Society). Among outer observers, the Venetian Soranzo deals with the Protectorate; and the despatches of Giovanni Michiel, published by Mr. Friedmann, with the events of Mary's reign. In spite of endless errors, of Puritan prejudices and deliberate suppressions of the truth (many of which will be found corrected by Dr. Maitland's "Essay on the Reformation,"), its mass of facts and wonderful charm of style will always give a great importance to the "Book of Martyrs" of Foxe. The story of the early Protestants has been admirably wrought up by Mr. Froude ("History of England," chap. vi.).]

At Cromwell's death the success of his policy was complete. The Monarchy had reached the height of its power. The old liberties of England lay prostrate at the feet of the King. The Lords were cowed and spiritless; the House of Commons was filled with the creatures of the Court and degraded into an engine of tyranny. Royal proclamations were taking the place of parliamentary legislation; benevolences were encroaching more and more on the right of parliamentary taxation. Justice was prostituted in the ordinary courts to the royal will, while the boundless and arbitrary powers of the royal Council were gradually superseding the slower processes of the Common Law. The new religious changes had thrown an almost sacred character over the "majesty" of the King. Henry was the Head of the Church. From the primate to the meanest deacon every minister of it derived from him his sole right to exercise spiritual powers. The voice of its preachers was the echo of his will. He alone could define orthodoxy or declare heresy. The forms of its worship and belief were changed and rechanged at the royal caprice. Half of its wealth went to swell the royal treasury, and the other half lay at the King's mercy. It was this unprecedented concentration of all power in the hands of a single man that overawed the imagination of Henry's subjects. He was regarded as something high above the laws which govern common men.

Cromwell and the Monarchy

Sec. I.

The Pro-
testants
1540
to
1553

Cromwell
and the
Parlia-
ment

The voices of statesmen and of priests extolled his wisdom and power as more than human. The Parliament itself rose and bowed to the vacant throne when his name was mentioned. An absolute devotion to his person replaced the old loyalty to the law. When the Primate of the English Church described the chief merit of Cromwell, it was by asserting that he loved the King "no less than he loved God."

It was indeed Cromwell, as we have seen, who more than any man had reared this fabric of king-worship; but he had hardly reared it before it began to give way. The very success of his measures indeed brought about the ruin of his policy. One of the most striking features of his system had been his revival of Parliaments. The great assembly which the Monarchy, from Edward the Fourth to Wolsey, had dreaded and silenced, was called to the front again by Cromwell, and turned into the most formidable weapon of despotism. He saw nothing to fear in a House of Lords whose nobles cowered helpless before the might of the Crown, and whose spiritual members his policy was degrading into mere tools of the royal will. Nor could he find anything to dread in a House of Commons which was crowded with members directly or indirectly nominated by the royal Council. With a Parliament such as this Cromwell might well trust to make the nation itself through its very representatives an accomplice in the work of absolutism. It was by parliamentary statutes that the Church was prostrated at the feet of the Monarchy. It was by bills of attainder that great nobles were brought to the block. It was under constitutional forms that freedom was gagged with new treasons and oaths and questionings. But the success of such a system depended wholly on the absolute servility of Parliament to the will of the Crown, and Cromwell's own action made the continuance of such a servility impossible. The part which the Houses were to play in after years shows the importance of clinging to the forms of constitutional freedom, even when their life is all but lost. In the inevitable reaction against tyranny they furnish centres for the reviving energies of the people, while the returning tide of liberty is enabled through their preservation to flow quietly and naturally along its traditional channels. On one occasion during Cromwell's own rule a "great debate" on the suppression of the lesser monasteries showed that elements of resistance still survived; and these elements developed rapidly as the power of the Crown declined under the minority of Edward and the unpopularity of Mary. To this revival of a spirit of independence the spoliation of the Church largely contributed. Partly from necessity, partly from a desire to build up a faction interested in the maintenance of their ecclesiastical policy, Cromwell and the King squandered the vast mass of wealth which flowed into the Treasury with reckless prodigality. Something like a fifth of the actual land in the kingdom was in this way transferred from the holding of the Church to that of nobles and gentry. Not only were the older houses enriched, but a new aristocracy was erected from among the dependants of the Court. The Russells and the Cavendishes are familiar instances of families which rose from obscurity through the enormous grants of Church-land made to Henry's courtiers. The old baronage was hardly crushed before a new aristocracy took its place. "Those families within or without the bounds of the peerage," observes Mr. Hallam, "who are now deemed the most considerable, will be found, with no great number of exceptions, to have first become conspicuous under the Tudor line of kings, and, if we could trace the title of their estates, to have acquired no small portion of them mediately or immediately from monastic or other ecclesiastical foundations." The leading part which the new peers took in the events which followed Henry's death gave a fresh strength and vigour to the whole order. But the smaller gentry shared in the general enrichment of the landed proprietors, and the new energy of the Lords was soon followed by a display of fresh political independence among the Commons themselves.

But it was above all in the new energy which the religious spirit of the people at large drew from the ecclesiastical changes which he had brought about, that the policy of Cromwell was fatal to the Monarchy. Lollardry, as a great social and popular movement, had ceased to exist, and little remained of the directly religious impulse given by Wyclif beyond a vague restlessness and discontent with the system of the Church. But weak and fitful as was the life of Lollardry, the prosecutions whose records lie scattered over the bishops' registers failed wholly to kill it. We see groups meeting here and there to read "in a great book of heresy all one night certain chapters of the Evangelists in English," while transcripts of Wyclif's tracts passed from hand to hand. The smouldering embers needed but a breath to fan them into flame, and the breath came from William Tyndale. He had passed from Oxford to Cambridge to feel the full impulse given by the appearance there of the New Testament of Erasmus. From that moment one thought was at his heart. "If God spare my life," he said to a learned controversialist, "ere many years I will cause a boy that driveth the plough shall know more of the scripture than thou dost." But he was a man of forty before his dream became fact. Drawn from his retirement in Gloucestershire by the news of Luther's protest at Wittemberg, he found shelter for a time in London, and then at Hamburg, before he found his way to the little town which had suddenly become the sacred city of the Reformation. Students of all nations were flocking there with an enthusiasm which resembled that of the Crusades. "As they came in sight of the town," a contemporary tells us, "they returned thanks to God with clasped hands, for from Wittemberg, as heretofore from Jerusalem, the light of evangelical truth had spread to the utmost parts of the earth." In 1525 his version of the New Testament was completed. Driven from Köln, he had to fly with his sheets to Worms, from whence six thousand copies of the New Testament were sent to English shores. But it was not as a mere translation of the Bible that Tyndale's work reached England. It came as a part of the Lutheran movement; it bore the Lutheran stamp in its version of ecclesiastical words; it came too in company with Luther's bitter invectives and reprints of the tracts of Wyclif. It was denounced as heretical, and a pile of books was burned before Wolsey in St. Paul's Churchyard. Bibles and pamphlets however were smuggled over to England and circulated among the poorer and trading classes through the agency of an association of " Christian Brethren," consisting principally of London tradesmen and citizens, but whose missionaries spread over the country at large. They found their way at once to the Universities, where the intellectual impulse given by the New Learning was quickening religious speculation. Cambridge had already won a name for heresy, and the Cambridge scholars whom Wolsey introduced into Cardinal College which he was founding spread the contagion through Oxford. A group of " Brethren " which was formed in Cardinal College for the secret reading and discussion of the Epistles soon included the more intelligent and learned scholars of the University. It was in vain that Clark, the centre of this group, strove to dissuade fresh members from joining it by warnings of the impending dangers. " I fell down on my knees at his feet," says one of them, Anthony Dalaber, " and with tears and sighs besought him that for the tender mercy of God he should not refuse me, saying that I trusted verily that He who had begun this on me would not forsake me, but would give me grace to continue therein to the end. When he heard me say so he came to me, took me in his arms, and kissed me, saying, ' The Lord God Almighty grant you so to do, and from henceforth ever take me for your father, and I will take you for my son in Christ.'" The excitement which followed on this rapid diffusion of Tyndale's works forced Wolsey to more vigorous action; many of the Oxford Brethren were thrown into prison and their books seized. But in spite of the panic of the Protestants, some of whom fled over sea, little severity was really exercised; and Wolsey remained steadily indifferent to all but political matters.

Henry's chief anxiety, indeed, was lest in the outburst against heresy the interest of the New Learning should suffer harm. This was remarkably shown in the protection he extended to one who was destined to eclipse even the fame of Colet as a popular preacher. Hugh Latimer was the son of a Leicestershire yeoman, whose armour the boy had buckled on ere he set out to meet the Cornish insurgents at Blackheath field. He has himself described the soldierly training of his youth. " My father was delighted to teach me to shoot with the bow. He taught me how to draw, how to lay my body to the bow, not to draw with strength of arm as other nations do, but with the strength of the body." At fourteen he was at Cambridge, flinging himself into the New Learning which was winning its way there with a zeal which at last told on his physical strength. The ardour of his mental efforts left its mark on him in ailments and enfeebled health, from which, vigorous as he was, his frame never wholly freed itself. But he was destined to be known, not as a scholar, but as a preacher. The sturdy good sense of the man shook off the pedantry of the schools as well as the subtlety of the theologian in his addresses from the pulpit. He had little turn for speculation, and in the religious changes of the day we find him constantly lagging behind his brother reformers. But he had the moral earnestness of a Jewish prophet, and his denunciations of wrong had a prophetic directness and fire. " Have pity on your soul," he cried to Henry, " and think that the day is even at hand when you shall give an account of your office, and of the blood that hath been shed by your sword." His irony was yet more telling than his invective. " I would ask you a strange question," he said once at Paul's Cross to a ring of Bishops, " who is the most diligent prelate in all England, that passeth all the rest in doing of his office? I will tell you. It is the Devil ! of all the pack of them that have cure, the Devil shall go for my money ; for he ordereth his business. Therefore, you unpreaching prelates, learn of the Devil to be diligent in your office. If you will not learn of God, for shame learn of the Devil." But he was far from limiting himself to invective. His homely humour breaks in with story and apologue ; his earnestness is always tempered with good sense ; his plain and simple style quickens with a shrewd mother-wit. He talks to his hearers as a man talks to his friends, telling stories such as we have given of his own life at home, or chatting about the changes and chances of the day with a transparent simplicity and truth that raises even his chat into grandeur. His theme is always the actual world about him, and in his homely lessons of loyalty, of industry, of pity for the poor, he touches upon almost every subject, from the plough to the throne. No such preaching had been heard in England before his day, and with the growth of his fame grew the danger of perse-cution. There were moments when, bold as he was, Latimer's heart failed him. " If I had not trust that God will help me," he wrote once, " I think the ocean sea would have divided my lord of London and me by this day." A citation for heresy at last brought the danger home. " I intend," he wrote with his peculiar medley of humour and pathos, " to make merry with my parishioners this Christmas, for all the sorrow, lest perchance I may never return to them again." But he was saved throughout by the steady protection of the Court. Wolsey upheld him against the threats of the Bishop of Ely ; Henry made him his own chaplain ; and the King's interposition at this

SEC. I.

THE PRO-
TESTANTS

1540
TO
1553
Crom-
well and
the Pro-
testants

critical moment forced Latimer's judges to content themselves with a few vague words of submission.

Henry's quarrel with Rome saved the Protestants from the keener persecution which troubled them after Wolsey's fall. The divorce, the renunciation of the Papacy, the degradation of the clergy, the suppression of the monasteries, the religious changes, fell like a series of heavy blows upon the priesthood. From persecutors they suddenly sank into men trembling for their very lives. Those whom they had threatened were placed at their head. Cranmer became Primate ; Shaxton, a favourer of the new changes, was raised to the see of Salisbury ; Barlow, a yet more extreme partizan, to that of St. David's ; Hilsey to that of Rochester ; Goodrich to that of Ely ; Fox to that of Hereford. Latimer himself became Bishop of Worcester, and in a

vehement address to the clergy in Convocation taunted them with their greed and superstition in the past, and with their inactivity when the King and his Parliament were labouring for the revival of religion. The aim of Cromwell, as we have seen, was simply that of the New Learning ; he desired religious reform rather than revolution, a simplification rather than a change of doctrine, the purification of worship rather than the introduction of a new ritual. But it was impossible to strike blow after blow at the Church without leaning instinctively to the party who sympathized with the German reformation, and were longing for a more radical change at home. Few as these " Lutherans " or " Protestants " still were in numbers, their new hopes made them a formidable force ; and in the school of persecution they had learned a violence which delighted in outrages on the faith which had so long trampled them under foot. At the very outset of Cromwell's

changes four Suffolk youths broke into the church at Dovercourt, tore down a wonder-working crucifix, and burned it in the fields. The suppression of the lesser monasteries was the signal for a new outburst of ribald insult to the old religion. The roughness, insolence, and extortion of the Commissioners sent to effect it drove the whole monastic body to despair. Their servants rode along the road with copes for doublets and tunicles for saddle-cloths, and scattered panic among the larger houses which were left. Some sold their jewels and relics to provide for the evil day they saw approaching. Some begged of their own will for dissolution. It was worse when fresh ordinances of the Vicar-General ordered the removal of objects of superstitious veneration. The removal, bitter enough to those whose religion twined itself around the image or the relic which was taken away, was yet more embittered by the insults with which it was accompanied. The miraculous rood at Boxley, which bowed its head and stirred its eyes, was paraded from market to market and exhibited as a juggle before the Court. Images of the Virgin were stripped of their costly vestments and sent to be publicly burnt at London. Latimer for-

warded to the capital the figure of Our Lady, which he had thrust out
of his cathedral church at Worcester, with rough words of scorn:
"She with her old sister of Walsingham, her younger sister of Ipswich, and their two other sisters of Doncaster and Penrice, would
make a jolly muster at Smithfield." Fresh orders were given to fling
all relics from their reliquaries, and to level every shrine with the
ground. The bones of St. Thomas of Canterbury were torn from the
stately shrine which had been the glory of his metropolitan church,
and his name was erased from the service-books as that of a traitor.

The introduction of the English Bible into churches gave a new opening for the zeal of the Protestants. In spite of royal injunctions that
it should be read decently and without comment, the young zealots of
the party prided themselves on shouting it out to a circle of excited
hearers during the service of mass, and accompanied their reading
with violent expositions. Protestant maidens took the new English
primer to church with them, and studied it ostentatiously during
matins. Insult passed into open violence when the Bishops' Courts
were invaded and broken up by Protestant mobs; and law and
public opinion were outraged at once when priests who favoured the
new doctrines began openly to bring home wives to their vicarages.
A fiery outburst of popular discussion compensated for the silence of
the pulpits. The new Scriptures, in Henry's bitter words of complaint,
were "disputed, rimed, sung, and jangled in every tavern and alehouse." The articles which dictated the belief of the English Church
roused a furious controversy. Above all, the Sacrament of the Mass,
the centre of the Catholic system of faith and worship, and which still
remained sacred to the bulk of Englishmen, was attacked with a
scurrility and profaneness which passes belief. The doctrine of
Transubstantiation, which was as yet recognized by law, was held up
to scorn in ballads and mystery plays. In one church a Protestant
lawyer raised a dog in his hands when the priest elevated the Host.
The most sacred words of the old worship, the words of consecration, "Hoc est corpus," were travestied into a nickname for jugglery
as "Hocus-pocus." It was by this attack on the Mass, even more
than by the other outrages, that the temper both of Henry and the
nation was stirred to a deep resentment; and the first signs of reaction were seen in the Act of the Six Articles, which was passed by
the Parliament with general assent. On the doctrine of Transubstan-

tiation, which was re-asserted by the first of these, there was no difference of feeling or belief between the men of the New Learning and the
older Catholics. But the road to a further instalment of even moderate
reform seemed closed by the five other articles which sanctioned communion in one kind, the celibacy of the clergy, monastic vows, private
masses, and auricular confession. A more terrible feature of the reaction was the revival of persecution. Burning was denounced as the

penalty for a denial of transubstantiation ; on a second offence it became the penalty for an infraction of the other five doctrines. A
refusal to confess or to attend Mass was made felony. It was in vain
that Cranmer, with the five bishops who partially sympathized with
the Protestants, struggled against the bill in the Lords : the Commons
were " all of one opinion," and Henry himself acted as spokesman on
the side of the Articles. In London alone five hundred Protestants
were indicted under the new act. Latimer and Shaxton were imprisoned, and the former forced into a resignation of his see.
Cranmer himself was only saved by Henry's personal favour. But
the first burst of triumph had no sooner spent itself than the strong
hand of Cromwell again made itself felt. Though his opinions remained those of the New Learning and differed little from the
general sentiment represented in the Act, he leaned instinctively to the
one party which did not long for his fall. His wish was to restrain the
Protestant excesses, but he had no mind to ruin the Protestants. The
bishops were quietly released. The London indictments were quashed.
The magistrates were checked in their enforcement of the law, while a
general pardon cleared the prisons of the heretics who had been
arrested under its provisions. A few months after the enactment of
the Six Articles we find from a Protestant letter that persecution had
wholly ceased, " the Word is powerfully preached and books of every
kind may safely be exposed for sale."

At Cromwell's fall his designs seemed to be utterly abandoned. The
marriage with Anne of Cleves was annulled, and a new Queen found
in Catharine Howard, a niece of the Duke of Norfolk. Norfolk himself returned to power, and resumed the policy which Cromwell had
interrupted. Like the King he looked to an Imperial alliance rather
than an alliance with Francis and the Lutherans. He still clung to
the dream of the New Learning, to a purification of the Church through
a general Council, and the reconciliation of England with the purified
body of Catholicism. For such a purpose it was necessary to vindicate
English orthodoxy ; and to ally England with the Emperor, by whose
influence alone the assembly of such a Council could be brought about.
To the hotter Catholics indeed, as to the hotter Protestants, the years
after Cromwell's fall seemed years of a gradual return to Catholicism.
There was a slight sharpening of persecution for the Protestants, and
restrictions were put on the reading of the English Bible. But neither
Norfolk nor his master desired any rigorous measure of reaction. There
was no thought of reviving the old superstitions, or undoing the work
which had been done, but simply of guarding the purified faith against
Lutheran heresy. The work of supplying men with means of devotion
in their own tongue was still carried on by the publication of an English
Litany and prayers, which furnished the germ of the national Prayer
Book of a later time. The greater abbeys which had been saved by

THE REFORMATION.

the energetic resistance of the Parliament in 1536 had in 1539 been involved in the same ruin with the smaller; but in spite of this confiscation the treasury was now empty, and by a bill of 1545 more than two thousand chauntries and chapels, with a hundred and ten hospitals, were suppressed to the profit of the Crown. If the friendship of England was offered to Charles, when the struggle between France and the House of Austria burst again for a time into flame, it was because Henry saw in the Imperial alliance the best hope for the reformation of the Church and the restoration of unity. But, as Cromwell had foreseen, the time for a peaceful reform and for a general reunion of Christendom was past. The Council, so passionately desired, met at Trent in no spirit of conciliation, but to ratify the very superstitions and errors against which the New Learning had protested, and which England and Germany had flung away. The long hostility of France and the House of Austria merged in the greater struggle which was opening between Catholicism and the Reformation. The Emperor allied himself definitely with the Pope. As their hopes of a middle course faded, the Catholic nobles themselves drifted unconsciously with the tide of reaction. Anne Ascue was tortured and burnt with three companions for the denial of Transubstantiation. Latimer was examined before the Council; and Cranmer himself, who in the general dissolution of the moderate party was drifting towards Protestantism as Norfolk was drifting towards Rome, was for a moment in danger. But at the last hours of his life Henry proved himself true to the work he had begun. His resolve not to bow to the pretensions of the Papacy sanctioned at Trent threw him, whether he would or no, back on the policy of the great minister whom he had hurried to the block. He offered to unite in a "League Christian" with the German Princes. He consented to the change, suggested by Cranmer, of the Mass into a Communion Service. He flung the Duke of Norfolk into the Tower as a traitor, and sent his son, the Earl of Surrey, to the block. The Earl of Hertford, the head of the "new men," and known as a patron of the Protestants, came to the front, and was appointed one of the Council of Regency which Henry nominated at his death.

Catharine Howard atoned like Anne Boleyn for her unchastity by a traitor's death; her successor on the throne, Catharine Parr, had the luck to outlive the King. But of Henry's numerous marriages only three children survived; Mary and Elizabeth, the daughters of Catharine of Aragon and of Anne Boleyn; and Edward, the boy who now ascended the throne as Edward the Sixth, his son by Jane Seymour. As Edward was but nine years old, Henry had appointed a carefully balanced Council of Regency; but the will fell into the keeping of Jane's brother, whom he had raised to the peerage as Lord Hertford, and who at a later time assumed the title of Duke of Somerset.

When the list of regents was at last disclosed Gardiner, who had till now been the leading minister, was declared to have been excluded from it; and Hertford seized the whole royal power with the title of Protector. His personal weakness forced him at once to seek for popular support by measures which marked the first retreat of the Monarchy from the position of pure absolutism which it had reached under Henry. The Statute which had given to royal proclamations the force of law was repealed, and several of the new felonies and treasons which Cromwell had created and used with so terrible an effect were erased from the Statute Book. The hope of support from the Protestants united with Hertford's personal predilections in his patronage of the innovations against which Henry had battled to the last. Cranmer had now drifted into a purely Protestant position; and his open break with the older system followed quickly on Hertford's rise to power. "This year," says a contemporary, "the Archbishop of Canterbury did eat meat openly in Lent in the Hall of Lambeth, the like of which was never seen since England was a Christian country." This significant act was followed by a rapid succession of sweeping changes. The legal prohibitions of Lollardry were removed; the Six Articles were repealed; a royal injunction removed all pictures and images from the churches; priests were permitted to marry; the new Communion which had taken the place of the Mass was ordered to be administered in both kinds, and in the English tongue; an English book of Common Prayer, the Liturgy which with slight alterations is still used in the Church of England, replaced the Missal and Breviary from which its contents are mainly drawn. These sweeping religious changes were carried through with the despotism, if not with the vigour, of Cromwell. Gardiner, who in his acceptance of the personal supremacy of the sovereign denounced all ecclesiastical changes made during the King's minority as illegal and invalid, was sent to the Tower. The power of preaching was restricted by the issue of licences only to the friends of the Primate. While all counter arguments were rigidly suppressed, a crowd of Protestant pamphleteers flooded the country with vehement invectives against the Mass and its superstitious accompaniments. The assent of noble and landowner was won by the suppression of chauntries and religious gilds, and by glutting their greed with the last spoils of the Church. German and Italian mercenaries were introduced to stamp out the wider popular discontent which broke out in the east, in the west, and in the midland counties. The Cornishmen refused to receive the new service "because it is like a Christmas game." Devonshire demanded in open revolt the restoration of the Mass and the Six Articles. The agrarian discontent, now heightened by economic changes, woke again in the general disorder. Twenty thousand men gathered round the "oak of Reformation" near Norwich, and repulsing the royal troops in a desperate engagement renewed the old cries for the removal of evil counsellors, a prohibition of enclosures, and redress for the grievances of the poor.

Sec. I.

The Pro-
testants
1540
to
1553
The Pro-
testant
Mis-rule

Revolt was stamped out in blood; but the weakness which the Protector had shown in presence of the danger, his tampering with popular demands, and the anger of the nobles at his resolve to enforce the laws against enclosures and evictions, ended in his fall. He was forced by the Council to resign, and his power passed to the Earl of Warwick, to whose ruthless severity the suppression of the revolt was mainly due. But the change of governors brought about no change of system. The rule of the upstart nobles who formed the Council of Regency became simply a rule of terror. "The greater part of the people," one of their creatures, Cecil, avowed, "is not in favour of defending this cause, but of aiding its adversaries; on that side are the greater part of the nobles, who absent themselves from Court, all the bishops save three or four, almost all the judges and lawyers, almost all the justices of the peace, the priests who can move their flocks any way, for the whole of the commonalty is in such a state of irritation that it will easily follow any stir towards change." But, heedless of danger from without or from within, Cranmer and his colleagues advanced yet more boldly in the career of innovation. Four prelates who adhered to the older system were deprived of their sees and committed on frivolous pretexts to the Tower. A new Catechism embodied the doctrines of the reformers; and a Book of Homilies, which enforced the chief Protestant tenets, was appointed to be read in churches. A crowning defiance was given to the doctrine of the Mass by an order to demolish the stone altars and replace them by wooden tables, which were stationed for the most part in the middle of the church. A revised Prayer-book was issued, and every change made in it leaned directly towards the extreme Protestantism which was at this time finding a home at Geneva. Forty-two Articles of Religion were introduced; and though since reduced by omissions to thirty-nine, these have remained to this day the formal standard of doctrine in the English Church. The sufferings of the Protestants had failed to teach them the worth of religious liberty; and a new code of ecclesiastical laws, which was ordered to be drawn up by a board of Commissioners as a substitute for the Canon Law of the Catholic Church, although it shrank from the penalty of death, attached that of perpetual imprisonment or exile to the crimes of heresy, blasphemy, and adultery, and declared excommunication to involve a severance of the offender from the mercy of God, and his deliverance into the tyranny of the devil. Delays in the completion of this Code prevented its legal establishment during Edward's reign; but the use of the new Liturgy and attendance at the new service was enforced by imprisonment, and subscription to the Articles of Faith was demanded by royal authority from all clergymen, churchwardens, and schoolmasters.

Warwick's Protectorate

Articles of Religion 1552

The distaste for changes so hurried and so rigorously enforced was increased by the daring speculations of the more extreme Protestants. The real value of the religious revolution of the sixteenth century to mankind lay, not in its substitution of one creed for another, but in the new spirit of inquiry, the new freedom of thought and of discussion, which was awakened during the process of change. But however familiar such a truth may be to us, it was absolutely hidden from the England of the time. Men heard with horror that the foundations of faith and morality were questioned, polygamy advocated, oaths denounced as unlawful, community of goods raised into a sacred obligation, the very Godhead of the Founder of Christianity denied. The repeal of the Statute of Heresy left the powers of the Common Law intact, and Cranmer availed himself of these to send heretics of the last class without mercy to the stake; but within the Church itself the Primate's desire for uniformity was roughly resisted by the more ardent members of his own party. Hooper, who had been named Bishop of Gloucester, refused to wear the episcopal habits, and denounced them as the livery of the "harlot of Babylon," a name for the Papacy which was supposed to have been discovered in the Apocalypse. Ecclesiastical order was almost at an end. Priests flung aside the surplice as superstitious. Patrons of livings presented their huntsmen or gamekeepers to the benefices in their gift, and kept the stipend. All teaching of divinity ceased at the Universities: the students indeed had fallen off in numbers, the libraries were in part scattered or burnt, the intellectual impulse of the New Learning died away. One noble measure indeed, the foundation of eighteen Grammar Schools, was destined to throw a lustre over the name of Edward, but it had no time to bear fruit in his reign. All that men saw was religious and political chaos, in which ecclesiastical order had perished and in which politics were dying down into the squabbles of a knot of nobles over the spoils of the Church and the Crown. The plunder of the chauntries and the gilds failed to glut the appetite of the crew of spoilers. Half the lands of every see were flung to them in vain: the wealthy see of Durham had been suppressed to satisfy their greed; and the whole endowments of the Church were threatened with confiscation. But while the courtiers gorged themselves with manors, the Treasury grew poorer. The coinage was again debased. Crown lands to the value of five millions of our modern money had been granted away to the friends of Somerset and Warwick. The royal expenditure had mounted in seventeen years to more than four times its previous total. It is clear that England must soon have risen against the misrule of the Protectorate, if the Protectorate had not fallen by the intestine divisions of the plunderers themselves.

Sec. II.

THE
MARTYRS

1553
TO
1558

Mary

Section II.—The Martyrs. 1553—1558.

[*Authorities*—As before.]

The waning health of Edward warned Warwick, who had now become Duke of Northumberland, of an unlooked-for danger. Mary, the daughter of Catharine of Aragon, who had been placed next to Edward by the Act of Succession, remained firm amidst all the changes of the time to the older faith; and her accession threatened to be the signal for its return. But the bigotry of the young King was easily brought to consent to a daring scheme by which her rights might be set aside. Edward's "plan," as Northumberland dictated it, annulled both the Statute of Succession and the will of his father, to whom the right of disposing of the Crown after the death of his own children had been entrusted by Parliament. It set aside both Mary and Elizabeth, who stood next in the Act. With this exclusion of the direct line of Henry the Eighth the succession would vest, if the rules of hereditary descent were observed, in the descendants of his elder sister Margaret, who had become by her first husband, James the Fourth of Scotland, the grandmother of the young Scottish Queen, Mary Stuart; and, by a second marriage with the Earl of Angus, was the grandmother of Henry Stuart, Lord Darnley. Henry's will, however, had passed by the children of Margaret, and had placed next to Elizabeth in the succession the children of his younger sister Mary, the wife of Charles Brandon, the Duke of Suffolk. Frances, Mary's child by this marriage, was still living, and was the mother of three daughters by her marriage with Grey, Lord Dorset, a hot partizan of the religious changes, who had been raised under the Protectorate to the Dukedom of Suffolk. Frances however was passed over, and Edward's "plan" named her eldest child Jane as his successor. The marriage of Jane Grey with Guildford Dudley, the fourth son of Northumberland, was all that was needed to complete the unscrupulous plot. The consent of the judges and council to her succession was extorted by the authority of the dying King, and the new sovereign was proclaimed on Edward's death. But the temper of the whole people rebelled against so lawless a usurpation. The eastern counties rose as one man to support Mary; and when Northumberland marched from London with ten thousand at his back to crush the rising, the Londoners, Protestant as they were, showed their ill-will by a stubborn silence. "The people crowd to look upon us," the Duke noted gloomily, "but not one calls 'God speed ye.'" The Council no sooner saw the popular reaction than they proclaimed Mary Queen; the fleet and the levies of the shires declared in her favour. Northumberland's courage suddenly gave way, and his retreat to Cambridge was the signal for a general defection. The Duke himself threw his cap into the air and shouted with his men for Queen Mary. But his submission failed to avert his doom ; and the death of Northumberland drew with it the imprisonment in the Tower of the hapless girl whom he had made the tool of his ambition. The whole system which had been pursued during Edward's reign fell with a sudden crash. London indeed retained much of its Protestant sympathy, but over the rest of the country the tide of reaction swept without a check. The married priests were driven from their churches, the images were replaced. In many parishes the new Prayer-book was set aside and the Mass restored. The Parliament which met in October annulled the laws made respecting religion during the past reign. Gardiner was drawn from the Tower. Bonner and the deposed bishops were restored to their sees. Ridley with the others who had displaced them were again expelled, and Latimer and Cranmer were sent to the Tower. But with the restoration of the system of Henry the Eighth the popular impulse was satisfied. The people had no more sympathy with Mary's leanings towards Rome than with the violence of the Protestants. The Parliament was with difficulty brought to set aside the new Prayer-book, and clung obstinately to the Church-lands and to the Royal Supremacy.

Nor was England more favourable to the marriage on which, from motives both of policy and religious zeal, Mary had set her heart. The Emperor had ceased to be the object of hope or confidence as a mediator who would at once purify the Church from abuses and restore the unity of Christendom : he had ranged himself definitely on the side of the Papacy and of the Council of Trent ; and the cruelties of the Inquisition which he introduced into Flanders gave a terrible in-dication of the bigotry which he was to bequeath to his House. The marriage with his son Philip, whose hand he offered to his cousin Mary, meant an absolute submission to the Papacy, and the undoing not only of the Protestant reformation, but of the more moderate reforms of the New Learning. On the other hand, it would have the political advantage of securing Mary's throne against the pretensions of the young Queen of Scots, Mary Stuart, who had become formidable by her marriage with the heir of the French Crown ; and whose adherents already alleged the illegitimate birth of both Mary and Elizabeth, through the annulling of their mothers' marriages, as a ground for denying their right of succession. To the issue of the marriage he proposed, Charles promised the heritage of the Low Countries, while he accepted the demand made by Mary's minister, Bishop Gardiner of Winchester, and by the Council, of complete inde-pendence both of policy and action on the part of England, in case of such a union. The temptation was great, and Mary's resolution overleapt all obstacles. But in spite of the toleration which she had promised, and had as yet observed, the announcement of her design drove the Protestants into a panic of despair. Risings which broke out in the west and centre of the country were quickly put down, and the Duke of Suffolk, who appeared in arms at Leicester, was sent to the Tower. The danger was far more formidable when the dread that Spaniards were coming "to conquer the realm" roused Kent into revolt under Sir Thomas Wyatt. The ships in the Thames submitted to be seized by the insurgents. A party of the trainbands of London, who marched under the Duke of Norfolk against them, deserted to the rebels in a mass with shouts of "A Wyatt! a Wyatt! we are all Englishmen!" Had the insurgents moved quickly on the capital, its gates would at once have been flung open and success would have been assured. But in the critical moment Mary was saved by her queenly courage. Riding boldly to the Guildhall she appealed with "a man's voice" to the loyalty of the citizens, and when Wyatt appeared on the Southwark bank the bridge was secured. The issue hung on the question which side London would take; and the insurgent leader pushed desperately up the Thames, seized a bridge at Kingston, threw his force across the river, and marched rapidly back on the capital. The night march along miry roads wearied and disorganized his men, the bulk of whom were cut off from their leader by a royal force which had gathered in the fields at what is now Hyde Park Corner, but Wyatt himself, with a handful of followers, pushed desperately on to Temple Bar. "I have kept touch," he cried as he sank exhausted at the gate; but it was closed, his adherents within were powerless to effect their promised diversion in his favour, and the daring leader was seized and sent to the Tower.

The courage of the Queen, who had refused to fly even while the rebels were marching beneath her palace walls, was only equalled by her terrible revenge. The hour was come when the Protestants were at her feet, and she struck without mercy. Lady Jane, her father, her husband, and her uncle atoned for the ambition of the House of Suffolk by the death of traitors. Wyatt and his chief adherents followed them to execution, while the bodies of the poorer insurgents were dangling on gibbets round London. Elizabeth, who had with some reason been suspected of complicity in the insurrection, was sent to the Tower; and only saved from death by the interposition of the Council. But the failure of the revolt not only crushed the Protestant party, it secured the marriage on which Mary was resolved. She used it to wring a reluctant consent from the Parliament, and meeting Philip at Winchester in the ensuing summer became his wife. The temporizing measures to which the Queen had been forced by the earlier difficulties of her reign could now be laid safely aside. Mary was resolved to bring about a submission to Rome; and her minister Gardiner fell back on the old ecclesiastical order, as the moderate party which had supported the policy of Henry the Eighth saw its hopes disappear, and ranged himself definitely on the side of a unity which could now only be brought about by a reconciliation with the Papacy. The

Spanish match was hardly concluded, when the negotiations with Rome were brought to a final issue. The attainder of Reginald Pole, who had been appointed by the Pope to receive the submission of the realm, was reversed ; and the Legate, who entered London by the river with his cross gleaming from the prow of his barge, was solemnly welcomed by a compliant Parliament. The two Houses decided by a formal vote to return to the obedience of the Papal See, and received on their knees the absolution which freed the realm from the guilt incurred by its schism and heresy. But, even in the hour of her triumph, the temper both of Parliament and the nation warned the Queen of the failure of her hope to bind England to a purely Catholic policy. The growing independence of the two Houses was seen in their rejection of measure after measure proposed by the Crown. A proposal to oust Elizabeth from the line of succession could not even be submitted to the Houses, nor could their assent be won to the postponing of her succession to that of Philip. Though the statutes abolishing Papal jurisdiction in England were repealed, they rejected all proposals for the restoration of Church-lands to the clergy. A proposal to renew the laws against heresy was thrown out by the Lords, even after the failure of Wyatt's insurrection, and only Philip's influence secured the re-enactment of the statute of Henry the Fifth in a later Parliament. Nor was the temper of the nation at large less decided. The sullen discontent of London compelled its Bishop, Bonner, to withdraw the inquisitorial articles by which he hoped to purge his diocese of heresy. Even the Council was divided on the question of persecution, and in the very interests of Catholicism the Emperor himself counselled prudence and delay. Philip gave the same counsel. But whether from without or from within, warning was wasted on the fierce bigotry of the Queen.

Rowland
Taylor

It was a moment when the prospects of the party of reform seemed utterly hopeless. Spain had taken openly the lead in the great Catholic movement, and England was being dragged, however reluctantly, by the Spanish marriage into the current of reaction. Its opponents were broken by the failure of their revolt, and unpopular through the memory of their violence and greed. Now that the laws against heresy were enacted, Mary pressed for their execution ; and in 1555 the opposition of her councillors was at last mastered, and the work of death began. But the cause which prosperity had ruined revived in the dark hour of persecution. If the Protestants had not known how to govern, they knew how to die. The story of Rowland Taylor, the Vicar of Hadleigh, tells us more of the work which was now begun, and of the effect it was likely to produce, than pages of historic dissertation. Taylor, who as a man of mark had been one of the first victims chosen for execution, was arrested in London, and condemned to suffer in his own parish. His wife, " suspecting that her husband should that night be carried away," had waited through the darkness with her children in the porch of St. Botolph's beside Aldgate. "Now when the sheriff his company came against St. Botolph's Church, Elizabeth cried, saying, 'O my dear father! Mother! mother! here is my father led away!' Then cried his wife, 'Rowland, Rowland, where art thou?'—for it was a very dark morning, that the one could not see the other. Dr. Taylor answered, 'I am here, dear wife,' and stayed. The sheriff's men would have led him forth, but the sheriff said, 'Stay a little, masters, I pray you, and let him speak to his wife.' Then came she to him, and he took his daughter Mary in his arms, and he and his wife and Elizabeth knelt down and said the Lord's prayer. At which sight the sheriff wept apace, and so did divers others of the company. After they had prayed he rose up and kissed his wife and shook her by the hand, and said, 'Farewell, my dear wife, be of good comfort, for I am quiet in my conscience! God shall still be a father to my children.' . . . Then said his wife, 'God be with thee, dear Rowland! I will, with God's grace, meet thee at Hadleigh.' . . . All the way Dr. Taylor was merry and cheerful as one that accounted himself going to a most pleasant banquet or bridal. . . . Coming within two miles of Hadleigh he desired to light off his horse, which done he leaped and set a frisk or twain as men commonly do for dancing. 'Why, master Doctor,' quoth the Sheriff, 'how do you now?' He answered, 'Well, God be praised, Master Sheriff, never better; for now I know I am almost at home. I lack not past two stiles to go over, and I am even at my Father's house!' . . . The streets of Hadleigh were beset on both sides with men and women of the town and country who waited to see him; whom when they beheld so led to death, with weeping eyes and lamentable voices, they cried, 'Ah, good Lord! there goeth our good shepherd from us!'" The journey was at last over. "'What place is this,' he asked, 'and what meaneth it that so much people are gathered together?' It was answered, 'It is Oldham Common, the place where you must suffer, and the people are come to look upon you.' Then said he, 'Thanked be God, I am even at home!' . . . . But when the people saw his reverend and ancient face, with a long white beard, they burst out with weeping tears and cried, saying, 'God save thee, good Dr. Taylor; God strengthen thee and help thee; the Holy Ghost comfort thee!' He wished, but was not suffered, to speak. When he had prayed, he went to the stake and kissed it, and set himself into a pitch-barrel which they had set for him to stand on, and so stood with his back upright against the stake, with his hands folded together and his eyes towards heaven, and so let himself be burned." One of the executioners "cruelly cast a fagot at him, which hit upon his head and brake his face that the blood ran down his visage. Then said Dr. Taylor, 'O friend, I have harm enough —what needed that?'" One more act of brutality brought his sufferings to an end.—"So stood he still without either crying or moving, with his

SEC. II.

THE
MARTYRS
1553
TO
1558
The
Martyrs

hands folded together, till Soyce with a halberd struck him on the head that the brains fell out, and the dead corpse fell down into the fire."

The terror of death was powerless against men like these. Bonner, the Bishop of London, to whom, as Bishop of the diocese in which the Council sate, its victims were generally delivered for execution, but who, in spite of the nickname and hatred which his official prominence in the work of death earned him, seems to have been naturally a good-humoured and merciful man, asked a youth who was brought before him whether he thought he could bear the fire. The boy at once held his hand without flinching in the flame of a candle which stood by. Rogers, a fellow-worker with Tyndale in the translation of the Bible, and one of the foremost among the Protestant preachers, died bathing his hands in the flame "as if it had been in cold water." Even the commonest lives gleamed for a moment into poetry at the stake. "Pray for me," a boy, William Hunter, who had been brought home to Brentwood to suffer, asked of the bystanders. "I will pray no more for thee," one of them replied, "than I will pray for a dog." "'Then,' said William, 'Son of God, shine upon me;' and immediately the sun in the elements shone out of a dark cloud so full in his face that he was constrained to look another way; whereat the people mused, be-cause it was so dark a little time before." The persecution fell heavily on London, and on Kent, Sussex, and the Eastern Counties, the homes of the mining and manufacturing industries; a host of Protestants were driven over sea to find refuge at Strasburg or Geneva. But the work of terror failed in the very ends for which it was wrought. The old spirit of insolent defiance, of outrageous violence, was roused again at the challenge of persecution. A Protestant hung a string of pud-dings round a priest's neck in derision of his beads. The restored images were grossly insulted. The old scurrilous ballads were heard again in the streets. One miserable wretch, driven to frenzy, stabbed the priest of St. Margaret's as he stood with the chalice in his hand. It was a more formidable sign of the times that acts of violence such as these no longer stirred the people at large to their former resent-ment. The horror of the persecution left no room for other feelings. Every death at the stake won hundreds to the cause of its victims. "You have lost the hearts of twenty thousands that were rank Papists," a Protestant wrote to Bonner, "within these twelve months." Bonner indeed, never a very zealous persecutor, was sick of his work; and the energy of the bishops soon relaxed. But Mary had no thought of hesitation in the course she had begun. "Rattling letters" from the council roused the lagging prelates to fresh activity and the mar-tyrdoms went steadily on. Two prelates had already perished; Hooper, the Bishop of Gloucester, had been burned in his own cathe-dral city; Ferrar, the Bishop of St. David's, had suffered at Caer-marthen. Latimer and Bishop Ridley of London were now drawn

from their prison at Oxford.   "Play the man, Master Ridley," cried
the old preacher of the Reformation as the flames shot up around him ;
" we shall this day light such a candle by God's grace in England as I
trust shall never be put out."   One victim remained, far beneath many
who had preceded him in character, but high above them in his position in the Church of England.   The other prelates who had suffered
had been created after the separation from Rome, and were hardly regarded as bishops by their opponents.   But, whatever had been his
part in the schism, Cranmer had received his Pallium from the Pope.
He was, in the eyes of all, Archbishop of Canterbury, the successor
of St. Augustine and of St. Thomas in the second see of Western
Christendom.   To burn the Primate of the English Church for heresy
was to shut out meaner victims from all hope of escape.   But revenge
and religious zeal alike urged Mary to bring Cranmer to the stake.
First among the many decisions in which the Archbishop had prostituted justice to Henry's will stood that by which he had annulled the
King's marriage with Catharine and declared Mary a bastard.   The
last of his political acts had been to join, whether reluctantly or no, in
the shameless plot to exclude Mary from the throne.   His great position too made him more than any man the representative of the religious revolution which had passed over the land.   His figure stood
with those of Henry and of Cromwell on the frontispiece of the
English Bible.   The decisive change which had been given to the
character of the Reformation under Edward was due wholly to
Cranmer.   It was his voice that men heard and still hear in the
accents of the English Liturgy.   As an Archbishop, Cranmer's judgment rested with no meaner tribunal than that of Rome, and his
execution had been necessarily delayed till its sentence could be
given.   But the courage which he had shown since the accession of
Mary gave way the moment his final doom was announced.   The
moral cowardice which had displayed itself in his miserable compliance with the lust and despotism of Henry displayed itself again
in six successive recantations by which he hoped to purchase pardon.
But pardon was impossible ; and Cranmer's strangely mingled nature
found a power in its very weakness when he was brought into the
church of St. Mary at Oxford to repeat his recantation on the way to
the stake.   "Now," ended his address to the hushed congregation
before him, "now I come to the great thing that troubleth my conscience more than any other thing that ever I said or did in my life,
and that is the setting abroad of writings contrary to the truth ; which
here I now renounce and refuse as things written by my hand contrary
to the truth which I thought in my heart, and written for fear of
death to save my life, if it might be.   And, forasmuch as my hand
offended in writing contrary to my heart, my hand therefore shall
be the first punished ; for if I come to the fire, it shall be the

SEC. II.

THE
MARTYRS
1553
TO
1558
The
Death of
Mary

first burned." "This was the hand that wrote it," he again exclaimed at the stake, "therefore it shall suffer first punishment;" and holding it steadily in the flame "he never stirred nor cried" till life was gone.

It was with the unerring instinct of a popular movement that, among a crowd of far more heroic sufferers, the Protestants fixed, in spite of his recantations, on the martyrdom of Cranmer as the death-blow to Catholicism in England. For one man who felt within him the joy of Rowland Taylor at the prospect of the stake, there were thousands who felt the shuddering dread of Cranmer. The triumphant cry of Latimer could reach only hearts as bold as his own; but the sad pathos of the Primate's humiliation and repentance struck chords of sympathy and pity in the hearts of all. It is from that moment that we may trace the bitter remembrance of the blood shed in the cause of Rome; which, however partial and unjust it must seem to an historic observer, still lies graven deep in the temper of the English people.

The overthrow of his projects for the permanent acquisition of England to the House of Austria had disenchanted Philip of his stay in the realm; and on the disappearance of all hope of a child, he had left the country in spite of Mary's passionate entreaties. But the Queen struggled desperately on. She did what was possible to satisfy the unyielding Pope. In the face of the Parliament's significant reluctance even to restore the first-fruits to the Church, she refounded all she could of the abbeys which had been suppressed; the greatest of these, that of Westminster, was re-established in 1556. Above all, she pressed on the work of persecution. It had spread now from bishops and priests to the people itself. The sufferers were sent in batches to the flames. In a single day thirteen victims, two of them women, were burnt at Stratford-le-Bow. Seventy-three Protestants of Colchester were dragged through the streets of London, tied to a single rope. A new commission for the suppression of heresy was exempted by royal authority from all restrictions of law which fettered its activity. The Universities were visited; and the corpses of foreign teachers who had found a resting place there under Edward were torn from their graves and reduced to ashes. The penalties of martial law were threatened against the possessors of heretical books issued from Geneva; the treasonable contents of which indeed, and their constant exhortations to rebellion and civil war, justly called for stern repression. But the work of terror broke down before the silent revolt of the whole nation. Open sympathy began to be shown to the sufferers for conscience' sake. In the three and a half years of the persecution nearly three hundred victims had perished at the stake. The people sickened at the work of death. The crowd round the fire at Smithfield shouted "Amen" to the prayer of seven martyrs whom Bonner had condemned, and prayed with them that God would strengthen them. A general discontent was roused when, in spite of the pledges given at her marriage, Mary dragged England into a war to support Philip—who on the Emperor's resignation had succeeded to his dominions of Spain, Flanders, and the New World —in a struggle against France. The war ended in disaster.. With characteristic secrecy and energy, the Duke of Guise flung himself upon Calais, and compelled it to surrender before succour could arrive "The chief jewel of the realm," as Mary herself called it, was suddenly reft away ; and the surrender of Guisnes, which soon followed, left England without a foot of land on the Continent. Bitterly as the blow was felt, the Council, though passionately pressed by the Queen, could find neither money nor men for any attempt to recover the town. The forced loan to which she resorted came in slowly. The levies mutinied and dispersed. The death of Mary alone averted a general revolt, and a burst of enthusiastic joy hailed the accession of Elizabeth.

Section III.—Elizabeth. 1558—1560.

[*Authorities.*—Camden's "Life of Elizabeth." For ecclesiastical matters, Strype's "Annals," his lives of Parker, Grindal, and Whitgift, and the "Zürich Letters" (Parker Society), are important. The State Papers are being calendared for the Master of the Rolls, and fresh light may be looked for from the Cecil Papers and the documents at Simancas, some of which are embodied in Mr. Froude's "History" (vols. vii. to xii.). We have also the Burleigh Papers, the Sidney Papers, the Sadler State Papers, the Hardwicke State Papers, letters published by Mr. Wright in his "Elizabeth and her Times," the collections of Murdin, the Egerton Papers, the "Letters of Elizabeth and James VI.," published by Mr. Bruce. The "Papiers d'Etat" of Cardinal Granvelle and the French despatches published by M. Teulet are valuable.]

Never had the fortunes of England sunk to a lower ebb than at the moment when Elizabeth mounted the throne. The country was humiliated by defeat and brought to the verge of rebellion by the bloodshed and misgovernment of Mary's reign. The old social discontent, trampled down for a time by the horsemen of Somerset, remained a menace to public order. The religious strife had passed beyond hope of reconciliation, now that the reformers were parted from their opponents by the fires of Smithfield and the party of the New Learning all but dissolved. The more earnest Catholics were bound helplessly to Rome. The temper of the Protestants, burned at home or driven into exile abroad, had become a fiercer thing, and the Calvinistic refugees were pouring back from Geneva with dreams of revolutionary change in Church and State. England, dragged at the heels of Philip into a useless and ruinous war, was left without an ally save Spain ; while France, mistress of Calais, became mistress of the Channel. Not only was Scotland a standing danger in the north, through the French marriage of its Queen Mary Stuart and its consequent bondage to French policy ; but Mary Stuart and her husband now assumed the style and arms of English sovereigns, and threatened to rouse every Catholic throughout the realm against Elizabeth's title. In presence of this host of dangers the country lay helpless, without army or fleet, or the means of manning one, for the treasury, already drained by the waste of Edward's reign, had been utterly exhausted by Mary's restoration of the Church-lands in possession of the Crown, and by the cost of her war with France.

England's one hope lay in the character of her Queen. Elizabeth was now in her twenty-fifth year. Personally she had more than her mother's beauty ; her figure was commanding, her face long but queenly and intelligent, her eyes quick and fine. She had grown up amidst the liberal culture of Henry's court a bold horsewoman, a good shot, a graceful dancer, a skilled musician, and an accomplished scholar. She studied every morning the Greek Testament, and followed this by the tragedies of Sophocles or orations of Demosthenes, and could " rub up her rusty Greek " at need to bandy pedantry with a Vice-Chancellor. But she was far from being a mere pedant. The new literature which was springing up around her found constant welcome in her court. She spoke Italian and French as fluently as her mother-tongue. She was familiar with Ariosto and Tasso. Even amidst the affectation and love of anagrams and puerilities which sullied her later years, she listened with delight to the " Faery Queen," and found a smile for " Master Spenser " when he appeared in her presence. Her moral temper recalled in its strange contrasts the mixed blood within her veins. She was at once the daughter of Henry and of Anne Boleyn. From her father she inherited her frank and hearty address, her love of popularity and of free intercourse with the people, her dauntless courage and her amazing self-confidence. Her harsh, manlike voice, her impetuous will, her pride, her furious outbursts of anger came to her with her Tudor blood. She rated great nobles as if they were schoolboys ; she met the insolence of Essex with a box on the ear ; she would break now and then into the gravest deliberations to swear at her ministers like a fishwife. But strangely in contrast with the violent outlines of her Tudor temper stood the sensuous, self-indulgent nature she derived from Anne Boleyn. Splendour and pleasure were with Elizabeth the very air she breathed. Her delight was to move in perpetual progresses from castle to castle through a series of gorgeous pageants, fanciful and extravagant as a caliph's dream. She loved gaiety and laughter and wit. A happy retort or a finished compliment never failed to win her favour. She hoarded jewels. Her dresses were innumerable. Her vanity remained, even to old age, the vanity of a coquette in her teens. No adulation was too fulsome for her, no flattery of her beauty too gross. " To see her was heaven," Hatton told her, " the lack of her was hell." She would play with her rings that her courtiers might note the delicacy of her hands; or dance a coranto that the French ambassador, hidden dexterously behind a curtain, might report her sprightliness to his master. Her levity, her frivolous laughter, her unwomanly jests gave colour to a thousand scandals. Her character in fact, like her portraits, was utterly without shade. Of womanly reserve or self-restraint she knew nothing. No instinct of delicacy veiled the voluptuous temper which had broken out in the romps of her girlhood and showed itself almost ostentatiously throughout her later life. Personal beauty in a man was a sure passport to her liking. She patted handsome young squires on the neck when they knelt to kiss her hand, and fondled her "sweet Robin," Lord Leicester, in the face of the court.

It was no wonder that the statesmen whom she outwitted held Elizabeth almost to the last to be little more than a frivolous woman, or that Philip of Spain wondered how "a wanton" could hold in check the policy of the Escurial. But the Elizabeth whom they saw was far from being all of Elizabeth. The wilfulness of Henry, the triviality of Anne Boleyn played over the surface of a nature hard as steel, a temper purely intellectual, the very type of reason untouched by imagination or passion. Luxurious and pleasure-loving as she seemed, Elizabeth lived simply and frugally, and she worked hard. Her vanity and caprice had no weight whatever with her in state affairs. The coquette of the presence-chamber became the coolest and hardest of politicians at the council-board. Fresh from the flattery of her courtiers, she would tolerate no flattery in the closet; she was herself plain and downright of speech with her counsellors, and she looked for a corresponding plainness of speech in return. If any trace of her sex lingered in her actual statesmanship, it was seen in the simplicity and tenacity of purpose that often underlies a woman's fluctuations of feeling. It was this in part which gave her her marked superiority over the statesmen of her time. No nobler group of ministers ever gathered round a council-board than those who gathered round the council-board of Elizabeth. But she was the instrument of none. She listened, she weighed, she used or put by the counsels of each in turn, but her policy as a whole was her own. It was a policy, not of genius, but of good sense. Her aims were simple and obvious: to preserve her throne, to keep England out of war, to restore civil and religious order. Something of womanly caution and timidity perhaps backed the passionless indifference with which she set aside the larger schemes of ambition which were ever opening before her eyes. She was resolute in her refusal of the Low Countries. She rejected with a laugh the offers of the Protestants to make her "head of the religion" and "mistress of the seas." But her amazing success in the end sprang mainly from this wise limitation of her aims. She had a finer sense than any of her counsellors of her real resources; she knew instinctively how far she could go, and what she could do.

Her cold, critical intellect was never swayed by enthusiasm or by panic either to exaggerate or to under-estimate her risks or her power.

Of political wisdom indeed in its larger and more generous sense Elizabeth had little or none ; but her political tact was unerring. She seldom saw her course at a glance, but she played with a hundred courses, fitfully and discursively, as a musician runs his fingers over the key-board, till she hit suddenly upon the right one. Her nature was essentially practical and of the present. She distrusted a plan in fact just in proportion to its speculative range or its out-look into the future. Her notion of statesmanship lay in watching how things turned out around her, and in seizing the moment for making the best of them. A policy of this limited, practical, tentative order was not only best suited to the England of her day, to its small resources and the transitional character of its religious and political belief, but it was one eminently suited to Elizabeth's peculiar powers. It was a policy of detail, and in details her wonderful readiness and ingenuity found scope for their exercise. " No War, my Lords," the Queen used to cry imperiously at the council-board, " No War ! " but her hatred of war sprang less from her aversion to blood or to expense, real as was her aversion to both, than from the fact that peace left the field open to the diplomatic manœuvres and intrigues in which she excelled. Her delight in the consciousness of her ingenuity broke out in a thousand puckish freaks, freaks in which one can hardly see any purpose beyond the purpose of sheer mystification. She revelled in "bye-ways" and " crooked ways." She played with grave cabinets as a cat plays with a mouse, and with much of the same feline delight in the mere embarrassment of her victims. When she was weary of mystifying foreign statesmen she turned to find fresh sport in mystifying her own ministers. Had Elizabeth written the story of her reign she would have prided herself, not on the triumph of England or the ruin of Spain, but on the skill with which she had hoodwinked and out-witted every statesman in Europe during fifty years. Nor was her trickery without political value. Ignoble, inexpressibly wearisome as the Queen's diplomacy seems to us now, tracing it as we do through a thousand despatches, it succeeded in its main end. It gained time, and every year that was gained doubled Elizabeth's strength. Nothing is more revolting in the Queen, but nothing is more characteristic, than her shameless mendacity. It was an age of political lying, but in the profusion and recklessness of her lies Elizabeth stood without a peer in Christendom. A falsehood was to her simply an intellectual means of meeting a difficulty ; and the ease with which she asserted or denied whatever suited her purpose was only equalled by the cynical indifference with which she met the exposure of her lies as soon as their purpose was answered. The same purely intellectual view of things showed itself in the dexterous use she made of her very faults. Her

VII.]

THE REFORMATION.

373

Sec. III.

Elizabeth

1558
TO
1560

levity carried her gaily over moments of detection and embarrassment where better women would have died of shame. She screened her tentative and hesitating statesmanship under the natural timidity and vacillation of her sex. She turned her very luxury and sports to good account. There were moments of grave danger in her reign when the country remained indifferent to its perils, as it saw the Queen give her days to hawking and hunting, and her nights to dancing and plays. Her vanity and affectation, her womanly fickleness and caprice, all had their part in the diplomatic comedies she played with the successive candidates for her hand. If political necessities made her life a lonely one, she had at any rate the satisfaction of averting war and conspiracies by love sonnets and romantic interviews, or of gaining a year of tranquillity by the dexterous spinning out of a flirtation.

As we track Elizabeth through her tortuous mazes of lying and intrigue, the sense of her greatness is almost lost in a sense of contempt. But wrapped as they were in a cloud of mystery, the aims of her policy were throughout temperate and simple, and they were pursued with a singular tenacity. The sudden acts of energy which from time to time broke her habitual hesitation proved that it was no hesitation of weakness. Elizabeth could wait and finesse ; but when the hour was come she could strike, and strike hard. Her natural temper indeed tended to a rash self-confidence rather than to self-distrust. She had, as strong natures always have, an unbounded confidence in her luck. "Her Majesty counts much on Fortune," Walsingham wrote bitterly ; "I wish she would trust more in Almighty God." The diplomatists who censured at one moment her irresolution, her delay, her changes of front, censure at the next her "obstinacy," her iron will, her defiance of what seemed to them inevitable ruin. "This woman," Philip's envoy wrote after a wasted remonstrance, "this woman is possessed by a hundred thousand devils." To her own subjects, indeed, who knew nothing of her manœuvres and retreats, of her "bye-ways" and "crooked ways," she seemed the embodiment of dauntless resolution. Brave as they were, the men who swept the Spanish Main or glided between the icebergs of Baffin's Bay never doubted that the palm of bravery lay with their Queen. Her steadiness and courage in the pursuit of her aims was equalled by the wisdom with which she chose the men to accomplish them. She had a quick eye for merit of any sort, and a wonderful power of enlisting its whole energy in her service. The sagacity which chose Cecil and Walsingham was just as unerring in its choice of the meanest of her agents. Her success indeed in securing from the beginning of her reign to its end, with the single exception of Leicester, precisely the right men for the work she set them to do sprang in great measure from the noblest characteristic of her intellect. If in loftiness of aim her temper fell below many of the tempers of her time, in the breadth of its range, in the universality of its sympathy it stood far above them all. Elizabeth could talk poetry with Spenser and philosophy with Bruno ; she could discuss Euphuism with Lyly, and enjoy the chivalry of Essex ; she could turn from talk of the last fashions to pore with Cecil over despatches and treasury books ; she could pass from tracking traitors with Walsingham to settle points of doctrine with Parker, or to calculate with Frobisher the chances of a north-west passage to the Indies. The versatility and many-sidedness of her mind enabled her to understand every phase of the intellectual movement of her day, and to fix by a sort of instinct on its higher representatives. But the greatness of the Queen rests above all on her power over her people. We have had grander and nobler rulers, but none so popular as Elizabeth. The passion of love, of loyalty, of admiration which finds its most perfect expression in the " Faery Queen," throbbed as intensely through the veins of her meanest subjects. To England, during her reign of half a century, she was a virgin and a Protestant Queen ; and her immorality, her absolute want of religious enthusiasm, failed utterly to blur the bright-ness of the national ideal. Her worst acts broke fruitlessly against the general devotion. A Puritan, whose hand she cut off in a freak of tyrannous resentment, waved his hat with the hand that was left, and shouted " God save Queen Elizabeth ! " Of her faults, indeed, England beyond the circle of her court knew little or nothing. The shiftings of her diplomacy were never seen outside the royal closet. The nation at large could only judge her foreign policy by its main outlines, by its temperance and good sense, and above all by its success. But every Englishman was able to judge Elizabeth in her rule at home, in her love of peace, her instinct of order, the firmness and moderation of her government, the judicious spirit of conciliation and compromise among warring factions which gave the country an unexampled tranquillity at a time when almost every other country in Europe was torn with civil war. Every sign of the growing prosperity, the sight of London as it became the mart of the world, of stately mansions as they rose on every manor, told, and justly told, in Elizabeth's favour. In one act of her civil administration she showed the boldness and originality of a great ruler ; for the opening of her reign saw her face the social difficulty which had so long impeded English progress, by the issue of a commission of inquiry which ended in the solution of the problem by the system of poor-laws. She lent a ready patronage to the new commerce ; she considered its extension and protection as a part of public policy, and her statue in the centre of the London Exchange was a tribute on the part of the merchant class to the interest with which she watched and shared personally in its enter-prises. Her thrift won a general gratitude. The memories of the Terror and of the Martyrs threw into bright relief the aversion from bloodshed which was conspicuous in her earlier reign, and never wholly wanting through its fiercer close. Above all there was a general confidence in her instinctive knowledge of the national temper. Her finger was always on the public pulse. She knew exactly when she could resist the feeling of her people, and when she must give way before the new sentiment of freedom which her policy unconsciously fostered. But when she retreated, her defeat had all the grace of victory; and the frankness and unreserve of her surrender won back at once the love that her resistance had lost. Her attitude at home in fact was that of a woman whose pride in the well-being of her subjects, and whose longing for their favour, was the one warm touch in the coldness of her natural temper. If Elizabeth could be said to love anything, she loved England. " Nothing," she said to her first Parliament in words of unwonted fire, " nothing, no worldly thing under the sun, is so dear to me as the love and good-will of my subjects." And the love and good-will which were so dear to her she fully won.

She clung perhaps to her popularity the more passionately that it hid in some measure from her the terrible loneliness of her life. She was the last of the Tudors, the last of Henry's children; and her nearest relatives were Mary Stuart and the House of Suffolk, one the avowed, the other the secret claimant of her throne. Among her mother's kindred she found but a single cousin. Whatever womanly tenderness she had, wrapt itself around Leicester; but a marriage with Leicester was impossible, and every other union, could she even have bent to one, was denied to her by the political difficulties of her position. The one cry of bitterness which burst from Elizabeth revealed her terrible sense of the solitude of her life. " The Queen of Scots," she cried at the birth of James, " has a fair son, and I am but a barren stock." But the loneliness of her position only reflected the loneliness of her nature. She stood utterly apart from the world around her, sometimes above it, sometimes below it, but never of it. It was only on its intellectual side that Elizabeth touched the England of her day. All its moral aspects were simply dead to her. It was a time when men were being lifted into nobleness by the new moral energy which seemed suddenly to pulse through the whole people, when honour and enthusiasm took colours of poetic beauty, and religion became a chivalry. But the finer sentiments of the men around her touched Elizabeth simply as the fair tints of a picture would have touched her. She made her market with equal indifference out of the heroism of William of Orange or the bigotry of Philip. The noblest aims and lives were only counters on her board. She was the one soul in her realm whom the news of St. Bartholomew stirred to no thirst for vengeance; and while England was thrilling with its triumph over the Armada, its Queen was coolly grumbling over the cost, and making her profit out of the spoiled provisions she had ordered for the fleet that saved her. To the voice of gratitude, indeed, she was for the most part deaf. She accepted services such as were never rendered to any other English sovereign without a thought of return. Walsingham spent his fortune in saving her life and her throne, and she left him to die a beggar. But, as if by a strange irony, it was to this very want of sympathy that she owed some of the grander features of her character. If she was without love she was without hate. She cherished no petty resentments; she never stooped to envy or suspicion of the men who served her. She was indifferent to abuse. Her good-humour was never ruffled by the charges of wantonness and cruelty with which the Jesuits filled every Court in Europe. She was insensible to fear. Her life became at last the mark for assassin after assassin, but the thought of peril was the one hardest to bring home to her. Even when the Catholic plots broke out in her very household she would listen to no proposals for the removal of Catholics from her court.

Elizabeth and the Church

It was this moral isolation which told so strangely both for good and for evil on her policy towards the Church. The young Queen was not without a sense of religion. But she was almost wholly destitute of spiritual emotion, or of any consciousness of the vast questions with which theology strove to deal. While the world around her was being swayed more and more by theological beliefs and controversies, Elizabeth was absolutely untouched by them. She was a child of the Italian Renascence rather than of the New Learning of Colet or Erasmus, and her attitude towards the enthusiasm of her time was that of Lorenzo de' Medici towards Savonarola. Her mind was unruffled by the spiritual problems which were vexing the minds around her; to Elizabeth indeed they were not only unintelligible, they were a little ridiculous. She had the same intellectual contempt for the superstition of the Romanist as for the bigotry of the Protestant. While she ordered Catholic images to be flung into the fire, she quizzed the Puritans as "brethren in Christ." But she had no sort of religious aversion from either Puritan or Papist. The Protestants grumbled at the Catholic nobles whom she admitted to the presence. The Catholics grumbled at the Protestant statesmen whom she called to her council-board. But to Elizabeth the arrangement was the most natural thing in the world. She looked at theological differences in a purely political light. She agreed with Henry the Fourth that a kingdom was well worth a mass. It seemed an obvious thing to her to hold out hopes of conversion as a means of deceiving Philip, or to gain a point in negotiation by restoring the crucifix to her chapel. The first interest in her own mind was the interest of public order, and she never could understand how it could fail to be first in every one's mind. Her ingenuity set itself to construct a system in which ecclesiastical unity should not jar against the rights of conscience; a compromise which merely required outer "conformity" to the established worship while, as she was never weary of repeating, it "left opinion free." She fell back from the very first on the system of Henry the Eighth. "I will do," she told the Spanish ambassador, "as my father did." She opened negotiations with the Papal See, till the Pope's summons to submit her claim of succession to the judgment of Rome made compromise impossible. The first work of her Parliament was to declare her legitimacy and title to the crown, to restore the royal supremacy, and to abjure all foreign authority and jurisdiction. At her entry into London Elizabeth kissed the English Bible which the citizens presented to her and promised "diligently to read therein." Further she had no personal wish to go. A third of the Council and at least two-thirds of the people were as opposed to any radical changes in religion as the Queen. Among the gentry the older and wealthier were on the conservative side, and only the younger and meaner on the other. But it was soon necessary to go further. If the Protestants were the less numerous, they were the abler and the more vigorous party; and the exiles who returned from Geneva brought with them a fiercer hatred of Catholicism. To every Protestant the Mass was identified with the fires of Smithfield, while Edward's Prayer-book was hallowed by the memories of the Martyrs. But if Elizabeth won the Protestants by an Act of Uniformity which restored the English Prayer-book and enforced its use on the clergy on pain of deprivation, the alterations she made in its language showed her wish to conciliate the Catholics as far as possible. She had no mind merely to restore the system of the Protectorate. She dropped the words "Head of the Church" from the royal title. The forty-two Articles which Cranmer had drawn up were left in abeyance. If Elizabeth had had her will, she would have retained the celibacy of the clergy and restored the use of crucifixes in the churches. In part indeed of her effort she was foiled by the increased bitterness of the reformers. The London mob tore down the crosses in the streets. Her attempt to retain the crucifix or enforce the celibacy of the priesthood fell dead before the opposition of the Protestant clergy. On the other hand, the Marian bishops, with a single exception, discerned the Protestant drift of the changes she was making, and bore imprisonment and deprivation rather than accept the oath required by the Act of Supremacy. But to the mass of the nation the compromise of Elizabeth seems to have been fairly acceptable. The bulk of the clergy, if they did not take the oath, practically submitted to the Act of Supremacy and adopted the Prayer-book. Of the few who openly refused only two hundred were deprived, and many went unharmed. No marked repugnance to the new worship was shown by the people at large; and Elizabeth was able to turn from questions of belief to the question of order.

She found in Matthew Parker, whom Pole's death enabled her to raise to the see of Canterbury, an agent in the reorganization of the Church whose patience and moderation were akin to her own. Theologically the Primate was a moderate man, but he was resolute to restore order in the discipline and worship of the Church. The whole machinery of English religion had been thrown out of gear by the rapid and radical changes of the past two reigns. The majority of the parish priests were still Catholic in heart; sometimes mass was celebrated at the parsonage for the more rigid Catholics, and the new communion in church for the more rigid Protestants. Sometimes both parties knelt together at the same altar-rails, the one to receive hosts consecrated by the priest at home after the old usage, the other wafers consecrated in Church after the new. In many parishes of the north no change of service was made at all. On the other hand, the new Protestant clergy were often unpopular, and roused the disgust of the people by their violence and greed. Chapters plundered their own estates by leases and fines and by felling timber. The marriages of the clergy became a scandal, which was increased when the gorgeous vestments of the old worship were cut up into gowns and bodices for the priests' wives. The new services sometimes turned into scenes of utter disorder where the clergy wore what dress they pleased and the communicant stood or sate as he liked; while the old altars were broken down and the communion-table was often a bare board upon trestles. The people, naturally enough, were found to be "utterly devoid of religion," and came to church "as to a May game." To the difficulties which Parker found in the temper of the reformers and their opponents new difficulties were added by the freaks of the Queen. If she had no convictions, she had tastes; and her taste revolted from the bareness of Protestant ritual and above all from the marriage of priests. "Leave that alone," she shouted to Dean Nowell from the royal closet as he denounced the use of images— "stick to your text, Master Dean, leave that alone!" When Parker was firm in resisting the introduction of the crucifix or of celibacy, Elizabeth showed her resentment at his firmness by an insult to his wife. Married ladies were addressed at this time as "Madam," unmarried ladies as "Mistress;" and when Mrs. Parker advanced at the close of a sumptuous entertainment at Lambeth to take leave of the Queen, Elizabeth feigned a momentary hesitation. "Madam," she said at last, "I may not call you, and Mistress I am loth to call you; however, I thank you for your good cheer." To the end of her reign indeed Elizabeth remained as bold a plunderer of the wealth of the bishops as either of her predecessors, and carved out rewards for her ministers from the Church-lands with a queenly disregard of the rights of property. Lord Burleigh built up the estate of the house of Cecil out of the demesnes of the see of Peterborough. The neighbourhood of Hatton Garden to Ely Place recalls the spoliation of another bishopric in favour of the Queen's sprightly chancellor. Her reply to the bishop's protest against this robbery showed what Elizabeth meant by her Ecclesiastical Supremacy. "Proud prelate," she wrote, "you know what you were before I made you what you are! If you do not immediately comply with my request, by God I will unfrock you." But freaks of this sort had little real influence beside the steady support which the Queen gave to the Primate in his work of order. She suffered no plunder save her own, and she was earnest for the restoration of order and decency in the outer arrangements of the Church. The vacant sees were filled for the most part with learned and able men ; and England seemed to settle quietly down in a religious peace.

The settlement of religion however was not the only pressing care which met Elizabeth as she mounted the throne. The country was drained by war ; yet she could only free herself from war, and from the dependence on Spain which it involved, by acquiescing in the loss of Calais. But though peace was won by the sacrifice, France remained openly hostile ; the Dauphin and his wife, Mary Stuart, had assumed the arms and style of King and Queen of England ; and their pretensions became a source of immediate danger through the presence of a French army in Scotland. To understand, however, what had taken place there we must cursorily review the past history of the Northern Kingdom. From the moment when England finally abandoned the fruitless effort to subdue it the story of Scotland had been a miserable one. Whatever peace might be concluded, a sleepless dread of the old danger from the south tied the country to an alliance with France, which dragged it into the vortex of the Hundred Years' War. But after the final defeat and capture of David in the field of Neville's Cross the struggle died down on both sides into marauding forays and battles, like those of Otterburn and Homildon Hill, in which alternate victories were won by the feudal lords of the Scotch or English border. The ballad of " Chevy Chase" brings home to us the spirit of the contest, the daring and defiance which stirred Sidney's heart " more than with a trumpet." But its effect on the internal developement of Scotland was utterly ruinous. The houses of Douglas and of March which it raised into supremacy only interrupted their strife with England to battle fiercely with one another or to coerce their King. The power of the Crown sank in fact into insignificance under the earlier sovereigns of the line of Stuart which had succeeded to the throne on the extinction of the male line of Bruce. Invasions and civil feuds not only arrested but even rolled back the national industry and prosperity. The country was a chaos of disorder and misrule, in which the peasant and the trader were the victims of feudal outrage. The Border became a lawless land, where robbery and violence reigned utterly without

SEC. III.

ELIZABETH

1558
TO
1560

1411

1424

1437

1502

1513

1542

1547

1558

check. So pitiable seemed the state of the kingdom that the clans of the Highlands drew together at last to swoop upon it as a certain prey; but the common peril united the factions of the nobles, and the victory of Harlaw saved the Lowlands from the rule of the Celt. A great name at last broke the line of the Scottish kings. Schooled by a long captivity in England, James the First returned to his realm to be the ablest of her rulers as he was the first of her poets. In the thirteen years of a short but wonderful reign justice and order were restored for a while, the Scotch Parliament organized, the clans of the Highlands assailed in their own fastnesses and reduced to swear fealty to the "Saxon" King. James turned to deal with the great houses, but feudal violence was still too strong for the hand of the law, and a band of ruffians who burst into the royal chamber left the King lifeless with sixteen stabs in his body. His death was the signal for a struggle between the House of Douglas and the Crown, which lasted through half a century. Order, however, crept gradually in; the exile of the Douglases left the Scottish monarchs supreme in the Lowlands; while their dominion over the Highlands was secured by the ruin of the Lords of the Isles. But in its outer policy the country still followed in the wake of France; every quarrel between French King and English King brought danger with it on the Scottish border; till Henry the Seventh bound England and Scotland together for a time by bestowing in 1502 the hand of his daughter Margaret on the Scottish king. The union was dissolved however by the strife with France which followed the accession of Henry the Eighth; war broke out anew, and the terrible defeat and death of James the Fourth at Flodden Field involved his realm in the turbulence and misrule of a minority. His successor James the Fifth, though nephew of the English King, from the outset of his reign took up an attitude hostile to England; and Church and people were ready to aid in plunging the two countries into a fresh struggle. His defeat at Solway Moss brought the young King broken-hearted to his grave. "It came with a lass, and it will go with a lass," he cried, as they brought him on his death-bed the news of Mary Stuart's birth. The hand of his infant successor at once became the subject of rivalry between England and France. Had Mary, as Henry the Eighth desired, been wedded to Edward the Sixth, the whole destinies of Europe might have been changed by the union of the two realms; but the recent bloodshed had embittered Scotland, and the high-handed way in which Somerset pushed the marriage project completed the breach. Somerset's invasion and victory at Pinkie Cleugh only enabled Mary of Guise, the French wife of James the Fifth, who had become Regent of the realm at his death, to induce the Scotch estates to consent to the union of her child with the heir of the French crown, the Dauphin Francis. From that moment, as we have seen, the claims of the Scottish Queen on

SEC. III.

ELIZABETH
1558
TO
1560

Elizabeth
and
Scotland

1559

the English throne became so formidable a danger as to drive Mary Tudor to her marriage with Philip of Spain. But the danger became a still greater one on the accession of Elizabeth, whose legitimacy no Catholic acknowledged, and whose religious attitude tended to throw the Catholic party into her rival's hands.

In spite of the peace with France, therefore, Francis and Mary persisted in their pretensions; and a French force landed at Leith, with the connivance of Mary of Guise. The appearance of this force on the Border was intended to bring about a Catholic rising. But the hostility between France and Spain bound Philip, for the moment, to the support of Elizabeth; and his influence over the Catholics secured quiet for a time. The Queen, too, played with their hopes of a religious reaction by talk of her own reconciliation with the Papacy and admission of a Papal legate to the realm, and by plans for her marriage with an Austrian and Catholic prince. Meanwhile she parried the blow in Scotland itself, where the Reformation had begun rapidly to gain ground, by secretly encouraging the "Lords of the Congregation," as the nobles who headed the Protestant party were styled, to rise against the Regent. Since her accession Elizabeth's diplomacy had gained her a year, and her matchless activity had used the year to good purpose. Order was restored throughout England, the Church was reorganized, the debts of the Crown were in part paid off, the treasury was recruited, a navy created, and a force ready for action in the north, when the defeat of her Scotch adherents forced her at last to throw aside the mask. As yet she stood almost alone in her self-reliance. Spain believed her ruin to be certain; France despised her chances; her very Council was in despair. The one minister in whom she dared to confide was Cecil, the youngest and boldest of her advisers, and even Cecil trembled for her success. But lies and hesitation were no sooner put aside than the Queen's vigour and tenacity came fairly into play. At a moment when D'Oysel, the French commander, was on the point of crushing the Lords of the Congregation, an English fleet appeared suddenly in the Forth and forced the Regent's army to fall back upon Leith. The Queen made a formal treaty with the Lords, and promised to assist them in the expulsion of the strangers. France was torn by internal strife, and could send neither money nor men. In March, Lord Grey moved over the border with 8,000 men to join the Lords of the Congregation in the siege of Leith. The Scots indeed gave little aid; and an assault on the town signally failed. Philip too in a sudden jealousy of Elizabeth's growing strength demanded the abandonment of the enterprise. But Elizabeth was immovable. Famine did its work better than the sword; and in two treaties with the Scotch and English, the envoys of Francis and Mary at last promised to withdraw the French, and leave the government to a Council of the Lords; and acknowledged

Sec. IV.

England
and Mary
Stuart

1560
to
1572

Elizabeth's title to her throne.   A Scotch Parliament at once declared
Calvinism the national religion.   Both Act and Treaty indeed were set
aside by Francis and Mary, but Elizabeth's policy had in fact broken
the dependence of Scotland on France, and bound to her side the
strongest and most vigorous party among its nobles.

Section IV.—England and Mary Stuart. 1560—1572.

[*Authorities.*—As before.   Ranke's "English History," "History of the Reformation," by Knox.   For Mary Stuart, the works of Buchanan and Leslie,
Melville's Memoirs, collections of Keith and Anderson.   For the Dutch revolt
Motley's "Rise of the Dutch Republic," and "History of the United Netherlands."]

**Mary
Stuart**

The issue of the Scotch war revealed suddenly to Europe the vigour
of Elizabeth, and the real strength of her throne.   She had freed
herself from the control of Philip, she had defied France, she had
averted the danger from the North by the creation of an English
party among the nobles of Scotland.   The same use of religious divisions gave her a similar check on the hostility of France.   The
Huguenots, as the French Protestants were called, had become a
formidable party under the guidance of the Admiral Coligni, and
the defeat of their rising against the family of the Guises, who stood
at the head of the French Catholics and were supreme at the Court
of Francis and Mary, threw them on the support and alliance of

1560

Elizabeth.   But if the decisive outbreak of the great religious struggle,
so long looked for between the Old Faith and the New, gave Elizabeth
strength abroad, it weakened her at home.   Her Catholic subjects lost
all hope of her conversion as they saw the Queen allying herself with
Scotch Calvinists and French Huguenots ; her hopes of a religious
compromise in matters of worship were broken by the issue of a Papal
brief which forbade attendance at the English service ; and Philip of
Spain, freed like herself from the fear of France by its religious divisions, had less reason to hold the English Catholics in check.   He
was preparing, in fact, to take a new political stand as the patron
of Catholicism throughout the world ; and his troops were directed
to support the Guises in the civil war which broke out after the death
of Francis the Second, and to attack the heretics wherever they
might find them.   "Religion," he told Elizabeth, "was being made
a cloak for anarchy and revolution."   It was at the moment when
the last hopes of the English Catholics were dispelled by the Queen's

1561

refusal to take part in the Council of Trent that Mary Stuart, whom
the death of her husband had left a stranger in France, landed
at Leith.   Girl as she was, and she was only nineteen, she was
hardly inferior in intellectual power to Elizabeth herself, while in fire
and grace and brilliancy of temper she stood high above her.   She

Sec. IV.

England
and Mary
Stuart

1560
to
1572

brought with her the voluptuous refinement of the French Renascence : she would lounge for days in bed, and rise only at night for dances and music. But her frame was of iron, and incapable of fatigue ; she galloped ninety miles after her last defeat without a pause save to change horses. She loved risk and adventure and the ring of arms ; as she rode in a foray to the north, the grim swordsmen beside her heard her wish she was a man, "to know what life it was to lie all night in the fields, or to walk on the cawsey with a Glasgow buckler and a broadsword." But in the closet she was as cool and astute a politician as Elizabeth herself ; with plans as subtle, but of a far wider and grander range than the Queen's. "Whatever policy is in all the chief and best practised heads of France," wrote an English envoy, "whatever craft, falsehood, and deceit is in all the subtle brains of Scotland, is either fresh in this woman's memory, or she can fetch it out with a wet finger." Her beauty, her exquisite grace of manner, her generosity of temper and warmth of affection, her frankness of speech, her sensibility, her gaiety, her womanly tears, her manlike courage, the play and freedom of her nature, the flashes of poetry that broke from her at every intense moment of her life, flung a spell over friend or foe which has only deepened with the lapse of years. Even to Knollys, the sternest Puritan of his day, she seemed in her captivity to be "a notable woman." "She seemeth to regard no ceremonious honour besides the acknowledgement of her estate royal. She showeth a disposition to speak much, to be bold, to be pleasant, to be very familiar. She showeth a great desire to be avenged on her enemies. She showeth a readiness to expose herself to all perils in hope of victory. She desireth much to hear of hardiness and valiancy, commending by name all approved hardy men of her country though they be her enemies, and she concealeth no cowardice even in her friends." As yet men knew nothing of the stern bigotry, the intensity of passion, which lay beneath the winning surface of Mary's woman-hood. But they at once recognized her political ability. She had seized eagerly on the new strength which was given her by her husband's death. Her cause was no longer hampered, either in Scotland or in England, by a national jealousy of French interference. It was with a resolve to break the league between Elizabeth and the Scotch Protestants, to unite her own realm around her, and thus to give a firm base for her intrigues among the English Catholics, that Mary landed at Leith. The effect of her presence was marvellous. Her personal fascination revived the national loyalty, and swept all Scotland to her feet. Knox, the greatest and sternest of the Calvinistic preachers, alone withstood her spell. The rough Scotch nobles owned that there was in Mary "some enchantment whereby men are bewitched." A promise of religious toleration united her subjects in support of the claim which she advanced to be named Elizabeth's successor. But

SEC. IV.

ENGLAND
AND MARY
STUART
1560
TO
1572

the question of the succession, like the question of her marriage, was with Elizabeth a question of life and death. Her wedding with a Catholic or a Protestant suitor would have been equally the end of her system of balance and national union, a signal for the revolt of the party which she disappointed and for the triumphant dictation of the party which she satisfied. "If a Catholic prince come here," a Spanish ambassador wrote while pressing an Austrian marriage, "the first Mass he attends will be the signal for a revolt." It was so with the question of the succession. To name a Protestant successor from the House of Suffolk would have driven every Catholic to insurrection. To name Mary was to stir Protestantism to a rising of despair, and to leave Elizabeth at the mercy of every fanatical assassin who wished to clear the way for a Catholic ruler. "I am not so foolish," was the Queen's reply to Mary, "as to hang a winding-sheet before my eyes."

But the pressure on her was great, and Mary looked to the triumph of Catholicism in France to increase the pressure. It was this which drove Elizabeth to listen to the cry of the Huguenots at the moment when they were yielding to the strength of the Guises. Hate war as she might, the instinct of self-preservation dragged her into the great struggle; and in spite of the menaces of Philip, money and six thousand men were promised to the aid of the Protestants under Condé. But a fatal overthrow of the Huguenot army at Dreux left the Guises masters of France, and brought the danger to the very doors of England. The hopes of the English Catholics rose higher. Though the Pope delayed to issue his Bull of Deposition, a Papal brief pronounced

joining in the Common Prayer schismatic, and forbade the attendance of Catholics at church. With the issue of this brief the conformity of worship which Elizabeth had sought to establish came to an end. The hotter Catholics withdrew from church. Heavy fines were laid on them as recusants; fines which, as their numbers increased, became a valuable source of supply for the exchequer. But no fines could compensate for the moral blow which their withdrawal dealt. It was the beginning of a struggle which Elizabeth had averted through three memorable years. Protestant fanaticism met Catholic fanaticism. The tidings of Dreux spread panic through the realm. Parliament showed its terror by measures of a new severity. "There has been enough of words," said the Queen's minister, Sir Francis Knollys; "it were time to draw

sword." The sword was drawn in a Test Act, the first in a series of penal statutes which weighed upon English Catholics for two hundred years. By this statute an oath of allegiance to the Queen and abjuration of the temporal authority of the Pope was exacted from all holders of office, lay or spiritual, with the exception of peers. Its effect was to place the whole power of the realm in the hands either of Protestants, or of Catholics who accepted Elizabeth's legitimacy and her ecclesiastical jurisdiction in the teeth of the Papacy. Caution indeed was used in applying this test to the laity, but pressure was more roughly put on the clergy. Many of the parish priests, though they had submitted to the use of the Prayer-book, had not taken the oath prescribed by the Act of Uniformity. As yet Elizabeth had cautiously refused to allow any strict inquiry into their opinions. But a commission was now opened by her order at Lambeth, with the Primate at its head, to enforce the Act, while thirty-nine of the Articles drawn up under Edward were adopted as a standard of faith, and acceptance of them demanded of the clergy.

SEC. IV.

ENGLAND
AND MARY
STUART

1560
TO
1572

It is possible that Elizabeth might have clung to her older policy of conciliation had she foreseen how suddenly the danger that appalled her was to pass away. At this crisis she was able, as usual, to "count on Fortune." The assassination of the Duke of Guise broke up his party; a policy of moderation and balance prevailed at the French Court; Catharine of Medicis was now supreme, and her aim was still an aim of peace. The Queen's good luck was chequered by a merited humiliation. She had sold her aid to the Huguenots in their hour of distress at the price of the surrender of Havre, and Havre was again wrested from her by the reunion of the French parties. Peace with France in the following spring secured her a year's respite in her anxieties; and Mary was utterly foiled in her plan for bringing the pressure of a united Scotland, backed by France, to bear upon her rival. But the defeat only threw her on a yet more formidable scheme. She was weary of the mask of religious indifference which her policy had forced her to wear with the view of securing the general support of her subjects. She resolved now to appeal to the English Catholics on the ground of Catholicism. Next to the Scottish Queen in the line of blood stood Henry Stuart, Lord Darnley, a son of the Countess of Lennox, and grandson of Margaret Tudor by her second marriage with the Earl of Angus, as Mary was her grandchild by Margaret's first marriage with James the Fourth. Though the house of Lennox conformed to the new system of English worship, its sympathies were known to be Catholic, and the hopes of the Catholics wrapped themselves round its heir. It was by a match with Henry Stuart that Mary now determined to unite the forces of Catholicism. The match was regarded on all sides as a challenge to Protestantism. Philip had till now looked upon Mary's system of toleration and on her hopes from France with equal suspicion. But he now drew slowly to her side. "She is the one gate," he owned, "through which Religion can be restored in England. All the rest are closed." It was in vain that Elizabeth strove to prevent the marriage by a threat of war, or by secret plots for the seizure of Mary and the driving of Darnley back over the border. The Lords of the Congregation woke with a start from their confidence in the Queen, and her half-brother, Lord James Stuart, better known as Earl of Murray, mustered his Protestant confederates. But their revolt was hardly

C C

SEC. IV.

ENGLAND
AND MARY
STUART

1560
TO
1572

declared when Mary marched on them with pistols in her belt, and drove their leaders helplessly over the border. A rumour spread that she was in league with Spain and with France, where the influences of the Guises was again strong. Elizabeth took refuge in the meanest dissimulation, while the announcement of Mary's pregnancy soon gave her a strength which swept aside Philip's counsels of caution and delay. "With the help of God and of your Holiness," Mary wrote to the Pope, "I will leap over the wall." Rizzio, an Italian who had counselled the marriage, still remained her adviser, and the daring advice he gave fell in with her natural temper. She demanded a recognition of her succession. She resolved in the coming Parliament to restore Catholicism in Scotland; and to secure the banishment of Murray and his companions. The English Catholics of the North were ready to revolt as soon as she was ready to aid them. No such danger had ever threatened Elizabeth as this, but again she could "trust to Fortune." Mary had staked all on her union with Darnley, and yet only a few months had passed since her wedding day when men saw that she "hated the King." The boy turned out a dissolute, insolent husband; and Mary's scornful refusal of his claim of the "crown matrimonial," a refusal which Darnley attributed to Rizzio's counsels, drove his jealousy to madness. At the very moment when the Queen revealed the extent of her schemes by her dismissal of the English ambassador, the young King, followed by his kindred the Douglases, burst into her chamber, dragged Rizzio from her presence, and stabbed him brutally in an outer chamber. The darker features of Mary's character were now to develope themselves. Darnley, keen as was her thirst for vengeance on him, was needful to the triumph of her political aims. She masked her hatred beneath a show of affection, which succeeded in severing the wretched boy from his fellow-conspirators, and in gaining his help in an escape to Dunbar. Once free, she marched in triumph on Edinburgh at the head of eight thousand men under the Earl of Bothwell, while Morton, Ruthven, and Lindesay fled in terror over the border. With wise dissimulation, however, she fell back on her system of religious toleration. But her intrigues with the English Catholics were never interrupted, and her Court was full of refugees from the northern counties. "Your actions," Elizabeth wrote in a sudden break of fierce candour, "are as full of venom as your words are of honey." The birth of her child, the future James the Sixth of Scotland and First of England, doubled Mary's strength. "Your friends are so increased," her ambassador wrote to her from England, "that many whole shires are ready to rebel, and their captains named by election of the nobility." The anxiety of the English Parliament which met at this crisis proved that the danger was felt to be real. The Houses saw but one way of providing against it; and they renewed their appeal for the Queen's marriage and for a settlement of the succession. As we have seen, both of these measures

1566

SEC. IV.

ENGLAND
AND MARY
STUART
1560
TO
1572

involved even greater dangers than they averted; but Elizabeth stood alone in her resistance to them. To settle the succession was at once to draw the sword. The Queen therefore on this point stood firm. The promise to marry, which she gave after a furious burst of anger, she was no doubt resolved to evade as she had evaded it before. But the quarrel with the Commons which followed on her prohibition of any debate on the succession, a quarrel to which we shall recur at a later time, hit Elizabeth hard. It was "secret foes at home," she told the Commons as their quarrel passed away in a warm reconciliation, "who thought to work me that mischief which never foreign enemies could bring to pass, which is the hatred of my Commons. Do you think that either I am so unmindful of your surety by succession, wherein is all my care, or that I went about to break your liberties? No! it never was my meaning; but to stay you before you fell into the ditch." It was impossible for her however to explain the real reasons for her course, and the dissolution of the Parliament left her face to face with a national discontent added to the ever-deepening peril from without.

One terrible event suddenly struck light through the gathering clouds. Mary had used Darnley as a tool to effect the ruin of his confederates and to further her policy, but since his share in Rizzio's murder she had loathed and avoided him. Ominous words dropped from her lips. "Unless she were freed of him some way," she said, "she had no pleasure to live." Her purpose of vengeance was quickened by her passion for the Earl of Bothwell, the boldest and most unscrupulous of the border nobles. The Earl's desperate temper shrank from no obstacles to a union with the Queen. Divorce would free him from his own wife. Darnley might be struck down by a conspiracy of the lords whom he had deserted and betrayed, and who still looked on him as their bitterest foe. The exiled nobles were recalled; there were dark whispers among the lords. The terrible secret of the deed which followed is still wrapt in a cloud of doubt and mystery which will probably never be wholly dispelled. The Queen's mood seemed suddenly to change. Her hatred to Darnley passed all at once into demonstrations of the old affection. He had fallen sick with vice and misery, and she visited him on his sick bed, and persuaded him to follow her to Edinburgh. She visited him again in a ruinous and lonely house near the palace, in which he was lodged by her order, kissed him as she bade him farewell, and rode gaily back to a wedding-dance at Holyrood. Two hours after midnight an awful explosion shook the city; and the burghers rushed out from the gates to find the house of Kirk o' Field destroyed, and Darnley's body dead beside the ruins. The murder was undoubtedly the deed of Bothwell. His servant, it was soon known, had stored the powder beneath the King's bed-chamber; and the Earl had watched without the walls till

Sec. IV.

England
and Mary
Stuart.
1560
to
1572

the deed was done. But, in spite of gathering suspicion and of a charge of murder made formally against him by Lord Lennox, no serious steps were taken to investigate the crime ; and a rumour that Mary proposed to marry the murderer drove her friends to despair. Her agent in England wrote to her that " if she married that man she would lose the favour of God, her own reputation, and the hearts of all England, Ireland, and Scotland." But every stronghold in the kingdom was soon placed in Bothwell's hands, and this step was the prelude to a trial and acquittal which the overwhelming force of his followers in Edinburgh turned into a bitter mockery. A shameless suit for his divorce removed the last obstacle to his ambition ; and a seizure of the Queen as she rode to Linlithgow was followed by a marriage. In a month more all was over. The horror at such a marriage with a man fresh from her husband's blood drove the whole nation to revolt. Its nobles, Catholic as well as Protestant, gathered in arms at Stirling ; and their entrance into Edinburgh roused the capital into insurrection. Mary and the Earl advanced with a fair force to Seton to encounter the Lords ; but their men refused to fight, and Bothwell galloped off into lifelong exile, while the Queen was brought back to Edinburgh in a frenzy of despair, tossing back wild words of defiance to the curses of the crowd. From Edinburgh she was carried a prisoner to the fortress of Lochleven ; as the price of her life she was forced to resign her crown in favour of her child, and to name her brother, the Earl of Murray, who was now returning from France, as regent. In July the babe was solemnly crowned as James the Sixth.

For the moment England was saved, but the ruin of Mary's hopes had not come one instant too soon. The great conflict between the two religions, which had begun in France, was slowly widening into a general struggle over the whole face of Europe. For four years the balanced policy of Catharine of Medicis had wrested a truce from both Catholics and Huguenots, but Condé and the Guises again rose in arms, each side eager to find its profit in the new troubles which now broke out in Flanders. For the long persecution of the Protestants there, and the unscrupulous invasion of the constitutional liberties of the Provinces by Philip of Spain, had at last stirred the Netherlands to revolt ; and the insurrection was seized by Philip as a pretext for dealing a blow he had long meditated at the growing heresy of this portion of his dominions. At the moment when Mary entered Lochleven, the Duke of Alva was starting with an army of ten thousand men on his march to the Low Countries ; and with his easy triumph over their insurgent forces began the terrible series of outrages and massacres which have made his name infamous in history. No event could be more embarrassing to Elizabeth than the arrival of Alva in Flanders. His extirpation of heresy there would prove the prelude for his

co-operation with the Guises in the extirpation of heresy in France.
Without counting, too, this future danger, the triumph of Catholicism
and the presence of a Catholic army in a country so closely connected
with England at once revived the dreams of a Catholic rising against
her throne ; while the news of Alva's massacres stirred in every one of
her Protestant subjects a thirst for revenge which it was hard to hold
in check.   Yet to strike a blow at Alva was impossible, for Antwerp
was the great mart of English trade, and a stoppage of the trade with
Flanders, such as war would bring about, would have broken half the
merchants in London.   Every day was deepening the perplexities of
Elizabeth, when Mary succeeded in making her escape from Lochleven.
Defeated at Langside, where the energy of Murray promptly crushed
the rising of the Catholic nobles in her support, she abandoned all
hope of Scotland ; and changing her designs with the rapidity of
genius, she pushed in a light boat across the Solway, and was safe
before evening fell in the castle of Carlisle.   The presence of Alva
in Flanders was a far less peril than the presence of Mary in Carlisle.
To retain her in England was to furnish a centre for revolt ; Mary
herself indeed threatened that " if they kept her prisoner they should
have enough to do with her."   Her ostensible demand was for English
aid in her restoration to the throne, or for a free passage to France : but
compliance with the last request would have given the Guises a terrible
weapon against Elizabeth and have ensured a new French intervention
in Scotland, while to restore her by arms to the crown she had lost
was impossible.   Till Mary was cleared of guilt, Murray would hear
nothing of her return, and Mary refused to submit to such a trial as
would clear her.   So eager, however, was Elizabeth to get rid of the
pressing peril of her presence in England, that Mary's refusal to submit
to any trial only drove her to fresh devices for her restoration.   She
urged upon Murray the suppression of the graver charges, and upon
Mary the leaving Murray in actual possession of the royal power as
the price of her return.   Neither however would listen to terms which
sacrificed both to Elizabeth's self-interest ; the Regent persisted in
charging the Queen with murder and adultery, while Mary refused
either to answer or to abdicate in favour of her infant son.   The
triumph indeed of her bold policy was best advanced, as the Queen of
Scots had no doubt foreseen, by simple inaction.   Her misfortunes,
her resolute denials, were gradually wiping away the stain of her guilt,
and winning back the Catholics of England to her cause.   Elizabeth
" had the wolf by the ears," while the fierce contest which Alva's
presence roused in the Netherlands and in France was firing the
temper of the two great parties in England.

In the Court, as in the country, the forces of progress and of
resistance stood at last in sharp and declared opposition to each other.
Cecil at the head of the Protestants demanded a general alliance

SEC. IV.

ENGLAND
AND MARY
STUART
1560
TO
1572

with the Protestant churches throughout Europe, a war in the Low
Countries against Alva, and the unconditional surrender of Mary to
her Scotch subjects for the punishment she deserved.   The Catholics
on the other hand, backed by the mass of the Conservative party with
the Duke of Norfolk at its head, and supported by the wealthier merchants who dreaded the ruin of the Flemish trade, were as earnest in
demanding the dismissal of Cecil and the Protestants from the council-
board, a steady peace with Spain, and, though less openly, a recognition
of Mary's succession.   Elizabeth was driven to temporize as before.
She refused Cecil's counsels ; but she sent money and arms to Condé,
and hampered Alva by seizing treasure on its way to him, and by
pushing the quarrel even to a temporary embargo on shipping either
side the sea.   She refused the counsels of Norfolk ; but she would hear
nothing of a declaration of war, or give any judgement on the charges
against the Scottish Queen, or recognize the accession of James in her
stead.   The effect of Mary's presence in England was seen in conspiracies
of Norfolk with the Northern Earls and with Spain.   Elizabeth, roused to
her danger, struck quick and hard.   Mary Stuart was given in charge
to Lord Huntingdon.   Arundel, Pembroke, and Lumley were secured,
and Norfolk sent to the Tower.   But the disasters of the Huguenots in

France, and the news brought by a papal envoy that a Bull of Deposition
against Elizabeth was ready at Rome. goaded the great Catholic
lords to action, and brought about the rising of the houses of Neville
and of Percy.   The entry of the Earls of Northumberland and Westmoreland into Durham proved the signal for revolt.   The Bible and
Prayer-book were torn to pieces, and Mass said once more at the altar
of Durham Cathedral, before the Earls pushed on to Doncaster with an
army which soon swelled to thousands of men.   Their cry was " to reduce all causes of religion to the old custom and usage ; " and the Earl
of Sussex, her general in the north, wrote frankly to Elizabeth that
" there were not ten gentlemen in Yorkshire that did allow [approve]
her proceedings in the cause of religion." But he was as loyal as he
was frank, and held York stoutly while the Queen ordered Mary's hasty
removal to a new prison at Coventry.   The storm however broke as
rapidly as it had gathered.   The mass of the Catholics throughout the
country made no sign ; and the Earls no sooner halted irresolute in
presence of this unexpected inaction than their army caught the panic
and dispersed.   Northumberland and Westmoreland fled, and were
followed in their flight by Leonard Dacres of Naworth, while their
miserable adherents paid for their disloyalty in bloodshed and ruin.
The ruthless measures of repression which closed this revolt were the
first breach in the clemency of Elizabeth's rule.   But they were signs
of terror which were not lost on her opponents.   It was the general
inaction of the Catholics which had foiled the hopes of the northern

Earls ; and Rome now did its best to stir them to activity by publishing the Bull of Excommunication and Deposition against the Queen, which had been secretly issued in the preceding year, and was found nailed in a spirit of ironical defiance on the Bishop of London's door. The Catholics of the north withdrew stubbornly from the national worship. Everywhere the number of recusants increased. Intrigues were busier than ever. The regent Murray was assassinated, and Scotland plunged into war between the adherents of Mary and those of her son. From the defeated Catholics Mary turned again to the Duke of Norfolk, who stood at the head of the Conservative peers. Norfolk had acquiesced in the religious compromise of the Queen, and professed himself a Protestant while he intrigued with the Catholic party. He trusted to carry the English nobles with him in pressing for his marriage with Mary, a marriage which should seem to take her out of the hands of French and Catholic intriguers, to make her an Englishwoman, and to settle the vexed question of the succession to the throne. His dreams of such a union with Mary in the preceding year had been detected by Cecil, and checked by a short sojourn in the Tower ; but his correspondence with the Queen was renewed on his release, and ended in an appeal to Philip for the intervention of a Spanish army. At the head of this appeal stood the name of Mary ; while Norfolk's name was followed by those of many lords of "the old blood," as the prouder peers styled themselves ; and the significance of the request was heightened by gatherings of Catholic refugees at Antwerp round the fugitive leaders of the Northern Revolt. Enough of these conspiracies was discovered to rouse a fresh ardour in the menaced Protestants. The Parliament met to pass an act of attainder against the Northern Earls, and to declare the introduction of Papal Bulls into the country an act of high treason. The rising indignation against Mary, as "the daughter of Debate, who discord fell doth sow," was shown in a statute, which declared any person who laid claim to the Crown during the Queen's life-time incapable of ever succeeding to it. The disaffection of the Catholics was met by imposing on all magistrates and public officers the obligation of subscribing to the Articles of Faith, a measure which in fact transferred the administration of justice and public order to their Protestant opponents. Meanwhile Norfolk's treason ripened into an elaborate plot. Philip had promised aid should the revolt actually break out ; but the clue to these negotiations had long been in Cecil's hands, and before a single step could be taken towards the practical realization of his schemes of ambition, they were foiled by Norfolk's arrest. With his death and that of Northumberland, who followed him to the scaffold, the dread of revolt within the realm which had so long hung over England passed quietly away. The failure of the two attempts not only showed the weakness and disunion of the party of discontent and reaction, but it revealed the weakness of all party feeling before the rise of a national temper which was springing

SEC. IV.

ENGLAND
AND MARY
STUART
1560
TO
1572

Treason of Norfolk

1571

SEC. V.

THE
ENGLAND
OF
ELIZABETH

naturally out of the peace of Elizabeth's reign, and which a growing sense of danger to the order and prosperity around it was fast turning into a passionate loyalty to the Queen. It was not merely against Cecil's watchfulness or Elizabeth's cunning that Mary and Philip and the Percies dashed themselves in vain; it was against a new England.

Section V.—The England of Elizabeth.

[*Authorities.*—For our constitutional history we have D'Ewes' Journals and Townshend's "Journal of Parliamentary Proceedings from 1580 to 1601," the first detailed account we possess of the proceedings of our House of Commons. The general survey given by Hallam ("Constitutional History") is as judicious as it is able. Macpherson in his "Annals of Commerce" gives details of the expansion of English trade; and Hakluyt's "Collection of Voyages" tells of its activity. Some valuable details are added by Mr. Froude. The general literary history is given by Craik ("History of English Literature"), who has devoted a separate work to Spenser and his times; and the sober but narrow estimate of Mr. Hallam ("Literary History") may be contrasted with the more brilliant though less balanced comments of M. Taine on the writers of the Renascence. A crowd of biographers mark the new importance of individual life and action.]

Elizabeth and the Poor Laws

"I have desired," Elizabeth said proudly to her Parliament, "to have the obedience of my subjects by love, and not by compulsion." It was a love fairly won by justice and good government. Buried as she seemed in foreign negotiations and intrigues, Elizabeth was above all an English sovereign. She devoted herself ably and energetically to the task of civil administration. At the first moment of relief from the pressure of outer troubles, she faced the two main causes of internal disorder. The debasement of the coinage was brought to an end in 1560. In 1561 a commission was issued to inquire into the best means of facing the problem of social discontent. Time, and the natural developement of new branches of industry, were working quietly for the relief of the glutted labour-market; but a vast mass of disorder still existed in England, which found a constant ground of resentment in the enclosures and evictions which accompanied the progress of agricultural change. It was on this host of "broken men" that every rebellion could count for support; their mere existence indeed was an encouragement to civil war; while in peace their presence was felt in the insecurity of life and property, in gangs of marauders which held whole counties in terror, and in "sturdy beggars" who stripped travellers on the road. Under Elizabeth as under her predecessors the terrible measures of repression, whose uselessness More had in vain pointed out, went pitilessly on: we find the magistrates of Somersetshire capturing a gang of a hundred at a stroke, hanging fifty at once on the gallows, and complaining bitterly to the Council of the necessity for waiting till the Assizes before they could enjoy the spectacle of the fifty others hanging beside them. But the Government were dealing with the difficulty in a wiser and more effectual way. The old powers to enforce labour on the idle and settlement on the vagrant class were continued; and each town and parish was held responsible for the relief of its indigent and disabled poor, as well as for the employment of able-bodied mendicants. But a more efficient machinery was gradually devised for carrying out the relief and employment of the poor. Funds for this purpose had been provided by the collection of alms in church; but the mayor of each town and the churchwardens of each country parish were now directed to draw up lists of all inhabitants able to contribute to such a fund, and on a persistent refusal the justices in sessions were empowered to assess the offender at a fitting sum and to enforce its payment by imprisonment. The principles embodied in these measures, that of local responsibility for local distress, and that of a distinction between the pauper and the vagabond, were more clearly defined in a statute of 1572. By this Act the justices in the country districts and mayors and other officers in towns were directed to register the impotent poor, to settle them in fitting habitations and to assess all inhabitants for their support. Overseers were appointed to enforce and superintend their labour, for which wool, hemp, flax, or other stuff was to be provided at the expense of the inhabitants; and houses of correction were established in every county for obstinate vagabonds or for paupers refusing to work at the overseer's bidding. A subsequent Act transferred to these overseers the collection of the poor rate, and powers were given to bind poor children as apprentices, to erect buildings for the improvident poor, and to force the parents and children of such paupers to maintain them. The well-known Act which matured and finally established this system, the 43rd of Elizabeth, remained the base of our system of pauper-administration until a time within the recollection of living men. Whatever flaws a later experience has found in these measures, their wise and humane character formed a striking contrast to the legislation which had degraded our statute-book from the date of the Statute of Labourers; and their efficacy at the time was proved by the cessation of the social danger against which they were intended to provide.

Its cessation however was owing, not merely to law, but to the natural growth of wealth and industry throughout the country. The change in the mode of cultivation, whatever social embarrassment it might bring about, undoubtedly favoured production. Not only was a larger capital brought to bear upon the land, but the mere change in the system introduced a taste for new and better modes of agriculture; the breed of horses and of cattle was improved, and a far greater use made of manure and dressings. One acre under the new system produced, it was said, as much as two under the old. As a more careful and constant cultivation was introduced, a greater number of hands were required on every farm; and much of the surplus labour which had been flung off the land in the commencement of the new system was thus recalled to it. But a far more efficient agency in absorbing the unemployed was found in the developement of manufactures. The linen trade was as yet of small value, and that of silk-weaving was only just introduced. But the woollen manufacture was fast becoming an important element in the national wealth. England no longer sent her fleeces to be woven in Flanders and to be dyed at Florence. The spinning of yarn, the weaving, fulling, and dyeing of cloth, was spreading rapidly from the towns over the country-side. The worsted trade, of which Norwich was the centre, extended over the whole of the Eastern counties. Farmers' wives began everywhere to spin their wool from their own sheep's backs into a coarse "home-spun." The South and the West, however, still remained the great seats of industry and of wealth, for they were the homes of mining and manufacturing activity. The iron manufactures were limited to Kent and Sussex, though their prosperity in this quarter was already threatened by the growing scarcity of the wood which fed their furnaces, and by the exhaustion of the forests of the Weald. Cornwall was then, as now, the sole exporter of tin; and the exportation of its copper was just beginning. The broadcloths of the West claimed the palm among the woollen stuffs of England. The Cinque Ports held almost a monopoly of the commerce of the Channel. Every little harbour from the Foreland to the Land's End sent out its fleet of fishing-boats, manned with the bold seamen who were to furnish crews for Drake and the Buccaneers. But in the reign of Elizabeth the poverty and inaction to which the North had been doomed for so many centuries began at last to be broken. We see the first signs of the revolution which has transferred English manufactures and English wealth to the north of the Mersey and the Humber in the mention which now meets us of the friezes of Manchester, the coverlets of York, the cutlery of Sheffield, and the cloth trade of Halifax.

The growth however of English commerce far outstripped that of its manufactures. We must not judge of it, indeed, by any modern standard; for the whole population of the country can hardly have exceeded five or six millions, and the burthen of all the vessels engaged in ordinary commerce was estimated at little more than fifty thousand tons. The size of the vessels employed in it would nowadays seem insignificant; a modern collier brig is probably as large as the biggest merchant vessel which then sailed from the port of London. But it was under Elizabeth that English commerce began the rapid career of developement which has made us the carriers of the world. The

foundation of the Royal Exchange by Sir Thomas Gresham was a mark of the commercial progress of the time. By far the most important branch of our trade was with Flanders; Antwerp and Bruges were in fact the general marts of the world in the early part of the sixteenth century, and the annual export of English wool and drapery to their markets was estimated at a sum of more than two millions in value. It was with the ruin of Antwerp at the time of its siege and capture by the Duke of Parma that the commercial supremacy of our own capital was first established. A third of the merchants and manufacturers of the ruined city are said to have found a refuge on the banks of the Thames. The export trade to Flanders died away as London developed into the general mart of Europe, where the gold and sugar of the New World were found side by side with the cotton of India, the silks of the East, and the woollen stuffs of England itself. Not only was much of the old trade of the world transferred by this change to English shores, but the sudden burst of national vigour found new outlets for its activity. The Venetian carrying fleet still touched at Southampton ; but as far back as the reign of Henry the Seventh a commercial treaty had been concluded with Florence, and the trade with the Mediterranean which had begun under Richard the Third constantly took a wider developement. The trade between England and the Baltic ports had hitherto been concluded by the Hanseatic merchants ; but the extinction at this time of their London depôt, the Steel Yard, was a sign that this trade too had now passed into English hands. The growth of Boston and Hull marked an increase of commercial intercourse with Scandinavia. The prosperity of Bristol, which depended in great measure on the trade with Ireland, was stimulated by the conquest and colonization of that island at the close of the Queen's reign and the beginning of her successor's. The dream of a northern passage to India opened up a trade with a land as yet unknown. Of three ships which sailed under Hugh Willoughby to realize this dream, two were found afterwards frozen with their crews and their hapless commander on the coast of Lapland ; but the third, under Richard Chancellor, made its way safely to the White Sea and by its discovery of Archangel created the trade with Russia. A more lucrative traffic had already begun with the coast of Guinea, to whose gold-dust and ivory the merchants of Southampton owed their wealth. The guilt of the Slave Trade which sprang out of it rests with John Hawkins, whose arms (a demi-moor, proper, bound with a cord) commemorated his priority in the transport of negroes from Africa to the labour-fields of the New World. The fisheries of the Channel and the German Ocean gave occupation to the numerous ports which lined the coast from Yarmouth to Plymouth Haven ; Bristol and Chester were rivals in the fisheries of Ulster; and the voyage of Sebastian Cabot from the former port to the mainland of North America had called English vessels to the stormy ocean of the North. From the time of Henry the Eighth the number of English boats engaged on the cod-banks of Newfoundland steadily increased, and at the close of Elizabeth's reign the seamen of Biscay found English rivals in the whale-fishery of the Polar seas.

1553

1562

SEC. V.

THE
ENGLAND
OF
ELIZABETH

**Wealth
and
Social
Progress**

What Elizabeth contributed to this upgrowth of national prosperity was the peace and social order from which it sprang, and the thrift which spared the purses of her subjects by enabling her in ordinary times to content herself with the ordinary resources of the Crown. She lent, too, a ready patronage to the new commerce, she shared in its speculations, she considered its extension and protection as a part of public policy, and she sanctioned the formation of the great Merchant Companies which could then alone secure the trader against wrong or injustice in distant countries. The Merchant-Adventurers of London, a body which had existed long before, and had received a charter of incorporation under Henry the Seventh, furnished a model for the Russian Company and the Company which absorbed the new commerce to the Indies. But it was not wholly with satisfaction that either Elizabeth or her ministers watched the social change which wealth was producing around them. They feared the increased expenditure and comfort which necessarily followed it, as likely to impoverish the land and to eat out the hardihood of the people. " England spendeth more on wines in one year," complained Cecil, "than it did in ancient times in four years." The disuse of salt-fish and the greater consumption of meat marked the improvement which was taking place among the country folk. Their rough and wattled farmhouses were being superseded by dwellings of brick and stone. Pewter was replacing the wooden trenchers of the earlier yeomanry ; there were yeomen who could boast of a fair show of silver plate. It is from this period indeed that we can first date the rise of a conception which seems to us now a peculiarly English one, the conception of domestic comfort. The chimney-corner, so closely associated with family life, came into existence with the general introduction of chimneys, a feature rare in ordinary houses at the beginning of this reign. Pillows, which had before been despised by the farmer and the trader as fit only " for women in child-bed," were now in general use. Carpets superseded the filthy flooring of rushes. The lofty houses of the wealthier merchants, their parapeted fronts and costly wainscoting, their cumbrous but elaborate beds, their carved staircases, their quaintly figured gables, not only contrasted with the squalor which had till then characterized English towns, but marked the rise of a new middle class which was to play its part in later history. A transformation of an even more striking kind proclaimed the extinction of the feudal character of the noblesse. Gloomy walls and serried battlements disappeared from the dwellings of the gentry. The strength of the mediæval fortress gave way to the pomp and grace of the Elizabethan Hall. Knole, Longleat, Burleigh and Hatfield, Hardwick and Audley End, are familiar instances of the social as well as architectural change which covered England with buildings where the thought of defence was abandoned for that of domestic comfort and refinement. We still gaze with pleasure on their picturesque line of gables, their fretted fronts, their gilded turrets and fanciful vanes, their castellated gateways, the jutting oriels from which the great noble looked down on his new Italian garden, on its stately terraces and broad flights of steps, its vases and fountains, its quaint mazes, its formal walks, its lines of yews cut into grotesque shapes in hopeless rivalry of the cypress avenues of the South. The Italian refinement of life which told on pleasaunce and garden told on the remodelling of the house within, raised the principal apartments to an upper floor—a change to which we owe the grand staircases of the time—surrounded the quiet courts by long " galleries of the presence," crowned the rude hearth with huge chimney-pieces adorned with fauns and cupids, with quaintly interlaced monograms and fantastic arabesques, hung tapestries on the walls, and crowded each chamber with quaintly-carved chairs and costly cabinets. The life of the Middle Ages concentrated itself in the vast castle hall, where the baron looked from his upper daïs on the retainers who gathered at his board. But the great households were fast breaking up ; and the whole feudal economy disappeared when the lord of the household withdrew with his family into his " parlour " or " withdrawing-room," and left the hall to his dependents. The prodigal use of glass became a marked feature in the domestic architecture of the time, and one whose influence on the general health of the people can hardly be overrated. Long lines of windows stretched over the fronts of the new manor halls. Every merchant's house had its oriel. " You shall have sometimes," Lord Bacon grumbled, " your houses so full of glass, that we cannot tell where to come to be out of the sun or the cold." But the prodigal enjoyment of light and sunshine was a mark of the temper of the age. The lavishness of a new wealth united with a lavishness of life, a love of beauty, of colour, of display, to revolutionize English dress. The Queen's three thousand robes were rivalled in their bravery by the slashed velvets, the ruffs, the jewelled purpoints of the courtiers around her. Men " wore a manor on their backs." The old sober notions of thrift melted before the strange revolutions of fortune wrought by the New World. Gallants gambled away a fortune at a sitting, and sailed off to make a fresh one in the Indies. Visions of galleons loaded to the brim with pearls and diamonds and ingots of silver, dreams of El Dorados where all was of gold, threw a haze of prodigality and profusion over the imagination of the meanest seaman. The wonders, too, of the New World kindled a burst of extravagant fancy in the Old. The strange medley of past and present which distinguishes its masques and feastings only reflected the medley of men's thoughts. Pedantry, novelty, the allegory of Italy, the chivalry of the Middle Ages, the mythology of Rome, the English bear-fight, pastorals, superstition. farce, all took their turn in the entertainment which Lord Leicester provided for the Queen at Kenilworth. A "wild man" from the Indies chanted her praises, and Echo answered him. Elizabeth turned from the greetings of sibyls and giants to deliver the enchanted lady from her tyrant " Sans Pitie." Shepherdesses welcomed her with carols of the spring, while Ceres and Bacchus poured their corn and grapes at her feet.

The Revival of English Literature

It was to this turmoil of men's minds, this wayward luxuriance and prodigality of fancy, that we owe the revival of English letters under Elizabeth. Here, as elsewhere, the Renascence found vernacular literature all but dead, poetry reduced to the doggrel of Skelton, history to the annals of Fabyan or Halle. It had however done little for English letters. The overpowering influence of the new models both of thought and style which it gave to the world in the writers of Greece and Rome was at first felt only as a fresh check to the dreams of any revival of English poetry or prose. Though England shared more than any European country in the political and ecclesiastical results of the New Learning, its literary results were far less than in the rest of Europe, in Italy, or Germany, or France. More alone ranks among the great classical scholars of the sixteenth century. Classical learning indeed all but perished at the Universities in the storm of the Reformation, nor did it revive there till the close of Elizabeth's reign. Insensibly however the influences of the Renascence fertilized the intellectual soil of England for the rich harvest that was to come. The court poetry which clustered round Wyatt and Surrey, exotic and imitative as it was, promised a new life for English verse. The growth of grammar schools realized the dream of Sir Thomas More, and brought the middle-classes, from the squire to the petty tradesman, into contact with the masters of Greece and Rome. The love of travel, which became so remarkable a characteristic of Elizabeth's day, quickened the intelligence of the wealthier nobles. " Home-keeping youths," says Shakspere in words that mark the time, "have ever homely wits ; " and a tour over the Continent was just becoming part of the education of a gentleman. Fairfax's version of Tasso, Harrington's version of Ariosto, were signs of the influence which the literature of Italy, the land to which travel led most frequently, exerted on English minds. The writers of Greece and Rome began at last to tell upon England when they were popularized by a crowd of translations. Chapman's noble version of Homer stands high above its fellows, but all the greater poets and historians of the classical world were turned into English before the close of the sixteenth century. It is characteristic of England that historical literature was the first to rise from its long death, though the form in which it rose marked the difference between the world in which it had perished and that in which it reappeared. During the Middle Ages the world had been without a past, save the shadowy and unknown past of early Rome ; and annalist

and chronicler told the story of the years which went before as a preface to his tale of the present without a sense of any difference between
them.   But the religious, social, and political change which had passed
over England under the New Monarchy broke the continuity of its
life ; and the depth of the rift between the two ages is seen by the way
in which History passes, on its revival under Elizabeth, from the
mediæval form of pure narrative to its modern form of an investigation
and reconstruction of the past.   The new interest which attached to
the bygone world led to the collection of its annals, their reprinting
and embodiment in an English shape.   It was his desire to give the
Elizabethan Church a basis in the past, as much as any pure zeal for
letters, which induced Archbishop Parker to lead the way in the first
of these labours.   The collection of historical manuscripts which, following in the track of Leland, he rescued from the wreck of the
monastic libraries created a school of antiquarian imitators, whose research and industry have preserved for us almost every work of permanent historical value which existed before the Dissolution of the
Monasteries.   To his publication of some of our earlier chronicles we
owe the series of similar publications which bear the names of Camden,
Twysden, and Gale.   But as a branch of literature, English History in
the new shape which we have noted began in the work of the poet
Daniel.   The chronicles of Stowe and Speed, who preceded him, are
simple records of the past, often copied almost literally from the annals
they used, and utterly without style or arrangement ; while Daniel, inaccurate and superficial as he is, gave his story a literary form and
embodied it in a pure and graceful prose.   Two larger works at the
close of Elizabeth's reign, the " History of the Turks " by Knolles, and
Ralegh's vast but unfinished plan of the " History of the World,"
showed the widening of historic interest beyond the merely national
bounds to which it had hitherto been confined.

A far higher developement of our literature sprang from the growing
influence which Italy, as we have seen, was exerting, partly through
travel and partly through its poetry and romances, on the manners and
taste of the time.   Men made more account of a story of Boccaccio's,
it was said, than of a story from the Bible.   The dress, the speech, the
manners of Italy became objects of almost passionate imitation, and
of an imitation not always of the wisest or noblest kind.   To Ascham
it seemed like " the enchantment of Circe brought out of Italy to
mar men's manners in England."   " An Italianate Englishman," ran
the harder proverb of Italy itself, " is an incarnate devil."   The literary
form which this imitation took seemed at any rate absurd.   John Lyly,
distinguished both as a dramatist and a poet, laid aside the tradition
of English style for a style modelled on the decadence of Italian prose.
Euphuism, as the new fashion has been styled from the prose romance
of Euphues in which Lyly originated it, is best known to modern

readers by the pitiless caricature in which Shakspere quizzed its pedantry, its affectation, the meaningless monotony of its far-fetched phrases, the absurdity of its extravagant conceits. Its representative, Armado in "Love's Labour's Lost," is "a man of fire-new words, fashion's own knight," "that hath a mint of phrases in his brain; one whom the music of his own vain tongue doth ravish like enchanting harmony." But its very extravagance sprang from the general burst of delight in the new resources of thought and language which literature felt to be at its disposal; and the new sense of literary beauty which it disclosed in its affectation, in its love of a "mint of phrases" and the "music of its own vain tongue," the new sense of pleasure in delicacy or grandeur of phrase, in the structure and arrangement of sentences, in what has been termed the atmosphere of words, was a sense out of which style was itself to spring. For a time Euphuism had it all its own way. Elizabeth was the most affected and detestable of Euphuists; and "that beauty in Court which could not parley Euphuism," a courtier of Charles the First's time tells us, "was as little regarded as she that now there speaks not French." The fashion however passed away, but the "Arcadia" of Sir Philip Sidney shows the wonderful advance which prose had made under its influence. Sidney, the nephew of Lord Leicester, was the idol of his time, and perhaps no figure reflects the age more fully and more beautifully. Fair as he was brave, quick of wit as of affection, noble and generous in temper, dear to Elizabeth as to Spenser, the darling of the court and of the camp, his learning and his genius made him the centre of the literary world which was springing into birth on English soil. He had travelled in France and Italy, he was master alike of the older learning and of the new discoveries of astronomy. Bruno dedicated to him as to a friend his metaphysical speculations; he was familiar with the drama of Spain, the poems of Ronsard, the sonnets of Italy. He combined the wisdom of a grave councillor with the romantic chivalry of a knight-errant. "I never heard the old story of Percy and Douglas," he says, "that I found not my heart moved more than with a trumpet." He flung away his life to save the English army in Flanders, and as he lay dying they brought a cup of water to his fevered lips. He bade them give it to a soldier who was stretched on the ground beside him. "Thy necessity," he said, "is greater than mine." The whole of Sidney's nature, his chivalry and his learning, his thirst for adventures, his tendency to extravagance, his freshness of tone, his tenderness and childlike simplicity of heart, his affectation and false sentiment, his keen sense of pleasure and delight, pours itself out in the pastoral medley, forced, tedious, and yet strangely beautiful, of his "Arcadia." In his "Defence of Poetry" the youthful exuberance of the romancer has passed into the earnest vigour and grandiose stateliness of the rhetorician. But whether in the one work

Sidney.

1590

or the other, the flexibility, the music, the luminous clearness of Sidney's style remains the same. The quickness and vivacity of English prose, however, was first developed in the school of Italian imitators who appeared in Elizabeth's later years. The origin of English fiction is to be found in the tales and romances with which Greene and Nash crowded the market, models for which they found in the Italian novels. The brief form of these novelettes soon led to the appearance of the "pamphlet;" and a new world of readers was seen in the rapidity with which the stories or scurrilous libels which passed under this name were issued, and the greediness with which they were devoured. It was the boast of Greene that in the eight years before his death he had produced forty pamphlets. "In a night or a day would he have yarked up a pamphlet, as well as in seven years, and glad was that printer that might be blest to pay him dear for the very dregs of his wit." Modern eyes see less of the wit than of the dregs in the works of Greene and his compeers; but the attacks which Nash directed against the Puritans and his rivals were the first English works which shook utterly off the pedantry and extravagance of Euphuism. In his lightness, his facility, his vivacity, his directness of speech, we have the beginning of popular literature. It had descended from the closet to the street, and the very change implied that the street was ready to receive it. The abundance indeed of printers and of printed books at the close of the Queen's reign shows that the world of readers and writers had widened far beyond the small circle of scholars and courtiers with which it began.

We shall have to review at a later time the great poetic burst for which this intellectual advance was paving the way, and the moral and religious change which was passing over the country through the progress of Puritanism. But both the intellectual and the religious impulses of the age united with the influence of its growing wealth to revive a spirit of independence in the nation at large, a spirit which it was impossible for Elizabeth to understand, but the strength of which her wonderful tact enabled her to feel. Long before any open conflict arose between the people and the Crown, we see her instinctive perception of the changes which were going on round her in the modifications, conscious or unconscious, which she introduced into the system of the monarchy. Of its usurpations on English liberty she abandoned none. But she curtailed and softened down almost all. She tampered, as her predecessors had tampered, with personal freedom; there was the same straining of statutes and coercion of juries in political trials as before, and an arbitrary power of imprisonment was still exercised by the Council. The duties she imposed on cloth and sweet wines were an assertion of her right of arbitrary taxation. Proclamations in Council constantly assumed the force of law. In one part of her policy indeed Elizabeth seemed to fall back from the constitutional attitude assumed by the Tudor sovereigns. Ever since Cromwell's time the Parliament had been convened almost year by year as a great engine of justice and legislation, but Elizabeth recurred to the older jealousy of the two Houses which had been entertained by Edward the Fourth, Henry the Seventh, and Wolsey. Her Parliaments were summoned at intervals of never less than three, and sometimes of five years, and never save on urgent necessity. Practically however the royal power was wielded with a caution and moderation that showed the sense of a gathering difficulty in the full exercise of it. The ordinary course of justice was left undisturbed. The jurisdiction of the Council was asserted almost exclusively over the Catholics ; and defended in their case as a precaution against pressing dangers. The proclamations issued were temporary in character and of small importance. The two duties imposed were so slight as to pass almost unnoticed in the general satisfaction at Elizabeth's abstinence from internal taxation. She abandoned the benevolences and forced loans which had brought home the sense of tyranny to the subjects of her predecessors. She treated the Privy Seals, which on emergencies she issued for advances to her Exchequer, simply as anticipations of her revenue (like our own Exchequer Bills), and punctually repaid them. The monopolies with which she fettered trade proved a more serious grievance ; but during her earlier reign they were looked on as a part of the system of Merchant Associations, which were at that time regarded as necessary for the regulation and protection of the growing commerce. Her thrift enabled her in ordinary times of peace to defray the current expenses of the Crown from its ordinary revenues. But the thrift was dictated not so much by economy as by the desire to avoid summoning fresh Parliaments. The Queen saw that the "management" of the two Houses, so easy to Cromwell, was becoming harder every day. The rise of a new nobility, enriched by the spoils of the Church and trained to political life by the stress of events around them, was giving fresh vigour to the Lords. The increased wealth of the country gentry, as well as their growing desire to obtain a seat in the Commons, brought about the cessation at this time of the old practice of payment of members by their constituencies. A change too in the borough representation, which had long been in progress but was now for the first time legally recognized, tended greatly to increase the vigour and independence of the Lower House. The members for boroughs had been required by the terms of the older writs to be chosen from the body of the burgesses ; and an Act of Henry the Fifth gave this custom the force of law. But the passing of the Act shows that the custom was already widely infringed ; and by the time of Elizabeth most borough seats were filled by strangers, often nominees of the great landowners round, but for the

*Changes in
the
Commons.*

most part men of wealth and blood, whose aim in entering Parliament was a purely political one, and whose attitude towards the Crown was far bolder and more independent than that of the quiet tradesmen who preceded them.   So changed, indeed, was the tone of the Commons, even as early as the close of Henry's reign, that Edward and Mary both fell back on the prerogative of the Crown to create boroughs, and summoned members from fresh constituencies, which were often mere villages, and wholly in the hands of the Crown.   But this " packing of the House " had still to be continued by their successor.   The large number of such members whom Elizabeth called into the Commons, sixty-two in all, was a proof of the increasing difficulty which the Government found in securing a working majority.

Had Elizabeth lived in quiet times her thrift would have saved her from the need of summoning Parliament at all.   But the perils of her reign drove her to renewed demands of subsidies, and at each demand the tone of the Houses rose higher and higher.   Constitutionally the policy of Cromwell had had this special advantage, that at the very crisis of our liberties it had acknowledged and confirmed by repeated instances, for its own purposes of arbitrary rule, the traditional right of Parliament to grant subsidies, to enact laws, and to consider and petition for the redress of grievances.   These rights remained, while the power which had turned them into a mere engine of despotism was growing weaker year by year.   Not only did the Parliament of Elizabeth exercise its powers as fully as the Parliament of Cromwell, but the forces, political and religious, which she sought stubbornly to hold in check pressed on irresistibly, and soon led to the claiming of new privileges.   In spite of the rarity of its assembling, in spite of high words and imprisonment and dexterous management, the Parliament quietly gained a power which, at her accession, the Queen could never have dreamed of its possessing.   Step by step the Lower House won the freedom of its members from arrest save by its own permission, the right of punishing and expelling members for crimes committed within the House, and of determining all matters relating to elections. The more important claim of freedom of speech brought on a series of petty conflicts which showed Elizabeth's instincts of despotism, as well as her sense of the new power which despotism had to face.   In the great crisis of the Darnley marriage Mr. Dalton defied a royal prohibition to mention the subject of the succession by denouncing the claim of the Scottish Queen.   Elizabeth at once ordered him into arrest, but the Commons prayed for leave " to confer upon their liberties," and the Queen ordered his release.   In the same spirit she commanded Mr. Strickland, the mover of a bill for the reform of the Common Prayer, to appear no more in Parliament ; but as soon as she perceived the House was bent upon his restoration the command was withdrawn. On the other hand the Commons still shrank from any consistent

Elizabeth
and the
Parlia-
ment

1566

1571

SEC. V.

THE
ENGLAND
OF
ELIZABETH

1575

1588

Claims of
the
Commons.

1559

repudiation of Elizabeth's assumption of control over freedom of speech. The bold protest of Peter Wentworth against it was met by the House itself with his committal to the Tower : and the yet bolder question which he addressed to a later Parliament, "Whether this Council is not a place for every member of the same freely and without control, by bill or speech, to utter any of the griefs of the Commonwealth," brought on him a fresh imprisonment at the hands of the Council, which lasted till the dissolution of the Parliament and with which the Commons declined to interfere. But while vacillating in its assertion of the rights of individual speakers, the House steadily asserted its claim to the wider powers which Cromwell's policy had given to Parliamentary action. In theory the Tudor statesmen regarded three cardinal subjects, matters of trade, matters of religion, and matters of State, as lying exclusively within the competence of the Crown. But in actual fact such subjects had been treated by Parliament after Parliament. The whole religious fabric of the realm, the very title of Elizabeth, rested on Parliamentary statutes. When the Houses petitioned at the outset of her reign for the declaration of a successor and for the Queen's marriage, it was impossible to deny their right to intermeddle with these "matters of State," though she rebuked the demand and evaded an answer. But the question of the succession became too vital to English freedom and English religion to remain confined within Elizabeth's council chamber. The Parliament which met in 1566 repeated the demand in a more imperative way. Her consciousness of the real dangers of such a request united with her arbitrary temper to move Elizabeth to a burst of passionate anger. The marriage indeed she promised, but she peremptorily forbade the subject of the succession to be approached. Wentworth at once rose in the Commons to know whether such a prohibition was not "against the liberties of Parliament?" and the question was followed by a hot debate. A fresh message from the Queen commanded "that there should be no further argument," but the message was met by a request for freedom of deliberation. Elizabeth's prudence taught her that retreat was necessary ; she protested that "she did not mean to prejudice any part of the liberties heretofore granted them ; " she softened the order of silence into a request ; and the Commons, won by the graceful concession to a loyal assent, received her message "most joyfully and with most hearty prayers and thanks for the same." But the victory was none the less a real one. No such struggle had taken place between the Commons and the Crown since the beginning of the New Monarchy ; and the struggle had ended in the virtual defeat of the Crown. It was the prelude to another claim equally galling to the Queen. Though the constitution of the Church rested in actual fact on Parliamentary enactments, Elizabeth, like the rest of the Tudor sovereigns, theoretically held her ecclesiastical supremacy to be a purely personal power, with her administration of which neither Parliament nor even her Council had any right to interfere. But the exclusion of the Catholic gentry through the Test Acts, and the growth of Puritanism among the landowners as a class, gave more and more a Protestant tone to the Commons and to the Council; and it was easy to remember that the Supremacy which was thus jealously guarded from Parliamentary interference had been conferred on the Crown by a Parliamentary statute. Here, however, the Queen, as the religious representative of the two parties who made up her subjects, stood on firmer ground than the Commons, who represented but one of them. And she used her advantage boldly. The bills proposed by the more advanced Protestants for the reform of the Common Prayer were at her command delivered up into her hands and suppressed. Wentworth, the most outspoken of his party, was, as we have seen, imprisoned in the Tower: and in a later Parliament the Speaker was expressly forbidden to receive bills "for reforming the Church, and transforming the Commonwealth." In spite of these obstacles, however, the effort for reform continued, and though crushed by the Crown or set aside by the Lords, ecclesiastical bills were presented in every Parliament. A better fortune awaited the Commons in their attack on the royal prerogative in matters of trade. Complaints made of the licences and monopolies by which internal and external commerce were fettered were at first repressed by a royal reprimand as matters neither pertaining to the Commons nor within the compass of their understanding. When the subject was again stirred nearly twenty years afterwards, Sir Edward Hoby was sharply rebuked by "a great personage" for his complaint of the illegal exactions made by the Exchequer. But the bill which he promoted was sent up to the Lords in spite of this, and at the close of Elizabeth's reign the storm of popular indignation which had been roused by the growing grievance nerved the Commons to a decisive struggle. It was in vain that the ministers opposed the bill for the Abolition of Monopolies, and after four days of vehement debate the tact of Elizabeth taught her to give way. She acted with her usual ability, declared her previous ignorance of the existence of the evil, thanked the House for its interference, and quashed at a single blow every monopoly that she had granted.

Section VI. The Armada. 1572—1588.

[*Authorities*.—The general history of the Catholics is given in the work of Dodd; see also "The Troubles of our Catholic Forefathers," published by Father Morris; and for the Jesuits, "More's Historia Provinciae Anglicanae Societatis Jesu;" to these may be added Mr. Simpson's life of Campian.]

The wonderful growth in wealth and social energy which we have described was accompanied by a remarkable change in the religious temper of the nation. Silently, almost unconsciously, England became Protestant, as the traditionary Catholicism which formed the religion of three-fourths of the people at the Queen's accession died quietly away. At the close of her reign the only parts of England where the old faith retained anything of its former vigour were the north and the extreme west, at that time the poorest and least populated parts of the kingdom. One main cause of the change lay undoubtedly in the gradual dying out of the Catholic priesthood and the growth of a new Protestant clergy who supplied their place. The older parish priests, though they had almost to a man acquiesced in the changes of ritual and doctrine which the various phases of the Reformation imposed upon them, remained in heart utterly hostile to its spirit. As Mary had undone the changes of Edward, they hoped for a Catholic successor to undo the changes of Elizabeth ; and in the meantime they were content to wear the surplice instead of the chasuble, and to use the Communion-office instead of the Mass-book. But if they were forced to read the Homilies from the pulpit, the spirit of their teaching remained unchanged ; and it was easy for them to cast contempt on the new services, till they seemed to old-fashioned worshippers a mere "Christmas game." But the lapse of twenty years did its work in emptying parsonage after parsonage. In 1579 the Queen felt strong enough to enforce for the first time a general compliance with the Act of Uniformity ; and the jealous supervision of Parker and the bishops ensured an inner as well as an outer conformity to the established faith in the clergy who took the place of the dying priesthood. The new parsons were for the most part not merely Protestant in belief and teaching, but ultra-Protestant. The old restrictions on the use of the pulpit were silently removed as the need for them passed away, and the zeal of the young ministers showed itself in an assiduous preaching which moulded in their own fashion the religious ideas of the new generation. But their character had even a greater influence than their preaching. Under Henry the priests had for the most part been ignorant and sensual men ; and the character of the clergy appointed by the greedy Protestants under Edward or in the first years of Elizabeth's reign was even worse than that of their Catholic rivals. But the energy of the successive Primates, seconded as it was by the general increase of zeal and morality at the time, did its work ; and by the close of Elizabeth's reign the moral temper as well as the social character of the clergy had greatly changed. Scholars like Hooker could now be found in the ranks of the priesthood, and the grosser scandals which disgraced the clergy as a body for the most part disappeared. It was impossible for a Puritan libeller to bring against the ministers of Elizabeth's reign the charges of drunkenness and immorality which Protestant libellers had been able to bring against the priesthood of Henry's. But the influence of the new clergy was backed by a general revolution

VII.]

THE REFORMATION.

407

SEC. VI.

THE
ARMADA
1572
TO
1588

in English thought. We have already watched the first upgrowth of the new literature which was to find its highest types in Shakspere and Bacon. The grammar schools were diffusing a new knowledge and mental energy through the middle classes and among the country gentry. The tone of the Universities, no unfair test of the tone of the nation at large, changed wholly as the Queen's reign went on. At its opening Oxford was "a nest of Papists," and sent its best scholars to feed the Catholic seminaries. At its close the University was a hot-bed of Puritanism, where the fiercest tenets of Calvin reigned supreme. The movement was no doubt hastened by the political circumstances of the time. Under the rule of Elizabeth loyalty became more and more a passion among Englishmen ; and the Bull of Deposition placed Rome in the forefront of Elizabeth's foes. The conspiracies which festered around Mary were laid to the Pope's charge ; he was known to be pressing on France and on Spain the invasion and conquest of the heretic kingdom ; he was soon to bless the Armada. Every day made it harder for a Catholic to reconcile Catholicism with loyalty to his Queen or devotion to his country ; and the mass of men, who are moved by sentiment rather than by reason, swung slowly round to the side which, whatever its religious significance might be, was the side of patriotism, of liberty against tyranny, of England against Spain. A new impulse was given to this silent drift of religious opinion by the atrocities which marked the Catholic triumph on the other side of the Channel. The horror of Alva's butcheries, or of the massacre in Paris on St. Bartholomew's day, revived the memories of the bloodshed under Mary. The tale of Protestant sufferings was told with a wonderful pathos and picturesqueness by John Foxe, an exile during the persecution ; and his "Book of Martyrs," which was set up by royal order in the churches for public reading, passed from the churches to the shelves of every English household. The trading classes of the towns had been the first to embrace the doctrines of the Reformation, but their Protestantism became a passion as the refugees of the Continent brought to shop and market their tale of outrage and blood. Thousands of Flemish exiles found a refuge in the Cinque Ports, a third of the Antwerp merchants were seen pacing the new London Exchange, and a Church of French Huguenots found a home which it still retains in the crypt of Canterbury Cathedral.

In her ecclesiastical policy Elizabeth trusted mainly to time ; and time, as we have seen, justified her trust. Her system of compromise both in faith and worship, of quietly replacing the old priesthood as it died out by Protestant ministers, of wearying recusants into at least outer conformity with the state-religion and attendance on the state-services by fines—a policy aided, no doubt, by the moral influences we have described—was gradually bringing England round to a new religious front. But the decay of Catholicism appealed

1576

strongly to the new spirit of Catholic zeal which, in its despair of aid from Catholic princes, was now girding itself for its own bitter struggle with heresy. Dr. Allen, a scholar who had been driven from Oxford by the test prescribed by the Act of Uniformity, had foreseen the results of the dying out of the Marian priests, and had set up a seminary at Douay to supply their place. The new college, liberally supported by the Catholic peers, and supplied with pupils by a stream of refugees from Oxford and the English grammar schools, soon landed its " seminary priests" on English shores ; and few as they were at first, their presence was at once felt in the check which it gave to the gradual reconciliation of the Catholic gentry to the English Church. No check could have been more galling to Elizabeth, and her resentment was quickened by the sense of danger. She had accepted the Bull of Deposition as a declaration of war on the part of the Papacy, and she viewed the Douay priests with some justice as its political emissaries. The comparative security of the Catholics from active persecution during the early part of her reign had arisen partly from the sympathy and connivance of the gentry who acted as justices of the peace, but still more from her own religious indifference. But the Test Act placed the magistracy in Protestant hands ; and as Elizabeth passed from indifference to suspicion and from suspicion to terror she put less restraint on the bigotry around her. In quitting Euston Hall, which she had visited in one of her pilgrimages, the Queen gave its master, young Rookwood, thanks for his entertainment and her hand to kiss. " But my Lord Chamberlain nobly and gravely understanding that Rookwood was excommunicate " for non-attendance at church, " called him before him, demanded of him how he durst presume to attempt her royal presence, he unfit to accompany any Christian person, forthwith said that he was fitter for a pair of stocks, commanded him out of Court, and yet to attend the Council's pleasure." The Council's pleasure was seen in his committal to the town prison at Norwich, while " seven more gentlemen of worship" were fortunate enough to escape with a simple sentence of arrest at their own homes. The Queen's terror became a panic in the nation at large. The few priests who landed from Douay were multiplied into an army of Papal emissaries despatched to sow treason and revolt throughout the land. Parliament, which the working of the Test Act had made a wholly Protestant body, save for the presence of a few Catholics among the peers, was summoned to meet the new danger, and declared the landing of these priests and the harbouring of them to be treason.

The Act proved no idle menace ; and the execution of Cuthbert Mayne, a young priest who was arrested in Cornwall with the Papal Bull of Deposition hidden about him, gave a terrible indication of the character of the struggle upon which Elizabeth was about to enter. She was far, indeed, from any purpose of religious persecution ; she boasted of her abstinence from any interference with men's consciences ; and Cecil, in his official defence of her policy, while declaring freedom of worship to be incompatible with religious order, boldly asserted the right of every English subject to perfect freedom of religious opinion. To modern eyes there is something even more revolting than open persecution in the policy which branded every Catholic priest as a traitor, and all Catholic worship as disloyalty ; but the first step towards toleration was won when the Queen rested her system of repression on purely political grounds. If Elizabeth was a persecutor, she was the first English ruler who felt the charge of religious persecution to be a stigma on her rule. Nor can it be denied that there was a real political danger in the new missionaries. Allen was a restless conspirator, and the work of his seminary priests was meant to aid a new plan of the Papacy for the conquest of England. And to the efforts of the seminary priests were now added those of Jesuit missionaries. A select few of the Oxford refugees at Douay joined the order of the Jesuits, whose members were already famous for their blind devotion to the will and judgements of Rome ; and the two ablest and most eloquent of these exiles, Campian, once a fellow of St. John's, and Parsons, once a fellow of Balliol, were chosen as the heads of a Jesuit mission in England. For the moment their success was amazing. The eagerness shown to hear Campian was so great that in spite of the denunciations of the Government he was able to preach with hardly a show of concealment to a large audience at Smithfield. From London the missionaries wandered in the disguise of captains or serving-men, sometimes even in the cassock of the English clergy, through many of the counties ; and wherever they went the zeal of the Catholic gentry revived. The list of nobles reconciled to the old faith by these wandering apostles was headed by the name of Lord Oxford, Cecil's own son-in-law and the proudest among English peers.

The success of the Jesuits in undoing Elizabeth's work of compromise was shown in a more public way by the growing withdrawal of the Catholics from attendance at the worship of the English Church. The panic of the Protestants and of the Parliament outran even the real greatness of the danger. The little group of missionaries was magnified by popular fancy into a host of disguised Jesuits ; and the invasion of this imaginary host was met by the seizure and torture of as many priests as the Government could lay hands on, the imprisonment of recusants, and the securing of the prominent Catholics throughout the country ; and by statutes which prohibited the saying of Mass even in private houses, increased the fine on recusants to twenty pounds a month, and enacted that "all persons pretending to any power of absolving subjects from their allegiance, or practising to withdraw them to the Romish religion, with all persons after the present session willingly so absolved or reconciled to the See of Rome, shall be guilty of High Treason." The way in which the vast powers conferred on the Crown by this statute were used by Elizabeth was not only characteristic in itself, but important as at once defining the policy to which, in theory at least, her successors adhered for more than a hundred years. Few laymen were brought to the bar and none to the block under its provisions. The oppression of the Catholic gentry was limited to an exaction, more or less rigorous at different times, of the fines for recusancy or non-attendance at public worship. The work of bloodshed was reserved wholly for priests, and under Elizabeth this work was done with a ruthless energy which for the moment crushed the Catholic reaction. The Jesuits were tracked by pursuivants and spies, dragged from their hiding-places, and sent in batches to the Tower. So hot was the pursuit that Parsons was forced to fly across the Channel; while Campian was brought a prisoner through the streets of London amidst the howling of the mob, and placed at the bar on the charge of treason. "Our religion only is our crime," was a plea which galled his judges; but the political danger of the Jesuit preaching was disclosed in his evasion of any direct reply when questioned as to his belief in the validity of the excommunication and deposition of the Queen by the Papal See. The death of Campian was the prelude to a steady, pitiless effort at the extermination of his class. If we adopt the Catholic estimate of the time, the twenty years which followed saw the execution of two hundred priests, while a yet greater number perished in the filthy and fever-stricken gaols into which they were plunged. The work of reconciliation to Rome was arrested by this ruthless energy; but, on the other hand, the work which the priests had effected could not be undone. The system of quiet compulsion and conciliation to which Elizabeth had trusted for the religious reunion of her subjects was foiled; and the English Catholics, fined, imprisoned at every crisis of national danger, and deprived of their teachers by the prison and the gibbet, were severed more hopelessly than ever from the national Church. A fresh impulse was thus given to the growing current of opinion which was to bring England at last to recognize the right of every man to freedom both of conscience and of worship. What Protestantism had first done under Mary, Catholicism was doing under Elizabeth. It was deepening the sense of personal religion. It was revealing in men who had cowered before the might of kingship a power greater than the might of kings. It was breaking the spell which the monarchy had laid on the imagination of the people. The Crown ceased to seem irresistible before a passion for religious and political liberty which gained vigour from the dungeon of the Catholic priest as from that of the Protestant zealot.

SEC. VI.

THE
ARMADA
1572
TO
1588
**Elizabeth
and
Philip**

But if a fierce religious struggle was at hand, men felt that behind this lay a yet fiercer political struggle. Philip's hosts were looming over sea, and the horrors of foreign invasion seemed about to be added to the horrors of civil war. Spain was at this moment the mightiest of European powers. The discoveries of Columbus had given it the New World of the West; the conquests of Cortes and Pizarro poured into its treasury the plunder of Mexico and Peru; its galleons brought the rich produce of the Indies, their gold, their jewels, their ingots of silver, to the harbour of Cadiz. To the New World its King added the fairest and wealthiest portions of the Old; he was master of Naples and Milan, the richest and the most fertile districts of Italy; of the busy provinces of the Low Countries, of Flanders, the great manufacturing district of the time, and of Antwerp, which had become the central mart for the commerce of the world. His native kingdom, poor as it was, supplied him with the steadiest and the most daring soldiers that the world had seen since the fall of the Roman Empire. The renown of the Spanish infantry had been growing from the day when it flung off the onset of the French chivalry on the field of Ravenna; and the Spanish generals stood without rivals in their military skill, as they stood without rivals in their ruthless cruelty. The whole, too, of this enormous power was massed in the hands of a single man. Served as he was by able statesmen and subtle diplomatists, Philip of Spain was his own sole minister; labouring day after day, like a clerk, through the long years of his reign, amidst the papers which crowded his closet; but resolute to let nothing pass without his supervision, and to suffer nothing to be done save by his express command. It was his boast that everywhere in the vast compass of his dominions he was "an absolute King." It was to realize this idea of unshackled power that he crushed the liberties of Aragon, as his father had crushed the liberties of Castille, and sent Alva to tread under foot the constitutional freedom of the Low Countries. His bigotry went hand in hand with his thirst for rule. Italy and Spain lay hushed beneath the terror of the Inquisition, while Flanders was being purged of heresy by the stake and the sword. The shadow of this gigantic power fell like a deadly blight over Europe. The new Protestantism, like the new spirit of political liberty, saw its real foe in Philip. It was Spain, rather than the Guises, against which Coligni and the Huguenots struggled in vain; it was Spain with which William of Orange was wrestling for religious and civil freedom; it was Spain which was soon to plunge Germany into the chaos of the Thirty Years' War, and to which the Catholic world had for twenty years been looking, and looking in vain, for a victory over heresy in England. Vast in fact as Philip's resources were, they were drained by the yet vaster schemes of ambition into which his religion and his greed of power, as well as the wide distribution of his dominions, perpetually drew him. To coerce the weaker States of Italy, to command the Mediterranean, to preserve his influence in Germany, to support Catholicism in France, to crush heresy in Flanders, to despatch one Armada against the Turk and another against Elizabeth, were aims mighty enough to exhaust even the power of the Spanish Monarchy. But it was rather on the character of Philip than on the exhaustion of his treasury that Elizabeth counted for success in the struggle which had so long been going on between them. The King's temper was slow, cautious even to timidity, losing itself continually in delays, in hesitations, in anticipating remote perils, in waiting for distant chances ; and on the slowness and hesitation of his temper his rival had been playing ever since she mounted the throne. The diplomatic contest between the two was like the fight which England was soon to see between the ponderous Spanish galleon and the light pinnace of the buccaneers. The agility, the sudden changes of Elizabeth, her lies, her mystifications, though they failed to deceive Philip, puzzled and impeded his mind. But amidst all this cloud of intrigue the actual course of their relations had been clear and simple. In her earlier days France rivalled Spain in its greatness, and Elizabeth simply played the two rivals off against one another. She hindered France from giving effective aid to Mary Stuart by threats of an alliance with Spain ; while she induced Philip to wink at her heresy, and to discourage the risings of the English Catholics, by playing on his dread of her alliance with France. But as the tide of religious passion which had so long been held in check broke at last over its banks, the political face of Europe changed. The Low Countries, driven to despair by the greed and persecution of Alva, rose in a revolt which after strange alternations of fortune gave to Europe the Republic of the United Provinces. The opening which their rising afforded was seized by the Huguenot leaders of France as a political engine to break the power which Catharine of Medicis exercized over Charles the Ninth, and to set aside her policy of religious balance by placing France at the head of Protestantism in the West. Charles listened to the counsels of Coligni, who pressed for war upon Philip and promised the support of the Huguenots in an invasion of the Low Countries. Never had a fairer prospect opened to French ambition. Catharine however saw ruin for the monarchy in a France at once Protestant and free. She threw herself on the side of the Guises, and ensured their triumph by lending herself to their massacre of the Protestants on St. Bartholomew's day. But though the long gathering clouds of religious hatred had broken, Elizabeth trusted to her dexterity to keep out of the storm. France plunged madly back into a chaos of civil war, and the Low Countries were left to cope single-handed with Spain. Whatever enthusiasm the heroic struggle of the Prince of Orange excited among ner subjects, it failed to move Elizabeth even for an instant from the path of cold self-interest. To her the revolt of the Netherlands was simply "a bridle of Spain, which kept war out of our own gate." At the darkest moment of the contest, when Alva had won back all but Holland and Zealand, and even William of Orange despaired, the Queen bent her energies to prevent him from finding succour in France. That the Provinces could in the end withstand Philip, neither she nor any English statesmen believed. They held that the struggle must close either in utter subjection of the Netherlands, or in their selling themselves for aid to France ; and the accession of power which either result must give to one of her two Catholic foes the Queen was eager to avert. Her plan for averting it was by forcing the Provinces to accept the terms offered by Spain—a restoration, that is, of their constitutional privileges on condition of their submission to the Church. Peace on such a footing would not only restore English commerce, which suffered from the war ; it would leave the Netherlands still formidable as a weapon against Philip. The freedom of the Provinces would be saved ; and the religious question involved in a fresh submission to the yoke of Catholicism was one which Elizabeth was incapable of appreciating. To her the steady refusal of William the Silent to sacrifice his faith was as unintelligible as the steady bigotry of Philip in demanding such a sacrifice. It was of more immediate consequence that Philip's anxiety to avoid provoking an intervention on the part of England which would destroy all hope of his success in Flanders, left her tranquil at home. Had revolt in England prospered he was ready to reap the fruits of other men's labours ; and he made no objection to plots for the seizure or assassination of the Queen. But his stake was too vast to risk an attack while she sate firmly on her throne ; and the cry of the English Catholics, or the pressure of the Pope, had as yet failed to drive the Spanish King into strife with Elizabeth.

The control of events was however passing from the hands of statesmen and diplomatists ; and the long period of suspense which their policy had won was ending in the clash of national and political passions. The rising fanaticism of the Catholic world was breaking down the caution and hesitation of Philip ; while England set aside the balanced neutrality of her Queen and pushed boldly forward to a contest which it felt to be inevitable. The public opinion, to which the Queen was so sensitive, took every day a bolder and more decided tone. Her cold indifference to the heroic struggle in Flanders was more than compensated by the enthusiasm it excited among the nation at large. The earlier Flemish refugees found a refuge in the Cinque Ports. The exiled merchants of Antwerp were welcomed by the merchants of London. While Elizabeth dribbled out her secret aid to the Prince of Orange, the London traders sent him half-a-million from their own purses, a sum equal to a year's revenue of the Crown.

Volunteers stole across the Channel in increasing numbers to the aid of the Dutch, till the five hundred Englishmen who fought in the beginning of the struggle rose to a brigade of five thousand, whose bravery turned one of the most critical battles of the war. Dutch privateers found shelter in English ports, and English vessels hoisted the flag of the States for a dash at the Spanish traders. Protestant fervour rose steadily as "the best captains and soldiers" returned from the campaigns in the Low Countries to tell of Alva's atrocities, or as privateers brought back tales of English seamen who had been seized in Spain and the New World, to linger amidst the tortures of the Inquisition, or to die in its fires. In the presence of this steady drift of popular passion the diplomacy of Elizabeth became of little moment. When she sought to put a check on Philip by one of her last matrimonial intrigues, which threatened England with a Catholic sovereign in the Duke of Anjou, a younger son of the hated Catharine

of Medicis, the popular indignation rose suddenly into a cry against "a Popish King" which the Queen dared not defy. If Elizabeth was resolute for peace, England was resolute for war. A new courage had arisen since the beginning of her reign, when Cecil and the Queen stood alone in their belief in England's strength, and when the diplo-matists of Europe regarded her obstinate defiance of Philip's counsels as "madness." The whole people had caught the self-confidence and daring of their Queen. The seamen of the southern coast had long been carrying on a half-piratical war on their own account. Four years after Elizabeth's accession the Channel swarmed with "sea-dogs," as they were called, who sailed under letters of marque from the Prince of Condé and the Huguenot leaders, and took heed neither of the complaints of the French Court nor of Elizabeth's own attempts at repression. Her efforts failed before the connivance of every man along the coast, of the very port-officers of the Crown who made profit out of the spoil, and of the gentry of the west, who were hand and glove with the adventurers. They broke above all against the national craving for open fight with Spain, and the Protestant craving for open fight with Catholicism. Young Englishmen crossed the sea to serve under Condé or Henry of Navarre. The war in the Nether-lands drew hundreds of Protestants to the field. The suspension of the French contest only drove the sea-dogs to the West Indies ; for the Papal decree which gave the New World to Spain, and the threats of Philip against any Protestant who should visit its seas, fell idly on the ears of English seamen. It was in vain that their trading vessels were seized, and the sailors flung into the dungeons of the Inquisition, "laden with irons, without sight of sun or moon." The profits of the trade were large enough to counteract its perils ; and the bigotry of Philip was met by a bigotry as merciless as his own. The Puritanism of the sea-dogs went hand in hand with their love of

Sec. VI.

The
Armada
1572
TO
1588
Francis
Drake
1577

adventure. To break through the Catholic monopoly of the New World, to kill Spaniards, to sell negroes, to sack gold-ships, were in these men's minds a seemly work for the "elect of God." The name of Francis Drake became the terror of the Spanish Indies. In Drake a Protestant fanaticism was united with a splendid daring. He conceived the design of penetrating into the Pacific, whose waters had never seen an English flag; and backed by a little company of adventurers, he set sail for the southern seas in a vessel hardly as big as a Channel schooner, with a few yet smaller companions who fell away before the storms and perils of the voyage. But Drake with his one ship and eighty men held boldly on; and passing the Straits of Magellan, untraversed as yet by any Englishman, swept the unguarded coast of Chili and Peru, loaded his bark with the gold-dust and silver-ingots of Potosi, and with the pearls, emeralds, and diamonds which formed the cargo of the great galleon that sailed once a year from Lima to Cadiz. With spoils of above half-a-million in value the daring adventurer steered undauntedly for the Moluccas, rounded the Cape of Good Hope, and after completing the circuit of the globe dropped anchor again in Plymouth harbour.

The romantic daring of Drake's voyage, as well as the vastness of his spoil, roused a general enthusiasm throughout England. But the welcome he received from Elizabeth on his return was accepted by Philip as an outrage which could only be expiated by war. Sluggish as it was, the blood of the Spanish King was fired at last by the de-fiance with which Elizabeth received all demands for redress. She met a request for Drake's surrender by knighting the freebooter, and by wearing in her crown the jewels he had offered her as a present. When the Spanish ambassador threatened that "matters would come to the cannon," she replied "quietly, in her most natural voice, as if she were telling a common story," wrote Mendoza, "that if I used threats of that kind she would fling me into a dungeon." Outraged as Philip was, she believed that with the Netherlands still in revolt and France longing for her alliance to enable it to seize them, the King could not afford to quarrel with her. But the sense of personal wrong, and the outcry of the Catholic world against his selfish reluctance to avenge the blood of its martyrs, at last told on the Spanish King, and the first vessels of an armada which was destined for the conquest of England began to gather in the Tagus. Resentment and fanaticism indeed were backed by a cool policy. His conquest of Portugal had almost doubled his power. It gave him the one navy that as yet rivalled his own. With the Portuguese colonies his flag claimed mastery in the Indian and the Pacific seas, as it claimed mastery in the Atlantic and Mediterranean; and he had now to shut Englishman and heretic not only out of the New World of the West but out of the lucrative traffic with the East. In the Netherlands too and in France all seemed

SEC. VI.

THE
ARMADA
1572
TO
1588

1584

to go well for Philip's schemes. His forces under Parma had steadily won their way in the Low Countries, and a more fatal blow had been dealt at his rebellious subjects in the assassination of William of Orange ; while all danger of French intervention passed away with the death of the Duke of Anjou, which left Henry of Navarre, the leader of the Huguenot party, heir of the crown of France. To prevent the triumph of heresy in the succession of a Protestant king, the Guises and the French Catholics rose at once in arms ; but the Holy League which they formed rested mainly on the support of Philip, and so long as he supplied them with men and money, he was secure on the side of France. It was at this moment that Parma won his crowning triumph in the capture of Antwerp ; its fall after a gallant resistance convinced even Elizabeth of the need for action if the one "bridle to Spain which kept war out of our own gate" was to be saved. Lord Leicester was hurried to the Flemish coast with 8,000 men. In a yet bolder spirit of defiance Francis Drake was suffered to set sail with a fleet of twenty-five vessels for the Spanish Main. Drake's voyage was a series of triumphs. The wrongs inflicted on English seamen by the Inquisition were requited by the burning of the cities of St. Domingo and Carthagena. The coasts of Cuba and Florida were plundered, and though the gold fleet escaped him, Drake returned with a heavy booty. But only one disastrous skirmish at Zutphen, the fight in which Sidney fell, broke the inaction of Leicester's forces, while Elizabeth strove vainly to use the presence of his army to negotiate a peace between Philip and the States. Meanwhile dangers thickened round her in England itself. Maddened by persecution, by the hopelessness of rebellion within or of deliverance from without, the fiercer Catholics listened to schemes of assassination to which the murder of William of Orange lent a terrible significance. The detection of Somerville, a fanatic who had received the Host before setting out for London "to shoot the Queen with his dagg," was followed by measures of natural severity, by the flight and arrest of Catholic gentry and peers, by a vigorous purification of the Inns of Court where a few Catholics lingered, and by the despatch of fresh batches of priests to the block. The trial and death of Parry, a member of the House of Commons who had served in the Queen's household, on a similar charge, fed the general panic. Parliament met in a transport of horror and loyalty. All Jesuits and seminary priests were banished from the realm on pain of death. A bill for the security of the Queen disqualified any claimant of the succession who instigated subjects to rebellion or hurt to the Queen's person from ever succeeding to the Crown. The threat was aimed at Mary Stuart. Weary of her long restraint, of her failure to rouse Philip or Scotland to aid her, of the baffled revolt of the English Catholics and the baffled intrigues of the Jesuits, she had bent for a

VII.]   THE REFORMATION.   417

SEC. VI.

THE
ARMADA
1572
TO
1588
1586

moment to submission. " Let me go," she wrote to Elizabeth ; " let me retire from this island to some solitude where I may prepare my soul to die. Grant this, and I will sign away every right which either I or mine can claim." But the cry was useless, and her despair found a new and more terrible hope in the plots against Elizabeth's life. She knew and approved the vow of Anthony Babington and a band of young Catholics, for the most part connected with the royal household, to kill the Queen ; but plot and approval alike passed through Walsingham's hands, and the seizure of Mary's correspondence revealed her guilt. In spite of her protest a Commission of Peers sate as her judges at Fotheringay Castle ; and their verdict of " guilty " annihilated under the provisions of the recent statute her claim to the Crown. The streets of London blazed with bonfires, and peals rang out from steeple to steeple at the news of her condemnation ; but, in spite of the prayer of Parliament for her execution, and the pressure of the Council, Elizabeth shrank from her death. The force of public opinion, however, was now carrying all before it, and the unanimous demand of her people wrested at last a sullen consent from the Queen. She flung the warrant signed upon the floor, and the Council took on themselves the responsibility of executing it. Mary died on a scaffold which was erected in the castle-hall at Fotheringay as dauntlessly as she had lived. " Do not weep," she said to her ladies, "I have given my word for you." " Tell my friends," she charged Melville, " that I die a good Catholic."

The blow was hardly struck before Elizabeth turned with fury on the ministers who had forced her hand. Cecil, who had now become Lord Burleigh, was for a while disgraced ; and Davison, who carried the warrant to the Council, was flung into the Tower to atone for an act which shattered the policy of the Queen. The death of Mary Stuart in fact seemed to remove the last obstacle out of Philip's way, by putting an end to the divisions of the English Catholics. To him, as to the nearest heir in blood who was of the Catholic Faith, Mary bequeathed her rights to the Crown, and the hopes of her adherents were from that moment bound up in the success of Spain. Philip no longer needed pressure to induce him to act. Drake's triumph had taught him that the conquest of England was needful for the security of his dominion in the New World. The presence of an English army in Flanders convinced him that the road to the conquest of the States lay through England itself. The operations of Parma therefore in the Low Countries were suspended with a view to the greater enterprise. Vessels and supplies for the fleet which had for three years been gathering in the Tagus were collected from every port of the Spanish coast. Only the dread of a counter-attack from France, where the fortunes of the League were wavering, held Philip back. But the news of the coming Armada called Drake again to action. He set

E E

sail with thirty small barks, burned the storeships and galleys in the
harbour of Cadiz, stormed the ports of the Faro, and was only foiled
in his aim of attacking the Armada itself by orders from home. A
descent upon Corunna however completed what Drake called his
" singeing of the Spanish King's beard." Elizabeth used the daring
blow to back her negotiations for peace ; but the Spanish pride had
been touched to the quick. Amidst the exchange of protocols Parma
gathered seventeen thousand men for the coming invasion, collected a
fleet of flat-bottomed transports at Dunkirk, and waited impatiently
for the Armada to protect his crossing. But the attack of Drake, the
death of its first admiral, and the winter storms delayed the fleet from
sailing. The fear of France held it back yet more effectually ; but in
the spring Philip's patience was rewarded. The League was triumphant, and the King a prisoner in its hands. The Armada at once
set sail from Lisbon, but it had hardly started when a gale in the Bay
of Biscay drove its scattered vessels into Ferrol. It was only on the

nineteenth of July that the sails of the Armada were seen from the
Lizard, and the English beacons flared out their alarm along the coast.
The news found England ready. An army was mustering under
Leicester at Tilbury, the militia of the midland counties were gathering
to London, while those of the south and east were held in readiness to
meet a descent on either shore. Had Parma landed on the earliest
day he purposed, he would have found his way to London barred by a
force stronger than his own, a force too of men in whose ranks were
many who had already crossed pikes on equal terms with his best
infantry in Flanders. "When I shall have landed," he warned
his master, " I must fight battle after battle, I shall lose men by
wounds and disease, I must leave detachments behind me to keep
open my communications ; and in a short time the body of my
army will become so weak that not only I may be unable to advance
in the face of the enemy, and time may be given to the heretics
and your Majesty's other enemies to interfere, but there may fall
out some notable inconvenience, with the loss of everything, and
I be unable to remedy it." Even had Parma landed, in fact, the only
real chance of Spanish success lay in a Catholic rising ; and at this
crisis patriotism proved stronger than religious fanaticism in the hearts
of the English Catholics. Catholic lords brought their vessels up
alongside of Drake and Lord Howard, and Catholic gentry led their
tenantry to the muster at Tilbury. But to secure a landing at all, the
Spaniards had to be masters of the Channel ; and in the Channel lay
an English fleet resolved to struggle hard for the mastery. As the
Armada sailed on in a broad crescent past Plymouth, moving towards
its point of junction with Parma at Calais, the vessels which had
gathered under Lord Howard of Effingham slipped out of the bay and
hung with the wind upon their rear. In numbers the two forces were

strangely unequal ; the English fleet counted only 80 vessels against the 149 which composed the Armada. In size of ships the disproportion was even greater. Fifty of the English vessels, including the squadron of the Lord Admiral and the craft of the volunteers, were little bigger than yachts of the present day. Even of the thirty Queen's ships which formed its main body, there were only four which equalled in tonnage the smallest of the Spanish galleons. Sixty-five of these galleons formed the most formidable half of the Spanish fleet ; and four galleys, four galleasses, armed with fifty guns apiece, fifty-six armed merchantmen, and twenty pinnaces, made up the rest. The Armada was provided with 2,500 cannons, and a vast store of provisions ; it had on board 8,000 seamen, and more than 20,000 soldiers ; and if a court-favourite, the Duke of Medina Sidonia, had been placed at its head, he was supported by the ablest staff of naval officers which Spain possessed. Small however as the English ships were, they were in perfect trim ; they sailed two feet for the Spaniards' one, they were manned with 9,000 hardy seamen, and their Admiral was backed by a crowd of captains who had won fame in the Spanish seas. With him was Hawkins, who had been the first to break into the charmed circle of the Indies ; Frobisher, the hero of the North-West passage ; and above all Drake, who held command of the privateers. They had won too the advantage of the wind, and, closing in or drawing off as they would, the lightly-handled English vessels, which fired four shots to the Spaniards' one, hung boldly on the rear of the great fleet as it moved along the Channel. "The feathers of the Spaniard," in the phrase of the English seamen, were "plucked one by one." Galleon after galleon was sunk, boarded, driven on shore ; and yet Medina Sidonia failed in bringing his pursuers to a close engagement. Now halting, now moving slowly on, the running fight between the two fleets lasted throughout the week, till the Armada dropped anchor in Calais roads. The time had now come for sharper work if the junction of the Armada with Parma was to be prevented ; for, demoralized as the Spaniards had been by the merciless chase, their loss in ships had not been great, while, though the numbers of English ships had grown, their supplies of food and ammunition were fast running out. Howard resolved to force an engagement, and, lighting eight fire-ships at midnight, sent them down with the tide upon the Spanish line. The galleons at once cut their cables, and stood out in panic to sea, drifting with the wind in a long line off Gravelines. Drake resolved at all costs to prevent their return. At dawn the English ships closed fairly in, and almost their last cartridge was spent ere the sun went down. Three great galleons had sunk, three had drifted helplessly on to the Flemish coast ; but the bulk of the Spanish vessels remained, and even to Drake the fleet seemed "wonderful great and strong." Within the Armada itself, however, all hope was gone. Huddled together by the wind and the deadly English fire, their sails torn, their masts shot away, the crowded galleons had become mere slaughter-houses. Four thousand men had fallen, and bravely as the seamen fought they were cowed by the terrible butchery. Medina himself was in despair. "We are lost, Señor Oquenda," he cried to his bravest captain ; "what are we to do?" "Let others talk of being lost," replied Oquenda, "your Excellency has only to order up fresh cartridge." But Oquenda stood alone, and a council of war resolved on retreat to Spain by the one course open, that of a circuit round the Orkneys. "Never anything pleased me better," wrote Drake, "than seeing the enemy fly with a southerly wind to the northwards. Have a good eye to the Prince of Parma, for, with the grace of God, if we like, I doubt not ere it be long so to handle the matter with the Duke of Sidonia, as he shall wish himself at St. Mary Port among his orange trees." But the work of destruction was reserved for a mightier foe than Drake. Supplies fell short and the English vessels were forced to give up the chase ; but the Spanish ships which remained had no sooner reached the Orkneys than the storms of the northern seas broke on them with a fury before which all concert and union disappeared. Fifty reached Corunna, bearing ten thousand men stricken with pestilence and death. Of the rest some were sunk, some dashed to pieces against the Irish cliffs. The wreckers of the Orkneys and the Faroes, the clansmen of the Scottish Isles, the kernes of Donegal and Galway, all had their part in the work of murder and robbery. Eight thousand Spaniards perished between the Giant's Causeway and the Blaskets. On a strand near Sligo an English captain numbered eleven hundred corpses which had been cast up by the sea. The flower of the Spanish nobility, who had been sent on the new crusade under Alonzo da Leyva, after twice suffering shipwreck, put a third time to sea to founder on a reef near Dunluce.

Section VII.—The Elizabethan Poets.

[*Authorities.*—For a general account of this period, see Mr. Morley's admirable " First Sketch of English Literature," Hallam's " Literary History," M. Taine's " History of English Literature," &c. Mr. Craik has elaborately illustrated the works of Spenser, and full details of the history of our early drama may be found in Mr. Collier's " History of English Dramatic Literature to the time of Shakspere." Malone's enquiry remains the completest investigation into the history of Shakspere's dramas ; and the works of Mr. Armytage Brown and Mr. Gerald Massey contain the latest theories as to the Sonnets. For Ben Jonson and his fellows, see their works with the notes of Gifford, &c. The fullest account of Lord Bacon will be found in his " Life and Letters," now published with his " Works," by Mr. Spedding, whose apologetic tones may be contrasted with the verdict of Lord Macaulay (" Essay on Lord Bacon ") and with the more judicious judgement of Mr. Gardiner (" History of England "). See also Mr. Lewes's " History of Philosophy."]

We have already watched the revival of English letters during the earlier half of Elizabeth's reign. The general awakening of national

VII.]

THE REFORMATION.

421

Sec. VII.

The Eliza-
bethan
Poets

life, the increase of wealth, of refinement and leisure, which marked that period, had been accompanied, as we have seen, by a quickening of English intelligence, which found vent in an upgrowth of grammar schools, in the new impulse given to classical learning at the Universities, in a passion for translations which familiarized all England with the masterpieces of Italy and Greece, and above all in the crude but vigorous efforts of Sackville and Lyly after a nobler poetry and prose. But to the national and local influences which were telling on English literature was added that of the restlessness and curiosity which characterized the age. The sphere of human interest was widened as it has never been widened before or since by the revelation of a new heaven and a new earth. It was only in the later years of the sixteenth century that the discoveries of Copernicus were brought home to the general intelligence of the world by Kepler and Galileo, or that the daring of the Buccaneers broke through the veil which the greed of Spain had drawn across the New World of Columbus. Hardly inferior to these revelations as a source of intellectual impulse was the sudden and picturesque way in which the various races of the world were brought face to face with one another through the universal passion for foreign travel. While the red tribes of the West were described by Amerigo Vespucci, and the strange civilization of Mexico and Peru disclosed by Cortes and Pizarro, the voyages of the Portuguese threw open the older splendours of the East, and the story of India and China was told for the first time to Christendom by Maffei and Mendoza. England took her full part in this work of discovery. Jenkinson, an English traveller, made his way to Bokhara. Willoughby brought back Muscovy to the knowledge of Western Europe. English mariners penetrated among the Esquimaux, or settled in Virginia. Drake circumnavigated the globe. The "Collection of Voyages," which was published by Hakluyt, not only disclosed the vastness of the world itself, but the infinite number of the races of mankind, the variety of their laws, their customs, their religions, their very instincts. We see the influence of this new and wider knowledge of the world, not only in the life and richness which it gave to the imagination of the time, but in the immense interest which from this moment attached itself to Man. Shakspere's conception of Caliban, like the questionings of Montaigne, marks the beginning of a new and a truer, because a more inductive, philosophy of human nature and human history. The fascination exercised by the study of human character showed itself in the essays of Bacon, and yet more in the wonderful popularity of the drama. And to these larger and world-wide sources of poetic powers was added in England the impulse which sprang from national triumph, from the victory over the Armada, the deliverance from Spain, the rolling away of the Catholic terror which had hung like a cloud over the hopes of the people. With its new sense of security, of national energy and national power, the whole aspect of England suddenly changed. As yet the interest of Elizabeth's reign had been political and material ; the stage had been crowded with statesmen and warriors, with Cecils and Walsinghams and Drakes. Literature had hardly found a place in the glories of the time. But from the moment when the Armada drifted back broken to Ferrol, the figures of warriors and statesmen were dwarfed by the grander figures of poets and philosophers. Amidst the throng in Elizabeth's ante-chamber the noblest form is that of the singer who lays the " Faerie Queen " at her feet, or of the young lawyer who muses amid the splen-dours of the presence over the problems of the " Novum Organum." The triumph at Cadiz, the conquest of Ireland, pass unheeded as we watch Hooker building up his " Ecclesiastical Polity " among the sheepfolds, or the genius of Shakspere rising year by year into supremer grandeur in a rude theatre beside the Thames.

Spenser
1552

The full glory of the new literature broke on England with Edmund Spenser. We know little of his life ; he was born in East London of poor parents, but connected with the Spencers of Althorpe, even then—as he proudly says—" a house of ancient fame." He studied as a sizar at Cambridge, and quitted the University while still a boy to live as a tutor in the north ; but after some years of obscure poverty the scorn of a fair " Rosalind " drove him again southwards. A college friendship with Gabriel Harvey served to introduce him to Lord Leicester, who sent him as his envoy into France, and in whose service he first became acquainted with Leicester's nephew, Sir Philip Sidney. From Sidney's house at Penshurst came his earliest work,

1579

the " Shepherd's Calendar ;" in form, like Sidney's own "Arcadia," a pastoral, where love and loyalty and Puritanism jostled oddly with the fancied shepherd life. The peculiar melody and profuse imagination which the pastoral disclosed at once placed its author in the forefront of living poets, but a far greater work was already in hand ; and from some words of Gabriel Harvey's we see Spenser bent on rivalling Ariosto, and even hoping "to overgo" the " Orlando Furioso," in his " Elvish Queen." The ill-will or indifference of Burleigh, however, blasted the expectations he had drawn from the patronage of Sidney or the Earl of Leicester, and the favour with which he had been welcomed by the Queen. Sidney, himself in disgrace with Elizabeth, withdrew to Wilton to write the " Arcadia," by his sister's side ; and "discontent of my long fruitless stay in princes' courts," the poet tells us, "and expectation vain of idle hopes," drove Spenser at last into exile. He followed Lord Grey as his secretary into Ireland, and remained there

1580

on the Deputy's recall in the enjoyment of an office and a grant of land from the forfeited estates of the Earl of Desmond. Spenser had thus enrolled himself among the colonists to whom England was looking at the time for the regeneration of Munster, and the practical interest he took in the "barren soil where cold and want and poverty do grow" was shown by the later publication of a prose tractate on the condition and government of the island. It was at Dublin or in his castle of Kilcolman, two miles from Doneraile, "under the foote of Mole, that mountain hoar," that he spent the ten years in which Sidney died and Mary fell on the scaffold and the Armada came and went; and it was in the latter home that Walter Ralegh found him sitting "alwaies idle," as it seemed to his restless friend, "among the cooly shades of the green alders by the Mulla's shore," in a visit made memorable by the poem of "Colin Clout's come home again." But in the "idlesse" and solitude of the poet's exile the great work begun in the two pleasant years of his stay at Penshurst had at last taken form, and it was to publish the first three books of the "Faerie Queen" that Spenser returned in Ralegh's company to London.

The appearance of the "Faerie Queen" is the one critical event in the annals of English poetry; it settled, in fact, the question whether there was to be such a thing as English poetry or no. The older national verse which had blossomed and died in Cædmon sprang suddenly into a grander life in Chaucer, but it closed again in a yet more complete death. Across the Border, indeed, the Scotch poets of the fifteenth century preserved something of their master's vivacity and colour, and in England itself the Italian poetry of the Renascence had of late found echoes in Surrey and Sidney. The new English drama too was beginning to display its wonderful powers, and the work of Marlowe had already prepared the way for the work of Shakspere. But bright as was the promise of coming song, no great imaginative poem had broken the silence of English literature for nearly two hundred years when Spenser landed at Bristol with the "Faerie Queen." From that moment the stream of English poetry has flowed on without a break. There have been times, as in the years which immediately followed, when England has "become a nest of singing birds;" there have been times when song was scant and poor; but there never has been a time when England was wholly without a singer. The new English verse has been true to the source from which it sprang, and Spenser has always been "the poet's poet." But in his own day he was the poet of England at large. The "Faerie Queen" was received with a burst of general welcome. It became "the delight of every accomplished gentleman, the model of every poet, the solace of every soldier." The poem expressed, indeed, the very life of the time. It was with a true poetic instinct that Spenser fell back for the framework of his story on the faery world of Celtic romance, whose wonder and mystery had in fact become the truest picture of the wonder and mystery of the world around him. In the age of Cortes and of Ralegh dreamland had ceased to be dreamland, and no marvel or adventure that befell lady or knight was stranger

than the tales which weather-beaten mariners from the Southern Seas
were telling every day to grave merchants upon 'Change. The very in-
congruities of the story of Arthur and his knighthood, strangely as it
had been built up out of the rival efforts of bard and jongleur and priest,
made it the fittest vehicle for the expression of the world of incongruous
feeling which we call the Renascence. To modern eyes perhaps there
is something grotesque in the strange medley of figures which crowd
the canvas of the " Faerie Queen," in its fauns dancing on the sward
where knights have hurtled together, in its alternation of the salvage-
men from the New World with the satyrs of classic mythology, in
the giants, dwarfs, and monsters of popular fancy, who jostle with
the nymphs of Greek legend and the damosels of mediæval romance.
But, strange as the medley is, it reflects truly enough the stranger
medley of warring ideals and irreconcileable impulses which made up
the life of Spenser's contemporaries. It was not in the "Faerie Queen"
only, but in the world which it pourtrayed, that the religious mysticism
of the Middle Ages stood face to face with the intellectual freedom of
the Revival of Letters, that asceticism and self-denial cast their spell
on imaginations glowing with the sense of varied and inexhaustible
existence, that the dreamy and poetic refinement of feeling which expressed itself in the fanciful unrealities of chivalry co-existed with the
rough practical energy that sprang from an awakening sense of human
power, or the lawless extravagance of an idealized friendship and love
lived side by side with the moral sternness and elevation which England
was drawing from the Reformation and the Bible. But strangely contrasted as are the elements of the poem, they are harmonized by the
calmness and serenity which is the note of the " Faerie Queen." The
world of the Renascence is around us, but it is ordered, refined, and
calmed by the poet's touch. The warmest scenes which he borrows
from the Italian verse of his day are idealized into purity ; the very
struggle of the men around him is lifted out of its pettier accidents,
and raised into a spiritual oneness with the struggle in the soul itself.
There are allusions in plenty to contemporary events, but the contest
between Elizabeth and Mary takes ideal form in that of Una and the
false Duessa, and the clash of arms between Spain and the Huguenots
comes to us faint and hushed through the serener air. The verse, like
the story, rolls on as by its own natural power, without haste or effort
or delay. The gorgeous colouring, the profuse and often complex
imagery which Spenser's imagination lavishes, leave no sense of
confusion in the reader's mind. Every figure, strange as it may be, is
seen clearly and distinctly as it passes by. It is in this calmness, this
serenity, this spiritual elevation of the " Faerie Queen," that we feel the
new life of the coming age moulding into ordered and harmonious
form the life of the Renascence. Both in its conception, and in the way
in which this conception is realized in the portion of his work which

Spenser completed, his poem strikes the note of the coming Puritanism. In his earlier pastoral, the "Shepherd's Calendar," the poet had boldly taken his part with the more advanced reformers against the Church policy of the Court.   He had chosen Archbishop Grindal, who was then in disgrace for his Puritan sympathies, as his model of a Christian pastor ; and attacked with sharp invective the pomp of the higher clergy.   His "Faerie Queen," in its religious theory, is Puritan to the core.   The worst foe of its "Red-cross Knight" is the false and scarlet-clad Duessa of Rome, who parts him for a while from Truth and leads him to the house of Pride.   Spenser presses strongly and pitilessly for the execution of Mary Stuart.   No bitter word ever breaks the calm of his verse save when it touches on the perils with which Catholicism was environing England, perils before which his knight must fall "were not that Heavenly Grace doth him uphold and steadfast Truth acquite him out of all."   But it is yet more in the temper and aim of his work that we catch the nobler and deeper tones of English Puritanism.   In his earlier musings at Penshurst the poet had purposed to surpass Ariosto, but the gaiety of Ariosto's song is utterly absent from his own.   Not a ripple of laughter breaks the calm surface of Spenser's verse.   He is habitually serious, and the seriousness of his poetic tone reflects the seriousness of his poetic purpose.   His aim, he tells us, was to represent the moral virtues, to assign to each its knightly patron, so that its excellence might be expressed and its contrary vice trodden under foot by deeds of arms and chivalry.   In knight after knight of the twelve he purposed to paint, he wished to embody some single virtue of the virtuous man in its struggle with the faults and errors which specially beset it ; till in Arthur, the sum of the whole company, man might have been seen perfected, in his longing and progress towards the "Faerie Queen," the Divine Glory which is the true end of human effort.   The largeness of his culture indeed, his exquisite sense of beauty, and above all the very intensity of his moral enthusiasm, saved Spenser from the narrowness and exaggeration which often distorted goodness into unloveliness in the Puritan.   Christian as he is to the core, his Christianity is enriched and fertilized by the larger temper of the Renascence, as well as by a poet's love of the natural world in which the older mythologies struck their roots.   Diana and the gods of heathendom take a sacred tinge from the purer sanctities of the new faith ; and in one of the greatest songs of the "Faerie Queen," the conception of love widens, as it widened in the mind of a Greek, into the mighty thought of the productive energy of Nature.   Spenser borrows in fact the delicate and refined forms of the Platonist philosophy to express his own moral enthusiasm.   Not only does he love, as others have loved, all that is noble and pure and of good report, but he is fired as none before or after him have been fired with a passionate sense of moral beauty. Justice, Temperance, Truth, are no mere names to him, but real existences to which his whole nature clings with a rapturous affection. Outer beauty he believed to spring, and loved because it sprang, from the beauty of the soul within. There was much in such a moral protest as this to rouse dislike in any age, but it is the glory of the age of Elizabeth that, "mad world" as in many ways it was, all that was noble welcomed the "Faerie Queen." Elizabeth herself, says Spenser, "to mine oaten pipe inclined her ear," and bestowed a pension on the poet. In 1595 he brought three more books of his poem to England. He returned to Ireland, to commemorate his marriage in Sonnets and the most beautiful of bridal songs, and to complete the "Faerie Queen" amongst love and poverty and troubles from his Irish neighbours. But these troubles soon took a graver form. In 1599 Ireland broke into revolt, and the poet escaped from his burning house to fly to England, and to die broken-hearted in an inn at Westminster.

If the "Faerie Queen" expressed the higher elements of the Elizabethan age, the whole of that age, its lower elements and its higher alike, was expressed in the English drama. We have already pointed out the circumstances which throughout Europe were giving a poetic impulse to the newly-aroused intelligence of men, and this impulse everywhere took a dramatic shape. The artificial French tragedy which began about this time with Garnier was not, indeed, destined to exert any influence over English poetry till a later age; but the influence of the Italian comedy, which had begun half a century earlier with Machiavelli and Ariosto, was felt directly through the Novelle, or stories, which served as plots for the dramatists. It left its stamp indeed on some of the worst characteristics of the English stage. The features of our drama that startled the moral temper of the time and won the deadly hatred of the Puritan, its grossness and profanity, its tendency to scenes of horror and crime, its profuse employment of cruelty and lust as grounds of dramatic action, its daring use of the horrible and the unnatural whenever they enable it to display the more terrible and revolting sides of human passion, were derived from the Italian stage. It is doubtful how much the English playwrights may have owed to the Spanish drama, that under Lope and Cervantes sprang suddenly into a grandeur which almost rivalled their own. In the intermixture of tragedy and comedy, in the abandonment of the solemn uniformity of poetic diction for the colloquial language of real life, the use of unexpected incidents, the complications of their plots and intrigues, the dramas of England and Spain are remarkably alike; but the likeness seems rather to have sprung from a similarity in the circumstances to which both owed their rise, than from any direct connection of the one with the other. The real origin of the English drama, in fact, lay not in any influence from without, but in the influence of England itself. The temper of the nation was dramatic. Ever since the Reformation, the Palace, the Inns of Court, and the University had been vyeing with one another in the production of plays; and so early was their popularity, that even under Henry the Eighth it was found necessary to create a " Master of the Revels " to supervise them. Every progress of Elizabeth from shire to shire was a succession of shows and interludes. Dian with her nymphs met the Queen as she returned from hunting; Love presented her with his golden arrow as she passed through the gates of Norwich. From the earlier years of her reign, the new spirit of the Renascence had been pouring itself into the rough mould of the Mystery Plays, whose allegorical virtues and vices, or scriptural heroes and heroines, had handed on the spirit of the drama through the Middle Ages. Adaptations from classical pieces soon began to alternate with the purely religious " Moralities ; " and an attempt at a livelier style of expression and invention appeared in the popular comedy of " Gammer Gurton's Needle ; " while Sackville, Lord Dorset, in his tragedy of " Gorboduc " made a bold effort at sublimity of diction, and introduced the use of blank verse as the vehicle of dramatic dialogue. But it was not to these tentative efforts of scholars and nobles that the English stage was really indebted for the amazing outburst of genius, which dates from the moment when " the Earl of Leicester's servants" erected the first public theatre in Blackfriars. It was the people itself that created its Stage. The theatre, indeed, was commonly only the courtyard of an inn, or a mere booth such as is still seen at a country fair ; the bulk of the audience sate beneath the open sky in the " pit " or yard, a few covered seats in the galleries which ran round it formed the boxes of the wealthier spectators, while patrons and nobles found seats upon the actual boards. All the appliances were of the roughest sort : a few flowers served to indicate a garden, crowds and armies were represented by a dozen scene-shifters with swords and bucklers, heroes rode in and out on hobby-horses, and a scroll on a post told whether the scene was at Athens or London. There were no female actors, and the grossness which startles us in words which fell from women's lips took a different colour when every woman's part was acted by a boy. But difficulties such as these were more than compensated by the popular character of the drama itself. Rude as the theatre might be, all the world was there. The stage was crowded with nobles and courtiers. Apprentices and citizens thronged the benches in the yard below. The rough mob of the pit inspired, as it felt, the vigorous life, the rapid transitions, the passionate energy, the reality, the lifelike medley and confusion, the racy dialogue, the chat, the wit, the pathos, the sublimity, the rant and buffoonery, the coarse horrors and vulgar bloodshedding, the immense range over all classes of society, the intimacy with the foulest as well as the fairest

1576

developements of human temper, which characterized the English stage. The new drama represented "the very age and body of the time, his form and pressure." The people itself brought its nobleness and its vileness to the boards. No stage was ever so human, no poetic life so intense. Wild, reckless, defiant of all past tradition, of all conventional laws, the English dramatists owned no teacher, no source of poetic inspiration, but the people itself.

The Earlier Drama-tists

Few events in our literary history are so startling as this sudden rise of the Elizabethan drama. The first public theatre, as we have seen, was erected only in the middle of the Queen's reign. Before the close of it eighteen theatres existed in London alone. Fifty dramatic poets, many of the first order, appeared in the fifty years which precede the closing of the theatres by the Puritans ; and great as is the number of their works which have perished, we still possess a hundred dramas, all written within this period, and of which at least a half are excellent. A glance at their authors shows us that the intellectual quickening of the age had now reached the mass of the people. Almost all of the new playwrights were fairly educated, and many were University men. But, instead of courtly singers of the Sidney and Spenser sort, we see the advent of the "poor scholar." The earlier dramatists, such as Nash, Peele, Kyd, Greene, or Marlowe, were for the most part poor, and reckless in their poverty ; wild livers, defiant of law or common fame, in revolt against the usages and religion of their day, "atheists" in general repute, "holding Moses for a juggler," haunting the brothel and the alehouse, and dying starved or in tavern brawls. But with their appearance began the Elizabethan drama. The few plays which have reached us of an earlier date are either cold imitations of the classical and Italian comedy, or rude farces like "Ralph Roister Doister," or tragedies such as "Gorboduc," where, poetic as occasional passages may be, there is little promise of dramatic developement. But in the year which preceded the coming of the Armada the whole aspect of the stage suddenly changes, and

1587

the new dramatists range themselves around two men of very different genius, Robert Greene and Christopher Marlowe. Of Greene, as the creator of our lighter English prose, we have already spoken. But his

Greene

work as a poet was of yet greater importance, for his keen perception of character and the relations of social life, the playfulness of his fancy, and the liveliness of his style exerted an influence on his contemporaries, which was equalled by that of none but Marlowe and Peele. No figure better paints the group of young playwrights. He left Cambridge to travel through Italy and Spain, and to bring back the debauchery of the one and the scepticism of the other. In the words of remorse he wrote before his death he paints himself as a drunkard and a roysterer, winning money only by ceaseless pamphlets and plays to waste it on wine and women, and drinking the cup of

life to the dregs.   Hell and the after-world were the butts of his
ceaseless mockery.   If he had not feared the judges of the Queen's
Courts more than he feared God, he said, in bitter jest, he should
often have turned cutpurse.   He married, and loved his wife, but she
was soon deserted ; and the wretched profligate found himself again
plunged into excesses which he loathed, though he could not live without them.   But wild as was the life of Greene, his pen was pure.   He
is steadily on virtue's side in the love pamphlets and novelettes he
poured out in endless succession, and whose plots were dramatized
by the school which gathered round him.   The life of Marlowe was
as riotous, his scepticism even more daring, than the life and scepticism of Greene.   His early death alone saved him, in all probability,
from a prosecution for atheism.   He was charged with calling Moses
a juggler, and with boasting that, if he undertook to write a new
religion, it should be a better religion than the Christianity he saw
around him.   But he stood far ahead of his fellows as a creator of
English tragedy.   Born at the opening of Elizabeth's reign, the son of
a Canterbury shoemaker, but educated at Cambridge, Marlowe burst
on the world in the year which preceded the triumph over the Armada,
with a play which at once wrought a revolution in the English stage.
Bombastic and extravagant as it was, and extravagance reached its
height in the scene where captive kings, the "pampered jades of Asia,"
drew their conqueror's car across the stage, "Tamburlaine" not only
indicated the revolt of the new drama against the timid inanities of
Euphuism, but gave an earnest of that imaginative daring, the secret
of which Marlowe was to bequeath to the playwrights who followed
him.   He perished at twenty-nine in a shameful brawl, but in his brief
career he had struck the grander notes of the coming drama.   His
Jew of Malta was the herald of Shylock.   He opened in "Edward the
Second" the series of historical plays which gave us "Cæsar" and
"Richard the Third."   Riotous, grotesque, and full of a mad thirst for
pleasure as it is, his "Faustus" was the first dramatic attempt to touch
the great problem of the relations of man to the unseen world, to paint
the power of doubt in a temper leavened with superstition, the daring
of human defiance in a heart abandoned to despair.   Extravagant,
unequal, stooping even to the ridiculous in his cumbrous and vulgar
buffoonery, there is a force in Marlowe, a conscious grandeur of tone,
a range of passion, which sets him above all his contemporaries
save one.   In the higher qualities of imagination, as in the majesty
and sweetness of his "mighty line," he is inferior to Shakspere alone.

A few daring jests, a brawl and a fatal stab, make up the life of
Marlowe ; but even details such as these are wanting to the life of
William Shakspere.   Of hardly any great poet, indeed, do we know
so little.   For the story of his youth we have only one or two trifling
legends, and these almost certainly false.   Not a single letter or

Marlowe

1593

**Shak-
spere**

characteristic saying, not one of the jests "spoken at the Mermaid,"
hardly a single anecdote, remain to illustrate his busy life in London.
His look and figure in later age have been preserved by the bust over
his tomb at Stratford, and a hundred years after his death he was
still remembered in his native town; but the minute diligence of the
enquirers of the Georgian time was able to glean hardly a single
detail, even of the most trivial order, which could throw light upon
the years of retirement before his death. It is owing perhaps to the
harmony and unity of his temper that no salient peculiarity seems to
have left its trace on the memory of his contemporaries; it is the
very grandeur of his genius which precludes us from discovering any
personal trait in his works. His supposed self-revelation in the
Sonnets is so obscure that only a few outlines can be traced even by
the boldest conjecture. In his dramas he is all his characters, and his
characters range over all mankind. There is not one, or the act or
word of one, that we can identify personally with the poet himself.

1564
He was born in the sixth year of Elizabeth's reign, twelve years
after the birth of Spenser, three years later than the birth of Bacon.
Marlowe was of the same age with Shakspere: Greene probably a few
years older. His father, a glover and small farmer of Stratford-on-
Avon, was forced by poverty to lay down his office of alderman, as his
son reached boyhood; and stress of poverty may have been the cause
which drove William Shakspere, who was already married at eighteen
to a wife older than himself, to London and the stage. His life in the
capital can hardly have begun later than in his twenty-third year, the
memorable year which followed Sidney's death, which preceded the
1587
coming of the Armada, and which witnessed the production of Marlowe's
"Tamburlaine." If we take the language of the Sonnets as a record
of his personal feeling, his new profession as an actor stirred in him
only the bitterness of self-contempt. He chides with Fortune, "that
did not better for my life provide than public means that public manners breed;" he writhes at the thought that he has "made himself a
motley to the view" of the gaping apprentices in the pit of Blackfriars.
"Thence comes it," he adds, "that my name receives a brand, and
almost thence my nature is subdued to that it works in." But the
application of the words is a more than doubtful one. In spite of
petty squabbles with some of his dramatic rivals at the outset of his
career, the genial nature of the new comer seems to have won him a
general love among his fellow actors. In 1592, while still a mere
fitter of old plays for the stage, a fellow playwright, Chettle, answered
Greene's attack on him in words of honest affection: "Myself have
seen his demeanour no less civil, than he excellent in the quality he
professes: besides, divers of worship have reported his uprightness of
dealing, which argues his honesty; and his facetious grace in writing,
that approves his art." His partner Burbage spoke of him after

death as a "worthy friend and fellow;" and Jonson handed down
the general tradition of his time when he described him as "indeed
honest, and of an open and free nature." His profession as an actor
was of essential service to him in his poetic career. Not only did it
give him the sense of theatrical necessities which makes his plays
so effective on the boards, but it enabled him to bring his pieces as he
wrote them to the test of the stage. If there is any truth in Jonson's
statement that Shakspere never blotted a line, there is no justice in
the censure which it implies on his carelessness or incorrectness.
The conditions of poetic publication were in fact wholly different from
those of our own day. A drama remained for years in manuscript
as an acting piece, subject to continual revision and amendment; and
every rehearsal and representation afforded hints for change which we
know the young poet was far from neglecting. The chance which has
preserved an earlier edition of his "Hamlet" shows in what an unsparing way Shakspere could recast even the finest products of his genius.
Five years after the supposed date of his arrival in London, he was
already famous as a dramatist. Greene speaks bitterly of him, under
the name of "Shakescene," as an "upstart crow beautified with our
feathers," a sneer which points either to his celebrity as an actor, or
to his preparation for loftier flights by fitting pieces of his predecessors
for the stage. He was soon partner in the theatre, actor, and playwright; and another nickname, that of "Johannes Factotum," or
Jack-of-all-Trades, shows his readiness to take all honest work which
came to hand.

With the poem of "Venus and Adonis," "the first heir of my invention," as Shakspere calls it, the period of independent creation fairly
began. The date of its publication was a very memorable one. The
"Faerie Queen" had appeared only three years before, and had placed
Spenser without a rival at the head of English poetry. On the
other hand, the two leading dramatists of the time passed at this
moment suddenly away. Greene died in poverty and self-reproach
in the house of a poor shoemaker. "Doll," he wrote to the wife he
had abandoned, " I charge thee, by the love of our youth and by my
soul's rest, that thou wilt see this man paid ; for if he and his wife had
not succoured me, I had died in the streets." " Oh, that a year were
granted me to live," cried the young poet from his bed of death—"but I
must die, of every man abhorred ! Time, loosely spent, will not again
be won ! My time is loosely spent—and I undone ! " A year later, the
death of Marlowe in a street brawl removed the only rival whose
powers might have equalled Shakspere's own. He was now about
thirty ; and the twenty-three years which elapsed between the appearance of the " Adonis " and his death were filled with a series of masterpieces. Nothing is more characteristic of his genius than its incessant
activity. Through the five years which followed the publication of his

early poem he seems to have produced on an average two dramas a
year.   When we attempt, however, to trace the growth and progress
of the poet's mind in the order of his plays, we are met, at least in the
case of many of them, by an absence of certain information as to the
dates of their appearance. The facts on which enquiry has to build are
extremely few.   " Venus and Adonis," with the " Lucrece," must have
been written before their publication in 1593-4 ; the Sonnets, though not
published till 1609, were known in some form among his private friends
as early as 1598.   His earlier plays are defined by a list given in the
" Wit's Treasury " of Francis Meres in 1598, though the omission of a
play from a casual catalogue of this kind would hardly warrant us in assuming its necessary non-existence at the time.   The works ascribed to
him at his death are fixed, in the same approximate fashion, through
the edition published by his fellow-actors. Beyond these meagre facts,
and our knowledge of the publication of a few of his dramas in his
lifetime, all is uncertain ; and the conclusions which have been drawn
from these, and from the dramas themselves, as well as from assumed
resemblances with, or references to, other plays of the period, can only
be accepted as approximations to the truth.   The bulk of his lighter
comedies and historical dramas can be assigned with fair probability
to the period from about 1593, when he was known as nothing more than
an adapter, to 1598, when they are mentioned in the list of Meres. They
bear on them indeed the stamp of youth.   In " Love's Labour's Lost "
the young playwright, fresh from his own Stratford, flings himself into
the midst of the brilliant England which gathered round Elizabeth,
busying himself as yet for the most part with the surface of it, with the
humours and quixotisms, the wit and the whim, the unreality, the fantastic extravagance, which veiled its inner nobleness.   Country lad as
he is, he can exchange quip and repartee with the best ; he quizzes the
verbal wit and high-flown extravagance of thought and phrase which
Euphues had made fashionable in the court world of the time.   He
shares the delight in existence which was so marked a feature of the age ;
he enjoys the mistakes, the contrasts, the adventures, of the men about
him ; his fun breaks almost riotously out in the practical jokes of the
" Taming of the Shrew " and the endless blunderings of the " Comedy
of Errors."   His work is as yet marked by little poetic elevation, or by
passion ; but the easy grace of the dialogue, the dexterous management
of a complicated story, the genial gaiety of his tone, and the music of
his verse, promised a master of social comedy as soon as Shakspere
turned from the superficial aspects of the world about him to find a new
delight in the character and actions of men.   In the " Two Gentlemen
of Verona," his painting of manners was suffused by a tenderness and
ideal beauty, which formed an effective protest against the hard though
vigorous character-painting which the first success of Ben Jonson in
" Every Man in his Humour " brought at the time into fashion.   But

quick on these lighter comedies followed two, in which his genius started fully into life. His poetic power, held in reserve till now, showed itself with a splendid profusion in the brilliant fancies of the "Midsummer Night's Dream;" and passion swept like a tide of resistless delight through "Romeo and Juliet." Side by side however with these passionate dreams, these delicate imaginings and piquant sketches of manners, had been appearing during this short interval of intense activity his historical dramas. No plays seem to have been more popular, from the earliest hours of the new stage, than dramatic representations of our history. Marlowe had shown in his "Edward the Second" what tragic grandeur could be reached in this favourite field; and, as we have seen, Shakspere had been led naturally towards it by his earlier occupation as an adapter of stock pieces like "Henry the Sixth" for the new requirements of the stage. He still to some extent followed in plan the older plays on the subjects he selected, but in his treatment of their themes he shook boldly off the yoke of the past. A larger and deeper conception of human character than any of the old dramatists had reached displayed itself in Richard the Third, in Falstaff, or in Hotspur; while in Constance and Richard the Second the pathos of human suffering was painted as even Marlowe had never dared to paint it. No dramas have done so much for Shakspere's enduring popularity with his countrymen as these historical plays. Nowhere is the spirit of our history so nobly rendered. If the poet's work echoes sometimes our national prejudice and unfairness of temper, it is instinct throughout with English humour, with our English love of hard fighting, our English faith in goodness and in the doom that waits upon triumphant evil, our English pity for the fallen.

Whether as a tragedian or as a writer of social comedy, Shakspere had now passed far beyond his fellows. "The Muses," said Meres, "would speak with Shakspere's fine filed phrase, if they would speak English." His personal popularity was at its height. His pleasant temper, and the vivacity of his wit, had drawn him early into contact with the young Earl of Southampton, to whom his "Adonis" and "Lucrece" are dedicated; and the different tone of the two dedications shows how rapidly acquaintance ripened into an ardent friendship. Shakspere's wealth and influence too were growing fast. He had property both in Stratford and London, and his fellow-townsmen made him their suitor to Lord Burleigh for favours to be bestowed on Stratford. He was rich enough to aid his father, and to buy the house at Stratford which afterwards became his home. The tradition that Elizabeth was so pleased with Falstaff in "Henry the Fourth" that she ordered the poet to show her Falstaff in love—an order which produced the "Merry Wives of Windsor"—whether true or false, proves his repute as a playwright. As the group of earlier poets passed away, they found successors in Marston, Dekker, Middleton,

Heywood, and Chapman, and above all in Ben Jonson.   But none of
these could dispute the supremacy of Shakspere.   The verdict of
Meres, that " Shakspere among the English is the most excellent in
both kinds for the stage," represented the general feeling of his contemporaries.   He was at last fully master of the resources of his art.
The " Merchant of Venice " marks the perfection of his developement
as a dramatist in the completeness of its stage effect, the ingenuity of
its incidents, the ease of its movement, the poetic beauty of its higher
passages, the reserve and self-control with which its poetry is used, the
conception and unfolding of character, and above all the mastery with
which character and event are grouped round the figure of Shylock.
But the poet's temper is still young ; the " Merry Wives of Windsor "
is a burst of gay laughter ; and laughter more tempered, yet full of a
sweeter fascination, rings round us in " As You Like It."   But in the
melancholy and meditative Jacques of the last drama we feel the touch
of a new and graver mood.   Youth, so full and buoyant in the poet till
now, seems to have passed almost suddenly away.   Though Shakspere
had hardly reached forty, in one of his Sonnets which cannot have
been written at a much later time than this, there are indications that
he already felt the advance of premature age.   The outer world suddenly darkened around him.   The brilliant circle of young nobles whose
friendship he had shared was broken up by the political storm which
burst in a mad struggle of the Earl of Essex for power.   Essex himself
fell on the scaffold ; his friend and Shakspere's idol, Southampton,
passed a prisoner into the Tower ; Herbert, Lord Pembroke, a younger
patron of the poet, was banished from Court.   While friends were
thus falling and hopes fading without, Shakspere's own mind
seems to have been going through a phase of bitter suffering and
unrest.   In spite of the ingenuity of commentators, it is difficult and
even impossible to derive any knowledge of his inner history from
the Sonnets ;   " the strange imagery of passion which passes over
the magic mirror," it has been finely said, " has no tangible evidence
before or behind it."   But its mere passing is itself an evidence
of the restlessness and agony within.   The change in the character
of his dramas gives a surer indication of his change of mood.
The joyousness which breathes through his early work disappears in
comedies such as "Troilus" and " Measure for Measure."   Failure seems
everywhere.   In " Julius Cæsar " the virtue of Brutus is foiled by its
ignorance of and isolation from mankind ; in Hamlet even penetrating
intellect proves helpless for want of the capacity of action ; the poison
of Iago taints the love of Desdemona and the grandeur of Othello ;
Lear's mighty passion battles helplessly against the wind and the rain ;
a woman's weakness of frame dashes the cup of her triumph from
the hand of Lady Macbeth ; lust and self-indulgence blast the heroism
of Antony ; pride ruins the nobleness of Coriolanus.   But the very

struggle and self-introspection that these dramas betray were to give a depth and grandeur to Shakspere's work such as it had never known before. The age was one in which man's temper and powers took a new range and energy. The daring of the adventurer, the philosophy of the scholar, the passion of the lover, the fanaticism of the saint, towered into almost superhuman grandeur. Man became conscious of the immense resources that lay within him, conscious of boundless powers that seemed to mock the narrow world in which they moved. It is this grandeur of humanity that spreads before us as the poet pictures the wide speculation of Hamlet, the awful convulsion of a great nature in Othello, the terrible storm in the soul of Lear which blends with the very storm of the heavens themselves, the fearful ambition that nerved a woman's hand to dabble itself with the blood of a murdered king, the reckless lust that " flung away a world for love." Amid the terror and awe of these great dramas we learn something of the vast forces of the age from which they sprang. The passion of Mary Stuart, the ruthlessness of Alva, the daring of Drake, the chivalry of Sidney, the range of thought and action in Ralegh or Elizabeth, come better home to us as we follow the mighty series of tragedies which began in " Hamlet " and ended in " Coriolanus."

Shakspere's last dramas, the three exquisite works in which he shows a soul at rest with itself and with the world, " Cymbeline," " The Tempest," " Winter's Tale," were written in the midst of ease and competence, in a house at Stratford, to which he withdrew a few years after the death of Elizabeth. In them we lose all relation with the world or the time and pass into a region of pure poetry. It is in this peaceful and gracious close that the life of Shakspere contrasts with that of his greatest contemporaries. Himself Elizabethan to the core, he stood at the meeting-point of two great epochs of our history. The age of the Renascence was passing into the age of Puritanism. A sterner Protestantism was invigorating and ennobling life by its morality, its seriousness, its intense conviction of God. But it was at the same time hardening and narrowing it. The Bible was superseding Plutarch. The " obstinate questionings " which haunted the finer souls of the Renascence were being stereotyped into the theological formulas of the Puritan. The sense of a divine omnipotence was annihilating man. The daring which turned England into a people of " adventurers," the sense of inexhaustible resources, the buoyant freshness of youth, the intoxicating sense of beauty and joy, which created Sidney and Marlowe and Drake, were passing away before the consciousness of evil and the craving to order man's life aright before God. A new political world, healthier, more really national, but less picturesque, less wrapt in the mystery and splendour which poets love, was rising with the new moral world. Rifts which were still little were widening hour by hour, and threatening ruin to the great fabric of Church and

State, which the Tudors had built up, and to which the men of the Renascence clung passionately. From this new world of thought and feeling Shakspere stood utterly aloof. Of the popular tendencies of Puritanism—and great as were its faults, Puritanism may fairly claim to be the first political system which recognized the grandeur of the people as a whole—Shakspere knew nothing. His roll of dramas is the epic of civil war. The Wars of the Roses fill his mind, as they filled the mind of his contemporaries. It is not till we follow him through the series of plays from "Richard the Second" to "Henry the Eighth" that we realize how profoundly the memory of the struggle between York and Lancaster had moulded the temper of the people, how deep a dread of civil war, of baronial turbulence, of disputes over the succession it had left behind it. From such a risk the Crown seemed the one security. With Shakspere as with his contemporaries the Crown is still the centre and safeguard of the national life. His ideal England is an England grouped round a king such as his own Henry V., a born ruler of men, with a loyal people about him, and his enemies at his feet. Socially too the poet reflects the aristocratic view of life which was shared by all the nobler spirits of the Elizabethan time. Coriolanus is the embodiment of a great noble ; and the taunts which Shakspere hurls in play after play at the rabble only echo the general temper of the Renascence. But he shows no sympathy with the struggle of feudalism against the Crown. He had grown up under the reign of Elizabeth ; he had known no ruler save one who had cast a spell over the hearts of Englishmen. The fear of misrule was dim and distant ; his thoughts were absorbed, as those of the country were absorbed, in the struggle for national existence, and the heat of such a struggle left no time for the thoughts of civil liberty. Nor were the spiritual sympathies of the poet those of the coming time. Turn as others might to the speculations of theology, man and man's nature remained with him an inexhaustible subject of interest. Caliban was among his latest creations. It is impossible to discover whether his faith, if faith there were, was Catholic or Protestant. It is hard, indeed, to say whether he had any religious belief or no. The religious phrases which are thinly scattered over his works are little more than expressions of a distant and imaginative reverence. But on the deeper grounds of religious faith his silence is significant. He is silent, and the doubt of Hamlet deepens his silence, about the after-world. "To die," it may be, was to him as to Claudio, "to go we know not whither." Often as his "questionings" turn to the riddle of life and death, he leaves it a riddle to the last, without heeding the common theological solutions around him. "We are such stuff as dreams are made of, and our little life is rounded with a sleep."

The contrast between the spirit of the Elizabethan drama and the new temper of the nation became yet stronger when the death of

SEC. VII.

THE ELIZA-
BETHAN
POETS

Jonson

1593

Shakspere left the sovereignty of the English stage to Ben Jonson. Jonson retained it almost to the moment when the drama itself perished in the storm of the Civil War. Webster and Ford, indeed, surpassed him in tragic grandeur, Massinger in facility and grace, Beaumont and Fletcher in poetry and inventiveness ; but in the breadth of his dramatic quality, his range over every kind of poetic excellence, Jonson was excelled by Shakspere alone. His life retained to the last the riotous, defiant colour of the earlier dramatic world, in which he had made his way to fame. The stepson of a bricklayer, he enlisted as a volunteer in the wars of the Low Countries, killed his man in single combat in sight of both armies, and returned at nineteen to London to throw himself on the stage for bread. At forty-five he was still so vigorous that he made his way to Scotland on foot. Even in old age his "mountain belly," his scarred face, and massive frame became famous among the men of a younger time, as they gathered at the "Mermaid" to listen to his wit, his poetry, his outbursts of spleen and generosity, of delicate fancy, of pedantry, of riotous excess. His entry on the stage was marked by a proud resolve to reform it. Already a fine scholar in early manhood, and disdainful of writers who, like Shakspere, "had small Latin and less Greek," Jonson aimed at a return to classic severity, to a severer criticism and taste. He blamed the extravagance which marked the poetry around him, he studied his plots, he gave symmetry and regularity to his sentences and conciseness to his phrase. But creativeness disappears : in his social comedies we are amongst qualities and types rather than men, amongst abstractions and not characters. His comedy is no genial reflection of life as it is, but a moral, satirical effort to reform manners. It is only his wonderful grace and real poetic feeling that lightens all this pedantry. He shares the vigour and buoyancy of life which distinguished the school from which he sprang. His stage is thronged with figures. In spite of his talk about correctness, his own extravagance is only saved from becoming ridiculous by his amazing force. If he could not create characters, his wealth of striking details gave life to the types which he substituted for them. His poetry, too, is of the highest order ; his lyrics of the purest, lightest fancy : his masques rich with gorgeous pictures ; his pastoral, the "Sad Shepherd," fragment as it is, breathes a delicate tenderness. But, in spite of the beauty and strength which lingered on, the life of our drama was fast ebbing away. The interest of the people was in reality being drawn to newer and graver themes, as the struggle of the Great Rebellion threw its shadow before it, and the efforts of the playwrights to arrest this tendency of the time by fresh excitement only brought about the ruin of the stage. The grossness of the later comedy is incredible. Almost as incredible is the taste of the later tragedians for horrors of incest and blood. The hatred of the Puritans to the stage was not a

mere longing to avenge the insults which it had levelled at Puritanism ; it was in the main the honest hatred of God-fearing men against
the foulest depravity presented in a poetic and attractive form.

If the imaginative resources of the new England were seen in the
creators of Hamlet and the Faerie Queen, its purely intellectual
capacity, its vast command over the stores of human knowledge, the
amazing sense of its own powers with which it dealt with them, were
seen in the work of Francis Bacon. Bacon was born at the opening
of Elizabeth's reign, three years before the birth of Shakspere. He
was the younger son of a Lord Keeper, as well as the nephew of Lord
Burleigh, and even in boyhood his quickness and sagacity won the
favour of the Queen. Elizabeth "delighted much to confer with him,
and to prove him with questions : unto which he delivered himself with
that gravity and maturity above his years that her Majesty would often
term him ' the young Lord Keeper.'" Even as a boy at college he had
expressed his dislike of the Aristotelian philosophy, as "a philosophy
only strong for disputations and contentions, but barren of the production of works for the benefit of the life of man." As a law-student
of twenty-one he sketched in a tract on the "Greatest Birth of Time"
the system of inductive enquiry he was already prepared to substitute
for it. The speculations of the young thinker were interrupted by
hopes of Court success ; but these were soon dashed to the ground.
He was left poor by his father's death ; the ill-will of the Cecils barred
his advancement with the Queen : and a few years before Shakspere's
arrival in London he entered as a barrister at Gray's Inn. He soon
became one of the most successful lawyers of the time. At twenty-
three he was a member of the House of Commons, and his judgement
and eloquence at once brought him to the front. "The fear of every
man that heard him was lest he should make an end," Ben Jonson tells
us. The steady growth of his reputation was quickened by the appearance of his "Essays," a work remarkable not merely for the condensation
of its thought and its felicity and exactness of expression, but for the
power with which it applied to human life that experimental analysis
which Bacon was at a later time to make the key of Science. His fame
at once became great at home and abroad, but with this nobler fame
Bacon could not content himself. He was conscious of great powers,
as well as great aims for the public good ; and it was a time when such
aims could hardly be realized save through the means of the Crown.
But political employment seemed further off than ever. At the outset
of his career in Parliament he had irritated Elizabeth by a firm opposition to her demand of a subsidy ; and though the offence was atoned
for by profuse apologies, and by the cessation of all further resistance
to the policy of the court, the law offices of the Crown were more than
once refused to him, and it was only after the publication of his
"Essays" that he could obtain some slight promotion as a Queen's

1561

1597

Counsel. The moral weakness which more and more disclosed itself is the best justification of the Queen in her reluctance—a reluctance so strangely in contrast with her ordinary course— to bring the wisest head in her realm to her Council-board. The men whom Elizabeth employed were for the most part men whose intellect was directed by a strong sense of public duty. Their reverence for the Queen, strangely exaggerated as it may seem to us, was guided and controlled by an ardent patriotism and an earnest sense of religion ; and with all their regard for the royal prerogative, they never lost their regard for the law. The grandeur and originality of Bacon's intellect parted him from men like these quite as much as the bluntness of his moral perceptions. In politics, as in science, he had little reverence for the past. Law, constitutional privileges, or religion, were to him simply means of bringing about certain ends of good government; and if these ends could be brought about in shorter fashion he saw only pedantry in insisting on more cumbrous means. He had great social and political ideas to realize, the reform and codification of the law, the civilization of Ireland, the purification of the Church, the union—at a later time—of Scotland and England, educational projects, projects of material improvement, and the like ; and the direct and shortest way of realizing these ends was in Bacon's eyes the use of the power of the Crown. But whatever charm such a conception of the royal power might have for her successor, it had little charm for Elizabeth ; and to the end of her reign Bacon was foiled in his efforts to rise in her service.

" For my name and memory," he said at the close of his life, " I leave it to men's charitable speeches, and to foreign nations, and the next age." Amid political activity and court intrigue he still found room for the philosophical speculation which had begun with his earliest years. At forty-four, after the final disappointment of his political hopes from Elizabeth, the publication of the " Advancement of Learning" marked the first decisive appearance of the new philosophy which he had been silently framing. The close of this work was, in his own words, " a general and faithful perambulation of learning, with an enquiry what parts thereof lie fresh and waste, and not improved and converted by the industry of man ; to the end that such a plot, made and recorded to memory, may both minister light to any public designation and also serve to excite voluntary endeavours." It was only by such a survey, he held, that men could be turned from useless studies, or ineffectual means of pursuing more useful ones, and directed to the true end of knowledge as " a rich storehouse for the glory of the Creator and the relief of man's estate." The work was in fact the preface to a series of treatises which were intended to be built up into an " Instauratio Magna," which its author was never destined to complete, and of which the parts that we possess were published in the following reign. The

" Cogitata et Visa " was a first sketch of the " Novum Organum," which in its complete form was presented to James in 1621. A year later Bacon produced his " Natural and Experimental History." This, with the " Novum Organum " and the " Advancement of Learning," was all of his projected " Instauratio Magna " which he actually finished ; and even of this portion we have only part of the last two divisions. The " Ladder of the Understanding," which was to have followed these and lead up from experience to science, the " Anticipations," or provisional hypotheses for the enquiries of the new philosophy, and the closing account of " Science in Practice," were left for posterity to bring to completion. " We may, as we trust," said Bacon, " make no despicable beginnings. The destinies of the human race must complete it, in such a manner perhaps as men looking only at the present world would not readily conceive. For upon this will depend, not only a speculative good, but all the fortunes of mankind, and all their power." When we turn from words like these to the actual work which Bacon did, it is hard not to feel a certain disappointment. He did not thoroughly understand the older philosophy which he attacked. His revolt from the waste of human intelligence, which he conceived to be owing to the adoption of a false method of investigation, blinded him to the real value of deduction as an instrument of discovery ; and he was encouraged in his contempt for it as much by his own ignorance of mathematics as by the non-existence in his day of the great deductive sciences of physics and astronomy. Nor had he a more accurate prevision of the method of modern science. The inductive process to which he exclusively directed men's attention bore no fruit in Bacon's hands. The " art of investigating nature " on which he prided himself has proved useless for scientific purposes, and would be rejected by modern investigators. Where he was on a more correct track he can hardly be regarded as original. " It may be doubted," says Dugald Stewart, " whether any one important rule with regard to the true method of investigation be contained in his works of which no hint can be traced in those of his predecessors." Not only indeed did Bacon fail to anticipate the methods of modern science, but he even rejected the great scientific discoveries of his own day. He set aside with the same scorn the astronomical theory of Copernicus and the magnetic investigations of Gilbert. The contempt seems to have been fully returned by the scientific workers of his day. " The Lord Chancellor wrote on science," said Harvey, the discoverer of the circulation of the blood, "like a Lord Chancellor."

In spite however of his inadequate appreciation either of the old philosophy or the new, the almost unanimous voice of later ages has attributed, and justly attributed, to the " Novum Organum " a decisive influence on the developement of modern science. If he failed in revealing the method of experimental research, Bacon was the first to proclaim the existence of a Philosophy of Science, to insist on the unity of knowledge and enquiry throughout the physical world, to give dignity by the large and noble temper in which he treated them to the petty details of experiment in which science had to begin, to clear a way for it by setting scornfully aside the traditions of the past, to claim for it its true rank and value, and to point to the enormous results which its culture would bring in increasing the power and happiness of mankind. In one respect his attitude was in the highest degree significant. The age in which he lived was one in which theology was absorbing the intellectual energy of the world. He was the servant, too, of a king with whom theological studies superseded all others. But if he bowed in all else to James, Bacon would not, like Casaubon, bow in this. He would not even, like Descartes, attempt to transform theology by turning reason into a mode of theological demonstration. He stood absolutely aloof from it. Though as a politician he did not shrink from dealing with such subjects as Church Reform, he dealt with them simply as matters of civil polity. But from his exhaustive enumeration of the branches of human knowledge he excluded theology, and theology alone. His method was of itself inapplicable to a subject, where the premisses were assumed to be certain, and the results known. His aim was to seek for unknown results by simple experiment. It was against received authority and accepted tradition in matters of enquiry that his whole system protested; what he urged was the need of making belief rest strictly on proof, and proof rest on the conclusions drawn from evidence by reason. But in theology—all theologians asserted—reason played but a subordinate part. "If I proceed to treat of it," said Bacon, "I shall step out of the bark of human reason, and enter into the ship of the Church. Neither will the stars of philosophy, which have hitherto so nobly shone on us, any longer give us their light." The certainty indeed of conclusions on such subjects was out of harmony with the grandest feature of Bacon's work, his noble confession of the liability of every enquirer to error. It was his especial task to warn men against the "vain shows" of knowledge which had so long hindered any real advance in it, the "idols" of the Tribe, the Den, the Forum, and the Theatre, the errors which spring from the systematizing spirit which pervades all masses of men, or from individual idiosyncrasies, or from the strange power of words and phrases over the mind, or from the traditions of the past. Nor were the claims of theology easily to be reconciled with the position which he was resolute to assign to natural science. "Through all those ages," Bacon says, "wherein men of genius or learning principally or even moderately flourished, the smallest part of human industry has been spent on natural philosophy, though this ought to be esteemed as the great mother of the sciences: for all the rest, if torn from this root, may perhaps be polished and formed for use, but can receive little increase." It was by the adoption of the method of inductive enquiry which physical science was to make its own, and by basing enquiry on grounds which physical science could supply, that the moral sciences, ethics and politics could alone make any real advance. "Let none expect any great promotion of the sciences, especially in their effective part, unless natural philosophy be drawn out to particular sciences; and, again, unless these particular sciences be brought back again to natural philosophy. From this defect it is that astronomy, optics, music, many mechanical arts, and (what seems stranger) even moral and civil philosophy and logic rise but little above the foundations, and only skim over the varieties and surfaces of things." It was this lofty conception of the position and destiny of natural science which Bacon was the first to impress upon mankind at large. The age was one in which knowledge was passing to fields of enquiry which had till then been unknown, in which Kepler and Galileo were creating modern astronomy, in which Descartes was revealing the laws of motion, and Harvey the circulation of the blood. But to the mass of men this great change was all but imperceptible; and it was the energy, the profound conviction, the eloquence of Bacon which first called the attention of mankind as a whole to the power and importance of physical research. It was he who by his lofty faith in the results and victories of the new philosophy nerved its followers to a zeal and confidence equal to his own. It was he who above all gave dignity to the slow and patient processes of investigation, of experiment, of comparison, to the sacrificing of hypothesis to fact, to the single aim after truth, which was to be the law of modern science.

Section VIII.—The Conquest of Ireland, 1588—1610.

[*Authorities*.—The materials for the early history of Ireland are described by Professor O'Curry in his "Lectures on the Materials of Ancient Irish History." They may be studied by the general reader in the compilation known as "The Annals of the Four Masters," edited by Dr. O'Donovan. Its ecclesiastical history is dryly but accurately told by Dr. Lanigan ("Ecclesiastical History of Ireland"). The chief authorities for the earlier conquest under Henry the Second are the "Expugnatio et Topographia Hibernica" of Gerald de Barri, edited for the Rolls series by Mr. Dimock, and the Anglo-Norman Poem edited by M. Francisque Michel (London, Pickering, 1857). Mr. Froude has devoted especial attention to the relations of Ireland with the Tudors; but both in accuracy and soundness of judgement his work is far inferior to Mr. Brewer's examination of them in his prefaces to the State Papers of Henry VIII., or to Mr. Gardiner's careful and temperate account of the final conquest and settlement under Mountjoy and Chichester ("History of England"). The two series of "Lectures on the History of Ireland" by Mr. A. G. Richey are remarkable for their information and fairness.]

While England became "a nest of singing birds" at home, the last years of Elizabeth's reign were years of splendour and triumph abroad.

Sec. VIII.

The
Conquest
of
Ireland
1588
to
1610

1589

The defeat of the Armada was the first of a series of defeats which broke the power of Spain, and changed the political aspect of the world. The next year fifty vessels and fifteen thousand men were sent under Drake and Norris against Lisbon. The expedition returned baffled to England, but it had besieged Corunna, pillaged the coast, and repulsed a Spanish army on Spanish ground. The exhaustion of the treasury indeed soon forced Elizabeth to content herself with issuing commissions to volunteers; but the war was a national one, and the nation waged it for itself. Merchants, gentlemen, nobles, fitted out privateers. The sea-dogs in ever growing numbers scoured the Spanish Main; Spanish galleons, Spanish merchant-ships, were brought month after month to English harbours. Philip meanwhile was held back from attack on England by the need of action in France. The Armada had hardly been dispersed when the assassination of Henry the Third, the last of the line of Valois, raised Henry of Navarre to the throne; and the accession of a Protestant sovereign at once ranged the Catholics of France to a man on the side of the League and its leaders, the Guises. The League rejected Henry's claims as those of a heretic, proclaimed the Cardinal of Bourbon King as Charles the Tenth, and recognized Philip as Protector of France. It received the support of Spanish soldiery and Spanish treasure: and this new effort of Spain, an effort whose triumph must have ended in her ruin, forced Elizabeth to aid Henry with men and money in his five years' struggle against the overwhelming odds which seemed arrayed against him. Torn by civil strife, it seemed as though France might be turned into a Spanish dependency; and it was from its coast that Philip hoped to reach England. But the day at last went against the Leaguers. On the death of their puppet king, their scheme of conferring the crown on Philip's daughter awoke jealousies in the house of Guise itself, while it gave strength to the national party who shrank from laying France at the feet of Spain. Henry's submission to the faith held by the bulk of his subjects at last destroyed all chance of Philip's success. "Paris is well worth a mass" was the famous phrase in which Henry explained his abandonment of the Protestant cause, but the step did more than secure Paris. It dashed to the ground all hopes of further resistance, it dissolved the League, and enabled the King at the head of a reunited people to force Philip to acknowledge his title and consent to peace in the Treaty of Vervins. The overthrow of Philip's hopes in France had been made more bitter by the final overthrow of his hopes at sea. In 1596 his threat of a fresh Armada was met by the daring descent of an English force upon Cadiz. The town was plundered and burned to the ground; thirteen vessels of war were fired in its harbour, and the stores accumulated for the expedition utterly destroyed. In spite of this crushing blow a Spanish fleet gathered in the following year and set sail for the English coast; but as in the case of its predecessor

SEC. VIII.

THE
CONQUEST
OF
IRELAND
1588
TO
1610

storms proved more fatal than the English guns, and the ships were wrecked and almost destroyed in the Bay of Biscay.

With the ruin of Philip's projects in France and the assertion of English supremacy at sea, all danger from Spain passed quietly away, and Elizabeth was able to direct her undivided energies to the last work which illustrates her reign.

To understand however the final conquest of Ireland, we must retrace our steps to the reign of Henry the Second. There had been little intercourse with England since Irish missionaries first brought religion and learning to the shores of Northumbria. The heathen

c. 800

hosts of Northmen and Danes had fallen on Ireland as on England with fierce destruction. After a century of ruin Irish kings led their people, as the kings of Wessex had done, in a succession of wars for

1014

the deliverance of their country, and Brian Borama, king of Munster, by his victory at Clontarf finally broke the power of the Danes in Ireland. There followed a time of slow recovery from the disorganization caused by perpetual warfare. The Danish settlers on the coasts had never conquered the inland country, where the Irish were grouped as of old in tribes loosely bound together in groups by the tie of kinship, and acknowledging by tribute, though scarcely obeying, the rule of a king. Wars between the clans were frequent, forays for cattle, or raids to secure hostages. Two hundred years of Danish invasions had intensified these evils, and established new causes of war. The coast-towns such as Dublin and Waterford and Limerick, which the invaders founded, remained Danish in blood and manners, and at feud with the Celtic tribes around them, though often forced by the fortunes of war to pay tribute, to seek Irish alliances, and to accept in name at least the over-lordship of the Irish kings. Also the Danes of the coast-cities, whose conversion had begun in England, applied to the see of Canterbury for the ordination of their bishops, and acknowledged in their own towns some right of spiritual supervision in Lanfranc and Anselm, which was rejected by the Irish Church. The petty "kingdoms" of the foreigners not only hindered the growth of a central rule, but multiplied occasions of conflict. On the other hand powerful forces were at work for prosperity and union. Irish life was not a mere scene of barbarous disorder. The Irish law which may be read in the Senchus Mor and other books was interpreted by hereditary and judicial authorities throughout the island, and exercised a civilizing force as regarded private rights, though the weakness of the central power made it less effective as an arbitrator in the disputes of the little kingdoms. Content and security were generally assured by the ordering of the land, held in common by the tribe. Schools illustrious in art and scholarship survived the Danish wars, and the strong influence of learning was marked by the rise of the literary clans. The Irish Church, in part organised in accordance with the

Sec. VIII.

The
Conquest
of
Ireland
1588
to
1610

X. Cent.

tribal system, nourished scholars and scribes of the highest learning, and artificers in every craft unsurpassed in skill. On their part the Danes had brought to Ireland a far-reaching commerce, in which the Irish took their share, and common interests led to a gradual fusion of the two peoples. Peaceful intercourse with England which had ceased since the eighth century was to some extent renewed as Irish traders carried their cloth as far as Ely, while closer relations with the Continent brought developments alike in Church and State. By visitations throughout the country of the archbishops of Armagh, and by a succession of councils, the Church was changed in many particulars of its earlier tribal character so as to correspond with the discipline of the European world. Moreover while the Irish Church drew the Danish sees from obedience to Canterbury under the rule of Armagh, there was in the State a determined effort to unite Danes and Irish in one commonwealth, under a high-king of increased authority, with a capital at Dublin and a university at Armagh. The island was losing something of its purely Celtic character. It was no wonder that such a time of transition should be marked by conflict and trouble. The state of the country afforded a pretext for war, had a pretext been needed by the ambition of Henry the Second; and within a few months of that king's coronation John of Salisbury was despatched to obtain the Papal sanction for an invasion of the island. The enterprise, as it was laid before Pope Hadrian the Fourth, took the colour of a crusade. The isolation of Ireland from the general body of Christendom, the supposed absence of learning and civilization, the scandalous vices of its people, were alleged as the grounds of Henry's action. It was the general belief of the time that all islands fell under the jurisdiction of the Papal See, and it was as a possession of the Roman Church that Henry sought Hadrian's permission to enter Ireland. His aim was "to enlarge the bounds of the Church, to restrain the progress of vices, to correct the manners of its people and plant virtue among them, and to increase the Christian religion." He engaged to "subject the people to laws, to extirpate vicious customs, to respect the rights of the native Churches, and to enforce the payment of Peter's pence" as a recognition of the overlordship of the Roman See. Hadrian by his bull approved the enterprise as one prompted by "the ardour of faith and love of religion," and declared his will that the people of Ireland should receive Henry with all honour, and revere him as their lord. The King's project was discussed in a great council of the English baronage, but the opposition of the Empress Matilda and the difficulties of the enterprise forced on Henry a temporary abandonment of his designs, and his energies were diverted for the moment to plans of Continental aggrandizement.

Twelve years had passed when an Irish chieftain, Dermot, King of

SEC. VIII.

THE
CONQUEST
OF
IRELAND
1588
TO
1610

1168

1169

1171

1176

1185

Leinster, presented himself at Henry's Court, and did homage to him for the dominions from which he had been driven in one of the endless civil wars which distracted the island. Dermot returned to Ireland with promises of aid from the English knighthood; and was soon followed by Robert FitzStephen, a son of the Constable of Cardigan, with a small band of a hundred and forty knights, sixty men-at-arms, and three or four hundred Welsh archers. Small as was the number of the adventurers, their horses and arms proved irresistible both to the Danish townsmen and the separate risings out of the clans. Wexford was taken. The arrival of fresh forces under Maurice Fitzgerald heralded the coming of Richard of Clare, earl of Pembroke and Striguil, a ruined baron later known by the nickname of Strongbow, who in defiance of Henry's prohibition landed near Waterford with a force of fifteen hundred men, as Dermot's mercenary. The city was at once stormed, and the united forces of the Earl and King marched to the siege of Dublin. In spite of a relief attempted by the King of Connacht, who was recognised as overking of the island by the rest of the tribes, Dublin was taken by surprise; and the marriage of Richard with Aife, Dermot's daughter, left him on the death of his father-in-law, which followed quickly on these successes, master of his kingdom of Leinster. The new lord had soon, however, to hurry back to England, and appease the jealousy of Henry by the surrender of Dublin to the Crown, by doing homage for Leinster as an English lordship, and by accompanying the King in his voyage to the new dominion which the adventurers had won. Had Henry been allowed by fortune to carry out his purpose, the conquest of Ireland would now have been accomplished. The King of Connacht indeed and the Irish chiefs owned his suzerainty; the bishops in synod at Cashel recognised him as their lord; and he was preparing to penetrate to the north and west, and to secure his conquest by a systematic erection of castles throughout the country, when the troubles which followed on the murder of Archbishop Thomas recalled him hurriedly to Normandy. The lost opportunity never returned. Connacht, indeed, bowed to a nominal acknowledgment of Henry's overlordship; John de Courcy penetrated into Ulster and established himself at Downpatrick; and the king planned for a while the establishment of his youngest son, John, as Lord of Ireland. But the levity of the young prince, who mocked the dresses of the native chieftains, and plucked them in insult by the beard, compelled his recall. The adventurers however were secure in their fortified towns on the sea coasts, Drogheda, Dublin, Wexford, Waterford, Cork, from which no inland power could dislodge them; and seizing the sites of churches and monasteries which were powerless to resist, they formed a series of strongholds from whence, by fostering and by using the dissensions of the clans, they could spread their power over the land.

SEC. VIII

THE
CONQUEST
OF
IRELAND
1588
TO
1610

Had the Irish driven their invaders into the sea, or the Normans succeeded in the complete conquest of Ireland, the misery of its after history might have been avoided. A struggle such as that in which Scotland drove out its conquerors might have produced a spirit of patriotism and national union, which would have formed a people out of the mass of warring clans. A conquest such as that of England by the Normans would have spread at any rate the law, the order, the peace and civilization of the conquering country over the length and breadth of the conquered. Unhappily Ireland, while powerless to effect its deliverance, was strong enough to hold its assailants partially at bay. The country was broken into two halves whose conflict has never ceased. The Irish clung to their ancient tradition and social system, even while the evils of tribal division were multiplied by the warring bands of Normans scattered through their land. All the lawlessness, the ferocity, the narrowness, of feudalism broke out unchecked in the horde of adventurers who held the land by their sword. The English kings, fearing the independence of the barons as much as that of the Irish, were at conflict with both. John and his successors created counties in the English march, and sent judges and sheriffs to administer English law, under English governors ruling from Dublin. But little real order was established. Every Irishman beyond the march was deemed an enemy and a robber, nor was his murder cognizable by the law. Half the subsistence of the barons was drawn from forays across the border, and these forays were avenged by incursions of native marauders, which carried havoc to the walls of Dublin. The settlers in the march itself were harried and oppressed by enemy and protector alike ; while the feuds of the Norman lords wasted their strength. The landing of a Scotch force after Bannockburn with Edward Bruce at its head, and a general rising of the Irish which welcomed this deliverer, drove indeed the barons of the march to a momentary union ; and in the bloody field of Athenry their valour was proved by the slaughter of eleven thousand of their foes, and the almost complete extinction of the sept of the O'Connors. In spite, however, of misgovernment and discord, Normans and Celts were drawn together by ties of marriage and fosterage, by joint interests in the land, above all by the enormous growth of manufactures and commerce and spread of inland trade which followed the Norman settlement. The invaders very rapidly adopted the language, the dress, and the laws of the country, and encouraged its arts and literature. Barons scattered through Irish territories took the position of Irish chieftains ; the FitzMaurices, for example, who became earls of Desmond, and whose great territory in the south was erected into a County Palatine, used the Irish methods of land tenure and taxation. A joint civilization grew up on Celtic lines, modified by the infiltration of feudal customs ; and the provisions of the Statute

Sec. VIII.

The
Conquest
of
Ireland
1588
to
1610

1366

1394
1395

1398

1494

1496

of Kilkenny were powerless to stop the movement. The Statute forbade the adoption by any man of English blood of the Irish language or name or dress; it enforced within the Pale the use of English law, and made that of the native or Brehon law, which was gaining ground, an act of treason; it made treasonable any marriage of the Englishry with persons of Irish blood, or any adoption of English children by Irish foster-fathers. But stern as they were, these provisions proved fruitless to check the fusion of the two races. Richard the Second was stirred to an effort for the conquest and organization of the island. He landed with an army at Waterford, made treaties, and received homage of the native chieftains. The lieutenant he left behind him, the earl of March, heir to the throne, was slain in battle with the Irish, and Richard resolved to complete his work by a fresh invasion; his breach of his treaty engagements alienated the Irish; disaster pursued his army; the troubles in England soon interrupted his efforts, and all traces of his work vanished with the embarkation of his soldiers.

With the renewal of the French wars, and the outburst of the Wars of the Roses, English sovereignty over the island dwindled to a shadow. But at last Henry the Seventh took the problem in hand. Sir Edward Poynings was despatched as Deputy; the Earl of Kildare, Deputy under three kings, was charged with treason and carried to the Tower; the district about Dublin which still obeyed English law was fortified by a double ditch from which it took the name of "the Pale"; the parliament in Ireland was forbidden by the famous Poynings' Act to treat of any matters save those first approved of by the English King and his Council. For a while, however, the feudal lords must still serve as the English garrison against the unconquered Irish, and Henry made his prisoner the Earl of Kildare once more Lord Deputy. "All Ireland cannot rule this man," grumbled his ministers. "Then shall he rule all Ireland," replied the King. But though Henry the Seventh had begun the work of bridling Ireland he had no strength for exacting a real submission; and the great Norman Lords of the Pale, the Butlers and Geraldines, the De la Poers and the Fitzpatricks, though subjects in name, were in fact defiant of royal authority. Norman feuds were as incessant as those of the Irish septs; and in the march lands the more violent could combine the horrors of feudal oppression with exactions of Celtic chieftains apart from the limits and control of Celtic law. Crushed by taxation, by oppression, by misgovernment, plundered alike by Celtic marauders and by the troops levied to disperse them, the wretched descendants of the first settlers found little safety in English "order." They found it better to live with their neighbours under Irish law; and the border of the march retreated steadily towards Dublin. The towns of the sea-board, sheltered by their walls and their municipal self-government, maintained a wealthy commerce in which Normans and Irish were united, and tended to increasing independence and jealousy of interference from England. Throughout its dominions the English Government, though still strong enough to break down any open revolt, was a mere phantom of rule. Among the Celtic tribes without the Pale its policy had ever been to maintain dissensions and strife, which saved it the necessity of self-defence, and weakened the enemy by civil war. The Geraldines sought to develop a larger statesmanship. Gerald, the Great Earl of Kildare, deputy for some thirty years, had worked toward a fusion of the races in a united Ireland; his son Gerald inherited his position, and his project of peace and conciliation. But times were changed. To Henry the Eighth the policy which had been pursued by his father, of ruling Ireland through the great Irish lords, was utterly hateful. His purpose was to rule in Ireland as thoroughly and effectively as he ruled in England, and during the latter half of his reign he bent his whole energies to accomplish this aim. Kildare was summoned to London and thrown into the Tower. A letter, forged it was said by his bitter enemy Alen, Archbishop of Dublin, was thrown in the way of his son, Silken Thomas, a youth of twenty, reporting that his father had been beheaded. In the madness of despair the boy called his followers to arms. Archbishop Alen was taken in flight and murdered. The insurgents, repulsed before the Castle, fell back into the country. At the news that his son was proclaimed a traitor Kildare died in the Tower of a broken heart. Henry had resolved to take Ireland seriously in hand, and he had Cromwell to execute his will. Skeffington, a new Lord Deputy, brought with him a train of artillery, which worked a startling change in the political aspect of the island. Maynooth, the stronghold of the Geraldines, was beaten down in a few days, and six months later Earl Thomas surrendered on promise of his life. He was carried to London; and with his five uncles hanged at Tyburn. The power of the great Norman house which had towered over Ireland was utterly broken, and only a young boy, who had escaped hidden in a turf-basket, remained to preserve its name.

With the fall of the Fitzgeralds Ireland felt itself in a master's grasp. "Irishmen," wrote one of the Lord Justices to Cromwell, "were never in such fear as now. The King's sessions are being kept in five shires more than formerly." Not only were the Englishmen of the Pale at Henry's feet, but the tribes of Wicklow and Wexford sent in their submission; and for the first time in men's memory an English army appeared in Munster and reduced the south to obedience. A castle of the O'Briens, which guarded the passage of the Shannon, was carried by assault, and its fall carried with it the submission of Clare. The capture of Athlone restored to Henry the key of Connacht, where the great Norman house of the De Burghs or

SEC. VIII

THE
CONQUEST
OF
IRELAND
1588
TO
1610

1477-151?

1512

1534

1535

1535

SEC. VIII.

THE
CONQUEST
OF
IRELAND
1588
TO
1610

1535-1542

Bourkes had assumed an almost royal authority. The tribes of the north yielded a vague submission to his army. In seven years, partly through the vigour of Skeffington's successor, Lord Leonard Grey, and still more through the resolute will of Henry and Cromwell, the power of the Crown, which had been limited to the walls of Dublin, was acknowledged over the length and breadth of Ireland. The King's aim was to rule not by force but by law. But the only conception of law which the King or his ministers could frame was that of English law. The customary law which prevailed without the Pale, the native system of clan government and common tenure of land by the tribe, as well as the poetry and literature which threw their lustre over the Irish tongue, were either unknown to the English statesmen, or despised by them as barbarous. The one mode of civilizing Ireland and redressing its chaotic misrule which presented itself to their minds was that of destroying the whole Celtic tradition of the Irish people—that of "making Ireland English" in manners, in law, and in tongue. The Deputy, Parliament, Judges, Sheriffs, which already existed within the Pale, furnished a faint copy of English institutions ; and these, it was hoped, might be gradually extended over the whole island. The English language and mode of life would follow, it was believed, the English law. The one effectual way of bringing about such a change as this lay in a complete conquest of the island, and in its colonization by English settlers ; but from this course, pressed on him as it was by his own lieutenants and by the settlers of the Pale, even the iron will of Cromwell shrank. It was at once too bloody and too expensive. To win over the chiefs, to turn them by policy into English nobles, to use the traditional devotion of their tribal dependents as a means of diffusing the English rule was a policy safer, cheaper, and more statesmanlike. " For now at the beginning," Henry wrote, " politic practices may do more good than the exploit of war, till such time as the strength of the Irish shall be enfeebled and diminished, as well by getting their captains from them, as by putting division amongst them, so that they join not together." It was this system which, even before the fall of the Geraldines, Henry had resolved to adopt ; and it was this which he pressed on Ireland when their ruin laid it at his feet. The chiefs were to be persuaded of the advantage of English justice and legal rule. Their fear of any purpose to " expel them from their lands and dominions lawfully possessed " was to be dispelled by a promise " to conserve them in their own." Even their remonstrances against the introduction of English law were to be regarded, and the course of justice to be enforced or mitigated according to the circumstances of the country. In the resumption of lands or rights which were claimed by the Crown, " sober ways, politic shifts, and amiable persuasions " were to be preferred to rigorous dealings. By these subtle means

SEC. VIII

THE
CONQUEST
OF
IRELAND
1588
TO
1610

Henry hoped without arousing suspicion to make a re-entry not only on the Crown lands such as the earldom of Ulster, but also on all the lands which had slipped from the hands of the great lords. It was this system which was in the main carried out by the English Government under Henry and his two successors. Chieftain after chieftain was won over to the acceptance of the indenture which guaranteed him in the possession of his lands. The test of loyalty demanded was the acceptance of an English title, the education of a son at the English Court, the rendering of tribute and service in war-time to the Crown, and in some cases, like that of the O'Neills, a promise to use the English language and dress. There was immediate profit for the chieftain himself. Not only did he secure the hereditary lordship of their territory to his house, but the English law-courts, ignoring the Irish custom by which the land belonged to the tribe at large, regarded the chief as sole proprietor of the soil.

The faults of the system a statesman of that day could hardly be expected to perceive. Tudor politicians held that the one hope for the regeneration of Ireland lay in its absorbing the civilization of England. The prohibition of the national dress, customs, laws, and language seemed to them merely the suppression of a barbarism which stood in the way of all improvement. At this moment, however, a fatal blunder plunged Ireland into religious strife. The religious aspect of Ireland was hardly less chaotic than its political aspect had been. Ever since Strongbow's landing there had been no one Irish Church, simply because there had been no one Irish nation. There was not the slightest difference in doctrine or discipline between the Church without the Pale and the Church within it. But within the Pale the clergy were exclusively of English blood and speech, and without it they were exclusively of Irish. Irishmen were shut out by law from abbeys and churches within the English boundary; and the ill-will of the natives shut out Englishmen from churches and abbeys outside it. As to the religious state of the country, it was much on a level with its political condition. Feuds and misrule had told fatally on ecclesiastical discipline. The bishops were political officers, or hard fighters like the chiefs around them; their sees were neglected, their cathedrals abandoned to decay. Through whole dioceses the churches lay in ruins and without priests. The English clergy spoke no Irish, and the only preaching, it was said, done in their districts was done by the begging friars. "If the King do not provide a remedy," it was said of the Pale, "there will be no more Christentie than in the middle of Turkey." Unfortunately the remedy which Henry provided was worse than the disease. Politically Ireland was one with England, and the great revolution which was severing the one country from the Papacy extended itself to the other. The Supremacy, a question which

Sec. VIII.
THE
CONQUEST
OF
IRELAND
1588
TO
1610

1537

had convulsed England, was passed by the Pale parliament with little difficulty. The bishops within the Pale bent to the King's will as easily as their fellows in England, and their example was followed by at least four prelates of dioceses without the Pale. Lords of the Council and State officials made no scruple in renouncing obedience to the Bishop of Rome, and in acknowledging Henry as the "Supreme Head of the Church of England and Ireland under Christ." The Act for the dissolution of the monasteries was forced on in face of bitter opposition in Parliament. In the course of a few years some seventy-eight houses in the English Pale were suppressed. In the Irish districts the process was slow and uncertain, and the work of destruction was not completed till the next century. The results of the measure were fatal to culture and religion. In the Pale there were no schools save those of the religious houses. The system of vicars, so general in England, was rare in Ireland; churches in the patronage of the abbeys were for the most part served by the religious themselves, and the dissolution of their houses suspended public worship over large districts of the country. The friars who continued to labour and teach in spite of the efforts of the Government, were thrown necessarily into a position of antagonism to the English rule.

In England the breach with Rome, the destruction of the monastic orders, and the establishment of the Supremacy, had roused in a portion of the people itself a desire for theological change which Henry shared, and was cautiously satisfying. In Ireland the spirit of the Reformation never existed among the people at all. They accepted the legislative measures passed in the English Parliament without any dream of theological consequences, or of any change in the doctrine or ceremonies of the Church. Not a single voice demanded the abolition of pilgrimages, or the destruction of images, or the reform of public worship. The mission of Archbishop Browne "for the plucking down of idols and extinguishing of idolatry" was a first step in the long effort of the English Government to force a new faith on a people who to a man clung passionately to their old religion. Browne's attempts at "tuning the pulpits" were met by a sullen and significant opposition. "Neither by gentle exhortation," the Primate wrote to Cromwell, "nor by evangelical instruction, neither by oath of them solemnly taken, nor yet by threats of sharp correction may I persuade or induce any, whether religious or secular, since my coming over, once to preach the Word of God nor the just title of our illustrious Prince." "In the Irishry," as Staples, bishop of Meath, reported, "the common voice runneth that the supremacy of our sovereign lord is maintained only by power and not reasoned by learning." The bishops abstained from compliance with the order to erase the Pope's name out of their mass-books. The pulpits remained steadily silent. When Browne ordered the destruction of the images and relics in his own

SEC. VIII.

THE
CONQUEST
OF
IRELAND
1588
TO
1610

cathedral, he had to report that the prior and canons "find them so sweet for their gain that they heed not my words." Cromwell, however, was resolute for a religious uniformity between the two islands, and the Primate borrowed some of his patron's vigour. Recalcitrant priests were thrown into prison, images were plucked down from the roodloft, and the most venerable of Irish relics, the Staff of St. Patrick, was burnt in the market-place. But he found no support in his vigour, save from across the Channel. The Irish Council was cold. The Lord Deputy knelt to say prayers before an image at Trim. A sullen, dogged opposition baffled Cromwell's efforts, and his fall was followed by a long respite in the religious changes which he was forcing on the conquered dependency. With the accession of Edward the Sixth, however, the system of change was renewed with all the energy of Protestant zeal. The bishops were summoned before the Deputy, Sir Anthony St. Leger, to receive the new English Liturgy, which, though written in a tongue as strange to the native Irish as Latin itself, was now to supersede the Latin service-book in every diocese. The order was the signal for an open strife. " Now shall every illiterate fellow read Mass," burst forth Dowdall, the Archbishop of Armagh, as he flung out of the chamber with all but one of his suffragans at his heels. Archbishop Browne, of Dublin, on the other hand, was followed in his profession of obedience by the Bishops of Meath, Limerick, and Kildare. The Government, however, was far from quailing before the division of the episcopate. Dowdall was driven from the country, and the vacant sees were filled with Protestants, like Bale, of the most advanced type. But no change could be wrought by measures such as these on the opinions of the people themselves. The new episcopal reformers spoke no Irish, and of their English sermons not a word was understood by the rude kernes around the pulpit. The native priests remained silent. " As for preaching we have none," reports a zealous Protestant, "without which the ignorant can have no knowledge." The prelates who used the new Prayer-book were simply regarded as heretics. The Bishop of Meath was assured by one of his flock that, " if the country wist how, they would eat you." Protestantism had failed to wrest a single Irishman from his older convictions, but it succeeded in uniting all Ireland against the Crown. The old political distinctions which had been produced by the conquest of Strongbow faded before the new struggle for a common faith. The population within the Pale and without it became one, " not as the Irish nation," it has been acutely said, " but as Catholics." A new sense of national identity was found in the identity of religion. " Both English and Irish begin to oppose your Lordship's orders," Browne had written years before to Cromwell, "and to lay aside their national old quarrels."

With the accession of Mary the shadowy form of this earlier Irish Protestantism melted quietly away. There were no Protestants in

SEC. VIII.

THE
CONQUEST
OF
IRELAND
1588
TO
1610

Ireland save the new bishops; and when Bale had fled over sea, and his fellow-prelates had been deprived, the Church resumed its old appearance. No attempt, indeed, was made to restore the monasteries; and Mary exercised her supremacy, deposed and appointed bishops, and repudiated Papal interference with her ecclesiastical acts, as vigorously as her father. But the Mass was restored, the old modes of religious worship were again held in honour, and religious dissension between the Government and its Irish subjects was for the time at an end. With the close, however, of one danger came the rise of another. England was growing tired of the policy of conciliation which had been steadily pursued by Henry the Eighth and his successor. As yet it had been rewarded with precisely the sort of success which Wolsey and Cromwell anticipated: the chiefs had come quietly in to the plan, and their septs had followed them in submission to the new order. "The winning of the Earl of Desmond was the winning of the rest of Munster with small charges. The making O'Brien an Earl made all that country obedient." MacUilliaim became Lord Clanrickard, and Macgiolla-Phadhruig Baron of Upper Ossory. A visit of the great northern chief who had accepted the title of Earl of Tyrone

to the English Court was regarded as a marked step in the subjection of the north. Some control had been established over the tribes between Limerick and Tipperary. "Men may pass quietly throughout these countries without danger of robbery or other displeasure." In the Clanrickard county, once wasted with war, "ploughing increaseth daily." In Tyrone and the north, indeed, the Irish chiefs ruled without a check, and everywhere the process of English occupation tried the temper of the Deputies by the slowness of its advance. The only hope of any real progress lay in patience; and there were signs that the Government at Dublin found it hard to wait. The "rough handling" of the chiefs by

Sir Edward Bellingham, a Lord Deputy under the Protector Somerset, roused a spirit of revolt that only subsided when the poverty of the Exchequer forced him to withdraw the garrisons he had planted in the heart of the country. His successor in Mary's reign, Lord Sussex, made raid after raid to no purpose on the obstinate tribes of the north, burning in one the Cathedral of Armagh and three other churches. A more serious breach in the system of conciliation was made when the project of English colonization which Henry had steadily rejected was adopted by the same Deputy, and the country of O'Connor Faly and of

the septs of Leix was assigned to English settlers, and made shire-land under the names of King's and Queen's Counties, in honour of Philip and Mary. A savage warfare began between the planters and the dispossessed septs, which only ended in the following reign in the utter defeat of the Irishmen. Commissioners were appointed to survey waste lands, with the aim of carrying the work of colonization into other districts, but the pressure of the French war put an end to these wider projects. Elizabeth at her accession recognized the risk of the policy of confiscation and colonization, and the prudence of Cecil fell back on the safer though more tedious methods of Henry.

The alarm however at English aggression had already spread among the natives : and its result was seen in a revolt of the north, and in the rise of a leader far more vigorous and able than any with whom the Government had had as yet to contend. An acceptance of the Earldom of Tyrone by the chief of the O'Neills brought about the inevitable conflict between the system of succession recognized by English and that recognized by Irish law. On the death of the Earl, England acknowledged his eldest son as the heir of his Earldom; while the sept maintained their older right of choosing a chief from the members of the family, and preferred Shane (Seaghan) O'Neill, a younger son of less doubtful legitimacy. Sussex marched northward to settle the question by force of arms; but ere he could reach Ulster the activity of Shane had quelled the disaffection of his rivals, the O'Donnells of Donegal, and won over the Scots of Antrim. "Never before," wrote Sussex, "durst Scot or Irishman look Englishman in the face in plain or wood since I came here;" but Shane had fired his men with a new courage, and charging the Deputy's army with a force hardly half its number, drove it back in rout on Armagh. A promise of pardon induced him to visit London, and make an illusory submission, but he was no sooner safe home again than its terms were set aside ; and after a wearisome struggle, in which Shane foiled the efforts of the Lord Deputy to entrap or to poison him, he remained virtually master of the north. His success stirred larger dreams of ambition ; he invaded Connacht, and pressed Clanrickard hard : while he replied to the remonstrances of the Council at Dublin with a bold defiance. "By the sword I have won these lands," he answered, "and by the sword will I keep them." But defiance broke idly against the skill and vigour of Sir Henry Sidney, who succeeded Sussex as Lord Deputy The rival septs of the north were drawn into a rising against O'Neill, while the English army advanced from the Pale. Shane, defeated by the O'Donnells, opened negotiations with the Scots for aid ; but fell slain in a sudden quarrel, through contrivance of a Scot employed for his murder by Sidney. The Deputy turned his arms to the subjection of Munster, where the great leader of the Desmonds, James Fitzmaurice, met English aggression by drawing together Anglo-Irish and Irish through the bond of their common religion. Ireland had already been fixed on by the Papacy as ground on which it could with advantage fight out its quarrel with Elizabeth. Practically indeed the religious question hardly existed there. The ecclesiastical policy of the Protestants had indeed been revived in name on the Queen's accession ; Rome was again renounced, the new Act of Uniformity forced the English Prayer-book on the island, and compelled

SEC. VIII.

THE
CONQUEST
OF
IRELAND
1588
TO
1610

**Ireland
and
Elizabeth**

1559

1567

Sec. VIII.

The
Conquest
of
Ireland
1588
to
1610

attendance at the services in which it was used. There was as before a general air of compliance with the law ; even in the districts without the Pale the bishops generally conformed, and the only exceptions of which we have any information were to be found in the extreme south and in the north, where resistance was distant enough to be safe. But the real cause of this apparent submission to the Act of Uniformity lay in the fact that it remained, and necessarily remained, a dead letter. It was impossible to find any considerable number of English ministers, or of Irish priests acquainted with English. Meath was one of the most civilized dioceses, and out of a hundred curates in it hardly ten knew any tongue save their own. The

1561

promise that the service-book should be translated into Irish was long unfulfilled, and the final clause of the Act itself authorized the use of a Latin rendering of it till further order could be taken. But this, like its other provisions, was ignored, and throughout Elizabeth's reign the gentry of the Pale went unquestioned to Mass. There was in fact no active religious persecution, and the conflict was waged on lines of political and racial supremacy. But this was not the view of Rome or of Spain, of the Catholic missionaries, or of the Irish exiles abroad. They represented, and perhaps believed, the Irish people to be writhing under a religious oppression which they were burning to shake off. They saw in the Irish loyalty to Catholicism a lever for overthrowing the heretic Queen when in 1579 the Papacy planned the greatest and most comprehensive of its attacks upon Elizabeth. While missionaries egged on the English Catholics to revolt, the Pope hastened to bring about a Catholic revolution in Scotland and

1571

in Ireland. Stukely, an Irish refugee, had long pressed on the Pope

1579

and Spain the policy of a descent on Ireland ; and his plans were carried out at last by the landing of a small force on the shores of Kerry. In spite of the arrival in the following year of two thousand Papal soldiers accompanied by a Legate, the attempt ended in a miserable failure. The fort of Smerwick, in which the invaders entrenched themselves, was forced by the new Deputy, Lord Grey, to surrender, and its garrison put ruthlessly to the sword. The Earl of Desmond, who after long indecision rose to support them, was defeated and hunted over his own country, which the panic-born cruelty of his pursuers harried into a wilderness. The settlement of Munster with English landlords followed the confiscation of the

1586

Desmond territory, which was parted out in estates for the new owners. Pitiless as it was, the work done in Munster spread a terror over the land which served England in good stead when the struggle

1588

with Catholicism culminated in the fight with the Armada.

The power of the Government was from this moment recognized

**Conquest
and
Settle-
ment**

everywhere throughout the land. But it was a power founded solely on terror ; and the outrages and exactions of the soldiery, who had been flushed with rapine and bloodshed in the south, sowed during the years which followed the reduction of Munster the seeds of a revolt more formidable than any which Elizabeth had yet encountered. The tribes of Ulster, divided by the policy of Sidney, were again united by the common hatred of their oppressors; and in Hugh O'Neill they found a leader of even greater ability than Shane. Hugh had been brought up at the English court, and while speaking and writing Irish perfectly was in manners and bearing an Englishman; he had been rewarded for loyalty in previous contests by the Earldom of Tyrone; and in his strife with a rival chieftain of his clan had won aid from the Government by an offer to introduce the English laws and shire-system into his new country. But he was no sooner undisputed master of the north than his tone gradually changed. Whether from a long-formed plan, or from suspicion of English designs upon himself, he at last took a position of open defiance. It was at the moment when the Treaty of Vervins, and the wreck of the second Armada, freed Elizabeth's hands from the struggle with Spain, that the revolt under Hugh O'Neill broke the quiet which had prevailed since the victories of Lord Grey. The Irish question again became the chief trouble of the Queen. The tide of her recent triumphs seemed at first to have turned. A defeat of the English forces in Tyrone caused a general rising of the northern tribes; and a great effort made in 1599 for the suppression of the growing revolt failed through the vanity and disobedience, if not the treacherous complicity, of the Queen's Lieutenant, the young Earl of Essex. His successor, Lord Mountjoy, found himself master on his arrival of only a few miles round Dublin. But in three years the revolt was at an end. A Spanish force which landed to support it at Kinsale was driven to surrender; a line of forts secured the country as the English mastered it; all open opposition was crushed out by the energy and the ruthlessness of the new Lieutenant; and a famine which followed on his ravages completed the devastating work of the sword. Hugh O'Neill was brought in triumph to Dublin; James Earl of Desmond, who had again roused Munster into revolt, fled for refuge to Spain; and the work of conquest was at last brought to a close. Under the administration of Mountjoy's successor, Sir Arthur Chichester, a determined and pitiless effort was made for the settlement of the conquered province by the general introduction of a purely English system of government, justice, and property. Every vestige of the old Celtic constitution of the country was rejected as "barbarous." The tribal authority of the chiefs was taken from them by law. They were reduced to the position of great landowners with tenants. The tribal system of property was set aside, and the communal holdings of the tribesmen turned into the copyholds of English law. In the same way the chieftains were stripped of their hereditary jurisdiction, and the English system of judges and trial by jury was substituted for their proceedings under Brehon or customary law. To

SEC. VIII.

THE
CONQUEST
OF
IRELAND

1588
TO
1610

1598

1601–1603

1605–1608

Sec. VIII.

The
Conquest
of
Ireland
1588
to
1610

all this the Celts opposed the tenacious devotion of their race to their ancient civilization. They held their chiefs for chieftains still. They preserved the tradition of the lands of the tribe and their boundaries. The attempt made by Chichester, under pressure from England, to introduce the English uniformity of religion ended in utter failure ; for the Englishry of the Pale remained as Catholic as the native Irishry ; and the sole result of the measure was to build up a new Irish people out of both on the common basis of religion. A final blow was struck at Irish hopes when Hugh O'Neill, Earl of Tyrone, and Ruadhri O'Donnell, Earl of Tyrconnel, who had submitted to the English Government, were driven into exile by the suspicions and dangers with which the Government surrounded them. The flight of

1607

the earls to the Continent closed the history of the Celtic tribes in Ireland. Signs were already appearing of a disposition on the part of the people to conform gradually to the new usages, when the English Council under Elizabeth's successor carried through on their territories the great revolutionary measure which is known as the

1608

Plantation of Ulster. A vast policy of spoliation was planned ; two-thirds of the north of Ireland was declared to have been confiscated to the Crown, though there had been no rising of the earls nor any evidence of conspiracy ; and the lands which were thus gained were allotted to new settlers of Scotch and English extraction. Farms and homesteads, churches and mills, rose fast amid the fertile land of Tyrone. The Corporation of London undertook the colonization of Derry, and gave to the little town the name which its heroic defence has made so famous. The foundations of the economic revival of Ulster were laid in the settlement of a people on the soil under terms from the Government—a race of tenants who fought stoutly to secure the tenant-right which was denied to the whole of the Irish outside Ulster. The evicted Irish withdrew sullenly to the mountain and boglands which had been left them by the spoiler; but all faith in English justice had been torn from the minds of the Irishry, and the seed had been sown of that fatal harvest of distrust and disaffection, which was to be reaped through tyranny and massacre in the age to come.

The plantation of Munster has carried us beyond the limits of our present story. The triumph of Mountjoy flung its lustre over the last days of Elizabeth, but no outer triumph could break the gloom which gathered round the dying Queen. Lonely as she had always been, her loneliness deepened as she drew towards the grave. The statesmen and warriors of her earlier days had dropped one by one from her Council-board ; and their successors were watching her last moments, and intriguing for favour in the coming reign. Her favourite,

1601

Lord Essex, was led into an insane outbreak of revolt which brought him to the block. The old splendour of her court waned and disappeared. Only officials remained about her, " the other of the Council and nobility

Sec. VIII.

The
Conquest
of
Ireland
1588
to
1610

estrange themselves by all occasions." As she passed along in her progresses, the people whose applause she courted remained cold and silent. The temper of the age, in fact, was changing, and isolating her as it changed. Her own England, the England which had grown up around her, serious, moral, prosaic, shrank coldly from this brilliant, fanciful, unscrupulous child of earth and the Renascence. She had enjoyed life as the men of her day enjoyed it, and now that they were gone she clung to it with a fierce tenacity. She hunted, she danced, she jested with her young favourites, she coquetted and scolded and frolicked at sixty-seven as she had done at thirty. "The Queen," wrote a courtier a few months before her death, "was never so gallant these many years, nor so set upon jollity." She persisted, in spite of opposition, in her gorgeous progresses from country-house to country-house. She clung to business as of old, and rated in her usual fashion "one who minded not to giving up some matter of account." But death crept on. Her face became haggard, and her frame shrank almost to a skeleton. At last her taste for finery disappeared, and she refused to change her dresses for a week together. A strange melancholy settled down on her : "she held in her hand," says one who saw her in her last days, "a golden cup, which she often put to her lips : but in truth her heart seemed too full to need more filling." Gradually her mind gave way. She lost her memory, the violence of her temper became unbearable, her very courage seemed to forsake her. She called for a sword to lie constantly beside her, and thrust it from time to time through the arras, as if she heard murderers stirring there. Food and rest became alike distasteful. She sate day and night propped up with pillows on a stool, her finger on her lip, her eyes fixed on the floor, without a word. If she once broke the silence, it was with a flash of her old queenliness. When Robert Cecil asserted that she "must" go to bed, the word roused her like a trumpet. "Must !" she exclaimed ; "is *must* a word to be addressed to princes ? Little man, little man ! thy father, if he had been alive, durst not have used that word." Then, as her anger spent itself, she sank into her old dejection. "Thou art so presumptuous," she said, "because thou knowest I shall die." She rallied once more when the ministers beside her bed named Lord Beauchamp, the heir to the Suffolk claim, as a possible successor. "I will have no rogue's son," she cried hoarsely, "in my seat." But she gave no sign, save a motion of the head, at the mention of the King of Scots. She was in fact fast becoming insensible ; and early the next morning the life of Elizabeth, a life so great, so strange and lonely in its greatness, passed quietly away.

CHAPTER VIII.

· PURITAN ENGLAND.

Section I.—The Puritans, 1583—1603.

[*Authorities.*—For the primary facts of the ecclesiastical history of this time, Strype's "Annals," and his lives of Grindal and Whitgift. Neal's "History of the Puritans," besides its inaccuracies, contains little for this period which is not taken from the more colourless Strype. For the origin of the Presbyterian movement, see the "Discourse of the Troubles at Frankfort, 1576," often republished; for its later contest with Elizabeth, Mr. Maskell's "Martin Marprelate," which gives copious extracts from the rare pamphlets printed under that name. Mr. Hallam's account of the whole struggle ("Constitutional History," caps. iv. and vii.) is admirable for its fulness, lucidity, and impartiality. Wallington's "Diary" gives us the common life of Puritanism; its higher side is shown in Mrs. Hutchinson's Memoirs of her husband, and in the early life of Milton, as told in Mr. Masson's biography.]

The Bible

NO GREATER moral change ever passed over a nation than passed over England during the years which parted the middle of the reign of Elizabeth from the meeting of the Long Parliament. England became the people of a book, and that book was the Bible. It was as yet the one English book which was familiar to every Englishman; it was read at churches and read at home, and everywhere its words, as they fell on ears which custom had not deadened, kindled a startling enthusiasm. When Bishop Bonner set up the first six Bibles in St. Paul's "many well-disposed people used much to resort to the hearing thereof, especially when they could get any that had an audible voice to read to them." . . . "One John Porter used sometimes to be occupied in that goodly exercise, to the edifying of himself as well as others. This Porter was a fresh young man and of a big stature; and great multitudes would resort thither to hear him, because he could read well and had an audible voice." But the "goodly exercise" of readers such as Porter was soon superseded by the continued recitation of both Old Testament and New in the public services of the Church; while the small Geneva Bibles carried the Scripture into every home. The popularity of the Bible was owing to other causes besides that of religion. The whole prose literature of England, save the forgotten tracts of Wyclif, has grown up since the translation of the Scriptures by Tyndale and Coverdale. So far as the nation at large was concerned, no history, no romance, hardly any poetry, save the little-known verse

of Chaucer, existed in the English tongue when the Bible was ordered
to be set up in churches. Sunday after Sunday, day after day, the
crowds that gathered round Bonner's Bibles in the nave of St. Paul's,
or the family group that hung on the words of the Geneva Bible in the
devotional exercises at home, were leavened with a new literature.
Legend and annal, war-song and psalm, State-roll and biography, the
mighty voices of prophets, the parables of Evangelists, stories of
mission journeys, of perils by the sea and among the heathen, philosophic arguments, apocalyptic visions, all were flung broadcast over
minds unoccupied for the most part by any rival learning. The disclosure of the stores of Greek literature had wrought the revolution of
the Renascence. The disclosure of the older mass of Hebrew literature wrought the revolution of the Reformation. But the one revolution
was far deeper and wider in its effects than the other. No version
could transfer to another tongue the peculiar charm of language which
gave their value to the authors of Greece and Rome. Classical letters,
therefore, remained in the possession of the learned, that is, of the
few ; and among these, with the exception of Colet and More, or of
the pedants who revived a Pagan worship in the gardens of the Florentine Academy, their direct influence was purely intellectual. But the
tongue of the Hebrew, the idiom of the Hellenistic Greek, lent themselves with a curious felicity to the purposes of translation. As a mere
literary monument, the English version of the Bible remains the
noblest example of the English tongue, while its perpetual use made
it from the instant of its appearance the standard of our language.
For the moment however its literary effect was less than its social.
The power of the book over the mass of Englishmen showed itself in
a thousand superficial ways, and in none more conspicuously than in
the influence it exerted on ordinary speech. It formed, we must
repeat, the whole literature which was practically accessible to ordinary Englishmen ; and when we recall the number of common phrases
which we owe to great authors, the bits of Shakspere, or Milton, or
Dickens, or Thackeray, which unconsciously interweave themselves in
our ordinary talk, we shall better understand the strange mosaic of
Biblical words and phrases which coloured English talk two hundred
years ago. The mass of picturesque allusion and illustration which
we borrow from a thousand books, our fathers were forced to borrow
from one ; and the borrowing was the easier and the more natural
that the range of the Hebrew literature fitted it for the expression
of every phase of feeling. When Spenser poured forth his warmest
love-notes in the " Epithalamion," he adopted the very words of the
Psalmist, as he bade the gates open for the entrance of his bride.
When Cromwell saw the mists break over the hills of Dunbar, he
hailed the sun-burst with the cry of David : " Let God arise, and let
his enemies be scattered. Like as the smoke vanisheth, so shalt thou

Sec. I.

The
Puritans
1583
to
1603
The
Puritans

drive them away!" Even to common minds this familiarity with
grand poetic imagery in prophet and apocalypse gave a loftiness and
ardour of expression, that with all its tendency to exaggeration and
bombast we may prefer to the slipshod vulgarisms of to-day.

But far greater than its effect on literature or social phrase was the
effect of the Bible on the character of the people at large. Elizabeth
might silence or tune the pulpits ; but it was impossible for her to
silence or tune the great preachers of justice, and mercy, and truth,
who spoke from the book which she had again opened for her people.
The whole moral effect which is produced now-a-days by the religious
newspaper, the tract, the essay, the lecture, the missionary report, the
sermon, was then produced by the Bible alone ; and its effect in this
way, however dispassionately we examine it, was simply amazing. One
dominant influence told on human action : and all the activities that
had been called into life by the age that was passing away were
seized, concentrated, and steadied to a definite aim by the spirit
of religion. The whole temper of the nation felt the change. A
new conception of life and of man superseded the old. A new moral
and religious impulse spread through every class. Literature reflected
the general tendency of the time ; and the dumpy little quartos of
controversy and piety, which still crowd our older libraries, drove
before them the classical translations and Italian novelettes of the age
of the Renascence. "Theology rules there," said Grotius of England
only two years after Elizabeth's death ; and when Casaubon, the last
of the great scholars of the sixteenth century, was invited to England
by King James, he found both King and people indifferent to pure
letters. "There is a great abundance of theologians in England," he
says, "all point their studies in that direction." Even a country
gentleman like Colonel Hutchinson felt the theological impulse.
"As soon as he had improved his natural understanding with the
acquisition of learning, the first studies he exercised himself in were
the principles of religion." The whole nation became, in fact, a
Church. The great problems of life and death, whose questionings
found no answer in the higher minds of Shakspere's day, pressed for
an answer not only from noble and scholar but from farmer and shop-

keeper in the age that followed him. We must not, indeed, picture
the early Puritan as a gloomy fanatic. The religious movement had
not as yet come into conflict with general culture. With the close of the
Elizabethan age, indeed, the intellectual freedom which had marked
it faded insensibly away ; the bold philosophical speculations which
Sidney had caught from Bruno, and which had brought on Marlowe
and Ralegh the charge of atheism, died, like her own religious indifference, with the Queen. But the lighter and more elegant sides of the
Elizabethan culture harmonized well enough with the temper of the
Puritan gentleman. The figure of Colonel Hutchinson, one of the

Regicides, stands out from his wife's canvas with the grace and tenderness of a portrait by Vandyck. She dwells on the personal beauty which distinguished his youth, on "his teeth even and white as the purest ivory," "his hair of brown, very thickset in his youth, softer than the finest silk curling with loose great rings at the ends." Serious as was his temper in graver matters, the young squire of Owthorpe was fond of hawking, and piqued himself on his skill in dancing and fence. His artistic taste showed itself in a critical love of "paintings, sculpture, and all liberal arts," as well as in the pleasure he took in his gardens, "in the improvement of his grounds, in planting groves and walks and forest trees." If he was "diligent in his examination of the Scriptures," "he had a great love for music, and often diverted himself with a viol, on which he played masterly." We miss, indeed, the passion of the Elizabethan time, its caprice, its largeness of feeling and sympathy, its quick pulse of delight; but, on the other hand, life gained in moral grandeur, in a sense of the dignity of manhood, in orderliness and equable force. The temper of the Puritan gentleman was just, noble, and self-controlled. The larger geniality of the age that had passed away was replaced by an intense tenderness within the narrower circle of the home. "He was as kind a father," says Mrs. Hutchinson of her husband, "as dear a brother, as good a master, as faithful a friend as the world had." The wilful and lawless passion of the Renascence made way for a manly purity. "Neither in youth nor riper years could the most fair or enticing woman ever draw him into unnecessary familiarity or dalliance. Wise and virtuous women he loved, and delighted in all pure and holy and unblameable conversation with them, but so as never to excite scandal or temptation. Scurrilous discourse even among men he abhorred; and though he sometimes took pleasure in wit and mirth, yet that which was mixed with impurity he never could endure." To the Puritan the wilfulness of life, in which the men of the Renascence had revelled, seemed unworthy of life's character and end. His aim was to attain self-command, to be master of himself, of his thought and speech and acts. A certain gravity and reflectiveness gave its tone to the lightest details of his converse with the world about him. His temper, quick as it might naturally be, was kept under strict control. In his discourse he was ever on his guard against talkativeness or frivolity, striving to be deliberate in speech and "ranking the words beforehand." His life was orderly and methodical, sparing of diet and of self-indulgence; he rose early, "he never was at any time idle, and hated to see any one else so." The new sobriety and self-restraint marked itself even in his change of dress. The gorgeous colours and jewels of the Renascence disappeared. Colonel Hutchinson "left off very early the wearing of anything that was costly, yet in his plainest negligent habit appeared very much a gentleman." The loss of colour and variety in costume

Sec. I.

The
Puritans
1583
TO
1603

*Puritanism
and society*

reflected no doubt a certain loss of colour and variety in life itself; but it was a loss compensated by solid gains. Greatest among these, perhaps, was the new conception of social equality. Their common calling, their common brotherhood in Christ, annihilated in the mind of the Puritans that overpowering sense of social distinctions which characterized the age of Elizabeth. The meanest peasant felt himself ennobled as a child of God. The proudest noble recognized a spiritual equality in the poorest "saint." The great social revolution of the Civil Wars and the Protectorate was already felt in the demeanour of gentlemen like Hutchinson. "He had a loving and sweet courtesy to the poorest, and would often employ many spare hours with the commonest soldiers and poorest labourers." "He never disdained the meanest nor flattered the greatest." But it was felt even more in the new dignity and self-respect with which the consciousness of their "calling" invested the classes beneath the rank of the gentry. Take such a portrait as that which Nehemiah Wallington, a turner in East-cheap, has left us of a London housewife, his mother. "She was very loving," he says, "and obedient to her parents, loving and kind to her husband, very tender-hearted to her children, loving all that were godly, much misliking the wicked and profane. She was a pattern of sobriety unto many, very seldom was seen abroad except at church; when others recreated themselves at holidays and other times, she would take her needle-work and say, 'here is my recreation.' . . . God had given her a pregnant wit and an excellent memory. She was very ripe and perfect in all stories of the Bible, likewise in all the stories of the Martyrs, and could readily turn to them; she was also perfect and well seen in the English Chronicles, and in the descents of the Kings of England. She lived in holy wedlock with her husband twenty years, wanting but four days."

The strength of the religious movement lay rather among the middle and professional classes than among the gentry; and it is in a Puritan of this class that we find the fullest and noblest expression of the new influence which was leavening the temper of the time. John Milton is not only the highest, but the completest type of Puritanism.

His life is absolutely contemporaneous with his cause. He was born when it began to exercise a direct power over English politics and English religion; he died when its effort to mould them into its own shape was over, and when it had again sunk into one of many influences to which we owe our English character. His earlier verse, the pamphlets of his riper years, the epics of his age, mark with a singular precision the three great stages in its history. His youth shows us how much of the gaiety, the poetic ease, the intellectual culture of the Renascence lingered in a Puritan home. Scrivener and "precisian" as his father was, he was a skilled musician; and the boy inherited his father's skill on lute and organ. One of the finest outbursts in the scheme of education which he put forth at a later time is a passage in which he vindicates the province of music as an agent in moral training. His home, his tutor, his school were all rigidly Puritan; but there was nothing narrow or illiberal in his early training. "My father," he says, "destined me while yet a little boy to the study of humane letters; which I seized with such eagerness that from the twelfth year of my age I scarcely ever went from my lessons to bed before midnight." But to the Greek, Latin, and Hebrew he learnt at school, the scrivener advised him to add Italian and French. Nor were English letters neglected. Spenser gave the earliest turn to his poetic genius. In spite of the war between play-wright and precisian, a Puritan youth could still in Milton's days avow his love of the stage, "if Jonson's learned sock be on, or sweetest Shakspere, Fancy's child, warble his native woodnotes wild," and gather from the "masques and antique pageantry" of the court-revel hints for his own "Comus" and "Arcades." Nor does any shadow of the coming struggle with the Church disturb the young scholar's reverie, as he wanders beneath "the high embowed roof, with antique pillars massy proof, and storied windows richly dight, casting a dim religious light," or as he hears "the pealing organ blow to the full-voiced choir below, in service high and anthem clear." His enjoy-ment of the gaiety of life stands in bright contrast with the gloom and sternness which strife and persecution fostered in the later Puritanism. In spite of "a certain reservedness of natural disposition," which shrank from "festivities and jests, in which I acknowledge my faculty to be very slight," the young singer could still enjoy the "jest and youthful jollity" of the world around him, its "quips and cranks and wanton wiles;" he could join the crew of Mirth, and look pleasantly on at the village fair, "where the jolly rebecks sound to many a youth and many a maid, dancing in the chequered shade." But his pleasures were "unreproved." There was nothing ascetic in his look, in his slender, vigorous frame, his face full of a delicate yet serious beauty, the rich brown hair which clustered over his brow; and the words we have quoted show his sensitive enjoyment of all that was beautiful. But from coarse or sensual self-indulgence the young Puritan turned with disgust: "A certain reservedness of nature, an honest haughtiness and self-esteem, kept me still above those low descents of mind." He drank in an ideal chivalry from Spenser, but his religion and purity disdained the outer pledge on which chivalry built up its fabric of honour. "Every free and gentle spirit," said Milton, "without that oath, ought to be born a knight." It was with this temper that he passed from his London school, St. Paul's, to Christ's College at Cambridge, and it was this temper that he preserved throughout his University career. He left Cambridge, as he said afterwards, "free from all reproach, and approved by all honest men," with a purpose of

SEC. I.

THE
PURITANS
1583
TO
1603
Cromwell
and
Bunyan

self-dedication "to that same lot, however mean or high, towards which time leads me, and the will of Heaven."

Even in the still calm beauty of a life such as this, we catch the sterner tones of the Puritan temper. The very height of its aim, the intensity of its moral concentration, brought with them a loss of the genial delight in all that was human which distinguished the men of the Renascence. "If ever God instilled an intense love of moral beauty into the mind of any man," said Milton, "he has instilled it into mine." "Love Virtue," closed his "Comus," "she alone is free!" But this passionate love of virtue and of moral beauty, if it gave strength to human conduct, narrowed human sympathy and human intelligence. Already in Milton we note a certain "reservedness of temper," a contempt for "the false estimates of the vulgar," a proud retirement from the meaner and coarser life around him. Great as was his love for Shakspere, we can hardly fancy him delighting in Falstaff. In minds of a less cultured order, this moral tension ended, no doubt, in a hard unsocial sternness of life. The ordinary Puritan "loved all that were godly, much misliking the wicked and profane." His bond to other men was not the sense of a common manhood, but the recognition of a brotherhood among the elect. Without the pale of the saints lay a world which was hateful to them, because it was the enemy of their God. It was this utter isolation from the "ungodly" that explains the contrast which startles us between the inner tenderness of the Puritans and the ruthlessness of so many of their actions. Cromwell, whose son's death (in his own words) went to his heart "like a dagger, indeed it did!" and who rode away sad and wearied from the triumph of Marston Moor, burst into horse-play as he signed the death-warrant of the King. A temper which had thus lost sympathy with the life of half the world around it could hardly sympathize with the whole of its own life. Humour, the faculty which above all corrects exaggeration and extravagance, died away before the new stress and strain of existence. The absolute devotion of the Puritan to a Supreme Will tended more and more to rob him of all sense of measure and proportion in common matters. Little things became great things in the glare of religious zeal ; and the godly man learnt to shrink from a surplice, or a mince-pie at Christmas, as he shrank from impurity or a lie. Life became hard, rigid, colourless, as it became intense. The play, the geniality, the delight of the Elizabethan age were exchanged for a measured sobriety, seriousness, and self-restraint. But the self-restraint and sobriety which marked the Calvinist limited itself wholly to his outer life. In his inner soul sense, reason, judgement, were too often overborne by the terrible reality of invisible things. Our first glimpse of Oliver Cromwell is as a young country squire and farmer in the marsh levels around Huntingdon and St. Ives, buried from time to time in a deep melancholy, and haunted by fancies of coming death.

" I live in Meshac," he writes to a friend, "which they say signifies Prolonging; in Kedar, which signifies Darkness; yet the Lord forsaketh me not." The vivid sense of a Divine Purity close to such men made the life of common men seem sin. "You know what my manner of life has been," Cromwell adds. "Oh, I lived in and loved darkness, and hated light. I hated godliness." Yet his worst sin was probably nothing more than an enjoyment of the natural buoyancy of youth, and a want of the deeper earnestness which comes with riper years. In imaginative tempers, like that of Bunyan, the struggle took a more picturesque form. John Bunyan was the son of a poor tinker at Elstow in Bedfordshire, and even in childhood his fancy revelled in terrible visions of Heaven and Hell. "When I was but a child of nine or ten years old," he tells us, "these things did so distress my soul, that then in the midst of my merry sports and childish vanities, amidst my vain companions, I was often much cast down and afflicted in my mind therewith; yet could I not let go my sins." The sins he could not let go were a love of hockey and of dancing on the village green; for the only real fault which his bitter self-accusation discloses, that of a habit of swearing, was put an end to at once and for ever by a rebuke from an old woman. His passion for bell-ringing clung to him even after he had broken from it as a "vain practice;" and he would go to the steeple-house and look on, till the thought that a bell might fall and crush him in his sins drove him panic-stricken from the door. A sermon against dancing and games drew him for a time from these indulgences; but the temptation again overmastered his resolve. "I shook the sermon out of my mind, and to my old custom of sports and gaming I returned with great delight. But the same day, as I was in the midst of a game of cat, and having struck it one blow from the hole, just as I was about to strike it the second time, a voice did suddenly dart from heaven into my soul, which said, ' Wilt thou leave thy sins and go to Heaven, or have thy sins and go to Hell?' At this I was put in an exceeding maze; wherefore, leaving my cat upon the ground, I looked up to heaven; and was as if I had with the eyes of my understanding seen the Lord Jesus looking down upon me, as being very hotly displeased with me, and as if He did severely threaten me with some grievous punishment for those and other ungodly practices."

John Bunyan b. 1628

Such was Puritanism, and it is of the highest importance to realize it thus in itself, in its greatness and its littleness, apart from the ecclesiastical system of Presbyterianism with which it is so often confounded. As we shall see in the course of our story, not one of the leading Puritans of the Long Parliament was a Presbyterian. Pym and Hampden had no sort of objection to Episcopacy, and the adoption of the Presbyterian system was only forced on the Puritan patriots in their later struggle by political considerations. But the

The Presbyterians

growth of the movement, which thus influenced our history for a time, forms one of the most curious episodes in Elizabeth's reign. Her Church policy rested on the Acts of Supremacy and of Uniformity; the first of which placed all ecclesiastical jurisdiction and legislative power in the hands of the State, while the second prescribed a course of doctrine and discipline, from which no variation was legally permissible. For the nation at large Elizabeth's system was no doubt a wise and healthy one. Single-handed, unsupported by any of the statesmen or divines about her, the Queen forced on the warring religions a sort of armed truce. The main principles of the Refor. mation were accepted, but the zeal of the ultra-reformers was held at bay. The Bible was left open, private discussion was unrestrained, but the warfare of pulpit against pulpit was silenced by the licensing of preachers. Outer conformity, attendance at the common prayer, was exacted from all; but the changes in ritual, by which the zealots of Geneva gave prominence to the radical features of the religious change which was passing over the country, were steadily resisted. While England was struggling for existence, this balanced attitude of the Crown reflected faithfully enough the balanced attitude of the nation; but with the declaration of war by the Papacy in the Bull of Deposition the movement in favour of a more pronounced Protestantism gathered a new strength. Unhappily the Queen clung obstinately to her system of compromise, weakened and broken as it was. With the religious enthusiasm which was growing up around her she had no sympathy whatever. Her passion was for moderation, her aim was simply civil order; and both order and moderation were threatened by the knot of clerical bigots who gathered under the banner of Presbyterianism. Of these Thomas Cartwright was the chief. He had studied at Geneva; he returned with a fanatical faith in Calvinism, and in the system of Church government which Calvin had devised; and as Margaret Professor of Divinity at Cambridge he used to the full the opportunities which his chair gave him of propagating his opinions. No leader of a religious party ever deserved less of after sympathy than Cartwright. He was unquestionably learned and devout, but his bigotry was that of a mediæval inquisitor. The relics of the old ritual, the cross in baptism, the surplice, the giving of a ring in marriage, were to him not merely distasteful, as they were to the Puritans at large, they were idolatrous and the mark of the beast. His declamation against ceremonies and superstition however had little weight with Elizabeth or her Primates; what scared them was his reckless advocacy of a scheme of ecclesiastical government which placed the State beneath the feet of the Church. The absolute rule of bishops, indeed, he denounced as begotten of the devil; but the absolute rule of Presbyters he held to be established by the word of God. For the Church modelled after the fashion of Geneva he claimed an authority which surpassed the wildest dreams of the masters of the Vatican. All spiritual authority and jurisdiction, the decreeing of doctrine, the ordering of ceremonies, lay wholly in the hands of the ministers of the Church. To them belonged the supervision of public morals. In an ordered arrangement of classes and synods these Presbyters were to govern their flocks, to regulate their own order, to decide in matters of faith, to administer "discipline." Their weapon was excommunication, and they were responsible for its use to none but Christ. The province of the civil ruler was simply to carry out the decisions of the Presbyters, "to see their decrees executed and to punish the contemners of them." The spirit of Calvinistic Presbyterianism excluded all toleration of practice or belief. Not only was the rule of ministers to be established as the one legal form of Church government, but all other forms, Episcopalian and Separatist, were to be ruthlessly put down. For heresy there was the punishment of death. Never had the doctrine of persecution been urged with such a blind and reckless ferocity. " I deny," wrote Cartwright, "that upon repentance there ought to follow any pardon of death. . . . Heretics ought to be put to death now. If this be bloody and extreme, I am content to be so counted with the Holy Ghost."

Opinions such as these might wisely have been left to the good sense of the people itself. Before many years they found in fact a crushing answer in the "Ecclesiastical Polity" of Richard Hooker, a clergyman who had been Master of the Temple, but whose distaste for the controversies of its pulpit drove him from London to a Wiltshire vicarage at Boscombe, which he exchanged at a later time for the parsonage of Bishopsbourne among the quiet meadows of Kent. The largeness of temper which characterized all the nobler minds of his day, the philosophic breadth which is seen as clearly in Shakspere as in Bacon, was united in Hooker with a grandeur and stateliness of style, which raised him to the highest rank among English prose writers. Divine as he was, his spirit and method were philosophical rather than theological. Against the ecclesiastical dogmatism of Presbyterian or Catholic he set the authority of reason. He abandoned the narrow ground of Scriptural argument to base his conclusions on the general principles of moral and political science, on the eternal obligations of natural law. The Puritan system rested on the assumption that an immutable rule for human action in all matters relating to religion, to worship, and to the discipline and constitution of the Church, was laid down, and only laid down, in Scripture. Hooker urged that a Divine order exists, not in written revelation only, but in the moral relations, the historical developement, and the social and political institutions of men. He claimed for human reason the province of determining the laws of this order; of distinguishing between what is changeable and unchangeable in them, between what is eternal and what is temporary in the Bible itself. It was easy for him to push on to the field of theological controversy where men like Cartwright were fighting the battle of Presbyterianism, to show that no form of Church government had ever been of indispensable obligation, and that ritual observances had in all ages been left to the discretion of churches, and determined by the differences of times. But the truth on which Hooker based his argument was of far higher value than his argument itself; and the acknowledgement of a divine order in human history, of a divine law in human reason, which found expression in his work, harmonized with the noblest instincts of the Elizabethan age. Against Presbyterianism, indeed, the appeal was hardly needed. Popular as the Presbyterian system became in Scotland, it never took any general hold on England; it remained to the last a clerical rather than a national creed, and even in the moment of its seeming triumph under the Commonwealth it was rejected by every part of England save London and Lancashire, and part of Derbyshire. But the bold challenge to the Government which was delivered by Cartwright's party in a daring " Admonition to the Parliament," which demanded the establishment of government by Presbyters, raised a panic among English statesmen and prelates which cut off all hopes of a quiet appeal to reason. It is probable that, but for the storm which Cartwright raised, the steady growth of general discontent with the ceremonial usages he denounced would have brought about their abolition. The Parliament of 1571 had not only refused to bind the clergy to subscription to three articles on the Supremacy, the form of Church government, and the power of the Church to ordain rites and ceremonies, but favoured the project of reforming the Liturgy by the omission of the superstitious practices. But with the appearance of the " Admonition" this natural progress of opinion abruptly ceased. The moderate statesmen who had pressed for a change in ritual withdrew from union with a party which revived the worst pretensions of the Papacy. As dangers from without and from within thickened round the Queen the growing Puritanism of the clergy stirred her wrath above measure, and she met the growth of " nonconforming" ministers by a measure which forms the worst blot on her reign.

The new powers which were conferred in 1583 on the Ecclesiastical Commission converted the religious truce into a spiritual despotism. From being a temporary board which represented the Royal Supremacy in matters ecclesiastical, the Commission was now turned into a permanent body wielding the almost unlimited powers of the Crown. All opinions or acts contrary to the Statutes of Supremacy and Uniformity fell within its cognizance. A right of deprivation placed the clergy at its mercy. It had power to alter or amend the statutes of colleges or schools. Not only heresy, and schism, and nonconformity, but incest or aggravated adultery were held to fall within its scope : its means of enquiry were left without limit, and it might fine or imprison at its will. By the mere establishment of such a Court half the work of the Reformation was undone. The large number of civilians on the board indeed seemed to furnish some security against the excess of ecclesiastical tyranny. Of its forty-four commissioners, however, few actually took any part in its proceedings ; and the powers of the Commission were practically left in the hands of the successive Primates. No Archbishop of Canterbury since the days of Augustine had wielded an authority so vast, so utterly despotic, as that of Whitgift and Bancroft and Abbot and Laud. The most terrible feature of their spiritual tyranny was its wholly personal character. The old symbols of doctrine were gone, and the lawyers had not yet stepped in to protect the clergy by defining the exact limits of the new. The result was that at the Commission-board at Lambeth the Primates created their own tests of doctrine with an utter indifference to those created by law. In one instance Parker deprived a vicar of his benefice for a denial of the verbal inspiration of the Bible. Nor did the successive Archbishops care greatly if the test was a varying or a conflicting one. Whitgift strove to force on the Church the Calvinistic supralapsarianism of his Lambeth Articles. Bancroft, who followed him, was as earnest in enforcing his anti-Calvinistic dogma of the Divine right of the episcopate. Abbot had no mercy for Arminianism. Laud had none for its opponents. It is no wonder that the Ecclesiastical Commission, which these men represented, soon stank in the nostrils of the English clergy. Its establishment however marked the adoption of a more resolute policy on the part of the Crown, and its efforts were backed by stern measures of repression. All preaching or reading in private houses was forbidden ; and in spite of the refusal of Parliament to enforce the requirement of them by law, subscription to the Three Articles was exacted from every member of the clergy.

For the moment these measures were crowned with success. The movement under Cartwright was checked ; Cartwright himself was driven from his Professorship ; and an outer uniformity of worship was more and more brought about by the steady pressure of the Commission. The old liberty which had been allowed in London and the other Protestant parts of the kingdom was no longer permitted to exist. The leading Puritan clergy, whose nonconformity had hitherto been winked at, were called upon to submit to the surplice, and to make the sign of the cross in baptism. The remonstrances of the country gentry availed as little as the protest of Lord Burleigh himself to protect two hundred of the best ministers from being driven from their parsonages on a refusal to subscribe to the Three Articles. But the persecution only gave fresh

Growth
of Puri-
tanism

life and popularity to the doctrines which it aimed at crushing, by drawing together two currents of opinion which were in themselves perfectly distinct. The Presbyterian platform of Church discipline had as yet been embraced by that of the clergy only, and by few among the clergy. On the other hand, the wish of the Puritans for a reform in the Liturgy, the dislike of "superstitious usages," of the use of the surplice, the sign of the cross in baptism, the gift of the ring in marriage, the posture of kneeling at the Lord's Supper, was shared by a large number of the clergy and laity alike. At the opening of Elizabeth's reign almost all the higher Churchmen save Parker were opposed to them, and a motion in Convocation for their abolition was lost but by a single vote. The temper of the country gentlemen on this subject was indicated by that of Parliament; and it was well known that the wisest of the Queen's Councillors, Burleigh, Walsingham, and Knollys, were at one in this matter with the gentry. If their common persecution did not wholly succeed in fusing these two sections of religious opinion into one, it at any rate gained for the Presbyterians a general sympathy on the part of the Puritans. which raised them from a clerical clique into a popular party. Nor were the consequences of the persecution limited to the strengthening of the Presbyterians.

The "Separatists" who were beginning to withdraw from attendance at public worship on the ground that the very existence of a national Church was contrary to the Word of God, grew quickly from a few scattered zealots to twenty thousand souls. Presbyterian and Puritan felt as bitter an abhorrence as Elizabeth herself of the "Brownists," as they were nicknamed after their founder Robert Brown. Parliament,

Puritan as it was, passed a statute against them. Brown himself was forced to fly to the Netherlands, and of his followers many were driven into exile. So great a future awaited one of these congregations that we may pause to get a glimpse of "a poor people" in Lincolnshire and the neighbourhood, who "being enlightened by the Word of God," and their members "urged with the yoke of subscription," had been led "to see further." They rejected ceremonies as relics of idolatry, the rule of bishops as unscriptural, and joined themselves, "as the Lord's free people," into "a church estate on the fellowship of the Gospel." Feeling their way forward to the great principle of liberty of conscience, they asserted their Christian right "to walk in all the ways which God had made known or should make known to them." Their meetings or "conventicles" soon drew down the heavy hand of the law, and the little company resolved to seek a refuge in other lands; but their first attempt at flight was prevented, and when they made another, their wives and children were seized at the very moment of entering the ship. At last, however, the magistrates gave a contemptuous assent to their project; they were in fact "glad to be rid of them at any price;" and the fugitives found shelter at Amsterdam, from whence some of them, choosing John Robinson as their minister, took refuge in 1609 at Leyden. "They knew they were pilgrims and looked not much on these things, but lifted up their eyes to Heaven, their dearest country, and quieted their spirits." Among this little band of exiles were those who were to become famous at a later time as the Pilgrim Fathers of the *Mayflower*.

It was easy to be "rid" of the Brownists; but the political danger of the course on which the Crown had entered was seen in the rise of a spirit of vigorous opposition, such as had not made its appearance since the accession of the Tudors. The growing power of public opinion received a striking recognition in the struggle which bears the name of the "Martin Marprelate controversy." The Puritans had from the first appealed by their pamphlets from the Crown to the people, and Whitgift bore witness to their influence on opinion by his efforts to gag the Press. The regulations of the Star-Chamber for this purpose are memorable as the first step in the long struggle of government after government to check the liberty of printing. The irregular censorship which had long existed was now finally organized. Printing was restricted to London and the two Universities, the number of printers reduced, and all candidates for licence to print were placed under the supervision of the Company of Stationers. Every publication too, great or small, had to receive the approbation of the Primate or the Bishop of London. The first result of this system of repression was the appearance, in the very year of the Armada, of a series of anonymous pamphlets bearing the significant name of "Martin Marprelate," and issued from a secret press which found refuge from the royal pursuivants in the country-houses of the gentry. The press was at last seized; and the suspected authors of these scurrilous libels, Penry, a young Welshman, and a minister named Udall, died, the one in prison, the other on the scaffold. But the virulence and boldness of their language produced a powerful effect, for it was impossible under the system of Elizabeth to "mar" the bishops without attacking the Crown; and a new age of political liberty was felt to be at hand when Martin Marprelate forced the political and ecclesiastical measures of the Government into the arena of public discussion. The suppression, indeed, of these pamphlets was far from damping the courage of the Presbyterians. Cartwright, who had been appointed by Lord Leicester to the mastership of an hospital at Warwick, was bold enough to organize his system of Church discipline among the clergy of that county and of Northamptonshire. His example was widely followed; and the general gatherings of the whole ministerial body of the clergy, and the smaller assemblies for each diocese or shire, which in the Presbyterian scheme bore the name of Synods and Classes, began to be held in many parts of England for

Sec. II.

The First
of the
Stuarts

1604
to
1628

the purposes of debate and consultation. The new organization was quickly suppressed indeed, but Cartwright was saved from the banishment which Whitgift demanded by a promise of submission; his influence steadily increased; and the struggle, transferred to the higher sphere of the Parliament, widened into the great contest for liberty under James, and the Civil War under his successor.

Section II.—The First of the Stuarts. 1604—1623.

[*Authorities.*—Mr. Gardiner's "History of England from the Accession of James I." is invaluable for its fairness and good sense, and for the fresh information collected in it. We have Camden's "Annals of James I.," Goodman's "Court of James I.," Weldon's "Secret History of the Court of James I.," Roger Coke's "Detection," the correspondence in the "Cabala," the letters in the "Court and Times of James I.," the documents in Winwood's "Memorials of State," and the reported proceedings of the last two Parliaments. The Camden Society has published the correspondence of James with Cecil, and Walter Yonge's "Diary." The letters and works of Bacon (fully edited by Mr. Spedding) are necessary for a knowledge of the period. Hacket's "Life of Williams," and Harrington's "Nugæ Antiquæ" throw valuable side-light on the politics of the time. But the Stuart system can only be fairly studied in the State-papers, calendars of which are being published by the Master of the Rolls.] [The State Papers are now carried on to 1644.—Ed.]

To judge fairly the attitude and policy of the English Puritans, that is of three-fourths of the Protestants of England, at this moment, we must cursorily review the fortunes of Protestantism during the reign of Elizabeth. At its opening the success of the Reformation seemed almost everywhere secure. Already triumphant in the north of Germany at the peace of Augsburg, it was fast advancing to the conquest of the south. The nobles of Austria as well as the nobles and the towns of Bavaria were forsaking the older religion. A Venetian ambassador estimated the German Catholics at little more than one-tenth of the whole population of Germany. The new faith was firmly established in Scandinavia. Eastward the nobles of Hungary and Poland became Protestants in a mass. In the west France was yielding more and more to heresy. Scotland flung off Catholicism under Mary, and England veered round again to Protestantism under Elizabeth. Only where the dead hand of Spain lay heavy, in Castille, in Aragon, or in Italy, was the Reformation thoroughly crushed out; and even the dead hand of Spain failed to crush heresy in the Low Countries. But at the very instant of its seeming triumph, the advance of the new religion was suddenly arrested. The first twenty years of Elizabeth's reign were a period of suspense. The progress of Protestantism gradually ceased. It wasted its strength in theological controversies and persecutions, and in the bitter and venomous discussions between the Churches which followed Luther and the Churches which followed

Sec. II.

The First
OF THE
Stuarts

1604
TO
1623

Zwingli or Calvin. It was degraded and weakened by the prostitution of the Reformation to political ends, by the greed and worthlessness of the German princes who espoused its cause, by the factious lawlessness of the nobles in Poland, and of the Huguenots in France. Meanwhile the Papacy succeeded in rallying the Catholic world round the Council of Trent. The Roman Church, enfeebled and corrupted by the triumph of ages, felt at last the uses of adversity. Her faith was settled and defined. The Papacy was owned afresh as the centre of Catholic union. The enthusiasm of the Protestants roused a counter enthusiasm among their opponents; new religious orders rose to meet the wants of the day; the Capuchins became the preachers of Catholicism, the Jesuits became not only its preachers, but its directors, its schoolmasters, its missionaries, its diplomatists. Their organization, their blind obedience, their real ability, their fanatical zeal galvanized the pulpit, the school, the confessional into a new life. If the Protestants had enjoyed the profitable monopoly of martyrdom at the opening of the century, the Catholics won a fair share of it as soon as the disciples of Loyola came to the front. The tracts which pictured the tortures of Campian and Southwell roused much the same fire at Toledo or Vienna as the pages of Foxe had roused in England. Even learning came to the aid of the older faith. Bellarmine, the greatest of controversialists at this time, Baronius, the most erudite of Church historians, were both Catholics. With a growing inequality of strength such as this, we can hardly wonder that the tide was seen at last to turn. A few years before the fight with the Armada Catholicism began definitely to win ground. Southern Germany, where Bavaria was restored to Rome, and where the Austrian House so long lukewarm in the faith at last became zealots in its defence, was re-Catholicized. The success of Socinianism in Poland severed that kingdom from any real communion with the general body of the Protestant Churches; and these again were more and more divided into two warring camps by the controversies about the Sacrament and Free Will. Everywhere the Jesuits won converts, and their peaceful victories were soon backed by the arms of Spain. In the fierce struggle which followed, Philip was undoubtedly worsted. England was saved by its defeat of the Armada; the United Provinces of the Netherlands rose into a great Protestant power through their own dogged heroism and the genius of William the Silent. France was rescued from the grasp of the Catholic League, at a moment when all hope seemed gone, by the unconquerable energy of Henry of Navarre. But even in its defeat Catholicism gained ground. In the Low Countries, the Reformation was driven from the Walloon provinces, from Brabant, and from Flanders. In France Henry the Fourth found himself obliged to purchase Paris by a mass; and the conversion of the King was followed by a quiet breaking up of the Huguenot party. Nobles and scholars alike forsook Protest-

SEC. II.

THE FIRST
OF THE
STUARTS

1604
TO
1623

Puritan-
ism
and the
Church

antism ; and though the Reformation remained dominant south of the Loire, it lost all hope of winning France as a whole to its side.

At the death of Elizabeth, therefore, the temper of every earnest Protestant, whether in England or abroad, was that of a man who, after cherishing the hope of a crowning victory, is forced to look on at a crushing and irremediable defeat. The dream of a Reformation of the universal Church was utterly at an end. The borders of Protestantism were narrowing every day, nor was there a sign that the triumph of the Papacy was arrested. As hope after hope died into defeat and disaster, the mood of the Puritan grew sterner and more intolerant. What intensified the dread was a sense of defection and uncertainty within the pale of the Church of England itself. As a new Christendom fairly emerged from the troubled waters, the Renascence again made its influence felt. Its voice was heard above all in the work of Hooker, and the appeal to reason and to humanity which there found expression coloured through its results the after history of the English Church. On the one hand the historical feeling showed itself in a longing to ally the religion of the present with the religion of the past, to claim part in the great heritage of Catholic tradition. Men like George Herbert started back

from the bare, intense spiritualism of the Puritan to find nourishment for devotion in the outer associations which the piety of ages had grouped around it, in holy places and holy things, in the stillness of church and altar, in the aweful mystery of sacraments. Men like Laud, unable to find standing ground in the purely personal relation between man and God which formed the basis of Calvinism, fell back on the consciousness of a living Christendom, which, torn and rent as it seemed, was soon to resume its ancient unity. On the other hand, the appeal which Hooker addressed to reason produced a school of philosophical thinkers whose timid upgrowth was almost lost in the clash of warring creeds about them, but who were destined—as the Latitudinarians of

later days—to make a deep impression on religious thought. As yet however this rationalizing movement limited itself to the work of moderating and reconciling, to recognizing with Calixtus the pettiness of the points of difference which parted Christendom, and the greatness of its points of agreement, or to revolting with Arminius from the more extreme tenets of Calvin and Calvin's followers. No men could be more opposed in their tendencies to one another than the later High Churchmen, such as Laud, and the later Latitudinarians, such as Hales. But to the ordinary English Protestant both Latitudinarian and High Churchman were equally hateful. To him the struggle with the Papacy was not one for compromise or comprehension. It was a struggle between light and darkness, between life and death. No innovation in faith or worship was of small account, if it tended in the direction of Rome. Ceremonies, which in an hour of triumph might have been allowed as solaces to weak brethren, he looked on as acts

of treason in this hour of defeat.   The peril was too great to admit of
tolerance or moderation.   Now that falsehood was gaining ground,
the only security for truth was to draw a hard and fast line between
truth and falsehood.   There was as yet indeed no general demand for
any change in the form of Church government, or of its relation to the
State, but for some change in the outer ritual of worship which should
correspond to the advance which had been made to a more pronounced
Protestantism.   We see the Puritan temper in the Millenary Petition
(as it was called), which was presented to James the First on his
accession by some eight hundred clergymen, about a tenth of the
whole number in his realm.   It asked for no change in the government or organization of the Church, but for a reform of its courts, the
removal of superstitious usages from the Book of Common Prayer, the
disuse of lessons from the apocryphal books of Scripture, a more
rigorous observance of Sundays, and the provision and training of
preaching ministers.   Even statesmen who had little sympathy with
the religious spirit about them pleaded for the purchase of religious
and national union by ecclesiastical reforms.   "Why," asked Bacon,
"should the civil state be purged and restored by good and wholesome
laws made every three years in Parliament assembled, devising remedies as fast as time breedeth mischief, and contrariwise the ecclesiastical state still continue upon the dregs of time, and receive no
alteration these forty-five years or more ?"   A general expectation, in
fact, prevailed that, now the Queen's opposition was removed, something would be done.   But, different as his theological temper was
from the purely secular temper of Elizabeth, her successor was equally
resolute against all changes in Church matters.

No sovereign could have jarred against the conception of an English
ruler which had grown up under Plantagenet or Tudor more utterly
than James the First.   His big head, his slobbering tongue, his quilted
clothes, his rickety legs, stood out in as grotesque a contrast with
all that men recalled of Henry or Elizabeth as his gabble and rhodo-
montade, his want of personal dignity, his buffoonery, his coarseness of speech, his pedantry, his contemptible cowardice.   Under this
ridiculous exterior however lay a man of much natural ability, a ripe
scholar, with a considerable fund of shrewdness, of mother-wit, and
ready repartee.   His canny humour lights up the political and theological
controversies of the time with quaint incisive phrases, with puns and
epigrams and touches of irony, which still retain their savour.   His
reading, especially in theological matters, was extensive ; and he was
a voluminous author on subjects which ranged from predestination to
tobacco.   But his shrewdness and learning only left him, in the phrase
of Henry the Fourth, "the wisest fool in Christendom."   He had the
temper of a pedant, a pedant's conceit, a pedant's love of theories, and a
pedant's inability to bring his theories into any relation with actual facts.

SEC. II.

THE FIRST
OF THE
STUARTS
1604
TO
1623

All might have gone well had he confined himself to speculations about witchcraft, about predestination, about the noxiousness of smoking. Unhappily for England and for his successor, he clung yet more passionately to theories of government which contained within them the seeds of a death-struggle between his people and the Crown. Even before his accession to the English throne, he had formulated his theory of rule in a work on "The True Law of Free Monarchy;" and announced that, "although a good King will frame his actions to be according to law, yet he is not bound thereto, but of his own will and for example-giving to his subjects." With the Tudor statesmen who used the phrase, "an absolute King," or "an absolute monarchy," meant a sovereign or rule complete in themselves, and independent of all foreign or Papal interference. James chose to regard the words as implying the monarch's freedom from all control by law, or from responsibility to anything but his own royal will. The King's theory however was made a system of government; it was soon, as the Divine Right of Kings, to become a doctrine which bishops preached from the pulpit, and for which brave men laid their heads on the block.

The Church was quick to adopt its sovereign's discovery. Convocation in its book of Canons denounced as a fatal error the assertion that "all civil power, jurisdiction, and authority were first derived from the people and disordered multitude, or either is originally still in them, or else is deduced by their consent naturally from them; and is not God's ordinance originally descending from Him and depending upon Him." In strict accordance with James's theory, these doctors declared sovereignty in its origin to be the prerogative of birthright, and inculcated passive obedience to the monarch as a religious obligation.

Cowell, a civilian, followed up the discoveries of Convocation by an announcement that "the King is above the law by his absolute power," and that "notwithstanding his oath he may alter and suspend any particular law that seemeth hurtful to the public estate." The book was suppressed on the remonstrance of the House of Commons, but the party of passive obedience grew fast. A few years before the death of James, the University of Oxford decreed solemnly that "it was in no case lawful for subjects to make use of force against their princes, or to appear offensively or defensively in the field against them." The King's "arrogant speeches," if they roused resentment in the Parliaments to which they were addressed, created by sheer force of repetition a certain belief in the arbitrary power they challenged for the Crown. We may give one instance of their tone from a speech delivered in the Star-Chamber. "As it is atheism and blasphemy to dispute what God can do," said James, "so it is presumption and a high contempt in a subject to dispute what a King can do, or to say that a King cannot do this or that." "If the practice should follow the positions," once commented a thoughtful observer on words such as these, "we are not likely to leave to our successors that freedom we received from our forefathers."

Sec. II.

The First
of the
Stuarts

1604
to
1623

The
Crown
and the
Bishops

It is necessary to weigh throughout the course of James's reign this aggressive attitude of the Crown, if we would rightly judge what seems at first sight to be an aggressive tone in some of the proceedings of the Parliaments. With new claims of power such as these before them, to have stood still would have been ruin. The claim, too, was one which jarred against all that was noblest in the temper of the time. Men were everywhere reaching forward to the conception of law. Bacon sought for law in material nature ; Hooker asserted the rule of law over the spiritual world. The temper of the Puritan was eminently a temper of law. The diligence with which he searched the Scriptures sprang from his earnestness to discover a Divine Will which in all things, great or small, he might implicitly obey. But this implicit obedience was reserved for the Divine Will alone ; for human ordinances derived their strength only from their correspondence with the revealed law of God. The Puritan was bound by his very religion to examine every claim made on his civil and spiritual obedience by the powers that be ; and to own or reject the claim, as it accorded with the higher duty which he owed to God. " In matters of faith," Mrs. Hutchinson tells us of her husband, " his reason always submitted to the Word of God ; but in all other things the greatest names in the world would not lead him without reason." It was plain that an impassable gulf parted such a temper as this from the temper of unquestioning devotion to the Crown which James demanded. It was a temper not only legal, but even pedantic in its legality, intolerant from its very sense of a moral order and law of the lawlessness and disorder of a personal tyranny ; a temper of criticism, of judgement, and, if need be, of stubborn and unconquerable resistance ; of a resistance which sprang, not from the disdain of authority, but from the Puritan's devotion to an authority higher than that of kings. But if the theory of a Divine Right of Kings was certain to rouse against it all the nobler energies of Puritanism, there was something which roused its nobler and its pettier instincts of resistance alike in the place accorded by James to Bishops. Elizabeth's conception of her ecclesiastical Supremacy had been a sore stumbling-block to her subjects, but Elizabeth at least regarded the Supremacy simply as a branch of her ordinary prerogative. The theory of James, however, was as different from that of Elizabeth, as his view of kingship was different from hers. It was the outcome of the bitter years of humiliation which he had endured in Scotland in his struggle with Presbyterianism. The Scotch presbyters had insulted and frightened him in the early days of his reign, and he chose to confound Puritanism with Presbyterianism. No prejudice, however, was really required to suggest his course. In itself it was logical, and consistent with the premisses from which it

SEC. II.

THE FIRST
OF THE
STUARTS
1604
TO
1623

started. If theologically his opinions were Calvinistic, in the ecclesiastical fabric of Calvinism, in its organization of the Church, in its annual assemblies, in its public discussion and criticism of acts of government through the pulpit, he saw an organized democracy which threatened his crown. The new force which had overthrown episcopacy in Scotland, was a force which might overthrow the monarchy itself. It was the people which in its religious or its political guise was the assailant of both. And as their foe was the same, so James argued with the shrewd short-sightedness of his race, their cause was the same. "No bishop," ran his famous adage, "no King!" Hopes of ecclesiastical change found no echo in a King who, among all the charms that England presented him, saw none so attractive as its ordered and obedient Church, its synods that met at the royal will, its courts that carried out the royal ordinances, its bishops that held themselves to be royal officers. If he accepted the Millenary Petition, and summoned a conference of prelates and Puritan divines at Hampton Court, he showed no purpose of discussing the grievances alleged. He revelled in the opportunity for a display of his theological reading; but he viewed the Puritan demands in a purely political light. The bishops declared that the insults he showered on their opponents were dictated by the Holy Ghost. The Puritans still ventured to dispute his infallibility. James broke up the conference with a threat which revealed the policy of the Crown. "I will make them conform," he said of the remonstrants, "or I will harry them out of the land."

*Hampton
Court Con-
ference*
1604

**The
Crown
and the
Parlia-
ment**

It is only by thoroughly realizing the temper of the nation on religious and civil subjects, and the temper of the King, that we can understand the long Parliamentary conflict which occupied the whole of James's reign. But to make its details intelligible we must briefly review the relations between the two Houses and the Crown. The wary prescience of Wolsey had seen in Parliament, even in its degradation under the Tudors, the memorial of an older freedom, and a centre of national resistance to the new despotism which Henry was establishing, should the nation ever rouse itself to resist. Never perhaps was English liberty in such deadly peril as when Wolsey resolved on the practical suppression of the two Houses. But the bolder genius of Cromwell set aside the traditions of the New Monarchy. His confidence in the power of the Crown revived the Parliament as an easy and manageable instrument of tyranny. The old forms of constitutional freedom were turned to the profit of the royal despotism, and a revolution which for the moment left England absolutely at Henry's feet was wrought out by a series of parliamentary statutes. Throughout Henry's reign Cromwell's confidence was justified by the spirit of slavish submission which pervaded the Houses. But the effect of the religious change for which his measures made room began to be felt during the minority of Edward the Sixth; and

SEC. II.

THE FIRST
OF THE
STUARTS

1604
TO
1623

the debates and divisions on the religious reaction which Mary pressed on the Parliament were many and violent. A great step forward was marked by the effort of the Crown to neutralize by "management" an opposition which it could no longer overawe. The Parliaments were packed with nominees of the Crown. Twenty-two new boroughs were created under Edward, fourteen under Mary; some, indeed, places entitled to representation by their wealth and population, but the bulk of them small towns or hamlets which lay wholly at the disposal of the royal Council. Elizabeth adopted the system of her two predecessors, both in the creation of boroughs and the recommendation of candidates; but her keen political instinct soon perceived the uselessness of both expedients. She fell back as far as she could on Wolsey's policy of practical abolition, and summoned Parliaments at longer and longer intervals. By rigid economy, by a policy of balance and peace, she strove, and for a long time successfully strove, to avoid the necessity of assembling them at all. But Mary of Scotland and Philip of Spain proved friends to English liberty in its sorest need. The struggle with Catholicism forced Elizabeth to have more frequent recourse to her Parliament, and as she was driven to appeal for increasing supplies the tone of the Houses rose higher and higher. On the question of taxation or monopolies her fierce spirit was forced to give way to their demands. On the question of religion she refused all concession, and England was driven to await a change of system from her successor. But it is clear, from the earlier acts of his reign, that James was preparing for a struggle with the Houses rather than for a policy of concession. During the Queen's reign, the power of Parliament had sprung mainly from the continuance of the war, and from the necessity under which the Crown lay of appealing to it for supplies. It is fair to the war party in Elizabeth's Council to remember that they were fighting, not merely for Protestantism abroad, but for constitutional liberty at home. When Essex overrode Burleigh's counsels of peace, the old minister pointed to the words of the Bible, "a bloodthirsty man shall not live out half his days." But Essex and his friends had nobler motives for their policy of war than a thirst for blood; as James had other motives for his policy of peace than a hatred of bloodshedding. The peace which he hastened to conclude with Spain was necessary to establish the security of his throne by depriving the Catholics, who alone questioned his title, of foreign aid. With the same object of averting a Catholic rising, he relaxed the penal laws against Catholics, and released recusants from payment of fines. But however justifiable such steps might be, the sterner Protestants heard angrily of negotiations with Spain and with the Papacy which seemed to show a withdrawal from the struggle with Catholicism at home and abroad.

The policy of James

The Parliament of 1604 met in another mood from that of any

II

Sec. II.

The First
of the
Stuarts

1604
to
1623

The Par-
liament
of 1604

Parliament which had met for a hundred years. Short as had been the time since his accession, the temper of the King had already disclosed itself; and men were dwelling ominously on the claims of absolutism in Church and State which were constantly on his lips. Above all, the hopes of religious concessions to which the Puritans had clung had been dashed to the ground in the Hampton Court Conference; and of the squires and merchants who thronged the benches at Westminster three-fourths were in sympathy Puritan. They listened with coldness and suspicion to the proposals of the King for the union of England and Scotland under the name of Great Britain. What the House was really set on was religious reform. The first step of the Commons was to name a committee to frame bills for the redress of the more crying ecclesiastical grievances; and the rejection of the measures they proposed was at once followed by an outspoken address to the King. The Parliament, it said, had come together in a spirit

of peace: " Our desires were of peace only, and our device of unity." Their aim had been to put an end to the long-standing dissension among the ministers, and to preserve uniformity by the abandonment of " a few ceremonies of small importance," by the redress of some ecclesiastical abuses, and by the establishment of an efficient training for a preaching clergy. If they had waived their right to deal with these matters during the old age of Elizabeth, they asserted it now. " Let your Majesty be pleased to receive public information from your Commons in Parliament, as well of the abuses in the Church, as in the civil state and government." The claim of absolutism was met in words which sound like a prelude to the Petition of Right. " Your Majesty would be misinformed," said the address, " if any man should deliver that the Kings of England have any absolute power in themselves either to alter religion, or to make any laws concerning the same, otherwise than as in temporal causes, by consent of Parliament." The address was met by a petulant scolding from James, and the Houses were adjourned. The support of the Crown emboldened the bishops to a fresh defiance of the Puritan pressure. The act of Elizabeth which sanctioned the Thirty-nine Articles compelled ministers to subscribe only to those which concerned the faith and the sacraments; but the Convocation of 1604 by its canons required subscription to the articles touching rites and ceremonies. The new archbishop, Bancroft, added a requirement of rigid conformity with the rubrics on the part of all beneficed clergymen. In the following spring three hundred of the Puritan clergy were driven from their livings for a refusal to comply with these demands.

The breach with the Puritans was followed by a breach with the Catholics. The increase in their numbers since the remission of fines had spread a general panic; and Parliament had re-enacted the penal laws. A rumour of his own conversion so angered the King that these

Sec. II.

The First
of the
Stuarts

1604
to
1623

were now put in force with even more severity than of old. The despair of the Catholics gave fresh life to a conspiracy which had long been ripening. Hopeless of aid from abroad, or of success in an open rising at home, a small knot of desperate men, with Robert Catesby, who had taken part in the rising of Essex, at their head, resolved to destroy at a blow both King and Parliament. Barrels of powder were placed in a cellar beneath the Parliament House; and while waiting for the fifth of November, when the Parliament was summoned to meet, the plans of the little group widened into a formidable conspiracy. Catholics of greater fortune, such as Sir Everard Digby and Francis Tresham, were admitted to their confidence, and supplied money for the larger projects they designed. Arms were bought in Flanders, horses were held in readiness, a meeting of Catholic gentlemen was brought about under show of a hunting party to serve as the beginning of a rising. The destruction of the King was to be followed by the seizure of his children and an open revolt, in which aid might be called for from the Spaniards in Flanders. Wonderful as was the secrecy with which the plot was concealed, the family affection of Tresham at the last moment gave a clue to it by a letter to Lord Monteagle, his relative, which warned him to absent himself from the Parliament on the fatal day; and further information brought about the discovery of the cellar and of Guido Fawkes, a soldier of fortune, who was charged with the custody of it. The hunting party broke up in despair, the conspirators were chased from county to county, and either killed or sent to the block, and Garnet, the Provincial of the English Jesuits, was brought to trial and executed. He had shrunk from all part in the plot, but its existence had been made known to him by another Jesuit, Greenway, and horror-stricken as he represented himself to have been he had kept the secret and left the Parliament to its doom.

Parliament was drawn closer to the King by deliverance from a common peril, and when the Houses met in 1606 the Commons were willing to vote a sum large enough to pay the debt left by Elizabeth after the war. But the prodigality of James was fast raising his peace expenditure to the level of the war expenditure of Elizabeth; and he was driven by the needs of his treasury, and the desire to free himself from Parliamentary control, to seek new sources of revenue. His first great innovation was the imposition of customs duties. It had long been declared illegal for the Crown to levy any duties ungranted by Parliament save those on wool, leather, and tin. A duty on imports indeed had been imposed in one or two instances by Mary, and this impost had been extended by Elizabeth to currants and wine; but these instances were too trivial and exceptional to break in upon the general usage. A more dangerous precedent lay in the duties which the great trading companies, such as those to the Levant and to the Indies, exacted from merchants, in exchange—as was held—for the protection they

SEC. II.

THE FIRST
OF THE
STUARTS

1604
TO
1623

Bates's case
1606

afforded them in far-off seas. The Levant Company was now dissolved, and James seized on the duties it had levied as lapsing to the Crown. Parliament protested in vain. James cared quite as much to assert his absolute authority as to fill his treasury. A case therefore was brought before the Exchequer Chamber, and the judgement of the Court asserted the King's right to levy what customs duties he would at his pleasure. " All customs," said the Judges, " are the effects of foreign commerce, but all affairs of commerce and treaties with foreign nations belong to the King's absolute power. He therefore, who has power over the cause, has power over the effect." The importance of a decision which would go far to free the Crown from the necessity of resorting to Parliament was seen keenly enough by James. English commerce was growing fast, and English merchants were fighting their way to the Spice Islands, and establishing settlements in the dominions of the Mogul. The judgement gave James a revenue which was sure to grow rapidly, and the needs of his treasury forced him to action. After two years' hesitation a royal proclamation imposed a system of customs duties on many articles of export and import. But if the new impositions came in fast, the royal debt grew faster. Every year the expenditure of James reached a higher level, and necessity forced on the King a fresh assembling of Parliament. The " great contract " drawn up by Cecil, now Earl of Salisbury, proposed that James should waive certain oppressive feudal rights, such as those of wardship and marriage, and the right of purveyance, on condition that the Commons raised the royal revenue by a sum of two hundred thousand a year. The bargain failed however before the distrust of the Commons : and the King's demand for a grant to pay off the royal debt was met by a petition of grievances. They had jealously watched the new character given by James to royal proclamations, by which he created new offences, imposed new penalties, and called offenders before courts which had no legal jurisdiction over them. The province of the spiritual courts had been as busily enlarged. It was in vain that the judges, spurred no doubt by the old jealousy between civil and ecclesiastical lawyers, entertained appeals against the High Commission, and strove by a series of decisions to set bounds to its limitless claims of jurisdiction, or to restrict its powers of imprisonment to cases of schism and heresy. The judges were powerless against the Crown ; and James was vehement in his support of courts which were closely bound up with his own prerogative. Were the treasury once full no means remained of redressing these evils. Nor were the Commons willing to pass over silently the illegalities of the past years. James forbade them to enter on the subject of the new duties, but their remonstrance was none the less vigorous. " Finding that your Majesty without advice or counsel of Parliament hath lately in time of peace set both greater impositions and more in number than any of your noble ancestors did ever in time of war," they prayed

SEC. II.

THE FIRST
OF THE
STUARTS

1604
TO
1623

"that all impositions set without the assent of Parliament may be quite abolished and taken away," and that "a law be made to declare that all impositions set upon your people, their goods or merchandise, save only by common consent in Parliament, are and shall be void." As to Church grievances their demands were in the same spirit. They prayed that the deposed ministers might be suffered to preach, and that the jurisdiction of the High Commission should be regulated by statute ; in other words, that ecclesiastical like financial matters should be taken out of the sphere of the prerogative and be owned as lying henceforth within the cognizance of Parliament. Whatever concessions James might offer on other subjects, he would allow no interference with his ecclesiastical prerogative ; the Parliament was dissolved, and three years passed before the financial straits of the Government forced James to face the two Houses again. But the spirit of resistance was now fairly roused. Never had an election stirred so much popular passion as that of 1614. In every case where rejection was possible, the court candidates were rejected. All the leading members of the popular party, or as we should now call it, the Opposition, were again returned. But three hundred of the members were wholly new men ; and among these we note for the first time the names of two leaders in the later struggle with the Crown. Yorkshire returned Thomas Wentworth ; St. Germans, John Eliot. Signs of an unprecedented excitement were seen in the vehement cheering and hissing which for the first time marked, the proceedings of the Commons. But the policy of the Parliament was precisely the same as that of its predecessors. It refused to grant supplies till it had considered public grievances, and it fixed on the impositions and the abuses of the Church as the first to be redressed. Unluckily the inexperience of the bulk of the House of Commons led it into quarrelling on a point of privilege with the Lords ; and the King, who had been frightened beyond his wont at the vehemence of their tone and language, seized on the quarrel as a pretext for their dissolution.

Four of the leading members in the dissolved Parliament were sent to the Tower ; and the terror and resentment which it had roused in the King's mind were seen in the obstinacy with which he long persisted in governing without any Parliament at all. For seven years he carried out with a blind recklessness his theory of an absolute rule, unfettered by any scruples as to the past, or any dread of the future. All the abuses which Parliament after Parliament had denounced were not only continued, but carried to a greater extent than before. The spiritual courts were encouraged in fresh encroachments. Though the Crown lawyers admitted the illegality of proclamations they were issued in greater numbers than ever. Impositions were strictly levied. But the treasury was still empty ; and a fatal necessity at last drove James to a formal breach of law. He fell back on a resource which

SEC. II.

THE FIRST
OF THE
STUARTS
1604
TO
1623

Benevolences

even Wolsey in the height of the Tudor power had been forced to abandon. But the letters from the Council demanding benevolences or gifts from the richer landowners remained generally unanswered. In the three years which followed the dissolution of 1614 the strenuous efforts of the sheriffs only raised sixty thousand pounds, a sum less than two-thirds of the value of a single subsidy; and although the remonstrances of the western counties were roughly silenced by the threats of the Council, two counties, those of Hereford and Stafford, sent not a penny to the last. In his distress for money James was driven to expedients which widened the breach between the gentry and the Crown. He had refused to part with the feudal rights which came down to him from the Middle Ages, such as his right to the wardship of young heirs and the marriage of heiresses, and these were steadily used as a means of extortion. He degraded the nobility by a shameless sale of peerages. Of the forty-five lay peers whom he added to the Upper House during his reign, many were created by sheer bargaining. A proclamation which forbade the increase of houses in London brought heavy fines into the treasury. By shifts such as these James put off from day to day the necessity for again encountering the one body which could permanently arrest his effort after despotic rule. But there still remained a body whose tradition

was strong enough, not indeed to arrest, but to check it. The lawyers had been subservient beyond all other classes to the Crown. In the narrow pedantry with which they bent before isolated precedents, without realizing the conditions under which these precedents had been framed, and to which they owed their very varying value, the judges had supported James in his claims. But beyond precedents even the judges refused to go. They had done their best, in a case that came before them, to restrict the jurisdiction of the ecclesiastical courts within legal and definite bounds: and when James asserted an inherent right in the King to be heard before judgement was delivered, whenever any case affecting the prerogative came before his courts, they timidly, but firmly, repudiated such a right as unknown to the law. James sent for them to the Royal closet, and rated them like school-boys, till they fell on their knees, and, with a single exception, pledged themselves to obey his will. The Chief-Justice, Sir Edward Coke, a narrow-minded and bitter-tempered man, but of the highest eminence as a lawyer, and with a reverence for the law that overrode every other instinct, alone remained firm. When any case came before him, he answered, he would act as it became a judge to act. Coke was at once dismissed from the Council, and a provision which made the judicial office tenable at the King's pleasure, but which had long fallen into disuse, was revived to humble the common law in the person of its chief officer; on the continuance of his resistance he was deprived of his post of Chief-Justice. No act of James seems to have stirred a deeper

SEC. II.

THE FIRST
OF THE
STUARTS

1604
TO
1623

The Court

resentment among Englishmen than this announcement of his will to tamper with the course of justice. It was an outrage on the growing sense of law, as the profusion and profligacy of the court were an outrage on the growing sense of morality. The treasury was drained to furnish masques and revels on a scale of unexampled splendour. Lands and jewels were lavished on young adventurers, whose fair faces caught the royal fancy. If the court of Elizabeth was as immoral as that of her successor, its immorality had been shrouded by a veil of grace and chivalry. But no veil hid the degrading grossness of the court of James. The King was held, though unjustly, to be a drunkard. Actors in a masque performed at court were seen rolling intoxicated at his feet. A scandalous trial showed great nobles and officers of state in league with cheats and astrologers and poisoners. James himself had not shrunk from meddling busily in the divorce of Lady Essex; and her subsequent bridal with one of his favourites was celebrated in his presence. Before scenes such as these, the half-idolatrous reverence with which the sovereign had been regarded throughout the period of the Tudors died away into abhorrence and contempt. The players openly mocked at the King on the stage. Mrs. Hutchinson denounced the orgies of Whitehall in words as fiery as those with which Elijah denounced the sensuality of Jezebel. But the immorality of James's court was hardly more despicable than the folly of his government. In the silence of Parliament, the royal Council, composed as it was not merely of the ministers, but of the higher nobles and hereditary officers of state, had served even under a despot like Henry the Eighth as a check upon the arbitrary will of the sovereign. But after the death of Lord Burleigh's son, Robert Cecil, the minister whom Elizabeth had bequeathed to him, and whose services in procuring his accession were rewarded by the Earldom of Salisbury, all real control over affairs was withdrawn by James from the Council, and entrusted to worthless favourites whom the King chose to raise to honour. A Scotch page named Carr was created Viscount Rochester and Earl of Somerset, and married after her divorce to Lady Essex. Supreme in State affairs, domestic and foreign, he was at last hurled from favour and power on the charge of a horrible crime, the murder of Sir Thomas Overbury by poison, of which he and his Countess were convicted of being the instigators. Another favourite was already prepared to take his place. George Villiers, a handsome young adventurer, was raised rapidly through every rank of the peerage, made Marquis and Duke of Buckingham, and entrusted with the appointment to high offices of state. The payment of bribes to him, or marriage with his greedy relatives, became the one road to political preferment. Resistance to his will was inevitably followed by dismissal from office. Even the highest and most powerful of the nobles were made to tremble at the nod of this young

SEC. II.

THE FIRST
OF THE
STUARTS
1604
TO
1623

upstart. " Never any man in any age, nor, I believe, in any country," says the astonished Clarendon, " rose in so short a time to so much greatness of honour, power, or fortune, upon no other advantage or recommendation than of the beauty or gracefulness of his person." Buckingham indeed had no inconsiderable abilities, but his self-confidence and recklessness were equal to his beauty ; and the haughty young favourite on whose neck James loved to loll, and whose cheek he slobbered with kisses, was destined to drag down in his fatal career the throne of the Stuarts.

The Spanish Policy

The new system was even more disastrous in its results abroad than at home.   The withdrawal of power from the Council left James in effect his own chief minister, and master of the control of affairs as no English sovereign had been before him.   At his accession he found the direction of foreign affairs in the hands of Salisbury, and so long as Salisbury lived the Elizabethan policy was in the main adhered to.   Peace, indeed, was made with Spain ; but a close alliance with the United Provinces, and a more guarded alliance with France, held the ambition of Spain in check almost as effectually as war.   When danger grew threatening in Germany from the Catholic zeal of the House of Austria, the marriage of the King's daughter, Elizabeth, with the heir

1612

of the Elector-Palatine promised English support to its Protestant powers.   But the death of Salisbury, and the dissolution of the Parliament of 1614, were quickly followed by a disastrous change.   James at once proceeded to undo all that the struggle of Elizabeth and the triumph of the Armada had done.   His quick, shallow intelligence held that in a joint action with Spain it had found a way by which the Crown might at once exert weight abroad, and be rendered independent of the nation at home.   A series of negotiations was begun for the marriage of his son with a Princess of Spain.   Each of his successive

1617

favourites supported the Spanish alliance ; and after years of secret intrigue the King's intentions were proclaimed to the world, at the moment when the policy of the House of Austria threatened the Protestants of Southern Germany with utter ruin or civil war.   From whatever quarter the first aggression should come, it was plain that a second great struggle in arms between Protestantism and Catholicism was to be fought out on German soil.   It was their prescience of the coming conflict which, on the very eve of the crisis, spurred a party among his ministers who still clung to the traditions of Salisbury to support an enterprise which promised to detach the King from his new policy by entangling him in a war with Spain.   Sir Walter Ralegh, the one great warrior of the Elizabethan time who still lingered on, had

Ralegh's death

been imprisoned ever since the beginning of the new reign in the Tower on a charge of treason.   He now disclosed to James his knowledge of a gold-mine on the Orinoco, and prayed that he might sail thither and work its treasures for the King.   The King was tempted by the bait **of** gold ; but he forbade any attack on Spanish territory, or the shedding of Spanish blood. Ralegh however had risked his head again and again, he believed in the tale he told, and he knew that if war could be brought about between England and Spain a new career was open to him. He found the coast occupied by Spanish troops ; evading direct orders to attack he sent his men up the country, where they plundered a Spanish town, found no gold-mine, and came broken and defeated back. The daring of the man saw a fresh resource ; he proposed to seize the Spanish treasure ships as he returned, and, like Drake, to turn the heads of nation and King by the immense spoil. But his men would not follow him, and he was brought home to face his doom. James at once put his old sentence in force ; and the death of the broken-hearted adventurer on the scaffold atoned for the affront to Spain. The failure of Ralegh came at a critical moment in German history. The religious truce which had so long preserved the peace of Germany was broken in 1618 by the revolt of Bohemia against the rule of the Catholic House of Austria ; and when the death of the Emperor Matthias raised his cousin Ferdinand in 1619 to the Empire and to the throne of Bohemia, its nobles declared the realm vacant and chose Frederick, the young Elector Palatine, as their King. The German Protestants were divided by the fatal jealousy between their Lutheran and Calvinist princes ; but it was believed that Frederick's election could unite them, and the Bohemians counted on England's support when they chose James's son-in-law for their king. A firm policy would at any rate have held Spain inactive, and limited the contest to Germany itself. But the "statecraft" on which James prided himself led him to count, not on Spanish fear, but on Spanish friendship. He refused aid to the Protestant Union of the German Princes when they espoused the cause of Bohemia, and threatened war against Holland, the one power which was earnest in the Palatine's cause. It was in vain that both court and people were unanimous in their cry for war. James still pressed his son-in-law to withdraw from Bohemia, and relied in such a case on the joint efforts of England and Spain to restore peace. But Frederick refused consent, and Spain quickly threw aside the mask. Her famous battalions were soon moving up the Rhine to the aid of the Emperor ; and their march turned the local struggle in Bohemia into a European war. While the Spaniards occupied the Palatinate, the army of the Catholic League under Maximilian of Bavaria marched down the Danube, reduced Austria to submission, and forced Frederick to battle before the walls of Prague. Before the day was over he was galloping off, a fugitive, to North Germany, to find the Spaniards encamped as its masters in the heart of the Palatinate.

James had been duped, and for the moment he bent before the burst of popular fury which the danger to German Protestantism called up. He had already been brought to suffer Sir Horace Vere to take some

SEC. II.

THE FIRST
OF THE
STUARTS

1604
TO
1623

1618

*The Thirty
Years' War*

Nov. 1620

**The Parliament
of 1621**

SEC. II.

THE FIRST
OF THE
STUARTS
1604
TO
1623

English volunteers to the Palatinate. But the succour had come too late. The cry for a Parliament, the necessary prelude to a war, overpowered the King's secret resistance; and the Houses were again called together. But the Commons were bitterly chagrined as they found only demands for supplies, and a persistence in the old efforts to patch up a peace. James even sought the good will of the Spaniards by granting license for the export of arms to Spain. The resentment of the Commons found expression in their dealings with home affairs. The most crying constitutional grievance arose from the revival of monopolies, in spite of the pledge of Elizabeth to suppress them. A parliamentary right which had slept ever since the reign of Henry VI., the right of the Lower House to impeach great offenders at the bar of the Lords, was revived against the monopolists; and James was driven by the general indignation to leave them to their fate. But the practice of monopolies was only one sign of the corruption of the court. Sales of peerages and offices of state had raised a general disgust; and this disgust showed itself in the impeachment of the highest among the officers of State, the Chancellor, Francis Bacon, the most distinguished man of his time for learning and ability. At the accession of James the rays of royal favour had broken slowly upon Bacon. He became successively Solicitor and Attorney-General; the year of Shakspere's death saw him called to the Privy Council; he verified Elizabeth's prediction by becoming Lord Keeper. At last the goal of his ambition was reached. He had attached himself to the rising fortunes of Buckingham, and the favour of Buckingham made him Lord Chancellor. He was raised to the peerage as Baron Verulam, and created, at a later time, Viscount St. Albans. But the nobler dreams for which these meaner honours had been sought escaped his grasp. His projects still remained projects, while to retain his hold on office he was stooping to a miserable compliance with the worst excesses of Buckingham and his royal master. The years during which he held the Chancellorship were the most disgraceful years of a disgraceful reign. They saw the execution of Ralegh, the sacrifice of the Palatinate, the exaction of benevolences, the multiplication of monopolies, the supremacy of Buckingham. Against none of the acts of folly and wickedness which distinguished James's government did Bacon do more than protest; in some of the worst, and above all in the attempt to coerce the judges into prostrating law at the King's feet, he took a personal part. But even his remonstrances were too much for the young favourite, who regarded him as the mere creature of his will. It was in vain that Bacon flung himself on the Duke's mercy, and begged him to pardon a single instance of opposition to his caprice. A Parliament was impending, and Buckingham resolved to avert from himself the storm which was gathering by sacrificing to it his meaner dependants. To ordinary eyes the Chancellor was at the summit of human success. Jonson had just sung of him as one "whose even thread the Fates spin round and full out of their choicest and their whitest wool," when the storm burst. The Commons charged Bacon with corruption in the exercise of his office. It had been customary among Chancellors to receive gifts from successful suitors after their suit was ended. Bacon, it is certain, had taken such gifts from men whose suits were still unsettled ; and though his judgement may have been unaffected by them, the fact of their reception left him with no valid defence. He at once pleaded guilty to the charge. "I do plainly and ingenuously confess that I am guilty of corruption, and do renounce all defence." "I beseech your Lordships," he added, "to be merciful to a broken reed." The heavy fine imposed on him was remitted by the Crown ; but the Great Seal was taken from him, and he was declared incapable of holding office in the State or of sitting in Parliament. Bacon's fall restored him to that position of real greatness from which his ambition had so long torn him away. "My conceit of his person," said Ben Jonson, "was never increased towards him by his place or honours. But I have and do reverence him for his greatness that was only proper to himself, in that he seemed to me ever by his work one of the greatest men, and most worthy of admiration, that had been in many ages. In his adversity I ever prayed that God would give him strength : for greatness he could not want." His intellectual activity was never more conspicuous than in the last four years of his life. He had presented "Novum Organum" to James in the year before his fall ; in the year after it he produced his "Natural and Experimental History." He began a digest of the laws, and a "History of England under the Tudors," revised and expanded his "Essays," dictated a jest book, and busied himself with experiments in physics. It was while studying the effect of cold in preventing animal putrefaction that he stopped his coach to stuff a fowl with snow and caught the fever which ended in his death.

James was too shrewd to mistake the importance of Bacon's impeachment ; but the hostility of Buckingham to the Chancellor, and Bacon's own confession of his guilt, made it difficult to resist his condemnation. Energetic too as its measures were against corruption and monopolists, the Parliament respected scrupulously the King's prejudices in other matters ; and even when checked by an adjournment, resolved unanimously to support him in any earnest effort for the Protestant cause. A warlike speech from a member before the adjournment roused an enthusiasm which recalled the days of Elizabeth. The Commons answered the appeal by a unanimous vote, "lifting their hats as high as they could hold them," that for the recovery of the Palatinate they would adventure their fortunes, their estates, and their lives. "Rather this declaration," cried a leader of the country party when it was read by the Speaker, "than ten thou-

SEC. II.

THE FIRST OF THE STUARTS

1604 TO **1623**

Death of Bacon 1626

Dissolution of the Parliament

June, **1621**

sand men already on the march." For the moment the resolve seemed to give vigour to the royal policy. James had aimed throughout at the restitution of Bohemia to Ferdinand, and at inducing the Emperor, through the mediation of Spain, to abstain from any retaliation on the Palatinate. He now freed himself for a moment from the trammels of diplomacy, and enforced a cessation of the attack on his son-in-law's dominions by a threat of war. The suspension of arms lasted through the summer ; but mere threats could do no more, and on the conquest of the Upper Palatinate by the forces of the Catholic League, James fell back on his old policy of mediation through the aid of Spain. The negotiations for the marriage with the Infanta were pressed more busily. Gondomar, the Spanish Ambassador, who had become all-powerful at the English court, was assured that no effectual aid should be sent to the Palatinate. The English fleet, which was cruising by way of menace off the Spanish coast, was called home. The King dismissed those of his ministers who still opposed a Spanish policy ; and threatened on trivial pretexts a war with the Dutch, the one great Protestant power that remained in alliance with England, and was ready to back the Elector. But he had still to reckon with his

Nov. 1621

Parliament ; and the first act of the Parliament on its re-assembling was to demand a declaration of war with Spain. The instinct of the nation was wiser than the statecraft of the King. Ruined and enfeebled as she really was, Spain to the world at large still seemed the champion of Catholicism. It was the entry of her troops into the Palatinate which had first widened the local war in Bohemia into a great struggle for the suppression of Protestantism along the Rhine ; above all it was Spanish influence, and the hopes held out of a marriage of his son with a Spanish Infanta, which were luring the King into his fatal dependence on the great enemy of the Protestant cause. In their petition the Houses coupled with their demands for war the demand of a Protestant marriage for their future King. Experience proved in later years how perilous it was for English freedom that the heir to the Crown should be brought up under a Catholic mother ; but James was beside himself at their presumption in dealing with mysteries of state. "Bring stools for the Ambassadors," he cried in bitter irony as their committee appeared before him. He refused the petition, forbade any further discussion of state policy, and threatened the speakers with the Tower. "Let us resort to our prayers," a member said calmly as the King's letter was read, "and then consider of this great business." The temper of the House

Protestation of the Commons

was seen in the Protestation which met the royal command to abstain from discussion. It resolved "That the liberties, franchises, privileges, and jurisdictions of Parliament are the ancient and undoubted birth-right and inheritance of the subjects of England ; and that the arduous and urgent affairs concerning the King, state, and defence of the realm, and of the Church of England, and the making and maintenance of laws, and redress of grievances, which daily happen within this realm, are proper subjects and matter of council and debate in Parliament. And that in the handling and proceeding of those businesses every member of the House hath, and of right ought to have, freedom of speech to propound, treat, reason, and bring to conclusion the same."

SEC. II.

THE FIRST
OF THE
STUART

1604
TO
1623

The King answered the Protestation by a characteristic outrage. He sent for the Journals of the House, and with his own hand tore out the pages which contained it. "I will govern," he said, "according to the common weal, but not according to the common will." A few days after he dissolved the Parliament. "It is the best thing that has happened in the interests of Spain and of the Catholic religion since Luther began preaching," wrote the Count of Gondomar to his master, in his joy that all danger of war had passed away. "I am ready to depart," Sir Henry Savile, on the other hand, murmured on his death-bed, "the rather that having lived in good times I foresee worse." Abroad indeed all was lost; and Germany plunged wildly and blindly forward into the chaos of the Thirty Years' War. But for England the victory of freedom was practically won. James had himself ruined the main bulwarks of the monarchy. In his desire for personal government he had destroyed the authority of the Council. He had accustomed men to think lightly of the ministers of the Crown, to see them browbeaten by favourites, and driven from office for corruption. He had disenchanted his people of their blind faith in the monarchy by a policy at home and abroad which ran counter to every national instinct. He had quarrelled with, and insulted the Houses, as no English sovereign had ever done before; and all the while the authority he boasted of was passing, without his being able to hinder it, to the Parliament which he outraged. There was shrewdness as well as anger in his taunt at its "ambassadors." A power had at last risen up in the Commons with which the Monarchy was henceforth to reckon. In spite of the King's petulant outbreaks, Parliament had asserted its exclusive right to the control of taxation. It had attacked monopolies. It had reformed abuses in the courts of law. It had revived the right of impeaching and removing from office the highest ministers of the Crown. It had asserted its privilege of free discussion on all questions connected with the welfare of the realm. It had claimed to deal with the question of religion. It had even declared its will on the sacred "mystery" of foreign policy. James might tear the Protestation from its Journals, but there were pages in the record of the Parliament of 1621 which he never could tear out.

Section III.—The King and the Parliament. 1623—1629.

[*Authorities.*— For the first part of this period we have still Mr. Gardiner's "History of England from the accession of James I.," which throws a full

SEC. III.

THE KING
AND THE
PARLIA-
MENT

1623
TO
1629

[and fresh light on one of the most obscure times in our history. His work is as valuable for the early reign of Charles, a period well illustrated by Mr. Forster's " Life of Sir John Eliot." Among the general accounts of the reign of Charles, Mr. Disraeli's " Commentaries on the Reign of Charles I." is the most prominent on the one side ; Brodie's " History of the British Empire," and Godwin's " History of the Commonwealth," on the other. M. Guizot's work is accurate and impartial, and Lingard of especial value for the history of the English Catholics, and for his detail of foreign affairs. For the ecclesiastical side see Laud's " Diary." The Commons' Journal gives the proceedings of the Parliaments. Throughout this period the Calendars of State Papers, now issuing under the direction of the Master of the Rolls, are of the greatest historic value. Ranke's " History of England in the Seventeenth Century " is important for the whole Stuart period.]

In the obstinacy with which he clung to his Spanish policy James stood absolutely alone ; for not only the old nobility and the statesmen who preserved the tradition of the age of Elizabeth, but even his own ministers, with the exception of Buckingham and the Treasurer, Cranfield, were at one with the Commons. The King's aim, as we have said, was to enforce peace on the combatants, and to bring about the restitution of the Palatinate to the Elector, through the influence of Spain. It was to secure this influence that he pressed for a closer union with the great Catholic power ; and of this union, and the success of the policy which it embodied, the marriage of his son Charles with the Infanta, which had been held out as a lure to his vanity, was to be the sign. But the more James pressed for this consummation of his projects, the more Spain held back. At last Buckingham proposed to force the Spaniard's hand by the arrival of Charles himself at the Spanish Court. The Prince quitted England in disguise, and appeared with Buckingham at Madrid to claim his bride. It was in

vain that Spain rose in its demands ; for every new demand was met by fresh concessions on the part of England. The abrogation of the penal laws against the Catholics, a Catholic education for the Prince's children, a Catholic household for the Infanta, all were no sooner asked than they were granted. But the marriage was still delayed, while the influence of the new policy on the war in Germany was hard to see. The Catholic League and its army, under the command of Count Tilly, won triumph after triumph over their divided foes. The reduction of Heidelberg and Mannheim completed the conquest of the Palatinate, whose Elector fled helplessly to Holland, while his Electoral dignity was transferred by the Emperor to the Duke of Bavaria. But there was still no sign of the hoped-for intervention on the part of Spain. At last the pressure of Charles himself brought about the disclosure of the secret of its policy. " It is a maxim of state with us," Olivares confessed, as the Prince demanded an energetic interference in Germany, " that the King of Spain must never fight against the Emperor. We cannot employ our forces against the Emperor." " If you hold to that," replied the Prince, " there is an end of all."

His return was the signal for a burst of national joy. All London was alight with bonfires, in her joy at the failure of the Spanish match, and of the collapse, humiliating as it was, of the policy which had so long trailed English honour at the chariot-wheels of Spain. Charles returned to take along with Buckingham the direction of affairs out of his father's hands. The journey to Madrid had revealed to those around him the strange mixture of obstinacy and weakness in the Prince's character, the duplicity which lavished promises because it never purposed to be bound by any, the petty pride that subordinated every political consideration to personal vanity or personal pique. He had granted demand after demand, till the very Spaniards lost faith in his concessions. With rage in his heart at the failure of his efforts, he had renewed his betrothal on the very eve of his departure, only that he might insult the Infanta by its withdrawal when he was safe at home. But to England at large the baser features of his character were still unknown. The stately reserve, the personal dignity and decency of manners which distinguished the Prince, contrasted favourably with the gabble and indecorum of his father. The courtiers indeed who saw him in his youth, would often pray God that "he might be in the right way when he was set; for if he was in the wrong he would prove the most wilful of any king that ever reigned." But the nation was willing to take his obstinacy for firmness; as it took the pique which inspired his course on his return for patriotism and for the promise of a nobler rule. Under the pressure of Charles and Buckingham the King was forced to call a Parliament, and to concede the point on which he had broken with the last, by laying before it the whole question of the Spanish negotiations. Buckingham and the Prince gave their personal support to Parliament in its demand for a rupture of the treaties with Spain and a declaration of war. A subsidy was eagerly voted; the persecution of the Catholics, which had long been suspended out of deference to Spanish intervention, began with new vigour. The head of the Spanish party, Cranfield, Earl of Middlesex, the Lord Treasurer, was impeached on a charge of corruption, and dismissed from office. James was swept along helplessly by the tide; but his shrewdness saw clearly the turn that affairs were taking; and it was only by hard pressure that the favourite succeeded in wresting his consent to the disgrace of Middlesex. "You are making a rod for your own back," said the King. But Buckingham and Charles persisted in their plans of war. A treaty of alliance was concluded with Holland; negotiations were begun with the Lutheran Princes of North Germany, who had looked coolly on at the ruin of the Elector Palatine; an alliance with France was proposed, and the marriage of Charles with Henrietta, a daughter of Henry the Fourth of France, and sister of its King. To restore the triple league was to restore the system of Elizabeth; but the first whispers of a Catholic Queen woke opposition in the Commons. At this juncture the death

SEC. III.

THE KING AND THE PARLIAMENT

1623 TO 1629

Charles the First

Breach with Spain 1624

1625

Death of James

SEC. III.

THE KING
AND THE
PARLIA-
MENT

1623
TO
1629

The
Policy of
Charles

of the King placed Charles upon the throne ; and his first Parliament met in May, 1625. " We can hope everything from the King who now governs us," cried Sir Benjamin Rudyerd in the Commons. But there were cooler heads in the Commons than Sir Benjamin Rudyerd's ; and enough had taken place in the few months since its last session to temper its loyalty with caution.

The war with Spain, it must be remembered, meant to the mass of Englishmen a war with Catholicism ; and the fervour against Catholicism without roused a corresponding fervour against Catholicism within the realm. Every English Catholic seemed to Protestant eyes an enemy at home. A Protestant who leant towards Catholic usage or dogma was a secret traitor in the ranks. But it was suspected, and suspicion was soon to be changed into certainty, that in spite of his pledge to make no religious concessions to France, Charles had on his marriage promised to relax the penal laws against Catholics, and that a foreign power had again been given the right of intermeddling in the civil affairs of the realm. And it was to men with Catholic leanings that Charles seemed disposed to show favour. Bishop Laud was recognized as the centre of that varied opposition to Puritanism, whose members were loosely grouped under the name of Arminians ; and Laud now became the King's adviser in ecclesiastical matters. With Laud at its head the new party grew in boldness as well as numbers. It naturally sought for shelter for its religious opinions by exalting the power of the Crown. A court favourite, Montague, ventured to slight the Reformed Churches of the Continent in favour of the Church of Rome, and to advocate as the faith of the Church the very doctrines rejected by the Calvinists. The temper of the Commons on religious matters was clear to every observer. " Whatever mention does break forth of the fears or dangers in religion, and the increase of Popery," wrote a member who was noting the proceedings of the House, " their affections are much stirred." Their first act was to summon Montague to the bar and to commit him to prison. But there were other grounds for their distrust besides the King's ecclesiastical tendency. The conditions on which the last subsidy had been granted for war with Spain had been contemptuously set aside ; in his request for a fresh grant Charles neither named a sum nor gave any indication of what war it was to support. His reserve was met by a corresponding caution. While voting a small and inadequate subsidy, the Commons restricted their grant of certain customs duties called tonnage and poundage, which had commonly been granted to the new sovereign for life, to a single year, so as to give time for consideration of the additional impositions laid by James on these duties. The restriction was taken as an insult ; Charles refused to accept the grant on such a condition, and adjourned the Houses. When they met again at Oxford it was

in a sterner temper, for Charles had shown his defiance of Parliament by drawing Montague from prison, by promoting him to a royal chaplaincy, and by levying the disputed customs without authority of law. "England," cried Sir Robert Phelips, "is the last monarchy that yet retains her liberties. Let them not perish now!" But the Commons had no sooner announced their resolve to consider public grievances before entering on other business than they were met by a dissolution. Buckingham, to whom the firmness of the Commons seemed simply the natural discontent which follows on ill success, resolved to lure them from their constitutional struggle by a great military triumph. His hands were no sooner free than he sailed for the Hague to conclude a general alliance against the House of Austria, while a fleet of ninety vessels and ten thousand soldiers left Plymouth in October for the coast of Spain. But these vast projects broke down before Buckingham's administrative incapacity. The plan of alliance proved fruitless. After an idle descent on Cadiz the Spanish expedition returned broken with mutiny and disease; and the enormous debt which had been incurred in its equipment forced the favourite to advise a new summons of the Houses. But he was keenly alive to the peril in which his failure had plunged him, and to a coalition which had been formed between his rivals at Court and the leaders of the last Parliament. His reckless daring led him to anticipate the danger, and by a series of blows to strike terror into his opponents. The Councillors were humbled by the committal of Lord Arundel to the Tower. Sir Robert Phelips, Coke, and four other leading patriots were made sheriffs of their counties, and thus prevented from sitting in the coming Parliament. But their exclusion only left the field free for a more terrible foe.

If Hampden and Pym are the great figures which embody the later national resistance, the earlier struggle for Parliamentary liberty centres in the figure of Sir John Eliot. Of an old family which had settled under Elizabeth near the fishing hamlet of St. Germans, and raised their stately mansion of Port Eliot, he had risen to the post of Vice-Admiral of Devonshire under the patronage of Buckingham, and had seen his activity in the suppression of piracy in the Channel rewarded by an unjust imprisonment. He was now in the first vigour of manhood, with a mind exquisitely cultivated and familiar with the poetry and learning of his day, a nature singularly lofty and devout, a fearless and vehement temper. There was a hot impulsive element in his nature which showed itself in youth in his drawing sword on a neighbour who denounced him to his father, and which in later years gave its characteristic fire to his eloquence. But his intellect was as clear and cool as his temper was ardent. In the general enthusiasm which followed on the failure of the Spanish marriage, he had stood almost alone in pressing for a recognition of the rights of Parliament, as a preliminary to any real reconciliation with the Crown. He fixed, from the very outset of his career, on the responsibility of the royal

SEC. III.

THE KING
AND THE
PARLIA-
MENT

1623
TO
1629

*Bucking-
ham's
designs*

Eliot

1624

SEC. III.

THE KING
AND THE
PARLIA-
MENT
1623
TO
1629

ministers to Parliament, as the one critical point for English liberty. It was to enforce the demand of this that he availed himself of Buckingham's sacrifice of the Treasurer, Middlesex, to the resentment of the Commons. "The greater the delinquent," he urged, "the greater the delict. They are a happy thing, great men and officers, if they be good, and one of the greatest blessings of the land : but power converted into evil is the greatest curse that can befall it." But the new Parliament had hardly met, when he came to the front to threaten a greater criminal than Middlesex. So menacing were his words, as he called for an inquiry into the failure before Cadiz, that Charles himself stooped to answer threat with threat. "I see," he wrote to the House, "you especially aim at the Duke of Buckingham. I must let you know that I will not allow any of my servants to be questioned among you, much less such as are of eminent place and near to me." A more direct attack on a right already acknowledged in the impeachment of Bacon and Middlesex could hardly be imagined, but Eliot refused to move from his constitutional ground. The King was by law irresponsible, he "could do no wrong." If the country therefore was to be saved from a pure despotism, it must be by enforcing the responsibility of the ministers who counselled and executed his acts. Eliot persisted in denouncing Buckingham's incompetence and corruption, and the Commons ordered the subsidy which the Crown had demanded to be brought in "when we shall have presented our grievances, and received his Majesty's answer thereto." Charles summoned them to Whitehall, and commanded them to cancel the condition. He would grant them "liberty of counsel, but not of control ;" and he closed the interview with a significant threat. "Remember," he said, "that Parliaments are altogether in my power for their calling, sitting, and dissolution : and, therefore, as I find the fruits of them to be good or evil, they are to continue or not to be." But the will of the Commons was as resolute as the will of the King. Buckingham's impeachment was voted and carried to the Lords. The favourite took his seat as a peer to listen to the charge with so insolent an air of contempt that one of the managers appointed by the Commons to conduct it turned sharply on him. "Do you jeer, my Lord !" said Sir Dudley Digges. "I can show you when a greater man than your Lordship—as high as you in place and power, and as deep in the King's favour—has been hanged for as small a crime as these articles contain." The "proud carriage" of the Duke provoked an invective from Eliot which marks a new era in Parliamentary speech. From the first the vehemence and passion of his words had contrasted with the grave, colourless reasoning of older speakers. His opponents complained that Eliot aimed to "stir up affections." The quick emphatic sentences he substituted for the cumbrous periods of the day, his rapid argument, his vivacious and caustic allusions, his passionate appeals, his fearless invective, struck a new note in English eloquence. The frivolous ostentation of Buckingham, his very figure blazing with jewels and gold, gave point to the fierce attack. "He has broken those nerves and sinews of our land, the stores and treasures of the King. There needs no search for it. It is too visible. His profuse expenses, his superfluous feasts, his magnificent buildings, his riots, his excesses, what are they but the visible evidences of an express exhausting of the State, a chronicle of the immensity of his waste of the revenues of the Crown?" With the same terrible directness Eliot reviewed the Duke's greed and corruption, his insatiate ambition, his seizure of all public authority, his neglect of every public duty, his abuse for selfish ends of the powers he had accumulated. "The pleasure of his Majesty, his known directions, his public acts, his acts of council, the decrees of courts—all must be made inferior to this man's will. No right, no interest may withstand him. Through the power of state and justice he has dared ever to strike at his own ends." "My Lords," he ended, after a vivid parallel between Buckingham and Sejanus, "you see the man! What have been his actions, what he is like, you know! I leave him to your judgment. This only is conceived by us, the knights, citizens, and burgesses of the Commons House of Parliament, that by him came all our evils, in him we find the causes, and on him must be the remedies! Pereat qui perdere cuncta festinat. Opprimatur ne omnes opprimat!"

The reply of Charles was as fierce and sudden as the attack of Eliot. He hurried to the House of Peers to avow as his own the deeds with which Buckingham was charged. Eliot and Digges were called from their seats, and committed prisoners to the Tower. The Commons, however, refused to proceed with public business till their members were restored; and after a ten-days' struggle Eliot was released. But his release was only a prelude to the close of the Parliament. "Not one moment," the King replied to the prayer of his Council for delay; and a final remonstrance in which the Commons begged him to dismiss Buckingham from his service for ever was met by their instant dissolution. The remonstrance was burnt by royal order; Eliot was deprived of his Vice-Admiralty; and an appeal was made to the nation to pay as a free gift the subsidies which the Parliament had refused to grant till their grievances were redressed. But the tide of public resistance was slowly rising. Refusals to give anything, "save by way of Parliament," came in from county after county. When the subsidy-men of Middlesex and Westminster were urged to comply, they answered with a tumultuous shout of "a Parliament! a Parliament! else no subsidies!" Kent stood out to a man. In Bucks the very justices neglected to ask for the "free gift." The freeholders of Cornwall only answered that, "if they had but two kine, they would sell one of them for supply to his Majesty—in a Parliamentary

SEC. III.

THE KING
AND THE
PARLIA-
MENT

**1623
TO
1629**

The King
and the
People

June 16,
1626

SEC. III.

THE KING
AND THE
PARLIA-
MENT
1623
TO
1629

*The Forced
Loan*
1627

way." The failure of the voluntary gift forced Charles to an open defiance of the law. He met it by the levy of a forced loan. Commissioners were named to assess the amount which every landowner was bound to lend, and to examine on oath all who refused. Every means of persuasion, as of force, was resorted to. The pulpits of the Laudian clergy resounded with the cry of " passive obedience." Dr. Mainwaring preached before Charles himself, that the King needed no Parliamentary warrant for taxation, and that to resist his will was to incur eternal damnation. Poor men who refused to lend were pressed into the army or navy. Stubborn tradesmen were flung into prison. Buckingham himself undertook the task of overawing the nobles and the gentry. Charles met the opposition of the judges by instantly dismissing from his office the Chief Justice, Crew. But in the country at large resistance was universal. The northern counties in a mass set the Crown at defiance. The Lincolnshire farmers drove the Commissioners from the town. Shropshire, Devon, and Warwickshire "refused utterly." Eight peers, with Lord Essex and Lord Warwick at their head, declined to comply with the exaction as illegal. Two hundred country gentlemen, whose obstinacy had not been subdued by their transfer from prison to prison, were summoned before the Council ;

and John Hampden, as yet only a young Buckinghamshire squire, appeared at the board to begin that career of patriotism which has made his name dear to Englishmen. " I could be content to lend," he said, " but fear to draw on myself that curse in Magna Charta, which should be read twice a year against those who infringe it." So close an imprisonment in the Gate House rewarded his protest, " that he never afterwards did look like the same man he was before." With gathering discontent as well as bankruptcy before him, nothing could save the Duke but a great military success ; and he equipped a force of six thousand men for the maddest and most profligate of all his enterprises. In the great struggle with Catholicism the hopes of every Protestant rested on the union of England with France against the House of Austria. But the blustering and blundering of the favourite had at last succeeded in plunging him into strife with his own allies, and England now suddenly found herself at war with France and Spain together. The French minister, Cardinal Richelieu, anxious as he was to maintain the English alliance, was convinced that the first step to any effective interference of France in a European war must be the restoration of order at home by the complete reduction of the Protestant town of Rochelle which had risen in revolt. In 1625 English aid had been given to the French forces, however reluctantly. But now Buckingham saw his way to win an easy popularity at home by supporting the Huguenots in their resistance. The enthu-

siasm for their cause was intense ; and he resolved to take advantage of this enthusiasm to secure such a triumph for the royal arms as should silence all opposition at home. A fleet of a hundred vessels sailed under his command for the relief of Rochelle. But imposing as was his force, the expedition was as disastrous as it was impolitic. After an unsuccessful siege of the castle of St. Martin, the English troops were forced to fall back along a narrow causeway to their ships ; and in the retreat two thousand fell, without the loss of a single man to their enemies.

The first result of Buckingham's folly was to force on Charles, overwhelmed as he was with debt and shame, the summoning of a new Parliament ; a Parliament which met in a mood even more resolute than the last. The Court candidates were everywhere rejected. The patriot leaders were triumphantly returned. To have suffered in the recent resistance to arbitrary taxation was the sure road to a seat. In spite of Eliot's counsel, even the question of Buckingham's removal gave place to the craving for redress of wrongs done to personal liberty. "We must vindicate our ancient liberties," said Sir Thomas Wentworth, in words soon to be remembered against himself : "we must reinforce the laws made by our ancestors. We must set such a stamp upon them, as no licentious spirit shall dare hereafter to invade them." Heedless of sharp and menacing messages from the King, of demands that they should take his "royal word" for their liberties, the House bent itself to one great work, the drawing up a Petition of Right. The statutes that protected the subject against arbitrary taxation, against loans and benevolences, against punishment, outlawry, or deprivation of goods, otherwise than by lawful judgment of his peers, against arbitrary imprisonment without stated charge, against billeting of soldiery on the people or enactment of martial law in time of peace, were formally recited. The breaches of them under the last two sovereigns, and above all since the dissolution of the last Parliament, were recited as formally. At the close of this significant list, the Commons prayed "that no man hereafter be compelled to make or yield any gift, loan, benevolence, tax, or such like charge, without common consent by Act of Parliament. And that none be called to make answer, or to take such oaths, or to be confined or otherwise molested or disputed concerning the same, or for refusal thereof. And that no freeman may in such manner as is before mentioned be imprisoned or detained. And that your Majesty would be pleased to remove the said soldiers and mariners, and that your people may not be so burthened in time to come. And that the commissions for proceeding by martial law may be revoked and annulled, and that hereafter no commissions of like nature may issue forth to any person or persons whatsoever to be executed as aforesaid, lest by colour of them any of your Majesty's subjects be destroyed and put to death, contrary to the laws and franchises of the land. All which they humbly pray of your most excellent Majesty, as their rights and liberties, according to the laws

SEC. III.

THE KING
AND THE
PARLIA-
MENT

1623
TO
1629

The
Petition
of Right

*The Parlia-
ment of*
1628

SEC. III.

THE KING
AND THE
PARLIA-
MENT
1623
TO
1629

and statutes of the realm. And that your Majesty would also vouchsafe to declare that the awards, doings, and proceedings to the prejudice of your people in any of the premisses shall not be drawn hereafter into consequence or example. And that your Majesty would be pleased graciously for the further comfort and safety of your people to declare your royal will and pleasure, that in the things aforesaid all your officers and ministers shall serve you according to the laws and statutes of this realm, as they tender the honour of your Majesty and the prosperity of the kingdom." It was in vain that the Lords desired to conciliate Charles by a reservation of his "sovereign power." "Our petition," Pym quietly replied, "is for the laws of England, and this power seems to be another power distinct from the power of the law." The Lords yielded, but Charles gave an evasive reply; and the failure of the more moderate counsels for which his own had been set aside, called Eliot again to the front. In a speech of unprecedented boldness he moved the presentation to the King of a Remonstrance on the state of the realm. But at the moment when he again touched on Buckingham's removal as the preliminary of any real improvement the Speaker of the House interposed. "There was a command laid on him," he said, "to interrupt any that should go about to lay an aspersion on the King's ministers." The breach of their privilege of free speech produced a scene in the Commons such as St. Stephen's had never witnessed before. Eliot sate abruptly down amidst the solemn silence of the House. "Then appeared such a spectacle of passions," says a letter of the time, "as the like had seldom been seen in such an assembly; some weeping, some expostulating, some prophesying of the fatal ruin of our kingdom, some playing the divines in confessing their sins and country's sins which drew these judgements upon us, some finding, as it were, fault with those that wept. There were above an hundred weeping eyes, many who offered to speak being interrupted and silenced by their own passions." Pym himself rose only to sit down choked with tears. At last Sir Edward Coke found words to blame himself for the timid counsels which had checked Eliot at the beginning of the Session, and to protest "that the author and source of all those miseries was the Duke of Buckingham."

Shouts of assent greeted the resolution to insert the Duke's name in their Remonstrance. But at this moment Charles gave way. To win supplies for a new expedition to Rochelle, Buckingham bent the King to consent to the Petition of Right. As Charles understood it, indeed the consent meant little. The point for which he really cared was the power of keeping men in prison without bringing them to trial or assigning causes for their imprisonment. On this he had consulted his judges; and they had answered that his consent to the Petition left his rights untouched; like other laws, they said, the Petition would have to be interpreted when it came before them, and the prerogative remained unaffected. As to the rest, while waiving all claim to levy taxes not granted by Parliament, Charles still reserved his right to levy impositions paid customarily to the Crown, and amongst these he counted tonnage and poundage. Of these reserves however the Commons knew nothing. The King's consent won a grant of subsidy from the Parliament, and such a ringing of bells and lighting of bonfires from the people "as were never seen but upon his majesty's return from Spain." But, like all Charles's concessions, it came too late to effect the end at which he aimed. The Commons persisted in presenting their Remonstrance. Charles received it coldly and ungraciously; while Buckingham, who had stood defiantly at his master's side as he was denounced, fell on his knees to speak. "No, George!" said the King as he raised him; and his demeanour gave emphatic proof that the Duke's favour remained undiminished. "We will perish together, George," he added at a later time, "if thou dost." No shadow of his doom, in fact, had fallen over the brilliant favourite, when, after the prorogation of the Parliament, he set out to take command of a new expedition for the relief of Rochelle. But a lieutenant in the army, John Felton, soured by neglect and wrongs, had found in the Remonstrance some fancied sanction for the revenge he plotted; and, mixing with the throng which crowded the hall at Portsmouth, he stabbed Buckingham to the heart. Charles flung himself on his bed in a passion of tears when the news reached him; but outside the Court it was welcomed with a burst of joy. Young Oxford bachelors, grave London aldermen, vied with each other in drinking healths to Felton. "God bless thee, little David," cried an old woman, as the murderer passed manacled by; "the Lord comfort thee," shouted the crowd, as the Tower gates closed on him. The very crews of the Duke's armament at Portsmouth shouted to the King, as he witnessed their departure, a prayer that he would "spare John Felton, their sometime fellow soldier." But whatever national hopes the fall of Buckingham had aroused were quickly dispelled. Weston, a creature of the Duke, became Lord Treasurer, and his system remained unchanged. "Though our Achan is cut off," said Eliot, "the accursed thing remains."

It seemed as if no act of Charles could widen the breach which his reckless lawlessness had made between himself and his subjects. But there was one thing dearer to England than free speech in Parliament, than security for property, or even personal liberty; and that one thing was, in the phrase of the day, "the Gospel." The gloom which at the outset of this reign we saw settling down on every Puritan heart had deepened with each succeeding year. The great struggle abroad had gone more and more against Protestantism, and at this moment the end of the cause seemed to have come. In Germany Lutheran and Calvinist alike lay at last beneath the heel of the Catholic

Sec. III.

THE KING
AND THE
PARLIA-
MENT
1623
TO
1629

1628

The
Quarrel
of
Religion

SEC. III.

THE KING
AND THE
PARLIA-
MENT
1623
TO
1629

*The
Laudian
Clergy*

House of Austria. The fall of Rochelle after Buckingham's death seemed to leave the Huguenots of France at the feet of a Roman Cardinal. While England was thrilling with excitement at the thought that her own hour of deadly peril might come again, as it had come in the year of the Armada, Charles raised Laud to the Bishopric of London, and entrusted him with the direction of ecclesiastical affairs. To the excited Protestantism of the country, Laud and the Churchmen whom he headed seemed a danger really more formidable than the Popery which was making such mighty strides abroad. To the Puritans they were traitors to God and their country at once. Their aim was to draw the Church of England farther away from the Protestant Churches and nearer to the Church which Protestants regarded as Babylon. They aped Roman ceremonies. Cautiously and tentatively they were introducing Roman doctrine. But they had none of the sacerdotal independence which Rome had at any rate preserved. They were abject in their dependence on the Crown. Their gratitude for the royal protection which enabled them to defy the religious instincts of the realm showed itself in their erection of the most dangerous pretensions of the monarchy into religious dogmas. Archbishop Whitgift declared James to have been inspired by God. They preached passive obedience to the worst tyranny. They declared the person and goods of the subject to be at the King's absolute disposal. They were turning religion into a systematic attack on English liberty. Up to this time they had been little more than a knot of courtly ecclesiastics, for the mass of the clergy, like their flocks, were steady Puritans ; but the energy of Laud, and the patronage of the Court, promised a speedy increase of their numbers and their power. Sober men looked forward to a day when every pulpit would be ringing with exhortations to passive obedience, with denunciations of Calvinism and apologies for Rome. Of all the members of the House of Commons Eliot was least fanatical in his natural bent, but the religious crisis swept away for the moment all other thoughts from his mind. " Danger enlarges itself in so great a measure," he wrote from the country, " that nothing but Heaven shrouds us from despair." The House met in the same temper. The first business called up was that of religion. "The Gospel," Eliot burst forth, "is that Truth in which this kingdom has been happy through a long and rare prosperity. This ground, therefore, let us lay for a foundation of our building, that that Truth, not with words, but with actions we will maintain!"

*The
Avowal*

" There is a ceremony," he went on, " used in the Eastern Churches, of standing at the repetition of the Creed, to testify their purpose to maintain it, not only with their bodies upright, but with their swords drawn. Give me leave to call that a custom very commendable!" The Commons answered their leader's challenge by a solemn avowal. They avowed that they held for truth that sense of the Articles is

SEC. III.

THE KING
AND THE
PARLIA-
MENT
1623
TO
1629

established by Parliament, which by the public act of the Church, and the general and current exposition of the writers of their Church, had been delivered unto them. But the debates over religion were suddenly interrupted. The Commons, who had deferred all grant of customs till the wrong done in the illegal levy of them was redressed, had summoned the farmers of those dues to the bar; but though they appeared, they pleaded the King's command as a ground for their refusal to answer. The House was proceeding to a protest, when the Speaker signified that he had received an order to adjourn. Dissolution was clearly at hand, and the long-suppressed indignation broke out in a scene of strange disorder. The Speaker was held down in the chair, while Eliot, still clinging to his great principle of ministerial responsibility, denounced the new Treasurer as the adviser of the measure. "None have gone about to break Parliaments," he added in words to which after events gave a terrible significance, "but in the end Parliaments have broken them." The doors were locked, and in spite of the Speaker's protests, of the repeated knocking of the usher at the door, and of the gathering tumult within the House itself, the loud "Aye, Aye" of the bulk of the members supported Eliot in his last vindication of English liberty. By successive resolutions the Commons declared whomsoever should bring in innovations in religion, or whatever minister endorsed the levy of subsidies not granted in Parliament, "a capital enemy to the kingdom and commonwealth," and every subject voluntarily complying with illegal acts and demands "a betrayer of the liberty of England and an enemy of the same."

Section IV.—New England.

[*Authorities.*—The admirable account of American colonization given by Mr. Bancroft ("History of the United States") may be corrected in some points of detail by Mr. Gardiner's History. For Laud himself, see his remarkable "Diary" and his Correspondence. His work at Lambeth is described in Prynne's scurrilous "Canterbury's Doom."] (Mr. Doyle's book "The English in America" has appeared since this list was drawn up.—ED.)

The dissolution of the Parliament of 1629 marked the darkest hour of Protestantism, whether in England or in the world at large. But it was in this hour of despair that the Puritans won their noblest triumph. They "turned," to use Canning's words in a far truer and grander sense than that which he gave to them, they "turned to the New World to redress the balance of the Old." It was during the years of tyranny which followed the close of the third Parliament of Charles that a great Puritan emigration founded the States of New England.

The Puritans were far from being the earliest among the English colonists of North America. There was little in the circumstances

which attended the first discovery of the Western world which promised well for freedom; its earliest result, indeed, was to give an
enormous impulse to the most bigoted and tyrannical among the
powers of Europe, and to pour the wealth of Mexico and Peru into the
treasury of Spain.   But while the Spanish galleons traversed the
Southern seas, and Spanish settlers claimed the southern part of the
great continent for the Catholic crown, a happy instinct drew Englishmen to the ruder and more barren districts along the shore of
Northern America.   England had reached the mainland even earlier
than Spain, for before Columbus touched its shores Sebastian Cabot,
a seaman of Genoese blood born and bred in England, sailed with an
English crew from Bristol in 1497, and pushed along the coast of
America to the south as far as Florida, and northward as high as
Hudson's Bay.   But no Englishman followed on the track of this bold
adventurer; and while Spain built up her empire in the New World,
the English seamen reaped a humbler harvest in the fisheries of
Newfoundland.   It was not till the reign of Elizabeth that the thoughts
of Englishmen turned again to the New World.   The dream of finding
a passage to Asia by a voyage round the northern coast of the American

1576

continent drew a west-country seaman, Martin Frobisher, to the coast
of Labrador, and the news which he brought back of the existence of
gold mines there set adventurers cruising among the icebergs of
Baffin's Bay.   Luckily the quest of gold proved a vain one; and the
nobler spirits among those who had engaged in it turned to plans of
colonization.   But the country, vexed by long winters and thinly
peopled by warlike tribes of Indians, gave a rough welcome to the
earlier colonists.   After a fruitless attempt to form a settlement, Sir

1584

Humphry Gilbert, one of the noblest spirits of his time, turned homewards again, to find his fate in the stormy seas.   "We are as near to
Heaven by sea as by land," were the famous words he was heard to
utter, ere the light of his little bark was lost for ever in the darkness
of the night.   An expedition sent by his half-brother, Sir Walter
Ralegh, explored Pamlico Sound; and the country they discovered,
a country where, in their poetic fancy, "men lived after the manner
of the Golden Age," received from Elizabeth, the Virgin Queen, the
name of Virginia.   The introduction of tobacco and of the potato into
Europe dates from Ralegh's discovery; but the energy of his settlers
was distracted by the delusive dream of gold, the hostility of the native
tribes drove them from the coast, and it is through the gratitude of
later times for what he strove to do, rather than for what he did, that
Raleigh, the capital of North Carolina, preserves his name.   The first

1606

permanent settlement on the Chesapeake was effected in the beginning
of the reign of James the First, and its success was due to the conviction of the settlers that the secret of the New World's conquest lay
simply in labour.   Among the hundred and five colonists who originally

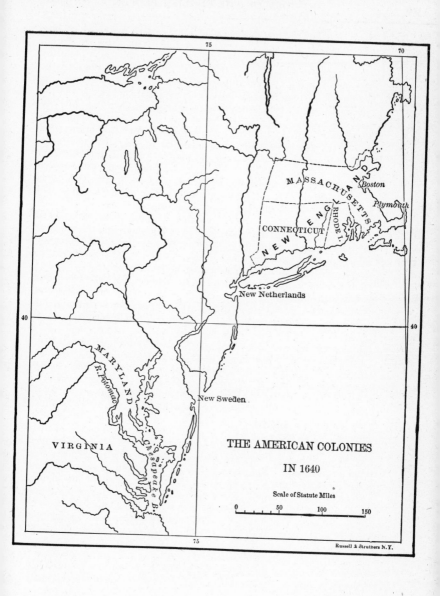

75

70

MASSACHUSETTS

Boston

Plymouth

CONNECTICUT

RHODE I.

NEW ENGLAND

New Netherlands

40

40

MARYLAND

R. Potomac

New Sweden

VIRGINIA

Chesapeake B.

THE AMERICAN COLONIES

IN 1640

Scale of Statute Miles

0   50   100   150

75

Russell & Struthers N.Y.

landed, forty-eight were gentlemen, and only twelve were tillers of the soil. Their leader, John Smith, however, not only explored the vast bay of Chesapeake and discovered the Potomac and the Susquehannah, but held the little company together in the face of famine and desertion till the colonists had learnt the lesson of toil. In his letters to the colonizers at home he set resolutely aside the dream of gold. "Nothing is to be expected thence," he wrote of the new country, "but by labour;" and supplies of labourers, aided by a wise allotment of lands to each colonist, secured after five years of struggle the fortunes of Virginia. "Men fell to building houses and planting corn;" the very streets of Jamestown, as their capital was called from the reigning sovereign, were sown with tobacco; and in fifteen years the colony numbered five thousand souls.

The laws and representative institutions of England were first introduced into the New World in the settlement of Virginia: some years later a principle as unknown to England as it was to the greater part of Europe found its home in another colony, which received its name of Maryland from Henrietta Maria, the Queen of Charles the First. Calvert, Lord Baltimore, one of the best of the Stuart counsellors, was forced by his conversion to Catholicism to seek a shelter for himself and colonists of his new faith in the district across the Potomac, and round the head of the Chesapeake. As a purely Catholic settlement was impossible, he resolved to open the new colony to men of every faith. "No person within this province," ran the earliest law of Maryland, "professing to believe in Jesus Christ, shall be in any ways troubled, molested, or discountenanced for his or her religion, or in the free exercise thereof." Long however before Lord Baltimore's settlement in Maryland, only a few years indeed after the settlement of Smith in Virginia, the church of Brownist or Independent refugees, whom we saw driven in the reign of James to Amsterdam, had resolved to quit Holland and find a home in the wilds of the New World. They were little disheartened by the tidings of suffering which came from the Virginian settlement. "We are well weaned," wrote their minister, John Robinson, "from the delicate milk of the mother-country, and inured to the difficulties of a strange land: the people are industrious and frugal. We are knit together as a body in a most sacred covenant of the Lord, of the violation whereof we make great conscience, and by virtue whereof we hold ourselves strictly tied to all care of each other's good and of the whole. It is not with us as with men whom small things can discourage." Returning from Holland to Southampton, they started in two small vessels for the new land: but one of these soon put back, and only its companion, the *Mayflower*, a bark of a hundred and eighty tons, with forty-one emigrants and their families on board, persisted in prosecuting its voyage. The little company of the " Pilgrim Fathers," as

after-times loved to call them, landed on the barren coast of Massachusetts at a spot to which they gave the name of Plymouth, in
memory of the last English port at which they touched. They had
soon to face the long hard winter of the north, to bear sickness
and famine : even when these years of toil and suffering had passed
there was a time when "they knew not at night where to have a bit in
the morning." Resolute and industrious as they were, their progress
was very slow ; and at the end of ten years they numbered only three
hundred souls. But small as it was, the colony was now firmly established and the struggle for mere existence was over. "Let it not be
grievous unto you," some of their brethren had written from England
to the poor emigrants in the midst of their sufferings, "that you have
been instrumental to break the ice for others. The honour shall be
yours to the world's end."

From the moment of their establishment the eyes of the English
Puritans were fixed on the little Puritan settlement in North America.
Through the early years of Charles projects were canvassed for a new
settlement beside the little Plymouth ; and the aid which the merchants of Boston in Lincolnshire gave to the realization of this project
was acknowledged in the name of its capital. At the moment when
he was dissolving his third Parliament, Charles granted the charter

which established the colony of Massachusetts ; and by the Puritans at
large the grant was at once regarded as a Providential call. Out of
the failure of their great constitutional struggle, and the pressing
danger to "godliness" in England, rose the dream of a land in the
West where religion and liberty could find a safe and lasting home.
The Parliament was hardly dissolved, when "conclusions" for the
establishment of a great colony on the other side the Atlantic were
circulating among gentry and traders, and descriptions of the new
country of Massachusetts were talked over in every Puritan household.
The proposal was welcomed with the quiet, stern enthusiasm which
marked the temper of the time ; but the words of a well-known emigrant show how hard it was even for the sternest enthusiasts to tear
themselves from their native land. "I shall call that my country,"
said the younger Winthrop, in answer to feelings of this sort, "where I
may most glorify God and enjoy the presence of my dearest friends."
The answer was accepted, and the Puritan emigration began on a
scale such as England had never before seen. The two hundred who
first sailed for Salem were soon followed by John Winthrop with eight
hundred men ; and seven hundred more followed ere the first year of the

king's personal rule had run its course. Nor were the emigrants, like
the earlier colonists of the South, "broken men," adventurers, bank-
rupts, criminals; or simply poor men and artisans, like the Pilgrim
Fathers of the *Mayflower*. They were in great part men of the professional and middle classes ; some of them men of large landed estate,

some zealous clergymen like Cotton, Hooker, and Roger Williams, some shrewd London lawyers, or young scholars from Oxford. The bulk were God-fearing farmers from Lincolnshire and the Eastern counties. They desired in fact "only the best" as sharers in their enterprise; men driven forth from their fatherland not by earthly want, or by the greed of gold, or by the lust of adventure, but by the fear of God, and the zeal for a godly worship. But strong as was their zeal, it was not without a wrench that they tore themselves from their English homes. "Farewell, dear England!" was the cry which burst from the first little company of emigrants as its shores faded from their sight. "Our hearts," wrote Winthrop's followers to the brethren whom they had left behind, "shall be fountains of tears for your everlasting welfare, when we shall be in our poor cottages in the wilderness."

During the next two years, as the sudden terror which had found so violent an outlet in Eliot's warnings died for the moment away, there was a lull in the emigration. But the measures of Laud soon revived the panic of the Puritans. The shrewdness of James had read the very heart of the man when Buckingham pressed for his first advancement to the see of St. David's. "He hath a restless spirit," said the old King, "which cannot see when things are well, but loves to toss and change, and to bring matters to a pitch of reformation floating in his own brain. Take him with you, but by my soul you will repent it." Cold, pedantic, superstitious as he was (he notes in his diary the entry of a robin-redbreast into his study as a matter of grave moment), William Laud rose out of the mass of court-prelates by his industry, his personal unselfishness, his remarkable capacity for administration. At a later period, when immersed in State-business, he found time to acquire so complete a knowledge of commercial affairs that the London merchants themselves owned him a master in matters of trade. Of statesmanship indeed he had none. But Laud's influence was really derived from the unity of his purpose. He directed all the power of a clear, narrow mind and a dogged will to the realization of a single aim. His resolve was to raise the Church of England to what he conceived to be its real position as a branch, though a reformed branch, of the great Catholic Church throughout the world; protesting alike against the innovations of Rome and the innovations of Calvin, and basing its doctrines and usages on those of the Christian communion in the centuries which preceded the Council of Nicæa. The first step in the realization of such a theory was the severance of whatever ties had hitherto united the English Church to the Reformed Churches of the Continent. In Laud's view episcopal succession was of the essence of a Church, and by their rejection of bishops, the Lutheran and Calvinistic Churches of Germany and Switzerland had ceased to be Churches at all. The freedom of worship therefore which had been allowed to the Huguenot refugees from France, or the Walloons from Flanders, was suddenly withdrawn ; and the requirement of conformity with the Anglican ritual drove them in crowds from the southern ports to seek toleration in Holland. The same conformity was required from the English soldiers and merchants abroad, who had hitherto attended without scruple the services of the Calvinistic churches. The English ambassador in Paris was forbidden to visit the Huguenot conventicle at Charenton. As Laud drew further from the Protestants of the Continent, he drew, consciously or unconsciously, nearer to Rome. His theory owned Rome as a true branch of the Church, though severed from that of England by errors and innovations against which Laud vigorously protested. But with the removal of these obstacles reunion would naturally follow, and his dream was that of bridging over the gulf which ever since the Reformation had parted the two Churches. The secret offer of a cardinal's hat proved Rome's sense that Laud was doing his work for her ; while his rejection of it, and his own reiterated protestations, prove equally that he was doing it unconsciously. Union with the great body of Catholicism, indeed, he regarded as a work which only time could bring about, but for which he could prepare the Church of England by raising it to a higher standard of Catholic feeling and Catholic practice. The great obstacle in his way was the Puritanism of nine-tenths of the English people, and on Puritanism he made war without mercy. No sooner

had his elevation to the see of Canterbury placed him at the head of the English Church, than he turned the High Commission into a standing attack on the Puritan ministers. Rectors and vicars were scolded, suspended, deprived for "Gospel preaching." The use of the surplice, and the ceremonies most offensive to Puritan feeling, were enforced in every parish. The lectures founded in towns, which were the favourite posts of Puritan preachers, were rigorously suppressed. They found a refuge among the country gentlemen, and the Archbishop withdrew from the country gentlemen the privilege of keeping chaplains, which they had till then enjoyed. As parishes became vacant the High Church bishops had long been filling them with men who denounced Calvinism, and declared passive obedience to the sovereign to be part of the law of God. The Puritans soon felt the stress of this process, and endeavoured to meet it by buying up the appropriations of livings, and securing through feoffees a succession of Protestant ministers in the parishes of which they were patrons : but Laud cited the feoffees before the Court of Exchequer, and roughly put an end to them. Nor was the persecution confined to the clergy. Under the two last reigns the small pocket-Bibles called the Geneva Bibles had become universally popular amongst English laymen ; but their marginal notes were found to savour of Calvinism, and their importation was prohibited. The habit of receiving the communion in a sitting posture

Sec. IV.

New
England

*Sunday
pastimes*

1633

had become common, but kneeling was now enforced, and hundreds were excommunicated for refusing to comply with the injunction. A more galling means of annoyance was found in the different views of the two religious parties on the subject of Sunday. The Puritans identified the Lord's day with the Jewish Sabbath, and transferred to the one the strict observances which were required for the other. The Laudian clergy, on the other hand, regarded it simply as one among the holidays of the Church, and encouraged their flocks in the pastimes and recreations after service which had been common before the Reformation. The Crown under James had taken part with the High Churchmen, and had issued a "Book of Sports" which recommended certain games as lawful and desirable on the Lord's day. The Parliament, as might be expected, was stoutly on the other side, and had forbidden Sunday pastimes by statute. The general religious sense of the country was undoubtedly tending to a stricter observance of the day, when Laud brought the contest to a sudden issue. He summoned the Chief-Justice, Richardson, who had enforced the statute in the western shires, to the Council-table, and rated him so violently that the old man came out complaining he had been all but choked by a pair of lawn sleeves. He then ordered every minister to read the declaration in favour of Sunday pastimes from the pulpit. One Puritan minister had the wit to obey, and to close the reading with the significant hint, "You have heard read, good people, both the commandment of God and the commandment of man. Obey which you please." But the bulk refused to comply with the Archbishop's will. The result followed at which Laud no doubt had aimed. Puritan ministers were cited before the High Commission, and silenced or deprived. In the diocese of Norwich alone thirty parochial ministers were expelled from their cures.

The suppression of Puritanism in the ranks of the clergy was only a preliminary to the real work on which the Archbishop's mind was set, the preparation for Catholic reunion by the elevation of the clergy to a Catholic standard in doctrine and ritual. Laud publicly avowed his preference of an unmarried to a married priesthood. Some of the bishops, and a large part of the new clergy who occupied the posts from which the Puritan ministers had been driven, advocated doctrines and customs which the Reformers had denounced as sheer Papistry; the practice, for instance, of auricular confession, a Real Presence in the Sacrament, or prayers for the dead. One prelate, Montague, was earnest for reconciliation with Rome. Another, Goodman, died acknowledging himself a Papist. Meanwhile Laud was indefatigable in his efforts to raise the civil and political status of the clergy to the point which it had reached ere the fatal blow of the Reformation fell on the priesthood. Among the archives of his see lies a large and costly volume in vellum, containing a copy of such records in the Tower as concerned the privileges of the clergy. Its compilation was entered in the Archbishop's diary as one among the "twenty-one things which I have projected to do if God bless me in them," and as among the fifteen to which before his fall he had been enabled to add his emphatic "done." The power of the Bishops' Courts, which had long fallen into decay, revived under his patronage. In 1636 he was able to induce the King to raise a prelate, Juxon, Bishop of London, to the highest civil post in the realm, that of Lord High Treasurer. "No Churchman had it since Henry the Seventh's time," Laud comments proudly. "I pray God bless him to carry it so that the Church may have honour, and the State service and content by it. And now, if the Church will not hold up themselves, under God I can do no more."

Laud and Ritual

As he aimed at a more Catholic standard of doctrine in the clergy, so he aimed at a nearer approach to the pomp of Catholicism in public worship. His conduct in his own house at Lambeth brings out with singular vividness the reckless courage with which he threw himself across the religious instincts of a time when the spiritual aspect of worship was overpowering in most men's minds its æsthetic and devotional sides. Men noted as a fatal omen the accident which marked his first entry into Lambeth; for the overladen ferry-boat upset in the passage of the river, and though the horses and servants were saved, the Archbishop's coach remained at the bottom of the Thames. But no omen, carefully as he might note it, brought a moment's hesitation to the bold, narrow mind of the new Primate. His first act, he boasted, was the setting about a restoration of his chapel; and, as Laud managed it, his restoration was the simple undoing of all that had been done there by his predecessors since the Reformation. The chapel of Lambeth House was one of the most conspicuous among the ecclesiastical buildings of the time; it had seen the daily worship of every Primate since Cranmer, and was a place "whither many of the nobility, judges, clergy, and persons of all sorts, as well strangers as natives, resorted." But all pomp of worship had gradually passed away from it. Under Cranmer the stained glass was dashed from its windows. In Elizabeth's time the communion table was moved into the middle of the chapel, and the credence table destroyed. Under James Archbishop Abbot put the finishing stroke on all attempts at a high ceremonial. The cope was no longer used as a special vestment in the communion. The Primate and his chaplains forbore to bow at the name of Christ. The organ and choir were alike abolished, and the service reduced to a simplicity which would have satisfied Calvin. To Laud the state of the chapel seemed intolerable. With characteristic energy he aided with his own hands in the replacement of the painted glass in its windows, and racked his wits in piecing the fragments together. The glazier was scandalized by the Primate's express command to repair and set up again the "broken crucifix" in the east window. The holy table was removed from the centre, and set altar-wise against the eastern wall, with a cloth of arras behind it, on which was embroidered the history of the Last Supper. The elaborate woodwork of the screen, the rich copes of the chaplain, the silver candlesticks, the credence table, the organ and the choir, the stately ritual, the bowings at the sacred name, the genuflexions to the altar, made the chapel at last such a model of worship as Laud desired. If he could not exact an equal pomp of devotion in other quarters, he exacted as much as he could. Bowing to the altar was introduced into all cathedral churches. A royal injunction ordered the removal of the communion table, which for the last half-century or more had in almost every parish church stood in the middle of the nave, back to its pre-Reformation position in the chancel, and secured it from pro-fanation by a rail. The removal implied, and was understood to imply, a recognition of the Real Presence, and a denial of the doctrine which Englishmen generally held about the Lord's Supper. But, strenuous as was the resistance Laud encountered, his pertinacity and severity warred it down. Parsons who denounced the change from their pulpits were fined, imprisoned, and deprived of their benefices. Church-wardens who refused or delayed to obey the injunction were rated at the Commission-table, and frightened into compliance.

In their last Remonstrance to the King the Commons had denounced Laud as the chief assailant of the Protestant character of the Church of England ; and every year of his Primacy showed him bent upon justify-ing the accusation. His policy was no longer the purely conservative policy of Parker or Whitgift ; it was aggressive and revolutionary. His "new counsels" threw whatever force there was in the feeling of conservatism into the hands of the Puritan, for it was the Puritan who now seemed to be defending the old character of the Church of England against its Primate's attacks. But backed as Laud was by the power of the Crown, the struggle became more hopeless every day. While the Catholics owned that they had never enjoyed a like tranquillity, while the fines for recusancy were reduced, and their worship suffered to go on in private houses, the Puritan saw his ministers silenced or deprived, his Sabbath profaned, the most sacred act of his worship brought near, as he fancied, to the Roman mass. Roman doctrine met him from the pulpit, Roman practices met him in the Church. We can hardly wonder that with such a world around them "godly people in England began to apprehend a special hand of Providence in raising this plantation" in Massachusetts ; "and their hearts were generally stirred to come over." It was in vain that weaker men returned to bring news of hardships and dangers, and told how two hundred of the new comers had perished with their first winter. A letter from Winthrop told how the rest toiled manfully on. "We now enjoy God and Jesus Christ," he wrote to those at home, "and is not that enough? I thank God I like so well to be here as I do not repent my coming. I would not have altered my course though I had foreseen all these afflictions. I never had more content of mind." With the strength and manliness of Puritanism, its bigotry and narrowness had crossed the Atlantic too. Roger Williams, a young minister who held the doctrine of freedom of conscience, was driven from the new settlement, to become a preacher among the settlers of Rhode Island. The bitter resentment stirred in the emigrants by persecution at home was seen in their rejection of Episcopacy and their prohibition of the use of the Book of Common Prayer. The intensity of its religious sentiments turned the colony into a theocracy. "To the end that the body of the Commons may be preserved of honest and good men, it was ordered and agreed that for the time to come no man shall be admitted to the freedom of the body politic but such as are members of some of the churches within the bounds of the same." As the contest grew hotter at home the number of Puritan emigrants rose fast. Three thousand new colonists arrived from England in a single year. The growing stream of emigrants marks the terrible pressure of the time. Between the sailing of Winthrop's expedition and the assembly of the Long Parliament, in the space, that is, of ten or eleven years, two hundred emigrant ships had crossed the Atlantic, and twenty thousand Englishmen had found a refuge in the West.

Section V.—The Personal Government. 1629—1640.

[*Authorities.*—For the general events of the time, see previous sections. The "Strafford Letters," and the Calendars of Domestic State Papers for this period give its real history. "Baillie's Letters" tell the story of the Scotch rising. Generally, Scotch affairs may be studied in Mr. Burton's "History of Scotland." Portraits of Weston, and most of the statesmen of this period, may be found in the earlier part of Clarendon's "History of the Rebellion."]

At the opening of his third Parliament Charles had hinted in ominous words that the continuance of Parliament at all depended on its compliance with his will. "If you do not your duty," said the King, "mine would then order me to use those other means which God has put into my hand." The threat, however, failed to break the resistance of the Commons, and the ominous words passed into a settled policy. "We have showed," said a proclamation which followed on the dissolution of the Houses, "by our frequent meeting our people, our love to the use of Parliament; yet, the late abuse having for the present driven us unwillingly out of that course, we shall account it presumption for any to prescribe any time unto us for Parliament."

No Parliament in fact met for eleven years. But it would be unfair to charge the King at the outset of this period with any definite scheme of establishing a tyranny, or of changing what he conceived to be the older constitution of the realm. He "hated the very

Sec. V.

The
Personal
Govern-
ment
1629
to
1640

name of Parliaments," but in spite of his hate he had as yet no settled purpose of abolishing them. His belief was that England would in time recover its senses, and that then Parliament might re-assemble without inconvenience to the Crown. In the interval, however long it might be, he proposed to govern single-handed by the use of "those means which God had put into his hands." Resistance, indeed, he was resolved to put down. The leaders of the popular party in the last Parliament were thrown into prison ; and Eliot died, the first martyr of English liberty, in the Tower. Men were forbidden to speak of the reassembling of a Parliament. But here the King stopped. The opportunity which might have suggested dreams of organized despotism to a Richelieu, suggested only means of filling his Exchequer to Charles. He had in truth neither the grander nor the meaner instincts of a born tyrant. He did not seek to gain an absolute power over his people, because he believed that his absolute power was already a part of the constitution of the country. He set up no standing army to secure it, partly because he was poor, but yet more because his faith in his position was such that he never dreamed of any effectual resistance. His expedients for freeing the Crown from that dependence on Parliaments against which his pride as a sovereign revolted were simply peace and economy. To secure the first he sacrificed an opportunity greater than ever his father had trodden under foot. The fortunes of the great struggle in Germany were suddenly reversed at this juncture by the appearance of Gustavus Adolphus, with a Swedish army, in the heart of Germany. Tilly was defeated and slain ; the Catholic League humbled in the dust ; Munich, the capital of its Bavarian leader, occupied by the Swedish army, and the Lutheran princes of North Germany freed from the pressure of the Imperial soldiery ; while the Emperor himself, trembling within the walls of Vienna, was driven to call for aid from Wallenstein, an adventurer whose ambition he dreaded, but whose army could alone arrest the progress of the Protestant conqueror. The ruin that James had wrought was suddenly averted ; but the victories of Protestantism had no more power to draw Charles out of the petty circle of his politics at home than its defeats had had power to draw James out of the circle of his imbecile diplomacy. When Gustavus, on the point of invading Germany, appealed for aid to England and France, Charles, left penniless by the dissolution of Parliament, resolved on a policy of peace, withdrew his ships from the Baltic, and opened negotiations with Spain, which brought about a treaty on the virtual basis of an abandonment of the Palatinate. Ill luck clung to him in peace as in war. The treaty was hardly concluded when Gustavus began his wonderful career of victory. Charles strove at once to profit by his success, and a few Scotch and English regiments followed Gustavus in his reconquest of the Palatinate. But the conqueror demanded, as the price of its restoration to Frederick, that

SEC. V.
THE
PERSONAL
GOVERN-
MENT
1629
TO
1640

Charles should again declare war upon Spain ; and this was a price that the King would not pay, determined as he was not to plunge into a combat which would again force him to summon Parliament. His whole attention was absorbed by the pressing question of revenue. The debt was a large one ; and the ordinary income of the Crown, unaided by parliamentary supplies, was inadequate to meet its ordinary expenditure. Charles himself was frugal and laborious ; and the economy of Weston, the new Lord Treasurer, whom he made Earl of Portland, contrasted advantageously with the waste and extravagance of the government under Buckingham. But economy failed to close the yawning gulf of the treasury, and the course into which Charles was driven by the financial pressure showed with how wise a prescience the Commons had fixed on the point of arbitrary taxation as the chief danger to constitutional freedom.

It is curious to see to what shifts the royal pride was driven in its effort at once to fill the Exchequer, and yet to avoid, as far as it could, any direct breach of constitutional law in the imposition of taxes by the sole authority of the Crown. The dormant powers of the prerogative were strained to their utmost. The right of the Crown to force knighthood on the landed gentry was revived, in order to squeeze them into composition for the refusal of it. Fines were levied on them for the redress of defects in their title-deeds. A Commission of the Forests exacted large sums from the neighbouring landowners for their encroachments on Crown lands. London, the special object of courtly dislike, on account of its stubborn Puritanism, was brought within the sweep of royal extortion by the enforcement of an illegal proclamation which James had issued, prohibiting its extension. Every house throughout the large suburban districts in which the prohibition had been disregarded was only saved from demolition by the payment of three years' rental to the Crown. Though the Catholics were no longer troubled by any active persecution, and the Lord Treasurer was in heart a Papist, the penury of the Exchequer forced the Crown to maintain the old system of fines for "recusancy." Vexatious measures of extortion such as these were far less hurtful to the State than the conversion of justice into a means of supplying the royal necessities by means of the Star Chamber. The jurisdiction of the King's Council had been revived by Wolsey as a check on the nobles ; and it had received great developement, especially on the side of criminal law, during the Tudor reigns. Forgery, perjury, riot, maintenance, fraud, libel, and conspiracy, were the chief offences cognizable in this court, but its scope extended to every misdemeanor, and especially to charges where, from the imperfection of the common law, or the power of offenders, justice was baffled in the lower courts. Its process resembled that of Chancery : in State trials it acted on an information laid before it by the King's Attorney. Both witnesses and accused

Sec. V.

The
Personal
Govern-
ment
1629
to
1640

were examined on oath by special interrogatories, and the Court was
at liberty to adjudge any punishment short of death.   However distinguished the Star Chamber was in ordinary cases for the learning
and fairness of its judgements, in political trials it was impossible to
hope for exact and impartial justice from a tribunal almost entirely
composed of privy councillors.   The possession of such a weapon
would have been fatal to liberty under a great tyrant; under Charles it
was turned freely to the profit of the Exchequer and the support of
arbitrary rule.   Enormous penalties were exacted for opposition to the
royal will, and though the fines imposed were often remitted, they served
as terrible engines of oppression.   Fines such as these however affected
a smaller range of sufferers than the financial expedient to which Weston
had recourse in the renewal of monopolies.   Monopolies, abandoned by
Elizabeth, and extinguished by Act of Parliament under James, were
again set on foot, and on a scale far more gigantic than had been
seen before; the companies who undertook them paying a fixed duty
on their profits as well as a large sum for the original concession of
the monopoly.   Wine, soap, salt, and almost every article of domestic
consumption fell into the hands of monopolists, and rose in price out of
all proportion to the profit gained by the Crown.   " They sup in our
cup," Colepepper said afterwards in the Long Parliament, " they dip in
our dish, they sit by our fire; we find them in the dye-fat, the wash
bowls, and the powdering tub.   They share with the cutler in his box.
They have marked and sealed us from head to foot."   But in spite of
these expedients the Treasury would have remained unfilled had not
the King persisted in those financial measures which had called forth
the protest of the Parliament.   The exaction of customs duties went on
as of old at the ports.   The resistance of the London merchants to their
payment was roughly put down; and one of them, Chambers, who
complained bitterly that merchants were worse off in England than in
Turkey, was brought before the Star Chamber and ruined by a fine of
two thousand pounds.   It was by measures such as these that Charles
gained the bitter enmity of the great city whose strength and resources
were fatal to him in the coming war.   The freeholders of the counties
were equally difficult to deal with.   On one occasion, when those of
Cornwall were called together at Bodmin to contribute to a voluntary
loan, half the hundreds refused, and the yield of the rest came to little
more than two thousand pounds.   One of the Cornishmen has left an
amusing record of the scene which took place before the Commissioners
appointed for assessment of the loan.   " Some with great words and
threatenings, some with persuasions," he says, " were drawn to it.   I
was like to have been complimented out of my money; but knowing
with whom I had to deal, I held, when I talked with them, my hands
fast in my pockets."

By such means as these the debt was reduced, and the annual

SEC. V.

THE
PERSONAL
GOVERN-
MENT

1629
TO
1640

General
Pros-
perity

revenue of the Crown increased.   Nor was there much sign of active discontent.   Vexatious indeed and illegal as were the proceedings of the Crown, there seems in these earlier years of personal rule to have been little apprehension of any permanent danger to freedom in the country at large.   To those who read the letters of the time there is something inexpressibly touching in the general faith of their writers in the ultimate victory of the Law.   Charles was obstinate, but obstinacy was too common a foible amongst Englishmen to rouse any vehement resentment.   The people were as stubborn as their King, and their political sense told them that the slightest disturbance of affairs must shake down the financial fabric which Charles was slowly building up, and force him back on subsidies and a Parliament. Meanwhile they would wait for better days, and their patience was aided by the general prosperity of the country.   The great Continental wars threw wealth into English hands.   The intercourse between Spain and Flanders was carried on solely in English ships, and the English flag covered the intercourse between Portuguese ports and the colonies in Africa, India, and the Pacific.   The long peace was producing its inevitable results in an extension of commerce and a rise of manufactures in the towns of the West Riding of Yorkshire.   Fresh land was being brought into cultivation, and a great scheme was set on foot for reclaiming the Fens.   The new wealth of the country gentry, through the increase of rent, was seen in the splendour of the houses which they were raising.   The contrast of this peace and prosperity with the ruin and bloodshed of the Continent afforded a ready argument to the friends of the King's system.   So tranquil was the outer appearance of the country that in Court circles all sense of danger had disappeared.   "Some of the greatest statesmen and privy councillors," says May, "would ordinarily laugh when the word, 'liberty of the subject,' was named."   There were courtiers bold enough to express their hope that "the King would never need any more Parliaments."   But beneath this outer calm "the country," Clarendon honestly tells us while eulogizing the peace, "was full of pride and mutiny and discontent."   Thousands were quitting England for America.   The gentry held aloof from the Court.   "The common people in the generality and the country freeholders would rationally argue of their own rights and the oppressions which were laid upon them."   If Charles was content to deceive himself, there was one man among his ministers who saw that the people were right in their policy of patience, and that unless other measures were taken the fabric of despotism would fall at the first breath of adverse fortune.

Sir Thomas Wentworth, a great Yorkshire landowner and one of the representatives of his county, had stood during the Parliament of 1628 among the more prominent members of the popular party in the Commons.   But from the first moment of his appearance in public his passionate desire had been to find employment in the service of the

Crown. At the close of the preceding reign he was already connected with the Court, he had secured a seat in Yorkshire for one of the royal ministers, and was believed to be on the high road to a peerage. But the consciousness of political ability which spurred his ambition roused the jealousy of Buckingham ; and the haughty pride of Wentworth was flung by repeated slights into an attitude of opposition, which his eloquence—grander in its sudden outbursts, though less earnest and sustained, than that of Eliot—soon rendered formidable. His intrigues at Court roused Buckingham to crush by a signal insult the rival whose genius he instinctively dreaded. While sitting in his court as sheriff of Yorkshire, Wentworth received the announcement of his dismissal from office, and of the gift of his post to Sir John Savile, his rival in the county. "Since they will thus weakly breathe on me a seeming disgrace in the public face of my country," he said with a characteristic outburst of contemptuous pride, " I shall crave leave to wipe it away as openly, as easily ! " His whole conception of a strong and able rule revolted against the miserable government of the favourite. Wentworth's aim was to force on the King, not such a freedom as Eliot longed for, but such a system as the Tudors had clung to, where a large and noble policy placed the sovereign naturally at the head of the people, and where Parliaments sank into mere aids to the Crown. But before this could be, Buckingham must be cleared away. It was with this end that Wentworth sprang to the front of the Commons in urging the Petition of Right. Whether in that crisis of Wentworth's life some nobler impulse, some true passion for the freedom he was to trample under foot mingled with his thirst for revenge, it is hard to tell. But his words were words of fire. "If he did not faithfully insist for the common liberty of the subject to be preserved whole and entire," it was thus he closed one of his speeches on the Petition, "it was his desire that he might be set as a beacon on a hill for all men else to wonder at."

It is as such a beacon that his name has stood from that time to this. The death of Buckingham had no sooner removed the obstacle that stood between his ambition and the end at which it had aimed throughout, than the cloak of patriotism was flung by. Wentworth was admitted to the royal Council, and he took his seat at the board determined, to use his own phrase, to "vindicate the Monarchy for ever from the conditions and restraints of subjects." So great was the faith in his zeal and power which he knew how to breathe into his royal master that he was at once raised to the peerage, and placed with Laud in the first rank of the King's councillors. Charles had good ground for this rapid confidence in his new minister. In Wentworth, or as he is known from the title he assumed at the close of his life, in the Earl of Strafford, the very genius of tyranny was embodied. If he shared his master's belief that the arbitrary power

SEC. V.

THE
PERSONAL
GOVERN-
MENT

1629
TO
1640

Went-
worth as
Minister
1629

SEC. V.

THE
PERSONAL
GOVERN-
MENT
1629
TO
1640

which Charles was wielding formed part of the old constitution of the country, and that the Commons had gone out of their "ancient bounds" in limiting the royal prerogative, he was clear-sighted enough to see that the only way of permanently establishing absolute rule in England was not by reasoning, or by the force of custom, but by the force of fear. His system was the expression of his own inner temper; and the dark gloomy countenance, the full heavy eye, which meet us in Strafford's portrait are the best commentary on his policy of "Thorough." It was by the sheer strength of his genius, by the terror his violence inspired amid the meaner men whom Buckingham had left, by the general sense of his power, that he had forced himself upon the Court. He had none of the small arts of a courtier. His air was that of a silent, proud, passionate man; when he first appeared at Whitehall his rough uncourtly manners provoked a smile in the royal circle. But the smile soon died into a general hate. The Queen, frivolous and meddlesome as she was, detested him; his fellow-ministers intrigued against him, and seized on his hot speeches against the great lords, his quarrels with the royal household, his transports of passion at the very Council-table, to ruin him in his master's favour. The King himself, while steadily supporting him against his rivals, was utterly unable to understand his drift. Charles valued him as an administrator, disdainful of private ends, crushing great and small with the same haughty indifference to men's love or hate, and devoted to the one aim of building up the power of the Crown. But in his purpose of preparing for the great struggle with freedom which he saw before him, of building up by force such a despotism in England as Richelieu was building up in France, and of thus making England as great in Europe as France had been made by Richelieu, he could look for little sympathy and less help from the King.

**Went-
worth in
Ireland**

Wentworth's genius turned impatiently to a sphere where it could act alone, untrammelled by the hindrances it encountered at home. His purpose was to prepare for the coming contest by the provision of a fixed revenue, arsenals, fortresses, and a standing army, and it was in Ireland that he resolved to find them. He saw in the country over which the English Government had now assumed full and undivided command the lever he needed for the overthrow of English freedom. The balance of Catholic against Protestant in Ireland might be used to make both parties dependent on the royal authority; the rights of conquest which by the Stuart theory vested the whole land in the absolute possession of the Crown, gave him a large field for his administrative ability; and for the rest he trusted, and trusted justly, to the force of his genius and of his will. In 1633 he was made Lord Deputy, and five years later his aim seemed all but realized. "The King," he wrote to Laud, "is as absolute here as any prince in the

Sec. V.

The
Personal
Govern-
ment
1629
to
1640

world can be." Wentworth's government was a rule of terror. Officials of Church and State such as Archbishop Usher and Lord Chancellor Loftus, or adventurers like Boyle Earl of Cork, were the objects of his insult and defiance. His tyranny strode over all legal bounds. A few insolent words, construed as mutiny, were enough to bring Lord Mountnorris before a council of war, and to inflict on him a sentence of death. But his tyranny aimed at public ends, and in Ireland the heavy hand of a single despot delivered the mass of the people at any rate from the local despotism of a hundred masters. The Irish land-owners were for the first time made to feel themselves amenable to the law. Justice was enforced, outrage was repressed, the condi-tion of the clergy was to some extent raised, the sea was cleared of the pirates who infested it. The encouragement of the linen manufac-ture which was to bring wealth to Ulster, and some revival of the ruined Irish commerce, date from the Lieutenancy of Wentworth. The noblest work for Ireland would have been a reconciliation between Catholic and Protestant, and an obliteration of the anger and thirst for vengeance raised by the Ulster Plantation. Wentworth, on the other hand, angered the Protestants by a toleration of Catholic worship ; while his perfidious scheme for the plantation of Connacht by Protestants taught the Irish that the suppression of their religion and the extermina-tion of their race from the soil was the settled policy of the Government, and that no submission could avert their doom. Meanwhile he en-couraged a disunion which left both parties dependent for support and protection on the Crown. It was a policy which was to end in bringing about the anguish of the Irish revolt, the vengeance of Cromwell, and the long series of atrocities which make the story of the country he ruined so terrible to tell. But for the hour it left Ireland helpless in his hands. He doubled the revenue. He reorganized the army. To provide for its support he ventured, in spite of the panic with which Charles heard his project, to summon an Irish Parliament. His aim was to read a lesson to England and the King, by showing how completely that dreaded thing, a Parliament, could be made the organ of the royal will ; and his success was complete. Two-thirds, indeed, of an Irish House of Commons consisted of the representatives of wretched villages, the pocket-boroughs of the Crown ; while absent peers were forced to entrust their proxies to the Council to be used at its pleasure. But precautions were hardly needed. The two Houses trembled at the stern master who bade their members not let the King "find them muttering, or, to speak it more truly, mutinying in corners," and voted with a perfect docility the means of maintaining an army of five thou-sand foot and five hundred horse. Had the subsidy been refused, the result would have been the same. "I would undertake," wrote Went-worth, "upon the peril of my head, to make the King's army able to subsist and provide for itself among them without their help."

Sec. V.
THE
PERSONAL
GOVERN-
MENT
1629
TO
1640

Charles
and
Scotland

While Wentworth was thus working out his system of "Thorough" on one side of St. George's Channel, it was being carried out on the other by a mind inferior, indeed, to his own in genius, but almost equal to it in courage and tenacity. On Weston's death in 1635, Laud became virtually first minister at the English Council-board. We have already seen with what a reckless and unscrupulous activity he was crushing Puritanism in the English Church, and driving Puritan ministers from English pulpits; and in this work his new position enabled him to back the authority of the High Commission by the terrors of the Star Chamber. It was a work, indeed, which to Laud's mind was at once civil and religious: he had allied the cause of ecclesiastical organization with that of absolutism in the State; and, while borrowing the power of the Crown to crush ecclesiastical liberty, he brought the influence of the Church to bear on the ruin of civil freedom. But his power stopped at the Scotch frontier. Across the Border stood a Church with bishops indeed, but without a ritual, modelled on the doctrine and system of Geneva, Calvinist in teaching and to a great extent in government. The mere existence of such a Church gave countenance to English Puritanism, and threatened in any hour of ecclesiastical weakness to bring a dangerous influence to bear on the Church of England. With Scotland, indeed, Laud could only deal indirectly through Charles, for the King was jealous of any interference of his English ministers or Parliament with his Northern Kingdom. But Charles was himself earnest to deal with it. He had imbibed his father's hatred of all that tended to Presbyterianism, and from the outset of his reign he had been making advance after advance towards the more complete establishment of Episcopacy. To understand, however, what had been done, and the relations which had by this time grown up between Scotland and its King, we must take up again the thread of its history which we broke at the moment when Mary fled for refuge over the English border.

After a few years of wise and able rule, the triumph of Protestantism under the Earl of Murray had been interrupted by his assassination, by the revival of the Queen's faction, and by the renewal of civil war. The next regent, the child-king's grandfather, was slain in a fray; but under the strong hand of Morton the land won a short breathing-space. Edinburgh, the last fortress held in Mary's name, surrendered to an English force sent by Elizabeth; and its captain, Kirkcaldy of Grange, was hanged for treason in the market-place; while the stern justice of Morton forced peace upon the warring lords. The people of the Lowlands, indeed, were now stanch for the new faith; and the Protestant Church rose rapidly after the death of Knox into a power which appealed at every critical juncture to the deeper feelings of the nation at large. In the battle with Catholicism the bishops had clung to the old religion; and the new faith, left without episcopal interfer-

SEC. V.

THE
PERSONAL
GOVERN-
MENT
1629
TO
1640

ence, and influenced by the Genevan training of Knox, borrowed from Calvin its model of Church government, as it borrowed its theology. The system of Presbyterianism, as it grew up at the outset without direct recognition from the law, not only bound Scotland together as it had never been bound before by its administrative organization, its church synods and general assemblies, but by the power it gave the lay elders in each congregation, and by the summons of laymen in an overpowering majority to the earlier Assemblies, it called the people at large to a voice, and as it proved, a decisive voice, in the administration of affairs. If its government by ministers gave it the outer look of an ecclesiastical despotism, no Church constitution has proved in practice so democratic as that of Scotland. Its influence in raising the nation at large to a consciousness of its own power is shown by the change which passes, from the moment of its final establishment, over the face of Scotch history. The sphere of action to which it called the people was in fact not a mere ecclesiastical but a national sphere ; and the power of the Church was felt more and more over nobles and King. When after five years the union of his rivals put an end to Morton's regency, the possession of the young sovereign, James the Sixth, and the exercise of the royal authority in his name, became the constant aim of the factions who were tearing Scotland to pieces. As James grew to manhood, however, he was strong enough to break the yoke of the lords, and to become master of the great houses that had so long overawed the Crown. But he was farther than ever from being absolute master of his realm. Amidst the turmoil of the Reformation a new force had come to the front. This was the Scotch people which had risen into being under the guise of the Scotch Kirk. Melville, the greatest of the successors of Knox, claimed for the ecclesiastical body an independence of the State which James hardly dared to resent, while he struggled helplessly beneath the sway which public opinion, expressed through the General Assembly of the Church, exercized over the civil government. In the great crisis of the Armada his hands were fettered by the league with England which it forced upon him. The democratic boldness of Calvinism allied itself with the spiritual pride of the Presbyterian ministers in their dealings with the Crown. Melville in open council took James by the sleeve, and called him "God's silly vassal." "There are two Kings," he told him, "and two kingdoms in Scotland. There is Christ Jesus the King, and His Kingdom the Kirk, whose subject James the Sixth is, and of whose kingdom not a king, nor a lord, nor a head, but a member." The words and tone of the great preacher were bitterly remembered when James mounted the English throne. "A Scottish Presbytery," he exclaimed years afterwards at the Hampton Court Conference, "as well fitteth with Monarchy as God and the Devil ! No Bishop, no King !" But Scotland was resolved

SEC. V.

THE
PERSONAL
GOVERN-
MENT
1629
TO
1640
*Presby-
terianism
established*
1592

on "no bishop." Episcopacy had become identified among the more zealous Scotchmen with the old Catholicism they had shaken off. When he appeared at a later time before the English Council-table, Melville took the Archbishop of Canterbury by the sleeves of his rochet, and, shaking them in his manner, called them Romish rags, and marks of the Beast. Four years therefore after the ruin of the Armada, Episcopacy was formally abolished, and the Presbyterian system established by law as the mode of government of the Church of Scotland. The rule of the Church was placed in a General Assembly, with subordinate Provincial Synods, Presbyteries, and Kirk Sessions, by which its discipline was carried down to every member of a congregation. All that James could save was the right of being present at the General Assembly, and of fixing a time and place for its annual meeting. But James had no sooner succeeded to the English throne than he used his new power in a struggle to undo the work which had been done. In spite of his assent to an act legalizing its annual convention, he hindered any meeting of the General Assembly for five successive years by repeated prorogations. The protests of the clergy were roughly met. When

nineteen ministers constituted themselves an Assembly they were banished as traitors from the realm. Of the leaders who remained the boldest were summoned with Andrew Melville to confer with the King in England on his projects of change. On their refusal to betray the freedom of the Church they were committed to prison ; and an epigram which Melville wrote on the usages of the English communion was seized on as a ground for bringing him before the English Privy Council. He was sent to the Tower, and released after some years of imprisonment only to go into exile. Deprived of their leaders, threatened with bonds and exile, deserted by the nobles, ill supported as yet by the mass of the people, the Scottish ministers bent before the pressure of the Crown. Bishops were allowed to act as presidents

in their synods ; and episcopacy was at last formally recognized in the Scottish Church. The pulpits were bridled. The General Assembly was brought to submission. The ministers and elders were deprived of their right of excommunicating offenders, save with a bishop's sanction. A Court of High Commission enforced the supremacy of the Crown. But with this assertion of his royal authority James was content. His aim was political rather than religious, and in seizing on the control of the Church through his organized prelacy, he held himself to have won back that mastery of his realm which the Reformation had reft from the Scottish Kings. The earlier policy of Charles followed his father's line of action. It effected little save a partial restoration of Church-lands,

which the lords were forced to surrender. But Laud's vigorous action soon made itself felt. His first acts were directed rather to points of outer observance than to any attack on the actual fabric of Presbyterian organization. The Estates were induced to withdraw the control of ecclesiastical apparel from the Assembly, and to commit it to the Crown ; a step soon followed by a resumption of their episcopal costume on the part of the Scotch bishops. When the Bishop of Moray preached before Charles in his rochet, on the King's visit to Edinburgh, it was the first instance of its use since the Reformation. The innovation was followed by the issue of a royal warrant which directed all ministers to use the surplice in divine worship. From costume, however, the busy minister soon passed to weightier matters. Many years had gone by since he had vainly invited James to draw his Scotch subjects " to a nearer conjunction with the liturgy and canons of this nation." " I sent him back again," said the shrewd old King, " with the frivolous draft he had drawn. For all that, he feared not my anger, but assaulted me again with another ill-fangled platform to make that stubborn Kirk stoop more to the English platform ; but I durst not play fast and loose with my word. He knows not the stomach of that people." But Laud knew how to wait, and his time had come at last. He was resolved to put an end to the Presbyterian character of the Scotch Church altogether, and to bring it to a uniformity with the Church of England. A book of canons issued by the sole authority of the King placed the government of the Church absolutely in the hands of its bishops ; no Church Assembly might be summoned but by the King, no alteration in worship or discipline introduced but by his permission. As daring a stretch of the prerogative superseded what was known as Knox's Liturgy—the book of Common Order drawn up on the Genevan model by that Reformer, and generally used throughout Scotland—by a new Liturgy based on the English Book of Common Prayer. The liturgy and canons drawn up by four Scottish bishops were laid before Laud ; in their composition the General Assembly had neither been consulted nor recognized ; and taken together they formed the code of a political and ecclesiastical system which aimed at reducing Scotland to an utter subjection to the Crown. To enforce them on the land was to effect a revolution of the most serious kind. The books however were backed by a royal injunction, and Laud flattered himself that the revolution had been wrought.

Triumphant in Scotland, with the Scotch Church—as he fancied —at his feet, Laud's hand still fell heavily on the English Puritans. There were signs of a change of temper which might have made even a bolder man pause. Thousands of " the best," scholars, merchants, lawyers, farmers, were flying over the Atlantic to seek freedom and purity of religion in the wilderness. Great landowners and nobles were preparing to follow. Ministers were quitting their parsonages rather than abet the royal insult to the sanctity of the Sabbath. The Puritans who remained among the clergy were giving

Sec. V.

The
Personal
Govern-
ment
1629
to
1640
1633

1636

*The new
Liturgy*

**Milton
at
Horton**

SEC. V.

THE
PERSONAL
GOVERN-
MENT
1629
TO
1640

up their homes rather than consent to the change of the sacred table into an altar, or to silence in their protests against the new Popery. The noblest of living Englishmen refused to become the priest of a Church whose ministry could only be "bought with servitude and forswearing." We have seen John Milton leave Cambridge, self-dedicated "to that same lot, however mean or high, to which time leads me and the will of Heaven." But the lot to which these called him was not the ministerial office to which he had been destined from his childhood. In later life he told bitterly the story, how he had been "Church-outed by the prelates." "Coming to some maturity of years, and perceiving what tyranny had invaded in the Church, that he who would take orders must subscribe slave, and take an oath withal, which unless he took with a conscience that would retch he must either straight perjure or split his faith, I thought it better to prefer a blameless silence before the sacred office of speaking, bought and begun with servitude and forswearing." In spite therefore of his father's regrets, he retired to a new home which the scrivener had found at Horton, a village in the neighbourhood of Windsor, and quietly busied himself with study and verse. The poetic impulse of the Renascence had been slowly dying away under the Stuarts. The stage was falling into mere coarseness and horror; Shakspere had died quietly at Stratford in Milton's childhood; the last and worst play of Ben Jonson appeared in the year of his settlement at Horton; and though Ford and Massinger still lingered on there were no successors for them but Shirley and Davenant. The philosophic and meditative taste of the age had produced indeed poetic schools of its own: poetic satire had become fashionable in Hall, better known afterwards as a bishop, and had been carried on vigorously by George Wither; the so-called "metaphysical" poetry, the vigorous and pithy expression of a cold and prosaic good sense, began with Sir John Davies, and buried itself in fantastic affectations in Donne; religious verse had become popular in the gloomy allegories of Quarles and the tender refinement which struggles through a jungle of puns and extravagances in George Herbert. But what poetic life really remained was to be found only in the caressing fancy and lively badinage of lyric singers like Herrick, whose grace is untouched by passion and often disfigured by coarseness and pedantry; or in the school of Spenser's more direct successors, where Browne in his pastorals, and the two Fletchers, Phineas and Giles, in their unreadable allegories, still preserved something of their master's sweetness, if they preserved nothing of his power. Milton was himself a Spenserian; he owned to Dryden in later years "that Spenser was his original," and in some of his earliest lines at Horton he dwells lovingly on "the sage and solemn tones" of the "Faerie Queen," its "forests and enchantments drear, where more is meant than meets the ear." But of the weakness and

affectation which characterized Spenser's successors he had not a trace.
In the "Allegro" and "Penseroso," the first results of his retirement
at Horton, we catch again the fancy and melody of the Elizabethan
verse, the wealth of its imagery, its wide sympathy with nature and
man.   There is a loss, perhaps, of the older freedom and spontaneity
of the Renascence, a rhetorical rather than passionate turn in the
young poet, a striking absence of dramatic power, and a want of subtle
precision even in his picturesque touches.   Milton's imagination is not
strong enough to identify him with the world which he imagines ; he
stands apart from it, and looks at it as from a distance, ordering it
and arranging it at his will.   But if in this respect he falls, both in his
earlier and later poems, far below Shakspere or Spenser, the deficiency
is all but compensated by his nobleness of feeling and expression, the
severity of his taste, his sustained dignity, and the perfectness and
completeness of his work.   The moral grandeur of the Puritan breathes,
even in these lighter pieces of his youth, through every line.   The
"Comus," planned as a masque for the festivities which the Earl of
Bridgewater was holding at Ludlow Castle, rises into an almost impassioned pleading for the love of virtue.

  The historic interest of Milton's "Comus" lies in its forming part of
a protest made by the more cultured Puritans at this time against the
gloomier bigotry which persecution was fostering in the party at large.
The patience of Englishmen, in fact, was slowly wearing out.   There
was a sudden upgrowth of virulent pamphlets of the old Martin Marprelate type.   Men, whose names no one asked, hawked libels, whose
authorship no one knew, from the door of the tradesman to the door of
the squire.   As the hopes of a Parliament grew fainter, and men despaired of any legal remedy, violent and weak-headed fanatics came, as
at such times they always come, to the front.   Leighton, the father of
the saintly Archbishop of that name, had given a specimen of their tone
at the outset of this period, by denouncing the prelates as men of blood,
Episcopacy as Antichrist, and the Popish queen as a daughter of Heth.
The "Histrio-mastix" of Prynne, a lawyer distinguished for his constitutional knowledge, but the most obstinate and narrow-minded of men,
marked the deepening of Puritan bigotry under the fostering warmth of
Laud's persecution.   The book was an attack on players as the ministers of Satan, on theatres as the devil's chapels, on hunting, maypoles,
the decking of houses at Christmas with evergreens, on cards, music,
and false hair.   The attack on the stage was as offensive to the more
cultured minds among the Puritan party as to the Court itself ; Selden
and Whitelock took a prominent part in preparing a grand masque by
which the Inns of Court resolved to answer its challenge, and in the following year Milton wrote his masque of "Comus" for Ludlow Castle.
To leave Prynne, however, simply to the censure of wiser men than himself was too sensible a course for the angry Primate.   No man was ever

Sec. V.

THE
PERSONAL
GOVERN-
MENT
1629
TO
1640

sent to prison before or since for such a sheer mass of nonsense; but a passage in the book was taken as a reflection on the Queen, and his sentence showed the hard cruelty of the Primate. Prynne was dismissed from the bar, deprived of his university degree, and set in the pillory. His ears were clipped from his head, and he was taken back to prison. But the storm of popular passion which was gathering was not so pressing a difficulty to the royal ministers at this time as the old difficulty of the exchequer. The ingenious devices of the Court lawyers, the revived prerogatives, the illegal customs, the fines and confiscations which were alienating one class after another and sowing in home after home the seeds of a bitter hatred to the Crown, were insufficient to meet the needs of the Treasury; and new exactions were necessary, at a time when the rising discontent made every new exaction a challenge to revolt. A fresh danger had suddenly appeared in an alliance of France and Holland which threatened English dominion over the Channel; and there were rumours of a proposed partition of the Spanish Netherlands between the two powers. It was necessary to put a strong fleet on the seas; and the money which had to

Ship-money
1634

be found at home was procured by a stretch of the prerogative which led afterwards to the great contest over ship-money. The legal research of Noy, one of the law officers of the Crown, found precedents among the records in the Tower for the provision of ships for the King's use by the port-towns of the kingdom, and for the furnishing of their equipment by the maritime counties. The precedents dated from times when no permanent fleet existed, and when sea warfare was waged by vessels lent for the moment by the various ports. But they were seized as a means of equipping a permanent navy without cost to the exchequer; the first demand for ships was soon commuted into a demand of money for the payment of ships; and the writs which were issued to London and the chief English ports were enforced by fine and imprisonment. When Laud took the direction of affairs a more vigorous and unscrupulous impulse made itself felt. To Laud as to Wentworth, indeed, the King seemed over-cautious, the Star Chamber feeble, the judges over-scrupulous. "I am for Thorough," the one writes to the other in alternate fits of impatience at the slow progress they are making. Wentworth was anxious that his good work might not "be spoiled on that side." Laud echoed the wish, while he envied the free course of the Lord Lieutenant. "You have a good deal of honour here," he writes, "for your proceeding. Go on a' God's name. I have done with expecting of Thorough on this side." The financial pressure was seized by both to force the King on to a bolder course. "The debt of the Crown being taken off," Wentworth urged, "you may govern at your will." All pretence of

*The new
Ship-money*
1635

precedents was thrown aside, and Laud resolved to find a permanent revenue in the conversion of the "ship-money," till now levied on ports and the maritime counties, into a general tax imposed by the royal will upon the whole country. "I know no reason," Wentworth had written significantly, "but you may as well rule the common lawyers in England as I, poor beagle, do here;" and the judges no sooner declared the new impost to be legal than he drew the logical deduction from their decision. "Since it is lawful for the King to impose a tax for the equipment of the navy, it must be equally so for the levy of an army: and the same reason which authorizes him to levy an army to resist, will authorize him to carry that army abroad that he may prevent invasion. Moreover what is law in England is law also in Scotland and Ireland. The decision of the judges will therefore make the King absolute at home and formidable abroad. Let him only abstain from war for a few years that he may habituate his subjects to the payment of that tax, and in the end he will find himself more powerful and respected than any of his predecessors." But there were men who saw the danger to freedom in this levy of ship-money as clearly as Wentworth himself. The bulk of the country party abandoned all hope of English freedom. There was a sudden revival of the emigration to New England; and men of blood and fortune now prepared to seek a new home in the West. Lord Warwick secured the proprietorship of the Connecticut valley. Lord Saye and Sele and Lord Brooke began negotiations for transporting themselves to the New World. Oliver Cromwell is said, by a doubtful tradition, to have only been prevented from crossing the seas by a royal embargo. It is more certain that Hampden purchased a tract of land on the Narragansett. John Hampden, a friend of Eliot's, a man of consummate ability, of unequalled power of persuasion, of a keen intelligence, ripe learning, and a character singularly pure and loveable, had already shown the firmness of his temper in his refusal to contribute to the forced loan of 1627. He now repeated his refusal, declared ship-money an illegal impost, and resolved to rouse the spirit of the country by an appeal for protection to the law.

The news of Hampden's resistance thrilled through England at a moment when men were roused by the news of resistance in the north. The patience of Scotland had found an end at last. While England was waiting for the opening of the great cause of ship-money, peremptory orders from the King forced the clergy of Edinburgh to introduce the new service into their churches. But the Prayer Book was no sooner opened at the church of St. Giles's than a murmur ran through the congregation, and the murmur soon grew into a formidable riot. The church was cleared, and the service read; but the rising discontent frightened the judges into a decision that the royal writ enjoined the purchase, and not the use, of the Prayer Book. Its use was at once discontinued, and the angry orders which came from England for its restoration were met by a shower of protests from every part of

Jan. 1636

The Resistance

July 23

M M

SEC. V.

THE
PERSONAL
GOVERN-
MENT
1629
TO
1640

Scotland.   The Duke of Lennox alone took sixty-eight petitions with
him to the court ; while ministers, nobles, and gentry poured into
Edinburgh to organize the national resistance.   The effect of these
events in Scotland was at once seen in the open demonstration of discontent south of the border.   The prison with which Laud had
rewarded Prynne's bulky quarto had tamed his spirit so little that a
new tract written within its walls attacked the bishops as devouring
wolves and lords of Lucifer.   A fellow-prisoner, John Bastwick,
declared in his " Litany " that " Hell was broke loose, and the Devils
in surplices, hoods, copes, and rochets, were come among us." Burton,
a London clergyman silenced by the High Commission, called on all
Christians to resist the bishops as "robbers of souls, limbs of the
Beast, and factors of Antichrist."   Raving of this sort might have been
passed by had not the general sympathy shown how fast the storm of
popular passion was rising.   Prynne and his fellow pamphleteers,
when Laud dragged them before the Star Chamber as "trumpets of
sedition," listened with defiance to their sentence of exposure in the
pillory and imprisonment for life ; and the crowd who filled Palace
Yard to witness their punishment groaned at the cutting off of their
ears, and "gave a great shout" when Prynne urged that the sentence
on him was contrary to the law.   A hundred thousand Londoners
lined the road as they passed on the way to prison ; and the journey
of these " Martyrs," as the spectators called them, was like a triumphal
progress.   Startled as he was at the sudden burst of popular feeling,
Laud remained dauntless as ever.   Prynne's entertainers as he
passed through the country were summoned before the Star Chamber,

while the censorship struck fiercer blows at the Puritan press.   But
the real danger lay not in the libels of silly zealots but in the attitude
of Scotland, and in the effect which was being produced in England
at large by the trial of Hampden.   For twelve days the cause of ship-
money was solemnly argued before the full bench of judges.   It was
proved that the tax in past times had been levied only in cases of
sudden emergency, and confined to the coast and port towns alone,
and that even the show of legality had been taken from it by formal
statute : it was declared a breach of the " fundamental laws " of England.   The case was adjourned, but the discussion told not merely on
England but on the temper of the Scots.   Charles had replied to their
petitions by a simple order to all strangers to leave the capital.   But
the Council at Edinburgh was unable to enforce his order ; and the
nobles and gentry before dispersing to their homes named a body of
delegates, under the odd title of " the Tables," who carried on through
the winter a series of negotiations with the Crown.   The negotiations
were interrupted in the following spring by a renewed order for their
dispersion, and for the acceptance of a Prayer Book ; while the judges

in England delivered at last their long-delayed decision on Hampden's

SEC. V.

THE
PERSONAL
GOVERN-
MENT
1629
TO
1640

case. Two judges only pronounced in his favour ; though three followed them on technical grounds. The majority, seven in number,
gave judgement against him. The broad principle was laid down that
no statute prohibiting arbitrary taxation could be pleaded against the
King's will. "I never read or heard," said Judge Berkley, "that lex
was rex, but it is common and most true that rex is lex." Finch, the
Chief-Justice, summed up the opinions of his fellow judges. "Acts of
Parliament to take away the King's royal power in the defence of his
kingdom are void," he said : . . . . "they are void Acts of Parliament
to bind the King not to command the subjects, their persons, and
goods, and I say their money too, for no Acts of Parliament make
any difference."

"I wish Mr. Hampden and others to his likeness," the Lord Deputy
wrote bitterly from Ireland, "were well whipt into their right senses."
Amidst the exultation of the Court over the decision of the judges,
Wentworth saw clearly that Hampden's work had been done. His
resistance had roused England to a sense of the danger to her freedom,
and forced into light the real character of the royal claims. How
stern and bitter the temper even of the noblest Puritans had become
at last we see in the poem which Milton produced at this time, his
elegy of "Lycidas." Its grave and tender lament is broken by a
sudden flash of indignation at the dangers around the Church, at the
"blind mouths that scarce themselves know how to hold a sheep-
hook," and to whom "the hungry sheep look up, and are not fed,"
while "the grim wolf" of Rome "with privy paw daily devours apace,
and nothing said!" The stern resolve of the people to deᵣ 1and justice
on their tyrants spoke in his threat of the axe. Wentworth and
Laud, and Charles himself, had yet to reckon with "that two-handed
engine at the door" which stood "ready to smite once, and smite no
more." But stern as was the general resolve, there was no need for
immediate action, for the difficulties which were gathering in the north
were certain to bring a strain on the Government which would force
it to seek support from the people. The King's demand for immediate
submission, which reached Edinburgh while England was waiting for
the Hampden judgment, at once gathered the whole body of remonstrants together round "the Tables" at Edinburgh; and a protestation,
read at Edinburgh and Stirling, was followed, on Johnston of Warris-
ton's suggestion, by a renewal of the Covenant with God which had
been drawn up and sworn to in a previous hour of peril, when Mary
was still plotting against Protestantism, and Spain was preparing its
Armada. "We promise and swear," ran the solemn engagement at
its close, "by the great name of the Lord our God, to continue in the
profession and obedience of the said religion, and that we shall defend
the same, and resist all their contrary errors and corruptions, according to our vocation and the utmost of that power which God has put

SEC. V.

THE
PERSONAL
GOVERN-
MENT
1629
TO
1640

into our hands all the days of our life." The Covenant was signed in the churchyard of the Grey Friars at Edinburgh, in a tumult of enthusiasm, "with such content and joy as those who, having long before been outlaws and rebels, are admitted again into covenant with God." Gentlemen and nobles rode with the documents in their pockets over the country, gathering subscriptions to it, while the ministers pressed for a general consent to it from the pulpit. But pressure was needless. "Such was the zeal of subscribers that for a while many subscribed with tears on their cheeks;" some were indeed reputed to have "drawn their own blood and used it in place of ink

The Scotch revolution

to underwrite their names." The force given to Scottish freedom by this revival of religious fervour was seen in the new tone adopted by the Covenanters. The Marquis of Hamilton, who came as Royal Commissioner to put an end to the quarrel, was at once met by demands for an abolition of the Court of High Commission, the withdrawal of the Books of Canons and Common Prayer, a free Parliament, and a free General Assembly. It was in vain that he threatened war; even the Scotch Council pressed Charles to give fuller satisfaction to the people. "I will rather die," the King wrote to Hamilton, "than yield to these impertinent and damnable demands;" but it was needful to gain time. "The discontents at home," wrote Lord Northumberland to Wentworth, "do rather increase than lessen:" and Charles was without money or men. It was in vain that he begged for a loan from Spain on promise of declaring war against Holland, or that he tried to procure two thousand troops from Flanders with which to occupy Edinburgh. The loan and troops were both refused, and some contributions offered by the English Catholics did little to recruit the Exchequer. Charles had directed the Marquis to delay any decisive breach till the royal fleet appeared in the Forth; but it was hard to equip a fleet at all. Scotland indeed was sooner ready for war than the King. The Scotch volunteers who had been serving in the Thirty

The Scotch war

Years' War streamed home at the call of their brethren. General Leslie, a veteran trained under Gustavus, came from Sweden to take the command of the new forces. A voluntary war tax was levied in every shire. The danger at last forced the King to yield to the Scotch demands; but he had no sooner yielded than the concession was withdrawn, and the Assembly hardly met before it was called upon to disperse. By an almost unanimous vote, however, it resolved to continue its session. The innovations in worship and discipline were abolished, episcopacy was abjured, the bishops deposed, and the system of Presbyterianism re-established in its fullest extent. The news that Charles was gathering an army at York, and reckoning for support on the scattered loyalists in Scotland itself, was answered by the

1639

seizure of Edinburgh, Dumbarton, and Stirling; while 10,000 well-equipped troops under Leslie and the Earl of Montrose entered Aber-

Sec. V.

The
Personal
Govern-
ment

1629
to
1640

The
Bishops'
War

deen, and brought the Catholic Earl of Huntly a prisoner to the south. Instead of overawing the country, the appearance of the royal fleet in the Forth was the signal for Leslie's march with 20,000 men to the Border. Charles had hardly pushed across the Tweed, when the "old little crooked soldier," encamping on the hill of Dunse Law, fairly offered him battle.

Charles however, without money to carry on war, was forced to consent to the gathering of a free Assembly and of a Scotch Parliament. But in his eyes the pacification at Berwick was a mere suspension of arms; his summons of Wentworth from Ireland was a proof that violent measures were in preparation, and the Scots met the challenge by seeking for aid from France. The discovery of a correspondence between the Scotch leaders and the French court raised hopes in the King that an appeal to the country for aid against Scotch treason would still find an answer in English loyalty. Wentworth, who was now made Earl of Strafford, had never ceased to urge that the Scots should be whipped back to their border; he now agreed with Charles that a Parliament should be called, the correspondence laid before it, and advantage taken of the burst of indignation on which the King counted to procure a heavy subsidy. While Charles summoned what from its brief duration is known as the Short Parliament, Strafford hurried to Ireland to levy forces. In fourteen days he had obtained money and men from his servile Parliament, and he came back flushed with his success, in time for the meeting of the Houses at Westminster. But the lesson failed in its effect. Every member of the Commons knew that Scotland was fighting the battle of English liberty. All hope of bringing them to any attack upon the Scots proved fruitless. The intercepted letters were quietly set aside, and the Commons declared as of old that redress of grievances must precede the grant of supplies. No subsidy could be granted till security was had for religion, for property, and for the liberties of Parliament. An offer to relinquish ship-money failed to draw Parliament from its resolve, and after three weeks' sitting it was dissolved. "Things must go worse before they go better" was the cool comment of St. John, one of the patriot leaders. But the country was strangely moved. "So great a defection in the kingdom," wrote Lord Northumberland, "hath not been known in the memory of man." Strafford alone stood undaunted. He urged that, by the refusal of the Parliament to supply the King's wants, Charles was "freed from all rule of government," and entitled to supply himself at his will. The Earl was bent upon war, and took command of the royal army, which again advanced to the north. But the Scots were ready to cross the border; forcing the passage of the Tyne in the face of an English detachment, they occupied Newcastle, and despatched from that town their proposals of peace. They prayed the King to consider their grievances, and, "with the advice

SEC. V.

THE
PERSONAL
GOVERN-
MENT
1626
TO
1640

and consent of the Estates of England convened in Parliament, to settle a firm and desirable peace." The prayer was backed by preparations for a march upon York, where Charles had abandoned himself to despair Strafford's troops were a mere mob; neither by threats nor prayers could he recall them to their duty, and he was forced to own that two months were required before they could be fit for action. It was in vain that Charles won a truce. Behind him in fact England was all but in revolt. The London apprentices mobbed Laud at Lambeth, and broke up the sittings of the High Commission at St. Paul's. The war was denounced everywhere as "the Bishops' War," and the new levies murdered officers whom they suspected of Papistry, broke down altar-rails in every church they passed, and deserted to their homes. Two peers, Lord Wharton and Lord Howard, ventured to lay before the King himself a petition for peace with the Scots; and though Strafford arrested and proposed to shoot them as mutineers, the English Council shrank from desperate courses. The King still strove to escape from the humiliation of calling a Parliament. He summoned a Great Council of the Peers at York. But his project broke down before its general repudiation by the nobles; and with wrath and shame at his heart Charles was driven to summon again the Houses to Westminster.

Section VI.—The Long Parliament. 1640—1644.

[*Authorities.*—Clarendon's "History of the Rebellion," as Hallam justly says, "belongs rather to the class of memoirs" than of histories, and the rigorous analysis of it by Ranke shows the very different value of its various parts. Though the work will always retain a literary interest from its nobleness of style and the grand series of character-portraits which it embodies, the worth of its account of all that preceded the war is almost destroyed by the contrast between its author's conduct at the time and his later description of the Parliament's proceedings, as well as by the deliberate and malignant falsehood with which he has perverted the whole action of his parliamentary opponents. May's "History of the Long Parliament" is fairly accurate and impartial; but the basis of any real account of it must be found in its own proceedings as they have been preserved in the notes of Sir Ralph Verney and Sir Simonds D'Ewes. The last remain unpublished; but Mr. Forster has drawn much from them in his two works, "The Grand Remonstrance" and "The Arrest of the Five Members." The collections of state-papers by Rushworth and Nalson are indispensable for this period. It is illustrated by a series of memoirs, of very different degrees of value, such as those of Whitelock, Ludlow, and Sir Philip Warwick, as well as by works like Mrs. Hutchinson's memoir of her husband, or Baxter's "Autobiography." For Irish affairs we have a vast store of materials in the Ormond papers and letters collected by Carte; for Scotland, "Baillie's Letters" and Mr. Burton's History. Lingard is useful for information as to intrigues with the Catholics in England and Ireland; and Guizot directs special attention to the relations with foreign powers. Pym has been fairly sketched with other statesmen of the time by Mr. Forster in his "Statesmen of the Commonwealth," and in an Essay on

SEC. VI.

THE
LONG PAR-
LIAMENT

1640
TO
1644

Pym

him by Mr. Goldwin Smith. A good deal of valuable research for the period in general is to be found in Mr. Sandford's "Illustrations of the Great Rebellion."] (Mr. Gardiner has now carried on his History to 1644.—*Ed*.)

If Strafford embodied the spirit of tyranny, John Pym, the leader of the Commons from the first meeting of the new houses at Westminster, stands out for all after time as the embodiment of law. A Somersetshire gentleman of good birth and competent fortune, he entered on public life in the Parliament of 1614, and was imprisoned for his patriotism at its close. He had been a leading member in that of 1620, and one of the "twelve ambassadors" for whom James ordered chairs to be set at Whitehall. Of the band of patriots with whom he had stood side by side in the constitutional struggle against the earlier despotism of Charles he was almost the sole survivor. Coke had died of old age ; Cotton's heart was broken by oppression ; Eliot had perished in the Tower ; Wentworth had apostatized. Pym alone remained, resolute, patient as of old ; and as the sense of his greatness grew silently during the eleven years of deepening misrule, the hope and faith of better things clung almost passionately to the man who never doubted of the final triumph of freedom and the law. At their close, Clarendon tells us, in words all the more notable for their bitter tone of hate, " he was the most popular man, and the most able to do hurt, that has lived at any time." He had shown he knew how to wait, and when waiting was over he showed he knew how to act. On the eve of the Long Parliament he rode through England to quicken the electors to a sense of the crisis which had come at last ; and on the assembling of the Commons he took his place, not merely as member for Tavistock, but as their acknowledged head. Few of the country gentlemen, indeed, who formed the bulk of the members, had sat in any previous House ; and of the few, none represented in so eminent a way the Parliamentary tradition on which the coming struggle was to turn. Pym's eloquence, inferior in boldness and originality to that of Eliot or Wentworth, was better suited by its massive and logical force to convince and guide a great party ; and it was backed by a calmness of temper, a dexterity and order in the management of public business, and a practical power of shaping the course of debate, which gave a form and method to Parliamentary proceedings such as they had never had before. Valuable, however, as these qualities were, it was a yet higher quality which raised Pym into the greatest, as he was the first, of Parliamentary leaders. Of the five hundred members who sate round him at St. Stephen's, he was the one man who had clearly foreseen, and as clearly resolved how to meet, the difficulties which lay before them. It was certain that Parliament would be drawn into a struggle with the Crown. It was probable that in such a struggle the House of Commons would be hampered, as it had been hampered before, by the House of Lords.

*His political
theory*

SEC. VI.

THE
LONG PAR-
LIAMENT
1640
TO
1644

The legal antiquaries of the older constitutional school stood helpless
before such a conflict of co-ordinate powers, a conflict for which no
provision had been made by the law, and on which precedents threw
only a doubtful and conflicting light. But with a knowledge of
precedent as great as their own, Pym rose high above them in his
grasp of constitutional principles. He was the first English statesman
who discovered, and applied to the political circumstances around
him, what may be called the doctrine of constitutional proportion.
He saw that as an element of constitutional life Parliament was of
higher value than the Crown; he saw, too, that in Parliament itself
the one essential part was the House of Commons. On these two
facts he based his whole policy in the contest which followed. When
Charles refused to act with the Parliament, Pym treated the refusal as
a temporary abdication on the part of the sovereign, which vested the
executive power in the two Houses until new arrangements were made.
When the Lords obstructed public business, he warned them that
obstruction would only force the Commons "to save the kingdom
alone." Revolutionary as these principles seemed at the time, they
have both been recognized as bases of our constitution since the days
of Pym. The first principle was established by the Convention and
Parliament which followed on the departure of James the Second; the
second by the acknowledgement on all sides since the Reform Bill of
1832 that the government of the country is really in the hands of the
House of Commons, and can only be carried on by ministers who
represent the majority of that House. Pym's temper, indeed, was the
very opposite of the temper of a revolutionist. Few natures have ever
His political been wider in their range of sympathy or action. Serious as his
genius purpose was, his manners were genial, and even courtly: he turned
easily from an invective against Strafford to a chat with Lady Carlisle;
and the grace and gaiety of his social tone, even when the care and
weight of public affairs were bringing him to his grave, gave rise
to a hundred silly scandals among the prurient royalists. It was this
striking combination of genial versatility with a massive force in his
nature which marked him out from the first moment of power as a
born ruler of men. He proved himself at once the subtlest of diplomatists and the grandest of demagogues. He was equally at home in
tracking the subtle intricacies of royalist intrigues, or in kindling
popular passion with words of fire. Though past middle life when
his work really began, for he was born in 1584, four years before the
coming of the Armada, he displayed from the first meeting of the
Long Parliament the qualities of a great administrator, an immense
faculty for labour, a genius for organization, patience, tact, a power of
inspiring confidence in all whom he touched, calmness and moderation
under good fortune or ill, an immovable courage, an iron will. No
English ruler has ever shown greater nobleness of natural temper or a

wider capacity for government than the Somersetshire squire whom his enemies, made clear-sighted by their hate, greeted truly enough as " King Pym."

His ride over England with Hampden on the eve of the elections had been hardly needed, for the summons of a Parliament at once woke the kingdom to a fresh life.   The Puritan emigration to New England was suddenly and utterly suspended; " the change," said Winthrop, " made all men to stay in England in expectation of a new world."   The public discontent spoke from every Puritan pulpit, and expressed itself in a sudden burst of pamphlets, the first-fruits of the thirty thousand which were issued in the next twenty years, and which turned England at large into a school of political discussion.   The resolute looks of the members as they gathered at Westminster contrasted with the hesitating words of the King, and each brought from borough or county a petition of grievances.   Fresh petitions were brought every day by bands of citizens or farmers.   Forty committees were appointed to examine and report on them, and their reports formed the grounds on which the Commons acted.   Prynne and his fellow "martyrs," recalled from their prisons, entered London in triumph amidst the shouts of a great multitude who strewed laurel in their path. The Commons dealt roughly with the agents of the royal system.   In every county a list of "delinquents," or officers who had carried out the plans of the government, was ordered to be prepared and laid before the House.   But their first blow was struck at the leading ministers of the King.   Even Laud was not the centre of so great and universal a hatred as the Earl of Strafford.   . Strafford's guilt was more than the guilt of a servile instrument of tyranny, it was the guilt of " that grand apostate to the Commonwealth who," in the terrible words which closed Lord Digby's invective, " must not expect to be pardoned in this world till he be despatched to the other."   He was conscious of his danger, but Charles forced him to attend the Court ; and with characteristic boldness he resolved to anticipate attack by accusing the Parliamentary leaders of a treasonable correspondence with the Scots.   He was just laying his scheme before Charles when the news reached him that Pym was at the bar of the Lords with his impeachment for high treason.   "With speed," writes an eye-witness, " he comes to the House : he calls rudely at the door," and, " with a proud glooming look, makes towards his place at the board-head.   But at once many bid him void the House, so he is forced in confusion to go to the door till he was called."   He was only recalled to hear his committal to the Tower.   He was still resolute to retort the charge of treason on his foes, and " offered to speak, but was commanded to be gone without a word."   The keeper of the Black Rod demanded his sword as he took him in charge.   " This done, he makes through a number of people towards his coach, no man capping to him, before

Sec. VI.

The
Long Par-
liament
1640
TO
1644
**The
Work of
the Par-
liament**

1640

*Impeach-
ment of
Strafford*

Nov. 11

SEC. VI.

THE
LONG PAR-
LIAMENT
1640
TO
1644
*Fall of the
Ministers*
Dec. 1640

whom that morning the greatest of all England would have stood uncovered." The blow was quickly followed up. Windebank, the Secretary of State, was charged with corrupt favouring of recusants, and escaped to France ; Finch, the Lord Keeper, was impeached, and fled in terror over-sea. Laud himself was thrown into prison. The shadow of what was to come falls across the pages of his diary, and softens the hard temper of the man into a strange tenderness. " I stayed at Lambeth till the evening," writes the Archbishop, " to avoid the gaze of the people. I went to evening prayer in my chapel. The Psalms of the day and chapter fifty of Isaiah gave me great comfort. God make me worthy of it, and fit to receive it. As I went to my barge, hundreds of my poor neighbours stood there and prayed for my safety and return to my house. For which I bless God and them." Charles was forced to look helplessly on at the wreck of the royal system, for the Scotch army was still encamped in the north ; and the Parliament, which saw in the presence of the Scots a security against its own dissolution, was in no hurry to vote the money necessary for their withdrawal. " We cannot do without them," Strode honestly confessed, " the Philistines are still too strong for us." One by one the lawless acts of Charles's government were undone. Ship-money was declared illegal, the judgement in Hampden's case annulled, and one of

the judges committed to prison. A statute declaring " the ancient right of the subjects of this kingdom that no subsidy, custom, impost, or any charge whatsoever, ought or may be laid or imposed upon any merchandize exported or imported by subjects, denizens, or aliens, without common consent in Parliament," put an end for ever to all pretensions to a right of arbitrary taxation on the part of the Crown. A Triennial Bill enforced the assembly of the Houses every three years, and bound the returning officers to proceed to election if the Royal writ failed to summon them. A Committee of Religion had been appointed to consider the question of Church Reform, and on its report the Commons passed a bill for the removal of bishops from the House of Lords.

The King made no sign of opposition. He was known to be resolute against the abolition of Episcopacy ; but he announced no purpose of resisting the expulsion of the bishops from the Peers. Strafford's life he was determined to save ; but he threw no obstacle in the way of his impeachment. The trial of the Earl

began in Westminster Hall, and the whole of the House of Commons appeared to support it. The passion which the cause excited was seen in the loud cries of sympathy or hatred which burst from the crowded benches on either side. For fifteen days Strafford struggled with a remarkable courage and ingenuity against the list of charges, and melted his audience to tears by the pathos of his defence. But the trial was suddenly interrupted. Though tyranny and misgovernment

Sec. VI.

THE
LONG PAR-
LIAMENT

1640
TO
1644

had been conclusively proved against him, the technical proof of treason was weak. " The law of England," to use Hallam's words, " is silent as to conspiracies against itself," and treason by the Statute of Edward the Third was restricted to a levying of war against the King or a compassing of his death. The Commons endeavoured to strengthen their case by bringing forward the notes of a meeting of a Committee of the Commons in which Strafford had urged the use of his Irish troops " to reduce this kingdom ; " but the Lords would only admit the evidence on condition of wholly reopening the case. Pym and Hampden remained convinced of the sufficiency of the impeachment ; but the Commons broke loose from their control, and, guided by St. John and Henry Marten, resolved to abandon these judicial proceedings, and fall back on the resource of a Bill of Attainder.

Their course has been bitterly censured by some whose opinion in such a matter is entitled to respect. But the crime of Strafford was none the less a crime that it did not fall within the scope of the Statute of Treasons. It is impossible indeed to provide for some of the greatest dangers which can happen to national freedom by any formal statute. Even now a minister might avail himself of the temper of a Parliament elected in some moment of popular panic, and, though the nation returned to its senses, might simply by refusing to appeal to the country govern in defiance of its will. Such a course would be technically legal, but such a minister would be none the less a criminal. Strafford's course, whether it fell within the Statute of Treasons or no, was from beginning to end an attack on the freedom of the whole nation. In the last resort a nation retains the right of self-defence, and the Bill of Attainder is the assertion of such a right for the punishment of a public enemy who falls within the scope of no written law. To save Strafford and Episcopacy Charles seemed to assent to a proposal for entrusting the offices of State to the leaders of the Parliament, with the Earl of Bedford as Lord Treasurer ; the only conditions he made were that Episcopacy should not be abolished nor Strafford executed. But the negotiations were interrupted by Bedford's death, and by the discovery that Charles had been listening all the while to counsellors who proposed to bring about his end by stirring the army to march on London, seize the Tower, free Strafford, and deliver the King from his thraldom to Parliament. The discovery of the Army Plot sealed Strafford's fate. The Londoners were roused to frenzy, and as the Peers gathered at Westminster crowds surrounded the House with cries of " Justice." On May 8 the Lords passed the Bill of Attainder. The Earl's one hope was in the King, but two days later the royal assent was given, and he passed to his doom. Strafford died as he had lived. His friends warned him of the vast multitude gathered before the Tower to witness his fall. " I know how to look death in the face, and the people too," he

SEC. VI.

THE
LONG PAR-
LIAMENT
1640
TO
1644

answered proudly. " I thank God I am no more afraid of death, but
as cheerfully put off my doublet at this time as ever I did when I went
to bed." As the axe fell, the silence of the great multitude was broken
by a universal shout of joy. The streets blazed with bonfires. The
bells clashed out from every steeple. " Many," says an observer, " that
came to town to see the execution rode in triumph back, waving their
hats, and with all expressions of joy through every town they went,
crying, ' His head is off! His head is off ! ' "

**The
Grand
Remon-
strance**

The failure of the attempt to establish a Parliamentary ministry, the
discovery of the Army Plot, the execution of Strafford, were the turning
points in the history of the Long Parliament. Till May there was
still hope for an accommodation between the Commons and the Crown
by which the freedom that had been won might have been taken as
the base of a new system of government. But from that hour little
hope of such an agreement remained. On the one hand, the air, since

The Panic

the army conspiracy, was full of rumours and panic ; the creak of a
few boards revived the memory of the Gunpowder Plot, and the
members rushed out of the House of Commons in the full belief that
it was undermined. On the other hand, Charles regarded his consent
to the new measures as having been extorted by force, and to be
retracted at the first opportunity. Both Houses, in their terror, swore
to defend the Protestant religion and the public liberties, an oath
which was subsequently exacted from every one engaged in civil
employment, and voluntarily taken by the great mass of the people.
The same terror of a counter-revolution induced Hyde and the
" moderate men " in the Commons to agree to a bill providing that
the present Parliament should not be dissolved but by its own consent.
Of all the demands of the Parliament this was the first that could be
called distinctly revolutionary. To consent to it was to establish a
power permanently co-ordinate with the Crown. Charles signed the
bill without protest, but he was already planning the means of breaking
the Parliament. Hitherto, the Scotch army had held him down, but
its payment and withdrawal could no longer be delayed, and a pacification was arranged between the two countries. The Houses hastened
to complete their task of reform. The irregular jurisdictions of the
Council of the North and the Court of the Marches of Wales had been

*Abolition of
the Star
Chamber*

swept away ; and the civil and criminal jurisdiction of the Star Chamber
and the Court of High Commission, the last of the extraordinary courts
which had been the support of the Tudor monarchy, were now summarily abolished. The work was pushed hastily on, for haste was
needed. The two armies had been disbanded ; and the Scots were no
sooner on their way homeward than the King resolved to bring them
back. In spite of prayers from the Parliament he left London for

*Charles in
Scotland*

Edinburgh, yielded to every demand of the Assembly and the Scotch
Estates, attended the Presbyterian worship, lavished titles and favours

on the Earl of Argyle and the patriot leaders, and gained for a few months a popularity which spread dismay in the English Parliament. Their dread of his designs was increased when he was found to have been intriguing all the while with the Earl of Montrose—who had seceded from the patriot party before his coming, and been rewarded for his secession with imprisonment in the castle of Edinburgh—and when Hamilton and Argyle withdrew suddenly from the capital, and charged the King with a treacherous plot to seize and carry them out of the realm. The fright was fanned to frenzy by news from Ireland, where the fall of Strafford left the power in bigoted Puritan hands. Foiled in every effort to secure through Parliament constitutional government, maddened by long misery and by the gloomy prospect of banishment from the land that yet remained and the extirpation of their religion, stirred by the homeless wanderers evicted from their lands, and by the disbanded soldiers of Strafford's army, the people sought a last hope in arms. A national rising was organised with wonderful power and secrecy by Rory O'More (Ruadhri O'Mordha) and Owen Roe (Eoghan ruadh) O'Neill. The military plans were frustrated at the last moment, and the revolt which broke out in Ulster, where the plantation had never been forgiven, was the insurrection of an evicted people against the confiscators. The clansmen drove the English out of their holdings, stripped them of all they possessed, poured into the little towns, seized the churches and public buildings, and captured all the arms they could lay hands on. Outrages of undisciplined bands were met by ferocious cruelty on the part of the Government—a cruelty which roused new districts to revolt. Frenzied tales were spread, by panic and malignity, of Irish atrocities ; they were alleged to have massacred more than three times the total number of English in Ireland, or ten times more than those living in the country parts. Parliament was bent on a war of extermination, and lands to be confiscated were openly sold in advance on the London market. A resolution of the English House of Commons that no toleration should be granted to the Catholic religion in Ireland drove the English Catholics of the Pale to join hands with the Irish. The revolt, unlike any earlier rising, was no longer wholly a struggle of Celt against Saxon, but of Catholic against Protestant. The "Confederate Catholics" resolved to defend " the public and free exercise of the true and Catholic Roman religion." English panic waxed greater when it was found they claimed to be acting by the King's commission, and in aid of his authority. The Commission they showed, purporting to have been issued by royal command at Edinburgh, was a forgery, but belief in it was quickened by the want of all sympathy with the national honour which Charles displayed. To him the revolt seemed a useful check on his opponents. "I hope," he wrote coolly, when the news reached him, "this ill news of Ireland may hinder some of these follies in

Sec. VI.

The
Long Par-
liament
1640
to
1644

Oct. 1641

Sec. VI.

THE
LONG PAR-
LIAMENT
1640
TO
1644

England." Above all, it would necessitate the raising of an army, and with an army at his command he would again be the master of the Parliament. The Parliament, on the other hand, saw in the Irish revolt the disclosure of a vast scheme for a counter-revolution, of which the withdrawal of the Scotch army, the reconciliation of Scotland, the intrigues at Edinburgh, were all parts. Its terror was quickened into panic by the exultation of the royalists at the King's return, and by the appearance of a royalist party in the Parliament itself. The new party had been silently organized by Hyde, the future Lord Clarendon. With him stood Lord Falkland, a man learned and accomplished, the centre of a circle which embraced the most liberal thinkers of his day, a keen reasoner and able speaker, whose intense desire for liberty of religious thought, which he now saw threatened by the dogmatism of the time, estranged him from Parliament, while his dread of a conflict with the Crown, his passionate longing for peace, his sympathy for the fallen, led him to struggle for a King whom he distrusted, and to die in a cause that was not his own. Behind Falkland and Hyde soon gathered a strong force of supporters; chivalrous soldiers like Sir Edmund Verney ("I have eaten the King's bread and served him now thirty years, and I will not do so base a thing as to desert him"), as well as men frightened by the rapid march of change or by the dangers which threatened Episcopacy and the Church, the partizans of the Court, and the time-servers who looked forward to a new triumph of the Crown. With a broken Parliament, and perils gathering without, Pym resolved to appeal for aid to the nation itself. The Grand Remonstrance which he laid before the House was a detailed narrative of the work which the Parliament had done, the difficulties it had surmounted, and the new dangers which lay in its path. The Parliament had been charged with a design to abolish Episcopacy, it declared its purpose to be simply that of reducing the power of bishops. Politically it repudiated the taunt of revolutionary aims. It demanded only the observance of the existing laws against recusancy, securities for the due administration of justice, and the employment of ministers who possessed the confidence of Parliament. The new King's party fought fiercely, debate followed debate, the sittings were prolonged till lights had to be brought in; and it was only at midnight, and by a majority of eleven, that the Remonstrance was finally adopted. On an attempt of the minority to offer a formal protest against a subsequent vote for its publication the slumbering passion broke out into a flame. "Some waved their hats over their heads, and others took their swords in their scabbards out of their belts, and held them by the pommels in their hands, setting the lower part on the ground." Only Hampden's coolness and tact averted a conflict. The Remonstrance was felt on both sides to be a crisis in the struggle. "Had it been rejected," said

SEC. VI.

THE
LONG PAR-
LIAMENT

1640
TO
1644

Arrest
of the
Five
Members

Cromwell, as he left the House, " I would have sold to-morrow all I possess, and left England for ever." Listened to sullenly by the King, it kindled afresh the spirit of the country. London swore to live and die with the Parliament ; associations were formed in every county for the defence of the Houses ; and when the guard which the Commons had asked for in the panic of the Army Plot was withdrawn by the King, the populace crowded down to Westminster to take its place.

The question which had above all broken the unity of the Parliament had been the question of the Church. All were agreed on the necessity of reform, and one of the first acts of the Parliament had been to appoint a Committee of Religion to consider the question. The bulk of the Commons as of the Lords were at first against any radical changes in the constitution or doctrines of the Church. But within as without the House the general opinion was in favour of a reduction of the power and wealth of the prelates, as well as of the jurisdiction of the Church Courts. Even among the bishops themselves, the more prominent saw the need for consenting to the abolition of Chapters and Bishops' Courts, as well as to the election of a council of ministers in each diocese, which had been suggested by Archbishop Usher as a check on episcopal autocracy. A scheme to this effect was drawn up by Bishop Williams of Lincoln ; but it was far from meeting the wishes of the general body of the Commons. Pym and Lord Falkland demanded, in addition to these changes, a severance of the clergy from all secular or state offices, and an expulsion of the bishops from the House of Lords. Such a measure seemed needed to restore the independence of the Peers ; for the number and servility of the bishops were commonly strong enough to prevent any opposition to the Crown. There was, however, a growing party which pressed for the abolition of Episcopacy altogether. The doctrines of Cartwright had risen into popularity under the persecution of Laud, and Presbyterianism was now a formidable force among the middle classes. Its chief strength lay in the eastern counties and in London, where a few ministers such as Calamy and Marshall had formed a committee for its diffusion ; while in Parliament it was represented by Lord Mandeville and some others. In the Commons Sir Harry Vane represented a more extreme party of reformers, the Independents of the future, whose sentiments were little less hostile to Presbyterianism than to Episcopacy, but who acted with the Presbyterians for the present, and formed a part of what became known as the " root and branch party," from its demand for the extirpation of prelacy. The attitude of Scotland in the great struggle against tyranny, and the political advantages of a religious union between the two kingdoms, as well as the desire to knit the English Church more closely to the general body of Protestantism, gave force to the Presbyterian party. Milton, who after the composition of his " Lycidas " had spent a year

SEC. VI.

THE
LONG PAR-
LIAMENT
1640
TO
1644

in foreign travel, returned to throw himself on this ground into the theological strife. He held it "an unjust thing that the English should differ from all Churches as many as be reformed." In spite of this pressure, however, and of a Presbyterian petition from London with fifteen thousand signatures to the same purport, the Committee of Religion reported in favour of the moderate reforms proposed by Falkland and Pym ; and a bill for the removal of bishops from the House of Peers passed the Commons almost unanimously. Rejected by the Lords on the eve of the King's journey to Scotland, it was again introduced on his return. Pym and his colleagues, anxious to close the disunion in their ranks, sought to end the pressure of the Presbyterian zealots, and the dread of the Church party, by taking their stand on the compromise suggested by the Committee of Religion in the spring. But in spite of violent remonstrances from the Commons the bill still hung fire among the Peers. The delay roused the excited crowd of Londoners who gathered round Whitehall ; the bishops' carriages were stopped, and the prelates themselves rabbled on their way to the House. The angry pride of Williams induced ten of his fellow bishops to declare themselves prevented from attendance in Parliament, and to protest against all acts done in their absence as null and void. The protest was met at once on the part of the Peers by the committal of the prelates who had signed it to the Tower. But

*Cavaliers
and
Roundheads*

the contest gave a powerful aid to the projects of the King. The courtiers declared openly that the rabbling of the bishops proved that there was "no free Parliament," and strove to bring about fresh outrages by gathering troops of officers and soldiers of fortune, who were seeking for employment in the Irish war, and pitting them against the crowds at Whitehall. The brawls of the two parties, who gave each other the nicknames of " Roundheads " and " Cavaliers," created fresh alarm in the Parliament ; but Charles persisted in refusing it a guard. " On the honour of a King," he engaged to defend them from violence as completely as his own children, but the answer had hardly been given when his Attorney appeared at the bar of the Lords, and accused Hampden, Pym, Hollis, Strode, and Haselrig of high treason in their correspondence with the Scots. A herald-at-arms appeared at the bar of the Commons, and demanded the surrender of the five members. If Charles believed himself to be within legal forms, the Commons saw a mere act of arbitrary violence in a charge which proceeded personally from the King, which set aside the most cherished privileges of Parliament, and summoned the accused before a tribunal which had no pretence to a jurisdiction over them. The Commons simply promised to take the demand into consideration, and again requested a guard. " I will reply to-morrow," said the King. On the morrow he summoned the gentlemen who clustered round Whitehall

*Jan. 4
1642*

to follow him, and, embracing the Queen, promised her that in an hour

Sec. VI.

The
Long Par-
liament

1640
to
1644

he would return master of his kingdom. A mob of Cavaliers joined him as he left the palace, and remained in Westminster Hall as Charles, accompanied by his nephew, the Elector-Palatine, entered the House of Commons. "Mr. Speaker," he said, "I must for a time borrow your chair!" He paused with a sudden confusion as his eye fell on the vacant spot where Pym commonly sate: for at the news of his approach the House had ordered the five members to withdraw. "Gentlemen," he began in slow broken sentences, "I am sorry for this occasion of coming unto you. Yesterday I sent a Sergeant-at-arms upon a very important occasion, to apprehend some that by my command were accused of high treason, whereunto I did expect obedience, and not a message." Treason, he went on, had no privilege, "and therefore I am come to know if any of these persons that were accused are here." There was a dead silence, only broken by his reiterated "I must have them where-soever I find them." He again paused, but the stillness was unbroken. Then he called out, "Is Mr. Pym here?" There was no answer; and Charles, turning to the Speaker, asked him whether the five members were there. Lenthall fell on his knees; "I have neither eyes to see," he replied, "nor tongue to speak in this place, but as this House is pleased to direct me." "Well, well," Charles angrily retorted, "'tis no matter. I think my eyes are as good as another's!" There was another long pause, while he looked carefully over the ranks of members. "I see," he said at last, "all the birds are flown. I do expect you will send them to me as soon as they return hither." If they did not, he added, he would seek them himself; and with a closing protest that he never intended any force, "he went out of the House," says an eye-witness, "in a more discontented and angry passion than he came in."

Nothing but the absence of the five members, and the calm dignity of the Commons, had prevented the King's outrage from ending in bloodshed. "It was believed," says Whitelock, who was present at the scene, "that if the King had found them there, and called in his guards to have seized them, the members of the House would have endeavoured the defence of them, which might have proved a very unhappy and sad business." Five hundred gentlemen of the best blood in England would hardly have stood tamely by while the bravoes of Whitehall laid hands on their leaders in the midst of the Parliament. But Charles was blind to the danger of his course. The five members had taken refuge in the city, and it was there that on the next day the King himself demanded their surrender from the aldermen at Guildhall. Cries of "Privilege" rang round him as he returned through the streets: the writs issued for the arrest of the five were disregarded by the Sheriffs, and a proclamation issued four days later, declaring them traitors, passed without notice. Terror drove the Cavaliers from Whitehall, and Charles stood absolutely alone; for the

SEC. VI.

THE
LONG PAR-
LIAMENT
1640
TO
1644

outrage had severed him for the moment from his new friends in the Parliament, and from the ministers, Falkland and Colepepper, whom he had chosen among them. But lonely as he was, Charles had resolved on war. The Earl of Newcastle was despatched to muster a royal force in the north ; and on the tenth of January news that the five members were about to return in triumph to Westminster drove Charles from Whitehall. He retired to Hampton Court and to Windsor, while the Trained Bands of London and Southwark on foot, and the London watermen on the river, all sworn " to guard the Parliament, the Kingdom, and the King," escorted Pym and his fellow-members along the Thames to the House of Commons. Both

*Prepara-
tions for
War*

sides prepared for the coming struggle. The Queen sailed from Dover with the Crown jewels to buy munitions of war. The Cavaliers again gathered round the King, and the royalist press flooded the country with State papers drawn up by Hyde. On the other hand, the Commons resolved by vote to secure the great arsenals of the kingdom, Hull, Portsmouth and the Tower ; while mounted processions of free-holders from Buckinghamshire and Kent traversed London on their way to St. Stephen's, vowing to live and die with the Parliament. The Lords were scared out of their policy of obstruction by Pym's bold announcement of the new position taken by the House of Commons. " The Commons," said their leader, " will be glad to have your concurrence and help in saving the kingdom ; but if they fail of it, it should not discourage them in doing their duty. And whether the kingdom be lost or saved, they shall be sorry that the story of this present Parliament should tell posterity that in so great a danger and extremity the House of Commons should be enforced to save the kingdom alone." The effect of Pym's words was seen in the passing of the bill for excluding bishops from the House of Lords. The great point, however, was to secure armed support from the nation at large, and here both sides were in a difficulty. Previous to the innovations introduced by the Tudors, and which had been already questioned by the Commons in a debate on pressing soldiers, the King in himself had no power of calling on his subjects generally to bear arms, save for purposes of restoring order or meeting foreign invasion. On the other hand, no one contended that such a power had ever been exercised by the two Houses without the King ; and Charles steadily refused to consent to a Militia bill, in which the command of the national force was given in every county to men devoted to the Parliamentary cause. Both parties therefore broke through constitutional precedent, the Parliament in appointing the Lord Lieutenants who commanded the Militia by ordinance of the two Houses, Charles in levying forces by royal commissions of array. The

*Outbreak
of War*

King's great difficulty lay in procuring arms, and on the twenty-third of April he suddenly appeared before Hull, the magazine of the north, and demanded admission. The new governor, Sir John Hotham, fell on his knees, but refused to open the gates : and the avowal of his act by the Parliament was followed by the withdrawal of the royalist party among its members from their seats at Westminster. Falkland, Colepepper and Hyde, with thirty-two peers and sixty members of the House of Commons, joined Charles at York ; and Lyttelton, the Lord Keeper, followed with the Great Seal. They aimed at putting a check on the King's projects of war, and their efforts were backed by the general opposition of the country. A great meeting of the Yorkshire freeholders which he convened on Heyworth Moor ended in a petition praying him to be reconciled to the Parliament, and in spite of gifts of plate from the Universities and nobles of his party, arms and money were still wanting for his new levies. The two Houses, on the other hand, gained in unity and vigour by the withdrawal of the royalists. The militia was rapidly enrolled, Lord Warwick named to the command of the fleet, and a loan opened in the city to which the women brought even their wedding rings. The tone of the two Houses had risen with the threat of force : and their last proposals demanded the powers of appointing and dismissing the royal ministers, naming guardians for the royal children, and of virtually controlling military, civil, and religious affairs. " If I granted your demands," replied Charles, " I should be no more than the mere phantom of a king."

SEC. VI.

THE
LONG PAR-
LIAMENT
1640
TO
1644
May 1642

Section VII.—The Civil War. July 1642—Aug. 1646.

[*Authorities.*—To those before given we may add Warburton's biography of Prince Rupert, Mr. Clements Markham's life of Fairfax, the Fairfax Correspondence, and Ludlow's " Memoirs." Sprigg's " Anglia Rediviva" gives an account of the New Model and its doings. For Cromwell, the primary authority is Mr. Carlyle's " Life and Letters," an invaluable store of documents, edited with the care of an antiquary and the genius of a poet. Clarendon, who now becomes of greater value, gives a good account of the Cornish rising.]

The breaking off of negotiations was followed on both sides by preparations for immediate war. Hampden, Pym, and Hollis became the guiding spirits of a Committee of Public Safety which was created by Parliament as its administrative organ ; English and Scotch officers were drawn from the Low Countries, and Lord Essex named commander of an army, which soon rose to twenty thousand foot and four thousand horse. The confidence on the Parliamentary side was great ; " we all thought one battle would decide," Baxter confessed after the first encounter ; for the King was almost destitute of money and arms, and in spite of his strenuous efforts to raise recruits he was embarrassed by the reluctance of his own adherents to begin the struggle. Resolved, however, to force on a contest, he raised the Royal Standard

Edgehill

Aug. 22

at Nottingham "on the evening of a very stormy and tempestuous day," but the country made no answer to his appeal; while Essex, who had quitted London amidst the shouts of a great multitude, with orders from the Parliament to follow the King, "and by battle or other way rescue him from his perfidious counsellors and restore him to Parliament," mustered his army at Northampton. Charles had but a handful of men, and the dash of a few regiments of horse would have ended the war; but Essex shrank from a decisive stroke, and trusted to reduce the King to submission by a show of force. As Charles fell back on Shrewsbury, Essex too moved westward and occupied Worcester. But the whole face of affairs suddenly changed. Catholics and royalists rallied fast to the King's standard, and a bold march on London drew Essex from Worcester to protect the capital. The two armies fell in with one another on the field of Edgehill, near Banbury. The encounter was a surprise, and the battle which followed was little more than a confused combat of horse. At its outset the desertion of Sir Faithful Fortescue with a whole regiment threw the Parliamentary forces into disorder, while the royalist horse on either wing drove the cavalry of the enemy from the field; but the foot soldiers of Lord Essex broke the infantry which formed the centre of the King's line, and though his nephew, Prince Rupert, brought back his squadrons in time to save Charles from capture or flight, the night fell on a drawn battle. The moral advantage, however, rested with the King. Essex had learned that his troopers were no match for the Cavaliers, and his withdrawal to Warwick left open the road to the capital. Rupert pressed for an instant march on London, but the proposal found stubborn opponents among the moderate royalists, who dreaded the complete triumph of Charles as much as his defeat. The King therefore paused for the time at Oxford, where he was received with uproarious welcome; and when the cowardice of its garrison delivered Reading to Rupert's horse, and his daring capture of Brentford drew the royal army in his support almost to the walls of the capital, the panic of the Londoners was already over, and the junction of their trainbands with the army of Essex forced Charles to fall back again on his old quarters. But though the Parliament rallied quickly from the blow of Edgehill, the war, as its area widened through the winter, went steadily for the King. The fortification of Oxford gave him a firm hold on the midland counties; while the balance of the two parties in the north was overthrown by the march of the Earl of Newcastle, with the force he had raised in Northumberland, upon York. Lord Fairfax, the Parliamentary leader in that county, was thrown back on the manufacturing towns of the West Riding, where Puritanism found its stronghold; and the arrival of the Queen with arms from Holland encouraged the royal army to push its scouts across the Trent, and threaten the eastern counties, which held firmly for the Parliament. The stress of the war was shown by the vigorous exertions of the two Houses. Some negotiations which had gone on into the spring were broken off by the old demand that the King should return to his Parliament; London was fortified; and a tax of two millions a year was laid on the districts which adhered to the Parliamentary cause. Essex, whose army had been freshly equipped, was ordered to advance upon Oxford; but though the King held himself ready to fall back on the west, the Earl shrank from again risking his raw army in an encounter. He confined himself to the recapture of Reading, and to a month of idle encampment round Brill.

But while disease thinned his ranks and the royalists beat up his quarters the war went more and more for the King. The inaction of Essex enabled Charles to send a part of his small force at Oxford to strengthen a royalist rising in the west. Nowhere was the royal cause to take so brave or noble a form as among the Cornishmen. Cornwall stood apart from the general life of England: cut off from it not only by differences of blood and speech, but by the feudal tendencies of its people, who clung with a Celtic loyalty to their local chieftains, and suffered their fidelity to the Crown to determine their own. They had as yet done little more than keep the war out of their own county; but the march of a small Parliamentary force under Lord Stamford upon Launceston forced them into action. A little band of Cornishmen gathered round the chivalrous Sir Bevil Greenvil, "so destitute of provisions that the best officers had but a biscuit a day," and with only a handful of powder for the whole force; but starving and outnumbered as they were, they scaled the steep rise of Stratton Hill, sword in hand, and drove Stamford back on Exeter, with a loss of two thousand men, his ordnance and baggage train. Sir Ralph Hopton, the best of the royalist generals, took the command of their army as it advanced into Somerset, and drew the stress of the war into the West. Essex despatched a picked force under Sir William Waller to check their advance; but Somerset was already lost ere he reached Bath, and the Cornishmen stormed his strong position on Lansdowne Hill in the teeth of his guns. But the stubborn fight robbed the victors of their leaders; Hopton was wounded, and Greenvil slain; while soon after, at the siege of Bristol, fell two other heroes of the little army, Sir Nicholas Slanning and Sir John Trevanion, "both young, neither of them above eight and twenty, of entire friendship to one another, and to Sir Bevil Greenvil." Waller, beaten as he was, hung on their weakened force as it moved for aid upon Oxford, and succeeded in cooping up the foot in Devizes. But the horse broke through, and joining a force which Charles had sent to their relief, turned back, and dashed Waller's army to pieces in a fresh victory on Roundway Down. The Cornish rising seemed to decide the fortune of the war; and the succours which his Queen was

SEC. VII.
THE CIVIL
WAR
1642
TO
1646

**The
Cornish
Rising**

May 1643

July 1643

*Death of
Hampden*

bringing him from the army of the North determined Charles to make a fresh advance upon London. He was preparing for this advance, when Rupert in a daring raid from Oxford on the Parliamentary army, met a party of horse with Hampden at its head, on Chalgrove field. The skirmish ended in the success of the royalists, and Hampden was seen riding off the field before the action was done, "which he never used to do," with his head bending down, and resting his hands upon the neck of his horse. He was mortally wounded, and his death seemed an omen of the ruin of the cause he loved. Disaster followed disaster. Essex, more and more anxious for a peace, fell back on Uxbridge; while a cowardly surrender of Bristol to Prince Rupert gave Charles the second city of the kingdom, and the mastery of the West. The news fell on the Parliament "like a sentence of death." The Lords debated nothing but proposals of peace. London itself was divided; " a great multitude of the wives of substantial citizens " clamoured at the door of the Commons for peace; and a flight of six of the few peers who remained at Westminster to the camp at Oxford proved the general despair of the Parliament's success.

**The
Covenant**

From this moment, however, the firmness of the Parliamentary leaders began slowly to reverse the fortunes of the war. If Hampden was gone, Pym remained. The spirit of the Commons was worthy of their great leader : and Waller was received on his return from Roundway Hill "as if he had brought the King prisoner with him." A new army was placed under the command of Lord Manchester to check the progress of Newcastle in the North. But in the West the danger was greatest. Prince Maurice continued his brother Rupert's career of success, and his conquest of Barnstaple and Exeter secured Devon for the King. Gloucester alone interrupted the communications between his forces in Bristol and in the north ; and Charles moved against the city, with hope of a speedy surrender. But the gallant

Sept. 6

resistance of the town called Essex to its relief. It was reduced to a single barrel of powder when the Earl's approach forced Charles to raise the siege ; and the Puritan army fell steadily back again on London, after an indecisive engagement near Newbury, in which Lord Falkland fell, "ingeminating 'Peace, peace!'" and the London trainbands flung Rupert's horsemen roughly off their front of pikes. In this posture of his affairs nothing but a great victory could have saved the King, for the day which witnessed the triumphant return of Essex witnessed the solemn taking of the Covenant. Pym had resolved at last to fling the Scotch sword into the wavering balance ; and in the darkest hour of the Parliament's cause Sir Harry Vane had been despatched

*League with
Scotland*

to Edinburgh to arrange the terms on which the aid of Scotland would be given. First amongst them stood the demand of a "unity in Religion ;" an adoption, in other words, of the Presbyterian system by the Church of England. Events had moved so rapidly since the earlier debates on Church government in the Commons that some arrangement of this kind had become a necessity. The bishops to a man, and the bulk of the clergy whose bent was purely episcopal, had joined the royal cause, and were being expelled from their livings as "delinquents." Some new system of Church government was imperatively called for by the religious necessities of the country ; and, though Pym and the leading statesmen were still in opinion moderate Episcopalians, the growing force of Presbyterianism, and still more the needs of the war, forced them to seek such a system in the adoption of the Scotch discipline. Scotland, for its part, saw that the triumph of the Parliament was necessary for its own security ; and whatever difficulties stood in the way of Vane's wary and rapid negotiations were removed by the King's policy. While Parliament looked for aid to the north, Charles had been seeking assistance from the Irish. Fables of massacre, exaggerated beyond any tragedy on record, had left them the objects of a vengeful hate such as England had hardly known before, but with Charles they were simply counters in his game of king-craft. The conclusion of a truce with the Confederate Catholics left the army under Ormond, now made marquis and Lord Lieutenant, at the King's disposal for service in England. With the promise of Catholic support Charles might even think himself strong enough to strike a blow at the Government in Edinburgh ; and negotiations were soon opened with the Irish Catholics to support by their landing in Argyleshire a rising of the Highlanders under Montrose. None of the King's schemes proved so fatal to his cause as these. As the rumour of his intentions spread, officer after officer in his own army flung down their commissions, the peers who had fled to Oxford fled back again to London, and the royalist reaction in the Parliament itself came utterly to an end. Scotland, anxious for its own safety, hastened to sign the Covenant ; and the Commons, "with uplifted hands," swore in St. Margaret's church to observe it. They pledged themselves to "bring the Churches of God in the three Kingdoms to the nearest conjunction and uniformity in religion, confession of faith, form of Church government, direction for worship and catechizing ; that we, and our posterity after us, may as brethren live in faith and love, and the Lord may delight to live in the midst of us" : to extirpate Popery, prelacy, superstition, schism, and profaneness ; to "preserve the rights and privileges of the Parliament, and the liberties of the Kingdom ;" to punish malignants and opponents of reformation in Church and State ; to "unite the two Kingdoms in a firm peace and union to all posterity." The Covenant ended with a solemn acknowledgement of national sin, and a vow of reformation. "Our true, unfeigned purpose, desire, and endeavour for ourselves and all others under our power and charge, both in public and private, in all duties we owe to God and man, is to amend

SEC. VII.

THE CIVIL
WAR

1642
TO
1646

Marston
Moor

our lives, and each one to go before another in the example of a real reformation."

The conclusion of the Covenant had been the last work of Pym. A "Committee of the Two Kingdoms" which was entrusted after his death in December with the conduct of the war and of foreign affairs did their best to carry out the plans he had formed for the coming year. The vast scope of these plans bears witness to his amazing ability. Three strong armies, comprising a force of fifty thousand men, had been raised for the coming campaign. Essex, with the army of the centre, was charged with the duty of watching the king at Oxford. Waller, with another army, was to hold Prince Maurice in check in the west. The force of fourteen thousand men which had been raised by the zeal of the eastern counties, and in which Cromwell's name was becoming famous as a leader, was raised into a third army under Lord Manchester, ready to co-operate in Yorkshire with Sir Thomas Fairfax. With Alexander Leslie, Lord Leven, at its head, the Scotch army crossed the border in January "in a great frost and snow," and Newcastle was forced to hurry northward to arrest its march. His departure freed the hands of Fairfax, who threw himself on the English troops from Ireland that had landed at Chester, and after cutting them to pieces marched as rapidly back to storm Selby. The danger in his rear called back Newcastle, who returned from confronting the Scots at Durham to throw himself into York, where he was besieged by Fairfax and by the Scotch army. The plans of Pym were now rapidly developed. While Manchester marched with the army of the Associated Counties to join the forces of Fairfax and Lord Leven under the walls of York, Waller and Essex gathered their troops round Oxford. Charles was thrown on the defensive. The troops from Ireland on which he counted had been cut to pieces by Fairfax or by Waller, and in North and South he seemed utterly overmatched. But he was far from despairing. He had already answered Newcastle's cry for aid by despatching Prince Rupert from Oxford to gather forces on the Welsh border ; and the brilliant partizan, after breaking the sieges of Newark and Lathom House, burst over the Lancashire hills into Yorkshire, slipped by the Parliamentary army, and made his way untouched into York. But the success of this feat of arms tempted him to a fresh act of daring ; he resolved on a decisive battle, and a discharge of musketry from the two armies as they faced each other on Marston Moor brought on, as evening gathered, a disorderly engagement. On the one flank a charge of the King's horse broke that of the enemy ; on the other, Cromwell's brigade won as complete a success over Rupert's troopers. "God made them as stubble to our swords," wrote the general at the close of the day ; but in the heat of victory he called back his men from the chase to back Manchester in his attack on the royalist foot, and to rout their other wing of horse as it returned breathless from pursuing the Scots. Nowhere had the fighting been so fierce. A young Puritan who lay dying on the field told Cromwell as he bent over him that one thing lay on his spirit. "I asked him what it was," Cromwell wrote afterwards. "He told me it was that God had not suffered him to be any more the executioner of His enemies." At night-fall all was over; and the royalist cause in the north had perished at a blow. Newcastle fled over sea: York surrendered, and Rupert, with about six thousand horse at his back, rode southward to Oxford. The blow was the more terrible that it fell on Charles at a moment when his danger in the south was being changed into triumph by a series of brilliant and unexpected successes. After a month's siege the King had escaped from Oxford followed by Essex and Waller; had waited till Essex marched to attack Prince Maurice at Lyme; and then, turning fiercely on Waller at Cropredy Bridge, had driven him back broken to London, two days before the battle of Marston Moor. Charles followed up his success by hurrying in the track of Essex, whom he hoped to crush between his own force and that under Maurice. By a fatal error, Essex plunged into Cornwall, where the country was hostile, and where the King hemmed him in among the hills, drew his lines tightly round his army, and forced the whole body of the foot to surrender at his mercy, while the horse cut their way through the besiegers, and Essex himself fled by sea to London. The day of the surrender was signalized by a royalist triumph in Scotland which promised to undo what Marston Moor had done. The Irish Catholics fulfilled their covenant with Charles by the landing of Irish soldiers in Argyle; and as had long since been arranged, Montrose, throwing himself into the Highlands, called the clans to arms. Flinging his new force on that of the Covenanters at Tippermuir, he gained a victory which enabled him to occupy Perth, to sack Aberdeen, and to spread terror to Edinburgh. The news fired Charles, as he came up from the west, to venture on a march upon London; but though the Scots were detained at Newcastle the rest of the victors at Marston Moor lay in his path at Newbury; and their force was strengthened by the soldiers who had surrendered in Cornwall, but who had been again brought into the field. The charges of the royalists failed to break the Parliamentary squadrons, and the soldiers of Essex wiped away the shame of their defeat by flinging themselves on the cannon they had lost, and bringing them back in triumph to their lines. Cromwell would have seized the moment of victory, but the darkness hindered his charging with his single brigade. Manchester, meanwhile, in spite of the prayers of his officers, refused to attack. Like Essex, he shrank from a crowning victory over the King. Charles was allowed to withdraw his army to Oxford, and even to reappear unchecked in the field of his defeat.

The quarrel of Cromwell with Lord Manchester at Newbury was

SEC. VII.

THE CIVIL
WAR

1642
TO
1646

Newbury
Oct. 27

Cromwell

SEC. VII.

THE CIVIL
WAR

1642
TO
1646

1599

destined to give a new colour and direction to the war.   Pym, in fact, had hardly been borne to his grave in Westminster Abbey before England instinctively recognized a successor of yet greater genius in the victor of Marston Moor.   Born in the closing years of Elizabeth's reign, the child of a cadet of the great house of the Cromwells of Hinchinbrook, and of kin through their mothers with Hampden and St. John, Oliver had been recalled by his father's death from a short stay at Cambridge to the little family estate at Huntingdon, which he quitted for a farm at St. Ives.   We have already seen his mood during the years of personal rule, as he dwelt in "prolonging" and "blackness" amidst fancies of coming death, the melancholy which formed the ground of his nature feeding itself on the inaction of the time.   But his energy made itself felt the moment the tyranny was over.   His father had sat, with three of his uncles, in the later Parliaments of Elizabeth.   Oliver had himself been returned to that of 1628, and the town of Cambridge sent him as its representative to the Short Parliament as to the Long.   It is in the latter that a courtier, Sir Philip Warwick, gives us our first glimpse of his actual appearance.   "I came into the House one morning, well clad, and perceived a gentleman speaking whom I knew not, very ordinarily apparelled, for it was a plain cloth suit, which seemed to have been made by an ill country tailor.   His linen was plain, and not very clean ; and I remember a speck or two of blood upon his little band, which was not much larger than his collar. His hat was without a hat-band.   His stature was of a good size ; his sword stuck close to his side ; his countenance swoln and reddish ; his voice sharp and untuneable, and his eloquence full of fervour."   He was already "much hearkened unto," but his power was to assert itself in deeds rather than in words.   Men of his own time marked him out

Cromwell's brigade

from all others by the epithet of Ironside.   He appeared at the head of a troop of his own raising at Edgehill ; but with the eye of a born soldier he at once saw the blot in the army of Essex.   "A set of poor tapsters and town apprentices," he warned Hampden, "would never fight against men of honour ;" and he pointed to religious enthusiasm as the one weapon which could meet the chivalry of the Cavalier.   Even to Hampden the plan seemed impracticable ; but the regiment of a thousand men which Cromwell raised for the Association of the Eastern Counties was formed strictly of "men of religion."   He spent his fortune freely on the task he set himself.   "The business . . . . hath had of me in money between eleven and twelve hundred pounds, therefore my private estate can do little to help the public. . . . I have little money of my own (left) to help my soldiers."   But they were "a lovely company," he tells his friends with soldierly pride.   No blasphemy, drinking, disorder, or impiety were suffered in their ranks.   "Not a man swears but he pays his twelve pence."   Nor was his choice of "men of religion" the only innovation Cromwell introduced into his new regiment.   The social traditions which restricted command to men of birth were disregarded. "It may be," he wrote, in answer to complaints from the committee of the Association, "it provokes your spirit to see such plain men made captains of horse. It had been well that men of honour and birth had entered into their employments; but why do they not appear? But seeing it is necessary the work must go on, better plain men than none: but best to have men patient of wants, faithful and conscientious in their employment, and such, I hope, these will approve themselves." The words paint Cromwell's temper accurately enough: he is far more of the practical soldier than of the reformer; though his genius already breaks in upon his aristocratic and conservative sympathies, and catches glimpses of the social revolution to which the war was drifting. "I had rather," he once burst out impatiently, "have a plain russet-coated captain, that knows what he fights for and loves what he knows, than what you call a gentleman, and is nothing else. I honour a gentleman that is so indeed!" he ends with a characteristic return to his more common mood of feeling. The same practical temper broke out in a more startling innovation. Bitter as had been his hatred of the bishops, and strenuously as he had worked to bring about a change in Church government, Cromwell, like most of the Parliamentary leaders, seems to have been content with the new Presbyterianism, and the Presbyterians were more than content with him. Lord Manchester "suffered him to guide the army at his pleasure." "The man, Cromwell," writes the Scotchman Baillie, "is a very wise and active head, universally well beloved as religious and stout." But against dissidents from the legal worship of the Church the Presbyterians were as bitter as Laud himself; and, as we shall see, Nonconformity was rising into proportions which made its claim of toleration, of the freedom of religious worship, one of the problems of the time. Cromwell met the problem in his unspeculative fashion. He wanted good soldiers and good men; and, if they were these, the Independent, the Baptist, the Leveller, found entry among his troops. "You would respect them, did you see them," he answered the panic-stricken Presbyterians who charged them with "Anabaptistry" and revolutionary aims: "they are no Anabaptists: they are honest, sober Christians; they expect to be used as men." He was soon to be driven—as in the social change we noticed before —to a far larger and grander point of view. But as yet he was busier with his new regiment than with theories of Church and State; and his horsemen were no sooner in action than they proved themselves such soldiers as the war had never seen yet. "Truly they were never beaten at all," their leader said proudly at its close. At Winceby fight they charged "singing psalms," cleared Lincolnshire of the Cavaliers, and freed the eastern counties from all danger from Newcastle's partizans. At Marston Moor they faced and routed Rupert's chivalry. At

SEC. VII.

THE CIVIL
WAR

1642
TO
1646
The New
Model

Newbury it was only Manchester's reluctance that hindered them from completing the ruin of Charles.

Cromwell had shown his capacity for organization in the creation of his regiment ; his military genius had displayed itself at Marston Moor. Newbury first raised him into a political leader. "Without a more speedy, vigorous, and effective prosecution of the war," he said to the Commons after his quarrel with Manchester, " casting off all lingering proceedings, like those of soldiers of fortune beyond sea to spin out a war, we shall make the kingdom weary of us, and hate the name of a Parliament." But under the leaders who at present conducted it a vigorous conduct of the war was hopeless. They were, in Cromwell's plain words, " afraid to conquer." They desired not to crush Charles, but to force him back, with as much of his old strength remaining as might be, to the position of a constitutional King. The old loyalty, too, clogged their enterprise ; they shrank from the taint of treason. " If the King be beaten," Manchester urged at Newbury, " he will still be king ; if he beat us he will hang us all for traitors." To a mood like this Cromwell's attitude seemed horrible: " If I met the King in battle," he answered, according to a later story, " I would fire my pistol at the King as at another." The army, too, as he long ago urged at Edge-hill, was not an army to conquer with. Now, as then, he urged that till the whole force was new modelled, and placed under a stricter discipline, "they must not expect any notable success in anything they went about." But the first step in such a re-organization must be a change of officers. The army was led and officered by members of the two Houses, and the Self-denying Ordinance, as it was intro-

duced by Cromwell and Vane, declared the tenure of military or civil offices incompatible with a seat in either. The long and bitter resistance which this measure met before it was finally passed in a modified form was justified at a later time by the political results which followed the rupture of the tie which had hitherto bound the army to the Parliament. But the drift of public opinion was too strong to be withstood. The passage of the Ordinance brought about the retirement of Essex, Manchester, and Waller ; and the new organization of the army went rapidly on under a new commander-in-chief, Sir Thomas Fairfax, the hero of the long contest in Yorkshire, and who had been raised into fame by his victory at Nantwich, and his bravery at Marston Moor. But behind Fairfax stood Cromwell ; and the principles on which Cromwell had formed his brigade were carried out on a larger scale in the " New Model." The one aim was to get together twenty thousand " honest " men. " Be careful," Cromwell had written, " what captains of horse you choose, what men be mounted. A few honest men are better than numbers. If you choose godly honest men to be captains of horse, honest men will follow them." The result was a curious medley of men of different ranks among the officers of the New

Model. The bulk of those in high command remained men of noble or gentle blood, Montagues, Pickerings, Fortescues, Sheffields, Sidneys, and the like. But side by side with these, though in far smaller proportion, were seen officers like Ewer, who had been a serving-man, like Okey, who had been a drayman, or Rainsborough, who had been a " skipper at sea." A result hardly less notable was the youth of the officers. Among those in high command there were few who, like Cromwell, had passed middle age. Fairfax was but thirty-three, and most of his colonels were even younger. Equally strange was the mixture of religions in its ranks ; though a large proportion of the infantry was composed of pressed recruits, the cavalry was for the most part strongly Puritan, and in that part of the army especially dissidence of every type had gained a firm foothold.

Of the political and religious aspect of the New Model we shall have to speak at a later time ; as yet its energy was directed solely to " the speedy and vigorous prosecution of the war." Fairfax was no sooner ready for action than the policy of Cromwell was aided by the policy of the King. From the hour when Newbury marked the breach between the peace and war parties in the Parliament, the Scotch Commissioners and the bulk of the Commons had seen that their one chance of hindering what they looked on as revolution in Church and State lay in pressing for fresh negotiations with Charles. Commissioners met at Uxbridge to draw up a treaty ; but the hopes of concession which Charles held out were suddenly withdrawn in the spring. He saw, as he thought, the Parliamentary army dissolved and ruined by its new modelling, at an instant when news came from Scotland of fresh successes on the part of Montrose, and of his overthrow of the Marquis of Argyle's troops in the victory of Inverlochy. " Before the end of the summer," wrote the conqueror, " I shall be in a position to come to your Majesty's aid with a brave army." The party of war gained the ascendant ; and in May the King opened his campaign by a march to the north. Leicester was stormed, the blockade of Chester raised, and the eastern counties threatened, until Fairfax, who had been unwillingly engaged in a siege of Oxford, hurried at last on his track. Cromwell, who had been suffered by the House to retain his command for a few days in spite of the Ordinance, joined Fairfax as he drew near the King, and his arrival was greeted by loud shouts of welcome from the troops. The two armies met near Naseby, to the north-west of Northampton. The King was eager to fight. " Never have my affairs been in as good a state," he cried ; and Prince Rupert was as impatient as his uncle. On the other side, even Cromwell doubted as a soldier the success of the newly-drilled troops, though religious enthusiasm swept away doubt in the assurance of victory. " I can say this of Naseby," he wrote soon after, " that when I saw the enemy draw up and march in gallant order towards us, and we a company of poor

SEC. VII.

THE CIVIL
WAR

1642
TO
1646

Naseby

June 14
1645

ignorant men, to seek to order our battle, the general having commanded me to order all the horse, I could not, riding alone about my business, but smile out to God in praises, in assurance of victory, because God would by things that are not bring to nought things that are. Of which I had great assurance, and God did it." The battle began with a furious charge of Rupert uphill, which routed the wing opposed to him under Ireton ; while the royalist foot, after a single discharge, clubbed their muskets and fell on the centre under Fairfax so hotly that it slowly and stubbornly gave way. But Cromwell's brigade were conquerors on the left. A single charge broke the northern horse under Langdale, who had already fled before them at Marston Moor ; and holding his troops firmly in hand, Cromwell fell with them on the flank of the royalist foot in the very crisis of its success. A panic of the King's reserve, and its flight from the field, aided his efforts : it was in vain that Rupert returned with forces exhausted by pursuit, that Charles, in a passion of despair, called on his troopers for " one charge more." The battle was over : artillery, baggage, even the royal papers, fell into the conquerors' hands ; five thousand men surrendered ; only two thousand followed the King in his headlong flight from the field. The war was ended at a blow.

While Charles wandered helplessly along the Welsh border in search of fresh forces, Fairfax marched rapidly into Somersetshire, and routed the royal forces at Langport. A victory at Kilsyth, which gave Scotland for the moment to Montrose, threw a transient gleam over the darkening fortunes of his master's cause ; but the surrender of Bristol to the Parliamentary army, and the dispersion of the last force Charles could collect in an attempt to relieve Chester, was followed by news of the

crushing and irretrievable defeat of the " Great Marquis " at Philiphaugh. In the wreck of the royal cause we may pause for a moment over an incident which brings out in relief the best temper of both sides. Cromwell " spent much time with God in prayer before the storm " of Basing House, where the Marquis of Winchester had held stoutly out through the war for the King. The storm ended its resistance, and the brave old royalist was brought in a prisoner with his house flaming around him. He " broke out," reports a Puritan bystander, " and said, 'that if the King had no more ground in England but Basing House he would adventure it as he did, and so maintain it to the uttermost,' comforting himself in this matter 'that Basing House was called Loyalty.' " Of loyalty such as this Charles was utterly unworthy. The seizure of his papers at Naseby had hardly disclosed his earlier intrigues with the Irish Catholics when the Parliament was able to reveal to England a fresh treaty with them, which purchased no longer their neutrality, but their aid, by the simple concession of every demand they had made. The shame was without profit, for whatever aid Ireland might have given came too late to be of service. The spring of 1646 saw the few troops who still clung to Charles surrounded and routed at Stow. "You have done your work now," their leader, Sir Jacob Astley, said bitterly to his conquerors, "and may go to play, unless you fall out among yourselves."

SEC. VIII.

THE ARMY
AND THE
PARLIA-
MENT

1646
TO
1649

Section VIII.—The Army and the Parliament. 1646–1649.

[*Authorities.*—Mainly as before, though Clarendon, invaluable during the war, is tedious and unimportant here, and Cromwell's letters become, unfortunately, few at the moment when we most need their aid. On the other hand Ludlow and Whitelock, as well as the passionate and unscrupulous "Memoirs" of Holles and Major Hutchinson, become of much importance. For Charles himself, we have Sir Thomas Herbert's "Memoirs" of the last two years of this reign. Burnet's "Lives of the Hamiltons" throw a good deal of light on Scotch affairs at this time, and Sir James Turner's "Memoir of the Scotch Invasion." The early history of the Independents, and of the principle of religious freedom, is told by Mr. Masson ("Life of Milton," vol. iii.).]

With the close of the Civil War we enter on a time of confused struggles, a time tedious and uninteresting in its outer details, but of higher interest than even the war itself in its bearing on our after history. Modern England, the England among whose thoughts and sentiments we actually live, began however dimly with the triumph of Naseby. Old things passed silently away. When Astley gave up his sword the "work" of the generations which had struggled for Protestantism against Catholicism, for public liberty against absolute rule, in his own emphatic phrase, was "done." So far as these contests were concerned, however the later Stuarts might strive to revive them, England could safely "go to play." But with the end of this older work a new work began. The constitutional and ecclesiastical problems which still in one shape or another beset us started to the front as subjects of national debate in the years between the close of the Civil War and the death of the King. The great parties which have ever since divided the social, the political, and the religious life of England, whether as Independents and Presbyterians, as Whigs and Tories, as Conservatives and Liberals, sprang into organized existence in the contest between the Army and the Parliament. Then for the first time began a struggle which is far from having ended yet, a struggle between political tradition and political progress, between the principle of religious conformity and the principle of religious freedom.

It was the religious struggle which drew the political in its train. We have already witnessed the rise under Elizabeth of sects who did not aim, like the Presbyterians, at a change in Church government, but rejected the notion of a national Church at all, and insisted on the right of each congregation to perfect independence of faith and worship. At the close of the Queen's reign, however, these "Brownists" had

SEC. VIII .

THE ARMY
AND THE
PARLIA-
MENT
1646
TO
1649

almost entirely disappeared. Some of the dissidents, as in the notable
instance of the congregation that produced the Pilgrim Fathers, had
found a refuge in Holland ; but the bulk had been driven by persecution to a fresh conformity with the Established Church. " As for
those which we call Brownists," says Bacon, " being when they were
at the best a very small number of very silly and base people, here and
there in corners dispersed, they are now, thanks to God, by the good
remedies that have been used, suppressed and worn out so that there
is scarce any news of them."   As soon, however, as Abbot's primacy
promised a milder rule, the Separatist refugees began to venture
timidly back again to England. During their exile in Holland the
main body had contented themselves with the free developement of
their system of independent congregations, each forming in itself a
complete Church, and to them the name of Independents attached
itself at a later time. A small part, however, had drifted into a more
marked severance in doctrine from the Established Church, especially
in their belief of the necessity of adult baptism, a belief from which
their obscure congregation at Leyden became known as that of the
Baptists.   Both of these sects gathered a church in London in the
middle of James's reign, but the persecuting zeal of Laud prevented
any spread of their opinions under that of his successor ; and it was
not till their numbers were suddenly increased by the return of a host
of emigrants from New England, with Hugh Peters at their head, on

1640   the opening of the Long Parliament, that the Congregational or Independent body began to attract attention.   Lilburne and Burton soon
declared themselves adherents of what was called " the New England
way ; " and a year later saw in London alone the rise of " four score
congregations of several sectaries," as Bishop Hall scornfully tells us,
" instructed by guides fit for them, cobblers, tailors, felt-makers,
and such-like trash."   But little religious weight however could be
attributed as yet to the Congregational movement.   Baxter at this
time had not heard of the existence of any Independents.   Milton in
his earlier pamphlets shows no sign of their influence.   Of the
hundred and five ministers present in the Westminster Assembly
only five were Congregational in sympathy, and these were all returned
refugees from Holland.   Among the one hundred and twenty London
ministers in 1643, only three were suspected of leanings towards the
Sectaries.

**Presby-
terian
England**
The struggle with Charles in fact at its outset only threw new
difficulties in the way of religious freedom.   It was with strictly conservative aims in ecclesiastical as in political matters that Pym and
his colleagues began the strife.   Their avowed purpose was simply to
restore the Church of England to its state under Elizabeth, and to free
it from " innovations," from the changes introduced by Laud and his
fellow prelates.   The great majority of the Parliament were averse to

SEC. VIII.

THE ARMY
AND THE
PARLIA-
MENT

1646
TO
1649

any alterations in the constitution or doctrine of the Church itself; and it was only the refusal of the bishops to accept any diminution of their power and revenues, the growth of a party hostile to Episcopalian government, the necessity for purchasing the aid of the Scots by a union in religion as in politics, and above all the urgent need of constructing some new ecclesiastical organization in the place of the older organization which had become impossible from the political attitude of the bishops, that forced on the two Houses the adoption of the Covenant. But the change to a Presbyterian system of Church government seemed at that time of little import to the bulk of Englishmen. The dogma of the necessity of bishops was held by few, and the change was generally regarded with approval as one which brought the Church of England nearer to that of Scotland and to the reformed Churches of the Continent. But whatever might be the change in its administration, no one imagined that it had ceased to be the Church of England, or that it had parted with its right to exact conformity to its worship from the nation at large. The Tudor theory of its relation to the State, of its right to embrace all Englishmen within its pale, and to dictate what should be their faith and form of worship, remained utterly unquestioned by any man of note. The sentiments on which such a theory rested indeed for its main support, the power of historical tradition, the association of "dissidence" with danger to the State, the strong English instinct of order, the as strong English dislike of "innovations," with the abhorrence of "indifferency," as a sign of lukewarmness in matters of religion, had only been intensified by the earlier incidents of the struggle with the King. The Parliament therefore had steadily pressed on the new system of ecclesiastical government in the midst of the troubles of the war. An Assembly of Divines which was called together at Westminster in 1643, and which sat in the Jerusalem Chamber during the five years which followed, was directed to revise the Articles, to draw up a Confession of Faith, and a Directory of Public Worship; and these with a scheme of Church government, a scheme only distinguished from that of Scotland by the significant addition of a lay court of superior appeal set by Parliament over the whole system of Church courts and assemblies, were accepted by the Houses and embodied in a series of Ordinances.

Had the change been made at the moment when "with uplifted hands" the Commons swore to the Covenant in St. Margaret's it would probably have been accepted by the country at large. But it met with a very different welcome when it came at the end of the war. In spite of repeated votes of Parliament for its establishment, the pure Presbyterian system took root only in London and Lancashire. While the Divines, indeed, were drawing up their platform of uniform belief and worship in the Jerusalem Chamber, dissidence had grown into a religious power. In the terrible agony of the struggle

SEC. VIII.

THE ARMY
AND THE
PARLIA-
MENT
1646
TO
1649

against Charles, individual conviction became a stronger force than religious tradition. Theological speculation took an unprecedented boldness from the temper of the times. Four years after the war had begun a horror-stricken pamphleteer numbered sixteen religious sects as existing in defiance of the law ; and, widely as these bodies differed among themselves, all were at one in repudiating any right of control in faith or worship by the Church or its clergy. Milton himself had left his Presbyterian stand-point, and saw that "new Presbyter is but old Priest writ large." The question of sectarianism soon grew into a practical one from its bearing on the war : for the class specially infected with the new spirit of religious freedom was just the class to whose zeal and vigour the Parliament was forced to look for success in its struggle. We have seen the prevalence of this spirit among the farmers from whom Cromwell drew his horsemen, and his enlistment of these "sectaries" was the first direct breach in the old system of conformity. The sentiments of the farmers indeed were not his own.

Cromwell and tolera- tion

Cromwell had signed the Covenant, and there is no reason for crediting him with any aversion to Presbyterianism as a system of doctrine or of Church organization. His first step was a purely practical one, a step dictated by military necessities, and excused in his mind by a sympathy with "honest" men, as well as by the growing but still vague notion of a communion among Christians wider than that of outer conformity in worship or belief. But the alarm and remonstrances of the Presbyterians forced his mind rapidly forward on the path of tole- ration. "The State in choosing men to serve it," Cromwell wrote before Marston Moor, "takes no notice of these opinions. If they be willing faithfully to serve it, that satisfies." Marston Moor spurred him to press on the Parliament the need of at least "tolerating" dissi- dents ; and he succeeded in procuring the appointment of a Committee of the Commons to find some means of effecting this. But the con- servative temper of the bulk of the Puritans was at last roused by his efforts. "We detest and abhor," wrote the London clergy in 1645, "the much endeavoured Toleration ; " and the Corporation of London petitioned Parliament to suppress all sects "without toleration." The Parliament itself too remained steady on the conservative side. But the fortunes of the war told for religious freedom. Essex and his Presbyterians only marched from defeat to defeat. In remodelling the army the Commons had rejected a demand made by the Lords that officers and men, besides taking the Covenant, should submit "to the form of Church government that was already voted by both Houses." The victory of Naseby raised a wider question than that of mere toleration. "Honest men served you faithfully in this action," Cromwell wrote to the Speaker of the House of Commons from the field. "Sir, they are trusty : I beseech you in the name of God not to discourage them. He that ventures his life for the liberty of his country, I wish he trust God for the liberty of his conscience." The storm of Bristol encouraged him to proclaim the new principles yet more distinctly. "Presbyterians, Independents, all here have the same spirit of faith and prayer, the same presence and answer. They agree here, have no names of difference; pity it is it should be otherwise anywhere. All that believe have the real unity, which is the most glorious, being the inward and spiritual, in the body and in the head. For being united in forms (commonly called uniformity), every Christian will for peace' sake study and do as far as conscience will permit. And from brethren in things of the mind we look for no compulsion but that of light and reason."

The increasing firmness of Cromwell's language was due to the growing irritation of his opponents. The two parties became every day more clearly defined. The Presbyterian ministers complained bitterly of the increase of the sectaries, and denounced the toleration which had come into practical existence without sanction from the law. Scotland, whose army was still before Newark, pressed for the execution of the Covenant and the universal enforcement of a religious uniformity. Sir Harry Vane, on the other hand, was striving to bring the Parliament round to less rigid courses by the introduction of two hundred and thirty new members, who filled the seats left vacant by royalist secessions, and the more eminent of whom, such as Ireton and Algernon Sidney, were inclined to support the Independents. But it was only the pressure of the New Model, and the remonstrances of Cromwell as its mouthpiece, which hindered any effective movement towards persecution. Amidst the wreck of his fortunes Charles intrigued busily with both parties, and promised liberty of worship to Vane and the Independents, at the moment when he was negotiating with the Parliament and the Scots. His negotiations were quickened by the march of Fairfax upon Oxford. Driven from his last refuge, the King after some aimless wanderings made his appearance in the camp of the Scots. Lord Leven at once fell back with his royal prize to Newcastle. The new aspect of affairs threatened the party of religious freedom with ruin. Hated as they were by the Scots, by the Lords, by the city of London, the apparent junction of Charles with their enemies destroyed their growing hopes in the Commons, where the prospects of a speedy peace on Presbyterian terms at once swelled the majority of their opponents. The two Houses laid their conditions of peace before the King without a dream of resistance from one who seemed to have placed himself at their mercy. They required for the Parliament the command of the army and fleet for twenty years; the exclusion of all "Malignants," or royalists who had taken part in the war, from civil and military office; the abolition of Episcopacy; and the establishment of a Presbyterian Church. Of toleration or liberty of conscience they said not a word. The Scots pressed these terms

Sec. VIII.

The Army
and the
Parlia-
ment
1646
to
1649

Charles
and the
Presby-
terians

*Charles in
the Scotch
Camp
May* 1646

SEC. VIII.

THE ARMY
AND THE
PARLIA-
MENT
1646
TO
1649

on the King "with tears;" his friends, and even the Queen, urged their acceptance. But the aim of Charles was simply delay. Time and the dissensions of his enemies, as he believed, were fighting for him. "I am not without hope," he wrote coolly, "that I shall be able to draw either the Presbyterians or the Independents to side with me for extirpating one another, so that I shall be really King again." His refusal of the terms offered by the Houses was a crushing defeat for the Presbyterians. "What will become of us," asked one of them, "now that the King has rejected our proposals?" "What would have become of us," retorted an Independent, "had he accepted them?" The vigour of Holles and the Conservative leaders in the Parliament rallied however to a bolder effort. The King's game lay in balancing the army against the Parliament; and while the Scotch army lay at Newcastle the Houses could not insist on dismissing their own. It was only a withdrawal of the Scots from England and their transfer of the King's person into the hands of the Houses that would enable them to free themselves from the pressure of their own soldiers by disbanding the New Model. Hopeless of success with the King, and unable to bring him into Scotland in face of the refusal of the General Assembly to receive a sovereign who would not swear to the Covenant, the Scottish army accepted £400,000 in discharge of its claims, handed Charles over to a committee of the Houses, and marched back over the Border. Masters of the King, the Presbyterian leaders at once moved boldly to their attack on the New Model and the Sectaries. They voted that the army should be disbanded, and that a new army should be raised for the suppression of the Irish rebellion with Presbyterian officers at its head. It was in vain that the men protested against being severed from "officers that we love," and that the Council of Officers strove to gain time by pressing on the Parliament the danger of mutiny. Holles and his fellow-leaders were resolute, and their ecclesiastical legislation showed the end at which their resolution aimed. Direct enforcement of conformity was impossible till the New Model was disbanded; but the Parliament pressed on in the work of providing the machinery for enforcing it as soon as the army was gone. Vote after vote ordered the setting up of Presbyteries throughout the country, and the first-fruits of these efforts were seen in the Presbyterian organization of London, and in the first meeting of its Synod at St. Paul's. Even the officers on Fairfax's staff were ordered to take the Covenant.

All hung however on the disbanding of the New Model, and the New Model showed no will to disband itself. Its attitude can only fairly be judged by remembering what many of the conquerors of Naseby really were. They were soldiers of a different class and of a different temper from the soldiers of any other army that the world has seen. They were for the most part young farmers and tradesmen of

SEC. VIII.

THE ARMY
AND THE
PARLIA-
MENT

1646
TO
1649

the lower sort, maintaining themselves, for the pay was twelve months in arrear, mainly at their own cost. The horsemen in many regiments had been specially picked as "honest," or religious men; and whatever enthusiasm or fanaticism they may have shown, their very enemies acknowledged the order and piety of their camp. They looked on themselves not as swordsmen, to be caught up and flung away at the will of a paymaster, but as men who had left farm and merchandise at a direct call from God. A great work had been given them to do, and the call bound them till it was done. Kingcraft, as Charles was hoping, might yet restore tyranny to the throne. A more immediate danger threatened that liberty of conscience which was to them "the ground of the quarrel, and for which so many of their friends' lives had been lost, and so much of their own blood had been spilt." They would wait before disbanding till these liberties were secured, and if need came they would again act to secure them. But their resolve sprang from no pride in the brute force of the sword they wielded. On the contrary, as they pleaded passionately at the bar of the Commons, "on becoming soldiers we have not ceased to be citizens." Their aims and proposals throughout were purely those of citizens, and of citizens who were ready the moment their aim was won to return peacefully to their homes. Thought and discussion had turned the army into a vast Parliament, a Parliament which regarded itself as representative of "godly" men in as high a degree as the Parliament at Westminster, and which must have become every day more conscious of its superiority in political capacity to its rival. Ireton, the moving spirit of the New Model, had no equal as a statesman in St. Stephen's: nor is it possible to compare the large and far-sighted proposals of the army with the blind and narrow policy of the two Houses. Whatever we may think of the means by which the New Model sought its aims, we must in justice remember that, so far as those aims went, the New Model was in the right. For the last two hundred years England has been doing little more than carrying out in a slow and tentative way the scheme of political and religious reform which the army propounded at the close of the Civil War. It was not till the rejection of the officers' proposals had left little hope of conciliation that the army acted, but its action was quick and decisive. It set aside for all political purposes the Council of Officers, and elected a new Council of Agitators or Agents, two members being named by each regiment, which summoned a general meeting of the army at Triploe Heath, where the proposals of pay and disbanding made by the Parliament were rejected with cries of "Justice." While the army was gathering, in fact, the Agitators had taken a step which put submission out of the question. A rumour that the King was to be removed to London, a new army raised, a new civil war begun, roused the soldiers to madness. Five hundred troopers suddenly

*The seizure
of the King*
June 1647

SEC. VIII.

THE ARMY
AND THE
PARLIA-
MENT
1646
TO
1649

appeared before Holmby House, where the King was residing in charge of Parliamentary Commissioners, and displaced its guards. "Where is your commission for this act?" Charles asked the cornet who commanded them. "It is behind me," said Joyce, pointing to his soldiers. "It is written in very fine and legible characters," laughed the King. The seizure had in fact been previously concerted between Charles and the Agitators. "I will part willingly," he told Joyce, "if the soldiers confirm all that you have promised me. You will exact from me nothing that offends my conscience or my honour." "It is not our maxim," replied the cornet, "to constrain the conscience of any one, still less that of our King." After a fresh burst of terror at the news, the Parliament fell furiously on Cromwell, who had relinquished his command and quitted the army before the close of the war, and had ever since been employed as a mediator between the two parties. The charge of having incited the mutiny fell before his vehement protest, but he was driven to seek refuge with the army, and on the 25th of June it was in full march upon London. Its demands were expressed with perfect clearness in an "Humble Representation" which it addressed to the Houses. "We desire a settlement of the Peace of the kingdom and of the liberties of the subject according to the votes and declarations of Parliament. We desire no alteration in the civil government: as little do we desire to interrupt or in the least to intermeddle with the settling of the Presbyterial government." They demanded toleration; but "not to open a way to licentious living under pretence of obtaining ease for tender consciences, we profess, as ever, in these things when the state has made a settlement we have nothing to say, but to submit or suffer." It was with a view to such a settlement that they demanded the expulsion of eleven members from the Commons, with Holles at their head, whom the soldiers charged with stirring up strife between the army and the Parliament, and with a design of renewing the civil war. After fruitless negotiations the terror of the Londoners forced the eleven to withdraw; and the Houses named Commissioners to treat on the questions at issue.

The
Army
and the
King

Though Fairfax and Cromwell had been forced from their position as mediators into a hearty co-operation with the army, its political direction rested at this moment with Cromwell's son-in-law, Henry Ireton, and Ireton looked for a real settlement, not to the Parliament, but to the King. "There must be some difference," he urged bluntly, "between conquerors and conquered;" but the terms which he laid before Charles were terms of studied moderation. The vindictive spirit which the Parliament had shown against the royalists and the Church disappeared in the terms exacted by the New Model; and the army contented itself with the banishment of seven leading "delinquents," a general Act of Oblivion for the rest, the withdrawal of all

Sec. VIII.

The Army
and the
Parlia-
ment
1646
to
1649

coercive power from the clergy, the control of Parliament over the military and naval forces for ten years, and its nomination of the great officers of State. Behind these demands however came a masterly and comprehensive plan of political reform which had already been sketched by the army in the "Humble Representation," with which it had begun its march on London. Belief and worship were to be free to all. Acts enforcing the use of the Prayer-book, or attendance at Church, or the enforcement of the Covenant were to be repealed. Even Catholics, whatever other restraints might be imposed, were to be freed from the bondage of compulsory worship. Parliaments were to be triennial, and the House of Commons to be reformed by a fairer distribution of seats and of electoral rights; taxation was to be re-adjusted; legal procedure simplified; a crowd of political, commercial, and judicial privileges abolished. Ireton believed that Charles could be "so managed" (says Mrs. Hutchinson) "as to comply with the public good of his people after he could no longer uphold his violent will." But Charles was equally dead to the moderation and to the wisdom of this great Act of Settlement. He saw in the crisis nothing but an opportunity of balancing one party against another; and be-lieved that the army had more need of his aid than he of the army's. "You cannot do without me—you are lost if I do not support you," he said to Ireton as he pressed his proposals. "You have an intention to be the arbitrator between us and the Parliament," Ireton quietly replied, "and we mean to be so between the Parliament and your Majesty." But the King's tone was soon explained. A mob of Londoners broke into the House of Commons, and forced its members to recall the eleven. While some fourteen peers and a hundred com-moners fled to the army, those who remained at Westminster prepared for an open struggle with it, and invited Charles to return to London. But the news no sooner reached the camp than the army was again on the march. "In two days," Cromwell said coolly, "the city will be in our hands." The soldiers entered London in triumph, and restored the fugitive members; the eleven were again expelled, and the army leaders resumed negotiations with the King. The indignation of the soldiers at his delays and intrigues made the task hourly more difficult; but Cromwell, who now threw his whole weight on Ireton's side, clung to the hope of accommodation with a passionate tenacity. His mind, conservative by tradition, and above all practical in temper, saw the political difficulties which would follow on the abolition of Monarchy, and in spite of the King's evasions he persisted in negotiating with him. But Cromwell stood almost alone; the Parliament refused to accept Ireton's proposals as a basis of peace, Charles still evaded, and the army grew restless and suspicious. There were cries for a wide reform, for the abolition of the House of Peers, for a new House of Commons; and the Agitators called on the Council of Officers to

Aug. 6

SEC. VIII.

THE ARMY
AND THE
PARLIA-
MENT
1646
TO
1649

discuss the question of abolishing royalty itself. Cromwell was never braver than when he faced the gathering storm, forbade the discussion, adjourned the Council, and sent the officers to their regiments. But the strain was too great to last long, and Charles was still resolute to "play his game." He was in fact so far from being in earnest in his negotiation with Cromwell and Ireton, that at the moment they were risking their lives for him he was conducting another and equally delusive negotiation with the Parliament, fomenting the discontent in London, preparing for a fresh royalist rising, and for an intervention of the Scots in his favour. "The two nations," he wrote joyously, "will soon be at war." All that was needed for the success of his schemes was his own liberty; and in the midst of their hopes of an accommodation the army leaders found with astonishment that they had been duped throughout, and that the King had fled.

Flight of the King Nov. 1647

The flight fanned the excitement of the New Model into frenzy, and only the courage of Cromwell averted an open mutiny in its gathering at Ware. But even Cromwell was powerless to break the spirit which now pervaded the soldiers, and the King's perfidy left him without resource. "The King is a man of great parts and great understanding," he said, "but so great a dissembler and so false a man that he is not to be trusted." The danger from his escape indeed soon passed away. By a strange error Charles had ridden from Hampton Court to the Isle of Wight, perhaps with some hope from the sympathy of Colonel Hammond, the Governor of Carisbrook Castle, and again found himself a prisoner. Foiled in his effort to put himself at the head of the new civil war, he set himself to organize it from his prison; and while again opening delusive negotiations with the Parliament, he signed a secret treaty with the Scots for the invasion of the realm. The practical suspension of the Covenant and the triumph of the party of religious liberty in England had produced a violent reaction across the Tweed. The moderate party had gathered round the Duke of Hamilton, and carried the elections against Argyle and the more zealous religionists; and on the King's consenting to a stipulation for the re-establishment of Presbytery in England, they ordered an army to be levied for his support. In England the whole of the conservative party, with many of the most conspicuous members of the Long Parliament at its head, was drifting, in its horror of the religious and political changes which seemed impending, towards the King; and the news from Scotland gave the signal for fitful insurrections in almost every quarter. London was only held down by main force, old officers of the Parliament unfurled the royal flag in South Wales, and surprised Pembroke. The seizure of Berwick and Carlisle opened a way for the Scotch invasion. Kent, Essex, and Hertford broke out in revolt. The fleet in the Downs sent their captains on shore, hoisted the King's pennon, and blockaded the Thames. "The hour

The Second Civil War

1648

is come for the Parliament to save the kingdom and to govern alone," cried Cromwell; but the Parliament only showed itself eager to take advantage of the crisis to profess its adherence to monarchy, to re-open the negotiations it had broken off with the King, and to deal the fiercest blow at religious freedom which it had ever received. The Presbyterians flocked back to their seats; and an " Ordinance for the suppression of Blasphemies and Heresies," which Vane and Cromwell had long held at bay, was passed by triumphant majorities. Any man —ran this terrible statute—denying the doctrine of the Trinity or of the Divinity of Christ, or that the books of Scripture are "the Word of God," or the resurrection of the body, or a future day of judgement, and refusing on trial to abjure his heresy, " shall suffer the pain of death." Any man declaring (amidst a long list of other errors) " that man by nature hath free will to turn to God,' that here is a Purgatory, that images are lawful, that infant baptism is unlawful; any one denying the obligation of observing the Lord's day, or asserting "that the Church government by Presbytery is anti-Christian or unlawful," shall on a refusal to renounce his errors "be commanded to prison." It was plain that the Presbyterians counted on the King's success to resume their policy of conformity, and had Charles been free, or the New Model disbanded, their hopes would probably have been realized. But Charles was still safe at Carisbrook; and the New Model was facing fiercely the danger which surrounded it. The wanton renewal of the war at a moment when all tended to peace swept from the mind of Fairfax and Cromwell, as from that of the army at large, every thought of reconciliation with the King. Soldiers and generals were at last bound together again in a stern resolve. On the eve of their march against the revolt all gathered in a solemn prayer-meeting, and came "to a very clear and joint resolution, 'That it was our duty, if ever the Lord brought us back again in peace, to call Charles Stuart, that man of blood, to account for the blood he has shed and mischief he has done to his utmost against the Lord's cause and people in this poor nation.'" In a few days Fairfax had trampled down the Kentish insurgents, and had prisoned those of the eastern countries within the walls of Colchester, while Cromwell drove the Welsh insurgents within those of Pembroke. Both towns however held stubbornly out; and though a rising under Lord Holland in the neighbourhood of London was easily put down, there was no force left to stem the inroad of the Scots, who poured over the border some twenty thousand strong. Luckily the surrender of Pembroke at this critical moment set Crom-well free. Pushing rapidly northward with five thousand men, he called in the force under Lambert which had been gallantly hanging on the Scottish flank, and pushed over the Yorkshire hills into the valley of the Ribble, where the Duke of Hamilton, reinforced by three thousand royalists of the north, had advanced as far as Preston. With

SEC. VIII.

THE ARMY
AND THE
PARLIA-
MENT
1646
TO
1649
*The Houses
and the
Army*

*The Scotch
Invasion*

SEC. VIII.

THE ARMY
AND THE
PARLIA-
MENT
1646
TO
1649
Aug. 17,
1648

an army which now numbered ten thousand men, Cromwell poured down on the flank of the Duke's straggling line of march, attacked the Scots as they retired behind the Ribble, passed the river with them, cut their rearguard to pieces at Wigan, forced the defile at Warrington, where the flying enemy made a last and desperate stand, and drove their foot to surrender, while Lambert hunted down Hamilton and the horse. Fresh from its victory, the New Model pushed over the Border, while the peasants of Ayrshire and the west rose in the " Whiggamore raid " (notable as the first event in which we find the name " Whig," which is possibly the same as our " Whey," and conveys a taunt against the " sour-milk " faces of the fanatical Ayrshiremen), and, marching upon Edinburgh, dispersed the royalist party and again installed Argyle in power.

Argyle welcomed Cromwell as a deliverer, but the victorious general had hardly entered Edinburgh when he was recalled by pressing news from the south. The temper with which the Parliament had met the royalist revolt was, as we have seen, widely different from that of the army. It had recalled the eleven members, and had passed the Ordinance against heresy. At the moment of the victory at Preston the Lords were discussing charges of treason against Cromwell, while commissioners were again sent to the Isle of Wight, in spite of the resistance of the Independents, to conclude peace with the King. Royalists and Presbyterians alike pressed Charles to grasp the easy terms which were now offered him. But his hopes from Scotland had only broken down to give place to hopes of a new war with the aid of an army from Ireland ; and the negotiators saw forty days wasted in useless chicanery. " Nothing," Charles wrote to his friends, " is changed in my designs." But the surrender of Colchester to Fairfax in August, and Cromwell's convention with Argyle, had now set free

the army, and petitions from its regiments at once demanded " justice on the King." A fresh " Remonstrance" from the Council of Officers called for the election of a new Parliament ; for electoral reform ; for the recognition of the supremacy of the Houses "in all things ; " for the change of kingship, should it be retained, into a magistracy elected by the Parliament, and without veto on its proceedings. Above all, they demanded "that the capital and grand author of our troubles, by whose commissions, commands, and procurements, and in whose behalf and for whose interest only, of will and power, all our wars and troubles have been, with all the miseries attending them, may be specially brought to justice for the treason, blood, and mischief he is therein guilty of." The demand drove the Houses to despair. Their reply was to accept the King's concessions, unimportant as they were, as a basis of peace. The step was accepted by the soldiers as a defiance : Charles was again seized by a troop of horse, and carried

off to Hurst Castle, while a letter from Fairfax announced the march of his army upon London. "We shall know now," said Vane, as the troops took their post round the Houses of Parliament, "who is on the side of the King, and who on the side of the people." But the terror of the army proved weaker among the members than the agonized loyalty which strove to save the monarchy and the Church, and a large majority in both Houses still voted for the acceptance of the terms which Charles had offered. The next morning saw Colonel Pride at the door of the House of Commons with a list of forty members of the majority in his hands. The Council of Officers had resolved to exclude them, and as each member made his appearance he was arrested, and put in confinement. "By what right do you act?" a member asked. "By the right of the sword," Hugh Peters is said to have replied. The House was still resolute, but on the following morning forty more members were excluded, and the rest gave way. The sword had fallen; and the two great powers which had waged this bitter conflict, the Parliament and the Monarchy, suddenly disappeared. The expulsion of one hundred and forty members, in a word of the majority of the existing House, reduced the Commons to a name. The remnant who remained to co-operate with the army were no longer representative of the will of the country; in the coarse imagery of popular speech they were but the "rump" of a Parliament. While the House of Commons dwindled to a sham, the House of Lords passed away altogether. The effect of "Pride's Purge" was seen in a resolution of the Rump for the trial of Charles and the nomination of a Court of one hundred and fifty Commissioners to conduct it, with John Bradshaw, a lawyer of eminence, at their head. The rejection of this Ordinance by the few peers who remained brought about a fresh resolution from members who remained in the Lower House, "that the People are, under God, the original of all just power; that the Commons of England in Parliament assembled—being chosen by, and representing, the People—have the supreme power in this nation; and that whatsoever is enacted and declared for law by the Commons in Parliament assembled hath the force of a law, and all the people of this nation are concluded thereby, although the consent and concurrence of the King or House of Peers be not had thereunto."

Charles appeared before Bradshaw's Court only to deny its competence and to refuse to plead; but thirty-two witnesses were examined to satisfy the consciences of his judges, and it was not till the fifth day of the trial that he was condemned to death as a tyrant, traitor, murderer, and enemy of his country. The popular excitement vented itself in cries of "Justice," or "God save your Majesty," as the trial went on, but all save the loud outcries of the soldiers was hushed as Charles passed to receive his doom. The dignity which he had failed to preserve in his long jangling with Bradshaw and the judges returned at the call of death. Whatever had been the faults and follies of his

SEC. VIII.

THE ARMY
AND THE
PARLIA-
MENT
1640
TO
1649
*Pride's
Purge*
Dec. 6

The
King's
Death

Jan. 30
1649

SEC. IX.

THE
COMMON-
WEALTH

1649
TO
1653

life, " he nothing common did nor mean, upon that memorable scene." Two masked executioners awaited the King as he mounted the scaffold, which had been erected outside one of the windows of the Banqueting House at Whitehall ; the streets and roofs were thronged with spectators, and a strong body of soldiers stood drawn up beneath.   His head fell at the first blow, and as the executioner lifted it to the sight of all a groan of pity and horror burst from the silent crowd.

Section IX.—The Commonwealth. 1649—1653.

[*Authorities.*—Rushworth's collection ceases with the King's Trial ; Whitelock and Ludlow continue as before, and must be supplemented by the Parliamentary History and the State Trials.   Special lives of Vane and Martyn will be found in Mr. Forster's " Statesmen of the Commonwealth," and a vigorous defence of the Council of State in the " History of the Commonwealth," by Mr. Bisset.   For Irish affairs see the Ormond Papers collected by Carte, and Cromwell's despatches in Carlyle's " Letters."   The account given by Mr. Carlyle of the Scotch war is perhaps the most valuable portion of his work. The foreign politics and wars of this period are admirably illustrated with a copious appendix of documents by M. Guizot ("Republic and Cromwell," vol. i.), whose account of the whole period is the fairest and best for the general reader.   Mr. Hepworth Dixon has published a biography of Blake.]   [Mr. Masson's " Life of Milton," vols. iv. and v., which illustrate this period, have been published since this list was drawn up.—ED.]

The news of the King's death was received throughout Europe with a thrill of horror.   The Czar of Russia chased the English envoy from his court.   The ambassador of France was withdrawn on the proclamation of the Republic.   The Protestant powers of the Continent seemed more anxious than any to disavow all connexion with the Protestant people who had brought their King to the block.   Holland took the lead in acts of open hostility to the new power as soon as the news of the execution reached the Hague ; the States-General waited solemnly on the Prince of Wales, who took the title of Charles the Second, and recognized him as " Majesty," while they refused an audience to the English envoys.   Their Stadtholder, his brother-in-law, the Prince of Orange, was supported by popular sympathy in the aid and encouragement he afforded to Charles ; and eleven ships of the English fleet, which had found a refuge at the Hague ever since their revolt from the Parliament, were suffered to sail under Rupert's command, and to render the seas unsafe for English traders.   The danger was far greater nearer home.   In Scotland Argyle and his party proclaimed Charles the Second King, and despatched an Embassy to the Hague to invite him to ascend the throne.   In Ireland Ormond, who had remained firm in his allegiance to the King, and acted as his viceroy, took the lead of the Confederate Catholics, drew into some kind of union royalists of both races and creeds, and entered into negotiations with

Owen Roe O'Neill. Ormond called on Charles to land in a country where he would find three-fourths of its people devoted to his cause. Nor was the danger from without met by resolution and energy on the part of the diminished Parliament which remained the sole depository of legal powers. The Commons entered on their new task with hesitation and delay. Six weeks passed after the King's execution before the monarchy was formally abolished, and the government of the nation provided for by the creation of a Council of State consisting of forty-one members selected from the Commons, who were entrusted with full executive power at home or abroad. Two months more elapsed before the passing of the memorable Act which declared "that the People of England and of all the dominions and territories thereunto belonging are, and shall be, and are hereby constituted, made, established, and confirmed to be a Commonwealth and Free State, and shall henceforward be governed as a Commonwealth and Free State by the supreme authority of this nation, the representatives of the People in Parliament, and by such as they shall appoint and constitute officers and ministers for the good of the people, and that without any King or House of Lords."

Of the dangers which threatened the new Commonwealth some were more apparent than real. The rivalry of France and Spain, both anxious for its friendship, secured it from the hostility of the greater powers of the Continent; and the ill-will of Holland could be delayed, if not averted, by negotiations. The acceptance of the Covenant was insisted on by Scotland before it would formally receive Charles as its ruler, and nothing but necessity would induce him to comply with such a demand. On the side of Ireland danger seemed pressing, and an army of twelve thousand men was set apart for the war ; but the Confederates had little cohesive force under Ormond, who was a Protestant, and who could not speak the Irish language. The real difficulties were the difficulties at home. The death of Charles gave fresh vigour to the royalist cause, and the new loyalty was stirred to enthusiasm by the publication of the "Eikon Basilike," a work really due to the ingenuity of Dr. Gauden, a Presbyterian minister, but which was believed to have been composed by the King himself in his later hours of captivity, and which reflected with admirable skill the hopes, the suffering, and the piety of the royal "martyr." The dreams of a rising were roughly checked by the execution of the Duke of Hamilton and Lords Holland and Capell, who had till now been confined in the Tower. But the popular disaffection told even on the Council of State. A majority of its members declined the oath offered to them at their earliest meeting, pledging them to an approval of the King's death and the establishment of the Commonwealth. Half the judges retired from the bench. Thousands of refusals met the demand of an engagement to be faithful to the Republic which was made to all beneficed clergymen and

Sec. IX.

The
Common-
wealth
1649
to
1653

*Abolition of
Monarchy*

May 19

**The
Rump
and the
Army**

SEC. IX.

THE
COMMON-
WEALTH

1649
TO
1653

public functionaries. It was not till May, and even then in spite of the ill-will of the citizens, that the Council ventured to proclaim the Commonwealth in London. The army indeed had no thought of setting up a mere military rule. Still less did it contemplate leaving the conduct of affairs to the small body of members, which still called itself the House of Commons, a body which numbered hardly a hundred, and whose average attendance was little more than fifty. In reducing it by "Pride's Purge" to the mere shadow of a House the army had never dreamed of its continuance as a permanent assembly: it had, in fact, insisted as a condition of even its temporary continuance that it should prepare a bill for the summoning of a fresh Parliament. The plan put forward by the Council of Officers is still interesting as the basis of many later efforts towards parliamentary reform. It advised a dissolution in the spring, the assembling every two years of a new Parliament consisting of four hundred members elected by all householders rateable to the poor, and a redistribution of seats which would have given the privilege of representation to every place of importance. Paid military officers and civil officials were excluded from election. The plan was apparently accepted by the Commons, and a bill based on it was again and again discussed, but there was a suspicion that no serious purpose of its own dissolution was entertained by the House. The popular discontent found a mouthpiece in John Lilburne, a brave, hot-headed soldier, and the excitement of the army appeared suddenly in a formidable mutiny in May. "You must cut these people in pieces," Cromwell broke out in the Council of State, "or they will cut you in pieces;" and a forced march of fifty miles to Burford enabled him to burst on the mutinous regiments at midnight, and to stamp out the revolt. But resolute as he was against disorder, Cromwell went honestly with the army in its demand of a new Parliament; he believed, and in his harangue to the mutineers he pledged himself to the assertion, that the House proposed to dissolve itself. Within the House, however, a vigorous knot of politicians was resolved to prolong its existence; in a witty paraphrase of the story of Moses, Henry Martyn was soon to picture the Commonwealth as a new-born and delicate babe, and hint that "no one is so proper to bring it up as the mother who has brought it into the world." As yet, however, their intentions were kept secret, and in spite of the delays thrown in the way of the bill for a new Representative body Cromwell entertained no serious suspicion of the Parliament's

design, when he was summoned to Ireland by a series of royalist successes which left only Dublin in the hands of the Parliamentary forces.

With Scotland threatening war, and a naval struggle impending with Holland, it was necessary that the work of the army in Ireland should be done quickly. The temper, too, of Cromwell and his soldiers was

SEC. IX.

THE
COMMON-
WEALTH
1649
TO
1653

Sept. 1649

one of vengeance, for legends of an Irish massacre remained living in every English breast, and the revolt was looked upon as a continuance of the massacre. "We are come," he said on his landing, "to ask an account of the innocent blood that hath been shed, and to endeavour to bring to an account all who by appearing in arms shall justify the same." A sortie from Dublin had already broken up Ormond's siege of the capital; and feeling himself powerless to keep the field before the new army, the Marquis had thrown his best troops, three thousand Englishmen under Sir Arthur Aston, as a garrison into Drogheda. The storm of Drogheda by Cromwell was the first of a series of awful massacres. The garrison fought bravely, and repulsed the first attack; but a second drove Aston and his force back to the Mill-Mount. "Our men getting up to them," ran Cromwell's terrible despatch, "were ordered by me to put them all to the sword. And indeed, being in the heat of action, I forbade them to spare any that were in arms in the town, and I think that night they put to death about two thousand men." A few fled to St. Peter's church, "whereupon I ordered the steeple to be fired, where one of them was heard to say in the midst of the flames: 'God damn me, I burn, I burn.'" "In the church itself nearly one thousand were put to the sword. I believe all their friars were knocked on the head promiscuously but two," but these were the sole exceptions to the rule of killing the soldiers only. At a later time Cromwell challenged his enemies to give "an instance of one man since my coming into Ireland, not in arms, massacred, destroyed, or banished." But for soldiers who refused to surrender on summons there was no mercy. Of the remnant who were driven to yield at last through hunger, "when they submitted, their officers were knocked on the head, every tenth man of the soldiers killed, and the rest shipped for the Barbadoes." "I am persuaded," the despatch ends, "that this is a righteous judgement of God upon these barbarous wretches who have imbrued their hands in so much innocent blood, and that it will tend to prevent the effusion of blood for the future." A detachment sufficed to relieve Derry, and to quiet Ulster; and Cromwell turned to the south, where as stout a defence was followed by as terrible a massacre at Wexford. A fresh success at Ross brought him to Waterford; but the city held stubbornly out, disease thinned his army, where there was scarce an officer who had not been sick, and the general himself was arrested by illness. At last the tempestuous weather drove him into winter quarters at Cork with his work half done. The winter was one of terrible anxiety. The Parliament was showing less and less inclination to dissolve itself, and was meeting the growing discontent by a stricter censorship of the press, and a fruitless prosecution of John Lilburne. English commerce was being ruined by the piracies of Rupert's fleet, which now anchored at Kinsale to support the royalist cause in Ireland.

SEC. IX.

THE
COMMON-
WEALTH
1649
TO
1653

*Charles and
the Scots*

1650

**Dunbar
and Wor-
cester**

July 1650

*Dunbar
Sept.* 3

The energy of Vane indeed had already re-created a navy, squadrons of which were being despatched into the British seas, the Mediterranean, and the Levant, and Colonel Blake, who had distinguished himself by his heroic defence of Taunton during the war, was placed at the head of a fleet which drove Rupert from the Irish coast, and finally blockaded him in the Tagus. But even the energy of Vane quailed before the danger from the Scots. "One must go and die there," the young King cried at the news of Ormond's defeat before Dublin, "for it is shameful for me to live elsewhere." But his ardour for an Irish campaign cooled as Cromwell marched from victory to victory ; and from the isle of Jersey, which alone remained faithful to him of all his southern dominions, Charles renewed the negotiations with Scotland which his hopes from Ireland had broken. They were again delayed by a proposal on the part of Montrose to attack the very Government with whom his master was negotiating ; but the failure and death of the Marquis in the spring forced Charles to accept the Presbyterian conditions. The news of the negotiations filled the English leaders with dismay, for Scotland was raising an army, and Fairfax, while willing to defend England against a Scotch invasion, scrupled to take the lead in an invasion of Scotland. The Council recalled Cromwell from Ireland, but his cooler head saw that there was yet time to finish his work in the west. During the winter he had been busily preparing for a new campaign, and it was only after the storm of Clonmell, and the overthrow of the Irish under Hugh O'Neil, that he embarked again for England.

Cromwell entered London amidst the shouts of a great multitude ; and a month after Charles had landed on the shores of Scotland the English army started for the north. It crossed the Tweed, fifteen thousand men strong ; but the terror of his massacres in Ireland hung round its leader, the country was deserted as he advanced, and he was forced to cling for provisions to a fleet which sailed along the coast. David Leslie, with a larger force, refused battle and lay obstinately in his lines between Edinburgh and Leith. A march of the English army round his position to the slopes of the Pentlands only brought about a change of the Scottish front ; and as Cromwell fell back baffled upon Dunbar, Leslie encamped upon the heights above the town, and cut off the English retreat along the coast by the seizure of Cockburnspath. His post was almost unassailable, while the soldiers of Cromwell were sick and starving ; and their general had resolved on an embarcation of his forces, when he saw in the dusk of evening signs of movement in the Scottish camp. Leslie's caution had at last been overpowered by the zeal of the preachers, and his army moved down to the lower ground between the hillside on which it was encamped and a little brook which covered the English front. His horse was far in advance of the main body, and it had hardly reached the level ground when

Sec. IX.

The
Common-
wealth

1649
TO
1653

Cromwell in the dim dawn flung his whole force upon it. "They run; I profess they run!" he cried as the Scotch horse broke after a desperate resistance, and threw into confusion the foot who were hurrying to its aid. Then, as the sun rose over the mist of the morning, he added in nobler words: "Let God arise, and let His enemies be scattered! Like as the mist vanisheth, so shalt Thou drive them away!" In less than an hour the victory was complete. The defeat at once became a rout; ten thousand prisoners were taken, with all the baggage and guns; three thousand were slain, with scarce any loss on the part of the conquerors. Leslie reached Edinburgh, a general without an army. The effect of Dunbar was at once seen in the attitude of the Continental powers. Spain hastened to recognize the Republic, and Holland offered its alliance. But Cromwell was watching with anxiety the growing discontent at home. The general amnesty claimed by Ireton, and the bill for the Parliament's dissolution, still hung on hand; the reform of the courts of justice, which had been pressed by the army, failed before the obstacles thrown in its way by the lawyers in the Commons. "Relieve the oppressed," Cromwell wrote from Dunbar, "hear the groans of poor prisoners. Be pleased to reform the abuses of all professions. If there be any one that makes many poor to make a few rich, that suits not a Commonwealth." But the House was seeking to turn the current of public opinion in favour of its own continuance by a great diplomatic triumph.

Break with Holland

It resolved secretly on the wild project of bringing about a union between England and Holland, and it took advantage of Cromwell's victory to despatch Oliver St. John with a stately embassy to the Hague. His rejection of an alliance and Treaty of Commerce which the Dutch offered was followed by the disclosure of the English proposal of union, but the proposal was at once refused. The envoys, who returned angrily to the Parliament, attributed their failure to the posture of affairs in Scotland, where Charles was preparing for a new campaign. Humiliation after humiliation had been heaped on Charles since he landed in his northern realm. He had subscribed to the Covenant; he had listened to sermons and scoldings from the ministers; he had been called on to sign a declaration that acknowledged the tyranny of his father and the idolatry of his mother. Hardened and shameless as he was, the young King for a moment recoiled. "I could never look my mother in the face again," he cried, "after signing such a paper;" but he signed. He was still, however, a King only in name, shut out from the Council and the army, with his friends excluded from all part in government or the war. But he was at once freed by the victory of Dunbar. "I believe the King will set up on his own score now," Cromwell wrote after his victory. With the overthrow of Leslie fell the power of Argyle and the narrow Presbyterians whom he led. Hamilton, the brother and successor of

Sec. IX.
The
Common-
wealth
1649
to
1653
1650–1651

the Duke who had been captured at Preston, brought back the royalists to the camp, and Charles insisted on taking part in the Council and on being crowned at Scone.   Master of Edinburgh, but foiled in an attack on Stirling, Cromwell waited through the winter and the long spring, while intestine feuds broke up the nation opposed to him, and while the stricter Covenanters retired sulkily from the royal army on the return of the " Malignants," the royalists of the earlier war, to its ranks.   With summer the campaign recommenced, but Leslie again fell back on his system of positions, and Cromwell, finding the Scotch camp at Stirling unassailable, crossed into Fife and left the road open to the south.   The bait was taken.   In spite of Leslie's counsels Charles resolved to invade England, and was soon in full march through Lancashire upon the Severn, with the English horse under Lambert hanging on his rear, and the English foot hastening by York and Coventry to close the road to London.   " We have done to the best of our judgement," Cromwell replied to the angry alarm of the Parliament, " knowing that if some issue were not put to this business it would occasion another winter's war."   At Coventry he learnt Charles's position, and swept round by Evesham upon Worcester,

where the Scotch King was encamped.   Throwing half his force across the river, Cromwell attacked the town on both sides on the anniversary of his victory at Dunbar.   He led the van in person, and was " the first to set foot on the enemy's ground."   When Charles descended from the cathedral tower to fling himself on the eastern division, Cromwell hurried back across the Severn, and was soon " riding in the midst of the fire."   For four or five hours, he told the Parliament, " it was as stiff a contest as ever I have seen ; " the Scots, outnumbered and beaten into the city, gave no answer but shot to offers of quarter, and it was not till nightfall that all was over.   The loss of the victors was as usual inconsiderable.   The conquered lost six thousand men, and all their baggage and artillery.   Leslie was among the prisoners : Hamilton among the dead.   Charles himself fled from the field ; and after months of wanderings made his escape to France.

" Now that the King is dead and his son defeated," Cromwell said gravely to the Parliament, " I think it necessary to come to a settlement."   But the settlement which had been promised after Naseby was still as distant as ever after Worcester.   The bill for dissolving the present Parliament, though Cromwell pressed it in person, was only passed, after bitter opposition, by a majority of two ; and even this success had been purchased by a compromise which permitted the House to sit for three years more.   Internal affairs were almost at a dead lock.   The Parliament appointed committees to prepare plans for legal reforms, or for ecclesiastical reforms, but it did nothing to carry them into effect.   It was overpowered by the crowd of affairs which the confusion of the war had thrown into its hands, by confiscations, sequestrations, appointments to civil and military offices, in fact, the whole administration of the state ; and there were times when it was driven to a resolve not to take any private affairs for weeks together in order that it might make some progress with public business. To add to this confusion and muddle there were the inevitable scandals which arose from it ; charges of malversation and corruption were hurled at the members of the house ; and some, like Haselrig, were accused with justice of using their power to further their own interests. The one remedy for all this was, as the army saw, the assembly of a new and complete Parliament in place of the mere " rump " of the old ; but this was the one measure which the House was resolute to avert. Vane spurred it to a new activity. The Amnesty Bill was forced through after fifteen divisions. A Grand Committee, with Sir Matthew Hale at its head, was appointed to consider the reform of the law. A union with Scotland was pushed resolutely forward ; eight English Commissioners convoked a Convention of delegates from its counties and boroughs at Edinburgh, and in spite of dogged opposition procured a vote in favour of the proposal. A bill was introduced which gave legal form to the union, and admitted representatives from Scotland into the next Parliament. A similar plan was proposed for a union with Ireland. But it was necessary for Vane's purposes not only to show the energy of the Parliament, but to free it from the control of the army. His aim was to raise in the navy a force devoted to the House, and to eclipse the glories of Dunbar and Worcester by yet greater triumphs at sea. With this view the quarrel with Holland had been carefully nursed ; a " Navigation Act'' prohibiting the importation in foreign vessels of any but the products of the countries to which they belonged struck a fatal blow at the carrying trade from which the Dutch drew their wealth ; and fresh debates arose from the English claim to salutes from all vessels in the Channel. The two fleets met before Dover, and a summons from Blake to lower the Dutch flag was met by the Dutch admiral, Van Tromp, with a broadside. The States-General attributed the collision to accident, and offered to recall Van Tromp ; but the English demands rose at each step in the negotiations till war became inevitable. The army hardly needed the warning conveyed by the introduction of a bill for its disbanding to understand the new policy of the Parliament. It was significant that while accepting the bill for its own dissolution the House had as yet prepared no plan for the assembly which was to follow it ; and the Dutch war had hardly been declared when, abandoning the attitude of inaction which it had observed since the beginning of the Commonwealth, the army petitioned, not only for reform in Church and State, but for an explicit declaration that the House would bring its proceedings to a close. The Petition forced the House to discuss a bill for " a New Representative," but the discussion soon brought out the resolve of the sitting members to

Sec. IX.

THE COMMON-WEALTH

1649
TO
1653.

Activity of the Parliament
1652

War with Holland

SEC. IX.

THE
COMMON-
WEALTH
1649
TO
1653

continue as a part of the coming Parliament without re-election. The officers, irritated by such a claim, demanded in conference after conference an immediate dissolution, and the House as resolutely refused. In ominous words Cromwell supported the demand of the army. "As for the members of this Parliament, the army begins to take them in disgust. I would it did so with less reason." There was just ground, he urged, for discontent in their selfish greed of houses and lands, the scandalous lives of many, their partiality as judges, their interference with the ordinary course of law in matters of private interest, their delay of law reform, above all in their manifest design of perpetuating their own power. "There is little to hope for from such men," he ended with a return to his predominant thought, "for a settlement of the nation."

The Ejection of the Rump

For the moment the crisis was averted by the events of the war. A terrible storm had separated the two fleets when on the point of engaging in the Orkneys, but Ruyter and Blake met again in the Channel, and after a fierce struggle the Dutch were forced to retire under cover of night. Since the downfall of Spain Holland had been the first naval power in the world, and the spirit of the nation rose gallantly with its earliest defeat. Immense efforts were made to strengthen the fleet, and the veteran, Van Tromp, who was replaced at its head, appeared in the

Blake

Channel with seventy-three ships of war. Blake had but half the number, but he at once accepted the challenge, and the unequal fight went on doggedly till nightfull, when the English fleet withdrew shattered into the Thames. Tromp swept the Channel in triumph, with a broom at his masthead ; and the tone of the Commons lowered with the defeat of their favourite force. A compromise seems to have been arranged between the two parties, for the bill providing a new Representative was again pushed on, and the Parliament agreed to retire in the coming November, while Cromwell offered no opposition to a reduction of the army. But the courage of the House rose afresh with a turn of fortune. The strenuous efforts of Blake enabled him again to put to sea in a few months after his defeat, and a running fight through

Feb. 1653

four days ended at last in an English victory, though Tromp's fine seamanship enabled him to save the convoy he was guarding. The House at once insisted on the retention of its power. Not only were the existing members to continue as members of the new Parliament, depriving the places they represented of their right of choosing representatives, but they were to constitute a Committee of Revision, to determine the validity of each election, and the fitness of the members returned. A conference took place between the leaders of the Commons and the Officers of the Army, who resolutely demanded not only the omission of these clauses, but that the Parliament should at once dissolve itself, and commit the new elections to the Council of State. "Our charge," retorted Haselrig, "cannot be transferred to any one." . The conference was adjourned till the next morning, on an understanding that no decisive step should be taken : but it had no sooner re-assembled than the absence of the leading members confirmed the news that Vane was fast pressing the bill for a new Representative through the House. "It is contrary to common honesty," Cromwell angrily broke out; and, quitting Whitehall, he summoned a company of musketeers to follow him as far as the door of the Commons. He sate down quietly in his place, "clad in plain grey clothes and grey worsted stockings," and listened to Vane's passionate arguments. "I am come to do what grieves me to the heart," he said to his neighbour, St. John ; but he still remained quiet, till Vane pressed the House to waive its usual forms and pass the bill at once. "The time has come," he said to Harrison. "Think well," replied Harrison, "it is a dangerous work !" and Cromwell listened for another quarter of an hour. At the question "that this Bill do pass," he at length rose, and his tone grew higher as he repeated his former charges of injustice, self-interest, and delay. "Your hour is come," he ended, "the Lord hath done with you !" A crowd of members started to their feet in angry protest. "Come, come," replied Cromwell, "we have had enough of this ; " and striding into the midst of the chamber, he clapt his hat on his head, and exclaimed, "I will put an end to your prating !" In the din that followed his voice was heard in broken sentences—"It is not fit that you should sit here any longer ! You should give place to better men ! You are no Parliament." Thirty musketeers entered at a sign from their General, and the fifty members present crowded to the door. "Drunkard !" Cromwell broke out as Wentworth passed him ; and Martin was taunted with a yet coarser name. Vane, fearless to the last, told him his act was "against all right and all honour." "Ah, Sir Harry Vane, Sir Harry Vane," Cromwell retorted in bitter indignation at the trick he had been played, "you might have prevented all this, but you are a juggler, and have no common honesty ! The Lord deliver me from Sir Harry Vane !" The Speaker refused to quit his seat, till Harrison offered to "lend him a hand to come down." Cromwell lifted the mace from the table. "What shall we do with this bauble?" he said. "Take it away !" The door of the House was locked at last, and the dispersion of the Parliament was followed a few hours after by that of its executive committee, the Council of State. Cromwell himself summoned them to withdraw. "We have heard," replied the President, John Bradshaw, "what you have done this morning at the House, and in some hours all England will hear it. But you mistake, sir, if you think the Parliament dissolved. No power on earth can dissolve the Parliament but itself, be sure of that ! "

Sec. IX.

The
Common-
wealth
1649
to
1653

April 20
1653

The
Parliament
driven out

Section X.—The Fall of Puritanism. 1653—1660.

[*Authorities*.—Many of the works mentioned before are still valuable, but the real key to the history of this period lies in Cromwell's remarkable series of Speeches (Carlyle, "Letters and Speeches," vol. iii.). Thurlow's State Papers furnish an immense mass of documents. For the Second Parliament of the Protector we have Burton's "Diary." For the Restoration, M. Guizot's "Richard Cromwell and the Restoration," Ludlow's "Memoirs," Baxter's "Autobiography," and the minute and accurate account given by Clarendon himself.]

The dispersion of the Parliament and of the Council of State left England without a government, for the authority of every official ended with that of the body from which his power was derived. Cromwell, in fact, as Captain-General of the forces, was forced to recognize his responsibility for the maintenance of public order. But no thought of military despotism can be fairly traced in the acts of the general or the army. They were in fact far from regarding their position as a revolutionary one. Though incapable of justification on any formal ground, their proceedings since the establishment of the Commonwealth had as yet been substantially in vindication of the rights of the country to representation and self-government; and public opinion had gone fairly with the army in its demand for a full and efficient body of representatives, as well as in its resistance to the project by which the Rump would have deprived half England of its right of election. It was only when no other means existed of preventing such a wrong that the soldiers had driven out the wrongdoers. "It is you that have forced me to this," Cromwell exclaimed, as he drove the members from the House; "I have sought the Lord night and day that He would rather slay me than put me upon the doing of this work." The act was one of violence to the members of the House, but the act which it aimed at preventing was one of violence on their part to the constitutional rights of the whole nation. The people had in fact been "dissatisfied in every corner of the realm" at the state of public affairs: and the expulsion of the members was ratified by a general assent. "We did not hear a dog bark at their going," the Protector said years afterwards. Whatever anxiety may have been felt at the use which was like to be made of "the power of the sword," was in great part dispelled by a proclamation of the officers. Their one anxiety was "not to grasp the power ourselves nor to keep it in military hands, no not for a day," and their promise to "call to the government men of approved fidelity and honesty" was to some extent redeemed by the nomination of a provisional Council of State, consisting of eight officers of high rank and four civilians, with Cromwell as their head, and a seat in which was offered, though fruitlessly, to Vane. The first business of such a body was clearly to summon a new Parliament and to resign its trust into its hands: but the bill for Parliamentary reform had dropped with the expulsion: and reluctant as the Council was to summon a new Parliament on the old basis of election, it shrank from the responsibility of effecting so fundamental a change as the creation of a new basis by its own authority. It was this difficulty which led to the expedient of a Constituent Convention. Cromwell told the story of this unlucky assembly some years after with an amusing frankness. "I will come and tell you a story of my own weakness and folly. And yet it was done in my simplicity—I dare avow it was. . . . It was thought then that men of our own judgment, who had fought in the wars, and were all of a piece on that account—why, surely, these men will hit it, and these men will do it to the purpose, whatever can be desired! And surely we did think, and I did think so—the more blame to me!" Of the hundred and fifty-six men, "faithful, fearing God, and hating covetousness," whose names were selected for this purpose by the Council of State, from lists furnished by the congregational churches, the bulk were men, like Ashley Cooper, of good blood and "free estates ;" and the proportion of burgesses, such as the leather-merchant, Praise-God Barebones, whose name was eagerly seized on as a nickname for the body to which he belonged, seems to have been much the same as in earlier Parliaments. But the circumstances of their choice told fatally on the temper of its members. Cromwell himself, in the burst of rugged eloquence with which he welcomed their assembling, was carried away by a strange enthusiasm. "Convince the nation," he said, "that as men fearing God have fought them out of their bondage under the regal power, so men fearing God do now rule them in the fear of God. . . . Own your call, for it is of God: indeed, it is marvellous, and it hath been unprojected. . . . Never was a supreme power under such a way of owning God, and being owned by Him." A spirit yet more enthusiastic appeared in the proceedings of the Convention itself. The resignation of their powers by Cromwell and the Council into its hands left it the one supreme authority ; but by the instrument which convoked it provision had been made that this authority should be transferred in fifteen months to another assembly elected according to its directions. Its work was, in fact, to be that of a constituent assembly, paving the way for a Parliament on a really national basis. But the Convention put the largest construction on its commission, and boldly undertook the whole task of constitutional reform. Committees were appointed to consider the needs of the Church and the nation. The spirit of economy and honesty which pervaded the assembly appeared in its redress of the extravagance which prevailed in the civil service, and of the inequality of taxation. With a remarkable energy it undertook a host of reforms, for whose execution England has had to wait to our own day. The Long Parliament had shrunk from any reform of the Court of Chancery, where twenty-three thousand cases were waiting unheard. The Convention proposed its abolition. The work of compiling a single

SEC. X.

THE FALL OF PURITANISM
1653
TO
1660

The Barebones Parliament
July 1653

The work of the Convention

SEC. X.

THE
FALL OF
PURITANISM

1653
TO
1660

code of laws, begun under the Long Parliament by a committee with Sir Matthew Hale at its head, was again pushed forward. The frenzied alarm which these bold measures aroused among the lawyer class was soon backed by that of the clergy, who saw their wealth menaced by the establishment of civil marriage, and by proposals to substitute the free contributions of congregations for the payment of tithes. The landed proprietors too rose against the scheme for the abolition of lay-patronage, which was favoured by the Convention, and predicted an age of confiscation. The " Barebones Parliament," as the assembly was styled in derision, was charged with a design to ruin property, the Church, and the law, with enmity to knowledge, and a blind and ignorant fanaticism. Cromwell himself shared the general uneasiness at its proceedings. His mind was that of an administrator, rather than that of a statesman, unspeculative, deficient in foresight, conservative, and eminently practical. He saw the need of administrative reform in Church and State ; but he had no sympathy whatever with the revolutionary theories which were filling the air around him. His desire was for " a settlement " which should be accompanied with as little disturbance of the old state of things as possible. If Monarchy had vanished in the turmoil of war, his experience of the Long Parliament only confirmed him in his belief of the need of establishing an executive power of a similar kind, apart from the power of the legislature, as a condition of civil liberty. His sword had won " liberty of conscience ; " but passionately as he clung to it, he was still for an established Church, for a parochial system, and a ministry maintained by tithes. His social tendencies were simply those of the class to which he belonged. " I was by birth a gentleman," he told a later Parliament, and in the old social arrangement of "a nobleman, a gentleman, a yeoman," he saw "a good interest of the nation and a great one." He hated "that levelling principle" which tended to the reducing of all to one equality. " What was the purport of it," he asks with an amusing simplicity, " but to make the tenant as liberal a fortune as the landlord ? Which, I think, if obtained, would not have lasted long. The men of that principle, after they had served their own turns, would then have cried up property and interest fast enough."

To a practical temper such as this the speculative reforms of the Convention were as distasteful as to the lawyers and clergy whom they attacked. " Nothing," said Cromwell, " was in the hearts of these men but ' overturn, overturn.' " But he was delivered from his embarrassment by the internal dissensions of the Assembly itself. The day after the decision against tithes the more conservative members snatched a vote by surprise "that the sitting of this Parliament any longer, as now constituted, will not be for the good of the Commonwealth, and that it is requisite to deliver up unto the Lord-General the

PURITAN ENGLAND.

SEC. X.

THE
FALL OF
PURITANISM

1653
TO
1660

powers we received from him." The Speaker placed their abdication in Cromwell's hands, and the act was confirmed by the subsequent adhesion of a majority of the members. The dissolution the Convention replaced matters in the state in which its assembly had found them; but there was still the same general anxiety to substitute some sort of legal rule for the power of the sword. The Convention had named during its session a fresh Council of State, and this body at once drew up, under the name of the Instrument of Government, a remarkable Constitution, which was adopted by the Council of Officers.

The Instrument of Government

They were driven by necessity to the step from which they had shrunk before, that of convening a Parliament on the reformed basis of representation, though such a basis had no legal sanction. The House was to consist of four hundred members from England, thirty from Scotland, and thirty from Ireland. The seats hitherto assigned to small and rotten boroughs were transferred to larger constituencies, and for the most part to counties. All special rights of voting in the election of members were abolished, and replaced by a general right of suffrage, based on the possession of real or personal property to the value of two hundred pounds. Catholics and " Malignants," as those who had fought for the King were called, were excluded for the while from the franchise. Constitutionally, all further organization of the form of government should have been left to this Assembly; but the dread of disorder during the interval of its election, as well as a longing for "settlement," drove the Council to complete their work by pressing the office of " Protector" upon Cromwell. " They told me that except I would undertake the government they thought things would hardly come to a composure or settlement, but blood and confusion would break in as before." If we follow however his own statement, it was when they urged that the acceptance of such a Protectorate actually limited his power as Lord-General, and "bound his hands to act nothing without the consent of a Council until the Parliament," that the post was accepted. The powers of the new Protector indeed were strictly limited. Though the members of the Council were originally named by him, each member was irremovable save by consent of the rest: their advice was necessary in all foreign affairs, their consent in matters of peace and war, their approval in nominations to the great offices of state, or the disposal of the military or civil power. With this body too lay the choice of all future Protectors. To the administrative check of the Council was added the political check of the Parliament. Three years at the most were to elapse between the assembling of one Parliament and another. Laws could not be made, nor taxes imposed but by its authority, and after the lapse of twenty days the statutes it passed became laws even if the Protector's assent was refused to them. The new Constitution was undoubtedly popular; and the promise of a real Parliament in a few

SEC. X.

THE
FALL OF
PURITANISM
1653
TO
1660

Parlia-
ment
of 1654

months covered the want of any legal character in the new rule. The Government was generally accepted as a provisional one, which could only acquire legal authority from the ratification of its acts in the coming session ; and the desire to settle it on such a Parliamentary basis was universal among the members of the new Assembly which met in the autumn at Westminster.

Few Parliaments have ever been more memorable, or more truly representative of the English people, than the Parliament of 1654. It was the first Parliament in our history where members from Scotland and Ireland sate side by side with those from England, as they sit in the Parliament of to-day. The members for rotten boroughs and pocket-boroughs had disappeared. In spite of the exclusion of royalists and Catholics from the polling-booths, and the arbitrary erasure of the names of a few ultra-republican members by the Council, the House had a better title to the name of a "free Parliament" than any which had sat before. The freedom with which the electors had exercized their right of voting was seen indeed in the large number of Presbyterian members who were returned, and in the reappearance of Haselrig and Bradshaw, with many members of the Long Parliament, side by side with Lord Herbert and the older Sir Harry Vane. The first business of the House was clearly to consider the question of government ; and Haselrig, with the fiercer republicans, at once denied the legal existence of either Council or Protector, on the ground that the Long Parliament had never been dissolved. Such an argument, however, told as much against the Parliament in which they sate as against the administration itself, and the bulk of the Assembly contented themselves with declining to recognize the Constitution or Protectorate as of more than provisional validity. They proceeded at once to settle the government on a Parliamentary basis. The "Instrument" was taken as the groundwork of the new Constitution, and carried clause by clause. That Cromwell should retain his rule as Protector was unanimously agreed ; that he should possess the right of veto or a co-ordinate legislative power with the Parliament was hotly debated, though the violent language of Haselrig did little to disturb the general tone of moderation. Suddenly, however, Cromwell interposed. If he had undertaken the duties of Protector with reluctance, he looked on all legal defects in his title as more than supplied by the consent of the nation. "I called not myself to this place," he urged, "God and the people of these kingdoms have borne testimony to it." His rule had been accepted by London, by the army, by the solemn decision of the judges, by addresses from every shire, by the very appearance of the members of the Parliament in answer to his writ. "Why may I not balance this Providence," he asked, "with any hereditary interest?" In this national approval he saw a call from God, a Divine Right of a higher order than that of the kings who had gone before.

But there was another ground for the anxiety with which he watched the proceedings of the Commons. His passion for administration had far overstepped the bounds of a merely provisional rule in the interval before the assembling of the Parliament. His desire for "settlement" had been strengthened not only by the drift of public opinion, but by the urgent need of every day; and the power reserved by the "Instrument" to issue temporary ordinances "until further order in such matters, to be taken by the Parliament," gave a scope to his marvellous activity of which he at once took advantage. Sixty-four Ordinances had been issued in the nine months before the meeting of the Parliament. Peace had been concluded with Holland. The Church had been set in order. The law itself had been minutely regulated. The union with Scotland had been brought to completion. So far was Cromwell from dreaming that these measures, or the authority which enacted them, would be questioned, that he looked to Parliament simply to complete his work. "The great end of your meeting," he said at the first assembly of its members, "is healing and settling." Though he had himself done much, he added, "there was still much to be done." Peace had to be made with Portugal, and alliance with Spain. Bills were laid before the House for the codification of the law. The plantation and settlement of Ireland had still to be completed. He resented the setting these projects aside for constitutional questions which, as he held, a Divine call had decided, but he resented yet more the renewed claim advanced by Parliament to the sole power of legislation. As we have seen, his experience of the evils which had arisen from the concentration of legislative and executive power in the Long Parliament had convinced Cromwell of the danger to public liberty which lay in such a union. He saw in the joint government of "a single person and a Parliament" the only assurance "that Parliaments should not make themselves perpetual," or that their power should not be perverted to public wrong. But whatever strength there may have been in the Protector's arguments, the act by which he proceeded to enforce them was fatal to liberty, and in the end to Puritanism. "If my calling be from God," he ended, "and my testimony from the People, God and the People shall take it from me, else I will not part from it." And he announced that no member would be suffered to enter the House without signing an engagement "not to alter the Government as it is settled in a single person and a Parliament." No act of the Stuarts had been a bolder defiance of constitutional law; and the act was as needless as it was illegal. One hundred members alone refused to take the engagement, and the signatures of three-fourths of the House proved that the security Cromwell desired might have been easily procured by a vote of Parliament. But those who remained resumed their constitutional task with unbroken firmness. They quietly asserted

SEC. X.

THE
FALL OF
PURITANISM
1653
TO
1660
Crom-
well's
Adminis-
tration

*Dissolution
of the
Parliament*

SEC. X.

THE
FALL OF
PURITANISM
1653
TO
1660

their sole title to government by referring the Protector's Ordinances to Committees for revision, and for conversion into laws. The "Instrument of Government" was turned into a bill, debated, and after some modifications read a third time. Money votes, as in previous Parliaments, were deferred till "grievances" had been settled. But Cromwell once more intervened. The royalists were astir again ; and he attributed their renewed hopes to the hostile attitude which he ascribed to the Parliament. The army, which remained unpaid while the supplies were delayed, was seething with discontent. " It looks," said the Protector, " as if the laying grounds for a quarrel had rather been designed than to give the people settlement. Judge yourselves whether the contesting of things that were provided for by this government hath been profitable expense of time for the good of this nation." In words of angry reproach he declared the Parliament dissolved.

Jan. 1655

**The New
Tyranny**

With the dissolution of the Parliament of 1654 ended all show of constitutional rule. The Protectorate, deprived by its own act of all chance of legal sanction, became a simple tyranny. Cromwell professed, indeed, to be restrained by the "Instrument": but the one great restraint on his power which the Instrument provided, the inability to levy taxes save by consent of Parliament, was set aside on the plea of necessity. "The People," said the Protector in words which Strafford might have uttered, "will prefer their real security to forms." That a danger of royalist revolt existed was undeniable, but the danger was at once doubled by the general discontent. From this moment, Whitelock tells us, "many sober and noble patriots," in despair of public liberty, "did begin to incline to the King's restoration." In the mass of the population the reaction was far more rapid. "Charles Stuart," writes a Cheshire correspondent to the Secretary of State, "hath five hundred friends in these adjacent counties for every one friend to you among them." But before the overpowering strength of the army even this general discontent was powerless. Yorkshire, where the royalist insurrection was expected to be most formidable, never ventured to rise at all. There were risings in Devon, Dorset, and the Welsh Marches, but they were quickly put down, and their leaders brought to the scaffold. Easily however as the revolt was suppressed, the terror of the Government was seen in the energetic measures to which Cromwell resorted in the hope of securing order. The country was divided into ten military governments, each with a major-general at its head, who was empowered to disarm all Papists and royalists, and to arrest suspected persons. Funds for the supports of this military despotism were provided by an Ordinance of the Council of State, which enacted that all who had at any time borne arms for the King should pay every year a tenth part of their income, in spite of the Act of Oblivion, as a fine for their royalist tendencies. The despotism

*The Major-
Generals*

of the major-generals was seconded by the older expedients of tyranny. The ejected clergy had been zealous in promoting the insurrection, and they were forbidden in revenge to act as chaplains or as tutors. The press was placed under a strict censorship. The payment of taxes levied by the sole authority of the Protector was enforced by distraint ; and when a collector was sued in the courts for redress, the counsel for the prosecution were sent to the Tower.

If pardon, indeed, could ever be won for a tyranny, the wisdom and grandeur with which he used the power he had usurped would win pardon for the Protector. The greatest among the many great enterprises undertaken by the Long Parliament had been the Union of the three Kingdoms : and that of Scotland with England had been brought about, at the very end of its career, by the tact and vigour of Sir Harry Vane. But its practical realization was left to Cromwell. In four months of hard fighting General Monk brought the Highlands to a new tranquillity ; and the presence of an army of eight thousand men, backed by a line of forts, kept the most restless of the clans in good order. The settlement of the country was brought about by the temperance and sagacity of Monk's successor, General Deane. No further interference with the Presbyterian system was attempted beyond the suppression of the General Assembly. But religious liberty was resolutely protected, and Deane ventured even to interfere on behalf of the miserable victims whom Scotch bigotry was torturing and burning on the charge of witchcraft. Even steady royalists acknowledged the justice of the Government and the wonderful discipline of its troops. "We always reckon those eight years of the usurpation," said Burnet afterwards, "a time of great peace and prosperity." There was sterner work in Ireland. The war of conquest had been continued by Ireton, and was completed after his death by General Ludlow. Thousands perished by famine, and a third of the population was blotted out. Shipload after shipload of those who surrendered were sent over sea for sale into forced labour in Jamaica and the West Indies. Slave-dealers were let loose, and orphan boys and girls and young widows of the slain sold in Barbadoes to the planters. More than forty thousand of the beaten Catholics were permitted to enlist for foreign service, and found a refuge in exile under the banners of France and Spain. The work of settlement turned out to be even more terrible than the work of the sword. It took as its model the Plantation of Ulster, the fatal measure which had destroyed all hope of a united Ireland, and had brought inevitably in its train the revolt and the war. The people were divided into classes in the order of their assumed guilt. All who had shared in the rising of 1641 were condemned to death and forfeiture of lands. Catholic proprietors who had borne arms against the Parliament forfeited all their estates :

SEC. X.

THE
FALL OF
PURITANISM

1653
TO
1660

Scotland
and
Ireland

1652

SEC. X.

THE
FALL OF
PURITANISM
1653
TO
1660

some were promised a third of their value in Connacht, carved out from the lands of the native clans ; others were banished. Papists who had not shown "a constant good affection" for the Parliament by actively taking arms for it, lost their estates and were allowed two-thirds of their value in Connacht. The confiscation was universal. Plough-men and labourers were alone permitted to remain to cultivate the land for the new masters, soldiers and adventurers. No such doom had ever fallen on a nation in modern times as fell upon Ireland in its new settlement. Among the bitter memories which part Ireland from England the memory of the bloodshed and confiscation which the Puritans wrought remains the bitterest ; and the worst curse an Irish peasant can hurl at his enemy is "the curse of Cromwell." But pitiless as the Protector's policy was, it was successful in the ends at which it aimed. The whole native population lay helpless and crushed. All or almost all the land in the three largest and richest provinces was confiscated and divided among English Protestants. The legislative union which had been brought about with Scotland was now carried out with Ireland, and thirty seats were allotted to its representatives in the general Parliament.

In England Cromwell dealt with the royalists as irreconcilable enemies ; but in every other respect he carried fairly out his pledge of "healing and settling." The series of administrative reforms planned by the Convention had been partially carried into effect before the meet-ing of Parliament in 1654; but the work was pushed on after the dissolu-tion of the House with yet greater energy. Nearly a hundred ordinances showed the industry of the Government. Police, public amusements, roads, finances, the condition of prisons, the imprisonment of debtors, were a few among the subjects which claimed Cromwell's attention. An ordinance of more than fifty clauses reformed the Court of Chancery. The anarchy which had reigned in the Church since the break-down of Episcopacy and the failure of the Presbyterian system to supply its place, was put an end to by a series of wise and temperate measures for its reorganization. Rights of patronage were left untouched ; but a Board of Triers, a fourth of whom were laymen, was appointed to examine the fitness of ministers presented to livings ; and a Church board of gentry and clergy was set up in every county to exercise a supervision over ecclesiastical affairs, and to detect and remove scandalous and ineffectual ministers. Even by the confession of Cromwell's opponents, the plan worked well. It furnished the country with "able, serious preachers," Baxter tells us, "who lived a godly life, of what tolerable opinion soever they were," and, as both Presbyterian and Independent ministers were presented to livings at the will of their patrons, it solved so far as practical working was con-cerned the problem of a religious union among the Puritans on the base of a wide variety of Christian opinion. From the Church which was

SEC. X.

THE
FALL OF
PURITANISM

1653
TO
1660

thus reorganized all power of interference with faiths differing from its own was resolutely withheld. Save in his dealings with the Episcopalians, whom he looked on as a political danger, Cromwell remained true throughout to the cause of religious liberty. Even the Quaker, rejected by all other Christian bodies as an anarchist and blasphemer, found sympathy and protection in the Protector. The Jews had been excluded from England since the reign of Edward the First; and a prayer which they now presented for leave to return was refused by the commission of merchants and divines to whom the Protector referred it for consideration. But the refusal was quietly passed over, and the connivance of Cromwell in the settlement of a few Hebrews in London and Oxford was so clearly understood that no one ventured to interfere with them.

No part of his policy is more characteristic of Cromwell's mind, whether in its strength or in its weakness, than his management of foreign affairs. While England had been absorbed in her long and obstinate struggle for freedom the whole face of the world around her had changed. The Thirty Years' War was over. The victories of Gustavus, and of the Swedish generals who followed him, had been seconded by the policy of Richelieu and the intervention of France. Protestantism in Germany was no longer in peril from the bigotry or ambition of the House of Austria: and the Treaty of Westphalia had drawn a permanent line between the territories belonging to the adherents of the old religion and the new. There was little danger, indeed, now to Europe from the great Catholic House which had threatened its freedom ever since Charles the Fifth. Its Austrian branch was called away from dreams of aggression in the west to a desperate struggle with the Turk for the possession of Hungary and the security of Austria itself. Spain was falling into a state of strange decrepitude. So far from aiming to be mistress of Europe, she was rapidly sinking into the almost helpless prey of France. It was France which had now become the dominant power in Christendom, though her position was far from being as commanding as it was to become under Lewis the Fourteenth. The peace and order which prevailed after the cessation of the religious troubles throughout her compact and fertile territory gave scope at last to the quick and industrious temper of the French people; while her wealth and energy were placed by the centralizing administration of Henry the Fourth, of Richelieu, and of Mazarin, almost absolutely in the hands of the Crown. Under the three great rulers who have just been named her ambition was steadily directed to the same purpose of territorial aggrandizement, and though limited as yet to the annexation of the Spanish and Imperial territories which still parted her frontier from the Pyrenees, the Alps, and the Rhine, a statesman of wise political genius would have discerned the beginning of that great struggle for supremacy over Europe at large which was

*Crom-
well and
Europe*

*Cromwell's
foreign
policy*

SEC. X.

THE
FALL OF
PURITANISM

1653
TO
1660

only foiled by the genius of Marlborough and the victories of the Grand Alliance. But in his view of European politics Cromwell was misled by the conservative and unspeculative temper of his mind as well as by the strength of his religious enthusiasm. Of the change in the world around him he seems to have discerned nothing. He brought to the Europe of Mazarin the hopes and ideas with which all England was thrilling in his youth at the outbreak of the Thirty Years' War. Spain was still to him "the head of the Papal Interest," whether at home or abroad. "The Papists in England," he said to the Parliament of 1656, "have been accounted, ever since I was born, Spaniolized; they never regarded France, or any other Papist state, but Spain only." The old English hatred of Spain, the old English resentment at the shameful part which the nation had been forced to play in the great German struggle by the policy of James and of Charles, lived on in Cromwell, and was only strengthened by the religious enthusiasm which the success of Puritanism had kindled within him. "The Lord Himself," he wrote to his admirals as they sailed to the West Indies, "hath a controversy with your enemies; even with that Romish Babylon of which the Spaniard is the great underpropper. In that respect we fight the Lord's battles." What Sweden had been under Gustavus, England, Cromwell dreamt, might be now—the head of a great Protestant League in the struggle against Catholic aggression. "You have on your shoulders," he said to the Parliament of 1654, "the interest of all the Christian people of the world. I wish it may be written on our hearts to be zealous for that interest."

**War with
Spain**

The first step in such a struggle was necessarily to league the Protestant powers together, and Cromwell's earliest efforts were directed to bring the ruinous and indecisive quarrel with Holland to an end. The fierceness of the strife had grown with each engagement; but the hopes of Holland fell with her admiral, Tromp, who received a mortal wound at the moment when he had succeeded in forcing the English line; and the skill and energy of his successor, De Ruyter, struggled in vain to restore her waning fortunes. She was saved by the expulsion of the Long Parliament, which had persisted in its demand of a political union of the two countries; and the new policy of Cromwell was seen in the conclusion of peace. The United Provinces recognized the supremacy of the English flag in the British seas, and submitted to the Navigation Act, while Holland pledged itself to shut out the House of Orange from power, and thus relieved England from the risk of seeing a Stuart restoration supported by Dutch forces. The peace with the Dutch was followed by the conclusion of like treaties with Sweden and with Denmark; and on the arrival of a Swedish envoy with offers of a league of friendship, Cromwell endeavoured to bring the Dutch, the Brandenburgers, and the Danes into a confederation of the Protestant powers. His efforts in this direction however, though they never

1654

Sec. X.

The
Fall of
Puritanism

1653
to
1660

1655

wholly ceased, remained fruitless ; but the Protector was resolute to carry out his plans single-handed. The defeat of the Dutch had left England the chief sea-power of the world ; and before the dissolution of the Parliament, two fleets put to sea with secret instructions. The first, under Blake, appeared in the Mediterranean, exacted reparation from Tuscany for wrongs done to English commerce, bombarded Algiers, and destroyed the fleet with which its pirates had ventured through the reign of Charles to insult the English coast. The thunder of Blake's guns, every Puritan believed, would be heard in the castle of St. Angelo, and Rome itself would have to bow to the greatness of Cromwell. But though no declaration of war had been issued against Spain, the true aim of both expeditions was an attack on that power ; and the attack proved singularly unsuccessful. Though Blake sailed to the Spanish coast, he failed to intercept the treasure fleet from America ; and the second expedition, which made its way to the West Indies, was foiled in a descent on St. Domingo. Its conquest of Jamaica, important as it really was in breaking through the monopoly of the New World in the South which Spain had till now enjoyed, seemed at the time but a poor result for a vast expenditure of blood and money. Its leaders were sent to the Tower on their return ; but Cromwell found himself at war with Spain, and thrown whether he would or no into the hands of the French minister Mazarin.

He was forced to sign a treaty of alliance with France ; while the cost of his abortive expeditions drove him again to face a Parliament. But Cromwell no longer trusted, as in his earlier Parliament, to freedom of elections. The sixty members sent from Ireland and Scotland under the Ordinances of union were simply nominees of the Government. Its whole influence was exerted to secure the return of the more conspicuous members of the Council of State. It was calculated that of the members returned one-half were bound to the Government by ties of profit or place. But Cromwell was still unsatisfied. A certificate of the Council was required from each member before admission to the House ; and a fourth of the whole number returned— one hundred in all, with Haselrig at their head—were by this means excluded on grounds of disaffection or want of religion. To these arbitrary acts of violence the House replied only by a course of singular moderation and wisdom. From the first it disclaimed any purpose of opposing the Government. One of its earliest acts provided securities for Cromwell's person, which was threatened by constant plots of assassination. It supported him in his war policy, and voted supplies of unprecedented extent for the maintenance of the struggle. It was this attitude of loyalty which gave force to its steady refusal to sanction the system of tyranny which had practically placed England under martial law. In his opening address Cromwell boldly took his stand in support of the military despotism wielded by the

SEC. X.
THE
FALL OF
PURITANISM
1653
TO
1660

major-generals. "It hath been more effectual towards the discountenancing of vice and settling religion than anything done these fifty years. I will abide by it," he said, with singular vehemence, "notwithstanding the envy and slander of foolish men. I could as soon venture my life with it as with anything I ever undertook. If it were to be done again, I would do it." But no sooner had a bill been introduced into Parliament to confirm the proceedings of the major-generals than a long debate showed the temper of the Commons. They had resolved to acquiesce in the Protectorate, but they were equally resolved to bring it again to a legal mode of government. This indeed was the aim of even Cromwell's wiser adherents. "What makes me fear the passing of this Act," one of them wrote to his son Henry, "is that thereby His Highness' government will be more founded in force, and more removed from that natural foundation which the people in Parliament are desirous to give him, supposing that he will become more theirs than now he is." The bill was rejected, and Cromwell bowed to the feeling of the nation by withdrawing the powers of the major-generals.

But the defeat of the tyranny of the sword was only a step towards a far bolder effort for the restoration of the power of the law. It was no mere pedantry, still less was it vulgar flattery, which influenced the Parliament in their offer to Cromwell of the title of King. The experience of the last few years had taught the nation the value of the traditional forms under which its liberties had grown up. A king was limited by constitutional precedents. "The King's prerogative," it was well urged, " is under the courts of justice, and is bounded as well as any acre of land, or anything a man hath." A Protector, on the other hand, was new in our history, and there were no traditional means of limiting his power. "The one office being lawful in its nature," said Glynne, "known to the nation, certain in itself, and confined and regulated by the law, and the other not so—that was the great ground why the Parliament did so much insist on this office and title." Under the name of Monarchy, indeed, the question really at issue between the party headed by the officers and the party led by the lawyers in the Commons was that of the restoration of constitutional and legal rule. The proposal was carried by an overwhelming majority, but a month passed in endless consultations between the Parliament and the Protector. His good sense, his knowledge of the general feeling of the nation, his real desire to obtain a settlement which should secure the ends for which Puritanism fought, political and religious liberty, broke in conference after conference through a mist of words. But his real concern throughout was with the temper of the army. Cromwell knew well that his government was a sheer government of the sword, and that the discontent of his soldiery would shake the fabric of his power. He vibrated to and fro between his sense of the political advan-

SEC. X.

THE
FALL OF
PURITANISM
1653
TO
1660

tages of such a settlement, and his sense of its impossibility in face of the mood of the army. His soldiers, he said, were no common swordsmen. They were "godly men, men that will not be beaten down by a worldly and carnal spirit while they keep their integrity;" men in whose general voice he recognized the voice of God. "They are honest and faithful men," he urged, "true to the great things of the Government. And though it really is no part of their goodness to be unwilling to submit to what a Parliament shall settle over them, yet it is my duty and conscience to beg of you that there may be no hard things put upon them which they cannot swallow. I cannot think God would bless an undertaking of anything which would justly and with cause grieve them." The temper of the army was soon shown. Its leaders, with Lambert, Fleetwood, and Desborough at their head, placed their commands in Cromwell's hands. A petition from the officers to Parliament demanded the withdrawal of the proposal to restore the Monarchy, "in the name of the old cause for which they had bled." Cromwell at once anticipated the coming debate on this petition, a debate which might have led to an open breach between the army and the Commons, by a refusal of the crown. "I cannot undertake this Government," he said, "with that title of King; and that is my answer to this great and weighty business."

Disappointed as it was, the Parliament with singular self-restraint turned to other modes of bringing about its purpose. The offer of the crown had been coupled with the condition of accepting a constitution which was a modification of the Instrument of Government adopted by the Parliament of 1654, and this constitution Cromwell emphatically approved. "The things provided by this Act of Government," he owned, "do secure the liberties of the people of God as they never before have had them." With a change of the title of King into that of Protector, the Act of Government now became law; and the solemn inauguration of the Protector by the Parliament was a practical acknowledgment on the part of Cromwell of the illegality of his former rule. In the name of the Commons the Speaker invested him with a mantle of State, placed the sceptre in his hand, and girt the sword of justice by his side. By the new Act of Government Cromwell was allowed to name his own successor, but in all after cases the office was to be an elective one. In every other respect the forms of the older Constitution were carefully restored. Parliament was again to consist of two Houses, the seventy members of "the other House" being named by the Protector. The Commons regained their old right of exclusively deciding on the qualification of their members. Parliamentary restrictions were imposed on the choice of members of the Council, and officers of State or of the army. A fixed revenue was voted to the Protector, and it was provided that no moneys should be raised but by assent of Parliament. Liberty of worship was secured

SEC. X.

THE
FALL OF
PURITANISM

1653
TO
1660

Crom-
well's
triumphs

for all but Papists, Prelatists, Socinians, or those who denied the inspiration of the Scriptures ; and liberty of conscience was secured for all.

The adjournment of the House after his inauguration left Cromwell at the height of his power. He seemed at last to have placed his government on a legal and national basis. The ill-success of his earlier operations abroad was forgotten in a blaze of glory. On the eve of the Parliament's assembly one of Blake's captains had managed to intercept a part of the Spanish treasure fleet. At the close of 1656 the Protector seemed to have found the means of realizing his schemes for rekindling the religious war throughout Europe in a quarrel between the Duke of Savoy and his Protestant subjects in the valleys of Piedmont. A ruthless massacre of these Vaudois by the Duke's troops roused deep resentment throughout England, a resentment which still breathes in the noblest of Milton's sonnets. While the poet called on God to avenge his " slaughtered saints, whose bones lie scattered on the Alpine mountains cold," Cromwell was already busy with the work of earthly vengeance. An English envoy appeared at the Duke's court with haughty demands of redress. Their refusal would have been followed by instant war, for the Protestant Cantons of Switzerland were bribed into promising a force of ten thousand men for an attack on Savoy. The plan was foiled by the cool diplomacy of Mazarin, who forced the Duke to grant Cromwell's demands ; but the apparent success of the Protector raised his reputation at home and abroad. The spring of 1657 saw the greatest as it was the last of the triumphs of Blake. He found the Spanish Plate fleet guarded by galleons in the strongly-armed harbour of Santa Cruz ; he forced an entrance into the harbour and burnt or sank every ship within it. Triumphs at sea were followed by a triumph on land. Cromwell's demand of Dunkirk, which had long stood in the way of any acceptance of his offers of aid, was at last conceded ; and a detachment of the Puritan army joined the French troops who were attacking Flanders under the command of Turenne. Their valour and discipline were shown by the part they took in the capture of Mardyke ; and still more by the victory of the Dunes, a victory which forced the Flemish towns to open their gates to the French, and gave Dunkirk to Cromwell.

Never had the fame of an English ruler stood higher ; but in the midst of his glory the hand of death was falling on the Protector. He had long been weary of his task. " God knows," he had burst out to the Parliament a year before, " I would have been glad to have lived under my woodside, and to have kept a flock of sheep, rather than to have undertaken this government." And now to the weariness of power was added the weakness and feverish impatience of disease. Vigorous and energetic as his life had seemed, his health was by no means as

Sec. X.

The
Fall of
Puritanism
1653
TO
1660
Jan. 1658

strong as his will ; he had been struck down by intermittent fever in the midst of his triumphs both in Scotland and in Ireland, and during the past year he had suffered from repeated attacks of it. " I have some infirmities upon me," he owned twice over in his speech at the re-opening of the Parliament after an adjournment of six months ; and his feverish irritability was quickened by the public danger. No supplies had been voted, and the pay of the army was heavily in arrear, while its temper grew more and more sullen at the appearance of the new Constitution and the re-awakening of the royalist intrigues. Under the terms of the new Constitution the members excluded in the preceding year took their places again in the House. The mood of the nation was reflected in the captious and quarrelsome tone of the Commons. They still delayed the grant of supplies. Meanwhile a hasty act of the Protector in giving to his nominees in "the other House," as the new second chamber he had devised was called, the title of " Lords," kindled a strife between the two Houses which was busily fanned by Haselrig and other opponents of the Government. It was contended that the " other House " had under the new Constitution simply judicial and not legislative powers. Such a contention struck at Cromwell's work of restoring the old political forms of English life ; and the reappearance of Parliamentary strife threw him at last, says an observer at his court, " into a rage and passion like unto madness." What gave weight to it was the growing strength of the royalist party, and its preparations for a coming rising. Charles himself with a large body of Spanish troops drew to the coast of Flanders to take advantage of it. His hopes were above all encouraged by the strife in the Commons, and their manifest dislike of the system of the Protectorate. It was this that drove Cromwell to action. Summoning his coach, by a sudden impulse, the Protector drove with a few guards to Westminster ; and setting aside the remonstrances of Fleetwood, summoned the two Houses to his presence. " I do dissolve this Parliament," he ended a speech of angry rebuke, " and let God be judge between you and me." Fatal as was the error, for the moment all went well. The army was reconciled by the blow levelled at its opponents, and the few murmurers were weeded from its ranks by a careful remodelling. The triumphant officers vowed to stand or fall with his Highness. The danger of a royalist rising vanished before a host of addresses from the counties. Great news too came from abroad, where victory in Flanders, and the cession of Dunkirk, set the seal on Cromwell's glory. But the fever crept steadily on, and his looks told the tale of death to the Quaker, Fox, who met him riding in Hampton Court Park. " Before I came to him," he says, " as he rode at the head of his Life Guards, I saw and felt a waft of death go forth against him, and when I came to him he looked like a dead man." In the midst of his triumph Cromwell's heart was in fact heavy with the sense of failure. He had no desire to

*Dissolution
of the
Parliament*

SEC X.

THE
FALL OF
PURITANISM
1653
TO
1660

play the tyrant; nor had he any belief in the permanence of a mere tyranny. He clung desperately to the hope of bringing the country to his side. He had hardly dissolved the Parliament before he was planning the summons of another, and angry at the opposition which his Council offered to the project. "I will take my own resolutions," he said gloomily to his household; "I can no longer satisfy myself to sit still, and make myself guilty of the loss of all the honest party and of the nation itself." But before his plans could be realized the over-

Aug. 1658

taxed strength of the Protector suddenly gave way. He saw too clearly the chaos into which his death would plunge England to be willing to die. "Do not think I shall die," he burst out with feverish energy to the physicians who gathered round him; "say not I have lost my reason! I tell you the truth. I know it from better authority than any you can have from Galen or Hippocrates. It is the answer of God Himself to our prayers!" Prayer indeed rose from every side for his recovery, but death drew steadily nearer, till even Cromwell felt that his hour was come. "I would be willing to live," the dying man murmured, "to be further serviceable to God and His people, but my work is done! Yet God will be with His people!" A storm which tore roofs from houses, and levelled huge trees in every forest, seemed a fitting prelude to the passing away of his mighty spirit. Three days later, on the third of September, the day which had witnessed his victories of Worcester and Dunbar, Cromwell quietly breathed his last.

**The Fall
of Puri-
tanism**

So absolute even in death was his sway over the minds of men, that, to the wonder of the excited royalists, even a doubtful nomina-tion on his death-bed was enough to secure the peaceful succession of his son, Richard Cromwell. Many, in fact, who had rejected the authority of his father submitted peaceably to the new Protector. Their motives were explained by Baxter, the most eminent among the Presbyterian ministers, in the address to Richard which announced his adhesion. "I observe," he says, "that the nation generally rejoice in your peaceable entrance upon the Government. Many are per-suaded that you have been strangely kept from participating in any of our late bloody contentions, that God might make you the healer of our breaches, and employ you in that Temple work which David him-self might not be honoured with, though it was in his mind, because

*Richard
Cromwell*

he shed blood abundantly and made great wars." The new Protector was a weak and worthless man, but the bulk of the nation were con-tent to be ruled by one who was at any rate no soldier, no Puritan, and no innovator. Richard was known to be lax and worldly in his con-duct, and he was believed to be conservative and even royalist in heart. The tide of reaction was felt even in his Council. Their first act was to throw aside one of the greatest of Cromwell's reforms,

Jan. 1659

and to fall back in the summons which they issued for the new Parliament on the old system of election.   It was felt far more keenly in the tone of the new House of Commons.   The republicans under Vane, backed adroitly by the secret royalists, fell hotly on Cromwell's system.   The fiercest attack of all came from Sir Ashley Cooper, a Dorsetshire gentleman who had changed sides in the civil war, had fought for the King and then for the Parliament, had been a member of Cromwell's Council, and had of late ceased to be a member of it.   His virulent invective on "his Highness of deplorable memory, who with fraud and force deprived you of your liberty when living, and entailed slavery on you at his death," was followed by an equally virulent invective against the army.   "They have not only subdued their enemies," said Cooper, "but the masters who raised and maintained them !   They have not only conquered Scotland and Ireland, but rebellious England too ; and there suppressed a Malignant party of magistrates and laws."   The army was quick with its reply.   It had already demanded the appointment of a soldier as its General in the place of the new Protector, who had assumed the command.   The tone of the Council of Officers now became so menacing that the Commons ordered the dismissal of all officers who refused to engage "not to disturb or interrupt the free meetings of Parliament." Richard ordered the Council of Officers to dissolve.   Their reply was a demand for the dissolution of the Parliament, a demand with which Richard was forced to comply.   The purpose of the army however was still to secure a settled government ; and setting aside the new Protector, whose weakness was now evident, they resolved to come to a reconciliation with the republican party, and to recall the fragment of the Commons whom they had expelled from St. Stephen's in 1653.   Of the one hundred and sixty members who had continued to sit after the King's death, about ninety returned to their seats, and resumed the administration of affairs.   But the continued exclusion of the members who had been "purged" from the House in 1648, proved that no real intention existed of restoring a legal rule.   The House was soon at strife with the soldiers.   In spite of Vane's counsels, it proposed a reform of the officers, and though a royalist rising in Cheshire during August threw the disputants for a moment together, the struggle revived as the danger passed away.   A new hope indeed filled men's minds.   Not only was the nation sick of military rule, but the army, unconquerable so long as it held together, at last showed signs of division.   In Ireland and Scotland the troops protested against the attitude of their English comrades ; and Monk, the commander of the Scottish army, threatened to march on London and free the Parliament from their pressure.   Their divisions encouraged Haselrig and his coadjutors to demand the dismissal of Fleetwood and Lambert from their commands.   They answered by driving the Parliament again from Westminster, and by marching under Lambert

SEC. X.

THE
FALL OF
PURITANISM

1653
TO
1660

*Return of
the Rump*

*Divisions in
the army*

SEC. X.
THE
FALL OF
PURITANISM
1653
TO
1660
Jan. 1660

to the north to meet Monk's army.   Negotiation gave Monk time to gather a Convention at Edinburgh and strengthen himself with money and recruits.   His attitude roused England to action.   So rapidly did the tide of feeling rise throughout the country that the army was driven to undo its work by recalling the Rump.   Monk however advanced rapidly to Coldstream, and crossed the border.   The cry of "A free Parliament" ran like fire through the country.   Not only Fairfax, who appeared in arms in Yorkshire, but the ships on the Thames and the mob which thronged the streets of London caught up the cry ; and Monk, who lavished protestations of loyalty to the Rump, while he accepted petitions for a " Free Parliament," entered London unopposed.   From the moment of his entry the restoration of the Stuarts became inevitable.   The army, resolute as it still remained for the maintenance of "the cause," was deceived by Monk's declarations of loyalty to it, and rendered powerless by his adroit dispersion of the troops over the country.   At the instigation of Ashley Cooper, those who re-

*The
Convention
April 25*

mained of the members who had been excluded from the House of Commons by Pride's Purge in 1648 again forced their way into Parliament, and at once resolved on a dissolution and the election of a new House of Commons.   The new House, which bears the name of the Convention, had hardly taken the solemn League and Covenant which showed its Presbyterian temper, and its leaders had only begun to draw up terms on which the King's restoration might be assented to, when they found that Monk was in negotiation with the exiled Court.   All exaction of terms was now impossible ; a Declaration from Breda in which Charles promised a general pardon, religious toleration, and satisfaction to the army was received with a burst of national enthusiasm ; and the old Constitution was restored by a solemn vote of the Convention, " that according to the ancient and fundamental laws of this Kingdom, the government is, and ought to be, by King, Lords, and

*Return of
Charles
May 25*

Commons."   The King was at once invited to hasten to his realm ; he landed at Dover, and made his way amidst the shouts of a great multitude to Whitehall.   " It is my own fault," laughed the new King, with characteristic irony " that I had not come back sooner ; for I find nobody who does not tell me he has always longed for my return."

Milton

Puritanism, so men believed, had fallen never to rise again.   As a political experiment it had ended in utter failure and disgust.   As a religious system of national life it brought about the wildest outbreak of moral revolt that England has ever witnessed.   And yet Puritanism was far from being dead ; it drew indeed a nobler life from suffering and defeat.   Nothing aids us better to trace the real course of Puritan influence since the fall of Puritanism than the thought of the two great works which have handed down from one generation to another its highest and noblest spirit.   From that time to this the most popular of all religious books has been the Puritan allegory of the " Pilgrim's Progress."

SEC. X.

THE
FALL OF
PURITANISM

1653
TO
1660

The most popular of all English poems has been the Puritan epic of the "Paradise Lost." Milton had been engaged during the civil war in strife with Presbyterians and with Royalists, pleading for civil and religious freedom, for freedom of social life, and freedom of the press. At a later time he became Latin Secretary to the Protector, in spite of a blindness which had been brought on by the intensity of his study. The Restoration found him of all living men the most hateful to the Royalists ; for it was his "Defence of the English People" which had justified throughout Europe the execution of the King. Parliament ordered his book to be burnt by the common hangman ; he was for a time imprisoned, and even when released he had to live amidst threats of assassination from fanatical Cavaliers. To the ruin of his cause were added personal misfortunes in the bankruptcy of the scrivener who held the bulk of his property, and in the Fire of London, which deprived him of much of what was left. As age drew on, he found himself reduced to comparative poverty, and driven to sell his library for subsistence. Even among the sectaries who shared his political opinions Milton stood in religious opinion alone, for he had gradually severed himself from every accepted form of faith, had embraced Arianism, and had ceased to attend at any place of worship. Nor was his home a happy one. The grace and geniality of his youth disappeared in the drudgery of a schoolmaster's life and amongst the invectives of controversy. In age his temper became stern and exacting. His daughters, who were forced to read to their blind father in languages which they could not understand, revolted utterly against their bondage. But solitude and misfortune only brought out into bolder relief Milton's inner greatness. There was a grand simplicity in the life of his later years. He listened every morning to a chapter of the Hebrew Bible, and after musing in silence for a while pursued his studies till midday. Then he took exercise for an hour, played for another hour on the organ or viol, and renewed his studies. The evening was spent in converse with visitors and friends. For, lonely and unpopular as Milton was, there was one thing about him which made his house in Bunhill Fields a place of pilgrimage to the wits of the Restoration. He was the last of the Elizabethans. He had possibly seen Shakspere, as on his visits to London after his retirement to Stratford the playwright passed along Bread Street to his wit combats at the Mermaid. He had been the contemporary of Webber and Massinger, of Herrick and Crashaw. His "Comus" and "Arcades" had rivalled the masques of Ben Jonson. It was with a reverence drawn from thoughts like these that men looked on the blind poet as he sate, clad in black, in his chamber hung with rusty green tapestry, his fair brown hair falling as of old over a calm, serene face that still retained much of its youthful beauty, his cheeks delicately coloured, his clear grey eyes showing no trace of their

SEC. X.

THE
FALL OF
PURITANISM

1653
TO
1660

The
Paradise
Lost

1667

blindness. But famous, whether for good or ill, as his prose writings had made him, during fifteen years only a few sonnets had broken his silence as a singer. It was now, in his blindness and old age, with the cause he loved trodden under foot by men as vile as the rabble in " Comus," that the genius of Milton took refuge in the great poem on which through years of silence his imagination had still been brooding.

On his return from his travels in Italy, Milton had spoken of himself as musing on " a work not to be raised from the heat of youth or the vapours of wine, like that which flows at waste from the pen of some vulgar amourist or the trencher fury of a rhyming parasite, nor to be obtained by the invocation of Dame Memory and her Siren daughters ; but by devout prayer to that Eternal Spirit who can enrich with all utterance and knowledge, and sends out His Seraphim, with the hallowed fire of His altar, to touch and purify the lips of whom He pleases." His lips were touched at last. In his quiet retreat he mused during these years of persecution and loneliness on his great work. Seven years after the Restoration appeared the " Paradise Lost," and four years later the " Paradise Regained" and " Samson Agonistes," in the severe grandeur of whose verse we see the poet himself " fallen," like Samson, " on evil days and evil tongues, with darkness and with danger compassed round." But great as the two last works were, their greatness was eclipsed by that of their predecessor. The whole genius of Milton expressed itself in the " Paradise Lost." The romance, the gorgeous fancy, the daring imagination which he shared with the Eliza-bethan poets, the large but ordered beauty of form which he had drunk in from the literature of Greece and Rome, the sublimity of conception, the loftiness of phrase, which he owed to the Bible, blended in this story " of man's first disobedience, and the fruit of that for-bidden tree, whose mortal taste brought death into the world and all our woe." It is only when we review the strangely mingled elements which make up the poem, that we realize the genius which fused them into such a perfect whole. The meagre outline of the Hebrew legend is lost in the splendour and music of Milton's verse. The stern idealism of Geneva is clothed in the gorgeous robes of the Renascence. If we miss something of the free play of Spenser's fancy, and yet more of the imaginative delight in their own creations which gives so exquisite a life to the poetry of the early dramatists, we find in place of these the noblest example which our literature affords of the ordered majesty of classic form. But it is not with the literary value of the " Paradise Lost " that we are here concerned. Its historic importance lies in this, that it is the Epic of Puritanism. Its scheme is the problem with which the Puritan wrestled in hours of gloom and darkness, the problem of sin and redemption, of the world-wide struggle of evil against good. The intense moral concen-tration of the Puritan had given an almost bodily shape to spiritual abstractions before Milton gave life and being to the forms of Sin and Death. It was the Puritan tendency to mass into one vast "body of sin" the various forms of human evil, and by the very force of a passionate hatred to exaggerate their magnitude and their power, to which we owe the conception of Milton's Satan. The greatness of the Puritan aim in the long and wavering struggle for justice and law and a higher good; the grandeur of character which the contest developed; the colossal forms of good and evil which moved over its stage; the debates and conspiracies and battles which had been men's life for twenty years; the mighty eloquence and mightier ambition which the war had roused into being—all left their mark on the "Paradise Lost." Whatever was highest and best in the Puritan temper spoke in the nobleness and elevation of the poem, in its purity of tone, in its grandeur of conception, in its ordered and equable realization of a great purpose. Even in his boldest flights, Milton is calm and master of himself. His touch is always sure. Whether he passes from Heaven to Hell, or from the council hall of Satan to the sweet conference of Adam and Eve, his tread is steady and unfaltering. But if the poem expresses the higher qualities of the Puritan temper, it expresses no less exactly its defects. Throughout it we feel almost painfully a want of the finer and subtler sympathies, of a large and genial humanity, of a sense of spiritual mystery. Dealing as Milton does with subjects the most awful and mysterious that poet ever chose, he is never troubled by the obstinate questionings of invisible things which haunted the imagination of Shakspere. We look in vain for any Æschylean background of the vast unknown. "Man's disobedience" and the scheme for man's redemption are laid down as clearly and with just as little mystery as in a Puritan discourse. On topics such as these, even God the Father (to borrow Pope's sneer) "turns a school divine." As in his earlier poems he had ordered and arranged nature, so in the "Paradise Lost" Milton orders and arranges Heaven and Hell. His mightiest figures, Angel or Archangel, Satan or Belial, stand out colossal but distinct. There is just as little of the wide sympathy with all that is human which is so loveable in Chaucer and Shakspere. On the contrary the Puritan individuality is nowhere so overpowering as in Milton. He leaves the stamp of himself deeply graven on all he creates. We hear his voice in every line of his poem. The cold, severe conception of moral virtue which reigns throughout it, the intellectual way in which he paints and regards beauty (for the beauty of Eve is a beauty which no mortal man may love) are Milton's own. We feel his inmost temper in the stoical self-repression which gives its dignity to his figures. Adam utters no cry of agony when he is driven from Paradise. Satan suffers in a defiant silence. It is to this intense self-concentration that we must attribute the strange deficiency of humour which Milton

SEC. X.

THE
FALL OF
PURITANISM

1653
TO
1660

Sec. X.
The
Fall of
Puritanism
1653
to
1660

Disband-
ing of
the Army

shared with the Puritans generally, and which here and there breaks the sublimity of his poem with strange slips into the grotesque. But it is above all to this Puritan deficiency in human sympathy that we must attribute his wonderful want of dramatic genius. Of the power which creates a thousand different characters, which endows each with its appropriate act and word, which loses itself in its own creations, no great poet ever had less.

The poem of Milton was the epic of a fallen cause. The broken hope, which had seen the Kingdom of the Saints pass like a dream away, spoke in its very name. Paradise was lost once more, when the New Model, which embodied the courage and the hope of Puritanism, laid down its arms. In his progress to the capital Charles passed in review the soldiers assembled on Blackheath. Betrayed by their general, abandoned by their leaders, surrounded as they were by a nation in arms, the gloomy silence of their ranks awed even the careless King with a sense of danger. But none of the victories of the New Model were so glorious as the victory which it won over itself. Quietly, and without a struggle, as men who bowed to the inscrutable will of God, the farmers and traders who had dashed Rupert's chivalry to pieces on Naseby field, who had scattered at Worcester the "army of the aliens," and driven into helpless flight the sovereign that now came "to enjoy his own again," who had renewed beyond sea the glories of Crécy and Agincourt, had mastered the Parliament, had brought a King to justice and the block, had given laws to England, and held even Cromwell in awe, became farmers and traders again, and were known among their fellow-men by no other sign than their greater soberness and industry. And, with them, Puritanism laid down the sword. It ceased from the long attempt to build up a kingdom of God by force and violence, and fell back on its truer work of building up a kingdom of righteousness in the hearts and consciences of men. It was from the moment of its seeming fall that its real victory began. As soon as the wild orgy of the Restoration was over, men began to see that nothing that was really worthy in the work of Puritanism had been undone. The revels of Whitehall, the scepticism and debauchery of courtiers, the corruption of statesmen, left the mass of Englishmen what Puritanism had made them, serious, earnest, sober in life and conduct, firm in their love of Protestantism and of freedom. In the Revolution of 1688 Puritanism did the work of civil liberty which it had failed to do in that of 1642. It wrought out through Wesley and the revival of the eighteenth century the work of religious reform which its earlier efforts had only thrown back for a hundred years. Slowly but steadily it introduced its own seriousness and purity into English society, English literature, English politics. The whole history of English progress since the Restoration, on its moral and spiritual sides, has been the history of Puritanism.

CHAPTER IX.

THE REVOLUTION.

Section I.—England and the Revolution.

[*Authorities.*—For the social change see Memoirs of Pepys and Evelyn, the dramatic works of Wycherly and Etherege, and Lord Macaulay's "Essay on the Dramatists of the Restoration." For the earlier history of English Science see Hallam's sketch ("Literary History," vol. iv.); the histories of the Royal Society by Thompson or Wade; and Sir D. Brewster's biography of Newton. Sir W. Molesworth has edited the works of Hobbes.]

THE entry of Charles the Second into Whitehall marked a deep and lasting change in the temper of the English people. With it modern England began. The influences which had up to this time moulded our history, the theological influence of the Reformation, the monarchical influence of the new kingship, the feudal influence of the Middle Ages, the yet earlier influence of tradition and custom, suddenly lost power over the minds of men. From the moment of the Restoration we find ourselves all at once among the great currents of thought and activity which have gone on widening and deepening from that time to this. The England around us becomes our own England, an England whose chief forces are industry and science, the love of popular freedom and of law, an England which presses steadily forward to a larger social justice and equality, and which tends more and more to bring every custom and tradition, religious, intellectual, and political, to the test of pure reason. Between modern thought, on some at least of its more important sides, and the thought of men before the Restoration there is a great gulf fixed. A political thinker in the present day would find it equally hard to discuss any point of statesmanship with Lord Burleigh or with Oliver Cromwell. He would find no point of contact between their ideas of national life or national welfare, their conception of government or the ends of government, their mode of regarding economical and social questions, and his own. But no gulf of this sort parts us from the men who followed the Restoration. From that time to this, whatever differences there may have been as to practical conclusions drawn from them, there has been a substantial agreement as to the grounds of our political, our social, our intellectual and religious life. Paley would have found no difficulty in understanding Tillotson: Newton and Sir

Modern England

SEC. I.

ENGLAND
AND THE
REVOLUTION

The
Puritan
Ideal

Humphry Davy could have talked without a sense of severance. There would have been nothing to hinder a perfectly clear discussion on government or law between John Locke and Jeremy Bentham.

The change from the old England to the new is so startling that we are apt to look on it as a more sudden change than it really was, and the outer aspect of the Restoration does much to strengthen this impression of suddenness. The aim of the Puritan had been to set up a visible Kingdom of God upon earth. He had wrought out his aim by reversing the policy of the Stuarts and the Tudors. From the time of Henry the Eighth to the time of Charles the First, the Church had been looked upon primarily as an instrument for securing, by moral and religious influences, the social and political ends of the State. Under the Commonwealth, the State, in its turn, was regarded primarily as an instrument for securing through its political and social influences the moral and religious ends of the Church. In the Puritan theory, Englishmen were " the Lord's people ; " a people dedicated to Him by a solemn Covenant, and whose end as a nation was to carry out His will. For such an end it was needful that rulers, as well as people, should be "godly men." Godliness became necessarily the chief qualification for public employment. The new modelling of the army filled its ranks with " saints." Parliament resolved to employ no man " but such as the House shall be satisfied of his real godliness." The Covenant which bound the nation to God bound it to enforce God's laws even more earnestly than its own. The Bible lay on the table of the House of Commons ; and its prohibition of swearing, of drunkenness, of fornication became part of the law of the land. Adultery was made felony without the benefit of clergy. Pictures whose subjects jarred with the new decorum were ordered to be burnt, and statues were chipped ruthlessly into decency. It was in the same temper that Puritanism turned from public life to private. The Covenant bound not the whole nation only, but every individual member of the nation, to "a jealous God," a God jealous of any superstition that robbed him of the worship which was exclusively his due, jealous of the distraction and frivolity which robbed him of the entire devotion of man to his service. The want of poetry, of fancy, in the common Puritan temper condemned half the popular observances of England as superstitions. It was superstitious to keep Christmas, or to deck the house with holly and ivy. It was superstitious to dance round the village May-pole. It was flat Popery to eat a mince-pie. The rough sport, the mirth and fun of " merry England," were out of place in an England called with so great a calling. Bull-baiting, bear-baiting, horse-racing, cock-fighting, the village revel, the dance under the May-pole, were put down with the same indiscriminating severity. The long struggle between the Puritans and the play-wrights ended in the closing of every theatre.

Sec. I.

ENGLAND
AND THE
REVOLUTION

**The
Revolt
of the
Restora-
tion.**

1663-1678

The Restoration brought Charles to Whitehall : and in an instant the whole face of England was changed. All that was noblest and best in Puritanism was whirled away with its pettiness and its tyranny in the current of the nation's hate. Religion had been turned into a system of political and social oppression, and it fell with their fall. Godliness became a by-word of scorn ; sobriety in dress, in speech, in manners was flouted as a mark of the detested Puritanism. Butler in his "Hudibras" poured insult on the past with a pedantic buffoonery for which the general hatred, far more than its humour, secured a hearing. Archbishop Sheldon listened to the mock sermon of a Cavalier who held up the Puritan phrase and the Puritan twang to ridicule in his hall at Lambeth. Duelling and raking became the marks of a fine gentleman ; and grave divines winked at the follies of "honest fellows," who fought, gambled, swore, drank, and ended a day of debauchery by a night in the gutter. Life among men of fashion vibrated between frivolity and excess. One of the comedies of the time tells the courtier that "he must dress well, dance well, fence well, have a talent for love-letters, an agreeable voice, be amorous and dis-creet—but not too constant." To graces such as these the rakes of the Restoration added a shamelessness and a brutality which passes belief. Lord Rochester was a fashionable poet, and the titles of some of his poems are such as no pen of our day could copy. Sir Charles Sedley was a fashionable wit, and the foulness of his words made even the porters of Covent Garden pelt him from the balcony when he ventured to address them. The Duke of Buckingham is a fair type of the time, and the most characteristic event in the Duke's life was a duel in which he consummated his seduction of Lady Shrewsbury by killing her hus-band, while the Countess in disguise as a page held his horse for him and looked on at the murder. Vicious as the stage was, it only re-flected the general vice of the time. The Comedy of the Restoration borrowed everything from the Comedy of France save the poetry, the delicacy, and good taste which veiled its grossness. Seduction, in-trigue, brutality, cynicism, debauchery, found fitting expression in dialogue of a studied and deliberate foulness, which even its wit fails to redeem from disgust. Wycherly, the popular play-wright of the time remains the most brutal among all writers of the stage ; and nothing gives so damning an impression of his day as the fact that he found actors to repeat his words and audiences to applaud them. Men such as Wycherly gave Milton models for the Belial of his great poem, " than whom a spirit more lewd fell not from Heaven, or more gross to love vice for itself." The dramatist piques himself on the frankness and "plain dealing" which painted the world as he saw it, a world of brawls and assignations, of orgies at Vauxhall, and fights with the watch, of lies and *double-entendres*, of knaves and dupes, of men who sold their daughters, and women who cheated their husbands.

SEC. I.

ENGLAND
AND THE
REVOLUTION

The
Earlier
Change

But the cynicism of Wycherly was no greater than that of the men about him ; and in mere love of what was vile, in contempt of virtue and disbelief in purity or honesty, the King himself stood ahead of any of his subjects.

It is however easy to exaggerate the extent of this reaction. So far as we can judge from the memoirs of the time, its more violent forms were practically confined to the capital and the court. The mass of Englishmen were satisfied with getting back their May-poles and mince-pies ; and a large part of the people remained Puritan in life and belief, though they threw aside many of the outer characteristics of Puritanism. Nor was the revolution in feeling as sudden as it seemed. Even if the political strength of Puritanism had remained unbroken, its social influence must soon have ceased. The young Englishmen who grew up in the midst of the civil war knew nothing of the bitter tyranny which gave its zeal and fire to the religion of their fathers. From the social and religious anarchy around them, from the endless controversies and discussions of the time, they drank in the spirit of scepticism, of doubt, of free inquiry. If religious enthusiasm had broken the spell of ecclesiastical tradition, its own extravagance broke the spell of religious enthusiasm ; and the new generation turned in disgust to try forms of political government and spiritual belief by the cooler and less fallible test of reason. The children even of the leading Puritans stood aloof from Puritanism. The eldest of Cromwell's sons made small pretensions to religion. Cromwell himself in his later years felt bitterly that Puritanism had missed its aim. He saw the country gentleman, alienated from it by the despotism it had brought in its train, alienated perhaps even more by the appearance of a religious freedom for which he was un-prepared, drifting into a love of the older Church that he had once opposed. He saw the growth of a dogged resistance in the people at large. The attempt to secure spiritual results by material force had failed, as it always fails. It broke down before the indifference and resentment of the great mass of the people, of men who were neither lawless nor enthusiasts, but who clung to the older traditions of social order, and whose humour and good sense revolted alike from the artificial conception of human life which Puritanism had formed and from its effort to force such a conception on a people by law. It broke down, too, before the corruption of the Puritans themselves. It was impossible to distinguish between the saint and the hypocrite as soon as godliness became profitable. Even amongst the really earnest Puritans prosperity disclosed a pride, a worldliness, a selfish hardness which had been hidden in the hour of persecution. The tone of Cromwell's later speeches shows his consciousness that the ground was slipping from under his feet. He no longer dwells on the dream of a Puritan England, of a nation rising as a whole into a people of God. He falls back on the

THE REVOLUTION.

SEC. I.

ENGLAND
AND THE
REVOLUTION

*The
intellectual
movement*

phrases of his youth, and the saints become again a "peculiar people," a remnant, a fragment among the nation at large. But the influences which were really foiling Cromwell's aim, and forming beneath his eyes the new England from which he turned in despair, were influences whose power he can hardly have recognized. Even before the outburst of the Civil War a small group of theological Latitudinarians had gathered round Lord Falkland at Great Tew. In the very year when the King's standard was set up at Nottingham, Hobbes published the first of his works on Government. The last royalist had only just laid down his arms when the little company who were at a later time to be known as the Royal Society gathered round Wilkins at Oxford. It is in this group of scientific observers that we catch the secret of the coming generation. From the vexed problems, political and religious, with which it had so long wrestled in vain, England turned at last to the physical world around it, to the observation of its phenomena, to the discovery of the laws which govern them. The pursuit of physical science became a passion ; and its method of research, by observation, comparison, and experiment, transformed the older methods of inquiry in matters without its pale. In religion, in politics, in the study of man and of nature, not faith but reason, not tradition but inquiry, were to be the watchwords of the coming time. The dead-weight of the past was suddenly rolled away, and the new England heard at last and understood the call of Francis Bacon.

Bacon had already called men with a trumpet-voice to such studies ; but in England at least Bacon stood before his age. The beginnings of physical science were more slow and timid there than in any country of Europe. Only two discoveries of any real value came from English research before the Restoration ; the first, Gilbert's discovery of terrestrial magnetism in the close of Elizabeth's reign ; the next, the great discovery of the circulation of the blood, which was taught by Harvey in the reign of James. Apart from these illustrious names England took little share in the scientific movement of the continent ; and her whole energies seemed to be whirled into the vortex of theology and politics by the Civil War. But the war had not reached its end when a little group of students were to be seen in London, men "inquisitive," says one of them, "into natural philosophy and other parts of human learning, and particularly of what hath been called the New Philosophy, . . . which from the times of Galileo at Florence, and Sir Francis Bacon (Lord Verulam) in England, hath been much cultivated in Italy, France, Germany, and other parts abroad, as well as with us in England." The strife of the time indeed aided in directing the minds of men to natural inquiries. " To have been always tossing about some theological question," says the first historian of the Royal Society, Bishop Sprat, " would have been to have made that their private diversion, the excess of which they disliked in the public. To have been eternally musing on civil business and the distresses of the country was too melancholy a reflection. It was nature alone which could pleasantly entertain them in that estate." Foremost in the group stood Doctors Wallis and Wilkins, whose removal to Oxford, which had just been reorganized by the Puritan Visitors, divided the little company into two societies. The Oxford society, which was the more important of the two, held its meetings at the lodgings of Dr. Wilkins, who had become Warden of Wadham College, and added to the names of its members that of the eminent mathematician Dr. Ward, and that of the first of English economists, Sir William Petty. "Our business," Wallis tells us, "was (precluding matters of theology and State affairs) to discourse and consider of philosophical inquiries and such as related thereunto, as Physick, Anatomy, Geometry, Astronomy, Navigation, Statics, Magnetics, Chymicks, Mechanicks, and Natural Experiments : with the state of these studies, as then cultivated at home and abroad. We then discoursed of the circulation of the blood, the valves in the *venæ lacteæ*, the lymphatic vessels, the Copernican hypothesis, the nature of comets and new stars, the satellites of Jupiter, the oval shape of Saturn, the spots in the sun and its turning on its own axis, the inequalities and selenography of the moon, the several phases of Venus and Mercury, the improvement of telescopes, the grinding of glasses for that purpose, the weight of air, the possibility or impossibility of vacuities, and Nature's abhorrence thereof, the Torricellian experiment in quicksilver, the descent of heavy bodies and the degree of acceleration therein, and divers other things of like nature."

The other little company of inquirers, who remained in London, was at last broken up by the troubles of the Second Protectorate ; but it was revived at the Restoration by the return to London of the more eminent members of the Oxford group. Science suddenly became the fashion of the day. Charles was himself a fair chymist, and took a keen interest in the problems of navigation. The Duke of Buckingham varied his freaks of riming, drinking, and fiddling by fits of devotion to his laboratory. Poets like Dryden and Cowley, courtiers like Sir Robert Murray and Sir Kenelm Digby, joined the scientific company to which in token of his sympathy with it the King gave the title of " The Royal Society." The curious glass toys called Prince Rupert's drops recall the scientific inquiries which, with the study of etching, amused the old age of the great cavalry-leader of the Civil War. Wits and fops crowded to the meetings of the new Society. Statesmen like Lord Somers felt honoured at being chosen its presidents. Its definite establishment marks the opening of a great age of scientific discovery in England. Almost every year of the half-century which followed saw some step made to a wider and truer knowledge. Our first national observatory rose at Greenwich, and modern astronomy began with the long series of astronomical observations which immortalized the name of Flamsteed. His successor, Halley, undertook the investigation of the tides, of comets, and of terrestrial magnetism. Hooke improved the microscope, and gave a fresh impulse to microscopical research. Boyle made the air-pump a means of advancing the science of pneumatics, and became the founder of experimental chymistry. Wilkins pointed forward to the science of philology in his scheme of a universal language. Sydenham introduced a careful observation of nature and facts which changed the whole face of medicine. The physiological researches of Willis first threw light upon the structure of the brain. Woodward was the founder of mineralogy. In his edition of Willoughby's "Ornithology," and in his own "History of Fishes," John Ray was the first to raise zoology to the rank of a science; and the first scientific classification of animals was attempted in his "Synopsis of Quadrupeds." Modern botany began with his "History of Plants," and the researches of an Oxford professor, Robert Morrison; while Grew divided with Malpighi the credit of founding the study of vegetable physiology. But great as some of these names undoubtedly are, they are lost in the lustre of Isaac Newton. Newton was born at Woolsthorpe in Lincolnshire, on Christmas-day, in the memorable year which saw the outbreak of the Civil War. In the year of the Restoration he entered Cambridge, where the teaching of Isaac Barrow quickened his genius for mathematics, and where the method of Descartes had superseded the older modes of study. From the close of his Cambridge career his life became a series of great physical discoveries. At twenty-three he facilitated the calculation of planetary movements by his theory of Fluxions. The optical discoveries to which he was led by his experiments with the prism, and which he partly disclosed in the lectures which he delivered as Mathematical Professor at Cambridge, were embodied in the theory of light which he laid before the Royal Society on becoming a Fellow of it. His discovery of the law of gravitation had been made as early as 1666; but the erroneous estimate which was then generally received of the earth's diameter prevented him from disclosing it for sixteen years; and it was not till the eve of the Revolution that the "Principia" revealed to the world his new theory of the Universe.

It is impossible to do more than indicate, in such a summary as we have given, the wonderful activity of directly scientific thought which distinguished the age of the Restoration. But the sceptical and experimental temper of mind which this activity disclosed was telling at the same time on every phase of the world around it. We see the attempt to bring religious speculation into harmony with the conclusions of reason and experience in the school of Latitudinarian theologians which sprang from the group of thinkers that gathered on the eve of the Civil War round Lord Falkland at Great Tew. Whatever

Hales

*Chilling-
worth*

Taylor

verdict history may pronounce on Falkland's political career, his name must ever remain memorable in the history of religious thought. A new era in English theology began with the speculations of the men he gathered round him. Their work was above all to deny the authority of tradition in matters of faith, as Bacon had denied it in matters of physical research ; and to assert in the one field as in the other the supremacy of reason as a test of truth. Of the authority of the Church, its Fathers, and its Councils, John Hales, a canon of Windsor, and a friend of Laud, said briefly " it is none." He dismissed with contempt the accepted test of universality. " Universality is such a proof of truth as truth itself is ashamed of. The most singular and strongest part of human authority is properly in the wisest and the most virtuous, and these, I trow, are not the most universal." William Chillingworth, a man of larger if not keener mind, had been taught by an early conversion to Catholicism, and by a speedy return, the insecurity of any basis for belief but that of private judgment. In his " Religion of Protestants " he set aside ecclesiastical tradition or Church authority as grounds of faith in favour of the Bible, but only of the Bible as interpreted by the common reason of men. Jeremy Taylor, the most brilliant of English preachers, a sufferer like Chillingworth on the royalist side during the troubles, and who was rewarded at the Restoration with the bishopric of Down, limited even the authority of the Scriptures themselves. Reason was the one means which Taylor approved of in interpreting the Bible ; but the certainty of the conclusions which reason drew from the Bible varied, as he held, with the conditions of reason itself. In all but the simplest truths of natural religion " we are not sure not to be deceived." The deduction of points of belief from the words of the Scriptures was attended with all the uncertainty and liability to error which sprang from the infinite variety of human understandings, the difficulties which hinder the discovery of truth, and the influences which divert the mind from accepting or rightly estimating it. It was plain to a mind like Chillingworth's that this denial of authority, this perception of the imperfection of reason in the discovery of absolute truth, struck as directly at the root of Protestant dogmatism as at the root of Catholic infallibility. " If Protestants are faulty in this matter [of claiming authority] it is for doing it too much and not too little. This presumptuous imposing of the senses of man upon the words of God, of the special senses of man upon the general words of God, and laying them upon men's consciences together under the equal penalty of death and damnation, this vain conceit that we can speak of the things of God better than in the words of God, this deifying our own interpretations and tyrannous enforcing them upon others, this restraining of the word of God from that latitude and generality, and the understandings of men from that liberty wherein Christ and His

Sec. I.

England
and the
Revolution

1647

The Latitu-
dinarian
Theology

apostles left them, is and hath been the only foundation of all the schisms of the Church, and that which makes them immortal." In his "Liberty of Prophesying" Jeremy Taylor pleaded the cause of toleration with a weight of argument which hardly required the triumph of the Independents and the shock of Naseby to drive it home. But the freedom of conscience which the Independent founded on the personal communion of each soul with God, the Latitudinarian founded on the weakness of authority and the imperfection of human reason. Taylor pleads even for the Anabaptist and the Romanist. He only gives place to the action of the civil magistrate in "those religions whose principles destroy government," and "those religions—if there be any such—which teach ill life." Hales openly professed that he would quit the Church to-morrow if it required him to believe that all that dissented from it must be damned. Chillingworth denounced persecution in words of fire. "Take away this persecution, burning, cursing, damning of men for not subscribing the words of men as the words of God : require of Christians only to believe Christ and to call no man master but Him ; let them leave claiming infallibility that have no title to it, and let them that in their own words disclaim it, disclaim it also in their actions. . . . . Protestants are inexcusable if they do offer violence to other men's consciences." From the denunciation of intolerance the Latitudinarians passed easily to the dream of comprehension which had haunted every nobler soul since the "Utopia" of More. Hales based his loyalty to the Church of England on the fact that it was the largest and the most tolerant Church in Christendom. Chillingworth pointed out how many obstacles to comprehension were removed by such a simplification of belief as flowed from a rational theology. Like More, he asked for "such an ordering of the public service of God as that all who believe the Scripture and live according to it might without scruple or hypocrisy or protestation in any part join in it." Taylor, like Chillingworth, rested his hope of union on the simplification of belief. He saw a probability of error in all the creeds and confessions adopted by Christian Churches. "Such bodies of confessions and articles," he said, "must do much hurt." "He is rather the schismatic who makes unnecessary and inconvenient impositions, than he who disobeys them because he cannot do otherwise without violating his conscience." The Apostles' Creed in its literal meaning seemed to him the one term of Christian union which the Church had any right to impose. With the Restoration the Latitudinarians came at once to the front. They were soon distinguished from both Puritans and High Churchmen by their opposition to dogma, by their preference of reason to tradition whether of the Bible or the Church, by their basing religion on a natural theology, by their aiming at rightness of life rather than at correctness of opinion, by their advocacy of toleration and comprehension as the

Hobbes

1588–1679

1642

1651

*His political
speculations*

grounds of Christian unity. Chillingworth and Taylor found successors in the restless good sense of Burnet, the enlightened piety of
Tillotson, and the calm philosophy of Bishop Butler. Meanwhile
the impulse which such men were giving to religious speculation was
being given to political and social inquiry by a mind of far greater
keenness and power.

Bacon's favourite secretary was Thomas Hobbes. " He was
beloved by his Lordship," Aubrey tells us, " who was wont to have
him walk in his delicate groves, where he did meditate ; and when
a notion darted into his mind, Mr. Hobbes was presently to write it
down. And his Lordship was wont to say that he did it better than
any one else about him ; for that many times when he read their notes
he scarce understood what they writ, because they understood it not
clearly themselves." The long life of Hobbes covers a memorable
space in our history. He was born in the year of the victory over the
Armada ; he died, at the age of ninety-two, only nine years before the
Revolution. His ability soon made itself felt, and in his earlier days he
was the secretary of Bacon, and the friend of Ben Jonson and Lord
Herbert of Cherbury. But it was not till the age of fifty-four, when he
withdrew to France on the eve of the Great Rebellion, that his speculations were made known to the world in his treatise " De Cive."
He joined the exiled Court at Paris, and became mathematical tutor
to Charles the Second, whose love and regard for him seem to have
been real to the end. But his post was soon forfeited by the appearance of his " Leviathan " ; he was forbidden to approach the Court,
and returned to England, where he seems to have acquiesced in the
rule of Cromwell. The Restoration brought him a pension ; but both
his works were condemned by Parliament, and " Hobbism " became,
ere he died, the popular synonym for irreligion and immorality. Prejudice of this kind sounded oddly in the case of a writer who had laid
down, as the two things necessary to salvation, faith in Christ and
obedience to the law. But the prejudice sprang from a true sense of
the effect which the Hobbist philosophy must necessarily have on the
current religion and the current notions of political and social morality.
Hobbes was the first great English writer who dealt with the science
of government from the ground, not of tradition, but of reason. It
was in his treatment of man in the stage of human development
which he supposed to precede that of society that he came most roughly
into conflict with the accepted beliefs. Men, in his theory, were by
nature equal, and their only natural relation was a state of war. It
was no innate virtue of man himself which created human society out
of this chaos of warring strengths. Hobbes in fact denied the existence
of the more spiritual sides of man's nature. His hard and narrow logic
dissected every human custom and desire, and reduced even the most
sacred to demonstrations of a prudent selfishness. Friendship was

simply a sense of social utility to one another.   The so-called laws of nature, such as gratitude or the love of our neighbour, were in fact contrary to the natural passions of man, and powerless to restrain them.   Nor had religion rescued man by the interposition of a Divine will.   Nothing better illustrates the daring with which the new scepticism was to break through the theological traditions of the older world than the pitiless logic with which Hobbes assailed the very theory of revelation.   "To say God hath spoken to man in a dream, is no more than to say man dreamed that God hath spoken to him." "To say one hath seen a vision, or heard a voice, is to say he hath dreamed between sleeping and waking."   Religion, in fact, was nothing more than "the fear of invisible powers;" and here, as in all other branches of human science, knowledge dealt with words and not with things.   It was man himself who for his own profit created society, by laying down certain of his natural rights and retaining only those of self-preservation.   A Covenant between man and man originally created "that great Leviathan called the Commonwealth or State, which is but an artificial man, though of greater stature and strength than the natural, for whose protection and defence it was intended."   The fiction of such an "original contract" has long been dismissed from political speculation, but its effect at the time of its first appearance was immense.   Its almost universal acceptance put an end to the religious and patriarchal theories of society, on which Kingship had till now founded its claim of a Divine right to authority which no subject might question.   But if Hobbes destroyed the old ground of royal despotism, he laid a new and a firmer one.   To create a society at all, he held that the whole body of the governed must have resigned all rights save that of self-preservation into the hands of a single ruler, who was the representative of all.   Such a ruler was absolute, for to make terms with him implied a man making terms with himself.   The transfer of rights was inalienable, and after generations were as much bound by it as the generation which made the transfer.   As the head of the whole body, the ruler judged every question, settled the laws of civil justice or injustice, or decided between religion and superstition.   His was a Divine Right, and the only Divine Right, because in him were absorbed all the rights of each of his subjects.   It was not in any constitutional check that Hobbes looked for the prevention of tyranny, but in the common education and enlightenment as to their real end and the best mode of reaching it on the part of both subjects and Prince.   And the real end of both was the weal of the Commonwealth at large.   It was in laying boldly down this end of government, as well as in the basis of contract on which he made government repose, that Hobbes really influenced all later politics. Locke, the foremost political thinker of the Restoration, derived political authority, like Hobbes, from the consent of the governed,

SEC. I.

ENGLAND
AND THE
REVOLUTION

*The Social
Contract*

John Locke

and adopted the common weal as the end of Government. But the practical temper of the time moulded the new theory into a form which contrasted strangely with that given to it by its first inventor. The political philosophy of Locke indeed was little more than a formal statement of the conclusions which the bulk of Englishmen had drawn from the great struggle of the Civil War. In his theory the people remain passively in possession of the power which they have delegated to the Prince, and have the right to withdraw it if it be used for purposes inconsistent with the end which society was formed to promote. To the origin of all power in the people, and the end of all power for the people's good—the two great doctrines of Hobbes—Locke added the right of resistance, the responsibility of princes to their subjects for a due execution of their trust, and the supremacy of legislative assemblies as the voice of the people itself. It was in this modified and enlarged form that the new political philosophy found general acceptance after the Revolution of 1688.

Section II.—The Restoration. 1660–1667.

[*Authorities.*—Clarendon's detailed account of his own ministry in his "Life," Bishop Kennet's " Register," and Burnet's lively " History of my own Times," are our principal sources of information. We may add fragments of the auto-biography of James the Second preserved in Macpherson's " Original Papers " (of very various degrees of value.) For the relations of the Church and the Dissenters, see Neal's " History of the Puritans," Calamy's " Memoirs of the Ejected Ministers," Mr. Dixon's " Life of William Penn," Baxter's " Auto-biography," and Bunyan's account of his sufferings in his various works. The social history of the time is admirably given by Pepys in his "Memoirs." Throughout the whole reign of Charles the Second, the "Constitutional History" of Mr. Hallam is singularly judicious and full in its information.]

When Charles the Second entered Whitehall, the work of the Long Parliament seemed undone. Not only was the Monarchy restored, but it was restored, in spite of the efforts of Sir Matthew Hale, without written restriction or condition on the part of the people, though with implied conditions on the part of Charles himself; and of the two great influences which had hitherto served as checks on its power, the first, that of Puritanism, had become hateful to the nation at large, while the second, the tradition of constitutional liberty, was discredited by the issue of the Civil War. But amidst all the tumult of demonstrative loyalty the great "revolution of the seventeenth century," as it has justly been styled, went steadily on. The supreme power was gradually transferred from the Crown to the House of Commons. Step by step, Parliament drew nearer to a solution of the political problem which had so long foiled its efforts, the problem how to make its will the law of administrative action without itself undertaking the task of administration. It is only

SEC. II.

THE
RESTORA-
TION

1660
TO
1667

by carefully fixing our eyes on this transfer of power, and by noting the successive steps towards its realization, that we can understand the complex history of the Restoration and the Revolution.

The first acts of the new Government showed a sense that, loyal as was the temper of the nation, its loyalty was by no means the blind devotion of the Cavalier. The chief part in the Restoration had in fact been played by the Presbyterians ; and the Presbyterians were still powerful from their almost exclusive possession of the magistracy and all local authority. The first ministry which Charles ventured to form bore on it the marks of a compromise between this powerful party and their old opponents. Its most influential member indeed was Sir Edward Hyde, the adviser of the King during his exile, who soon became Earl of Clarendon and Lord Chancellor. Lord Southampton, a steady royalist, accepted the post of Lord Treasurer ; and the devotion of Ormond was rewarded with a dukedom and the dignity of Lord Steward. But the purely Parliamentary interest was represented by Monk, who remained Lord-General of the army with the title of Duke of Albemarle ; and though the King's brother, James, Duke of York, was made Lord Admiral, the administration of the fleet was virtually in the hands of one of Cromwell's followers, Montagu, the new Earl of Sandwich. An old Puritan, Lord Say and Sele, was made Lord Privy Seal. Sir Ashley Cooper, a leading member of the same party, was rewarded for his activity in bringing about the Restoration first by a Privy Councillorship, and soon after by a barony and the office of Chancellor of the Exchequer. Of the two Secretaries of State, the one, Nicholas, was a devoted royalist ; the other, Morice, was a steady Presbyterian. Of the thirty members of the Privy Council, twelve had borne arms against the King.

It was clear that such a ministry was hardly likely to lend itself to a mere policy of reaction, and the temper of the new Government therefore fell fairly in with the temper of the Convention when that body, after declaring itself a Parliament, proceeded to consider the measures which were requisite for a settlement of the nation. The Convention had been chosen under the ordinances which excluded royalist "Malignants" from the right of voting ; and the bulk of its members were men of Presbyterian sympathies, loyalist to the core, but as averse to despotism as the Long Parliament itself. In its earlier days a member who asserted that those who had fought against the King were as guilty as those who cut off his head was sternly rebuked from the Chair. The first measure which was undertaken by the House, the Bill of Indemnity and Oblivion for all offences committed during the recent troubles, showed at once the moderate character of the Commons. In the punishment of the Regicides indeed, a Presbyterian might well be as zealous as a Cavalier. In spite of a Proclamation he had issued in the first days of his return, in which **mercy was**

Sec. II.

The
Restora-
tion
1660
to
1667

virtually promised to all the judges of the late King who surrendered themselves to justice, Charles pressed for revenge on those whom he regarded as his father's murderers, and the Lords went hotly with the King. It is to the credit of the Commons that they steadily resisted the cry for blood. By the original provisions of the Bill of Oblivion and Indemnity only seven of the living regicides were excluded from pardon ; and though the rise of royalist fervour during the three months in which the bill was under discussion forced the House in the end to leave almost all to the course of justice, the requirement of a special Act of Parliament for the execution of those who had surrendered under the Proclamation protected the lives of most of them. Twenty-eight of the King's judges were in the end arraigned at the bar of a court specially convened for their trial, but only thirteen were executed, and only one of these, General Harrison, had played any conspicuous part in the rebellion. Twenty others, who had been prominent in what were now called " the troubles " of the past twenty years, were declared incapable of holding office under the State : and by an unjustifiable clause which was introduced into the Act before its final adoption, Sir Harry Vane and General Lambert, though they had taken no part in the King's death, were specially exempted from the general pardon. In dealing with the questions of property which arose from the confiscations and transfers of estates during the Civil Wars the Convention met with greater difficulties. No opposition was made to the resumption of all Crown-lands by the State, but the Convention desired to protect the rights of those who had purchased Church property, and of those who were in actual possession of private estates which had been confiscated by the Long Parliament, or by the Government which succeeded it. The bills however which they prepared for this purpose were delayed by the artifices of Hyde ; and at the close of the session the bishops and the evicted royalists quietly re-entered into the occupation of their old possessions. The royalists indeed were far from being satisfied with this summary confiscation. Fines and sequestrations had impoverished all the steady adherents of the royal cause, and had driven many of them to forced sales of their estates ; and a demand was made for compensation for their losses and the cancelling of these sales. Without such provisions, said the frenzied Cavaliers, the bill would be " a Bill of Indemnity for the King's enemies, and of Oblivion for his friends." But here the Convention stood firm. All transfers of property by sale were recognized as valid, and all claims of compensation for losses by sequestration were barred by the Act. From the settlement of the nation the Convention passed to the settlement of the relations between the nation and the Crown. So far was the constitutional work of the Long Parliament from being undone, that its more important measures were silently accepted as the base of future government. Not a voice demanded the restoration

Sec. II.

The
Restora-
tion

1660
to
1667

of the Star Chamber, or of monopolies, or of the Court of High Commission; no one disputed the justice of the condemnation of Ship-money, or the assertion of the sole right of Parliament to grant supplies to the Crown. The Militia, indeed, was placed in the King's hands; but the army was disbanded, though Charles was permitted to keep a few regiments for his guard. The revenue was fixed at £1,200,000; and this sum was granted to the King for life, a grant which might have been perilous for freedom had not the taxes provided to supply the sum fallen constantly below this estimate, while the current expenses of the Crown, even in time of peace, greatly exceeded it. But even for this grant a heavy price was exacted. Though the rights of the Crown over lands held, as the bulk of English estates were held, in military tenure, had ceased to be of any great pecuniary value, they were indirectly a source of considerable power. The right of wardship and of marriage, above all, enabled the sovereign to exercise a galling pressure on every landed proprietor in his social and domestic concerns. Under Elizabeth, the right of wardship had been used to secure the education of all Catholic minors in the Protestant faith; and under James and his successor the charge of minors had been granted to court favourites or sold in open market to the highest bidder. But the real value of these rights to the Crown lay in the political pressure which it was able to exert through them on the country gentry. A squire was naturally eager to buy the good will of a sovereign who might soon be the guardian of his daughter and the administrator of his estate. But the same motives which made the Crown cling to this prerogative made the Parliament anxious to do away with it. Its efforts to bring this about under James the First had been foiled by the King's stubborn resistance; but the long interruption of these rights during the wars made their revival almost impossible at the Restoration. One of the first acts therefore of the Convention was to free the country gentry by abolishing the claims of the Crown to reliefs and wardship, purveyance, and pre-emption, and by the conversion of lands held till then in chivalry into lands held in common socage. In lieu of his rights, Charles accepted a grant of £100,000 a year; a sum which it was originally purposed to raise by a tax on the lands thus exempted from feudal exactions; but which was provided for in the end, with less justice, by a general excise.

Successful as the Convention had been in effecting the settlement of political matters, it failed in bringing about a settlement of the Church. In his proclamation from Breda Charles had promised to respect liberty of conscience, and to assent to any Acts of Parliament which should be presented to him for its security. The Convention was in the main Presbyterian; but it soon became plain that the continuance of a purely Presbyterian system was impossible. "The generality of the people," wrote Sharpe, a shrewd Scotch observer, from London,

The
Cavalier
Parlia-
ment

The Church
question

SEC. II.

THE
RESTORA-
TION
1660
TO
1667

"are doting after Prelacy and the Service-book." The Convention, however, still hoped for some modified form of Episcopalian government which would enable the bulk of the Puritan party to remain within the Church. A large part of the existing clergy, indeed, were Independents, and for these no compromise with Episcopacy was possible: but the greater number were moderate Presbyterians, who were ready "for fear of worse" to submit to such a plan of Church government as Archbishop Usher had proposed, a plan in which the bishop was only the president of a diocesan board of presbyters, and to accept the Liturgy with a few amendments and the omission of the "superstitious practices." It was to a compromise of this kind that the King himself leant at the beginning; and a royal declaration which announced his approval of the Puritan demands was read at a conference of the two parties, and with it a petition from the Independents praying for religious liberty. The King proposed to grant the prayer of the petition, not for the Independents only but for all Christians; but on the point of tolerating the Catholics, Churchmen and Puritans were at one, and a bill which was introduced into the House of Commons by Sir Matthew Hale to turn the declaration into a law was thrown out. A fresh conference was promised, but in the absence of any Parliamentary action the Episcopal party boldly availed themselves of their legal rights. The ejected clergy who still remained alive entered again into their parsonages, the bishops returned to their sees, and the dissolution of the Convention-Parliament destroyed the last hope of an ecclesiastical compromise. The tide of loyalty had in fact been rising fast during its session, and its influence was already seen in a shameful outrage wrought under the very orders of the Convention itself. The bodies of Cromwell, Bradshaw, and Ireton were torn from their graves and hung on gibbets at Tyburn, while those of Pym and Blake were cast out of Westminster Abbey into St. Margaret's churchyard. But in the elections for the new Parliament the zeal for Church and King swept all hope of moderation and compromise before it. "Malignity" had now ceased to be a crime, and voters long deprived of the suffrage, vicars, country gentlemen, farmers,· with the whole body of the Catholics, rushed again to the poll. The Presbyterians sank in the Cavalier Parliament to a handful of fifty members. The new House of Commons was made up for the most part of young men, of men, that is, who had but a faint memory of the Stuart tyranny of their childhood, but who had a keen memory of living from manhood beneath the tyranny of the Commonwealth. Their very bearing was that of wild revolt against the Puritan past. To a staid observer, Roger Pepys, they seemed a following of "the most profane, swearing fellows that ever I heard in my life." The zeal of the Parliament at its outset, indeed, far outran that of Charles or his ministers. Though it confirmed the other acts of the Convention, it could with diffi-

Sec. II.
THE
RESTORA-
TION
1660
TO
1667

culty be brought to confirm the Act of Indemnity. The Commons pressed for the prosecution of Vane. Vane was protected alike by the spirit of the law and by the King's pledge to the Convention that, even if convicted of treason, he would not suffer him to be brought to the block. But he was now brought to trial on the charge of treason against a King "kept out of his royal authority by traitors and rebels," and his spirited defence served as an excuse for his execution. "He is too dangerous a man to let live," Charles wrote with characteristic coolness, "if we can safely put him out of the way." But the new members were yet better churchmen than loyalists. A common suffering had thrown the squires and the Episcopalian clergy together, and for the first time since the Reformation the English gentry were ardent not for King only, but for Church and King. At the opening of their session the Commons ordered every member to receive the communion, and the League and Covenant to be solemnly burnt by the common hangman in Westminster Hall. The bill excluding bishops from the House of Lords was repealed. The conference at the Savoy between the Episcopalians and Presbyterians broke up in anger, and the few alterations made in the Liturgy were made with a view to disgust rather than to conciliate the Puritan party.

The temper of the new Parliament, however, was not a mere temper of revenge. Its wish was to restore the constitutional system which the civil war had violently interrupted, and the royalists were led by the most active of the constitutional loyalists who had followed Falkland in 1642, Hyde, now Earl of Clarendon and Lord Chancellor. The Parliament and the Church were in his conception essential parts of the system of English government, through which the power of the Crown was to be exercized; and under his guidance Parliament turned to the carrying out of the principle of uniformity in Church as well as in State on which the minister was resolved. The chief obstacle to such a policy lay in the Presbyterians, and the strongholds of this party were in the corporations of the boroughs, which practically returned the borough members. An attempt was made to drive the Presbyterians from municipal posts by a severe Corporation Act, which required a reception of the Communion according to the rites of the Anglican Church, a renunciation of the League and Covenant, and a declaration that it was unlawful on any grounds to take up arms against the King, before admission to municipal offices. A more deadly blow was dealt at the Puritans in the renewal of the Act of Uniformity. Not only was the use of the Prayer-book, and the Prayer-book only, enforced in all public worship, but an unfeigned consent and assent was demanded from every minister of the Church to all which was contained in it; while, for the first time since the Reformation, all orders save those conferred by the hands of bishops were legally disallowed. The declaration exacted from corporations was exacted from the clergy,

Clarendon

Corporation Act

Act of Uniformity

SEC. II.

THE
RESTORA-
TION
1660
TO
1667

and a pledge was required that they would seek to make no change in Church or State. It was in vain that Ashley opposed the bill fiercely in the Lords, that the peers pleaded for pensions to the ejected ministers and for the exemption of schoolmasters from the necessity of subscription, and that even Clarendon, who felt that the King's word was at stake, pressed for the insertion of clauses enabling the Crown to grant dispensations from its provisions. Every suggestion of compromise was rejected by the Commons ; and Charles at last assented to the bill, while he promised to suspend its execution by the exercize of his prerogative.

St.
Bartho-
lomew's
Day
1662

The Anglican Parliament however was resolute to enforce the law ; and on St. Bartholomew's day, the last day allowed for compliance with its requirements, nearly two thousand rectors and vicars, or about a fifth of the English clergy, were driven from their parishes as Nonconformists. No such sweeping alteration in the religious aspect of the Church had ever been seen before. The changes of the Reformation had been brought about with little change in the clergy itself. Even the severities of the High Commission under Elizabeth ended in the expulsion of a few hundreds. If Laud had gone zealously to work in emptying Puritan pulpits, his zeal had been to a great extent foiled by the restrictions of the law and by the growth of Puritan sentiment in the clergy as a whole. A far wider change had been brought about by the Civil War ; but the change had been gradual, and had ostensibly been wrought for the most part on political or moral rather than on religious grounds. The parsons expelled were expelled as " malignants " or as unfitted for their office by idleness or vice or inability to preach. But the change wrought by St. Bartholomew's day was a distinctly religious change, and it was a change which in its suddenness and completeness stood utterly alone. The rectors and vicars who were driven out were the most learned and the most active of their order. The bulk of the great livings throughout the country were in their hands. They stood at the head of the London clergy, as the London clergy stood in general repute at the head of their class throughout England. They occupied the higher posts at the two Universities. No English divine, save Jeremy Taylor, rivalled Howe as a preacher. No parson was so renowned a controversialist, or so indefatigable a parish priest, as Baxter. And behind these men stood a fifth of the whole body of the clergy, men whose zeal and labour had diffused throughout the country a greater appearance of piety and religion than it had ever displayed before. But the expulsion of these men was far more to the Church of England than the loss of their individual services. It was the definite expulsion of a great party which from the time of the Reformation had played the most active and popular part in the life of the Church. It was the close of an effort which had been going on ever since Elizabeth's accession to bring the English Communion into closer relations with the Reformed

*Its religious
results*

SEC. II.

THE
RESTORA-
TION
1660
TO
1667

Communions of the Continent, and into greater harmony with the religious instincts of the nation at large. The Church of England stood from that moment isolated and alone among all the Churches of the Christian world. The Reformation had severed it irretrievably from those which still clung to the obedience of the Papacy. By its rejection of all but episcopal orders, the Act of Uniformity severed it as irretrievably from the general body of the Protestant Churches, whether Lutheran or Reformed. And while thus cut off from all healthy religious communion with the world without, it sank into immobility within. With the expulsion of the Puritan clergy, all change, all efforts after reform, all national developement, suddenly stopped. From that time to this the Episcopal Church has been unable to meet the varying spiritual needs of its adherents by any modification of its government or its worship. It stands alone among all the religious bodies of Western Christendom in its failure through two hundred years to devise a single new service of prayer or of praise. But if the issues of St. Bartholomew's day have been harmful to the spiritual life of the English Church, they have been in the highest degree advantageous to the cause of religious liberty. At the Restoration religious freedom seemed again to have been lost. Only the Independents and a few despised sects, such as the Quakers, upheld the right of every man to worship God according to the bidding of his own conscience. The bulk of the Puritan party with the Presbyterians at its head, was at one with its opponents in desiring a uniformity of worship, if not of belief, throughout the land ; and, had the two great parties within the Church held together, their weight would have been almost irresistible. Fortunately the great severance of St. Bartholomew's day drove out the Presbyterians from the Church to which they clung, and forced them into a general union with sects which they had hated till then almost as bitterly as the bishops themselves. A common suffering soon blended the Nonconformists into one. Persecution broke down before the numbers, the wealth, and the political weight of the new sectarians ; and the Church, for the first time in its history, found itself confronted with an organized body of Dissenters without its pale. The impossibility of crushing such a body as this wrested from English statesmen the first legal recognition of freedom of worship in the Toleration Act ; their rapid growth in later times has by degrees stripped the Church of almost all the exclusive privileges which it enjoyed as a religious body, and now threatens what remains of its official connexion with the State. With these remoter consequences however we are not as yet concerned. It is enough to note here that with the Act of Uniformity and the expulsion of the Puritan clergy a new element in our religious and political history, the element of Dissent, the influence of the Nonconformist churches, comes first into play.

SEC. II.

THE
RESTORA-
TION
1660
TO
1667
The
Persecu-
tion

*First
Declaration
of
Indulgence*
1662

The sudden outbreak and violence of the persecution turned the disappointment of the Presbyterians into despair. Many were for retiring to Holland, others proposed flight to New England and the American colonies. Charles however was anxious to use the strife between the two great bodies of Protestants so as to secure toleration for the Catholics, and revive at the same time his prerogative of dispensing with the execution of laws ; and fresh hopes of protection were raised by a royal proclamation, which expressed the King's resolve to exempt from the penalties of the Act, " those who, living peaceably, do not conform themselves thereunto, through scruple and tenderness of misguided conscience, but modestly and without scandal perform their devotions in their own way." A bill introduced in 1663, in redemption of a pledge in the declaration itself, gave Charles the power to dispense, not only with the provisions of the Act of Uniformity, but with the penalties provided by all laws which enforced religious conformity, or which imposed religious tests. But if the Presbyterian leaders in the council had stooped to accept the aid of the declaration, the bulk of the Dissidents had no mind to have their grievances used as a means of procuring by a side wind toleration for Roman Catholics, or of building up again that dispensing power which the civil wars had thrown down. The Churchmen, too, whose hatred for the Dissidents had been embittered by suspicions of a secret league between the Dissidents and the Catholics in which the King was taking part, were resolute in opposition. The Houses therefore struck simultaneously at both their opponents. They forced Charles by an address to withdraw his pledge of toleration.

They then extorted from him a proclamation for the banishment of all Catholic priests, and followed this up by a Conventicle Act, which punished with fine, imprisonment, and transportation on a third offence all persons who met in greater number than five for any religious worship save that of the Common Prayer ; while return, or escape from banishment was punished by death. The Five Mile Act, a year

later, completed the code of persecution. By its provisions, every clergyman who had been driven out by the Act of Uniformity was called on to swear that he held it unlawful under any pretext to take up arms against the King, and that he would at no time " endeavour any alteration of government in Church and State." In case of refusal, he was forbidden to go within five miles of any borough, or of any place where he had been wont to minister. As the main body of the Nonconformists belonged to the city and trading classes, the effect of this measure was to rob them of any religious teaching at all. A motion to impose the oath of the Five Mile Act on every person in the nation was rejected in the same session by a majority of only six. The sufferings of the Nonconformists indeed could hardly fail to tell on the sympathies of the people. The thirst for revenge, which had been roused by the violence of the Presbyterians in their hour of triumph, was satisfied by

Sec. II.

The
Restora-
tion
1660
to
1667

their humiliation in the hour of defeat. The sight of pious and learned clergymen driven from their homes and their flocks, of religious meetings broken up by the constables, of preachers set side by side with thieves and outcasts in the dock, of gaols crammed with honest enthusiasts whose piety was their only crime, pleaded more eloquently for toleration than all the reasoning in the world. We have a clue to the extent of the persecution from what we know to have been its effect on a single sect. The Quakers had excited alarm by their extravagances of manner, their refusal to bear arms or to take oaths ; and a special Act was passed for their repression. They were one of the smallest of the Nonconformist bodies, but more than four thousand were soon in prison, and of these five hundred were imprisoned in London alone. The King's Declaration of Indulgence, twelve years later, set free twelve hundred Quakers who had found their way to the gaols. Of the sufferings of the expelled clergy one of their own number, Richard Baxter, has given us an account. " Many hundreds of them, with their wives and children, had neither house nor bread. . . . Their congregations had enough to do, besides a small maintenance, to help them out of prisons, or to maintain them there. Though they were as frugal as possible they could hardly live ; some lived on little more than brown bread and water, many had but eight or ten pounds a year to maintain a family, so that a piece of flesh has not come to one of their tables in six weeks' time ; their allowance could scarce afford them bread and cheese. One went to plow six days and preached on the Lord's Day. Another was forced to cut tobacco for a livelihood." But poverty was the least of their sufferings. They were jeered at by the players. They were hooted through the streets by the mob. " Many of the ministers, being afraid to lay down their ministry after they had been ordained to it, preached to such as would hear them in fields and private houses, till they were apprehended and cast into gaols, where many of them perished." They were excommunicated in the Bishops' Court, or fined for non-attendance at church ; and a crowd of informers grew up who made a trade of detecting the meetings they held at midnight. Alleyn, the author of the well-known "Alarm to the Unconverted," died at thirty-six from the sufferings he endured in Taunton Gaol. Vavasour Powell, the apostle of Wales, spent the eleven years which followed the Restoration in prisons at Shrewsbury, Southsea, and Cardiff, till he perished in the Fleet. John Bunyan was for twelve years a prisoner at Bedford.

We have already seen the atmosphere of excited feeling in which the youth of Bunyan had been spent. From his childhood he heard heavenly voices, and saw visions of heaven ; from his childhood, too, he had been wrestling with an overpowering sense of sin, which sickness and repeated escapes from death did much as he grew up to deepen. But in spite of his self-reproaches his life was a religious one ;

s s

SEC. II.

THE
RESTORA-
TION
1660
TO
1667
1645

and the purity and sobriety of his youth was shown by his admission at seventeen into the ranks of the "New Model." Two years later the war was over, and Bunyan though hardly twenty found himself married to a "godly" wife, as young and penniless as himself. So poor were the young couple that they could scarce muster a spoon and a plate between them; and the poverty of their home deepened, perhaps, the gloom of the young tinker's restlessness and religious depression. His wife did what she could to comfort him, teaching him again to read and write, for he had forgotten his school-learning, and reading with him in two little "godly" books which formed his library. But the darkness only gathered the thicker round his imaginative soul. "I walked," he tells us of this time, "to a neighbouring town; and sate down upon a settle in the street, and fell into a very deep pause about the most fearful state my sin had brought me to; and after long musing I lifted up my head; but methought I saw as if the sun that shineth in the heavens did grudge to give me light; and as if the very stones in the street and tiles upon the houses did band themselves against me. Methought that they all combined together to banish me out of the world. I was abhorred of them, and wept to dwell among them, because I had sinned against the Saviour. Oh, how happy now was every creature over I! for they stood fast and kept their station. But I was gone and lost." At last, after more than

two years of this struggle, the darkness broke. Bunyan felt himself "converted," and freed from the burthen of his sin. He joined a Baptist church at Bedford, and a few years later he became famous as a preacher. As he held no formal post of minister in the congregation, his preaching even under the Protectorate was illegal and "gave great offence," he tells us, "to the doctors and priests of that county," but he persisted with little real molestation until the Restoration. Six months however after the King's return he was committed to Bedford Gaol on a charge of preaching in unlicensed conventicles; and his refusal to promise to abstain from preaching kept him there twelve years. The gaol was crowded with prisoners like himself, and amongst them he continued his ministry, supporting himself by making tagged thread laces, and finding some comfort in the Bible, the "Book of Martyrs," and the writing materials which he was suffered to have with him in his prison. But he was in the prime of life, his age was thirty-two when he was imprisoned; and the inactivity and severance from his wife and little children was hard to bear. "The parting with my wife and poor children," he says in words of simple pathos, "hath often been to me in this place as the pulling of the flesh from the bones, and that not only because I am somewhat too fond of those great mercies, but also because I should have often brought to my mind the many hardships, miseries, and wants that my poor family was like to meet with should I be taken from them, especially my poor blind child, who lay nearer to my heart than all besides. Oh, the thoughts of the hardships I thought my poor blind one might go under would break my heart to pieces. 'Poor child,' thought I, 'what sorrow art thou like to have for thy portion in this world! Thou must be beaten, must beg, suffer hunger, cold, nakedness, and a thousand calamities, though I cannot now endure the wind should blow upon thee.'" But suffering could not break his purpose, and Bunyan found compensation for the narrow bounds of his prison in the wonderful activity of his pen. Tracts, controversial treatises, poems, meditations, his "Grace Abounding," and his "Holy City," followed each other in quick succession. It was in his gaol that he wrote the first and greatest part of his "Pilgrim's Progress." Its publication was the earliest result of his deliverance at the Declaration of Indulgence, and the popularity which it enjoyed from the first proves that the religious sympathies of the English people were still mainly Puritan. Before Bunyan's death in 1688 ten editions of the "Pilgrim's Progress" had already been sold; and though even Cowper hardly dared to quote it a century later for fear of moving a smile in the polite world about him its favour among the middle classes and the poor has grown steadily from its author's day to our own. It is now the most popular and the most widely known of all English books. In none do we see more clearly the new imaginative force which had been given to the common life of Englishmen by their study of the Bible. Its English is the simplest and the homeliest English which has ever been used by any great English writer; but it is the English of the Bible. The images of the "Pilgrim's Progress" are the images of prophet and evangelist; it borrows for its tenderer outbursts the very verse of the Song of Songs, and pictures the Heavenly City in the words of the Apocalypse. But so completely has the Bible become Bunyan's life that one feels its phrases as the natural expression of his thoughts. He has lived in the Bible till its words have become his own. He has lived among its visions and voices of heaven till all sense of possible unreality has died away. He tells his tale with such a perfect naturalness that allegories become living things, that the Slough of Despond and Doubting Castle are as real to us as places we see every day, that we know Mr. Legality and Mr. Worldly Wiseman as if we had met them in the street. It is in this amazing reality of impersonation that Bunyan's imaginative genius specially displays itself. But this is far from being his only excellence. In its range, in its directness, in its simple grace, in the ease with which it changes from lively dialogue to dramatic action, from simple pathos to passionate earnestness, in the subtle and delicate fancy which often suffuses its childlike words, in its playful humour, its bold character-painting, in the even and balanced power which passes without effort from the Valley of the Shadow of Death to the land "where the Shining Ones commonly

Sec. II.

The
Restora-
tion

1660
to
1667

1672

SEC. II.

THE
RESTORA-
TION

1660
TO
1667

walked, because it was on the borders of heaven," in its sunny kindli-
ness unbroken by one bitter word, the "Pilgrim's Progress" is among
the noblest of English poems. For if Puritanism had first discovered
the poetry which contact with the spiritual world awakes in the
meanest soul, Bunyan was the first of the Puritans who revealed this
poetry to the outer world. The journey of Christian from the City of
Destruction to the Heavenly City is simply a record of the life of such
a Puritan as Bunyan himself, seen through an imaginative haze of
spiritual idealism in which its commonest incidents are heightened and
glorified. He is himself the pilgrim who flies from the City of Destruction, who climbs the hill Difficulty, who faces Apollyon, who sees his
loved ones cross the river of Death towards the Heavenly City, and
how, because "the hill on which the City was framed was higher than
the clouds, they therefore went up through the region of the air,
sweetly talking as they went."

The success, however, of the system of religious repression rested
mainly on the maintenance of peace; and while Bunyan was lying in
Bedford Gaol, and the Church was carrying on its bitter persecution
of the Nonconformists, England was plunging into a series of bitter
humiliations and losses abroad. The old commercial jealousy between
the Dutch and English, which had been lulled by a formal treaty in
1662, but which still lived on in petty squabbles at sea, was embittered
by the cession of Bombay—a port which gave England an entry into
the profitable trade with India—and by the establishment of a West
Indian Company in London which opened a traffic with the Gold
Coast of Africa. The quarrel was fanned into a war. Parliament voted a
large supply unanimously; and the King was won by hopes of the ruin
of the Dutch presbyterian and republican government, and by his resentment at the insults he had suffered from Holland in his exile. The war at
sea which followed was a war of giants. An obstinate battle off Lowestoft

ended in a victory for the English fleet; but in an encounter the next
year with De Ruyter off the North Foreland Monk and his fleet after
two day's fighting were only saved from destruction by the arrival of
Prince Rupert. The dogged admiral renewed the fight, but the combat
again ended in De Ruyter's favour and the English took refuge in the
Thames. Their fleet was indeed ruined, but the losses of the enemy

had been hardly less. "English sailors may be killed," said De Witt,
"but they cannot be conquered;" and the saying was as true of one
side as the other. A third battle, as hard-fought as its predecessors,
ended in the triumph of the English, and their fleet sailed along the
coast of Holland, burning ships and towns. But Holland was as unconquerable as England herself, and the Dutch fleet was soon again
refitted and was joined in the Channel by the French. Meanwhile,

calamity at home was added to the sufferings of the war. In the preceding year a hundred thousand Londoners had died in six months of

SEC. III.

CHARLES
THE
SECOND
1667
TO
1673

1667

the Plague which broke out in the crowded streets of the capital ; and the Plague was followed now by a fire, which, beginning in the heart of London, reduced the whole city to ashes from the Tower to the Temple. Thirteen thousand houses and ninety churches were destroyed. The loss of merchandise and property was beyond count. The Treasury was empty, and neither ships nor forts were manned when the Dutch fleet appeared at the Nore, advanced unopposed up the Thames to Gravesend, forced the boom which protected the Medway, burned three men-of-war which lay anchored in the river, and withdrew only to sail proudly along the coast, the masters of the Channel.

Section III.—Charles the Second. 1667—1673.

[*Authorities.*—To the authorities already mentioned, we may add the Memoirs of Sir William Temple, with Lord Macaulay's well-known Essay on that states-man, Reresby's Memoirs, and the works of Andrew Marvell. The "Memoirs of the Count de Grammont," by Anthony Hamilton, give a witty and amusing picture of the life of the court. Lingard becomes important from the original materials he has used, and from his clear and dispassionate statement of the Catholic side of the question. Ranke's "History of the XVII. Century" throws great light on the diplomatic history of the later Stuart reigns ; on in-ternal and constitutional points he is dispassionate but of less value. Dalrymple, in his "Memoirs of Great Britain and Ireland," was the first to discover the real secret of the negotiations with France ; but all previous researches have been superseded by those of M. Mignet, whose "Négociations relatives à la Succession d'Espagne" is indispensable for a knowledge of the time.]

The thunder of the Dutch guns in the Medway and the Thames woke England to a bitter sense of its degradation. The dream of loyalty was over. "Everybody now-a-days," Pepys tells us, "reflect upon Oliver and commend him, what brave things he did, and made all the neighbour princes fear him." But Oliver's successor was coolly watching this shame and discontent of his people with the one aim of turning it to his own advantage. To Charles the Second the degrada-tion of England was only a move in the political game which he was playing, a game played with so consummate a secrecy and skill that it deceived not only the closest observers of his own day but still mis-leads historians of ours. What his subjects saw in their King was a pleasant, brown-faced gentleman playing with his spaniels, or drawing caricatures of his ministers, or flinging cakes to the water-fowl in the park. To all outer seeming Charles was the most consummate of idlers. "He delighted," says one of his courtiers, "in a bewitching kind of pleasure called sauntering." The business-like Pepys soon discovered that "the King do mind nothing but pleasures, and hates the very sight or thoughts of business." He only laughed when Tom Killigrew frankly told him that badly as things were going there was one man whose industry could soon set them right, "and this is one

Sec. III.

Charles
the
Second
1667
to
1673

Charles Stuart, who now spends his time in using his lips about the Court, and hath no other employment." That Charles had great natural parts no one doubted. In his earlier days of defeat and danger he showed a cool courage and presence of mind which never failed him in the many perilous moments of his reign. His temper was pleasant and social, his manners perfect, and there was a careless freedom and courtesy in his address which won over everybody who came into his presence. His education indeed had been so grossly neglected that he could hardly read a plain Latin book; but his natural quickness and intelligence showed itself in his pursuit of chymistry and anatomy, and in the interest he showed in the scientific inquiries of the Royal Society. Like Peter the Great his favourite study was that of naval architecture, and he piqued himself on being a clever ship-builder. He had some little love too for art and poetry, and a taste for music. But his shrewdness and vivacity showed itself most in his endless talk. He was fond of telling stories, and he told them with a good deal of grace and humour. His humour indeed never forsook him: even on his death-bed he turned to the weeping courtiers around and whispered an apology for having been so unconscionable a time in dying. He held his own fairly with the wits of his Court, and bandied repartees on equal terms with Sedley or Buckingham. Even Rochester in his merciless epigram was forced to own that Charles "never said a foolish thing." He had inherited in fact his grandfather's gift of pithy sayings, and his habitual irony often gave an amusing turn to them. When his brother, the most unpopular man in England, solemnly warned him of plots against his life, Charles laughingly bade him set all fear aside. "They will never kill me, James," he said, "to make you king." But courage and wit and ability seeme   o have been bestowed on him in vain. Charles hated business. He   to outer observers no sign of ambition. The one thing he seemed n.   rnest about was sensual pleasure, and he took his pleasure with a c nical shamelessness which roused the disgust even of his shameless courtiers. Mistress followed mistress, and the guilt of a troop of profligate women was blazoned to the world by the gift of titles and estates. The royal bastards were set amongst English nobles. The ducal house of Grafton springs from the King's adultery with Barbara Palmer, whom he created Duchess of Cleveland. The Dukes of St. Albans owe their origin to his intrigue with Nell Gwynn, a player and a courtezan. Louise de Quérouaille, a mistress sent by France to win him to its interests, became Duchess of Portsmouth and ancestress of the house of Richmond. An earlier mistress, Lucy Walters, was mother of a boy whom he raised to the Dukedom of Monmouth, and to whom the Dukes of Buccleuch trace their line; but there is good reason for doubting whether the King was actually his father. But Charles was far from

Sec. III.

Charles
the
Second
1667
to
1673

being content with these recognized mistresses, or with a single form of self-indulgence. Gambling and drinking helped to fill up the vacant moments when he could no longer toy with his favourites or bet at Newmarket. No thought of remorse or of shame seems ever to have crossed his mind. "He could not think God would make a man miserable," he said once, "only for taking a little pleasure out of the way." From shame indeed he was shielded by his cynical disbelief in human virtue. Virtue he regarded simply as a trick by which clever hypocrites imposed upon fools. Honour among men seemed to him as mere a pretence as chastity among women. Gratitude he had none, for he looked upon self-interest as the only motive of men's actions, and though soldiers had died and women had risked their lives for him, he "loved others as little as he thought they loved him." But if he felt no gratitude for benefits he felt no resentment for wrongs. He was incapable either of love or of hate. The only feeling he retained for his fellow-men was that of an amused contempt.

It was difficult for Englishmen to believe that any real danger to liberty could come from an idler and a voluptuary such as Charles the Second. But in the very difficulty of believing this lay half the King's strength. He had in fact no taste whatever for the despotism of the Stuarts who had gone before him. His shrewdness laughed his grandfather's theory of Divine Right down the wind, while his indolence made such a personal administration as that which his father delighted in burthensome to him. He was too humorous a man to care for the pomp and show of power, and too good-natured a man to play the tyrant. But he believed as firmly as his father or his grandfather had believed in the older prerogatives of the Crown ; and, like them, he looked on Parliaments with suspicion and jealousy. "He told Lord Essex," Burnet says, "that he did not wish to be like a Grand Signior, with some mutes about him, and bags of bowstrings to strangle men ; but he did not think he was a king so long as a company of fellows were looking into his actions, and examining his ministers as well as his accounts." "A king," he thought, "who might be checked, and have his ministers called to an account, was but a king in name." In other words, he had no settled plan of tyranny, but he meant to rule as independently as he could, and from the beginning to the end of his reign there never was a moment when he was not doing something to carry out his aim. But he carried it out in a tentative, irregular fashion which it was as hard to detect as to meet. Whenever there was any strong opposition he gave way. If popular feeling demanded the dismissal of his ministers, he dismissed them. If it protested against his declaration of indulgence, he recalled it. If it cried for victims in the frenzy of the Popish Plot, he gave it victims till the frenzy was at an end. It was easy for Charles to yield and to wait, and just as easy for him to take up the thread of his purpose again the moment the pressure was over.

Sec. III.

Charles
THE
Second
1667
TO
1673

The one fixed resolve which overrode every other thought in the King's mind was a resolve "not to set out on his travels again." His father had fallen through a quarrel with the two Houses, and Charles was determined to remain on good terms with the Parliament till he was strong enough to pick a quarrel to his profit. He treated the Lords with an easy familiarity which robbed opposition of its seriousness. "Their debates amused him," he said in his indolent way; and he stood chatting before the fire while peer after peer poured invectives on his ministers, and laughed louder than the rest when Shaftesbury directed his coarsest taunts at the barrenness of the Queen. Courtiers were entrusted with the secret "management" of the Commons: obstinate country gentlemen were brought to the royal closet to kiss the King's hand and listen to the King's pleasant stories of his escape after Worcester; and still more obstinate country gentlemen were bribed. Where bribes, flattery, and management failed, Charles was content to yield and to wait till his time came again. Meanwhile he went on patiently gathering up what fragments of the old royal power still survived, and availing himself of whatever new resources offered themselves. If he could not undo what Puritanism had done in England, he could undo its work in Scotland and in Ireland. Before the Civil War these kingdoms had served as useful checks on English liberty, and by simply regarding the Union which the Long Parliament and the Protector had brought about as a nullity in law it was possible they might become checks again. In his refusal to recognize the Union Charles was supported by public opinion among his English subjects, partly from sheer abhorrence of changes wrought during "the troubles," and partly from a dread that the Scotch and Irish members would form a party in the English Parliament which would always be at the service of the Crown. In both the lesser kingdoms too a measure which seemed to restore somewhat of their independence was for the moment popular. But the results of this step were quick in developing themselves. In Scotland the Covenant was at once abolished. The new Scotch Parliament at Edinburgh, the Drunken Parliament, as it was called, outdid the wildest loyalty of the English Cavaliers by annulling in a single Act all the proceedings of its predecessors during the last eight-and-twenty years. By this measure the whole existing Church system of Scotland was deprived of legal sanction. The General Assembly had already been prohibited from meeting by Cromwell; the kirk-sessions and ministers' synods were now suspended. The Scotch bishops were again restored to their spiritual pre-eminence, and to their seats in Parliament. An iniquitous trial sent the Marquis of Argyle, the only noble strong enough to oppose the royal will, to the block, and the government was entrusted to a knot of profligate statesmen till it fell into the hands of Lauderdale, one of the ablest and most unscrupulous of the King's ministers.

SEC.III.

CHARLES
THE
SECOND
1667
TO
1673

Their policy was steadily directed to the two purposes of humbling Presbyterianism—as the force which could alone restore Scotland to freedom, and enable her to lend aid as before to English liberty in any struggle with the Crown—and that of raising a royal army which might be ready in case of need to march over the border to the King's support. In Ireland the dissolution of the Union brought back the bishops to their sees; but whatever wish Charles may have had to restore the balance of Catholic and Protestant as a source of power to the Crown was baffled by the Protestant resistance to any plans for redressing the confiscations of Cromwell. If one interest or other must suffer, Charles "thought it most for the good of the kingdom, advantage of the Crown, and security of his Government, that the loss should fall on the Irish. This was the opinion of his council, and a contrary conduct would have been matter of discontent to the Parliament of England." A new Bill of Settlement excluded without trial over three thousand old proprietors from their estates; it was estimated that four-fifths of the kingdom, or more than two-thirds of the good land, was secured to the Protestants. The downfall of the old race was all but accomplished. But the severance of the two kingdoms from England was in itself a gain to the royal authority; and Charles turned quietly to the building up of a royal army at home. A standing army had become so hateful a thing to the body of the nation, and above all to the royalists whom the New Model had trodden under foot, that it was impossible to propose its establishment. But in the mind of Charles and his brother James, their father's downfall had been owing to the want of a disciplined force which would have trampled out the first efforts of national resistance; and while disbanding the New Model, Charles availed himself of the alarm created by a mad rising of some Fifth-Monarchy men in London under an old soldier called Venner to retain five thousand horse and foot in his service under the name of his guards. A body of "gentlemen of quality and veteran soldiers, excellently clad, mounted, and ordered," was thus kept ready for service near the royal person; and in spite of the scandal which it aroused the King persisted, steadily but cautiously, in gradually increasing its numbers. Twenty years later it had grown to a force of seven thousand foot and one thousand seven hundred horse and dragoons at home, with a reserve of six fine regiments abroad in the service of the United Provinces.

But Charles was too quick-witted a man to believe, as his brother James believed, that it was possible to break down English freedom by the royal power or by a few thousand men in arms. It was still less possible by such means to break down, as he wished to break down, English Protestantism. In heart, whether the story of his renunciation of Protestantism during his exile be true or no, he had long ceased to be a Protestant. Whatever religious feeling he had was on

SEC. III.

CHARLES
THE
SECOND
1667
TO
1673

Charles and Catholicism

the side of Catholicism; he encouraged conversions among his courtiers, and the last act of his life was to seek formal admission into the Roman Church. But his feelings were rather political than religious. The English Roman Catholics formed a far larger part of the population then than now; their wealth and local influence gave them a political importance which they have long since lost, and every motive of gratitude as well as self-interest led him to redeem his pledge to procure toleration for their worship. But he was already looking, however vaguely, to something more than Catholic toleration. He saw that despotism in the State could hardly co-exist with free inquiry and free action in matters of the conscience, and that government, in his own words, "was a safer and easier thing where the authority was believed infallible and the faith and submission of the people were implicit." The difficulties in the way of such a religious change probably seemed the less to him from his long residence in Roman Catholic countries, and from his own religious scepticism. Two years indeed after his restoration he had already despatched an agent to Rome to arrange the terms of a reconciliation between the Anglican Church and the Papacy. But though he counted much for the success of his project of toleration on taking advantage of the dissensions between Protestant Churchmen and Protestant Dissenters he soon discovered that for any real success in his political or religious aims he must seek resources elsewhere than at home. At this moment France was the dominant power in Europe. Its young King, Lewis the Fourteenth, was the champion of Catholicism and despotism against civil and religious liberty throughout the world. France was the wealthiest of European powers, and her subsidies could free Charles from dependence on his Parliament. Her army was the finest in the world, and French soldiers could put down, it was thought, any resistance from English patriots. The aid of Lewis could alone realize the aims of Charles, and Charles was willing to pay the price which Lewis demanded for his aid, the price of concurrence in his designs on Spain. Spain at this moment had not only ceased to threaten Europe but herself trembled at the threats of France; and the aim of Lewis was to complete her ruin, to win the Spanish provinces in the Netherlands, and ultimately to secure the succession to the Spanish throne for a French prince. But the presence of the French in Flanders was equally distasteful to England and to Holland, and in such a contest Spain might hope for the aid of these states and of the Empire. For some years Lewis contented himself with perfecting his army and preparing by skilful negotiations to make such a league of the great powers against him impossible. His first success in England was in the marriage of the King. Portugal, which had only just shaken off the rule of Spain, was really dependent upon France; and in accepting the hand of Catharine of Braganza in spite of the protests of Spain, Charles

Marriage of Charles

SEC. III.

CHARLES
THE
SECOND

1667
TO
1673

announced his adhesion to the alliance of Lewis. Already English opinion saw the danger of such a course, and veered round to the Spanish side. As early as 1661 the London mob backed the Spanish ambassador in a street squabble for precedence with the ambassador of France. "We do all naturally love the Spanish," says Pepys, "and hate the French." The marriage of Catharine, the sale of Dunkirk, the one result of Cromwell's victories, to France, aroused the national jealousy and suspicion of French influence; and the war with Holland seemed at one time likely to end in a war with Lewis. The Dutch war was in itself a serious stumblingblock in the way of French projects. To aid either side was to throw the other on the aid of the House of Austria, and to build up a league which would check France in its aim. Only peace could keep the European states disunited, and enable Lewis by their disunion to carry out his design of seizing Flanders. His attempt at mediation was fruitless; the defeat of Lowestoft forced him to give aid to Holland, and the news of his purpose at once roused England to a hope of war. When Charles announced it to the Houses, "there was a great noise," says Louvois, "in the Parliament to show the joy of the two Houses at the prospect of a fight with us." Lewis, however, cautiously limited his efforts to narrowing the contest to a struggle at sea, while England, vexed with disasters at home and abroad, could scarcely maintain the war. The appearance of the Dutch fleet in the Thames was followed by the sudden conclusion of peace which again left the ground clear for the diplomatic intrigues of Lewis.

*Peace of
Breda*
1667

**The
Fall of
Clarendon**

In England the irritation was great and universal, but the public resentment fell on Clarendon alone. Charles had been bitterly angered when in 1663 his bill to vest a dispensing power in the Crown had been met by Clarendon's open opposition. The Presbyterian party, represented by Ashley, and the Catholics, led by the Earl of Bristol, alike sought his overthrow; in the Court he was opposed by Bennet, afterwards Earl of Arlington, a creature of the King's. But Clarendon was still strong in his intimate connexion with the King's affairs, in the marriage of his daughter, Anne Hyde, to the Duke of York, in his capacity for business, above all in the support of the Church, and the confidence of the royalist and orthodox House of Commons. Foiled in their efforts to displace him, his rivals had availed themselves of the jealousy of the merchant-class to drive him against his will into the war with Holland; and though the Chancellor succeeded in forcing the Five Mile Act through the Houses in the teeth of Ashley's protests, the calculations of his enemies were soon verified The union between Clarendon and the Parliament was broken by the war. The Parliament was enraged by his counsel for its dissolution, and by his proposal to raise troops without a Parliamentary grant, and his opposition to the inspection of accounts, in which they saw an attempt

SEC. III.

CHARLES
THE
SECOND
1667
TO
1673

The Cabal

1668

*The policy
of France*

1667

to re-establish the one thing they hated most, a standing army. Charles could at last free himself from the minister who had held him in check so long ; the Chancellor was dismissed from office, and driven to take refuge in France.   By the exile of Clarendon, the death of South-ampton, and the retirement of Ormond and Nicholas, the party of constitutional loyalists in the Council ceased to exist ; and the section which had originally represented the Presbyterians, and which under the guidance of Ashley had bent to purchase toleration even at the cost of increasing the prerogatives of the Crown, came to the front of affairs.   The religious policy of Charles had as yet been defeated by the sturdy Churchmanship of the Parliament, the influence of Clarendon, and the reluctance of the Presbyterians as a body to accept the Royal "indulgence" at the price of a toleration of Catholicism and a recognition of the King's power to dispense with Parliamentary statutes.   The first steps of the new ministry in releasing Noncon-formists from prison, in suffering conventicles to reopen, and suspending the operation of the Act of Uniformity, were in open defiance of the known will of the two Houses.   But when Charles again proposed to his counsellors a general toleration he no longer found himself supported by them as in 1663.   Even Ashley's mood was changed.   Instead of toleration they pressed for a union of Protestants which would have utterly foiled the King's projects ; and a scheme of Protestant compre-hension which had been approved by the moderate divines on both sides, by Tillotson and Stillingfleet on the part of the Church as well as by Manton and Baxter on the part of the Nonconformists, was laid before the House of Commons.   Even its rejection failed to bring Ashley and his party back to their old position.   They were still for toleration, but only for a toleration the benefit of which did not extend to Catholics, "in respect the laws have determined the principles of the Romish religion to be inconsistent with the safety of your Majesty's person and government."   The policy of the Council in fact was determined by the look of public affairs abroad.   Lewis had quickly shown the real cause of the eagerness with which he had pressed on the Peace of Breda between England and the Dutch.   He had secured the neutrality of the Emperor by a secret treaty which shared the Spanish dominions between the two monarchs in case the King of Spain died without an heir.   England, as he believed, was held in check by Charles, and like Holland was too exhausted by the late war to meddle with a new one.   On the very day therefore on which the treaty was signed he sent in his formal claims on the Low Countries, and his army at once took the field.   The greater part of Flanders was occupied and six great fortresses secured in two months. Franche Comté was overrun in seventeen days.   Holland protested and appealed to England for aid ; but her appeals remained at first unanswered.   England sought in fact to tempt Holland, Spain, and

France in turn by secret offers of alliance. From France she demanded, as the price of her aid against Holland and perhaps Spain, a share in the eventual partition of the Spanish dominions, and an assignment to her in such a case of the Spanish Empire in the New World. But all her offers were alike refused. The need of action became clearer every hour to the English ministers, and wider views gradually set aside the narrow dreams of merely national aggrandizement. The victories of Lewis, the sudden revelation of the strength of France, roused even in the most tolerant minds a dread of Catholicism. Men felt instinctively that the very existence of Protestantism and with it of civil freedom was again to be at stake. Arlington himself had a Dutch wife and had resided in Spain ; and Catholic as in heart he was, thought more of the political interests of England, and of the invariable resolve of its statesmen since Elizabeth's day to keep the French out of Flanders, than of the interests of Catholicism. Lewis, warned of his danger, strove to lull the general excitement by offers of peace to Spain, while he was writing to Turenne, " I am turning over in my head things that are far from impossible, and go to carry them into execution whatever they may cost." Three armies were, in fact, ready to march on Spain, Germany, and Flanders, when Arlington despatched Sir William Temple to the Hague, and the signature of a Triple Alliance between England, Holland, and Sweden bound Lewis to the terms he had offered as a blind, and forced on him the Peace of Aix-la-Chapelle.

Few measures have won a greater popularity than the Triple Alliance. " It is the only good public thing," says Pepys, " that hath been done since the King came to England." Even Dryden, writing at the time as a Tory, counted among the worst of Shaftesbury's crimes that "the Triple Bond he broke." In form indeed the Alliance simply bound Lewis to adhere to terms of peace proposed by himself, and those advantageous terms. But in fact it utterly ruined his plans. It brought about too that union of the powers of Europe against which, as Lewis felt instinctively, his ambition would dash itself in vain. It was Arlington's aim to make the Alliance the nucleus of a greater confederation ; and he tried not only to perpetuate it, but to include within it the Swiss Cantons, the Empire, and the House of Austria. His efforts were foiled ; but the " Triple Bond" bore within it the germs of the Grand Alliance which at last saved Europe. To England it at once brought back the reputation which she had lost since the death of Cromwell. It was a sign of her re-entry on the general stage of European politics, and of the formal adoption of the balance of power as a policy essential to the welfare of Europe at large. But it was not so much the action of England which had galled the pride of Lewis, as the action of Holland. That "a nation of shopkeepers" (for Lewis applied the phrase to Holland long before Napoleon applied it to England) should

SEC. III.

CHARLES
THE
SECOND

1667
TO
1673

have foiled his plans at the very moment of their realization, "stung him," he owned, "to the quick." If he refrained from an instant attack it was to nurse a surer revenge. His steady aim during the four years which followed the Peace of Aix-la-Chapelle was to isolate the United Provinces, to bring about the neutrality of the Empire in any attack on them, to break the Triple Alliance by detaching Sweden from it and securing Charles, and to leave the Dutch without help, save from the idle goodwill of Brandenburg and Spain. His diplomacy was everywhere successful, but it was nowhere so successful as with England. Charles had been stirred to a momentary pride by the success of the Triple Alliance, but he had never seriously abandoned his policy, and he was resolute at last to play an active part in realizing it. It was clear that little was to be hoped for from his old plans of winning toleration for the Catholics from his new ministers, and that in fact they were resolute to bring about such a union of Protestants as would have been fatal to his designs. From this moment

Charles turns to France

he resolved to seek for his advantage from France. The Triple Alliance was hardly concluded when he declared to Lewis his purpose of entering into an alliance with him, offensive and defensive. He owned to being the only man in his kingdom who desired such a league, but he was determined to realize his desire, whatever might be the sentiments of his ministers. His ministers, indeed, he meant either to bring over to his schemes or to outwit. Two of them, Arlington and Sir Thomas Clifford, were Catholics in heart like the King; and they were summoned, with the Duke of York, who had already secretly embraced Catholicism, and two Catholic nobles, to a conference in which Charles, after pledging them to secrecy, declared himself a Catholic, and asked their counsel as to the means of establishing the Catholic religion in

1669

his realm. It was resolved to apply to Lewis for aid in this purpose; and Charles proceeded to seek from the King a "protection," to use the words of the French ambassador, "of which he always hoped to feel the powerful effects in the execution of his design of changing the present state of religion in England for a better, and of establishing his authority so as to be able to retain his subjects in the obedience they owe him." The fall of Holland was as needful for the success of the plans of Charles as of Lewis; and with the ink of the Triple Alliance hardly dry, Charles promised help in Lewis's schemes for the ruin of Holland and the annexation of Flanders. He offered therefore to declare his religion and to join France in an attack on Holland, if Lewis would grant him a subsidy equal to a million a year. In the event of the King of Spain's death without a son Charles pledged himself to support France in her claims upon Flanders, while Lewis promised to assent to the designs of England on the Spanish dominions in America. On this basis, after a year's negotiations, a secret treaty

May 1670

was concluded at Dover in an interview between Charles and his sister Henrietta, the Duchess of Orleans. It provided that Charles should announce his conversion, and that in case of any disturbance arising from such a step he should be supported by a French army and a French subsidy. War was to be declared by both powers against Holland, England furnishing a small land force, but bearing the chief burthen of the contest at sea, on condition of an annual subsidy of three hundred thousand pounds.

Nothing marks better the political profligacy of the age than that Arlington, the author of the Triple Alliance, should have been chosen as the confidant of Charles in his treaty of Dover. But to all save Arlington and Clifford the King's change of religion or his political aims remained utterly unknown. It would have been impossible to obtain the consent of the party in the royal council which represented the old Presbyterians, of Ashley or Lauderdale or the Duke of Buckingham, to the Treaty of Dover. But it was possible to trick them into approval of a war with Holland by playing on their desire for a toleration of the Nonconformists. The announcement of the King's Catholicism was therefore deferred ; and a series of mock negotiations, carried on through Buckingham, ended in the conclusion of a sham treaty which was communicated to Lauderdale and to Ashley, a treaty which suppressed all mention of the religious changes or of the promise of French aid in bringing them about, and simply stipulated for a joint war against the Dutch. In such a war there was no formal breach of the Triple Alliance, for the Triple Alliance only guarded against an attack on the dominions of Spain, and Ashley and his colleagues were lured into assent to it in 1671 by the promise of a toleration on their own terms. Charles in fact yielded the point to which he had hitherto clung, and, as Ashley demanded, promised that no Catholic should be benefited by the Indulgence. The bargain once struck, and his ministers outwitted, it only remained for Charles to outwit his Parliament. A large subsidy had been demanded in 1670 for the fleet, under the pretext of upholding the Triple Alliance ; and the subsidy was granted. In the spring the two Houses were adjourned. So great was the national opposition to his schemes that Charles was driven to plunge hastily into hostilities. An attack on a Dutch convoy was at once followed by a declaration of war, and fresh supplies were obtained for the coming struggle by closing the Exchequer, and suspending under Clifford's advice the payment of either principal or interest on loans advanced to the public Treasury. The suspension spread bankruptcy among half the goldsmiths of London ; but with the opening of the war Ashley and his colleagues gained the toleration they had bought so dear. By virtue of his ecclesiastical powers the King ordered "that all manner of penal laws on matters ecclesiastical against whatever sort of Nonconformists or recusants should be from that day suspended," and gave liberty of public worship to all

SEC. III.

CHARLES
THE
SECOND
1667
TO
1673

The
Declara-
tion of
Indul-
gence

*The Cabal
and the war*

1671

1672

SEC. III.

CHARLES
THE
SECOND
1667
TO
1673

dissidents save Catholics, who were allowed to say mass only in private houses. The effect of the Declaration went far to justify Ashley and his colleagues (if anything could justify their course) in the bargain by which they purchased toleration. Ministers returned, after years of banishment, to their homes and their flocks. Chapels were reopened. The gaols were emptied. Bunyan left his prison at Bedford ; and hundreds of Quakers, who had been the special objects of persecution, were set free to worship God after their own fashion.

The War with Holland

The Declaration of Indulgence however failed to win any expression of gratitude from the bulk of the Nonconformists. Dear as toleration was to them, the general interests of religion were dearer, and not only these but national freedom was now at stake. The success of the Allies seemed at first complete. The French army passed the Rhine, overran three of the States without opposition, and pushed its outposts to within sight of Amsterdam. It was only by skill and desperate courage that the Dutch ships under De Ruyter held the English fleet under the Duke of York at bay in an obstinate battle off the coast of Suffolk. The triumph of the English cabinet was shown in the elevation of the leaders of both its parties. Ashley was made Chancellor and Earl of Shaftesbury, and Clifford became Lord Treasurer. But the Dutch were saved by the stubborn courage which awoke before the arrogant demands of the conqueror. The plot of the two Courts hung for success on the chances of a rapid surprise ; and with the approach of winter which suspended military operations, all chance of a surprise was over. The death of De Witt, the leader of the great merchant class, called William the Prince of Orange to the head of the Republic. Young as he was, he at once displayed the cool courage and tenacity of his race. " Do you not see your country is lost ? " asked the Duke of Buckingham, who had been sent to negotiate at the Hague. " There is a sure way never to see it lost," replied William, " and that is, to die in the last ditch." With the spring the tide began to turn. Holland was saved and province after province won back from France by William's dauntless resolve. In England the delay of winter had exhausted the supplies which had been so unscrupulously procured, while the closing of the Treasury had shaken credit and rendered it impossible to raise a loan. It was necessary in 1673 to appeal to the Commons, but the Commons met in a mood of angry distrust. The war, unpopular as it was, they left alone. What overpowered all other feelings was a vague sense, which we know now to have been justified by the facts, that liberty and religion were being unscrupulously betrayed. There was a suspicion that the whole armed force of the nation was in Catholic hands. The Duke of York was suspected of being in heart a Papist, and he was in command of the fleet. Catholics had been placed as officers in the force which was being raised for the war in Holland. Lady Castlemaine, the King's

Sec. III.

Charles
the
Second
1667
to
1673

mistress, paraded her conversion ; and doubts were fast gathering over the Protestantism of the King. There was a general suspicion that a plot was on foot for the establishment of Catholicism and despotism, and that the war and the Indulgence were parts of the plot. The change of temper in the Commons was marked by the appearance of what was from that time called the Country party, with Lord Russell, Lord Cavendish, and Sir William Coventry at its head, a party which sympathized with the desire of the Nonconformists for religious toleration, but looked on it as its first duty to guard against the designs of the Court. As to the Declaration of Indulgence, however, all parties in the House were at one. The Commons resolved "that penal statutes in matters ecclesiastical cannot be suspended but by consent of Parliament," and refused supplies till the Declaration was recalled. The King yielded ; but the Declaration was no sooner recalled than a Test Act was passed through both Houses without opposition, which required from every one in the civil and military employment of the State the oaths of allegiance and supremacy, a declaration against transubstantiation, and a reception of the sacrament according to the rites of the Church of England. It was known that the Protestant dissidents were prepared to waive all objection to oath or sacrament, while the Bill would wholly exclude Catholics from share in the government. Clifford at once counselled resistance, and Buckingham talked flightily about bringing the army to London. But the grant of a subsidy was still held in suspense ; and Arlington, who saw that all hope of carrying the " great plan " through was at an end, pressed Charles to yield. A dissolution was the King's only resource, but in the temper of the nation a new Parliament would have been yet more violent than the present one ; and Charles sullenly gave way. Few measures have ever brought about more startling results. The Duke of York owned himself a Catholic, and resigned his office as Lord High Admiral. Throngs of excited people gathered round the Lord Treasurer's house at the news that Clifford, too, had owned to being a Catholic and had laid down his staff of office. Their resignation was followed by that of hundreds of others in the army and the civil service of the Crown. On public opinion the effect was wonderful. " I dare not write all the strange talk of the town," says Evelyn. The resignations were held to have proved the existence of the dangers which the Test Act had been framed to meet. From this moment all trust in Charles was at an end. " The King," Shaftesbury said bitterly, "who if he had been so happy as to have been born a private gentleman had certainly passed for a man of good parts, excellent breeding, and well natured, hath now, being a Prince, brought his affairs to that pass that there is not a person in the world, man or woman, that dares rely upon him or put any confidence in his word or friendship."

The Test Act

SEC. IV.

DANBY
1673
TO
1678

Shaftes-
bury

Section IV.—Danby. 1673—1678.

[*Authorities*.—As before. Mr. Christie's "Life of Shaftesbury," a defence, and in some respects a successful defence, of that statesman's career, throws a fresh light on the policy of the Whig party during this period.]

The one man in England on whom the discovery of the King's perfidy fell with the most crushing effect was the Chancellor, Lord Shaftesbury. Ashley Cooper had piqued himself on a penetration which read the characters of men around him, and on a political instinct which discerned every coming change. His self-reliance was wonderful. In mere boyhood he saved his estate from the greed of his guardians by boldly appealing in person to Noy, who was then Attorney-General. As an undergraduate at Oxford he organized a rebellion of the freshmen against the oppressive customs which were enforced by the senior men of his college, and succeeded in abolishing them. At eighteen he was a member of the Short Parliament. On the outbreak of the Civil War he took part with the King ; but in the midst of the royal successes he foresaw the ruin of the royal cause, passed to the Parliament, attached himself to the fortunes of Cromwell, and became member of the Council of State. Before all things a strict Parliamentarian, however, he was alienated by Cromwell's setting up of absolute rule without Parliament ; and a temporary disgrace during the last years of the Protectorate only quickened him to an active opposition which did much to bring about its fall. His bitter invectives against the dead Protector, his intrigues with Monk, and the active part which he took, as member of the Council of State, in the King's recall, were rewarded at the Restoration with a peerage, and with promotion to a foremost share in the royal councils. Ashley was then a man of forty, and under the Commonwealth he had been, in the contemptuous phrase of Dryden when writing as a Tory, "the loudest bagpipe of the squeaking train ;" but he was no sooner a minister of Charles than he flung himself into the debauchery of the Court with an ardour which surprised even his master. "You are the wickedest dog in England!" laughed Charles at some unscrupulous jest of his counsellor's. "Of a subject, Sir, I believe I am!" was the unabashed reply. But the debauchery of Ashley was simply a mask. He was in fact temperate by nature and habit, and his ill-health rendered any great excess impossible. Men soon found that the courtier who lounged in Lady Castlemaine's boudoir, or drank and jested with Sedley and Buckingham, was a diligent and able man of business. "He is a man," says the puzzled Pepys, three years after the Restoration, "of great business, and yet of pleasure and dissipation too." His rivals were as envious of the ease and mastery with which he dealt with questions of finance, as of the "nimble wit" which won the favour of the King. Even in later years his industry earned the grudging praise of his enemies. Dryden owned that as Chancellor he was "swift to despatch and easy of access," and wondered at the restless activity which "refused his age the needful hours of rest." His activity indeed was the more wonderful that his health was utterly broken. An accident in early days left behind it an abiding weakness, whose traces were seen in the furrows which seared his long pale face, in the feebleness of his health, and the nervous tremor which shook his puny frame. The "pigmy body" was "fretted to decay" by the "fiery soul" within it. But pain and weakness brought with them no sourness of spirit. Ashley was attacked more unscrupulously than any statesman save Walpole ; but Burnet, who did not love him, owns that he was never bitter or angry in speaking of his assailants. Even the wit with which he crushed them was commonly good-humoured. "When will you have done preaching ?" a bishop murmured testily, as Shaftesbury was speaking in the House of Peers. "When I am a bishop, my Lord ! " was the laughing reply.

As a statesman Ashley not only stood high among his contemporaries from his wonderful readiness and industry, but he stood far above them in his scorn of personal profit. Even Dryden, while raking together every fault in his character, owns that his hands were clean. As a political leader his position was to modern eyes odd enough. In religion he was at best a Deist, with some fanciful notions "that after death our souls lived in stars." But Deist as he was, he remained the representative of the Presbyterian and Nonconformist party in the royal council. He was the steady and vehement advocate of toleration, but his advocacy was based on purely political grounds. He saw that persecution would fail to bring back the Dissenters to the Church, and that the effort to recall them only left the country disunited, and thus exposed English liberty to invasion from the Crown, and robbed England of all influence in Europe. The one means of uniting Churchmen and Dissidents was by a policy of toleration, but in the temper of England after the Restoration he saw no hope of obtaining toleration save from the King. Wit, debauchery, rapidity in the despatch of business, were all therefore used as a means to gain influence over the King, and to secure him as a friend in the struggle which Ashley carried on against the intolerance of Clarendon. Charles, as we have seen, had his own game to play and his own reasons for protecting Ashley during his vehement but fruitless struggle against the Test and Corporation Act, the Act of Uniformity, and the persecution of the Dissidents. Fortune at last smiled on the unscrupulous ability with which he entangled Clarendon in the embarrassments of the Dutch war of 1664, and took advantage of the alienation of the Parliament to ensure his fall. By a yet more unscrupulous bargain

Ashley had bought, as he believed, the Declaration of Indulgence, the release of the imprisoned Nonconformists, and freedom of worship for all dissidents, at the price of a consent to the second attack on Holland ; and he was looked on by the public at large as the minister most responsible both for the measures he advised and the measures he had nothing to do with. But while facing the gathering storm of unpopularity Ashley learnt in a moment of drunken confidence the secret of the King's religion. He owned to a friend " his trouble at the black cloud which was gathering over England ; " but, troubled as he was, he still believed himself strong enough to use Charles for his own purposes. His acceptance of the Chancellorship and of the Earldom of Shaftesbury, as well as his violent defence of the war on opening the Parliament, identified him yet more with the royal policy. It was

*Shaftes-
bury's
change of
policy*

after the opening of the Parliament, if we credit the statement of the French Ambassador, that he learnt from Arlington the secret of the Treaty of Dover. Whether this were so, or whether suspicion, as in the people at large, deepened into certainty, Shaftesbury saw he had been duped. To the bitterness of such a discovery was added the bitterness of having aided in schemes which he abhorred. His change of policy was rapid and complete. He pressed in the royal council for the withdrawal of the Declaration of Indulgence. In Parliament he supported the Test Act with extraordinary vehemence. The displacement of James and Clifford by the Test left him, as he thought, dominant in the royal council, and gave him hopes of revenging the deceit which had been practised on him by forcing his policy on the King. He was resolved to end the war. He had dreams of meeting the danger of a Catholic successor by a dissolution of the King's marriage and by a fresh match with a Protestant princess. For the moment indeed Charles was helpless. He found himself, as he had told Lewis long before, alone in his realm. The Test Act had been passed unanimously by both Houses. Even the Nonconformists deserted him, and preferred persecution to the support of his plans. The dismissal of the Catholic officers made the employment of force, if he ever contemplated it, impossible, while the ill success of the Dutch war robbed him of all hope of aid from France. The firmness of the Prince of Orange had roused the stubborn energy of his countrymen. The French conquests on land were slowly won back, and at sea the fleet of the allies was still held in check by the fine seamanship of De Ruyter. Nor was William less successful in diplomacy than in war. The House of Austria was at last roused to action by the danger which threatened Europe, and its union with the United Provinces laid the foundation of the Grand Alliance. If Charles was firm to continue the war, Shaftesbury, like the Parliament itself, was resolved on peace ; and for this purpose he threw himself into hearty alliance with the Country party in the Commons, and welcomed the Duke of Ormond and Prince

SEC. IV.

DANBY
1673
TO
1678

Shaftes-
bury's
Dismissal
1673

Charles
and
Shaftes-
bury

Rupert, who were looked upon as "great Parliament men," back to the royal council. It was to Shaftesbury's influence that Charles attributed the dislike which the Commons displayed to the war, and their refusal of a grant of supplies until fresh religious securities were devised. It was at his instigation that an address was presented by both Houses against the plan of marrying James to a Catholic princess, Mary of Modena. But the projects of Shaftesbury were suddenly interrupted by an unexpected act of vigour on the part of the King. The Houses were no sooner prorogued in November than the Chancellor was ordered to deliver up the Seals.

"It is only laying down my gown and buckling on my sword," Shaftesbury is said to have replied to the royal bidding; and, though the words were innocent enough, for the sword was part of the usual dress of a gentleman which he must necessarily resume when he laid aside the gown of the Chancellor, they were taken as conveying a covert threat. He was still determined to force on the King a peace with the States. But he looked forward to the dangers of the future with even greater anxiety than to those of the present. The Duke of York, the successor to the throne, had owned himself a Catholic, and almost every one agreed that securities for the national religion would be necessary in the case of his accession. But Shaftesbury saw, and it is his especial merit that he did see, that with a king like James, convinced of his Divine Right and bigoted in his religious fervour, securities were valueless. From the first he determined to force on Charles his brother's exclusion from the throne, and his resolve was justified by the Revolution which finally did the work he proposed to do. Unhappily he was equally determined to fight Charles with weapons as vile as his own. The result of Clifford's resignation, of James's acknowledgement of his conversion, had been to destroy all belief in the honesty of public men. A panic of distrust had begun. The fatal truth was whispered that Charles himself was a Catholic. In spite of the Test Act, it was suspected that men Catholics in heart still held high office in the State, and we know that in Arlington's case the suspicion was just. Shaftesbury seized on this public alarm, stirred above all by a sense of inability to meet the secret dangers which day after day was disclosing, as the means of carrying out his plans. He began fanning the panic by tales of a Papist rising in London, and of a coming Irish revolt with a French army to back it. He retired to his house in the City to find security against a conspiracy which had been formed, he said, to cut his throat. Meanwhile he rapidly organized the Country party in the Parliament, and placed himself openly at its head. An address for the removal of ministers "popishly affected or otherwise obnoxious or dangerous" was presented on the reassembling of the Houses. The Commons called on the King to dismiss Lauderdale, Buckingham, and Arlington, and to disband the troops raised since 1664. A bill was brought in to prevent all Catholics from approaching the Court, in other words for removing James from the King's councils. A far more important bill was that of the Protestant Securities, which was pressed by Shaftesbury, Halifax, and Carlisle, the leaders of the new Opposition in the House of Lords, a bill which enacted that any prince of the blood should forfeit his right to the Crown on his marriage with a Catholic. The bill, which was the first sketch of the later Exclusion Bill, failed to pass, but its failure left the Houses excited and alarmed. Shaftesbury intrigued busily in the City, corresponded with William of Orange, and pressed for a war with France which Charles could only avert by an appeal to Lewis, a subsidy from whom enabled him to prorogue the Parliament. But Charles saw that the time had come to give way. "Things have turned out ill," he said to Temple with a burst of unusual petulance, "but had I been well served I might have made a good business of it." His concessions however were as usual complete. He dismissed Buckingham and Arlington. He made peace with the Dutch. But Charles was never more formidable than in the moment of defeat, and he had already resolved on a new policy by which the efforts of Shaftesbury might be held at bay. Ever since the opening of his reign he had clung to a system of balance, had pitted Churchman against Nonconformist, and Ashley against Clarendon, partly to preserve his own independence, and partly with a view of winning some advantage to the Catholics from the political strife. The temper of the Commons had enabled Clarendon to baffle the King's efforts ; and on his fall Charles felt strong enough to abandon the attempt to preserve a political balance, and had sought to carry out his designs with the single support of the Nonconformists. But the new policy had broken down like the old. The Noncon-formists refused to betray the cause of Protestantism, and Shaftesbury, their leader, was pressing on measures which would rob Catholicism of the hopes it had gained from the conversion of James. In straits like these Charles resolved to win back the Commons by boldly adopting the policy on which the House was set. The majority of its members were Cavalier Churchmen, who regarded Sir Thomas Osborne, a dependant of Arlington's, as their representative in the royal councils. The King had already created Osborne Earl of Danby, and made him Lord Treasurer in Clifford's room. In 1674 he frankly adopted the policy of Danby and his party in the Parliament.

The policy of Danby was in the main that of Clarendon. He had all Clarendon's love of the Church, his equal hatred of Popery and Dissent, his high notions of the prerogative tempered by a faith in Parliament and the law. His first measures were directed to allay the popular panic, and strengthen the position of James. Mary, the Duke's eldest child and after him the presumptive heir to the Crown, was confirmed by the royal order as a Protestant. Secret negotiations were opened for her marriage with William of Orange, the son of the King's sister Mary, who if James and his house were excluded stood next in succession to the crown. Such a marriage secured James against the one formidable rival to his claims, while it opened to William a far safer chance of mounting the throne at his father-in-law's death. The union between the Church and the Crown was ratified in conferences between Danby and the bishops; and its first fruits were seen in the rigorous enforcement of the law against conventicles, and the exclusion of all Catholics from court; while the Parliament which was assembled in 1675 was assured that the Test Act should be rigorously enforced. The change in the royal policy came not a moment too soon. As it was, the aid of the Cavalier party which rallied round Danby hardly saved the King from the humiliation of being forced to recall the troops he still maintained in the French service. To gain a majority on this point Danby was forced to avail himself of a resource which from this time played for nearly a hundred years an important part in English politics. He bribed lavishly. He was more successful in winning back the majority of the Commons from their alliance with the Country party by reviving the old spirit of religious persecution. He proposed that the test which had been imposed by Clarendon on municipal officers should be extended to all functionaries of the State; that every member of either House, every magistrate and public officer, should swear never to take arms against the King or to "endeavour any alteration of the Protestant religion now established by law in the Church of England, or any alteration in the Government in Church and State as it is by law established." The Bill was forced through the Lords by the bishops and the Cavalier party, and its passage through the Commons was only averted by a quarrel on privilege between the two Houses which Shaftesbury dexterously fanned into flame. On the other hand the Country party remained strong enough to hamper their grant of supplies with conditions unacceptable to the King. Eager as they were for the war with France which Danby promised, the Commons could not trust the King; and Danby was soon to discover how wise their distrust had been. For the Houses were no sooner prorogued than Charles revealed to him the negotiations he had been all the while carrying on with Lewis, and required him to sign a treaty by which, on consideration of a yearly pension guaranteed on the part of France, the two sovereigns bound themselves to enter into no engagements with other powers, and to lend each other aid in case of rebellion in their dominions. Such a treaty not only bound England to dependence on France, but freed the King from all Parliamentary control. But his minister pleaded in vain for delay and for the advice of the Council. Charles answered his entreaties by signing the treaty with his own hand. Danby found himself duped by the King as Shaftesbury had found himself duped;

but his bold temper was only spurred to fresh plans for rescuing Charles from his bondage to Lewis. To do this the first step was to reconcile the King and the Parliament, which met after a prorogation of fifteen months. The Country party stood in the way of such a reconciliation, but Danby resolved to break its strength by measures of unscrupulous vigour, for which a blunder of Shaftesbury's gave an opportunity. Shaftesbury despaired of bringing the House of Commons, elected as it had been fifteen years before in a moment of religious and political reaction, to any steady opposition to the Crown. He had already moved an address for a dissolution ; and he now urged that as a statute of Edward the Third ordained that Parliaments should be held " once a year or oftener if need be," the Parliament by the recent prorogation of a year and a half had ceased legally to exist. The Triennial Act deprived such an argument of any force. But Danby represented it as a contempt of the House, and the Lords at his bidding committed its supporters, Shaftesbury, Buckingham, Salisbury, and Wharton, to the Tower. While the Opposition cowered under the blow, Danby pushed on a measure which was designed to win back alarmed Churchmen to confidence in the Crown. By the Bill for the security of the Church it was provided that on the succession of a king not a member of the Established Church the appointment of bishops should be vested in the existing prelates, and that the King's children should be placed in the guardianship of the Archbishop of Canterbury.

The bill however failed in the Commons ; and a grant of supply was only obtained by Danby's profuse bribery. The progress of the war abroad, indeed, was rousing panic in England faster than Danby could allay it. New successes of the French arms in Flanders, and a defeat of the Prince of Orange at Cassel, stirred the whole country to a cry for war. The two Houses echoed the cry in an address to the Crown ; but Charles parried the blow by demanding a supply before the war was declared, and on the refusal of the still suspicious House prorogued the Parliament. Fresh and larger subsidies from France enabled him to continue this prorogation for seven months. But the silence of the Parliament did little to silence the country ; and Danby took advantage of the popular cry for war to press an energetic course of action on the King. In its will to check French aggression the Cavalier party was as earnest as the Puritan, and Danby aimed at redeeming his failure at home by uniting the Parliament through a vigorous policy abroad. As usual, Charles appeared to give way. He was himself for the moment uneasy at the appearance of the French on the Flemish coast, and he owned that " he could never live at ease with his subjects " if Flanders were abandoned. He allowed Danby, therefore, to press on both parties the necessity for mutual concessions, and to define the new attitude of England by a step which was to produce momentous results. The Prince of Orange was invited to England, and wedded to Mary, the presumptive heiress of the Crown. The marriage promised a close political union in the future with Holland, and a corresponding opposition to the ambition of France. With the country it was popular as a Protestant match, and as ensuring a Protestant successor to James. But Lewis was bitterly angered; he rejected the English propositions of peace, and again set his army in the field. Danby was ready to accept the challenge, and the withdrawal of the English ambassador from Paris was followed by an assembly of the Parliament. A warlike speech from the throne was answered by a warlike address from the House, supplies were voted, and an army raised. But the actual declaration of war still failed to appear. While Danby threatened France, Charles was busy turning the threat to his own profit, and gaining time by prorogations for a series of base negotiations. At one stage he demanded from Lewis a fresh pension for the next three years as the price of his good offices with the allies. Danby stooped to write the demand, and Charles added, "This letter is written by my order, C.R." A force of three thousand English soldiers were landed at Ostend; but the allies were already broken by their suspicions of the King's real policy, and Charles soon agreed for a fresh pension to recall the brigade. The bargain was hardly struck when Lewis withdrew the terms of peace he had himself offered, and on the faith of which England had ostensibly retired from the scene. Once more Danby offered aid to the allies, but all faith in England was lost. One power after another gave way to the new French demands, and though Holland, the original cause of the war, was saved, the Peace of Nimeguen made Lewis the arbiter of Europe.

Disgraceful as the peace was to England, it left Charles the master of a force of twenty thousand men levied for the war he refused to declare, and with nearly a million of French money in his pocket. His course had roused into fresh life the old suspicions of his perfidy, and of a secret plot with Lewis for the ruin of English freedom and of English religion. That there was such a plot we know; and from the moment of the Treaty of Dover the hopes of the Catholic party mounted even faster than the panic of the Protestants. But they had been bitterly disappointed by the King's withdrawal from his schemes after his four years ineffectual struggle, and by his seeming return to the policy of Clarendon. Their anger and despair were revealed in letters from English Jesuits, and the correspondence of Coleman. Coleman, the secretary of the Duchess of York, and a busy intriguer, had gained sufficient knowledge of the real plans of the King and of his brother to warrant him in begging for money from Lewis for the work of saving Catholic interests from Danby's hostility by intrigues in the Parliament. A passage from one of his letters gives us a glimpse of the

Sec. IV.

DANBY
1673
TO
1678
*Marriage of
William
and Mary*
1678

July 1678

The
Popish
Plot

wild dreams which were stirring among the hotter Catholics of the time. "They had a mighty work on their hands," he wrote, "no less than the conversion of three kingdoms, and by that perhaps the utter subduing of a pestilent heresy which had so long domineered over a great part of the northern world. Success would give the greatest blow to the Protestant religion that it had received since its birth." The suspicions which had been stirred in the public mind mounted into alarm when the Peace of Nimeguen suddenly left Charles master—as it seemed—of the position ; and it was of this general panic that one of the vile impostors who are always thrown to the surface at times of great public agitation was ready to take advantage by the invention of *Titus Oates* a Popish plot. Titus Oates, a Baptist minister before the Restoration, a curate and navy chaplain after it, but left penniless by his infamous character, had sought bread in a conversion to Catholicism, and had been received into Jesuit houses at Valladolid and St. Omer. While he remained there, he learnt the fact of a secret meeting of the Jesuits in London, which was probably nothing but the usual congregation of the order. On his expulsion for misconduct this single fact widened in his fertile brain into a plot for the subversion of Protestantism and the death of the King. His story was laid before Charles, and received with cool *Aug.* 1678 incredulity ; but Oates made affidavit of its truth before a London magistrate, Sir Edmondsbury Godfrey, and at last managed to appear before the Council. He declared that he had been trusted with letters which disclosed the Jesuit plans. They were stirring rebellion in Ireland ; in Scotland they disguised themselves as Cameronians ; in England their aim was to assassinate the King, and to leave the throne open to the Papist Duke of York. The extracts from Jesuit letters however which he produced, though they showed the disappointment and anger of the writers, threw no light on the monstrous charges of a plot for assassination. Oates would have been dismissed indeed with contempt but for the seizure of Coleman's correspondence. His letters gave a new colour to the plot. Danby himself, conscious of the truth that there were designs which Charles dared not avow, was shaken in his rejection of the disclosures, and inclined to use them as weapons to check the King in his Catholic policy. But a more dexterous hand had already seized on the growing panic. Shaftesbury, released after a long imprisonment and hopeless of foiling the King's policy in any other way, threw himself into the plot. "Let the Treasurer cry as loud as he pleases against Popery," he laughed, "I will cry a note louder." But no cry was needed to heighten the popular frenzy from the moment when Sir Edmondsbury Godfrey, the magistrate before whom Oates had laid his information, was found in a field near London with his sword run through his heart. His death was assumed to be murder, and the murder to be an attempt of the Jesuits to "stifle the plot." A solemn funeral added to public agitation ; and the two Houses named committees to investigate the charges made by Oates.

SEC. IV.

DANBY
1673
TO
1678
**The
Fall of
Danby**

In this investigation Shaftesbury took the lead. Whatever his personal ambition may have been, his public aims in all that followed were wise and far-sighted. He aimed at forcing Charles to dissolve Parliament and appeal to the nation. He aimed at driving Danby out of office and at forcing on Charles a ministry which should break his dependence on France and give a constitutional turn to his policy. He saw that no security would really avail to meet the danger of a Catholic sovereign, and he aimed at excluding James from the throne. But in pursuing these aims he rested wholly on the plot. He fanned the popular panic by accepting without question some fresh depositions in which Oates charged five Catholic peers with part in the Jesuit conspiracy. The peers were sent to the Tower, and two thousand suspected persons were hurried to prison. A proclamation ordered every Catholic to leave London. The trainbands were called to arms, and patrols paraded through the streets, to guard against the Catholic rising which Oates declared to be at hand. Meanwhile Shaftesbury turned the panic to political account by forcing through Parliament a bill which excluded Catholics from a seat in either House. The exclusion remained in force for a century and a half; but it had really been aimed against the Duke of York, and Shaftesbury was defeated by a proviso which exempted James from the operation of the bill. The plot, which had been supported for four months by the sole evidence of Oates, began to hang fire; but a promise of reward brought forward a villain, named Bedloe, with tales beside which those of Oates seemed tame. The two informers were now pressed forward by an infamous rivalry to stranger and stranger revelations. Bedloe swore to the existence of a plot for the landing of a Catholic army and a general massacre of the Protestants. Oates capped the revelations of Bedloe by charging the Queen herself, at the bar of the Lords, with knowledge of the plot to murder her husband. Monstrous as such charges were, they revived the waning frenzy of the people and of the two Houses. The peers under arrest were ordered to be impeached. A new proclamation enjoined the arrest of every Catholic in the realm. A series of judicial murders began with the trial and execution of Coleman, which even now can only be remembered with horror. But the alarm must soon have worn out had it only been supported by perjury. What gave force to the false plot was the existence of a true one. Coleman's letters had won credit for the perjuries of Oates, and a fresh discovery now won credit for the perjuries of Bedloe. From the moment when the pressure of the Commons and of Danby had forced Charles into a position of seeming antagonism to France, Lewis had resolved to bring about the dissolution of the Parliament, the fall of the Minister, and the disbanding of the army which Danby still looked on as a weapon against him. For this purpose the

French ambassador had entered into negotiations with the leaders of the Country party. The English ambassador at Paris, Ralph Montagu, now returned home on a quarrel with Danby, obtained a seat in the House of Commons, and in spite of the seizure of his papers, laid on the table of the House the despatch which had been forwarded to Lewis, demanding payment for the King's services to France during the late negotiations. The House was thunderstruck; for strong as had been the general suspicion, the fact of the dependence of England on a foreign power had never before been proved. Danby's name was signed to the despatch, and he was at once impeached on a charge of high treason. But Shaftesbury was more eager to secure the election of a new Parliament than to punish his rival, and Charles was resolved to prevent at any price a trial which could not fail to reveal the disgrace-

*Dissolution
of the
Parliament*

ful secret of his foreign policy. Charles was in fact at Shaftesbury's mercy, and the end for which Shaftesbury had been playing was at last secured. In January, 1679, the Parliament of 1661, after the longest unbroken life in our Parliamentary annals, was at last dissolved.

Section V.—Shaftesbury. 1679—1682.

[*Authorities.*—As before. We may add for this period Earl Russell's Life of his ancestor, William, Lord Russell.]

**Sir
William
Temple**

The new Parliament was elected in a tumult of national excitement. The members were for the most part Churchmen and country gentle-men, but they shared the alarm of the country, and even before their assembly in March their temper had told on the King's policy. James was sent to Brussels. Charles began to disband the army and promised that Danby should soon withdraw from office. In his speech from the throne he asked for supplies to maintain the Pro-testant attitude of his Government in foreign affairs. But it was impossible to avert Danby's fall. The Commons insisted on carrying his impeachment to the bar of the Lords. It was necessary to dismiss

*The new
ministry*

him from his post of Treasurer and to construct a new ministry. Shaftesbury became President of the Council. The chiefs of the Country party, Lord Russell and Lord Cavendish, took their seats at the board with Lords Holles and Roberts, the older representatives of the Presbyterian party which had merged in the general Opposition. Savile, Lord Halifax, as yet known only as a keen and ingenious speaker, entered the ministry in the train of Shaftesbury, with whom he was connected; Lord Sunderland was admitted to the Council; while Lord Essex and Lord Capel, two of the most popular among the Country leaders, went to the Treasury. The recall of Sir William Temple, the negotiator of the Triple Alliance, from his embassy at the Hague to fill the post of Secretary of State, promised a foreign policy which would again place England high among the European powers. Temple returned with a plan of administration which, fruitless as it directly proved, is of great importance as marking the silent change which was passing over the Constitution. Like many men of his time, he was equally alarmed at the power both of the Crown and of the Parliament. In moments of national excitement the power of the Houses seemed irresistible. They had overthrown Clarendon. They had overthrown Clifford and the Cabal. They had just overthrown Danby. But though they were strong enough in the end to punish ill government, they showed no power of securing good government or of permanently influencing the policy of the Crown. For nineteen years, with a Parliament always sitting, Charles as far as foreign policy went had it pretty much his own way. He had made war against the will of the nation and he had refused to make war when the nation demanded it. While every Englishman hated France, he had made England a mere dependency of the French King. The remedy for this state of things, as it was afterwards found, was a very simple one. By a change which we shall have to trace, the Ministry has now become a Committee of State-officers, named by the majority of the House of Commons from amongst the more prominent of its representatives in either House, whose object in accepting office is to do the will of that majority. So long as the majority of the House of Commons itself represents the more powerful current of public opinion it is clear that such an arrangement makes government an accurate reflection of the national will. But obvious as such a plan may seem to us, it had as yet occurred to no English statesman. Even to Temple the one remedy seemed to lie in the restoration of the Royal Council to its older powers. This body, composed as it was of the great officers of the Court, the royal Treasurer and Secretaries, and a few nobles specially summoned to it by the sovereign, formed up to the close of Elizabeth's reign a sort of deliberative assembly to which the graver matters of public administration were commonly submitted by the Crown. A practice, however, of previously submitting such measures to a smaller body of the more important councillors must always have existed ; and under James this secret committee, which was then known as the Cabala or Cabal, began almost wholly to supersede the Council itself. In the large and balanced Council which was formed after the Restoration all real power rested with the " Cabala " of Clarendon, Southampton, Ormond, Monk, and the two Secretaries ; and on Clarendon's fall these were succeeded by Clifford, Arlington, Buckingham, Ashley, and Lauderdale. By a mere coincidence the initials of the latter names formed the word " Cabal," which has ever since retained the sinister meaning their unpopularity gave to it. The effect of these smaller committees had undoubtedly been to remove the check which the larger numbers

Sec. V.

Shaftes-
bury

1679
to
1682

*Temple
and his
Council*

and the more popular composition of the Royal Council laid upon the Crown. The unscrupulous projects which made the Cabal of Clifford and his fellows a by-word among Englishmen could never have been laid before a Council of great peers and hereditary officers of State. To Temple therefore the organization of the Council seemed to furnish a check on mere personal government which Parliament was unable to supply. For this purpose the Cabala, or Cabinet, as it was now becoming the fashion to term the confidential committee of the Council, was abolished. The Council itself was restricted to thirty members, and their joint income was not to fall below £300,000, a sum little less than what was estimated as the income of the whole House of Commons. A body of great nobles and proprietors, not too numerous for secret deliberation, and wealthy enough to counterbalance either the Commons or the Crown, would form, Temple hoped, a barrier against the violence and aggression of the one power, and a check on the mere despotism of the other.

**The
Exclusion
Bill**

The new Council and the new ministry gave fair hope of a wise and patriotic government. But the difficulties were still great. The nation was frenzied with suspicion and panic. The elections to the Parliament had taken place amidst a whirl of excitement which left no place for candidates of the Court. The appointment of the new ministry, indeed, was welcomed with a general burst of joy. But the question of the Succession threw all others into the shade. At the bottom of the national panic lay the dread of a Catholic King, a dread which the after history of James fully justified. Shaftesbury was earnest for the exclusion of James, but as yet the majority of the Council shrank from the step, and supported a plan which Charles brought forward for preserving the rights of the Duke of York while restraining his powers as sovereign. By this project the

*The Bill of
Securities*

presentation to Church livings was to be taken out of his hands on his accession. The last Parliament of the preceding reign was to continue to sit ; and the appointment of all Councillors, Judges, Lord-Lieutenants, and officers in the fleet, was vested in the two Houses so long as a Catholic sovereign was on the throne. The extent of these provisions showed the pressure which Charles felt, but Shaftesbury was undoubtedly right in setting the plan aside as at once insufficient and impracticable. He continued to advocate the Exclusion in the royal Council ; and a bill for depriving James of his right to the Crown, and for devolving it on the next Protestant in the line of succession was introduced into the Commons by his adherents, and passed the House by a large majority. It was known that Charles would use his influence with the Peers for its rejection, and the Earl therefore fell back on the tactics of Pym. A bold Remonstrance was prepared in the Commons. The City of London was ready with an address to the two Houses in favour of the bill. All Charles could do

SEC. V.

SHAFTES-
BURY

1679
TO
1682

Mon-
mouth

was to gain time by the prorogation of the Parliament, and by its dissolution in May.

But delay would have been useless had the Country party remained at one. The temper of the nation and of the House of Commons was so hotly pronounced in favour of the exclusion of the Duke, that union among the ministers must in the end have secured it and spared England the necessity for the Revolution of 1688. The wiser leaders of the Country party, indeed, were already leaning to the very chang which that Revolution brought about. If James were passed over, his daughter Mary, the wife of the Prince of Orange, stood next in the order of succession : and the plan of Temple, Essex, and Halifax after the failure of their bill of Securities, was to bring the Prince over to England during the prorogation, to introduce him into the Council, and to pave his way to the throne. Unhappily Shaftesbury was contemplating a very different course. He distrusted the Prince of Orange as a mere adherent of the royal house, and as opposed to any weakening of the royal power or invasion of the royal prerogative. His motive for setting aside William's claims is probably to be found in the maxim ascribed to him, that " a bad title makes a good king." Whatever were his motives, however, he had resolved to set aside the claims of James and his children, as well as William's own claim, and to place the Duke of Monmouth on the throne. Monmouth was reputed to be the eldest of the King's bastards, a weak and worthless profligate in temper, but popular through his personal beauty and his reputation for bravery. The tale was set about of a secret marriage between the King and his mother ; Shaftesbury induced Charles to put the Duke at the head of the troops sent to repress a rising of the Covenanters in the west of Scotland, and on his return pressed the King to give him the command of the Guards, which would have put the only military force possessed by the Crown in Monmouth's hands.

Sunderland, Halifax, and Essex, however, were not only steadily opposed to Shaftesbury's project, but saw themselves marked out for ruin in the event of Shaftesbury's success. They had advised the dissolution of the last Parliament ; and the Earl's anger had vented itself in threats that the advisers of the dissolution should pay for it with their heads. The danger came home to them when a sudden illness of the King and the absence of James made Monmouth's accession a possible contingency. The three ministers at once induced Charles to recall the Duke of York ; and though he withdrew to Scotland on the King's recovery, Charles deprived Monmouth of his charge as Captain-General of the Forces and ordered him like James to leave the realm. Left alone in his cause by the opposition of his colleagues, Shaftesbury threw himself more and more on the support of the Plot. The prosecution of its victims was pushed recklessly on. Three

Catholics were hanged in London. Eight priests were put to death in the country. Pursuivants and informers spread terror through every Catholic household. He counted on the reassembling of the Parliament to bring all this terror to bear upon the King. But Charles had already marked the breach which the Earl's policy had made in the ranks of the Country party. He saw that Shaftesbury was unsupported by any of his colleagues save Russell. To Temple, Essex, or Halifax it seemed possible to bring about the succession of Mary without any violent revolution; but to set aside not only the right of James but the right of his Protestant children, and even of the Prince of Orange, was to ensure a civil war. It was with their full support

therefore that Charles deprived Shaftesbury of his post of Lord President of the Council. The dismissal was the signal for a struggle to whose danger Charles was far from blinding himself. What had saved him till now was his cynical courage. In the midst of the terror and panic of the Plot men "wondered to see him quite cheerful amidst such an intricacy of troubles," says the courtly Reresby, "but it was

not in his nature to think or perplex himself much about anything." Even in the heat of the tumult which followed on Shaftesbury's dismissal, Charles was seen fishing and sauntering as usual in Windsor Park. But closer observers than Reresby saw beneath this veil of indolent unconcern a consciousness of new danger. "From this time," says Burnet, "his temper was observed to change very visibly." He became in fact "sullen and thoughtful; he saw that he had to do with a strange sort of people, that could neither be managed nor frightened." But he faced the danger with his old unscrupulous coolness. He reopened secret negotiations with France. Lewis was as alarmed as Charles himself at the warlike temper of the nation, and as anxious to prevent the assembly of a Parliament; but the terms on which he offered a subsidy were too humiliating even for the King's acceptance. The failure forced him to summon a new Parliament; and the panic, which Shaftesbury was busily feeding with new tales of massacre and invasion, returned members even more violent than the members of the House he had just dismissed. A host of petitions called on the King to suffer Parliament to meet at the opening of 1680. Even the Council shrank from the King's proposal to prorogue its assembly to November, 1680, but Charles persisted. Alone as he stood, he was firm in his resolve to gain time, for time, as he saw, was working in his favour. The tide of public sympathy was beginning to turn. The perjury of Oates proved too much at last for the credulity of juries; and the acquittal of four of his victims was a sign that the panic was beginning to ebb. A far stronger proof of this was seen in the immense efforts which Shaftesbury made to maintain it. Fresh informers were brought forward to swear to a plot for the assassination of the Earl himself, and to the share of the Duke of York in the con-

SEC. V.

SHAFTES-
BURY

**1679
TO
1682**
**Peti-
tioners
and Ab-
horrers**

spiracies of his fellow-religionists. A paper found in a meal-tub was produced as evidence of the new danger. Gigantic torch-light processions paraded the streets of London, and the effigy of the Pope was burnt amidst the wild outcry of a vast multitude.

Acts of yet greater daring showed the lengths to which Shaftesbury was ready to go. He had grown up amidst the tumults of civil war, and, greyheaded as he was, the fire and vehemence of his early days seemed to wake again in the singular recklessness with which he drove on the nation to a struggle in arms. Early in 1680 he formed a committee for promoting agitation throughout the country ; and the petitions which it drew up for the assembly of the Parliament were sent to every town and grand jury, and sent back again with thousands of signatures. Monmouth, in spite of the King's orders, returned at Shaftesbury's call to London ; and a daring pamphlet pointed him out as the nation's leader in the coming struggle "against Popery and tyranny." So great was the alarm of the Council that the garrison in every fortress was held in readiness for instant war. But the danger was really less than it seemed. The tide of opinion had fairly turned. Acquittal followed acquittal. A reaction of horror and remorse at the cruelty which had hurried victim after victim to the gallows succeeded to the pitiless frenzy which Shaftesbury had fanned into a flame. Anxious as the nation was for a Protestant sovereign, its sense of justice revolted against the wrong threatened to James's Protestant children ; and every gentleman in the realm felt insulted at the project of setting Mary aside to put the crown of England on the head of a bastard. The memory too of the Civil War was still fresh and keen, and the rumour of an outbreak of revolt rallied men more and more round the King. The host of petitions which Shaftesbury procured from the counties was answered by a counter host of addresses from thousands who declared their "abhorrence" of the plans against the Crown. The country was divided into two great factions of "petitioners" and "abhorrers," the germs of the two great parties of "Whigs" and "Tories" which have played so prominent a part in our political history from the time of the Exclusion Bill. Charles at once took advantage of this turn of affairs. He recalled the Duke of York to the Court. He received the resignations of Russell and Cavendish, as well as of the Earl of Essex, who had at last gone over to Shaftesbury's projects "with all his heart." Shaftesbury met defiance with defiance. Followed by a crowd of his adherents he attended before the Grand Jury of Middlesex, to indict the Duke of York as a Catholic recusant, and the King's mistress, the Duchess of Portsmouth, as a national nuisance, while Monmouth made a progress through the country, and gained favour everywhere by his winning demeanour. Above all, Shaftesbury relied on the temper of the Commons, elected as they had been in the very heat of the panic and irritated by the long delay in calling them together. The first act of the House on meeting in October was to vote that their care should be "to suppress Popery and prevent a Popish successor." Rumours of a Catholic plot in Ireland were hardly needed to push the Exclusion Bill through the Commons without a division. So resolute was the temper of the Lower House that even Temple and Essex now gave their adhesion to it as a necessity, and Sunderland himself wavered towards accepting it. Halifax, whose ability and eloquence had now brought him fairly to the front, opposed it resolutely and successfully in the Lords; but Halifax was

*William
and the
Exclusion*
1680

only the mouthpiece of William. "My Lord Halifax is entirely in the interest of the Prince of Orange," the French ambassador, Barillon, wrote to his master, "and what he seems to be doing for the Duke of York is really in order to make an opening for a compromise by which the Prince of Orange may benefit." The Exclusion Bill once rejected, Halifax followed up the blow by bringing forward a plan of Protestant securities, which would have taken from James on his accession the right of veto on any bill passed by the two Houses, the right of negotiating with foreign states, or of appointing either civil or military officers save with the consent of Parliament. This plan also was no doubt prompted by the Prince of Orange; and the States of Holland supported it by pressing Charles to come to an accommodation with his subjects which would enable them to check the perpetual aggressions which France was making on her neighbours.

*The
Oxford
Parlia-
ment*

But if the Lords would have no Exclusion Bill the Commons with as good reason would have no Securities Bill. They felt—as one of the members for London fairly put it—that such securities would break down at the very moment they were needed. A Catholic king, should he ever come to the throne, would have other forces besides those in England to back him. "The Duke rules over Scotland; the Irish and the English Papists will follow him; he will be obeyed by the officials of high and low rank whom the King has appointed; he will be just such a king as he thinks good." Shaftesbury however was far from resting in a merely negative position. He made a despairing effort to do the work of exclusion by a Bill of Divorce, which would have enabled Charles to put away his Queen on the ground of barrenness, and by a fresh marriage to give a Protestant heir to the throne. The Earl was perhaps already sensible of a change in public feeling, and this he resolved to check and turn by a great public impeachment

*Trial of
Lord
Stafford*

which would revive and establish the general belief in the Plot. Lord Stafford, who from his age and rank was looked on as the leader of the Catholic party, had lain a prisoner in the Tower since the first outburst of popular frenzy. He was now solemnly impeached; and his trial in December 1680 mustered the whole force of informers to prove the truth of a Catholic conspiracy against the King and the realm. The evidence was worthless; but the trial revived, as Shaftesbury had hoped, much of the old panic, and the condemnation of the prisoner by a majority of his peers was followed by his death on the scaffold. The blow produced its effect on all but Charles. Sunderland again pressed the King to give way. But deserted as he was by his ministers, and even by his mistress, for the Duchess of Portsmouth had been cowed into supporting the exclusion by the threats of Shaftesbury, Charles was determined to resist. On the coupling of a grant of supplies with demands for a voice in the appointment of officers of the royal garrisons he prorogued the Parliament. The truth was that he was again planning an alliance with France. With characteristic subtlety, however, he dissolved the existing Parliament, and called a new one to meet in March. The act was a mere blind. The King's aim was to frighten the country into reaction by the dread of civil strife ; and his summons of the Parliament to Oxford was an appeal to the country against the disloyalty of the capital, and an adroit means of reviving the memories of the Civil War. With the same end he ordered his guards to accompany him, on the pretext of anticipated disorder ; and Shaftesbury, himself terrified at the projects of the Court, aided the King's designs by appearing with his followers in arms on the plea of self-protection. Monmouth renewed his progresses through the country. Riots broke out in London. Revolt seemed at hand, and Charles hastened to conclude his secret negotiations with France. He verbally pledged himself to a policy of peace, in other words to withdrawal from any share in the Grand Alliance which William was building up, while Lewis promised a small subsidy which with the natural growth of the royal revenue sufficed to render Charles, if he remained at peace, independent of Parliamentary aids. The violence of the new Parliament played yet more effectually into the King's hands. The members of the House of Commons were the same as those who had been returned to the Parliaments he had just dissolved, and their temper was naturally embittered by the two dissolutions. Their rejection of a new Limitation Bill brought forward by Halifax, which while granting James the title of King would have vested the actual functions of government in the Prince and Princess of Orange, alienated the more moderate and sensible of the Country party. The attempt of the Lower House to revive the panic by impeaching an informer named Fitzharris before the House of Lords, in defiance of the constitutional rule which entitled him as a commoner to a trial by his peers in the course of common law, did still more to throw public opinion on the side of the Crown. Shaftesbury's course, in fact, went wholly on a belief that the penury of the Treasury left Charles at his mercy, and that a refusal of supplies must wring from the King his assent to the Exclusion. But the gold of France had freed the King from his thraldom. He had used the Parliament simply to exhibit himself as a sovereign whose patience and con-

SEC. V.

SHAFTES-
BURY

1679
TO
1682

Shaftes-
bury's
Death

ciliatory temper was rewarded with insult and violence; and now that his end was accomplished, he no sooner saw the Exclusion Bill re-introduced, than he suddenly dissolved the Houses after a month's sitting, and appealed in a royal declaration to the justice of the nation at large.

The appeal was met by an almost universal burst of loyalty. The Church rallied to the King; his declaration was read from every pulpit; and the Universities solemnly decided that "no religion, no law, no fault, no forfeiture," could avail to bar the sacred right of hereditary succession. The arrest of Shaftesbury on a charge of suborning false witnesses to the Plot marked the new strength of the Crown. London indeed was still true to him; the Middlesex Grand Jury ignored the bill of his indictment; and his discharge from the Tower was welcomed in every street with bonfires and ringing of bells. But a fresh impulse was given to the loyal enthusiasm of the country at large by the publication of a plan said to have been found among his papers, the plan of a secret association for the furtherance of the Exclusion, whose members bound themselves to obey the orders of Parliament even after its prorogation or dissolution by the Crown. So general was the reaction that Halifax advised the calling of a new Parliament in the belief that it would be a loyal one. William of Orange too visited England to take advantage of the turn of affairs to pin Charles to the policy of the Alliance; but the King met both counsels with evasion. He pushed boldly on in his new course. He confirmed the loyalty of the Church by a renewed persecution of the Nonconformists, which drove Penn from England and thus brought about the settlement of Pennsylvania as a refuge for his fellow Quakers. He was soon strong enough to call back James to Court. Monmouth, who had resumed his progresses through the country as a means of checking the tide of reaction, was arrested. The friendship of a Tory mayor secured the nomination of Tory sheriffs in London, and the juries they packed left the life of every Exclusionist at the mercy of the Crown. Shaftesbury, alive to the new danger, plunged madly into conspiracies with a handful of adventurers as desperate as himself, hid himself in the City, where he boasted that ten thousand "brisk boys" were ready to appear at his call, and urged his friends to rise in arms. But their delays drove him to flight; and two months after his arrival in Holland, the soul of the great leader, great from his immense energy and the wonderful versatility of his genius, but whose genius and energy had ended in wrecking for the time the fortunes of English freedom, and in associating the noblest of causes with the vilest of crimes, found its first quiet in death.

Section VI.—The Second Stuart Tyranny, 1682—1688.

[*Authorities.*—To those given before we may add Welwood's "Memoirs," Luttrell's "Diary," and above all Lord Macaulay's "History of England."]

Sec. VI.

The
Second
Stuart
Tyranny
1682
to
1688
**The
Royal
Triumph**

The flight of Shaftesbury proclaimed the triumph of the King. His marvellous sagacity had told him when the struggle was over and further resistance useless. But the country leaders, who had delayed to answer the Earl's call, still believed opposition possible ; and Monmouth, with Lord Essex, Lord Howard of Ettrick, Lord Russell, Hampden, and Algernon Sidney held meetings with the view of founding an association whose agitation should force on the King the assembly of a Parliament. The more desperate spirits who had clustered round him as he lay hidden in the City took refuge in plots of assassination, and in a plan for murdering Charles and his brother as they passed the Rye-house on their road from London to Newmarket. Both projects were betrayed, and though they were wholly distinct from one another the cruel ingenuity of the Crown lawyers blended them into one. Lord Essex saved himself from a traitor's death by suicide in the Tower. Lord Russell, convicted on a charge of sharing in the Rye-house plot, was beheaded in Lincoln's Inn Fields. The same fate awaited Algernon Sidney. Monmouth fled in terror over sea, and his flight was followed by a series of prosecutions for sedition directed against his followers. In 1683 the Constitutional opposition which had held Charles so long in check lay crushed at his feet. A weaker man might easily have been led into a wild tyranny by the mad outburst of loyalty which greeted his triumph. On the very day when the crowd around Russell's scaffold were dipping their handkerchiefs in his blood, as in the blood of a martyr, the University of Oxford solemnly declared that the doctrine of passive obedience, even to the worst of rulers, was a part of religion. But Charles saw that immense obstacles still lay in the road of a mere tyranny. The great Tory party which had rallied to his succour against the Exclusionists were still steady for parliamentary and legal government. The Church was as powerful as ever, and the mention of a renewal of the Indulgence to Nonconformists had to be withdrawn before the opposition of the bishops. He was careful therefore during the few years which remained to him to avoid the appearance of any open violation of public law. He suspended no statute. He imposed no tax by royal authority. Nothing indeed shows more completely how great a work the Long Parliament had done than a survey of the reign of Charles the Second. "The King," Hallam says very truly, "was restored to nothing but what the law had preserved to him." No attempt was made to restore the abuses which the patriots of 1641 had swept away. Parliament was continually summoned. In spite of

SEC. VI.

THE
SECOND
STUART
TYRANNY

1682
TO
1688

*Freedom
of the
Press*

its frequent refusal of supplies, no attempt was ever made to raise money by unconstitutional means. The few illegal proclamations issued under Clarendon ceased with his fall. No effort was made to revive the Star Chamber and the Court of High Commission; and if judges were servile and juries sometimes packed, there was no open interference with the course of justice. In two remarkable points freedom had made an advance even on 1641. From the moment when printing began to tell on public opinion, it had been gagged by a system of licences. The regulations framed under Henry the Eighth subjected the press to the control of the Star Chamber, and the Martin Marprelate libels brought about a yet more stringent control under Elizabeth. Even the Long Parliament laid a heavy hand on the press, and the great remonstrance of Milton in his "Areopagitica" fell dead on the ears of his Puritan associates. But the statute for the regulation of printing which was passed immediately after the Restoration expired finally in 1679, and the temper of the Parliament at once put an end to any attempt at re-establishing the censorship. To the new freedom of the press the Habeas Corpus Act added a new security for the personal freedom of every Englishman. Against arbitrary imprisonment provision had been made in the earliest ages by a famous clause in the Great Charter. No free man could be held in prison save on charge or conviction of crime or for debt, and every prisoner on a criminal charge could demand as a right from the Court of King's Bench the issue of a writ of "habeas corpus," which bound his gaoler to produce both the prisoner and the warrant on which he was imprisoned, that the court might judge whether he was imprisoned according to law. In ▒▒▒ ▒▒▒ ▒▒▒ever of imprisonment on a warrant of the royal Council it had ▒▒en sometimes held by judges that the writ could not be issued, and under Clarendon's administration instances had in this way occurred of imprisonment without legal remedy. But his fall was quickly followed by the introduction of a bill to secure this right of the subject, and after a long struggle the Act which is known as the Habeas Corpus Act passed finally in 1679. By this great statute the old practice of the law was freed from all difficulties and exceptions. Every prisoner committed for any crime save treason or felony was declared entitled to his writ even in the vacations of the courts, and heavy penalties were enforced on judges or gaolers who refused him this right. Every person committed for felony or treason was entitled to be released on bail, unless indicted at the next session of gaol delivery after his commitment, and to be discharged if not indicted at the sessions which followed. It was forbidden under the heaviest penalties to send a prisoner into any places or fortresses beyond the seas.

Galling to the Crown as the freedom of the press and the Habeas Corpus Act were soon found to be, Charles made no attempt to curtail the one or to infringe the other.   But while cautious to avoid rousing popular resistance, he moved coolly and resolutely forward on the path of despotism.   It was in vain that Halifax pressed for energetic resistance to the aggressions of France, for the recall of Monmouth, or for the calling of a fresh Parliament.   Like every other English statesman he found he had been duped, and that now his work was done he was suffered to remain in office but left without any influence in the government.   Hyde, who was created Earl of Rochester, still remained at the head of the Treasury ; but Charles soon gave more of his confidence to the supple and acute Sunderland.   Parliament, in defiance of the Triennial Act, which after having been repealed had been re-enacted but without the safeguards of the original act, remained unassembled during the remainder of the King's reign.   His secret alliance with France furnished Charles with the funds he immediately required, and the rapid growth of the customs through the increase of English commerce promised to give him a revenue which, if peace were preserved, would save him from the need of a fresh appeal to the Commons.   All opposition was at an end.   The strength of the Country party had been broken by its own dissensions over the Exclusion Bill, and by the flight or death of its more prominent leaders.   Whatever strength it retained lay chiefly in the towns, and these were now attacked by writs of "quo warranto," which called on them to show cause why their charters should not be declared forfeited on the ground of abuse of their privileges.   A few verdicts on the side of the Crown brought about a general surrender of municipal liberties ; and the grant of fresh charters, in which all but ultra-loyalists were carefully excluded from their corporations, placed the representation of the boroughs in the hands of the Crown.   Against active discontent Charles had long been quietly providing by the gradual increase of his Guards.   The withdrawal of its garrison from Tangier enabled him to raise their force to nine thousand well-equipped soldiers, and to supplement this force, the nucleus of our present standing army. by a reserve of six regiments, which were maintained till they should be needed at home in the service of the United Provinces.   But great as the danger really was, it lay not so much in isolated acts of tyranny as in the character and purpose of Charles himself.   His death at the very moment of his triumph saved English freedom.   He had regained his old popularity, and at the news of his sickness crowds thronged the churches, praying that God would raise him up again to be a father to his people.   But the one anxiety of the King was to die reconciled to the Catholic Church.   His chamber was cleared and a priest named Huddleston, who had saved his life after the battle of Worcester, received his confession and administered the last sacraments.   Not a word of this ceremony was whispered when the nobles and bishops were recalled into the

SEC. VI.

THE
SECOND
STUART
TYRANNY
1682
TO
1688

*New Town
Charters*

1685

SEC. VI.

THE
SECOND
STUART
TYRANNY
1682
TO
1688

royal presence. All the children of his mistresses save Monmouth were gathered round the bed. Charles "blessed all his children one by one, pulling them on to his bed; and then the bishops moved him, as he was the Lord's anointed and the father of his country, to bless them also and all that were there present, and in them the general body of his subjects. Whereupon, the room being full, all fell down upon their knees, and he raised himself in his bed and very solemnly blessed them all." The strange comedy was at last over. Charles died as he had lived: brave, witty, cynical, even in the presence of death. Tortured as he was with pain, he begged the bystanders to forgive him for being so unconscionable a time in dying. One mistress, the Duchess of Portsmouth, hung weeping over his bed. His last thought was of another mistress, Nell Gwynn. "Do not," he whispered to his successor ere he sank into a fatal stupor, "do not let poor Nelly starve!"

**James
the
Second**

The first words of James on his accession in February 1685, his promise "to preserve the Government both in Church and State as it is now by law established," were welcomed by the whole country with enthusiasm. All the suspicions of a Catholic sovereign seemed to have disappeared. "We have the word of a King!" ran the general cry, "and of a King who was never worse than his word." The conviction of his brother's faithlessness stood James in good stead. He was looked upon as narrow, impetuous, stubborn, and despotic in heart, but even his enemies did not accuse him of being false. Above all he was believed to be keenly alive to the honour of his country, and resolute to free it from foreign dependence. It was necessary to summon a Parliament, for the royal revenue ceased with the death of Charles; but the elections, swayed at once by the tide of loyalty and by the command of the boroughs which the surrender of their charters had given to the Crown, sent up a House of Commons in which James found few members who were not to his mind. The question of religious security was waived at a hint of the royal displeasure. A revenue of nearly two millions was granted to the King for life. All that was wanted to rouse the loyalty of the country into fanaticism was supplied by a rebellion in the North, and by another under Monmouth in the West. The hopes of Scotch freedom had clung ever since the Restoration to the house of Argyll. The great Marquis, indeed, had been brought to the block at the King's return. His son, the Earl of Argyll, had been unable to save himself even by a life of singular caution and obedience from the ill-will of the vile politicians who governed Scotland. He was at last convicted of treason in 1682 on grounds at which every English statesman stood aghast. "We should not hang a dog here," Halifax protested, "on the grounds on which my lord Argyll has been sentenced to death." The Earl escaped however to Holland, and lived peacefully there during the last years of the reign of Charles.

*Argyll's
rising*

Sec. VI.

The
Second
Stuart
Tyranny

1682
to
1688

Monmouth had found the same refuge at the Hague, where a belief in the King's purpose to recall him secured him a kindly reception from William of Orange. But the accession of James was a death-blow to the hopes of the Duke, while it stirred the fanaticism of Argyll to a resolve of wresting Scotland from the rule of a Catholic king. The two leaders determined to appear in arms in England and the North, and the two expeditions sailed within a few days of each other. Argyll's attempt was soon over. His clan of the Campbells rose on his landing in Cantyre, but the country had been occupied for the King, and quarrels among the exiles who accompanied him robbed his effort of every chance of success. His force scattered without a fight; and Argyll, arrested in an attempt to escape, was hurried to a traitor's death. Monmouth for a time found brighter fortune. His popularity in the West was great, and though the gentry held aloof when he landed at Lyme, and demanded effective parliamentary government and freedom of worship for Protestant Nonconformists, the farmers and traders of Devonshire and Dorset flocked to his standard. The clothier-towns of Somerset were true to the Whig cause, and on the entrance of the Duke into Taunton the popular enthusiasm showed itself in flowers which wreathed every door, as well as in a train of young girls who presented Monmouth with a Bible and a flag. His forces now amounted to six thousand men, but whatever chance of success he might have had was lost by his assumption of the title of king. The Houses supported James, and passed a bill of attainder against the Duke. The gentry, still true to the cause of Mary and of William, held stubbornly aloof; while the Guards hurried to the scene of the revolt, and the militia gathered to the royal standard. Foiled in an attempt on Bristol and Bath, Monmouth fell back on Bridge-water, and flung himself in the night of the sixth of July, 1685, on the King's forces, which lay encamped on Sedgemoor. The surprise failed; and the brave peasants and miners who followed the Duke, checked in their advance by a deep drain which crossed the moor, were broken after a short resistance by the royal horse. Their leader fled from the field, and after a vain effort to escape from the realm, was captured and sent pitilessly to the block.

Monmouth's rising

Never had England shown a firmer loyalty; but its loyalty was changed into horror by the terrible measures of repression which followed on the victory of Sedgemoor. Even North, the Lord Keeper, a servile tool of the Crown, protested against the license and bloodshed in which the troops were suffered to indulge after the battle. His protest however was disregarded, and he withdrew broken-hearted from the Court to die. James was, in fact, resolved on a far more terrible vengeance; and the Chief-Justice Jeffreys, a man of great natural powers but of violent temper, was sent to earn the Seals by a series of judicial murders which have left his name a byword for cruelty. Three

The Bloody Circuit

SEC. VI.

THE
SECOND
STUART
TYRANNY
1682
TO
1688

hundred and fifty rebels were hanged in the "Bloody Circuit," as Jeffreys made his way through Dorset and Somerset. More than eight hundred were sold into slavery beyond sea. A yet larger number were whipped and imprisoned. The Queen, the maids of honour, the courtiers, even the Judge himself, made shameless profit from the sale of pardons. What roused pity above all were the cruelties wreaked upon women. Some were scourged from market-town to market-town. Mrs. Lisle, the wife of one of the Regicides, was sent to the block at Winchester for harbouring a rebel. Elizabeth Gaunt, for the same act of womanly charity, was burned at Tyburn. Pity turned into horror when it was found that cruelty such as this was avowed and sanctioned by the King. Even the cold heart of General Churchill, to whose energy the victory at Sedgemoor had mainly been owing, revolted at the ruthlessness with which James turned away from all appeals for mercy. "This marble," he cried as he struck the chimney-piece on which he leant, "is not harder than the King's heart." But it was soon plain that the terror which the butchery was meant to strike into the people was part of a larger purpose. The revolt was made a pretext for a vast increase of the standing army. Charles, as we have seen, had silently and cautiously raised it to nearly ten thousand men; James raised it at one swoop to twenty thousand. The employment of this force was to be at home, not abroad, for the hope of an English policy in foreign affairs had already faded away. In the designs which James had at heart he could look for no consent from Parliament; and however his pride revolted against a dependence on France, it was only by French gold and French soldiers that he could hope to hold the Parliament permanently at bay. A week therefore after his accession he assured Lewis that his gratitude and devotion to him equalled that of Charles himself. "Tell your master," he said to the French ambassador, "that without his protection I can do nothing. He has a right to be consulted, and it is my wish to consult him, about everything." The pledge of subserviency was rewarded with the promise of a subsidy, and the promise was received with the strongest expressions of delight and servility.

The Tyranny

Never had the secret league with France seemed so full of danger to English religion. Europe had long been trembling at the ambition of Lewis; it was trembling now at his bigotry. He had proclaimed warfare against civil liberty in his attack upon Holland; he declared war at this moment upon religious freedom by revoking the Edict of Nantes, the measure by which Henry the Fourth after his abandonment of Protestantism secured toleration and the free exercise of their worship for his Protestant subjects. It had been respected by Richelieu even in his victory over the Huguenots, and only lightly tampered with by Mazarin. But from the beginning of his reign Lewis had resolved to set aside its provisions, and his revocation of it in 1685 was only the natural close of a progressive system of persecution. The Revocation was followed by outrages more cruel than even the bloodshed of Alva. Dragoons were quartered on Protestant families, women were flung from their sick-beds into the streets, children were torn from their mothers' arms to be brought up in Catholicism, ministers were sent to the galleys. In spite of the royal edicts, which forbade even flight to the victims of these horrible atrocities, a hundred thousand Protestants fled over the borders, and Holland, Switzerland, the Palatinate, were filled with French exiles. Thousands found refuge in England, and their industry founded in the fields east of London the silk trade of Spitalfields. But while Englishmen were looking with horror on these events in France, James drew from them new hopes. In defiance of the law he was filling his fresh regiments with Catholic officers. He dismissed Halifax from the Privy Council on his refusal to consent to a plan for repealing the Test Act. He met the Parliament with a haughty declaration that whether legal or no his grant of commissions to Catholics must not be questioned, and with a demand of supplies for his new troops. Loyal as was the temper of the Houses, their alarm for the Church, their dread of a standing army, was yet stronger than their loyalty. The Commons by the majority of a single vote deferred the grant of supplies till grievances were redressed, and demanded in their address the recall of the illegal commissions. The Lords took a bolder tone; and the protest of the bishops against any infringement of the Test Act was backed by the eloquence of Halifax. But both Houses were at once prorogued. The King resolved to obtain from the judges what he could not obtain from Parliament. He remodelled the bench by dismissing four judges who refused to lend themselves to his plans; and their successors decided in the case of Sir Edward Hales, a Catholic officer in the army, that a royal dispensation could be pleaded in bar of the Test Act. The principle laid down by the judges asserted the right of the King to dispense with penal laws according to his own judgement, and it was applied by James with a reckless impatience of all decency and self-restraint. Catholics were admitted into civil and military offices without stint, and four Catholic peers were sworn as members of the Privy Council. The laws which forbade the presence of Catholic priests in the realm, or the open exercise of Catholic worship, were set at nought. A gorgeous chapel was opened in the palace of St. James for the worship of the King. Carmelites, Benedictines, Franciscans, appeared in their religious garb in the streets of London, and the Jesuits set up a crowded school in the Savoy.

The quick growth of discontent at these acts would have startled a wiser man into prudence, but James prided himself on an obstinacy

Sec. VI.

The
Second
Stuart
Tyranny
1682
to
1688

1686

*The
Test Act
set aside*

James
and the
Church

SEC. VI.

THE
SECOND
STUART
TYRANNY

1682
TO
1688

which never gave way ; and a riot which took place on the opening of a fresh Catholic chapel in the City was followed by the establishment of a camp of thirteen thousand men at Hounslow to overawe the capital. The course which James intended to follow in England was shown by the course he was following in the sister kingdoms. In Scotland he acted as a pure despot. He placed its government in the hands of two lords, Melfort and Perth, who had embraced his own religion, and put a Catholic in command of the Castle of Edinburgh. The Scotch Parliament had as yet been the mere creature of the Crown, but servile as were its members there was a point at which their servility stopped. When James boldly required them to legalize the toleration of Catholics, they refused to pass such an Act. It was in vain that the King tempted them to consent by the offer of a free trade with England. "Shall we sell our God?" was the indignant reply. James at once ordered the Scotch judges to treat all laws against Catholics as null and void, and his orders were obeyed. In Ireland his policy threw off even the disguise of law. Catholics were admitted by the King's command to the Council and to civil offices. A Catholic, Lord Tyrconnell, was put at the head of the army, and set instantly about its re-organization by cashiering Protestant officers and by admitting two thousand Catholic natives into its ranks. Meanwhile James had begun in England a bold and systematic attack upon the Church. He regarded his ecclesiastical supremacy as a weapon providentially left to him for undoing the work which it had enabled his predecessors to do. Under Henry and Elizabeth it had been used to turn the Church of England from Catholic to Protestant. Under James it should be used to turn it back again from Protestant to Catholic. The High Commission indeed had been declared illegal by an Act of the Long Parliament, and this Act had been confirmed by the Parliament of the Restoration. But it was thought possible to evade this Act by omitting from the instructions on which the Commission acted the extraordinary

powers and jurisdictions by which its predecessor had given offence. With this reserve, seven commissioners were appointed for the government of the Church, with Jeffreys at their head ; and the first blow of the Commission was at the Bishop of London. James had forbidden the clergy to preach against "the King's religion," and ordered Bishop Compton to suspend a London vicar who set this order at defiance. The Bishop's refusal was punished by his own suspension. But the pressure of the Commission only drove the clergy to a bolder defiance of the royal will. Sermons against superstition were preached from every pulpit ; and the two most famous divines of the day, Tillotson and Stillingfleet, put themselves at the head of a host of controversialists who scattered pamphlets and tracts from every printing press.

SEC. VI.

THE
SECOND
STUART
TYRANNY
1682
TO
1688
Declara-
tion of
Indul-
gence

It was in vain that the bulk of the Catholic gentry stood aloof and predicted the inevitable reaction his course must bring about, or that Rome itself counselled greater moderation. James was infatuated with what seemed to be the success of his enterprises. He looked on the opposition he experienced as due to the influence of the High Church Tories who had remained in power since the reaction of 1681, and these he determined "to chastise." The Duke of Queensberry, the leader of this party in Scotland, was driven from office. Tyrconnell, as we have seen, was placed as a check on Ormond in Ireland. In England James resolved to show the world that even the closest ties of blood were as nothing to him if they conflicted with the demands of his faith. His earlier marriage with Anne Hyde, the daughter of Clarendon, bound both the Chancellor's sons to his fortunes; and on his accession he had sent his elder brother-in-law, Henry, Earl of Clarendon, as Lord Lieutenant to Ireland, and raised the younger, Laurence, Earl of Rochester, to the post of Lord Treasurer. But Rochester was now told that the King could not safely entrust so great a charge to any one who did not share his sentiments on religion, and on his refusal to abandon his faith he was deprived of the White Staff. His brother, Clarendon, shared his fall. A Catholic, Lord Bellasys, became First Lord of the Treasury, which was put into commission after Rochester's removal; and another Catholic, Lord Arundel, became Lord Privy Seal, while Father Petre, a Jesuit, was called to the Privy Council. One official after another who refused to aid in the repeal of the Test Act was dismissed. In defiance of the law the Nuncio of the Pope was received in state at Windsor. But even James could hardly fail to perceive the growth of public discontent. If the great Tory nobles were staunch for the Crown, they were as resolute Englishmen in their hatred of mere tyranny as the Whigs themselves. James gave the Duke of Norfolk the sword of State to carry before him as he went to Mass. The Duke stopped at the Chapel door. "Your father would have gone further," said the King. "Your Majesty's father was the better man," replied the Duke, "and he would not have gone so far." The young Duke of Somerset was ordered to introduce the Nuncio into the Presence Chamber. "I am advised," he answered, "that I cannot obey your Majesty without breaking the law." "Do you not know that I am above the law?" James asked angrily. "Your Majesty may be, but I am not," retorted the Duke. He was dismissed from his post; but the spirit of resistance spread fast. In spite of the King's letters the governors of the Charter House, who numbered among them some of the greatest English nobles, refused to admit a Catholic to the benefits of the foundation. The most devoted loyalists began to murmur when James demanded apostasy as a proof of their loyalty. He had soon in fact to abandon all hope of bringing the Church or the Tories over to his will. He

*The Tory
nobles*

*The Non-
conformists*

SEC. VI.

THE
SECOND
STUART
TYRANNY
1682
TO
1688

turned, as Charles had turned, to the Nonconformists, and published in 1687 a Declaration of Indulgence which suspended the operation of the penal laws against Nonconformists and Catholics alike, and of every Act which imposed a test as a qualification for office in Church or State. The temptation to accept the Indulgence was great, for since the fall of Shaftesbury persecution had fallen heavily on the Protestant dissidents, and we can hardly wonder that the Nonconformists wavered for a time, or that numerous addresses of thanks were presented to James. But the great body of them, and all the more venerable names among them, remained true to the cause of freedom. Baxter, Howe, and Bunyan all refused an Indulgence which could only be purchased by the violent overthrow of the law. It was plain that the attempt to divide the forces of Protestantism had utterly failed, and that the only mode of securing his end was to procure a repeal of the Test Act from Parliament itself.

The temper of the existing Houses however remained absolutely opposed to the King's project. He therefore dissolved the Parliament, and summoned a new one. But no free Parliament could be brought, as he knew, to consent to the repeal. The Lords indeed could be swamped by lavish creations of new peers. "Your troop of horse," his minister, Lord Sunderland, told Churchill, "shall be called up into the House of Lords." But it was a harder matter to secure a compliant House of Commons. The Lord-Lieutenants were directed to bring about such a "regulation" of the governing body in boroughs as would ensure the return of candidates pledged to the repeal of the Test, and to question every magistrate in their county as to his vote. Half of them at once refused, and a long list of great nobles—the Earls of Oxford, Shrewsbury, Dorset, Derby, Pembroke, Rutland, Abergavenny, Thanet, Northampton, and Abingdon—were dismissed from their Lord-Lieutenancies. The justices when questioned simply replied that they would vote according to their consciences, and send members to Parliament who would protect the Protestant religion. After repeated "regulations" it was found impossible to form a corporate body which would return representatives willing to comply with the royal will. All thought of a Parliament had to be abandoned; and even the most bigoted courtiers counselled moderation at this proof of the stubborn opposition which James must prepare to encounter from the peers, the gentry, and the trading classes. The clergy alone still hesitated in any open act of resistance. Even the tyranny of the Commission failed to rouse into open disaffection men who had been preaching Sunday after Sunday the doctrine of passive obedience to the worst of kings. But James cared little for passive obedience. He looked on the refusal of the clergy to support his plans as freeing him from his pledge to maintain the Church as established by law; and he resolved to attack it in the great institutions which had till now been its

Sec. VI.

The
Second
Stuart
Tyranny
1682
to
1688

strongholds. To secure the Universities for Catholicism was to seize the only training schools which the clergy possessed. Cambridge indeed escaped easily. A Benedictine monk who presented himself with royal letters recommending him for the degree of a Master of Arts was rejected on his refusal to sign the Articles: and the Vice-Chancellor paid for the rejection by dismissal from his office. But a violent and obstinate attack was directed against Oxford. The Master of University College, who declared himself a convert, was authorized to retain his post in defiance of the law. Massey, a Roman Catholic, was presented by the Crown to the Deanery of Christ Church. Magdalen was the wealthiest Oxford College, and James in 1687 recommended one Farmer, a Catholic of infamous life and not even qualified by statute for the office, to its vacant headship. The Fellows remonstrated, and on the rejection of their remonstrance chose Hough, one of their own number, as their President. The Ecclesiastical Commission declared the election void; and James, shamed out of his first candidate, recommended a second, Parker, Bishop of Oxford, a Catholic in heart and the meanest of his courtiers. But the Fellows held stubbornly to their legal head. It was in vain that the King visited Oxford, summoned them to his presence, and rated them as they knelt before him like schoolboys. "I am King," he said, "I will be obeyed! Go to your chapel this instant, and elect the Bishop! Let those who refuse look to it, for they shall feel the whole weight of my hand!" It was seen that to give Magdalen as well as Christ Church into Catholic hands was to turn Oxford into a Catholic seminary, and the King's threats were disregarded. But they were soon carried out. A special Commission visited the University, pronounced Hough an intruder, set aside his appeal to the law, burst open the door of his President's house to install Parker in his place, and on their refusal to submit deprived the Fellows of their fellowships. The expulsion of the Fellows was followed on a like refusal by that of the Demies. Parker, who died immediately after his installation, was succeeded by a Roman Catholic bishop *in partibus*, Bonaventure Giffard, and twelve Catholics were admitted to fellowships in a single day.

Meanwhile James clung to the hope of finding a compliant Parliament, from which he might win a repeal of the Test Act. In face of the dogged opposition of the country the elections had been adjourned; and a renewed Declaration of Indulgence was intended as an appeal to the nation at large. At its close he promised to summon a Parliament in November, and he called on the electors to choose such members as would bring to a successful end the policy he had begun. His resolve, he said, was to establish universal liberty of conscience for all future time. It was in this character of a royal appeal that he ordered every clergyman to read the declaration during divine service

Sec. VI.

The
Second
Stuart
Tyranny
1682
to
1688

on two successive Sundays. Little time was given for deliberation, but little time was needed. The clergy refused almost to a man to be the instruments of their own humiliation. The Declaration was read in only four of the London churches, and in these the congregation flocked out of church at the first words of it. Nearly all of the country clergy refused to obey the royal orders. The Bishops went with the rest of the clergy. A few days before the appointed Sunday Archbishop Sancroft called his suffragans together, and the six who were able to appear at Lambeth signed a temperate protest to the King, in which they declined to publish an illegal Declaration. " It is a standard of rebellion," James exclaimed as the Primate presented the paper ; and the resistance of the clergy was no sooner announced to him than he determined to wreak his vengeance on the prelates who had signed the protest. He ordered the Ecclesiastical Commissioners to deprive them of their sees, but in this matter even the Commissioners shrank from obeying him. The Chancellor, Lord Jeffreys, advised a prosecution for libel as an easier mode of punishment ; and the bishops, who refused to give bail, were committed on this charge to the Tower. They passed to their prison amidst the shouts of a great multitude, the sentinels knelt for their blessing as they entered its gates, and the soldiers of the garrison drank their healths. So threatening was the temper of the nation that his ministers pressed James to give way. But his obstinacy grew with the danger. "Indulgence," he said, "ruined my father ;" and on the 29th of June the bishops appeared as criminals at the bar of the King's Bench. The jury had been packed, the judges were mere tools of the Crown, but judges and jury were alike overawed by the indignation of the people at large. No sooner had the foreman of the jury uttered the words "Not guilty" than a roar of applause burst from the crowd, and horsemen spurred along every road to carry over the country the news of the acquittal.

Trial of the Bishops 1688

Section VII.—William of Orange.

[*Authorities.*—As before.]

William and Europe

Amidst the tumult of the Plot and the Exclusion Bill the wiser among English statesmen had fixed their hopes steadily on the succession of Mary, the elder daughter and heiress of James. The tyranny of her father's reign made this succession the hope of the people at large. But to Europe the importance of the change, whenever it should come about, lay not so much in the succession of Mary, as in the new power which such an event would give to her husband, William Prince of Orange. We have come in fact to a moment when the struggle of England against the aggression of its King blends with the larger struggle of Europe against the aggression of Lewis the Fourteenth, and it is only by a rapid glance at the political state of the Continent that we can understand the real nature and results of the Revolution which drove James from the throne.

SEC. VII

WILLIAM
OF
ORANGE

The
Great-
ness of
France

At this moment France was the dominant power in Christendom. The religious wars which began with the Reformation had broken the strength of the nations around her. Spain was no longer able to fight the battle of Catholicism. The Peace of Westphalia, by the independence it gave to the German princes and the jealousy it kept alive between the Protestant and Catholic powers of Germany, destroyed the strength of the Empire. The German branch of the House of Austria, spent with the long struggle of the Thirty Years' War, had enough to do in battling hard against the advance of the Turks from Hungary on Vienna. The victories of Gustavus and of the generals whom he formed had been dearly purchased by the exhaustion of Sweden. The United Provinces were as yet hardly regarded as a great power, and were trammelled by their contest with England for the empire of the seas. France alone profited by the general wreck. The wise policy of Henry the Fourth in securing religious peace by a grant of toleration to the Protestants had undone the ill effects of its religious wars. The Huguenots were still numerous south of the Loire, but the loss of their fortresses had turned their energies into the peaceful channels of industry and trade. Feudal disorder was roughly put down by Richelieu, and the policy which gathered all local power into the hands of the crown, though fatal in the end to the real welfare of France, gave it for the moment an air of good government, and a command over its internal resources which no other country could boast. Its compact and fertile territory, the natural activity and enterprise of its people, and the rapid growth of its commerce and manufactures, were sources of natural wealth which even its heavy taxation failed to check. In the latter half of the seventeenth century France was looked upon as the wealthiest power in Europe. The yearly income of the French crown was double that of England, and even Lewis the Fourteenth trusted as much to the credit of his treasury as to the glory of his arms. "After all," he said, when the fortunes of war began to turn against him, "it is the last louis d'or which must win!" It was in fact this superiority in wealth which enabled France to set on foot forces such as had never been seen in Europe since the downfall of Rome. At the opening of the reign of Lewis the Fourteenth its army mustered a hundred thousand men. With the war against Holland it rose to nearly two hundred thousand. In the last struggle against the Grand Alliance there was a time when it counted nearly half a million of men in arms. Nor was France content with these enormous land forces. Since the ruin of Spain the fleets of Holland and of England had alone disputed the empire of

SEC. VII.

WILLIAM
OF
ORANGE

Lewis
the Four-
teenth

the seas.   Under Richelieu and Mazarin France could hardly be looked upon as a naval power.   But the early years of Lewis saw the creation of a navy of 100 men-of-war, and the fleets of France soon held their own against England or the Dutch.

Such a power would have been formidable at any time ; but it was doubly formidable when directed by statesmen who in knowledge and ability were without rivals in Europe.   No diplomatist could compare with Lionne, no war minister with Louvois, no financier with Colbert. Their young master, Lewis the Fourteenth, bigoted, narrow-minded, commonplace as he was, without personal honour or personal courage, without gratitude and without pity, insane in his pride, insatiable in his vanity, brutal in his selfishness, had still many of the qualities of a great ruler : industry, patience, quickness of resolve, firmness of purpose, a capacity for discerning greatness and using it, an immense self-belief and self-confidence, and a temper utterly destitute indeed of real greatness, but with a dramatic turn for seeming to be great. As a politician Lewis had simply to reap the harvest which the two great Cardinals who went before him had sown.   Both had used to the profit of France the exhaustion and dissension which the wars of religion had brought upon Europe.   Richelieu turned the scale against the House of Austria by his alliance with Sweden, with the United Provinces, and with the Protestant princes of Germany ; and the two great treaties by which Mazarin ended the Thirty Years' War, the Treaty of Westphalia and the Treaty of the Pyrenees, left the Empire disorganized and Spain powerless.   From that moment indeed Spain

sank into a strange decrepitude.   Robbed of the chief source of her wealth by the independence of Holland, weakened at home by the revolt of Portugal, her infantry annihilated by Condé in his victory of Rocroi, her fleet ruined by the Dutch, her best blood drained away to the Indies, the energies of her people destroyed by the suppression of all liberty, civil or religious, her intellectual life crushed by the Inquisition, her industry crippled by the expulsion of the Moors, by financial oppression, and by the folly of her colonial system, the kingdom which under Philip the Second had aimed at the empire of the world lay helpless and exhausted under Philip the Fourth.   The aim of Lewis from 1661, the year when he really became master of France, was to carry on the policy of his predecessors, and above all to complete the ruin of Spain. The conquest of the Spanish provinces in the Netherlands would carry his border to the Scheldt.   A more distant hope lay in the probable extinction of the Austrian line which now sat on the throne of Spain. By securing the succession to that throne for a French prince, not only Castille and Aragon with the Spanish dependencies in Italy and the Netherlands, but the Spanish empire in the New World would be added to the dominions of France.   Nothing could save Spain but a union of the European powers, and to prevent this union by his negotiations was a work at which Lewis toiled for years. The intervention of the Empire was guarded against by a renewal of the old alliances between France and the lesser German princes. A league with the Turks gave Austria enough to do on her eastern border. The old league with Sweden, the old friendship with Holland were skilfully maintained. The policy of Charles the Second bound England to the side of Lewis. At last it seemed that the moment for which he had waited had come, and the signing of the Treaty of Breda gave an opportunity for war of which Lewis availed himself in 1667. But the suddenness and completeness of the French success awoke a general terror before which the skilful diplomacy of Charles gave way. Holland was roused to a sense of danger at home by the appearance of French arms on the Rhine. England woke from her lethargy on the French seizure of the coast-towns of Flanders. Sweden joined the two Protestant powers in the Triple Alliance ; and the dread of a wider league forced Lewis to content himself with the southern half of Flanders and the possession of a string of fortresses which practically left him master of the Netherlands.

Lewis was maddened by the check. He had always disliked the Dutch as Protestants and Republicans ; he hated them now as an obstacle which must be taken out of the way ere he could resume his projects upon Spain. Four years were spent in preparations for a decisive blow. The French army was gradually raised to a hundred and eighty thousand men. Colbert created a fleet which rivalled that of Holland in number and equipment. Sweden was again won over. England was again secured by the Treaty of Dover. Meanwhile Holland lay wrapped in a false security. The French alliance had been its traditional policy since the days of Henry the Fourth, and it was especially dear to the party of the great merchant class which had mounted to power on the fall of the House of Orange. John de Witt, the leader of this party, though he had been forced to conclude the Triple Alliance by the advance of Lewis to the Rhine, still clung blindly to the friendship of France. His trust only broke down when the French army crossed the Dutch border in 1672, and the glare of its watch-fires was seen from the walls of Amsterdam. For the moment Holland lay crushed at the feet of Lewis, but the arrogance of the conqueror roused again the stubborn courage which had wrung victory from Alva and worn out the pride of Philip the Second. De Witt was murdered in a popular tumult, and his fall called William, the Prince of Orange, to the head of the Republic. Though the new Stadholder had hardly reached manhood, his great qualities at once made themselves felt. His earlier life had schooled him in a wonderful self-control. He had been left fatherless and all but friendless in childhood, he had been bred among men who looked on his very existence as a danger to the State, his words had been watched, his

SEC. VII.

WILLIAM
OF
ORANGE

looks noted, his friends jealously withdrawn. In such an atmosphere the boy grew up silent, wary, self-contained, grave in temper, cold in demeanour, blunt and even repulsive in address. He was weak and sickly from his cradle, and manhood brought with it an asthma and consumption which shook his frame with a constant cough; his face was sullen and bloodless and scored with deep lines which told of ceaseless pain. But beneath this cold and sickly presence lay a fiery and commanding temper, an immoveable courage, and a political ability of the highest order. William was a born statesman. Neglected as his education had been in other ways, for he knew nothing of letters or of art, he had been carefully trained in politics by John De Witt: and the wide knowledge with which in his first address to the States-General the young Stadholder reviewed the general state of Europe, the cool courage with which he calculated the chances of the struggle, at once won him the trust of his countrymen. Their trust was soon rewarded. Holland was saved, and province after province won back from the arms of France, by William's dauntless resolve. Like his great ancestor, William the Silent, he was a luckless commander, and no general had to bear more frequent defeats. But he profited by defeat as other men profit by victory. His bravery indeed was of that nobler cast which rises to its height in moments of ruin and dismay. The coolness with which, boy-general as he was, he rallied his broken squadrons amidst the rout of Seneff, and wrested from Condé at the last the fruits of his victory, moved his veteran opponent to a generous admiration. It was in such moments indeed that the real temper of the man broke through the veil of his usual reserve. A strange light flashed from his eyes as soon as he was under fire, and in the terror and confusion of defeat his manners took an ease and gaiety that charmed every soldier around him.

William
and
Charles
II.

The political ability of William was seen in the skill with which he drew Spain and the House of Austria into a coalition against France, a union which laid the foundation of the Grand Alliance. But France was still matchless in arms, and the effect of her victories was seconded by the selfishness of the allies, and above all by the treacherous diplomacy of Charles the Second. William was forced to consent in 1678 to the Treaty of Nimeguen, which left France dominant over Europe as she had never been before. Holland indeed was saved from the revenge of Lewis, but fresh spoils had been wrested from Spain, and Franche-Comté, which had been restored at the close of the former war, was retained at the end of this. Above all France overawed Europe by the daring and success with which she had faced single-handed the wide coalition against her. Her King's arrogance became unbounded. Lorraine was turned into a subject-state. Genoa was bombarded, and its Doge forced to seek pardon in the antechambers of Versailles. The Pope was humiliated by the march of an army upon Rome to avenge a slight offered to the French ambassador. The Empire was outraged by a shameless seizure of Imperial fiefs in Elsass and elsewhere. The whole Protestant world was defied by the persecution of the Huguenots which was to culminate in the revocation of the Edict of Nantes. In the mind of Lewis peace meant a series of outrages on the powers around him ; but every outrage helped the cool and silent adversary who was looking on from the Hague to build up that Great Alliance of all Europe from which alone he looked for any effectual check to the ambition of France. The experience of the last war had taught William that of such an alliance England must form a part, and the efforts of the Prince ever since the peace had been directed to secure her co-operation. A reconciliation of the King with his Parliament was an indispensable step towards freeing Charles from his dependence on France, and it was such a reconciliation that William at first strove to bring about ; but he was for a long time foiled by the steadiness with which Charles clung to the power whose aid was needful to carry out the schemes which he was contemplating. The change of policy however which followed on the fall of the Cabal and the entry of Danby into power raised new hopes in William's mind ; and his marriage with Mary dealt Lewis what proved to be a fatal blow. James was without a son, and the marriage with Mary would at any rate ensure William the aid of England in his great enterprise on his father-in-law's death. But it was impossible to wait for that event, and though the Prince used his new position to bring Charles round to a decided policy his efforts remained fruitless. The storm of the Popish Plot complicated his position. In the earlier stages of the Exclusion Bill, when the Parliament seemed resolved simply to pass over James and to seat Mary at once on the throne after her uncle's death, William stood apart from the struggle, doubtful of its issue, though prepared to accept the good luck if it came to him. But the fatal error of Shaftesbury in advancing the claims of Monmouth forced him into action. To preserve his wife's right of succession, with all the great issues which were to come of it, no other course was left than to adopt the cause of the Duke of York. In the crisis of the struggle, therefore, William threw his whole weight on the side of James. The eloquence of Halifax secured the rejection of the Exclusion Bill, and Halifax was but the mouthpiece of William.

But while England was seething with the madness of the Popish Plot and of the royalist reaction, the great European struggle was drawing nearer and nearer. The patience of Germany was worn out by the ceaseless aggressions of Lewis, and in 1686 its princes had bound themselves at Augsburg to resist all further encroachments on the part of France. From that moment war became inevitable, and William watched the course of his father-in-law with redoubled anxiety. His efforts to ensure English aid had utterly failed. James had renewed his brother's secret treaty with France, and plunged into a quarrel with his people which of itself would have prevented him from giving any aid in a struggle abroad. The Prince could only silently look on, with a desperate hope that James might yet be brought to a nobler policy. He refused all encouragement to the leading malcontents who were already calling on him to interfere in arms. On the other hand he declined to support the King in his schemes for the abolition of the Test. If he still cherished hopes of bringing about a peace between the King and people which might enable him to enlist England in the Grand Alliance, they vanished in 1687 before the Declaration of Indulgence. It was at this moment that James called on him to declare himself in favour of the abolition of the penal laws and of the Test. But simultaneously with the King's appeal came letters of warning and promises of support from the leading English nobles. Some, like the Hydes, simply assured him of their friendship. The Bishop of London added promises of support. Others, like Devonshire, Nottingham, and Shrewsbury, cautiously or openly warned the Prince against compliance with the King's demand. Lord Churchill announced the resolve of Mary's sister Anne to stand by the cause of Protestantism. Danby, the leading representative of the great Tory party, sent urgent warnings. The letters dictated William's answer. No one, he truly protested, loathed religious persecution more than he himself did, but in relaxing political disabilities James called on him to countenance an attack on his own religion. "I cannot," he ended, "concur in what your Majesty desires of me." But William still shrank from the plan of an intervention in arms. General as the disaffection undoubtedly was, the position of James seemed fairly secure. He counted on the aid of France. He had an army of twenty thousand men. Scotland, disheartened by the failure of Argyll's rising, could give no such aid as it gave to the Long Parliament. Ireland was ready to throw a Catholic army on the western coast. It was doubtful if in England itself disaffection would turn into actual rebellion. The "Bloody Circuit" had left its terror on the Whigs. The Tories and the Churchmen, angered as they were, were hampered by their doctrine of non-resistance. William's aim therefore was to discourage all violent counsels, and to confine himself to organizing such a general opposition as would force James by legal means to reconcile himself to the country, to abandon his policy at home and abroad, and to join the alliance against France.

But at this moment the whole course of William's policy was changed by an unforeseen event. His own patience and that of the nation rested on the certainty of Mary's succession. But in the midst of the King's struggle with the Church it was announced that the Queen was again with child. The news was received with general unbelief, for five years had passed since the last pregnancy of Mary of Modena. But it at once forced on a crisis. If, as the Catholics joyously fore-told, the child turned out a boy, and, as was certain, was brought up a Catholic, the highest Tory had to resolve at last whether the tyranny under which England lay should go on for ever. The hesitation of the country was at an end. Danby, loyal above all to the Church and firm in his hatred of subservience to France, answered for the Tories; Compton for the High Churchmen, goaded at last into re-bellion by the Declaration of Indulgence. The Earl of Devonshire, the Lord Cavendish of the Exclusion struggle, answered for the Non-conformists, who were satisfied with William's promise to procure them toleration, as well as for the general body of the Whigs. The announcement of the birth of a Prince of Wales was followed ten days after by a formal invitation to William to intervene in arms for the restoration of English liberty and the protection of the Protestant religion; it was signed by the representatives of the great parties now united against a common danger, and by some others, and was carried to the Hague by Herbert, the most popular of English seamen, who had been deprived of his command for a refusal to vote against the Test. The Invitation called on William to land with an army strong enough to justify those who signed it in rising in arms. It was sent from London on the day after the acquittal of the Bishops. The general excitement, the shouts of the boats which covered the river, the bonfires in every street, showed indeed that the country was on the eve of revolt. The army itself, on which James had implicitly relied, suddenly showed its sympathy with the people. James was at Hounslow when the news of the verdict reached him, and as he rode from the camp he heard a great shout behind him. "What is that?" he asked. "It is nothing," was the reply, "only the soldiers are glad that the Bishops are acquitted!" "Do you call that nothing?" grumbled the King. The shout told him that he stood utterly alone in his realm. The peerage, the gentry, the Bishops, the clergy, the Univer-sities, every lawyer, every trader, every farmer, stood aloof from him. And now his very soldiers forsook him. The most devoted Catholics pressed him to give way. But to give way was to change the whole nature of his government. All show of legal rule had disappeared. Sheriffs, mayors, magistrates, appointed by the Crown in defiance of a parliamentary statute, were no real officers in the eye of the law. Even if the Houses were summoned, members returned by officers such as these could form no legal Parliament. Hardly a Minister of the Crown or a Privy Councillor exercised any lawful authority. James had brought things to such a pass that the restoration of legal govern-ment meant the absolute reversal of every act he had done. But he was in no mood to reverse his acts. His temper was only spurred to a more dogged obstinacy by danger and remonstrance. He broke up the camp at Hounslow and dispersed its troops in distant cantonments. He dismissed the two judges who had favoured the acquittal of the Bishops. He ordered the chancellor of each diocese to report the names of the clergy who had not read the Declaration of Indulgence. But his will broke fruitlessly against the sullen resistance which met him on every side. Not a chancellor made a return to the Commissioners, and the Commissioners were cowed into inaction by the temper of the nation. When the judges who had displayed their servility to the Crown went on circuit the gentry refused to meet them. A yet fiercer irritation was kindled by the King's resolve to supply the place of the English troops, whose temper proved unserviceable for his purposes, by draughts from the Catholic army which Tyrconnell had raised in Ireland. Even the Roman Catholic peers at the Council table protested against this measure; and six officers in a single regiment laid down their commissions rather than enroll the Irish recruits among their men. The ballad of "Lillibullero," a scurrilous attack on the Irish recruits, was sung from one end of England to the other.

William's Landing 1688

An outbreak of revolt was in fact inevitable. William was straining all his resources to gather a fleet and sufficient forces, while noble after noble made their way to the Hague. The Earl of Shrewsbury brought £2,000 towards the expenses of the expedition. Edward Russell, the representative of the Whig Earl of Bedford, was followed by the representatives of great Tory houses, by the sons of the Marquis of Winchester, of Lord Danby, of Lord Peterborough, and by the High Church Lord Macclesfield. At home the Earls of Danby and Devonshire prepared silently with Lord Lumley for a rising in the North. In spite of the profound secrecy with which all was conducted, the keen instinct of Sunderland, who had stooped to purchase continuance in office at the price of a secret apostasy to Catholicism, detected the preparations of William; and the sense that his master's ruin was at hand encouraged him to tell every secret of James on the promise of a pardon for the crimes to which he had lent himself. James alone remained stubborn and insensate as of old. He had no fear of a revolt unaided by the Prince of Orange, and he believed that the threat of a French attack on Holland would render William's departure impossible. But in September the long-delayed war began, and by the greatest political error of his reign Lewis threw his forces not on Holland, but on Germany. The Dutch at once felt themselves secure; the States-General gave their sanction to William's project, and the armament he had prepared gathered rapidly in the Scheldt. The news no sooner reached England than the King passed from obstinacy to panic. By draughts from Scotland and Ireland he had

James gives way

mustered forty thousand men, but the temper of the troops robbed him of all trust in them. Help from France was now out of the question.

He could only fall back on the older policy of a union with the Tory party and the party of the Church. He personally appealed for support to the Bishops. He dissolved the Ecclesiastical Commission. He replaced the magistrates he had driven from office. He restored their franchises to the towns. The Chancellor carried back the Charter of London in state into the City. The Bishop of Winchester was sent to replace the expelled Fellows of Magdalen. Catholic chapels and Jesuit schools were ordered to be closed. Sunderland pressed for the instant calling of a Parliament, but to James the counsel seemed treachery, and he dismissed Sunderland from office. In answer to a declaration from the Prince of Orange, which left the question of the legitimacy of the Prince of Wales to Parliament, he produced before the peers who were in London proofs of the birth of his child. But concessions and proofs came too late. Detained by ill winds, beaten back on its first venture by a violent storm, William's fleet of six hundred transports, escorted by fifty men-of-war, anchored on the fifth of November in Torbay; and his army, thirteen thousand men strong, entered Exeter amidst the shouts of its citizens. His coming had not been looked for in the West, and for a week no great landowner joined him. But nobles and squires soon flocked to his camp, and the adhesion of Plymouth secured his rear. Insurrection broke out in Scotland. Danby, dashing at the head of a hundred horsemen into York, gave the signal for a rising. The militia met his appeal with shouts of "A free Parliament and the Protestant religion!" Peers and gentry flocked to his standard; and a march on Nottingham united his forces to those under Devonshire, who had mustered at Derby the great lords of the midland and eastern counties. Everywhere the revolt was triumphant. The garrison of Hull declared for a free Parliament. The Duke of Norfolk appeared at the head of three hundred gentlemen in the market-place at Norwich. At Oxford townsmen and gownsmen greeted Lord Lovelace with uproarious welcome. Bristol threw open its gates to the Prince of Orange, who advanced steadily on Salisbury, where James had mustered his forces. But the King's army, broken by dissensions and mutual suspicions among its leaders, fell back in disorder; and the desertion of Lord Churchill was followed by that of so many other officers that James abandoned the struggle in despair. He fled to London to hear that his daughter Anne had left St. James's to join Danby at Nottingham. "God help me," cried the wretched King, "for my own children have forsaken me!" His spirit was utterly broken; and though he promised to call the Houses together, and despatched commissioners to Hungerford to treat with William on the terms of a free Parliament, in his heart he had resolved on flight. Parliament, he said to the few who still clung to him, would force on him concessions he could not endure; and he only waited for news of the escape of his wife and child to make his way to the Isle of Sheppey, where a hoy lay ready to carry him to France. Some rough fishermen, who took him for a Jesuit, prevented his escape, and a troop of Life Guards brought him back in safety to London : but it was the policy of William and his advisers to further a flight which removed their chief difficulty out of the way. It would have been hard to depose James had he remained, and perilous to keep him prisoner : but the entry of the Dutch troops into London, the silence of the Prince, and an order to leave St. James's, filled the King with fresh terrors, and taking advantage of the means of escape which were almost openly placed at his disposal, James a second time quitted London and embarked on the 23rd of December unhindered for France.

Before flying James had burnt most of the writs convoking the new Parliament, had disbanded his army, and destroyed so far as he could all means of government. For a few days there was a wild burst of panic and outrage in London, but the orderly instinct of the people soon reasserted itself. The Lords who were at the moment in London provided on their own authority as Privy Councillors for the more pressing needs of administration, and resigned their authority into William's hands on his arrival. The difficulty which arose from the absence of any person legally authorized to call Parliament together was got over by convoking the House of Peers, and forming a second body of all members who had sat in the Commons in the reign of Charles the Second, with the Aldermen and Common Councillors of London. Both bodies requested William to take on himself the pro-

visional government of the kingdom, and to issue circular letters inviting the electors of every town and county to send up representatives to a Convention which met in January, 1689. In the new Convention both Houses were found equally resolved against any recall of or negotiation with the fallen King. They were united in entrusting a provisional authority to the Prince of Orange. But with this step their unanimity ended. The Whigs, who formed a majority in the Commons, voted a resolution which, illogical and inconsistent as it seemed, was well adapted to unite in its favour every element of the opposition to James : the Churchman who was simply scared by his bigotry, the Tory who doubted the right of a nation to depose its King, the Whig who held the theory of a contract between King and People. They voted that King James, "having endeavoured to subvert the constitution of this kingdom by breaking the original contract between King and People, and by the advice of Jesuits and other wicked persons having violated the fundamental laws, and having withdrawn himself out of the kingdom, has abdicated the Government, and that the throne is thereby vacant." But in the Lords, where the Tories were still in the ascendant, the resolution was fiercely debated. Archbishop Sancroft with the high Tories held that no crime could bring about a forfeiture of the crown, and that James still remained King, but that his tyranny had given the nation a right to withdraw from him the actual exercise of government and to entrust his functions to a Regency. The moderate Tories under Danby's guidance admitted that James had ceased to be King, but denied that the throne could be vacant, and contended that from the moment of his abdication the sovereignty vested in his daughter Mary. It was in vain that the eloquence of Halifax backed the Whig peers in struggling for the resolution of the Commons as it stood. The plan of a Regency was lost by a single vote, and Danby's scheme was adopted by a large majority. But both the Tory courses found a sudden obstacle in William. He declined to be Regent. He had no mind, he said to Danby, to be his wife's gentleman-usher. Mary, on the other hand, refused to accept the crown save in conjunction with her husband. The two declarations put an end to the question. It was agreed that William and Mary should be acknowledged as joint sovereigns, but that the actual administration should rest with William alone. A Parliamentary Committee in which the most active member was John Somers, a young lawyer who had distinguished himself in the trial of the Bishops and who was destined to play a great part in later history, drew up a Declaration of Rights which was presented on February 13th to William and Mary by the two Houses in the banqueting-room at Whitehall. It recited the misgovernment of James, his abdication, and the resolve of the Lords and Commons to assert the ancient rights and liberties of English subjects. It condemned as illegal his establishment of an ecclesiastical commission, and his raising an army without Parliamentary sanction. It denied the right of any king to suspend or dispense with laws, or to exact money, save by consent of Parliament. It asserted for the subject a right to petition, to a free choice of representatives in Parliament, and to a pure and merciful administration of justice. It declared the right of both Houses to liberty of debate. It demanded securities for the free exercise of their religion by all Protestants, and bound the new sovereign to maintain the Protestant religion and the law and liberties of the realm. In full faith that these principles would be accepted and maintained by William and Mary, it ended with declaring the Prince and Princess of Orange King and Queen of England. At the close of the Declaration, Halifax, in the name of the Estates of the Realm, prayed them to receive the crown. William accepted the offer in his own name and his wife's, and declared in a few words the resolve of both to maintain the laws and to govern by advice of Parliament.

Sec. VIII.

The Grand
Alliance
1689
to
1697
The
Grand
Alliance

Section VIII.—The Grand Alliance. 1689—1697.

[*Authorities.*—As before.]

The blunder of Lewis in choosing Germany instead of Holland for his point of attack was all but atoned for by the brilliant successes with which he opened the war. The whole country west of the Rhine was soon in his hands; his armies were masters of the Palatinate, and penetrated even to Würtemberg. His hopes had never been higher than at the moment when the arrival of James at St. Germain dashed all hope to the ground. Lewis was at once thrown back on a war of defence, and the brutal ravages which marked the retreat of his armies from the Rhine revealed the bitterness with which his pride stooped to the necessity. The Palatinate was turned into a desert. The same ruin fell on the stately palace of the Elector at Heidelberg, on the venerable tombs of the Emperors at Speyer, on the town of the trader, on the hut of the vine-dresser. In accepting the English throne William had been moved not so much by personal ambition as by the prospect of firmly knitting together England and Holland, the two great Protestant powers whose fleets held the mastery of the sea, as his diplomacy had knit all Germany together a year before in the Treaty of Augsburg. But the advance from such a union to the formation of the European alliance against France was still delayed by the reluctance of the two branches of the House of Austria in Germany and Spain to league with Protestant States against a Catholic King, while England cared little to join in an attack on France with the view of saving the liberties of Europe. All hesitation, however, passed away when the reception of James as still King of England at St. Germain gave England just ground for a declaration of war, a step in which it was soon followed by Holland, and the two countries at once agreed to stand by one another in their struggle against France. The adhesion of Spain and the Court of Vienna in 1689 to this agreement completed the Grand Alliance which William had designed; and when Savoy joined the allies France found herself girt in on every side save that of Switzerland with a ring of foes. The Scandinavian kingdoms alone stood aloof from the confederacy of Europe, and their neutrality was unfriendly to France. Lewis was left without a single ally save the Turk: but the energy and quickness of movement which sprang from the concentration of the power of France in a single hand still left the contest an equal one. The Empire was slow to move; the Court of Vienna was distracted by a war with the Turks; Spain was all but powerless; Holland and England were alone earnest in the struggle, and England could as yet give little aid in the war. One English brigade, indeed, formed from the regiments raised by James, joined the Dutch army on the Sambre, and distinguished itself under

Churchill, who had been rewarded for his treason by the title of Earl of Marlborough, in a brisk skirmish with the enemy at Walcourt. But William had as yet grave work to do at home.

In England not a sword had been drawn for James. In Scotland his tyranny had been yet greater than in England, and so far as the Lowlands went the fall of his tyranny was as rapid and complete. No sooner had he called his troops southward to meet William's invasion than Edinburgh rose in revolt. The western peasants were at once up in arms, and the Episcopalian clergy who had been the instruments of the Stuart misgovernment ever since the Restoration were rabbled and driven from their parsonages in every parish. The news of these disorders forced William to act, though he was without a show of legal authority over Scotland. On the advice of the Scotch Lords present in London, he ventured to summon a Convention similar to that which had been summoned in England, and on his own responsibility to set aside the laws which excluded Presbyterians from the Scotch Parliament. This Convention resolved that James had forfeited the crown by misgovernment, and offered it to William and Mary. The offer was accompanied by a Claim of Right framed on the model of the Declaration of Rights to which they had consented in England, but closing with a demand for the abolition of Prelacy. Both crown and claim were accepted, and the arrival of the Scotch regiments which William had brought from Holland gave strength to the new Government. Its strength was to be roughly tested. John Graham of Claverhouse, whose cruelties in the persecution of the Western Covenanters had been rewarded by high command in the Scotch army, and the title of Viscount Dundee, withdrew with a few troopers from Edinburgh to the Highlands, and appealed to the clans. In the Highlands nothing was known of English government or misgovernment: all that the Revolution meant to a Highlander was the restoration of the House of Argyll. To many of the clans it meant the restoration of lands which had been granted them on the Earl's attainder; and the Macdonalds, the Macleans, the Camerons, were as ready to join Dundee in fighting the Campbells and the Government which upheld them as they had been ready to join Montrose in the same cause forty years before. They were soon in arms. As William's Scotch regiments under General Mackay climbed the pass of Killiecrankie, Dundee charged them at the head of three thousand clansmen and swept them in headlong rout down the glen. But his death in the moment of victory broke the only bond which held the Highlanders together, and in a few weeks the host which had spread terror through the Lowlands melted helplessly away. In the next summer Mackay was able to build the strong post of Fort William in the very heart of the disaffected country, and his offers of money and pardon brought about the submission of the clans. Sir John

SEC. VIII.

THE GRAND ALLIANCE

1689
TO
1697

William and Scotland

Killie-crankie

July 1689

Dalrymple, the Master of Stair, in whose hands the government of Scotland at this time mainly rested, had hoped that a refusal of the oath of allegiance would give grounds for a war of extermination, and free Scotland for ever from its terror of the Highlanders. He had provided for the expected refusal by orders of a ruthless severity. "Your troops," he wrote to the officer in command, "will destroy entirely the country of Lochaber, Lochiel's lands, Keppoch's, Glengarry's, and Glencoe's. Your powers shall be large enough. I hope the soldiers will not trouble the Government with prisoners." But his hopes were disappointed by the readiness with which the clans accepted the offers of the Government. All submitted in good time save Macdonald of Glencoe, whose pride delayed his taking of the oath till six days after the latest date fixed by the proclamation. Foiled in his larger hopes of destruction, Dalrymple seized eagerly on the pretext given by Macdonald, and an order "for the extirpation of that sect of robbers" was laid before William and received the royal signature. "The work," wrote the Master of Stair to Colonel Hamilton who undertook it, "must be secret and sudden." The troops were chosen from among the Campbells, the deadly foes of the clansmen of Glencoe, and quartered peacefully among the Macdonalds for twelve days, till all suspicion of their errand disappeared. At daybreak they fell on their hosts, and in a few moments thirty of the clansfolk lay dead on the snow. The rest, sheltered by a storm, escaped to the mountains to perish for the most part of cold and hunger. "The only thing I regret," said the Master of Stair when the news reached him, "is that any got away." Whatever horror the Massacre of Glencoe has roused in later days, few save Dalrymple knew of it at the time. The peace of the Highlands enabled the work of reorganization to go on quietly at Edinburgh. In accepting the Claim of Right with its repudiation of Prelacy, William had in effect restored the Presbyterian Church, and its restoration was accompanied by the revival of the Westminster Confession as a standard of faith, and by the passing of an Act which abolished lay patronage. Against the Toleration Act which the King proposed, the Scotch Parliament stood firm. But the King was as firm in his purpose as the Parliament. So long as he reigned, William declared in memorable words, there should be no persecution for conscience' sake. "We never could be of that mind that violence was suited to the advancing of true religion, nor do we intend that our authority shall ever be a tool to the irregular passions of any party."

*Massacre of
Glencoe*

Feb. 13,
1692

*The
Irish
Revolt*

It was not in Scotland, however, but in Ireland that James and Lewis hoped to arrest William's progress. In the middle of his reign, when his chief aim was to provide against the renewed depression of his fellow religionists at his death by any Protestant successor, James had resolved (if we may trust the statement of the French ambassador) to place Ireland in such a position of independence that she might serve as a refuge for his Catholic subjects. Lord Clarendon was dismissed from the Lord-Lieutenancy and succeeded in the charge of the island by the Catholic Earl of Tyrconnel. The army, purged of its Protestant soldiers, was entrusted to Catholic officers. Catholics were introduced into the Council, and made judges, sheriffs, and magistrates. The settlers were disarmed, and excluded from the public service. The towns, which had been made wholly Protestant by the settlement of James the First, were compelled to accept new charters providing that two-thirds in their corporations should be Catholic. In a brief time the English ascendancy was overthrown, and the life and fortune of the English settlers were at the mercy of the natives on whom they had trampled since Cromwell's day. Panic spread through the island. When Lord Clarendon left the Lord-Lieutenancy, fifteen hundred Protestant families fled in terror oversea. Wild rumours spread, and a massacre was believed to be at hand. The Protestants of the north drew together at Enniskillen and Londonderry, and prepared for self-defence. The King's flight raised the agitation in Ireland to its height. The English of the north proclaimed William King. Tyrconnel, who had raised an army of nearly forty thousand men, scarcely clothed or armed, called on James to return to Ireland, and at the news of his coming with officers, ammunition, and a supply of money provided by the French King, Tyrconnel met him at Cork, and was raised to a dukedom. On James' entry into Dublin, a flag was hoisted over the Castle with the words embroidered on its folds, "Now or never, now and for ever." The aim of James was to carry out an invasion of England with the army that Tyrconnel was said to have at his disposal. But his hopes were ruined by the conflict between his English and Irish supporters. To Tyrconnel and the Irish leaders the King's plans were utterly distasteful. Their policy was that of Ireland for the Irish, and the first step was to drive out the adherents of William who still stood at bay in Ulster. James called a Parliament to Dublin, and meanwhile marched with the troops to Londonderry, where seven thousand five hundred trained soldiers and some four thousand volunteers found shelter behind a weak wall, manned by a few old guns, and destitute even of a ditch. But the desperate Englishmen behind the wall made up for its weakness. So fierce were their sallies, so crushing the repulse of his attack, that the King's general, Hamilton, at last turned the siege into a blockade. The Protestants died of hunger in the streets, and of the fever which comes of hunger, but the cry of the town was still "No Surrender." The siege had lasted a hundred and five days, and only two days' food remained in Londonderry, when on the 28th of July an English ship broke the boom across the river, and the besiegers sullenly withdrew. Their defeat was turned into a rout by the men of Enniskillen, who struggled

SEC. VIII.

THE GRAND
ALLIANCE
1689
TO
1697

1687

1688

Jan. 1,
1689

Mar. 1689

SEC. VIII.

THE GRAND
ALLIANCE
1689
TO
1694

May 7–
July 20

through a bog to charge an Irish force of double their number at Newtown Butler, and drove horse and foot before them in a panic which soon spread through Hamilton's whole army. The routed soldiers fell back on Dublin, where James was holding the Parliament he had summoned. Nearly all the members were Irishmen and Catholics, and their aim was to undo the confiscations of the last forty-eight years which had given the soil to English settlers, and to get back Ireland for the Irish. An Act declared that the proprietors of 1641 whose lands had been confiscated by Cromwell's Government had received the King's solemn pledge of restoration, and enacted that where the pledge had been broken by the Act of Settlement, they should now at once enter on their old lands. An Act of Attainder proclaimed more than two thousand landowners to be conditionally attainted of treason ; hastily and clumsily drawn up, launched in the panic of civil war, its object was to restore by a new forfeiture lands which the English had confiscated, and to find resources to carry on the war. Complete religious equality was proclaimed by a statute far in advance of the age. By another it was ordered that Catholics should pay tithes to their own priests, and Protestants to their clergy, who were left full liberty of teaching. A further Act claimed for Ireland her ancient constitutional right to be governed by laws made in her own Parliament under the King, and not by legislation of the English Parliament.

**England
and the
Revolu-
tion**

Through the long agony of Londonderry, through the proscription and forfeitures of the new Irish rule, William was forced to look helplessly on. The best troops in the army which had been mustered at Hounslow had been sent with Marlborough to the Sambre ; and the political embarrassments which grew up around the Government made it impossible to spare a man of those who remained. The great ends of the Revolution were indeed secured, even amidst the confusion and intrigue which we shall have to describe, by the common consent of all. On the great questions of civil liberty Whig and Tory were now at one.

*Bill of
Rights*

The Declaration of Rights was turned into the Bill of Rights by the Convention which had now become a Parliament, and the passing of this measure in 1689 restored to the monarchy the character which it had lost under the Tudors and the Stuarts. The right of the people through its representatives to depose the King, to change the order of succession, and to set on the throne whom they would, was now established. All claim of Divine Right, or hereditary right independent of the law, was formally put an end to by the election of William and Mary. Since their day no English sovereign has been able to advance any claim to the crown save a claim which rested on a particular clause in a particular Act of Parliament. William, Mary, and Anne were sovereigns simply by virtue of the Bill of Rights. George the First and his successors have been sovereigns solely by virtue of the Act of Settlement. An English monarch is now as much the creature of an Act of Parliament as the pettiest tax-gatherer in his realm. Nor was the older character of the kingship alone restored. The older constitution returned with it. Bitter experience had taught England the need of restoring to the Parliament its absolute power over taxation. The grant of revenue for life to the last two kings had been the secret of their anti-national policy, and the first act of the new legislature was to restrict the grant of the royal revenue to a term of four years. William was bitterly galled by the provision. "The gentlemen of England trusted King James," he said, "who was an enemy of their religion and their laws, and they will not trust me, by whom their religion and their laws have been preserved." But the only change brought about in the Parliament by this burst of royal anger was a resolve henceforth to make the vote of supplies an annual one, a resolve which, in spite of the slight changes introduced by the next Tory Parliament, soon became an invariable rule. A change of almost as great importance established the control of Parliament over the army. The hatred to a standing army which had begun under Cromwell had only deepened under James; but with the continental war the existence of an army was a necessity. As yet, however, it was a force which had no legal existence. The soldier was simply an ordinary subject; there were no legal means of punishing strictly military offences or of providing for military discipline : and the assumed power of billeting soldiers in private houses had been taken away by the law. The difficulty both of Parliament and the army was met by the Mutiny Act. The powers requisite for discipline in the army were conferred by Parliament on its officers, and provision was made for the pay of the force, but both pay and disciplinary powers were granted only for a single year. The Mutiny Act, like the grant of supplies, has remained annual ever since the Revolution ; and as it is impossible for the State to exist without supplies, or for the army to exist without discipline and pay, the annual assembly of Parliament has become a matter of absolute necessity. The greatest constitutional change which our history has witnessed was thus brought about in an indirect but perfectly efficient way. The dangers which experience had lately shown lay in the Parliament itself were met with far less skill. Under Charles, England had seen a Parliament, which had been returned in a moment of reaction, maintained without fresh election for eighteen years. A Triennial Bill, which limited the duration of a Parliament to three, was passed with little opposition, but fell before the dislike and veto of William. To counteract the influence which a king might obtain by crowding the Commons with officials proved a yet harder task. A Place Bill, which excluded all persons in the employment of the State from a seat in Parliament, was defeated, and wisely defeated, in the Lords. The

Sec. VIII
THE GRAND ALLIANCE
1689 TO **1697**
Taxation

The Army

The Parliament

modern course of providing against a pressure from the Court or the administration by excluding all minor officials, but of preserving the hold of Parliament over the great officers of State by admitting them into its body, seems as yet to have occurred to nobody. It is equally strange that while vindicating its right of Parliamentary control over the public revenue and the army, the Bill of Rights should have left by its silence the control of trade to the Crown. It was only a few years later, in the discussions on the charter granted to the East India Company, that the Houses silently claimed and obtained the right of regulating English commerce.

Tolera-tion and the Church

The religious results of the Revolution were hardly less weighty than the political. In the common struggle against Catholicism Churchman and Nonconformist had found themselves, as we have seen, strangely at one; and schemes of Comprehension became suddenly popular. But with the fall of James the union of the two bodies abruptly ceased : and the establishment of a Presbyterian Church in Scotland, together with the " rabbling " of the Episcopalian clergy in its western shires, revived the old bitterness of the clergy towards the dissidents. The Convocation rejected the scheme of the Latitudinarians for such modifications of the Prayer-book as would render possible a return of the Nonconformists, and a Comprehension Bill which was introduced into Parliament failed to pass in spite of the King's strenuous support. William's attempt to partially admit Dissenters to civil equality by a repeal of the Corporation Act proved equally fruitless ; but the passing

Toleration Act

of a Toleration Act in 1689 practically established freedom of worship. Whatever the religious effect of the failure of the Latitudinarian schemes may have been, its political effect has been of the highest value. At no time had the Church been so strong or so popular as at the Revolu-tion, and the reconciliation of the Nonconformists would have doubled its strength. It is doubtful whether the disinclination to all political change which has characterized it during the last two hundred years would have been affected by such a change ; but it is certain that the power of opposition which it has wielded would have been enormously increased. As it was, the Toleration Act established a group of religious bodies whose religious opposition to the Church forced them to support the measures of progress which the Church opposed. With religious forces on the one side and on the other England has es-caped the great stumbling-block in the way of nations where the cause of religion has become identified with that of political reaction. A secession from within its own ranks weakened the Church still more.

The Non jurors

The doctrine of Divine Right had a strong hold on the body of the clergy, though they had been driven from their other favourite doctrine of passive obedience, and the requirement of the oath of allegiance to the new sovereigns from all persons in public functions was resented as an intolerable wrong by almost every parson. Sancroft, the Archbishop of Canterbury, with a few prelates and a large number of the higher clergy, absolutely refused the oath, treated all who took it as schismatics, and on their deprivation by Act of Parliament regarded themselves and their adherents, who were known as Nonjurors, as the only members of the true Church of England. The bulk of the clergy bowed to necessity, but their bitterness against the new Government was fanned into a flame by the religious policy announced in this assertion of the supremacy of Parliament over the Church, and the deposition of bishops by an act of the legislature. The new prelates, such as Tillotson, the Archbishop of Canterbury, and Burnet, Bishop of Salisbury, were men of learning and piety ; but it was only among Whigs and Latitudinarians that William and his successors could find friends among the clergy, and it was mainly to these that they were driven to entrust the higher offices of the Church. The result was a severance between the higher dignitaries and the mass of the clergy which broke the strength of the Church ; and till the time of George the Third its fiercest strife was waged within its own ranks. But the resentment at the measure which brought this strife about already added to the difficulties which William had to encounter.

Yet greater difficulties arose from the temper of his Parliament. In the Commons the bulk of the members were Whigs, and their first aim was to redress the wrongs which the Whig party had suffered during the last two reigns. The attainder of Lord Russell was reversed. The judgements against Sidney, Cornish, and Alice Lisle were annulled. In spite of the opinion of the judges that the sentence on Titus Oates had been against law, the Lords refused to reverse it, but even Oates received a pardon and a pension. The Whigs however wanted not merely the redress of wrongs but the punishment of the wrong-doers. Whig and Tory had been united, indeed, by the tyranny of James ; both parties had shared in the Revolution, and William had striven to prolong their union by joining the leaders of both in his first Ministry. He named the Tory Earl of Danby Lord President, made the Whig Earl of Shrewsbury Secretary of State, and gave the Privy Seal to Lord Halifax, a trimmer between the one party and the other. But save in a moment of common oppression or common danger union was impossible. The Whigs clamoured for the punishment of Tories who had joined in the illegal acts of Charles and of James, and refused to pass the Bill of General Indemnity which William laid before them. William on the other hand was resolved that no bloodshed or proscription should follow the revolution which had placed him on the throne. His temper was averse from persecution ; he had no great love for either of the battling parties ; and above all he saw that internal strife would be fatal to the effective prosecution of the war. While the cares of his new throne were chaining him to England, the confederacy of which he was the guiding spirit was proving too slow and

too loosely compacted to cope with the swift and resolute movements
of France. The armies of Lewis had fallen back within their own
borders, but only to turn fiercely at bay. Even the junction of the
English and Dutch fleets failed to assure them the mastery of the
seas. The English navy was paralyzed by the corruption which prevailed in the public service, as well as by the sloth and incapacity of
its commander. The services of Admiral Herbert at the Revolution
had been rewarded by the Earldom of Torrington and the command
of the fleet ; but his indolence suffered the seas to be swept by French
privateers, and his want of seamanship was shown in an indecisive
engagement with a French squadron in Bantry Bay. Meanwhile
Lewis was straining every nerve to win the command of the Channel ;
the French dockyards were turning out ship after ship, and the
galleys of the Mediterranean fleet were brought round to reinforce the
fleet at Brest. A French victory off the English coast would have
brought serious political danger, for the reaction of popular feeling
which had begun in favour of James had been increased by the pressure of the war, by the taxation, by the expulsion of the Non-jurors
and the discontent of the clergy, by the panic of the Tories at the
spirit of vengeance which broke out among the triumphant Whigs, and

*The
Jacobites*

above all by the presence of James in Ireland. A new party, that of
the Jacobites or adherents of King James, was just forming ; and it
was feared that a Jacobite rising would follow the appearance of a
French fleet on the coast. In such a state of affairs William judged
rightly that to yield to the Whig thirst for vengeance would have
been to ruin his cause. He dissolved the Parliament, which had

1690

refused to pass a Bill of Indemnity for all political offences, and called
a new one to meet in March. The result of the election proved that
he had only expressed the general temper of the nation. The
boroughs had been alienated from the Whigs by their refusal to
pass the Indemnity, and their attempts to secure the Corporations
for their own party ; while in the counties parson after parson led his
flock to the poll against the Whigs. In the new Parliament the bulk
of the members proved Tories. William accepted the resignation of
the more violent Whigs among his councillors, and placed Danby at
the head of affairs. In May the Houses gave their assent to the Act
of Grace. The King's aim in this sudden change of front was not only
to meet the change in the national spirit, but to secure a momentary
lull in English faction which would suffer him to strike at the rebellion
in Ireland. While James was King in Dublin it was hopeless to crush
treason at home ; and so urgent was the danger, so precious every
moment in the present juncture of affairs, that William could trust no
one to bring the work as sharply to an end as was needful save himself.

**Battle of
the
Boyne**

In the autumn of the year 1689 the Duke of Schomberg, an exiled
Huguenot who had followed William to England, had been sent with

a small force to Ulster, but his landing had only roused Ireland to a fresh enthusiasm. The ranks of the Irish army were filled up at once, and James was able to face the Duke at Drogheda with a force double that of his opponent. Schomberg, whose men were all raw recruits whom it was hardly possible to trust at such odds in the field, entrenched himself at Dundalk, in a camp where pestilence soon swept off half his men, till winter parted the two armies. During the next six months James, whose treasury was utterly exhausted, sought to fill it by a coinage of brass money; his soldiers lacked war material, arms, and stores. William meanwhile was toiling hard on the other side of the Channel to bring the Irish war to an end. Schomberg was strengthened during the winter with men and stores, and when the spring came his force reached thirty thousand men. Lewis too felt the importance of the coming struggle; and seven thousand picked Frenchmen, under the Count of Lauzun, were despatched to reinforce the army of James. They had hardly arrived when William himself landed at Carrickfergus, and pushed rapidly to the south. His columns soon caught sight of the Irish forces, posted strongly behind the Boyne. "I am glad to see you, gentlemen," William cried with a burst of delight; "and if you escape me now the fault will be mine." Early next morning the whole English army plunged into the river. The Irish foot broke in a sudden panic, but the horse made so gallant a stand that Schomberg fell in repulsing its charge, and for a time the English centre was held in check. With the arrival of William, however, at the head of the left wing all was over. James, who had throughout been striving to secure the withdrawal of his troops rather than frankly to meet William's onset, forsook his troops as they fell back in retreat upon Dublin, and took ship at Kinsale for France.

But though the beaten army was forced by William's pursuit to abandon the capital, it was still resolute to fight. The incapacity of the Stuart sovereign moved the scorn even of his followers. "Change kings with us," an Irish officer replied to an Englishman who taunted him with the panic of the Boyne, "change kings with us and we will fight you again." They did better in fighting without a king. The French, indeed, withdrew scornfully from the routed army as it stood at bay beneath the walls of Limerick. "Do you call these ramparts?" sneered Lauzun: "the English will need no cannon; they may batter them down with roasted apples." But twenty thousand men remained with Sarsfield, a brave and skilful officer who had seen service in England and abroad; and his daring surprise of the English ammunition train, his repulse of a desperate attempt to storm the town, and the approach of the winter, forced William to raise the siege. The course of the war abroad recalled him to England, and he left his work to one who was quietly proving himself a master in the art of war. Churchill, now Earl of Marlborough, had been recalled from

*Ireland
conquered*

Oct. 1691

Flanders to command a division which landed in the south of Ireland. Only a few days remained before the operations were interrupted by the coming of winter, but the few days were turned to good account. Cork, with five thousand men behind its walls, was taken in forty-eight hours. Kinsale a few days later shared the fate of Cork. Winter indeed left Connacht and the greater part of Munster in Irish hands; the French force remained untouched, and the coming of a new French general, St. Ruth, with arms and supplies encouraged the insurgents. But the summer of 1691 had hardly opened when Ginkell, the new English general, by his seizure of Athlone forced on a battle with the combined French and Irish forces at Aughrim, in which St. Ruth fell on the field and his army was utterly broken. The defeat left Limerick alone in its revolt, and even Sarsfield bowed to the necessity of a surrender. Two treaties were drawn up between the Irish and English generals. By the first it was stipulated that the Catholics of Ireland should enjoy such privileges in the exercise of their religion as were consistent with law, or as they had enjoyed in the reign of Charles the Second. The Crown pledged itself also to summon a Parliament as soon as possible, and to endeavour to procure to the good Roman Catholics security "from any disturbance upon the account of the said religion." By the military treaty those of Sarsfield's soldiers who would were suffered to follow him to France ; and ten thousand men, the whole of his force, chose exile rather than life in a land where all hope of national freedom was lost. When the wild cry of the women who stood watching their departure was hushed, the silence of death settled down upon Ireland. For a hundred years the country remained at peace, but the peace was a peace of despair. The most terrible legal tyranny under which a nation has ever groaned avenged the rising under Tyrconnel. The conquered people, in Swift's bitter words of contempt, became "hewers of wood and drawers of water" to their conquerors. With a people held in close bondage by a series of atrocious penal laws, all dream of a national revolt passed away ; and till the eve of the French Revolution Ireland ceased to be a source of political danger to England.

**The
Jacobite
Plots**

June 30,
1690

Short as the struggle of Ireland had been, it had served Lewis well, for while William was busy at the Boyne a series of brilliant successes was restoring the fortunes of France. In Flanders the Duke of Luxembourg won the victory of Fleurus. In Italy Marshal Catinat defeated the Duke of Savoy. A success of even greater moment, the last victory which France was fated to win at sea, placed for an instant the very throne of William in peril. William never showed a cooler courage than in quitting England to fight James in Ireland at a moment when the Jacobites were only looking for the appearance of a French fleet on the coast to rise in revolt. He was hardly on his way in fact when Tourville, the French admiral, put to sea with strict orders to fight. He was met by the English and Dutch fleet at Beachy Head, and the Dutch division at once engaged. Though utterly outnumbered, it fought stubbornly in hope of Herbert's aid; but Herbert, whether from cowardice or treason, looked idly on while his allies were crushed, and withdrew at nightfall to seek shelter in the Thames. The danger was as great as the shame, for Tourville's victory left him master of the Channel, and his presence off the coast of Devon invited the Jacobites to revolt. But whatever the discontent of Tories and Non-jurors against William might be, all signs of it vanished with the landing of the French. The burning of Teignmouth by Tourville's sailors called the whole coast to arms; and the news of the Boyne put an end to all dreams of a rising in favour of James. The natural reaction against a cause which looked for foreign aid gave a new strength for the moment to William in England; but ill luck still hung around the Grand Alliance. So urgent was the need for his presence abroad that William left, as we have seen, his work in Ireland undone, and crossed in the spring of 1691 to Flanders. It was the first time since the days of Henry the Eighth that an English king had appeared on the Continent at the head of an English army. But the slowness of the allies again baffled William's hopes. He was forced to look on with a small army while a hundred thousand Frenchmen closed suddenly around Mons, the strongest fortress of the Netherlands, and made themselves masters of it in the presence of Lewis. The humiliation was great, and for the moment all trust in William's fortune faded away. In England the blow was felt more heavily than elsewhere. The Jacobite hopes which had been crushed by the indignation at Tourville's descent woke up to a fresh life. Leading Tories, such as Lord Clarendon and Lord Dartmouth, opened communications with James; and some of the leading Whigs, with the Earl of Shrewsbury at their head, angered at what they regarded as William's ingratitude, followed them in their course. In Lord Marlborough's mind the state of affairs raised hopes of a double treason. His design was to bring about a revolt which would drive William from the throne without replacing James, and give the crown to his daughter Anne, whose affection for Marlborough's wife would place the real government of England in his hands. A yet greater danger lay in the treason of Admiral Russell, who had succeeded Torrington in command of the fleet. Russell's defection would have removed the one obstacle to a new attempt which James was resolved to make for the recovery of his throne, and which Lewis had been brought to support. In the beginning of 1692 an army of thirty thousand troops was quartered in Normandy in readiness for a descent on the English coast. Transports were provided for their passage, and Tourville was ordered to cover it with the French fleet at Brest. Though Russell had twice as many ships as his opponent, the

SEC. VIII.

THE GRAND ALLIANCE

1689
TO
1697

French descent on England

Intrigues in England

SEC. VIII

THE GRAND
ALLIANCE

1689
TO
1697
*Battle of
La Hogue*

belief in his purpose of betraying William's cause was so strong that Lewis ordered Tourville to engage the allied fleets at any disadvantage. But whatever Russell's intrigues may have meant, he was no Herbert. "Do not think I will let the French triumph over us in our own seas," he warned his Jacobite correspondents. "If I meet them I will fight them, even though King James were on board." When the allied fleets met the French off the heights of Barfleur his fierce attack proved Russell true to his word. Tourville's fifty vessels were no match for the ninety ships of the allies, and after five hours of a brave struggle the French were forced to fly along the rocky coast of the Cotentin. Twenty-two of their vessels reached St. Malo; thirteen anchored with Tourville in the bays of Cherbourg and La Hogue; but their pursuers were soon upon them, and in a bold attack the English boats burnt ship after ship under the eyes of the French army. All dread of the invasion was at once at an end; and the throne of William was secured by the detection and suppression of the Jacobite conspiracy at home which the invasion was intended to support. But the overthrow of the Jacobite hopes was the least result of the victory of La Hogue. France ceased from that moment to exist as a great naval power; for though her fleet was soon recruited to its former strength, the confidence of her sailors was lost, and not even Tourville ventured again to tempt in battle the fortune of the seas. A new hope, too, dawned on the Grand Alliance. The spell of French triumph was broken. Namur indeed surrendered to Lewis, and the Duke of Luxembourg maintained the glory of the French arms by a victory over William at Steinkirk. But the battle was a useless butchery in which the conquerors lost as many men as the conquered. France felt herself disheartened and exhausted by the vastness of her efforts. The public misery was extreme. "The country," Fénelon wrote frankly to Lewis, "is a vast hospital." In 1693 the campaign of Lewis in the Netherlands proved a fruitless one, and Luxembourg was hardly able to beat off the fierce attack of William at Neerwinden. For the first time in his long career of prosperity Lewis bent his pride to seek peace at the sacrifice of his conquests, and though the effort was vain it told that the daring hopes of French ambition were at an end, and that the work of the Grand Alliance was practically done.

In outer seeming, the Revolution of 1688 had only transferred the sovereignty over England from James to William and Mary. In actual fact it had given a powerful and decisive impulse to the great constitutional progress which was transferring the sovereignty from the King to the House of Commons. From the moment when its sole right to tax the nation was established by the Bill of Rights, and when its own resolve settled the practice of granting none but annual supplies to the Crown, the House of Commons became the supreme power in the State. It was impossible permanently to

SEC. VIII.

THE GRAND
ALLIANCE

1689
TO
1697

*The
sovereignty
of the
Commons*

suspend its sittings, or in the long run to oppose its will, when either course must end in leaving the Government penniless, in breaking up the army and navy, and in suspending the public service. But though the constitutional change was complete, the machinery of government was far from having adapted itself to the new conditions of political life which such a change brought about. However powerful the will of the House of Commons might be, it had no means of bringing its will directly to bear upon the conduct of public affairs. The Ministers who had charge of them were not its servants, but the servants of the Crown; it was from the King that they looked for direction, and to the King that they held themselves responsible. By impeachment or more indirect means the Commons could force a King to remove a Minister who contradicted their will; but they had no constitutional power to replace the fallen statesman by a Minister who would carry out their will. The result was the growth of a temper in the Lower House which drove William and his Ministers to despair. It became as corrupt, as jealous of power, as fickle in its resolves and factious in spirit, as bodies always become whose consciousness of the possession of power is untempered by a corresponding consciousness of the practical difficulties or the moral responsibilities of the power which they possess. It grumbled at the ill-success of the war, at the suffering of the merchants, at the discontent of the Churchmen; and it blamed the Crown and its Ministers for all at which it grumbled. But it was hard to find out what policy or measures it would have preferred. Its mood changed, as William bitterly complained, with every hour. It was, in fact, without the guidance of recognized leaders, without adequate information, and destitute of that organization out of which alone a definite policy can come. Nothing better proves the inborn political capacity of the English mind than that it should at once have found a simple and effective solution of such a difficulty as this. The credit of the solution belongs to a man whose political character was of the lowest type. Robert, Earl of Sunderland, had been a Minister in the later days of Charles the Second; and he had remained Minister through almost all the reign of James. He had held office at last only by compliance with the worst tyranny of his master, and by a feigned conversion to the Roman Catholic faith; but the ruin of James was no sooner certain than he had secured pardon and protection from William by the betrayal of the master to whom he had sacrificed his conscience and his honour. Since the Revolution Sunderland had striven only to escape public observation in a country retirement, but at this crisis he came secretly forward to bring his unequalled sagacity to the aid of the King. His counsel was to recognize practically the new power of the Commons by choosing the Ministers of the Crown exclusively from among the members of the party which was strongest in the Lower House. As yet no

Ministry in the modern sense of the term had existed.   Each great officer of state Treasurer or Secretary or Lord Privy Seal, had in theory been independent of his fellow-officers ; each was the " King's servant" and responsible for the discharge of his special duties to the King alone.   From time to time one Minister, like Clarendon, might tower above the rest and give a general direction to the whole course of government, but the predominance was merely personal and never permanent ; and even in such a case there were colleagues who were ready to oppose or even impeach the statesman who overshadowed them.   It was common for a King to choose or dismiss a single Minister without any communication with the rest ; and so far was even William from aiming at ministerial unity, that he had striven to reproduce in the Cabinet itself the balance of parties which prevailed outside it.   Sunderland's plan aimed at replacing these independent Ministers by a homogeneous Ministry, chosen from the same party, representing the same sentiments, and bound together for common action by a sense of responsibility and loyalty to the party to which it belonged.   Not only would such a plan secure a unity of administration which had been unknown till then, but it gave an organization to the House of Commons which it had never had before.   The Ministers who were representatives of the majority of its members became the natural leaders of the House.   Small factions were drawn together into the two great parties which supported or opposed the Ministry of the Crown.   Above all it brought about in the simplest possible way the solution of the problem which had so long vexed both King and Commons.   The new Ministers ceased in all but name to be the King's servants.   They became simply an executive Committee representing the will of the majority of the House of Commons, and capable of being easily set aside by it and replaced by a similar Committee whenever the balance of power shifted from one side of the House to the other.

The Junto

Such was the origin of that system of representative government which has gone on from Sunderland's day to our own.   But though William showed his own political genius in understanding and adopting Sunderland's plan, it was only slowly and tentatively that he ventured to carry it out in practice.   In spite of the temporary reaction Sunderland believed that the balance of political power was really on the side of the Whigs.   Not only were they the natural representatives of the principles of the Revolution, and the supporters of the war, but they stood far above their opponents in parliamentary and administrative talent.   At their head stood a group of statesmen, whose close union in thought and action gained them the name of the Junto. Russell, as yet the most prominent of these, was the victor of La Hogue ; John Somers was an advocate who had sprung into fame by his defence of the Seven Bishops ; Lord Wharton was known as the

SEC. VIII.

THE GRAND
ALLIANCE
1689
TO
1697
1694

most dexterous and unscrupulous of party managers ; and Montague was fast making a reputation as the ablest of English financiers. In spite of such considerations, however, it is doubtful whether William would have thrown himself into the hands of a purely Whig Ministry but for the attitude which the Tories took towards the war. Exhausted as France was the war still languished, and the allies failed to win a single victory. Meanwhile English trade was all but ruined by the French privateers, and the nation stood aghast at the growth of taxation. The Tories, always cold in their support of the Grand Alliance, now became eager for peace. The Whigs, on the other hand, remained resolute in their support of the war. William, in whose mind the contest with France was the first object, was thus driven slowly to follow Sunderland's advice. Montague had already met the strain of the war by bringing forward a plan which had been previously suggested by a Scotchman, William Paterson, for the creation of a National Bank. While serving as an ordinary bank for the supply of capital, the Bank of England, as the new institution was called, was in reality an instrument for procuring loans from the people at large by the formal pledge of the State to repay the money advanced on the demand of the lender. A loan of £1,200,000 was thrown open to public subscription ; and the subscribers to it were formed into a chartered company in whose hands the negotiations of all after loans was placed. In ten days the list of subscribers was full. The discovery of the resources afforded by the national wealth revealed a fresh source of power ; and the rapid growth of the National Debt, as the mass of these loans to the State came to be called, gave a new security against the return of the Stuarts, whose first work would have been the repudiation of the claims of the lenders or "fundholders." The evidence of the public credit gave strength to William abroad, while at home a new unity of action followed the change which Sunderland counselled and which was quietly carried out. One by one the Tory Ministers, already weakened by Montague's success, were replaced by members of the Junto. Russell went to the Admiralty ; Somers was named Lord Keeper ; Shrewsbury, Secretary of State ; Montague, Chancellor of the Exchequer. Even before this change was completed its effect was felt. The House of Commons took a new tone. The Whig majority of its members, united and disciplined, moved quietly under the direction of their natural leaders, the Whig Ministers of the Crown. It was this which enabled William to face the shock which was given to his position by the death of Queen Mary. The renewed attacks of the Tories showed what fresh hopes had been raised by William's lonely position. The Parliament, however, whom the King had just conciliated by assenting at last to the Triennial Bill, went steadily with the Ministry ; and its fidelity was rewarded by triumph abroad. In 1695 the Alliance succeeded for the

first time in winning a great triumph over France in the capture of
Namur. The King skilfully took advantage of his victory to call a
new Parliament, and its members at once showed their temper by a
vigorous support of the war. The Houses, indeed, were no mere tools
in William's hands. They forced him to resume prodigal grants of
lands made to his Dutch favourites, and to remove his ministers in
Scotland who had aided in a wild project for a Scotch colony on the
Isthmus of Darien. They claimed a right to name members of the

1696

new Board of Trade, established for the regulation of commercial
matters. They rejected a proposal, never henceforth to be revived,
for a censorship of the Press. But there was no factious opposition.
So strong was the ministry that Montague was enabled to face the
general distress that was caused for the moment by a reform of the
currency, which had been reduced by clipping to far less than its
nominal value ; and in spite of the financial embarrassments created
by the reform, William was able to hold the French at bay.

**Peace of
Ryswick**

But the war was fast drawing to a close. Lewis was simply fighting
to secure more favourable terms, and William, though he held that
"the only way of treating with France is with our swords in our
hands," was almost as eager as Lewis for a peace. The defection of
Savoy made it impossible to carry out the original aim of the Alliance,
that of forcing France back to its position at the Treaty of Westphalia, and the question of the Spanish succession was drawing closer
every day. The obstacles which were thrown in the way of an accommodation by Spain and the Empire were set aside in a private

1697

negotiation between William and Lewis, and the year 1697 saw the
conclusion of the Peace of Ryswick. In spite of failure and defeat in
the field William's policy had won. The victories of France remained
barren in the face of a United Europe ; and her exhaustion forced
her, for the first time since Richelieu's day, to consent to a disadvan-
tageous peace. On the side of the Empire France withdrew from
every annexation save that of Strassburg which she had made since
the Treaty of Nimeguen, and Strassburg would have been restored
but for the unhappy delays of the German negotiators. To Spain
Lewis restored Luxemburg and all the conquests he had made during
the war in the Netherlands. The Duke of Lorraine was replaced
in his dominions. A far more important provision of the peace pledged
Lewis to an abandonment of the Stuart cause and a recognition of
William as King of England. For Europe in general the Peace of
Ryswick was little more than a truce. But for England it was the
close of a long and obstinate struggle and the opening of a new
æra of political history. It was the final and decisive defeat of the
conspiracy which had gone on between Lewis and the Stuarts ever
since the Treaty of Dover, the conspiracy to turn England into a
Roman Catholic country and into a dependency of France. But it

was even more than this. It was the definite establishment of England as the centre of European resistance against all attempts to overthrow the balance of power.

Section IX.—Marlborough. 1698—1712.

[*Authorities.*—Lord Macaulay's great work, which practically ends at the Peace of Ryswick, has been continued by Lord Stanhope ("History of England under Queen Anne") during this period. For Marlborough himself the main authority must be the Duke's biography by Archdeacon Coxe, with his "Despatches." The French side of the war and negotiations has been carefully given by M. Martin ("Histoire de France") in what is the most accurate and judicious portion of his work. Swift's Journal to Stella, and his political tracts and Bolingbroke's correspondence shew the character of the Tory opposition.]

What had bowed the pride of Lewis to the humiliating terms of the Peace of Ryswick was not so much the exhaustion of France as the need of preparing for a new and greater struggle. The death of the King of Spain, Charles the Second, was known to be at hand; and with him ended the male line of the Austrian princes, who for two hundred years had occupied the Spanish throne. How strangely Spain had fallen from its high estate in Europe the wars of Lewis had abundantly shown, but so vast was the extent of its empire, so enormous the resources which still remained to it, that under a vigorous ruler men believed its old power would at once return. Its sovereign was still master of some of the noblest provinces of the Old World and the New, of Spain itself, of the Milanese, of Naples and Sicily, of the Netherlands, of Southern America, of the noble islands of the Spanish Main. To add such a dominion as this to the dominion either of Lewis or of the Emperor would be to undo at a blow the work of European independence which William had wrought; and it was with a view to prevent either of these results that William freed his hands by the Peace of Ryswick. At this moment the claimants of the Spanish succession were three: the French Dauphin, a son of the Spanish King's elder sister; the Electoral Prince of Bavaria, a grandson of his younger sister; and the Emperor, who was a son of Charles's aunt. In strict law—if there had been any law really applicable to the matter—the claim of the last was the strongest of the three; for the claim of the Dauphin was barred by an express renunciation of all right to the succession at his mother's marriage with Lewis the Fourteenth, a renunciation which had been ratified at the Treaty of the Pyrenees; and a similar renunciation barred the claim of the Bavarian candidate. The claim of the Emperor was more remote in blood, but it was barred by no renunciation at all. William, however, was as resolute in the interests of Europe to repulse the claim of the Emperor as to repulse that of Lewis; and it was the consciousness

SEC. IX.

MARL-
BOROUGH

1698
TO
1712

The
Spanish
Succes-
sion

that the Austrian succession was inevitable if the war continued and Spain remained a member of the Grand Alliance, in arms against France and leagued with the Emperor, which made him suddenly conclude the Peace of Ryswick. Had England and Holland shared William's temper he would have insisted on the succession of the Electoral Prince to the whole Spanish dominions. But both were weary of war. In England the peace was at once followed by the reduction of the army at the demand of the House of Commons to fourteen thousand men ; and a clamour had already begun for the disbanding even of these. It was necessary to bribe the two rival claimants to a waiver of their claims ; and by the First Partition Treaty, concluded in 1698, between England, Holland, and France, the succession of the Electoral Prince was recognized on condition of the cession by Spain of its Italian possessions to his two rivals. The Milanese was to pass to the Emperor ; the Two Sicilies, with the border province of Guipuzcoa, to France. But the arrangement was hardly concluded when the death of the Bavarian prince made the Treaty waste paper. Austria and France were left face to face, and a terrible struggle, in which the success of either would be equally fatal to the independence of Europe, seemed unavoidable. The peril was greater that the temper of England left William without the means of backing his policy by arms. The suffering which the war had caused to the merchant class, and the pressure of the debt and taxation it entailed, were waking every day a more bitter resentment in the people, and the general discontent avenged itself on William and the party who had backed his policy. The King's natural partiality to his Dutch favourites, the confidence he gave to Sunderland, his cold and sullen demeanour, his endeavours to maintain the standing army, robbed him of popularity. In the elections held at the close of 1698 a Tory majority pledged to peace was returned to the House of Commons. The Junto lost all hold on the new Parliament. The resignation of Montague and Russell was followed by the dismissal of the Whig ministry, and Somers and his friends were replaced by an administration composed of moderate Tories, with Lords Rochester and Godolphin as its leading members. The fourteen thousand men who still remained in the army were cut down to seven. William's earnest entreaty could not turn the Parliament from its resolve to send his Dutch guards out of the country. The navy, which had numbered forty thousand sailors during the war, was cut down to eight. How much William's hands were weakened by this peace-temper of England was shown by the Second Partition Treaty which was concluded between the two maritime powers and France. The demand of Lewis that the Netherlands should be given to the Elector of Bavaria, whose political position left him a puppet in the French King's hands, was resisted. Spain, the Netherlands, and the Indies were assigned to the second son of the Emperor, the Archduke Charles of Austria. But the whole of the Spanish territories in Italy were now granted to France; and it was provided that Milan should be exchanged for Lorraine, whose Duke was to be summarily transferred to the new Duchy. If the Emperor persisted in his refusal to come into the Treaty, the share of his son was to pass to another unnamed prince, who was probably the Duke of Savoy.

The Emperor still protested, but his protest was of little moment so long as Lewis and the two maritime powers held firmly together. Nor was the bitter resentment of Spain of more avail. The Spaniards cared little whether a French or an Austrian prince sat on the throne of Charles the Second, but their pride revolted against the dismemberment of the monarchy by the loss of its Italian dependencies. Even the dying King shared the anger of his subjects, and a will wrested from him by the factions which wrangled over his death-bed bequeathed the whole monarchy of Spain to a grandson of Lewis, the Duke of Anjou, the second son of the Dauphin. The Treaty of Partition was so recent, and the risk of accepting this bequest so great, that Lewis would hardly have resolved on it but for his belief that the temper of England must necessarily render William's opposition a fruitless one. Never in fact had England been so averse from war. So strong was the antipathy to William's foreign policy that men openly approved the French King's course. Hardly any one in England dreaded the succession of a boy who, French as he was, would as they believed soon be turned into a Spaniard by the natural course of events. The succession of the Duke of Anjou was generally looked upon as far better than the increase of power which France would have derived from the cessions of the last Treaty of Partition, cessions which would have turned the Mediterranean, it was said, into a French lake, imperilled the English trade with the Levant and America, and raised France into a formidable power at sea. "It grieves me to the heart," William wrote bitterly, "that almost every one rejoices that France has preferred the Will to the Treaty." Astonished and angered as he was at his rival's breach of faith, he had no means of punishing it. The Duke of Anjou entered Madrid, and Lewis proudly boasted that henceforth there were no Pyrenees. The life-work of William seemed undone. He knew himself to be dying. His cough was incessant, his eyes sunk and dead, his frame so weak that he could hardly get into his coach. But never had he shown himself so great. His courage rose with every difficulty. His temper, which had been heated by the personal affronts lavished on him through English faction, was hushed by a supreme effort of his will. His large and clear-sighted intellect looked through the temporary embarrassments of French diplomacy and English party strife to the great interests which he knew must in the end determine the course of European politics. Abroad and at home all seemed to go against him. For the moment he had no ally save Holland, for Spain was now united with Lewis, while the attitude of Bavaria divided Germany and held the House of Austria in check. The Bavarian Elector indeed, who had charge of the Spanish Netherlands and on whom William had counted, openly joined the French side from the first and proclaimed the Duke of Anjou as King in Brussels. In England the new Parliament was crowded with Tories who were resolute against war. The Tory Ministry pressed him to acknowledge the new King of Spain ; and as even Holland did this, William was forced to submit. He could only count on the greed of Lewis to help him, and he did not count in vain. The approval of the French King's action had sprung from the belief that he intended to leave Spain to the Spaniards under their new King. Bitter too as the strife of Whig and Tory might be in England, there were two things on which Whig and Tory were agreed. Neither would suffer France to occupy the Netherlands. Neither would endure a French attack on the Protestant succession which the Revolution of 1688 had established. But the arrogance of Lewis blinded him to the need of moderation in his hour of good-luck. In the name of his grandson he introduced French troops into the seven fortresses known as the Dutch barrier, and into Ostend and the coast towns of Flanders. Even the

England and the war

Peace-Parliament at once acquiesced in William's demand for their withdrawal, and authorized him to conclude a defensive alliance with Holland. The King's policy indeed was bitterly blamed, while the late ministers, Somers, Russell, and Montague (now become peers), were impeached for their share in the treaties. But outside the House of Commons the tide of national feeling rose as the designs of Lewis grew clearer. He refused to allow the Dutch barrier to be re-established ; and a great French fleet gathered in the Channel to support, it was believed, a fresh Jacobite descent, which was proposed by the ministers of James in a letter intercepted and laid before Parliament. Even the House of Commons took fire at this, and the fleet was raised to thirty thousand men, the army to ten thousand. Kent sent up a remonstrance against the factious measures by which the Tories still struggled against the King's policy, with a prayer that addresses might be turned into Bills of Supply ; and William was encouraged by these signs of a change of temper to despatch an English force to Holland, and to conclude a secret treaty with the United Provinces for the recovery of the Netherlands from Lewis, and for their transfer with the Milanese to the house of Austria as a means of counter-balancing the new power added to France. But England was still clinging

Death of James

desperately to a hope of peace, when Lewis by a sudden act forced it into war. He had acknowledged William as King in the Peace of

Sept. 1701

Ryswick, and pledged himself to oppose all attacks on his throne. He now entered the bed-chamber at St. Germain where James was breathing his last, and promised to acknowledge his son at his death as King of England, Scotland, and Ireland. The promise was in fact a declaration of war, and in a moment all England was at one in accepting the challenge. The issue Lewis had raised was no longer a matter of European politics, but the question whether the work of the Revolution should be undone, and whether Catholicism and despotism should be replaced on the throne of England by the arms of France. On such a question as this there was no difference between Tory and Whig. When the death, in 1700, of the last child of the Princess Anne had been followed by a new Act of Succession, not a voice had been raised for James or his son ; and the descendants of the daughter of Charles the First, Henrietta of Orleans, whose only child had married the Catholic Duke of Savoy, were passed over in the same silence. The Parliament fell back on the line of James the First. His daughter Elizabeth had married the Elector Palatine, and her only surviving child, Sophia, was the wife of the late and the mother of the present Elector of Hanover. It was in Sophia and her heirs, being Protestants, that the Act of Settlement vested the Crown. It was enacted that every English sovereign must be in communion with the Church of England as by law established. All future kings were forbidden to leave England without consent of Parliament, and foreigners were excluded from all public posts. The independence of justice was established by a clause which provided that no judge should be removed from office save on an address from Parliament to the Crown. The two principles that the King acts only through his ministers, and that these ministers are responsible to Parliament, were asserted by a requirement that all public business should be formally done in the Privy Council, and all its decisions signed by its members—provisions which went far to complete the parliamentary Constitution which had been drawn up by the Bill of Rights. The national union which had already been shown in this action of the Tory Parliament, now showed itself in the King's welcome on his return from the Hague, where the conclusion of a new Grand Alliance between the Empire, Holland, and the United Provinces, had rewarded William's patience and skill. The Alliance was soon joined by Denmark, Sweden, the Palatinate, and the bulk of the German States. The Parliament of 1702, though still Tory in the main, replied to William's stirring appeal by voting forty thousand soldiers and as many sailors for the coming struggle. A Bill of Attainder was passed against the new Pretender ; and all members of either House and all public officials were sworn to uphold the succession of the House of Hanover.

Act of Settlement 1701

But the King's weakness was already too great to allow of his taking the field ; and he was forced to entrust the war in the Netherlands to the one Englishman who had shown himself capable of a great command. John Churchill, Earl of Marlborough, was born in 1650, the

Marl-borough

son of a Devonshire Cavalier, whose daughter became at the Restoration mistress of the Duke of York. The shame of Arabella did more perhaps than her father's loyalty to win for her brother a commission in the royal Guards ; and, after five years' service abroad under Turenne, the young captain became colonel of an English regiment which was retained in the service of France. He had already shown some of the qualities of a great soldier, an unruffled courage, a bold and venturous temper held in check by a cool and serene judgment, a vigilance and capacity for enduring fatigue which never forsook him. In later years he was known to spend a whole day in reconnoitring, and at Blenheim he remained on horseback for fifteen hours. But courage and skill in arms did less for Churchill on his return to the English court than his personal beauty. In the French camp he had been known as "the handsome Englishman ; " and his manners were as winning as his person. Even in age his address was almost irresistible : "he engrossed the graces," says Chesterfield ; and his air never lost the careless sweetness which won the favour of Lady Castlemaine. A present of £5,000 from the King's mistress laid the foundation of a fortune which grew rapidly to greatness, as the prudent forethought of the handsome young soldier hardened into the avarice of age. But it was to the Duke of York that Churchill looked mainly

*Churchill
and
James*

for advancement, and he earned it by the fidelity with which as a member of his household he clung to the Duke's fortunes during the dark days of the Popish Plot. He followed James to the Hague and to Edinburgh, and on his master's return he was rewarded with a peerage and the colonelcy of the Life Guards. The service he rendered James after his accession by saving the royal army from a surprise at Sedgemoor would have been yet more splendidly acknowledged but for the King's bigotry. In spite of his master's personal solicitations Churchill remained true to Protestantism ; but he knew James too well to count on further favour. Luckily he had now found a new groundwork for his fortunes in the growing influence of his wife over the King's second daughter, Anne ; and at the crisis of the Revolution the adhesion of Anne to the cause of Protestantism was of the highest value. No sentiment of gratitude to his older patron hindered Marlborough from corresponding with the Prince of Orange, from promising Anne's sympathy to William's effort, or from deserting the ranks of the King's

*Churchill
and
William*

army when it faced William in the field. His desertion proved fatal to the royal cause ; but great as this service was it was eclipsed by a second. It was by his wife's persuasion that Anne was induced to forsake her father and take refuge in Danby's camp. Unscrupulous as his conduct had been, the services which he rendered to William were too great to miss their reward. He became Earl of Marlborough ; he was put at the head of a force during the Irish war where his rapid successes won William's regard ; and he was given high command in the army of Flanders. But the sense of his power over Anne soon turned Marlborough from plotting treason against James to plot treason against William. Great as was his greed of gold, he had married Sarah Jennings, a penniless beauty of Charles's court, in whom a violent and malignant temper was strangely combined with a power of winning and retaining love. Churchill's affection for her ran like a thread of gold through the dark web of his career. In the midst of his marches and from the very battle-field he writes to his wife with the same passionate tenderness. The composure which no danger or hatred could ruffle broke down into almost womanish depression at the thought of her coldness or at any burst of her violent humour. He never left her without a pang. " I did for a great while with a perspective glass look upon the cliffs," he once wrote to her after setting out on a campaign, " in hopes that I might have had one sight of you." It was no wonder that the woman who inspired Marlborough with a love like this bound to her the weak and feeble nature of the Princess Anne. The two friends threw off the restraints of state, and addressed each other as " Mrs. Freeman " and " Mrs. Morley." It was on his wife's influence over her friend that the Earl's ambition counted in its designs against William. His plan was to drive the King from the throne by backing the Tories in their opposition to the war as well as by stirring to frenzy the English hatred of foreigners, and to seat Anne in his place. The discovery of his designs roused the King to a burst of unusual resentment. " Were I and my Lord Marlborough private persons," William exclaimed, " the sword would have to settle between us." As it was, he could only strip the Earl of his offices and command, and drive his wife from St. James's. Anne followed her favourite, and the court of the Princess became the centre of the Tory opposition ; while Marlborough opened a correspondence with James. So notorious was his treason that on the eve of the French invasion of 1692 he was one of the first of the suspected persons sent to the Tower.

The death of Mary forced William to recall Anne, who became by this event his successor ; and with Anne the Marlboroughs returned to court. The King could not bend himself to trust the Earl again ; but as death drew near he saw in him the one man whose splendid talents fitted him, in spite of the baseness and treason of his life, to rule England and direct the Grand Alliance in his stead. He employed Marlborough therefore to negotiate the treaty of alliance with the Emperor, and put him at the head of the army in Flanders. But the Earl had only just taken the command when a fall from his horse proved fatal to the broken frame of the King. " There was a time when I should have been glad to have been delivered out of my troubles," the dying man whispered to Portland, " but I own I see another scene, and could wish to live a little longer." He knew, however, that the wish was vain, and commended Marlborough to Anne as the fittest person to lead her armies and guide her counsels. Anne's zeal needed no quickening. Three days after her accession the Earl was named Captain-General of the English forces at home and abroad, and entrusted with the entire direction of the war. His supremacy over home affairs was secured by the construction of a purely Tory administration with Lord Godolphin, a close friend of Marlborough's, as Lord Treasurer at its head. The Queen's affection for his wife ensured him the support of the Crown at a moment when Anne's personal popularity gave the Crown a new weight with the nation. In England, indeed, party feeling for the moment died away. All save the extreme Tories were won over to the war now that it was waged on behalf of a Tory queen by a Tory general, while the most extreme of the Whigs were ready to back even a Tory general in waging a Whig war. Abroad, however, William's death shook the Alliance to its base ; and even Holland wavered in dread of being deserted by England in the coming struggle. But the decision of Marlborough soon did away with this distrust. Anne was made to declare from the throne her resolve to pursue with energy the policy of her predecessor. The Parliament was brought to sanction vigorous measures for the prosecution of the war. The new general hastened to the Hague, received the command of the Dutch as well as of the English forces, and drew the German powers into the Confederacy with a skill and adroitness which even William might have envied. Never was greatness more quickly recognized than in the case of Marlborough. In a few months he was regarded by all as the guiding spirit of the Alliance, and princes whose jealousy had worn out the patience of the King yielded without a struggle to the counsels of his successor. His temper fitted him in an especial way to be the head of a great confederacy. Like William, he owed little of his power to any early training. The trace of his neglected education was seen to the last in his reluctance to write. " Of all things," he said to his wife, " I do not love writing." To pen a despatch indeed was a far greater trouble to him than to plan a campaign. But nature had given him qualities which in other men spring specially from culture. His capacity for business was immense. During the next ten years he assumed the general direction of the war in Flanders and in Spain. He managed every negotiation with the courts of the allies. He watched over the shifting phases of English politics. He crossed the Channel to win over Anne to a change in the Cabinet, or hurried to Berlin to secure the due contingent of Electoral troops from Brandenburg. At one and the same moment men saw him reconciling the Emperor with the Protestants of Hungary, stirring the Calvinists of the Cévennes into revolt, arranging the affairs of Portugal, and providing for the protection of the Duke of Savoy. But his air showed no trace of fatigue or haste or vexation.   He retained to the last the indolent grace of his youth.   His natural dignity was never ruffled by an outbreak of temper.   Amidst the storm of battle his soldiers saw their leader " without fear of danger or in the least hurry, giving his orders with all the calmness imaginable."   In the cabinet he was as cool as on the battle-field.   He met with the same equable serenity the pettiness of the German princes, the phlegm of the Dutch, the ignorant opposition of his officers, the libels of his political opponents. There was a touch of irony in the simple expedients by which he sometimes solved problems which had baffled Cabinets.   The touchy pride of the King of Prussia made him one of the most vexatious among the allies, but all difficulty with him ceased when Marlborough rose at a state banquet and handed him a napkin.   Churchill's composure rested partly indeed on a pride which could not stoop to bare the real self within to the eyes of meaner men.   In the bitter moments before his fall he bade Godolphin burn some querulous letters which the persecution of his opponents had wrung from him.   " My desire is that the world may continue in their error of thinking me a happy man, for I think it better to be envied than pitied."   But in great measure it sprang from the purely intellectual temper of his mind. His passion for his wife was the one sentiment which tinged the colourless light in which his understanding moved.   In all else he was without love or hate, he knew neither doubt nor regret.   In private life he was a humane and compassionate man ; but if his position required it he could betray Englishmen to death, or lead his army to a butchery such as that of Malplaquet.   Of honour or the finer sentiments of mankind he knew nothing ; and he turned without a shock from guiding Europe and winning great victories to heap up a matchless fortune by peculation and greed.   He is perhaps the only instance of a man of real greatness who loved money for money's sake.   The passions which stirred the men around him, whether noble or ignoble, were to him simply elements in an intellectual problem which had to be solved by patience.   " Patience will overcome all things," he writes again and again.   " As I think most things are governed by destiny, having done all things we should submit with patience."

As a statesman the high qualities of Marlborough were owned by his bitterest foes.   " Over the Confederacy," says Bolingbroke, " he, a new, a private man, acquired by merit and management a more decided influence than high birth, confirmed authority, and even the crown of Great Britain, had given to King William."   But great as he was in the council, he was even greater in the field.   He stands alone amongst the masters of the art of war as a captain whose victories began at an age when the work of most men is done.   Though he served as a young officer under Turenne and for a few months in Ireland and the Netherlands, he had held no great command till he took the field in

*Opening of
the war*

Flanders at the age of fifty-two. He stands alone, too, in his unbroken good fortune. Voltaire notes that he never besieged a fortress which he did not take, or fought a battle which he did not win. His difficulties came not so much from the enemy, as from the ignorance and timidity of his own allies. He was never defeated in the field, but victory after victory was snatched from him by the incapacity of his officers or the stubbornness of the Dutch. What startled the cautious strategists of his day was the vigour and audacity of his plans. Old as he was, Marlborough's designs had from the first all the dash and boldness of youth. On taking the field in 1702 he at once resolved to force a battle in the heart of Brabant. The plan was foiled by the timidity of the Dutch deputies. But his resolute advance across the Meuse drew the French forces from that river, and enabled him to reduce fortress after fortress in a series of sieges, till the surrender of Liége closed a campaign which cut off the French from the Lower Rhine, and freed Holland from all danger of an invasion. The successes of Marlborough had been brought into bolder relief by the fortunes of the war in other quarters. Though the Imperialist general, Prince Eugene of Savoy, showed his powers by a surprise of the French army at Cremona, no real successes had been won in Italy. An English descent on the Spanish coast ended in failure. In Germany the Bavarians joined the French, and the united armies defeated the forces of the Empire. It was in this quarter that Lewis resolved to push his fortunes. In the spring of 1703 a fresh army under Marshal Villars again relieved the Bavarian Elector from the pressure of the Imperial forces, and only a strife which arose between the two commanders hindered the joint armies from marching on Vienna. Meanwhile the timidity of the Dutch deputies served Lewis well in the Low Countries. The hopes of Marlborough, who had been raised to a Dukedom for his services in the previous year, were again foiled by the deputies of the States-General. Serene as his temper was, it broke down before their refusal to co-operate in an attack on Antwerp and French Flanders; and the prayers of Godolphin and of the pensionary Heinsius alone induced him to withdraw his offer of resignation. But in spite of his victories on the Danube, of the blunders of his adversaries on the Rhine, and the sudden aid of an insurrection which broke out in Hungary, the difficulties of Lewis were hourly increasing. The accession of Savoy to the Grand Alliance threatened his armies in Italy with destruction. That of Portugal gave the allies a base of operations against Spain. The French King's energy however rose with the pressure; and while the Duke of Berwick, a natural son of James the Second, was despatched against Portugal, and three small armies closed round Savoy, the flower of the French troops joined the army of Bavaria on the Danube; for the bold plan of Lewis was to decide the fortunes of the

SEC. IX.

MARL-
BOROUGH
1698
TO
1712
Blenheim

war by a victory which would wrest peace from the Empire under the walls of Vienna.

The master-stroke of Lewis roused Marlborough at the opening of 1704 to a master-stroke in return ; but the secresy and boldness of the Duke's plans deceived both his enemies and his allies. The French army in Flanders saw in his march upon Maintz only a design to transfer the war into Elsass. The Dutch were lured into suffering their troops to be drawn as far from Flanders as Coblentz by proposals for an imaginary campaign on the Moselle. It was only when Marlborough crossed the Neckar and struck through the centre of Germany for the Danube that the true aim of his operations was revealed. After struggling through the hill country of Würtemberg, he joined the Imperial army under the Prince of Baden, stormed the heights of Donauwerth, crossed the Danube and the Lech, and penetrated into the heart of Bavaria. The crisis drew the two armies which were facing one another on the Upper Rhine to the scene. The arrival of Marshal Tallard with thirty thousand French troops saved the Elector of Bavaria for the moment from the need of submission ; but the junction of his opponent, Prince Eugene, with Marlborough raised the contending forces again to an equality. After a few marches the armies met on the north bank of the Danube, near the little town of Hochstadt and the village of Blindheim or Blenheim, which have given their names to one of the most memorable battles in the history of the world. In one respect the struggle which followed stands almost unrivalled, for the whole of the Teutonic race was represented in the strange medley of Englishmen, Dutchmen, Hanoverians, Danes, Wurtembergers and Austrians who followed Marlborough and Eugene. The French and Bavarians, who numbered like their opponents some fifty thousand men, lay behind a little stream which ran through swampy ground to the Danube. Their position was a strong one, for its front was covered by the swamp, its right by the Danube, its left by the hill-country in which the stream rose ; and Tallard had not only entrenched himself, but was far superior to his rival in artillery. But for once Marlborough's hands were free. " I have great reason," he wrote calmly home, " to hope that everything will go well, for I have the pleasure to find all the officers willing to obey without knowing any other reason than that it is my desire, which is very different from what it was in Flanders, where I was obliged to have the consent of a council of war for everything I undertook." So formidable were the obstacles, however, that though the allies were in motion at sunrise, it was not till midday that Eugene, who commanded on the right, succeeded in crossing the stream. The English foot at once forded it on the left and attacked the village of Blindheim in which the bulk of the French infantry were entrenched ; but after a furious struggle the attack was repulsed, while as gallant a resistance at the other end of the line held Eugene in check.   The centre, however, which the French believed to be unassailable, had been chosen by Marlborough for the chief point of attack ; and by making an artificial road across the morass he was at last enabled to throw his eight thousand horsemen on the French cavalry which occupied this position.   Two desperate charges which the Duke headed in person decided the day.   The French centre was flung back on the Danube and forced to surrender. Their left fell back in confusion on Hochstadt : while their right, cooped up in Blindheim and cut off from retreat, became prisoners of war.   Of the defeated army only twenty thousand escaped.   Twelve thousand were slain, fourteen thousand were captured.   Germany was finally freed from the French ; and Marlborough, who followed the wreck of the French host in its flight to Elsass, soon made himself master of the Lower Moselle.   But the loss of France could not be measured by men or fortresses.   A hundred victories since Rocroi had taught the world to regard the French army as invincible, when Blenheim and the surrender of the flower of the French soldiery broke the spell.   From that moment the terror of victory passed to the side of the allies, and " Malbrook " became a name of fear to every child in France.

Ramillies   In England itself the victory of Blenheim aided to bring about a great change in the political aspect of affairs.   The Tories were resolved to create a permanent Tory majority in the Commons by excluding Nonconformists from the municipal corporations, which returned the bulk of the borough members.   The Protestant Dissenters, while adhering to their separate congregations, in which they were now protected by the Toleration Act, " qualified for office " by the " occasional conformity " of receiving the sacrament at Church once

*Occasional
conformity*

in the year.   It was against this " occasional conformity " that the Tories introduced a test to exclude the Nonconformists ; and this test at first received Marlborough's support.   But it was steadily rejected by the Lords as often as it was sent up to them, and it was soon guessed that their resistance was secretly backed by both Marlborough and Godolphin.   Tory as he was, in fact, Marlborough had no mind for an unchecked Tory rule, or for a revival of religious strife which would be fatal to the war.   But he strove in vain to propitiate his party by inducing the Queen to set aside the tenths and first-fruits hitherto paid by the clergy to the Crown as a fund for the augmentation of small benefices, a fund which still bears the name of Queen Anne's Bounty.   The Commons showed their resentment by refusing to add a grant of money to the grant of a Dukedom after his first campaign ; and the higher Tories, with Lord Nottingham at their head, began to throw every obstacle they could in the way of the continuance of the war.   At last they quitted office in 1704, and Marlborough replaced them by Tories of a more moderate stamp who were still in favour of the war: by Robert Harley, who became Secretary of State, and Henry St. John, a man of splendid talents, who was named Secretary at War. The Duke's march into Germany, which pledged England to a struggle in the heart of the Continent, embittered the political strife. The high Tories and Jacobites threatened, if Marlborough failed, to bring his head to the block, and only the victory of Blenheim saved him from political ruin. Slowly and against his will the Duke drifted from his own party to the party which really backed his policy. He availed himself of the national triumph over Blenheim to dissolve Parliament; and when the election of 1705, as he hoped, returned a majority in favour of the war, his efforts brought about a coalition between the moderate Tories who still clung to him and the Whig Junto, whose support was purchased by making a Whig, William Cowper, Lord Keeper, and by sending Lord Sunderland as envoy to Vienna. The bitter attacks of the peace party were entirely foiled by this union, and Marlborough at last felt secure at home. But he had to bear disappointment abroad. His plan of attack along the line of the Moselle was defeated by the refusal of the Imperial army to join him. When he entered the French lines across the Dyle, the Dutch generals withdrew their troops; and his proposal to attack the Duke of Villeroy in the field of Waterloo was rejected in full council of war by the deputies of the States with cries of "murder" and "massacre." Even Marlborough's composure broke into bitterness at the blow. "Had I had the same power I had last year," he wrote home, "I could have won a greater victory than that of Blenheim." On his complaint the States recalled their commissaries, but the year was lost; nor had greater results been brought about in Italy or on the Rhine. The spirits of the allies were only sustained by the romantic exploits of Lord Peterborough in Spain. Profligate, unprincipled, flighty as he was, Peterborough had a genius for war, and his seizure of Barcelona with a handful of men, his recognition of the old liberties of Aragon, roused that province to support the cause of the second son of the Emperor, who had been acknowledged as King of Spain by the allies under the title of Charles the Third. Catalonia and Valencia soon joined Aragon in declaring for Charles: while Marlborough spent the winter of 1705 in negotiations at Vienna, Berlin, Hanover, and the Hague, and in preparations for the coming campaign. Eager for freedom of action, and sick of the Imperial generals as of the Dutch, he planned a march over the Alps and a campaign in Italy; and though his designs were defeated by the opposition of the allies, he found himself unfettered when he again appeared in Flanders in 1706. The French marshal Villeroy was as eager as Marlborough for an engagement; and the two armies met on the 23rd of May at the village of Ramillies on the undulating plain which forms the highest ground in Brabant. The French were drawn up in a wide curve with morasses covering their front. After a feint on their left, Marlborough flung himself on their right wing at Ramillies, crushed it in a brilliant charge that he led in person, and swept along their whole line till it broke in a rout which only ended beneath the walls of Louvain. In an hour and a half the French had lost fifteen thousand men, their baggage, and their guns ; and the line of the Scheldt, Brussels, Antwerp and Bruges became the prize of the victors. It only needed four successful sieges which followed the battle of Ramillies to complete the deliverance of Flanders.

**The
Union
with
Scotland**

The year which witnessed the victory of Ramillies remains yet more memorable as the year which witnessed the final Union of England with Scotland. As the undoing of the earlier union had been the first work of the Government of the Restoration, its revival was one of the first aims of the Government which followed the Revolution. But the project was long held in check by religious and commercial jealousies. Scotland refused to bear any part of the English debt. England would not yield any share in her monopoly of trade with the colonies. The English Churchmen longed for a restoration of Episcopacy north of the border, while the Scotch Presbyterians would not hear even of the legal toleration of Episcopalians. In 1703, however, an Act of Settlement which passed through the Scotch Parliament at last brought home to English statesmen the dangers of further delay. In dealing with this measure the Scotch Whigs, who cared only for the independence of their country, joined hand in hand with the Scotch Jacobites, who looked only to the interests of the Pretender. The Jacobites excluded from the Act the name of the Princess Sophia ; the Whigs introduced a provision that no sovereign of England should be recognized as sovereign of Scotland save upon security given to the religion, freedom, and trade of the Scottish people. Great as the danger arising from such a measure undoubtedly was, for it pointed to a recognition of the Pretender in Scotland on the Queen's death, and such a recognition meant war between Scotland and England, it was only after three years' delay that the wisdom and

1706

resolution of Lord Somers brought the question to an issue. The Scotch proposals of a federative rather than a legislative union were set aside by his firmness ; the commercial jealousies of the English trader were put by ; and the Act of Union provided that the two kingdoms should be united into one under the name of Great Britain, and that the succession to the crown of this United Kingdom should be ruled by the provisions of the English Act of Settlement. The Scotch Church and the Scotch Law were left untouched : but all rights of trade were thrown open, and a uniform system of coinage adopted. A single Parliament was henceforth to represent the United Kingdom, and for this purpose forty-five Scotch members were added to the five hundred and thirteen English members of the House of Commons, and sixteen

IX.] THE REVOLUTION. 715

SEC. IX.

MARL-
BOROUGH

1698
TO
1712

representative peers to the one hundred and eight who formed the English House of Lords. In Scotland the opposition was bitter and almost universal. The terror of the Presbyterians indeed was met by an Act of Security which became part of the Treaty of Union, and which required an oath to support the Presbyterian Church from every sovereign on his accession. But no securities could satisfy the enthusiastic patriots or the fanatical Cameronians. The Jacobites sought troops from France, and plotted a Stuart restoration. The nationalists talked of seceding from the Houses which voted for the Union, and of establishing a rival Parliament. In the end, however, good sense and the loyalty of the trading classes to the cause of the Protestant succession won their way. The measure was adopted by the Scotch Parliament, and the Treaty of Union became in 1707 a legislative Act to which Anne gave her assent in noble words. " I desire," said the Queen, " and expect from my subjects of both nations that from henceforth they act with all possible respect and kindness to one another, that so it may appear to all the world they have hearts disposed to become one people." Time has more than answered these hopes. The two nations whom the Union brought together have ever since remained one. England gained in the removal of a constant danger of treason and war. To Scotland the Union opened up new avenues of wealth which the energy of its people turned to wonderful account. The farms of Lothian have become models of agricultural skill. A fishing town on the Clyde has grown into the rich and populous Glasgow. Peace and culture have changed the wild clansmen of the Highlands into herdsmen and farmers. Nor was the change followed by any loss of national spirit. The world has hardly seen a mightier and more rapid development of national energy than that of Scotland after the Union. All that passed away was the jealousy which had parted since the days of Edward the First two peoples whom a common blood and common speech proclaimed to be one. The Union between Scotland and England has been real and stable simply because it was the legislative acknowledgment and enforcement of a national fact.

Its results

With the defeat of Ramillies the fortunes of France reached their lowest ebb. The loss of Flanders was followed by the loss of Italy after a victory by which Eugene relieved Turin ; and not only did Peterborough hold his ground in Spain, but Charles the Third with an army of English and Portuguese entered Madrid. Marlborough was at the height of his renown. Ramillies gave him strength enough to force Anne, in spite of her hatred of the Whigs, to fulfil his compact with them by admitting Lord Sunderland, the bitterest leader of their party, to office. But the system of political balance which he had maintained till now began at once to break down. Constitutionally, Marlborough's was the last attempt to govern England on other terms

**Marl-
borough
and the
Whigs**

1706

than those of party government, and the union of parties to which he
had clung ever since his severance from the extreme Tories soon
became impossible. The growing opposition of the Tories to the war
threw the Duke more and more on the support of the Whigs, and the
Whigs sold their support dearly. Sunderland, who had inherited his
father's conceptions of party government, was resolved to restore
a strict party administration on a purely Whig basis, and to drive
the moderate Tories from office in spite of Marlborough's desire to
retain them. The Duke wrote hotly home at the news of the
pressure which the Whigs were putting on him. "England," he

1706   said, "will not be ruined because a few men are not pleased." Nor
was Marlborough alone in his resentment. Harley foresaw the danger
of his expulsion from office, and began to intrigue at court, through
Mrs. Masham, a bedchamber woman of the Queen, who was supplant-
ing the Duchess in Anne's favour, against the Whigs and against
Marlborough. St. John, who owed his early promotion to office to the
Duke's favour, was driven by the same fear to share Harley's schemes.
Marlborough strove to win both of them back, but he was helpless in
the hands of the only party that steadily supported the war. A
factious union of the Whigs with their opponents, though it roused the
Duke to a burst of unusual passion in Parliament, effected its end by
convincing him of the impossibility of further resistance. The opposition of the Queen indeed was stubborn and bitter. Anne was at
heart a Tory, and her old trust in Marlborough died with his submission to the Whig demands. It was only by the threat of resignation
that he had forced her to admit Sunderland to office ; and the violent
outbreak of temper with which the Duchess enforced her husband's
will changed the Queen's friendship for her into a bitter resentment.
Marlborough was driven to increase this resentment by fresh com-

*Triumph
of the
Whigs*
1708
pliances with the conditions which the Whigs imposed on him, by
removing Peterborough from his command as a Tory general, and by
wresting from Anne her consent to the dismissal from office of Harley
and St. John with the moderate Tories whom they headed. Their
removal was followed by the complete triumph of the Whigs. Somers
became President of the Council, Wharton Lord-Lieutenant of Ireland,
while lower posts were occupied by men destined to play a great part
in our later history, such as the young Duke of Newcastle and Robert
Walpole. Meanwhile, the great struggle abroad went on, with striking
alternations of success. France rose with singular rapidity from the
crushing blow of Ramillies. Spain was recovered for Philip by a victory
of Marshal Berwick at Almanza. Villars won fresh triumphs on the

1707   Rhine, while Eugene, who had penetrated into Provence, was driven
back into Italy. In Flanders, Marlborough's designs for taking advantage of his great victory were foiled by the strategy of the Duke
of Vendôme and by the reluctance of the Dutch, who were now

wavering towards peace. In the campaign of 1708, however, Vendôme, in spite of his superiority in force, was attacked and defeated at
Oudenarde; and though Marlborough was hindered from striking at
the heart of France by the timidity of the English and Dutch statesmen,
he reduced Lille, the strongest of its frontier fortresses, in the face of
an army of relief which numbered a hundred thousand men. The
pride of Lewis was at last broken by defeat and by the terrible
suffering of France. He offered terms of peace which yielded all that
the allies had fought for. He consented to withdraw his aid from
Philip of Spain, to give up ten Flemish fortresses to the Dutch, and to
surrender to the Empire all that France had gained since the Treaty of
Westphalia. He offered to acknowledge Anne, to banish the Pretender
from his dominions, and to demolish the fortifications of Dunkirk, a
port hateful to England as the home of the French privateers.

To Marlborough peace now seemed secure; but in spite of his
counsels, the allies and the Whig Ministers in England demanded
that Lewis should with his own troops compel his grandson to give up
the crown of Spain. "If I must wage war," replied the King, "I had
rather wage it against my enemies than against my children." In a
bitter despair he appealed to France; and exhausted as it was, the
campaign of 1709 proved how nobly France answered his appeal.
The terrible slaughter which bears the name of the battle of Malplaquet showed a new temper in the French soldiers. Starving as
they were, they flung away their rations in their eagerness for the
fight, and fell back at its close in serried masses that no efforts of
Marlborough could break. They had lost twelve thousand men, but
the forcing their lines of entrenchment had cost the allies a loss of
double that number. Horror at such a "deluge of blood" increased
the growing weariness of the war; and the rejection of the French offers
was unjustly attributed to a desire on the part of Marlborough of
lengthening out a contest which brought him profit and power. A
storm of popular passion burst suddenly on the Whigs. Its occasion
was a dull and silly sermon in which a High Church divine, Dr.
Sacheverell, maintained the doctrine of non-resistance at St. Paul's.
His boldness challenged prosecution; but in spite of the warning of
Marlborough and of Somers the Whig Ministers resolved on his impeachment before the Lords, and the trial at once widened into a great
party struggle. An outburst of popular enthusiasm in Sacheverell's
favour showed what a storm of hatred had gathered against the Whigs
and the war. The most eminent of the Tory Churchmen stood by his
side at the bar, crowds escorted him to the court and back again, while
the streets rang with cries of "The Church and Dr. Sacheverell." A
small majority of the peers found the preacher guilty, but the light
sentence they inflicted was in effect an acquittal, and bonfires and
illuminations over the whole country welcomed it as a Tory triumph.

Sec. IX.

MARL-
BOROUGH
1698
TO
1712
Oudenarde

**England
and the
War**

Malplaquet

Sacheverell

Sec. IX.

Marl-
borough
1698
to
1712
Fall of
Marl-
borough

The party whom the Whigs had striven to crush were roused to new life. The expulsion of Harley and St. John from the Ministry had given the Tories leaders of a more subtle and vigorous stamp than the High Churchmen who had quitted office in the first years of the war, and St. John brought into play a new engine of political attack whose powers soon made themselves felt. In the *Examiner* and in a crowd of pamphlets and periodicals which followed in its train, the humour of Prior, the bitter irony of Swift, and St. John's own brilliant sophistry spent themselves on the abuse of the war and of its general. "Six millions of supplies and almost fifty millions of debt!" Swift wrote bitterly; "the High Allies have been the ruin of us!" Marlborough was ridiculed and reviled, he was accused of insolence, cruelty and ambition, of corruption and greed. Even his courage was called in question. The turn of popular feeling freed Anne at once from the pressure beneath which she had bent: and the subtle intrigue of Harley was busy in undermining the Ministry. The Whigs, who knew the Duke's alliance with them had simply been forced on him by the war, were easily persuaded that the Queen had no aim but to humble him, and looked coolly on at the dismissal of his son-in-law, Sunderland, and his friend, Godolphin. Marlborough on his part was lured by hopes of reconciliation with his old party, and looked on as coolly while

Anne dismissed the Whig Ministers and appointed a Tory Ministry in their place, with Harley and St. John at its head. But the intrigues of Harley paled before the subtle treason of St. John. Resolute to drive Marlborough from his command, he fed the Duke's hopes of reconciliation with the Tories, till he led him to acquiesce in his wife's dismissal, and to pledge himself to a co-operation with the Tory policy. It was the Duke's belief that a reconciliation with the Tories was effected that led him to sanction the despatch of troops which should have strengthened his army in Flanders on a fruitless expedition against Canada, though this left him too weak to carry out a masterly plan which he had formed for a march into the heart of France in the opening of 1711. He was unable even to risk a battle or to do more than to pick up a few seaboard towns, and St. John at once turned the small results of the campaign into an argument for the conclusion of peace. In defiance of an article of the Grand Alliance which pledged its members not to carry on separate negotiations with France, St. John, who now became Lord Bolingbroke, pushed forward

a secret accommodation between England and France. It was for this negotiation that he had crippled Marlborough's campaign; and it was the discovery of his perfidy which revealed to the Duke how utterly he had been betrayed, and forced him at last to break with the Tory Ministry. He returned to England; and his efforts induced the House of Lords to denounce the contemplated peace; but the support of the Commons and the Queen, and the general hatred of the war among the people, enabled Harley to ride down all resistance. At the opening of 1712 the Whig majority in the House of Lords was swamped by the creation of twelve Tory peers. Marlborough was dismissed from his command, charged with peculation, and condemned as guilty by a vote of the House of Commons. The Duke at once withdrew from England, and with his withdrawal all opposition to the peace was at an end.

Marlborough's flight was followed by the conclusion of a Treaty at Utrecht between France, England, and the Dutch ; and the desertion of his allies forced the Emperor at last to make peace at Rastadt. By these treaties the original aim of the war, that of preventing the possession of France and Spain by the House of Bourbon, was abandoned. No precaution was taken against the dangers it involved to the "balance of power," save by a provision that the two crowns should never be united on a single head, and by Philip's renunciation of all right of succession to the throne of France. The principle on which the Treaties were based was in fact that of the earlier Treaties of Partition. Philip retained Spain and the Indies : but he ceded his possessions in Italy and the Netherlands with the island of Sardinia to Charles of Austria, who had now become Emperor, in satisfaction of his claims ; while he handed over Sicily to the Duke of Savoy. To England he gave up not only Minorca but Gibraltar, two positions which secured her the command of the Mediterranean. France had to consent to the re-establishment of the Dutch barrier on a greater scale than before ; to pacify the English resentment against the French privateers by the dismantling of Dunkirk ; and not only to recognize the right of Anne to the crown, and the Protestant succession in the House of Hanover, but to consent to the expulsion of the Pretender from her soil. The failure of the Queen's health made the succession the real question of the day, and it was a question which turned all politics into faction and intrigue. The Whigs, who were still formidable in the Commons, and who showed the strength of their party in the Lords by defeating a Treaty of Commerce, in which Bolingbroke anticipated the greatest financial triumph of William Pitt and secured freedom of trade between England and France, were zealous for the succession of the Elector ; nor did the Tories really contemplate any other plan. But on the means of providing for his succession Harley and Bolingbroke differed widely. Harley inclined to an alliance between the moderate Tories and the Whigs. The policy of Bolingbroke, on the other hand, was so to strengthen the Tories by the utter overthrow of their opponents, that whatever might be the Elector's sympathies they could force their policy on him as King. To ruin his rival's influence he introduced a Schism Bill, which hindered any Nonconformist from acting as a schoolmaster or a tutor ; and which broke Harley's plans by creating a more bitter division than ever between Tory and

Whig. But its success went beyond his intentions. The Whigs regarded the Bill as the first step in a Jacobite restoration. The Electress Sophia was herself alarmed, and the Hanoverian ambassador demanded for the son of the Elector, the future George the Second, who had been created Duke of Cambridge, a summons as peer to the coming Parliament, with the aim of securing the presence in England of a Hanoverian Prince in case of the Queen's death. The Queen's anger, fanned by Bolingbroke, broke out in a letter to the Electress which warned her that " such conduct may imperil the succession itself ; " and in July Anne was brought to dismiss Harley, now Earl of Oxford, and to construct a strong and united Tory Ministry which would back her in her resistance to the Elector's demand. As the crisis grew nearer, both parties prepared for civil war. In the beginning of 1714 the Whigs had made ready for a rising on the Queen's death, and invited Marlborough from Flanders to head them, in the hope that his name would rally the army to their cause. Bolingbroke, on the other hand, intent on building up a strong Tory party, made the Duke of Ormond, whose sympathies were known to be in favour of the Pretender's succession, Warden of the Cinque Ports, the district in which either claimant of the crown must land, while he gave Scotland in charge to the Jacobite Earl of Mar. But events moved faster than his plans. Anne was suddenly struck with apoplexy. The Privy Council at once assembled, and at the news the Whig Dukes of Argyll and Somerset entered the Council Chamber without summons and took their places at the board. The step had been taken in secret concert with the Duke of Shrewsbury, who was President of the Council in the Tory Ministry, but a rival of Bolingbroke and an adherent of the Hanoverian succession. The act was a decisive one. The right of the House of Hanover was at once acknowledged, Shrewsbury was nominated as Lord Treasurer by the Council, and the nomination was accepted by the dying Queen. Bolingbroke, though he remained Secretary of State, suddenly found himself powerless and neglected, while the Council took steps to provide for the emergency. Four regiments were summoned to the capital in the expectation of a civil war. But the Jacobites were hopeless and unprepared ; and on the death of Anne the Elector George of Hanover, who had become heir to the throne by his mother's death, was proclaimed King of England without a show of opposition.

Section X.—Walpole, 1712—1742.

[*Authorities.*—Coxe's Life of Sir Robert Walpole, Horace Walpole's " Memoirs of the Reign of George II.," and Lord Hervey's amusing Memoirs from the accession of George II. to the death of Queen Caroline, give the main materials on one side ; Bolingbroke's Letter to Sir William Wyndham, his " Patriot King," and his correspondence afford some insight into the other. Horace Walpole's Letters to Sir Horace Mann give a minute account of his father's fall. A sober and judicious account of the whole period may be found in Lord Stanhope's " History of England from the Peace of Utrecht."]

The accession of George the First marked a change in the position of England in the European Commonwealth. From the age of the Plantagenets the country had stood apart from more than passing contact with the fortunes of the Continent. But the Revolution had forced her to join the Great Alliance of the European peoples ; and shameful as were some of its incidents, the Peace of Utrecht left her the main barrier against the ambition of the House of Bourbon. And not only did the Revolution set England irrevocably among the powers of Europe, but it assigned her a special place among them. The result of the alliance and the war had been to establish what was then called a " balance of power " between the great European states ; a balance which rested indeed not so much on any natural equilibrium of forces as on a compromise wrung from warring nations by the exhaustion of a great struggle ; but which, once recognized and established, could be adapted and readjusted, it was hoped, to the varying political conditions of the time. Of this balance of power, as recognized and defined in the Treaty of Utrecht and its successors, England became the special guardian. The stubborn policy of the Georgian statesmen has left its mark on our policy ever since. In struggling for peace and for the sanctity of treaties, even though the struggle was one of selfish interest, England took a ply which she has never wholly lost. Warlike and imperious as is her national temper, she has never been able to free herself from a sense that her business in the world is to seek peace alike for herself and for the nations about her, and that the best security for peace lies in her recognition, amidst whatever difficulties and seductions, of the force of international engagements and the sanctity of treaties.

At home the new King's accession was followed by striking political results. Under Anne the throne had regained much of the older influence which it lost through William's unpopularity ; but under the two sovereigns who followed Anne the power of the Crown lay absolutely dormant. They were strangers, to whom loyalty in its personal sense was impossible ; and their character as nearly approached insignificance as it is possible for human character to approach it. Both were honest and straightforward men, who frankly accepted the irksome position of constitutional kings. But neither had any qualities which could make their honesty attractive to the people at large. The temper of George the First was that of a gentleman usher ; and his one care was to get money for his favourites and himself. The temper of George the Second was that of a drill-

Margin notes:

SEC. X.

WALPOLE

1712
TO
1742

England and Europe

England and the House of Hanover

Decline of the royal influence

sergeant, who believed himself master of his realm while he repeated the lessons he had learnt from his wife, and which his wife had learnt from the Minister. Their Court is familiar enough in the witty memoirs of the time; but as political figures the two Georges are almost absent from our history. William of Orange had not only used the power of rejecting bills passed by the two Houses, but had kept in his own hands the control of foreign affairs. Anne had never yielded even to Marlborough her exclusive right of dealing with Church preferment, and had presided to the last at the Cabinet Councils of her ministers. But with the accession of the Georges these reserves passed away. No sovereign since Anne's death has appeared at a Cabinet Council, or has ventured to refuse his assent to an Act of Parliament. As Elector of Hanover indeed the King still dealt with Continental affairs: but his personal interference roused an increasing jealousy, while it affected in a very slight degree the foreign policy of his English counsellors. England, in short, was governed not by the King, but by the Whig ministers of the Crown. Nor had the Whigs to fear any effective pressure from their political opponents. "The Tory party," *Withdrawal of the Tories* Bolingbroke wrote after Anne's death, "is gone." In the first House of Commons indeed which was called by the new King, the Tories hardly numbered fifty members; while a fatal division broke their strength in the country at large. In their despair the more vehement among them turned to the Pretender. Lord Oxford was impeached and sent to the Tower; Bolingbroke and the Duke of Ormond fled from England to take office under the son of King James. At home Sir William Wyndham seconded their efforts by building up a Jacobite faction out of the wreck of the Tory party. The Jacobite secession gave little help to the Pretender, while it dealt a fatal blow to the Tory cause. England was still averse from a return of the Stuarts; and the suspicion of Jacobite designs not only alienated the trading classes, who shrank from the blow to public credit which a Jacobite repudiation of the debt would bring about, but deadened the zeal even of the parsons and squires; while it was known to have sown a deep distrust of the whole Tory party in the heart of the new *Rule of the Whigs* sovereign. The Crown indeed now turned to the Whigs; while the Church, which up to this time had been the main stumbling-block of their party, was sinking into political insignificance, and was no longer a formidable enemy. For more than thirty years the Whigs ruled England. But the length of their rule was not wholly due to the support of the Crown or the secession of the Tories. It was in some measure due to the excellent organization of their party. While their adversaries were divided by differences of principle and without leaders of real eminence, the Whigs stood as one man on the principles of the Revolution and produced great leaders who carried them into effect. They submitted with admirable discipline to the guidance of a knot of great nobles, to the houses of Bentinck, Manners, Campbell, and Cavendish, to the Fitzroys and Lennoxes, the Russells and Grenvilles, families whose resistance to the Stuarts, whose share in the Revolution, whose energy in setting the line of Hanover on the throne, gave them a claim to power. It was due yet more largely to the activity with which the Whigs devoted themselves to the gaining and preserving an ascendency in the House of Commons. The support of the commercial classes and of the great towns was secured not only by a resolute maintenance of public credit, but by the special attention which each ministry paid to questions of trade and finance. Peace and the reduction of the land-tax conciliated the farmers and the landowners, while the Jacobite sympathies of the bulk of the squires, and their consequent withdrawal from all share in politics, threw even the representation of the shires for a time into Whig hands. Of the county members, who formed the less numerous but the weightier part of the lower House, nine-tenths were for some years relatives and dependents of the great Whig families. Nor were coarser means of controlling Parliament neglected. The wealth of the Whig houses was lavishly spent in securing a monopoly of the small and corrupt constituencies which made up a large part of the borough representation. It was spent yet more unscrupulously in parliamentary bribery. Corruption was older than Walpole or the Whig Ministry, for it sprang out of the very transfer of power to the House of Commons which had begun with the Restoration. The transfer was complete, and the House was supreme in the State; but while freeing itself from the control of the Crown, it was as yet imperfectly responsible to the people. It was only at election time that a member felt the pressure of public opinion. The secrecy of parliamentary proceedings, which had been needful as a safeguard against royal interference with debate, served as a safeguard against interference on the part of constituencies. This strange union of immense power with absolute freedom from responsibility brought about its natural results in the bulk of members. A vote was too valuable to be given without recompense; and parliamentary support had to be bought by places, pensions, and bribes in hard cash. But dexterous as was their management, and compact as was their organization, it was to nobler qualities than these that the Whigs owed their long rule over England. They were true throughout to the principles on which they had risen into power, and their unbroken administration converted those principles into national habits. Before their long rule was over, Englishmen had forgotten that it was possible to persecute for difference of opinion, or to put down the liberty of the press, or to tamper with the administration of justice, or to rule without a Parliament.

That this policy was so firmly grasped and so steadily carried out was due above all to the genius of Robert Walpole. Born in 1676, he entered

Parliament two years before William's death as a young Norfolk land-owner of fair fortune, with the tastes and air of the class from which he sprang. His big square figure, his vulgar good-humoured face were those of a common country squire. And in Walpole the squire underlay the statesman to the last. He was ignorant of books, he "loved neither writing nor reading," and if he had a taste for art, his real love was for the table, the bottle, and the chase. He rode as hard as he drank. Even in moments of political peril, the first despatch he would open was the letter from his gamekeeper. There was the temper of the Norfolk fox-hunter in the "doggedness" which Marlborough noted as his characteristic, in the burly self-confidence which declared "If I had not been Prime Minister I should have been Archbishop of Canterbury," in the stubborn courage which conquered the awkward-ness of his earlier efforts to speak, or met single-handed at the last the bitter attacks of a host of enemies. There was the same temper in the genial good-humour which became with him a new force in politics. No man was ever more fiercely attacked by speakers and writers, but he brought in no "gagging Act" for the press; and though the lives of most of his assailants were in his hands through their intrigues with the Pretender, he made little use of his power over them. Where his country breeding showed itself most, however, was in the shrewd, narrow, honest character of his mind. Though he saw very clearly, he could not see far, and he would not believe what he could not see. He was thoroughly straightforward and true to his own convictions, so far as they went. "Robin and I are two honest men," the Jacobite Shippen owned in later years, when contrasting him with his factious opponents: "he is for King George and I am for King James, but those men with long cravats only desire place either under King George or King James." He saw the value of the political results which the Revolution had won, and he carried out his "Revolution principles" with a rare fidelity through years of unquestioned power. But his prosaic good sense turned sceptically away from the poetic and passionate sides of human feeling. Appeals to the loftier or purer motives of action he laughed at as "school-boy flights." For young members who talked of public virtue or patriotism he had one good-natured answer: "You will soon come off that and grow wiser."

How great a part Walpole was to play no one could as yet foresee. Though his vigour in the cause of his party had earned him the bitter hostility of the Tories in the later years of Anne, and a trumped-up charge of peculation had served in 1712 as a pretext for expelling him from the House and committing him to the Tower, at the accession of George the First Walpole was far from holding the commanding position he was soon to assume. The first Hanoverian Ministry was drawn wholly from the Whig party, but its leaders and Marlborough found themselves alike set aside. The direction of affairs was entrusted to the new Secretary of State, Lord Townshend; his fellow Secretary was General Stanhope, who was raised to the peerage. It was as Townshend's brother-in-law, rather than from a sense of his actual ability, that Walpole successively occupied the posts of Paymaster of the Forces, Chancellor of the Exchequer, and First Lord of the Treasury, in the new administration. The first work of the Ministry was to meet a desperate attempt of the Pretender to gain the throne. There was no real prospect of success, for the active Jacobites in England were few, and the Tories were broken and dispirited by the fall of their leaders. The death of Lewis ruined all hope of aid from France; the hope of Swedish aid proved as fruitless; but in spite of Bolingbroke's counsels James Stuart resolved to act alone. Without informing his new minister, he ordered the Earl of Mar to give the signal for revolt in the North. In Scotland the triumph of the Whigs meant the continuance of the House of Argyll in power, and the rival Highland clans were as ready to fight the Campbells under Mar as they had been ready to fight them under Dundee or Montrose. But Mar was a leader of different stamp from these. Six thousand Highlanders joined him at Perth, but his cowardice or want of conduct kept his army idle, till Argyll had gathered forces to meet it in an indecisive engagement at Sheriffmuir. The Pretender, who arrived too late for the action, proved a yet more sluggish and incapable leader than Mar: and at the close of 1715 the advance of fresh forces drove James over-sea again and dispersed the clans to their hills. In England the danger passed away like a dream. The accession of the new King had been followed by some outbreaks of riotous discontent; but at the talk of Highland risings and French invasions Tories and Whigs alike rallied round the throne; while the army went hotly for King George. The suspension of the Habeas Corpus Act, and the arrest of their leader, Sir William Wyndham, cowed the Jacobites; and not a man stirred in the west when Ormond appeared off the coast of Devon, and called on his party to rise. Oxford alone, where the University was a hotbed of Jacobitism, showed itself restless; and a few of the Catholic gentry rose in Northumberland, under Lord Derwentwater and Mr. Forster. The arrival of two thousand Highlanders who had been sent to join them by Mar spurred them to a march into Lancashire, where the Catholic party was strongest; but they were soon cooped up in Preston, and driven to a surrender. The Ministry availed itself of its triumph to gratify the Nonconformists by a repeal of the Schism and Occasional Conformity Acts, and to venture on a great constitutional change. Under the Triennial Bill in William's reign the duration of a Parliament was limited to three years. Now that the House of Commons however was become the ruling power in the State, a change was absolutely required to secure steadiness and fixity of political action; and in

The Rising of 1715

The Septennial Bill

1716 this necessity coincided with the desire of the Whigs to maintain in power a thoroughly Whig Parliament. The duration of Parliament was therefore extended to seven years by the Septennial Bill. But the Jacobite rising brought about a yet more momentous change in English policy abroad. At the moment when the landing of James in Scotland had quickened the anxiety of King George that France should be wholly detached from his cause, the actual state of European politics aided to bring about a new triple alliance between France, England, and Holland.

Since the death of Lewis the Fourteenth in 1715 France had been ruled by the Duke of Orleans as Regent for the young King, Lewis the Fifteenth. The Duke stood next in the succession to the crown, if Philip of Spain observed the renunciation of his rights which he had made in the Treaty of Utrecht. It was well known, however, that Philip had no notion of observing this renunciation, and the constant dream of every Spaniard was to recover all that Spain had given up. To attempt this was to defy Europe; for Savoy had gained Sicily; the Emperor held the Netherlands, Naples, and the Milanese; Holland looked on the Barrier fortresses as vital to its own security; while England clung tenaciously to the American trade. But the boldness of Cardinal Alberoni, who was now the Spanish Minister, accepted the risk; and while his master was intriguing against the Regent in France, Alberoni promised aid to the Jacobite cause as a means of preventing the interference of England with his designs. His first attempt was to recover the Italian provinces which Philip had lost, and armaments greater than Spain had seen for a century reduced

Sardinia in 1717. England and France at once drew together and entered into a compact by which France guaranteed the succession of the House of Hanover in England, and England the succession of the House of Orleans, should Lewis the Fifteenth die without heirs; and the two powers were joined, though unwillingly, by Holland. When in the summer of 1718 a strong Spanish force landed in Sicily, and made itself master of the island, the appearance of an English squadron in the Straits of Messina was followed by an engagement in which the Spanish fleet was all but destroyed. Alberoni strove to avenge the blow by fitting out an armament which the Duke of Ormond was to command for a revival of the Jacobite rising in Scotland. But the ships were wrecked in the Bay of Biscay; and the accession of Austria with Savoy to the Triple Alliance left Spain alone in the face of Europe. The progress of the French armies in the north of Spain forced Philip at last to give way. Alberoni was dismissed; and the Spanish forces were withdrawn from Sardinia and Sicily. The last of these islands now passed to the Emperor, Savoy being compensated for its loss by the acquisition of Sardinia, from which its Duke took the title of King; while the work of the

Treaty of Utrecht was completed by the Emperor's renunciation of his claims on the crown of Spain, and Philip's renunciation of his claims on the Milanese and the two Sicilies.

The struggle however had shown the difficulties which the double position of its sovereign was to bring on England. In his own mind George cared more for the interests of his Electorate of Hanover than of his kingdom; and these were now threatened by Charles XII. of Sweden, whose anger had been roused at the cession to Hanover of the Swedish possessions of Bremen and Verden by the King of Denmark, who had seized them while Charles was absent in Turkey. The despatch of a British fleet into the Baltic to overawe Sweden identified England with the policy of Hanover, and Charles retorted by joining with Alberoni, and by concluding an alliance with the Czar, Peter the Great, for a restoration of the Stuarts. Luckily for the new dynasty his plans were brought to an end by his death at the siege of Frederickshall; but the policy which provoked them had already brought about the dissolution of the Ministry. In assenting to a treaty of alliance with Hanover against Sweden, they had yielded to the fact that Bremen and Verden were not only of the highest importance to Hanover, which was thus brought into contact with the sea, but of hardly less value to England, as they secured the mouths of the Elbe and the Weser, the chief inlets for British commerce into Germany, in the hands of a friendly state. But they refused to go further in carrying out a Hanoverian policy; the anger of the King was seconded by intrigues among the ministers; and in 1717 Townshend and Walpole had been forced to resign their posts. In the reconstituted cabinet Lords Sunderland and Stanhope remained supreme; and their first aim was to secure the maintenance of the Whig power by a constitutional change. Harley's creation of twelve peers to ensure the sanction of the Lords to the Treaty of Utrecht showed that the Crown possessed a power of swamping the majority in the House of Peers. In 1720 therefore the Ministry introduced a bill, suggested as was believed by Sunderland, which professed to secure the liberty of the Upper House by limiting the power of the Crown in the creation of fresh Peers. The number of Peers was permanently fixed at the number then sitting in the House; and creations could only be made when vacancies occurred. Twenty-five hereditary Scotch Peers were substituted for the sixteen elected Peers for Scotland. The bill however was strenuously opposed by Walpole. It would in fact have rendered representative government impossible. For representative government was now coming day by day more completely to mean government by the will of the House of Commons, carried out by a Ministry which served as the mouthpiece of that will. But it was only through the prerogative of the Crown, as exercized under the advice of such a Ministry, that the Peers could be forced to bow to the

SEC. X.
WALPOLE
1712
TO
1742
The
Stanhope
Ministry

1718

*England
and
Hanover*

*The Peerage
Bill*

*South Sea
Bubble*

will of the Lower House in matters where their opinion was adverse to it ; and the proposal of Sunderland would have brought legislation and government to a dead lock.   The Peerage Bill owed its defeat to Walpole's opposition ; and his rivals were forced to admit him, with Townshend, into the Ministry, though they held subordinate places. But this soon gave way to a more natural arrangement.   The sudden increase of English commerce begot at this moment the mania of speculation.   Ever since the age of Elizabeth the unknown wealth of Spanish America had acted like a spell upon the imagination of Englishmen ; and Harley gave countenance to a South Sea Company, which promised a reduction of the public debt as the price of a monopoly of the Spanish trade.   Spain however clung jealously to her old prohibitions of all foreign commerce ; and the Treaty of Utrecht only won for England the right of engaging in the negro slave-trade, and of despatching a single ship to the coast of Spanish America.   But in spite of all this, the Company again came forward, offering in exchange for new privileges to pay off national burdens which amounted to nearly a million a year.   It was in vain that Walpole warned the Ministry and the country against this " dream." Both went mad ; and in 1720 bubble Company followed bubble Company, till the inevitable reaction brought a general ruin in its train. The crash brought Stanhope to the grave.   Of his colleagues, many were found to have received bribes from the South Sea Company to back its frauds.   Craggs, the Secretary of State, died of terror at the investigation ; Aislabie, the Chancellor of the Exchequer, was sent to the Tower ; and in the general wreck of his rivals Walpole mounted again into power.   In 1721 he became First Lord of the Treasury, while Townshend returned to his post of Secretary of State.   But their relative position was now reversed.   Townshend had been the head in their earlier administration : in this Walpole was resolved, to use his own characteristic phrase, that " the firm should be Walpole and Townshend and not Townshend and Walpole."

*Walpole's
Ministry*

**Walpole's
Peace
Policy**

If no Minister has fared worse at the hands of poets and historians, there are few whose greatness has been more impartially recognized by practical statesmen.   The years of his power indeed are years without parallel in our history for political stagnation.   His long administration of more than twenty years is almost without a history.   All legislative and political activity seemed to cease with his entry into office.   Year after year passed by without a change.   In the third year of his Ministry there was but one division in the House of Commons.   The Tory members were so few that for a time they hardly cared to attend its sittings ; and in 1722 the loss of Bishop Atterbury of Rochester, who was convicted of correspondence with the Pretender, deprived of his bishopric, and banished by Act of Parliament, deprived the Jacobites of their only remaining leader.   Walpole's one care was to maintain the quiet which was reconciling the country to the system of the Revolution. But this inaction fell in with the temper of the nation at large. It was popular with the class which commonly presses for political activity. The energy of the trading class was absorbed in the rapid extension of commerce and accumulation of wealth. So long as the country was justly and temperately governed the merchant and shopkeeper were content to leave government in the hands that held it. All they asked was to be let alone to enjoy their new freedom, and develope their new industries. And Walpole let them alone. Progress became material rather than political, but the material progress of the country was such as England had never seen before. The work of keeping England quiet and of giving quiet to Europe, was in itself a noble one ; and it is the temper with which he carried on this work which gives Walpole his place among English statesmen. He was the first and he was the most successful of our Peace Ministers. " The most pernicious circumstances," he said, " in which this country can be are those of war ; as we must be losers while it lasts, and cannot be great gainers when it ends." It was not that the honour or influence of England suffered in his hands, for he won victories by the firmness of his policy and the skill of his negotiations as effectual as any which are won by arms. But in spite of the complications of foreign affairs, and the pressure from the Court and the Opposition, it is the glory of Walpole that he resolutely kept England at peace. Peace indeed was hard to maintain. The Emperor Charles the Sixth had issued a Pragmatic Sanction, by which he provided that his hereditary dominions should descend unbroken to his daughter, Maria Theresa ; but no European State had yet consented to guarantee her succession. Spain, still resolute to regain her lost possessions, and her old monopoly of trade with her American colonies, seized the opportunity of detaching the Emperor from the alliance of the Four Powers, which left her isolated in Europe. She promised to support the Pragmatic Sanction in return for a pledge from Charles to aid in wresting Gibraltar and Minorca from England, and in securing to a Spanish prince the succession to Parma, Piacenza, and Tuscany. A grant of the highest trading privileges in her American dominions to a commercial company which the Emperor had established at Ostend, in defiance of the Treaty of Westphalia and the remonstrances of England and Holland, revealed this secret alliance ; and there were fears of the adhesion of Russia. The danger was met for a while by an alliance of England, France, and Prussia ; but the withdrawal of the last Power again gave courage to the confederates, and in 1727 the Spaniards besieged Gibraltar, while Charles threatened an invasion of Holland. The moderation of Walpole alone averted a European war. While sending British squadrons to the Baltic, the Spanish coast, and America, he succeeded by diplomatic pressure in again forcing the Emperor to inaction ; Spain was at last brought to sign

SEC. X.

WALPOLE
1712
TO
1742
Walpole's
Finance

the Treaty of Seville, and to content herself with a promise of the succession of a Spanish prince to the Duchies of Parma and Tuscany; and the discontent of Charles at this concession was allayed in 1731 by giving the guarantee of England to the Pragmatic Sanction.

As Walpole was the first of our Peace Ministers, so he was the first of our Financiers. He was far indeed from discerning the powers which later statesmen have shown to exist in a sound finance, but he had the sense to see, what no minister had till then seen, that the wisest course a statesman can take in presence of a great increase in national industry and national wealth is to look quietly on and let it alone. At the outset of his rule he declared in a speech from the Throne that nothing would more conduce to the extension of commerce " than to make the exportation of our own manufactures, and the importation of the commodities used in the manufacturing of them, as practicable and easy as may be." The first act of his financial administration was to take off the duties from more than a hundred British exports, and nearly forty articles of importation. In 1730 he broke in the same enlightened spirit through the prejudice which restricted the commerce of the colonies to the mother-country alone, by allowing Georgia and the Carolinas to export their rice directly to any part of Europe. The result was that the rice of America soon drove that of Italy and Egypt from the market. His Excise Bill, defective as it was, was the first measure in which an English Minister showed any real grasp of the principles of taxation. The wisdom of Walpole was rewarded by a quick up-growth of prosperity. Our exports, which were six millions in value at the beginning of the century, had doubled by the middle of it. The rapid developement of the Colonial trade gave England a new wealth. In Manchester and Birmingham, whose manufactures were now becoming of importance, population doubled in thirty years. Bristol, the chief seat of the West Indian trade, rose into new prosperity. Liverpool, which owes its creation to the new trade with the West, sprang up from a little country town into the third port in the kingdom. With peace and security, and the wealth that they brought with them, the value of land, and with it the rental of every country gentleman, rose fast. But this up-growth of wealth around him never made Walpole swerve from a rigid economy, from the steady reduction of the debt, or the diminution of fiscal duties. Even before the death of George the First the public burdens were reduced by twenty millions.

The accession of George the Second in 1727 seemed to give a fatal shock to Walpole's power; for the new King was known to have hated his father's Minister hardly less than he had hated his father. But hate Walpole as he might, the King was absolutely guided by the adroitness of his wife, Caroline of Anspach; and Caroline had resolved

that there should be no change in the Ministry. The years which followed were in fact those in which Walpole's power reached its height. He gained as great an influence over George the Second as he had gained over his father. His hold over the House of Commons remained unshaken. The country was tranquil and prosperous. The prejudices of the landed gentry were met by a steady effort to reduce the land-tax. The Church was quiet. The Jacobites were too hopeless to stir. A few trade measures and social reforms crept quietly through the Houses. An inquiry into the state of the gaols showed that social thought was not utterly dead. A bill of great value enacted that all proceedings in courts of justice should henceforth be in the English language. Only once did Walpole break this tranquillity by an attempt at a great measure of statesmanship. No tax had from the first moment of its introduction been more unpopular than the Excise. Its origin was due to Pym and the Long Parliament, who imposed duties on beer, cyder, and perry, which at the Restoration produced an annual income of more than six hundred thousand pounds. The war with France brought with it the malt-tax, and additional duties on spirits, wine, tobacco, and other articles. So great had been the increase in the public wealth that the return from the Excise amounted at the death of George the First to nearly two millions and a half a year. But its unpopularity remained unabated, and even philosophers like Locke contended that the whole public revenue should be drawn from direct taxes upon the land. Walpole, on the other hand, saw in the growth of indirect taxation a means of winning over the country gentry to the new dynasty of the Revolution by freeing the land from all burdens whatever. Smuggling and fraud diminished the revenue by immense sums. The loss on tobacco alone amounted to a third of the whole duty. The Excise Bill of 1733 met this evil by the establishment of bonded warehouses, and by the collection of the duties from the inland dealers in the form of Excise and not of Customs. The first measure would have made London a free port, and doubled English trade. The second would have so largely increased the revenue, without any loss to the consumer, as to enable Walpole to repeal the land-tax. In the case of tea and coffee alone, the change in the mode of levying the duty was estimated to bring in an additional hundred thousand pounds a year. The necessaries of life and the raw materials of manufacture were in Walpole's plan to remain absolutely untaxed. The scheme was an anticipation of the principles which have guided English finance since the triumph of free trade; but in 1733 Walpole stood ahead of his time. A violent agitation broke out; riots almost grew into revolt; and in spite of the Queen's wish to put down resistance by force, Walpole withdrew the bill. "I will not be the Minister," he said with noble self-command, "to enforce taxes at the expense of blood." What had fanned popular prejudice into a flame during the uproar was the violence of the

Excise Bill

The Patriots

so-called "Patriots." In the absence of a strong opposition and of great impulses to enthusiasm a party breaks readily into factions; and the weakness of the Tories joined with the stagnation of public affairs to breed faction among the Whigs. Walpole too was jealous of power; and as his jealousy drove colleague after colleague out of office, they became leaders of a party whose sole aim was to thrust him from his post. Greed of power indeed was the one passion which mastered his robust common-sense. Townshend was turned out of office in 1730, Lord Chesterfield in 1733; and though he started with the ablest administration the country had known, Walpole was left after twenty years of supremacy with but one man of ability in his cabinet, the Chancellor, Lord Hardwicke. With the single exception of Townshend, the colleagues whom his jealousy dismissed plunged into an opposition more factious and unprincipled than has ever disgraced English politics. The "Patriots," as they called themselves, owned Pulteney as their head; they were reinforced by a band of younger Whigs—the "Boys," as Walpole named them—whose temper revolted alike against the inaction and cynicism of his policy, and whose spokesman was a young cornet of horse, William Pitt; and they rallied to these the fragment of the Tory party which still took part in politics, and which was guided for a while by the virulent ability of Bolingbroke, whom Walpole had suffered to return from exile, but to whom he had refused the restoration of his seat in the House of Lords. But Walpole's defeat on the Excise Bill had done little to shake his power, and Bolingbroke withdrew to France in despair at the failure of his efforts.

**The
Spanish
War**

Abroad the first signs of a new danger showed themselves in 1733, when the peace of Europe was broken afresh by disputes which rose out of a contested election to the throne of Poland. Austria and France were alike drawn into the strife; and in England the awakening jealousy of French designs roused a new pressure for war. The new King too was eager to fight, and her German sympathies inclined even Caroline to join in the fray. But Walpole stood firm for the observance of neutrality. "There are fifty thousand men slain this year in Europe," he boasted as the strife went on, "and not one Englishman." The intervention of England and Holland succeeded in 1736 in restoring peace; but the country noted bitterly that peace was bought by the triumph of both branches of the House of Bourbon. A new Bourbon monarchy was established at the cost of the House of Austria by the cession of the Two Sicilies to a Spanish Prince, in exchange for his right of succession to Parma and Tuscany. On the other hand, Lorraine passed finally into the hands of France. The birth of children to Lewis the Fifteenth had settled all questions of succession in France, and no obstacle remained to hinder their family sympathies from uniting the Bourbon Courts in a common action. As early as 1733

*The Family
Compact*

a Family Compact had been secretly concluded between France and Spain, the main object of which was the ruin of the maritime supremacy of Britain. Spain bound herself to deprive England gradually of its commercial privileges in her American dominions, and to transfer them to France. France in return engaged to support Spain at sea, and to aid her in the recovery of Gibraltar. The caution with which Walpole held aloof from the Polish war rendered this compact inoperative for the time ; but neither of the Bourbon courts ceased to look forward to its future execution. No sooner was the war ended than France strained every nerve to increase her fleet; while Spain steadily tightened the restrictions on British commerce with her American colonies.

The trade with Spanish America, which, illegal as it was, had grown largely through the connivance of Spanish port-officers during the long alliance of England and Spain in the wars against France, had at last received a legal recognition in the Peace of Utrecht. It was indeed left under narrow restrictions ; but these were evaded by a vast system of smuggling which rendered what remained of the Spanish monopoly all but valueless. The efforts of Philip however to bring down English intercourse with his colonies to the importation of negroes and the despatch of a single ship, as stipulated by the Treaty of Utrecht, brought about collisions which made it hard to keep the peace. The ill-humour of the trading classes rose to madness in 1738 when a merchant captain named Jenkins told at the bar of the House of Commons the tale of his torture by the Spaniards, and produced an ear which, he said, they had cut off with taunts at the English king. It was in vain that Walpole strove to do justice to both parties, and that he battled stubbornly against the cry for an unjust and impolitic war. The Emperor's death was now close at hand ; and at such a juncture it was of the highest importance that England should be free to avail herself of every means to guard the European settlement. But his efforts were in vain. His negotiations were foiled by the frenzy of the one country and the pride of the other. At home his enemies assailed him with a storm of abuse. Ballad-singers trolled out their rimes to the crowd on " the cur-dog of Britain and spaniel of Spain." His position had been weakened by the death of the Queen ; and it was now weakened yet more by the open hostility of the Prince of Wales. His mastery of the House of Commons too was no longer unquestioned. The Tories were slowly returning to Parliament. The numbers and the violence of the " Patriots " had grown with the open patronage of Prince Frederick. The country was slowly turning against him. With the cry for a commercial war the support of the trading class failed him. But it was not till he stood utterly alone that Walpole gave way and that he consented in 1739 to a war against Spain.

" They may ring their bells now," the great minister said bitterly, as peals and bonfires welcomed his surrender; "but they will soon be wringing their hands." His foresight was at once justified. No sooner had Admiral Vernon appeared off the coast of South America with an English fleet, and captured Porto Bello, than France formally declared that she would not consent to any English settlement on the mainland of South America, and despatched two squadrons to the West Indies. At this crisis the death of Charles the Sixth forced on the European struggle which Walpole had dreaded. France saw her opportunity for finishing the work which Henry the Second had begun of breaking up the Empire into a group of powers too weak to resist French aggression. While the new King of Prussia, Frederick the Second, claimed Silesia, Bavaria claimed the Austrian Duchies, which passed with the other hereditary dominions, according to the Pragmatic Sanction, to the Queen of Hungary, Maria Theresa. In union therefore with Spain, which aimed at the annexation of the Milanese, France promised her aid to Prussia and Bavaria; while Sweden and Sardinia allied themselves to France. In the summer of 1741 two French armies entered Germany, and the Elector of Bavaria appeared unopposed before Vienna. Never had the House of Austria stood in such peril. Its opponents counted on a division of its dominions. France claimed the Netherlands, Spain the Milanese, Bavaria the kingdom of Bohemia, Frederick the Second Silesia. Hungary and the Duchy of Austria alone were left to Maria Theresa. Walpole, though still true to her cause, advised her to purchase Frederick's aid against France and her allies by the cession of part of Silesia; but the "Patriots" spurred her to refusal by promising her the aid of England. Walpole's last hope of rescuing Austria was broken, and Frederick was driven to conclude an alliance with France. But the Queen refused to despair. She won the support of Hungary by restoring its constitutional rights; and British subsidies enabled her to march at the head of a Hungarian army to the rescue of Vienna, to overrun Bavaria, and repulse an attack of Frederick on Moravia in the spring of 1742. On England's part, however, the war was waged feebly and ineffectively. Admiral Vernon was beaten before Carthagena; and Walpole was charged with thwarting and starving the war. He still repelled the attacks of the "Patriots" with wonderful spirit; but in a new Parliament his majority dropped to sixteen, and in his own cabinet he became almost powerless. The buoyant temper which had carried him through so many storms broke down at last. "He who was asleep as soon as his head touched the pillow," writes his son, "now never sleeps above an hour without waking: and he who at dinner always forgot his own anxieties, and was more gay and thoughtless than all the company, now sits without speaking, and with his eyes fixed for an hour together." The end was in fact near; and in the opening of 1742 the dwindling of his majority to three forced Walpole to resign.

CHAPTER X.

MODERN ENGLAND.

Section I.—William Pitt, 1742–1762.

[*Authorities.*—Lord Stanhope and Horace Walpole, as before. Southey's biography, or the more elaborate life by Mr. Tyerman, gives an account of Wesley. For Pitt himself, the Chatham correspondence, his life by Thackeray, and Lord Macaulay's two essays on him. The Annual Register begins with 1758; its earlier portion has been attributed to Burke. Carlyle's "Frederick the Great" gives a picturesque account of the Seven Years' War. For Clive, see the biography by Sir John Malcolm, and Lord Macaulay's essay.]

THE fall of Walpole revealed a change in the temper of England which was to influence from that time to this its social and political history. New forces, new cravings, new aims, which had been silently gathering beneath the crust of inaction, began at last to tell on the national life. The stir showed itself markedly in a religious revival which dates from the later years of Walpole's ministry. Never had religion seemed at a lower ebb. The progress of free inquiry, the aversion from theological strife which had been left by the Civil Wars, the new political and material channels opened to human energy, had produced a general indifference to all questions of religious speculation or religious life. The Church, predominant as its influence seemed at the close of the Revolution, had sunk into political insignificance. The bishops, who were now chosen exclusively from among the small number of Whig ecclesiastics, were left politically powerless by the estrangement and hatred of their clergy; while the clergy themselves, drawn by their secret tendencies to Jacobitism, stood sulkily apart from any active interference with public affairs. The prudence of the Whig statesmen aided to maintain this ecclesiastical immobility. They were careful to avoid all that could rouse into life the slumbering forces of bigotry and fanaticism. When the Dissenters pressed for a repeal of the Test and Corporation Acts, Walpole openly avowed his dread of awaking the passions of religious hate by such a measure, and satisfied them by an annual act of indemnity for any breach of these penal statutes; while a suspension of the meetings of Convocation deprived the clergy of their natural centre of agitation and opposition. Nor was this political inaction compensated by any religious activity. A large number of prelates were mere Whig partizans with no higher aim than that of promotion. The levees of the

The Church and the Georges

Ministers were crowded with lawn sleeves.   A Welsh bishop avowed
that he had seen his diocese but once, and habitually resided at the
lakes of Westmoreland.   The system of pluralities turned the wealthier
and more learned of the priesthood into absentees, while the bulk of
them were indolent, poor, and without social consideration.   A shrewd,
if prejudiced, observer brands the English clergy of the day as the
most lifeless in Europe, "the most remiss of their labours in private,
and the least severe in their lives."   There was a revolt against
religion and against churches in both the extremes of English
society.   In the higher circles of society "every one laughs," said
Religious indifference Montesquieu on his visit to England, "if one talks of religion."   Of
the prominent statesmen of the time the greater part were unbelievers
in any form of Christianity, and distinguished for the grossness and
immorality of their lives.   Drunkenness and foul talk were thought no
discredit to Walpole.   A later prime minister, the Duke of Grafton,
was in the habit of appearing with his mistress at the play.   Purity
and fidelity to the marriage vow were sneered out of fashion ; and
Lord Chesterfield, in his letters to his son, instructs him in the art of
seduction as part of a polite education.   At the other end of the social
scale lay the masses of the poor.   They were ignorant and brutal to a
degree which it is hard to conceive, for the increase of population
which followed on the growth of towns and the developement of commerce had been met by no effort for their religious or educational
improvement.   Not a new parish had been created.   Schools there
were none, save the grammar schools of Edward and Elizabeth, and
some newly established "circulating schools" in Wales, for religious
education.   The rural peasantry, who were fast being reduced to
pauperism by the abuse of the poor-laws, were left without much
moral or religious training of any sort.   "We saw but one Bible in the
parish of Cheddar," said Hannah More at a far later time, "and that
was used to prop a flower-pot."   Within the towns things were worse.
There was no effective police ; and in great outbreaks the mob of
London or Birmingham burnt houses, flung open prisons, and sacked
and pillaged at their will.   The criminal class gathered boldness and
numbers in the face of ruthless laws which only testified to the terror
of society, laws which made it a capital crime to cut down a cherry
tree, and which strung up twenty young thieves of a morning in front
of Newgate ; while the introduction of gin gave a new impetus to
drunkenness.   In the streets of London at one time gin-shops invited
every passer-by to get drunk for a penny, or dead drunk for twopence.

The Religious Revival   In spite however of scenes such as this, England remained at heart
religious.   In the middle class the old Puritan spirit lived on unchanged,
and it was from this class that a religious revival burst forth at the close
of Walpole's administration, which changed after a time the whole tone
of English society.   The Church was restored to life and activity.

Religion carried to the hearts of the people a fresh spirit of moral zeal, while it purified our literature and our manners. A new philanthropy reformed our prisons, infused clemency and wisdom into our penal laws, abolished the slave trade, and gave the first impulse to popular education. The revival began in a small knot of Oxford students, whose revolt against the religious deadness of their times showed itself in ascetic observances, an enthusiastic devotion, and a methodical regularity of life which gained them the nickname of "Methodists."

Three figures detached themselves from the group as soon as, on its transfer to London in 1738, it attracted public attention by the fervour and even extravagance of its piety ; and each found his special work in the task to which the instinct of the new movement led it from the first, that of carrying religion and morality to the vast masses of population which lay concentrated in the towns, or around the mines and collieries of Cornwall and the north. Whitefield, a servitor of Pembroke College, was above all the preacher of the revival. Speech was

governing English politics ; and the religious power of speech was shown when a dread of "enthusiasm" closed against the new apostles the pulpits of the Established Church, and forced them to preach in the fields. Their voice was soon heard in the wildest and most barbarous corners of the land, among the bleak moors of Northumberland, or in the dens of London, or in the long galleries where in the pauses of his labour the Cornish miner listens to the sobbing of the sea. Whitefield's preaching was such as England had never heard before, theatrical, extravagant, often commonplace, but hushing all criticism by its intense reality, its earnestness of belief, its deep tremulous sympathy with the sin and sorrow of mankind. It was no common enthusiast who could wring gold from the close-fisted Franklin and admiration from the fastidious Horace Walpole, or who could look down from the top of a green knoll at Kingswood on twenty thousand colliers, grimy from the Bristol coal-pits, and see as he preached the tears "making white channels down their blackened cheeks." On the rough and ignorant masses to whom they spoke the effect of Whitefield and his fellow Methodists was mighty both for good and ill. Their preaching stirred a passionate hatred in their opponents. Their lives were often in danger, they were mobbed, they were ducked, they were stoned, they were smothered with filth. But the enthusiasm they aroused was equally passionate. Women fell down in convulsions ; strong men were smitten suddenly to the earth ; the preacher was interrupted by bursts of hysteric laughter or of hysteric sobbing. All the phenomena of strong spiritual excitement, so familiar now, but at that time strange and unknown, followed on their sermons ; and the terrible sense of a conviction of sin, a new dread of hell, a new hope of heaven, took forms at once grotesque and sublime. Charles Wesley, a Christ Church student, came to add sweetness to this sudden and startling

SEC. I.

WILLIAM
PITT

1742
TO
1762

John
Wesley

light. He was the "sweet singer" of the movement. His hymns expressed the fiery conviction of its converts in lines so chaste and beautiful that its more extravagant features disappeared. The wild throes of hysteric enthusiasm passed into a passion for hymn-singing, and a new musical impulse was aroused in the people which gradually changed the face of public devotion throughout England.

But it was his elder brother, John Wesley, who embodied in himself not this or that side of the new movement, but the movement itself. Even at Oxford, where he resided as a fellow of Lincoln, he had been looked upon as head of the group of Methodists, and after his return from a quixotic mission to the Indians of Georgia he again took the lead of the little society, which had removed in the interval to London. In power as a preacher he stood next to Whitefield ; as a hymn-writer he stood second to his brother Charles. But while combining in some degree the excellences of either, he possessed qualities in which both were utterly deficient ; an indefatigable industry, a cool judgement, a command over others, a faculty of organization, a singular union of patience and moderation with an imperious ambition, which marked him as a ruler of men. He had besides a learning and skill in writing which no other of the Methodists possessed ; he was older than any of his colleagues at the start of the movement, and he outlived them all.

His life indeed almost covers the century, and the Methodist body had passed through every phase of its history before he sank into the grave at the age of eighty-eight. It would have been impossible for Wesley to have wielded the power he did had he not shared the follies and extravagance as well as the enthusiasm of his disciples. Throughout his life his asceticism was that of a monk. At times he lived on bread only, and he often slept on the bare boards. He lived in a world of wonders and divine interpositions. It was a miracle if the rain stopped and allowed him to set forward on a journey. It was a judgement of Heaven if a hailstorm burst over a town which had been deaf to his preaching. One day, he tells us, when he was tired and his horse fell lame, " I thought—cannot God heal either man or beast by any means or without any ?—immediately my headache ceased and my horse's lameness in the same instant." With a still more childish fanaticism he guided his conduct, whether in ordinary events or in the great crises of his life, by drawing lots or watching the particular texts at which his Bible opened. But with all this extravagance and superstition, Wesley's mind was essentially practical, orderly, and conservative. No man ever stood at the head of a great revolution whose temper was so anti-revolutionary. In his earlier days the bishops had been forced to rebuke him for the narrowness and intolerance of his churchmanship. When Whitefield began his sermons in the fields, Wesley "could not at first reconcile himself to that strange way." He condemned and fought against the admission of laymen as preachers till he found himself left with none but laymen to preach. To the last he clung passionately to the Church of England, and looked on the body he had formed as but a lay society in full communion with it. He broke with the Moravians, who had been the earliest friends of the new movement, when they endangered its safe conduct by their contempt of religious forms. He broke with Whitefield when the great preacher plunged into an extravagant Calvinism. But the same practical temper of mind which led him to reject what was unmeasured, and to be the last to adopt what was new, enabled him at once to grasp and organize the novelties he adopted. He became himself the most unwearied of field preachers, and his journal for half a century is little more than a record of fresh journeys and fresh sermons. When once driven to employ lay helpers in his ministry he made their work a new and attractive feature in his system. His earlier asceticism only lingered in a dread of social enjoyments and an aversion from the gayer and sunnier side of life which links the Methodist movement with that of the Puritans. As the fervour of his superstition died down into the calm of age, his cool common sense discouraged in his followers the enthusiastic outbursts which marked the opening of the revival. His powers were bent to the building up of a great religious society which might give to the new enthusiasm a lasting and practical form. The Methodists were grouped into classes, gathered in love-feasts, purified by the expulsion of unworthy members, and furnished with an alternation of settled ministers and wandering preachers; while the whole body was placed under the absolute government of a Conference of ministers. But so long as he lived, the direction of the new religious society remained with Wesley alone. " If by arbitrary power," he replied with charming simplicity to objectors, " you mean a power which I exercise simply without any colleagues therein, this is certainly true, but I see no hurt in it."

The great body which he thus founded numbered a hundred thousand members at his death, and now counts its members in England and America by millions. But the Methodists themselves were the least result of the Methodist revival. Its action upon the Church broke the lethargy of the clergy; and the " Evangelical " movement, which found representatives like Newton and Cecil within the pale of the Establishment, made the fox-hunting parson and the absentee rector at last impossible. In Walpole's day the English clergy were the idlest and most lifeless in the world. In our own time no body of religious ministers surpasses them in piety, in philanthropic energy, or in popular regard. In the nation at large appeared a new moral enthusiasm which, rigid and pedantic as it often seemed, was still healthy in its social tone, and whose power was seen in the disappearance of the profligacy which had disgraced the upper classes, and the foulness which had infested literature, ever since the Restoration. A

3 B 2

*John
Howard*

yet nobler result of the religious revival was the steady attempt, which has never ceased from that day to this, to remedy the guilt, the ignorance, the physical suffering, the social degradation of the profligate and the poor. It was not till the Wesleyan impulse had done its work that this philanthropic impulse began. The Sunday Schools established by Mr. Raikes of Gloucester at the close of the century were the beginnings of popular education. By writings and by her own personal example Hannah More drew the sympathy of England to the poverty and crime of the agricultural labourer. A passionate impulse of human sympathy with the wronged and afflicted raised hospitals, endowed charities, built churches, sent missionaries to the heathen, supported Burke in his plea for the Hindoo, and Clarkson and Wilberforce in their crusade against the iniquity of the slave-trade. It is only the moral chivalry of his labours that amongst a crowd of philanthropists draws us most, perhaps, to the work and character of John Howard. The sympathy which all were feeling for the sufferings of mankind he felt for the sufferings of the worst and most hapless of men. With wonderful ardour and perseverance he devoted himself to the cause of the debtor, the felon, and the murderer. An appointment to the office of High Sheriff of Bedfordshire in 1774 drew his attention to the state of the prisons which were placed under his care ; and from that time the quiet country gentleman, whose only occupation had been reading his Bible and studying his thermometer, became the most energetic and zealous of reformers. Before a year was over he had personally visited almost every English gaol, and he found in nearly all of them frightful abuses which had been noticed half a century before, but left unredressed by Parliament. Gaolers who bought their places were paid by fees, and suffered to extort what they could. Even when acquitted, men were dragged back to their cells for want of funds to discharge the sums they owed to their keepers. Debtors and felons were huddled together in the prisons which Howard found crowded by the cruel legislation of the day. No separation was preserved between different sexes, no criminal discipline enforced. Every gaol was a chaos of cruelty and the foulest immorality, from which the prisoner could only escape by sheer starvation, or through the gaol-fever that festered without ceasing in these haunts of wretchedness. Howard saw everything with his own eyes, he tested every suffering by his own experience. In one gaol he found a cell so narrow and noisome that the poor wretch who inhabited it begged as a mercy for hanging. Howard shut himself up in the cell and bore its darkness and foulness till nature could bear no more. It was by work of this sort, and by the faithful pictures of such scenes which it enabled him to give, that he brought about their reform. The book in which he recorded his terrible experience, and the plans which he submitted for the reformation of criminals made him the father, so far as England is concerned, of prison discipline. But his labours were far from being confined to England. In journey after journey he visited the gaols of Holland and Germany, till his longing to discover some means of checking the fatal progress of the plague led him to examine the lazarettos of Europe and the East. He was still engaged in this work of charity when he was seized by a malignant fever at Cherson in Southern Russia, and "laid quietly in the earth," as he desired.

While the revival of the Wesleys was stirring the very heart of England, its political stagnation was unbroken. The fall of Walpole made no change in English policy, at home or abroad. The bulk of his ministry, who had opposed him in his later years of office, resumed their posts, simply admitting some of the more prominent members of opposition, and giving the control of foreign affairs to Lord Carteret, a man of great power, and skilled in continental affairs. Carteret mainly followed the system of his predecessor. It was in the union of Austria and Prussia that he looked for the means of destroying the hold France had now established in Germany by the election of her puppet, Charles of Bavaria, as Emperor ; and the pressure of England, aided by a victory of Frederick at Chotusitz, forced Maria Theresa to consent to Walpole's plan of a peace with Prussia at Breslau on the terms of the cession of Silesia. The peace enabled the Austrian army to drive the French from Bohemia at the close of 1742 ; an English fleet blockaded Cadiz, and another anchored in the bay of Naples and forced Don Carlos by a threat of bombarding his capital to conclude a treaty of neutrality, while English subsidies detached Sardinia from the French alliance. Unfortunately Carteret and the Court of Vienna now determined not only to set up the Pragmatic Sanction, but to undo the French encroachments of 1736. Naples and Sicily were to be taken back from their Spanish King, Elsass and Lorraine from France ; and the imperial dignity was to be restored to the Austrian House. To carry out these schemes an Austrian army drove the Emperor from Bavaria in the spring of 1743 ; while George the Second, who warmly supported Carteret's policy, put himself at the head of a force of 40,000 men, the bulk of whom were English and Hanoverians, and marched from the Netherlands to the Main. His advance was checked and finally turned into a retreat by the Duc de Noailles, who appeared with a superior army on the south bank of the river, and finally throwing 31,000 men across it, threatened to compel the King to surrender. In the battle of Dettingen which followed, however, not only was the allied army saved from destruction by the impetuosity of the French horse and the dogged obstinacy with which the English held their ground, but their opponents were forced to recross the Main. Small as was the victory, it produced amazing results. The French evacuated Germany. The English and Austrian armies appeared on the Rhine ; and a league between England, Prussia, and the Queen of

SEC. I.

WILLIAM
PITT

1742
TO
1762

Carteret

*England
and Austria*

*Dettingen
June 27,
1743*

SEC. I.

WILLIAM
PITT

1742
TO
1762

Fontenoy

Hungary, seemed all that was needed to secure the results already gained.

But the prospect of peace was overthrown by the ambition of the House of Austria. In the spring of 1744 an Austrian army marched upon Naples, with the purpose of transferring it after its conquest to the Bavarian Emperor, whose hereditary dominions in Bavaria were to pass in return to Maria Theresa. If however Frederick had withdrawn from the war on the cession of Silesia, he was resolute to take up arms again rather than suffer so great an aggrandisement of the House of Austria in Germany. His sudden alliance with France failed at first to change the course of the war ; for though he was successful in seizing Prague and drawing the Austrian army from the Rhine, Frederick was driven from Bohemia, while the death of the Emperor forced Bavaria to lay down its arms and to ally itself with Maria Theresa. So high were the Queen's hopes at this moment that she formed a secret alliance with Russia for the division of the Prussian monarchy. But in 1745 the tide turned, and the fatal results of Carteret's weakness in assenting to the change from a war of defence into one of attack became manifest. The French King, Lewis the Fifteenth, led an army into the Netherlands ; and the refusal of Holland to act against him left their defence wholly in the hands of England. The general anger at this widening of the war proved fatal to Carteret, or, as he now became, Earl Granville. His imperious temper had rendered him odious to his colleagues, and he was driven from office by the Duke of Newcastle and his brother Henry Pelham. Of the

reconstituted ministry which followed Henry Pelham became the head. His temper, as well as a consciousness of his own mediocrity, disposed him to a policy of conciliation which reunited the Whigs. Chesterfield and the Whigs in opposition, with Pitt and "the Boys," all found room in the new administration ; and even a few Tories found admittance. The bulk of the Whigs were true to Walpole's policy ; and it was to pave the way to an accommodation with Frederick and a close of the war that the Pelhams forced Carteret to resign. But their attention had first to be given to the war in Flanders, where Marshal Saxe had established the superiority of the French army by his defeat of the Duke of Cumberland. Advancing to the relief of Tournay with a force of English, Hanoverians, and Dutch—for Holland had at last been dragged into the war—the Duke on the 31st of May 1745 found the French covered by a line of fortified villages and redoubts with but a single narrow gap near the hamlet of Fontenoy. Into this gap, however, the English troops, formed in a dense column, doggedly thrust themselves in spite of a terrible fire ; but at the moment when the day seemed won the French guns, rapidly concentrated in their front, tore the column in pieces and drove it back in a slow and orderly retreat. The blow was quickly followed up in

Sec. I.
William
Pitt
1742
to
1762
Charles
Edward
Stuart

June by a victory of Frederick at Hohenfriedburg which drove the Austrians from Silesia, and by a landing of a Stuart on the coast of Scotland at the close of July.

The war with France had at once revived the hopes of the Jacobites; and as early as 1744 Charles Edward, the grandson of James the Second, was placed by the French Government at the head of a formidable armament. But his plan of a descent on Scotland was defeated by a storm which wrecked his fleet, and by the march of the French troops which had sailed in it to the war in Flanders. In 1745, however, the young adventurer again embarked with but seven friends in a small vessel and landed on a little island of the Hebrides. For three weeks he stood almost alone; but on the 29th of August the clans rallied to his standard in Glenfinnan, and Charles found himself at the head of fifteen hundred men. His force swelled to an army as he marched through Blair Athol on Perth, entered Edinburgh in triumph, and proclaimed "James the Eighth" at the Town Cross: and two thousand English troops who marched against him under Sir John Cope were broken and cut to pieces on the 21st of September by a single charge of the clansmen at Preston Pans. Victory at once doubled the forces of the conqueror. The Prince was now at the head of six thousand men; but all were still Highlanders, for the people of the Lowlands held aloof from his standard, and it was with the utmost difficulty that he could induce them to follow him to the south. His tact and energy however at last conquered every obstacle, and after skilfully evading an army gathered at Newcastle he marched through Lancashire, and pushed on the 4th of December as far as Derby. But here all hope of success came to an end. Hardly a man had risen in his support as he passed through the districts where Jacobitism boasted of its strength. The people flocked to see his march as if to see a show. Catholics and Tories abounded in Lancashire, but only a single squire took up arms. Manchester was looked on as the most Jacobite of English towns, but all the aid it gave was an illumination and two thousand pounds. From Carlisle to Derby he had been joined by hardly two hundred men. The policy of Walpole had in fact secured England for the House of Hanover. The long peace, the prosperity of the country, and the clemency of the Government, had done their work. The recent admission of Tories into the administration had severed the Tory party finally from the mere Jacobites. Jacobitism as a fighting force was dead, and even Charles Edward saw that it was hopeless to conquer England with five thousand Highlanders. He soon learned too that forces of double his own strength were closing on either side of him, while a third army under the King and Lord Stair covered London. Scotland itself, now that the Highlanders were away, quietly renewed in all the districts of the Lowlands its allegiance to the House of Hanover. Even in the

Highlands the Macleods rose in arms for King George, while the
Gordons refused to stir, though roused by a small French force which
landed at Montrose. To advance further south was impossible, and
Charles fell rapidly back on Glasgow ; but the reinforcements which
he found there raised his army to nine thousand men, and on the
23rd January, 1746, he boldly attacked an English army under General
Hawley which had followed his retreat and had encamped near Falkirk.
Again the wild charge of his Highlanders won victory for the Prince,
but victory was as fatal as defeat. The bulk of his forces dispersed
with their booty to the mountains, and Charles fell sullenly back to
the north before the Duke of Cumberland. On the 16th of April the

*Culloden
Moor*

armies faced one another on Culloden Moor, a few miles eastward of
Inverness. The Highlanders still numbered six thousand men, but
they were starving and dispirited, while Cumberland's force was nearly
double that of the Prince. Torn by the Duke's guns, the clansmen
flung themselves in their old fashion on the English front ; but they
were received with a terrible fire of musketry, and the few that broke
through the first line found themselves fronted by a second. In a few
moments all was over, and the Stuart force was a mass of hunted
fugitives. Charles himself after strange adventures escaped to France.

*Conquest
of the
Highlands*

In England fifty of his followers were hanged ; three Scotch lords,
Lovat, Balmerino, and Kilmarnock, brought to the block ; and forty
persons of rank attainted by Act of Parliament. More extensive
measures of repression were needful in the Highlands. The feudal
tenures were abolished. The hereditary jurisdictions of the chiefs
were bought up and transferred to the Crown. The tartan, or garb of
the Highlanders, was forbidden by law. These measures, followed by a
general Act of Indemnity, proved effective for their purpose. The dread
of the clansmen passed away, and the Sheriff's writ soon ran through
the Highlands with as little resistance as in the streets of Edinburgh.

*Peace of
Aix-la-
Chapelle*

Defeat abroad and danger at home only quickened the resolve of
the Pelhams to bring the war with Prussia to an end. When England
was threatened by a Catholic Pretender, it was no time for weakening
the chief Protestant power in Germany. On the refusal of Maria

1745

Theresa to join in a general peace, England concluded the Convention
of Hanover with Prussia, and withdrew so far as Germany was concerned from the war. Elsewhere however the contest lingered on.
The victories of Maria Theresa in Italy were balanced by those of
France in the Netherlands, where Marshal Saxe inflicted new defeats
on the English and Dutch at Roucoux and Lauffeld. The danger of
Holland and the financial exhaustion of France at last brought about

1748

the conclusion of a peace at Aix-la-Chapelle, by which England surrendered its gains at sea, and France its conquests on land. But the
peace was a mere pause in the struggle, during which both parties
hoped to gain strength for a mightier contest which they saw impend·

ing.　The war was in fact widening far beyond the bounds of Germany or of Europe.　It was becoming a world-wide duel which was to settle the destinies of mankind.　Already France was claiming the valleys of the Ohio and the Mississippi, and mooting the great question whether the fortunes of the New World were to be moulded by Frenchmen or Englishmen.　Already too French adventurers were driving English merchants from Madras, and building up, as they trusted, a power which was to add India to the dominions of France.

The early intercourse of England with India gave little promise of the great fortunes which awaited it.　It was not till the close of Elizabeth's reign, a century after Vasco da Gama had crept round the Cape of Good Hope and founded the Portuguese settlement on the Goa coast, that an East India Company was established in London.　The trade, profitable as it was, remained small in extent ; and the three early factories of the Company were only gradually acquired during the century which followed.　The first, that of Madras, consisted of but six fishermen's houses beneath Fort St. George ; that of Bombay was ceded by the Portuguese as part of the dowry of Catharine of Braganza ; while Fort William, with the mean village which has since grown into Calcutta, owes its origin to the reign of William the Third.　Each of these forts was built simply for the protection of the Company's warehouses, and guarded by a few " sepahis," sepoys, or paid native soldiers ; while the clerks and traders of each establishment were under the direction of a President and a Council.　One of these clerks in the middle of the eighteenth century was Robert Clive, the son of a small proprietor near Market Drayton in Shropshire, an idle dare-devil of a boy whom his friends had been glad to get rid of by packing him off in the Company's service as a writer to Madras.　His early days there were days of wretchedness and despair.　He was poor and cut off from his fellows by the haughty shyness of his temper, weary of desk-work, and haunted by home-sickness.　Twice he attempted suicide ; and it was only on the failure of his second attempt that he flung down the pistol which baffled him with a conviction that he was reserved for higher things.

A change came at last in the shape of war and captivity.　As soon as the war of the Austrian Succession broke out, the superiority of the French in power and influence tempted them to expel the English from India.　Labourdonnais, the governor of the French colony of the Mauritius, besieged Madras, razed it to the ground, and carried its clerks and merchants prisoners to Pondicherry.　Clive was among these captives, but he escaped in disguise, and returning to the settlement, threw aside his clerkship for an ensign's commission in the force which the Company was busily raising.　For the capture of Madras had not only established the repute of the French arms, but had roused Dupleix, the governor of Pondicherry, to conceive plans for the

creation of a French empire in India. When the English merchants
of Elizabeth's day brought their goods to Surat, all India, save the
south, had just been brought for the first time under the rule of a
single great power by the Mogul Emperors of the line of Akbar. But
with the death of Aurungzebe, in the reign of Anne, the Mogul Empire
fell fast into decay. A line of feudal princes raised themselves to
independence in Rajpootana. The lieutenants of the Emperor founded
separate sovereignties at Lucknow and Hyderabad, in the Carnatic,
and in Bengal. The plain of the Upper Indus was occupied by a race
of religious fanatics called the Sikhs. Persian and Affghan invaders
crossed the Indus, and succeeded even in sacking Delhi, the capital of
the Moguls. Clans of systematic plunderers, who were known under
the name of Mahrattas, and who were in fact the natives whom conquest had long held in subjection, poured down from the highlands
along the western coast, ravaged as far as Calcutta and Tanjore, and
finally set up independent states at Poonah and Gwalior. Dupleix
skilfully availed himself of the disorder around him. He offered his
aid to the Emperor against the rebels and invaders who had reduced
his power to a shadow ; and it was in the Emperor's name that he
meddled with the quarrels of the states of Central and Southern India,
made himself virtually master of the Court of Hyderabad, and seated
a creature of his own on the throne of the Carnatic. Trichinopoly, the
one town which held out against this Nabob of the Carnatic, was all
but brought to surrender when Clive, in 1751, came forward with a
daring scheme for its relief. With a few hundred English and sepoys

Arcot

he pushed through a thunderstorm to the surprise of Arcot, the Nabob's
capital, entrenched himself in its enormous fort, and held it for fifty
days against thousands of assailants. Moved by his gallantry, the
Mahrattas, who had never believed that Englishmen would fight
before, advanced and broke up the siege ; but Clive was no sooner
freed than he showed equal vigour in the field. At the head of raw
recruits who ran away at the first sound of a gun, and sepoys who hid
themselves as soon as the cannon opened fire, he twice attacked and
defeated the French and their Indian allies, foiled every effort of
Dupleix, and razed to the ground a pompous pillar which the French
governor had set up in honour of his earlier victories.

**The
American
Colonies**

Clive was recalled by broken health to England, and the fortunes
of the struggle in India were left for decision to a later day. But
while France was struggling for the Empire of the East she was
striving with even more apparent success for the command of the new
world of the West. Populous as they had become, the English settlements in America still lay mainly along the sea-board of the Atlantic ;
for only a few exploring parties had penetrated into the Alleghanies
before the Seven Years' War ; and Indian tribes wandered unquestioned along the lakes. It was not till the peace of Aix-la-Chapelle

Sec. I.

WILLIAM
PITT

1742
TO
1762

1748

that the pretensions of France drew the eyes of the colonists and of English statesmen to the interior of the Western Continent. Planted firmly in Louisiana and Canada, France openly claimed the whole country west of the Alleghanies as its own, and its governors now ordered all English settlers or merchants to be driven from the valleys of Ohio or Mississippi which were still in the hands of Indian tribes. Even the inactive Pelham revolted from pretensions such as these. The original French settlers were driven from Acadia or Nova Scotia, and an English colony founded the settlement of Halifax. An Ohio Company was formed, and its agents made their way to the valleys of that river and the Kentucky; while envoys from Virginia and Pennsylvania drew closer the alliance between their colonies and the Indian tribes across the mountains. Nor were the French slow to accept the challenge. Fighting began in Acadia. A vessel of war appeared in Ontario, and Niagara was turned into a fort. A force of 1,200 men despatched to Erie drove the few English settlers from their little colony on the fork of the Ohio, and founded there a fort called Duquesne, on the site of the later Pittsburg. The fort at once gave this force command of the river valley. After a fruitless attack on it under George Washington, a young Virginian, the colonists were forced to withdraw over the mountains, and the whole of the west was left in the hands of France. The bulk of the Indian tribes from Canada as far as the Mississippi attached themselves to the French cause, and the value of their aid was shown in 1755, when General Braddock led a force of English soldiers and American militia to an attack upon Fort Duquesne. The force was utterly routed and Braddock slain. The Marquis of Montcalm, who in 1756 commanded the French forces in Canada, was gifted with singular powers of administration. He carried out with even more zeal than his predecessor the plans of annexation; and the three forts of Duquesne on the Ohio, of Niagara on the St. Lawrence, and of Ticonderoga on Lake Champlain, were linked together by a chain of lesser forts, which cut off the English colonists from all access to the west. The defeat of Braddock had already roused England to its danger, for it was certain that war in America would be followed by war in Europe. The ministers looked on a league with Prussia, as the only means of checking France; but Frederick held cautiously aloof, while the advances of England to Prussia only served to alienate Maria Theresa, whose one desire was to regain Silesia. The two powers of the House of Bourbon were still bound by the Family Compact; and as early as 1752 Maria Theresa by a startling change of policy drew to their alliance. The jealousy which Russia entertained of the growth of a strong power in North Germany brought the Czarina Elizabeth to promise aid to the schemes of the Queen of Hungary; and in 1755 the league of the four powers and of Saxony was practically completed. So secret were these nego-

Sec. I.

William
Pitt

1742
TO
1762

The
Seven
Years'
War

tiations that they remained unknown to Henry Pelham and to his brother the Duke of Newcastle, who succeeded him on his death in 1754 as the head of the Ministry. But they were detected from the first by the keen eye of Frederick of Prussia, who saw himself fronted by a line of foes that stretched from Paris to St. Petersburg.

The danger to England was hardly less; for France appeared again on the stage with a vigour and audacity which recalled the days of Lewis the Fourteenth. The weakness and corruption of the French government were screened for a time by the daring and scope of its plans, as by the ability of the agents it found to carry them out. In England, on the contrary, all was vagueness and indecision. It was

not till the close of the year that a treaty was at last concluded with the Prussian King. With this treaty between England and Frederick began the Seven Years' War. No war has had greater results on the history of the world or brought greater triumphs to England; but few have had more disastrous beginnings. Newcastle was too weak and ignorant to rule without aid, and yet too greedy of power to purchase aid by sharing it with more capable men. His preparations for the gigantic struggle before him may be guessed from the fact that there were but three regiments fit for service in England at the opening of 1756. France, on the other hand, was quick in her attack. Port Mahon in Minorca, the key of the Mediterranean, was besieged by the Duke of Richelieu and forced to capitulate. To complete the shame of England, a fleet sent to its relief under Admiral Byng retreated before the French. In Germany Frederick seized Dresden at the outset of the war and forced the Saxon army to surrender; and in 1757 a victory at Prague made him master for a while of Bohemia; but his success was transient, and a defeat at Kolin drove him to retreat again into Saxony. In the same year the Duke of Cumberland, who had taken post on the Weser with an army of fifty thousand men for the defence of Hanover, fell back before a French army to the mouth of the Elbe, and engaged by the Convention of Closter-Seven to disband his forces. In America things went even worse than in Germany. The inactivity of the English generals was contrasted with the genius and activity of Montcalm. Already masters of the Ohio by the

defeat of Braddock, the French drove the English garrison from the forts which commanded Lake Ontario and Lake Champlain, and their empire stretched without a break over the vast territory from Louisiana to the St. Lawrence. A despondency without parallel in our history took possession of our coolest statesmen, and even the impassive Chesterfield cried in despair, "We are no longer a nation."

But the nation of which Chesterfield despaired was really on the eve of its greatest triumphs, and the miserable incapacity of the Duke of Newcastle only called to the front the genius of William Pitt.   Pitt was the grandson of a wealthy governor of Madras, who had entered Parliament in 1735 as member for one of his father's pocket boroughs, and had headed the younger "patriots" in their attack on Walpole. The dismissal from the army by which Walpole met his attacks turned his energy wholly to politics. His fiery spirit was hushed in office during the "broad-bottom administration" which followed Walpole's fall, but after the death of Henry Pelham, Newcastle's jealousy of power threw him into an attitude of opposition and he was deprived of his place. When the disasters of the war however drove Newcastle from office in November 1756, Pitt became Secretary of State ; but in four months the enmity of the King and of Newcastle's party drove him to resign. In July 1757, however, it was necessary to recall him. The failure of Newcastle to construct an administration forced the Duke to a junction with his rival ; and fortunately for their country, the character of the two statesmen made the compromise an easy one. For all that Pitt coveted, for the general direction of public affairs, the control of foreign policy, the administration of the war, Newcastle had neither capacity nor inclination. On the other hand, his skill in parliamentary management was unrivalled. If he knew little else, he knew better than any living man the price of every member and the intrigues of every borough. What he cared for was not the control of affairs, but the distribution of patronage and the work of corruption, and from this Pitt turned disdainfully away. "Mr. Pitt does everything," wrote Horace Walpole, "and the Duke gives everything. So long as they agree in this partition they may do what they please." Out of the union of these two strangely-contrasted leaders, in fact, rose the greatest, as it was the last, of the purely Whig administrations. But its real power lay from beginning to end in Pitt himself. Poor as he was, for his income was little more than two hundred a year, and springing as he did from a family of no political importance, it was by sheer dint of genius that the young cornet of horse, at whose youth and inexperience Walpole had sneered, seized a power which the Whig houses had ever since the Revolution kept jealously in their grasp. His ambition had no petty aim. "I want to call England," he said as he took office, " out of that enervate state in which twenty thousand men from France can shake her." His call was soon answered. He at once breathed his own lofty spirit into the country he served, as he communicated something of his own grandeur to the men who served him. "No man," said a soldier of the time, "ever entered Mr. Pitt's closet who did not feel himself braver when he came out than when he went in." Ill-combined as were his earlier expeditions, many as were his failures, he roused a temper in the nation at large which made ultimate defeat impossible. "England has been a long time in labour," exclaimed Frederick of Prussia as he recognized a greatness like his own, " but she has at last brought forth a man."

Sec. I.

William
Pitt

1742
to
1762

Pitt and
the Age

It is this personal and solitary grandeur which strikes us most as we look back to William Pitt. The tone of his speech and action stands out in utter contrast with the tone of his time. In the midst of a society critical, polite, indifferent, simple even to the affectation of simplicity, witty and amusing but absolutely prosaic, cool of heart and of head, sceptical of virtue and enthusiasm, sceptical above all of itself, Pitt stood absolutely alone. The depth of his conviction, his passionate love for all that he deemed lofty and true, his fiery energy, his poetic imaginativeness, his theatrical airs and rhetoric, his haughty self-assumption, his pompousness and extravagance, were not more puzzling to his contemporaries than the confidence with which he appealed to the higher sentiments of mankind, the scorn with which he turned from a corruption which had till then been the great engine of politics, the undoubting faith which he felt in himself, in the grandeur of his aims, and in his power to carry them out. "I know that I can save the country," he said to the Duke of Devonshire on his entry into the Ministry, "and I know no other man can." The groundwork of Pitt's character was an intense and passionate pride ; but it was a pride which kept him from stooping to the level of the men who had so long held England in their hands. He was the first statesman since the Restoration who set the example of a purely public spirit. Keen as was his love of power, no man ever refused office so often, or accepted it with so strict a regard to the principles he professed. "I will not go to Court," he replied to an offer which was made him, "if I may not bring the Constitution with me." For the corruption about him he had nothing but disdain. He left to Newcastle the buying of seats and the purchase of members. At the outset of his career Pelham appointed him to the most lucrative office in his administration, that of Paymaster of the Forces ; but its profits were of an illicit kind, and poor as he was Pitt refused to accept one farthing beyond his salary. His pride never appeared in loftier and nobler form than in his attitude towards the people at large. No leader had ever a wider popularity than "the great commoner," as Pitt was styled, but his air was always that of a man who commands popularity, not that of one who seeks it. He never bent to flatter popular prejudice. When mobs were roaring themselves hoarse for "Wilkes and liberty," he denounced Wilkes as a worthless profligate ; and when all England went mad in its hatred of the Scots, Pitt haughtily declared his esteem for a people whose courage he had been the first to enlist on the side of loyalty. His noble figure, the hawk-like eye which flashed from the small thin face, his majestic voice, the fire and grandeur of his eloquence, gave him a sway over the House of Commons far greater than any other minister has possessed. He could silence an opponent with a look of scorn, or hush the whole House with a single word. But he never stooped to the arts by which men form a political party, and at the height

*His public
spirit*

of his power his personal following hardly numbered half a dozen members.

SEC. I.

WILLIAM
PITT

1742
TO
1762

**The
Great
Com-
moner**

His real strength indeed lay not in Parliament but in the people at large. His significant title of "the great commoner" marks a political revolution. "It is the people who have sent me here," Pitt boasted with a haughty pride when the nobles of the Cabinet opposed his will. He was the first to see that the long political inactivity of the public mind had ceased, and that the progress of commerce and industry had produced a great middle class, which no longer found its representatives in the legislature. "You have taught me," said George the Second when Pitt sought to save Byng by appealing to the sentiment of Parliament, "to look for the voice of my people in other places than within the House of Commons." It was this unrepresented class which had forced him into power. During his struggle with Newcastle the greater towns backed him with the gift of their freedom and addresses of confidence. "For weeks," laughs Horace Walpole, "it rained gold boxes." London stood by him through good report and evil report, and the wealthiest of English merchants, Alderman Beckford, was proud to figure as his political lieutenant. The temper of Pitt indeed harmonized admirably with the temper of the commercial England which rallied round him, with its energy, its self-confidence, its pride, its patriotism, its honesty, its moral earnestness. The merchant and the trader were drawn by a natural attraction to the one statesman of their time whose aims were unselfish, whose hands were clean, whose life was pure and full of tender affection for wife and child. But there was a far deeper ground for their enthusiastic reverence and for the reverence which his country has borne Pitt ever since. He loved England with an intense and personal love. He believed in her power, her glory, her public virtue, till England learned to believe in herself. Her triumphs were his triumphs, her defeats his defeats. Her dangers lifted him high above all thought of self or party-spirit. "Be one people," he cried to the factions who rose to bring about his fall: "forget everything but the public! I set you the example!" His glowing patriotism was the real spell by which he held England. But even the faults which chequered his character told for him with the middle classes. The Whig statesmen who preceded him had been men whose pride expressed itself in a marked simplicity and absence of pretence. Pitt was essentially an actor, dramatic in the cabinet, in the House, in his very office. He transacted business with his clerks in full dress. His letters to his family, genuine as his love for them was, are stilted and unnatural in tone. It was easy for the wits of his day to jest at his affectation, his pompous gait, the dramatic appearance which he made on great debates with his limbs swathed in flannel and his crutch by his side. Early in life Walpole sneered at him for bringing into the House of Commons "the gestures and emotions of

Sec. I.

WILLIAM
PITT

1742
TO
1762

Pitt's
Elo-
quence

the stage." But the classes to whom Pitt appealed were classes not easily offended by faults of taste, and saw nothing to laugh at in the statesman who was borne into the lobby amidst the tortures of the gout, or carried into the House of Lords to breathe his last in a protest against national dishonour.

Above all Pitt wielded the strength of a resistless eloquence. The power of political speech had been revealed in the stormy debates of the Long Parliament, but it was cramped in its utterance by the legal and theological pedantry of the time. Pedantry was flung off by the age of the Revolution, but in the eloquence of Somers and his rivals we see ability rather than genius, knowledge, clearness of expression, precision of thought, the lucidity of the pleader or the man of business, rather than the passion of the orator. Of this clearness of statement Pitt had little or none. He was no ready debater like Walpole, no speaker of set speeches like Chesterfield. His set speeches were always his worst, for in these his want of taste, his love of effect, his trite quotations and extravagant metaphors came at once to the front. That with defects like these he stood far above every orator of his time was due above all to his profound conviction, to the earnestness and sincerity with which he spoke. " I must sit still," he whispered once to a friend, " for when once I am up everything that is in my mind comes out." But the reality of his eloquence was transfigured by a large and poetic imagination, and by a glow of passion which not only raised him high above the men of his own day but set him in the front rank among the orators of the world. The cool reasoning, the wit, the common sense of his age made way for a splendid audacity, a sympathy with popular emotion, a sustained grandeur, a lofty vehemence, a command over the whole range of human feeling. He passed without an effort from the most solemn appeal to the gayest raillery, from the keenest sarcasm to the tenderest pathos. Every word was driven home by the grand self-consciousness of the speaker. He spoke always as one having authority. He was in fact the first English orator whose words were a power, a power not over Parliament only but over the nation at large. Parliamentary reporting was as yet unknown, and it was only in detached phrases and half-remembered outbursts that the voice of Pitt reached beyond the walls of St. Stephen's. But it was especially in these sudden outbursts of inspiration, in these brief passionate appeals, that the power of his eloquence lay. The few broken words we have of him stir the same thrill in men of our day

*His states-
manship*

which they stirred in the men of his own. But passionate as was Pitt's eloquence, it was the eloquence of a statesman, not of a rhetorician. Time has approved almost all his greater struggles, his defence of the liberty of the subject against arbitrary imprisonment under "general warrants," of the liberty of the press against Lord Mansfield, of the rights of constituencies against the House of Commons, of the constitutional rights of America against England itself. His foreign policy was directed to the preservation of Prussia, and Prussia has vindicated his foresight by the creation of Germany. We have adopted his plans for the direct government of India by the Crown, which when he proposed them were regarded as insane. Pitt was the first to recognize the liberal character of the Church of England. He was the first to sound the note of Parliamentary reform. One of his earliest measures shows the generosity and originality of his mind. He quieted Scotland by employing its Jacobites in the service of their country, and by raising Highland regiments among its clans. The selection of Wolfe and Amherst as generals showed his contempt for precedent and his inborn knowledge of men.

But it was fortune rather than his genius which showered on Pitt the triumphs which signalized the opening of his ministry. In the East the daring of a merchant's clerk made a company of English traders the sovereigns of Bengal, and opened that wondrous career of conquest which has added the Indian peninsula, from Ceylon to the Himalayas, to the dominion of the British crown. Recalled by broken health to England, Clive returned at the outbreak of the Seven Years' War to win for England a greater prize than that which his victories had won for it in the supremacy of the Carnatic. He had been only a few months at Madras when a crime whose horror still lingers in English memories called him to Bengal. Bengal, the delta of the Ganges, was the richest and most fertile of all the provinces of India. Its rice, its sugar, its silk, and the produce of its looms, were famous in European markets. Its viceroys, like their fellow lieutenants, had become practically independent of the Emperor, and had added to Bengal the provinces of Orissa and Behar. Surajah Dowlah, the master of this vast domain, had long been jealous of the enterprise and wealth of the English traders ; and, roused at this moment by the instigation of the French, he appeared before Fort William, seized its settlers, and thrust a hundred and fifty of them into a small prison called the Black Hole of Calcutta. The heat of an Indian summer did its work of death. The wretched prisoners trampled each other under foot in the madness of thirst, and in the morning only twenty-three remained alive. Clive sailed at the news with a thousand Englishmen and two thousand sepoys to wreak vengeance for the crime. He was no longer the boy-soldier of Arcot ; and the tact and skill with which he met Surajah Dowlah in the negotiations by which the Viceroy strove to avert a conflict were sullied by the Oriental falsehood and treachery to which he stooped. But his courage remained unbroken. When the two armies faced each other on the plain of Plassey the odds were so great that on the very eve of the battle a council of war counselled retreat. Clive withdrew to a grove hard by, and after an hour's lonely musing gave the word to fight.

**Pitt and
Frederick**

*Rossbach
Nov.* 1757

Courage, in fact, was all that was needed. The fifty thousand foot
and fourteen thousand horse who were seen covering the plain at daybreak on the 23rd of June, 1757, were soon thrown into confusion by
the English guns, and broke in headlong rout before the English
charge. The death of Surajah Dowlah enabled the Company to place
a creature of its own on the throne of Bengal; but his rule soon
became a nominal one. With the victory of Plassey began in fact
the Empire of England in the East.

The year of Plassey was the year of a victory hardly less important
in the West. There was little indeed in the military expeditions which
marked the opening of Pitt's ministry to justify the trust of his country;
for money and blood were lavished on buccaneering descents upon the
French coasts which did small damage to the enemy. But incidents
such as these had little weight in the minister's general policy. His
greatness lies in the fact that he recognized the genius of Frederick
the Great, and resolved to give him an energetic support. On his
entry into office he refused to ratify the Convention of Closter-Seven,
which had reduced Frederick to despair by throwing open his realm
to a French advance; protected his flank by gathering an English
and Hanoverian force on the Elbe, and on the counsel of the Prussian
King placed the best of his generals, the Prince of Brunswick, at its
head; while subsidy after subsidy were poured into Frederick's exhausted treasury. Pitt's trust was met by the most brilliant display of
military genius which the modern world had as yet witnessed. Two
months after his repulse at Kolin, Frederick flung himself on a French
army which had advanced into the heart of Germany, and annihilated
it in the victory of Rossbach. Before another month had passed he
hurried from the Saale to the Oder, and by a yet more signal victory
at Leuthen cleared Silesia of the Austrians. The victory of Rossbach
was destined to change the fortunes of the world by bringing about
the unity of Germany; its immediate effect was to force the French
army on the Elbe to fall back on the Rhine. Here Ferdinand of
Brunswick, reinforced with twenty thousand English soldiers, held
them at bay during the summer, while Frederick, foiled in an attack
on Moravia, drove the Russians back on Poland in the battle of Zorndorf. His defeat however by the Austrian General Daun at Hochkirch proved the first of a series of terrible misfortunes; and the year
1759 marks the lowest point of his fortunes. A fresh advance of the
Russian army forced the King to attack it at Kunersdorf in August, and
Frederick's repulse ended in the utter rout of his army. For the moment
all seemed lost, for even Berlin lay open to the conqueror. A few
days later the surrender of Dresden gave Saxony to the Austrians;
and at the close of the year an attempt upon them at Plauen was
foiled with terrible loss. But every disaster was retrieved by the
indomitable courage and tenacity of the King, and winter found him

as before master of Silesia and of all Saxony save the ground which Daun's camp covered. The year which marked the lowest point of Frederick's fortunes was the year of Pitt's greatest triumphs, the year of Minden and Quiberon and Quebec. France aimed both at a descent upon England and at the conquest of Hanover, and gathered a naval armament at Brest, while fifty thousand men under Contades and Broglie united on the Weser. Ferdinand with less than forty thousand met them on the field of Minden. The French marched along the Weser to the attack, with their flanks protected by that river and a brook which ran into it, and with their cavalry, ten thousand strong, massed in the centre. The six English regiments in Ferdinand's army fronted the French horse, and, mistaking their general's order, marched at once upon them in line, regardless of the batteries on their flank, and rolled back charge after charge with volleys of musketry. In an hour the French centre was utterly broken. "I have seen," said Contades, "what I never thought to be possible—a single line of infantry break through three lines of cavalry, ranked in order of battle, and tumble them to ruin!" Nothing but the refusal of Lord John Sackville to complete the victory by a charge of the horse which he headed saved the French from utter rout. As it was, their army again fell back broken on Frankfort and the Rhine. The project of an invasion of England met with like success. Eighteen thousand men lay ready to embark on board the French fleet, when Admiral Hawke came in sight of it at the mouth of Quiberon Bay. The sea was rolling high, and the coast where the French ships lay was so dangerous from its shoals and granite reefs that the pilot remonstrated with the English admiral against his project of attack. "You have done your duty in this remonstrance," Hawke coolly replied; "now lay me alongside the French admiral." Two English ships were lost on the shoals, but the French fleet was ruined and the disgrace of Byng's retreat wiped away.

It was not in the Old World only that the year of Minden and Quiberon brought glory to the arms of England. In Europe, Pitt had wisely limited his efforts to the support of Prussia, but across the Atlantic the field was wholly his own, and he had no sooner entered office than the desultory raids, which had hitherto been the only resistance to French aggression, were superseded by a large and comprehensive plan of attack. The sympathies of the colonies were won by an order which gave their provincial officers equal rank with the royal officers in the field. They raised at Pitt's call twenty thousand men, and taxed themselves heavily for their support. Three expeditions were simultaneously directed against the French line—one to the Ohio valley, one against Ticonderoga on Lake Champlain, while a third under General Amherst and Admiral Boscawen sailed to the mouth of the St. Lawrence. The last was brilliantly successful.

Sec. I.

WILLIAM
PITT

1742
TO
1762

*Minden
Aug.* 1,
1759

*Quiberon
Nov.* 20

**The
Conquest
of
Canada**

1758

Louisburg, though defended by a garrison of five thousand men, was taken with the fleet in its harbour, and the whole province of Cape Breton reduced. The American militia supported the British troops in a vigorous campaign against the forts ; and though Montcalm, with a far inferior force, was able to repulse General Abercromby from Ticonderoga, a force from Philadelphia and Virginia, guided and inspired by the courage of George Washington, made itself master of Duquesne. The name of Pittsburg which was given to their new conquest still commemorates the enthusiasm of the colonists for the great Minister who first opened to them the West. The next year saw the evacuation of Ticonderoga before the advance of Amherst, and the capture of Fort Niagara after the defeat of an Indian force which marched to its relief. The capture of the three forts was the close of the French effort to bar the advance of the colonists to the valley of the Mississippi, and to place in other than English hands the destinies of North America. But Pitt had resolved, not merely to foil the ambition of Montcalm, but to destroy the French rule in America altogether ; and while Amherst was breaking through the line of forts, an expedition under General Wolfe entered the St. Lawrence and anchored below Quebec. Wolfe had already fought at Dettingen, Fontenoy, and Laffeldt, and had played the first part in the capture of Louisburg. Pitt had discerned the genius and heroism which lay hidden beneath the awkward manner and the occasional gasconade of the young soldier of thirty-three whom he chose for the crowning exploit of the war, but for a while his sagacity seemed to have failed. No efforts could draw Montcalm from the long line of inaccessible cliffs which at this point borders the river, and for six weeks Wolfe saw his men wasting away in inactivity while he himself lay prostrate with sickness and despair. At last his resolution was fixed, and in a long line of boats the army dropped down the St. Lawrence to a point at the base of the Heights of Abraham, where a narrow path had been discovered to the summit. Not a voice broke the silence of the night save the voice of Wolfe himself, as he quietly repeated the stanzas of Gray's " Elegy in a Country Churchyard," remarking as he closed, " I had rather be the author of that poem than take Quebec." But his nature was as brave as it was tender ; he was the first to leap on shore and to scale the narrow path where no two men could go abreast. His men followed, pulling themselves to the top by the help of bushes and the crags, and at daybreak on the 12th of September the whole army stood in orderly formation before Quebec. Montcalm hastened to attack, though his force, composed chiefly of raw militia, was far inferior in discipline to the English ; his onset however was met by a steady fire, and at the first English advance his men gave way. Wolfe headed a charge which broke the French line, but a ball pierced his breast in the moment of victory. " They run," cried an officer who held the dying

Sec. II.

The Inde-
pendence
of America

**1761
to
1782**

man in his arms—" I protest they run." Wolfe rallied to ask who they were that ran, and was told " The French." " Then," he murmured, " I die happy ! " The fall of Montcalm in the moment of his defeat completed the victory ; and the submission of Canada, on the capture of Montreal by Amherst in 1760, put an end to the dream of a French empire in America.

Section II.—The Independence of America. 1761—1782.

[*Authorities.*—The two sides of the American quarrel have been told with the same purpose of fairness and truthfulness, though with a very different bias, by Lord Stanhope (" History of England from the Peace of Utrecht "), and Mr. Bancroft (" History of the United States "). The latter is by far the more detailed and picturesque, the former perhaps the cooler and more impartial of the two narratives. For England see Mr. Massey's " History of England from the Accession of George the Third ;" Walpole's " Memoirs of the Early Reign of George the Third ;" the Rockingham Memoirs ; the Grenville Papers ; the Bedford Correspondence ; the correspondence of George the Third with Lord North ; the Letters of Junius ; and Lord Russell's " Life and Correspondence of C. J. Fox." Burke's speeches and pamphlets during this period, above all his " Thoughts on the Causes of the Present Discontents," are indispensable for any real knowledge of it. The Constitutional History of Sir Erskine May all but compensates us, in its fulness and impartiality, for the loss of Mr. Hallam's comments.] [Mr. Lecky's " History of England in the Eighteenth Century " was published after this book was written ; and his " History of Ireland in the Eighteenth Century," all-important for Irish affairs.—*Ed.*]

Never had England played so great a part in the history of mankind as in the year 1759. It was a year of triumphs in every quarter of the world. In September came the news of Minden, and of a victory off Lagos. In October came tidings of the capture of Quebec. November brought word of the French defeat at Quiberon. " We are forced to ask every morning what victory there is," laughed Horace Walpole, " for fear of missing one." But it was not so much in the number as in the importance of its triumphs that the Seven Years' War stood and remains still without a rival. It is no exaggeration to say that three of its many victories determined for ages to come the destinies of mankind. With that of Rossbach began the re-creation of Germany, the revival of its political and intellectual life, the long process of its union under the leadership of Prussia and Prussia's kings. With that of Plassey the influence of Europe told for the first time since the days of Alexander on the nations of the East. The world, in Burke's gorgeous phrase, " saw one of the races of the north-west cast into the heart of Asia new manners, new doctrines, new institutions." With the triumph of Wolfe on the heights of Abraham began the history of the United States. By removing an enemy whose dread had knit the colonists to the mother country, and by breaking through the line with which France had barred them from the basin of the Mississippi, Pitt laid the founda-

SEC. II.

THE INDE-
PENDENCE
OF AMERICA

1761
TO
1782

tion of the great republic of the west. Nor were these triumphs less momentous to Britain. The Seven Years' War is a turning-point in our national history, as it is a turning-point in the history of the world. Till now the relative weight of the European states had been drawn from their possessions within Europe itself. But from the close of the war it mattered little whether England counted for less or more with the nations around her. She was no longer a mere European power, no longer a mere rival of Germany or Russia or France. Mistress of Northern America, the future mistress of India, claiming as her own the empire of the seas, Britain suddenly towered high above the nations whose position in a single continent doomed them to comparative insignificance in the after history of the world. The war indeed was hardly ended when a consciousness of the destinies that lay before the English people showed itself in the restlessness with which our seamen penetrated into far-off seas. The Atlantic was dwindling into a mere strait within the British Empire ; but beyond it to the westward lay a reach of waters where the British flag was almost unknown. In the year which followed the Peace of Paris two English ships were sent on a cruise of discovery to the Straits of Magellan ; three years later Captain Wallis reached the coral reefs of Tahiti ; and in 1768 Captain Cook traversed the Pacific from end to end, and wherever he touched, in New Zealand, in Australia, he claimed the soil for the English Crown, and opened a new world for the expansion of the English race. Statesmen and people alike felt the change in their country's attitude. In the words of Burke, the Parliament of Britain claimed " an imperial character in which as from the throne of heaven she superintends all the several inferior legislatures, and guides and controls them all, without annihilating any." Its people, steeped in the commercial ideas of the time, saw in the growth of their vast possessions, the monopoly of whose trade was reserved to the mother country, a source of boundless wealth. The trade with America alone was in 1772 nearly equal to what England carried on with the whole world at the beginning of the century. To guard and preserve so vast and lucrative a dominion became from this moment not only the aim of British statesmen but the resolve of the British people.

*Britain
and its
empire*

1764

*The
American
Colonies*

From the time when the Puritan emigration added the four New England States, Massachusetts, New Hampshire, Connecticut, and Rhode Island to those of Maryland and Virginia the progress of the English colonies in North America had been slow, but it had never ceased. Settlers still came, though in smaller numbers, and two new colonies south of Virginia received from Charles the Second their name of the Carolinas. The war with Holland transferred to British rule a district claimed by the Dutch from the Hudson to the inner Lakes ; and this country, which was granted by Charles to his brother, received from him the name of New York. Portions were soon broken off from

1664

SEC. II.

THE INDE-
PENDENCE
OF AMERICA
1761
TO
1782

its vast territory to form the colonies of New Jersey and Delaware. In 1682 a train of Quakers followed William Penn across the Delaware into the heart of the primæval forest, and became a colony which recalled its founder and the woodlands among which he planted it in its name of Pennsylvania. A long interval elapsed before a new settlement, which received its title of Georgia from the reigning sovereign, George the Second, was established by General Oglethorpe on the Savannah as a refuge for English debtors and for the persecuted Protestants of Germany. Slow as this progress seemed, the colonies were really growing fast in numbers and in wealth. Their whole population amounted in the middle of the eighteenth century to about 1,200,000 whites and a quarter of a million of negroes ; nearly a fourth of that of the mother country. The wealth of the colonists was growing even faster than their numbers. As yet the southern colonies were the more productive. Virginia boasted of its tobacco plantations, Georgia and the Carolinas of their maize and rice and indigo crops, while New York and Pennsylvania, with the colonies of New England, were restricted to their whale and cod fisheries, their corn harvests and their timber trade. The distinction indeed between the Northern and Southern colonies was more than an industrial one. In the Southern States the prevalence of slavery produced an aristocratic spirit and favoured the creation of large estates ; even the system of entails had been introduced among the wealthy planters of Virginia, where many of the older English families found representatives in houses such as those of Fairfax and Washington. Throughout New England, on the other hand, the characteristics of the Puritans, their piety, their intolerance, their simplicity of life, their love of equality and tendency to democratic institutions, remained unchanged. In education and political activity New England stood far ahead of its fellow colonies, for the settlement of the Puritans had been followed at once by the establishment of a system of local schools which is still the glory of America. " Every township," it was enacted, " after the Lord hath increased them to the number of fifty householders, shall appoint one to teach all children to write and read ; and when any town shall increase to the number of a hundred families, they shall set up a grammar school."

Their progress

Great however as these differences were, and great as was to be their influence on American history, they were little felt as yet. In the main features of their outer organization the whole of the colonies stood fairly at one. In religious and in civil matters alike all of them contrasted sharply with the England at home. Religious tolerance had been brought about by a medley of religious faiths such as the world had never seen before. New England was still a Puritan stronghold. In all the Southern colonies the Episcopal Church was established by law, and the bulk of the settlers clung to it ; but Roman Catholics formed a large part of the population of Maryland. Pennsylvania was a State

England and the Colonies

SEC. II.

THE INDE-
PENDENCE
OF AMERICA
1761
TO
1782

of Quakers. Presbyterians and Baptists had fled from tests and persecutions to colonize New Jersey. Lutherans and Moravians from
Germany abounded among the settlers of Carolina and Georgia. In
such a chaos of creeds religious persecution became impossible. There
was the same outer diversity and the same real unity in the political
tendency and organization of the States. Whether the spirit of the
colony was democratic, moderate, or oligarchical, its form of government was pretty much the same. The original rights of the proprietor,
the projector and grantee of the earliest settlement, had in all cases,
save in those of Pennsylvania and Maryland, either ceased to exist or
fallen into desuetude. The government of each colony lay in a House
of Assembly elected by the people at large, with a Council sometimes
elected, sometimes nominated by the Governor, and a Governor either
elected, or appointed by the Crown. With the appointment of these
Governors all administrative interference on the part of the Government at home practically ended. The colonies were left by a happy
neglect to themselves. It was wittily said at a later day that " Mr.
Grenville lost America because he read the American despatches, which
none of his predecessors ever did." There was little room indeed for
any interference within the limits of the colonies. Their privileges
were secured by royal charters. Their Assemblies alone exercised the
right of internal taxation, and they exercised it sparingly. Walpole,
like Pitt afterwards, set roughly aside the project for an American
excise. "I have Old England set against me," he said, "by this
measure, and do you think I will have New England too?" Even in
matters of trade the supremacy of the mother country was far from
being a galling one. There were some small import duties, but they
were evaded by a well-understood system of smuggling. The restriction of trade with the colonies to Great Britain was more than
compensated by the commercial privileges which the Americans enjoyed as British subjects. As yet, therefore, there was nothing to
break the good will which the colonists felt towards the mother
country, while the danger of French aggression drew them closely to
it. But strong as the attachment of the Americans to Britain seemed
at the close of the war, keen lookers-on saw in the very completeness of Pitt's triumph a danger to their future union. The
presence of the French in Canada, their designs in the west, had
thrown America for protection on the mother-country. But with the
conquest of Canada all need of this protection was removed. The
attitude of England towards its distant dependency became one of
mere possession : and differences of temper, which had till now been
thrown into the background by the higher need for union, started
into a new prominence. If questions of trade and taxation awoke
murmurings and disputes, behind these grievances lay an uneasy
dread at the democratic form which the government and society

*English
control*

of the colonies had taken, and at the "levelling principles" which prevailed.

Sec. II.

The Inde-
pendence
of America
1761
to
1782
**George
the
Third**

To check this republican spirit, to crush all dreams of severance, and to strengthen the unity of the British Empire was one of the chief aims of the young sovereign who mounted the throne on the death of his grand-father in 1760. For the first and last time since the accession of the House of Hanover England saw a King who was resolved to play a part in English politics ; and the part which George the Third succeeded in playing was undoubtedly a memorable one. In ten years he reduced government to a shadow, and turned the loyalty of his subjects at home into disaffection. In twenty he had forced the American colonies into revolt and independence, and brought England to what then seemed the brink of ruin. Work such as this has sometimes been done by very great men, and often by very wicked and profligate men ; but George was neither profligate nor great. He had a smaller mind than any English king before him save James the Second. He was wretchedly educated, and his natural powers were of the meanest sort. Nor had he the capacity for using greater minds than his own by which some sovereigns have concealed their natural littleness. On the contrary, his only feeling towards great men was one of jealousy and hate. He longed for the time when "decrepitude or death" might put an end to Pitt ; and even when death had freed him from "this trumpet of sedition," he denounced the proposal for a public monument to the great statesman as "an offensive measure to me per-sonally." But dull and petty as his temper was, he was clear as to his purpose and obstinate in the pursuit of it. And his purpose was to rule. "George," his mother, the Princess of Wales, had continually repeated to him in youth, "George, be king." He called himself always "a Whig of the Revolution," and he had no wish to undo the work which he believed the Revolution to have done. But he looked on the subjection of his two predecessors to the will of their ministers as no real part of the work of the Revolution, but as a usurpation of that authority which the Revolution had left to the crown. And to this usurpation he was determined not to submit. His resolve was to govern, not to govern against law, but simply to govern, to be freed from the dictation of parties and ministers, and to be in effect the first Minister of the State. How utterly incompatible such a dream was with the Parliamentary constitution of the country as it had received its final form from Sunderland it is easy to see ; but George was re-solved to carry out his dream. And in carrying it out he was aided by the circumstances of the time. The spell of Jacobitism was broken by the defeat of Charles Edward, and the later degradation of his life wore finally away the thin coating of disloyalty which clung to the clergy and the squires. They were ready again to take part in politics, and in the accession of a king who, unlike his two predecessors, was no

SEC. II.

THE INDE-
PENDENCE
OF AMERICA

1761
TO
1782

*The King's
Friends*

Pitt
resigns

stranger but an Englishman, who had been born in England and spoke English, they found the opportunity they desired. From the opening of the reign Tories gradually appeared again at court. It was only slowly indeed that the party as a whole swung round to a steady support of the Government; but their action told at once on the complexion of English politics. Their withdrawal from public affairs had left them untouched by the progress of political ideas since the Revolution of 1688, and when they returned to political life it was to invest the new sovereign with all the reverence which they had bestowed on the Stuarts. A "King's party" was thus ready made to his hand; but George was able to strengthen it by a vigorous exertion of the power and influence which was still left to the Crown. All promotion in the Church, all advancement in the army, a great number of places in the civil administration and about the court, were still at the King's disposal. If this vast mass of patronage had been practically usurped by the ministers of his predecessors, it was resumed and firmly held by George the Third; and the character of the House of Commons made patronage, as we have seen, a powerful engine in its management. George had one of Walpole's weapons in his hands, and he used it with unscrupulous energy to break up the party which Walpole had held so long together. He saw that the Whigs were divided among themselves by the factious spirit which springs from a long hold of office, and that they were weakened by the rising contempt with which the country at large regarded the selfishness and corruption of its representatives. More than thirty years before, Gay had set the leading statesmen of the day on the public stage under the guise of highwaymen and pickpockets. " It is difficult to determine," said the witty playwright, "whether the fine gentlemen imitate the gentlemen of the road, or the gentlemen of the road the fine gentlemen." And now that the "fine gentlemen" were represented by hoary jobbers such as Newcastle, the public contempt was fiercer than ever, and men turned sickened from the intrigues and corruption of party to a young sovereign who aired himself in a character which Bolingbroke had invented, as a Patriot King.

Had Pitt and Newcastle held together, supported as the one was by the commercial classes, the other by the Whig families and the whole machinery of Parliamentary management, George must have struggled in vain. But the ministry was already disunited. The Whigs, attached to peace by the traditions of Walpole, dismayed at the enormous expenditure, and haughty with the pride of a ruling oligarchy, were in silent revolt against the war and the supremacy of the Great Commoner. It was against their will that he rejected proposals of peace from France which would have secured to England all her conquests on the terms of a desertion of Prussia, and that his steady support enabled Frederick still to hold out against the terrible exhaustion of

Sec. II.

The Inde-
pendence
of America

1761
to
1782

an unequal struggle. The campaign of 1760 indeed was one of the grandest efforts of Frederick's genius. Foiled in an attempt on Dresden, he again saved Silesia by a victory at Liegnitz, and hurled back an advance of Daun by a victory at Torgau; while Ferdinand of Brunswick held his ground as of old along the Weser. But even victories drained Frederick's strength. Men and money alike failed him. It was impossible for him to strike another great blow, and the ring of enemies again closed slowly round him. His one remaining hope lay in the firm support of Pitt, and triumphant as his policy had been, Pitt was tottering to his fall. The envy and resentment of his colleagues at his undisguised supremacy found a supporter in the young King. The Earl of Bute, a mere Court favourite, with the temper and abilities of a gentleman usher, was forced into the Cabinet. As he was known to be his master's mouthpiece, a peace-party was at once formed; but Pitt showed no signs of giving way. In 1761 he proposed a vast extension of the war. He had learnt the signature of a treaty which brought into force the Family Compact between the Courts of Paris and Madrid, and of a special convention which bound the last to declare war on England at the close of the year. Pitt proposed to anticipate the blow by an instant seizure of the treasure fleet which was on its way from the Indies to Cadiz, by occupying the Isthmus of Panama, and by an attack on the Spanish dominions in the New World. But his colleagues shrank from plans so vast and daring; and Newcastle was backed in his resistance by the bulk of the Whigs. The King openly supported them. It was in vain that Pitt enforced his threat of resignation by declaring himself responsible to "the people"; and the resignation of his post in October changed the face of European affairs.

"Pitt disgraced!" wrote a French philosopher, "it is worth two victories to us!" Frederick on the other hand was almost driven to despair. But George saw in the removal of his powerful minister an opening for the realization of his long-cherished plans. Pitt's appeal had been heard by the people at large. When he went to Guildhall the Londoners hung on his carriage wheels, hugged his footmen, and even kissed his horses. Their break with Pitt was in fact the death-blow of the Whigs. Newcastle found he had freed himself from the great statesman only to be driven from office by a series of studied mortifications from his young master; and the more powerful of his Whig colleagues followed him into retirement. George saw himself triumphant over the two great forces which had hampered the free action of the Crown, "the power which arose," in Burke's words, "from popularity, and the power which arose from political connexion;" and the rise of Lord Bute to the post of First Minister marked the triumph of the King. He took office simply as an agent of the King's will; and the King's will was to end the war. In the spring of 1762

Close
of the
Seven
Years'
War

Bute's
Ministry

SEC. II.

THE INDE-
PENDENCE
OF AMERICA
1761
TO
1782

Frederick, who still held his ground stubbornly against fate, was brought to the brink of ruin by a withdrawal of the English subsidies ; it was in fact only his dogged resolution and a sudden change in the policy of Russia, which followed on the death of his enemy the Czarina Elizabeth, that enabled him at last to retire from the struggle in the Treaty of Hubertsberg without the loss of an inch of territory. George and Lord Bute had already purchased peace at a very different price. With a shameless indifference to the national honour they not only deserted Frederick, but they offered to negotiate a peace for him on the basis of a cession of Silesia to Maria Theresa and East Prussia to the Czarina. The issue of the strife with Spain saved England from humiliation such as this. Pitt's policy of instant attack had been justified by a Spanish declaration of war three weeks after his fall ; and the year 1762 saw triumphs which vindicated his confidence in the issue of the new struggle. Martinico, the strongest and wealthiest of the French West Indian possessions, was conquered at the opening of the year, and its conquest was followed by those of Grenada, St. Lucia, and St. Vincent. In the summer the reduction of Havana brought with it the gain of the rich Spanish colony of Cuba. The Philippines, the wealthiest of the Spanish colonies in the Pacific, yielded to a British fleet. It was these losses that brought about the

*Peace of
Paris
Feb.* 1763

Peace of Paris. So eager was Bute to end the war that he contented himself in Europe with the recovery of Minorca, while he restored Martinico to France, and Cuba and the Philippines to Spain. The real gains of Britain were in India and America. In the first the French abandoned all right to any military settlement. From the second they wholly withdrew. To England they gave up Canada, Nova Scotia, and Louisiana as far as the Mississippi, while they resigned the rest of that province to Spain, in compensation for its surrender of Florida to the British Crown.

**The
House of
Commons**

The anxiety which the young King showed for peace abroad sprang mainly from his belief that peace was needful for success in the struggle for power at home. So long as the war lasted Pitt's return to office and the union of the Whigs under his guidance was an hourly danger. But with peace the King's hands were free. He could count on the dissensions of the Whigs, on the new-born loyalty of the Tories, on the influence of the Crown patronage which he had taken into his own hands. But what he counted on most of all was the character of the House of Commons. At a time when it had become all-powerful in the State, the House of Commons had ceased in any real and effective sense to be a representative body at all. That changes in the distribution of seats were called for by the natural shiftings of population and wealth since the days of Edward the First had been recognized as early as the Civil Wars ; but the reforms of the Long Parliament were cancelled at the Restoration. From the time of Charles the Second to that of George

Sec. II.

The Inde-
pendence
of America

1761
to
1782

the Third not a single effort had been made to meet the growing abuses of our parliamentary system. Great towns like Manchester or Birmingham remained without a member, while members still sat for boroughs which, like Old Sarum, had actually vanished from the face of the earth. The effort of the Tudor sovereigns to establish a Court party in the House by a profuse creation of boroughs, most of which were mere villages then in the hands of the Crown, had ended in the appropriation of these seats by the neighbouring landowners, who bought and sold them as they bought and sold their own estates. Even in towns which had a real claim to representation, the narrowing of municipal privileges ever since the fourteenth century to a small part of the inhabitants, and in many cases the restriction of electoral rights to the members of the governing corporation, rendered their representation a mere name. The choice of such places hung simply on the purse or influence of politicians. Some were "the King's boroughs," others obediently returned nominees of the Ministry of the day, others were "close boroughs" in the hands of jobbers like the Duke of Newcastle, who at one time returned a third of all the borough members in the House. The counties and the great commercial towns could alone be said to exercise any real right of suffrage, though the enormous expense of contesting such constituencies practically left their representation in the hands of the great local families. But even in the counties the suffrage was ridiculously limited and unequal. Out of a population of eight millions, only a hundred and sixty thousand were electors at all. How far such a House was from really representing English opinion we see from the fact that in the height of his popularity Pitt could hardly find a seat in it. Purchase was becoming more and more the means of entering Parliament. Seats were bought and sold in the open market at a price which rose to four thousand pounds, and we can hardly wonder that a reformer could allege without a chance of denial, "This House is not a representative of the people of Great Britain. It is the representative of nominal boroughs, of ruined and exterminated towns, of noble families, of wealthy individuals, of foreign potentates." The meanest motives naturally told on a body returned by such constituencies, cut off from the influence of public opinion by the secrecy of Parliamentary proceedings, and yet invested with almost boundless authority. Walpole and Newcastle had made bribery and borough-jobbing the base of their power. George the Third seized it in his turn as a base of the power he proposed to give to the Crown. The royal revenue was employed to buy seats and to buy votes. Day by day George himself scrutinized the voting-list of the two Houses, and distributed rewards and punishments as members voted according to his will or no. Promotion in the civil service, preferment in the Church, rank in the army, was reserved for "the King's friends." Pensions and court places were

SEC. II.

THE INDE-
PENDENCE
OF AMERICA

1761
TO
1782

**Fall of
Bute**

used to influence debates. Bribery was employed on a scale never known before. Under Bute's ministry an office was opened at the Treasury for the purchase of members, and twenty-five thousand pounds are said to have been spent in a single day.

The result of these measures was soon seen in the tone of the Parliament. Till now it had bowed beneath the greatness of Pitt ; but in the teeth of his denunciation the provisions of the Peace of Paris were approved by a majority of five to one. "Now indeed," cried the Princess Dowager, "my son is king." But the victory was hardly won when King and minister found themselves battling with a storm of popular ill-will such as never since the overthrow of the Stuarts assailed the throne. Violent and reckless as it was, the storm only marked a fresh advance in the re-awakening of public opinion. The Parliament indeed had become supreme, and in theory the Parliament was a representative of the whole English people. But in actual fact the bulk of the English people found itself powerless to control the course of English government. For the first and last time in our history Parliament was unpopular and its opponents sure of popularity. The House of Commons was more corrupt than ever, and it was the slave of the King. The King still called himself a Whig, yet he was reviving a system of absolutism which Whiggism had long made impossible. His minister was a mere favourite, and in Englishmen's eyes a foreigner. The masses saw this, but they saw no way of mending it. They had no means of influencing the Government they hated save by sheer violence. They came therefore to the front with their old national and religious bigotry, their long-nursed dislike of the Hanoverian Court, their long-nursed habits of violence and faction, their long-nursed hatred of Parliament, but with no means of expressing them save riot and uproar. Bute found himself the object of a sudden and universal hatred ; and in 1763 he withdrew from office as a means of allaying the storm of popular indignation. But the King was made of more stubborn stuff than his minister. If he suffered his favourite to resign he still regarded him as the real head of administration ; for the ministry which Bute left behind him consisted simply of the

*George
Grenville*

more courtly of his colleagues. George Grenville was its nominal chief, but its measures were still secretly dictated by the favourite. Charles Townshend and the Duke of Bedford, the two ablest of the Whigs who had remained with Bute after Newcastle's dismissal, refused to join it ; and its one man of ability was Lord Shelburne, a young Irishman. It was in fact only the disunion of its opponents which allowed it to hold its ground. Townshend and Bedford remained apart from the main body of the Whigs, and both sections held aloof from Pitt. George had counted on the divisions of the opposition in forming such a ministry ; and he counted on the weakness of the ministry to make it the creature of his will. But Grenville had no mind to be a puppet either of the King or of Bute; and the conflicts between the King and his minister soon became so bitter that George appealed in despair to Pitt to form a ministry. Never had Pitt shown a nobler patriotism or a grander self-command than in the reception he gave to this appeal. He set aside all resentment at his own expulsion from office by Newcastle and the Whigs, and made the return to office of the whole party, with the exception of Bedford, a condition of his own. George however refused to comply with terms which would have defeated his designs. The result left Grenville as powerful as he had been weak. Bute ceased to exercise any political influence. On the other hand, Bedford joined Grenville with his whole party, and the ministry thus became strong and compact.

SEC. II.

THE INDE-
PENDENCE
OF AMERICA

1761
TO
1782

Aug. 1763

Grenville's one aim was to enforce the supremacy of Parliament over subject as over King. He therefore struck fiercely at the new force of opinion which had just shown its power in the fall of Bute. The opinion of the country no sooner found itself unrepresented in Parliament than it sought an outlet in the Press. In spite of the removal of the censorship after the Revolution the Press had been slow to attain any political influence. Under the first two Georges its progress had been hindered by the absence of great topics for discussion, the worthlessness of the writers, and above all the lethargy of the time. It was in fact not till the accession of George the Third that the impulse which Pitt had given to the national spirit, and the rise of a keener interest in politics, raised the Press into a political power. The nation found in it a court of appeal from the Houses of Parliament. The journals became organs for that outburst of popular hatred which drove Lord Bute from office; and in the *North Briton* John Wilkes led the way by denouncing the Cabinet and the Peace with peculiar bitterness, and venturing to attack the hated minister by name. Wilkes was a worthless profligate, but he had a remarkable faculty of enlisting popular sympathy on his side, and by a singular irony of fortune he became the chief instrument in bringing about three of the greatest advances which our Constitution has ever made. He woke the nation to a conviction of the need for Parliamentary reform by his defence of the rights of constituencies against the despotism of the House of Commons. He took the lead in the struggle which put an end to the secrecy of Parliamentary proceedings. He was the first to establish the right of the Press to discuss public affairs. In his attack on the ministry of Lord Bute, however, he was simply an organ of the general discontent. It was indeed his attack which more than all else determined Bute to withdraw from office. But Grenville was of stouter stuff than the court favourite, and his administration was hardly reformed when he struck at the growing opposition to Parliament by a blow at its leader. In " Number 45 " of the *North Briton* Wilkes had censured the speech from the throne at the opening of Parliament, and

SEC. II.

THE INDE-
PENDENCE
OF AMERICA

1761
TO
1782

a " general warrant" by the Secretary of State was issued against the " authors, printers, and publishers of this seditious libel." Under this warrant forty-nine persons were seized for a time ; and in spite of his privilege as a member of Parliament Wilkes himself was sent to the Tower. The arrest however was so utterly illegal that he was at once released by the Court of Common Pleas; but he was immediately prosecuted for libel. While the paper which formed the subject for prosecution was still before the courts of justice it was condemned by the House of Commons as a "false, scandalous, and seditious libel." The House of Lords at the same time voted a pamphlet found among Wilkes's papers to be blasphemous, and advised a prosecution. Wilkes

*Wilkes
expelled*

fled to France, and was in 1764 expelled from the House of Commons. But the assumption of an arbitrary judicial power by both Houses, and the system of terror which Grenville put in force against the Press by issuing two hundred injunctions against different journals, roused a storm of indignation throughout the country. Every street resounded with cries of " Wilkes and Liberty." It was soon clear that opinion had been embittered rather than silenced by the blow at Wilkes ; and six years later, the failure of the prosecution directed against an anonymous journalist named " Junius " for his Letter to the King established the right of the Press to criticize the conduct not of ministers or Parliament only, but of the sovereign himself.

**The
Stamp
Act**

The same narrowness of view, the same honesty of purpose, the same obstinacy of temper, were shown by Grenville in a yet more important struggle, a struggle with the American Colonies. Pitt had waged war with characteristic profusion, and he had defrayed the cost of the war by enormous loans. At the time of the Peace of Paris the public debt stood at a hundred and forty millions. The first need therefore which met Bute after the conclusion of the Peace was that of making provision for the new burthens which the nation had incurred, and as these had been partly incurred in the defence of the American Colonies it was the general opinion of Englishmen that the Colonies should bear a share

*Bute and
America*

of them. In this opinion Bute and the King concurred. But their plans went further than mere taxation. The new minister declared himself resolved on a rigorous execution of the Navigation laws, laws by which a monopoly of American trade was secured to the mother-country, on the raising of a revenue within the Colonies for the discharge of the debt, and above all on impressing upon the colonists a sense of their dependence upon Britain. The direct trade between America and the French or Spanish West Indian islands had hitherto been fettered by prohibitory duties, but these had been easily evaded by a general system of smuggling. The duties were now reduced, but the reduced duties were rigorously exacted, and a considerable naval force was despatched to the American coast with a view of suppressing the clandestine trade with the foreigner. The revenue which was expected from this measure was to be supplemented by an internal Stamp Tax, a tax on all legal documents issued within the Colonies. The plans of Bute had fallen to the ground on his retirement from office. But Grenville had fully concurred in the financial part at least of Bute's designs ; and, now that he found himself at the head of a strong administration, he proceeded to carry out the plans which had been devised for the purpose of raising both an external and an internal revenue from America. One of his first steps was to suppress, by a rigid enforcement of the Navigation laws, the contraband trade which had grown up between American ports and the adjacent Spanish islands. Harsh and unwise as these measures seemed, the colonists owned their legality ; and their resentment only showed itself in a pledge to use no British manufactures till the restrictions were relaxed. But the next scheme of the Minister —his proposal to introduce internal taxation within the bounds of the Colonies themselves by reviving the project of an excise or stamp duty, which Walpole's good sense had rejected—was of another order from his schemes for suppressing the contraband traffic. Unlike the system of the Navigation Acts, it was a gigantic change in the whole actual relations of England and its Colonies. They met it therefore in another spirit. Taxation and representation, they asserted, went hand in hand. America had no representatives in the British Parliament. The representatives of the colonists met in their own colonial assemblies, and all save the Pennsylvanians protested strongly against the interference of Parliament with their right of self-taxation. Massachusetts marked accurately the position she took. "Prohibitions of trade are neither equitable nor just ; but the power of taxing is the grand barrier of British liberty. If that is once broken down, all is lost." The distinction was accepted by the assembly of every colony ; and it was with their protest that they despatched Benjamin Franklin, who had risen from his position of a working printer in Philadelphia to high repute among scientific discoverers, as their agent to England. In England however Franklin found few who recognized the distinction which the colonists had drawn. Grenville had no mind to change his plans without an assurance, which Franklin could not give, of a union of the Colonies to tax themselves ; and the Stamp Act was passed through both Houses with less opposition than a turnpike bill.

The Stamp Act was hardly passed when an insult offered to the Princess Dowager, by the exclusion of her name from a Regency Act, brought to a head the quarrel which had long been growing between the ministry and the King. George again offered power to William Pitt. But Pitt stood absolutely alone. The one friend who remained to him, his brother-in-law, Lord Temple, refused to aid in an attempt to construct a Cabinet ; and he felt himself too weak, when thus deserted, to hold his ground in any ministerial combination with the Whigs. The King turned for help to the main body of the Whigs,

SEC. II.

THE INDE-
PENDENCE
OF AMERICA
1761
TO
1782
*Grenville's
policy*

*Franklin's
mission*
1765

**The
Rock-
ingham
Ministry**

3 D

SEC. II.

THE INDE-
PENDENCE
OF AMERICA

1761
TO
1782

now headed by the Marquis of Rockingham. The weakness of the
ministry which Rockingham formed in July, 1765, was seen in its slowness to deal with American affairs. Franklin had seen no other course
for the Colonies, when the obnoxious Acts were passed, but that of submission. But submission was the last thing the colonists dreamed of.
Everywhere through New England riots broke out on the news of the
arrival of the stamped paper ; and the frightened collectors resigned
their posts. Northern and Southern States were drawn together by
the new danger. The assembly of Virginia was the first to formally
deny the right of the British Parliament to meddle with internal
taxation, and to demand the repeal of the acts. Massachusetts not
only adopted the denial and the demand as its own, but proposed a
Congress of delegates from all the colonial assemblies to provide for
common and united action ; and in October 1765 this Congress met to
repeat the protest and petition of Virginia. The news of its assembly
reached England at the end of the year, and at once called Pitt to the
front when the Houses met in the spring of 1766. As a minister he
had long since rejected a similar scheme for taxing the colonies. He
had been ill and absent from Parliament when the Stamp Act was
passed, but he adopted to the full the constitutional claim of America.
He gloried in a resistance which was denounced in Parliament as
rebellion. " In my opinion," he said, " this kingdom has no right to
lay a tax on the colonies. . . America is obstinate ! America is almost
in open rebellion ! Sir, I rejoice that America has resisted. Three
millions of people so dead to all the feelings of liberty as voluntarily to
submit to be slaves would have been fit instruments to make slaves of
the rest."

Repeal
of the
Stamp
Act

Edmund
Burke

There was a general desire that Pitt should return to office ; but the
negotiations for his union with the Whigs broke down. The radical
difference between their policy and that of Pitt was now in fact defined for them by the keenest political thinker of the day. Edmund
Burke had come to London in 1750 as a poor and unknown Irish
adventurer. The learning which at once won him the friendship of
Johnson, and the imaginative power which enabled him to give his
learning a living shape, promised him a philosophical and literary
career : but instinct drew Burke in politics ; he became secretary to
Lord Rockingham, and in 1765 entered Parliament under his patronage. His speeches on the Stamp Acts at once lifted him into fame.
The heavy Quaker-like figure, the scratch wig, the round spectacles,
the cumbrous roll of paper which loaded Burke's pocket, gave little
promise of a great orator and less of the characteristics of his oratory
—its passionate ardour, its poetic fancy, its amazing prodigality of
resources; the dazzling succession in which irony, pathos, invective,
tenderness, the most brilliant word-pictures, the coolest argument
followed each other. It was an eloquence indeed of a wholly new

Sec. II.

The Inde-
pendence
of America

1761
to
1782

order in English experience.   Walpole's clearness of statement, Pitt's appeals to emotion, were exchanged for the impassioned expression of a distinct philosophy of politics.   " I have learned more from him than from all the books I ever read," Fox cried at a later time, with a burst of generous admiration.   The philosophical cast of Burke's reasoning was unaccompanied by any philosophical coldness of tone or phrase. The groundwork indeed of his nature was poetic.   His ideas, if conceived by the reason, took shape and colour from the splendour and fire of his imagination.   A nation was to him a great living society, so complex in its relations, and whose institutions were so interwoven with glorious events in the past, that to touch it rudely was a sacrilege. Its constitution was no artificial scheme of government, but an exquisite balance of social forces which was in itself a natural outcome of its history and developement.   His temper was in this way conservative, but his conservatism sprang not from a love of inaction but from a sense of the value of social order, and from an imaginative reverence for all that existed.   Every institution was hallowed to him by the clear insight with which he discerned its relations to the past, and its subtle connexion with the social fabric around it.   To touch even an anomaly seemed to Burke to be risking the ruin of a complex structure of national order which it had cost centuries to build up. " The equilibrium of the Constitution," he said, " has something so delicate about it, that the least displacement may destroy it."   " It is a difficult and dangerous matter even to touch so complicated a machine."   Perhaps the readiest refutation of such a theory was to be found in its influence on Burke's practical dealing with politics.   In the great question indeed which fronted him as he entered Parliament, it served him well.   No man has ever seen with deeper insight the working of those natural forces which build up communities, or which group communities into empires ; and in the actual state of the American Colonies he saw a result of such forces which only madmen and pedants would disturb.   But Burke's theory was less fitted to the state of politics at home.   He looked on the Revolution of 1688 as the final establishment of English institutions.   His aim was to keep England as the Revolution had left it, and under the rule of the great nobles who were faithful to the Revolution.   He gave his passionate adhesion to the inaction of the Whigs.   He made an idol of Lord Rockingham, an honest man, but the weakest of party leaders.   He strove to check the corruption of Parliament by a bill for civil retrenchment, but he took the lead in defeating all plans for its reform.   Though he was one of the few men in England who understood with Pitt the value of free industry, he struggled bitterly against the young Minister's proposals to give freedom to Irish trade, and against his Commercial Treaty with France.   His work seemed to be that of investing with a gorgeous poetry the policy of timid content which the Whigs believed they

Burke and politics

SEC. II.

THE INDE-
PENDENCE
OF AMERICA

1761
TO
1782

inherited from Sir Robert Walpole ; and the very intensity of his trust in the natural developement of a people rendered him incapable of understanding the good that might come from particular laws or from special reforms.   At this crisis then the temper of Burke squared with the temper of the Whig party.   Rockingham and his fellow-ministers were driven, whether they would or no, to a practical acknowledgement of the policy which Pitt demanded ; but they resolved that the repeal of the Stamp Acts should be accompanied by a formal repudiation of the principles of colonial freedom which Pitt had laid down.   A declaratory act was brought in, which asserted the supreme power of Parliament over the Colonies " in all cases whatsoever."   The passing of this act was followed by the introduction of a bill for the repeal of the Stamp Acts ; and in spite of the resistance of the King's friends, a resistance instigated by George himself, the bill was carried by a large majority.

Feb. 1766

From this moment the Ministry was unable to stand against the general sense that the first man in the country should be its ruler, and bitter as was the King's hatred of him, he was forced to call Pitt into office.   Pitt's aim was still to unite the Whig party, and though forsaken by Lord Temple, he succeeded to a great extent in the administration which he formed in the summer of 1766.   Though Rockingham stood coldly aside, some of his fellow ministers accepted office, and they were reinforced by the few friends who clung to Pitt ; while Pitt stooped to strengthen his Parliamentary support by admitting some even of the " King's friends " to a share in the administration.   But its life lay really in Pitt himself, in his immense popularity, and in the command which his eloquence gave him over the House of Commons.   His acceptance of the Earldom of Chatham removed him to the House of Lords, and for a while ruined the confidence which his reputation for unselfishness had aided him to win.   But it was from no vulgar ambition that Pitt laid down his title of the Great Commoner.   It was the consciousness of failing strength which made him dread the storms of debate, and in a few months the dread became a certainty.   A painful and overwhelming illness, the result of nervous disorganization, withdrew him from public affairs ; and his withdrawal robbed his colleagues of all vigour or union.   The plans which Chatham had set on foot for the better government of Ireland, the transfer of India from the Company to the Crown, and the formation of an alliance with Prussia and Russia to balance the Family Compact of the House of Bourbon, were suffered to drop.   The one aim of the ministry which bore his name, and which during his retirement looked to the Duke of Grafton as its actual head, was simply to exist.   But even existence was difficult ; and Grafton saw himself forced to a union with the faction which was gathered under the Duke of Bedford, and to the appointment of a Tory noble as Secretary of State.

Sec. II.

The Inde-
pendence
of America

1761
to
1782

**Wilkes
and the
Parlia-
ment**

1768

The force of public opinion on which Pitt had relied turned at once against the ministry which had so drifted from its former position. The elections for the new Parliament were more corrupt than any that had been yet witnessed. How bitter the indignation of the country had grown was seen in its fresh backing of Wilkes. He seized on the opening afforded by the elections to return from France, and was elected member for Middlesex, a county the large number of whose voters made its choice a real expression of public opinion. The choice of Wilkes was in effect a public condemnation of the House of Commons and the ministerial system. The ministry however and the House alike shrank from a fresh struggle with the agitator ; but the King was eager for the contest. After ten years of struggle and disappointment George had all but reached his aim. The two forces which had as yet worsted him were both of them paralyzed. The Whigs were fatally divided, and discredited in the eyes of the country by their antagonism to Pitt. Pitt, on the other hand, was suddenly removed from the stage. The ministry was without support in the country ; and for Parliament-ary support it was forced to lean more and more on the men who looked for direction to the King himself. One form of opposition alone remained in the public discontent ; and at this he struck more fiercely than ever. " I think it highly expedient to apprise you," he wrote to Lord North, " that the expulsion of Mr. Wilkes appears to be very essential, and must be effected." The Ministers and the House of Commons bowed to his will. By his non-appearance in court when charged with libel, Wilkes had become an outlaw, and he was now thrown into prison on his outlawry. Dangerous riots broke out in London and over the whole country. The Ministry were torn with dissensions. The announcement of Lord Shelburne's purpose to resign office was followed by the resignation of Chatham himself ; and his withdrawal from the Cabinet which traded on his name left the Ministry wholly dependent on the King. In 1769 Wilkes was brought before the bar of the House of Commons on a charge of libel, a crime which was cognizable in the ordinary courts of law ; and was expelled from Parliament. He was at once re-elected by the shire of Middlesex. Violent and oppressive as the course of the House of Commons had been, it had as yet acted within its strict right, for no one questioned its possession of a right of expulsion. But the defiance of Middlesex led it now to go further. It resolved, " That Mr. Wilkes having been in this session of Parliament expelled the House, was and is incapable of being elected a member to serve in the present Parliament ; " and it issued a writ for a fresh election. Middlesex answered this insolent claim to limit the free choice of a constituency by again returning Wilkes ; and the House was driven by its anger to a fresh and more outrageous usurpation. It again expelled the member for Middlesex : and on his return for

SEC. II.

THE INDE-
PENDENCE
OF AMERICA

1761
TO
1782

the third time by an immense majority, it voted that the candidate whom he had defeated, Colonel Luttrell, ought to have been returned, and was the legal representative of Middlesex. The Commons had not only limited at their own arbitrary discretion the free election of the constituency, but they had transferred its rights to themselves by seating Luttrell as member in defiance of the deliberate choice of Wilkes by the freeholders of Middlesex. The country at once rose indignantly against this violation of constitutional law. Wilkes was elected an Alderman of London ; and the Mayor, Aldermen, and Livery petitioned the King to dissolve the Parliament. A remonstrance from London and Westminster said boldly that "there is a time when it is clearly demonstrable that men cease to be representatives. That time is now arrived. The House of Commons do not represent the people." Meanwhile a writer who styled himself Junius attacked the Government in letters, which, rancorous and unscrupulous as was their tone, gave a new power to the literature of the Press by their clearness and terseness of statement, the finish of their style, and the terrible vigour of their invective.

The storm however beat idly on the obstinacy of the King. The printer of the letters was prosecuted, and the petitions and remonstrances of London were haughtily rejected. At the beginning of 1770 a cessation of the disease which had long held him prostrate enabled Chatham to reappear in the House of Lords. He at once denounced the usurpations of the Commons, and brought in a bill to declare them illegal. But his genius made him the first to see that remedies of this sort were inadequate to meet evils which really sprang from the fact that the House of Commons no longer represented the people of England ; and he mooted a plan for its reform by an increase of the county members, who then formed the most independent portion of the House. Further he could not go, for even in the proposals he made he stood almost alone. The Tories and the King's friends were not likely to welcome schemes which would lessen the King's influence. The Whigs under Lord Rockingham had no sympathy with Parliamentary reform ; and they shrank with haughty disdain from the popular agitation in which public opinion was forced to express itself, and which Chatham, while censuring its extravagance, deliberately encouraged. It is from the quarrel between Wilkes and the House of Commons that we may date the influence of public meetings on English politics. The gatherings of the Middlesex electors in his support were preludes to the great meetings of Yorkshire freeholders in which the question of Parliamentary reform rose into importance ; and it was in the movement for reform, and the establishment of corresponding committees throughout the country for the purpose of promoting it, that the power of political agitation first made itself felt. Political societies and clubs took their part in this quickening and organization of public opinion : and the spread of discussion, as well as the influence which now began to be exercised by the appearance of vast numbers of men in support of any political movement, proved that Parliament would soon have to reckon with the sentiments of the people at large.

Sec. II.

The Inde-
pendence
of America

1761
to
1782

Power
of the
Press

But an agent far more effective than popular agitation was preparing to bring the force of public opinion to bear on Parliament itself. We have seen how much of the corruption of the House of Commons sprang from the secrecy of Parliamentary proceedings, but this secrecy was the harder to preserve as the nation woke to a greater interest in its own affairs. From the accession of the Georges imperfect reports of the more important discussions began to be published under the title of "The Senate of Lilliput," and with feigned names or simple initials to denote the speakers. Obtained by stealth and often merely recalled by memory, such reports were naturally inaccurate ; and their inaccuracy was eagerly seized on as a pretext for enforcing the rules which guarded the secrecy of proceedings in Parliament. In 1771 the Commons issued a proclamation forbidding the publication of debates ; and six printers, who set it at defiance, were summoned to the bar of the House. One who refused to appear was arrested by its messenger ; but the arrest at once brought the House into conflict with the magistrates of London. They set aside the proclamation as without legal force, released the printers, and sent the messenger to prison for an unlawful arrest. The House sent the Lord Mayor to the Tower, but the cheers of the crowds which followed him on his way told that public opinion was again with the Press, and the attempt to hinder its publication of Parliamentary proceedings dropped silently on his release at the next prorogation. Few changes of equal importance have been so quietly brought about. Not only was the responsibility of members to their constituents made constant and effective by the publication of their proceedings, but the nation itself was called in to assist in the deliberations of its representatives. A new and wider interest in its own affairs was roused in the people at large, and a new political education was given to it through the discussion of every subject of national importance in the Houses and the Press. Public opinion, as gathered up and represented on all its sides by the journals of the day, became a force in practical statesmanship, influenced the course of debates, and controlled in a closer and more constant way than even Parliament itself had been able to do the actions of the Government. The importance of its new position gave a weight to the Press which it had never had before. The first great English journals date from this time. With the *Morning Chronicle*, the *Morning Post*, the *Morning Herald*, and the *Times*, all of which appeared in the interval between the opening years of the American War and the beginning of the war with the French Revolution, journalism took a new tone of

SEC. II.

THE INDE-
PENDENCE
OF AMERICA

1761
TO
1782

George
III. and
America

responsibility and intelligence. The hacks of Grub Street were superseded by publicists of a high moral temper and literary excellence;
and philosophers like Coleridge or statesmen like Canning turned to
influence public opinion through the columns of the Press.

But as yet these influences were feebly felt, and George the Third
was able to set Chatham's policy disdainfully aside, and to plunge into
a contest far more disastrous than his contest with the Press. In all
the proceedings of the last few years, what had galled him most had
been the act which averted a war between England and her colonies.
To the King the Americans were already "rebels," and the great
statesman whose eloquence had made their claims irresistible was a
"trumpet of sedition." George deplored in his correspondence with
his ministers the repeal of the Stamp Acts. "All men feel," he wrote,
"that the fatal compliance in 1766 has increased the pretensions
of the Americans to absolute independence." In America itself the
news of the repeal had been received with universal joy, and taken as
a close of the strife. But on both sides there remained a pride and
irritability which only wise handling could have allayed; and in the
present state of English politics wise handling was impossible. Only
a few months indeed passed before the quarrel was re-opened; for no
sooner had the illness of Lord Chatham removed him in 1767 from any
real share in public affairs, than the wretched administration which
bore his name suspended the Assembly of New York on its refusal to
provide quarters for English troops, and resolved to assert British
sovereignty by levying import duties of trivial amount at American
ports. The Assembly of Massachusetts was dissolved on a trifling
quarrel with its Governor, and Boston was occupied for a time by
British soldiers. The remonstrances of the Legislatures of Massachusetts and Virginia, however, coupled with a fall in the funds, warned
the Ministers of the dangerous course on which they had entered; and
in 1769 the troops were withdrawn, and all duties, save one, abandoned.
But the King insisted on retaining the duty on tea; and its retention
was enough to prevent any thorough restoration of good feeling. A
series of petty quarrels went on in almost every colony between the
popular Assemblies and the Governors appointed by the Crown, and
the colonists persisted in their agreement to import nothing from the
mother country. As yet however there was no prospect of serious
strife. In America the influence of George Washington allayed the
irritation of Virginia. Massachusetts contented itself with quarrelling
with its Governor, and refusing to buy tea so long as the duty was
levied. In England, even Grenville, though approving the retention
of the duty in question, abandoned all dream of further taxation.

But the King was now supreme. The attack of Chatham in 1770
had completed the ruin of the Ministry. Those of his adherents who
still clung to it resigned their posts; and were followed by the Duke of

Sec. II.

The Inde-
pendence
of America

1761
TO
1782

Grafton. All that remained were the Bedford faction and the dependents of the King; these were gathered under the former Chancellor of the Exchequer, Lord North, into a ministry which was in fact a mere cloak for the direction of public affairs by George himself. " Not only did he direct the minister," a careful observer tells us, " in all important matters of foreign and domestic policy, but he instructed him as to the management of debates in Parliament, suggested what motions should be made or opposed, and how measures should be carried. He reserved for himself all the patronage, he arranged the whole cast of administration, settled the relative place and pretensions of ministers of State, law officers, and members of the household, nominated and promoted the English and Scotch judges, appointed and translated bishops and deans, and dispensed other preferments in the Church. He disposed of military governments, regiments, and commissions, and himself ordered the marching of troops. He gave and refused titles, honours, and pensions." All this immense patronage was steadily used for the creation and maintenance in both Houses of Parliament of a majority directed by the King himself; and its weight was seen in the steady action of such a majority. It was seen yet more in the subjection to which the ministry that bore North's name was reduced. George was in fact the minister through the twelve years of its existence, from 1770 till the close of the American war; and the shame of the darkest hour of English history lies wholly at his door.

His fixed purpose was to seize on the first opportunity of undoing the "fatal compliance of 1766." A trivial riot gave him the handle he wanted. In December 1773 the arrival of some English ships laden with tea kindled fresh irritation in Boston, where the non-importation agreement was strictly enforced. A mob in the disguise of Indians boarded the vessels and flung their contents into the sea. The outrage was deplored alike by the friends of America in England and by its own leading statesmen; and both Washington and Chatham were prepared to support the Government in its looked-for demand of redress. But the thought of the King was not of redress but of repression, and he set roughly aside the more conciliatory proposals of Lord North and his fellow-ministers. They had already rejected as " frivolous and vexatious " a petition of the Assembly of Massachusetts for the dismissal of two public officers whose letters home advised the withdrawal of free institutions from the Colonies. They now seized on the riot as a pretext for rigorous measures. A bill introduced into Parliament in the beginning of 1774 punished Boston by closing its port against all commerce. Another punished the State of Massachusetts by withdrawing the liberties it had enjoyed ever since the Pilgrim Fathers landed on its soil. Its charter was altered. The choice of its Council was transferred from the people to the Crown, and the nomination of its judges was transferred to the Governor. In the

SEC. II.

THE INDE-
PENDENCE
OF AMERICA

1761
TO
1782

Governor, too, by a provision more outrageous than even these, was vested the right of sending all persons charged with a share in the late disturbances to England for trial. To enforce these measures of repression troops were sent to America, and General Gage, the commander-in-chief there, was appointed Governor of Massachusetts. The King's exultation at the prospect before him was unbounded. "The die," he wrote triumphantly to his minister, "is cast. The Colonies must either triumph or submit." Four regiments would be enough to bring the Americans to their senses. They would only be lions while we are lambs." "If we take the resolute part," he decided solemnly, "they will undoubtedly be very meek." Unluckily, the blow at Massachusetts was received with anything but meekness.

Resistance of America

The jealousies between State and State were hushed by the sense that the liberties of all were in danger. If the British Parliament could cancel the charter of Massachusetts and ruin the trade of Boston, it could cancel the charter of every colony and ruin the trade of every port from the St. Lawrence to the coast of Georgia. All therefore adopted the cause of Massachusetts; and all their Legislatures, save that of Georgia, sent delegates to a Congress which assembled on the 4th of September at Philadelphia. Massachusetts took a yet bolder course. Not a citizen would act under the new laws. Its Assembly met in defiance of the Governor, called out the militia of the State, and provided arms and ammunition for it. But there was still room for reconciliation. The resolutions of the Congress had been moderate; for Virginia was the wealthiest and most influential among the States who sent delegates; and though resolute to resist the new measures of the Government, Virginia still clung to the mother country. At home, the merchants of London and Bristol pleaded loudly for reconciliation; and in January 1775 Chatham again came forward to avert a strife he had once before succeeded in preventing. With characteristic largeness of feeling he set aside all half-measures or proposals of compromise. "It is not cancelling a piece of parchment," he insisted, "that can win back America: you must respect her fears and her resentments." The bill which he introduced in concert with Franklin provided for the repeal of the late acts and for the security of the colonial charters, abandoned the claim to taxation, and ordered the recall of the troops. A colonial assembly was directed to meet and provide means by which America might contribute towards the payment of the public debt.

The Independence of America

Chatham's measure was contemptuously rejected by the Lords, as was a similar measure of Burke's by the Commons, and a petition of the City of London in favour of the Colonies by the King himself. With the rejection of these efforts at reconciliation began the great struggle which ended eight years later in the severance of the American Colonies from the British Crown. The Congress of delegates from

SEC. II.

THE INDE-
PENDENCE
OF AMERICA

1761
TO
1782

*George
Washington*

the Colonial Legislatures at once voted measures for general defence, ordered the levy of an army, and set George Washington at its head. No nobler figure ever stood in the forefront of a nation's life. Washington was grave and courteous in address ; his manners were simple and unpretending ; his silence and the serene calmness of his temper spoke of a perfect self-mastery ; but there was little in his outer bearing to reveal the grandeur of soul which lifts his figure, with all the simple majesty of an ancient statue, out of the smaller passions, the meaner impulses of the world around him. What recommended him for command was simply his weight among his fellow landowners of Virginia, and the experience of war which he had gained by service in border contests with the French and the Indians, as well as in Braddock's luckless expedition against Fort Duquesne. It was only as the weary fight went on that the colonists learned little by little the greatness of their leader, his clear judgment, his heroic endurance, his silence under difficulties, his calmness in the hour of danger or defeat, the patience with which he waited, the quickness and hardness with which he struck, the lofty and serene sense of duty that never swerved from its task through resentment or jealousy, that never through war or peace felt the touch of a meaner ambition, that knew no aim save that of guarding the freedom of his fellow countrymen, and no personal longing save that of returning to his own fireside when their freedom was secured. It was almost unconsciously that men learned to cling to Washington with a trust and faith such as few other men have won, and to regard him with a reverence which still hushes us in presence of his memory. Even America hardly recognized his real greatness till death set its seal on "the man first in war, first in peace, and first in the hearts of his fellow countrymen." Washington more than any of his fellow colonists represented the clinging of the Virginian landowners to the mother country, and his acceptance of the command proved that even the most moderate among them had no hope now save in arms. The struggle opened with a skirmish between a party of English troops and a detachment of militia at Lexington, and in a few days twenty thousand colonists appeared before Boston. The Congress re-assembled, declared the States they represented "The United Colonies of America," and undertook the work of government. Meanwhile ten thousand fresh troops landed at Boston ; but the provincial militia seized the neck of ground which joins it to the mainland, and though they were driven from the heights of Bunker's Hill which commanded the town, it was only after a desperate struggle in which their bravery put an end for ever to the taunts of cowardice which had been levelled against the colonists. "Are the Yankees cowards?" shouted the men of Massachusetts, as the first English attack rolled back baffled down the hill-side. But a far truer courage was shown in the stubborn endurance with which Washington's raw militiamen,

*Opening of
the war
April* **1775**

June **17**

Sec. II.

The Inde-
pendence
of America

1761
to
1782

who gradually dwindled from sixteen thousand to ten, ill fed, ill armed, and with but forty-five rounds of ammunition to each man, cooped up through the winter a force of ten thousand veterans in the lines of Boston. The spring of 1776 saw them force these troops to withdraw from the city to New York, where the whole British army, largely reinforced by mercenaries from Germany, was concentrated under General Howe. Meanwhile a raid of the American General, Arnold, nearly drove the British troops from Canada ; and though his attempt broke down before Quebec, it showed that all hope of reconciliation was over. The Colonies of the south, the last to join in the struggle, had in fact expelled their Governors at the close of 1775 ; at the opening of the next year Massachusetts instructed its delegates to support a complete repudiation of the King's government by the Colonies ; while the American ports were thrown open to the world in defiance of the Navigation Acts. These decisive steps were followed by the great act with which American history begins, the adoption on the 4th of July, 1776, by the delegates in Congress of a Declaration of Independence. "We," ran its solemn words, "the representatives of the United States of America in Congress assembled, appealing to the Supreme Judge of the world for the rectitude of our intentions, solemnly publish and declare that these United Colonies are, and of right ought to be, Free and Independent States."

*Declaration
of Inde-
pendence*

**Death of
Chatham**

The earlier successes of the Colonists were soon followed by suffering and defeat. Howe, an active general with a fine army at his back, cleared Long Island in August by a victory at Brooklyn ; and Washington, whose army was weakened by withdrawals and defeat, and disheartened by the loyal tone of the State in which it was encamped, was forced to evacuate New York and New Jersey, and to fall back first on the Hudson and then on the Delaware. The Congress prepared to fly from Philadelphia, and a general despair showed itself in cries of peace. But a well-managed surprise and a daring march on the rear of Howe's army restored the spirits of Washington's men, and forced the English general in his turn to fall back on New York. The campaign of 1777 opened with a combined effort for the suppression of the revolt. An army assembled in Canada under General Burgoyne marched by way of the Lakes to seize the line of the Hudson, and with help from the army at New York to cut off New England from her sister provinces. Howe meanwhile sailed up the Chesapeake, and advanced on Philadelphia, the temporary capital of the United States and the seat of the Congress. The rout of his little army of seven thousand men at Brandywine forced Washington to abandon Philadelphia, and, after a bold but unsuccessful attack on his victors, to retire into winter quarters on the banks of the Schuylkill ; where the unconquerable resolve with which he nerved his handful of beaten and half-starved troops to face Howe's army in their camp at Valley Forge is the noblest of his triumphs. But in the north the war had taken another colour. When Burgoyne appeared on the Upper Hudson he found the road to Albany barred by an American force under General Gates. The spirit of New England, which had grown dull as the war rolled away from its borders, quickened again at the news of invasion and of the outrages committed by the Indians whom Burgoyne employed among his troops.   Its militia hurried from town and homestead to the camp ; and after a fruitless attack on the American lines, Burgoyne saw himself surrounded on the heights of Saratoga.   On the 17th of October he was compelled to surrender.   The news of this calamity gave force to the words with which Chatham at the very time of the surrender was pressing for peace. " You cannot conquer America," he cried when men were glorying in Howe's successes. " If I were an American as I am an Englishman, while a foreign troop was landed in my country, I never would lay down my arms—never, never, never ! "   Then in a burst of indignant eloquence he thundered against the use of the Indian and his scalping-knife as allies of England against her children.   The proposals which Chatham brought forward might perhaps, in his hands, even yet have drawn America and the mother country together.   His plan was one of absolute conciliation, and of a federal union between the settlements and Great Britain which would have left the Colonies absolutely their own masters in all matters of internal government, and linked only by ties of affection and loyalty to the general body of the Empire.   But it met with the same fate as his previous proposals. Its rejection was at once followed by the news of Saratoga, and by the yet more fatal news that this disaster had roused the Bourbon Courts to avenge the humiliation of the Seven Years' War.   In February 1778 France concluded an alliance with the States.   Lord North strove to meet the blow by fresh offers of conciliation, and by a pledge to renounce for ever the right of direct taxation over the Colonies ; but he felt that the time for conciliation was past, while all hope of reducing America by force of arms had disappeared.   George indeed was as obstinate for war as ever ; and the country, stung to the quick by the attack of France, backed passionately the obstinacy of the King.   But unlike George the Third, it instinctively felt that if a hope still remained of retaining the friendship of the Colonies, and of baffling the efforts of the Bourbons, it lay in Lord Chatham ; and in spite of the King's resistance the voice of the whole country called him back to power. But on the eve of his return to office this last chance was shattered by the hand of death.   Broken with age and disease, the Earl was borne to the House of Lords to utter in a few broken words his protest against the proposal to surrender America.   " I rejoice," he murmured, " that I am still alive to lift up my voice against the dismemberment of this ancient and noble monarchy.   His Majesty succeeded to an Empire as great in extent as its reputation was unsullied.   Seventeen years

Sec. II.

The Inde-
pendence
of America
1761
to
1782

Saratoga

*Chatham's
proposals*

April 7

Sec. II

The Inde-
pendence
of America

1761
to
1782

Progress
of the
War

ago this people was the terror of the world." He listened impatiently to the reply of the Duke of Richmond, and again rose to his feet. But he had hardly risen when he pressed his hand upon his heart, and falling back in a swoon was borne home to die.

From the hour of Chatham's death England entered on a conflict with enemies whose circle gradually widened till she stood single-handed against the world. At the close of 1778 Spain joined the league of France and America against her; and in the next year the joint fleets of the two powers rode the masters of the Channel. They even threatened a descent on the English coast. But dead as Chatham was, his cry woke a new life in England. "Shall we fall prostrate," he exclaimed with his last breath, "before the House of Bourbon?" and the divisions which had broken the nation in its struggle with American liberty were hushed in the presence of this danger to its own existence. The weakness of the Ministry was compensated by the energy of England itself. For three years, from 1779 to 1782, General Elliott held against famine and bombardment the rock fortress of Gibraltar. Although a quarrel over the right of search banded Holland and the Courts of the North in an armed neutrality against her, and added the Dutch fleet to the number of her assailants, England held her own at sea. Even in America the fortune of the war seemed to turn. After Burgoyne's surrender the English generals had withdrawn from Pennsylvania, and bent all their efforts on the South where a strong Royalist party still existed. The capture of Charlestown and the successes of Lord Cornwallis in 1780 were rendered fruitless by the obstinate resistance of General Greene; but the States were weakened by bankruptcy, and unnerved by hopes of aid from France. Meanwhile England was winning new triumphs in the East.

Since the day of Plassey, India had been fast passing into the hands of the merchant company whose traders but a few years before held only three petty factories along its coast. The victory which laid Bengal at the feet of Clive had been followed in 1760 by a victory at Wandewash, in which Colonel Coote's defeat of Lally, the French Governor of Pondicherry, established British supremacy over Southern India. The work of organization had soon to follow on that of conquest; for the tyranny and corruption of the merchant-clerks who suddenly found themselves lifted into rulers was fast ruining the province of Bengal; and although Clive had profited more than any other by the spoils of his victory, he saw that the time had come when greed must give way to the responsibilities of power. In 1765 he returned to India, and the two years of his rule were in fact the most glorious years in his life. In the teeth of opposition from every clerk and of mutiny throughout the army, he put down the private trading of the Company's servants and forbade their acceptance of gifts from the natives. Clive set an example of disinterestedness by handing over to public uses a legacy which had been left him by the prince he had raised to the throne of Bengal ; and returned poorer than he went to face the storm his acts had roused among those who were interested in Indian abuses at home. His unsparing denunciations of the misgovernment of Bengal at last stirred even Lord North to interfere ; and when the financial distress of the Company drove it for aid to Government, the grant of aid was coupled with measures of administrative reform. The Regulating Act of 1773 established a Governor-General and a Supreme Court of Judicature for all British possessions in India, prohibited judges and members of Council from trading, forbade any receipt of presents from natives, and ordered that every act of the Directors should be signified to the Government to be approved or disallowed. The new interest which had been aroused in the subject of India was seen in an investigation of the whole question of its administration by a Committee of the House of Commons. Clive's own early acts were examined with unsparing severity. His bitter complaint in the Lords that, Baron of Plassey as he was, he had been arraigned like a sheep-stealer, failed to prevent the passing of resolutions which censured the corruption and treachery of the early days of British rule in India. Here, however, the justice of the House stopped. When his accusers passed from the censure of Indian misgovernment to the censure of Clive himself, the memory of his great deeds won from the House of Commons a unanimous vote, " That Robert Lord Clive did at the same time render great and meritorious services to his country."

By the Act of 1773 Warren Hastings was named Governor-General of Bengal, with powers of superintendence and control over the other presidencies. Hastings was sprung of a noble family which had long fallen into decay, and poverty had driven him in boyhood to accept a writership in the Company's service. Clive, whose quick eye discerned his merits, drew him after Plassey into political life ; and the administrative ability he showed, during the disturbed period which followed, raised him step by step to the post of Governor of Bengal. No man could have been better fitted to discharge the duties of the new office which the Government at home had created without a thought of its real greatness. Hastings was gifted with rare powers of organization and control. His first measure was to establish the direct rule of the Company over Bengal by abolishing the government of its native princes, which, though it had become nominal, hindered all plans for effective administration. The Nabob sank into a pensionary, and the Company's new province was roughly but efficiently organized. Out of the clerks and traders about him Hastings formed that body of public servants which still remains the noblest product of our rule in India. The system of law and finance which he devised, hasty and imperfect as it necessarily was, was far superior

SEC. II.

THE INDE-
PENDENCE
OF AMERICA
1761
TO
1782

SEC. II.

THE INDE-
PENDENCE
OF AMERICA

1761
TO
1782

to any that India had ever seen. Corruption he put down with as firm a hand as Clive's, but he won the love of the new "civilians" as he won the love of the Hindoos. Although he raised the revenue of Bengal and was able to send home every year a surplus of half a million to the Company, he did this without laying a fresh burden on the natives or losing their good will. His government was guided by an intimate knowledge of and sympathy with the people. At a time when their tongue was looked on simply as a medium of trade and business, Hastings was skilled in the languages of India ; he was versed in native customs, and familiar with native feeling. We can hardly wonder that his popularity with the Bengalees was such as no later ruler has ever attained, or that after a century of great events Indian mothers still hush their infants with the name of Warren Hastings.

India in the American War

As yet, though English influence was great in the south, Bengal alone was directly in English hands. Warren Hastings recognized a formidable danger to the power of Britain in that of the Mahrattas, freebooters of Hindoo blood whose tribes had for a century past carried their raids over India from the hills of the western coast, and founded sovereignties in Guzerat, Malwa, and Tanjore, and who were bound by a slight tie of subjection to the Mahratta chief who reigned at Poonah. The policy of Hastings was to prevent the Mahrattas from over-running the whole of India, and taking the place which the Mogul Emperors had occupied. He bound native princes, as in Oudh or Berar, by treaties and subsidies, crushed without scruple the Rohillas to strengthen his ally the Nabob Vizier of Oudh, and watched with incessant jealousy the growth of powers even as distant as the Sikhs. The jealousy of France sought in the Mahrattas a counterpoise to the power of Britain, and through their chieftain the French envoys were able to set the whole confederacy in motion against the English presidencies. The danger was met by Hastings with characteristic swiftness of resolve. His difficulties were great. For two years he had been rendered powerless through the opposition of his Council ; and when freed from this obstacle the Company pressed him incessantly for money, and the Crown more than once strove to recall him. His own general, Sir Eyre Coote, was miserly, capricious, and had to be humoured like a child. Censures and complaints reached him with every mail. But his calm self-command never failed. No trace of his embarrassments showed itself in his work. The war with the Mahrattas was pressed with a tenacity of purpose which the blunders of subordinates and the inefficiency of the soldiers he was forced to use never shook for a moment. Failure followed failure, and success had hardly been wrung from fortune when a new and overwhelming danger

Hyder Ali

threatened from the south. A military adventurer, Hyder Ali, had built up a compact and vigorous empire out of the wreck of older principalities on the table-land of Mysore. Tyrant as he was, no

SEC. II.

THE INDE-
PENDENCE
OF AMERICA
1761
TO
1782

native rule was so just as Hyder's, no statesmanship so vigorous. He was quickwitted enough to discern the real power of Britain, and only the wretched blundering of the Council of Madras forced him at last to the conclusion that war with the English was less dangerous than friendship with them. Old as he was, his generalship retained all its energy; and a disciplined army, covered by a cloud of horse and backed by a train of artillery, poured down in 1780 on the plain of the Carnatic. The small British force which met him was driven into Madras, and Madras itself was in danger. The news reached Hastings when he was at last on the verge of triumph over the Mahrattas; but his triumph was instantly abandoned, a peace was patched up, and every soldier hurried to Madras. The appearance of Eyre Coote checked the progress of Hyder, and after a campaign of some months he was hurled back into the fastnesses of Mysore. India was the one quarter of the world where Britain lost nothing during the American war; and in the annexation of Benares, the extension of British rule along the Ganges, the reduction of Oudh to virtual dependence, the appearance of English armies in Central India, and the defeat of Hyder, the genius of Hastings laid the foundation of an Indian Empire

But while England triumphed in the East, the face of the war in America was changed by a terrible disaster. Foiled in an attempt on North Carolina by the refusal of his fellow general, Sir Henry Clinton, to assist him, Lord Cornwallis fell back in 1781 on Virginia, and entrenched himself in the lines of York Town. A sudden march of Washington brought him to the front of the English troops at a moment when the French fleet held the sea, and the army of Cornwallis was driven by famine to a surrender as humiliating as that of Saratoga. The news fell like a thunderbolt on the wretched Minister who had till now suppressed at his master's order his own conviction of the uselessness of further bloodshed. Opening his arms and pacing wildly up and down his room, Lord North exclaimed "It is all over," and resigned. England in fact seemed on the brink of ruin. In the crisis of the American struggle Ireland itself turned on her. A force of forty thousand volunteers had been raised in 1779 for the defence of the island against a French invasion. Threats of an armed revolt backed the eloquence of two Parliamentary leaders, Grattan and Flood, in their demand for the repeal of Poynings' Act and their assertion that, while Ireland and England were united under one Crown, no power was competent to make laws for Ireland save the Irish Parliament. The demands were in effect a claim for national independence; but there were no means of resisting them, for England was without a soldier to oppose the volunteers. The fall of Lord North recalled the Whigs under Lord Rockingham to office; and on Rockingham fell the double task of satisfying Ireland and of putting an end, at any cost, to the war with the United States. The task involved in both quarters a humiliating surrender; and it needed the bitter stress of

SEC. II.

THE INDE-
PENDENCE
OF AMERICA
1761
TO
1782

necessity to induce the Houses to follow his counsels. The English Parliament abandoned by a formal statute the judicial and legislative supremacy it had enacted a century before over the Parliament of Ireland ; and negotiations were begun with America and its allies. In the difficulties of England the hopes of her enemies rose high. Spain refused to suspend hostilities at any other price than the surrender of Gibraltar. France proposed that England should give up all her Indian conquests save Bengal. But the true basis of her world-power lay on the sea ; and at this moment the command of the seas again became her own. Admiral Rodney, the greatest of English seamen save Nelson and Blake, had in January, 1780, encountered the

Jan. 16,
1780

Spanish fleet off Cape St. Vincent, and only four of its vessels escaped to Cadiz. Two years later the triumphs of the French Admiral De Grasse called him to the West Indies, and in April 1782, a manœuvre which he was the first to introduce broke his opponent's line, and drove the French fleet shattered from the Atlantic. In September a last attack of the joint force gathered against Gibraltar was repulsed by the heroism of Elliott. Nor would America wait any longer for the

*Treaties of
peace*

satisfaction of her allies. In November her commissioners signed the preliminaries of a peace, in which Britain reserved to herself on the American continent only Canada and the island of Newfoundland, and acknowledged without reserve the independence of the United States. The treaty of peace with the United States was a prelude to treaties of peace with the Bourbon powers. France indeed won nothing in the treaties with which the war ended ; Spain gained only Florida and Minorca. England, on the other hand, had won ground in India ; she had retained Canada ; her West Indian islands were intact ; she had asserted her command of the seas. But at the close of the war there was less thought of what she had retained than of what she had lost. The American Colonies were irrecoverably gone. It is no wonder that in the first shock of such a loss England looked on herself as on the verge of ruin, or that the Bourbon Courts believed her position as a world-power to be practically at an end. How utterly groundless such a conception was the coming years were to show.

Section III.—The Second Pitt. 1783—1793.

[*Authorities*.— Mr. Massey's account of this period may be supplemented by Lord Stanhope's "Life of Pitt," Lord Russell's "Memoirs of Fox," and the Correspondence of Lord Malmesbury, Lord Auckland, and Mr. Rose. For the Slave Trade, see the Memoirs of Wilberforce by his sons. Burke may be studied in his Life by Macknight, in Mr. Morley's valuable essay on him, and above all in his own works. The state of foreign affairs in 1789 is best seen in Von Sybel's "History of the French Revolution."]

**England
and the
World**

That in the creation of the United States the world had reached one of the turning points in its history seems at the time to have

Sec. III.

The
Second
Pitt
1783
to
1793

entered into the thought of not a single European statesman. What startled men most at the moment was the discovery that England herself was far from being ruined by the greatness of her defeat. She rose from it indeed stronger and more vigorous than ever. Never had she shown a mightier energy than in the struggle against France which followed only ten years after her loss of America, nor did she ever stand higher among the nations than on the day of Waterloo. Her real greatness, however, lay not in the old world but in the new. She was from that hour a mother of nations. In America she had begotten a great people, and her emigrant ships were still to carry on the movement of the Teutonic race from which she herself had sprung. Her work was to be colonization. Her settlers were to dispute Africa with the Kaffir and the Hottentot; they were to build up in the waters of the Pacific colonies as great as those which she had lost in America. And to the nations that she founded she was to give not only her blood and her speech, but the freedom which she had won. It is the thought of this which flings its grandeur round the pettiest details of our story in the past. The history of France has little result beyond France itself. German or Italian history has no direct issue outside the bounds of Germany or Italy. But England is only a small part of the outcome of English history. Its greater issues lie not within the narrow limits of the mother island, but in the destinies of nations yet to be. The struggles of her patriots, the wisdom of her statesmen, the steady love of liberty and law in her people at large, were shaping in the past of our little island the future of mankind.

Meanwhile the rapid developement of industrial energy and industrial wealth in England itself was telling on the conditions of English statesmanship. Though the Tories and "King's friends" had now grown to a compact body of a hundred and fifty members, the Whigs, who held office under Lord Rockingham, were superior to their rivals in numbers and political character, now that the return of the Bedford section to the general body of the party during its steady opposition to the American war had restored much of its old cohesion. But this reunion only strengthened their aristocratic and exclusive tendencies, and widened the breach which was steadily opening on questions such as Parliamentary Reform, between the bulk of the Whig party and the small fragment which remained true to the more popular sympathies of Chatham. Lord Shelburne stood at the head of the Chatham party, and it was reinforced at this moment by the entry into Parliament of the second son of Chatham himself. William Pitt had hardly reached his twenty-second year; but he left college with the learning of a ripe scholar, and his ready and sonorous eloquence had been matured by his father's teaching. "He will be one of the first men in Parliament," said a member to the Whig leader, Charles Fox, after Pitt's first

SEC. III.

THE
SECOND
PITT

1783
TO
1793

speech in the House of Commons. "He is so already," replied Fox. The haughty self-esteem of the new statesman breathed in every movement of his tall, spare figure, in the hard lines of a countenance which none but his closer friends saw lighted by a smile, in his cold and repulsive address, his invariable gravity of demeanour, and his habitual air of command. How great the qualities were which lay beneath this haughty exterior no one knew; nor had any one guessed how soon this "boy," as his rivals mockingly styled him, was to crush every opponent and to hold England at his will. He refused any minor post in the Rockingham Administration, claiming, if he took office at all, to be at once admitted to the Cabinet. But Pitt had no desire to take office under Rockingham. To him as to Chatham the main lesson of the war was the need of putting an end to those abuses in the composition of Parliament by which George the Third had been enabled to plunge the country into it. A thorough reform of the House of Commons was the only effectual means of doing this, and Pitt brought forward a bill founded on his father's plans for that purpose. But the great bulk of the Whigs could not resolve on the sacrifice of property and influence which such a reform would involve. Pitt's bill was thrown out; and in its stead the Ministry endeavoured to weaken the means of corrupt influence which the King had unscrupulously used, by disqualifying persons holding government contracts from sitting in Parliament, by depriving revenue officers of the elective franchise (a measure which diminished the influence of the Crown in seventy boroughs), and above all by a bill for the reduction of the civil establishment, of the pension list, and of the secret service fund, which was brought in by Burke. These measures were to a great extent effectual in diminishing the influence of the Crown over Parliament, and they are memorable as marking the date when the direct bribery of members absolutely ceased. But they were absolutely inoperative in rendering the House of Commons really representative of or responsible to the people of England. The jealousy which the mass of the Whigs entertained of the Chatham section and its plans was more plainly shown on the death of Lord Rockingham in July. Shelburne was no sooner called to the head of the Ministry than Fox, who acted on personal grounds, and the bulk of Rockingham's followers resigned. Pitt on the other hand accepted office as Chancellor of the Exchequer.

The Shelburne Ministry only lasted long enough to conclude the final peace with the United States; for in the opening of 1783 it was overthrown by the most unscrupulous coalition known in our history, that of the Whig followers of Fox with the Tories who still clung to Lord North. Never had the need of representative reform been more clearly shown than by a coalition which proved how powerless was the force of public opinion to check even the most shameless faction in

Parliament, how completely the lessening of the royal influence by the measures of Burke and Rockingham had tended to the profit, not of the people, but of the borough-mongers who usurped its representation. Pitt's renewed proposal of Parliamentary Reform was rejected by a majority of two to one.   Secure in their Parliamentary majority, and heedless of the power of public opinion without the walls of the House of Commons, the new Ministers entered boldly on a greater task than had as yet taxed the constructive genius of English statesmen.   To leave such a dominion as Warren Hastings had built up in India to the control of a mere company of traders was clearly impossible; and Fox proposed to transfer the political government from the Directors of the Company to a board of seven Commissioners.   The appointment of the seven was vested in the first instance in Parliament, and afterwards in the Crown; their office was to be held for five years, but they were removeable on address from either House of Parliament.   The proposal was at once met with a storm of opposition.   The scheme indeed was an injudicious one; for the new Commissioners would have been destitute of that practical knowledge of India which belonged to the Company, while the want of any immediate link between them and the actual Ministry of the Crown would have prevented Parliament from exercising an effective control over their acts.   But the real faults of this India Bill were hardly noticed in the popular outcry against it. The merchant-class was galled by the blow levelled at the greatest merchant-body in the realm: corporations trembled at the cancelling of a charter; the King viewed the measure as a mere means of transferring the patronage of India to the Whigs.   With the nation at large the faults of the bill lay in the character of the Ministry which proposed it.   To give the rule and patronage of India over to the existing House of Commons was to give a new and immense power to a body which misused in the grossest way the power it possessed.   It was the sense of this popular feeling which encouraged the King to exert his personal influence to defeat the measure in the Lords, and on its defeat to order his Ministers to deliver up the seals.   In December 1783 Pitt accepted the post of First Lord of the Treasury; but his position would at once have been untenable had the country gone with its nominal representatives.   He was defeated again and again by large majorities in the Commons; but the majorities dwindled as a shower of addresses from every quarter, from the Tory University of Oxford as from the Whig Corporation of London, proved that public opinion went with the Minister and not with the House.   It was the general sense of this which justified Pitt in the firmness with which, in the teeth of addresses for his removal from office, he delayed the dissolution of Parliament for five months, and gained time for that ripening of national sentiment on which he counted for success. When the elections of 1784 came the struggle was at once at an end.

SEC. III.

THE
SECOND
PITT

1783
TO
1793
**William
Pitt**

The public feeling had become strong enough to break through the corrupt influences which commonly governed its representation. Every great constituency returned supporters to Pitt; of the majority which had defeated him in the Commons a hundred and sixty members were unseated; and only a fragment of the Whig party was saved by its command of nomination boroughs.

When Parliament came together after the overthrow of the Coalition, the Minister of twenty-five was master of England as no Minister had been before. Even the King yielded to his sway, partly through gratitude for the triumph he had won for him over the Whigs, partly from a sense of the madness which was soon to strike him down, but still more from a gradual discovery that the triumph which he had won over his political rivals had been won, not to the profit of the crown, but of the nation at large. The Whigs, it was true, were broken, unpopular, and without a policy, while the Tories clung to the Minister who had "saved the King." But it was the support of a new political power that really gave his strength to the young Minister. The sudden rise of English industry was pushing the manufacturer to the front; and all that the trading classes loved in Chatham, his nobleness of temper, his consciousness of power, his patriotism, his sympathy with a wider world than the world within the Parliament-house, they saw in his son. He had little indeed of the poetic and imaginative side of Chatham's genius, of his quick perception of what was just and what was possible, his far-reaching conceptions of national policy, his outlook into the future of the world. Pitt's flowing and sonorous commonplaces rang hollow beside the broken phrases which still make his father's eloquence a living thing to Englishmen. On the other hand he possessed some qualities in which Chatham was utterly wanting. His temper, though naturally ardent and sensitive, had been schooled in a proud self-command. His simplicity and good taste freed him from his father's ostentation and extravagance. Diffuse and commonplace as his speeches seem, they were adapted as much by their very qualities of diffuseness and commonplace as by their lucidity and good sense to the intelligence of the middle classes whom Pitt felt to be his real audience. In his love of peace, his immense industry, his despatch of business, his skill in debate, his knowledge of finance, he recalled Sir Robert Walpole; but he had virtues which Walpole never possessed, and he was free from Walpole's worst defects. He was careless of personal gain. He was too proud to rule by corruption. His lofty self-esteem left no room for any jealousy of subordinates. He was generous in his appreciation of youthful merits; and the "boys" he gathered round him, such as Canning and Lord Wellesley, rewarded his generosity by a devotion which death left untouched. With Walpole's cynical inaction Pitt had no sympathy whatever. His

SEC. III.

THE
SECOND
PITT

1783
TO
1793

policy from the first was one of active reform, and he faced every one of the problems, financial, constitutional, religious, from which Walpole had shrunk. Above all he had none of Walpole's scorn of his fellow-men. The noblest feature in his mind was its wide humanity. His love for England was as deep and personal as his father's love, but of the sympathy with English passion and English prejudice which had been at once his father's weakness and strength he had not a trace. When Fox taunted him with forgetting Chatham's jealousy of France and his faith that she was the natural foe of England, Pitt answered nobly that "to suppose any nation can be unalterably the enemy of another is weak and childish." The temper of the time and the larger sympathy of man with man, which especially marks the eighteenth century as a turning-point in the history of the human race, was everywhere bringing to the front a new order of statesmen, such as Turgot and Joseph the Second, whose characteristics were a love of mankind, and a belief that as the happiness of the individual· can only be secured by the general happiness of the community to which he belongs, so the welfare of individual nations can only be secured by the general welfare of the world. Of these Pitt was one. But he rose high above the rest in the consummate knowledge, and the practical force which he brought to the realization of his aims.

Pitt's strength lay in finance ; and he came forward at a time when the growth of English wealth made a knowledge of finance essential to a great minister. The progress of the nation was wonderful. Population more than doubled during the eighteenth century, and the advance of wealth was even greater than that of population. The war had added a hundred millions to the national debt, but the burden was hardly felt. The loss of America only increased the commerce with that country ; and industry had begun that great career which was to make Britain the workshop of the world. Though England already stood in the first rank of commercial states at the accession of George the Third, her industrial life at home was mainly agricultural. The wool-trade had gradually established itself in Norfolk, the West Riding of Yorkshire, and the counties of the south-west ; while the manufacture of cotton was still almost limited to Manchester and Bolton, and remained so unimportant that in the middle of the eighteenth century the export of cotton goods hardly reached the value of fifty thousand a year. There was the same slow and steady progress in the linen trade of Belfast and Dundee, and the silks of Spitalfields. The processes of manufacture were too rude to allow any large increase of production. It was only where a stream gave force to turn a mill-wheel that the wool-worker could establish his factory ; and cotton was as yet spun by hand in the cottages, the " spinsters " of the family sitting with their distaffs round the weaver's handloom. But had the processes of manufacture been more efficient, they would have been ren-

**English
Industry**

*Manufac-
tures*

*Roads and
canals*

SEC. III.

THE
SECOND
PITT

1783
TO
1793

dered useless by the want of a cheap and easy means of transport.
The older main roads, which had lasted fairly through the middle
ages, had broken down in later times before the growth of traffic
and the increase of wagons and carriages. The new lines of trade
lay often along mere country lanes which had never been more than
horse-tracks. Much of the woollen trade therefore had to be carried
on by means of long trains of pack-horses; and in the case of yet
heavier goods, such as coal, distribution was almost impracticable,
save along the greater rivers or in districts accessible from the sea.
A new æra began when the engineering genius of Brindley joined
Manchester with its port of Liverpool in 1767 by a canal which
crossed the Irwell on a lofty aqueduct; the success of the experiment
soon led to the universal introduction of water-carriage, and Great
Britain was traversed in every direction by three thousand miles
of navigable canals. At the same time a new importance was

Coal and Iron

given to the coal which lay beneath the soil of England. The
stores of iron which had lain side by side with it in the northern
counties had lain there unworked through the scarcity of wood,
which was looked upon as the only fuel by which it could be smelted.
In the middle of the eighteenth century a process for smelting iron
with coal turned out to be effective; and the whole aspect of the
iron-trade was at once revolutionized. Iron was to become the
working material of the modern world; and it is its production of
iron which more than all else has placed England at the head of
industrial Europe. The value of coal as a means of producing
mechanical force was revealed in the discovery by which Watt in

The Steam-Engine

1765 transformed the Steam-Engine from a mere toy into the most
wonderful instrument which human industry has ever had at its
command. The invention came at a moment when the existing
supply of manual labour could no longer cope with the demands of
the manufacturers. Three successive inventions in twelve years, that
of the spinning-jenny in 1764 by the weaver Hargreaves, of the
spinning-machine in 1768 by the barber Arkwright, of the "mule" by
the weaver Crompton in 1776, were followed by the discovery of the
power-loom. But these would have been comparatively useless had it
not been for the revelation of a new and inexhaustible labour-force in
the steam-engine. It was the combination of such a force with such
means of applying it that enabled Britain during the terrible years of
her struggle with France and Napoleon to all but monopolize the
woollen and cotton trades, and raised her into the greatest manufacturing country that the world had seen.

Adam Smith

    To deal wisely with such a growth required a knowledge of the
laws of wealth which would have been impossible at an earlier time.
But it had become possible in the days of Pitt. If books are to be
measured by the effect which they have produced on the fortunes of

Sec. III.

The
Second
Pitt

1783
to
1793

mankind, the "Wealth of Nations" must rank among the greatest of books. Its author was Adam Smith, an Oxford scholar and a professor at Glasgow. Labour, he contended, was the one source of wealth, and it was by freedom of labour, by suffering the worker to pursue his own interest in his own way, that the public wealth would best be promoted. Any attempt to force labour into artificial channels, to shape by laws the course of commerce, to promote special branches of industry in particular countries, or to fix the character of the intercourse between one country and another, is not only a wrong to the worker or the merchant, but actually hurtful to the wealth of a state. The book was published in 1776, at the opening of the American war, and studied by Pitt during his career as an undergraduate at Cambridge. From that time he owned Adam Smith for his master. He had hardly become Minister before he took the principles of the "Wealth of Nations" as the groundwork of his policy. The ten earlier years of his rule marked a new point of departure in English statesmanship. Pitt was the first English Minister who really grasped the part which industry was to play in promoting the welfare of the world. He was not only a peace Minister and a financier, as Walpole had been, but a statesman who saw that the best security for peace lay in the freedom and widening of commercial intercourse between nations; that public economy not only lessened the general burdens but left additional capital in the hands of industry; and that finance might be turned from a mere means of raising revenue into a powerful engine of political and social improvement.

That little was done by Pitt himself to carry these principles into effect was partly owing to the mass of ignorance and prejudice with which he had to contend, and still more to the sudden break of his plans through the French Revolution. His power rested above all on the trading classes, and these were still persuaded that wealth meant gold and silver, and that commerce was best furthered by jealous monopolies. It was only by patience and dexterity that the mob of merchants and country squires who backed him in the House of Commons could be brought to acquiesce in the changes he proposed. How small his power was when it struggled with the prejudices around him was seen in the failure of the first great measure he brought forward. The question of parliamentary reform which had been mooted during the American war had been steadily coming to the front. Chatham had advocated an increase of county members, who were then the most independent part of the Lower House. The Duke of Richmond talked of universal suffrage, equal electoral districts, and annual Parliaments. Wilkes anticipated the Reform Bill of a later time by proposing to disfranchise the rotten boroughs, and to give members in their stead to the counties and to the more populous and wealthy towns. William Pitt had made the question his own by

SEC. III.

THE
SECOND
PITT

1783
TO
1793

bringing forward a motion for reform on his first entry into the House, and one of his first measures as Minister was to bring in a bill in 1785 which, while providing for the gradual extinction of all decayed boroughs, disfranchised thirty-six at once, and transferred their members to counties. He brought the King to abstain from opposition, and strove to buy off the borough-mongers, as the holders of rotten boroughs were called, by offering to compensate them for the seats they lost at their market value. But the bulk of his own party joined the bulk of the Whigs in a steady resistance to the bill. The more glaring abuses, indeed, within Parliament itself, the abuses which stirred Chatham and Wilkes to action, had in great part disappeared. The bribery of members had ceased. Burke's Bill of Economical Reform had just dealt a fatal blow at the influence which the King exercised by suppressing a host of useless offices, household appointments, judicial and diplomatic charges, which were maintained for the purposes of corruption. Above all, the recent triumph of public opinion to which Pitt owed his power had done much to diminish the sense of any real danger from the opposition which Parliament had shown till now to the voice of the nation. "Terribly disappointed and beat" as Wilberforce tells us Pitt was by the rejection of his measure, the temper of the House and of the people was too plain to be mistaken, and though his opinion remained unaltered, he never brought it forward again.

**Pitt's
Finance**

The failure of his constitutional reform was more than compensated by the triumphs of his finance. When he entered office public credit was at its lowest ebb. The debt had been doubled by the American war, yet large sums still remained unfunded, while the revenue was reduced by a vast system of smuggling which turned every coast-town into a nest of robbers. The deficiency was met for the moment by new taxes, but the time which was thus gained served to change the whole face of public affairs. The first of Pitt's financial measures —his plan for gradually paying off the debt by a sinking fund—was undoubtedly an error; but it had a happy effect in restoring public confidence. He met the smuggler by a reduction of Custom-duties which made his trade unprofitable. He revived Walpole's plan of an Excise. Meanwhile the public expenses were reduced, and commission after commission was appointed to introduce economy into every department of the public service. The rapid developement of the national industry which we have already noted no doubt aided the success of these measures. Credit was restored. The smuggling trade was greatly reduced. In two years there was a surplus of a million, and though duty after duty was removed the revenue rose steadily with every remission of taxation. Meanwhile Pitt was showing the political value of the new finance in a wider field. Ireland, then as now, was England's difficulty. The tyrannous misgovernment under

Sec. III.

The
Second
Pitt
1783
to
1793

which she had groaned ever since the battle of the Boyne was producing its natural fruit in universal discontent. All alike suffered from a plundered treasury, a ruined trade, a corrupted Parliament ; and so threatening had the attitude of the Protestant party which ruled it become during the American war that they had forced the English Parliament to relinquish its control over their Parliament in Dublin. Pitt saw that much at least of the misery and disloyalty of Ireland sprang from its poverty. The population had grown rapidly while culture remained stationary and commerce perished. And of this poverty much was the direct result of unjust law. Ireland was a grazing country, but to protect the interests of English graziers the import of its cattle into England was forbidden. To protect the interests of English clothiers and weavers, its manufactures were loaded with duties. To redress this wrong was the first financial effort of Pitt, and the bill which he introduced in 1785 did away with every obstacle to freedom of trade between England and Ireland. It was a measure which, as he held, would "draw what remained of the shattered empire together," and repair in part the loss of America by creating a loyal and prosperous Ireland ; and struggling almost alone in face of a fierce opposition from the Whigs and the Manchester merchants, he dragged it through the English Parliament, only to see amendments forced into it which ensured its rejection by the Irish Parliament. But the defeat only spurred him to a greater effort elsewhere. France had been looked upon as England's natural enemy ; but in 1787 he concluded a Treaty of Commerce with France which enabled the subjects of both countries to reside and travel in either without license or passport, did away with all prohibition of trade on either side, and reduced every import duty.

India owes to Pitt's triumph a form of government which remained unchanged to our own day. The India Bill which he carried in 1784 preserved in appearance the political and commercial powers of the Directors, while establishing a Board of Control, formed from members of the Privy Council, for the approval or annulling of their acts. Practically, however, the powers of the Board of Directors were absorbed by a secret committee of three elected members of that body, to whom all the more important administrative functions had been reserved by the bill, while those of the Board of Control were virtually exercised by its President. As the President was in effect a new Secretary of State for the Indian Department, and became an important member of each Ministry, responsible like his fellow-members for his action to Parliament, the administration of India was thus made a part of the general system of the English Government ; while the secret committee supplied the experience of Indian affairs in which the Minister might be deficient. Meanwhile the new temper that was growing up in the English people told on the attitude of England towards its great depend-

SEC. III.

THE
SECOND
PITT
1783
TO
1793
1786

ency. Discussions over rival plans of Indian administration diffused a sense of national responsibility for its good government, and there was a general resolve that the security against injustice and misrule which was enjoyed by the poorest Englishman should be enjoyed by the poorest Hindoo. This resolve expressed itself in the trial of Warren Hastings. Hastings returned from India at the close of the war with the hope of rewards as great as those of Clive. He had saved all that Clive had won. He had laid the foundation of a vast empire in the East. He had shown rare powers of administration, and the foresight, courage, and temperance which mark the born ruler of men. But the wisdom and glory of his rule could not hide its terrible ruthlessness. He was charged with having sold for a vast sum the services of British troops to crush the free tribes of the Rohillas, with having wrung half a million by extortion from the Rajah of Benares, with having extorted by torture and starvation more than a million from the Princesses of Oudh. He was accused of having kept his hold upon power by measures as unscrupulous, and with having murdered a native who opposed him by an abuse of the forms of English law. On almost all these charges the cooler judgement of later enquirers has acquitted Warren Hastings of guilt. Personally there can be little doubt that he had done much to secure to the new subjects of Britain a just and peaceable government. What was hardest and most pitiless in his rule had been simply a carrying out of the system of administration which was native to India and which he found existing there. But such a system was alien from the new humanity of Englishmen ; and few dared to vindicate Hastings when Burke in words of passionate earnestness moved for his impeachment. The great trial lingered on for years, and in the long run Hastings secured an acquittal. But the end at which the impeachment aimed had really been won. The attention, the sympathy of Englishmen had been drawn across distant seas to a race utterly strange to them ; and the peasant of Cornwall or Cumberland had learned how to thrill at the suffering of a peasant of Bengal.

The Slave Trade

Even while the trial was going on a yet wider extension of English sympathy made itself felt. In the year which followed the adoption of free trade with France the new philanthropy allied itself with the religious movement created by the Wesleys in an attack on the Slave Trade. One of the profits which England bought by the triumphs of Marlborough was a right to a monopoly of the slave trade between Africa and the Spanish dominions ; and it was England that had planted slavery in her American colonies and her West Indian islands. But the horrors and iniquity of the trade, the ruin and degradation of Africa which it brought about, the oppression of the negro himself, were now felt widely and deeply. "After a conversation in the open air at the root of an old tree, just above the steep descent

Sec. III.

The
Second
Pitt

1783
to
1793

into the Vale of Keston," with the younger Pitt, his friend, William Wilberforce, whose position as a representative of the evangelical party gave weight to his advocacy of such a cause, resolved in 1788 to bring in a bill for the abolition of the slave trade. But the bill fell before the opposition of the Liverpool slave merchants and the general indifference of the House of Commons. The spirit of humanity which breathed through Pitt's policy had indeed to wrestle with difficulties at home and abroad ; and his efforts to sap the enmity of nation against nation by a freer intercourse encountered a foe even more fatal than English prejudice, in the very movement of which his measures formed a part. Across the Channel this movement was growing into a revolution which was to change the face of the world.

So far as England was concerned the Puritan resistance of the seventeenth century had in the end succeeded in checking the general tendency of the time to religious and political despotism. Since the Revolution of 1688 freedom of conscience and the people's right to govern itself through its representatives in Parliament had been practically established. Social equality had begun long before. Every man from the highest to the lowest was subject to, and protected by, the same law. The English aristocracy, though exercising a powerful influence on government, were possessed of few social privileges, and prevented from forming a separate class in the nation by the legal and social tradition which counted all save the eldest son of a noble house as commoners. No impassable line parted the gentry from the commercial classes, and these again possessed no privileges which could part them from the lower classes of the community. Public opinion, the general sense of educated Englishmen, had established itself after a short struggle as the dominant element in English government. But in all the other great states of Europe the wars of religion had left only the name of freedom. Government tended to a pure despotism. Privilege was supreme in religion, in politics, in society. Society itself rested on a rigid division of classes from one another, which refused to the people at large any equal rights of justice or of industry. We have already seen how alien such a conception of national life was from the ideas which the wide diffusion of intelligence during the eighteenth century was spreading throughout Europe ; and in almost every country some enlightened rulers endeavoured by administrative reforms in some sort to satisfy the sense of wrong which was felt around them. The attempts of sovereigns like Frederick the Great in Prussia, and Joseph the Second in Austria and the Netherlands, were rivalled by the efforts of statesmen such as Turgot in France. It was in France indeed that the contrast between the actual state of society and the new ideas of public right was felt most keenly. Nowhere had the victory of the Crown been more complete. The aristocracy had been robbed of all share in public affairs ; it enjoyed social privileges and exemption from any

SEC. III.

THE
SECOND
PITT

1783
TO
1793

**State of
France**

contribution to the public burdens, without that sense of public duty which a governing class to some degree always possesses. Guilds and monopolies fettered the industry of the trader and the merchant, and cut them off from the working classes, as the value attached to noble blood cut off both from the aristocracy.

If its political position indeed were compared with that of most of the countries round it, France stood high. Its government was less oppressive, its general wealth was larger and more evenly diffused, there was a better administration of justice, and greater security for public order. Poor as its peasantry seemed to English eyes, they were far above the peasants of Germany or Spain. Its middle class was the quickest and most intelligent in Europe. Under Lewis the Fifteenth opinion was practically free ; and a literary class had sprung up which devoted itself with wonderful brilliancy and activity to popularizing the ideas of social and political justice which it learned from English writers, and in the case of Montesquieu and Voltaire from personal contact with English life. The moral conceptions of the time, its love of mankind, its sense of human brotherhood, its hatred of oppression, its pity for the guilty and the poor, its longing after a higher and nobler standard of life and action, were expressed by a crowd of writers, and above all by Rousseau, with a fire and eloquence which carried them to the heart of the people. But this new force of intelligence only jostled roughly with the social forms with which it found itself in contact. The philosopher denounced the tyranny of the priesthood. The peasant grumbled at the lord's right to judge him in his courts and to exact feudal services from him. The merchant was galled by the trading restrictions and the heavy taxation. The country gentry rebelled against their exclusion from public life and from the government of the country. Its powerlessness to bring about any change at home turned all this new energy into sympathy with a struggle against tyranny abroad. Public opinion forced France to ally itself with America in its contest for liberty, and French volunteers under the Marquis de Lafayette joined Washington's army. But while the American war spread more widely throughout the nation the craving for freedom, it brought on the Government financial embarrassment from which it could only free itself by an appeal to the country at large. Lewis the Sixteenth resolved to summon the States-General, which had not met since the time of Richelieu, and to appeal to the nobles to waive their immunity from taxation. His resolve at once stirred into vigorous life every impulse and desire which had been seething in the minds of the people ; and the States-General no sooner met at Versailles in May 1789 than the fabric of depotism and privilege began to crumble. A rising in Paris destroyed the Bastille, and the capture of this fortress was taken for the sign of a new æra of constitutional freedom in France and through Europe. Even in England men

Sec. III.

The
Second
Pitt

1783
to
1793
**Pitt and
Russia**

thrilled with a strange joy at the tidings of its fall. "How much is this the greatest event that ever happened in the world," Fox cried with a burst of enthusiasm, "and how much the best!"

Pitt regarded the approach of France to sentiments of liberty which had long been familiar to England with greater coolness, but with no distrust. For the moment indeed his attention was distracted by an attack of madness which visited the King in 1788, and by the claim of a right to the Regency which was at once advanced by the Prince of Wales. The Prince belonged to the Whig party; and Fox, who was travelling in Italy, hurried home to support his claim, in full belief that the Prince's Regency would be followed by his own return to power. Pitt successfully resisted it on the constitutional ground that in such a case the right to choose a temporary regent, under what limitations it would, lay with Parliament; and a bill which conferred the Regency on the Prince, in accordance with this view, was already passing the Houses when the recovery of the King put an end to the long dispute. Foreign difficulties, too, absorbed Pitt's attention. Russia had risen into greatness under Catharine the Second; and Catharine had re-solved from the first on the annexation of Poland, the expulsion of the Turks from Europe, and the setting up of a Russian throne at Con-stantinople. In her first aim she was baffled for the moment by Frederick the Great. She had already made herself virtually mistress of the whole of Poland, her armies occupied the kingdom, and she had seated a nominee of her own on its throne, when Frederick in union with the Emperor Joseph the Second forced her to admit Germany to a share of the spoil. If the Polish partition of 1773 brought the Russian frontier westward to the upper waters of the Dwina and the Dnieper, it gave Galicia to Maria Theresa, and West Prussia to Frederick himself. Foiled in her first aim, she waited for the realiza-tion of her second till the alliance between the two German powers was at an end through the resistance of Prussia to Joseph's schemes for the annexation of Bavaria, and till the death of Frederick removed her most watchful foe. Then in 1788 Joseph and the Empress joined hands for a partition of the Turkish Empire. But Prussia was still watchful, and England was no longer fettered as in 1773 by troubles with America. The friendship established by Chatham between the two countries, which had been suspended by Bute's treachery and all but destroyed during the Northern League of Neutral Powers, had been restored by Pitt through his co-operation with Frederick's suc-cessor in the restoration of the Dutch Statholderate. Its political weight was now seen in an alliance of England, Prussia, and Holland in 1789 for the preservation of the Turkish Empire. A great European struggle seemed at hand; and in such a struggle the sympathy and aid of France was of the highest importance. But with the treaty the danger passed away. In the spring of 1790 Joseph died broken-

SEC. III.

THE
SECOND
PITT

1783
TO
1793
Pitt and
France

hearted at the failure of his plans and the revolt of the Netherlands against his innovations; and Austria practically withdrew from the war with the Turks.

Meanwhile in France things moved fast. By breaking down the division between its separate orders the States-General became a National Assembly, which abolished the privileges of the provincial parliaments, of the nobles, and the Church. In October the mob of Paris marched on Versailles and forced the King to return with them to the capital; and a Constitution hastily put together was accepted by Lewis the Sixteenth in the stead of his old despotic power. To Pitt the tumult and disorder with which these great changes were wrought seemed transient matters. In January 1790 he still believed that " the present convulsions in France must sooner or later culminate in general harmony and regular order," and that when her own freedom was established, " France would stand forth as one of the most brilliant powers of Europe." But the coolness and good-will with which Pitt looked on the Revolution was far from being universal in the nation at large. The cautious good sense of the bulk of Englishmen, their love of order and law, their distaste for violent changes and for abstract theories, as well as their reverence for the past, were fast rousing throughout the country a dislike of the revolutionary changes which were hurrying on across the Channel; and both the political sense and the political prejudice of the nation were being fired by the warnings of Edmund Burke. The fall of the Bastille, though it kindled enthusiasm in Fox, roused in Burke only distrust. " Whenever a separation is made between liberty and justice," he wrote a few weeks later, " neither is safe." The night of the fourth of August, when the privileges of every class were abolished, filled him with horror. He saw, and rightly saw, in it the critical moment which revealed the character of the Revolution, and his part was taken at once. " The French," he cried in January, while Pitt was foretelling a glorious future for the new Constitution, " the French have shown themselves the ablest architects of ruin who have hitherto existed in the world. In a short space of time they have pulled to the ground their army, their navy, their commerce, their arts and their manufactures." But in Parliament Burke stood alone. The Whigs, though distrustfully, followed Fox in his applause of the Revolution. The Tories, yet more distrustfully, followed Pitt; and Pitt warmly expressed his sympathy with the constitutional government which was ruling France. At this moment indeed the revolutionary party gave a signal proof of its friendship for England. Irritated by an English settlement at Nootka Sound in California, Spain appealed to France for aid in accordance with the Family Compact: and the French Ministry, with a party at its back which believed things had gone far enough, resolved on a war as the best means of checking the progress of the Revolution and restoring the power of the Crown. The revolutionary party naturally opposed this design; after a bitter struggle the right of declaring war, save with the sanction of the Assembly, was taken from the King; and all danger of hostilities passed away. "The French Government," Pitt asserted, "was bent on cultivating the most unbounded friendship for Great Britain," and he saw no reason in its revolutionary changes why Britain should not return the friendship of France. He was convinced that nothing but the joint action of France and England would in the end arrest the troubles of Eastern Europe. His intervention foiled for the moment a fresh effort of Prussia to rob Poland of Dantzig and Thorn. But though Russia was still pressing Turkey hard, a Russian war was so unpopular in England that a hostile vote in Parliament forced Pitt to discontinue his armaments; and a fresh union of Austria and Prussia, which promised at this juncture to bring about a close of the Turkish struggle, promised also a fresh attack on the independence of Poland.

SEC. III.

THE
SECOND
PITT
1783
TO
1793

But while Pitt was pleading for friendship between the two countries, Burke was resolved to make friendship impossible. He had long ceased, indeed, to have any hold over the House of Commons. The eloquence which had vied with that of Chatham during the discussions on the Stamp Act had become distasteful to the bulk of its members. The length of his speeches, the profound and philosophical character of his argument, the splendour and often the extravagance of his illustrations, his passionate earnestness, his want of temper and discretion, wearied and perplexed the squires and merchants about him. He was known at last as "the dinner-bell of the House," so rapidly did its benches thin at his rising. For a time his energies found scope in the impeachment of Hastings; and the grandeur of his appeals to the justice of England hushed detraction. But with the close of the impeachment his repute had again fallen; and the approach of old age, for he was now past sixty, seemed to counsel retirement from an assembly where he stood unpopular and alone. But age and disappointment and loneliness were all forgotten as Burke saw rising across the Channel the embodiment of all that he hated—a Revolution founded on scorn of the past, and threatening with ruin the whole social fabric which the past had reared; the ordered structure of classes and ranks crumbling before a doctrine of social equality; a State rudely demolished and reconstituted; a Church and a Nobility swept away in a night. Against the enthusiasm of what he rightly saw to be a new political religion he resolved to rouse the enthusiasm of the old. He was at once a great orator and a great writer; and now that the House was deaf to his voice, he appealed to the country by his pen. The "Reflections on the French Revolution" which he published in October 1790 not only denounced the acts of rashness and violence which sullied the great change that France had wrought, but the very

Sec. III.

The
Second
Pitt
1783
to
1793

principles from which the change had sprung. Burke's deep sense of the need of social order, of the value of that continuity in human affairs "without which men would become like flies in a summer," blinded him to all but the faith in mere rebellion, and the yet sillier faith in mere novelty, which disguised a real nobleness of aim and temper even in the most ardent of the revolutionists. He would see no abuses in the past, now that it had fallen, or anything but the ruin of society in the future. He preached a crusade against men whom he regarded as the foes of religion and civilization, and called on the armies of Europe to put down a Revolution whose principles threatened every state with destruction.

Pitt and the Re-volution

The great obstacle to such a crusade was Pitt: and one of the grandest outbursts of the "Reflections" closed with a bitter taunt at the Minister's policy. "The age of chivalry," Burke cried, "is gone; that of sophisters, economists, and calculators has succeeded, and the glory of Europe is extinguished for ever." But neither taunt nor invective moved Pitt from his course. At the moment when the "Reflections" appeared he gave a fresh assurance to France of his resolve to have nothing to do with any crusade against the Revolution. "This country," he wrote, "means to persevere in the neutrality hitherto scrupulously observed with respect to the internal dissensions of France; and from which it will never depart unless the conduct held there makes it indispensable as an act of self-defence." So far indeed was he from sharing the reactionary panic which was spreading around him that he chose this time for supporting Fox in his Libel Act, a measure which, by transferring the decision on what was libellous in any publication from the judge to the jury, completed the freedom of the press; and himself passed a Bill which, though little noticed among the storms of the time, was one of the noblest of his achieve-

Constitution given to Canada
1791

ments. He boldly put aside the dread which had been roused by the American war, that the gift of self-government to our colonies would serve only as a step towards their secession from the mother-country, and established a House of Assembly and a Council in the two Canadas. "I am convinced," said Fox (who, however, differed from Pitt as to the nature of the Constitution to be given to Canada), "that the only method of retaining distant colonies with advantage is to enable them to govern themselves;" and the policy of the one statesman and the foresight of the other have been justified by the later history of our dependencies. Nor had Burke better success with his own party. Fox remained an ardent lover of the Revolution, and answered a fresh attack of Burke upon it with more than usual warmth. A close affection had bound till now the two men together; but the fanaticism of Burke declared it at an end. "There is no loss of friendship," Fox exclaimed, with a sudden burst of tears. "There is!" Burke repeated. "I know the price of my conduct. Our friendship is at an end."

SEC. III.

THE
SECOND
PITT

1783
TO
1793

*Burke's
success with
the country*

Within the walls of Parliament, Burke stood utterly alone. His "Appeal from the New to the Old Whigs," in June 1791, failed to detach a follower from Fox. Pitt coldly counselled him rather to praise the English Constitution than to rail at the French. "I have made many enemies and few friends," Burke wrote sadly to the French princes who had fled from their country and were gathering in arms at Coblentz, "by the part I have taken." But the opinion of the people was slowly drifting to his side. A sale of thirty thousand copies showed that the "Reflections" echoed the general sentiment of Englishmen. The mood of England indeed at this moment was unfavourable to any fair appreciation of the Revolution across the Channel. Her temper was above all industrial. Men who were working hard and fast growing rich, who had the narrow and practical turn of men of business, looked angrily at this sudden disturbance of order, this restless and vague activity, these rhetorical appeals to human feeling, these abstract and often empty theories. In England it was a time of political content and social well-being, of steady economic progress, and of a powerful religious revival; and an insular lack of imaginative interest in other races hindered men from seeing that every element of this content, of this order, of this peaceful and harmonious progress, of this reconciliation of society and religion, was wanting abroad. The sympathy which the Revolution had roused at first among Englishmen died away before the violence of its legislative changes, and the growing anarchy of the country. Sympathy in fact was soon limited to a few groups of reformers who gathered in "Constitutional Clubs," and whose reckless language quickened the national reaction. But in spite of Burke's appeals and the cries of the nobles who had fled from France and longed only to march against their country, Europe held back from war, and Pitt preserved his attitude of neutrality, though with a greater appearance of reserve.

So anxious, in fact, did the aspect of affairs in the East make Pitt for the restoration of tranquillity in France, that he foiled a plan which its emigrant nobles had formed for a descent on the French coast, and declared formally at Vienna that England would remain absolutely neutral should hostilities arise between France and the Emperor. But the Emperor was as anxious to avoid a French war as Pitt himself. Though Catharine, now her strife with Turkey was over, wished to plunge the two German Powers into a struggle with the Revolution which would leave her free to annex Poland single-handed, neither Leopold nor Prussia would tie their hands by such a contest. The flight of Lewis the Sixteenth from Paris in June 1791 brought Europe for a moment to the verge of war; but he was intercepted and brought back; and for a while the danger seemed to incline the revolutionists in France to greater moderation. Lewis too not only accepted the Constitution, but pleaded earnestly with the Emperor against any armed

SEC. III.

THE
SECOND
PITT
1783
TO
1793
*Coalition
against
France*

intervention as certain to bring ruin to his throne. In their conference at Pillnitz therefore, in August, Leopold and the King of Prussia contented themselves with a vague declaration inviting the European powers to co-operate in restoring a sound form of government in France, availed themselves of England's neutrality to refuse all military aid to the French princes, and dealt simply with the affairs of Poland. But the peace they desired soon became impossible. The Constitutional Royalists in France availed themselves of the irritation caused by the Declaration of Pillnitz to rouse again the cry for a war which, as they hoped, would give strength to the throne. The more violent revolutionists, or Jacobins, on the other hand, under the influence of the "Girondists," or deputies from the south of France, whose aim was a republic, and who saw in a great national struggle a means of overthrowing the monarchy, decided in spite of the opposition of their leader, Robespierre, on a contest with the Emperor. Both parties united to demand the breaking up of an army which the emigrant princes had formed on the Rhine; and though Leopold assented to this demand, France declared war against his successor, Francis, in April 1792.

Misled by their belief in a revolutionary enthusiasm in England, the French had hoped for her alliance in this war; and they were astonished and indignant at Pitt's resolve to stand apart from the struggle. It was in vain that Pitt strove to allay this irritation by demanding only that Holland should remain untouched, and promising neutrality even though Belgium should be occupied by a French army, or that he strengthened these pledges by a reduction of military forces, and by bringing forward a peace-budget which rested on a large

remission of taxation. The revolutionists still clung to the hope of England's aid in the emancipation of Europe, but they came now to believe that England must itself be emancipated before such an aid could be given. Their first work therefore they held to be the bringing about a revolution in England which might free the people from the aristocracy which held it down, and which oppressed, as they believed, great peoples beyond the bounds of England itself. To rouse India, to rouse Ireland to a struggle which should shake off the English yoke, became necessary steps to the establishment of freedom in England. From this moment therefore French agents were busy "sowing the revolution" in each quarter. In Ireland they entered into communication with the United Irishmen. In India they appeared at the courts of the native princes. In England itself they strove through the Constitutional Clubs to rouse the same spirit which they had roused in France; and the French envoy, Chauvelin, protested warmly against a proclamation which denounced this correspondence as seditious. The effect of these revolutionary efforts on the friends of the Revolution was seen in a declaration which they wrested from Fox, that at such a moment even the discussion of parliamentary reform was inexpedient. Meanwhile Burke was working hard, in writings whose extravagance of style was forgotten in their intensity of feeling, to spread alarm throughout Europe. He had from the first encouraged the emigrant princes to take arms, and sent his son to join them at Coblentz. " Be alarmists," he wrote to them ; " diffuse terror ! " But the royalist terror which he sowed had roused a revolutionary terror in France itself. At the threat of war against the Emperor the two German Courts had drawn together, and reluctantly abandoning all hope of peace with France, gathered eighty thousand men under the Duke of Brunswick, and advanced slowly in August on the Meuse. France, though she had forced on the struggle, was really almost defenceless ; her forces in Belgium broke at the first shock of arms into shameful rout ; and the panic spreading from the army to the nation at large, took violent and horrible forms. At the first news of Brunswick's advance the mob of Paris broke into the Tuileries on the 10th of August ; and at its demand Lewis, who had taken refuge in the Assembly, was suspended from his office and imprisoned in the Temple. In September, while General Dumouriez by boldness and adroit negotiations arrested the progress of the allies in the defiles of the Argonne, bodies of paid murderers butchered the royalist prisoners who crowded the gaols of Paris, with a view of influencing the elections to a new Convention which met to proclaim the abolition of royalty. The retreat of the Prussian army, whose numbers had been reduced by disease till an advance on Paris became impossible, and a brilliant victory won by Dumouriez at Jemappes which laid the Netherlands at his feet, turned the panic of the French into a wild self-confidence. In November the Convention decreed that France offered the aid of her soldiers to all nations who would strive for freedom. " All Governments are our enemies," said its President ; " all peoples are our allies." In the teeth of treaties signed only two years before, and of the stipulation made by England when it pledged itself to neutrality, the French Government resolved to attack Holland, and ordered its generals to enforce by arms the opening of the Scheldt.

To do this was to force England into war. Public opinion was pressing harder day by day upon Pitt. The horror of the massacres of September, the hideous despotism of the Parisian mob, had done more to estrange England from the Revolution than all the eloquence of Burke. But even while withdrawing our Minister from Paris on the imprisonment of the King, Pitt clung stubbornly to the hope of peace. His hope was to bring the war to an end through English mediation, and to "leave France, which I believe is the best way, to arrange its own internal affairs as it can." No hour of Pitt's life is so great as the hour when he stood alone in England, and refused to bow to the growing cry of the nation for war. Even the news of the Septem-

SEC. III.

THE SECOND PITT

1783 TO **1793**

The Coalition attacks France

1792

France declares War on England

SEC. III.

THE
SECOND
PITT

1783
TO
1793

ber massacres could only force from him a hope that France might abstain from any war of conquest, and escape from its social anarchy. In October the French agent in England reported that Pitt was about to recognize the Republic. At the opening of November he still pressed on Holland a steady neutrality. It was France, and not England, which at last wrenched from his grasp the peace to which he clung so desperately. The decree of the Convention and the attack on the Dutch left him no choice but war, for it was impossible for England to endure a French fleet at Antwerp, or to desert allies like the United Provinces. But even in December the news of the approaching partition of Poland nerved him to a last struggle for peace; he offered to aid Austria in acquiring Bavaria if she would make terms with France, and pledged himself to France to abstain from war if that power would cease from violating the independence of her neighbour states. But across the Channel his moderation was only taken for fear, while in England the general mourning which followed on the news of the French King's execution showed the growing ardour for the contest. The rejection of his last offers indeed made a contest inevitable. Both sides ceased from diplomatic communications, and in February, 1793, France issued her Declaration of War.

Section IV.—The War with France. 1793—1815.

[*Authorities.*—To those mentioned before we may add Moore's Life of Sheridan; the Lives of Lord Castlereagh, Lord Eldon, and Lord Sidmouth; Romilly's Memoirs; Lord Cornwallis's Correspondence; Mr. Yonge's Life of Lord Liverpool; the Diaries and Correspondence of Lord Malmesbury, Lord Colchester, and Lord Auckland. For the general history of England at this time, see Alison's " History of Europe;" for its military history, Sir William Napier's " History of the Peninsular War."]

Pitt and the War

From the moment when France declared war against England Pitt's power was at an end. His pride, his immoveable firmness, and the general confidence of the nation still kept him at the head of affairs; but he could do little save drift along with a tide of popular feeling which he never fully understood. The very excellences of his character unfitted him for the conduct of a war. He was in fact a Peace Minister, forced into war by a panic and enthusiasm which he shared in a very small degree, and unaided by his father's gift of at once entering into the sympathies and passions around him, and of rousing passions and sympathies in return. Around him the country broke out in a fit of frenzy and alarm which rivalled the passion and panic over-sea. The confidence of France in its illusions as to opinion in England deluded for the moment even Englishmen themselves. The partizans of Republicanism were in reality but a few handfuls of men who played at gathering Conventions, and at calling themselves citizens and patriots,

The English panic

SEC. IV.

THE
WAR WITH
FRANCE
1793
TO
1815

in childish imitation of what was going on across the Channel. But in the mass of Englishmen the dread of revolution passed for the hour into sheer panic. Even the bulk of the Whig party forsook Fox when he still proclaimed his faith in France and the Revolution. The "Old Whigs," as they called themselves, with the Duke of Portland, Earls Spencer and Fitzwilliam, and Mr. Windham at their head, followed Burke in giving their adhesion to the Government. Pitt himself, though little touched by the political reaction around him, was shaken by the dream of social danger, and believed in the existence of "thousands of bandits," who were ready to rise against the throne, to plunder every landlord, and to sack London. "Paine is no fool," he said to his niece, who quoted to him a passage from the "Rights of Man," in which that author had vindicated the principles of the Revolution ; "he is perhaps right ; but if I did what he wants, I should have thousands of bandits on my hands to-morrow, and London burnt." It was this sense of social danger which alone reconciled him to the war. Bitter as the need of the struggle which was forced upon England was to him, he accepted it with the less reluctance that war, as he trusted, would check the progress of "French principles" in England itself. The worst issue of this panic was the series of legis-lative measures in which it found expression. The Habeas Corpus Act was suspended, a bill against seditious assemblies restricted the liberty of public meeting, and a wider scope was given to the Statute of Treasons. Prosecution after prosecution was directed against the Press ; the sermons of some dissenting ministers were indicted as seditious ; and the conventions of sympathizers with France were roughly broken up. The worst excesses of the panic were witnessed in Scotland, where young Whigs, whose only offence was an advocacy of Parliamentary reform, were sentenced to transportation, and where a brutal judge openly expressed his regret that the practice of torture in seditious cases should have fallen into disuse. The panic indeed soon passed away for sheer want of material to feed on. In 1794 the leaders of the Corresponding Society, a body which professed sympathy with France, were brought to trial on a charge of high treason, but their acquittal proved that all active terror was over. Save for occasional riots, to which the poor were goaded by sheer want of bread, no social disturbance troubled England through the twenty years of the war. But the blind reaction against all reform which had sprung from the panic lasted on when the panic was forgotten. For nearly a quarter of a century it was hard to get a hearing for any measure which threatened change to an existing institution, beneficial though the change might be. Even the philanthropic movement which so nobly characterized the time found itself checked and hampered by the dread of revolution.

Results of the panic

At first indeed all seemed to go ill for France. She was girt in

Sec. IV.

The
War with
France

1793
to
1815

France
and the
Coalition

by a ring of enemies; the Empire, Austria, Prussia, Sardinia, Spain, and England were leagued in arms against her; and their efforts were seconded by civil war.   The peasants of Poitou and Britanny rose in revolt against the government at Paris, while Marseilles and Lyons were driven into insurrection by the violent leaders who now seized on power in the capital.   The French armies were driven back from the Netherlands when ten thousand English soldiers, under the Duke of York, joined the Austrians in Flanders in 1793.   But the chance of crushing the Revolution was lost by the greed of the two German powers.   Russia, as Pitt had foreseen, was now free to carry out her schemes in the East; and Austria and Prussia saw themselves forced, in the interest of a balance of power, to share in her annexations at the cost of Poland.   But this new division of Poland would have become impossible had France been enabled by a restoration of its monarchy to take up again its natural position in Europe, and to accept the alliance which Pitt would in such a case have offered her.   The policy of the German courts therefore was to prolong an anarchy which left them free for the moment to crush Poland : and the allied armies which might have marched upon Paris were purposely frittered away in sieges in the Netherlands and the Rhine.   Such a policy gave

France time to recover from the shock of her disasters.   Whatever were the crimes and tyranny of her leaders, France felt in spite of them the value of the Revolution, and rallied enthusiastically to its support.   The revolts in the West and South were crushed.   The Spanish invaders were held at bay at the foot of the Pyrenees, and the Piedmontese were driven from Nice and Savoy.   The great port of Toulon, which called for foreign aid against the government of Paris, and admitted an English garrison within its walls, was driven to surrender by measures counselled by a young artillery officer from Corsica, Napoleon Buonaparte.   At the opening of 1794 a victory at Fleurus which again made the French masters of the Netherlands showed that the tide had turned.   France was united within by the cessation of the Terror and of the tyranny of the Jacobins, while on every border victory followed the gigantic efforts with which she met the coalition against her. Spain sued for peace; Prussia withdrew her armies from the Rhine; the Sardinians were driven back from the Maritime Alps; the Rhine provinces were wrested from the Austrians; and before the year ended Holland was lost.   Pichegru crossed the Waal in mid-winter with an overwhelming force, and the wretched remnant of ten thousand men who had followed the Duke of York to the Netherlands, thinned by disease and by the hardships of retreat, re-embarked for England.

The victories of France broke up the confederacy which had threatened it with destruction.   The Batavian republic which Pichegru had set up after his conquest of Holland was now an ally of France. Prussia bought peace by the cession of her possessions west of the

Rhine. Peace with Spain followed in the summer, while Sweden and the Protestant cantons of Switzerland recognized the Republic. In France itself discord came well-nigh to an end. The fresh severities against the ultra-republicans which followed on the establishment of a Directory indicated the moderate character of the new government, and Pitt seized on this change in the temper of the French government as giving an opening for peace. Pitt himself was sick of the strife. England had maintained indeed her naval supremacy. The triumphs of her seamen were in strange contrast with her weakness on land ; and at the outset of the contest, in 1794, the French fleet was defeated off Brest by Lord Howe in a victory which bore the name of the day on which it was won, the First of June. Her colonial gains too had been considerable. Most of the West Indian islands which had been held by France, and the far more valuable settlements of the Dutch, the Cape of Good Hope, Ceylon, and the famous Spice Islands of the Malaccas and Java had been transferred to the British Crown. But Pitt was without means of efficiently carrying on the war. The army was small and without military experience, while its leaders were utterly incapable. "We have no General," wrote Lord Grenville, "but some old woman in a red riband." Wretched too as had been the conduct of the war, its cost was already terrible. If England was without soldiers, she had wealth, and Pitt had been forced to turn her wealth into an engine of war. He became the paymaster of the coalition, and his subsidies kept the allied armies in the field. But the immense loans which these called for, and the quick growth of expenditure, undid all his financial reforms. Taxation, which had reached its lowest point under Pitt's peace administration, mounted to a height undreamt of before. The public debt rose by leaps and bounds. In three years nearly eighty millions had been added to it.

But though the ruin of his financial hopes, and his keen sense of the European dangers which the contest involved, made Pitt earnest to close the struggle with the Revolution, he stood almost alone in his longings for peace. The nation at large was still ardent for war, and its ardour was fired by Burke in his "Letters on a Regicide Peace," the last outcry of that fanaticism which had done so much to plunge the world in blood. Nor was France less ardent for war than England. At the moment when Pitt sought to open negotiations, her victories had roused hopes of wider conquests, and though General Moreau was foiled in a march on Vienna, the wonderful successes of Napoleon Buonaparte, who now took the command of the army of the Alps, laid Piedmont at her feet. Lombardy was soon in the hands of the French, the Duchies south of the Po pillaged, and the Pope driven to purchase an armistice. Fresh victories enabled Buonaparte to wring a peace from Austria in the treaty of Campo Formio, which not only gave France the Ionian Islands, a part of the old territory of Venice, as

Sec. IV.

The War with France
1793 to 1815

1795

Progress of the War

1796

Oct. 1797

SEC. IV.

THE
WAR WITH
FRANCE
1793
TO
1815

well as the Netherlands and the whole left bank of the Rhine, but united Lombardy with the Duchies south of the Po, and the Papal States as far as the Rubicon, into a " Cisalpine Republic," which was absolutely beneath her control. The withdrawal of Austria left France without an enemy on the Continent, and England without an ally. The stress of the war was pressing more heavily on her every day. The alarm of a French invasion of Ireland brought about a suspension of specie payments on the part of the Bank. A mutiny in the fleet was suppressed with difficulty. It was in this darkest hour of the struggle that Burke passed away, protesting to the last against the peace which, in spite of his previous failure, Pitt tried in 1797 to negotiate at Lille. Peace seemed more needful to him than ever ; for the naval supremacy of Britain was threatened by a coalition such as had all but crushed her in the American War. Again the Dutch and Spanish fleets were allied with the fleets of France, and if they gained command of the Channel, it would enable France to send overwhelming forces in aid of the rising which was planned in Ireland. But the danger had hardly threatened when it was dispelled by two great victories. When in 1797 the Spanish fleet put out to sea, it was attacked by Admiral Jervis off Cape St. Vincent and driven back to Cadiz with the loss of four of its finest vessels ; while the Dutch fleet from the Texel, which was to protect a French force in its descent upon Ireland, was met by a far larger fleet under Admiral Duncan, and almost annihilated in a battle off Camperdown, after an obstinate struggle which showed the Hollanders still worthy of their old renown. The ruin of its hopes in the battle of Camperdown drove Ireland to a rising of despair ; but the revolt was crushed by the defeat of the insurgents at Vinegar Hill in May, 1798, and the surrender of General Humbert, who landed in August with a French force. Of the threefold attack on which the Directory relied, two parts had now broken down. England still held the seas, and the insurrection in Ireland had failed. The next year saw the crowning victory of the Nile. The genius of Buonaparte had seized on the schemes for a rising in India, where Tippoo Sahib, the successor of Hyder Ali in Mysore, had vowed to drive the English from the south ; and he laid before the Directory a plan for the conquest of Egypt as a preliminary to a campaign in Southern India. In 1798 he landed in Egypt ; and its conquest was rapid and complete. But the thirteen men-of-war which had escorted his expedition were found by Admiral Nelson in Aboukir Bay, moored close to the coast in a line guarded at either end by gun-boats and batteries. Nelson resolved to thrust his own ships between the French and the shore ; his flagship led the way ; and after a terrible fight of twelve hours, nine of the French vessels were captured and destroyed, two were burnt, and five thousand French seamen were killed or made prisoners. All communication between France and

*Cape St.
Vincent
Feb.* 14

*Camper-
down
Oct.* 11

*Battle of
the Nile
Aug.* 1,
1798

Buonaparte's army was cut off; and his hopes of making Egypt a starting-point for the conquest of India fell at a blow.

Freed from the dangers that threatened her rule in Ireland and in India, and mistress of the seas, England was free to attack France; and in such an attack she was aided at this moment by the temper of the European powers, and the ceaseless aggressions of France. Russia formed a close alliance with Austria; and it was with renewed hope that Pitt lavished subsidies on the two allies. A union of the Russian and Austrian armies drove the French back again across the Alps and the Rhine; but the stubborn energy of General Massena enabled his soldiers to hold their ground in Switzerland; and the attempt of a united force of Russians and English to wrest Holland from its French masters was successfully repulsed. In the East, however, England was more successful. Foiled in his dreams of Indian conquests, Buonaparte conceived the design of the conquest of Syria, and of the creation of an army among its warlike mountaineers, with which he might march upon Constantinople or India at his will. But Acre, the key of Syria, was stubbornly held by the Turks, the French battering train was captured at sea by an English captain, Sir Sidney Smith, whose seamen aided in the defence of the place, and the besiegers were forced to fall back upon Egypt. The French general despairing of success left his army and returned to France. His arrival in Paris was soon followed by the overthrow of the Directors. Three consuls took their place; but under the name of First Consul Buonaparte became in effect sole ruler of the country. His energy at once changed the whole face of European affairs. The offers of peace which he made to England and Austria were intended to do little more than to shake the coalition, and gain breathing time for the organization of a new force which was gathering in secrecy at Dijon, while Moreau with the army of the Rhine pushed again along the Danube. The First Consul crossed the Saint Bernard in 1800, and a victory at Marengo forced the Austrians to surrender Lombardy; while a truce arrested the march of Moreau, who had captured Munich and was pushing on to Vienna. On the resumption of the war in the autumn the Austrians were driven back on Vienna; and Moreau crushed their army on the Iser in the victory of Hohenlinden. In February, 1801, the Continental War was brought suddenly to an end by the Peace of Luneville.

It was but a few months before the close of the war that Pitt brought about the Union of Ireland with England. The history of Ireland, during the fifty years that followed its conquest by William the Third, is one which no Englishman can recall without shame. After the surrender of Limerick every Catholic Irishman, and there were five Irish Catholics to every Irish Protestant, was treated as a stranger and a foreigner in his own country. The House of Lords, the House

Sec. IV.

The War with France

1793 to 1815

The Peace of Luneville

Nov. 10, 1799

June 14, 1800

Dec. 2

Ireland under the Georges

SEC. IV.

THE
WAR WITH
FRANCE
1793
TO
1815

of Commons, the magistracy, all corporate offices in towns, all ranks in the army, the bench, the bar, the whole administration of government or justice, were closed against Catholics. The very right of voting for their representatives in Parliament was denied them. Few Catholic landowners had been left by the sweeping confiscations which had followed the successive revolts of the island, and oppressive laws forced even these few with scant exceptions to profess Protestantism. Necessity, indeed, had brought about a practical toleration of their religion and their worship; but in all social and political matters the native Catholics, in other words the immense majority of the people of Ireland, were simply hewers of wood and drawers of water to their Protestant masters, who looked on themselves as mere settlers, who boasted of their Scotch or English extraction, and who regarded the name of " Irishman " as an insult. But small as was this Protestant body, one half of it fared little better, as far as power was concerned, than the Catholics; for the Presbyterians, who formed the bulk of the Ulster settlers, were shut out by law from all

Government in Ireland

civil, military, and municipal offices. The administration and justice of the country were thus kept rigidly in the hands of members of the Established Church, a body which comprised about a twelfth of the population of the island; while its government was practically monopolized by a few great Protestant landowners. The rotten boroughs, which had originally been created to make the Irish Parliament dependent on the Crown, had fallen under the influence of the adjacent landlords, who were thus masters of the House of Commons, while they formed in person the House of Peers. During the first half of the eighteenth century two thirds of the House of Commons, in fact, was returned by a small group of nobles, who were recognized as " parliamentary undertakers," and who undertook to "manage" Parliament on their own terms. Irish politics were for these men a means of public plunder; they were glutted with pensions, preferments, and bribes in hard cash in return for their services; they were the advisers of every Lord-Lieutenant, and the practical governors of the country. The first check was dealt to their power when the party of

1768

reform won the election of a new Parliament every eight years. To counteract popular influence which might threaten the subservience of Ireland to England, the Lord Lieutenant was charged to reside constantly and concentrate all political power in the Crown. The Irish Parliament had no power of originating legislative or financial measures, and could only say " yes " or " no " to Acts submitted to it by the Privy Council in England. The English Parliament, too, had

1693

asserted a statutory right of binding Ireland by its laws, and transferred the appellate jurisdiction of the Irish Peerage to the English House of Lords. Its power was used to annihilate Irish commerce and to ruin Irish agriculture. Statutes passed by the jealousy of English land-

Sec. IV.

The
War with
France
1793
to
1815

Pitt and
Ireland

owners forbade the export of Irish cattle or sheep to English ports. The export of wool was forbidden, lest it might interfere with the profits of English wool-growers. Poverty was thus added to the curse of misgovernment; and poverty deepened with the rapid growth of the native population, till famine turned the country into a hell.

The bitter lesson of the last conquest, however, long sufficed to check all dreams of revolt among the natives, and the outbreaks which sprang from time to time out of the general misery and discontent were purely social in their character, and were roughly repressed by the ruling class. When political revolt threatened at last, the threat came from the ruling class itself. At the very outset of the reign of George the Third, the Irish Parliament insisted on its claim to the exclusive control of money bills, and a cry was raised for the removal of the checks imposed on its independence. But it was not till the American war that this cry became a political danger, a danger so real that England was forced to give way. From the close of the war, when the Irish Volunteers wrung legislative independence from the Rockingham Ministry, Great Britain and Ireland were held together by the fact that the sovereign of the one island was also the sovereign of the other. During the next eighteen years Ireland was nominally "independent," but its independence was a mere name for the uncontrolled rule of an Executive which was appointed by England, and worked in strict concert with the English Privy Council and the English Ministers. By a highly artificial system, in fact, the Government of Ireland was kept in permanent subjection to the English Executive. To such a length had the whole system of monopoly and patronage been carried under this rule, that at the time of the Union more than sixty seats were in the hands of three families alone, those of the Hills, the Ponsonbys, and the Beresfords; while the dominant influence in the Parliament now lay with the Treasury boroughs at the disposal of the Government. The victory of the Volunteers immediately produced measures in favour of the Catholics and Presbyterians. The Volunteers had already in 1780 won for the Presbyterians, who formed a good half of their force, full political liberty by the abolition of the Sacramental Test; and the Irish Parliament of 1782 removed at once the last grievances of the Protestant Dissenters. The Catholics were rewarded for their aid by the repeal of the more grossly oppressive enactments of the penal laws. But when Grattan, supported by the bulk of the Irish party, pleaded for Parliamentary reform, and for the grant of equal rights to the Catholics, he was utterly foiled by the opposition of the Executive, which, entirely independent of Parliament, controlled the administration in the interests of English supremacy. The ruling class found government too profitable to share it with other possessors, and by hard bribery the English Viceroys could always secure for their measures the co-operation of the small group of borough owners.

SEC. IV.

THE
WAR WITH
FRANCE
1793
TO
1815

Though the Irish Catholics were held down by the brute force of their Protestant rulers, the general discontent of the middle class, Protestant and Catholic, was growing fast ; and in Pitt's eyes one secret of discontent lay in a poverty increased if not originally brought about by the jealous exclusion of Irish products from their natural markets in England itself. In 1779 Ireland had won from Lord North large measures of free-trade abroad ; but the heavy duties laid by the English Parliament on all Irish manufactures save linen and woollen yarn still shut them out of England. One of Pitt's first commercial

1785

measures aimed at putting an end to this exclusion by a Bill which established freedom of trade between the two islands ; he hoped thus to unite the two islands indissolubly for military and commercial purposes, and obtain from Ireland a fixed contribution to the defence of the Empire. His first proposals were accepted in the Irish Parliament ; but the fears and jealousies of the English farmers and manufacturers forced into the Bill amendments which gave to the British Parliament powers over Irish navigation and commerce, thus over-riding their newly-won independence, and the measure in its new form was rejected in Ireland. The outbreak of the revolutionary struggle, and the efforts which the French revolutionists at once made to excite rebellion amongst the Irish, roused Pitt

1793

to fresh measures of conciliation. He forced the Irish Administration to abandon a resistance which had wrecked his projects the previous year ; and the Irish Parliament passed without opposition measures for the admission of Catholics to the electoral franchise, and to civil and military office, which promised to open a new era of religious

1795

liberty. But the abrupt recall by the English Government of Lord Fitzwilliam, when he proposed to complete the work of emancipation, flung the country again into disorder. The hope of conciliation was lost in the fast rising tide of political passion. The Society of "United Irish-

1791

men," which was founded at Belfast by Wolfe Tone with a view of forming a union between Protestants and Catholics to win Parliamentary reform, drifted into a correspondence with France and projects of insurrection. The peasantry, brooding over their misery and their wrongs, were equally stirred by the news from France ; and their discontent broke out in outrages of secret societies which spread panic among the ruling classes. The misery was increased by faction fights between the Protestants and Catholics, which had already broken out before the French Revolution. The Catholics banded themselves together as " Defenders " against the outrages of the " Peep-o'-day Boys," who were mainly drawn from the more violent Presbyterians; and these factions became later merged in the larger associations of the " United Irishmen " and the " Orange-men."

**The
Union**

At last the smouldering discontent and disaffection burst into flame. The panic roused in 1796 by an attempted French invasion under Hoche woke passions of cruelty and tyranny which turned Ireland

SEC. IV.

THE
WAR WITH
FRANCE
1793
TO
1815

into a hell. Soldiers and yeomanry marched over the country torturing and scourging the "croppies," as the Irish peasantry were
called in derision from their short-cut hair, robbing, ravishing, and
murdering. Their outrages were sanctioned by the landowners who
formed the Irish Parliament in a Bill of Indemnity, and protected
for the future by an Insurrection Act. Meanwhile the United Irishmen prepared for an insurrection, which was delayed by the failure
of the French expeditions, on which they counted for support, and
above all by the victory of Camperdown. Atrocities were answered
by atrocities when the revolt at last broke out in 1798. Loyalists were
lashed and tortured in their turn, and every soldier taken was butchered
without mercy. The rebels however no sooner mustered fourteen
thousand men strong in a camp on Vinegar Hill, near Enniscorthy,
than the camp was stormed by the English troops, and the revolt
utterly suppressed. A few weeks after the close of the rebellion nine
hundred French soldiers under General Humbert landed in Mayo,
broke a force of thrice their number in a battle at Castlebar, and only
surrendered when the Lord-Lieutenant, Lord Cornwallis, faced them
with thirty thousand men. Pitt's disgust at "the bigoted fury of Irish
Protestants" backed Cornwallis in checking the ferocious reprisals of
the troops and the Orangemen; but the rebellion gave to the Chancellor
FitzGibbon, the implacable foe of Irish Catholics, created Earl of Clare
for his part in the recall of FitzWilliam, the opportunity of pressing
on Pitt a long discussed plan for ending Irish independence by a
legislative Union with England. The necessity of such a union had
been brought home to every English statesman during the disputes
over the Regency; for while England repelled the claims of the
Prince of Wales to the Regency as of right, the legislature of Ireland
admitted them. As the link between the two peoples was their
obedience to a common ruler, such an act might conceivably have
ended in their entire severance; and the sense of this danger secured
a welcome in England for Pitt's proposal to unite the two Parliaments.
The opposition of the Irish Parliament was stubborn. But Parliament was purged of irreconcilable members, and the borough-
mongers with whom it was a sheer question of gold were bought
with over a million of money, and a liberal distribution of pensions
and peerages. Base and shameless as were such means, Pitt may
plead that they were the only means by which the Union could
have been passed. As the matter was finally arranged, one hundred
and twenty-eight temporal with four spiritual peers, chosen for each
Parliament by their fellows, took their seats in the House of Lords.
Commerce between the two countries was freed from all restrictions, and every trading privilege of the one thrown open to the
other; while taxation was proportionately distributed between the
two peoples.

May 21,
1798

1795
1798

1788

June 1800

Pitt
and the
Peerage
SEC. IV.

THE
WAR WITH
FRANCE

1793
TO
1815

The lavish creation of peers which formed a part of the price paid for the Union of Ireland brought about a practical change in our constitution. Few bodies have varied more in the number of their members than the House of Lords. At the close of the Wars of the Roses the lay lords who remained numbered fifty-two ; in Elizabeth's reign they numbered only sixty ; the prodigal creations of the Stuarts raised them to one hundred and seventy-six. At this point, however, they practically remained stationary during the reigns of the first two Georges ; and, as we have seen, only the dogged opposition of Walpole prevented Lord Stanhope from limiting the peerage to the number it had at that time reached. Mischievous as such a measure would have been, it would at any rate have prevented the lavish creation of peerages on which George the Third relied in the early days of his reign as one of his means of breaking up the party government which restrained him. But what was with the King a mere means of corruption became with Pitt a settled purpose of bringing the peerage into closer relations with the landowning and opulent classes, and rendering the Crown independent of factious combinations among the existing peers. While himself disdainful of hereditary honours, *Increase of the peers* he lavished them as no Minister had lavished them before. In his first five years of rule he created forty-eight new peers. In two later years alone, 1796-7, he created thirty-five. By 1801 the peerages which were the price of the Union with Ireland had helped to raise his creations to upwards of one hundred and forty. So busily was his example followed by his successors that at the end of George the Third's reign the number of hereditary peers had become double what it was at his accession. The whole character of the House of Lords was changed. Up to this time it had been a small assembly of great nobles, bound together by family or party ties into a distinct power in the State. From this time it became the stronghold of property, the representative of the great estates and great fortunes which the vast increase of English wealth was building up. For the first time, too, in our history it became the distinctly conservative element in our constitution. The full import of Pitt's changes has still to be revealed, but in some ways their results have been clearly marked. The larger number of the peerage, though due to the will of the Crown, has practically freed the House from any influence which the Crown can exert by the distribution of honours. This change, since the power of the Crown has been practically wielded by the House of Commons, has rendered it far harder to reconcile the free action of the Lords with the regular working of constitutional government. On the other hand, the increased number of its members has rendered the House more responsive to public opinion, when public opinion is strongly pronounced ; and the political tact which is inherent in great aristocratic assemblies has hitherto prevented any collision with the Lower House from being pushed to an irreconcilable quarrel.

But the legislative union of the two countries was only part of the plan which Pitt had conceived for the conciliation of Ireland. With the conclusion of the Union his projects of free trade between the countries, which had been defeated a few years back, came into play. The change which brought Ireland directly under the common Parliament was very tardily followed by a gradual revision of its oppressive laws, and an amendment in their administration ; and a faint beginning was made of public instruction. But in Pitt's mind the great means of conciliation was the concession of religious equality. In proposing to the English Parliament the union of the two countries he pointed out that when thus joined to a Protestant country like England all danger of a Catholic supremacy in Ireland, should Catholic disabilities be removed, would be practically at an end ; and had suggested that in such a case "an effectual and adequate provision for the Catholic clergy" would be a security for their loyalty. His words gave strength to the hopes of "Catholic Emancipation," or the removal of what remained of the civil disabilities of Catholics, which were held out by the viceroy, Lord Castlereagh, in Ireland itself, as a means of hindering any opposition to the project of Union on the part of the Catholics. It was agreed on all sides that their opposition would have secured its defeat ; but no Catholic opposition showed itself. After the passing of the bill, Pitt prepared to lay before the Cabinet a measure which would have raised the Irish Catholic to perfect equality of civil rights. He proposed to remove all religious tests which limited the exercise of the franchise, or were required for admission to Parliament, the magistracy, the bar, municipal offices, or posts in the army, or the service of the State. An oath of allegiance and of fidelity to the Constitution was substituted for the Sacramental test ; while the loyalty of the Catholic and Dissenting clergy was secured by a grant of some provision to both by the State. To win over the Episcopal Church, measures were added for strengthening its means of discipline, and for increasing the stipends of its poorer ministers. A commutation of tithes was to remove a constant source of quarrel in Ireland between the Protestant clergy and the Irish people. The scheme was too large and statesmanlike to secure the immediate assent of the Cabinet ; and before that assent could be won the plan was communicated through the treachery of the Chancellor, Lord Loughborough, to George the Third. "I count any man my personal enemy," the King broke out angrily to Dundas, "who proposes any such measure." Pitt answered this outburst by submitting his whole plan to the King. "The political circumstances under which the exclusive laws originated," he wrote, "arising either from the conflicting powers of hostile and nearly balanced sects, from

Sec. IV.

THE
WAR WITH
FRANCE
1793
TO
1815

**Catholic
Eman-
cipation**

Pitt's policy

Its defeat

3 G

SEC. IV.

THE
WAR WITH
FRANCE
1793
TO
1815

the apprehension of a Popish Queen as successor, a disputed succession and a foreign pretender, a division in Europe between Catholic
and Protestant Powers, are no longer applicable to the present state
of things." But argument was wasted upon George the Third. In
spite of the decision of the lawyers whom he consulted, the King held
himself bound by his Coronation Oath to maintain the tests. On this
point his bigotry was at one with the bigotry of the bulk of his subjects,
as well as with their political distrust of Catholics and Irishmen ; and
his obstinacy was strengthened by a knowledge that his refusal must
drive Pitt from office. In February 1801, the month of the Peace of

Pitt resigns

Luneville, Pitt resigned, and was succeeded by the Speaker of the
House of Commons, Mr. Addington, a weak and narrow-minded man,
and as bigoted as the King himself. Of Lord Hawkesbury, who succeeded Lord Grenville in the conduct of foreign affairs, nothing was
known outside the House of Commons.

**The
Adding-
ton
Ministry**

It was with anxiety that England found itself guided by men like
these at a time when every hour brought darker news. The scarcity
of bread was mounting to a famine. Taxes were raised anew, and
yet the loan for the year amounted to five and twenty millions. The
country stood utterly alone ; while the peace of Luneville secured
France from all hostility on the Continent. And it was soon plain
that this peace was only the first step in a new policy on the part
of the First Consul. What he had done was to free his hands for
a decisive conflict with Britain itself, both as a world-power and as
a centre of wealth. England was at once the carrier of European
commerce, and the workshop of European manufactures. While her
mines, her looms, her steam-engines, were giving her almost a
monopoly of industrial production, the carrying trade of France
and Holland alike had been transferred to the British flag, and the
conquest during the war of their richer settlements had thrown into
British hands the whole colonial trade of the world. In his gigantic

*The
Continental
System*

project of a " Continental System " the aim of Buonaparte was to strike
at the trade of England by closing the ports of Europe against her ships.
By a league of the Northern powers he sought to wrest from her the command of the seas. Denmark and Sweden, who resented the severity
with which Britain enforced that right of search which had brought
about their armed neutrality at the close of the American war, were
enlisted in a league of neutrals which was in effect a declaration of
war against England, and which Prussia was prepared to join. The
Czar Paul of Russia on his side saw in the power of Britain the
chief obstacle to his designs upon Turkey. A squabble over Malta,
which had been taken from the Knights of St. John by Buonaparte on his way to Egypt, and had ever since been blockaded by
English ships, but whose possession the Czar claimed as his own
on the ground of an alleged election as Grand Master of the Order,

served him as a pretext for a quarrel with England, and Paul openly prepared for hostilities. It was plain that as soon as spring opened the Baltic, the fleets of Russia, Sweden, and Denmark would act in practical union with those of France and Spain. But dexterous as the combination was it was shattered at a blow. In April a British fleet appeared before Copenhagen, and after a desperate struggle silenced the Danish batteries, captured six Danish ships, and forced Denmark to conclude an armistice which enabled English ships to enter the Baltic. The Northern Coalition too was broken up by the death of the Czar. In June a Convention between England and Russia settled the vexed questions of the right of search and contraband of war, and this Convention was accepted by Sweden and Denmark. Meanwhile, at the very moment of the attack on Copenhagen, a stroke as effective had wrecked the projects of Buonaparte in the East. The surrender of Malta to the English fleet left England the mistress of the Mediterranean ; and from Malta she now turned to Egypt itself. A force of 15,000 men under General Abercromby anchored in Aboukir Bay. The French troops that Buonaparte had left in Egypt rapidly concentrated, and on the 21st of March their general attacked the English army. After a stubborn battle, in which Abercromby fell mortally wounded, the French drew off with heavy loss ; and at the close of June the capitulation of the 13,000 soldiers who remained closed the French rule over Egypt.

Both parties in this gigantic struggle however were at last anxious to suspend the war. It was to give time for such an organization of France and its resources as might enable him to reopen the struggle with other chances of success that Buonaparte opened negotiations for peace at the close of 1801. His offers were at once met by the English Government. The terms of the Peace of Amiens which was concluded in March 1802 were necessarily simple, for England had no claim to interfere with the settlement of the Continent. France promised to retire from Southern Italy, and to leave to themselves the republics it had set up along its border in Holland, Switzerland and Piedmont. England recognized the French Government, gave up her newly conquered colonies save Ceylon and Trinidad, acknowledged the Ionian Islands as a free Republic, and engaged to replace the Knights of St. John in the isle of Malta. There was a general sense of relief at the close of the long struggle ; and the new French ambassador was drawn in triumph on his arrival through the streets of London. But shrewd observers saw the dangers that lay in the temper of the First Consul. Whatever had been the errors of the French revolutionists, even their worst attacks on the independence of the nations around them had been veiled by a vague notion of freeing the peoples whom they invaded from the yoke of their rulers. But the aim of Buonaparte was simply that of a vulgar

SEC. IV.

THE
WAR WITH
FRANCE
1793
TO
1815

*The
Coalition
broken up*
1801

**The
Peace of
Amiens**

*Designs of
Napoleon*

SEC. IV.

THE
WAR WITH
FRANCE
1793
TO
1815

conqueror.   He was resolute to be master of the Western world, and no notions of popular freedom or sense of national right interfered with his resolve.   The means at his command were immense.   The political life of the Revolution had been cut short by his military despotism, but the new social vigour which it had given to France through the abolition of privileges and the creation of a new middle class on the ruins of the clergy and the nobles still lived on.   While the dissensions which tore France asunder were hushed by the policy of the First Consul, by his restoration of the Church as a religious power, his recall of the exiles, and the economy and wise administration which distinguished his rule, the centralized system of government bequeathed by the Monarchy to the Revolution, and by the Revolution to Buonaparte, enabled him easily to seize this national vigour for the profit of his own despotism.   The exhaustion of the brilliant hopes raised by the Revolution, the craving for public order, the military enthusiasm and the impulse of a new glory given by the wonderful victories France had won, made a Tyranny possible ; and in the hands of Buonaparte this tyranny was supported by a secret police, by the suppression of the press and of all freedom of opinion, and above all by the iron will and immense ability of the First Consul himself.   Once chosen Consul for life, he felt himself secure at home, and turned restlessly to the work of outer aggression.   The pledges given at Amiens were set aside.   The republics established on the borders of France were brought into mere dependence on his will.   Piedmont and Parma were annexed to France ; and a French army occupied

Declaration of war

Switzerland.   The temperate protests of the English Government were answered by demands for the expulsion of the French exiles who had been living in England ever since the Revolution, and for its surrender of Malta, which was retained till some security could be devised against a fresh seizure of the island by the French fleet.   It was plain that a struggle was inevitable ; huge armaments were preparing in the French ports, and a new activity was seen in those of Spain.   In May 1803 the British Government anticipated Buonaparte's attack by a declaration of war.

Trafalgar

The breach only quickened Buonaparte's resolve to attack the enemy at home.   The difficulties in his way he set contemptuously aside.   " Fifteen millions of people," he said, in allusion to the disproportion between the population of England and France, " must give way to forty millions " ; and an invasion of England itself was planned on a gigantic scale.   A camp of one hundred thousand

The Camp at Boulogne

men was formed at Boulogne, and a host of flat-bottomed boats gathered for their conveyance across the Channel.   The peril of the nation forced Addington from office and recalled Pitt to power. His health was broken, and as the days went by his appearance became so haggard and depressed that it was plain death was drawing near. But dying as he really was, the nation clung to him with all its old faith. He was still the representative of national union; and he proposed to include Fox and the leading Whigs in his new ministry, but he was foiled by the bigotry of the King; and the refusal of Lord Grenville and of Windham to take office without Fox, as well as the loss of his post at a later time by his ablest supporter, Dundas, left him almost alone. But lonely as he was, he faced difficulty and danger with the same courage as of old. The invasion seemed imminent when Buonaparte, who now assumed the title of the Emperor Napoleon, appeared in the camp at Boulogne. "Let us be masters of the Channel for six hours," he is reported to have said, "and we are masters of the world." A skilfully combined plan by which the British fleet would have been divided, while the whole French navy was concentrated in the Channel, was delayed by the death of the admiral destined to execute it. But the alliance with Spain placed the Spanish fleet at Napoleon's disposal, and in 1805 he planned its union with that of France, the crushing of the squadron which blocked the ports of the Channel before the English ships which were watching the Spanish armament could come to its support, and a crossing of the vast armament thus protected to the English shore. The three hundred thousand volunteers mustered in England to meet the coming attack would have offered small hindrance to the veterans of the Grand Army, had they once crossed the Channel. But Pitt had already found work for France elsewhere. The alarm of the Continental Powers had been brought to a head by Napoleon's annexation of Genoa; Pitt's subsidies had removed the last obstacle in the way of a league; and Russia, Austria, and Sweden joined in an alliance to wrest Italy and the Low Countries from the grasp of the French Emperor. Napoleon meanwhile swept the sea in vain for a glimpse of the great armament whose assembly in the Channel he had so skilfully planned. Admiral Villeneuve, uniting the Spanish ships with his own squadron from Toulon, drew Nelson in pursuit to the West Indies, and then, suddenly returning to Cadiz, hastened to form a junction with the French squadron at Brest and crush the English fleet in the Channel. But a headlong pursuit brought Nelson up with him ere the manœuvre was complete, and the two fleets met on the 21st of October, 1805, off Cape Trafalgar. "England," ran Nelson's famous signal, "expects every man to do his duty;" and though he fell himself in the hour of victory, twenty French sail had struck their flag ere the day was done. "England has saved herself by her courage," Pitt said in what were destined to be his last public words: "she will save Europe by her example!" But even before the victory of Trafalgar Napoleon had abandoned the dream of invading England to meet the coalition in his rear; and swinging round his forces on the Danube he forced an Austrian army to capitulation in Ulm three days before his

SEC. IV.

THE
WAR WITH
FRANCE
1793
TO
1815

*League
against
France*

Sec. IV.

The
War with
France

1793
to
1815

*Death of
Pitt*

naval defeat. From Ulm he marched on Vienna, and crushed the combined armies of Austria and Russia in the battle of Austerlitz. "Austerlitz," Wilberforce wrote in his diary, "killed Pitt." Though he was still but forty-seven, the hollow voice and wasted frame of the great Minister had long told that death was near ; and the blow to his hopes proved fatal. "Roll up that map," he said, pointing to a map of Europe which hung upon the wall : " it will not be wanted these ten years ! " Once only he rallied from stupor ; and those who bent over him caught a faint murmur of " My country ! How I leave my country ! " On the 23rd of January, 1806, he breathed his last ; and was laid in Westminster Abbey in the grave of Chatham. " What grave," exclaimed Lord Wellesley, " contains such a father and such a son ! What sepulchre embosoms the remains of so much human excellence and glory ! "

**The
Grenville
Ministry**

So great was felt to be the loss that nothing but the union of parties, which Pitt had in vain desired during his lifetime, could fill up the gap left by his death. In the new Ministry Fox, with the small body of popular Whigs who were bent on peace and internal reform, united with the aristocratic Whigs under Lord Grenville and with the Tories under Lord Sidmouth. All home questions in fact were subordinated to the need of saving Europe from the ambition of France, and in the resolve to save Europe, Fox was as resolute as Pitt himself. His hopes of peace, indeed, were stronger ; but they were foiled by the evasive answer which Napoleon gave to his overtures, and by a new war which he undertook against Prussia, the one power which seemed able to resist his arms. On the 14th of October, 1806, a decisive victory

Jena

at Jena laid North Germany at Napoleon's feet. Death only a month before saved Fox from witnessing the overthrow of his hopes ; and his loss weakened the Grenville Cabinet at the opening of a new and more desperate struggle with France. Napoleon's earlier attempt at the enforcement of a Continental System had broken down with the failure of the Northern League ; but in his mastery of Europe he now saw a more effective means of realizing his dream ; and he was able to find a pretext for his new attack in England's own action. By a violent stretch of her rights as a combatant she had declared the whole coast occupied by France and its allies, from Dantzig to Trieste, to be in a state of blockade. It was impossible to enforce such a " paper blockade," even with the immense force at her disposal ; and Napoleon seized on the opportunity to retaliate by the entire exclusion of British commerce from the Continent, an exclusion which he trusted would end the war by the ruin it would bring on the English

*The Berlin
Decree

Nov.* 1806

manufacturers. A decree was issued from Berlin which—without a single ship to carry it out—placed the British Islands in a state of blockade. All commerce or communication with them was prohibited ; all English goods or manufactures found in the territory of France or

Sec. IV.

THE
WAR WITH
FRANCE
1793
TO
1815

its allies were declared liable to confiscation; and their harbours were closed, not only against vessels coming from Britain, but against all who had touched at her ports. The attempt to enforce such a system was foiled indeed by the rise of a widespread contraband trade, by the reluctance of Holland to aid in its own ruin, by the connivance of officials along the Prussian and Russian shores, and by the pressure of facts. It was impossible even for Napoleon himself to do without the goods he pretended to exclude; an immense system of licences soon neutralized his decree; and the French army which marched to Eylau was clad in great-coats made at Leeds, and shod with shoes made at Northampton. But if it failed to destroy British industry, it told far more fatally on British commerce. Trade began to move from English vessels, which were subject to instant confiscation, and to pass into the hands of neutrals, and especially of the Americans. The merchant class called on the Government to protect it, and it was to this appeal that the Grenville Ministry replied in January, 1807, by an Order in Council which declared all the ports of the coast of France and her allies under blockade, and any neutral vessels trading between them to be good prize. Such a step was far from satisfying the British merchants. But their appeal was no longer to Lord Grenville. The forces of ignorance and bigotry which had been too strong for Pitt were too strong for the Grenville Ministry. Its greatest work, the abolition of the slave trade, in February, was done in the teeth of a vigorous opposition from the Tories and the merchants of Liverpool; and in March the first indication of its desire to open the question of religious equality by allowing Catholic officers to serve in the army was met on the part of the King by the demand of a pledge not to meddle with the question. On the refusal of this pledge the Ministry was dismissed.

Its fall was the final close of the union of parties brought about by the peril of French invasion; and from this time to the end of the war England was wholly governed by the Tories. The nominal head of the Ministry which succeeded that of Lord Grenville was the Duke of Portland; its guiding spirit was the Foreign Secretary, George Canning, a young and devoted adherent of Pitt, whose brilliant rhetoric gave him power over the House of Commons, while the vigour and breadth of his mind gave a new energy and colour to the war. At no time had opposition to Napoleon seemed so hopeless. From Berlin the Emperor marched into the heart of Poland, and though checked in the winter by the Russian forces in the hard-fought battle of Eylau, his victory of Friedland brought the Czar Alexander in the summer of 1807 to consent to the Peace of Tilsit. From foes the two Emperors of Western and Eastern Europe became friends, and the hope of French aid in the conquest of Turkey drew Alexander to a close alliance with

SEC. IV.

THE
WAR WITH
FRANCE
1793
TO
1815

Napoleon. Russia not only enforced the Berlin decrees against British commerce, but forced Sweden, the one ally that England still retained on the Continent, to renounce her alliance. The Russian and Swedish fleets were thus placed at the service of France; and the two Emperors counted on securing the fleet of Denmark, and again threatening by this union the maritime supremacy which formed England's real defence. The hope was foiled by the appearance off Elsinore in July 1807 of an expedition, promptly and secretly equipped by Canning, with a demand for the surrender of the Danish fleet into the hands of England, on pledge of its return at the close of the war. On the refusal of the Danes the demand was enforced by a bombardment of Copenhagen; and the whole Danish fleet, with a vast mass of naval stores, was carried into British ports. It was in the same spirit of almost reckless decision that Canning turned to meet Napoleon's Continental System. In November he issued fresh Orders in Council. By these France, and every Continental state from which the British flag was excluded, was put in a state of blockade, and all vessels bound for their harbours were held subject to seizure unless they had touched at a British port. The orders were at once met by another decree of Napoleon issued at Milan in December, which declared every vessel, of whatever nation, coming from or bound to Britain or any British colony, to have forfeited its character as a neutral, and to be liable to seizure.

The Milan Decree

The Peninsular War

Meanwhile the effect of the Continental System upon Napoleon was to drive him to aggression after aggression in order to maintain the material union of Europe against Britain. He was absolutely master of Western Europe, and its whole face changed as at an enchanter's touch. Prussia was occupied by French troops. Holland was changed into a monarchy by a simple decree of the French Emperor, and its crown bestowed on his brother Louis. Another brother, Jerome, became King of Westphalia, a new realm built up out of the Electorates of Hesse Cassel and Hanover. A third brother, Joseph, was made King of Naples; while the rest of Italy, and even Rome itself, was annexed to the French Empire. It was the hope of effectually crushing the world power of Britain which drove him to his worst aggression, the aggression upon Spain. He acted with his usual subtlety. In October 1807 France and Spain agreed to divide Portugal between them; and on the advance of their forces the reigning House of Braganza fled helplessly from Lisbon to a refuge in Brazil. But the seizure of Portugal was only a prelude to the seizure of Spain. Charles the Fourth, whom a riot in his capital drove at this moment to abdication, and his son, Ferdinand the Seventh, were drawn to Bayonne in May, 1808, and forced to resign their claims to the Spanish crown; while a French army entered Madrid and proclaimed Joseph Buonaparte King of Spain. But this high-handed act of aggression was hardly completed

Sec. IV.

The
War with
France
1793
to
1815
*The rising
of Spain*

when Spain rose as one man against the stranger ; and desperate as the effort of its people seemed, the news of the rising was welcomed throughout England with a burst of enthusiastic joy. " Hitherto," cried Sheridan, a leader of the Whig opposition, "Buonaparte has contended with princes without dignity, numbers without ardour, or peoples without patriotism. He has yet to learn what it is to combat a people who are animated by one spirit against him." Tory and Whig alike held that " never had so happy an opportunity existed in Britain to strike a bold stroke for the rescue of the world;" and Canning at once resolved to change the system of desultory descents on colonies and sugar islands for a vigorous warfare in the Peninsula. Supplies were sent to the Spanish insurgents with reckless profusion, and two small armies placed under the command of Sir John Moore and Sir Arthur Wellesley for service in the Peninsula. In July 1808 the surrender at Baylen of a French force which had invaded Andalusia gave the first shock to the power of Napoleon, and the blow was followed by one almost as severe. Landing at the Mondego with fifteen thousand men, Sir Arthur Wellesley drove the French army of Portugal from the field of Vimiera, and forced it to surrender in the Convention of Cintra on the 30th of August. But the tide of success was soon roughly turned. Napoleon appeared in Spain with an army of two hundred thousand men ; and Moore, who had advanced from Lisbon to Salamanca to support the Spanish armies, found them crushed on the Ebro, and was driven to fall hastily back on the coast. His force saved its honour in a battle before Corunna, which enabled it to embark in safety ; but elsewhere all seemed lost. The whole of northern and central Spain was held by the French armies ; and even Zaragoza, which had once heroically repulsed them, submitted after a second equally desperate resistance.

The landing of the wreck of Moore's army and the news of the Spanish defeats turned the temper of England from the wildest hope to the deepest despair ; but Canning remained unmoved. On the day of the evacuation of Corunna he signed a treaty of alliance with the Spanish Junta at Cadiz ; and the English force at Lisbon, which had already prepared to leave Portugal, was reinforced with thirteen thousand fresh troops and placed under the command of Sir Arthur Wellesley. " Portugal," Wellesley wrote coolly, " may be defended against any force which the French can bring against it." At this critical moment the best of the French troops with the Emperor himself were drawn from the Peninsula to the Danube ; for the Spanish rising had roused Austria as well as England to a renewal of the struggle. When Marshal Soult therefore threatened Lisbon from the north, Wellesley marched boldly against him, drove him from Oporto in a disastrous retreat, and suddenly changing his line of operations, pushed with twenty thousand men by Abrantes on Madrid. He was joined on the march by a Spanish force of thirty thousand men ; and

Sec. IV.

The
War with
France
1793
to
1815

a bloody action with a French army of equal force at Talavera in July, 1809, restored the renown of English arms. The losses on both sides were enormous, and the French fell back at the close of the struggle ; but the fruits of the victory were lost by a sudden appearance of Soult on the English line of advance, and Wellesley was forced to retreat hastily on Badajoz. His failure was embittered by heavier disasters elsewhere. Austria was driven to sue for peace by Napoleon's victory at Wagram ; and a force of forty thousand English soldiers which had been despatched against Antwerp returned home baffled after losing half its numbers in the marshes of Walcheren.

**Torres
Vedras**

The failure at Walcheren brought about the fall of the Portland Ministry. Canning attributed the disaster to the incompetence of Lord Castlereagh, an Irish peer who after taking the chief part in bringing about the union between England and Ireland had been raised by the Duke of Portland to the post of Secretary at War ; and the quarrel between the two Ministers ended in a duel, and in their resignation of their offices. The Duke of Portland retired with Canning ; and a new ministry was formed out of the more Tory members of the late administration under the guidance of Spencer Perceval, an industrious mediocrity of the narrowest type ; the Marquis of Wellesley, a brother of the English general in Spain, becoming Foreign Secretary. But if Perceval and his colleagues possessed few of the higher qualities of statesmanship, they had one characteristic which in the actual position of English affairs was beyond all price. They were resolute to continue the war. In the nation at large the fit of enthusiasm had been followed by a fit of despair ; and the City of London even petitioned for a withdrawal of the English forces from the Peninsula. Napoleon seemed irresistible, and now that Austria was crushed and England stood alone in opposition to him, the Emperor resolved to put an end to the strife by a vigorous prosecution of the war in Spain. Andalusia, the one province which remained independent, was invaded in the opening of 1810, and with the exception of Cadiz reduced to submission ; while Marshal Massena with a fine army of eighty thousand men marched upon Lisbon. Even Perceval abandoned all hope of preserving a hold on the Peninsula in face of these new efforts, and threw on Wellesley, who had been raised to the peerage as Lord Wellington after Talavera, the responsibility of resolving to remain there. But the cool judgement and firm temper which distinguished Wellington enabled him to face a responsibility from which weaker men would have shrunk. " I conceive," he answered, " that the honour and interest of our country require that we should hold our ground here as long as possible ; and, please God, I will maintain it as long as I can." By the addition of Portuguese troops who had been trained under British officers, his army was now raised to fifty thousand men ; and though his inferiority in force com-

SEC. IV.

THE
WAR WITH
FRANCE
1793
TO
1815

pelled him to look on while Massena reduced the frontier fortresses of Ciudad Rodrigo and Almeida, he inflicted on him a heavy check at the heights of Busaco, and finally fell back in October, 1810, on three lines of defence which he had secretly constructed at Torres Vedras, along a chain of mountain heights crowned with redoubts and bristling with cannon. The position was impregnable ; and able and stubborn as Massena was he found himself forced after a month's fruitless efforts to fall back in a masterly retreat ; but so terrible were the privations of the French army in passing again through the wasted country that it was only with forty thousand men that he reached Ciudad Rodrigo in the spring of 1811. Reinforced by fresh troops, Massena turned fiercely to the relief of Almeida, which Wellington had besieged ; but two days' bloody and obstinate fighting in May, 1811, failed to drive the English army from its position at Fuentes d'Onore, and the Marshal fell back on Salamanca and relinquished his effort to drive Wellington from Portugal.

Great as was the effect of Torres Vedras in restoring the spirit of the English people and in reviving throughout Europe the hope of resistance to the tyranny of Napoleon, its immediate result was little save the deliverance of Portugal. The French remained masters of all Spain save Cadiz and the eastern provinces, and even the east coast was reduced in 1811 by the vigour of General Suchet. While England thus failed to rescue Spain from the aggression of Napoleon, she was suddenly brought face to face with the result of her own aggression in America. The Orders in Council with which Canning had attempted to prevent the transfer of the carrying trade from English to neutral ships, by compelling all vessels on their way to ports under blockade to touch at British harbours, had at once created serious embarrassments with America. In the long strife between France and England, America had already borne much from both combatants, but above all from Britain. Not only had the English Government exercized its right of search, but it asserted a right of seizing English seamen found in American vessels ; and as there were few means of discriminating between English seamen and American, the sailor of Maine or Massachusetts was often impressed to serve in the British fleet. Galled however as was America by outrages such as these, she was hindered from resenting them by her strong disinclination to war, as well as by the profit which she drew from the maintenance of her neutral position. But the Orders in Council and the Milan Decree forced her into action, and she at once answered them by an embargo of trade with Europe. After a year's trial, however, America found it impossible to maintain the embargo ; and at the opening of 1809 she exchanged the embargo for an Act of Non-Intercourse with France and England alone. But the Act was equally ineffective. The American Government was utterly with-

Sec. IV.

The
War with
France
1793
to
1815
May 1810

out means of enforcing it on its land frontier ; and it had small means of enforcing it at sea. Vessels sailed daily for British ports ; and at last the Non-Intercourse Act was repealed altogether. All that America persisted in maintaining was an offer that if either Power would repeal its edicts, it would prohibit American commerce with the other. Napoleon seized on this offer, and after promising to revoke his Berlin and Milan Decrees he called on America to redeem her pledge. In February 1811, therefore, the United States announced that all intercourse with Great Britain and her dependencies was at an end. The effect of this step was seen in a reduction of English exports during this year by a third of their whole amount. It was in vain that Britain pleaded that the Emperor's promises remained unfulfilled, and that the enforcement of non-intercourse with England was thus an unjust act, and an act of hostility. The pressure of the American policy, as well as news of the warlike temper which had at last grown up in the United States, made submission inevitable ; for the industrial state of England was now so critical that to expose it to fresh shocks was to court the very ruin which Napoleon had planned.

State of England

During the earlier years of the war indeed the increase of wealth had been enormous. England was sole mistress of the seas. The war gave her possession of the colonies of Spain, of Holland, and of France ; and if her trade was checked for a time by the Berlin Decree, the efforts of Napoleon were soon rendered fruitless by the vast smuggling system which sprang up along the southern coasts and the coast of North Germany. English exports had nearly doubled since the opening of the century. Manufactures profited by the discoveries of Watt and Arkwright ; and the consumption of raw cotton in the mills of Lancashire rose during the same period from fifty to a hundred millions of pounds. The vast accumulation of capital, as well as the vast increase of the population at this time, told upon the land, and forced agriculture into a feverish and unhealthy prosperity. Wheat rose to famine prices, and the value of land rose in proportion with the price of wheat. Inclosures went on with prodigious rapidity ; the income of every landowner was doubled, while the farmers were able to introduce improvements into the processes of agriculture which changed the whole face of the country. But if the increase of wealth was enormous, its distribution was partial. During the fifteen years which preceded Waterloo, the number of the population rose from ten to thirteen millions, and this rapid increase kept down the rate of wages, which would naturally have advanced in a corresponding degree with the increase in the national wealth. Even manufactures, though destined in the long run to benefit the labouring classes, seemed at first rather to depress them ; for one of the earliest results of the introduction of machinery was the ruin of a number of

Sec. IV.

The
War with
France
1793
to
1815

small trades which were carried on at home, and the pauperization of families who relied on them for support. In the winter of 1811 the terrible pressure of this transition from handicraft to machinery was seen in the Luddite, or machine-breaking, riots which broke out over the northern and midland counties ; and which were only suppressed by military force. While labour was thus thrown out of its older grooves, and the rate of wages kept down at an artificially low figure by the rapid increase of population, the rise in the price of wheat, which brought wealth to the landowner and the farmer, brought famine and death to the poor, for England was cut off by the war from the vast corn-fields of the Continent or of America, which now-a-days redress from their abundance the results of a bad harvest. Scarcity was followed by a terrible pauperization of the labouring classes. The amount of the poor-rate rose fifty per cent. ; and with the increase of poverty followed its inevitable result, the increase of crime.

The natural relation of trade and commerce to the general wealth of the people at large was thus disturbed by the peculiar circumstances of the time. The war enriched the landowner, the farmer, the merchant, the manufacturer ; but it impoverished the poor. It is indeed from these fatal years which lie between the Peace of Luneville and Waterloo that we must date that war of classes, that social severance between employers and employed, which still forms the main difficulty of English politics. But it is from these years too that we must date the renewal of that progressive movement in politics which had been suspended since the opening of the war. The publication of the *Edinburgh Review* in 1802 by a knot of young lawyers at Edinburgh marked a revival of the policy of constitutional and administrative progress which had been reluctantly abandoned by William Pitt. Jeremy Bentham gave a new vigour to political speculation by his advocacy of the doctrine of Utility, and his definition of "the greatest happiness of the greatest number" as the aim of political action. In 1809 Sir Francis Burdett revived the question of Parliamentary Reform. Only fifteen members supported his motion ; and a reference to the House of Commons, in a pamphlet which he subsequently published, as "a part of our fellow-subjects collected together by means which it is not necessary to describe" was met by his committal to the Tower, where he remained till the prorogation of the Parliament. A far greater effect was produced by the perseverance with which Canning pressed year by year the question of Catholic Emancipation. So long as Perceval lived both efforts at Reform were equally vain ; but on the accession of Lord Liverpool to power the advancing strength of a more liberal sentiment in the nation was felt by the policy of "moderate concession" which was adopted by the new ministry. Catholic Emancipation became an open question in the Cabinet itself, and was adopted in 1812 by a triumphant majority in the House of Commons, though still rejected by the Lords.

SEC. IV.

THE
WAR WITH
FRANCE
1793
TO
1815
**War with
America**

With social and political troubles thus awaking about them, even Tory statesmen were not willing to face the terrible consequences of a ruin of English industry, such as might follow from the junction of America with Napoleon. They were, in fact, preparing to withdraw the Orders in Council when their plans were arrested by the dissolution of the Perceval Ministry. Its position had from the first been a weak one. A return of the King's madness had made it necessary in the beginning of 1811 to confer the Regency by Act of Parliament on the Prince of Wales ; and the Whig sympathies of the Prince threatened the Perceval Cabinet with dismissal. The insecurity of their position told on the conduct of the war ; for the apparent inactivity of Wellington during 1811 was really due to the hesitation and timidity of the ministers at home. In May, 1812, the assassination of Perceval by a maniac named Bellingham brought about the fall of his ministry ; and fresh efforts were made by the Regent to install the Whigs in office. Mutual distrust however foiled his attempts ; and the old

ministry was restored under the headship of Lord Liverpool, a man of no great abilities, but temperate, well informed, and endowed with a remarkable skill in holding discordant colleagues together. The most important of these colleagues was Lord Castlereagh, who became Secretary for Foreign Affairs. His first work was to meet the danger in which Canning had involved the country by his Orders in Council. At the opening of 1812 America, in despair of redress, had resolved on war ; Congress voted an increase of both army and navy, and laid an embargo on all vessels in American harbours. Actual hostilities might still have been averted by the repeal of the Orders, on which the English Cabinet was resolved, but in the confusion which followed the murder of Perceval the opportunity was lost. On the 23rd of June, only twelve days after the Ministry had been formed, the Orders were repealed ; but when the news of the repeal reached America, it came six weeks too late. On the 18th of June an Act of Congress had declared America at war with Great Britain.

The moment when America entered into the great struggle was a critical moment in the history of mankind. Six days after President Madison issued his declaration of war, Napoleon crossed the Niemen on his march to Moscow. Successful as his policy had been in stirring up war between England and America, it had been no less successful in breaking the alliance which he had made with the Emperor Alexander at Tilsit and in forcing on a contest with Russia. On the one hand, Napoleon was irritated by the refusal of Russia to enforce strictly the suspension of all trade with England, though such a suspension would have ruined the Russian landowners. On the other, the Czar saw with growing anxiety the advance of the French Empire which sprang from Napoleon's resolve to enforce his system by a seizure of the northern coasts. In 1811 Holland, the Hanseatic towns, part of Westphalia, and the Duchy of Oldenburg were successively annexed, and the Duchy of Mecklenburg threatened with seizure.   A peremptory demand on the part of France for the entire cessation of intercourse with England brought the quarrel to a head; and preparations were made on both sides for a gigantic struggle.   The best of the French soldiers were drawn from Spain to the frontier of Poland; and Wellington, whose army had been raised to a force of forty thousand Englishmen and twenty thousand Portuguese, profited by the withdrawal to throw off his system of defence and to assume an attitude of attack.   Ciudad Rodrigo and Badajoz were taken by storm during the spring of 1812; and three days before Napoleon crossed the Niemen in his march on Moscow, Wellington crossed the Agueda in a march on Salamanca.   After a series of masterly movements on both sides, Marmont with the French army of the North attacked the English on the hills in the neighbourhood of that town.   While he was marching round the right of the English position, his left wing remained isolated; and with a sudden exclamation of " Marmont is lost!" Wellington flung on it the bulk of his force, crushed it, and drove the whole army from the field.   The loss on either side was nearly equal, but failure had demoralized the French army; and its retreat forced Joseph to leave Madrid, and Soult to evacuate Andalusia and to concentrate the southern army on the eastern coast.   While Napoleon was still pushing slowly over the vast plains of Poland, Wellington made his entry into Madrid in August, and began the siege of Burgos. The town however held out gallantly for a month, till the advance of the two French armies, now concentrated in the north and south of Spain, forced Wellington in October to a hasty retreat on the Portuguese frontier.   If he had shaken the rule of the French in Spain in this campaign, his ultimate failure showed how firm a military hold they still possessed there.   But the disappointment was forgotten in the news which followed it.   At the moment when the English troops fell back from Burgos began the retreat of the Grand Army from Moscow.   Victorious in a battle at Borodino, Napoleon had entered the older capital of Russia in triumph, and waited impatiently to receive proposals of peace from the Czar, when a fire kindled by its own inhabitants reduced the city to ashes.   The French army was forced to fall back amidst the horrors of a Russian winter. Of the four hundred thousand combatants who formed the Grand Army at its first outset, only a few thousand recrossed the Niemen in December.

In spite of the gigantic efforts which Napoleon made to repair the loss of the Grand Army, the spell which he had cast over Europe was broken by the retreat from Moscow.   Prussia rose against him as the Russians crossed the Niemen in the spring of 1813; and the forces which held it were at once thrown back on the Elbe.   In this

SEC. IV.

THE
WAR WITH
FRANCE
1793
TO
1815
*Wellington
in Spain*

July 22

*The Retreat
from
Moscow*

**Fall of
Napoleon**

SEC. IV.

THE
WAR WITH
FRANCE
1793
TO
1815

emergency the military genius of the French Emperor rose to its height. With a fresh army of two hundred thousand men whom he had gathered at Mainz he marched on the allied armies of Russia and Prussia in May, cleared Saxony by a victory over them at Lutzen, and threw them back on the Oder by a fresh victory at Bautzen. Disheartened by defeat, and by the neutral attitude which Austria still preserved, the two powers consented in June to an armistice, and negotiated for peace. But Austria, though unwilling to utterly ruin France to the profit of her great rival in the East, was as resolute as either of the allies to wrest from Napoleon his supremacy over Europe; and at the moment when it became clear that Napoleon was only bent on playing with her proposals, she was stirred to action by news that his army was at last driven from Spain. Wellington had left Portugal in May with an army which had now risen to ninety thousand men;

and overtaking the French forces in retreat at Vitoria he inflicted on them a defeat which drove them in utter rout across the Pyrenees. Madrid was at once evacuated; and Clauzel fell back from Zaragoza into France. The victory not only freed Spain from its invaders; it restored the spirit of the Allies. The close of the armistice was followed by a union of Austria with the forces of Prussia and the Czar; and in October a final overthrow of Napoleon at Leipzig forced the French army to fall back in rout across the Rhine. The war now hurried to its close. Though held at bay for a while by the sieges of San Sebastian and Pampeluna, as well as by an obstinate defence of the Pyrenees, Wellington succeeded in the very month of the triumph at Leipzig in winning a victory on the Bidassoa, which enabled him to enter France. He was soon followed by the Allies. On the last day of 1813 their forces crossed the Rhine; and a third of France passed, without opposition, into their hands. For two months more Napoleon maintained a wonderful struggle with a handful of raw conscripts against their overwhelming numbers; while in the south, Soult, forced from his entrenched camp near Bayonne and defeated at Orthes, fell back before Wellington on Toulouse. Here their two armies met in April in a stubborn and indecisive engagement. But though neither leader knew it, the war was even then at an end. The struggle of Napoleon himself had ended at the close of March with the surrender of Paris; and the submission of the capital was at once followed by the abdication of the Emperor and the return of the Bourbons.

England's triumph over its enemy was dashed by the more doubtful fortunes of the struggle across the Atlantic. The declaration of war by America seemed an act of sheer madness; for its navy consisted of a few frigates and sloops; its army was a mass of half-drilled and half-armed recruits; while the States themselves were divided on the question of the war, and Connecticut with Massachusetts refused to send either money or men. Three attempts to penetrate into Canada during the summer and autumn were repulsed with heavy loss. But these failures were more than redeemed by unexpected successes at sea. In two successive engagements between English and American frigates, the former were forced to strike their flag. The effect of these victories was out of all proportion to their real importance ; for they were the first heavy blows which had been dealt at England's supremacy over the seas. In 1813 America followed up its naval triumphs by more vigorous efforts on land. Its forces cleared Lake Ontario, captured Toronto, destroyed the British flotilla on Lake Erie, and made themselves masters of Upper Canada. An attack on Lower Canada, however, was successfully beaten back ; and a fresh advance of the British and Canadian forces in the heart of the winter again recovered the Upper Province. The reverse gave fresh strength to the party in the United States which had throughout been opposed to the war, and whose opposition to it had been embittered by the terrible distress brought about by the blockade and the ruin of American commerce. Cries of secession began to be heard, and Massachusetts took the bold step of appointing delegates to confer with delegates from the other New England States "on the subject of their grievances and common concerns." In 1814, however, the war was renewed with more vigour than ever ; and Upper Canada was again invaded. But the American army, after inflicting a severe defeat on the British forces in the battle of Chippewa in July, was itself defeated a few weeks after in an equally stubborn engagement, and thrown back on its own frontier ; while the fall of Napoleon enabled the English Government to devote its whole strength to the struggle with an enemy which it had ceased to despise. General Ross, with a force of four thousand men, appeared in the Potomac, captured Washington, and before evacuating the city burnt its public buildings to the ground. Few more shameful acts are recorded in our history ; and it was the more shameful in that it was done under strict orders from the Government at home. The raid upon Washington, however, was intended simply to strike terror into the American people ; and the real stress of the war was thrown on two expeditions whose business was to penetrate into the States from the north and from the south. Both proved utter failures. A force of nine thousand Peninsular veterans which marched in September to the attack of Plattsburg on Lake Champlain was forced to fall back by the defeat of the English flotilla which accompanied it. A second force under General Packenham appeared in December at the mouth of the Mississippi and attacked New Orleans, but was repulsed by General Jackson with the loss of half its numbers. Peace, however, had already been concluded. The close of the French war, if it left untouched the grounds of the struggle, made the United States sensible of the danger of pushing it further ;

SEC. IV.

THE
WAR WITH
FRANCE
1793
TO
1815
**Return
of
Napoleon**

Britain herself was anxious for peace ; and the warring claims, both of England and America, were set aside in silence in the treaty of 1814.

The close of the war with America freed England's hands at a moment when the reappearance of Napoleon at Paris called her to a new and final struggle with France. By treaty with the Allied Powers Napoleon had been suffered to retain a fragment of his former empire —the island of Elba off the coast of Tuscany ; and from Elba he had looked on at the quarrels which sprang up between his conquerors as soon as they gathered at Vienna to complete the settlement of Europe. The most formidable of these quarrels arose from the claim of Prussia to annex Saxony, and that of Russia to annex Poland ; but their union for this purpose was met by a counter-league of England and Austria with their old enemy France, whose ambassador, Talleyrand, laboured vigorously to bring the question to an issue by force of arms. At the moment, however, when a war between the two leagues seemed close at hand, Napoleon quitted Elba, landed on the coast near Cannes, and, followed only by a thousand of his guards, marched over the mountains of Dauphiné upon Grenoble and Lyons. He counted, and counted justly, on the indifference of the country to its new Bourbon rulers, on the longing of the army for a fresh struggle which should restore its glory, and above all on the spell of his name over soldiers whom he had so often led to victory. In twenty days from his landing he reached the Tuileries unopposed, while Lewis the Eighteenth fled helplessly to Ghent. But whatever hopes he had drawn from the divisions of the Allied Powers were at once dispelled by their resolute action on the news of his descent upon France. Their strife was hushed and their old union restored by the consciousness of a common danger. An engagement to supply a million of men for the purposes of the war, and a recall of their armies to the Rhine, answered Napoleon's efforts to open negotiations with the Powers. England furnished subsidies to the amount of eleven millions, and hastened to place an army on the frontier of the Netherlands. The best troops of the force which had been employed in the Peninsula, however, were still across the Atlantic ; and of the eighty thousand men who gathered round Wellington only about a half were Englishmen, the rest principally raw levies from Belgium and Hanover. The Duke's plan was to unite with the one hundred and fifty thousand Prussians under Marshal Blucher who were advancing on the Lower Rhine, and to enter France by Mons and Namur, while the forces of Austria and Russia closed in upon Paris by way of Belfort and Elsass.

March 1,
1815

Waterloo

1815

But Napoleon had thrown aside all thought of a merely defensive war. By amazing efforts he had raised an army of two hundred and fifty thousand men in the few months since his arrival in Paris ; and in the opening of June one hundred and twenty thousand Frenchmen were concentrated on the Sambre at Charleroi, while Wellington'-

troops still lay in cantonments on the line of the Scheldt from Ath to Nivelle, and Blucher's on that of the Meuse from Nivelle to Liége. Both the allied armies hastened to unite at Quatre Bras; but their junction was already impossible. Blucher with eighty thousand men was himself attacked by Napoleon at Ligny, and after a desperate contest driven back with terrible loss upon Wavre. On the same day Ney with twenty thousand men, and an equal force under D'Erlon in reserve, appeared before Quatre Bras, where as yet only ten thousand English and the same force of Belgian troops had been able to assemble. The Belgians broke before the charges of the French horse; but the dogged resistance of the English infantry gave time for Wellington to bring up corps after corps, till at the close of the day Ney saw himself heavily outnumbered, and withdrew baffled from the field. About five thousand men had fallen on either side in this fierce engagement: but heavy as was Wellington's loss, the firmness of the English army had already done much to foil Napoleon's effort at breaking through the line of the Allies. Blucher's retreat however left the English flank uncovered; and on the following day, while the Prussians were falling back on Wavre, Wellington with nearly seventy thousand men—for his army was now well in hand—withdrew in good order upon Waterloo, followed by the mass of the French forces under the Emperor himself. Napoleon had detached Marshal Grouchy with thirty thousand men to hang upon the rear of the beaten Prussians, while with a force of eighty thousand he resolved to bring Wellington to battle. On the morning of the 18th of June the two armies faced one another on the field of Waterloo in front of the Forest of Soignies, on the high road to Brussels. Napoleon's one fear had been that of a continued retreat. "I have them!" he cried, as he saw the English line drawn up on a low rise of ground which stretched across the high road from the château of Hougomont on its right to the farm and straggling village of La Haye Sainte on its left. He had some grounds for his confidence of success. On either side the forces numbered between seventy and eighty thousand men: but the French were superior in guns and cavalry, and a large part of Wellington's force consisted of Belgian levies who broke and fled at the outset of the fight. A fierce attack upon Hougomont opened the battle at eleven; but it was not till midday that the corps of D'Erlon advanced upon the centre near La Haye Sainte, which from that time bore the main brunt of the struggle. Never has greater courage, whether of attack or endurance, been shown on any field than was shown by both combatants at Waterloo. The columns of D'Erlon, repulsed by the English foot, were hurled back in disorder by a charge of the Scots Greys; but the victorious horsemen were crushed in their turn by the French cuirassiers, and the mass of the French cavalry, twelve thousand strong, flung itself in charge after charge on the English front, carrying the

SEC. IV.

THE
WAR WITH
FRANCE

1793
TO
1815
June 16

SEC. IV.

THE
WAR WITH
FRANCE
1793
TO
1815

English guns and sweeping with desperate bravery round the unbroken squares whose fire thinned their ranks. With almost equal bravery the French columns of the centre again advanced, wrested at last the farm of La Haye Sainte from their opponents, and pushed on vigorously though in vain under Ney against the troops in its rear. But meanwhile every hour was telling against Napoleon. To win the battle he must crush the English army before Blucher joined it ; and the English army was still uncrushed. Terrible as was his loss, and many of his regiments were reduced to a mere handful of men, Wellington stubbornly held his ground while the Prussians, advancing from Wavre through deep and miry forest roads, were slowly gathering to his support, disregarding the attack on their rear by which Grouchy strove to hold them back from the field. At half-past four their advanced guard deployed at last from the woods ; but the main body was far behind, and Napoleon was still able to hold his ground against them till their increasing masses forced him to stake all on a desperate effort against the English front. The Imperial Guard—his only reserve, and which had as yet taken no part in the battle—was drawn up at seven in two huge columns of attack. The first, with Ney himself at its head, swept all before it as it mounted the rise beside La Haye Sainte, on which the thin English line still held its ground, and all but touched the English front when its mass, torn by the terrible fire of musketry with which it was received, gave way before a charge. The second, three thousand strong, advanced with the same courage over the slope near Hougomont, only to be repulsed and shattered in its turn. At the moment when these masses fell slowly and doggedly back down the fatal rise, the Prussians pushed forward on Napoleon's right, their guns swept the road to Charleroi, and Wellington seized the moment for a general advance. From that hour all was lost. Only the Guard stood firm in the wreck of the French army ; and though darkness and exhaustion checked the English in their pursuit of the broken troops as they hurried from the field, the Prussian horse continued the chase through the night. Only forty thousand Frenchmen with some thirty guns recrossed the Sambre, while Napoleon himself fled hurriedly to Paris. His second abdication was followed by the triumphant entry of the English and Prussian armies into the French capital ; and the long war ended with his exile to St. Helena, and the return of Lewis the Eighteenth to the throne of the Bourbons.

EPILOGUE.[1]

Section I.—The Social Revolution, 1815—1914.

It is impossible to relate here the crowded events of the century that followed the battle of Waterloo. The Napoleonic war itself was not more critical for the fortunes of England, nor more passionate in its conduct, than the desperate struggle of the nation to direct the industrial revolution into the way of freedom, and to unite the whole people in full rights of citizenship. In that hundred years every order and class in the State has been profoundly changed, and with these the State itself transformed in the theory of government, the source of power, and the exercise of authority. The whole body of Statutes has been changed in form or in substance till but few laws on the statute-book in 1804 now remain unaltered. English life had twice before been given a new direction in character through legislation imposed by powerful rulers, Henry II. and Henry VIII.; but this third age of legislative change, this series of reforms unparalleled in English history, was the work of the nation itself. The undiminished force of the old English tradition of self-government and the spirit of freedom have directed the growth of national life at home, the shaping of the colonial empire, and in some degree the foreign policy of the country.

Social reform had all but ceased in an England deeply occupied with the struggle in America and the conflict with France. But throughout the century to come no grave outward danger threatened her. Through the sufferings of the long war, England had asserted her own independence and that of the European peoples. From all sides opened a great prosperity. Left without a rival by the destruction of the navies of France, Spain, Denmark, she absorbed the carrying trade of two continents, and shipped her own wares to be flung broadcast in the United States and in Germany, and as far as India itself, to undersell every competitor. Once more, as after the Armada, a lofty pride stirred the nation. "England," it was said, "seems destined by Providence to lead the moral condition of the world. Year after year we are sending forth thousands and hundreds of thousands of our citizens to people the vast solitudes and islands of another hemisphere; the Anglo-Saxon race will shortly overspread half the habitable globe. What a mighty and what a rapid addition to the happiness of mankind, if these thousands should carry with them, and plant in those distant regions, our freedom, our laws, our morality, and our religion!" The hereditary faith of the governing

The peace

---

[1] Copyright, 1916, by Alice Stopford Green.

Sec. I.

The Social
Revolu-
tion
1815
to
1914

classes in the Constitution, built up through long ages of effort, was
unabated. "To sustain, to repair, to beautify this noble pile," Black-
stone had written in 1765, "is a charge intrusted principally to the
nobility, and such gentlemen of the kingdom as are delegated by
their country to parliament"; and in 1830 Wellington, in the same
spirit, declared that no improvement was needed—if he had to form a
legislature for England, he did not mean to assert he could form such a
legislature as they possessed now, for the nature of man was incapable
of reaching such excellence at once; but he would try to form one
that would produce the same results. The only fear of the old aristocracy was a dread of change. The terror of the French revolution
had doubled their anxiety to maintain undisturbed the form of government which gave to them unchallenged security of political power and
of property. With the fall of the ancient principle of primogeniture,
they held, the pillars of the State would crumble—the parliamentary
government of the landed magnates, and their command of county
administration. With the division of great hereditary estates on which
their power rested, the food of the country must perish.

The ideal of the Tory aristocracy was a world where the rich
should guide and protect the poor, who under this guardianship
should obediently labour for a modest customary wage, while the
welfare of all was secured by a changeless Constitution. They were
confronted with new problems when the industrial revolution turned
Great Britain from a thinly peopled agricultural land into a crowded
workshop, and created a society unknown before—a middle class of
prodigious wealth and activity, and a vast working class on the
borders of starvation. Neither the leaders of industry nor the factory
workers, alike shut out from a voice in the government of the country,
saw any grounds of reverence for the "great juggle of the English
constitution, a thing of monopolies and churchcraft and sinecures."
The new industrial world had the confidence of pre-eminent ability.
On the manufacturers depended the restoration of the country's wealth,
and the payment of its enormous war debt. The men of science were
with them, Davy, Herschell, Watt, Stephenson; religious philanthropists such as Zachary Macaulay, Clarkson, Wilberforce; and
secular reformers, James Mill, Sir Samuel Romilly, Mackintosh,
Huskisson, Jeremy Bentham, and many more, discussing universal
suffrage, the ballot, reform of Parliament, freedom of the Press,

just and equal laws. Above all the rest the call of Bentham rang
out to free men through the country. Born of the middle classes he
shared their ideals, and became at last their prophet. The end of all

government, he proclaimed, must be utility, or the good of the governed. "The greatest happiness of the greatest number," such was
the generous passion that was to direct his life: "At the sight of it
I cried out, as it were in an inward ecstasy." Before the public need

the long apathy of legislative stagnation must end: and reform of
the whole law of England must be by act of the people, the guardians
of their own welfare, in an omnipotent Parliament—a Parliament
holding a real sovereignty.   Legislation must henceforth be a
science with fixed principles, and a legal procedure that would
give to every man a certainty of protection. All laws must be open
to free inquiry, and "the principle of utility" the sole test of worth.
This principle was to strike at all abuses and selfish interests, at
all offices or institutions which brought no benefit to the public. It
was to abolish every needless restraint which limited the freedom of
human existence.   Such was the revolution that Bentham in his
ecstasy foresaw, and preached with all the fervour of his original
genius and lofty devotion.   "Has a man talents?" he wrote; "he
owes them to his country in every way in which they can be
serviceable."

"To the Tories," said Bentham, "the principle of utility is a
dangerous principle." There were other heralds of revolution. Never
before had such misery been known among the English poor. Half
a million of men cast adrift at the end of the war wandered through
the country, dying by hundreds and thousands of hunger.   A more
prolonged and universal agony followed the destruction of the old
industrial system through the rapid development of machinery driven
by steam.   Ruin fell on the master craftsman—a manual worker
employing his family or a few journeymen and apprentices in his home,
owning his plant, and selling for his own profit—as labour was swept
into new factories, and the factories gathered into hastily created
towns, till by 1826 not a third of the population was left to live on the
land.   In eighteen years the power-looms increased from 3,000 to
100,000; and the hand-loom weavers, once an aristocracy as it were
of labour, sank through extremity of want into the undistinguished
mass of hired workers—life-long wage-earners with no economic
interest in the product of their labour, and helpless under the
autocracy of the all-powerful capitalist of the new industry.   The
simple local government of older days broke down; with the new
doctrines of unlimited competition and every man for himself alone,
the ancient protecting customs of the craftsmen disappeared.   Economists contemplating the greatest national debt that any country had
ever incurred, dazzled by the prospects of England in the world's
market, fearful of foreign rivalry, proclaimed the making of wealth
and the full use of labour to be the first duty and right of the citizen, and the first necessity for the permanence of the State.   The
prosperity of the country, the virtue of its people, must depend on the
competitive struggle for life, and the freedom of every man in whatever estate to make his own contract as best he could.   The profit of
a cotton mill, declared one, was obtained out of the work of the last

SEC. I.

THE SOCIAL
REVOLU-
TION
1815
TO
1914

Indus-
trial
Revolu-
tion

1816–1834

*The new
economics*

Sec. I.

The Social
Revolu-
tion
1815
to
1914

hour. It was commonly averred that "in the lower orders the deterioration of morals increases with the quantity of unemployed time." On every plea, moral and economical, the day of labour was lengthened and the wage cheapened. There was not a single Act on the statute books to protect the worker in his bargain. While the employer was practically beyond the reach of the law, the worker accused of breaking contract could be sentenced, in a magistrate's private house, and without being allowed to say a word in his own defence, to three months' imprisonment. He had no remedy if he was defrauded of his wretched wage, and paid in food from the master's shop, and at his price; or was given at cost price some of the goods he had made to sell as best he could for a livelihood. A few sanitary and moral rules were laid down for workers in factories—the washing of the rooms twice a year with quick-lime, the limit of twelve hours' work for child apprentices, separate dormitories for men and women, and the teaching to apprentices for one hour on Sunday the principles of the Christian religion; but the Act provided no means to carry out this advice. Later Acts forbade children under nine to work in a cotton factory, and under sixteen to work more than twelve hours a day; and limited young persons under eighteen to sixty-nine hours of labour a week. There was little means of enforcing such rules. Toil went on through day and night. Men were kept in at meal times to clean machinery. They were forbidden to carry watches, lest they should check the factory clock that prolonged the natural hours. There were frequent floggings, distortions from painful disease, accidents from unfenced machinery. Managers urged in defence of the system that thus alone could England defy the foreigner and keep her place in the world. As the growth of machinery for the first time brought in the labour of women and children to supersede that of men, they too were caught into the circle of misery. Their situation was one of unrelieved woe. Women toiled in coal-mines, chained like beasts of burden to carts which they dragged on all fours through the long galleries, traversing from seventeen to thirty miles a day. Children from five years old were sent into the darkness of the mines. In the model mill of David Dale children from five to eight worked from 6 a.m. to 7 p.m., after which they went into school. When a child reached nine the parish cut off relief, as it could then legally earn its own living by work for twelve hours, or often fourteen or sixteen. Children might be seen lying on the factory floors at night to be ready for work in the morning. Orphans and destitute infants were practically bought and sold as apprentices. We hear of blacksmiths kept at work forging fetters for them if they tried to escape, and of horses kept saddled to hunt down those who fled.

Nor was there relief for the workers in their homes; where in the "dolorous chaos" of the new-made towns they were crowded under the most forlorn conditions, huddled in houses run up by speculators in tiny courts, in alleys like gutters, in lanes where a wheelbarrow could not pass, crammed with dunghills and human beings, the air tainted by perpetual exhalations, the pavement never dry, without water supply, or drainage, or scavengers' carts. Mounds of filth were sold as manure to the farmers; and as late as 1844 only two towns were known where refuse was removed at the public expense from the quarters of the poor. Fever never left the courts, where the feeble waited for a "slow, mouldering, and putrefying death." Municipal bodies that had taken shape in another age and world were helpless before the new conditions. Each borough had its special customs, its peculiar way of conferring the freedom and the right to vote, its own form of Council. But all were alike in the original tradition carried down from merchant and trade guilds, which taught them to seek first and last the trade interests of their own members, and to exclude "strangers" from every privilege. As for the town property, said one of the Cambridge corporation, he thought it "belonged *bona-fide* to the corporation, and they had a right to do what they pleased with their own." Their finance was secret. There was no public control, and no representation on town councils, to protect the incoming multitude of workers—aliens crowded in the courts of death.

In 1816 agriculture was at the head of all other industries: while incomes from trade, handicrafts, and manufactures were reckoned at nearly 34½ millions, the rents paid by occupiers of land approached 37 millions. But while agriculture advanced, while vast fields of wheat supplied ninety per cent. of the corn used in England, the rural labourers who formed the greatest industry in the country sank into abject dependence. A secular revolution had slowly transformed country life by the steady increase of great estates worked by landless labourers. After the judges of the seventeenth century yielded to landowners the right of tying up their estates by settlements the numbers of small holdings steadily decreased. There was no land to purchase. The "enclosures" of waste, forest, or common lands cut off the people's last hold on the soil. These changes proceeded rapidly under the rule of a landed aristocracy which from the seventeenth century had absolute control of legislation. Primogeniture with its aggregation of great estates held necessary for the stability of the State, was considered no less necessary for the economic production of food for the country. From the time of Anne when enclosures, once a matter of voluntary assent or arbitrary action, were carried out by private Acts, the anxiety of the legislature was to cheapen and facilitate the process, which was thought to be a national benefit. The need of food supply in war time, the demands of an increasing population, the cost of scientific farming,

SEC. I.

THE SOCIAL
REVOLU-
TION
1815
TO
1914

1795–1800

1800

1801–45

1828

The
rural
labourer

1795

the new teaching of experimental economists—all these influences came to the aid of the powerful landed interest in their struggle to secure greater rapidity in enclosures, to lessen expenses, and overcome opposition. If reasons of State would have preserved a peasantry with a hold on the soil, all the reasons of class interest were for dissolving it. After a sharp parliamentary conflict a general Act to simplify and make uniform the working of private Acts granted under it marked the triumph of those who desired to force enclosure in all directions and on all lands, and the crushing defeat of their opponents. Two thousand Acts for fencing in commons followed in swift succession. Under the laws of settlement and of enclosures, the landlords' hold on the soil was secure. Royal Commissioners appointed to report on Real Property declared that "the law of England except in a few unimportant particulars appears to come almost as near perfection as can be expected in any human institution."

No doubt of the public advantage of enclosures, or consideration of the claims of the poor, arose till the middle of the nineteenth century. The great proprietors who made and administered the laws, and could alone bear the costs of parliamentary action and of fencing enclosures, had of necessity the determining voice. Compensation to the old commoners was often given in a form that did not alleviate their suffering: nor could any compensation ultimately atone for entire severance from the soil, and the sinking of the whole rural population into a body of mere wage-earners, owning less land than the labourers of any country in Europe; and by that fact, as we shall see, rendered more incapable of combination and resistance than even the wretched Irish cottiers. The destruction of cottage industries completed the ruin of the country people. Yeomen farmers and peasant proprietors practically ceased to exist: they drifted to the towns, or sank into workers at a daily wage. Not only small holdings but the lesser tenancies gradually vanished in a universal system of large estates and farms. On these the tillers of the soil fell into practical servitude. When with rising prices a wage of five shillings or so could not support life, a custom began of giving allowances of food to eke out the pay, and prevent wages from rising "to a height from which it would be difficult to reduce them"; and these pauperising doles from the parish came to be a part of the industrial system. Every labourer was tied to the place where he was born, and where he could be put on the rates. There, unchecked by any central control, village churchwardens and overseers had opportunity to abuse their power to private advantage; and the peasant had no appeal save to magistrates who were themselves landlords and employers. Fear and hunger were his lot. "I see scores of men," wrote Cobbett, "framed by nature to be rosy-cheeked, athletic, bold. . . I see them as thin as herrings, dragging their feet after them, pale as a ceiling, and sneaking about like beggars." Many "are actually become a sort of skeleton." The workhouse which provided for the last extremity was worse than the prison. The sick and feeble there had no helpers. The children were sold out as apprentices, or given, with 3s. 4d. a week each for food, to a contractor to make what he could of them.

If no relief was given by statute to the workers severer laws were still invented to repress their discontent. Two hundred offences were accumulated for which a man could be hanged, and it is reckoned that from 1810 to 1845 more than fourteen hundred persons were executed for crimes that are no longer punished with death. Murderers swung in chains on gibbets. For stealing five shillings, or for burning a rick of hay, the bodies of men were left for hours on gallows in the market places as a warning. The punishment for picking a pocket of a handkerchief was seven years' transportation, and that after a few minutes' undefended trial; for even in 1824 and 1826 the House of Commons still refused to allow prisoners tried for murder or larceny defence by counsel. Perjurers in the pillory slowly revolved before the crowd. Landowners used spring-guns and man-traps, rating the life of a poacher below that of a hare; and gave sentence of seven years' transportation for stealing a pheasant. In vain Sir Samuel Romilly, known for his "anti-hanging laws," fought to bring some humanity into the code; at his death all his efforts had only exempted from capital punishment picking pockets and stealing from bleaching grounds. " Neither in private nor in public was there any refuge or kindness for an evangelical man " ; nor could " Human-itarians " hope for toleration, even if Dr. Parr "was more shocked as a grammarian at the word than as a divine at the sect."

Workers so harshly trained from infancy learned often a fathomless resignation: and many were illumined by an impassioned piety nourished in the chapel and the Sunday school where they were consoled by humble ministers who had suffered the same tribulations. In the darkest courts and alleys we find records of a spiritual enthusiasm which, ignored by the Established Church, called men to an amazing heroism and tenderness to suffering. Parliament had constantly rejected bills to provide a system of national education, and not a penny was spent by the State for the instruction of the people. Philanthropic and ecclesiastical efforts were few and perverted in intention. A Friend, Lancaster, with the help of some Quaker philanthropists and Nonconformist ministers, proposed a scheme of " Schools for all " ; and this was followed by the " National Society for the Education of the Poor in the principles of the Established Church." Their plan was to obtain some disused workshop which could contain a thousand children; to give to a sensible master a month's training;

Sec. I.

The Social Revolution
1815
to
1914

Law and Crime

1818

1819

Education

1807
1820

1810
1811

Sec. I.

The Social
Revolu-
tion
1815
to
1914

on opening the school to choose thirty intelligent children, who for half an hour before the rest of the school should be taught the day's lesson; after which each little monitor should instruct a class of thirty; while the master kept order over the whole. Mrs. Hannah More, a famous writer and philanthropist of her time, pointed out how an all-wise Providence showed to the poor by times of scarcity the advantages of the Government and Constitution of this country, and of the distinctions of rank and fortune which enabled the rich so liberally to assist the needy placed in their dependence. "We trust," she said, "the poor in general, especially those that are well instructed, have received what has been done for them as a matter of favour, not of right—if so the same kindness will, I doubt not, always be extended to them." In spite of all difficulties never had such a roll of distinguished men risen from the poor as at this time. Gifford, son of a small tradesman, was to lead Conservatives as editor of the Quarterly Review ; Dalton, a weaver's son, was a famous man of science ; and another weaver's son, White, was professor of Arabic at Oxford. Any real education the poor created for themselves in working-men's clubs, mechanics' institutes, debating societies, industrial classes, Sunday schools, or little libraries where the student paid a shilling a month for books and conferences. They learned to read, and had political tracts and newspapers. "Get knowledge," was the cry of the working-classes for the next fifty years, "for in getting knowledge you get power." They discussed political economy, and the new social order which was to put an end to the calamities and humiliations inflicted by the current system. Ministers sprung from their own class denounced the influence of the State Church, and the aristocracy that upheld it as a political force. Through the dark underworld of toilers, oppressed, miserably poor, feared and despised, there ran a ferment of thought, a passionate idealism, dreams of a new society, a richer education, a larger humanitarianism, and the hopes of a national fellowship of all who laboured. Not a single theory or scheme of reform emerged in the coming century that we do not find in these early years, the full seed-time of the coming harvest. Cartwright, who had spent his life since 1776 for parliamentary reform, opened Hampden clubs to advocate universal suffrage. Thomas Spence, a poor man, once a schoolmaster, preached that the land in every village should belong to all the inhabitants. William Lovett, born in a Cornish fishing village in great poverty, claimed for the poor "bread, knowledge, and liberty" ; and with unquenchable courage and perseverance organised co-operative societies and associations to fight for political equality. Hodgskin argued that all products of labour should be distributed among labourers, manual or mental. Thompson of Cork, the most eminent founder of scientific socialism, urged that the worker should have the value he creates.

*The new
thought*

1815
1817

1819

1825

1824

Place, a tailor, who in youth had suffered poverty and want, made his shop in Westminster the headquarters of radicals working for universal suffrage, annual parliaments, financial reform, freedom of speech and of assembly. Robert Owen, whose own energy had raised him from an apprentice to a wealthy factory owner, rejected such reforms as these to become the apostle of communism. His "new system of society" was to be an industrial democracy with co-operative owner-ship and control of industry. It was he who first put forward the idea of a factory act to limit hours of labour, of the "right to work," of a minimum wage, of the housing of the poor by provincial authorities, of a national system of free and compulsory education, of free libraries. He believed with an apostle's ardour that if he could win respite from poverty to give to but one generation of children a true education, they would form a new moral world, and carry out the emancipation of the working classes.

But it was from the country-side that came the greatest tribune the English poor ever possessed, William Cobbett, "born in a farmhouse, bred up at the plough-tail, with a smock-frock on my back." He had for twenty years toiled in vain to get possession of his holding; he had saved from his scanty food farthings to buy candles and paper, and in his hunger had cried like a child at the loss of a half-penny, the price of a red herring for his dinner. Serving as a common soldier he had trained himself by writing out an entire grammar three times, and reciting it once each time he stood sentry. In pity for the poor he abandoned his Tory creed to open a long fight with the possessing and educated classes—"the race that plunder the people." "England," he cried, "now contains the most miserable people that ever trod the earth." Penetrated by passion for the country-side, his indignant alarm was lest the poor should grow accustomed to their dependence and accept their degradation. The poor man must be freed from fear. He ought to have help as his "legal due." The domination of the aristocracy must be destroyed with all that lay behind it—the superstitious reverence for its capacity and public spirit, the habit of supposing that any country could live creditably which left the rich to think and act for the poor. The Duke's word of command, he insisted, had no effect on wheat, nor could his army of a hundred thousand men make it 10s. a bushel. In capital he saw only money taken from the labouring classes. Up and down the country, year after year, with a fury of eloquence, he drove home the lesson so that Englishmen could never again forget it, that for a people who had lost the right of voting taxes, and were denied free assembly and speech and combination, there was no hope save by reform of parliament and universal suffrage. "We must have that first or we shall have nothing good." The working classes as a body must unite in self-

Sec. I.

The Social
Revolu-
tion
1815
to
1914

1816

Cobbett

1807–35

1820

Sec. I.

The Social
Revolu-
tion
1815
to
1914

1816

The Tory
Govern-
ment

1818

1821

1815

1817-18

defence against the two great parties in the State. Cobbett formed, it was said, a Fourth Estate in himself; he first gave to the people a journal written by one of themselves, and by his literary genius taught them the power of the Press. When he reduced "The Weekly Political Register" from a shilling and a halfpenny to two-pence, 50,000 copies were scattered over the country, and everywhere men gathered in clubs to hear the paper read by one of them who had schooling.

Thus the old aristocracy found themselves confronted in the middle classes and in the workers alike with a new intelligence, an ardent questioning of the old traditions. It must, said one, "make those in higher regions look about them and be on the alert; every man now feels that warning from the man immediately beneath him, and the stimulus is propagated. What it will come to God knows." "The same impulse of the times that makes one man a reformer will make others revolutionists." No one at that time, neither landlord, nor capitalist, nor economist, could understand the revolution that was overturning the old society and fashioning a new democracy. But already at the close of the Napoleonic war the social problem which was to fill the coming century confronted England. After the peace, government was carried on, under Lord Liverpool, by Wellington victor of Waterloo, and Castlereagh plenipotentiary at the Congress of Vienna. They brought to a country where statecraft and sound finance were needed the habits learned in war of wasteful expenditure, and a dependence on armed force. The French Revolution had bequeathed alike to aristocrats and plutocrats an abiding panic as to the security of property, and a terror of the working classes—"the basest of the populace." To save the State their own power must be maintained. Parliament was surrounded by troops while the landlords, who in the war had ploughed up their fields for tillage, passed a corn-law in their own relief, forbidding corn to be imported till it had reached eighty shillings a quarter. The successful agitation of Brougham against the income-tax, a move-ment supported by the plutocracy and the industrialists, and the repeal of the malt-tax, left a heavier burden of the national debt on the people. While the rich paid twenty per cent. on their wine, the poor paid two hundred per cent. on their beer; and landed property passed without any charges, when duty was levied on the money and effects of tradesmen and farmers. Agitations of starving men demanding bread at a fixed price or wages to buy food, or assemblies for the suffrage and the ballot, were to the rulers crimes against the State; they encouraged informers; their secret committees of enquiry drew up terrifying reports of Radical schemes for new division of wealth and land. The Habeas Corpus Act was suspended, meetings forbidden, and Press laws issued against blasphemy and sedition. Five hundred writers suffered fine and imprisonment between 1800 and 1832. In the hunger riots of 1818 fifteen hundred famishing men marched under a banner "Bread or Blood," demanding that the price of bread should be fixed: twenty-four were condemned to death, and five hanged at Ely. When the most powerful of the popular speakers, "Orator" Hunt, held a meeting at St. Peter's Fields, Manchester, fifty thousand people gathered with banners flying—"Equal Representation or Death," "Liberty or Death"; in a charge of the yeomanry on the unarmed crowd a man was killed and forty injured. The dark day of "Peterloo" was followed by legislation of sheer panic. The "Six Acts" commonly known as the "Gagging Acts," gave new powers to suppress meetings and freedom of speech or writing. Since Cobbett avoided the stamp of fourpence on newspapers by printing no news in his Political Register, an Act was passed to subject certain publications to the duties on newspapers, so as to ruin the cheap circulation and influence of his "Twopenny Trash." Orator Hunt with other leaders was thrown into prison. Cobbett fled to America. Executions, transportations, military force, silenced the deep indignation of the working classes, and no serious disturbance troubled the rulers for ten years. It was almost safer to be a felon than a reformer, said Sidney Smith. So great was the terror that no Whig would join the Reformers in asserting the right of public meeting; nor stir a finger nor subscribe a shilling to help reform. No private person without the utmost danger could attempt to remove even the smallest public grievance.

It was the last triumph of the old Tory despotism. In the face of the new England the Habeas Corpus Act was never again suspended there. With the death of George III., and of Castlereagh, came the stirrings of a great change. Steadily the power of the monarch was limited. The peers had given to the Cabinet of 1815 more than three-fourths of its number; in 1823 nearly half the ministers sat in the House of Commons. Terror of progress no longer ruled among younger men who had forgotten the French Revolution. Even Tories themselves were drifting towards imminent change under ministers of the unavowed and painful transition: Canning, who succeeded Castlereagh as Foreign Secretary, and Peel the Home Secretary. Although he was a defender of the Six Acts, an enemy of Jacobinism, Canning's glowing imagination saw the coming of a new world: by the force of his lofty genius, his compelling enthusiasm and eloquence, he dominated the House of Commons, and in the five brief years before his death formed, out of Tories and Whigs, a group ready to move in the way of reform. Peel for thirty years stood before England as the tragic figure of the transition. "Leader," as he boasted, "of the gentlemen of England," proud, sensitive, hostile to every proposal for civil and religious equality, he yet by the tact in public affairs that made

Sec. I.
The Social Revolution
1815 TO 1914
Peterloo

1820

The First Conservatives
1820
1822

Canning and Peel
1822–1827
1819–1850

Sec. I.

The Social
Revolu-
tion
1815
TO
1914

1824-5

1827

1819
1823

1828

Catholic
Emanci-
pation

1817

1828

1829

him "the greatest member of Parliament that ever lived," saw himself compelled to sacrifice tradition to the final authority of the public will, and the necessity of the public good: and more than once used his absolute mastery over the House to drive through it the liberating bills that he had most desperately denounced. Under leaders such as these the first movements towards reform were slow, halting and reluctant. Working-men and masters were allowed a limited right to meet together and agree on rates of wages and terms of work: but beyond these limits any trade combination was punished as "conspiracy," and trade unions were outside the protection of law. In a revision of the disordered State finance and taxation by Peel and Huskisson, who knew the middle classes well, a dim beginning of free trade was made by amending tariffs and navigation laws, and proposing a revision of the Corn Laws. There was a first attempt to check cruelty to animals. Landlords were forbidden to use spring-guns against poachers. Mackintosh, who had taken up the question of capital punishment, moved Peel to abolish sentence of death for about a hundred felonies, and wholly or partially repealed nearly three hundred Acts relating to the criminal law. He "could almost think that he had lived in two different countries and conversed with people who spoke two different languages," said Mackintosh, remembering his old battle against flogging of women, and death on the gallows for shoplifting to the value of five shillings.

When Canning died and Wellington became Prime Minister, he was in fact confronted by a new country. All seemed unchanged. The fundamental laws and constitution of England stood in 1828 exactly as they had been in 1800, and the old complacency was undiminished. But within three years the ancient constitution was in fact new-made, and the modern world as we know it had begun.

The first trial of strength was a demand for the civil equality of all creeds. Catholic emancipation, first proposed in 1778, was passionately refused for fifty years. Since 1805 Parliament had fourteen times rejected bills for Catholic relief; for twenty years the Whigs had fought for it, and Canning had given his life for it in vain. Catholics and Dissenters might die for their country since army and navy had been opened to them; but no Catholic might serve it in a civil post, and no Dissenter save under the protection of an annual Indemnity bill. The manufacturing classes now procured repeal of the Test and Corporation Acts to free Dissenters from the sacramental test for civil office. Peel, "spokesman of the intolerant faction," vehemently led the opposition to Catholic relief, and Wellington declared it fatal to the best interests of the country. The next year they united to force through Parliament a bill admitting Catholics to Parliament and to nearly all civil and political offices. The first great victory of freedom was won. But no spirit of liberality had moved the government. It was Ireland, long defrauded of the emancipation promised at the Union, that by an immense organization of a whole people compelled a hearing. The Catholic peasantry of Clare broke from the control of their Protestant landlords, and in a solemn national demonstration elected Daniel O'Connell as their member. Wellington was warned by his brother, Wellesley, Lord Lieutenant of Ireland, that he might expect not only a general rising but a mutiny of the Catholic soldiers, unless the will of the people was heard. The Ministers' resistance broke down. The authority of Wellington and Peel alone could have forced the Tories to accept the bill. But Peel's anger was hot against the independent Irish tenantry. The franchise was to him a weapon of class ascendancy, and that weapon, as he said, "which the landlord has forged with so much care, and has heretofore wielded with such success, had broken short in his hands." In the same bill therefore by which he granted emancipation he abolished the franchise of the forty shilling freeholders, and threw Ireland yet more completely under the political power of the Protestant landlord. The Irish however had shown on their side the power of a national democracy in shaking the very foundations of English tradition in Church and State, and putting to the question its social order, and the power of parliament itself. From this time Irish influence was a potent factor in English politics. The liberalising spirit of the Celtic peoples, nourished in traditions of an old democracy, and in the pains of persecution, was strong in years to come to enfranchise thought and give a glowing life to social and political agitation in England.

The Catholic Relief Act, if it wrecked the Tory party, showed that after two hundred years the doctrine of philosophers such as Hales and Chillingworth was passing into common men's thought— "Protestants are inexcusable if they do offer violence to other men's consciences." At the same time the teaching of Hobbes had sprung into new life—that the end of all government was the weal of the Commonwealth. For if in the Emancipation Act the old Tories met their first defeat, they found their overthrow in the Reform Act. The control of the legislature by the hereditary landowners of England was by them held to be the only security for a stable government. During two centuries and a half Parliamentary representation had been untouched. For eighty-five years all protests had been successfully broken down. The urging of reform was judged sedition; five leading men of position and character, pleading "the eternal basis of justice," were tried and transported for this offence: "we were all mad," one of the jurymen said, looking back from thirty-five years later. On the renewal of the struggle a score of attempts for some degree of reform were defeated in twenty-two years. The landowners felt secure in their ancient authority. Supreme in the House of Lords, in the Commons they appointed the county members, and nearly all the

SEC. I.

THE SOCIAL REVOLUTION

1815 TO **1914**

1828

1829

Reform of Parliament

1745–1830

1793–4

1809–31

SEC. I.

THE SOCIAL
REVOLU-
TION
1815
TO
1914

1829

1831

boroughs were in their hands. There were "nomination boroughs" where the member was elected by the patron—possibly an uninhabited green mound, a ruined wall, a town no longer visible under invading tides; and there were "rotten boroughs" where the candidate was chosen by the lord's influence. In Newark, for example, on the defeat of his candidate the Duke of Newcastle evicted every tenant who had given a hostile vote—"Have I not a right," said the Duke, "to do what I like with my own?" The cost of elections kept representation in the hands of the wealthy. Lord Ashley spent £15,600 in Dorsetshire. There were towns where the patron or member was required to defray the municipal expenses. Some boroughs had for centuries been bought and used by magnates to pack the House in their own interest. Others had a tradition of four hundred years of restriction and privilege. Everywhere bribery, "more lamentable than all the other evils," cried Cobbett, could work its deep demoralisation. The established authority of the landed classes was however now threatened by the accumulating wealth of the commercial world, and by the rising multitude of workers—an urban population which from the beginning of the century grew at the rate of thirty per cent. every ten years. Their agitations continued for lightening of taxation, bread at fixed price, reform of justice, universal suffrage, and annual parliaments. With schemes of communistic settlements and modes of production, the word Socialism now came first into use. Grand General Unions of the several trades were formed to unite workers over the whole kingdom. An Irish Roman Catholic, Doherty, put forward the far-reaching idea of a Trades Union which should unite the different trades in one gigantic association; and half a century before the idea of a general strike had taken root in France it was preached to English workmen as the central idea of their movement. The terror felt by Whig and Tory alike was seen in barbarous prosecutions and attempts to gag the newspapers. Unorganised rural labourers who protested by rick-burning against starvation wages and pauper allowances, were broken by ferocious punishment. In 1830 there were wage-riots in which one rioter lost his life, while no one on the side of authority was seriously wounded: in expiation of their disorder nine men and boys were hanged, four hundred and fifty-seven were transported, and four hundred imprisoned at home. Through all agitations, however, Lord John Russell had since 1819 incessantly renewed the demand for some representation of the new commercial classes and the rising towns—a steadfast and passionless debater who admitted no check or defeat. As the movement grew the Canningites became reformers under Lord Palmerston. Lord Grey and Lord Lansdowne led the Whigs. Sharing the Tory fear of the "lower orders," they proposed a moderate reform to enfranchise "all the intelligence and respectability

Organiza-
tion of
working
classes

1829
1832

1828

SEC. I.

THE SOCIAL
REVOLU-
TION
1815
TO
1914

of the independent class." " By the people," said Brougham, " I mean the middle classes, the wealth and intelligence of the country, the glory of the British name " ; and Macaulay urged that such a scheme, safe, moderate, and final, would keep at bay the perils of universal suffrage. " Shufflers and cowards," retorted the working-men, " mere drawling Whigs." For fifteen years their clubs had taught universal suffrage. They were on the verge of revolution. But in this crisis the artisans showed a sound political instinct, and amid their bitter disappointment loyally supported the middle class rather than lose the beginning of reform. The workers were formidable in the unrepresented towns such as Birmingham, Leeds, or Manchester. In Birmingham where the population had risen from 90,000 in 1815 to 150,000 in 1832—a town denied even a single voice in Parliament, with no powers to preserve order, fight disease, or protect its workers—

1830

arose the first " Political Union of the Middle and Lower classes " for household suffrage; which became the model for others up and

1831

down the country. A " National Union of the Working Classes " advocated manhood suffrage as the only means for a true division of

1832

wealth : when the government ordered a fast to ward off cholera the members marched in procession, carrying a slice of bread and a piece of beef with the inscription " The true remedy against cholera."

Reform Act
July 1830

It was at this moment that Wellington, through the speech of the new king William IV. at the opening of Parliament, threatened the seditious and disaffected, and praised the constitution which gave to England more true liberty and social happiness than had fallen to the lot of any country in the world. To the last Wellington protested against tampering with a perfect Constitution : he had to barricade himself in his house behind bullet-proof shutters. The King and ministers dared not drive through the streets to the Lord Mayor's dinner. When the Duke was forced to resign,

Nov. 1830

his place was taken by the Whig leader Lord Grey, a reformer for more than forty years. Lord Palmerston joined him at the head of the Canningites. Lord John Russell introduced into the House of Commons the first Reform Bill, which swept away decayed

Mar. 1
1831

boroughs, enfranchised the rising towns, and fixed for all a uniform £20 household franchise. Scoffing jeers of the Tories interrupted the reading of a bill which was to renew and repair the constitutional liberties first created by the genius of Earl Simon and Edward I. The second reading was carried by one vote. A month later an

Mar. 21

amendment was passed in Committee against the bill, and the King hastened to Westminster to dissolve Parliament. At the roaring of the guns that announced to the Commons his hurried approach there broke out an indescribable scene of violence, such a scene as had marked the memorable struggle of 1641 — shouts of fury,

April 22

hats waved aloft, and deep threatenings. The next time the guns

SEC. I.

THE SOCIAL
REVOLU-
TION
1815
TO
1914
Sept. 22
Oct. 8
1832
March
April
May

were heard, a member cried to the Ministers, "they will be shotted and take off some of your heads." In the country the passion of the people swept aside all the old influences of corruption, and sent back the ministers with a majority of over a hundred. At the reading of the second Reform Bill the majority rose to 109. When it was rejected by the Lords popular fury broke out in riots and burnings. In Birmingham blacksmiths worked all night preparing arms, and balls with steel points to throw under the feet of cavalry. The third Bill won a majority of 162. The Lords by nine votes passed the second reading, and threw out the bill in committee. Wellington at the King's orders attempted to form a ministry, which scarcely lasted a week. The people threatened barricades and open war. Political clubs and unions ordered their members to pay no taxes unless the bill passed. The temper of the soldiers was doubtful. To force a failure of the banks placards lined the London streets: "To stop the Duke go for gold." Confronted with a nation in opposition, the King bowed to a final and complete submission. Grey was recalled, with power to create as many peers as he needed to pass the bill through the House

of Lords. The peers sullenly yielded to the threat so far that 278 absented themselves from the House, while 106 Lords appeared to vote for the bill, and 22 against it.

"The King has thrown his crown into the gutter," cried the Czar of Russia. Englishmen were astounded at the vastness of a scheme which destroyed the old monoply of power. The Tories lamented their "falling country": thirty years, they thought, might bring the imminent catastrophes of the bill, changes in hereditary estates, overthrow of the established Church, destruction of an independent House of Lords, or even annihilation of its existence. The working-men no less than the Tories foresaw a future that bore in it revolution. They knew that by "their manly, steady, and courageous conduct," the victory had been won. "This," said Place, "was indeed the first time they ever combined of their own free will for a really national purpose, and this it is which marks the era as of more importance than any former proceeding;" in a few years' time a new race of young men would have sprung up, "brought up very generally without reverence for authority, and imbued with notions of representative government," and by their moral power a wider Reform would at last satisfy the expectations of the people. "There must be a decisive quarrel with the Lords some day and the Lords will in the end be beaten."

Such hopes and fears gathered indeed round the principle of the Reform Bill rather than its bare facts. The Act abolished fifty-six nomination or rotten boroughs, and left thirty others with only one member. A hundred and forty-three seats were set free for distribution, sixty-five new representatives were thus given to the counties, and the rest divided among Manchester, Leeds, Birmingham, and forty other rising towns. A £10 household franchise was established in the boroughs, and the rights of freemen to vote were restricted. In the counties copy-holders and lease-holders for years were added to the forty-shilling freeholders, and tenants-at-will paying £50 a year. The propertied classes in the House, however, with the design of protecting property and vested interests, and checking revolutionary ideas, had combined to make as little change as possible in the old order. The Act that enfranchised the commercial classes did not add 500,000 voters in the three countries, and the distribution of seats was so arranged that more than half the members were returned by three per cent. of the grown men in the kingdom. Five out of six of the people were still without a vote. The middle class was practically defrauded by a system which left half of them unenfranchised. As for the working-men, by whose aid the bill had been carried, they found themselves roughly and insolently thrown aside. The new Constitution proved to them in fact less democratic than the old. Many had lost the franchise they once possessed, and few indeed could find a place among the new £10 householders. They were utterly exhausted by their immense efforts; their leaders bankrupt, impoverished, or worn out by incessant labour. The House of Commons seemed in fact but little changed. The landed gentry still commanded the House by their numbers. Even half the boroughs were represented by them as before. For the next thirty-six years all ministries, Whig and Tory, were led from the House of Lords (save for five years when Lord John Russell was Prime Minister). But both friends and foes of reform were right in acknowledging the triumph of a revolution. The fetish of the fixed Constitution was gone. All was flung open to criticism and change. The "principle of utility," the reasoned good of the Commonwealth, had replaced the divine right of the ruling classes, and at the day of his death Bentham had reached the height of his success. The balance of power was changed. The last Act ever introduced by the personal will of the sovereign was the Bill demanded by George IV. for his divorce from Queen Caroline: it was almost the first measure which had to be abandoned before the popular fury. After William IV. no sovereign ventured to claim the right to dismiss Ministers. The "King's Ministers," who till then had been practically chosen by royal influence, were transformed into Ministers selected and dismissed by the House of Commons alone. For the first time in the history of England a Ministry was compelled to resign office as the direct result of a general election. The new sense of responsibility was shown when the House of Commons began itself to publish its division lists. Up to this time, as Gladstone noted, the peers by their command of the close boroughs had as it were "cushioned off" conflict between the Houses; but as

SEC. I.

THE SOCIAL
REVOLU-
TION
1815
TO
1914

*New House
of Commons*
1833

1832

1834

1836

Sec. I.

The Social
Revolu-
tion
1815
TO
1914

The
Reform
Parlia-
ment
1833

Religious
equality
1833

1835

1833
Legal
reform

1836
1837
1837-69

1833

Education

1839

this control vanished and the lower House gained in independence, there appeared a new opposition of the Lords to the Commons unknown before the Reform Act. That Act had, in fact, made of the House of Commons "the ruling and the choosing House"; and the daring principle laid down by Pym two hundred years before was now finally asserted as one of the bases of the Constitution—that in case of obstruction the Commons would "save the kingdom alone."

Ten years of office save for a few months lay before the Whigs—years of crowded legislation. Their first great Act, the Emancipation of Slaves in all British Colonies, was the triumph of Evangelicals of the older school. In home reforms the early ardour of the Commons was seen in a number of enactments, small in themselves, but each one establishing a principle which was to direct the action of the State for the coming century. The new influence of the middle class was seen in efforts to free Dissenters and Jews from religious restrictions, and to reform administration of the Established Churches in England and Ireland. When the House of Lords refused to open Oxford and Cambridge, the new-made London University was empowered to grant degrees to men of all creeds. Nonconformists for the first time since 1753 were allowed to celebrate marriages in their own churches. The work thus begun, the essential freeing of the spiritual life of the country from the bondage of political service, and the habit of worldly authority, was carried on through the century. No less honourable was the determination to give to every member of the Commonwealth equal justice and protection of law. A series of enactments secured evidence of competent witnesses on behalf of people accused, and gave all prisoners the right to defence by counsel. Before long the shameful pillory was abolished, with the barbarities of gibbets and common floggings; the death punishment still allowed for thirty-seven crimes was finally restricted to murder; public executions forbidden; and wide improvements made in courts of law to bring their remedies within reach of all. In the first year too the Reform Parliament discovered a dim sense that the State would have to answer for the education of its people—a duty long refused, whether from fear of the populace or from deference to employers and economists: "Men in power," wrote Place, "dread the consequences of teaching the people more than they dread the effect of their ignorance." Now for the first time a State grant was given, a sort of subscription of £20,000 divided between two societies representing the established Church and the dissenting bodies. Later a Board of Education was appointed with £30,000 to distribute among all denominations, including those that used the Roman Catholic Bible, and it was ordered that children should be taught for two hours a week. Even if busy districts with hundreds of thousands of people remained for long years without one school for poor children; even if

Sec. I.
The Social
Revolu-
tion
1815
to
1914
*Factory
laws*
1831
1833

only one half of those that were taught could read when they left school, one in four could write, and two per cent. learned a moderate degree of arithmetic; still a principle of State obligation had been established which has never been lost. Factory legislation, revived by Michael Sadler, was forced on the House of Commons by a Committee of which he was chairman, and an Act introduced by Lord Ashley was carried which forbade the work of children under nine, and limited to twelve hours the work of all under eighteen. Through the influence of Edwin Chadwick the Act appointed four travelling inspectors from the Home Office for five years; thus inaugurating the first attempt, regarded as purely experimental and temporary, to establish the new and vital principle of central control. The zeal of the inspectors won for children some effective protection, the beginning of new hope. But this Act is further remembered as the opening of a controversy which was to fill the century. All economists of that day maintained the right of every English-man to do his own business without any meddling, aid, or hindrance; so that the manufacturer should suffer from no ominous interference of the State; and that the worker should make his bargain as a free man, looking not to parliament but to his own manhood for success. There were others living closer to the poor, who saw in the "freedom" offered to an enslaved and famishing people a thing of words and delusion. Lord Ashley (better known as Lord Shaftesbury from 1851) in pity for the suffering, and overwhelmed by the magnitude of the despair he witnessed, became the im-passioned apostle of the interference of the State. "Let your laws, we say to the Parliament, assume the proper function of law; protect those for whom neither wealth, nor station, nor age, has raised a bulwark against Tyranny." When the government sought to lower the age of protection, urging that children of twelve should be allowed to judge for themselves like their elders, and that sixty-nine hours of work a week would do them no harm, Ashley scornfully de-manded why a Parliament which condemned slave labour and allowed no adult negro to work more than forty-five hours a week, should fling back into slavery children of the British Empire. His Factory Act marked the beginning of the battle between the Individualists taught by Bentham, and the State Socialists who held that every citizen of the State should of right claim the protection of the whole nation through its Government.

This year in fact may be taken as the starting-point of a new age. The Parliament, fresh from the amazing impulse of the country, breathed a spirit of liberty and justice. However timid and in-significant the first measures were, they heralded a time of brave thought and endeavour. The Poor Law of the next year, as it was a more ambitious effort, so it revealed more clearly the virtues and the

Sec. I.

The Social
Revolu-
tion
1815
to
1914

vices of the legislators. Here, too, as in the Factory Act, they set up a central control over local officials for the first time since 1640, cautiously proposed in an experiment for five years. They laid down principles of administration both original and beneficent—grouping the small and inadequate parishes into the larger union, and creating a new salaried class of officials wholly occupied in public work instead of the old voluntary guardians and overseers. On the other hand the theory and method of relief, in which the working-classes had no voice, only deepened their sufferings. The views of economists who then ruled opinion were bounded by certain fixed theories which, amid the bewildering changes of their time, they believed themselves to have discovered. They were obsessed with the fear that population would increase beyond the means of subsistence. They averred that wages, if not interfered with, obeyed natural "laws" which would not allow them to sink below the minimum of subsistence, nor to rise beyond what the trade of the country could fairly bear, but would fairly adjust their level according to the price of corn. They could allow no limitation or exception to their doctrine that economic success depended on the personal freedom of action of every individual, and the unaided efforts of his own capacity. On these principles it was held injurious to give poor relief save with the utmost parsimony, in cases of imminent starvation, and under conditions so harsh as to deter all but the despairing and desperate. Outdoor relief was ended, and pauperising doles of corn in aid of low wages. The labourer was thus enabled to move about more freely in search of work. His freedom was but nominal. Wages did not rise because doles were taken away, and when corn was over sixty shillings a quarter the people starved as before for lack of bread. Workhouses were multiplied, more forbidding and terrible than the gaol. It seemed to doctrinaires good business to combine the principles of economy and representation, by giving to those who held rateable property votes for the Board of Guardians in proportion to their rates, with the result that the first care of the Guardians was directed, as was said, not to the poor but to the poor-rates. The labourer met the harsh administration of the Poor Law with savage revolt, and a bitter class hatred which left a long legacy of evil. There was wild rick-burning in the country, and repression by authority as cruel as of old.

A work less marred by error was the Municipal Reform Act—the great grant of local self-government, which was practically to end the long civic struggle by which the English towns had won their way, with many a failure and backsliding, from serfage to independence and social freedom. The measure was immensely more democratic than the Reform Act of three years before; it doubtless seemed less formidable to entrust the local concerns of a borough to the people than to allow them entry into affairs of State. Old outworn privileges and cherished monopolies were swept away, as merchant guilds and trade corporations disappeared before the new incorporated body of the burgesses, the general association of the householders, whose concern was to promote the common interests of all the inhabitants. Both the representative Councils elected by household suffrage for the common business, and the town officials, were now considered the servants of the ratepayers; so much so that a borough treasurer is legally bound to disregard even an order of the council to appropriate moneys out of the borough fund, unless the appropriation is authorised by the municipal laws and the constitution of the borough. It was many years before the new powers were fully used. We can only view with consternation the long agony of a few brave heroes such as Edwin Chadwick and Lord Shaftesbury struggling with indomitable faith against apathy, prejudice, and administrative difficulties, in their fight with pestilence and mortality, with ignorance and cruelty. A bill for ventilation, drainage, and building in the poor quarters of the towns was refused by Government, and there was scarcely an effort for housing the poor. But hope broadened for workers in the enfranchised towns. Municipalities, vying with one another in local zeal, began from the middle of the century to provide for the citizens water, light, paving, houses, libraries, transit, medical care, and to concentrate under democratic control the means of health and of education.

The impulse and inspiration of reform had so far sustained the Whigs. But their betrayal of the working-men brought its sure consequence, blunting their own sense of justice and honour, and destroying their good fame in the country. In two years the Liberal majority fell from 314 to 107. Meanwhile Sir Robert Peel rallied the moderate Tories under the new name of "Conservatives," first indicated by Canning and gradually coming into use: and led them towards a "middle-class Toryism," with a careful finance, an efficient machinery of government against popular agitation, and proposals for cautious amendment of such abuses as threatened danger to Church or State. In a series of weak Governments Whigs and moderate Tories or Conservatives were scarcely to be distinguished: both alike distrusted popular institutions, and greatly feared Radical agitation. The Reform Act of the upper classes proved to be no settlement, and for the next thirty years every popular association moved with fixed purpose to the one end—the bringing of the people within the constitution of their country. When Cobbett in 1818 roused the poor to the need of the vote there were 57,000 workers in the cotton factories; in 1839 there were 469,000, more crowded than ever, flung aside by the Reform bill. The artisans in fierce discontent and sullen anger drew apart. Henceforth, their leaders cried, they need

Sec. I.

The Social Revolu-tion

1815 to 1914

1841
1842

The Con-servative Party

1835

1832-38

Revolt of the artisans

Sec. I.

The Social
Revolu-
tion
1815
to
1914
1834

1833
1834

look for no help save in their own united strength ; and their sense of organised fellowship was seen in a marvellous growth of benefit societies, industrial associations, co-operative societies, trade clubs and unions. Co-operative societies (opened in 1828 by the first "Union shop" with a capital of £5) increased to some hundreds. In 1829 an Irish Roman Catholic, Doherty, had led the first effort to unite the trades into a federation or national association for the protection of workers ; and Robert Owen, a Welshman, followed with his "Society for National Regeneration" and his "Grand National Consolidated Trades Union," a federation of separate lodges of the various trades to secure an eight hours' day, a wage sufficient to keep the worker in comfort, the right to employment, a share in the profit of whatever his hands had been employed on. Within a few weeks half a million members, artisans, and women, and rural labourers in tens of thousands had joined the Union—a gigantic enlistment such as had never before been known either in England or any country of Europe. Ministers, Whig and Tory, spoke of the new Unions as "the most formidable difficulty and danger with which they had to contend." Rules of law were scandalously stretched to compass the ruin of the "Grand National," till the perversion of justice reached its height in the condemnation of six Dorsetshire labourers to seven years' transportation for forming a village lodge of the Union. London was filled with troops when a vast procession of Trade Unionists marched under thirty-three banners to carry to the Government a remonstrance and petition for the labourers—the first of the great demonstrations we now know so well—and were turned back unheard. Undaunted by the failure of the "Grand National" adventure, a "Working Men's Association" developed the scheme of a society where the artisans should shape their own education and produce their own leaders, and thus evolve a true working class policy. It opened the way moreover for the first time to international action, by introducing a system of messages between the workers of all countries. Penny papers for the people were started in various forms, and between 1830 and 1836 there were 728 prosecutions for selling these without the fourpenny government tax—219 of them in the one year of 1835. Though public outcry forced Lord Melbourne to lower the stamp duty to a penny, yet with the charge on advertisements and a duty on paper of £770,000 (or more than half the value of the paper produced by the English makers) the poor man's legal newspaper cost $2\frac{1}{2}d.$ for the next twenty-five years, and by strict prosecution he was effectively denied a free press. We can but wonder at the temerity of the workers' new idealism. But whatever their courage, universal combination was in fact beyond the resources of a working-class still in a state of serfage, without a cheap press, a penny postage, railway communication or convenience of travel and change of employers. A series of State trials for sedition, conspiracy, or treason showed the temper of the government, the misery of the people, and the fast-widening separation between the democracy outside Parliament and the Whig ministry within it.   By experience the workers had learned how newly-enfranchised classes, busied in redressing their own grievances, could silence the cry of those outside.   Henceforth Chartists, Anti-Corn Law Leaguers, Trade Unionists, Co-operators, Factory Reformers—under whatever name the working-classes were grouped—inevitably ranged themselves as so many regiments in the great army that demanded the emancipation of the people.

In the next decade every one of these associations was drawn into the battle.   Lord John Russell, now leader of the House, that ardent reformer to whose incessant work the country owed the Reform Act, the Bill for municipal reform, the repeal of tests, much softening of the penal laws and religious disabilities, and the stirring of education—who in the House of Commons was for more than ten years Peel's chief antagonist, and for more than twenty years the dominant force in the Whig party—held that the Reform of 1832 was final, and the Constitution once more complete   In that same year the Chartists, led by Feargus O'Connor, flung themselves into the political struggle : " we will avenge ourselves on the Whigs," was the cry.   The betrayal of Reform, the hated Poor Law, the severity of hunger in a falling trade, united radicals, socialists, trade unionists, and the considerable women's suffrage clubs, in a pledge to put aside all other questions till they had won the vote.   When Peel's opposition to Factory Acts robbed the working-classes of all hope from the Conservatives, they saw no remedy for their distress save through the political movement of Chartism.   The *Charter*, as O'Connell named it, demanded six points—vote by ballot ; abolition of property qualification for a member of Parliament ; payment of members ; manhood suffrage ; the division of the country into equal electoral districts ; and annual elections. Peaceful meetings, monster petitions to Parliament (whose importance fraudulent signatures could not wholly destroy), a paper to urge their cause, by such means the constitutional Chartists hoped to persuade the Government, while through temperance societies and popular universities the people were to become their own regenerators and win for themselves true liberty.   Another section, desperate from excessive poverty, turned to revolution and physical force.   The ruling orders simply classed the whole of them together as infidel Communists, bent on destroying the throne, the Church, and the family : " Two great demons in morals and politics, Socialism and Chartism, are stalking through the land," lamented Lord Shaftesbury.   Themselves weakened by divided counsels, ill-compacted under doubtful leaders, the Chartists were confronted with a highly developed military administration, with barracks ranged through the industrial districts,

Sec. I.

The Social
Revolu-
tion
1815
to
1914

The
Chartists

1837

1838–48

1840

SEC. I.

THE SOCIAL
REVOLU-
TION
1815
TO
1914

and with a newly created and well drilled police force. The Government, after all sections of the Chartists had been goaded into violence
by the harsh imprisonment of their most pious and high-minded
leaders, repressed them with cruel severity.

1848

Their effort crumbled away, to awaken once more in 1848—a
recrudescence due to distress at home and to contagion of Continental
revolutions. The suffering of the poor had reached its extreme point
when the last Chartist convention met in London, and as one after
another rose to recount the intolerable misery of the people the
Chartists again, after many trials and errors, renewed the passion and
ardour of their earlier days. Their procession to carry a petition to
Parliament failed before the military precautions of the Duke of
Wellington and the London police. Chartism disappeared as the
crowd turned hopelessly away. But its work had not been in vain.
Ten years of struggle had revealed the growth of a new class, and
united the workers as they had never before been united by common
effort and endurance. Their word, too, had gone out beyond England,

Nov. 1847

carried by Karl Marx, who had watched the preparations for the last
convention: the Chartists of England, he said, were the real
democrats, and by winning their six points they would open the way
of liberty to the universe.

**The Corn
Laws**

1836–46

The Chartists in fact had been pushed aside by another upheaval
of the people in these same years—the resounding conflict of the
industrial classes against the landed proprietors and their corn
laws. The fields of England could no longer provide bread for
the crowded multitudes of the famished cities. Population was increasing by some 2,000,000 in every decade, and the mass of the
people were living on barley and potatoes. Cobden declared that more
goods were exported to Brazil in one year than were consumed by
the whole agricultural peasantry in England. A series of bad seasons
from 1837 brought general ruin; while wages were falling the price
of food was mounting: and the increase by 1840 was put down at
£36,000,000 a year, which was chiefly borne by the poor. Meanwhile the value of exports was less in 1830–34 than it had been in
1816–20, and with the decline of commerce the manufacturers'
trade was dying. The Corn Laws, imposed by the landed class
in 1815 and 1825, were denounced by the industrial leaders as the
cause of the general ruin, of capital without profit and labour

*Cobden and
Bright*

1838

1841

without wages. Richard Cobden, son of a farmer who had been
ruined in the agricultural disasters of 1814, joined the Anti-
Corn-Law League, with John Bright, a Quaker manufacturer of
Rochdale. The two missionaries carried far and wide their burning
message of Free Trade. They moved in a storm of political
controversy. In their campaign organisation was given to classes
hitherto unheard in the national councils: the gathering of seven

hundred representatives of the Nonconformist clergy was to the
Times a "freak and drollery." Before this time politicians seldom
spoke outside the House except on the hustings at elections, and
members never appeared outside their own constituencies, but
Cobden, who entered Parliament in 1841, and Bright in 1843, gave
their finest powers to addressing mass meetings, where the people
gathered in multitudes to find a political education which was not
less important than the Chartist movement in preparing a new
democracy and a new Reform bill. They called employers and
employed to unite for the first time in a common interest. "The
people of England," Cobden insisted, were "not the country party,
but the people who live in towns, and will govern this country."
Languishing industries, growing poverty, the needs of the hungry
and the dying, the redemption of the labourer, the profit of the
manufacturer, the wealth of oversea trade, the lifting of the people
from feudal bondage into a free nation, the spread of peace and good
will among all countries, arguments of business, aspiration, and
philanthropy, met in the rich appeal of the Free Traders. The
Chartists retorted that cheap bread would be cheap labour, that
over-production brought uncertainty of wage, that the Whigs had
already given them the Poor Law, sent their children to death in
factories, cast their leaders into prison, and left them still burdened
by a debt of £800,000,000, a load of pensions, an established church,
hosts of officials and salaries, army and navy, local taxes, and
landlordism. The impassioned answer was ready: "That which
is the greatest enemy of the remorseless aristocracy of Britain must
also of necessity be your greatest friend," cried Bright. A tenth of
the people were in fact paupers, with poor relief at £7,000,000 a year.
Distress as of old brought riots and a reign of terror; in one gaol
alone 500 prisoners were tried by special commissioners.

During eight years of power the Whigs, deplorably ignorant of
finance and economics, had piled up taxation without revision, only to
increase year by year the deficit in their budgets. Sir Robert Peel
returning to office once more took up the work he had begun in
1819; strengthened the revenue by relief of taxation, and restored
the income tax abolished in 1816. To revive commerce and cheapen
living he abated or repealed duties on 769 articles. But the duty on
corn, by which the landed gentry had protected agriculture in 1816,
was only slightly modified. The landed interest was powerful and
party ties were strong. But as proof accumulated that the wages of
labour did not vary with the price of corn, and that disorder followed
starvation, Peel's opposition weakened. He measured the force and
direction of the rising popular gale: and the approach of the Irish
Famine became the occasion to overcome the force of old theories and
associations. From the Tory benches he proposed a bill to repeal

SEC. I.

THE SOCIAL
REVOLU-
TION
1815
TO
1914

1842

1841
**Free
Trade**

1841–6

SEC. I.

THE SOCIAL
REVOLU-
TION
1815
TO
1914

New
Commer-
cial con-
ditions

1815–48

1848
1830
1838

1838

1840

Trade
Unions

1844

1851

the Corn Laws. After a discussion of furious excitement, the division was called at 4 o'clock on a Saturday morning, and Free Trade in corn was carried. Once more, as in 1829, Peel averted a revolution, but it was his last service to his country. In that " sad fierce session " the vengeance of his party threw him from office on the day the Queen gave her assent to the bill.

Thus, after a ten years' fury of battle over the Corn Laws, the country party suffered their second great defeat, as significant as their overthrow in the Reform Bill. The exhaustion of the artisan by sheer hunger was lessened when in the next score of years food to the value of nearly £500,000,000 was brought into the country. New victories awaited them. By the Free Trade triumph, Great Britain was definitely and finally changed from an agricultural country which raised almost all the corn it used into a mainly industrial country fed by foreign wheat. In thirty-three years houses, factories, and warehouses had increased £26,000,000 in annual value. The revolution was quickened by gold discoveries in California and Australia, which raised the production of the world's gold from 5½ millions to over 30 millions; by the railways that linked every corner of England with the sea-ports, and the Cunard steamers that opened a new traffic across the Atlantic. Scientific invention had so multiplied man's powers of production that while the number of the people rose between 1811 and 1900 from 10 to 41 millions the average production was perhaps ten times as great. "What a nation is this!" exclaimed Lord Shaftesbury. "What materials for happiness and power!" It seemed, in the unexampled prosperity of some thirty years, that Great Britain was to become the workshop of the world. Old forces must decline, and the power of the artisan increase. Widespread and lasting combinations were encouraged by the new means of travel. The Act to carry mails by railroad drew together all parts of the country, and made possible the " nonsensical penny postage scheme," as it was called, which was " forced on an unwilling Liberal ministry by the clamour of a nation," and opened to the people unimagined opportunities of intercourse. Trade Unionists stood at the gates of a new world. The English working-men had already astonished Europe by the magnitude of their organisations and mass-meetings. A vital instinct of self-government, changing with each generation, shaping itself to meet successive difficulties, lifted Trade Unionism out of every crisis stronger, more highly organised and disciplined, democratic in a larger sense, and more conscious of its power. Two million workers had already united to throw back a reactionary government bill framed to widen the powers of justices in cases where masters had a dispute with their servants and artificers. But now was the moment of their great enlargement. From this time the Unions ordered themselves after a new plan, no longer directed by the old casual and amateur leaders, but by genuine working-men who were paid a salary and specially trained. The Amalgamated Society of Engineers, with 11,000 members, an income of £500 a week, a reserve fund and an admirable financial and administrative system, remained the model of new societies for the next twenty years. When working-men for whom their societies had gained security and good wages could become £10 householders and electors, artisans for the first time touched political power. Trade Unions began to discuss direct labour representation for winning through Parliament better laws, education, and larger opportunities. Parliament itself no longer despised a population which could begin to make itself felt at elections, and the notion prevailed that at least highly skilled artisans might be safely admitted to the vote. Other working-class organisations stood side by side with the Trade Unions, no less admirable in management—the Co operative Associations. The Stores of the "Rochdale Pioneers," which according to the law of the time had no legal status, found their sole and sufficient security against fraud and theft in the personal honour of members and officials, and in the spirit of enthusiasm and public service which illuminated the dawning communal life. In a few years hundreds of small Co-operative Societies were formed. Unlike guilds and trade unions of producers the co-operative associations of consumers had no vested interests to protect, and were open to the whole body of citizens. Every man who paid his shilling shared in the advantages and government of this working-class democracy, with its organised hierarchy of artisan committees elected quarter by quarter at open meetings of all the members, on the basis of one member one vote, men and women, whatever their stake, whatever their time of membership; the committee-men in their turn choosing the departmental managers. Not only did these pioneers of self-dependence reveal an amazing capacity for business, but in days when local self-government was little known they carried a new sense of communal life to remote villages and mining districts where the co-operative store was in effect the only school of citizenship—the school where the commonalty was trained in the use of free and deliberate choice, and the elected officers learned the pride of public service. The power of these trained masses of citizens was before long to be shown in the public affairs of the State.

While Trade Unionists and Co-operators, Chartists and Free Traders, were being driven into the conflict for the franchise, the struggle over the factory laws added to all workers a sharper and more poignant resolution. The artisans had neither voice nor influence in the laws which were to carry to them life or death. A demand for legislation to lessen their suffering had risen among

SEC. I.

THE SOCIAL
REVOLU-
TION
1815
TO
1914

1844
*Co-operative
Associations*

1844-50

**Factory
Legisla-
tion**

Sec. I.

The Social
Revolu-
tion
1815
to
1914

humane men of all creeds and opinions. Michael Sadler, their chief leader before the Reform Act, was a reactionary, opposed to Emancipation and Reform, a forerunner of Tory and Christian Socialists; Southey, a preacher of Tory philanthropy; Oastler, a land-agent, Churchman, Tory, and Protectionist; with them was Edwin Chadwick once secretary to Bentham; Fielden, a Radical member; and Radical manufacturers and artisans, Anglican clergy, Wesleyan ministers, Quakers, Freethinkers, journalists, all stirred by a common pity. "We are just now," grumbled a spectator, "overrun with philanthropy, and God knows where it will stop or whither it will lead us." In Parliament however the workers had for long years one leading advocate, Lord Shaftesbury. A fervent Tory, an Evangelical of the old school, detesting alike Catholicism and infidelity, Republicanism and Socialism, he stood in the Commons till 1851 in daily conflict with capitalists, economists, mill-owners, doctrinaires, haters of "humanity-mongers," "not having in the House even a bulrush to rest upon"; alone to "attack every interest and one half of mankind" on behalf of the helpless who had neither voice nor influence. Liberals, who were willing to aid in protecting children, were united against any suggestions of State interference with the "liberty" to work of young persons and women. John Bright threatened to turn the key on his mills and throw on the legislators the responsibility of "feeding the millions whom they will not allow us to employ with a profit." Cobden maintained that workers should make their own bargains. Pease of Darlington proposed to close his factory if the labour of young persons was shortened to fifty-eight hours. The whole of the aristocracy held aloof: so did the clergy, "cowed by capital and power," and the evangelicals. Peel as Prime Minister put every obstacle in his way—"all Peel's affinities are towards wealth and capital"; the Home Secretary scoffed at "a Jack Cade legislation"; Gladstone, vice-president of the Board of Trade, never attempted to keep the House together for Shaftesbury, nor gave him a vote, nor said a word in his support. "I neither express or feel despair," Shaftesbury wrote in the darkest days. Of very singular distinction of mind, living in the Divine presence, he freely sacrificed ease, power, social ties, a place in the Cabinet, to the cause of the poor. "Should I deceive them, they will never henceforward believe that there exists a single man of station or fortune who is worthy to be trusted." Long effort was needed to get some relief (which Parliament had for forty years refused) for the "climbing" boys and girls, sometimes five years old or less, stolen, sold, or entrapped as sweeps, driven up narrow tortuous chimneys by wisps of lighted straw to put out fires, lying naked on the soot-heap all the night, and perishing of horrible diseases. He gave twenty-two years of labour on behalf of lunatics chained and starved, to carry a very imperfect lunacy bill; seventeen years to secure laws forbidding night work. Partial attention had been awakened in those years, he said, "to the wants and rights of the poor; to the powers and duties of the rich." "The labour of 300,000 persons has been reduced within reasonable limits, and full 40,000 children under thirteen years of age attend school for three hours every day." But twenty years after the first effective Factory Act, Lord Shaftesbury was still pleading for 1,600,000 operatives shut out from any benefit of legislation: "until they are brought under the protection of the law I cannot take office."

So grudging a progress of Factory Acts, a bitter experience of Poor-law, the complicated strife of conflicting interests, ideals, and opinions, deepened the determination of the workers to redress the wrong done them in 1832. A dozen years of confused strife had brought a strange medley of success and failure: the Individualists had won their chief triumph in Free Trade, and the State Socialists their first success in a Factory Act; while in the Chartist failure the democracy was again thrust back from the polls. But in the same year, with the call of Karl Marx for union among the workers of all countries, Socialism began its modern work. Leaving behind the effort to secure reform by establishing separate societies and colonies, it henceforth aimed at renewing the whole social and industrial order by the power of democratic government. Current economic theories taught that men must inevitably choose either relief by legislation of the suffering poor or the welfare of the State, but could not secure both; since the source of all hope, and cure of social misery, must lie in the freedom of individuals liberated from restrictions and left to take their interests into their own hand. These doctrines were now challenged with increasing energy and passion. If the capitalist enjoyed such freedom through the enormous power given him by the industrial changes, against his autocracy Trade Unionists and Socialists were alike battling, whether by combinations of labour, or by State legislation, to recover in some degree freedom of labour for the hired worker — the life-long wage-earner now wholly cut off from any economic interest in the product of his labour. Amid problems transcending experience there was no certainty of guidance, nor any common consent as to remedies for distress. Groups formed and re-formed as friends and foes found themselves in shifting camps and met in strange alliances. John Stuart Mill, the prophet of the new age, was feeling his way to the conviction that since the struggle of individuals must deepen misery, the Commonwealth should provide for the good of all, restraining the power of the strong and shielding the helplessness of the weak, protecting children, controlling contracts, joint-stock companies, railway monopolies, and the like, aiding associations of people united for common benefit, and giving help to public services such

SEC. I.

THE SOCIAL REVOLUTION

1815
TO
1914

1866

Rise of Socialism

1846
1847
1848

Economic theories

Confusion of opinions
1848

Sec. I.
The Social
Revolu-
tion
1815
to
1914
1843

as scientific expeditions and colonisation. Place on the other hand, in his zeal for free bargaining, would even have left the work-men at the mercy of the employer in the truck system. Both Bright and Cobden denounced Trade Unions; "they are founded upon principles of brutal tyranny and monopoly"; but while Cobden resisted household suffrage, Bright thought it essential to healthy national life. Conservatives such as Peel and Gladstone joined with Radicals like Cobden and Bright to oppose the bill of a Tory Lord Shaftesbury delivering women and children from mines and pits: and united with them again to secure free trade. Radicals and "Christian Socialists" supported Trade Unions, which Liberals condemned as bringing in a new despotism no less ominous, perhaps more formidable, than the tyranny of the State. Shaftesbury, friend of the people, resisted Socialism, the vote, and the ballot, gave a humbler place to Nonconformist ministers of the poor below the Anglican clergy, and opposed State aid in education to the most needy schools where the Roman Catholic Bible was allowed. When Gladstone advocated the opening of the Civil Service to free com-petition, Bright objected. Toleration was in men's minds, but

every separate advance in religious equality—a grant to Maynooth, the election of a Rothschild, the allowing of Roman Catholic bishops in England, roused a new storm of excitement, and was denounced as the disintegration of English character and of the British Empire. Only amid harsh controversy were Nonconformists and Catholics freed by 1854 from most of their political disabilities; Jews admitted to municipal office in 1844, and in 1859 to Parliament; and Universities gradually thrown open in 1854 and 1871.

It was in a world shaken to its depths that the first International Exhibition opened, marking the mid-way of the century. Englishmen hailed it as a pledge that free trade would appease the discord of nations, and endow their country with unbroken prosperity. They recognised with pride that English Liberalism had become the hope and model of the Continent. In England Cavour learnt his political lessons for Italy. From England Karl Marx took his ideas. Prussia recognised the better organisation of English labour by her system of protection, and had adopted for her workers the very factory law which Peel rejected. But the "Great Exhibition," inaugurated with such high hopes, was in fact to mark the end of the long peace, and the close of the legislative work of the reformed Parliament. After battles won and lost, there had come a pause with the passing of the

old world, and the waiting for the new. Sir Robert Peel was dead, and Wellington dying—the leader of the old Toryism and the founder of modern Conservatism. The end of the Whig activity was marked

by the resignation of the reformer Lord John Russell; since their refusal to lead the democracy against the peers in the free-trade campaign, power had passed from the Whigs, and no leader of Cabinets rose out of their decline. For ten years of slow transition the country was ruled by the last representative of the older world. Lord Palmerston had entered Parliament in 1806, and held office under the Tories from 1809 to 1828, when he became leader of the Canningites. He was adored by the mob for his love of sport, his reputation for liberalism, and the position he maintained on the Continent as the advocate of freedom and defender of rising nationalities. But to reformers at home he seemed, with no distinct policy or lofty teaching, a cynical degrader of public life. The young men growing up around him were held back by his " repressive force." No other chief, Bright declared, would again be found to keep as many people quiet as Lord Palmerston had been able to do. His traditions came from an age of immobility when the Parliamentary record was monotonously blank. In later times the statute-book had come to contain more new laws yearly than that of any other country : but under Lord Palmerston's rule the stir of legislation ceased. The House of Lords was known as the " dormitory." It acted as the mere registration office for the decrees of a House of Commons from which it had nothing to fear. Meetings no longer assembled to call for redress of grievances : " there is no worse trade than agitation at this time," said one. Formal Bills to enfranchise a few skilled artisans were from time to time brought in and dismissed with equal indifference. When Bright pleaded for household suffrage he compared his labours to flogging a dead horse. " We live in anti-reforming times," said Gladstone. No doubt the perils of the Crimean War and the Indian Mutiny drew men's attention abroad : but the ten years of political stagnation was perhaps mainly due to the entire absorption of the whole people in commercial and financial questions. With the diffusion of wealth a haste of speculation spread to classes never touched before, and the country was terrified by recurring financial catastrophes—in 1836 from the growing numbers of joint-stock banks unregulated by any public law ; in 1847 from a frenzy of railway speculation ; in 1857 from reckless overtrading abroad ; in 1866 from an outburst of senseless speculation, commercial fraud, and banking incapacity. So great was public alarm that a Select Committee was formed to consider " investments for the savings of the middle and working classes " ; another to examine into the law of partnership on a large scale ; and a Mercantile Law Commission for smaller associations or business firms. Men now began to demand of the State protection for the thrifty, and laws to prevent wrong doing and not simply patch up the consequences when it has been committed. In the interests of the working-classes co-operative associations were granted legal protection ; and after a series of conferences were grouped into general confederations.

Sec. I.

The Social Revolution

1815 to 1914

Lord Palmerston

1859

1850
1851
1852

Trading and banking laws

1852

Sec. I.

The Social
Revolu-
tion
1815
to
1914
1863
1872

the English and Scottish Wholesale Societies and the Co-operative Union, into which thousands of citizens were gathered up—an army of organised and intelligent workers. The Co-operative Wholesale Society, originated by a little group of artisans who met in Manchester over a " sixpenny tea," expanded during the next fifty years into a commercial enterprise exceeding any effort of private capitalism in its continuous success. Beginning with 24,000 members, it was in nine years serving 100,000 families; had started its own banking department which has now an annual turnover of nearly £ 20,000,000, and opened a boot factory with a present annual manufacture of nearly £ 8,000,000. It now manages five of the largest flour mills, and one of the largest tobacco factories; owns agricultural land in England and tea plantations in Ceylon: and is said to buy goods—and this for cash—at the rate of something like a thousand pounds in every minute of the working year. A scheme to

protect the savings of the poor was inaugurated by Gladstone in the Post-Office Savings Banks, in which a fifth of the whole population now invest their economies: he also made it for the first time

possible for the working-classes to acquire small annuities without risk of fraud or bankruptcy. The creation of Limited Liability

Companies, instead of the old joint-stock companies and banking associations, was so effectually carried out by a series of Acts that the laid up capital of these Companies under the Act of 1862 increased to 307 millions by 1877, and by the end of the century to over 2,000 millions. The whole company law was amended. The new notion that law should not only punish fraud but protect the public

was seen in the Bankruptcy Act, which for the first time treated the merchant prince who fell into debt on the same terms as the

small trader. With these innovations a silent reconstruction of society began. Wealth which had once gone to a score of men was diffused among hundreds of thousands, to the increase of small incomes, and the general rise of moderate comfort. The limiting of liability, which enabled individuals to trade without exposing all their property to the risk of loss, opened new opportunities for middle class business and investment. Year by year a larger number of men became practically traders, and as shareholders in companies had their part in the profits of the vast industrial and commercial activity of the country. Through the working of the limited liability system large shops replaced the smaller independent tradesmen. An immense army of men passed from a life of competition, risk, and independent private venture, into the new multitude of salaried clerks and officials of large companies and business firms—a class now so vast in numbers (with the addition of those in public employment) as to give a new tone to

national character and policy.

These years were indeed full of significance. By the genius of

SEC. I.

THE SOCIAL
REVOLU-
TION

1815
TO
1914

Gladstone the whole of public finance and account-keeping was revised, while the nation was called to a graver concern in the conduct of public business. Opening an attack on the system of political patronage and family influences under which the Civil Service had become a secure asylum for those debarred by incompetence from all other professions, he urged the throwing open of appointments to competition and promotion by merit—a revolution of the first importance for the public welfare, which was slowly carried out against powerful opposition. Reforms of taxation and finance begun by Peel were developed in the astonishing series of budgets which revealed Gladstone as the greatest financier in English history, and which by completing free trade, by lightening the burdens of taxation, and by giving a powerful stimulus to commerce, won for him the devotion of the merchants, of the severely-taxed ten-pound householders who had no power to protect themselves financially, and of the unrepresented working-men. Another searching reform followed. A Bill to rescind the paper duties, and thus make possible a cheap press for the people, was rejected by the Lords. Such a claim to "a revising power over the House of Commons in its most vital function" of finance was to Gladstone a "gigantic innovation on the constitution," a very "quarrel of the Lords with the nation." In spite of Palmerston's strong opposition he asserted the authority of the Commons by a new practice of combining the financial measures of the year in a single Bill; and the paper duties were abolished. But the privileges of the House were from this time to be balanced by its obligations. Till now there had been no exact accounts of expenditure laid before the Commons, no serious examination of them, and no security for the orderly administration of finance. A real control was now established by the creation of a Committee of the House of Commons—the Committee of Public Accounts—and the appointment of a great Parliamentary official independent of the Government—the Comptroller and Auditor-General—who were charged to inspect and report to the House on past expenditure of every State department, to scrutinise the propriety of payments made out of parliamentary grants, and to call to account any official concerned in misappropriation. In this manner an effective power over finance, and the responsibility of Ministers and their officers to the House of Commons, was for the first time demanded and achieved.

"The English are a nation of shopkeepers" was the taunt of Napoleon I. In their intense concentration on business, no dim prevision of the advent of democracy now disturbed the commercial mind. Whigs and Tories were alike satisfied with the constitutional equilibrium which they had set up. "The working classes contribute almost nothing to our corporate public opinion," Bagehot noted. The

*Civil
Service*
1853-76
1853-9

1860

1861

1862
*Charter of
the Com-
mons in
finance*

1866

**The New
Age**

Sec. I.

The Social
Revolu-
tion
1815
to
1914
1861

electors, awed by the great proprietors and capitalists, had proved
" deferential. They have deferred to their representatives." The
balance of the constitution seemed again fixed, and there was once
more a complacent sense of security. " The great ends of freedom,"
wrote Erskine May, " have been attained, in an enlightened and
responsible rule, approved by the judgment of the governed. The
constitution, having worked out the aims, and promoted the just
interests of society, has gained upon democracy." Suddenly from the
gathering clouds fire fell and ran along the ground, consuming the
stubble, preparing for a harvest to come. The voice of Gladstone
called with its lofty utterance to the new society that unnoticed had
been slowly taking form over the land. With the death of Palmerston
the bands were loosed, and the old system crumbled into dust.
" There is not a brick of the Palmerston house standing," men said
astonished.

A world in fact had arisen which was not as the old world—a
world changed in spirit and outlook. Faith in unlimited competition weakened as one trade after another passed from the
management of private persons into that of corporate bodies created
and regulated by the Government. The new laws of partnership
under keeping and control of the State; the recognition of working-
men's associations and co-operative societies for the common advantage; the grant of monopolies to special bodies (as for example
railway companies) under vigilant public control; the authority given
to municipal corporations to replace the slow and painful efforts of
individuals by communal services paid for out of the public property
or general taxes, voted by the people themselves, and aided by
State loans—such changes as these turned thought in a new direction.
The Benthamite idea of a Government concerned only to abolish restriction sank out of sight, and a new socialistic vision arose of a State
actively charged with securing the public good. How rapid was the
change we may see in Mill's apology for speaking of the " labouring
classes." Deeply influenced in turn by the Utilitarians and Individualists of the first half of the century and by the rising Socialism
of its close, holding the Liberal doctrine of the uses of competition to
force men to activity and intelligence, with the Socialists he forecast a
time when industrial life would take new forms, when there would be
no more " labouring classes," since all classes must in the end labour,
and the produce of work be divided by consent; when the bitterness
of strife between employers and employed parted into hostile camps
should no longer endure. Already democracy was at the door.
" The poor have come out of leading strings, and cannot any longer be
governed or treated like children. To their own qualities must now
be commended the care of their destiny." So wrote John Stuart Mill,
standing between the old world and the new. Two leaders stood

ready for the duel of giants which was to absorb the next generation. "Genius better is than birth," was the refrain of later Tyneside workers when Gladstone came among them in his triumph as leader of the people. For the first time in English history the heads of the two parties were men born outside the old governing caste, William Gladstone, of Scotch descent, the son of a West Indian merchant, Benjamin Disraeli, son of a Jewish man of letters. Their rivalry, begun five years after Gladstone's election to the first reformed Parliament, at the entry of Disraeli to the first parliament of Queen Victoria, was pursued when Disraeli as Chancellor of the Exchequer framed his budget, and Gladstone the next year produced his own from the same place; across the contest in successive years of their rival Reform bills; and to the rise within a year of the two leaders to the place of Prime Minister. Each of the new statesmen was destined, forsaking his early allies, to re-organize and lead the opposite party; for now again, as in the days of Canning and Peel, older groups were disintegrating under the rise of a new social force—the organized workingclasses—and Tories and Whigs, who at the first Reform bill had united to keep the wage earners at bay, became as the second reform drew near rivals for popular support. Gladstone, a Conservative follower of Peel, had supported coercion, defended the corn-law, maintained sinecures in army and navy, resisted religious equality, opposed the ballot and every effort to broaden the popular control of Parliament, refused lightening of the window tax and abolition of flogging in the army. Like his master he was swept from his old bearings by the rising tide of passion in the people, but more than Peel by the ardour of his own nature—a statesman in whom the spirit of improvement was incarnate, said Mill; who did not wait to be pressed or driven, but sought out what might be bettered. A high Anglican, he boasted of Nonconformist ancestors, and drew the Dissenters into the movements of national life: the "old, old Whigs" were induced by his amazing authority of intellect and character to enter with the Radicals into untried paths of reform; business men admired him for his public thrift and his creed of peace and retrenchment as against ostentation of military adventure; by his generous hopes for mankind he stirred deeply the hearts of the multitude, and new life was kindled in minds long arid as with his fervid energy, his glowing intelligence, his voice so rich in cadences, he pictured the spiritual destinies of England, the august spectacle of a nation called to the great and responsible duty of pronouncing a verdict on governments, the consecration of the weak things of the world to war on injustice in high places. Such a strain of moral and religious emotion was entirely distasteful to his rival, Benjamin Disraeli. Of devouring ambition ("We come here for fame," he cried to Bright), a cynical opportunist, his adventurous spirit could have feared no bold

Sec. I.

The Social
Revolu-
tion

1815
to
1914

1832
1837
1852–3

1866–7
1868

Gladstone

Disraeli

SEC. I.

THE SOCIAL
REVOLU-
TION
1815
TO
1914

1846

1847-8

1852

1872

Second
Reform
Act
1866

1867

1861

1867

advance. His intellectual force, his discriminating outlook over public affairs, were unrivalled in his time, and his Radical criticism of the state of England and Ireland, so far as words alone went, was penetrating, vigorous, and detached. But of more than intellectual perception he shewed no sign; nor did he seek in power to carry the reforms he preached in opposition. In the hour of their shattering defeat, he rallied for battle the disheartened Protectionists and extreme Tories, and bitterly pursued Peel to his ruin in the corn-laws controversy. With patient skill, as leader of the Tory opposition, he created a party out of the wreckage left by Peel, and after some thirty years of discomfiture, in which the Tories had but once a fleeting majority of their own, in which at dissolutions of Parliament demanded by them (1852, 1859, 1868) they never won a victory from the people, he raised them to power and authority. When he was forced to abandon a policy of protection, he turned to a vague programme of social reform to be controlled by national and historic considerations, as opposed to the philosophic and logical reforms of the Radicals. The aristocracy he led, anxious to wipe off the accusation of being "hostile to the working classes," were ready for a time to accept the grandiose idea of a disciplined democracy led by the Crown and the House of Lords, in which the landed gentry, as guardians of the people, should maintain their power against the commercial classes: but hereditary alarms of the peers and country gentry revived at the risks of socialism and of perilous encroachments by the populace. Devoid of any conspicuous power in finance or constructive policy, Disraeli finally turned from home affairs to kindle the enthusiasm of the country by the dazzling alternative of a new "Imperialism."

No sooner was Palmerston dead than Gladstone, Chancellor of the Exchequer under Lord Russell, advanced a Reform bill. "Every man," he had already said, "who is not presumably incapacitated by some consideration of personal unfitness or of political danger is morally entitled to come within the pale of the Constitution": but though the cautious compromise he proposed left out more than four millions of working-men, and would have given to the wage-earning class, three-fourths of the whole population, only one-fourth of the electoral power in the boroughs and scarcely any in the counties, yet a timid Liberal parliament rejected even this meagre bill. A Tory government was formed by Lord Derby with Disraeli as his Chancellor of the Exchequer. Now it was that the artisans showed the strength they had built up in years of organization. The cotton famine of the American war had brought its harsh reminder of what workers might suffer under a Poor Law imposed by the upper classes alone. The importance of the vote for the working-man was newly demonstrated when a decision in the courts of law revealed that there was no reality in their legal status and protection for their funds which the Trade Unions supposed to have been won. Mill was teaching them that whatever might be the benevolence of Parliament the views of the working-man himself must be heard there, and must influence legislation. Bright reiterated the cry of Cobbett fifty years before. "If," he told the people, "a class has failed, let us try the nation." "The nation in every country are the dwellers in the cottages." The London Trade Societies marched through the capital. Mass meetings of working-men stirred tremendous agitation in the country and provincial towns; trade unions and co-operative societies paraded in their ordered ranks before Bright—a serried army to win enfranchisement. The failure of the Chartists twenty years before had turned to triumph. Disraeli, bending to necessity, or hoping to secure the working-men for the Tories as against the Benthamites, after many strange shiftings finally passed in a Parliament that showed more surprise than pleasure the most sweeping and Radical Reform Bill that had ever been proposed—to add over a million voters from the great body of artisans in the towns. At the next election the new voters lifted Gladstone to power with a passion of personal popularity such as had not been known in England since the time of William Pitt. He stood to them as the finance minister who had tripled trade with France, as the giver of cheap food, the friend and defender of the common people, the minister of peace, the preacher of piety and righteousness. The cynicism of Palmerston was changed to an exaltation of enthusiasm as massed crowds heard the rallying battle-cry of Gladstone to virtue and civil duty, to a high place in the great affairs of nations, to the unbounded hope of the future; as they listened to the wrath of the prophet denouncing injustice; and bent awed before the noble music of his voice, and the commanding power of his gesture. Old antagonisms, he declared, were henceforth submerged in the new revelation of the State, in the latter-day confidence of the working-man in the law, in parliament, even in the executive government. All lovers of freedom in England, Wales, Scotland, or Ireland were to be called into the new fellowship of liberty, in a union of free will instead of the bondage of political subjection.

The story of 1833 was repeated in 1868. "The new voters," men complained, "have returned the old kinds of men," men who could spend vast sums on elections, sons of great families—not a single member of extreme democratic views among them. And yet, as in 1833, all was changed. Both Tories and Whigs stood "exceedingly afraid of the ignorant multitude of the new constituencies" whose combination might make them supreme in the country—a supremacy of ignorance over instruction and of numbers over knowledge. And

SEC. I.
THE SOCIAL REVOLUTION
1815 TO 1914

1868

The new parliament

Sec. I.
The Social
Revolu-
tion
1815
to
1914

in fact the great Whig families, who had led the Liberals for thirty-four years, saw their reign at an end. For the first time there was an altered social tone in the House, with the election of a troop of able young men not necessarily aristocrats. New boroughs sent Liberal members. The Scotch elected forty-six Liberals to seven Conservatives—a people, said Bright, perfectly instructed on the working-man's questions, "the people who should have repeal of the Union, for that if they were separate from England they might have a government wholly popular and intelligent to a degree which, I believe, does not exist in any other country on the face of the earth." "The working classes," Lord Shaftesbury noted, "have become patrons instead of clients, and they both can and do fight their own battles." In 1869 John Bright entered the Cabinet, the first Nonconformist there, and the first nominee of the working-men ; in 1870 the first working-man sat on a Royal Commission ; in 1874 the first labour member was elected to the House of Commons ; in 1875 Trade Union officials were called to sit on School Boards, and working-men were appointed Factory inspectors in 1882. But the pressure of the rising democracy had more profound results than these. Since the first Reform Act ministers had been chosen, not by royal influence, but by the House of Commons ; after the second Reform Act, by a new development, the Prime Minister was understood on both sides to be the "elect of the nation." Disraeli admitted the direct verdict of the people when, beaten at the polls, he resigned without meeting Parliament. At the same time, as the power of the Crown lessened and the power of the House increased, the Ministers were bound in a closer discipline than of old. Queen Victoria had been taught to look on the Cabinet as the ministers not of Parliament but of the sovereign, and to regard the defeat of a minister as an "affront to the Crown," and a dissolution as a personal exercise of royal power. Under that older system Earl Grey in 1829 contended that a minister brought in a Bill merely as an ordinary member, and that the failure of such a Bill could not therefore decide the fate of the Government ; and there were later cases when the Ministry was changed without any dissolution of Parliament, and when a Prime Minister ruled without a majority in the House. The Premiers however had steadily won the right to claim a dissolution not only against a hostile House of Commons but against an obstructive House of Lords. Through the assertion that Ministers acted, not from the sovereign's permission but by the will of the people, and by the strict enforcing of the authority of the House, the Cabinet was compacted into a body united in responsibility.

The new reformed Parliament recalled the unfulfilled pledges of 1833. A motion to repeal the Corn Laws had been defeated in 1834 ; the last remnant of duty, the shilling on every quarter of wheat, was now abolished. England was still behind every other great country in the world, with two million of her children, two-thirds of the whole, left outside the schools; under a paid Minister of Education (1856), a scheme of national and compulsory education was now set up. Competitive examination for the Civil Service was established by Order in Council. A Local Government Board was set up charged with care of the public health and control of the Poor Law system. The sole influence of the aristocracy in the army was checked by abolishing the purchase of commissions and bringing the military force under the undivided control of the House of Commons. After years of conflict religious tests were abolished for students enjoying the privileges of Oxford and Cambridge; and for the first time a peerage was given to a Jew, and for the first time in living memory to a Roman Catholic. The Ballot Act finally closed the burning controversy by which throughout the century the people had been vainly demanding protection for those whose daily bread might depend on the secrecy of their vote: "the desire to conceal votes is a bad sign of the times," was the old answer: "it would destroy their character as Englishmen," and turn them into pitiful figures, ashamed to confess their political creed, "sneaking up to the ballot-box." A long series of reforms to end the extravagance, the inequality, and the delays of the law, were consummated by the Judicature Act, the constitution of a High Court of Justice, and a Supreme Court of Criminal Appeal.

But amid these changes, carrying out old pledges, two new Acts stood out—the Irish Church Act and the Irish Land Act. They marked a new stage in the controversy of Ireland with England. The disestablishment of the Irish Church, the Church of the minority and the ascendancy, sounded the doom of the old political theory (carefully preserved in 1833) of ecclesiastical authority as a necessary adjunct of the secular government of the State. A struggle with the Upper Chamber, which had already opened with the University Tests bill of 1866, was renewed with more intense animosity. "Never," writes Lord Morley, "was the political system more strained" than in the sharpness of the conflict with the Lords, who only yielded when the danger became acute. The Land Act, by which Gladstone boldly sought to assure to Irish tenants the Ulster tenant right, opened a controversy yet more prolonged and violent. "Tenant-right is landlord-wrong," Palmerston had exclaimed amid the cheers of a House mainly composed of landlords; but the first Irish Land Act was the death-knell of the landlord monopoly not only in Ireland but in England. Since the transportation of the Dorsetshire labourers in 1834 agricultural workers in England had known no change in their state; once more, led by Joseph Arch, a labourer and Methodist preacher, they began to form unions, asking sixteen shillings a week and an eleven hours day, and in a

Sec. I.

The Social
Revolu-
tion
1815
to
1914
1871

1871

1871-4

1872

1869-1873
1907
**Reforms
for
Ireland**

1856

1870

1872

SEC. I.

THE SOCIAL
REVOLU-
TION

1815
TO
1914

**Victory
of the
Tories
1874**

1875

1874

1875

*Imperialism
and
Democracy*

1875

1876

**Parlia-
ment and
people**

year had gathered nearly a hundred thousand members, meeting
often by moonlight, facing dangers and sacrifices and universal
opposition.

Energy of reform was followed, as in 1835, by quick reaction; and
the Trade Unionists felt their own special claims neglected. The party
reconstructed by Disraeli triumphed in the first Parliament of the twelve
since the Reform Act that remained Tory from beginning to end.
Two years before he had proclaimed the new mission of Toryism:
"the maintenance of our institutions, the preservation of our empire,
and the improvement of the condition of the people." To use a
phrase of the time, "All social questions had now advanced into
regions of Imperialism." But his party was not yet one for revolutionary adventure. For Ireland there was the usual Coercion Act.
The iniquity of "climbing children" was ended, after an agitation of
a hundred and fifteen years. A Factory Bill for the health of women
was added to a series of statutes which had gradually brought
2,500,000 workers under the protection of law. To the Trade Unions
who had won his election Disraeli granted two Acts—one of which
made the employer and the workman equal parties in a civil contract,
while the other gave legal recognition to the function of Trade
Unionism and to collective bargaining and peaceful picketing. Thus
was ended the long conflict begun in 1824–5 to free Trade Unions
from the law of conspiracy and its penalties. For the farmers there
was an Act of Compensation for improvements, provided the landlord
consented to come under the Act—a perfectly ineffectual measure.
From social questions Disraeli rapidly turned to measures less
contentious for his party—"the preservation of our Empire." He met
the fears of manufacturers, alarmed at the competition of other lands
which through their arts and arms, enterprise and wealth, skill, industry and freedom, might threaten the pre-eminence of England, by
schemes of Imperial consolidation, an imperial tariff, imperial representation, an imperial military code of defence. Through Colonial
expansion, and the pressure, not to say ascendancy of England in the
councils of Europe, the glory of Elizabethan days was to be revived.
A spirited foreign policy was to show the Continent that nothing
could be done there without the authority of England. The purchase of the Suez Canal shares for four million pounds indicated a
new departure. The next year England was magnified as an "Asiatic
Power," and an "Oriental Empire" by giving to the Queen the title
of "Empress of India"; and Disraeli as Lord Beaconsfield entered
the House of Lords.

Thus the modern Imperialism, as defined by the Tory Minister's
glowing imagination and his dazzling vision of the imperial destiny of
the island of Great Britain over the broad earth and in command
of every ocean, went out over the country to become a new creed

of popular enthusiasm, and an all-important force in directing the course of English history in our time. Radicals and Socialists on the other hand contended that only by internal reform could England hold a high and secure place among the nations. They demanded that the people, lifted above destitution, should have the independence of free men, knowledge to use their liberty, and power to enforce their will. The whole country rang with the public controversy. "What was outside Parliament," Gladstone observed, "had mounted to an importance far exceeding what was inside." New weapons of war were forged. Mr. Joseph Chamberlain, the ardent leader of the Radical reformers, found in Birmingham material waiting for his shrewd business capacity. A new town of small masters and unorganized labour, without tradition of wealthy manufacturers, without effective Trade Unions, it was a society which he could exactly "hammer and mould into an electoral instrument at once more pliable and more dependable than any ever controlled by the borough-mongers of the eighteenth century." The Liberals of Birmingham were ranged under a rigid discipline, in which every candidate pledged himself to abide by the decision of the "caucus," as Lord Beaconsfield called it; every symptom of revolt was suppressed, and individual opinion subdued to an ordered plan of conflict. The "Birmingham plan" of Mr. Chamberlain's ingenious and despotic mind was extended to other towns: on his election to Parliament he grouped these associations into a National Liberal Federation with a central Council, and thus stood at the head of a democracy united for battle. While the caucus suppressed individual opinion among the voters, candidates for election were forced by the mere size of the new constituencies to accept submissively the authorized party programme as the only means of gaining a common consent. The Tories, overthrown in a general election by Mr. Chamberlain's driving force, copied in their turn the "Birmingham plan," when Lord Randolph Churchill as leader of the "Tory Democracy" formed a federation of Conservative Associations. In the passion of public debate both agitators called on the voters outside to support them by their drilled organizations in forcing on popular reform against the opposition of slower-moving leaders of their own parties within the House. Interest shifted from the House of Commons to the electors themselves, and the public quickly learned that for a political champion success in the country was more needful than success in the House itself. In former times no minister ever made important announcements outside the House, or laid proposals for legislation before electors devoid of any share in the initiation of laws; and as late as 1886 Queen Victoria objected to a Minister speaking outside his own constituency as tending to popular agitation. But the new classes that had entered political life were no longer to be shepherded

Sec. I.

The Social Revolution

1815 to 1914

The caucus

1876
1877

1880

1883

Appeal to the people

Sec. I.

The Social
Revolu-
tion
1815
to
1914
1879

behind such barriers. Gladstone, who on a public platform had announced to an astonished nation his intention of carrying his Reform bill (1866), and had amazed the country by speeches defining a popular budget (1874) not yet introduced into the House of Commons, now led the first campaign among the masses which had ever been undertaken by any leader of the government. It was in this "Midlothian campaign," "a romance of politics," as Gladstone called it, that in deep winter snow the old man of seventy, preparing for his twelfth election, moved in triumphant progress, and with an unexampled fervour of oratory called on serried masses of weavers, miners, artizans, farmers, to weigh their obligations in foreign affairs and home policy. Tories denounced this passionate pilgrimage of democracy as "an innovation on the constitution," "a positive danger to the commonwealth." But henceforth neither party could live save by direct appeal to the people. The Marquis of Salisbury himself, as Gladstone wrote to the Queen, "established a

1880

rule of what may be called popular agitation" by general public meetings. But all other efforts were surpassed by Gladstone's later processional progresses through England and Scotland in his crusade

1886

for the Home Rule bill, and his assertion to the Queen of his right to "the use of any means requisite in order to place (what he thinks) the true issue before the country."

The Liberal Parliament elected after the stupendous excitement of the Midlothian campaign, and led by the most intrepid reformer that had ever been Prime Minister, opened wide the road along which modern England, the England that we know, was to advance, and hewed out for Ireland a way of hope. For a dozen years, since 1872, Mr. Trevelyan had year by year vainly proposed the enfranchisement of the multitude of householders who lay outside the Parliamentary boroughs. Obstruction was swept aside as the power of Gladstone

1884

drove a new Reform bill through the House. In 1832 less than 500,000 voters had been added to the entire constituency of the three countries; and 1,364,000 in 1867-9: but 2,000,000 new voters were now brought in; and yet more remarkable, by the sheer force of Gladstone's fervour, Parliament was persuaded to raise the number of Irish voters from 200,000 to 500,000. The working classes of Great Britain, after a conflict of fifty years, had won the full citizenship denied them in 1832. As for the mass of the Irish people, it was their first admission to representation in the Parliament of the United Kingdom.

A sense of imminent change was in the air—the beginning of the effective Socialist movement in England. Henry George had started a new agricultural agitation, and had driven home among tillers of the soil and workers in the towns the Ricardian theory of economic rent and the landlords' appropriation of it in town or country.

Quickened by the teaching of Karl Marx on the industrial revolution, and by the fervour of revivalist leaders, the workers were breaking through years of quiescent Liberalism and moving fast towards a "New Unionism." Trade Unions, once held to be an impenetrable barrier against Socialism, themselves insisted on the power and duty of the State to compel reform. Their Congress accepted Land Nationalisation, and an Eight Hour Day to be enforced by law. Since the first days of factory legislation the world had moved on, and the State was now neither "invoked as a parent nor as a beneficent master; it is invoked as the agent, aye, as the servant of the people's will." In municipal government the democracy entered on a new range of power. Rapidly gathering into their hands all outlying and scattered remnants of local administration, widening their franchise to the single-room tenant and the independent woman, the towns carried beyond all experience the use of communal property and public taxes for the general benefit. The dream of Robert Owen became a reality. It is calculated that local bodies now administer for the public good, and by the will of the community, property of a capital value not far short of a thousand million sterling; and that the services organised by the people for themselves and under their own control, whether in voluntary associations of co-operators, or in public bodies of borough and county councils, represent "an annual expenditure of something like two hundred millions sterling, or approximately an eighth of the whole personal expenditure of the United Kingdom." On all sides the principles that had guided the decisions of Parliament for fifty years were discarded. The modern demand was not for the mere abolition of privilege and protection of individual liberty, whether against the State or any form of combination; it was for the active construction of a new society. Men were shaking themselves free from the old authority of economic doctrine; Bentham was discredited; havoc had been made of the teaching of Mill, the autocrat of his own time. But among the contending series of new doctrines sent abroad not one attained a recognised supremacy. Philosophic Liberals, struggling in the midst of economic anarchy, might protest in vain against the growing habit of political experiments, apart from any clear system of thought: "It is futile," wrote Jevons, "to attempt to uphold in regard to social legislation any theory of eternal fixed principles or abstract rights. All is a question of probability and degree." Mr. Chamberlain, then dominated by ideals of a reformed social State, gave to these for the first time the authority of a minister of the Crown, impetuously pouring forth from the Board of Trade one "unauthorized programme" after another—manhood suffrage, no plural voting, payment of members, free education, small holdings, the re-housing of the urban poor, the

Sec. I.

The Social Revolution

1815 to 1914

1887

1885

1880-5

Sec. I.

The Social
Revolu-
tion
1815
to
1914

right of the State to take land for public purposes at the lowest
market price, a graduated income tax, the breaking up of great estates,
the "ransom" of the landed rich who would "neither toil nor spin."
England was no longer to be "the purgatory of the poor." Swiftly
the revolution spread beyond social reform, to the very foundations of
the English constitution.   All statesmen from the middle of the
eighteenth century down to Palmerston had been agreed on the
necessity of hereditary succession to unbroken masses of landed
property, so as to protect by extensive agriculture the food of the
country, and to maintain by primogeniture the constitution of the
kingdom—in other words the position of the landed aristocracy.
Half the land of England was in the possession of fewer than a
hundred and fifty men, Bright told the people, and half the land of
Scotland was held by ten or twelve. So carefully were the means of
tying up property favoured that two-thirds of the land of England
were said to be in strict settlement.   Soon after the first Reform Act
Lord Shaftesbury in a visit to Chatsworth had felt intimations of the
end of the old order, and in that ultimate magnificence had seen his
vision of "probably the last great effort of hereditary wealth, of
aristocratical competition with the splendour of kings " and had known
that the acquiring of immense properties by primogeniture "has
reached the full and is now upon the wane."   But under the second
Reform Act even economists began to put in question the agricultural
value of great estates, and proposed that land should be as freely sold
and dispersed as personal property, and that primogeniture and
entail should disappear.   Moreover, those who denied that primogeniture was the pillar of agricultural prosperity were ultimately to
question whether it was the necessary mainstay of the Constitution.

Conflict in fact had begun to harden between the two Houses of
Parliament.   After the Reform Act the Lords, unable to realise the
new strength of the Commons, had sought by strategy to secure their
old position and exercise their accustomed powers ; but there had been
gradual accommodation to the altered conditions.   Under Lord
Palmerston the Commons, in the absence of any serious strife, were
accepted without question as "the depository of power."   "The
peers act as breakwaters and think as such," Lord Shaftesbury had
said. "This is their office and they never rise beyond it."   Lords
and Commons, fearful that if they had a controversy "the great body
of ignorant poor " would be called in to decide between them, long
maintained a carefully balanced equilibrium through the family groups
which till 1867 practically occupied both Houses.   But immediately
on Palmerston's death the controversy began which was to culminate
forty years later.   So long as the two Houses were similar in their
essence, taken from the same class of the English gentry of ancient

descent, no differences arose between them.   The abolition of the old property qualification had made no real change in the Commons; and the landed gentry had easily come to terms with the plutocracy. But with the entry of new men carrying into the Lower House a spirit and tradition formed outside the old governing classes, strife became inevitable. The growing temper of the democracy, the revolt of the Commons against "our masters in the other House," found voice in the curt warning flung to the Lords by John Bright: "In harmony with the nation they may go on for a long time, but throwing themselves athwart its course they may meet with accidents not pleasant for them to think of." As the contrast between the Upper and Lower Chambers became more marked, the Lords tended to identify themselves with one party in the State. While conflicts with the Liberals increased, the peers only twice in the course of twenty years carried a vote against Conservatives—in defence of Palmerston in the China war, and in the reluctant consent to the Church Act. In spite of occasions of friction and delay, however, it was of advantage to the country that the House which represented the great body of landed proprietors should, by its separate consent, record their adherence to new measures, and that this powerful interest should thus formally associate itself with the general movement of the people. But the drift of the Lords to a permanent Tory alliance rapidly became a serious constitutional difficulty. At the death of Lord Beaconsfield the leadership of the Tories passed back to an ancient aristocratic house, and their fortunes were for over thirty years shaped by the Marquis of Salisbury and his nephew, Mr. Balfour. The great revising Chamber became, according to Goschen, "a simple Tory club," so that "if the country looks to the peers for their decision, it knows beforehand precisely on the lines of party what that decision will be." When their bitter and prolonged resistance to the Reform Bill was met by Gladstone's ominous threat of "organic changes in the House of Lords," the final conflict of the Houses was clearly shadowed out.

With this Act began the modern history of the United Kingdom. The double force of the two new democracies, English and Irish, was the measure of the coming revolution. Since 1815 the democrats had urged their propaganda. Nowhere else in Europe had they moved such masses of men, nor given such a spectacle of gigantic demonstrations and agitations, nor of such resource in practical organization. But in spite of enormous efforts their progress halted. Slow and partial reforms were grudgingly meted out to them only after repression had driven the populace to the utmost limit of patience. Fifty years of conflict trailed on before the town artizans were partially admitted to the vote; seventy years before the country folk were recognised as citizens. Seventy years in fact might be taken as the normal time for carrying any popular reform. Emancipation, free trade, household suffrage, the ballot, were won by violent agitation.

SEC. I.

THE SOCIAL REVOLUTION

1815
TO
1914

1869

Policy of the Lords

1857
1869

1881

1885

Ireland and England

Sec. I.

The Social
Revolu-
tion

1815
to
1914

June 1885
Jan. 1886
July 1886

**Ireland
under the
Union**

and conceded only when danger had become extreme. The dominant influence in the country was still the old England of the south, the centre of the court, the aristocracy, the law, the established church, a powerful press, high finance, the military forces of the crown, all the social powers of conservatism. This aristocratic England, severed in interests from the industrial population of the north, stood yet more aloof from Scotland, Wales, and Ireland, which had remained distinct by their social organisation, tradition, and religion. The Reform Act of 1884 not only created a new balance of powers, but brought a force into English politics which was to change the order of battle and accelerate the advance. The Celtic race, " the Celtic Fringe," as Lord Salisbury termed it, was reckoned an alien and inferior people. It was this despised race that now appeared to reinforce the English democracy. The Irish brought with them a problem already centuries old—the place allotted to Ireland in the Empire. The fall of three governments in a year marked the energy of their onset, and the confusion with which the new order was ushered in. As the conflict widened the fierce vigour of attack and defence recalled, as in 1832, precedents of the Great Rebellion both in violence of repression and in ardour of liberty.

The Union had left the Protestant landowners in unchecked ascendancy. With all the wealth and prestige that the sole possession of land could give, they were backed by the might of England, whose garrison they were; by the House of Lords, in which the Irish people had not a single advocate: by the House of Commons, to which members were sent at the bidding of landlords who at elections locked their tenants in outhouses and marched them under guards of soldiers to the poll; by the military forces of the crown, always at their call; by the press, which their influence controlled; and by the old English tradition of inveterate hostility to the Irish, flavoured with contempt. A wealthy Established Church was at their bidding, long trained in politics, officered by their sons and nominees. Special laws, unknown in England, to make eviction cheap and rapid, and perpetual coercion-acts (over and above sharp severity of the old English law) were administered by the landed class; who, themselves, their sons and their agents, filled all the posts of judges, magistrates, grand juries, sheriffs, bailiffs, police officers, and officials of all public departments. This unexampled power was used to maintain a land system utterly wasteful of human life and labour, under which four millions of peasants, tenants-at-will, lay in a more abject state of poverty than human nature could be supposed able to bear, rented to starvation point, fed on potatoes, housed in dwellings more wretched than any found by travellers among savages of the Arctic circle or the tribes of Asia; while they watched the fruits of their toil transported oversea to absentee landlords in England. Peel's corn-law was no remedy for the hunger of a population that never tasted bread. The free corn which gave cheap loaves to the English only doubled to the Irish the labour-rent for his patch of ground. In a land of abundant harvests, among a laborious people, recurring dearths culminated in the Great Famine, long foreseen and foretold. A million of people lay dead, and that in years when abundant harvest of the corn they had grown was being shipped to England under military guard to pay the rent of the absentees. "Monster evictions" cleared another million from the land. From the thousands of houses that were "tumbled" outcasts fled to the bog or ditch, or to the "coffin ships" that carried them to America. Lamentation and mourning filled the air as the shifting of a whole people began— an incredible funeral procession of a nation turning empty away from its holy places, its language and tradition and culture—a transplantation such as the world had not known since the feats of pagan kings of Assyria and consuls of Rome, and the onrush of Attila the Scourge of God. "The Celts are going, and going with a vengeance," said the *Times*. Ruin waited on the landlord as on the tenant, and the English remedy of an Act for the sale of Encumbered Estates completed the misfortunes of the country. The union of the two countries had brought immediate bankruptcy to Irish finances, and the course of taxation, invariably planned at Westminster to relieve the tax-payer of Great Britain, did as invariably increase the burdens of Ireland, where the conditions were wholly different. With the people flying from the stricken land, the Government added £2,500,000 to the permanent taxation of the country, an increase of 40% in ten years; and a Royal Commission recorded that in Great Britain the revenue raised per head on commodities was about half that raised in 1819, while in Ireland it had doubled. Nor were the taxes as in England spent at home. Three millions a year of Irish money remained in the English exchequer over and above what was spent on Ireland, till in ninety-three years no less than three hundred and twenty-five millions, "an Empire's ransom," had passed over the channel without return. The reign of Queen Victoria, to England a time of vaunted prosperity and progress, was to Ireland an age of unmitigated national disaster only to be compared to the reign of Queen Elizabeth. All forms of popular protest failed in turn. There had been deep religious resignation and fidelity. There were savage outbursts of local violence—cries of maddened suffering and despair which the ruling classes branded as "disloyalty" and "rebellion." Daniel O'Connell, in European opinion the greatest popular orator since Demosthenes, led a political agitation against the infamous system of tithes, the exclusion of Catholics from the vote, the whole method of the Union.

SEC. I.

THE SOCIAL REVOLUTION

1815 TO **1914**

The Famine 1846–51

1847

1817 *Financial relations*

1850–60

1896

1823–46

Irish protests

Sec. I.

The Social
Revolu-
tion
1815
TO
1914

1851
1865
1870

Thomas Davis created a "Young Ireland" movement (1842–6) to revive the intellectual life of the country and unite all classes and creeds in the claim for national freedom. Smith O'Brien, driven to despair by the apathy in Parliament to appeals of a famine-stricken Ireland (1848), tried and failed to arouse attention by an insufficient rising in arms. A League of Tenants in north and south was formed. The Fenians planned a campaign in Canada and in Ireland, to shake off by open war a dependence made odious by tyranny and insufferable by misery. Isaac Butt led a party of constitutional Home Rule. To all these the English answer was the eighty-six Crimes or Coercion Acts that marked the century after the Union. Englishmen looked back with shame on the black reaction of 1819 under which the Habeas Corpus Act, the proud charter of British liberty, had been suspended in their own island; through the wide British Empire it had once been set aside for a few weeks in Jamaica : but in Ireland during the hundred years after the Union it was suspended no less than thirteen times. Law became a mere "course of discretion" under packed juries, political judges, partial magistrates, police shadowing, and informers. There was no constitutional remedy. The country people since Peel's legislation in 1829 were wholly unrepresented; the 30,700 borough electors were increased in 1868, by a reform very different from that of England or Scotland, to no more than 40,000. For nearly seventy years, till death and emigration had reduced the people from eight millions to five, the members allotted to Ireland by the Union were below the number° allowed to the same population in England. In a permanent minority at Westminster of one to six, their entire helplessness was demonstrated when Irish Bills supported by all the Irish members for dealing with the land, with municipalities, parliamentary reform, finance, or education, were indifferently thrown out by the English majority. The hours at or after midnight were all that could be got for Irish Bills, nor did that country ever obtain any share in the Government time. Every Irish question as it entered the House of Commons was transformed into a mere matter of English party politics. "Ireland had had no rulers who ruled for Ireland," said Bright. "I have not observed since I have been in Parliament anything on this Irish question that approaches the dignity of statesmanship"—men the most clumsy and brutal might suspend the Habeas Corpus Act, but for real government men of higher temper, genius, and patriotism were needed. Irish affairs always remained remote, unfamiliar, and distasteful to Englishmen, who cherished the constant belief that Home Rule was no more than "a little cauldron simmering."

1851

1875

Parnell
1875

"Ireland is a nation," Charles Stewart Parnell declared in his first speech to the Commons. In the name of a dying country, where the

Sec. I.

The Social
Revolu-
tion
1815
to
1914

remnant of the Irish population was still being flung out of their cabins
to a "sentence of death" on the road-side, he demanded a National
Parliament and a free people established in security on their own land.
Elected President of the Home Rule Confederation, he repudiated the
efforts at "conciliation" which had so notoriously failed: "policy
must be pushed to extremes" to compel the attention of an indifferent
and contemptuous England. By skilled obstruction he paralysed the
House of Commons, forced it to shape the first rule for "Order in
debate" that limited the ancient freedom of its members, and established a compact Irish Party in the House to threaten the old two-
party system. In Ireland meanwhile the Fenian organization and the
Land League opened war on the autocracy of the landlords. Evictions
were raging as in the Great Famine; in 1880 10,657 persons were
ejected, 17,641 in 1881, at the rate of nearly fifty for every day of the
year; 7,000 for the first three months of 1882, and 15,000 awaiting
eviction in the next quarter. In three days 750 persons were turned
out on the bogs and rocks of Connemara. Their state in the west,
said General Gordon, was worse than that of any people in the
world: along the Atlantic shore gunboats might be seen carrying
armed police to evict the inhabitants, and hurrying to the next harbour
for charitable food-stuffs to maintain the people in the houses which
were already levelled. Home Rule was pronounced by Lord Beaconsfield the issue of the next election: and in the new Parliament Parnell
stood leader of 35 out of 103 Irish members. The House of
Lords threw out a Compensation for Disturbance Bill passed by the
Commons to mitigate the tenants' danger and distress. The peers
had called the battle, and violence answered violence. Parnell
and the Land League stood in the fore-front of an indignant
people. The Government suspended the Habeas Corpus Act, and
gave the Viceroy a power of random arrest and imprisonment on mere
suspicion. For nine weeks Parnell and his followers fought the
monstrous scheme with every insolence and violence of obstruction;
nor were they defeated till the old liberty of the House was overturned
by the "new and exceptional course" of the "closure," and the
suspension of the Irish members from the House. In a few months
over a thousand men, Parnell himself and many Irish members among
them, lay in prison under the Act thus passed to suppress "village
ruffians." Thence they issued the "No Rent" manifesto. It was
amid this frenzy of popular rage that Gladstone, stirred by a nobler
sense of statesmanship, framed a new Land Bill to secure for the Irish
tenant fixity of tenure, fair rents, and free sale of his rights in his
holding. It was "the single measure of a single man" in that session,
none but the Irish shewing the slightest care or interest. He faced
the entire apathy and indifference of the House; he met "difficulties
such as no other bill of this country has ever encountered"; though

Sec. I.

The Social
Revolu-
tion
1815
TO
1914

1882

**Home
Rule**
1884

June 1885

Nov. 1885

Jan. 1886

Jan. 1886

April

his scheme abounded in faults and needed much later repair, yet by his courage and authority Gladstone gave to the Irish tenant "the fundamental charter of his redemption." The gleam of hope was darkened by the murder of a new Chief Secretary, Lord Frederic Cavendish, and the Under Secretary, Burke, by a small group of desperate men; new coercion for Ireland brought fresh coercion of the House of Commons, suspension of Irish members, and more emphatic rules for closure of debate.

Such was the situation when, in a speech that formed a turning-point in English history, Gladstone in the name of justice demanded for the Irish people the same franchise as the English: and in the Reform Act of 1884 gave them for the first time since the Union the chance of making their voice effectively heard at Westminster. Mr. Chamberlain desired to come to terms with the actual Irish members through a scheme of Local Government by National Councils, and a land settlement, but his plan was rejected by the peers in the Cabinet and by Lord Hartington, and at the threat of renewing the Crimes Act the Liberal Government fell. The Tories immediately passed a Land Act with Purchase provisions, and abandoned coercion. To demonstrate to England that the newly enfranchised Irish voters had through these favours lost their pretended desire for Home Rule, seventy-seven Tory candidates stood forward confidently at the election under the new Act, and five Liberals, to win Ireland from the Nationalists. Only a score of seats were left uncontested. Their rout was final and complete. By overwhelming majorities in Munster, Leinster, Connacht, every county, every borough, was carried by Nationalists, and half of Ulster. Nothing was left to the Tories but the north-east corner of Ulster and Dublin University, held by eighteen members. Parnell, "the uncrowned king of Ireland," led back a party of 85 members out of 103, returned by an almost unanimous vote, pledged not to take office under an English Government till Home Rule was won — a party which has remained unchallenged at elections for thirty years. Since in England the Liberal majority over the Conservatives was 86, Parnell held the balance between the parties; and the fundamental problem supposed to have been settled once for all at the Union again confronted England. The Tory Government, on the same day that it announced a Bill to suppress the National League, fell, as the last Government had fallen, before the Irish vote. In Gladstone's view it was "the office of law and institutions to reflect the wants and wishes of the country." When there was no longer possibility of doubt, when by their votes the people of Ireland had openly given their decision for the national cause, the question of Home Rule was to his mind settled. In a House thronged beyond all example, and stilled by suspense, he proposed his Bill to create anew an Irish Parliament. The willingness of the public outside to grant Home Rule took everyone by surprise. But other influences dominated Westminster. England saw herself at the beginning of an unexampled prosperity. The new pride of Empire was at the height of its power, and men were intolerant of any apparent rift in the majestic scheme, and confident in the military force of England to compel the obedience of an Ireland depopulated and enfeebled. The maintenance of the Union in its actual form was held essential for the preservation of the Empire. It was believed that Protestant government and control was necessary to hold in check a Catholic population. Fear and anger had been awakened by the land war, the outrages, the revolutionary aspect of the island, the fiery denunciations of English administration there; and old hostilities and contempts of the Celt were intensified in England. Ninety-three Liberals voted against their party and Home Rule was lost by thirty votes. Ireland sifted and winnowed the forces of Liberalism, already divided and terrified in England by the Radical campaign of Mr. Chamberlain and his doctrine of "ransom." The great Whig magnates renounced their old tradition and secular alliance with the Liberal party, and at the Marquis of Hartington's secession they passed out of its counsels: as their power slipped away, and the Whig influence of the Liberal peers was no longer a force to be considered, the "ending or mending" of the House of Lords became inevitable. Plutocrats and commercial men followed, and with them went the tradesmen. The economists joined them, and the intellectual classes. The two external forces which were to mould the course of English history for the next generation, the Empire and Ireland, were sharply confronted in the general election that followed.

For twenty years, with one brief interruption (1892–5), the Conservatives ruled. The significance of the "Celtic Fringe" had been demonstrated in the elections, when Scotland approved the Bill by 3 to 2, Wales by 5 to 1, Ireland by 4½ to 1, while England rejected it by 2½ to 1; and from this time Unionists adjudged a different value to the representatives of various parts of the United Kingdom, giving to the English votes a predominant importance. Lord Salisbury's Cabinet, the most aristocratic of modern times, with its ten members in the House of Lords, was forced into new paths by the pressure of the Liberals and Radicals who had placed it in power, and gave to it the new inclusive name of the "Unionist" party. Lord Halsbury introduced a Land Transfer Bill, left by Lord Cairns, to abolish primogeniture and put real property on the same footing as personal property—a Bill rejected by the peers as "a sop to the Cerberus of Socialism" and "tantamount to a sentence of death and extinction for many ancient families." Parliament, which had once bent its energies to the increase of enclosures,

SEC. I.

THE SOCIAL REVOLUTION

1815
TO
1914
Ireland and Empire

June 1886

End of the Whigs

July

Country Reforms

1887

Sec. I.

The Social
Revolu-
tion
1815
to
1914

1845-69
1865

1887-93

1900

1888

responded slowly to a "new and special feeling" that stirred the public. Forty years earlier the growing idea of central control had led to the appointment of commissioners for enclosures, and a rule to make allotments for recreation and for labourers showed the first recognition of the people's needs. But in practice this Act only served to facilitate enclosures, and in twenty-four years out of 614,800 acres enclosed only some 2,200 had been set apart for the public. A Society formed to protect legal common rights, the public interest, and the needs of the labouring poor against wholesale encroachments, carried on intrepid war in Parliament, in the Law Courts, on the very ground of the Commons themselves; battling against decisions of the judges that the public, not being a person, was incapable of rights and could never assert any claim to customary use of the open lands. The lords of the manors were gradually forced to recognise the new principle that their property in commons was subject to the general interest, so that no enclosure could take place without open proof of benefit to the public. The old system was felt to have become "practically obsolete" when, a hundred years after the Enclosure Act, the last sanction was given to fence in a common as private property. In other matters the influence of the Liberals on the new Conservative Cabinet might be seen. Free Education, so long promised by Mr. Chamberlain, was granted. A Local Government Act, which also had been urged by Mr. Chamberlain for years, transferred rural administration from the county magnates to the people themselves, and the country folk at last entered on the democratic privileges for which Bentham had pleaded, and which the towns had enjoyed since 1835. Inhabitants of a house or room, without restriction or qualification, might henceforth elect by ballot the Council which taxed them and expended the money for the common good. A Liberal government completed later the whole hierarchy of county administration by adding district and parish councils (1894), and the old life of township and vill, which had lingered on as a mere shadow of earlier custom, was given a chance to revive the sense of local pride and responsibility.

1887

In Ireland Tory rule opened with a third rejection of a Tenants' Relief Bill, though at the bidding of Ulster Lord Salisbury was forced to accept revision of rents and admission of leaseholders, which a few months before he had denounced as dishonest and inexpedient. The tenants' "Plan of Campaign" and the "National League" were met by the remedy of "twenty years resolute government." A perpetual Coercion Act gave the Lord Lieutenant power to "proclaim" any district at his will, and thus at the discretion of the Executive to vary the criminal law in any part of Ireland; to decide what were to be counted crimes; what the legal procedure should be; and whether the prisoner should be allowed a jury. Mr. Balfour's proposal to

carry prisoners in certain cases to London for trial—a proposal
invented against "rebels" of the American war of independence—
failed ; and the Bill was driven through the Commons against Irish
opposition by the developed closure nick-named the "guillotine."
Its provisions were put to use by Mr. Balfour as Chief Secretary, a
post of more unrestrained authority than any other in the Empire.
Convictions in land cases rose to 2,805, in more than half of which
the rights of the prisoner would in England have been guarded by a
jury. The battering ram became notorious. Eighteen counties were
"proclaimed," and twenty-five members of parliament imprisoned. A
charge of complicity in crime was launched against Parnell by the
Times, and repeated in the House of Commons by the Government.
The accused was denied the constitutional remedy of a select committee of the Commons, and compelled to face a trial before a
tribunal constituted and chosen by his bitterest political foes.
"Other persons," members of parliament and all sorts of patriots,
peaceful and militant, were by the government's decree joined with
him in this general compulsory investigation, this unlimited inquisition. Political passion ran high as it had done in the seventeenth century, and Liberals protested that "for the first time in
England since the Great Rebellion men were practically put upon
their trial on a political charge without giving them the protection of
a jury. For the first time in that period judges were to find a verdict
on the facts of crime." The proceedings dragged on for a hundred
and twenty-eight days, to end with the suicide of the perjured
impostor Pigott on whose forgeries the charges had been brought.

Calamity deepened over Ireland when a divorce suit against Parnell
was followed by the demand of the Liberals that he should lay down
his leadership. A tragic struggle was only ended by his death. But
he had lifted Ireland to a place in politics which she was never again
to lose. The Liberal Federation at Newcastle announced a policy of
Home Rule, with disestablishment of the Welsh Church, electoral
reform, payment of members, land reform, temperance and local veto,
taxation of land values, and "ending or mending" of the House of
Lords. The next year Gladstone, with a majority of forty for Home
Rule, took office to plead again the cause of Irish nationality. In
his last desperate fight for a people's freedom he stood majestic at the
age of eighty-three, with "that white-hot face, stern as a covenanter's
yet mobile as a comedian's, those restless flashing eyes, that wondrous
voice . . . the masterly gestures." With deep indignation the
Unionists saw the closure, framed to suppress Irish Nationalists,
turned against themselves. The Home Rule Bill, accepted by a
majority of 44 in the Commons, was summarily rejected in the
Lords by 419 to 41. In the universal and humiliating wreck of all the
other Government bills through the Lords' resistance, the Commons

Sec. I.
The Social Revolution
1815 to 1914

The Parnell Commission

Sept. 1888

Death of Parnell

1891

Second Home Rule Bill

1892

1893-5

Sec. I.

The Social
Revolu-
tion
1815
to
1914

could find but one point of advantage, and used their supremacy in money matters to introduce high death duties on estates, graduated according to wealth. Sir William Harcourt thus for the first time placed land on the same footing as other property, and established the principle that the greater inheritance should pay duty to the State on a higher scale than the smaller. Torn by divisions, disorganized by continuous defeat, without any constructive programme to follow their work of emancipation, the Liberals disappeared from power, their fortunes fallen lower than they had been for the last century.

1894

Gladstone had already left in gloom and defeat the House to which his labours had been given for sixty-one years, throwing his last passionate warning to the Lords that a power so recklessly used "will demand a settlement from the highest authority."

Reforms
for
Ireland

During the next ten years of Tory power all questions of reform were adjourned, and there was little legislation for England. In Ireland, after twice rejecting self-government, the Unionists sought

1893
1891

by reforms to exorcise the spirit of Home Rule. The last Tory Government had created a Congested Districts Board to improve the lot of the forlorn tenants of bog and rock on the Atlantic shore; light railways traversed the waste regions of the west to open

1896
1897

communications and markets; a new Land Act was devised to adjust rent, and aid the tenants to purchase; an Agricultural Board was formed to develope the resources of the country; popular local

1898

government was for the first time instituted by the creation of County and District Councils after the English model, with added compensation to the landed classes; technical instruction was encouraged. Irish revenue, after a century of confiscation, was at last directed to Ireland. On the other hand when a Royal Commis-

1896

sion reported that Ireland, contrary to the provisions of the Treaty of Union, was overtaxed in proportion to her resources by some two millions a year or more, and that her administration was the most wasteful of any European country, the Report was silently ignored and no remedy proposed. The Irish race was kept in tutelage under an administration which remained wholly in the hands of the Protestant minority, a fourth of the people, and the system of Boards and doles was still directed to serve the political ends of England. In direct succession to the old Whig doctrine of 1843, "to purchase not to prosecute repeal," the Tory policy of "resolute government" balanced by the "killing of Home Rule with kindness" rested on the belief that national fidelity was but a fiction of agitators, and material prosperity the chief end of peoples. The system proved without power to check the flight of the people from their home-land in an emigration which was the wonder and scandal of Christendom: the exiles who sought refuge under the American flag from 1846 to 1900 cannot have numbered fewer than 5,000,000: and the 30,000 or more young men and women in their best strength, now sent yearly across the Ocean from a still diminishing population of four and a quarter millions, surpass in numbers the emigration from the whole seventy millions of the German Empire. The very habit of tillage declined in a country which has in little more than the last generation lost 300,000 agricultural labourers. In an Irish phrase the people were "over-boarded and underfed." Nor did the national idea disappear. Fresh coercion opened the century, and under renewed "strong government" the greater part of the country was "proclaimed," and ten Irish members lay in prison. The declaration of Sir Antony MacDonnell, sent as Under Secretary, that "Irish ideas" must guide Irish administration, was resented with a fierce outcry of indignation by the ruling classes; but the Government decided by a great and courageous Act of Land Purchase to close for ever the devastating land war in Ireland. Through that Act the soil of Ireland is rapidly passing to peasant proprietors, and the older race, emerging from the barren uplands and bogs to which they had been driven, are creeping over their ancient plains and pastures. Such a close of the land conflict revealed how far the Irish landlord in his security had fallen behind his class in England in practical instinct. In the developed English system of enclosures and large farms the battle of the labourer, landless and working for a wage, was very different from that of the Irish tenant renting his patch of ground. The labourer could only refuse his labour and starve; the tenant could withhold his rent and live. Thus the Irish landlord, seeking the highest profits with the least responsibility, had himself established by his scheme of competitive rents the power that was to overthrow him.

England meanwhile had marvellously increased in wealth and in national self-confidence. The figures of modern trade are too prodigious to convey a clear meaning to the mind—the six thousand millions' worth of cheques that passed through the London Bankers' Clearing House in 1886 rising by 1913 to between sixteen and seventeen thousand millions; the capital supplied from the City of London for the opening of four hundred thousand miles of railway in the new countries of the industrial world; the volume of foreign trade increasing in the last eight years by more than forty-four per cent., to reach in 1913 the sum of over fourteen hundred million pounds sterling; the wresting from the earth about two hundred and eighty million tons of coal, over ninety-eight millions of which were carried to foreign lands. In the era of prosperity from 1846 to 1866, the Liberals have been in power, and by their commercial legislation the general wealth was still enabled to advance, in Gladstone's phrase, "by leaps and bounds." In this twenty years, from 1886 to 1906, presided over by the Tories, a broadening diffusion of wealth and comfort brought to the prosperous part of the population a vast

SEC. I.

THE SOCIAL REVOLUTION

1815
TO
1914

1902

1903

Land Purchase Act

Wealth of England

SEC. I.

THE SOCIAL
REVOLU-
TION
1815
TO
1914

national complacency. Two Jubilees of the Queen, in the fiftieth and sixtieth years of her reign, were celebrated with a pomp of Colonial and Imperial ceremony such as England had never before seen; and the policy left by Disraeli to Lord Salisbury in the triumphant vision of a vast and world-controlling Empire, for whose safeguard and advancement no cost should be counted, held men's minds with a powerful fascination as Mr. Chamberlain called on citizens of the Empire to throw off entanglement in parochial politics, to "think imperially," and to realise the magnitude of their Colonial might. Movements of great significance were at the same time proceeding unobserved at home. The phrase "Tory Democracy" was the recognition of forces emerging from the deep. Scientific investigation revealed an underlying world of the darkest misery when Mr. Charles Booth, by his exhaustive census of London, shewed that in the wealthiest city of the world thirty-two per cent. of the whole population were forced by industrial conditions to endure a life of chronic poverty and want, lacking the first necessities of physical health and capacity for work; and when Parliamentary Commissions over the country extended before the public view the circle of misery, without discovering a remedy. Many experiments failed to solve the question of how workers might acquire a share in the profits of their labour and in the control of their industries, and the problem of a more equal distribution of the ever increasing national wealth remained as obscure and undetermined as it had been fifty years before. But the old doctrine was discounted that the making of riches was the first duty of the citizen. Vital fervour was breathed into the "New Unionism" by young enthusiasts. They achieved the organization of unskilled workers. Turning from revolutionary socialism to constitutional action, they strengthened all working-men's organizations and spread among them new literature. As the wave of trade unionism spread into every corner of British industry, the half million members of thirty years ago have now increased to three and a quarter millions, with an income of over four million pounds, and an annual outlay on the sick or unemployed sometimes beyond a million pounds. It formed in fact a State within the State, governing itself by Congresses after the model of Parliament. The Workmen's Compensation Act showed their power. So greatly did their solidarity and independence develope, that while the London dockers' strike was supported by general subscriptions of which about a tenth only came from trade and co-operative societies, the strike of workers in Dublin was fought with funds from the trade unions of the United Kingdom—some £80,000, of which less than £10,000 came from outside sources. The formidable organization of the unions was shown in an increasing number of strikes; while in 1894, 1896, and 1911 there were

1886–1893

*The Poverty
Line*

1889

*The new
Trade
Unionism*

1897

1889

1913

something under 1,000 trade disputes in each year, in 1913 the number has risen to 1,462 : in 1911 nearly a million workers were involved, and in 1912 nearly a million and a half. The main difficulty of the unions lies in fact in the vastness of the problem, and general perplexity as to the true road of constructive reform. Immersed in laborious detail the working-class lacks thinkers. A system of education accepted from reformers of the middle class has tended, instead of raising the position of the crafts, to draw the more intelligent youths away from productive enterprise, and from the intellectual leadership of their own fellows, and add them to the amorphous middle world of salaried clerks and teachers. New forms of intellectual training may possibly be forced on the workers of this country by the stress of foreign competition. Their political activity has so far outstripped their zeal for education. They were careful to secure the election of working-men on municipal and other local bodies, where they have now a thousand labour members. They demanded a more adequate power in Parliament. A Labour Electoral Association of the trade unions was followed by the drawing together of various socialistic and other organizations in an Independent Labour Party ; but neither of these groups gained much authority until a Trade Union Congress and a general Convention of all working-class associations united their common interests in a Labour Representation Committee to secure the election of labour members to Parliament. The influence of the working-class begins even now to reach beyond the borders of Great Britain. Already a Working Men's Association had attempted to establish international communications : and Karl Marx had sent out his appeal for the union of workers in all countries ; once more projects were renewed for emancipation of labour through the union of " every trade, skilled and unskilled, of every nationality under the sun," and after twenty-six years of effort, an International Congress in London, and one in Paris, and the establishment at Basel of an International Union for Labour Legislation, to secure a uniform code for the workers in all civilised countries, affirmed a new brotherhood of labour. Such events have given to the people a wider outlook, have led to embassies, as we may say, of working-men from nation to nation, and have for the first time in history offered to the inhabitants of a country a concern in its foreign relations and a share of responsibility for peace or war.

Discordance between an advancing democracy and an aristocratic Cabinet became suddenly manifest when the Boer War ended and Mr. Balfour took the place of Lord Salisbury. An Act to reform the educational system raised the yearly cost to the country to nearly £30,000,000 : but the provisions which allowed Church schools, while maintained from the rates, to remain outside complete national

Margin notes:

Sec. I.

The Social Revolution 1815 to 1914

1888

1893
1899
1900
1906

1836
1848

1862

1888-9

End of the Boer War 1902

SEC. I.

THE SOCIAL
REVOLU-
TION

1815
TO
1914

control in management and religious instruction, revived Nonconformist antagonism to a State Church in political relations with the
Government; and was only forced through the Commons by the
"guillotine" which the Conservatives had so vehemently denounced
when used in 1893 to pass the Home Rule Bill. Thus a measure,
no longer needed to enforce Irish coercion since the permanent Act of
1887, was revived to suppress English opposition to an English Bill; and
for the next seven years the closure, highly developed, appeared in every
session, and was used by each Government in turn to carry party legis-

1903

lation. A second struggle followed when Mr. Chamberlain gave to
the spirit of Imperialism, then intensified by the South African war,
a new direction; sending out his rallying cry of Protection for

*Tariff
Reform*

English manufactures against foreign competition, and an Imperial
Tariff to attach the Colonies by a commercial bond to England.
All other national concerns were merged in the passionate war of
Protection and Free Trade. Legislation ceased in the fury of con-

1905

troversy, and fewer Bills were passed into law than in any other year
for a century. Parties were rent asunder by the contest. The
shipping industry, the coal industry, the textile industry, the banking
industry stood to lose by protection: while the agricultural workers
in England, a class not of proprietors but of day labourers, had no
advantage in selling corn dear, but a decided concern in buying it
cheap. When Mr. Balfour resigned, his challenge was answered by
the greatest defeat inflicted on either party since the Reform Bill: in
1833 there were elected 172 Tories, but in 1906 only 158 Unionists
entered the House of Commons.

**Power
of the
People**

Problems old and new stood at the door of the Liberal
Parliament, imminent, no longer to be denied, diverse and inextricably
linked together, grave beyond all former experience. The working-
classes, co-operators and trade unionists, had demonstrated their
political strength. The gigantic working-class organization of co-
operators, which through its three millions of members represents a
fifth of the whole population, had created the largest general supply
business in the world, with a trade exceeding a hundred and twenty
millions annually. Its fifteen hundred societies administered by
30,000 elected committee-men, and employing 50,000 salaried officials,
proved in fact the most successful commercial venture of our time.

1914

In its factories the Wholesale Society has established a standard of
minimum wages and hours of work more liberal than any decreed by
law in 1912. The triumph of democratic industry, the training in
affairs represented by yearly purchases of £80,000,000, the solidarity
of interests, and habit of joint action, made this association of
working-men a potent influence in the commercial controversy of
parties. They were not only consumers but traders: their fleet bore
from over sea the products of ten different countries; their whole-

sale society had sent the largest cheque ever paid in customs duties; with a keen sense of prices they refused to believe that import duties were paid by the foreigner, and their two million voters were powerful in breaking Tariff reform. A Labour Party sat for the first time in the House; thirty three-cornered elections, and the entry of twenty-nine labour representatives into Parliament, gave ominous warning to the settled order of parties and to old established interests. When a Trades Dispute Act (to remedy a decision of the House of Lords in 1901 on the Taff Vale case) was brought forward, the trade unions, throwing their entire force on the side of the Labour Party, rejected the Bill of the Attorney-General, and extorted from the Government a measure which put the unions outside the jurisdiction of the law in so far as to exempt them from being sued for torts, and their funds from claims for damages. Public opinion forced labour questions into the first rank of State affairs. A population which we have seen a hundred years ago hardened by suffering has become distinguished for compassion to misery and aversion from pain, as a new consciousness arose of the commonwealth as a whole, which must suffer with the weakness of any part. In 1842 it was thought an intolerable drain on the country to spend seven millions in saving the destitute from starvation: the public money now spent for the poorer classes reaches seventy millions a year, and two-thirds of that sum is separated from any association with pauperism or Poor Law relief. Medical inspection was given to children in schools, pensions decreed for the aged, compulsory State-aided insurance for all workers, special aid for the unemployed, sanatoria for the sick, new cottages and allotments for rural labourers. New grants for extended education gave a quarter of the accommodation in 885 secondary schools as "free places" for candidates from elementary schools. Arbitration in trade disputes became a duty of the Government. The old authoritative doctrine that the legislature had no power over wages, implicitly accepted for generations, was thrown over when Parliament accepted the principle of the legal Minimum Wage by establishing Trade Boards for certain trades, and by the Coal Miners' Minimum Wage Act—a principle adumbrated by Robert Owen in 1818; discussed since 1874; demanded in the strike and lock-out of 1893, the greatest dispute of modern times; renewed in the great strike of 1912; and enlarged into a claim for a universal minimum wage by the two million co-operative voters in their Congress of 1913. The special difficulties of women as workers and as citizens were insistently urged on the Government. Economic pressure had driven women increasingly into daily toil. By the industrial changes and commercial legislation of the century they too were pressed into the democracy of hired workers. They too paid their price for Empire, as the men poured out to the new colonies or

SEC. I.

THE SOCIAL REVOLUTION

1815
TO
1914

1906

The new Legislation

1906-11

1902-12

1912

Place of Women

Sec. I.
The Social
Revolu-
tion
1815
to
1914

1854

1847–8

1869–80

1876

1878–9

1857–1893

1867

territories and the proportion of single and self-dependent women increased at home, till more than four millions of women over eighteen, almost a third of the whole number, are engaged in money-making occupations, and have become personally concerned in all social, financial, and labour legislation. Their trade unions, begun in the cotton industry, were of slow and difficult growth: but have extended rapidly in the last twenty years, and the number of members almost doubled since 1906. Meanwhile the old civic franchise by which women householders had a right to vote on vestries was extended to the new Boards of Health and Town improvement; and later to the Municipal and County Councils. They were allowed to serve on School Boards, as Poor Law Guardians, as members of District and Parish Councils, and were admitted to the Civil Service. The new consciousness of a class pressing on to a more varied and independent life was shown by a vigorous movement for education and by the foundation of Women's Colleges. An opening to the professions was found by gaining a right to practise medicine. The London University and the Royal University of Ireland conceded to them degrees. An ever increasing body of trained women lavished their labour on public matters, and their influence throughout the range of social and industrial problems was recognised by the appointments of women as Factory Inspectors and on Royal Commissions. The growing importance of this army of workers during the last fifty years may be traced in a series of laws to secure to women their property and their earnings; and in the reiterated demand for the full rights of citizens. As long ago as 1776 Cartwright brought in a scheme of parliamentary reform which included women; and their claims were again urged with considerable strength by the Women's Clubs in the Chartist movement, which were however closed lest they should retard the universal suffrage for men. Twenty years later the most ardent advocate of the enfranchisement of women, John Stuart Mill, revived their neglected cause in the House of Commons itself: and in these last years the repeated Bills introduced into the House have shown the urgency of the problem. The hundred thousand pounds a year spent by the suffrage societies is an outlay far greater than that of any public movement of the time. Factory workers, women employed in a host of minor occupations, and practically all the brain-workers in responsible posts and professions, have been united in the suffrage agitation, and as the struggle for enfranchisement draws this mass of active and intelligent women for the first time into alliance with the Socialists and the Labour Party, a new force is being added to the revolutionary movement of our day.

**Consti-
tutional
Changes**

The pressure of social movements had meanwhile forced on grave constitutional changes. Party strife was intensified, and in a sense justified, by the growing subjection of the House of Commons to the

Government in office. Each Ministry in turn awakened by its absolutism new fears, and by its social legislation new resentments. In
stress of battle all questions were treated as a test of confidence in the
Cabinet. " The time and strength of the House of Commons came
to be more and more regarded as the time and strength of the
Government"; and the liberty of members, so scrupulously preserved by the old rules of the House, was gradually limited—by the
" Rule of Progress" applied first to the Committee stage of Bills
and later to Supply; by disuse of certain forms of motion that the
Speaker do leave the Chair; by rejection of proposals that redress
of grievances should precede Supply as no longer in consonance
with constitutional conditions, " inasmuch as the Government were
now the servants of the House"; and by restrictions in debates.
The accumulation of party funds, the defraying of election expenses
of favoured candidates, the power of the Whips in selection of
speakers, the necessity of obedience in every detail to secure the
strategy of the whole campaign, even the newly decreed payment of members—all combined to force all parties alike under
a military discipline. Further strength was added to the Cabinet
by the ever widening powers of the State departments. Foreign
affairs were practically withdrawn by Lord Salisbury from the House
of Commons, and the naval and military defence of the country: and
government by departments generally established. We have seen
in 1834-5 the first cautious and tentative efforts to establish a new
principle of State control in factory and Poor Law, and how the
experiment for five years became a lasting rule, and widened out
to cover the whole of urban and county administration, till in the
course of two generations every local authority was brought under
direct control of the Government. The highly centralised administration of home affairs was recognised by Parliament when
it placed the heads of the Board of Trade and the Local Government
Board on financial equality with the Secretaries of State. When the
sums allotted to local bodies from the national exchequer and
parliamentary grants in aid rose in fifty years from less than a
million to twenty millions (in addition to the forty millions raised
by local rates), the central authorities gained further rights of inspection, advice, and control. With this increase of statutory duties,
the departments acquired also large and arbitrary powers, both
judicial and legislative, which were extended in turn to every
Government office. To the bureaucracy has been given the whole
administration of all social reforms inaugurated in the last years,
from which local bodies have been excluded. Former checks imposed
on officials by courts of law or by Parliament in important questions
both of law and policy have been overcome or evaded, and the State
departments, with power themselves to interpret and judge what the law

Sec. I.

The Social
Revolu-
tion
1815
to
1914

1909

is, and to make their own statutory rules and orders, have been enabled to exercise authority over property and rights till now almost exclusively reserved for Parliament. With the practical introduction of "administrative law" into this country various encroachments have been made on the rights of subjects and the control of the House of Commons. The Treasury refusal to admit supervision by the Auditor-General or the Public Accounts Committee in administration of the Old Age Pensions (where in two years fifteen thousand disputed claims have arisen), was received with silent acquiescence. Every influence combined to depress the in-

The Cabinet

dependence of the members and to elevate the Ministers as the sole source of authority and the only spring of legislation. In the complexity of modern affairs the drafting of Bills became too intricate a business for any but official experts, and the Commons, who had practically lost all opportunity of initiating laws, presently lost control even over the form of new Acts. As new authority was pressed on him from every side, the Prime Minister became the most powerful Minister of any modern State. He found profit even in the demo-cratic movement to lessen the power of the Crown : for, if jealousy of Royal interference had through the reign of Queen Victoria constantly curtailed the personal action of the sovereign, the people had wel-comed Royal privilege when it passed from the Crown to the Minister to be held in trust for the nation. With the growth of democracy the actual power of the Crown was increased, but its exercise was altered. Old prerogatives were revived, and new were granted, till the English executive has now become legally the most powerful Government in the world. Sovereignty, Sir William Anson has said, now lies in the Cabinet. Through the nineteenth century the head of the Cabinet had no formal recognition as such among his fellow-citizens, and in the case of Gladstone, for example, stood in the social order as a commoner with the sole rank of a privy coun-cillor. For the first time the Prime Minister was given a status

by royal proclamation of Edward VII., that he should henceforth share the dignity, as ancient as the British Constitution, of the two Archbishops and the Lord Chancellor, in taking precedence, after the Royal Family, of the officers of the Household and the whole peerage.

Meanwhile the conflict of Lords and Commons was accelerated by new disputes. The Tories, who throughout the century had stood as a bulwark to guard the ancient constitution from change—a break-water to check too violent an inrush of new thought—had turned to an active policy of innovation, advocating a new fiscal system, and even beginning to move in the direction of a modified Con-stitution. As the sense of tradition and its ancient authority de-clined, the term Conservative gave place to the word Unionist, the aristocratic conduct of the party weakened, and the most powerful influences tended to fall back from the landed to the commercial classes—a transformation typified by the choice of Mr. Bonar Law, Canadian by birth, Presbyterian by religion, and manufacturer by profession, as leader in the place of Mr. Balfour. At the same time the House of Lords, radically transformed by the frequent creation of peers from another class, and by the militant energy which followed the alliance of the Tory magnates with the Whig aristocracy and the mercantile plutocracy, had become completely identified with the new Unionist policy. Abandoning their constitutional attitude of impartial revision, the peers for the first time in their history cast their whole force invariably on the side of one political party. The old defence of the House of Lords, in which Whigs and Tories had agreed, that its function was to maintain a check on democracy, was set aside for a new theory: that the office of the Lords was to give effect to the considered will of the people, even against their parliamentary representatives. Burke had reckoned the House of Lords in his time as " by itself the feeblest part of the Constitution." "The Lower House is the ruling and the choosing House . . . . . the Government that can rest on it has nine-tenths of what it needs . . . . the support of the Lords is an aid and a luxury": so Bagehot had recorded in 1872. Now, however, the peers claimed to be not merely a constitutional revising chamber, but as it were a political Court of Appeal; asserting the right, as guardians of the democracy, to judge of the representative value of the popular verdict at the polls, and to refuse any important alteration in the law without compelling a dissolution from which they themselves would return unchanged. Thus to all the other crowding controversies of the time there was added the menacing conflict between the two Houses of Parliament, foreseen at the Reform Act, and steadily drawing nearer for the last forty years.

"The parts of our Constitution," said Burke, "whilst they are balanced as opposing interests, are also connected as friends: otherwise nothing but confusion could be the result of such a complex Constitution." This confusion had now arisen, full of peril and disturbance to the State. The doctrine that the government held its authority from the direct will of the people had been carried beyond all precedent by Mr. Balfour's sudden resignation during the recess after hostile bye-elections. There remained the question of how the will of the people was to be discovered, and how enforced. During the last ten years no government bill passed by a Conservative House of Commons was rejected by the Lords, nor was any amendment pressed which Conservative ministers disliked. But a Liberal Government, fresh from the greatest Liberal victory since the Reform Act, found itself in four years of " rebuffs and humiliations " unable

Sec. I.
The Social
Revolu-
tion
1815
to
1914

to pass a single measure, even if carried by majorities of from one to two hundred, which the Conservative minority opposed. By the alliance between the peers and the Tory party, it was possible for the Tory leader in the Commons, in or out of office, to decide in consultation with the Lords the fate of any contested bill. The claim of the peers put in jeopardy the dignity of the House of Commons and the authority of representative government. The Liberal Cabinet made proposals to strengthen representative institutions by electoral reforms and short Parliaments, but their Bills, passed by enormous majorities, were uniformly rejected. The answer of the Commons,

June 1907 under Sir Henry Campbell Bannerman, was a Resolution that the veto of the Lords must be so curtailed that the final decision of the Commons should prevail within the limits of a single Parliament. Under the new Prime Minister, Mr. Asquith, the unwelcome conflict was still delayed. There were sharper retaliations, aggressions, and the stretching of privileges on both sides beyond all precedent. A government which was refused legislation in the customary way was tempted to increase, as we have seen, the legislative and judicial functions of the departments it controlled outside the House. Within the House it introduced Bills in which political matters were inextricably interwoven with financial questions. Revision of any Bill became a farce on the part of either Chamber. The rights of the subject and the rights of members of the House were crushed aside in the confusion of strife. Battle was finally joined on a question of finance. The Unionist proposal to benefit the working-classes by a

*Rejection
of the
budget* protective system which, they alleged, would tax the foreigner on his manufactured goods and provide full employment for British workers, was met by the Liberal budget, which offered to find money for social reforms by a fresh incidence of taxation to fall on the unearned increment of building-land values—a value unexpectedly created by the rise of towns after the industrial revolution. Mr. Chamberlain from his sick-bed protested that the passing of this financial scheme, the Free Trade answer to Protection, must indefinitely postponed the triumph of Tariff Reform ; and the Lords, claiming an impregnable position behind the ancient constitution,

1909 rejected by 350 votes to 75 the budget which the Commons after a session of extraordinary length had passed by a majority of 230. Never in English history had such a power been exercised or even claimed. It had moreover been supposed that Gladstone in 1860 had asserted once for all the power to impose and remit taxes in such manner "that the right of the Commons as to the matter, manner, measure, and time, might be maintained inviolate." In the public

Jan., Dec.
1910 excitement two elections were held within the year. The first Parliament met to repudiate any right in the Lords to throw the finance of the year into confusion, bring the administration of the country to ?

SEC. I.

THE SOCIAL
REVOLU-
TION
1815
TO
1914

standstill, and force a dissolution. A Bill was introduced that the House of Lords should henceforth be disabled by law from rejecting or amending a money bill, and that for all other bills their right of veto should be restricted to a single Parliament: while the preamble stated that in due time the Upper Chamber should be reconstituted on a popular and not a hereditary basis. The Budget once more sent up was passed by the peers. The second Parliament was required to express the national consent to the Parliament Bill. As the battle developed the Lords, by a series of bills and resolutions, sought too late to meet attack by hurried schemes of reform. Renouncing the principle of primogeniture, once held as of the very essence of the Constitution, the assurance of its existence, and the basis of the English land system, they introduced a scheme of combined birth and public service, of election and nomination. They urged a right to reject or amend such financial bills as were " bills producing social and political effects," a claim which would have given them equal control with the Commons over finance. They proposed to decide contested questions by joint sittings of Lords and Commons. They desired to call for a " referendum" whenever the Lords, or a combination of malcontents in the two Houses, required the special verdict of the people on any point—a grave innovation and full of menace to the whole system of representative government. But the time for such proposals had passed. The exasperation of feeling over the rejection of the Budget had left no room for discussion or compromise. The Parliament Act was sent up to the Lords with the threat, as in 1832, that if necessary sufficient new peers would be created to overwhelm opposition. In a House packed to the doors, fevered with excitement, the result was doubtful even at the very last moment. Out of six hundred and thirty-six Peers seventy-eight Liberals voted for the Bill, and a hundred and fourteen extreme Tories against it: some fifty moderate Tories gave their votes on the Liberal side, as many as were necessary to avert the swamping of their order by the creation of five hundred new Lords. The Act was passed amid shouts of reproach and indignation such as had never been heard within that Chamber. As the clamour penetrated into the House of Commons new vociferations rang beyond the walls of Parliament, to acclaim this final proof that the supreme prerogative of forcing the Lords to yield to the will of the Commons remained in the hands of the people, and was held in trust for them by the Prime Minister, the " elect of the nation."

The House of Lords, the oldest assembly in the world, saw at once the loss of its independent power, and the doom of its ancient hereditary tradition. The full circle of change had come. Men were at last confronted with the issues foretold by opponents of the first Reform Act, that it must bring large and organic changes, and destroy

Sec. I.

The Social
Revolu-
tion
1815
to
1914

the independence of the House of Lords, if not altogether annihilate its existence. At the second Reform Act Bagehot had warned the peers that the storm which should destroy the House of Lords would carry away with it both hereditary estates and great aggregations of property and social power: "the whole body of the Lords have an incalculably greater influence over society while there is still a House of Lords than they would have if the House of Lords were abolished." Like prophecies had attended the third Reform—"a measure which will affect the tenure and transmission of property in every form, as the other measures have affected the principle and action of political institutions."

A change so prodigious might even at the last moment have been still deferred if the decision had been left to England alone. The difficulty of getting from the country a separate sanction for any single act of legislation was shown in the confused result of the elections of 1910, when the voters divided their interest between the Second Chamber, Tariff Reform, the Union, and a Budget raising the whole question of social legislation. In England parties stood balanced between the industrial districts and the rural counties— 274 Liberals and 272 Tories, with an outlying group of 41 Labour members. Scotland and Wales supported the Government, but on different grounds. Various interpretations were given of the verdict of the people. In this confusion of interest and balance of forces, Ireland accelerated and determined the conflict. Before they would give

consent to passing the Budget, now a year delayed, the Nationalists joined the extreme Radicals in demanding that abolition of the veto

should precede all other business, and that the Government should pledge itself irrevocably to carry through the Parliament Bill and leave the way open for Home Rule. By one of the revenges of history, a people cut off from self-government at home had long held power to direct and confound English politics across the sea. From 1801 to 1886 ten British Ministries fell on the Irish question. After the enactment of a Union designed in the darkest period of political reaction and panic, Irishmen had wandered among the English working-classes as missionaries of democratic liberty, had given them models of popular organization, had provided leaders to plan the first "National Trades Union," and to inspire a Chartist agitation. It was the Irish who in the Emancipation Act struck the first tremendous blow at the dominance of the Established Church, in the Tithe war at its extravagant claims to property, and in the Disestablishment Act at its political importance. In the Land question

the Irish had forced the order of battle. They gave to English farmers and labourers a new motive and impetus by the spectacle in Ireland of an unrestrained landlordism, of its political and social bankruptcy, and of the power of a national movement; while they compelled the English aristocracy to enter the lists crippled by their alliance with an agrarian system in Ireland developed under penal laws and maintained by coercion. In fourteen years the power of the landed gentry in Ireland was shattered, and the reverberations of the battle were felt in England. The first Irish Land Act was followed by the first agitation among English rural labourers since 1834, and by a first vain attempt to give English farmers compensation for disturbance. The second Act was followed by the first lightening of the game-laws under which, Bright had told the country-people in 1845 five thousand of them were yearly fined, imprisoned, or transported; and by a more effectual compensation for farmers—with no voice now raised for "the sacred right of freedom of contract." Into the chasm that yawned between England and Ireland, England had thrown, said Mr. Goschen, "concession after concession . . . . We have toppled into it great boulders of principle: we have made gigantic Parliamentary sacrifices." It was not eternal principles that had gone; it was but the form of constitution which England had established for herself before the Union, and thought to maintain unchanged after it. A century of Irish coercion obscured in the governing country Bentham's teaching of a scientific procedure and regular method of law as the subject's best protection, and allowed to creep into popular opinion a notion of legal administration as a course of discretion, and of resistance to law as carrying with it no crime. Ireland cost the Commons loss of old liberties through the "rules of debate" to carry coercion, the closure to suspend the Habeas Corpus Act, and the guillotine to enact a perpetual Crimes Act, and to force the Commission for the Parnell trial. The system of two-party government, which England had evolved to suit her own conditions, was overturned in the more complex State created by the Union, when the Irish Party, representing separate interests, became the model for new groups. Irish passion was enlisted against their old antagonist the House of Lords, to which their people had ever appealed in vain, and within a generation the hereditary authority of the aristocracy was broken, and the dominant power of their House. Before the union of the Irish people with the working classes of Great Britain fell the ascendancy of primogeniture and the power of great estates, shaking to its foundations the old English Constitution. Ireland had not ceased to put in question her relations under the Union with Great Britain, and to rend English parties by her re-iterated demand of Home Rule. A fourth attempt in the course of twelve years was made to solve the problem, by a scheme of Devolution embodied in an Irish Councils Bill; and when this was overthrown as inadequate, it was followed by a new Bill to restore an Irish Parliament and Executive responsible to it, which now stands before Parliament. Such a project of Home Rule has opened discussion,

Sec. I.

The Social Revolution

1815 TO **1914**

1875
1881

1885

1878-91

1877

1907

1911-14

Sec. I.

The Social
Revolu-
tion
1815
to
1914

**English
self-
govern-
ment**

not only of a new government for Ireland, but of a Federal Constitution for all the members of the United Kingdom. The great Earl
of Chatham in the eighteenth century had repeatedly refused to entertain the idea of a Union which must deluge the British legislature by
an addition of Irish peers and commoners. It would not be easy for
modern observers to say which class ultimately proved the most
dangerous to the old balance of the State.

Thus the Irish, flinging into England their separate problems and
their imported energies, might accelerate or even deflect its progress,
and confuse the grave political issues of the United Kingdom and the
Empire. But, as we have seen, the steady movement of the English
people towards the full accomplishment of democratic self-government had pressed on through the century by its own resistless force.
The main achievement of that hundred years on the people's side had
not been the lessening of suffering (however great that was) but
rather the lifting of every rank into the dignity of full citizenship,
till the people of Great Britain stood forth as the foremost pioneers
in the world of popular government. The instinct of self-government,
fostered and trained among the voluntary associations of the
working-classes, developed in the middle-classes through local
administration in town and country, and reaching on to the control
of Parliament and Cabinets, has been far beyond the power of
Ministries to check or to direct. While governments and parliaments
hovered on the edge of the future in an uncertain opportunism, unable
to foresee their destination, the revolution of the last century pursued
its unchanging course, whatever might be the ignorances, perplexities,
or projects of men. Among English leaders in that age of change
Gladstone alone may be said by his personal energy to have
compelled the events of his time and left on them the mark of his
dominating will; forcing England into the centre of the torrent, to learn
the full power and velocity of the popular and national demand. The
efforts of political parties indeed have not turned aside the current; it
has broken them. It turned the Tories into Conservatives, and the
Conservatives into Unionists, while they seek a more permanent name.
It turned Whigs into Liberals, and Liberals into Radicals, about to
fall into new groups. Labour has offered to all in turn its formidable
alliance. All classes, overwhelmed by changes unprecedented in
English history, have been moving among issues hidden and
unknown. The landlords of a hundred years ago, engrossed in
their scientific cultivation and their enclosures, felt no warning
that a system which broke down among the rural labourers the
old hereditary attachment to the ancestral cottage and the village
common, and turned the yeoman into a hired labourer, was to
end in the doom of their ancient House of Lords. If the political
economy of the day was justified, the Tory principle of heredity

SEC. I.

THE SOCIAL
REVOLU-
TION

1815
TO
1914

and the pride of ancient rights was severed at its deepest roots in the national life. So also the plutocrat saw no omens in the future from the huge accession of personal power brought to him by the industrial revolution. Wealth indeed might accumulate while the master-craftsman and the journeyman were alike joined to the undistinguished mass of hired workers; but the solidarity of these life-long wage-earners in their multiplied necessity, and in the effort to recover power over their own lives, has created a new House of Commons, the end of whose present transformation we cannot foretell. If the Upper Chamber has to discover a power of impartial revision, the Lower Chamber has still to find safeguards for the free and independent expression of the will of the people through freely chosen representatives. The past offers no guidance in such problems of the future. Never perhaps in English history has the reverence for tradition fallen so low, nor has pride in the ancient State been abandoned with so little questioning. Conservative classes who a century ago upheld the English Constitution as a well-nigh perfect creation of man, are now eager advocates of revolutionary change. The labour world, refusing to accept the tradition of those who claim their title of rights from the past, asserts a power of the people based on the foundations of the present, and declares the millions of the nameless and obscure to be the true and veritable framers of the new world. Dangers that shadow the advance into the future are contemplated with the unquestioning confidence of men who have behind them a long tale of difficulties surmounted: they count on the discipline of their trained organizations, on the habit of public work, on the enlargement of the corporate sense of common interests and responsibilities, to carry democratic government through the perilous tests that lie before it. It may be by a virile self-confidence, or it may be by the new-bred habit of change, that men find emancipation from the concentrated devotion and anxious fears which swayed an older House of Commons when it was threatened with a breach of its privileges: "there were a hundred weeping eyes, many who offered to speak being interrupted and silenced by their own passions."

A hundred years ago when the call of great principles was sounding, and insurgent masses were storming the gates of freedom, there were impassioned poets to inaugurate the passing of darkness and triumph of a new age. As the century advanced, the militant note disappeared amid the general prosperity, and the satisfaction of the middle-class in the liberty and progress they had achieved for themselves was reflected in a gentler poetry, where the tone of revolt was no longer heard. In later years when the idea of equal liberty and opportunity for all citizens was secured in theory by the common consent, the national task became one of elaborate detail, of mechanical

Sec. I.

The Social
Revolu-
tion
1815
TO
1914

adjustment so as to give effect to accepted doctrines. The aspect of life took on a duller hue. Material considerations filled the foreground, and the very mass of detail blotted out from view the enthusiasms and passions of the earlier fight for glowing ideals of freedom. Literature was not concerned with such details of humdrum toil. But if inspiring motives of action shine with a lesser brilliance in the material business of to-day, the range of moral ardour and conviction has gained with the ever-increasing number of devoted workers in the public cause, and with the incessant effort and vigilance demanded in these years of preparation for the next scene in the great transition. At no time in the history of England were the issues of constitutional changes so momentous, or the claims so great on the wisdom and mutual allegiance of the English people. The defection of any class may ensure failure. If it is left to the working population alone to supply the higher impulse and the driving power for progress, if the demand for a larger measure of material comfort and ease is pursued without intellectual insight and direction, if it is met only by distrust and reaction on the part of the wealthy and leisured classes, if these fail to infuse into modern civilization a finer intelligence of social interests, all alike will have had their share in the triumph of materialism. We are approaching dangers foreseen by a great ruler of a free people, President Lincoln: "It has long been a grave question whether any government, not too strong for the liberties of the people, can be strong enough to maintain its existence in great emergencies." The world has yet to see how many trials, catastrophes, and rebirths lie before the peoples who are determined to discover the ultimate secret of human liberty.

Section II.—Foreign and Colonial Policy, 1815 to 1914.

After Waterloo the social and political progress of Britain was no longer carried on under the old national conditions, and the influences that were shaping the new England were profoundly changed. As at the end of the war she took her way over the great oceans, and detached herself from European affairs, interest in continental thought also declined, and its higher literature had perhaps less effect on the English mind than in any former century; till with the passage of a hundred years it was revealed how deep were the ignorances of the country as to the vital forces which were about to transform the European scene. Two conflicting streams of political influence meanwhile were perpetually beating on the island from the farthest places of the world, as the empire extended over a fifth of the globe. The ever-increasing number of administrators from distant dependencies, trained on lines of paternal government by a higher race, carried back an experience and a habit of mind opposed to the democratic tendencies at home. On the other hand was the unceasing pressure from the colonial democracies, where the great wind of freedom swept with violence, overturning old conventions — a pressure whose vigour England now begins to understand. With the congress of Vienna in fact England entered on an age vast and crowded beyond any that had gone before, incomparable in its tangled complexity; and to meet new emergencies her whole foreign and colonial policy was recast.

There ended in 1815 an era of war and revolution which had lasted for nearly thirty years. The nineteenth century opened amid unwonted disorder; boundaries had shifted like the sands; there were thrones without sovereigns, and sovereigns without thrones. Faced by this aftermath of a desperate conflict, statesmen had to effect the reconstruction of a continent where the people were powerless, bewildered, and inert. The time proved unpropitious for the conclusion of a lasting peace. Passion burned fiercely, distrust was rife; questions of boundaries, indemnities, and safeguards absorbed attention. Calm consideration was prevented by the return of Napoleon from Elba. The Congress of Vienna concluded its work in haphazard fashion, and a series of treaties were hurriedly sealed. Kant had propounded a project for perpetual peace, and the Emperor of Russia, Alexander I., had suggested the establishment of a general system of public law, but with the renewal of strife which ended at Waterloo all such schemes were brushed aside. Our representative, Lord Castlereagh, who had hoped for a permanent Concert, rejected an international police; he foresaw that it must be mainly Russian, and feared lest Alexander should prove a second Napoleon. Statesmen were divided in interests; though a declaration of the congress announced the abolition of the slave-trade, "the affair of the negroes," as Talleyrand, called it, was postponed through the jealousy entertained of our sea-power and the distrust of our claims to a right of search. Talleyrand, the most experienced and subtle diplomatist of the time, took advantage of the general mistrust to press his definition of a "legitimate" government as one whose possessions had an historic basis; by this means the Bourbons were restored in France, in Spain, and in Naples, and the "people were penned like so many cattle." The doctrine ignored nationality and destroyed the hopes of smaller nations, who, having helped to overthrow the common tyrant, were made once again the victims of dynastic ambitions. The dreaded national unity of Germany was set back by forming a loose Confederation of thirty-

SEC. II.

FOREIGN
AND
COLONIAL
POLICY

1815
TO
1914

**The
Congress
of
Vienna**

1795

1801–1825

Sec. II.

Foreign
AND
Colonial
Policy
1815
TO
1914

nine German states under the leadership of Austria, who was to hold
the perpetual presidency in the federal Diet of Frankfort, closing the
way to national union or to a strong central government; thus the
Catholic south and Protestant north were thrown into antagonism,
and Prussia was driven into her fifty years' contest with Austria for
the headship of the German people. Finns were handed over to
Russia, Norwegians to Sweden, Belgians to Holland; Italians were
left subject to Austria, or to the temporal power of the Pope, and
the Poles remained the victims of an iniquitous partition. The fire
of revolt was stamped out, though some small sparks escaped the
trampling of the feet.

**England
and
Europe**

Under Castlereagh's guidance England was connected more closely
with the continent than ever before or since. In the wars with the
French Republic she had frankly allied herself with the principle of
reaction; but the later struggle of Napoleon was of a more complex
character, when side by side with the insistence of despotism had
arisen movements of national life in Germany and Spain, bringing
elements of Liberalism into the new conflict. After Waterloo, however,
the triumph of reaction was complete. England at the Congress of
Vienna raised no protest on behalf of the subject nationalities, she
helped to restore the Pope to temporal power, allowed the worst forms
of clerical reaction in Italy and Spain, and admitted the petty despotism of the German settlement decreed by Prince Metternich, the
Austrian Chancellor. She was pledged to the Bourbon monarchy; for
Louis XVIII., smuggled back to the throne "in the baggage of the
Allies," was imposed on the French by British soldiers, and ruled on
the lines of our constitution. But in spite of failures, the Congress
had accustomed men to talk of a Concert of Europe, and thus set a
precedent for later hopes. For seven years the effort persisted to
direct the relations of the European peoples and the fortunes of the
various states by common action of the great powers. But two imminent dangers threatened the Concert. The passion for liberty, the
ceaseless protest of peoples condemned to servitude, which had been
the motive force of the revolution, was ready to break forth anew,
intensified by faith in national rights. But this danger was less feared
by European governments than the menace of England herself—an
England lying outside the continental circle, individualistic and self-
dependent, with her outlook far beyond the bounds of Europe. Great
Britain was indeed the first to break from the European circle; she
was the strong forerunner of a new imperialism which in the following
century was to spread among the nations, shattering the European
concert and overthrowing the balance of European powers by the
ambition of world-empire.

**Empire
and Sea-
power**

From the Napoleonic wars England had emerged with so gigantic
a reputation for sea-power that for a hundred years no country

ventured to challenge her navy. To her older possessions the wars
of the Revolution had added Heligoland in the North Sea; in the
Mediterranean a new footing at Malta; in the Indian Ocean the
Cape Colony, the island of Mauritius, and Ceylon, with its landlocked harbour of Trincomalee; while Trinidad and Demerara gave
her valuable stations in South America. After the peace Singapore
was annexed, and a series of wars added Lower Burmah and Assam.
While conquest was pushed forward in the East to establish secure
frontiers, to quell border tribes, or to protect missionaries and
traders, a second empire was being created by the colonization of
new territories hitherto untouched by white traders, as in Australasia,
or by peopling vacant lands in Canada and South Africa, where
French and Dutch had already led the way. Five thousand colonists
were sent to South Africa, and with the annulling of old restrictions
imposed when soldiers were needed at home, a long line of emigrants
escaped from poverty and tyranny to the lands oversea. Cobbett
noted that already under George IV. the word " empire " began
to replace "kingdom," and the title "sovereign" that of "king":
and papers which had once been " submitted to the King " were now
"laid at His Majesty's feet." On the seas England alone owned
as many trading vessels as all other nations together, while her harbours were the international market for the produce of the outer
world. Every bale of Australian and South African wool passed
through London: all Europe took its cotton from Liverpool: manufactures from Lancashire looms were poured out over India. The tea
of China, the tropical produce of the East and West Indies, the riches
of South America, were carried in English ships. For the protection
of these world-wide interests every route was guarded, every point of
vantage watched. At the outlet of the North Sea Belgium, the old
"counterscarp of England," was no less jealously observed than the
coast of Ireland; it was the same in every country on the European
seaboard. Lisbon was a naval base of the first importance, for the
routes to Brazil and to the Cape and the defence of Gibraltar; Spain
had traditional rights in Morocco, commanding the entry to the
Mediterranean; Naples held the passage of the narrow seas; Austria
controlled the commerce of the Levant; Turkey, as lord of Egypt
and Syria, commanded the routes to the Persian Gulf and the
Red Sea, by which the sea-borne trade of India poured into the
Mediterranean. But no power was feared like Russia, as she advanced towards the passes of Afghanistan or, pressing southwards
over the Caucasus, threatened to intercept the trade of the Persian
Gulf, where for three hundred years English ships had policed, for a
distance greater than that from Plymouth to Gibraltar, those distant
waters lying between fiery stretches of desert gaunt and sun-scorched,
had put down pirates, set buoys and beacons, and guarded the lines

Sec. II.

Foreign
AND
Colonial
l olicy

1815
TO
1914

1819–1826

1819

1824
1836

Sec. II.
Foreign
AND
Colonial
Policy
1815
TO
1914

of her old commerce with Persia and the direct way to the harbour of Karrachi and Bombay. England was forced to recognize that her existence depended on the sea. The industrial revolution which had transformed a nation of farmers into a manufacturing people. made new markets necessary for their produce and for the supply of raw material and food; and the European seas became the passage of England to the world beyond. Her vast territories, her command of the oceans, the scarcity of food for her industrial workers at home and their tumultuous discontent, all causes combined to the same end; and in the next hundred years led to the building up of the greatest dominion which it has yet come within the power of man to accomplish, and the development of a government which in its originality and variety has no example.

**Castle-
reagh**

1814–1822

In the European settlement meanwhile Castlereagh, architect of peace, was resolved that no accident should destroy the fabric. At the Congress of Vienna his just and sober attitude made a considerable impression, and he was admired for his dignity of manner and simplicity of dress. Though some foreign statesmen accused him of fear of parliamentary criticism and of British disregard and misunderstanding of continental affairs, he was in fact, as conciliator and arbiter, the most effective guardian of the peace of Europe. He furnished the Congress with a plan of action, and enforced on Europe the Grand Alliance of Great Britain, Russia, Austria, and Prussia. In Castlereagh's view peace, the first necessity of Europe, was to be secured by a just equilibrium of states, by the support of those powers whose exertions had "saved Europe," and by indulgence even to the offending peoples. It was his desire to bind together the great powers with a more enduring sanction than a treaty, and pledge them by a

1815

general accord and guarantee to unite their arms against any mutineer or disturber of the continental settlement. His hopes were thwarted when Austria, Russia, and Prussia joined in a pact of Christian sovereigns designed by the visionary Alexander I. In the "sublime mysticism" of the Holy Alliance the dogmas of religion were mingled with the elements of Rousseau's Social Contract; the princes were to be as brothers, their peoples as their children, and their acts founded on the principles of the Gospel of Christ. At periodical meetings they were to consider salutary measures for the repose and prosperity of the nations and for the peace of Europe. The grandiose intentions of the Alliance were soon perverted. Despotism was provided with the garment of religion, and under the cloak of Christianity Metternich attacked constitutional and national aspirations. He stifled Alexander's Liberal sympathies by playing on his fears; the conversion of the

**1817
1818
1820**

Tsar was rendered more easy by acts of violence—a riot of students at the Wartburg, the murder of a Russian agent in Saxe-Weimar, the assassination of the Duc de Berri, and the Cato Street conspiracy.

Sec. II.

Foreign
AND
Colonial
Policy

1815
TO
1914

At each successive outbreak Metternich strengthened the system by which he strangled Liberalism in its cradle ; he suppressed the gatherings and dissolved the societies of students, forbade their songs and the wearing of their colours, and sent his secret police to invade the lecture-rooms of the Universities. Castlereagh, convinced that our constitution satisfied every need, was determined not " to let his country burn for the sake of a few poets." But while England exercised at home the utmost rigour, she used, as Metternich said, " two weights and two measures," and where her interests were involved condemned extreme repression abroad. The Holy Alliance had agreed that in case of a revolution a German State could invoke help from the armed forces of the whole confederation—a measure which caused a speaker in Parliament to picture the day when Hyde Park would be crowded with Cossacks to prevent the agitation for reform. But when the lesser German states were threatened, Castlereagh's protests were precise ; he could not allow his sovereign to connive at the overthrow of Liberal constitutions in Germany, since George IV. was also king of Hanover, the gate through which the German markets were supplied with English goods. On the other hand he declined to defend the constitutional hopes of the Neapolitans against the special interest claimed by Austria in Italian affairs. His attitude to the Alliance was one of deprecation rather than protest, and there were Whigs who grumbled that England was reduced to the position of a second-rate power.

Castlereagh's first concern in fact was for the British Empire, whose power had excited enemies and rivals on every side. He had inherited from Pitt a lively jealousy of Russia, and his suspicions were quickened by reports of her designs on Asiatic Turkey and her intrigues at Madrid, threatening two main centres of English influence in the Mediterranean ; in every maritime and colonial question Russia raised her hostile challenge. France was equally suspect for her relations to Spain and Portugal, and her colonial aspirations. The central powers seemed to offer an alliance against both dangers. To Prussia, the point of contact of Hanover with Europe, England looked to guard the Rhine and protect Holland, to hold the Baltic ports and the Polish frontier, and on east and west to raise an impenetrable barrier against French and Russian aggression. In hope of German support Castlereagh gave to Austria Lombardy and Venetia, and desired to give Saxony to Prussia if she would have allowed the restoration of the Polish kingdom in agreement with Austria. He would even have ceded Hanover in order to check France and Russia. Thwarted in his schemes by Russian influence over Prussia, he drew closer to Austria and France—an uncertain alliance with two powers whose interests conflicted with those of England—Austria in Naples and France in Spain. For it was Castlereagh's aim to establish English

HISTORY OF THE ENGLISH PEOPLE.

Sec. II.

Foreign
and
Colonial
Policy

1815
to
1914

The
Spanish
colonies

1815-1825

influence as supreme in all the peninsulas of southern Europe—a policy which he handed down to Canning and Palmerston. To safeguard the Balkans he had attempted at Vienna, though in vain, to bring the Porte into the circle of the Allied powers; and when the Greeks revolted against Turkey he held that the only interest of England lay in maintaining the integrity of the Ottoman Empire. As regarded Italy he refused, amid much obloquy, to join the Holy Alliance in their proposed coercion of Piedmont. In the case of Spain he was prepared to defy Europe. During the wars an enfeebled Spain had lost the greater part of her possessions in South America; one by one Bolivia, Chile, Colombia, and Peru asserted their independence, with support from the United States, who proposed to exclude Europeans from the new continent and themselves secure its wealthy commerce. Castlereagh was at all times willing to mediate between Spain and her revolted colonies, on the terms that no force should be used, that an amnesty should be granted to the people of South America, and their commerce opened to all nations, with moderate duties and a reasonable preference for Spain. The colonial empire of Spain had been an old offence to England, and her determination was fixed to secure against all rivals her own trading pre-eminence. Russia and France were vehemently hostile, and Spain sought her profit in dividing the European powers   With all the continental statesmen Castlereagh dreaded that the United States, propelled by the more ardent revolutionists, would foster new republics. He staved off American recognition of the colonies by skilfully concealing from Washington the dissensions of the powers, while he hoped that the persuasion of the Tories might win the revolted provinces for the principles of monarchy. But in his anxiety not to leave to the United States the credit and influence of first recognizing the aspirations of the colonies, Castlereagh was gradually forced along the new road of Liberalism, till he contemplated not only admitting the independence of the new nations, but even assisting constitutional revolutionists, if in no other way he could safeguard British interests. By what right, he wrote, could an English government force a population freed from an oppressive government to replace itself under the domination of that same government?

When the Holy Alliance assembled at Verona to discuss the disorders in Greece, Italy, and Spain, Castlereagh protested against interference in the internal affairs of Spain, and resolved to break with the Alliance over the South American Republics. Before his death he knew that the European system which he had endeavoured to uphold was perverted and outworn.

His successor, George Canning, breaking away from the reactionary bonds of the last thirty years of English history, burst upon Europe, in Metternich's words, "like a malevolent meteor." Like Castlereagh, he was of the planters of Ireland, but to his English stock was added

SEC. II.

FOREIGN
AND
COLONIAL
POLICY

1815
TO
1914

the blood of an ancient Irish race. In his defiance of despotic courts on behalf of constitutional liberty, he "inspired foreign powers with respect, domestic Tories with hatred." His brilliant personality of body and mind won to him many of the younger Whigs; but when Canning raised his toast in the Whig Club: "The cause of civil and religious liberty all over the world," he was no mere knight-errant of freedom. If liberty was his guiding intention, he never failed to regard England's commercial interests, and followed Castlereagh in his imperial policy. Foreign statesmen distrusted the growing isolation of the English temper, a habit of thought more insular than European. "Every nation for itself and God for us all," said Canning. In a brief four years he defined the independent policy of England, and admitted the principle of national revolt. When Spain refused to admit trade with her colonies, or abate a rigid protection, Canning, who had no panic about revolution and cared little whether South American states were republican or not, decided that the commerce and maritime power of his country would gain by their complete emancipation. The crisis came when the Holy Alliance, acting through Louis XVIII., restored to Spain the exiled Bourbon king, Ferdinand VII.; and Ferdinand proposed that the powers who had made him king should call a congress to recover his American colonies. English merchants and shipowners petitioned Canning for aid, and the Whigs demanded war. He refused intervention in the Peninsula. "We had disappointed the hopes and excited the indignation of every man who loved freedom and independence throughout Europe," complained Russell. But Canning struck hard for English interests in another hemisphere. "We will trade," he said, "with the late Spanish American colonies, whether France likes it or not." He made a meeting of the Holy Alliance impossible by refusing to share or take part in it; and he boldly accepted the policy of the United States. His open rupture of the solidarity of Europe alone made possible the declaration of the new American departure. President Monroe in his famous message to Congress recognized the southern republics, denied the continent of America to the colonization of European powers, and renounced interference of the United States in European affairs. The Monroe doctrine, vague as it was, asserted the right of South America to a deliberately chosen form of government, and certain Tories looked askance at the encouragement thus given "to every disaffected Irishman by recognizing rebellion in the New World." Canning had no such fears. First among European statesmen he accepted the independence of the South American peoples, and signed commercial treaties with the new sovereign states. "I resolved," he said, "that if France had Spain it should not be Spain with the Indies; I called the New World into existence to redress the balance of the Old." Nor did he favour any extension of a Portuguese empire in America. When Dom Miguel was driven

SEC. II.

FOREIGN
AND
COLONIAL
POLICY

1815
TO
1914

The
Whig
policy

from his country it was arranged that Dom Pedro, son of John VI., should have the remote heritage of an independent Brazil, while his young daughter, Dona Maria, was maintained as queen in her unstable inheritance at home. Portugal was thus at once guarded from foreign adventure and protected in her dependent state of tutelage; and the naval base of Lisbon, so necessary for Canning's Mediterranean policy, was secured against France.

The revolution thus openly begun gave its character to English foreign policy for the coming century. The might which Nelson and the Tories had carried to its culmination, and invested with the monopoly of sea power, was under Liberal influence mainly turned to support the cause of constitutional freedom. Englishmen recalled the promise of the Allies: " The object of the war, and of the peace, is to secure the rights, the freedom, and the independence of all nations." The Congress of Vienna left two great problems, constitutional and national, which overlap at times; and Englishmen, while they failed to appreciate or understand the new ideal of nationality, were deeply interested in political freedom. The Whigs attacked systems of government which suppressed popular liberty and checked reform. England had saved herself by her exertions, and they would now have her save Europe by her example; the words of the younger Pitt were transfused with a constitutional meaning. From 1815 England provided the political pattern for reforming states who battled for free institutions and sought to enlist her sympathy. The word Liberal crept into party politics—at first as a term of reproach, hurled at those who denied that it was the business of the smaller nations to wear " one universal grin," and who preferred a balance of power to a uniform agreement for suppression. The true Liberal, such as Brougham, saw in England and her legislature the succour and solace of the oppressed wherever tyranny was rampant. The word stood for a principle of foreign policy, identified with the struggle for self-government. At times their intervention appeared aggressive—the help proffered by a nation confident of its own security and mindful of its own importance; to continental statesmen our posture seemed capricious, while the antagonistic aims of Whig and Tory, and the ruthless coercion of Ireland, gave force to the taunt of " perfidious Albion," and to the continental comment that English doctrines of liberty were " for export." But the Whig was consistent in supporting a policy of freedom which accorded with the political spirit of the English people.

This new spirit of sympathy with suffering peoples was lifted to a height of romantic passion in the cause of Greece. The Balkan States had long been inspired by the dream of emancipation from Turkey and of a new Byzantine Empire. Serbia was first in revolt

SEC. II.

FOREIGN
AND
COLONIAL
POLICY

1815
TO
1914

and, unaided by the powers, had won a measure of freedom. But as the other states were severally defeated Greece alone remained to fight, not for an empire but for a nation. She fought single-handed, for Metternich, in the name of the Holy Alliance, persuaded the Tsar Alexander to support the doctrine of legitimacy rather than that of the Cross against the Crescent. In the first war of independence Castlereagh regarded the insurrection as a matter to be left to the Turkish government. But the struggle against the Mohammedan tyrant caught the popular imagination and volunteers streamed from every country in Europe. On all sides lovers of democracy and freedom hoped that Greece would renew her ancient glories, and saw visions of an ideal republic taking shape under her clear skies. Shelley extolled the cause of the Greeks in impassioned lyrics; Byron set aside his detestation of their intrigues and jealousies, raised a considerable loan, enrolled volunteers, and sailed to Greece only to die at Missolonghi. Lord Erskine, a lover of liberty, appealed to England's honour in an eloquent pamphlet. The advanced Liberals demanded immediate intervention and accused the ministry of lowering the lofty and independent character of this country in pursuing a neutral policy which was a disgrace to Christianity and a discredit to their manhood. But Turkey had her defenders; men of the older school regarded her as an "ancient and faithful ally," and a Tory told the House that he had always found the Turks "very honest fellows, although they had a way of governing people by taking off their heads." Canning had no wish to embark on a "wild crusade," but when, to protect English commerce from lawless piracy in the Levant, he recognized the Greek flag and the Greeks as belligerents, he took the first step towards the recognition of a new nation. In the darkest hour of the Greek fortunes he sought by untiring negotiations to win Russia to the cause of her liberation, determined, as he said, to avoid war and "to save Greece through the agency of the Russian name." Such a policy foreshadowed later projects for the Balkans. It was in part the outcome of a hope that in an independent Greece, which aspired to restore the empire not of Athens but of Byzantium, there would be found an Orthodox power able to counteract Russian influence in the Turkish Empire. But Wellington, whom Canning chose as envoy to the new Tsar Nicholas I., belonged to Castlereagh's day, and carried on the tradition that the menace of Russia must be met by maintaining unbroken the integrity and strength of the Ottoman empire. The protocol he signed gave self-government to Greece, but left Turkey as suzerain. Metternich characterized the document as a "feeble and ridiculous production," but was bound to admit that it had dissolved the Holy Alliance. Austria and Prussia withdrew from such a crazy scheme: "the thicker the darkness," said a statesman, "the sooner will the meddlers in it

Sec. II.

Foreign
and
Colonial
Policy

1815
to
1914

1827

break their heads." Russia, France, and England alone met at a conference in London to convert the protocol into a treaty. In the protracted anxieties of this arduous settlement Canning gave his last services to the cause of " liberty all over the world." His death came a week before the treaty was presented to the Porte, and with it ended the hope of peace and of a permanent settlement. Turks and Greeks alike refused to lay down arms, and when the ships of Russia, France, and England followed the Turkish fleet commanded by Ibrahim Pasha, into the bay of Navarino to demand securities for peace, the aggressive movements of a Turkish fireship brought about a desultory cannonade, which developed into a naval engagement. In a few hours the Turkish fleet was sunk. The disastrous news raised a bitter conflict in England. Liberals claimed Navarino as an honest victory, a necessary consequence of the treaty of London, and a manifestation of the brilliant success which had attended the introduction of a Liberal system into foreign affairs. But the Tory government under Wellington was aghast at the tidings, and urged that such an " untoward event " should not disturb the traditional relations between Great Britain and the Porte. Canning's work was undone by the withdrawal of the English fleet. Political troubles hampered France, and Russia alone remained the guardian of the Greeks. Enraged by the disaster of Navarino, Turkey declared war upon the Tsar. After two years of desperate fighting she was forced to accept

1829

the treaty of Adrianople, through which Greece obtained her independence under the guarantee of England, France, and Russia. But the

1833

Greece for which the Bavarian prince Otto, a lad of seventeen, was provided as king, was a Greece disappointed through Wellington's determined support of Turkey of her richest province, Thessaly — a Greece but half delivered, and purposely left at the mercy of the Porte. Russia regained all her influence, and England found herself driven to the old policy from which Canning had attempted to escape. English sympathy however remained true to Greece, and thirty

1863

years later, when Otto's incompetence and errors led to his deposition, and a prince of the House of Denmark was elected as King George I., England voluntarily ceded the Ionian Islands to Greece, on condition that constitutional government should be preserved.

Belgium
and
Holland

Canning's work indeed could not be wholly destroyed. He stood forth as a statesman who had broken the despotism of the Holy Alliance, and supported the first national revolution against the settlement of the Congress. The task that lay before England was the endeavour to work out new principles of public action to take the place of those which had guided her regrettable alliance with the reactionary monarchs ; and from the stubborn situations as they arose to hew out some sort of purpose and method for the defence and the advance of freedom in Europe. A second rising of a small nation for independence renewed the controversy among English statesmen as to the true direction of their continental policy. The grant of Belgium to Holland as compensation for some of her lost colonies had been designed at Vienna as a barrier to France. But the union had already broken down before inherent differences of race, religion, and language, aggravated by unequal administration. The freedom of the Scheldt and the prosperity due to expanding colonial markets failed to reconcile the Belgians, while the revolution by which the French cast out the Bourbons and installed their "citizen king" raised excitement in Brussels to the highest point. An opera teeming with revolutionary sentiment was staged amid frenzied applause, and the next day the standard of Brabant was raised. Nobles and merchants joined the popular rising and threw back the Dutch troops. Bitter disappointment awaited the king of Holland when he appealed to the five great Powers to defend the "stability of all thrones and powers" and maintain the "political system" of the Congress. The principles of the Holy Alliance failed before the revolution that blazed across Europe. Russia was faced by a national rising in Poland. Outbreaks in Brunswick, Hanover, Hesse Cassel, and Saxony, and a threat of war from France, checked Prussian aid to the Dutch. Before the end of the year Austria had to meet a revolt in Italy. France, the exemplar of the Belgian revolution, was wholly sympathetic; and England, having broken with the Holy Alliance, found herself the ally, hesitating and mistrustful, of a liberal France which had escaped from the servitude imposed on her at Vienna. Both countries felt the gravest preoccupation at the Russian protectorate of Turkey, and each desired the other's help. Both needed peace, whether to secure Liberal reforms in England or to establish the new monarchy in France, and Talleyrand was determined on alliance with England whether under Whig or Tory. A common wave of thought had drawn the two peoples together, for the study of our economic conditions formed a bond between the Liberals, and Guizot, statesman and historian, had expounded our constitutional history at the Sorbonne. The "July revolution" which set Louis Philippe on the throne was a compromise not unlike that which England had framed in the Bill of Rights. By many influences the minds of the two countries had been prepared for their first partnership in the cause of liberty.

Thus secure from interference Belgium in a national congress proclaimed its independence. The question aroused in England sharp party conflict. The Tories, who had gained repose for Europe, deplored any sign of change; their prime minister, Wellington, regarded the recurrence of revolution as a "devilish bad business," and when William IV. met his first parliament, the speech from the throne threatened all disturbers of the peace. The Belgians were described

Sec. II.

Foreign
and
Colonial
Policy

1815
to
1914

1830

Belgium[1]
a nation

Sec. II.

Foreign
AND
Colonial
Policy

1815
TO
1914

as "revolted subjects"; the Whigs resented the phrase and ardently adopted their cause. Constitutional aspirations and foreign policy were linked together; the reform bill and the independence of Belgium became a single purpose. Hume declared that the greater portion of the people rejoiced over the revolution; Cobbett, unsympathetic to Greece, was loudly in favour of the union of Belgium with the great democracy of France; Brougham resisted interference on behalf of tyrants—"the people of England," he said, "are enamoured of their own liberties and they are friends to the liberty of others." O'Connell, famous throughout Europe as orator and champion of nationality, protested that, excepting the union of Great Britain and Ireland, there was no fouler blot in the page of history than the annexation of Belgium by Holland. The Tories replied that England was bound to uphold the treaty of Vienna; a country, they said, which had so often been the arena on which the great powers of Europe decided their quarrels, "should have learned by the sad experience of former calamities to seek all other means of redress before turning to the power of arms." Had Wellington remained in office, Belgium would have found neither help nor sympathy; but within two months the Tories were defeated, and scarcely had the Belgian Congress met when the friends of the Reform Bill returned to power. The foreign minister, Lord Palmerston, had learned much from Canning, if he was without his passion or his genius, and under his influence the conference of the powers which had assembled in London for the settlement of the Greek question proclaimed the dissolution of the United Kingdom of Holland and Belgium. The triumph of the Anglo-French alliance was marred by jealousies and fears. Palmerston's main dread was the absorption or occupation of Belgium by France and the possibility that the accession of the Orleanist dynasty might be celebrated by a revision of the French frontier. When the Belgians elected as king a son of Louis Philippe, he refused to admit so close a family bond; at his warning that "our desire for peace would never lead us to submit to an affront either in language or in act," Louis Philippe withdrew his son's candidature, and a German prince, Leopold of Saxe-Coburg, reigned in Belgium. Indignant at the liberal terms granted to the new king by the London conference—contrary, they said, to the "irrevocable" promises of the powers—the Dutch sent an army which in ten days overwhelmed the Belgians and occupied Liége and Louvain. French troops hastened to drive them out; but the moment the French stepped upon Belgian soil England was up in arms. No accusation was too extravagant for the Tories. They suggested that Belgian disturbances were used to prepare a way for the freedom of Ireland: "the centre of the bigoted army was in Paris," said one, "the right wing was in Brussels, while the left wing was looking on in Dublin." They demanded that all correspondence should be laid upon the table of the House so that Parliament might have its part in matters of peace and war. Peel protested against secrecy, though he offered to sacrifice his desire for information "in the public interest." During an angry debate Palmerston stated the constitutional functions of his office; maintaining that decisions on war and peace belonged solely to the royal prerogative, and that any power to conduct negotiations was vested in the Crown. He therefore refused papers until the matter was settled. In this sharp conflict the cabinet, and with it the Reform Bill, were saved from defeat by Talleyrand, who dreaded the downfall of the Whigs and persuaded his unwilling government to withdraw the French troops. Belgium was established under the guarantee of the Powers as an independent and perpetually neutral State, its neutrality being made a foremost clause in the constitution. But harder terms than before were dealt out to a defeated people, stripped of part of Luxemburg and Limburg, and forced to pay dues to Holland on the Scheldt; while the Dutch refused to give up the citadel of Antwerp. Palmerston dared not let France alone drive them out, nor dared to join with her against the will of the merchants, who opposed war with Holland. William IV. meanwhile, with his "Jack Tar animosity," deplored a tendency to subscribe to democratic theories current in Paris and cursed his advisers for taking the hand of France. Only when the desperate struggle at home ended in the triumph of the Reform Bill was Palmerston strong enough to take his own way in foreign affairs. A French army at Antwerp and an English fleet in the Scheldt scourged the Dutch back "to their phlegmatic swamps," declaimed an Irish patriot, "knocked their flag and sceptre, their laws and bayonets into the sluggish waters of the Scheldt," and "on the ramparts of Antwerp" taught "the right of a nation to govern itself." But as with Greece the settlement was marred. The king of Holland long refused to recognize a free Belgium. Six years later, seizing his opportunity when its only supporters France and England had quarrelled, he persuaded the powers to enforce the harsh terms of 1831. Palmerston, who was then negotiating with Metternich, demanded immediate submission of the Belgians, and only through the mediation of France was some alleviation granted. By the treaty of London the neutrality and independence of Belgium were again placed under the guarantee of the five great powers.

The settlement of Vienna had within seven years begun to crumble under the pressure of national revolts and of rivalry for oversea commerce. In a single generation every problem which now confronts the nations had taken form. Decrees which fixed a few proprietary dynasties for Europe, and artificial boundaries for their peoples, were challenged. The Prussian Zollverein slowly broadened into a commercial agreement which included some thirty-eight

SEC. II.

FOREIGN AND COLONIAL POLICY

1815 TO **1914**

1831

1832

1833
1839

Nationality in Europe

1830–1832

Sec. II.

Foreign
AND
Colonial
Policy

1815
TO
1914

German States and foreshadowed the national union of Germany under Prussian leadership. At the same moment Mazzini inspired the "Young Italy" movement, and raised the banner of "Unity and Independence"; and Charles Albert came to the throne of Sardinia with a mission to end the rule of Austria. The kingdom of Russian Poland, reconstituted at Vienna from the old Duchy of Warsaw, and given by Alexander a brief hope of life, was thrust into subjection by Nicholas; and thousands of Poles, the remnants of a nation, were dispersed through Europe to preach revolution. Magyar nationalists in the fight with Metternich turned back to their history and the memory of their heroes: "an independent nation we mean to live with our own language." In their revival of literature and tradition the Slavs were moved by a common impulse, and each isolated group of their scattered peoples felt itself to be part of a mighty race. Bohemia pointed to the example of Ireland and O'Connell as a call to national liberty. The Croatians and Southern Slavs dreamed of the "Illyria" planned by Napoleon, the home of a liberated race. In the Balkans after the Serbian example Bulgaria and the Danubian States demanded from Turkey, and in part secured, some form of autonomy and national privilege. Roumania already aimed at the union of all her peoples of Bessarabia, Transylvania, and Bukovina.

1826–1833 During the wars of liberation Russia made her formal entry into the Balkans as the protector of the Slavonic races as well as the head of the Orthodox Church; with Russian influence established on the lower Danube, the monopoly of Austria disappeared, and the conflict opened between the Teutons and the Slavs for leadership of the peninsula. The "mouldering empire" of the Ottomans, shorn of a province by the Greek rising, entered on its long period of slow dismemberment and political dependence; and the threat of an independent Egypt, and the closing of the Dardanelles to foreign warships, brought Europe to the verge of war. Prussia took up her part of military instructor to the Sultan by sending to his army von

1835
The
Imperial
rivalry

Moltke with other officers, who first proposed the exploitation by Germany of Asia Minor. Beyond Europe, meanwhile, another struggle had begun, to some extent in emulation of the British Empire, for race dominion in the world. Russia had entered on her Asiatic empire: she had crossed the Caucasus, contested Armenia,

1828–1834 and fortified the Caspian; her wares reached Lahore; she excited suspicion and apprehension by her trade rivalry, her exclusion of British vessels from the Circassian coast, her opposition to efforts for a mail route to India by steamers on the Euphrates, her intrigues in Persia. A few years later she had pushed to the Pacific coast in Kamschatka and on the Amur. France, meanwhile, turned to Africa and the Pacific for the creation of a new colonial empire. She celebrated

1830–1834 her resurrection from a long abasement when Louis Philippe opened the Arc de Triomphe and consecrated Versailles to the glorious deeds of France. Enthusiasts believed that the winning of Algeria would be to her what India was to England, and when Lord Grey demanded its evacuation, colonization was carried on half secretly to avoid hostility. The new-made "Government of French Possessions in North Africa" penetrated from the littoral to the interior, and presently menaced Morocco. "I desire the French to restore Roman Africa," said Marshal Valée; "wherever at my bidding France sets her foot, I shall form lasting stations." Since Napoleon's time she had kept watch on the gate of the East; her officers had trained the army and the navy of Mehemet Ali, viceroy of Egypt, and England feared her growing influence in this richest province of the Ottoman empire. In the Pacific her patrols, protectorates, and schemes of settlement startled England into the colonization of New Zealand. Already in Asia, Africa, and the Pacific, the European powers learned the risks of colonial rivalry, which henceforth gave to alliances a suspicious, temporary, and uncertain character; for the relations of the home governments were at best insecure while a dispute on the other side of the globe could threaten to wreck their understanding.

In this world of universal agitation and revolution Palmerston, equally ready to make British power felt and to profit by the quarrels of other peoples, opened his vigorous policy of intervention on behalf of English interests. For thirty-five years, with but one considerable interval, he guided our foreign policy; admired by the trader, for whose glory or fortune he was prepared to throw down the gage of battle; by the sportsman, who followed his colours at Epsom or gazed on the fine horses that champed their bits outside the Foreign Office; by the democrat, who forgave a want of interest in reform to such a doughty assailant of despotism. Abroad he was looked on as a dictator— brusque, violent, and fearless. Not to count upon the foreigner, but to make the foreigner count upon England; such was said to be the programme he designed for a great industrial people protected by its isolation. Regardless of the name of "Jacobin," and of his opponents' charge that he made us "generally detested by the nations of Europe," he constituted his country the champion of the smaller states. His partnership with France in the liberation of Belgium was felt as an outrage by the Tsar, who renewed at Münchengrätz with Austria and Prussia a Holy Alliance in support of "divine right" against the two powers which had "the courage to profess aloud rebellion and the overthrow of all stability." But Palmerston, pupil of Canning and Castlereagh, followed a single guiding line of policy— the imperial interests of England. He viewed with suspicion French advance in Algeria and French influence beyond the Pyrenees; incessantly on guard lest Spain should become a satellite of France and draw Portugal into her orbit, thus shutting English ships out

SEC. II.

FOREIGN
AND
COLONIAL
POLICY

1815
TO
1914

1827–1842

**England
and
Spain**
1830

1833

Sec. II.
Foreign
AND
Colonial
Policy
1815
TO
1914

1834

1835

of their strategic position in the Tagus. Each country had the same dynastic misfortunes—child queens crowned at the ages of three and seven and supported by Liberals, while Absolutists and Clericals rallied round the two Pretenders. In Portugal they favoured Dom Miguel; in Spain Don Carlos. After ten years of reaction, in which Spanish Liberals had suffered the vengeance of the "Society of the Exterminating Angel," followed the "seven years' war" of factions. Talleyrand thought of intervention; but Palmerston's "great stroke" was a treaty of alliance with the Liberals of Portugal and Spain which he suddenly presented to the Cabinet. With the later adhesion of France it became the Quadruple Alliance. The moral effect of the treaty, in Palmerston's boast, intimidated the pretenders. On the other hand, France saw in it a definite purpose to fetter French policy, to forbid her assertion of any authority beyond the Pyrenees, and to turn the Spanish troubles to the exclusive advantage of English power. Louis Philippe deserted his headstrong partner, while Palmerston went forward alone. Without committing his government to intervention he suspended the Foreign Enlistment Act, and a legion was raised in aid of the Liberals. Tempted by high but precarious pay, the adventurers fought with great gallantry until, destitute of stores and ill-supported by the Spaniards, they were with difficulty extricated. Exhaustion alone brought about the downfall of the Carlists and the close of the civil war. Against critics of his intervention in a domestic affair, Palmerston contended that commercial and political interests would profit by constitutional government, and claimed that he had prevented the dictation of other powers. "Spain for the Spaniards is the maxim upon which we proceed," said he, "and we considered that the independence of Spain was more likely to be secured by a government controlled by a representative and national assembly than by a government purely arbitrary." His arguments could not conceal the danger of his policy, and how gravely he had prejudiced the relations of England and France.

England
and
Turkey

1808

1808-1824

A new conflict intensified the French view of Palmerston as an enemy bent on checking their country at every outlet. In the east the French had long been patrons of the famous Mehemet Ali. He had served with the English against Napoleon; but as Pasha of Egypt he defeated an English force that attacked Alexandria, and exhibited in Cairo an avenue of posts bearing the heads of a thousand British slain; while by the advice of the French consul the prisoners were returned without ransom. With the aid of French officers he created a navy and an army and built up a dominion from Crete to Khartoum. His powerful help alone enabled the Sultan to hold out against the Greek revolt. To exact his promised reward—the Pashalics of Damascus and Syria—he sent his son Ibrahim to conquer the whole of Syria and advance over

SEC. II.

FOREIGN
AND
COLONIAL
POLICY

1815
TO
1914

Asia Minor. The English envoy to the Porte, Sir Stratford Canning, a believer in the possible reform of Turkey and in a nascent Young Turk party, desired help from England; but the English fleet was occupied on the Dutch coast in defence of Belgium, nor could the French interfere, since their troops were besieging Antwerp. Mehemet might have ruled in Constantinople, but for a Russian army which landed at the Bosporus. From the grateful Sultan the Tsar wrested the treaty of Unkiar Skelessi, by which in effect the warships of every nation but his own were excluded from the Black Sea. England and France protested in vain against handing over the keys of the Black Sea to a rival power, while Turkey remained little better than " vassal to the Russian Government." On the other hand the Tsar, deeply incensed at the two revolutionary countries of the West, whom he considered outside the Concert of Europe, refused to allay their fears by communicating to England the decision of Münchengrätz which bound him to maintain the integrity of Turkey. Mehemet, meanwhile, proposing to set up his independent rule from Egypt over Syria and Arabia, stood across the two routes to India, the Red Sea, and the Euphrates valley to which the invention of steamers had given increased commercial importance. Copying Western methods, he had trifled with the idea of a parliament, but to prevent inconvenience he selected both the government and the opposition. As an industrial and commercial reformer he set up huge cotton mills, whose expensive machinery fell to pieces through want of care; and bound down every profitable industry from silk to vegetable gardens under his government monopolies. To defeat his system of protection Palmerston won from the Sultan a commercial treaty of free trade throughout the Ottoman empire, and to enforce it required the cession of Aden—a sun-scorched fort which from the crater of an extinct volcano dominated the entrance to the Red Sea— the first new territory of Queen Victoria's reign and the forecast of a greater harvest to come. The commercial treaty was the turning point of the struggle. Mehemet threatened to declare himself independent and the Sultan answered by war. A vast army (with von Moltke among other Prussian officers), hurled against Ibrahim, was annihilated in the battle of Nezib. Within six days the Sultan was dead, and his fleet had sailed from the Dardanelles to join Mehemet Ali. A year of embittered controversy followed. Palmerston had a single purpose—so to restore the old boundaries of the Turkish empire that it should remain in occupation of the roads to India. The French, on the other hand, whose influence was powerful in the eastern Mediterranean, and throughout Greece, Egypt, and Mesopotamia, saw in Mehemet an invincible bulwark against English power; believing that the Turkish empire must inevitably be dismembered, they advocated the independence of its detached provinces

Sec. II.

Foreign
AND
Colonial
, olicy

1815
TO
1914

1840

and the union of Egypt and Syria. Casting France aside, Palmerston entered into mysterious dealings not only with Austria and Prussia but with Russia, and received the Tsarevitch in England. In the Convention of London the four powers pledged themselves to secure the integrity of Turkey by maintaining the neutrality of the Dardanelles, and required Mehemet to renounce Crete, northern Syria, and the holy cities of Arabia; if his answer was delayed for twenty days, all his other possessions might be withdrawn. As six years before Palmerston had sprung on the country a Quadruple Alliance to secure its hold on the west Mediterranean, so to protect her place in the east he now threw England into a Quadrilateral arrangement with the despotic powers under Metternich's influence.

*Convention
of London*

France was neither informed of the treaty nor invited to sign; she had now to choose between the desertion of her old ally Mehemet and a conflict with all Europe. The Tsar detested the government of Louis Philippe. Throughout Germany passions of hatred and vengeance sprang to life with the revival of the Napoleonic legend in France, the second landing of Louis Napoleon in the moment of the most intense exasperation at the affronts of the London conference, and the bringing of the great Emperor's bones to Paris from St. Helena amid the tears and acclamations of a people. Prussia professed a fear of French revenge for 1815. The anniversary of the battle of Leipsic was in its ardent celebration like the birth of a new nation. The isolation of France gave Palmerston his opportunity. " If Mehemet Ali would not yield he must be chucked into the Nile," he declared : it was " to England's interest " that the Sultan should retake Syria and Egypt. He had already in June prepared a rising in Syria. Now, before it was possible to have an answer from Mehemet to the terms offered, he sent a fleet, aided by Austria and Turkey, to bombard Beirut. The excitement in Paris was extreme, and inflammatory denunciations of England were shouted at every street corner. " I know your king better than you," said Palmerston to a Frenchman; " he will never make war." He spoke truly. In an outburst of national rage Louis Philippe was christened " the Napoleon of Peace." Thiers was forced to resign. The fall of Acre, till then held impreg‧ nable, cut Mehemet off from Syria, and Napier sailed to bombard Alexandria. But Palmerston's pertinacity was at last checked by the

1841

intervention of France and the other powers. In a new conference of Five Powers at London Mehemet's hereditary possession of Egypt was asserted, and in spite of Palmerston's prolonged resistance and many intrigues was established; while he was presently given for his life the basin of the Nile into the far Sudan. France in vain proposed the freedom or the neutrality of the Suez and Euphrates routes, or pleaded the wretched case of the Syrian Christians thrown back under the savage rule of Turkey.

England was now the leading power in the Levant, having thrown back France and Russia and secured her way to India. In the capitals of Europe and throughout the East the fame of Palmerston resounded for his alert diplomacy and the vigour of his blow, while Englishmen in general agreed that the foiling of French policy and a naval victory had raised the honour of the country higher than it had been since Waterloo. He had, however, to meet strong opposition in Parliament. The Radicals condemned a policy which caused the "signal calamity" of a rupture with France and made England an accomplice of the "sinister motives" of Russia. Monckton Milnes cried out against "an armed people, a peace without its profits, a war without its stimulants, and without any of those circumstances which could make war tolerable." Disraeli, insisting on the value of alliance with France, declared that since 1830 England had witnessed her foreign system changed and reconstructed, while Parliament, absorbed in domestic affairs, had not a single debate to discuss the principles of her action abroad. But Palmerston never trimmed his foreign policy to the pattern of the House of Commons; his support was outside its walls. He could rely on the traditional hatred of France. He caught the ear of the people, and flattered them by his assertions of the power of Great Britain. They loved his racy speeches and the boasts of his least scrupulous intrigues. "How was it we did drive him out of Syria?" he told his constituents. "Merely by giving a few muskets to the people of the country; by sending a few hundred marines on shore to aid them and saying, 'Go it, my boys; if you want to get rid of Mehemet Ali, here we are to back you; if you intend to act, now's your time.' They took us at our word; they kicked him out neck and crop, and his army too; they hailed us as their deliverers." Later years were to show the cost of Palmerston's success. The Ottoman empire was now under the joint protection of all the great powers; henceforth it would be the battlefield of them all. Mehemet Ali ruled in Egypt by the will of Europe—a new diplomatic situation. The case of the Syrian Christians held already the menace of a great war. An attempt by the Porte at internal reform succeeded at least in organizing a powerful military force against the Christian subjects. As for the neutrality of the Dardanelles, in a dozen years the fleets of France and England, whatever the protocol might say, were to pass into the Black Sea. Russia, fully sensible that it was through England she had lost the position won in 1833, was determined to regain her predominant influence at Constantinople, even if she had to break with her dangerous ally. Another sinister change appeared in Europe from the moment when France, betrayed by England, turned to Austria; for Prussia, threatened on her western and southern frontiers by the alliance she most feared, prepared her weapon for self-defence by closer

Sec. II.

Foreign
AND
Colonial
Policy

1815
TO
1914

Palmer=
ston's
policy

SEC. II.

FOREIGN
AND
COLONIAL
POLICY

1815
TO
1914

union of the German states. All Europe was convulsed with fears and ambitions, and a settlement of the "Eastern question" in which each power, with narrow and short-sighted outlook, was bent on its sole interests, regardless of the ultimate peace of the continent—such a settlement could only be the prelude of new wars to come.

The Tory policy

There was a change in foreign policy when the Liberals fell, defeated on a budget which attempted some concessions to free-traders. Since Wellington the Tory policy was that of peace and friendliness to the autocratic sovereigns of the Continent. Sir Robert Peel, the new premier, inculcated on his ministers "strong aversion to extension of territorial responsibilities, and a frank admission of the equal rights of foreign countries." Reversing the system of Palmerston, which he abhorred, he introduced relations with foreign powers more sedate and conciliatory. A series of disputes into which Palmerston had entered with the United States were settled so as to secure American friendship. Since 1812 relations had been courteous: the two countries had joined hands over the Monroe doctrine; the Ashburton-Webster treaty solved an old dispute dating from 1783 over the frontier of Maine and New Brunswick, and other misunderstandings, and Peel's proposals stilled the cry for war over the boundary of Oregon. In Europe the Queen's favourite minister, Lord Aberdeen, had but a lukewarm sympathy with oppressed nationalities, and saw no bulwark against war save the treaties of Vienna; under him England drew to a better understanding with Austria and Prussia. Intent on resuming good relations with France, he refused to regard the clamour of rage when a French admiral, exceeding his instructions, annexed Tahiti, or when the French war in Algiers widened into Morocco and threatened the transport trade between Tangier and Gibraltar. Louis Philippe, uneasy about the security of his throne, welcomed the renewal of English friendship, marked by two meetings with Queen Victoria in France, and a visit to Windsor. An attempt was made towards a joint settlement of the perennial problem of the Spanish succession; the young Queen Isabella was allotted to a Bourbon prince, and her sister to the youngest son of Louis Philippe, provided that an heir to the throne was previously born. But the chosen Bourbon was so depraved and effete that the accidents of revolution or lack of issue might have given the throne to the grandson of Louis Philippe. Three years of sordid intrigue came to a sudden end when Palmerston returned to power, with his known determination to prevent the Orleanist alliance. Spain and France—alike alienated by his dictatorial dispatch on the marriages, which directed the Spanish government to abandon at once arbitrary rule and return to the ways of the constitution—agreed to have the two marriages celebrated on the same day.

Once more Palmerston had severed the understanding between England and France. Alarmed at the growth of a republican party, Guizot restricted the freedom of the press and of meetings; while, as if by contrast, Palmerston extended his patronage broadcast to Liberal ideas. He sent a mission of sympathy to Italian States struggling for reform, hoping in fact to counsel prudence and to check the wearing of the red cap of liberty—"to teach diplomacy," scoffed Disraeli, "to the country where Machiavelli was born." His action led to an alliance between Metternich and Guizot when the people of Switzerland broke into revolution. Seven Catholic cantons threw off their allegiance to the Federation, formed the Sonderbund, and appealed to arms; on their defeat by the Federal Diet in a brisk campaign, Guizot endeavoured by means of a European Conference to bring about intervention in favour of the Catholics. But Palmerston, upholding the right of the Swiss nation to control its own affairs, did little to further the Conference until the war was at an end. The powers were soon engaged with greater issues, for in a few months the example of Switzerland was universal. "Liberty," said Bright, "is on the march." Nationalists and democrats asserted their claims throughout Europe. The risings began in Sicily, and every post brought news of a revolution or a dethronement. Radicals and republicans expelled the house of Orleans, and Louis Philippe fled to our shores; Metternich escaped to London in fear of his life; the Emperor Ferdinand abdicated, and was succeeded by Francis Joseph who links the revolution of 1848 with the war of 1914. Encouraged by this turmoil the Magyars revolted, and within a year Louis Kossuth had proclaimed the independence of Hungary. The Czechs rallied the "South Slavonic nations," and the Slav congress at Prague, and the Croatians at Agram, demanded their constitutional rights; Rome ejected the Pope, and Mazzini and Garibaldi set up a Roman Republic. Sardinia endeavoured to drive the Austrians from the north of Italy; Prussia demanded a constitution. Of the great powers England alone, confident in such political and economic freedom as she had won, afforded a shelter to the refugees, king, statesman, and revolutionist alike. Beyond this Palmerston remained a "passive spectator"; intervention would have had no limit, and common action was impossible. At length authority gained the upper hand, and rebellion was slowly crushed. The Socialists of France tried a series of experiments, which led to disastrous conflicts, and paved the way for the rule of Louis Buonaparte. Austria defeated Sardinia at Novara; with the help of Russia, she drove Kossuth from the plains of Hungary, and forced him to take refuge in Turkey. The Republicans were thrust out of Rome. For nearly two years panic and violence possessed every court in Europe and reigned

Sec. II.

Foreign
and
Colonial
Policy

1815
to
1914

**Revolu-
tion in
Europe**

1847

1848

1849

Sec. II.

Foreign
AND
Colonial
Policy

1815
TO
1914

in every mob. Though Great Britain sternly held down a famine-stricken Ireland, and suppressed the Chartists, Palmerston was not indifferent to the Liberals of other nations; he supplied arms to the Sicilians, protested against Russia's intervention in Hungary, and denounced the atrocities of Austria. No answer was sent when the Austrian minister, in a pungent retort to Palmerston's admonitions, reminded him of "unhappy Ireland" and of the empire throughout whose vast extent England was accustomed to maintain "the authority of law, were it even at the price of torrents of blood. It is not for us to blame her." From advice Palmerston proceeded to action. When the despots tried to force the Sultan to expel Kossuth and the Hungarian refugees, the British fleet was sent to demonstrate in support of Turkey. To admonish King Otto for his hostility to

Turkey and friendship for France and Russia, he diverted the fleet to the Piræus and exacted exorbitant compensations for a strip of land taken from Finlay, the historian, and for the depredations of a mob in the house of Don Pacifico, a Jew born in Gibraltar. The protests of France and Russia, our co-guarantors of the kingdom of Greece, were alike neglected, and war appeared possible. A violence so overbearing was repudiated by the Lords, and their censure compelled Lord John

Russell to discard his foreign minister, to justify his policy, or to resign. A motion was brought forward expressing confidence in the spirit and principle upon which our affairs were conducted; "its defeat," said Russell, "would inspire joy in the hearts of all the lovers of despotism, and all the haters of liberty throughout Europe." Palmerston's work for the past twenty years was reviewed in all its phases. The Conservatives abjured "the alluring and dangerous doctrine" of intervention, and affirmed that Palmerston's interference was capricious; they attacked his provocative language, declaring that by encouraging "what were called Liberal principles" he "paved the way for Jacobinism and anarchy, which eventually led to reaction." England's mission, said Gladstone, was not that of a "universal schoolmaster": he denied to any one country a position of peculiar privilege, and raised the debate to a higher plane when he associated all Europe with the obligations of Christendom. Peel, unconscious that he was addressing the House for the last time, denounced aggressive diplomacy as costly and mischievous, and asserted that constitutional liberty was best ensured by the efforts of those who aspired to freedom. Russell in reply defended intervention: "Besides the general interest of mankind," he said, "it is our particular interest with regard to Europe that freedom should be extended." A display of enthusiasm beyond example in that generation burst forth at the premier's closing words: "So long as we continue the government of this country, I can answer for my noble friend that he will act not as the minister of Austria, or as the minister of Russia, or of France, or of any other country,

Sec. II.

Foreign
AND
Colonial
Policy

1815
TO
1914

but as the minister of England." But the most vigorous defence came from Palmerston himself, who appealed confidently to the principles of justice and freedom which had actuated his general policy. Denying that the Greek affair was a matter of intervention, he claimed that the Briton abroad, "whether his house be a palace or a cabin," should have the protection of the flag, rather than submit to the indifferent justice of foreign tribunals. He invoked the remembrance of Roman citizenship, and affirmed that "a British subject, in whatever land he may be, shall feel confident that the watchful eye and the strong arm of England will protect him against injustice and wrong." The cheers which greeted his bold peroration echoed throughout the land; the vote of confidence was carried and Palmerston's popularity assured.

The
Man-
chester
School

1847
1850

It was in this debate that Richard Cobden appeared as pioneer of that school of thought which embodied the doctrines of Kant and the aims of the Congress of Vienna. Cobden possessed a considerable, though biassed, knowledge of foreign affairs; he had studied the Egyptian question while Mehemet Ali was still a power; had visited America and Prussia; had discussed the state of Ireland with Metternich, and economics with Bastiat; he was an active member of the peace conferences held in Paris and Frankfort; and was an advocate of arbitration. In the Greek debate he displayed a "sovereign contempt for diplomacy" with its superfine distinctions of terms; had the people, he said, been fully acquainted with the contents of the blue-books, they would have subscribed the money necessary to compensate British subjects in Greece, rather than coerce a small country. "If I have one conviction stronger than another," he declared, "it is in favour of the principle of non-intervention in the domestic concerns of other nations." His hopes were centred in international law; since it was seldom easy to be sure of the rights of a quarrel in foreign countries, and the heat of contention, and the platforms of "ignorant and excitable constituencies," were the worst time and place in which to arrive at a correct judgment. The keystone of his political arch was free trade. On that he based his confidence, and regarded the exchange of goods as an object-lesson in the benefits and practice of peace. He brought the aspirations of the Abbé de St. Pierre into the House of Commons, and though he reluctantly admitted war in defence of honour and interests, he looked forward to a day when it should become as obsolete as the duel. Towards this consummation the English people were to lead the way. "It is precisely because Great Britain is strong in resources, in courage, in institutions, in geographical position," he wrote, "that she can before all other Powers afford to be moral, and to set the example of a mighty nation walking in the paths of justice and peace." But peace had to contend with many enemies;

SEC. II.
FOREIGN
AND
COLONIAL
POLICY
1815
TO
1914

and Cobden lived to see slavery abolished by force of arms in the country which next to his own he regarded as a pattern to the world. While he was at the height of his power, Italy was still a "geographical expression," and the German empire was a medley of races preparing for unity through a policy of "blood and iron." Cobden ignored the danger of being unarmed in a world of armaments. His theories were stoutly assailed. "Whatever can be called principle in the Manchester school," said a politician, "depends upon the price of cotton"; and Tennyson ridiculed "the huckster" who would put down war. More cogent was Disraeli's criticism that it was madness to think of universal peace because America and England were rich and prosperous, since "wars are made not by the powers which are contented and satisfied, but by the race or prince who agitates for a position." But a peace party steadily grew, educated either on economic lines by Cobden, or by a friend of humanity like the Quaker John Bright; and foreign policy had henceforth to reckon with criticism from the standpoint of ethics. The Liberals held fast their right of interference for Liberal ideas, the Conservatives advocated peace with security, but the Radicals unfurled a new banner, inscribed with a message of goodwill between nations, and endeavoured to give effect to international law.

**Palmer-
ston's
fall**

The Manchester school built vain hopes of peace on the success of the Great Exhibition, and on the sudden downfall of Palmerston from the height of his triumph. For the last four years he had been in conflict with the court, where the Queen asserted a new authority in the direction of foreign affairs, and where all influences were German in character and reactionary in sentiment. Palmerston's neglect to submit to the sovereign the final drafts of his dispatches; his high-handed rebuffs to Austrian, Greek, and Prussian ambassadors; his open sympathy with Louis Kossuth, had already offended the Queen, the Prince Consort, and the Premier. At length, without the consent of his colleagues, he gave official approval to Louis Napoleon,

Dec. 1851

whose *coup d'état* had made him President of the French Republic. Palmerston believed the new ruler to be no despot, but willing to restore constitutional government. He foresaw in him one of the dominant forces of the next generation, and in face of dangers threatening England's policy in the East a power whose support she would need. From the court and the cabinet came angry demands for a foreign minister who could act "without offering the right hand to rampant despotism, and the left to democratic conspirators," and Palmerston was dismissed. His downfall was regarded throughout Europe as equally grateful to despots and dangerous to liberalism.

1852

Russell's government survived his resignation for a few weeks only, and his successor Lord Derby fell a few months later. As the panic spread that France under the new despotism would become once

Sec. II.

Foreign
AND
Colonial
Policy

1815
TO
1914

more a powerful military state, a war-fever swept through the country, and Wellington's last speech in the Lords, in support of the Militia Bill to arm England against a new Napoleon, marked the height of the agitation. Before the year was out however Queen and ministers were obliged to reverse their policy, and to give public recognition to Napoleon III. as Emperor of the French. The court soon found that the fallen minister had not lost his influence. Palmerston had left a tradition which criticism could not destroy, and the lapse of time cannot wholly obscure. Since England was to him the champion of justice he interpreted intervention as a right, and was always on the side of the people when democracy and despotism fought out their battles abroad. When a mob of draymen at a brewery assaulted Haynau, "the butcher of Hungary," Palmerston laughed at the outrage, and prepared so haughty an explanation for the Austrian Ambassador that Russell was forced to tone it down. The Radicals who presented addresses to Louis Kossuth, with "too much gunpowder" for Cobden and too much "knight-errantry" for Bright, knew that Palmerston had dismayed the government by proposing to receive Kossuth, and had allowed a deputation at the Foreign Office to denounce the emperors of Russia and Austria as odious assassins. So complete were the admiration and trust won from the Radicals by his democratic sympathies, that his colleagues as a whole preferred to cling to the coach rather than dispense with a reckless driver. The middle class saw in "Pam" a statesman prepared at all hazards to defend their country's rights; and the merchant repaid the minister by earning a reputation for commercial integrity. Though the Queen was convinced that he exposed the court to constant risk of alarming complications, there came a time when she realized that her later advisers obliged her to take the military measures which Palmerston refused to threaten. He accorded well with an age in which violent action and humanitarian sentiment contrived an odd companionship: they met in what he looked upon as his "greatest achievement," the forcing of the Brazilians to give up their slave-trade. Though at times opposing arbitration, as contrary to our honour, he suggested a treaty with the United States by which, if a quarrel arose, the two nations should have recourse to the mediation of some friendly Power. At the same time he saw that our navy and our colonies excited such jealousy that it would be difficult to discover impartial arbiters. Even as a staunch free-trader, he had no delusions as to perpetual peace in a world untuned to its reception. Unlike Cobden he would arm first and talk afterwards; he exhorted his country to remember that England, unarmed and unprepared, betrayed her friends, proved unjust to herself, and was unworthy of her mission. The flag was in his eyes an emblem of freedom, and a guarantee of protection. "I look only to the honour and advantage

Sec. II.

Foreign
AND
Colonial
Policy

1815
TO
1914

The
Eastern
Problem

1852

of England," said Palmerston frankly, "and to what offers the fairest prospect of extending her commercial relations, and the system of her influence and power."

Since the great peace the foreign policy of England had been guided according to principles of party, Whig or Tory. But in the confusion and general disruption which followed Peel's acceptance of free trade, the breaking of all ties of party allegiance, and the failure of traditional rules left Russell's ministry without solid support—"a government on sufferance." After its fall the Conservatives lingered a few months in office, till they in their turn were displaced by a coalition of Whigs and Peelites under Lord Aberdeen. Palmerston was relegated to the Home Office, while Russell, and after him Clarendon, conducted foreign affairs. With opposing ideals, and distracted by dissensions, the ill-assorted Cabinet made a sincere effort for the next two years to guide the country through an uneasy period of transition. Within a year the ministry had involved England in a great war, and broken the forty years' peace. The problem of the Ottoman empire, half buried ten years before, was rising in a more ominous form. The Tsar Nicholas believed that the time had now come to recover the predominant position in Turkey which he had won at Unkiar Skelessi and lost at the Conference of London. An excuse for acting was at hand. Since 1774 Russia had claimed the right to protect the Orthodox Faith within the Turkish Empire; dignitaries of the Greek Church guarded the tombs of the Christian kings, appointed the door-keeper for the Holy Sepulchre, or tended the roof of the Chapel of the Nativity. France, on behalf of Latin Christians in Palestine, had a claim of over twelve hundred years to similar privileges, which had been practically lost in the Napoleonic wars. Louis Napoleon, as President or Emperor, was determined to abandon none of these historic rights:

and the duel between France and Russia begun at Constantinople was urged on by the clerical party, and embittered by Napoleon's anger at the Tsar's contempt for his imperial title. To give the Latin monks a key to the Shrine of the Sacred Manger, a cupboard and a lamp in the Virgin's tomb, three great powers were dragged into war. Nothing seemed more remote than the participation of Great Britain. But the government was undecided; to support Turkey was an article of political faith, and the fear of Russian menace to the British position in India was now the dominating influence in foreign policy. The Tsar was misled by the reports of his ambassador and by the speeches of public men as to the will of England to go to war on behalf of a moribund empire; while he himself had long been under the illusion that a permanent conciliation between Russia and England might be effected by a division of power in the east, which would allow to Russia an issue for her ships from the Black Sea, and to

England control of the Red Sea route to India. His proposals to divide the inheritance of the Turk, the "sick man of Europe," were practically the same as he had urged on Aberdeen in his visit nine years before. For a free hand in the Danubian provinces, he offered to England Crete and Egypt. His prevision was remarkable, but we mistrusted the giver. An effort to stave off war by urging moderation on France, and on the Porte reform, was vitiated by the choice of a mediator. Russell, before giving up the Foreign Office to Clarendon, appointed as ambassador to the Porte Lord Stratford de Redcliffe, the Stratford Canning of earlier times. Clarendon distrusted Stratford, but could not recall him; Stratford had a grievance against the Tsar, and had no faith in Russia. Menschikoff, Russian Ambassador at Constantinople, assumed that Russia and Turkey were alone concerned in the dispute, and demanded a protectorate over all Greek Christians which would have given his country a pretext for interference in any part of the Turkish Empire. At Stratford's instigation, the Porte resisted a proposal which left it but a fragment of sovereignty. Russia retorted with an ultimatum, withdrew her ambassador, and occupied Moldavia and Wallachia. British and French ships were dispatched at once to the Dardanelles, and warlike preparations, which tended to inflame rather than allay the crisis, were hurried on. In a last attempt to avert disaster the representatives of Austria, France, Prussia, and Great Britain met at Vienna, and drew up a note for presentation at St. Petersburg and Constantinople; but the diplomats failed at their own trade, for the note was couched in such ambiguous terms as to be of little value. Russia accepted an arrangement which could be interpreted in her favour; Turkey suggested amendments, and had the secret support of Stratford. Feeling assured of English help, an assurance strengthened by the presence of the fleet, she demanded the withdrawal of the Russian forces from the Danubian provinces, and sent troops to enforce the demands. Tentative engagements took place, while the diplomats worked for a settlement. But Napoleon had determined to defy Russia, and we had as much to apprehend from our ally as from our enemy. Aberdeen and Clarendon desired peace, though they saw England "drifting towards war." No resolute word was spoken, but the British fleet was ordered, in spite of the treaty of 1841, to pass through the Bosporus for "defensive operations" in any part of the Black Sea. Measures vacillating yet provocative failed, as they failed at the time of Navarino. Another "untoward event" confounded diplomacy. In reply to an attack upon their army near Bucharest the Russian fleet sank a Turkish squadron in the bay of Sinope. At the news all hope of peace was destroyed. Troops were moved to Malta, and the British and French fleets sailed into the Black Sea. Diplomacy made its final effort, but on Russia's refusal to evacuate the

SEC. II.

FOREIGN AND COLONIAL POLICY

1815 TO **1914**

1853

Nov. 30

SEC. II.

FOREIGN
AND
COLONIAL
POLICY

**1815
TO
1914**

Mar. 27,
1854

**The
Crimean
War**

provinces war was declared. Such was the effect of divided counsels; Aberdeen was irresolute while Palmerston was determined, and an aggressive and uncontrolled Liberalism hastened a conflict with the champion of autocracy — a contest not for the Holy Places, but against the remnants of the Holy Alliance, and the despotic principle which had triumphed in 1849. Russia's attack upon Hungary, her treatment of Poland were counts in a long indictment; but above all these was jealousy at her steady approach towards India and her designs upon the Dardanelles.

War was opened with a light heart. Immense crowds cheered the soldiers and hardly gave them room to pass; the navy left Spithead escorted by the royal yacht. It was soon seen that the Foreign Office and the War Office had failed to work together. The navy was well over the two-power standard, but the army was scarcely larger than that of Belgium. With ill-timed zeal the government separated the departments of Colonies and War. The Duke of Newcastle began work with an entirely new staff; mobilization was a farce; there were no reserves; arms and clothing were insufficient, and no preparation was made for a winter campaign. In four months 11,000 men were landed in Turkey, to fight side by side with the Turks and the French. There was jealousy in the chief command; the active and brilliant St. Arnaud did not see eye to eye with Raglan, whose experience dated back to the Peninsular war, and who was close on seventy. To threaten the communications of the Russian army and force it to fall back, troops were landed at Varna. The next step was to secure a base for operations in Russia and to destroy her naval power by the capture of Sebastopol. At the opening of the war its fall was a daily rumour, but the Allies were far from success. The first engagement took place at the river Alma, north of the fortress. The Russians were posted upon the heights above the stream, and were dislodged after a tremendous struggle. They retreated in good order and were unpursued. In the time gained Menschikoff rendered an attack from the north almost impossible, blocked the harbour by sinking his own ships, and brought up reinforcements. Taking the offensive, he endeavoured to break up the British position at Balaclava. The resistance of our infantry was clinched by a dauntless charge of the heavy cavalry, who routed many times their number. To crown the day by a further success, Raglan sent the Light Cavalry Brigade into action. His orders were misunderstood, and six hundred and seventy-three troopers dashed through a valley towards the Russian batteries. One hundred and ninety-five survived the famous charge. The officers and men were magnificent in daring, and in the next engagement they displayed astounding valour. A sortie was made against the British lines at Inkerman, a position held by the Guards. Masses of Russians came on in the grey dawn, only to be driven back ; when ammunition failed our men clubbed their rifles or used the bayonet, and some even fought with their fists. Yet owing to the numbers of the enemy no assault could be made upon Sebastopol, and the soldiers' battle remained a pointless sacrifice. A winter of arctic severity found the troops totally unprepared. The picturesque uniforms were in rags ; there was neither food nor forage, no shelter, no succour for the wounded ; disease and death were everywhere. A terrific storm tore up the tents, destroyed vast quantities of provisions, and caused incredible suffering. The state of the men leaked out through the correspondent of the *Times* newspaper : " Sharp misery has worn them to the bone ; they have lost all the bravery of war. They are ragged, shoeless, besmeared with mud, infested by vermin, and tortured by scorbutic disease. Their life has been one long troubled miserable dream." Florence Nightingale, by her labours to alleviate their sufferings, became the heroine of the soldiers. The unflinching gallantry of the troops was recognized by the Victoria Cross with its motto " For Valour." But the country, appalled by the revelations of incompetence and mis-management, called for an inquiry into the conduct of the war. The ministry, involved in disputes and recriminations with the military and naval leaders, at length resigned, and after some hesitation the Queen was compelled by public opinion to send for Palmerston. From the pitch of expectation to which it had been led, the country fell into a corresponding gloom. Peace seemed impossible until some of the disgrace was wiped away, and the pacifists, Cobden and Bright, were burned in effigy. Negotiations opened at Vienna broke down upon the neutrality of the Black Sea, but the prolongation of the war called out no protest from the public. The command of the sea enabled a steady stream of men and supplies to reach headquarters, and the Allies were reinforced by fifteen thousand troops from Piedmont. The chief officers were changed, there were gallant attacks on the various redoubts by French and Sardinians : and while the English troops were repulsed in an assault on the Redan, military pride was saved by the heroic defence of Kars under General Fenwick Williams. He had held the town from the beginning of the war, and the flag was still flying when Sebastopol fell, after a year's siege, though he was forced at last to surrender. From the destruction of Russia's naval base on the Black Sea England would have proceeded to destroy Cronstadt, bombard St. Petersburg, restore Finland to Sweden in return for her alliance, and utterly break the power of Russia in the Baltic. But Napoleon refused to hear of a diversion of the war from its first purpose, and insisted on ceasing hostilities.

The popular war produced an unpopular peace : " There was no indication," said a Frenchman, " as to which was the victor and which the vanquished." Reviews and illuminations could not obscure the

SEC. II.

FOREIGN
AND
COLONIAL
POLICY

1815
TO
1914

Nov. 14

Jan. 1855

Sept.

**The
Treaty of
Paris**

SEC. II.

FOREIGN
AND
COLONIAL
POLICY

1815
TO
1914

1856

truth; Britain had sacrificed lives and treasure and obtained little in return, while France secretly concerted with Austria the terms of peace which with slight changes were accepted at the treaty of Paris. For the first time in the nineteenth century the Sultan signed a treaty which did not diminish his territory or authority; on his mere promise to grant to his Christian subjects equality with the Mussulmans, they were left absolutely at his mercy; the neutrality of the Straits and the Black Sea was guaranteed by the great powers. Turkey, secured within and without from European interference, or from Russian attack at sea, obtained what Castlereagh would have given her at Vienna, a place in the concert of the Powers and in the public law of Europe. By the forbidding of all vessels of war and arsenals on the Black Sea, England secured the abolition of a Russian navy which might some day have passed into the Mediterranean. Austria gained the withdrawal of a Russian protectorate in Wallachia and Moldavia, and their independence under Turkish suzerainty; by her insistence a strip of Bessarabia was added to Moldavia. Little did Austria know, commented the Russian ambassador, how many tears and how much blood this altered frontier would cost her. In twenty years the treaty was a dead letter. Turkish reform died. Russia sailed her ships on the Black Sea, fortified its shores, and took back Bessarabia. Guarantees of integrity for Turkey were forgotten. England accepted, not Crete but Cyprus, and occupied Egypt. The only relic of the Conference was the Declaration of Paris, which laid down laws for maritime warfare. England had always asserted, contrary to the general opinion, a right to confiscate enemy goods in neutral vessels. On the invitation of France an attempt was made at an international system. It was agreed that privateering should be abolished; that the neutral flag covers the enemy's goods, except contraband of war; that neutral goods, except contraband of war, are not liable to capture under enemy's flags; that a blockade, to be binding, must be maintained by a force sufficient to prevent access to the enemy's coastline. Such a code chiefly affected Great Britain, whose islands form the heart of a diffuse empire, and whose only safeguard is a navy which in time of war should have the fullest scope. With other nations it was different; each had an interest in the diminution of British sea power, and welcomed a code which effected it. Clarendon signed the Declaration without consulting the government, and though it was never formally ratified by Great Britain nor by the United States, its principles were accepted. The omission to define contraband left us entangled in a net of "juridical niceties." Naval experts deplored a step which made our position insecure, and journals announced the news with their pages in mourning.

The results as well as the motives of the Crimean war were in many respects a gain for liberal principles. The profits of the war had

Sec. II.

Foreign
AND
Colonial
Policy

1815
TO
1914

indeed fallen to Napoleon III. From his place at the head of the Congress of Paris he might look back proudly to the Congress of Vienna. After the struggle, in which England had helped him to win military prestige, largely at the expense of her own, he stood forth as a brilliant leader in European politics, inspired by romantic visions of knightly deeds from Circassia to Mexico, and by his imperial obligation to renew for his country an age of glory. The dread of France, which corresponded to the dread of Russia in the next generation, and to that of Germany to-day, reached its height after the Crimean war. Fear of Napoleon's aggrandizement, which was shared alike by Liberal and Tory, by the court and the whole nation, culminated in the universal panic at the increase of the French fleet, and in the Volunteer movement to avert a dreaded invasion. But France under Napoleon's rule was in the main a liberal power with regard to lesser nationalities. And not the least result of the Crimean war was his success in breaking the alliance of Russia, Prussia, and Austria, and thus preparing the way for the liberation of Italy. In Russia, meanwhile, the corrupt and reactionary system gave way before the anger of the people, who believed it to be the cause of their failure in the war. Moved by the popular impulse, the new Tsar Alexander proceeded to free the serfs and gradually to liberalize the government. Deeply angered at the "ingratitude" of Austria in standing aloof during the Crimean war, Russia denied to her in 1859 the aid to crush Italy which she had given in 1849. With Great Britain a long and embittered hostility had begun. Arbiter of Europe in 1849, Russia now saw her power decrease; against England her bitterness remained. The Tsar resented English friendship with a Mohammedan potentate, and distrusted her obstinate blindness towards the corruptions of Turkish rule. Checked in her march towards Constantinople, Russia bided her time until the Black Sea could be reopened, and turned with the steady pressure of a glacier towards India and the Persian Gulf.

The reverberation of the Crimean war was first felt in India. In that strangely isolated country, cut off by the desert and high lands of Baluchistan, by the Himalayas, and the forested hills of Burmah, the only external attack that could threaten English dominion was from Russia. Afghanistan was the sole road by land to India, and behind its mountains and valleys the steppes and deserts and hills of Turkestan, Khorassan, and north-east Persia were themselves a formidable barrier. At the first advance of Russia towards the deep
passages of the north-west England had sent a small army and a few civilians to occupy Kabul, and having expelled the Amir, Dost Mohammed, the friend of Russia, restored his rival to the throne. An insurrection of the Afghans drove out the foreigners, and in that terrible retreat a single survivor escaped through the snow-covered

Sec. II.
Foreign
and
Colonial
Policy
1815
to
1914

passes to carry the news to the nearest English post. After a few months the tragedy was partially avenged; and an ostentatious triumph was announced with "prancing" proclamations. But Dost Mohammed returned in peace to his throne in Kabul; and the practical defeat of British policy and action lessened British prestige in India. It was somewhat restored by the military successes which followed on Sir Charles Napier's unprovoked aggression on Sind; and by the victories over the Mahratta chief of Gwalior. A more important matter was the Sikh war. Ranjit Sing, the ruler of Lahore, had died, and his Sikh generals were anxious to measure their strength

1845

against the British. They crossed the Sutlej into English territory; but within a brief period their military power was broken at the pitched battles of Moodke, Ferozeshah, Aliwal, and Sabraon, and Lahore was occupied. Peace was made at the cost of Sikh territory

1848-1856

and a limitation of their military forces. The arrival of Lord Dalhousie as Governor-General was the turning point of Anglo-Indian history. Well-intentioned and masterful, he believed that the extension of British rule was the true remedy for all the ills of India. His annexation of the Punjab was forced on him by the Sikh soldiery, who again challenged the British power at Chilienwalah and Goojerat; his annexation of Lower Burmah was the consequence of the ill-treatment of British merchants and insults offered to the captain of a frigate sent to remonstrate; but the annexation of Oudh and of the State of Satara as an escheat to the British Crown was in pursuance of his

Reforms in India

policy of expansion. Dalhousie improved the administration, adjusted the finances, and organized irrigation; but shocked the native princes by forbidding the immemorial custom of adoption where a ruler had no son to inherit his principality and perform the religious rites for the dead father. His successor, a son of George Canning, responding to a demand by the more advanced Indians, offended the feelings of the orthodox by permitting the marriage of widows. In the coast fringe Indians sought western education as the surest passport to government employment and professional success, but throughout native society the effervescence of the new learning produced doubt, suspicion, and dissension; men were shaken by the clash of eastern and western knowledge. In the isolation of India her people had preserved ancient rites and their own peculiar life, differing in tradition and domestic organization from any other community in Asia. They were attached to their civilization, which, though gradually overlaid with gross superstition and monstrous practice, was distinguished by its sacred writings and philosophy, and had a noble tradition of architecture, painting, and skilled crafts. In the foreigner's reforms the orthodox Indian was less pleased by material comfort than displeased by the shocks to his strong conservative instinct which many of the administrative improvements entailed. The people were ignorant, and found continued regulation irksome. These and other causes of dissatisfaction more recondite gathered force with the conviction that an old Asiatic civilization could find no appeal to European rulers but by the sword.

While India was shaken by this contest of ideals and interests the events of the Crimean war furnished insidious gossip for the bazaars and diminished the dread of English power. Hostility to alien rule was intensified by the humiliating sense that the will of the foreigner was enforced by an insignificant army, which had been depleted by the troops withdrawn to the Crimea and China till the English soldiers were outnumbered by eight to one. In the native army religious excitement had been roused by the distribution of a new rifle with cartridges, part of which had to be bitten off before use; the story spread that in their manufacture the grease of cattle or of swine was used, the touching of which was an abomination to Hindus and Mohammedans respectively. The Indian government at once issued new cartridges for the troops, but suspicion still haunted the soldiers. Rumours and prophecies were spread abroad, and mysterious messages passed from hand to hand. Local mutinies began with the outbreak in Meerut and spread to the cantonments in Hindustan. The mutineers made for Delhi, where the last of the Moghuls kept a precarious state — a city which in their hopes was again to be the glorious centre of a Moghul empire. From Delhi the insurrection swept down the valley of the Jumna by Agra, over Central India and Bundelkhand, and reached its greatest force in Oudh, annexed only a year before, and along the valley of the sacred Ganges by Cawnpore and Benares. Traditions of old dynasties, the ambitions of local chieftains, and religious fanaticism, were united against the foreigner. A few instances alone can be given of the peril and heroism of those tragic days. In Cawnpore 800 Europeans were shut in a temporary fortification with a garrison of 210; after a fatal siege in the summer heat, almost starving, they surrendered on the promise of a safe conduct by the Rajah of Bithoor, commonly known as Nana Sahib, and claiming to be the adopted heir of the last Mahratta Peishwa, whose adoption had been disallowed under Dalhousie's edict; but the fugitives had hardly embarked upon the Ganges when the mutineers opened fire, killed a large number, and hacked most of the survivors in pieces. The women and children were massacred in cold blood and their bodies thrown into a well, only just before forces arrived for their relief. British troops supported by Sikhs were sent to relieve Delhi, but were themselves besieged on the awful ridge they held, and for three months suffered every horror of exposure to the Indian sun, of cholera and disease, of assaults day and night, and a deluge of fire from the fortifications, till reinforcements arrived, and the city and palace were occupied. Havelock and Outram hastened on to the

SEC. II.

FOREIGN
AND
COLONIAL
POLICY

1815
TO
1914

**The
Indian
Mutiny**

1856

June 6–27

July 15

Sept. 21

Sec. II.

Foreign
AND
Colonial
Policy

1815
to
1914

Sept. 25

help of Lucknow, the second city after Calcutta, filled with mutinous soldiers, where almost a thousand Europeans, men, women, and children, and the bulk of the 32nd Regiment, with some loyal native troops, were gathered in the Residency and a group of houses in a small park below it — buildings never intended for defence. On the second day of the siege Sir Henry Lawrence, Governor of Oudh, had been killed, but in their absolute isolation the garrison held out for three months under General Inglis until aid came, and a month later the city was retaken by Colin Campbell. The government hurriedly diverted troops from the China war, from Persia, from Madras, and Ceylon; and by the end of the year the danger to England had passed away. The revolt had been mostly limited to the army and the troops of native princes. India was preserved to the Empire by the gallantry of the British army, the fidelity of most of the native princes and of the Sikh soldiers, and the assistance lent by the Maharajah of Nepal, from whose hill state came the hardy Gurkha soldiers.

India under the Crown

For a time the terror and rage kindled by the revolt broke out in deeds of vengeance, and extreme excesses were indulged in on both sides. The Governor, dreading the dangers of an embittered conflict, sought to mitigate these passions, and by his courage and magnanimity earned the honourable nickname of " Clemency Canning." While the mutiny still raged, he issued a proclamation exhorting the East India Company to refrain from unreasoning vengeance. " We have had bloody enmities with every tribe and race in India," he wrote, " but we have never yet treated them when vanquished with sweeping contempt and hatred. It will be a bad day for us when that word becomes naturalized in India." His attitude was condemned by those who demanded " Saxon domination," stringent laws for the natives, and the exclusion of the Indian from all places of trust and authority. If that is " Saxon domination," said Canning, " the less we have of it the better. Justice, and that as stern and inflexible as law and might can make it, I will deal out. But I will never allow an angry or discriminating act or word to proceed from the Government of India so long as I am responsible for it." His own policy of confiscating to the State the soil of the entire province of Oudh was vehemently impugned in England, but he justified himself by re-granting it to the proprietors on condition of payment of the revenue and of loyalty to the British Crown. These grants are now prized by the proprietors, or Talukdars, as their indefeasible title deeds, and Canning's policy would have been admirable if it had only been accompanied by adequate provision for the cultivators of the soil. This omission was not rectified till very recent times. Not only the dangers of the mutiny, but the rapid accessions of territory, and the new problems of government, forced Englishmen to feel their grave responsibility

Sec. II.

Foreign
AND
Colonial
Policy

1815
TO
1914

for so vast a dependency. The whole extent of subject India, with two or three hundred millions of inhabitants, forty-three separate races, and twenty-one languages in common use, was still governed by Pitt's India Bill, and her trade by the directors of the East India Company. Palmerston brought in a Bill for the better government of India, and at his temporary fall from power the Conservatives assured Canning of their support. They framed the final bill by which the Court of Directors and the Board of Control were abolished, and the powers and territory of the East India Company were at length vested in the Crown. The Queen was proclaimed Sovereign of India. Her first Viceroy ruled in Calcutta, and at Westminster a Secretary of State was made responsible to Parliament. In the later development of this great dependency the officials of Irish and Scottish origin played a prominent part in the work of peaceful and humane government, winning for themselves a high position as administrators, nearer in comprehension to the subject peoples, and intelligent in softening the more rigid lines of rule imposed by conquest.

Scarcely was the mutiny ended when Indian troops were hurried to the China coast, where England had lately made Hong-Kong her farthest station in the east. One of Palmerston's earliest acts had been to admit English merchants to the China trade, until then a monopoly of the East India Company. Stripped of its old prudent regulations, the new trade was carried on with grave disorders and complications. The Chinese, resentful of intrusion, forbade the import of opium, "the foreign curse," amid protests of the Indian government at their loss of revenue, and angry outcries from the merchants, nine-tenths of them engaged in the opium trade, who declared that the Chinese only closed their harbours to opium as a crafty excuse to bar out all trade with foreigners. An opium war became in the popular view a war for the "open door" to commerce. Confused and unequal conflicts followed the coast-guards and smugglers, Chinese officials and British agents. Palmerston, with his brisk methods of coercion, demanded of China a commercial treaty, or the cession of one or more islands from which Great Britain could trade, and sent a naval force to blockade the rivers and secure the necessary islands; with such success in assault and capture that the treaty of Nanking ceded to England Hong-Kong, opened five other ports to her trade, and granted rich indemnities. Britain required only such trading rights as should be extended to other nations. America hastened to make a treaty, and to stipulate that if ministers of European peoples were allowed at Peking her envoy too should be received. France with a powerful squadron obtained her commercial treaty and a protectorate of Roman Catholic converts. The whole world, Shaftesbury said, "was intoxicated with the

Sec. II.

Foreign
AND
Colonial
Policy

1815
TO
1914

1856

1857

1858

1860

1861–1869

Euro-
pean
wars

1859–1878

prospect of the China trade." One war led to another. The Chinese, regarding the English as the source of all trouble, imprisoned their
seamen and murdered their missionaries. A Chinese lorcha, the
Arrow, flying the British flag, was seized by Chinese authorities who
declared the crew to be pirates. The English representative, Sir John
Bowring, required the release of the men and ordered the bombardment of Canton. France joined with England; the United States
and Russia helped to keep the ring. In Parliament Cobden condemned the course of action as violent and arbitrary, and the Government was defeated—"a discussion," said Gladstone, "doing more
honour to the House of Commons than any I can remember." But
Palmerston appealed to the country in defence of Bowring, whose life,
he said, "an insolent barbarian" had attempted. The merchants
once more rallied to the cry of British interests, and with such alacrity
that Palmerston for the first time in his life stood at the head of a
compact majority in the new Parliament. A Sepoy army crossed the
seas to the assault and capture of Canton; and the British envoy,
Lord Elgin, in the treaty of Tientsin, forced on the Chinese a legalized
trade in opium, with other terms yet more obnoxious—the admission
of foreign legations to Peking, toleration of native Christians, and their
uncontrolled protection by foreign powers. The resistance of China,
as fierce and cruel as it was patriotic, was broken by the pillage and
burning of the palace at Peking and the levying of a huge indemnity.
In the rebellions that followed the American Ward was as famous an
officer of Chinese Government as the English Gordon; an Irishman,
Sir Robert Hart, organized the new customs in faithful service to
China. All European nations hastened to profit by like treaties,
Prussia the first, then Denmark, Spain, Holland, Belgium, Italy, and
Austria. China, in the words of her greatest statesman, seemed about
to be sliced like a water-melon. At the same time foreign trade was
forced on Japan by the powers that had imposed it on China—
England, France, and Russia following the United States—with a
corresponding tale of outrages, revolt, wars, and compensations to
the invaders. The competing powers had now laid their several
claims to the wealth of the Pacific shores.

The conflict for world-empire however was delayed for twenty
years by a series of five great wars within Europe itself. The
congress of Vienna had left some ten peoples, or groups of peoples,
without national life or security, and of these only two small powers,
Greece and Belgium, had as yet won independence. The Crimean
war, which ended the long peace, and the imperfect settlement of the
treaty of Paris, let loose the fears and jealousies of Europe, and
opened a new era of conflict and reconstruction. England stood
aloof; but as the determination to accomplish the national ideal
passed from country to country, the boundaries of peoples were

SEC. II.

FOREIGN
AND
COLONIAL
POLICY

1815
TO
1914

The Rise
of Italy

remade, their ambitions recast, and in the overturning of the old balance of power the European concert was swept aside.

"All the territorial arrangements on this side of the Alps are complete," wrote Castlereagh in 1815. Beyond the mountains Italy was still struggling for unity. The "cry of woe" which echoed throughout Europe was due to mediæval forms of misgovernment in the Papal states, the hard hand of Austria in Lombardy, and the scandalous rule of the Bourbon kings in Sicily and Naples. The aspirations of Italy centred round the kingdom of Piedmont-Sardinia, with its liberal institutions and its small but gallant army. The republicanism of Mazzini, and the work of the secret societies, had been discredited by the failure of forlorn revolts. On the other hand Cavour, the prime minister of Sardinia, was a statesman of the first rank. Some of his most impressionable years were spent in England; he had written upon the Irish question, and studied English methods of agriculture. He saw in the power of industry and science the source of political freedom; "railways," said he, "were to stitch up the boot." Eager to cultivate English support, he sent Italian goods to the Great Exhibition, lured the Liberals with a promise of free trade, and furthered his cause by supplying our writers with material, our press with facilities. King Victor Emmanuel visited Windsor and impressed the Court by his courage and honesty. Panizzi, librarian of the British Museum, laboured to create a public opinion favourable to "that most interesting and unfortunate country." Piedmont was made an example; her leaders were neither republicans nor advocates of assassination, but Liberals, who paid their debts and conducted the government upon a sound financial basis. Such a combination of ideals and efficiency won English sympathy. Palmerston and Russell were pronounced adherents, and the minister at Turin, Sir James Hudson, was "more Italian than the Italians themselves." Gladstone had witnessed political trials in Naples, and proclaimed Neapolitan misrule, with all its horrors, as "the negation of God erected into a system of government." The English Whig recalled his contests for Belgium and Greece; the Radical supported a small state which in the name of freedom attacked the outworks of clerical privilege; Protestant zeal approved a movement which challenged the Pope, and even Lord Shaftesbury "the Huguenot," though no radical, welcomed an anti-papal rising. Cavour in return encouraged the Bible Society, provided its agents did not excite disorder in ardent endeavours to convert the Piedmontese. Step by step the cause of the "noble little country" gained ground. The utmost enthusiasm was aroused when, at the invitation of Napoleon, Cavour sent an army to the Crimea, and by this courageous act allied himself with the democratic powers and established his position in the councils of Europe. ·He obtained at the congress of

1851

1855

1856

SEC. II.

FOREIGN
AND
COLONIAL
POLICY

1815
TO
1914

Paris a discussion on the affairs of Italy. Our envoy, Lord Clarendon, spoke with warmth and indignation, but when on his return Lord Lyndhurst, a true friend to Italy, moved to condemn the Austrian occupation the motion was withdrawn at Clarendon's request, as though, said a statesman, we had barked and then not ventured to bite. Cavour indeed, by revealing his desire for war against Austria, had alarmed Clarendon, who hoped that the pressure of France and England could provide a peaceful solution of the Italian question. "If our Allies desert us," said Cavour, in an outburst of disappointment, "the triumph of Austria and the Pope will be complete."

This danger was increased by the fall of the Whigs. Frequent shelter given to political refugees, from Kossuth and Mazzini to lesser fugitives, had made London in the eyes of foreign sovereigns "a den of conspirators." An Italian exile, Orsini, well known in society, attempted to assassinate Napoleon by bombs made in Birmingham; the indignation of France forced Palmerston to frame a Bill which, preserving the right of asylum, converted conspiracy from misdemeanour to a felony; but public resentment at any alteration of the law on the behest of a foreign power drove the Whigs from office. The Tory government and the Court, clinging to their tradition of "peace and order," dreaded the tearing up of the treaties of 1815 in Italy or elsewhere, as certain to lead to war and to another period of Napoleonic ambitions,—fears which were realized in the wars of 1859, 1866, and 1870, though these did not end in Napoleonic aggrandizement. Lord Derby, like Castlereagh, hoped by agreement with the central states of Prussia and Austria to maintain a balance of power against danger. But this renewal, in a more peaceful way, of Pitt's policy involved leaving Austria mistress of Italy, and compelled English opposition to the Italian liberal movement. Queen Victoria supported the view of Lord Malmesbury, the foreign secretary, that Austria's title to Lombardy was as good as that of England to Ireland, "quivering in our grasp," and that the Neapolitan government had a right to deal with revolutionaries in its own manner. Dreading the consequences of Cavour's "diabolic energy," the Conservatives sought rather to palliate the grievances of Italy than to aid her by arms or diplomacy. Cavour turned to Napoleon, who dramatically pledged his support. While preparations for war were accelerated, Malmesbury urged a conference to enforce disarmament. France wavered, and Cavour in despair accepted the proposal. But Austria, confident of victory, played into his hands; the Emperor hurled an ultimatum at Piedmont and declared war upon the combined forces of France and Sardinia. One province after another rallied to the cause of Italian unity. The rapid success of the allies amazed and disconcerted the whole of Europe. Prussia, restless upon the Rhine, threatened to take up arms in defence of a German state. Not only was Napoleon fearful for France, but he saw that his retainer might fast become an independent colleague. The French reproached him with raising a possible rival in the Mediterranean. After the victories of Magenta and Solferino he deserted his ally, and concluded a truce with Francis Joseph at Villafranca. Lombardy alone was freed. The great betrayal forced Cavour to resign; and Italy, confronted with Austria and France, could not hope to achieve alone her unity and independence. In her extreme peril she found help in England. When the downfall of Derby's ministry was announced the representative of Sardinia, waiting in the lobby, threw up his hat with joy. The papers which might have justified their foreign policy were withheld from the House in inscrutable fashion by Disraeli. In June, at the very crisis of Italy's fate, Palmerston barely scraped back into power with a majority of only thirteen votes. Instantly his foreign minister Russell rejected the proposal of a European conference, proclaimed the Italians to be the best judges of their own affairs, and asserted that the British government viewed with sympathy the prospect of a people building up the edifice of their independence amid the good wishes of Europe. "You are blessed night and morning," said his nephew, "by twenty millions of Italians."

It was England's view that the various provinces should confirm their union by a popular vote, and Napoleon, whose power rested on universal suffrage, could not well resist. He was paid for his help by the cession of Savoy and Nice, a sacrifice so great that only the timely return of Cavour rendered it possible. Bologna and Parma, Tuscany and Emilia voted with scarce a dissentient voice for union with Piedmont. But the south was yet to be won, and Russell supported Cavour in frustrating the intervention of the Powers. It had been Napoleon's object to establish in north Italy a weak liberal state dependent on himself against Austria, and to reform the governments of the Pope and the Neapolitan Bourbons under French influence. Palmerston and Russell, on the other hand, proposed to check the dreaded power of Napoleon III. by raising up a liberal kingdom strong enough to drive both France and Austria beyond its frontiers. They accepted Hudson's view that a united Italy would gravitate to alliance with Austria and Prussia against France—a prophecy fulfilled later in the Triple Alliance. Sicily and Naples were liberated by Garibaldi and his thousand volunteers, part of the papal territory was annexed, and Victor Emmanuel was hailed king of Italy. The British fleet, which under Nelson had aided the excesses of the Neapolitan court, now as a friendly neutral at Naples gave moral support to the King and to Garibaldi: when Napoleon threatened to retain the Bourbons in Sicily, a strong remonstrance from England compelled the French admiral to withdraw his squadron from Gaeta. The success of Palmerston and Russell in defeating the schemes of

Sec. II.

Foreign
AND
Colonial
Policy

1815
to
1914

The
Italian
nation

1860

1861

SEC. II.
FOREIGN
AND
COLONIAL
POLICY
1815
TO
1914

Napoleon III., and establishing a united Italy able to stand alone, remains the greatest achievement of English diplomacy in the century. Within a month the Parliament elected by various states met at Turin, and England was the first power which accorded recognition to the monarchy. The death of Cavour called forth a tribute in Parliament such as is rarely given to a foreign statesman, and cries of applause greeted the eulogies spoken by Palmerston and Russell. Robert and Elizabeth Browning and George Meredith gave noble expression to the feeling of the country. No sovereign

1864

could have met with a more royal reception than did Garibaldi when he came to our shores. He was accorded a gala night at the opera and given the freedom of the City of London. But the most striking tribute came from the English people. Trade unions and benefit societies escorted him through London; miles of human beings lined the streets and flags decorated every window. "I like to be called the brother of the working-man," said their guest, "in every part of the world." So striking was the evidence of democratic feeling that when his visit terminated abruptly there were politicians who said that he was hurried out of the country. Thousands of those who welcomed the "pure patriot" lived to see the fulfilment of his

1866

dreams. During the struggle between Prussia and Austria, Italy, though defeated on land and sea, obtained Venetia, and it was only the greater issue of the Franco-Prussian war which obscured the

1870

importance of the silent conquest of Rome and the withdrawal of the French troops. "The people of England," said Victor Emmanuel, "that home of liberty, nobly affirmed our right to be the arbiters of our own fate, and they were liberal to us in their good offices, the memory of which will endure for ever."

**The
Rise of
Prussia**

The union of Italy quickened the imagination and hopes of the German nation, as the Napoleonic empire in France had already deeply stirred national rivalries. Prussia, inspired by the memory of Frederick the Great, resolved to revoke the dual confederation made at Vienna and to challenge Austria for the leadership of the German race. Her great future had already been predicted. "The Allies," said Talleyrand at the Congress, "have pledged themselves to leave Prussia with ten millions of her people. If she be so left she will soon have twenty millions of her people, and all Germany will be subject to her." Heeren, a Göttingen

1821

professor, apprehended that a united German monarchy seeking to attain that preponderance which her central situation demanded would dig the grave of European liberty. Prussia steadily pursued

1844

her aims; her Zollverein gradually drew into its sphere all the states north of Austria, blending commercial interests with national ideals. Aspirations for a united Germany resounded in the triumphant

1840

songs, "Die Wacht am Rhein" and "Deutchland über Alles." England thought of her as a homely and peaceful nation nurtured

SEC. II.

FOREIGN
AND
COLONIAL
POLICY

1815
TO
1914

on music and philosophy, a misconception fostered by the German influence so powerful at Court. Cobden regarded the mild form of absolutism practised in Prussia as the best government in Europe for the mass of the people; and Russell, in spite of Disraeli's scoff at his "mystical hallucination of German nationality," was convinced that she would "establish representative institutions." But Prussia had not forgiven Castlereagh for thwarting her aims at the Congress, she had been angered by the Monroe doctrine which hampered her growing trade with South America, and she was attacking the liberal constitution granted by William IV. to Hanover at the time when his death severed it from the English crown. English diplomatists were suspicious of her bearing; Stratford Canning resented the fictitious interviews which the Prussian minister at the Porte put into his mouth, "a scheme of treachery almost unparalleled even in diplomacy"; and Malmesbury declared that the Prussian government circulated false reports of his conversations over Schleswig-Holstein. The necessity of understanding her aims was urged by Robert Morier, a diplomatist who was in Germany when a trivial incident aroused bitter feeling. An English officer, equally ignorant of Prussian law and the German language, became involved in a dispute about a seat in a railway carriage. Neither side would tender an apology, and the affair assumed an international importance justifying the publication of a blue-book. An indignant speech of the Prime Minister led to recriminations in the Prussian Parliament. "Has the devil a son?" said a German rhymester, "he is assuredly Palmerston." The press did "enormous and wanton mischief" by a series of attacks upon everything Prussian. A quarrel so easily misunderstood and exaggerated had far-reaching effects. The Crown Prince had in 1858 married our Princess Royal; and England's reputation for arrogance was increased, and her influence at Berlin lessened, at the very moment when Prussian Liberalism was making a last struggle for power, and a strong party favoured an Anglo-Prussian alliance. But all hopes of constitutional government were extinguished by the army bill which Otto von Bismarck forced on the nation; the state of Prussia, he affirmed, was too critical to venture a constitution; great questions were not decided by speeches and votes, but by "blood and iron." His single purpose was to beat back the dangers that threatened every German frontier. To protect the east, and secure his country against France on the west, he gained the alliance of Russia by a signal service The constitution granted to the Poles at the Congress of Vienna was revoked in 1832, and their hopes now rested on the liberal policy which the Tsar had inaugurated after the Crimean War. "Enemies from abroad" procured their ruin; a new and harsh system of conscription in Poland for the Russian army led to a desperate revolt, encouraged from Prussia. Confidential correspondence lately discovered at Cracow

1837

1855

1858

1861

1862

The Polish revolt

1863

SEC. II.
FOREIGN
AND
COLONIAL
POLICY
1815
TO
1914
has revealed the mistrust and jealousy which prevented common action by the powers. Napoleon suggested a congress. " If the congress had been a house of Babel," said the Queen of Holland, " at least it would have taught to lurking democracy the sincere desire of the governments to do something to settle claims and wrongs which are growing daily more clamorous." English sympathy was largely with the Poles; but intervention was impossible without the support of France, and Napoleon was engaged in a fantastic attempt to create a Catholic Empire in Mexico. Austria feared the revolution as an example to her own possessions. Bismarck, in spite of the liberals, threw his country on the side of the Tsar and secured the triumph of Russia. His eastern frontier safe, he turned to make Prussia a maritime power commanding, and linking together, ports on the Baltic

The Danish war

and the North Sea. The duchies of Schleswig and Holstein were united to Denmark by a vague personal tie, and when in 1848 they revolted against a threat of incorporation they were assisted by Prussian troops. Disraeli alone in England protested against this attempt to convert the " dreamy and dangerous nonsense " of nationality into an excuse for Prussia to take the Baltic ports and the mouth of the Elbe.

1850

Before long Prussia was forced by Austria to withdraw her army from Schleswig-Holstein, whose relations with Denmark, and whose com-

1852

plications of succession, were regulated by the Protocol of London. But Bismarck still regarded the " liberation of the Duchies " as a means for Prussian aggrandizement. The quarrel burst out again

1863

with the accession of a new king of Denmark. In return for his support to the dynasty Bismarck demanded a marine station at Kiel, and the right to construct a Prussian canal between the two seas. The aggressions of Denmark on the liberties of the provinces, and its dynastic disputes, enabled him to lure Austria into a scheme for a united invasion of the duchies. Fired by their success in Italy, Palmerston and Russell desired intervention, and in their speeches pledged the government to maintain, even by arms, the integrity of Denmark. But Napoleon, who had proposed a congress, refused to join, and Russia held to her new ally. The navy alone could not affect the issue, and the army was inadequate. While the country sympathized with a small nation, the Queen supported Prussia, and asserted that " any encouragement to Denmark would be fatal." A conference was unsuccessful, for the Danes trusting to English help refused compromise, and England had to stand aside while the

1864

duchies were overrun by the joint armies of Austria and Prussia. The government had pledged her good name in foreshadowing engagements she was compelled to disown. Had England been impartial she might have acted as mediator, but as a partisan she was out of court. Disraeli lamented the harm which was done, and taunted the government with its want of system in foreign affairs.

Even Cobden, who welcomed the blow given to intervention, condemned our policy. After fifty-eight years of public life, in which only nine had been spent out of office, Palmerston was now by his death spared the spectacle of an advancing rival whose great destiny he had not foreseen. His system of foreign policy died with him, and the helplessness of England in the matter of the duchies made Bismarck regard her as a nation negligible in continental affairs. "The theory of the balance of power," said Bright, "is pretty nearly dead and buried." For two years Europe was entangled in intrigues. Bismarck pacified Austria by proposing to divide the duchies; he bribed Italy to neutrality by promising possession of Venetia, drawing her towards the German alliance foreseen by Hudson; he secured the acquiescence of France by deceptive offers to Napoleon of illusory frontiers on the Rhine and Belgium. When his plans were completed he suddenly denounced the action of Austria in the duchies, demanded of the Frankfort Diet reform of the federal constitution of Germany, ordered his troops to occupy Holstein, and finally declared the German federation dissolved. A war of seven weeks ended with the triumph of Sadowa. Austria ceded Venetia to Italy, and withdrew from Germany. Prussia gained her coveted position on the sea, and took her place as head of a newly created "North German Confederation"—henceforth the greatest military power in Europe. The stupendous revolution was little observed in England by a people wholly occupied in Hyde Park riots, in a reconstruction of public finance, and in projects for a wider reform bill. Tories and Whigs saw in a greater Prussia increased security against Russia and France, while to the Court it gave added brilliance to a royal alliance.

Bismarck and Napoleon now remained the chief figures on the European stage. France represented the last menace to a Prussian frontier, and the menace increased after the expulsion of Austria from the German Confederation, when the South German Catholic states, in their hatred of the hegemony of Protestant Prussia, turned to Napoleon III. in secret negotiations. Bismarck saw his opportunity to consolidate German unity, and define a military frontier to the west. The failure of Napoleon's romantic adventure to set up a Catholic and Latin empire in Mexico had diminished his prestige; he had alienated the sympathies of Italy and England; the weakness of Austria had deprived him of a possible ally; and he was lured to a fatal step over the old question of the Spanish succession. When he resented the candidature of a prince of the House of Hohenzollern it was withdrawn, but in a rash attempt to obtain further assurances a French envoy was dispatched to Ems, and the account of his interview with the king of Prussia was distorted by Bismarck and sent to the press. At a moment when Europe appeared supremely tranquil the telegram was answered by a declaration of war. Ten days later Bismarck announced through

SEC. II.

FOREIGN
AND
COLONIAL
POLICY

1815
TO
1914

1865

*The
Austrian
war*

1866

July 3

Aug. 24

**The
French
war**

1865

1870

Sec. II.

Foreign
and
Colonial
Policy

1815
to
1914

the *Times* that Napoleon had recently plotted to annex Belgium; the English government, deeply concerned by the revelation, decided that if either combatant crossed the Belgian frontier, Great Britain would assist the other in defending neutral territory, but would not engage in further operations. Important declarations were appended. Gladstone affirmed that our action was voluntary, that a guarantor might weigh the circumstances of a case before honouring his security, but he considered that England was not forced to stand aside because neither Austria nor Russia chose to intervene. A vote increasing the army and navy showed Belgium that England was in earnest, but to the bitter disappointment of the French her sympathies leaned at first in favour of Prussia from the belief that France had provoked the conflict expecting an easy invasion of Germany. The course of the war soon showed that one combatant was prepared and united, the other unprepared and the victim of her dynasty.

Within six weeks Sedan was fought and France defeated. After the fall of Napoleon Gladstone and Lord Granville refused the appeal made by Thiers to England first among the powers, for mediation on behalf of the French in their extremity; and in spite of his remonstrances against their abdication of any part in continental affairs, they left France to deal alone with Germany. The severity of her punishment, the cession of Alsace-Lorraine, the ruthlessness of the Prussian troops, combined to react on public opinion. England had maintained her neutrality amid the indignation of both sides—"too holy to fight," wrote Morier, "but rubbing our hands at the roaring trade we are driving in cartridges and ammunition. We are heaping up to ourselves the undying hatred of this German race that will henceforth rule the world." The proximity of France enabled her to buy from us coal, munitions, and horses. Prussians reproached our government, and recalled the day when Wellington and Blücher joined hands at Waterloo; we allowed free trade, they said, in instruments of slaughter, though we could always prevent the sale of arms to the Fenians. "The English are more hated at this moment than the French," wrote the Crown Princess, and the warning was repeated by countless diplomats and correspondents. A further danger was disclosed in the discovery that Bismarck had ensured Russia's neutrality by a promise to refrain from protest when his

ally violated the treaty of Paris and reopened the Black Sea to her warships. Palmerston had seen, as Gladstone saw, that the restriction could hardly be permanent, but the deliberate breach of a treaty without the consent of the signatories was of evil omen. Menaced as England was by disputes with the United States, and hampered by the helplessness of France, she found herself in a

dangerous position, but a threat of war won for her a conference in London. Though Russia's action received formal sanction, the

Sec. II.

Foreign
AND
Colonial
Policy

1815
to
1914

The
British
Empire

principle was affirmed that no power could alter a treaty or liberate itself from an engagement without the consent of the European concert.

The elevation at Versailles of the king of Prussia to the place of German Emperor, and the Treaty of Frankfort dismembering and humiliating France, changed the course of European history. The rise of an overpowering military nation, prophesied by every continental statesman since Talleyrand, was accepted in England with satisfaction. " A strong Germany under Prussian leadership," said an observer, " had been the life-long dream of Baron Stockmar, under whose influence Queen Victoria and Prince Albert had placed this fundamental idea as their chief hope for the new Europe which was to arise from the ashes of 1848." " So if Sadowa and Sedan had gone amiss," wrote Lord Morley later, " the resplendent orb of German radiance and intellectual power would never have broken through the nebulous skies of a disunited fatherland and diffused its beams over the civilized world." The English in general watched almost as disinterested spectators the fall and rise of continental empires. England, in fact, stood apart from the European conflicts that followed the Crimean war. Her concern lay beyond the European border. From 1856 onwards there was scarcely a year in which Great Britain was not at war in some far region of the globe, pushing out her frontiers over ever-increasing territories, or defending her settlements. An empire had arisen from the sea, the first island empire in the world's history. If its swift expansion, and the complicated administration of subject peoples, exceeded in extent and degree all former records, those did not constitute its original character or its ultimate strength. They were of less significance than the steady movement of self-government by which England was establishing a power wholly new in the tale of empires ancient or modern. The development of the German state and of the British dominions moved forward step by step during the same years. Europe watched the deliberate creation of a typical military empire, of single design and marvellous organization, an empire inspired by traditions from the past of Charlemagne, and of Barbarossa. The work of England lay in half-consciously moulding her own scattered colonies on the other side of the world along peaceful and democratic lines into a confederation of common consent—a bold advance into the future, where the past could give neither pattern nor experience, and where the design and organization of statesmen were subordinated to the living spirit of free peoples. Twenty years before the Crimean war she had begun to convert the colonies of English race into the " five free nations " of an empire planted in the great oceans. While Palmerston busied himself with China or Spain, the colonists were preparing the way for the independence to which the bolder

HISTORY OF THE ENGLISH PEOPLE.

SEC. II.

FOREIGN
AND
COLONIAL
POLICY

1815
TO
1914

*The old
imperialism*

1837

1840

**Freedom
of
Canada**

1837-1839

spirits aspired. "Emancipate your colonies," wrote Bentham in 1793, and pointed the way to a new policy. The mercantile system had been discredited by the loss of America, and a new empire slowly took shape, rising from the ruins of the old. The terror of the American revolt and of the Napoleonic wars had imposed strict military discipline and command; and during the first half of the nineteenth century imperialism stood for rigid and centralized control. As a measure of greater security Parliament took the place of the Crown as supreme authority. No new territory was granted a local legislature: in all the governor was absolute, subject only to the minister at home. The colonies, in complete commercial and financial subjection, suffered at times considerable loss and inconvenience. Ministers who encouraged a tentative growth of democratic principles in England were fearful lest colonial democracy might become a menace to the Mother country. Whigs and Tories alike opposed the doctrine of freedom; even Russell held that extended self-government was outside the pale of practical politics, and Wellington persisted that "responsible government and the sovereignty of Great Britain were completely incompatible." But the same spirit of freedom which by the Reform bill had captured the outworks of responsible government in England against all obstacles and prejudices was also astir in colonial life.

A small band of men endowed with imagination determined to show the truth of Bentham's prophecy that empire was not inconsistent with self-government. Charles Buller and Edward Gibbon Wakefield—"a democratic man in all fibres of him," said Carlyle—were the apostles of a new age and a noble future. They foresaw the opportunities which the colonies would give to the wealth of England, to her industries and shipping, and to the vigour and daring of her people. They deplored the slowness of politicians to grasp the importance of the new lands, and decried the rigidity and lack of sympathy shown by "Mr. Mothercountry," the embodiment of Downing Street rule; their remedy was to train the colonies themselves by control of municipal affairs to wider duties. They soon had occasion to test their creed. "You have got another Ireland growing up in every colony you possess," said Peel, and the issue bore witness to the truth of his warning. Canada had in her representative assemblies a shadow of self-government; but the reality of power lay with a Governor and an administrative Council responsible only to Downing Street. To the jealousy between the council and the assemblies was added the racial strife of English and French Canadians, and a conflict between the democracy and the local oligarchy, or "family compact" of the church, magistracy, and banks. At length the provinces of Upper and Lower Canada broke into open revolt, and for two years political passion drove insurgents to resist the law, while the ruling class perverted justice in the name of order. Refugees crossed the frontier and mingled with the wild and lawless men who lived near the Great Lakes. America justly complained of disturbance so near her borders. At the same time the strong ties of the frontier colonists with their neighbours in the United States foreshadowed a powerful agitation for the absorption of Canada. Loyalists, suspicious of every mark of sympathy as an attempt to seduce Canada, cried for vengeance on the French Canadians, and for war with the United States. Both countries threatened a campaign of plunder and reprisal. In this tragic and disastrous confusion Lord Durham was sent to Canada as High Commissioner, and with him went Buller and Wakefield. " Never, I believe, " wrote Buller, " did men embark in any public undertaking with more singleness and honesty of purpose." Durham's first step was daring and conciliatory; he proclaimed an amnesty and released the prisoners. The effect in the United States was instantaneous, and for a time jealousy was forgotton in admiration for his boldness. He had rallied Canada to the Crown. But at home Melbourne's ministry was divided; it failed to support him in the amnesty; and within six months of his departure Durham returned to England baffled and heartbroken. In his passion of imperial patriotism he sent to the press, as a matter of " grave urgency," his report drawn up by Buller and Wakefield. " It needs no change in the principles of government," ran the report, " no invention of a new constitutional theory. . . . It needs but to follow out consistently the principles of the British constitution." Many detailed reforms were insisted on, but above all was the principle of responsible government as the Magna Charta of the colonies, coupled with " a good system of municipal institutions." The Crown should " henceforth consult the wishes of the people in the choice of its servants "; the executive Council should no longer retain office when they lost the confidence of the representative Assembly. Lord Durham and his helpers left their mark on imperial affairs by their bold spirit of constitutional liberty. They foretold the future great. ness of the dominions, the pride of nationality within the colonies, and the need of giving to the new peoples a country of their own, a country whose course they would themselves direct, and whose free existence they would defend against all enemies. Though Durham's mind was concentrated on Canada and its dangers, he laid down principles which made his report " the text-book of every advocate of colonial freedom." Russell accepted his advice, and Canada received representative government, with a single Parliament and a legislative Council.

" British America is lost ! " was the cry of the Tories, and in this " rank and infectious report " they saw only an excuse for future

SEC. II.

FOREIGN AND COLONIAL POLICY

1815 TO **1914**

1838

1839

1840

The Federation of Canada

Sec. II.

Foreign
and
Colonial
Policy

1815
TO
1914

rebellions : at any sacrifice England was bound, in their view, to keep
complete command over the colonies "as an integral part of the
Empire." The Whigs, in their fervour for free trade, insisted on
commercial control while allowing political liberty. The Radicals
believed that complete freedom and the growth of common interests
would alone secure imperial union. But, as the colonies complained,
the general indifference of English people "abandoned them entirely
to Downing Street." Save when a party vote was involved, imperial
questions were discussed in an empty and inattentive House. An
endeavour to educate the country was made by the Society for

1850
Colonial Reform, founded by William Molesworth. He recognized
that a Colonial Office which undertook the care of forty communities had set itself an impossible task. England had to meet
the " vast expenditure " of their internal administration, the protection
of their interests in a world-wide diplomacy, and the military defence
of a hundred frontiers, mountain ranges lost in snow, parched deserts
of sand, rivers, seas, or a bare line of latitude ruled across the prairie.
The colonies paid but a tenth of their expenses; they yielded no
tribute; it was doubted whether they offered any important commercial
advantages; and there was a common opinion that the adoption
of free trade had destroyed the only motive for retaining them
under control. As responsibility grew enthusiasm declined. Carlyle's
satire broke forth : " 'If you want to go from us, go ; we by no means
want you to stay : you cost us money, which is scarce ; desperate
quantities of trouble too : why not go if you wish it?' Such is the
humour of British statesmen at this time." Molesworth for his part
urged faith in the colonists : and showed that with the expansion of
self-government they would gradually shoulder their own burdens.
While politicians argued, Canada was leading the colonies towards a
new position in the Empire. She owed much to the guidance of Lord
Elgin, who launched responsible government. Though mobbed by a

1847
minority, who burned down the Parliament House at Montreal, he
insisted on giving his assent to an unpopular Bill, and urged Canada
to grip her own administration. When her farmers were faced with
ruin by the repeal of the Corn Laws he struck off the shackles of

1854
1859
the Navigation Act, thus preparing a reciprocal treaty with the United
States ; and five years later Canada established her own protective
tariff and founded the fiscal independence of the colonies. Her
statesmen foresaw the day when the inhabited plots should be pieced
together and a greater Canada should stretch, like the States, in
unbroken political unity from the Atlantic to the Pacific Ocean. They
desired a boundless expanse of territory to provide for the needs of a
fast increasing population, which the certainty of freedom and the
hopes of fortune attracted from Europe. Above all they feared the
activity of a powerful and aggressive neighbour ; for Polk, President

of the United States, after annexing Texas, had attempted to push his claims across the vulnerable Canadian border, where the advent of alien traders or the raids of alien armies might intercept the road to the Pacific, and wreck not only their hopes but their very independence. Moreover the progress of the Civil War in the United States involved them in the grave risks which threatened England. Dangerous questions had arisen as to the definition of belligerents and of rebels, of blockade, contraband, "continuous voyage." Two envoys from the southern states who sailed for London in a British steamer, the *Trent*, were arrested by an officer of the Northern navy. Palmerston sent a force to be held ready in Canada, and demanded instant apology for a violation of international law. For some weeks peace hung in the balance; the press was violent; prayers for war were said in the States Senate, and a resolution was passed in favour of a navy sufficient to "defend the seas from the sway of an arbitrary trident." By wise counsel war was averted; but scarcely had the envoys been given up than a new peril arose. The Confederates having bought a British vessel fitted her as a privateer, and while the government was inquiring into the rights of the enterprise the *Alabama* slipped out of the Mersey, and delivered a series of attacks upon Northern commerce. In the height of excitement at her extraordinary success, Gladstone made his famous declaration as to the Confederates of the South : their leaders had made an army, they are making a navy, and what is more than either, he said, " they have made a nation." Thousands of Englishmen echoed his words, for they regarded the South as fighting for its constitutional life. But there was a sudden revulsion of feeling with President Lincoln's proclamation of freedom to the slaves. All other matters forgotten, Englishmen refused to recognize a State " based on the foundation of human bondage." They came to think as Manchester had thought for many months. The mills had long been deprived of raw material, but even in face of starvation the cotton-workers refused to take a single bale from slave-owning states. Rich and poor, Whig and Tory, hastened to subscribe for the relief of Lancashire. President Lincoln sent cargoes of flour for the workers whose attitude had helped to maintain peace between the countries. A section of opinion in the Northern States indeed was eager for war with Great Britain, and the hotheads urged an attack on Canada or on English commerce, while English merchants on their side proposed to break the irregular blockade of the Southern States, and two ironclads were built in English yards for the Confederates. The government however checked every breach of neutrality, detained the ships, and resisted Napoleon's project for joint mediation. The close of the war brought new difficulties. Hundreds of thousands of Irish fugitives from famine and eviction had sought in the States, beyond the British

SEC. II.

FOREIGN
AND
COLONIAL
POLICY

1815
TO
1914

*American
Civil War*
1861

1862

Sec. II.

Foreign
AND
Colonial
Policy

1815
TO
1914

1866

Empire, liberty, home, and opportunity. They lay outside the current theories of "Anglo-Saxon kinship." Many thousands had joined the American army. A Fenian rising was planned on both sides of the Atlantic; at the peace, soldiers of Irish birth, set free from the army, were joined in a raid across the Canadian frontier by American comrades eager for war with England. A member suggested in Congress that Ireland should be recognized as a belligerent; rumours of political dissensions in Canada and doubts of its loyalty gained some credence; while even in England fear of entanglement in war with the States led to a talk of separation. A flood of pamphlets showed the popular excitement. Meanwhile the States denounced the reciprocal treaty of 1854 in the hope that commercial pressure would force Canada into the Union, an end desired by her own republicans. But the covert threat stimulated the Canadian spirit of nationality. Already the approaching victory of the Federals under President Lincoln had quickened the demand for Federal union of

the provinces, and at a meeting in Quebec the delegates mapped out a Constitution. On the threat of coercion or of war a deputation of Ministers carried their scheme to London and triumphantly con-cluded their Treaty. The British North America Act created a

Parliament for the Dominion of Canada, with a Governor and a Ministry supreme over the provincial legislatures. Without realizing the greatness of her deed, England had overturned her old colonial system; and while many hailed a step towards "amicable separation" she had forged the stoutest link in the chain of empire. When

"Dominion Day" witnessed the opening of the first Parliament at Ottawa a mighty nation sprang into life. As the remoter parts, one

by one, came into the Union, the Dominion was extended to the Rocky Mountains and to the Arctic Ocean. By the accession of British Columbia, a province twice the size of France, Canada bordered on the Pacific. Seven states and several territories were united under its rule. A railway built with British capital soon spanned the Dominion from sea to sea, and opened a route from England to Hong-Kong half as long as the journey by the Suez Canal. The vast distances which by dividing the eastern and western provinces formed a bar to federation, were conquered by railway development without parallel. With the means of transport her trade in wheat and cattle, furs and fruit, increased a thousandfold; her products were turned to the English markets, and her prosperity encouraged a rapid extension of settlements beyond all example. The word colony has long been proudly rejected by this first of nations within the Empire.

Newfoundland, refusing to enter the Canadian Union, maintained the constitution given it in 1855; but the example of Canada inspired the settlers of the Pacific. When the United States were lost, England

turned to colonize Australia. With the coming of the earliest
convicts and their guards the first plough was driven into Australian
soil at Parramatta; and John Macarthur soon planted the first vineyard and imported merino sheep. From that time the squatter
began to feed our woollen industries with abundant raw material.
The first free colony was established as a warning to French
explorers. A vast continent equal in size to Europe was dotted
with tiny settlements, and separate bands of colonists pressed
from the sea to the heated and parched interior. Searching for
pasture-land, explorers rowed up the broad rivers or toiled across
illimitable deserts which yielded neither water, shade, nor sus-
tenance. For fifty years the squatters composed Australia's chief
population, but the discovery of gold brought new problems;
shepherds and labourers rushed to the gold-fields, and crowds of
immigrants flooded the land. Hitherto each colony, ruled by autocratic governors and councils, fought for its own hand; there was
no racial question, no indefensible boundary, no powerful neighbour to
emphasize the need for union. Contests for irrigation or the control
of navigable rivers, for tariffs or boundaries, were embittered by
animosities between colonies formed by emigration and those whose
origin lay in convict settlements where men were drilled and brutalized
under penal discipline. Amid the dangers of the wilderness and the
sufferings of frequent years of drought, settlers were hardened in
mind and body; they endured the evils of alternate hoarding or
waste and instability, due to speculation in land or metals; their
opportunities for worship or education were scant. Australia, like
Canada, owed a debt to Edward Gibbon Wakefield. While imprisoned
for elopement with a ward in Chancery he talked in Newgate with
felons condemned to Botany Bay, bought books, and emerged from
confinement a colonial reformer, indignant at the scandal of transporting convicts, the iniquity of simply "shovelling out paupers," the
numbing effect of the want of schools and the dearth of religion.
Though his schemes for the disposal of land were a failure, he
stimulated thought upon the whole range of the problem, and it was
largely due to him that an end was put to transportation. Its firmest
opponent was Henry Parkes; a farm labourer from Warwickshire,
he set out with his wife "to unlock a door," and landed in Sydney
without a friend to meet him, to become at first keeper of a toy
shop, then journalist, and later a dominating parliamentary leader.
The passionate energy of the new settlers made Australia. Ignorance
was stamped out, political life lost much of its factiousness, a
"constituted anarchy" lost its power, the brutality and violence of the
press were mitigated. The slow evolution of order forms one of
the finest tributes to the virtue of self-government. But under the
guidance of self-made men each colony preserved a strong sense of its

Sec. II.

Foreign
AND
Colonial
Policy
1815
TO
1914

1817–1829

1849

1830

1848

Sec. II.

Foreign
AND
Colonial
Policy

1815
TO
1914

1846–1850
1856–1880

ᴜwn importance. Varieties of climate and products led to conflicting problems of labour and development. New South Wales was inclined to free trade, Victoria was wholly for protection, South Australia was mainly pastoral, Queensland had abundance of gold, while Western Australia imported convicts until compelled to desist by the anger of its rivals. Isolated by vast tracts of waste and desert, each State was content with its separate constitution, and though the British Government urged Federal Union the question was pushed aside. Its most powerful advocate was an Irish emigrant, Gavan Duffy, who had barely escaped a rebel's doom in the cause of "Ireland a nation," and now worked ardently for the national idea in his adopted country: "In the eyes of Europe and America what was a few years ago known to them only as an obscure penal settlement in some uncertain position in the Southern Ocean begins to be recognized as a fraternity of wealthy and important States capable of immense development." But in vain he warned the colonists that "neighbouring States of the second rank inevitably become confederates or enemies." The first proposal for federation was received with shouts of laughter. His great effort failed. A later conference and Bill for a Federal Council came to nothing. The strong pressure of external danger could alone put a check on internecine war and fratricidal struggles. There had been occasional alarm when the French patrolled the Pacific, annexing Tahiti and other stations, or seized New Caledonia; and the Australian demand for possession of the Oceanic archipelago against all other European Powers was met by Disraeli in his annexation of the Fiji Islands. But the first effective shock towards union was given when France planted a penal settlement in one of the islands, and Germany entered on New Guinea and the "Bismarck Archipelago." In their remote and isolated position the colonies consented to a general conference for defence; and asserted an Australian Monroe doctrine, that no foreign power should establish itself in their western waters. But the Act to create a federal council for the protection of their interests was a scanty and imperfect sketch of union for definite effort; and when a wider scheme was supported by Sir Henry Parkes, a national convention at Sydney still failed to construct a constitution.

1880

1882

1883–1885

1889
1891

1840
1852
1876

New Zealand, in the very centre of the water hemisphere, 1,200 miles from Australia, had taken form as a British colony under the same sense of jealous independence. From 1814 English subjects had settled there, but the British Government, 11,000 miles away, had disavowed sovereignty, till French activity in the Pacific and their efforts to establish a colony in New Zealand and make it a dependency of France hastened our annexation of the islands. Six provinces were united under a Governor and Parliament, and the provincial governments presently sank into County Councils. After ten years' fighting with the Maoris, English troops were withdrawn, and the country was left to its own resources. In the planting of the islands Wakefield's intense hostility to Ireland had left New Zealand the most purely English and Scotch in blood of all the colonies. The little community of half a million white people were confident of their own vigour, proud of the wonders of their country, with its snow-clad mountains fuming with volcanic heat, its glaciers and abundant rivers, its ice-cold lakes towards the Antarctic zone, and towards the tropics sheets of water heated to boiling-point by hidden geysers. A people ambitious and self-dependent refused to merge their colony by federation in the Commonwealth of Australia; the two countries in fact find their market on the other side of the world, and have no need to look to each other for raw material. The aim of New Zealand was to become a sister State in an Imperial Confederation, and trust for the protection of its isolated settlement to the central government, under whose guardianship the colony worked out her experiments in social reform.

It was by no road of peaceful development that South Africa entered into the circle of the free States of the Empire, but by a way of sorrow, violence, and storm. When Cape Town was taken from the Dutch in 1806, South Africa was mainly regarded as a stepping-stone to the East, and the Cape as a half-way house on the route to India. At first a mere outpost of empire, this harbour of call soon became the chief town of a new and expanding settlement. When finally the Cape became a Crown Colony immigrants poured in from Great Britain, and the Dutchman saw himself gradually ousted from a land he had marked for his own by a race equally insistent upon expansion, with whose language and law he was unfamiliar, and with whose methods of dealing he was justly dissatisfied. The Dutch courts of *Landroost* and *Heemraden* were abolished, their places being taken by resident migistrates; judicial proceedings were to be in English; equality of rights between the white and the coloured population was established. But a predominating grievance in connexion with the emancipation of the slaves determined the Dutchmen to cast off for ever English law and government. They considered the compensation to be inadequate; the order that it should be paid in London alone threw the Dutch slave-proprietors into the hands of English agents who basely defrauded them. Indignation at the treatment to which they were subjected drove them to the Great Trek. Northwards lay the unbounded veldt; harnessing their oxen to cumbrous wagons, some seven thousand, Paul Kruger among them, set out for new soil, and founded the Transvaal and the Orange Free State. By continued wars against fierce tribes of Zulus and Matabele, they maintained a precarious independence. But each move was countered by the British, who by the annexation of Natal cut off the Dutchmen

Sec. II.

Foreign
and
Colonial
Policy

1815
to
1914

**South
Africa**

1834

*The Great
Trek*
1836

1844

SEC. II.
FOREIGN
AND
COLONIAL
POLICY
1815
TO
1914
1852

from the sea.   At length the home government, reluctant to bear for
an obstinate and disaffected neighbour the cost and risk of defence,
signed the Sand River Convention, by which the Boers were allowed
to assume their independence.   Two years later the Orange Free
State obtained a like agreement at Bloemfontein.   Thus, with the
consent of the home government, South Africa had been divided into
provinces of different allegiance.   The rivalry of the old Dutch and
French settlers with the incoming and dominating English was
aggravated by feuds both within and without the borders of the
several states.   The Boer Republics saw in the provinces under
English dominion a perpetual threat.   Cape Colony, practically partitioned between Dutch and English, was divided against itself, contemptuous of the Boers beyond its borders, and opposed to Natal,
which was intensely British.   In one danger South Africa stood alone.
No other colony had to face the problem of a native race which did
not disappear before the European advance, and where the existence
of the scanty white population was continually menaced by powerful
military tribes.   Besides recurrent wars with Kaffirs and Basutos, the
settlers were confronted with the even more ominous problems of a
community dependent on native labour, and the relations of a white
race to a subject population of Africans within their borders.   To

meet the danger of the encompassing tribes Sir George Grey urged
a system of common defence by a federal union of the various
states, united under British rule, but so as to leave great individual
freedom of action to each province.   His scheme was wrecked by
the home government; and a new proposal sent out from London
was refused in South Africa on the question of the native vote.
From Canada the colonies had learned that the question of their
federal union must be a purely colonial question to be decided among
themselves.

**Empire
and De-
mocracy**

While the colonies acquired political self-consciousness England
was gradually awakening to the range and importance of her vast
heritage.   Ocean steamers were now carrying out emigrants from
every class in the country; and travellers such as Sir Charles Dilke,
a statesman of unrivalled knowledge and sympathy with the rising
fortunes of the colonies, endeavoured to inform public ignorance and
compel the attention of Parliament.   A new world had arisen where
our language, laws, and customs were now supreme, and whose people
were justly proud of their achievements.   Literature, art, and music
had in towns toned down the roughness of the earlier settler.   The
countryman bred in toil, in adventure, in daily conflict with nature,
had gained an astonishing physical vigour and endurance, and skill in
every sport.   Confident in his freedom and strength, rapid in resource,
stern and even ruthless in purpose, he was little disposed to subject
either himself or his country to discipline or control.   When Canada

imposed her first protective tariff the protest of the Colonial Office was met by a curt answer: "Self-government would be utterly annihilated if the views of the Imperial Government were to be preferred to those of the people of Canada." Thus at a blow ended the old theory of Empire. With the development of colonial institutions a stalwart independence grew up side by side with imperial sentiment. Pioneers of freedom, encouraged by some small successes, boldly questioned the right of Great Britain to dictate fiscal treaties and decide foreign relations; it was suggested that the colonies should become like Hanover, an apanage of the Crown, but not necessarily involved in her wars. But colonials in the main extolled "the crimson thread of kinship," and claimed the right to maintain their position and privileges as Englishmen; like Queensland they refused to be "thrust out of the Empire." In England itself all parties had abandoned "the hated name of force and coercion exercised by us." Sir Charles Dilke proposed through Imperial Councils to admit the colonies to a share in the common defence. Disraeli had in fact preceded him with a scheme of colonial representation in the Imperial Parliament, and for over a quarter of a century advocated a customs union. But politicians shirked a problem perplexed and tangled, until pressing needs of imperial defence forced them to take a wider outlook. The Maori wars in New Zealand, a futile invasion of Canada by Fenians, the Red River rebellion led by the half-caste Louis Riel, the native troubles in Natal, illustrated the expediency of leaving to the colonies their own defence. Liberals regarded the withdrawal of imperial troops as a pursuance of their general "principle of freedom," and claimed that self-government was the cure for disturbance and unrest. The system, in fact, of throwing on the colonies that managed their own affairs the entire cost of their own support enabled Britain to maintain an empire ten times as large as that of France at a third of the expense. To Conservatives the measure seemed a signal of dissolution—the final slackening of the old imperial bond. Their only alternative to separation was federation of the empire, and extremists sought in premature fashion to introduce "in black and white" a definite federal tie, alien and abhorrent to the traditions of English political life. Ardent imperialists regarded the day of small nationalities as past, and pointed to the German empire and Italy as examples of the strength which federation produced. But neither England nor the colonies were as yet prepared for the administrative difficulties of such a union. In the main all sides accepted the actual situation. Separation might come, colonials admitted, but the general feeling was that the colonies themselves were moving in the other direction. They predicted a day when Great Britain would define her wishes and duties and the colonies would accept their obligations.

Sec. II.

Foreign
and
Colonial.
Policy

1815
to
1914

1869

1870

SEC. II.

FOREIGN
AND
COLONIAL
POLICY

1815
TO
1914

The new
im-
perialism

Not only in colonial questions, but in foreign affairs, the country was torn by rival policies. After Palmerston's death English Liberals shunned intervention in Europe; Gladstone, schooled by Peel and supported by Granville, a foreign minister who loved peace, reverted to an unaggressive and conciliatory attitude. He had carried out the cession of the Ionian Islands to Greece, and had made the Treaty of Washington, to adjust many old and long-drawn-out disputes with America. Six months later he accepted arbitration to end the five years' dangerous quarrel over the *Alabama* question. The award was given by a composite tribunal sitting at Geneva. American statesmen assessed English liabilities, not at the damage that the *Alabama* had done, but at all she had cost by prolonging the war; the "indirect claims," said Disraeli, were like a tribute levied on a conquered nation. At length America reduced her terms to nine millions, and obtained three. Great Britain expressed regret for the damage done; and certain conditions were laid down governing the conduct of neutrals. The enthronement of "public right as the governing idea of European policy," together with peace and economy, were Gladstone's guiding principles. England, he wrote, could never be unfaithful to her great tradition, nor forswear her interest in the common transactions and general interests of Europe. "But her credit and her power form a fund, which in order that they may be made the most of should be thriftily used." He urged the country not to encourage the weak by expectation, but to deter the strong from aggression. Disraeli, on the other hand, represented the change of outlook in England, the distrust of a cosmopolitan view, a jealous imperialism, and the superseding of home affairs by an imaginative and striking eastern policy. In his earlier spell of power he had made war in Abyssinia and reduced Magdala. His return to office on the fall of Gladstone was marked by the annexation of the Fiji Islands, and he appealed to the pride of the country by a dramatic purchase of the Suez Canal shares that had been allotted to Egypt at its opening six years before. The magnitude of English trade through the Canal, which exceeded tenfold that of any other nation, had made a revolution in shipbuilding, and the excitement in Liverpool as the new model vessels arrived to load up in the Mersey gave force to his imperial ideas. At the same moment the brilliant tour planned for the Prince of Wales to India brought home to the general public the importance of the highways to the east, and the interest of England in the Ottoman Empire, whose "dominion is recognized at the head of the Persian Gulf, on the shores of the Levant, and in the immediate neighbourhood of the Suez Canal." Disraeli's Asiatic policy caught the imagination and satisfied the ambitions of the country, and invested the empire with a new glamour. Under his guidance the peaceful Tory tradition was transformed into an ostentatious and aggressive

Sec. II.

Foreign
AND
Colonial
Policy

1815
TO
1914

Imperialists
and
Liberals

imperialism, marked on distant frontiers by a new "forward policy." The expansion of British dominions was at all times pushed on with equal energy and success by both parties, and in the winning of new territories neither side had the slightest pre-eminence. The causes of difference lay deeper. All the nations now stood at the outset of a new age of conquest unparalleled in the world, for the first time made possible by the exaltation of man's power through scientific and mechanical discoveries. England with her coal-fields and her iron, her fleets of steamers and her ocean cables, was inevitably in the forefront of the struggle; and her leaders in enterprise, looking at past efforts and future endeavour, saw no limits to her material triumph if her spirit rose to the great occasion. On the other side were men deeply impressed by difficulties of a different order—men who saw as yet no certain solution to the grave problems of colonial government, and who questioned whether the resources of a small island were sufficient for the responsibilities it was assuming to administer, control, and defend a quarter of the earth's surface. The democracy on its part justly demanded that imperialism should mean not only foreign undertakings but a home policy, that before English resources were lavished on the outermost regions of the empire slums should be cleared from England, health given to her people, and a fitting education to her children—a policy which, if the ruling classes had understood the great issues involved, would indeed have made their country the first in the world and impregnable to all attack. The instinct of the English people, very nobly reinforced in this controversy by the Celtic races, remained true to the spirit of liberty. To Liberals the name of imperialism was justly suspect. It was the denial of a generous tradition handed down since Canning, that in Britain small and oppressed nationalities ought to find a liberal support. The word carried the implications of reactionary oppression in Russia, of government by massacre in Turkey, of the vast pretensions and corruptions of the fallen empire of Napoleon, and the military rule of that which was rising in Germany. Before the title of imperial could be accepted by a free people it had to receive after long effort a new British interpretation, as yet hidden from the Tory party of that day, and almost beyond the hopes of the Liberals themselves.

The policies represented by the two mighty antagonists, Disraeli and Gladstone, were brought into the sharpest contrast, and invested with intense popular emotion during a new crisis of the eastern danger. The problem of the Ottoman Empire after every supposed settlement reappeared more threatening than before. It took its most ominous form after the defeat of France. Alarmed at the French power of recovery, and fearful of her alliance with Russia, Bismarck almost precipitated a second war, which was only averted by the personal

Sec. II.
Foreign
and
Colonial
Policy
1815
to
1914

July.

The rival
policies

Dec.

1876

efforts of the Tsar and Queen Victoria. To prevent any union between Russia and France, he pressed the Tsar to push his conquests round the Black Sea; while he encouraged Austria, now barred out from Germany, and expelled from Italy, to repair her fortunes by a Balkan empire. The old duel between Russia seeking an outlet to the sea, and England guarding the way to India, became a conflict among the leading European powers for dominance in the East. England was isolated by the fall of France. The Sultan on the other hand gained strength by the check given to the influence of French thought, which had penetrated the Ottoman Empire, stimulating among its peoples, and even among the Moslems, aspirations of nationality; and he was now prepared to assert his mastery with a powerful army, reorganized on western lines. Turkish bankruptcy added an argument for extortion from the subject Christians. Their misery was extreme; and a rising in Herzegovina and Bosnia, planned or encouraged by Prussia, set the whole peninsula in a blaze of revolt. Three years followed of massacre and war within, and ceaseless intrigue without. Europe was divided by rival policies. The powers demanded a system of local reforms suited to the needs of the various provinces and guaranteed by Europe; England advocated the integrity of Turkey and her absolute rule, admitting no local autonomy, but giving to the Christians the protection of the European concert to prevent Russia from claiming their guardianship in the Balkans and Armenia, and France in Syria and Egypt. When therefore Austria offered the mediation of the three imperial courts, the Sultan threw aside the proposal by an announcement that he was considering a universal reform in the Ottoman Empire—a proposal in great part inspired by Disraeli and the English government. To this Austria answered by the famous "Andrassy Note," which presented terms of immediate and definite relief for the special Balkan provinces, agreed upon by the three Emperors, by France and Italy, and half accepted by England. Since there was no hint of real pressure Turkey might acquiesce in reforms which she could "accept with reluctance and neglect with impunity." But a new outbreak of Mohammedan fanaticism, and the murder of the French and German consuls at Salonica, forced from the three Emperors the "Berlin Note," shorter and more decisive than the last, and threatening "efficacious measures." Though France and Italy signed, Disraeli—who had sent a fleet to Besika Bay to protect British interests—refused joint action, offered no alternative policy, and broke up the last hope of peace enforced by the will of a united Europe. For Disraeli the day of small nations was over, while his foreign minister, Lord Derby, held that Turkey had as much right to deal in her own fashion with rebellion in the Balkans as England in Ireland, then shaken by Parnell's demands for "Ireland a nation." The Sultan mocked at powers in discord.

From Bulgaria came news of a month of massacre, when 10,000 bashi-bazouks were let loose to slaughter and burn—in Batak not 2,000 left from a population of 7,000, in the Philippopolis district alone some 12,000 hideously tortured and massacred—"horror which turns one's blood to flame," said Lord Carnarvon. In their fury Serbians and Montenegrins declared war. Overrun by Turkish forces, Serbia appealed to Europe. Disraeli scoffed at his own consul's reports as "coffee-house babble"; he professed his faith in a Young Turk constitution; which, after two Sultans had disappeared in a few weeks, finally vanished under the notorious Abd-ul-Hamid, nominee of the Old Turks. Gladstone's indignation glowed with a white heat. He made the question one of humanity and the Christian faith. Russell, now at eighty-one of the last links between the old and the new Whigs, declared that, like Canning, he was for making friends with Russia and Greece and turning the Turk out of Europe; it was Gladstone's policy—joint intervention, and the expulsion of the Turk from Europe "bag and baggage." "The unspeakable Turk," wrote Carlyle, "should be immediately struck out of the question, and the country left to honest European guidance." Meetings of protest were supported by Browning and Burne Jones, Froude and Freeman, Ruskin and Morris. In the height of this public excitement Disraeli was given the title of Lord Beaconsfield by the Queen, who six months before had become at his advice Empress of India. Lord Derby appealed to the Turks to make peace with the Serbians as an "urgent necessity," but knowing that his government would apply no force they pressed on the war. Meanwhile Russia had completed her preparations. At Reichstadt the Tsar and the Austrian emperor made a compact that Russia should have a free hand in the Danubian provinces, and that in case of war with Turkey Austria should remain neutral, and for her reward should occupy Bosnia and Herzegovina. Thus fortified, and moved by the approaching extinction of the Serbian people, Russia sent an ultimatum to the Porte, obtained an armistice for Serbia, and saved the country. Her ambassador Ignatief had restored even more than the prestige of Menschikoff. Beaconsfield retorted by instantly ordering the English fleet to Besika Bay, and by a menacing speech at the Lord Mayor's banquet; and his threat of war was repeated in every music-hall by the "Jingoes" in the blatant rhyme that gave them their name. To support "our traditional policy" appeals were made to the hatreds and prejudices of the Crimean war. England proposed a conference at Constantinople, where Lord Salisbury, "with no Disraelite prejudice," was sent as representative; but immediately before the first formal meeting a telegram from the Cabinet assured the Porte that it would never countenance coercive measures against Turkey. As the full conference opened, salvoes of artillery rang out

SEC. II.

FOREIGN AND COLONIAL POLICY

1815 TO **1914**

The Bulgarian atrocities

Aug.

July

Conference at Constantinople

Sec. II.

Foreign
AND
Colonial
Policy
1815
TO
1914

to announce "the promulgation of an Ottoman constitution" by Abd-ul-Hamid. The audacious renewal of an old device for exploiting the dissensions of the Powers could deceive no one; but it enabled the Sultan, confident of English support, to refuse the terms offered him, and to reject the later proposals which the baffled diplomats drew up in the Protocol of London. Russia, tired of delays, ordered her troops across the frontier. Osman Pasha's brilliant defence of Plevna long delayed their advance, but at length Roumania came to the rescue, and Russia obtained her terms almost at the gates of

Constantinople. The treaty of San Stefano recognized the independence of Serbia, Montenegro, and Roumania, and created a new Bulgaria—a Christian state which stretched from the Archipelago to the Black Sea, dividing in two the empire left to the Sultan. It restored to Russia the strip of Bessarabia taken from her in 1856, and gave her the mountain land of Armenia, commanding the descent to Mesopotamia, with a part of the caravan road from Trebizond to the heart of Persia. As alarm at Russia's success spread through Tory and Liberal ranks the storm of passion at Turkish atrocities died down. Early in the war, in spite of Gladstone's prophetic denunciations, Parliament had given to Beaconsfield full freedom to conduct affairs as he saw best. His cabinet was hesitating. Twice the fleet had been ordered to pass the Dardenelles, and twice recalled on threats of resignations. But when a misleading telegram from the British Minister at the Porte announced a menacing Russian advance on Constantinople, English ships were hurried to the Bosporus and off the island of Prinkipo confronted the Russian army at San Stefano. War seemed imminent. Liberals wavered in the House of Commons and joined in passing a vote of credit. Gladstone's windows were broken by a "Jingo" mob. The impression was false, but panic remained. Beaconsfield seized the opportunity, called out the reserves, and on Lord Derby's resignation made Lord Salisbury his foreign minister. In a famous dispatch he struck the alarm of a shattered Turkey, a Canal in danger, and an omnipotent Russia in command of "the unrivalled situation and resources which Europe had entrusted to the Porte." He carried with him the stockbrokers and soldiers, and by a dramatic stroke announced an order, unknown to Parliament, to bring 7,000 Indian troops to Malta. Finally, supported by Austria, he refused to recognize the treaty of San Stefano, and forced Russia to submit to a general congress, on the ground that the eastern question was one for Europe, not for Russia alone.

The Congress of Berlin assembled under the presidency of Bismarck, who offered himself as the "honest broker," to revise the treaty of San Stefano. It met only to find itself already superfluous. Beaconsfield came, as he said, not to partition a worn-out state, but to strengthen an ancient empire. But an evening paper published the terms, revealed by a temporary clerk, of a secret agreement already concluded between Salisbury and Shuvaloff. Russia was promised the lands she had won, renouncing only the caravan route from the Black Sea towards Persia; and Austria received the protectorate of Bosnia and Herzegovina, where she stood as " sentinel of the Balkans." The boundaries of the proposed "greater Bulgaria" were redrawn, dividing it into three states, Bulgaria, Eastern Rumelia, and Macedonia, the diplomatists supposing that the danger of reunion would be averted by lack of a common name: thus Beaconsfield sought to avert the danger he feared, of a Bulgaria whose gratitude might yield to Russia a harbour on the Ægean from which she could threaten the Suez Canal. The frontiers of these states, like those of Serbia and Montenegro, were so amended as to weaken the power of each, and the Slav peoples were broken into groups between which Austria held the ways of communication. At the last moment Shuvaloff found himself outwitted. For by a secret treaty of "defensive alliance" with Turkey a week before the Congress, Beaconsfield had secured possession of Cyprus in payment for his pledge to defend Asia Minor against any further advance by Russia. The Congress had little to do but register these secret agreements. The two great powers who had not struck a blow nor sacrificed a man in the war seized their prize of territory. France was confidentially assured that Great Britain would accept her occupation of Tunis. Bismarck suggested that England should acquire Egypt. Italy alone went away empty-handed, and alarmed at the advance of Austria over Bosnia: like France, she saw beyond the Mediterranean "the last door open" for compensation and expansion, and was ultimately to receive the offer of Tripoli. The integrity of Turkey had disappeared. Few treaties indeed have been more cynical in spirit or more cruel in its provisions than the treaty of Berlin. Excepting Russia, the one supporter of the Orthodox Slavs, the powers had repudiated belief in the solidarity of Christian nations. Great Britain, whose people could not, as in the Crimean war, plead ignorance of Turkish atrocities, had taken a culpable part in forcing Macedonians and Armenians, whom Russia proposed to emancipate, under the Porte, with cynical advice to trust in the Sultan's reforms. On the other hand Russia, whose enthusiastic crusade, heavy sufferings, and sweeping victory had begun the redemption of the Slavs, saw her work destroyed. For sixty years Europe had been occupied in undoing the settlement of Vienna: the Berlin Congress turned back all aid to subject nationalities for a generation to come. Beaconsfield's policy shattered the hopes of liberty, not only in the Balkans, but in Russia. The diplomatic defeat inflicted on the country by England—the darkest page, said Gortschakoff, in his career—threw disgrace on the new Liberalism, and a long reaction, strengthened by the assassination of

Sec. II.

Foreign
and
Colonial
Policy

1815
to
1914

Sec. II.

Foreign
AND
Colonial
Policy

1815
TO
1914

The
European
Powers

the Liberal Tsar, settled down upon Russia, a reaction which lasted to our own day. The powers bequeathed to later generations problems which their contempt of national life and unscrupulous diplomacy had aggravated and embittered.

In England an exultant enthusiasm swept over the country at the triumphal return of Beaconsfield from Berlin, with his defiant cry of "peace with honour." All opposition was silenced as the Tory imperialism sprang to its full strength, ready for every enterprise, brave in expansion, confident of English force of dominion, sceptical of Liberal traditions as to "free" peoples or of the virtue of small nationalities, and contemptuous of the "parish pump politics of a democratic nation." Societies and institutes took the title of "Imperial"; and "Liberal Imperialists" disputed with the Tories the glory of empire and the pride of conquest. Lord Salisbury indeed lived to confess that in Turkey we had "put our money on the wrong horse"; while Lord Beaconsfield in a few months recanted his sensational description of the Russian advance. One result of his work remained. He had called in Bismarck to arbitrate in the Balkans, and after the congress Germany, arbiter of Europe, stood at the height of her diplomatic power, assured at once of the friendship of England and the gratitude of Austria. The initials of the Emperor Francis Joseph on the hill-side at Plevlye marked the advance of Austria, backed by Germany, in the "corridor" leading to Salonica. Russia, who had pledged herself not to enter Constantinople, saw Austria advanced nearer to the Mediterranean than herself, while her own communications with the sea were barred by a string of small states at the mercy of surrounding intrigues. Ambitions and disappointments ranged the European powers in a new order. The informal "League of the Three Emperors," Teuton and Slav, was broken up as Russia, duped at Berlin, slowly fell away, and in consequence of the Tsar's alienation the alliance of the "Two Emperors" was made. With subtle diplomacy Bismarck drew Italy into the Teutonic system, and by her union with her hereditary Austrian enemy the "Triple Alliance" was formed, which for over thirty years set its barrier from sea to sea between eastern and western Europe. France and Russia approached each other, and by gradual steps a "Dual Alliance" of east and west was established. Instead of the concert of Europe, there arose a system of opposing groups of nations, from which there could scarcely be any final issue but war. Meanwhile the new grouping of the powers, the suspension of national struggles in Europe, and the fresh direction given to political ambitions, foreshadowed an age of military dangers, of imperial contempt of national claims, and of a stupendous race conflict for dominion of the world. The Congress of Berlin was followed by the most astounding scheme that history has known for dividing up an entire continent among the powers of Europe—the partition of Africa.

So far European settlements had but touched the fringe of the "dark continent," a land of mystery and terror, untraversed and unmapped. Explorers from every country were seeking the sources of the Nile, or tracking the Niger basin. Britain had sent Burton and Speke, and above all the Highlander McLeay, known as David Livingstone, explorer, philanthropist, scholar, and missionary, true representative after a thousand years of the old Celtic wanderers. His noble and tragic story fired the imagination of Englishmen, and concentrated the attention of the world upon the possibilities of Africa. A vast continent rich in untilled tracts promised for Europe supplies of cotton and food: the abundant yield of rubber and ivory attracted the merchant, while the missionary was stirred by the horrors of slavery and by the heathen masses yet to be won for Christianity. A Conference of statesmen and merchants, missionaries and scientists, assembled at Brussels under Leopold II. and founded an International Association to conduct "a crusade worthy of this century of progress." Committees were formed and expeditions sent out from France, Germany, and Belgium. Suddenly there came news that Henry Stanley had traversed the continent, fighting against man and nature, and for the first time revealed the majestic course of the Congo through the vast basin left by some ancient sea. Messengers from King Leopold met him as he landed at Marseilles, and secured his services. As envoy of the King he was sent out to guide a "great philanthropic enterprise," later known as the International Association of the Congo. Those who foresaw the dreary future were misrepresented and attacked. Amid projects of unknown wealth to be exploited "the scramble for Africa" began. From her western colonies, France endeavoured to control the basin of the Congo ; but her noblest African explorer, de Brazza, was by Stanley's enterprise held back to the northern bank of the river. Portugal, established for centuries near the mouth of the river, put in her claim for the territories that stretched across the continent to her dominions on the east coast, and signed with Great Britain a convention which secured to her Angola and cut off Leopold's Association from the sea. For the first time Germany, from her place as arbiter of Europe, formally interfered in colonial affairs. She led a protest of France and the United States against the check by England to the "friends of humanity," and called a Conference of the Powers at Berlin.

It was not the ownership of the Congo basin alone that was now put in question, but the fate of the entire continent. Along the outer borders of Africa the European powers had already marked claims and seized positions for further advance. England had led the way alike in north and south. The semi-independence of Egypt won

SEC. II.

FOREIGN AND COLONIAL POLICY

1815 TO 1914

Partition of Africa

1876

1878

1884

English in Egypt

Sec. II.

Foreign
AND
Colonial
Policy

1815
TO
1914

by Mehemet Ali, and the opening of the Suez Canal, had magnified the importance of the Nile valley to English commerce. "We want to trade with Egypt," wrote Palmerston in 1857, "but we do not want the burden of governing Egypt." That burden was now undertaken. Egypt had won a sudden prosperity by supplying English mills with cotton during the American war, but her newly won wealth was squandered by the Khedive Ismail with oriental extravagance. The national debt mounted rapidly; loans were floated in England and France, but the interest remained unpaid

until the two powers established a dual control of administration and finance — an unworkable arrangement, as events speedily proved. The extravagance of a decadent Khedive had ruined the peasant and bade fair to ruin the bond-holder. False accounts were issued, sources of revenue suppressed. Beaconsfield distrusted Bismarck's offer at the Congress of Berlin to connive at England's annexation of

Egypt; and the suzerainty of the Sultan, a mere name since the days of Mehemet Ali, was called into use to depose the Khedive. Tewfik Pasha succeeded to an impoverished State with half his revenue pledged to creditors, a people oppressed and discontented, and an army unpaid. A nationalist movement, directed in part against Turkey, in part against the numerous officials and stock-jobbers who served the Dual

Control, was led by Arabi Bey, who had risen from lowly position to be minister of war and Pasha. With the malcontents of the army behind him he helped to establish a Chamber of Notables and advanced schemes for a democracy; but when he claimed to touch the Budget, and the debt was in danger, the bond-holder called for action. The Sultan was persuaded to send a tardy mission to Egypt, and English and French warships anchored off the coast, while the other Powers proposed a Congress. But Arabi had prepared batteries, and popular resentment against the foreigner broke out in attack on Europeans in Alexandria. The Sultan would neither decide to restore order, nor give a free hand to the representatives of the Powers assembled at Constantinople. Gladstone yielded to the cry of protection for British subjects, and the British admiral, seeing his warships threatened, demanded the surrender of the forts, and bombarded Alexandria. The premier was severely criticized, and to his great grief Bright left the Cabinet. But criticism was silenced when Arabi's troops fired the town, and a mob completed the work of rapine and plunder. England acted alone, for the French withdrew, willing to aid in protecting the Canal, but refusing to share in intervention. The remaining Powers protested. An expedition under Wolseley (who to the chagrin of the Powers used the Suez Canal as his base) routed the Egyptian army at Tel-el-kebir; when it occupied Cairo Arabi surrendered. His trial and banishment left England in sole command. The dual control was abolished, and France refused an offer that

Sec. II.

Foreign
and
Colonial
Policy

1815
to
1914

she should appoint a financial adviser. A circular dispatch to explain the English position was sent to the Powers. The occupation, said Granville in the Lords, was to last until "a stable, a permanent, and a beneficial government" could be established. But Gladstone had prophesied that our first site in Egypt would be "the almost certain egg of a North African Empire," and fate forced his steps in the direction which he feared. The Sudan, a tributary state of Egypt misruled by bashi-bazouks and renegade Pashas, stretched southward, a land half rich, half barren, a home of the slave trade. There a Mohammedan leader calling himself the Mahdi proclaimed a holy war of liberation, and was joined by discontented troops who had fought with Arabi. An inadequate force under an Englishman, Hicks Pasha, was sent by the Khedive to defend the outposts of Egypt. Hicks Pasha hoped for help from home, but Granville, who would not prevent the expedition, denied our responsibility for the inevitable disaster. After other reverses under other leaders it was decided to abandon a "useless possession," and to withdraw from the Sudan the Egyptian garrisons surrounded by fanatical hordes. For this arduous task the choice fell upon General Gordon, who had previously governed the province on behalf of the Khedive and had zealously attacked the slave-trade. He was a strange combination of saint and hero. Misgivings as to the appointment of a man whose devout Christianity might alienate the friendly tribes were overruled by the Cabinet. "Are you sure," said Granville next day, "that we did not commit a gigantic folly?" On his way to Khartoum Gordon received incoherent instructions from the Khedive, who cherished thoughts of retaining the Sudan and appointed him Governor-General "for the time necessary." His impulsive nature led Gordon astray; remote from authority, he changed his mind. He had first told the Sudanese of the intended evacuation; he now began to talk of "smashing the Mahdi"; he dreamed of reconquest, and selected a governor to succeed him—an able ruler, but a notorious slave-trader. The Cabinet were sharply divided, some desiring Gordon's recall, others approving of his plan. Suddenly came news that hordes of Arabs had surrounded Gordon and his garrison in Khartoum. The Cabinet began to discuss whether he should be relieved, while their military advisers were unable to agree on the time, the force, or the route. Never were ministers more ill at ease, and never was a decision upon foreign policy made the object of so many barbed shafts. Late in the year Wolseley was dispatched with an army of rescue, but gallantry and determination availed them little in face of tropical heat, lack of water, and difficulties of transport. They were harassed by dervishes, delayed by accidents. And in Khartoum, among hundreds starving or dead and hundreds ready to desert, the means of defence were

Sec. II.

Foreign
AND
Colonial
Policy

1815
TO
1914

1892

exhausted. The city was taken by assault and Gordon slain. Few events have so stirred the heart of the English people as the last isolation and mysterious death of this singular leader, whose impassioned sympathy had made him a romantic hero both of the Egyptians and of his own countrymen. Throughout the Empire there rose a bitter cry of anger and humiliation. For many years advance southwards failed before the triumphant hosts of the Mahdi and his successor. But England kept firm control of the government of Egypt, even when at the news that Gladstone had replaced Lord Salisbury as prime minister the popular cry was raised of "Egypt for the Egyptians," with the encouragement of the Sultan, nominal suzerain of the country.

English
in South
Africa

1871

1872

1875

1877

In South Africa, as in the north, Gladstone was the unwilling heir to an imperial policy which embarrassed the Liberal party. The English had already pushed their eastern sea-board from Cape Colony to Natal, and beyond the Orange River had absorbed the diamond mines of Griqualand West: while the arrival of Cecil Rhodes heralded new schemes of conquest. A proposed federation of the provinces, English and Dutch, was hindered by the jealousy of Cape Colony in the pride of its newly won responsible government, and by the commercial independence of the Transvaal; in 1868 it had annexed Delagoa Bay, and when by arbitration of the President of the French Republic Delagoa was allotted to the Portuguese, the Boers still enjoyed by treaty with Portugal an outlet to the sea that lay outside British rule. But the Transvaal was weakly defended, factiously governed, and financially in disorder, and when the federation of South Africa seemed imminent a minority of Boers appeared favourable to union. Their voice was eagerly accepted as the voice of the republic, and in accordance with the imperial policy of Beaconsfield, his government annexed the Transvaal, and the responsibility for its defence again fell on the empire. The Dutch, however, had not abated their hostility to British rule, nor their distrust of English interference with the native question. The Boer resented the counsels of the English missionary and the philanthropist. In his lonely farm he knew the menace of the surrounding tribes, and ruled his servant with the sjambok. It was only immediate danger from the Zulus under King Cetewayo, who threatened alike Natal and the Transvaal, that wrung a partial and sullen assent to annexation. Sir Bartle Frere, Governor of the Cape, demanded from Cetewayo the disbandment of his savage hordes, to whom marriage was not allowed until their assegais were washed in blood. The Zulu chief did not deign to reply. Immediately the British troops invaded Zululand, but no adequate reinforcements were sent from home, and many of the Boers who were half-hearted hung back. The general, Lord Chelmsford, was new to South African warfare;

Sec. II.

Foreign
AND
Colonial
Policy

1815
TO
1914

he divided his army: his scouting was defective, his camps undefended. One of his forces was annihilated at Isandhlwana, and Natal was only saved by the gallant defence of Rorke's Drift, where two lieutenants, Bromhead and Chard, with eighty men behind a barricade of sandbags and empty cans, held the Zulu host at bay. But before Sir Garnet Wolseley arrived from England with reinforcements Chelmsford had already defeated the Zulus at Ulundi. Their territory was divided; and at Pretoria, Wolseley as victor proclaimed the Transvaal a Crown Colony, denied any form of representative institutions to this vigorous and independent democracy, and installed an English government, announcing that British sovereignty would endure there as long as the sun shone or the rivers flowed into the sea. Already however during the Zulu War the Dutch had appealed to the Sand River Convention and demanded their independence. They awaited the return of Gladstone to office, regarding him as pledged to their freedom by his denunciations in the Midlothian campaign of Beaconsfield's annexation of the Transvaal. But they grew impatient as the Liberals dallied with a scheme of federation, and hesitated over the treatment of the natives. Hoisting the flag of the republic they proclaimed their independence and called their commandos to arms. The Cabinet renounced their pledge and postponed self-government till they had vindicated the Queen's authority. Once again a peace party drifted into war. The power of the Boers had been under-estimated; Sir George Colley's army was inadequate, and his gallantry alone could not stave off disaster. Parties of Boers besieged our garrisons, the rest invaded Natal and repulsed a relieving force at Laing's Nek. A month later in the surprise of Majuba Hill, Colley was killed and his men defeated by a band of two hundred. The disaster, slight as it was from a military point of view, had great political consequences. Peace was made by a government which had first encouraged the Boers and then declared for a fight. Gladstone had been as vacillating in action as he was magnanimous in speech. The British were angered and the Boers encouraged by an apparent surrender to force. After heated discussion, both in the Cabinet and in the Transvaal, self-government was granted; but the control of foreign policy was retained for the Crown, and a British resident was placed at Pretoria. Three years later the Convention of London restored the title of "South African Republic," and the word "suzerainty" was omitted. With new confidence the Boers held out against projects of federation put forward by the Dutch of Cape Colony in their Afrikander Bond; in face of all imperial schemes they clung desperately to the little country they had defended, and continued to wring their living from its ungenerous soil.

Meanwhile a rival power had approached the English borders. For the last ten years Germany had been sending out her pioneers to

1879

1880

1881

1884

German
and
French
Colonies

SEC. II.

FOREIGN
AND
COLONIAL
POLICY

1815
TO
1914

1883

Africa, and the growth of a colonial party forced Bismarck, who had till now opposed foreign adventure, and "wished only for coaling stations acquired by treaty," to a change of policy. Traders entered Damaraland, which the British had looked on as their own sphere of influence while they had done nothing to make the occupation effective. Alarmed at last by the growth of German settlements and intrigues for union with the Boers, Cape Colony which had just won self-government occupied Walfisch Bay; but Downing Street was indifferent, and left the inland district to German penetration. Their traders crept still nearer and acquired the bay of Angra Pequeña with a strip of hinterland, confining Cape Colony to the south of the Orange River. A new and delicate imperial problem was created. The colonies could only protest through the colonial office, and Bismarck refused communication with any department except the foreign office which had made the concessions. "England," he said, "establishes a sort of Monroe doctrine in Africa against the vicinage of other nations." The problem raised a grave warning as to the dangers of international agreements on colonial questions made in London by the cabinet and the foreign office. Gladstone hailed Germany as a colonizing power, "our ally and partner in the execution of the great purposes of Providence." Granville, occupied with the critical question of the Sudan, had not "the slightest jealousy of the Germans acquiring colonial possessions." A barren strip of coast seemed a small price to pay for their goodwill and the peaceful tenure of Egypt. But the Cape Colony took another view. They saw that as the Germans advanced they could almost join hands with the Boers who were pushing westwards over the Harts river; at the rumour of a German occupation of the bay of St. Lucia on the Zulu coast a cruiser was dispatched to unfurl the British flag. Their alarms were excited by reports of skilled German agents on their borders, active and tortuous in their methods, alike with native chiefs and with the British consuls who gave them hospitality. On the west coast the Germans wedged themselves between France and England in the Cameroons and Togoland; following a proposal of 1867 they entered the east coast at Zanzibar to establish a colony. Within a few years they could boast that "the large pudding of Africa was dotted with German peppercorns." The French, pushing from Senegal to the Niger and over the Sahara, had taken north-west Africa for their dominion. From Lake Chad their way lay open to the Sudan and to the English colonies of the west coast; and by the Ubanghi into the Congo basin.

1884

Confer-
ence of
Berlin
1884

Such was the clash of conflicting interests when Bismarck summoned the Conference of Berlin. The powers agreed to define their claims, and laid down rules for "lawful and valid annexation," with other new doctrines of the "hinterland," and of "spheres of influence",

Sec. II.

Foreign
and
Colonial
Policy

1815
to
1914

where annexation was not required; and of free trade and free navigation of the great rivers. The International Association of the Congo was formally allotted the vast domain it demanded in central Africa, on condition of the forbidding of trade monopolies and suppression of slavery. Scarcely had the act of Berlin been signed when King Leopold announced his personal proprietorship of the lands Stanley had annexed, and his sole sovereignty over the Congo Free State. Maxims of the conference were cast aside in the haste of ruthless exploitation, and the "great philanthropic enterprise" ended in a scramble for possession. The nations flung themselves into Africa; explorers were turned into conquerors, and in twenty years Europe by hurried strokes had carved up an entire continent, pushing vague frontiers into the unknown, till at last there was nothing left to divide save at the cost of the weakest of the conquerors. Germany emerged from the conference a colonial power, owner of the Cameroons and Togoland, with the Emperor's charter of protection for a colony in East Africa, and with South-West Africa already secured. France gained dominion over a homogeneous block of territory nearly a million square miles larger than the area of the United States—from Algeria and Tunis to the Congo, and from Senegal to Bahr-el-Ghazal. Portugal, with the consent of Germany and France, claimed the whole course of the Zambesi, to establish her empire across South Africa from Mozambique to Angola—a claim disallowed by the English. Italy extended her influence along the Red Sea coast. England revived her lapsed system of trading Companies; the Niger Company disputed the progress of the French in the west; an East African Company blocked German advance across the lakes and to the Nile valley; while Cecil Rhodes, defying all rivals with his loud-sounding formula " From the Cape to Cairo "— a watchword already ringing through the imperialist ranks—founded the South African, or Chartered, Company, to seize the Zambesi. Bechuanaland was annexed, the great tract known as Rhodesia was seized; and holding the whole of the rich central territory from Cape Colony to the Congo State, the British cut off all hope of expansion for Boer, German, or Portuguese. The European powers proceeded to regulate their respective boundaries by a series of agreements. Secret treaties with England and the Chartered Company gave to Germany rights of purchase in case Portugal should ever be forced to sell her colonies. In return for possession of Zanzibar and Uganda, she admitted a French protectorate over Madagascar, and ceded to Germany Heligoland—a post long desired by Bismarck, who proposed to crown his annexation of Kiel by opening the Baltic Canal, and threw out the bait of advantage to England from an easier route to Russia, and of the strengthening of good feeling by the cession. Granville dryly replied that the cession of Gibraltar would strengthen

Sec. II.
Foreign
AND
Colonial
Policy
1815
TO
1914

our good relations with Spain. He was willing to give "friendly consideration" to the question, but the transfer was left to Lord Salisbury. The War Office saw no advantage in its retention, the Admiralty insisted upon its strategical importance, and Parliament after long debate veered suddenly from strong opposition to consent. By the same treaty England secured a right of free transit over German land to connect her territories from the Cape to Cairo; and established the frontiers of the Sudan on the Congo State, and the watershed of the Nile. It was by this treaty that she claimed the right to repel, almost at the cost of war with France, a French

1898

force led by Marchand to Fashoda, in the very month of the English reconquest of the Sudan. A railway had been pushed from cataract to cataract towards Khartoum, and British troops were joined by Egyptian in the battles of Atbara and of Omdurman. There the Dervishes, clad in mediæval armour or in linen, charged with the utmost bravery again and again, to be mown down by the deadly Maxim. Two days later the British and Egyptian flags were unfurled over the place where Gordon died. Protests of the powers against occupation were met by the promise of free trade, and payment of interest on the debt, and the Sudan became a protectorate of England. The northern littoral alone remained for partition, and in a series of negotiations Morocco was allotted to France by England in 1904 and by Germany in 1911: while Lord Salisbury's unofficial offer of Tripoli to Italy in 1880 was ratified by France in 1900. Nothing was left of Africa but the mountain fastness of Abyssinia. In some dozen years the vast continent had been scored by European nations with the boundaries of their foreign sovereignty. Henceforth its interests were intermingled and confounded with the chances of European politics, and Africa lay at the peril of every war which the conflicts of Europe might fling on its remote and unconscious peoples.

England and foreign affairs

The race for conquest, the secret treaties, the successive threats of war which were only revealed after the danger was passed, alarmed thoughtful men in England. "We should have a manlier and plainer way of dealing with foreign policy," wrote Bagehot, "if ministers were obliged to explain clearly their foreign contracts before they were valid, just as they have to explain their domestic problems before they can become laws." He saw that foreigners were often puzzled by our institutions, vexed at our statesmen, and angry with our newspapers, and that ambiguities might be avoided by open discussion between nations. But apart from the evident difficulty of dealing in the open between parliamentary governments and despotic courts where discussion is not practised, there was a further problem in the temper of England herself. The high tide of imperialism had lifted her people above the sense of national risk, and left them generally indifferent to European developments. Their eyes were upon the ends of the earth.

SEC. II.

FOREIGN
AND
COLONIAL
POLICY

1815
TO
1914

At the third Reform bill the ruling classes had apprehended some disturbing influence of the new democracy on the conduct or continuity of foreign affairs, and had come to a tacit compact that foreign policy should be removed from party strife, and decided by agreement between the two front benches. Foreign ministers since Palmerston had been mostly members of the House of Lords, and this custom was continued until 1905. The conduct of external affairs was in fact practically withdrawn from Parliament. The matter passed unobserved among a people confident in their insular security: the system had the practical convenience of allowing them to choose and dismiss their ministers on questions of home policy alone, without interference of foreign questions. This lack of responsibility in its turn increased the popular detachment from foreign affairs. When a private member moved that "it is not just or expedient to embark in war, contract engagements involving grave responsibilities for the nation, and add territories to the Empire without the consent of Parliament," Gladstone as prime minister declined to settle so far-reaching a change on a single vote of the House : delicate negotiations could not be carried on in the face of the whole world, and since a secret committee would be necessary, matters of foreign policy must be trusted to the executive. As to annexation he was decided : enlargement of the empire was fraught with danger, even if the risk was not immediate. But there had been no agreement to withdraw imperial, like foreign, affairs from public contention, and problems of the empire were presently to cleave the Liberal party in two. In controversies between aggressive Imperialists or "Jingoes," and Liberals or "Little Englanders," the few Radicals who adhered to Cobden's tenets were overborne ; and a Liberal Imperialist party arose under the guidance of Lord Rosebery, and the dominating influence of Joseph Chamberlain, whose exhortations to "think imperially" rang through the country. The divisions of the Liberals left Lord Salisbury dictator. Though he suggested a committee on foreign affairs, he emphasized the need of unanimity so that England could speak with a decisive voice. A strong imperialist, Lord Salisbury's view of our foreign policy was subordinated to the empire; when a disagreement with the United States over the boundaries of British Guiana and Venezuela led to a sharp assertion of the Monroe doctrine by President Cleveland, good sense on both sides made war impossible, and the dispute was committed to arbitration. Amid the vast obligations now borne by the British islands peace became the first of British interests, and both parties were agreed on abstention from continental politics. Without a single ally Great Britain stood in a so-called "splendid isolation."

The Imperial system had been laid down in years of British security and peace. It was to be tested in a world of war in which the whole balance of power was changed. The Conference of Berlin

SEC. II.

FOREIGN
AND
COLONIAL
POLICY

1815
TO
1914

had opened the gigantic conflict for the division of world-dominion.
While Africa was still being parcelled out the battle for position and
for new markets swung eastward to Asia. France had under
Napoleon III. begun imperial expansion in the East, and closed thirty
years of war by securing Cochin China, Cambodia, Annam, and
Tonkin. She was feeling her way to a footing in Upper Burmah
when the Viceroy of India answered by annexing that country. The
"intoxication of the nations at the China trade" inflamed them with
schemes of ambition more immense than any that had been projected
since the great Napoleon. The Chino-Japanese war gave to Japan
Formosa and the Pescadores. The union of France, Russia, and
Germany to force her to give back to China the peninsula of Liao-Tung,
was the beginning of vast European encroachments. In payment for
the murder of two missionaries Germany extracted a lease of the
district of Kiao-Chou, fortified a harbour at Tsing-Chou, and developed
her naval and military "sphere of influence." Russia followed with a
lease of Port Arthur and Talien-wan, winning at last an ice-free port
on a temperate sea. As a make-weight Great Britain acquired the
lease of Wei-hai-wei and Kowloon, together with the extension of the
Shanghai settlement, the opening of new treaty ports inland, and
recognition of her interests in the Yang-tsze valley. France in her
turn demanded a lease of Kwang Chow Wan, and "a zone of influence" as far as the Yang-tsze, with railway, mining, and postal
privileges. The resentment of China led to the Boxer risings and
attacks on the foreign legations, and the spirit of the European troops
sent to exact vengeance against "a barbarous foe" was illustrated by
the charge of the German emperor to his troops: "Wield your
weapons to such effect that for a thousand years no Chinaman shall
ever again dare to look askance at a German." The United States
signalized their new position in the Pacific as masters of the Philippines
by joining the other Powers in the retributive march on Peking. "We
are in desperate straits indeed," wrote the greatest of Chinese statesmen, Li Hung Chang. He judged that the division of China was only
averted because the European nations could not agree upon their
respective shares.

In central Asia meanwhile Russia and Great Britain waged their
perennial conflict. Checked in the Balkans, Russia turned again
with sullen mien towards expansion in Asia. For twenty years
India had been undisturbed, while relays of civilians wrestled with
frequent famine, built roads and railways, grappled with the complications of finance or the problems of justice, and returned to
an England which was little curious and little informed on the gravest
problems of the empire. Beaconsfield had travelled in the East and
its blood was in his veins; he determined to emphasize the grandeur of
our administration, to revive the Empire of the Great Moghul, and

enhance the setting of the "most costly jewel" in the crown. The Queen was acclaimed as Empress amid the pomp of a Durbar at Delhi; while the strong opposition aroused at home was only overcome by a pledge that the title should never be used in England. For the last three years Lord Salisbury, Secretary for India, had been seeking a "scientific frontier" to bar the Russian advance. Lonely outposts guarded each pass which threaded the hills of the northwest. Beyond was the scene of conflict, where Afghanistan lay "like an earthen pipkin between two iron pots." When the Amir, Shere Ali, desired closer relations with Great Britain Granville, preferring a "masterly inactivity," had refused his advances, and made an agreement with Russia. Still the shifting policy of the East saw Russia entangle the Amir in a diplomatic net as she wove protectorates closer to our frontier. Under Lord Salisbury a "forward policy" was adopted and carried out by Lord Lytton. The first sign was the occupation of Quetta, the second a request that the Amir would receive British officers as residents in his chief cities. Shere Ali, fearful and suspicious, "slipped out of our hands." No sooner had England denounced the treaty of San Stefano than the Russians sent a mission to Afghanistan; and on the refusal of Shere Ali to receive a British mission, Lytton closed twenty years of peace by a declaration of war. In Parliament a fierce conflict arose. When the Indian estimates were presented, Beaconsfield declaimed against the deleterious and mischievous doctrine of peace at any price, which occasioned wars and destroyed political equilibrium. Gladstone attacked the government's policy: it was Russia, he averred, and not Afghanistan, which should be called to account. But Shere Ali had already paid. His army had been defeated, and he died a fugitive. His crafty son, Yakub Khan, signed a treaty by which, in return for a subsidy, he pretended to cede the Khyber Pass and accepted a British envoy in Kabul. Six weeks later Sir Lewis Cavagnari and his staff were massacred. An army of occupation entered Kandahar, a punitive expedition advanced to Kabul, and the Amir was dethroned. In England the "forward policy" of the Tories was shattered with Beaconsfield's defeat at a general election; but Gladstone had to meet the difficulties bequeathed to him. The succession of Abdur Rahman, grandson of Dost Mohammed, was disputed by Ayub Khan. At Maiwand he inflicted a bloody defeat upon British and Indian troops, only half of whom returned to Kandahar and were there surrounded by hordes of Afghans. Sir Frederick Roberts set out from Kabul to their relief, following the road which had been cleared shortly before by his companion in arms, Sir Donald Stewart, in his famous march from Kandahar to Kabul. After three weeks of burning heat by day and icy cold by night Roberts's force emerged at Kandahar and routed the

SEC. II.

FOREIGN
AND
COLONIAL
POLICY

1815
TO
1914

1878

1880

SEC. II.

FOREIGN
AND
COLONIAL
POLICY

1815
TO
1914

1885

1907

The
Pacific

1899

The
Japanese
advance

1896
1906

enemy. So brilliant a victory enabled the evacuation of Afghanistan to be carried through by the Liberal government without loss of dignity. But Russia had now to seek compensation not only for her diplomatic reverse in the Balkans but for England's occupation of Egypt. From a railhead at Merv the Russians marched upon the outlying stronghold of Pendjeh. Using every form of tortuous delay to arrest the decisions of a boundary commission, they routed at Pendjeh the Afghans who had resisted their advance. A challenge so direct united every party in the House, and Gladstone was able to carry a vote of eleven millions. The unanimity of Parliament impressed the Russians, and the Pendjeh incident was ended by the delimitation of the Russian boundary. For the next twenty years of Russian progress over central Asia, England stood at guard, and was involved in conflicts with frontier tribes, in the barren territory of the Wakkan valley, in unknown Thibet to the gates of the sacred city of Lhassa, among the mountains of Chitral, in Persia and the passages to the Persian Gulf. Not till the Russo-Japanese war for possession of the Far East was the rivalry with England definitely postponed, and a mutual agreement defined the relations of the two countries in Afghanistan, Thibet, and Persia.

Not only in Africa and Asia, but in the Pacific also, "spheres of influence" were mapped out for the colonizing Powers. France after sixty years' effort gained Tahiti and a position in the New Hebrides. Germany established her position in the Polynesian Sea by buying the remaining possessions of Spain, while her earlier settlements in New Guinea and the Solomon and Marshall Islands were assured by a treaty with England, who retired from Samoa during the Boer war. The United States also had entered into the world-policy. When war had given them the outlying remnants of the Spanish empire, the American line of naval bases reached from New York to Peking. By Cuba, Puerto Rico, and other islands, she was established in the Caribbean Sea and the Gulf of Mexico; the Philippines lay on the trade route from Europe to China; stations in the Pacific were secured by treaties—Hawaii with the impregnable base of Honolulu, "the Gibraltar of the Pacific," the islands of Wake and Guam, and a post in the Samoan group. Finally Japan, conqueror of Korea and Formosa, took her place as the greatest military and naval force in the Pacific. Her coming was a new challenge. In 1885 Victoria had forbidden Asiatic immigration—a law which was adopted later by all the Australian colonies, by New Zealand, Canada, and South Africa. But if at the outset Japan consented to a treaty which excluded her immigrants from British dominions, ten years later she refused even to consider the idea, and demanded for her citizens the same terms as the members of white communities. Her subsidized schooners, carrying

SEC. II.

FOREIGN
AND
COLONIAL
POLICY

1815
TO
1914

highly skilled shipowners and fishermen, explorers and traders, all trained to war, penetrated among the islands, and left thousands of skilled workers in naval stations such as Hawaii, or Naumea in New Caledonia, whose harbour could hold half a dozen Japanese fleets, with one of the finest coalfields in the world close at hand. In the storm-centre of the future Australia and New Zealand lay as isolated outposts of Great Britain, among Asiatic peoples whose multitudes were breaking through old boundaries. Here less than five millions of the British race (and their members do not increase) held territory almost as large as Europe. The lands of the colonies were still unfilled: they had not been finally won for England nor for the white race while their shores remained unprotected and their scanty population might be submerged by a more numerous people. Moreover while Great Britain was no longer unchallenged on the far seas, a change had come too in the balance of imperial commerce. Once the whole produce of the colonies had been distributed from English ports, and external colonial trade rested upon London as its financial base. But while England still held the first place in international trade, foreign competitors were attacking the markets of the empire: Germany had risen to the second place, while American trusts pushed a world-wide activity. A new element of distrust had been added to this competition. For fifty years the British empire had held an open door to the world, and the peoples who had free access to its markets felt the less alarm at its huge expansion. There was a quick revulsion of feeling when, under pressure from Canada, England denounced her old free trade treaties with Germany and Belgium, and a preferential tariff with Canada was established, amid rumours of an imperial customs union to extend all over the colonies—a new " isolation " for the British Empire. Each self-governing Colony hastened to set up its own protective tariff. The Tory party, backed by traders eager to monopolize the colonial markets, declared for commercial " preference " throughout the empire as against the outside world. France and the United States had already hedged round their possessions by tariff and shipping restrictions; and Germany, the chief international trader after Britain, had no guarantee that England, possessing territory nearly five times the size of Europe, and half the sea-borne trade of the world, might not at last shut the door in all her dependencies, and that German trade would find itself banished from a quarter of the earth's surface. Hence the efforts made by Germany to maintain free trade in England. Men foresaw a world divided into spheres of influence, where neutral markets would dwindle and disappear, where each nation would be denied free entry and competition except in dominions under its own sway, and the entire globe would be dominated by great powers as jealous for their trading monopoly as for their territorial rights. An economic world-struggle had begun for the possession of

*Imperial
trade*

1895

*Tariff
reform*

Sec. II.

Foreign
AND
Colonial
Policy

1815
TO
1914

land and the appropriation of neutral markets. Instead of the old trade wars of cities, states, and countries, the threat hung over the nations of the monstrous clash of empires; and the problem of Europe—the balance of power among half a dozen states—broadened into the wider problem of equilibrium among the world-empires, and the complex alliances and counter-alliances needed to buttress an unstable and precarious peace.

Amid these conditions the imperialism propounded by Disraeli was before long to exhibit in its foreign policy the gravest elements of danger. At home his view of colonial empire was received with enthusiasm by his party, and his early impatient outbreak at the burden of the colonies was forgotten. He was the first prime minister to extol Canada in a speech. Self-government he accepted, but contended that all grants of liberty should have been limited by provisions for a customs union or imperial tariff, by a military code imposing the duties of common defence, and by a representative council in London. Chamberlain followed him as prophet of a united Empire with its ruling centre, its brain and its heart, in London. The majestic scheme was inaugurated by Lord Salisbury when, with a pomp beyond example,

he celebrated the Queen's Jubilee at the Foreign Office by the first assemblage of representatives of the free nations from oversea. But even the first Colonial Conference demonstrated that the imperial idea as conceived in England—the scheme of an empire under strict central control—was not easily reconciled with the temper of the dominions. These had now more than doubled in population. Each boasted of its own history, more original than that of many independent states. The supremacy of the Imperial Parliament, so cautiously established to ward off revolt, had vanished, and a new nationalism, distrustful and half mutinous, might even threaten to disrupt the empire. The "free nations" made their own laws, controlled at will citizenship, immigration, and trade; and asserted their national duty to allow no sacrifice of their prospects or privileges for any advantage to England or the Empire. Divergent interests led them to political isolation and to their own "Monroe doctrine," the doctrine of non-commitment to imperial responsibilities. Lord Salisbury justly warned the country of difficulties that must emerge from a state of things perfectly new to the world, the slow rise of an empire out of the sea, without territorial contiguity, held together merely by the necessities of naval defence, and resting on the feelings and affections of some of the most vehement races upon the face of the earth. If in conference the colonies admitted the principle of common obligation for defence, they rejected the idea of an imperial army as derogatory to their independence, and very doubtfully allowed an imperial navy. Australia's consent to contribute to an imperial squadron was denounced by Canada as a poor-spirited and non-national "hiring of defence." Seddon, the popular Minister of Defence in New Zealand, told a country audience, "What does a man hunting the country with a swag upon his back want with armed cruisers and a torpedo corps?" In a like spirit the Colonies resisted Chamberlain's proposal for a customs union after the German example: "if there is no fiscal autonomy," they insisted, "there cannot for long be an empire of free nations." Led by Canada, the dominions questioned the authority of the Foreign Office to conclude any treaty drawn·up without their consent, on the ground that English interests must be protected by the free will of free nations, and that each dominion must have the right to choose its part in the shifting diplomacy of England and of Europe. At the second Conference the Prime Ministers of the dominions were for the first time assembled; but behind the triumphant display of imperial might in honour of the Queen's second Jubilee rose more urgently the problem of defence. The Triple Alliance, hitherto regarded as a land power, was now threatening a formidable rivalry on the sea. For the first time advancing Asiatic immigration, even as far as African shores, forced discussion; if Indian emigrants could raise the claim of Imperial citizenship, the Japanese might justify their expansion by the force of fifty million people. But when Chamberlain, as Colonial Secretary, asked their aid in bearing the burden of empire—("The weary Titan staggers under the too vast orb of his fate")—the colonies showed no alacrity for a joint organization of defence; they gave their voice rather for commercial union by preferential duties, and asserted their financial independence by repealing the provisions for imperial free trade, and by making among themselves such fiscal treaties as they chose. At the third conference, after fifteen years of controversy, the Colonial Office scheme of federation under London control disappeared. The Boer War had proved its destruction.

The discovery of the richest gold mines in the world had drawn to the Transvaal adventurers from all countries, crowding to Johannesburg. There a medley of races found themselves under a primitive form of government originally framed for a pastoral and united people. Heavily taxed, vexed by partial laws and monopolies, and hampered by inexperienced and hostile officials, they demanded a share in government through the vote. The Boer refused it, and went his way. His one desire was to be left alone, and not to be disturbed by interlopers. Petitions and protests were unheeded. "You have not got the guns," said President Kruger, "and I have." It was at first supposed that the exhaustion of the mines might lead to the dispersion of the Uitlanders from a land so arid and ungrateful; but when the discovery of new deposits revealed that the gold of the Transvaal was equal to that of the British Empire or of the United States, it was

SEC. II.

FOREIGN
AND
COLONIAL
POLICY

1815
TO
1914

1899–1900

1897

**Second
Boer War**

1894

SEC. II.

FOREIGN
AND
COLONIAL
POLICY

1815
TO
1914

*The
Jameson
raid*
1896

1899

Oct. 9

plain that the foreigners had come to stay. The strife took fresh intensity. By annexing the coast the British took from the Boers all hope of securing a sea-port. The Uitlanders renewed their agitation for political rights. Rhodes, Premier of Cape Colony, secretly offered them assistance for an armed raid on the Transvaal under Dr. Jameson, the Administrator of Rhodesia—a treacherous and discreditable conspiracy. At the last moment divisions between the English and foreign Uitlanders disturbed the plan of attack and the raid ended with the capture of Jameson and his six hundred horsemen at Doornkop. No serious censure of Rhodes, the prime mover, came from the Tory government, who were believed to fear inquiry and even graver implications. Henceforth all hope of voluntary reform and conciliation disappeared in the tumult of race hostility and suspicion that were to throw the country into war. The Boers, convinced that future violence was intended, hurried on their preparation of armaments, while the Orange Free State, hitherto a faithful friend of England, joined their cause. All Europe was indignant and hostile. Arms were smuggled from Germany and France, and volunteers from every country streamed into the Transvaal. Kruger offered a form of franchise with conditions that diminished its value, and claimed for his Republic, in whose founding he had shared at the Great Trek, the status of a sovereign state. The High Commissioner, Sir Alfred Milner, insisted upon suzerainty, and the conference broke up. "The co-existence of ideas so repugnant," reported a Commission, "might at any time lead to an armed collision." The Afrikander Bond, a powerful union of the Cape Dutch, urged the Republic to carry a franchise bill; but the reactionary clauses of the draft made it of little value. England proposed arbitration, but included outstanding questions which the Boer regarded as an increase of the original demands. On the suzerainty neither side would yield. Repeated and emphatic warnings by Sir William Butler, the experienced general in command at the Cape, both as to the aggressive policy of the Uitlanders, and the inadequacy of the military forces for active operations, were met by his removal. Alarmed at the military preparations in Cape Colony and Natal, at the landing of troops from India, the surrounding of the Transvaal by armed forces—but above all at the calling out of the reserves in England—President Kruger demanded the withdrawal of British troops and the turning back of reinforcements. It was a demand "such as Her Majesty's Government deem it impossible to discuss." Three days later the Boers invaded Natal. "Before the diplomat proceeds to an ultimatum," said General Buller, "the military should be in a position to enforce it." But with a fatal contempt of the enemy there was neither plan of campaign nor any reliable maps, while the Boer knew every stream and kopje; and due provision of stores, hygiene, and sanitation were

Sec. II.

Foreign
and
Colonial
Policy

1815
to
1914

Dec. 11
Dec. 15

*Landing of
colonial
troops*
1900

*The
republics
annexed*

1901

alike neglected. The Boers surrounded Ladysmith, Kimberley, and Mafeking, and annexed Bechuanaland; and three separate lines of advance were ordered. The British troops, inferior in numbers to the Boers, had to meet marvellous marksmen, men trained on the veldt to peril, to hardship, to all craft and self-reliance of the fighter. Lord Methuen's way to Kimberley was barred by Boer commandos. Cronje, a veteran of former wars, defended the Modder River, and an attempt to surprise him at Magersfontein failed with heavy loss; on that day there was a disaster at Stormberg; and in the same week Buller on his march to Ladysmith was checked at the Tugela River, where the enemy under Louis Botha waited at Colenso, and the English lost eleven hundred killed and wounded. Since the loss of the American colonies no such week of humiliation had confounded England. Immense reinforcements were hurried out under Lord Roberts, with Lord Kitchener as chief of the staff. A storm of enthusiasm swept over the "free nations" of the Empire, and the astonishing sight was seen of troops landing in South Africa from Canada, Australia, and New Zealand to support the English armies. Lord Roberts's new host overtook the army of Cronje at Paardeberg and forced it to surrender. General French relieved Kimberley, the long siege of Ladysmith was raised by General Buller, and two months later a Rhodesian force went to the relief of Mafeking. Lord Roberts was advancing by rapid marches on Bloemfontein when a message from Kruger asked for peace with independence. The Boers, Lord Salisbury answered, must take the consequences of the war they had made; they had invaded our lands, and while success seemed possible had given no sign of conciliation. The Orange Free State was annexed, and once more a general at the head of an English army at Pretoria formally annexed the Transvaal. President Kruger fled to Holland to die in exile. But the Boers, led by Botha, Delarey, and de Wet, being now rid of every general over fifty years of age, maintained the war for two years, and even invaded Cape Colony. In Lord Kitchener's new campaign block-houses lined the railways and wire entanglements spread over the country, while women and children were collected in concentration camps, and Boer prisoners removed by thousands oversea. The method of conducting the campaign was vigorously condemned by the Liberal party in England. Sir Henry Campbell-Bannerman denounced warfare carried on by "methods of barbarism": "The whole country outside the mining towns is a howling wilderness. The farms are burned, the country is wasted. The flocks and herds are either butchered or driven off; the mills are destroyed, furniture and implements of agriculture are smashed." The conflict had become as deplorable as civil war. A strong feeling grew up for conciliation, and the Unionists were urged to revert to those generous traditions which had so often

Sec. II.
Foreign
AND
Colonial
Policy
1815
TO
1914

1902

The
Empire
and
nation-
ality

brought colonial peace. "My function," said Sir Alfred Milner, "is to destroy the domination of Afrikanderism." The Boers on their side fought with desperation. Whole districts were swept clear by overwhelming force before the peace of Vereeniging put an end to the misery. England undertook to restore to the country representative institutions, and the prisoners and women returned to their farms. Chamberlain as Minister of the Colonies travelled over the ravaged land to urge imperial federation, but the Tory Government was tottering, and the Boers waited for the promise of the Liberals.

Little as it was understood in England at the time, the Colonial troops that landed in Africa had changed the outlook of the Empire. Elated with the sudden sense of the forces at their command and the services they could render, the dominions looked forward to winning a status no lower than that of England herself. The policy of imperial concentration under the colonial and foreign office fell into the background, and a new scheme took its place, that of co-operation and equal alliance, and of defence founded on the principle of "future Dominion Navies." The Boer war had started nationalism on its victorious way, and the dominions entered on a new stage of their history. By a strange irony, unexpected and almost unperceived in England, the forces that had poured into South Africa to assert imperial rule over the Boers established for the whole Colonial world a measure of independence which English imperialists had not foreseen. The third conference, which followed the war, was the first to obtain absolute recognition from England of "national" aspirations. The occasion was favourable to their claims, for after the Jameson raid England was left without a friend, and exposed to extraordinary rancour from the governments and the press of Europe. "We are in bitter need of a strong German navy," said the Kaiser. The South African campaign, as well as the voyage of his squadrons to China, had afforded him a lesson in the resources of sea-power and the chain of coaling stations which linked the British Empire, and a new navy bill presented to the Reichstag was accompanied by the Kaiser's ringing words: "Our future lies upon the water." The challenge of the bill was made more definite by the Emperor's stirring visions of the "trident in our fist," and of the new division of the oceans, with "Germany to be Admiral of the Atlantic," even as "Russia of the Pacific." Nothing in English history has so suddenly changed the outlook of the people. Chamberlain apprehended the new issues of the future, and after his failure to bring about a Teutonic alliance between England, Germany, and the United States, he turned to the nations of the Empire: "More important than the goodwill of foreign nations was the confidence and affection of our kinsmen beyond the seas." Meanwhile the colonies were being forced into closer internal union. Within ten years three federated nations were formed after the example of Canada. Australia, watching the entry of one foreign power after another into the Pacific, cast off her hesitations of fifty years, and called a convention to frame a federal constitution. Every sentence of the new scheme was scrutinized in assemblies of the leading men of every profession and party. Approved in a meeting of prime ministers, and accepted in a referendum to the people, the Bill was carried to England. They rejected the term colony or dominion, and proclaimed a Commonwealth. A proposal of the Colonial Office to allow appeals to the Privy Council in constitutional disputes between the Commonwealth and the States after the example of Canada was refused. The first great act of the new nation was to assert a "white" Australia and exclude coloured immigration; the next was to take over the national defence. New Zealand stood apart, still aiming at the hegemony of the Southern Pacific and the island groups of Polynesia, which Sir George Grey had long before (1830) sought to establish by a customs union after the German example. Refusing to federate with Australia, she preferred to become a sister State in an Imperial system; and various islands were annexed to the Dominion. The latest entry into the "five nations," and the most stormy, was the Union of South Africa. Here the Liberals vindicated their principles of freedom when Sir Henry Campbell-Bannerman took office. The South African Customs Union was the first step towards a new federation. Prodigious difficulties lay in the way. Since the nearest outlet for the Transvaal mines was through a Portuguese port, and their chief supply of labour from Portuguese territory, many questions concerning the internal relations of the States must be dealt with by the Foreign Office. Commercial quarrels aggravated racial hostilities. The Transvaal by its railway to Delagoa had the traffic interests of South Africa at its mercy, and could threaten Cape Colony with ruin. The railways that connected the several states cut across frontiers arbitrarily ruled on the map corresponding to no political or physical lines of division; and communities that owned competing sections were in chronic hostility. Memories of the Raid and the concentration camps had united the Boer of the veldt with the French Huguenot of Cape Colony; while the English feared the betrayal of their interests or of their ascendancy. Above all rose the unsolved problem of the coloured races. From the Transvaal to Cape Colony the various states had pursued their separate policies, inconsistent and uncontrolled, towards the native Africans. Natal for her part had imported indentured labour of Indian coolies till in some twenty years she had nearly as many Indian as white men, and the black race outnumbered the European by ten to one; but after she became responsible for her own government and defence, she shut out Indian immigrants by law, and raised a formidable imperial problem.

SEC. II.

FOREIGN
AND
COLONIAL
POLICY

1815
TO
1914

1901

1907

1897

SEC. II.

FOREIGN
AND
COLONIAL
POLICY

1815
TO
1914

1909

Problems
of federa-
tion

Chinese labour in the gold mines added a later difficulty. The Liberal government determined to relieve a situation so desperate by the grant of Home Rule to the broken provinces and a place among the free nations of the Empire. Denounced as a "reckless experiment," the project, which might have failed in the House of Lords, was courageously launched by an Order in Council. By a scheme of self-government for the Transvaal and the Orange River Colony the way was prepared for a South African constitution. While the new Union was still in the making the Prime Minister welcomed the delegates of South Africa at a Colonial Conference in London. "I can assure you," he said, "the feeling of affectionate interest and pride entertained within the shores of the Old Country is not to be surpassed even by your warmest sentiments." A convention of members of the South African Government met to frame a constitution, which was amended and accepted by the four Colonies, and passed into law by the Imperial Parliament. The two races stood on equal terms, with both languages recognized, and with Pretoria as the centre of administration, and Cape Town as the seat of Parliament.

The constitutional experiments of the new Empire were as varied as the Colonies themselves. In Canada the federating provinces had suffered a complete loss of status, and had been re-created by the instrument which united them; a careful distribution of legislative power was made between the provinces and the new Dominion Parliament, which exercised all powers not expressly reserved to the local legislatures. Lieutenant-governors of the provinces are appointed by the Governor-General in Council, who can thereby exercise a veto in the name of the Dominion Cabinet upon all provincial legislatures, and who is given special powers to protect in regard to education the interests of religious minorities. Even the members of the Senate, supposed to represent the provinces, are the life-nominees of the Governor-General; this grave defect lowered their prestige, which was further diminished by their refusal of the commons' proposals to admit the western provinces to equality of representation in the Senate. The predominance of the central government in Canada is in striking contrast to the Australian commonwealth. Here the States, which had developed a strong provincial character, proudly refused to surrender their independence at federation, and continued under governors appointed by the Crown and responsible to it alone. It was not only by rejecting the interference of the Privy Council that Australia broke away from the Canadian precedent; another notable departure was the power to amend the constitution by a referendum to the Australian people themselves, whereas in British North America the constitution can only be altered through the imperial parliament. In both these respects the Australian Commonwealth Act is the high water mark of colonial "nationalism," and approaches nearer to the

United States constitution than that of any other Dominion. There
are other points of likeness, in the insistence on equality of State
rights as represented in the Senate; and in the restriction, contrary
to the Canadian system, of the Federal legislature within carefully defined limits, the residuary powers falling to the States. In
South Africa all these conditions were reversed. The relics of past
errors in allowing provinces of different allegiance to grow up, the
sudden changes by which the wealth of gold and diamonds had turned
old pastoral communities into new towns, the consequent revolution
in local government, the presence across the frontier of the greatest
military power of Europe—these were considerations that led South
African statesmen to exclude the federation adopted elsewhere. More
far-reaching than all these was the world-problem of the future, the
relation between the white and coloured races. Its presence, more
acute here than in any other country, is the clue to the history of
South Africa, where a million and a quarter white men were intermingled with an African and coloured population of nearly five times
their number, and two white nations looked upon the natives from
two entirely different standpoints, and Downing Street and Exeter
Hall from a third. In face of these complicated difficulties unity was
preferred to federal union and the constituent colonies were required
to surrender their legislative powers and to sink to the level of
administrative councils for the conduct of local government, under one
single and supreme parliament—a system by which highly centralized
government has been, it is thought, carried too far. In the various
Dominions every variety of political theory has thus been given a
trial, and to them falls the task of adapting their several constitutions
to their actual needs. South Africa may yet find means to reach her
full national life by developing under the Union more liberal scope
for local interests, and greater freedom of activity in her states. In
Canada, notwithstanding the power of the central government, the
balance in the distribution of legislative power has been carefully
maintained by the judicial decisions of the Privy Council, even if it is
only secured at the cost of an enormous amount of litigation and not
a little friction. Australia, with its larger democratic independence,
is in perpetual oscillation between the party of " State rights " and the
party in favour of enlarging the Federal power—a party chiefly
recruited from the ranks of labour, who desire to exercise effective
control over the far-reaching industrial questions which by the terms
of the Constitution are confided to the States. So far the weight of
judicial decisions has been against any disturbance in the actual
decision of power; and the States party have not succeeded in winning
their victory through the referendum. The end is not yet, and the
question remains in acute controversy. Federation in fact is no
mechanical scheme. In no dominion have all adjustments yet been

Sec. II.

Foreign
and
Colonial
Policy

1815
to
1914

*Federal
changes*

Sec. II.

Foreign
and
Colonial
Policy

1815
to
1914

Imperial
federa-
tion

1897

1911

Future
dominion
navies

1902–1914

completed between local vigour and central uniformity, and still less has the final solution been found for the Empire. It was necessary for the dominions first to solve their own internal problem.

The absorbing question henceforth was how to strengthen the imperial organization. Bentham's plan of allowing the colonies to find their own way to national independence, and the attempt of Disraeli and Chamberlain to unite the forces of the Empire in a scheme of Imperial concentration, had been set aside. To divert trade by a British tariff-league or commercial bond in supposed imperial interests was felt to be but a milder form of the old colonial system. The colonies, suspicious of general trade preference to the Mother Country, declared that "their fiscal policy is a matter on which the Dominions will never surrender their autonomy. Preferences must be purely voluntary." They especially resented the control of foreign policy from London. In the early days of Imperialism the English government, in the name of foreign policy, could forbid Queensland to enforce her law against Chinese immigrants. But, led by Canada, the Dominions denied that any foreign treaty, whether as to trade or immigration, made by Britain without their consent, could be forced on them, and claimed both the right of making their own treaties and a controlling diplomatic influence in treaties made by England. Mr. Asquith emphatically warned the third Colonial Conference that the conduct of foreign policy must rest absolutely with the Foreign Office. But the pressure of imminent danger allowed a significant precedent; and the third Japanese treaty (which safeguarded the Empire from the possibility of being drawn by Japan into war with America) was the first occasion on which all the Prime Ministers in Council approved of a solemn international agreement. On the question of defence the Dominions were equally rigid. After the scare of the German navy bill controversy was carried on through a dozen years of growing perils. While the colonies discussed their future national navies, and the Japanese fleet asserted its strength in the Pacific, England was forced to withdraw her effective battleships to meet threatened dangers in the North Sea. Intensely occupied with their own social and industrial affairs the Dominions but dimly perceived the gravity of foreign problems, till these were forced on them by the threat of a European war on the question of Bosnia, by a third German navy bill, and by Sir Edward Grey's statement to the House of Commons that to meet the new dangers the British fleet must be rebuilt on *Dreadnought* lines. The Conference of 1909 hastened to give contributions to the imperial navies, and to increase greatly their own military burdens. As to naval defence the Dominions were divided between two schools of thought. The New Zealand government and one of the great parties in Canada, now led by Sir Robert Borden, support the principle of a contribution of ships and men which shall at all times form an integral part of a homogeneous Imperial navy. Australia, and Sir Wilfrid Laurier's followers in Canada, preferred the system of national navies to be stationed in local waters, and to be subject to the Admiralty only in time of war. This agreement was the boldest recognition yet given by any Conference in London to national sentiment as one of the sure foundations of the Empire. But the scheme broke down before a menace of war such as had not threatened England since 1815. In the crises of Algeciras and Agadir the Dominions read the warning that their very existence was at stake; and felt the approach of peril at a rumour that France would cede Tahiti to Germany. By a hurried compromise they consented to unity of control and concentration of the fleet in the place of danger, while Britain agreed to maintain a squadron in the east. Excitement was increased by a fifth German navy bill. England, which in 1902 had 147 ships in the Atlantic, Pacific, and Mediterranean, had now but thirty-six. Without imperial help, "our seas are defenceless and our trade routes unprotected," said the Australians. "The dangers which face Australia are unique: they affect no other nation in the world in the same degree." The more ardent looked forward to ultimate control of the Pacific fleet by the Dominions' navies. "We are asking for a trust in us and for privileges which no Empire in history has yet accorded to its constituents." They needed "a great fighting navy" in what might "yet become the battle-ground of the nations." The building of their own ships was begun.

The Australian peoples, more than all others, are concerned with problems completely of the modern world. The most democratic part of the empire, carrying no burdens from a long past, they have made Australia and New Zealand the ground of experiments in social legislation more advanced and daring than any in the world. Except in Tasmania, church and state are absolutely separated; labour is everywhere powerful in parliaments, and labour governments hold office in Commonwealth and states; the public departments exceed those of European countries; and the statute-books teem with laws to assure material well-being and social equality. Nowhere in any land have the workers fewer hours, or more pay and holidays. In New Zealand the average wealth of the people is the highest in the world, and here the rule of radical and labour governments has been longer than in any other colony. The influence of Sir George Grey, governor first and then leader of the Liberal revolt and prime minister, may be seen in the fearless democratic legislation of the colony. New Zealand was first in adult suffrage, which included even Maori women; it led the advance in factory and shipping laws, in laws to subdivide great estates and establish the principle of state-ownership of the soil, in industrial arbitration, in life insurance, and in the

SEC. II.

FOREIGN AND COLONIAL POLICY

1815 TO 1914

1911

1912

The Free Peoples

1876

1893

Sec. II.

Foreign
AND
Colonial
Policy

1815
TO
1914

admirable care of the citizens' interests by a public trustee. It has shared indeed with other new countries the dangerous effects of interests narrowed to material development and local problems, and subjected to the enormous influence of the borrowing and spending of money, and the doling out of grants for industrial and sectional purposes. But in the least of the free dominions as in the greatest, the peoples have shown how a virile race, with the certain assurance of genuine and honourable self-government under the protection of an imperial peace, and with "habits equal to their birth," can justify the spirit of democratic responsibility. By a strange destiny the proof of the new Empire, slowly working out its problem of equal rights and free consent, was swift and sudden. Its casual conferences of delegates had but just begun to foreshadow a Council of the Empire. The South African Union had only existed long

enough to take part in one Conference. Australia had scarcely prepared her first manifest signs of national union—the inauguration of railway connection for all the provinces, a postage stamp for the whole Commonwealth, and agreement for a federal capital in the desolate locality of Yass Canberra. Canada of east and west had not long been connected by three trans-continental railways over lonely prairies and lofty and unexplored mountain ranges. The Dominions in general, absorbed in rapid internal development, had but newly proclaimed their national consciousness, discussion on imperial organization had hardly begun, a plan of defence was still in hot debate, when the catastrophe of universal war fell on the world. Never was there a test of Empire so sudden in its blow, so fierce in its trial of a system still in the eyes of critics almost in chaos, haphazard and unscientific. But in the gathering of scattered colonists into self-governing nations, and of these again into an Imperial Commonwealth based on free consent, Englishmen proudly recognize the most gigantic experiment in government and the most stirring effort after human liberty that the world has known.

If the English settlers of the empire look back to Bentham, the races of other blood may look back to Wilberforce and Clarkson as their apostles of freedom. Beyond the fifty-six million subjects of the British crown who are of European descent lie the three hundred or more millions of other races whose administration Great Britain has taken in charge. This vast enterprise, without parallel in the world, is rather a study in governments than in the development of the English people. Every form of rule is represented, from the free colonial system at one end to the "political despotism" of the "protectorates" at the other, in which the Crown, without claiming ownership, can exercise absolute authority and set up whatever jurisdiction it pleases. In spite of deviations, failures, and human errors, there has been a growing purpose to protect the interests

Sec. II.

Foreign
and
Colonial
Policy

1815
to
1914

of each state or territory as against the old notion of exploiting the inhabitants for profit. And with this has gone a series of experiments in broadening the share of the various peoples in their own government. During the last thirty years liberties have been enlarged in the empire of India. Not only is there a tendency to lessen the checks upon the power of the Princes in their own states, but in territories under British rule the attempt has been made throughout the whole administration to advance representative government: first by municipalities and district boards, then by a reform of provincial councils so that the majority shall be elected by the lower representative bodies, and finally by admitting to the imperial legislative council members largely elected by the provincial councils. The demand for fiscal and financial liberty has been recognized in the powers given to discuss the annual budget, and to interpellate officials, foreshadowing some ultimate abatement of a control from England which is essentially financial. It is the pride of Great Britain that she has won her way in Asia and Africa to a higher general standard of humanity and justice than any other rulers of alien peoples. Her advance may perhaps be best measured in the protectorate of northern Nigeria, where a company of devoted officials have illustrated how far the guardianship of native civilization can be made the purpose and the triumph of imperial rule. Everywhere, save in Canada and Australia, Englishmen have come into contact with the problem of governing and judging men of a lower or a different civilization from their own. It is evident that if their rule has meant the carrying of Indian troops to China, Somaliland, Crete, Persia, and at last to France, if it involves the planting of Indians and Chinese coolies in South America, of Indians in Africa, and of Chinese in islands of the Pacific, the problems of the future must be yet more intricate than in the past. For Englishmen, with their world-wide engagements, it is not possible to aspire to a Monroe doctrine of setting a boundary round any region of the earth within which they shall perfect their own civilization, and limit their obligations to external peoples. The duty of Great Britain and her fate are linked with the world universal. Within her empire her work has been to establish a wide peace, under one overshadowing authority, among peoples of every diversity of climate and conditions, of speech, tradition, and religion. By a just instinct she has seen in the free interchange of commerce the first means of intercourse and mutual comprehension among men of all nations and races, and has rejected the manipulation of tariffs on any plea whatever as "a fertile, frequent, and almost inexhaustible source of friction." Her policy has been justified, for England still carries half the produce of the whole world, and moreover provides for it the capital, and transacts in London half its business. It was in the midst of a development so engrossing that the English were called

Imperial obligations

Sec. II.

Foreign
and
Colonial
Policy

1815
to
1914

The
German
policy

back into the circle of European conflicts which since Waterloo they had sought to avoid or to forget.

The lingering authority of the Concert of Europe had presided over the colonial expansion of the nations. While the powers were occupied in partitioning the world they ceased to arouse old quarrels at home, and more or less amicably adjusted their new boundaries in Asia, Africa, and the Pacific. But the failure of the most stupendous project yet imagined—the dividing of China into spheres of influence— checked foreign adventure. Europe was thrown back on herself. Her governments, entangled in confused disputes and indiscriminate ententes, endeavoured by means of independent and secret agreements to gain their several advantages, pushing back general perils and responsibilities to some later time : and the peoples, at the mercy of a secret diplomacy, became involved in engagements, responsibilities, and dangers of which they knew nothing, though they must ultimately assume the burden. While France, England, and Russia pursued their separate and uncertain paths, Germany steadily strengthened the Triple Alliance and determined her own policy. Soon after

William II. received the imperial crown, not, as he claimed, conferred by parliament or popular decisions but by the grace of God only,

Bismarck was dismissed, and the young emperor's romantic, vehement, and versatile nature had full scope. "Germany," said Bismarck, "as a unit is only a new nation ; but the time will come when the German empire will dominate Europe." The Kaiser looked beyond Europe. In emulation of the vastness of British power he resolved that Germany should be not only first among military nations on land, but powerful enough at sea to command a great colonial future. On

the twenty-fifth anniversary of the inaugural ceremony at Versailles he proclaimed that the German empire was now a world-empire : world power and influence, he told his people, were theirs by the will of Providence. "Nothing must henceforth be settled in the world without the intervention of Germany and the German emperor." "My cause is the right one, and I shall follow it." "Those who oppose me I shall dash in pieces." The colonial party determined to outvie the splendours of India. The whole people were united in the sense of their mission, by the supremacy of German thought and German organization, to lead and benefit the nations of the earth. Endowed with energy, resources, and government, trained to the virtues of labour and thrift, educated to fulfil their allotted parts in the great scheme, they followed leaders who never lost sight of a fixed plan of aggrandizement. To the German accepting the rigorous training necessary for his gigantic task the impression of England was one of indiscipline, disorder, and ignorance. "A thing that is wholly a sham," said Treitschke, "cannot in this universe of ours endure for ever." The British empire, some five times as great as Europe, scattered through the oceans, was a standing outrage to the Prussian sense of organization; there was no conscript army for its defence, no fiscal agreement, and no unquestioned control, and in a hundred weak points Bismarck foresaw the undoing of the "boastful Englanders, even though German blood rules from the throne." Germany had in view a more compact and scientific dominion. The year after his accession the young emperor William II. visited the Sultan at Constantinople. There he looked out on a new world. In western Asia were lands rich in metals, with oil-wells more abundant than those of Russia and North America, vast forests, and fertile soil which could produce cotton, wool, and wheat. The exploitation of Babylonia and the valleys of the Euphrates and Tigris had been suggested by an English general, Francis Chesney, who surveyed the country for a railway, but English capitalists were diffident, and the project was abandoned. Von Moltke while training the Turkish army advocated the foundation of a protectorate in Palestine, and the day was predicted when German statesmen would be as powerful in the east as Palmerston, Thiers, or Menschikoff. German economists had urged for fifty years the scheme which was to be taken up finally by William II.—a scheme of reclamation equal to any in the British empire. A great railway contract between the Porte and France ended with the defeat of Sedan. The congress of Berlin opened new chances. Confronted with the Christian kingdoms sliced from his territory, Abd-ul-Hamid called in Prussian generals to make him an army. German interests in the Balkans were further advanced when Rumelia and Bulgaria came together in a single principality under Alexander of Battenberg, France and England consenting, and Lord Salisbury's ambassador at Constantinople now deprecating needless references to the treaty of Berlin. The Tsar however in his anger forced Alexander to resign; and German influence persuaded Bulgaria to elect in his stead prince Ferdinand of Saxe-Coburg-Gotha, officer in the Austro-Hungarian army. Friendship with Turkey was confirmed; Abd-ul-Hamid, the first Sultan to realize the value of Pan-islamism as a political weapon, and to exploit the spiritual sovereignty of the Caliphate, had led a Mohammedan revival which spread as far as the tribes of the Indian border. Feuds and local disturbances in Armenia were suppressed by massacres exceeding anything registered in the past: some 150,000 Christians perished. Gladstone with a last effort denounced to an indignant England the "Great Assassin": to the French he was the "Red Assassin." Lord Salibury, returning to power, threatened the Ottoman empire with extinction under the fiat of divine justice; English vessels lay in wait at Salonica, Russian at Sebastopol, French at Smyrna, while in words that seemed to threaten war he demanded expiation for public crime. For the first time the

SEC. II.

FOREIGN AND COLONIAL POLICY

1815 TO **1914**

1889
Asia Minor

1839

1836

1868

1883

1885

1887
The Turkish revival

1894-1895

SEC. II.

FOREIGN
AND
COLONIAL
POLICY

1815
TO
1914

1897

1898

*The Bagdad
railway*
1899–1902

Sultan could do as he chose unharmed in presence of six great powers so hampered by pledges, by distrust, or by ambitions that no common action was possible. After a new Armenian massacre in Constantinople he turned to forbid the withdrawal from the Turkish empire of Crete—the last relic of Ottoman sea-power since the overthrow of Navarino, the only link with Tripoli and the Mohammedans of North Africa, the chief naval base between Malta and Suez. The powers were called in to prevent the union of Crete with Greece: and when the Greeks declared war, the overwhelming victory of Turkey asserted Mohammedan strength. The memory of Armenian massacres was still fresh when the Kaiser, detaching himself from the universal condemnation of Europe, visited the "Red Assassin" at Constantinople. In Syria he proclaimed himself the protector of Moslem peoples, the immense majority of whom were citizens of the British and French empires, while there was not one under German rule. "May the Sultan and the three hundred million Mussulmans scattered over the earth," he said at Damascus, "be assured that the German emperor will always be their friend." It was the beginning of a momentous alliance. Germany foresaw with her entry into Asia Minor "a German Suez Canal," and German culture in the Orient dominant over the whole Mohammedan world. Prince Ferdinand of Coburg readily gave permission for direct communication through Bulgaria from Berlin to Constantinople, while the Sultan granted a concession to a German company for a railway from Konieh to Koweit, one of the most important routes of his empire. Thus opened the scheme which strategic and commercial experts in Germany had prepared—a scheme as grandiose and more solidly based on fact that the "Cape to Cairo" catchword of Rhodes; they looked forward to a Bremen, Byzantium, and Bagdad line, an overland route to India, trains for a thousand miles to coal a German fleet in the Persian Gulf, a railway from Damascus to Cairo, another from Angora to Erzerum and Tiflis. Branch lines were to link Constantinople with the Holy Cities of Islam. Russia was threatened on her Caucasian frontier, and Italy in her trade from Brindisi; while French traders were ousted from Syria, and the traffic from Marseilles endangered. It was intended to emigrate thousands of Prussian peasants to Mesopotamia, and a scientific survey prepared for the irrigation of enormous tracts of land. "If one can speak of boundless prospects anywhere," said von Bülow, "it is in Mesopotamia." Throughout the nineteenth century the Ottoman empire had suffered from every incitement to war, international, national, racial, and religious, but a final passion was now added—the competition of the colonizing empires for possession of Asia Minor and Egypt, the lands in which all conquerors, from Alexander to Napoleon, have seen the keys of the world.

Sec. II.

Foreign
AND
Colonial
Policy

1815
TO
1914

England
and
Europe
1899

England, emerging from the Boer war into a changed world, was
led to reverse her attitude to the European powers. France and
Russia had been of old the enemy. Extreme bitterness had followed
the Fashoda quarrel, and Chamberlain had rudely warned France
to mend her manners. "Who sups with the devil must have a long
spoon," he had exclaimed when Russia took Port Arthur. Both
court and nation had been favourable to Germany; in the seizure of
New Guinea Chamberlain saw "an unconsidered trifle of territory,"
and believed the cession of Heligoland outweighed by "vast advantages"; after the agreement over Samoa he suggested an alliance
between Great Britain, Germany, and the United States, as a "potent
influence in the future of the world." There began friendly discussions
over colonial concessions. The English socialists admired and
trusted their German brethren. But there was no real understanding.
Germany held back from English advances, lest she should become
"the sword of England on the continent." Chamberlain was made
to see that he was "biting granite." His programme of fiscal reform
and an imperial customs union, and Canada's preferential tariff,
roused the suspicion of Germany and brought a threat of reprisals;
and a second navy bill practically doubled her fleet. Her hostility was
increased when England refused assistance for the Bagdad railway.
At this moment the accession of Edward VII. gave the court a wholly

new outlook on foreign affairs, and facilitated a reversal of English
policy. So long as Lord Salisbury guided English affairs he maintained her "isolation." The Bagdad line was to him primarily a
German-Russian matter. One startling innovation he admitted.
England still controlled commerce by her carrying trade, her
wealth, and her prestige, but France, who before 1870 had been
second, sank to the fourth rank, while the United States and Germany
stood second and third; it was no longer possible to maintain against
all rivals a preponderant English navy on every ocean, and the
government secured peace for Australasia by an alliance with Japan,
the leading power in the Pacific. Under Mr. Balfour as premier,

with Lord Lansdowne as foreign secretary, a revolution in
policy was inaugurated, to meet the formidable menaces and the
universal fears arising in Europe. Since Waterloo England had held
her separate place, aloof from the alliances and disputes of European
states; and her naval and military forces had been adjusted to that
understanding. With Edward VII. there came a change. By a
series of agreements the cabinet gradually reverted to the balance of
power in the hope of preserving the European peace. The advances
of French ministers to secure English support were no longer
treated with reserve, and the first official visit of the new king
to Paris led to an understanding with France closer than Palmerston

had ever admitted. England, abandoning the system of Castlereagh

SEC. II.

FOREIGN
AND
COLONIAL
POLICY

1815
TO
1914

*The Anglo-
French
entente*

1904

1905

June

Jan.
1906

and Canning, closed her seventy years' opposition to the spread of
French power in Morocco; and Lord Rosebery alone denounced the
new convention as carrying a grave military danger. By the bargain
the English gained trading privileges and the neutralization of Tangier,
a free course in Egypt, control of the Newfoundland fisheries, and
settlement of disputes in Siam and West Africa, New Hebrides and
Madagascar. Tripoli was left to Italy. This treaty was accepted by
Germany as " very natural and perfectly justified." But while France
and Spain had openly guaranteed the integrity of Morocco they had
made a secret treaty, only revealed seven years later, for a division of
the country which was to leave to Spain the extreme northern sea-
board, including Tangier. When France proceeded to impose on
the Sultan a radical scheme of reforms to be carried out by French
loans, she was met by a dramatic German challenge. Suddenly
landing in his yacht at Tangier, the Kaiser accentuated his new
position as protector of the Moslems, announcing that no power
should come between him and the free sovereign of a free country.
Germany claimed the right to be consulted in the affairs of Morocco,
where she had commercial interests affirmed by treaty, lest she should
suffer " detriment in other questions, perhaps more important." The
emperor's denunciations of a slight to the " world-wide dominion of
the Hohenzollerns " rang out. " Powder dry, sword keen, eyes on the
goal, muscles taut," he said to his army. The great controversy had
begun whose issue is still unknown. From that time Germany
believed, with intensity of apprehension and anger, that a plan
existed to " hem her in." France and England on their side were
convinced of a deliberate German intention to shatter the Anglo-
French agreement, and make a trial of strength in an affair " under
which lurked the deepest and most difficult problems of power."
The Emperor had landed at Tangier at the moment when Russia,
the only ally of France, was falling back before the Japanese after
her crushing defeat at Mukden; and it was four days after the
Russian fleet had been broken at Tsushima that he demanded an
international conference on the Moroccan question. Delcassé, the
foreign minister who had carried the Anglo-French entente, would
have taken up the abrupt challenge to French claims, but he stood
alone in a cabinet which refused to risk war without an ally, and was
forced to resign. Germany triumphed in his fall, and in the calling
of the Algeciras conference. There the powers (the United States
among them) arranged a compromise, confirming the integrity of
Morocco, but authorizing France and Spain to police the coast towns.
The blow against the entente had failed; but neither side could claim
success, and bitter passions remained. Delcassé's threats of the
power of the entente for war on Germany, and of England's willingness
for a formidable naval attack, roused intense German excitement.

Wild rumours were dictated by anger and suspicion, and lay in men's minds. It was not till over eight years after, on the outbreak of the European war, that it was made known to England how far her honour had been engaged by secret negotiations. When the French asked for an assurance of armed support in case of war Sir Edward Grey had refused a promise, but had admitted the possibility that if war were forced on France the British would rally to its material support: and had authorized secret naval and military "conversations" to prepare for such a contingency, on the condition that these discussions should not pledge or restrict either government.

There could be no doubt that the first and absorbing object of the Liberal government under Sir Henry Campbell-Bannerman, with Sir Edward Grey as foreign minister, was peace. The traditional free-trade policy of the Liberals removed a dangerous source of friction with foreign states, and schemes for imperial preference were buried. The grant of self-government to the Transvaal won admiration and sympathy. An agreement with Russia in Central Asia tended to assuage the jealousy which for seventy years had prevented any loyal understanding between the two greatest Asiatic empires. It seemed that with the close of England's isolation the balance of power might again hang fairly equal, and the European concert have its resurrection; and in an exuberance of prosperity and of self-confidence difficulties were overlooked. On the one side was the Triple Alliance of the central states, compacted by thirty years of discipline, with an overpowering military force and a definite policy. On the other side were countries till lately hostile and suspicious, now drawn together by separate and local understandings concerning Africa and Asia, but without any common policy in Europe. The prime minister pointed to the parting of the roads—the broad and easy way to protection, military service, and the degradation of England's liberal institutions; and the path of free trade and larger liberties, leading to peace, retrenchment, and reform. His followers, burning with a long-restrained zeal, and autocratic by virtue of their huge majority, determined to push through their long-deferred schemes of social reform at home, outreaching the projects of any European country. A fervent energy pervaded the incongruous elements of the party—the preponderant body of lawyers in Parliament confident in the power of international law, the liberals believing in open and faithful agreements of the nations but maintaining an avowed distrust of reactionary Russia, the labour party in strong sympathy with German socialists and the international ideal of a "new brotherhood of labour," by whom war would be brought to an end, and whose messages of goodwill carried from country to country would reveal the power of the democracy to purge foreign policy and banish secret diplomacy. But their work for peace was hampered by narrowness of

SEC. II.

FOREIGN
AND
COLONIAL
POLICY

1815
TO
1914

outlook and ignorance of foreign history and politics, the flagrant defect of England during this century. Cobbett had once regarded English interest in Greek independence as little but a manœuvre to obtain the advantages of a loan. Cobden and Bright often spoiled their case through overstatement, and Liberals who inherited their tradition were liable to misinterpret both their faults and their merits. Bright, an ardent pacifist, thought that the cause of liberty justified the American Civil war. Cobden was an advocate of naval supremacy, and offered to vote a hundred million pounds rather than see another navy on a level with that of England, since "any attempt of that sort would argue some sinister design upon this country." Mill desired a strong navy, and deplored the Declaration of Paris: "We have put away the natural weapon of a maritime nation," he said, "because we have abandoned the right of warring against the commerce of our enemies."

When England proposed retrenchment of armaments, and set the hazardous example of cutting down her shipbuilding, Germany, recalling her struggle with Austria in 1850, replied that an agreement to limit her navy would be another Convention of Olmütz, and the reply was no mere rhetoric: "to ask from an independent power that it should limit its force is to assail its rights of sovereignty on its own territory"—so spoke Bright in 1855. Germany increased the number of her battleships, condemned academic discussions, and made it a condition of joining a Peace Conference at The Hague that there should be no proposal for disarmament. This second Conference, following that called by Nicholas II. in 1899 to mitigate the barbarity of war, accepted the rules of the Geneva Convention of 1864 for relief of wounded and prisoners; sought to protect neutral trade, and neutral lands under an occupying army; and attempted to frame rules for naval war, to form an international prize court, and to create a permanent judicial court of arbitration. Difficulties arose in defining the position of neutrals, in drawing up an accepted code of arbitration and of prize; even in the dubious authority of the Hague conference itself with its forty-four represented states. The South American continent had been taken into the European circle as professing the same civilization; but the great powers who refused to recognize the equality of small nations in debate, still less admitted that their ancient interests could be decided by a casting vote of Ecuador. The New World could not yet, a century after Canning's dream, redress the balance of the Old.

The prime minister, a dying man, made his last effort for peace by a new reduction of shipbuilding, and by an open letter to the world urging disarmament in the interests of humanity and civilization. Mr. Asquith took his place, and with Sir Edward Grey consistently laboured for peace amid fresh threats of war. The controversy which opened at Tangier passed to the Balkans, and the menace of

European war swung from the western to the eastern Mediterranean. If Morocco, commanding the double routes of the Mediterranean and the Atlantic, seemed twice in the next five years the point of danger, the true centre of peril remained in the Ottoman empire. Austria extolled the mission of the future to open up Asia Minor as a worthy exploit of the German spirit, and received from Berlin help (in spite of engagements with Russia ten years before) to secure a railway through Novi-bazar opening on the valley of the Vardar towards Salonica, the true commercial outlet from the Danube for the whole German world. Serbia, supported by Russia, demanded a compensating railway to the Adriatic. The Novi-bazar project was suddenly replaced by a proposal formally to annex Bosnia and Herzegovina, as a suitable Jubilee offering to Francis Joseph in the sixtieth year of his reign—a conception of kings and peoples worthy of Metternich of a hundred years before. Already Austria and Hungary, alarmed at the growing unity of the Southern Slavs, were looking forward to a punitive expedition and the annexation of Serbia—the Piedmont of the Balkan states, the country which had been the first in revolt against tyranny in 1804, and had won its freedom with less help than any other people of the Balkans. Finally came rumours that at King Edward's visit to the Tsar at Reval England and Russia had proposed the administration of Macedonia by the six powers. The answer to these predatory schemes was the revolution of the Young Turks at Salonica. Reviving Midhat Pasha's famous constitution of 1876, they once more confronted Europe with "the integrity of the Ottoman empire." The German powers, checked for a moment, adopted the policy that Bismarck had pointed out—a Balkan confederation under Austrian leadership. There was a rapid "entente" with Bulgaria, and secret understandings with Roumania and Greece. The Protestant prince Ferdinand had in 1895 made his astute bargain for a possible entry some day into Constantinople by having his son baptized in the Orthodox Greek church: and now throwing off Ottoman lordship, he significantly proclaimed himself Tsar of Bulgaria. Austria formally annexed the provinces she had for thirty years administered. In the general excitement sinister rumours embittered every nation, and extraordinary unrest troubled men's minds. The Kaiser sowed distrust by a statement that in the Boer war France and Russia had proposed to him an alliance against England and had been repulsed. There was a war panic over the arrest of German deserters by the French at Casablanca, until the question was referred to arbitration at The Hague. As the Germans watched the agreements on African questions among the Latin powers of the Mediterranean, and the new cordiality between the Russian and English governments, they recalled the French phrase of "encirclement." The idea of the "circle" closing around

SEC. II.

FOREIGN
AND
COLONIAL
POLICY

1815
TO
1914

SEC. II.

FOREIGN
AND
COLONIAL
POLICY

1815
TO
1914

1909

them became a fixed and fanatical prepossession. Competition for sea-power grew more intense. The German programme for thirty-three Dreadnoughts was hastened in the North Sea, while Austria and Italy and France prepared to launch battleships in the Mediterranean. Already the supremacy of the great Armada that had gathered at Portsmouth for the Jubilee of 1897 was passing, and Sir Edward Grey announced that the fleet must be rebuilt and eight Dreadnoughts laid down that year. The astounding naval and military preparations of Germany, the vast increase of workmen in Krupp's factory, with new engines of war, gave the Triple Alliance a more aggressive character. German pressure tightened on Italy. When Austria hesitated to defy Russia to war on the question of annexation, the Kaiser proposed to garrison Bohemia and Galicia while Bosnia and Herzegovina were taken over; and on Austria's refusal he sent an ultimatum to Russia, forestalled her capitulation to Austria alone, and announced to the world that it was he in "shining armour" who had made the great success. Since the other powers were too much divided to insist on a conference, the annexation was carried through without protest. The same month Abd-ul-Hamid was deposed and the Young Turks opened their ill-starred rule. German influence overspread the Balkans, and Prussian officers reconstructed the Turkish army. A Turkish loan was raised in Germany and Austria. The Bagdad railway was pushed on rapidly. The Kaiser met the Tsar at Potsdam, when Nicholas agreed to withdraw his army to a fixed distance behind the Russo-German frontier, recognized the control of the German government over the Bagdad line, and consented to build a railway which would have opened the markets of Persia to German goods.

The grief of England for the death of Edward "the peacemaker," as he was called, intensified the desire for general conciliation. A convention had already met in London to continue the work of the Hague Conference; and the Declaration of London, which elaborated the Declaration of Paris, was an attempt to define the high-water mark of common agreement in a code of maritime war. The govern-ment, faithful to the cause of international right, passed the Declara-tion through the House of Commons. It was rejected by the Lords; the Colonial conference was doubtful of its provisions; the United States, with their enormous coast-line and interests on two oceans refused their signature. Ten years of effort at The Hague had borne little fruit. Meanwhile the press and the pulpit were pouring out promises of a speedy disarmament and universal peace. A new Japanese treaty provided against the possibility of England being involved in any dispute between Japan and America. The warm reception to the German Emperor on his visit to England; the amicable arrangement that the Bagdad railway should be given an opening on the Mediterranean and not carried to the Persian Gulf;

the large colonial concessions to Germany adumbrated in friendly discussion; the settlement of outstanding disputes in Persia and the Mediterranean—all these encouraged high hopes. Germany, it is true, rejected proposals put forward by President Taft to discuss a system of general arbitration, observing that if a country would not spend enough on armaments to make its way in the world it would sink to the *rôle* of super on the world's stage. And in England a powerful imperialist opposition challenged the peace party in office, and Lord Roberts declared that "its armed force should be the measure of the nation's devotion to whatever end it pursued"; called England to recognize in war the road by which, sword in hand, she had climbed to her unmatched eminence, the road by which had gone "all nations and cities that have ever added the lustre of their name to human annals"; and desired his countrymen to admit the maxims of German statesmen and of General Bernhardi. But in his scheme of a voluntary army, with compulsory training for home defence, no sufficient thought had been given to the problem of the military necessities of England across the seas, nor had there been any effort to meet the practical question of how to adapt the soldier's training to the conditions of the industrial workers at home, to whom the leaders of the movement had no access either by knowledge or by experience. The system was not endorsed by a single responsible statesman on either side, nor by the War Office, who saw in it grave danger to the English army in India and the dependencies. English-men meanwhile still concentrated their attention on internal problems, and left European concerns to a foreign office which, in spite of the democratic inrush, had for a generation neither sought to inform the people nor to win their support. When a threat of war sounded once more from Morocco the country was distracted by an internal revolution which astonished Europe with the range and audacity of its movement, national, social, constitutional, and financial, and by an intense preoccupation with home problems, which ministers charged with the European policy had left undisturbed. The French, in spite of their twofold guarantee of the "integrity of Morocco," occupied Fez on the pretext of danger to European residents; and the answer was a German gunboat, the *Panther*, at Agadir. Germany demanded a full understanding with France on the Moroccan question; her share in the scheme of compensations arranged in 1904, when the northern littoral of Africa had been divided between France, Spain, Italy, and England; and a close to the long and discreditable disputes on the Franco-German border in the Congo basin. England entered the lists with the declaration that she must take part in any discussion on Morocco, that she would not stand aside if the cession of the French Congo were asked, nor submit to any German proposal to make Agadir a naval base. The

SEC. II.

FOREIGN
AND
COLONIAL
POLICY

1815
TO
1914

1911
July

SEC. II.

FOREIGN
AND
COLONIAL
POLICY

1815
TO
1914

fleet, with sealed orders, lay prepared to put to sea; and the Chancellor of the Exchequer, Mr. Lloyd George, announced that at all hazards Great Britain would maintain her place and her commerce among the great powers of the world. The speech exasperated German feeling beyond measure, but once more, as in 1905, war was averted by leaving all direct negotiations to France and Germany. Germany recognized the protectorate of France over Morocco, and in the name of "African equilibrium" obtained in the Congo basin a substantial part of the lands which had been won by de Brazza, the noble champion who had once represented the French ideals of liberty and chivalry. The dispute, sordid in its history and in its close, threw a gloomy light on the course of the partition of Africa which for thirty years had embittered the relations of the European powers. But Africa was no longer the real question between the continental states; and Europe turned from the problems left by the Berlin conference to those which had been bequeathed by the leaders of the Berlin congress, the Prussian Bismarck, the Magyar Andrássy, and the Jew Beaconsfield. National passions were again concentrated on the fate of the Balkans, the blood-stained battle-ground of the rising nationalities and the surrounding empire-builders. There remained the question of Serbia.

Since Bismarck and Andrássy in 1879 had laid the foundations of an alliance by which Germany could use Austria-Hungary as her outpost in the Balkans, the Magyars held the leadership in the Dual Monarchy. Their publicists and politicians claimed that no national culture of Serbs, Roumanians, or Slovaks did or could exist on Hungarian soil, while their men of business were assured of support in breaking every economic effort of the Slavs. Count Aerenthal, the Austro-Hungarian Foreign Minister, seeking a convenient justification for the annexation of Bosnia, connived at and encouraged the notorious high-treason trial at Agram, which dragged on for seven months.

Its sequel was the even more scandalous trial of Aerenthal's publicist Dr. Friedjung, which established the fact of an extensive traffic in documents forged in the Austro-Hungarian embassy at Belgrade to discredit the Serbian government, with the complicity of the Legation, and indirectly of its chiefs in the Austrian foreign office. The

Croatian constitution was abolished, the charter of the Serb Orthodox Church suspended, the "preventive" censorship imposed, among other harsh measures. Meanwhile in Macedonia the Christian races united to throw off the Ottoman yoke. Caught between Austro-Magyar oppression and the violence and disorder of Young Turk rule, and encouraged by Russia, they banded together in a Balkan League against the Turks—an ill-assorted group in which Montenegro and Serbia hated above all Austria, while Greece and Bulgaria never forgot their mutual distrust and hatred even in their joint assault on

Turkey. The campaign confounded the prophecies of the military theorists. While the Bulgarians were threatening Constantinople, the Greeks entered Salonica, and the Serbs recovered the capital of their mediæval empire. The German powers, whose future plans depended on the destruction of the Balkan League and the military reform of the Ottoman empire under Prussian officers, now saw a Turkey weakened and defeated, and a barrier of Slav states lying across their road. The belief that Russia was marshalling the peoples to drive Austria from the sea embittered the conflict of Teuton and Slav. And in the Balkans national consciousness was excited beyond measure. "The Bulgarian nation has need of three seas," it was said. Greece aimed at Salonica and Kavalla. Young enthusiasts of the "Greater Serbia" read of the Italian war of liberation and took the name of the "Piedmontese Party." But when the Serb army, cut off from the Ægean, entered Albania to win a port on the Adriatic, Austria mobilized to forbid her access to the coast. In the name of peace the powers interfered: Sir Edward Grey presided over a congress in London, and by his spirit of conciliation terms were arranged which Serbia was persuaded to accept. Amid the intrigues of rival empires the Balkan peoples were incited to a second war. The quarrel between Serbia and Bulgaria, envenomed by Austria, broke out in a midnight raid by the Bulgarians. From Vienna, Budapest, Constantinople, and St. Petersburg strife was actively encouraged. Serbians fought in greatcoats supplied by Russians for the last conflict, and had help from French banks; munitions poured from Austria-Hungary into Bulgaria, where the Tsar Ferdinand (who obtained from his parliament in 1912 sole control of foreign policy) had kept up secret relations with Vienna and Budapest in the fond hope of aid to establish his dominion from the Black Sea to the Ægean and the Adriatic. There was a second surprise for the powers. Serbia and Greece, with help of Roumania, stood stronger than before, while Bulgaria was left with an inadequate opening to the sea, and saw the greater part of Macedonia partitioned among her rivals. In this crisis Austria invited Italy to join her in a "defensive" war against the Serbians, and on Italy's refusal the German emperor came to the help of Francis Joseph in drawing up the treaty of Bucharest. Once more a settlement was planned under which no future agreement of the Balkan States was possible. The powers of the entente weakly allowed the treaty of London to be torn up. Adrianople was left once more in the hands of the Turks; Serbia and Greece retained the lion's share of Macedonia; but by the creation of an autonomous Albania under the German prince William of Wied, Serbia was excluded from the Adriatic.

A time of dark confusion followed, massacre, violence, and vengeance. The Tsar Ferdinand rejected the principle of "the Balkans

SEC. II.

FOREIGN
AND
COLONIAL
POLICY

1815
TO
1914

*Congress of
London*

June
1913

*Treaty of
Bucharest*

**European
war**

Sec. II.

Foreign
AND
Colonial
Policy

1815
TO
1914

June 28

July 23

July 28

Demo-
cracy and
nation-
ality

for the Balkan people" and the solidarity of the Slavs; if he could gain Salonica, and amicably ensure Austria's road to the sea, he believed Austria would aid him to crush their common enemy Serbia. His cynical *Realpolitik* ended any hope of reconstructing the Balkan League, and small states, all but one ruled by foreign dynasties and all divided by unnational and fratricidal wars, lay at the mercy of surrounding empires. Out of the thickening gloom, a young fanatic of Bosnia stood forth at Serajevo to murder the heir of the Austrian empire, the archduke Francis Ferdinand. Never did guilt precipitate such vengeance and such ruin. The emperor Francis Joseph, with the strong support of Germany, answered by an ultimatum and manifesto to Serbia singularly alike in its charges and in its very terms to the ultimatum he had hurled against Piedmont fifty-five years before. Serbia was given forty-eight hours to accept demands that menaced her existence as an independent state. No time was allowed for diplomacy or mediation of the other European nations. On the declaration of war all the great powers of Europe one after another were swept into the prodigious conflict—driven by powerful ambitions, by patriotism, by panic of final destruction, entangled in the web of old diplomacies, or blinded by the swift uprising of a primæval instinct that machines of death could subjugate the spirit of freedom, or could vindicate honour, chivalry, and justice, notwithstanding that every nation, so long as it had life, would refuse to accept against it as authoritative any decision of war. The incalculable forces which had been revealed in the modern world transcended the measure of statesmen and the inherited traditions of the chancelleries.

Thus the hundred years, which began with the loftiest expectations from a European congress, ended with the hopes of peace utterly wrecked under a balance of powers so hazardous that a chance bomb could overthrow the whole crazy equilibrium and plunge three continents into war. This century too had seen the disappearance of the old belief in Christendom as a commonwealth charged with the highest mission of civilization. A new ideal had in its turn caught the heart of the peoples—the doctrine of nationality—and had fired men with an exalted resolve that, delivered from the abasement of servitude, the nations should be free to carry on the spiritual tradition of their fathers, in religion, in literature, in the shaping of their social life, even in the conduct of their trade for the advantage and uplifting of their own lands. The most democratic call yet heard, it summoned men of every class and degree to give their service to the land and people of their birth, and as it bound the whole community in one purpose of large emancipation, it opened to them wider issues than any industrial struggle to win material advantage for a single class. By reverent memory of ancient human conflicts, by the sense of obligations to an unknown future, imagination was lifted beyond the bonds of the present. Democracy as the spiritual union of an entire people was exalted in noble devotion and courage, and in a revelation of intellectual energy; and through the western half of Europe the cause of freedom had its triumphs and public acclamations. The English people had in the main been the upholders of popular government and the refuge of those under constraint, and in alliance with France had vindicated national liberties. A more disastrous epoch opened after the defeat of France, when nationality became identified less with liberty than with aggression and power. Conditions were greatly altered. Mechanical and scientific discovery had from the middle of the century prodigiously increased the range of the power, and with it the expanding ambition, of man. The material strength of the proprietary dynasties was raised to such a height by the development of military weapons, and by the State control of vast mechanical resources, that no subject people could stand against them in rebellion, nor any small nationality in war. The rights of emperors claiming world-dominion superseded those of European kings, and old ideals lost their value in the mirage of new immensities. Even in England the subtle effect of empire might be seen in accustoming men's minds to the idea of law less as the protection of the subject than as the means of repressing the unruly. Above all, the dynasties were trebly secured in power when the new territorial ambitions passed from rulers to peoples, and nations themselves, intoxicated like the kings with the passion of aggrandizement, abandoned the ideal of liberation for that of dominion, and repeated the violences of the old despots under the plea of national life. The problems of the new age assumed a magnitude and a complexity beyond the skill of statesmen to compass; the bureaucracies with all their conventional resources failed in their tasks. There followed an age of excitement beyond what Europe had ever seen—the greater States fevered by rivalry and dread, the lesser buffeted between their powerful neighbours. In the passion of the time imperialism and nationalism were set in sharpest conflict. Under the fatal sense of advancing doom the generous ardours of freedom were overlaid by the selfishness of panic and of ambition, and nationalism became the plea for violence, treachery, and hate. So times of war and danger confuse human virtues, and install the instincts of primitive man as the leading forces in human action. To some it seemed that nationalism had "spent its force," and that the lesser peoples disheartened and exhausted would now learn "the larger patriotism" of empire. But national life, though it has been turned out of its course, will not fail, so deep does it lie in the nature of man. A time of peace and sufficient security is needed for the higher law to assert its power, and for men to find assurance that in the virtue of freedom, and not in the glory of dominion, lies the way of human progress. It may well be that the majesty of empires will

Sec. II.

Foreign
and
Colonial
Policy

1815
to
1914

SEC. II.

FOREIGN
AND
COLONIAL
POLICY

1815
TO
1914

not foster the highest developments of genius, when men gifted with intellect and energy recognize the discouragement of strength dissipated in boundless extension of space, or broken against the stupendous machinery of government on the imperial scale. Even though the several nations, without experience, knowledge, or habit of affairs, have to hew out their way against old traditions and diplomacies, and may too easily fall on this side or on that, their faith is steadfast. Liberty, and along with it a spirit of international solidarity, or greater still of human fraternity—these together can alone save and develop civilization; and a new concert of Europe will one day establish the principles of loyalty to the nation and " allegiance to humanity." A hundred years have passed since England at the congress of Vienna ignored the rights of nations. Through a century she has been slowly learning, in a sense that the old Whigs and Radicals but dimly felt after, the power of national freedom as something greater than constitutional reform. For long ages the English people have been winning their own privileges under the protection of an assured national security such as was granted to no other people in Europe. Their history will have its justification when in confident faith of freedom they desire to extend the benefits they have themselves enjoyed; and when with resolution worthy of the matchless opportunities conferred on them, and with knowledge equal to their power, they set the high example of ordered liberty, of national emancipation, and of loyalty to mankind.

" The sympathies of peoples with peoples, the sense of a common humanity between nations, the aspirations of nationalities after freedom and independence, *are* real political forces."

Feb., 1877.

" The great force which has transformed Europe, which has been the secret of its history ever since 1815, is a political 'sentiment'—that of Nationality."

April, 1880.

(*Letters of J. R. Green*, pp. 447, 480.)

INDEX.

ABBO of Fleury, 58
Abbot, Archbishop of Canterbury, 471, 512
Abd-ul-Aziz, Sultan of Turkey, 964
Abd-ul-Hamid, the Second, Sultan of Turkey, 965, 966, 970, 995, 996, 1002
Abd-ul-Medjid, Sultan of Turkey, 924, 936
Abercorn, see of, 34, 36, 185
Abercromby, General, 756, 819
Aberdeen, Earl of," 926, 932–934
Aberffraw, princes of, 164, 167
"Abhorrers," 657
Aboukir, battle of, 819
Aclea, battle of, 46
Acre, siege of, 811
Addington's Ministry, 818, 820
Adelard of Bath, 132, 137
Admonition, the, 470
Adrianople, treaty of, 916
Aehrenthal, Count, 1004
Ælfheah, Archbishop of Canterbury, 62, 65
Ælfred, King of Wessex, 47
    his rule, 48–50
    character, 50, 51
    literary work, 51, 52
    struggle with Danes, 48, 50, 53
    death, 53
    "Sayings of," 121
Ælfred, the Ætheling, 67
Ælle, King of Deira, 18
Ælle, King of the South Saxons, 11
Æthelbald, King of Mercia, 38, 41
Æthelberht, King of Kent, 17–19
Æthelflæd, Lady of the Mercians, 49, 54
Æthelfrith, King of Northumbria, 19, 20
Æthelgifu, mother-in-law of Eadwig, 57
Æthelred, King of Mercia, 35–37
Æthelred the First, King of Wessex, 46, 47
Æthelred the Unready, King of Wessex, 61
    marriage, 62
    flight to Normandy, ib., 78
    death, 65
Æthelred, Ealdorman of Mercia, 49, 53, 54
Æthelric, King of Bernicia, 13, 17
Æthelstan, King of Wessex, 54, 55
Æthelthryth (Etheldreda), S., 33
Æthelwold, Bishop of Winchester, 58
Æthelwulf, King of Wessex, 46
Afghan wars, 937–938, 979–980
Afrikander Bond, 973–984
Agincourt, battle of, 268
Agitators, Council of, 565

Agricultural labourers, 842, 858
Agriculture, changes in, 245–247, 292, 393, 838, 841, 861, 890
Aidan, S., 24, 25
Aislabie, Chancellor of the Exchequer, 728
Aix-la-Chapelle, Peace of, 637, 744
Alabama arbitration, 955, 962
Albemarle, Stephen of, 89
Alberoni, Cardinal, 726
Alcluyd, 41
Alcuin, 43
Aldgate, Priory of Holy Trinity at, 95
Aldfrith the Learned, King of Northumbria, 38
Alexander the First, Tsar (or Czar) of Russia, 823, 907, 910, 915, 920
Alexander the Second, Tsar of Russia, 937, 947, 948, 964, 965, 967
Alexander the Third, Tsar of Russia, 995
Alexander the Third, King of Scots, 188
Alexandria, bombardment of, 970
Aliwal, battle of, 938
Allen, Dr., 408, 409
Alliance, Dual, 968
    Grand, 684, 705, 910
    Holy, 910–917, 921, 934
    Quadrilateral, 924
    Quadruple, 922
    Triple, 637, 726, 968, 983, 994, 999, 1002
Alma, battle of the, 934
Almanza, battle of, 716
Almeida, siege of, 827
Alva, Duke of, 388, 389
America, English settlements in, 506, 746, 758, 759
    rivalry with the French, 747, 748, 755–757
    religion and government, 759, 760
    relations with England, 760, 768
    struggle for self-taxation, 769, 776, 777
    Congress, 770, 778–780
    Declaration of Independence, 780
    alliance with France, 781
    war with England, 779–782, 785, 786
    embargo and non-intercourse, 827, 828
    war with England, 830, 832, 834
    Spanish settlements, 506
    their trade with English, 733
American Civil War, 955
Amherst, General, 755–757
Amiens, Mise of, 156
    Peace of, 819
Anderida, 11

Andrássy, Count Julius, 964, 1004
Andredsweald, 11
Angeln, 1
Anglesey conquered by Eadwine, 21
Anglia, East, settlement of the Engle in, 11
  submits to Penda, 22
  seized by Offa, 43
  conquered by Danes, 46, 47
  earldom of, 65
Anglo-French entente, 998
Anglo-Japanese treaty, 990, 997, 1002
Anglo-Russian agreement, 980, 999
Anjou, Duke of, suitor of Elizabeth, 414, 416
Anjou, Counts of, 98–100
Anne, daughter of James the Second, deserts him, 681
  her relations with the Marlboroughs, 695, 707, 716
  Queen, 708
  her Bounty, 712
  death, 720
Anne of Bohemia, wife of Richard the Second, 263
Anselm, S., 73, 74
  Archbishop of Canterbury, 90
  exiled, ib.
  recalled, 91
  supports Henry the First, 96
Anti-Corn-Law League, 860
Appeal, Henry the Second's court of, 111
Aquitaine, loss of, 233, 234
Arabi Bey, 970
Arch, Joseph, 875
Arcot, Clive's capture of, 746
Argyll, Earl and Marquis of, Presbyterian leader, 541, 570, 572, 577
  beheaded, 632, 664
Argyll, Earl of, his condemnation, rebellion and death, 664, 665
Aristotle, study of, in Middle Ages, 135, 137, 138, 151
Arkwright invents spinning-machine, 792
Arlington, Bennet, Earl of, 635
  forms Triple Alliance, 637
  share in Treaty of Dover, 638, 639
  dismissed, 646
Arlotta, mother of William the Conqueror, 75
Armada, Spanish, 418–420
  second, 443–444
Armenian massacres, 995
Arminians or Latitudinarians, 476
Arms, Assize of, 110
Army, standing, its origin, 633
  increased by James the Second, 666
  subject to control of Parliament, 689
  see Model, New
Army Plot, 539
Arrow, affair of the, 942
Arthur, romances and legends of, 119, 120, 166
Arthur of Brittany, 115
Arthur, son of Henry the Seventh, 311
Articles of Religion, 340
  the Six, 355
  repealed, 358
  Forty-two, 359
  Forty-two, 359
  Thirty-nine, 385
  Three, 470
Artillery, results of its introduction, 301

Arundel, Archbishop of Canterbury, 262, 263
Arundel, Earl of, patron of Caxton, 298
Arundel, Earl of, Lord Privy Seal, 669
Ascue, Anne, 357
Ashburton-Webster treaty, 926
Ashdown, battle of, 47
Ashley, Lord, see Cooper
  opposes Act of Uniformity, 622
  heads the Presbyterians, 635
  his scheme of Protestant comprehension, 636
  terms of toleration, 639
  Chancellor, 640, see Shaftesbury
Asquith, Herbert Henry, 900, 990, 1000
Assandun, battle of, 65
Asser, 51
Assize of Arms, 110
  of Clarendon, ib., 111
  of Northampton, 111
Astley, Sir Jacob, 559
Aston, Sir Arthur, 579
Atbara, battle of, 976
Athelney, 48, 52
Athenree, battle of, 447
Atterbury, Bishop of Rochester, 728
Aughrim, battle of, 694
Augsburg, league of, 677
Augustine, his mission to England, 18, 19
Austerlitz, battle of, 822
Australia, 956–958, 980–982, 985, 987–989, 991, 992
Austria joins the Grand Alliance, 684
  war of succession in, 734
  policy during French war, 799, 801, 811, 821, 832
Austro-Italian war, 944
Austro-Prussian war, 949
Avaux, Count of, 688
Aylesford, battle of, 9

Babington's Plot, 417
Bacon, Francis, 438–442
  his plea for Church reform, 477
  fall, 490, 491
  death, 491
Bacon, Roger, 137–141
Badby, John, 265
Badajoz stormed, 831
Badon, Mount, battle of, 12
Bæda, 39–41
  Ælfred's translation of, 52
Bagdad Railway, 996, 997, 1002
Bagehot, Walter, 869, 902, 976
Balaclava, battle of, 934
"Balance of power," 721
Balfour, Arthur James, 881, 888, 889, 893, 894, 899, 997
Balkan League, 1004–1006
  wars, 1004–1005
Ball, John, 240, 250–252
Balliol, Edward, 214, 216
Balliol, John, 188–190
Ballot Act, 875, 881
Balmerino, Earl of, 744
Baltimore, Calvert, Lord, 507
Bamborough, 13, 25
Bancroft, Archbishop of Canterbury, 471, 482
Bangor, monks of, slain, 19, 20
Bank of England founded, 699
Bankruptcy Act, 868

Bannerman, Sir Henry Campbell-, 900, 985, 987, 988, 999, 1000
Bannockburn, battle of, 213, 214
Bantry Bay, battle in, 692
Baptists, 560
Barbury Hill, battle of, 12
Bards, the Welsh, 166
Barebones, Praise-God, 583
Barlow, Bishop of St. David's, 354
Barnet, battle of, 288
Barons, their relations with the Conqueror, 84, 85, 88
  with Henry the First, 96
  with Henry the Second, 109
  with John, 124, 126, 127
  council of, appointed to enforce the Charter, 130
  offer the crown to Lewis, ib.
  quarrel with Henry the Third, 154, 155
  war with him, 156, 157
  greater and lesser, 174
  their rule, 203
  struggle with Edward the First, 203–207
  effects of Hundred Years' War on, 273, 274
  their decline, 290, 291
  Henry the Seventh's dealings with, 302
  Northern, rise against Elizabeth, 390
Barrier, the Dutch, 704
Bartholomew's Day, S., massacre of, 412
  the English, 622, 623
Basing House, siege of, 558
Bastille destroyed, 798
Bates's case, 484
Bath, Henry de, 145
Bautzen, battle of, 832
Baxter, Richard, 622, 625, 636, 670
Baylen, French surrender at, 825
Beachy Head, battle of, 695
Beaufort, Henry, Bishop of Winchester, 273
  Cardinal, 280
Beaufort, Margaret, see Richmond
Beaufort, house of, its claims to the Crown, 282
Beaumont, palace of, 133
Bec, abbey of, 72
Beckford, Alderman, 751
Bedford, John, Duke of, Regent of France, 275, 279, 280
Bedford, Duke of, minister of George the Third, 766, 767, 772
Bedloe, 651
Beket, Gilbert, 92
  site of his house, 103
Beket, Thomas, 103, 104
  Chancellor, 106
  Archbishop of Canterbury, ib.
  quarrel with Henry the Second, 107, 108
  death, 108, 109
  canonized, 109
  desecration of his shrine, 335
Belesme, Robert of, 96, 164
Belgium, neutrality of, 919, 950
Bellahoe, battle of, 449
Bellasys, Lord, 669
Benedict Biscop, 29, 30, 39
"Benedict of Peterborough," 118
"Benevolences" under Edward the Fourth, 293
  under Wolsey, 325
  under James the First, 486

Bensington, battle of, 41
Bentham, Jeremy, 829, 838, 839, 853, 879, 888, 952, 990
Beorhtric, King of Wessex, 42, 43
Beornwulf, King of Mercia, 44
Berlin, Act of, 975
  Conference of, 969, 974, 978
  Congress of, 966, 967
  Note, 964
  treaty of, 967, 995
Bernicia, kingdom of, 13
  joined with Deira, ib., 17
Bertha, wife of Æthelberht of Kent, 17
Berwick stormed by Edward the First, 190
  taken by Bruce, 209, 214
  its peculiar position, 216
  pacification at, 533
Berwick, Duke of, 710, 716
Beverley, Alfred of, 119
Bible, Wyclif's translation of, 244
  its effects, 259
  in Bohemia, 263
  translation promised by Henry the Eighth, 334
  Tyndale's, 334, 351, 352
  forbidden, 334
  Coverdale's, 341
  the Geneva, forbidden, 510
  effects of, on England, 460–462
Bigod, Hugh, Earl of Norfolk, 154, 155
Bigod, Earl of Norfolk, defies Edward the First, 206
Birinus, 24
Bishops, mode of appointing, 338
  James the First's theory of, 479, 480
  expelled from House of Lords, 538
  restored, 621
  position under the Georges, 735, 736
  the Seven, 672
Bismarck, Prince, 947–950, 963, 966, 967, 968, 974, 975, 994, 995, 1001, 1004
Black Death, the, 248
Blake defends Taunton, 576
  blockades Rupert in the Tagus, ib.
  struggle with Tromp, 579, 580
  with Spain, 593, 596
  his corpse outraged, 620
Blenheim, battle of, 711, 712
Bloreheath, battle of, 283
Blucher, Marshal, 834–836
Boer War, First, 973; Second, 983–986
  Republics, annexation of, 985
Bohemia, effects of Wyclif's writings in, 263
  struggle against Austria, 489
Boleyn, Anne, 328, 329, 337, 348
Bolingbroke, Viscount (see St. John), 718
  rivalry with Harley, 719
  joins the Pretender, 722
  returns, 732
Bombay ceded to England, 628, 745
Boniface, S. (Winfrith), 43
Boniface VIII., Pope, 192, 206
Bonner, Bishop of London, 362, 364, 366, 460
Booth, Charles, 892
Born, Bertrand de, 113
Borodino, battle of, 831
Boroughbridge, battle of, 209
Boroughs, early English, 194
  their representation in Parliament, 158, 177

Boroughs — *Continued.*
  restriction of franchise in, 272
  changes in representation, 402
  new, created under the Tudors, 481
  the Five, 49, 54
  social revolution (1815–1914), 841, 850, 852, 853, 874, 886
Boscawen, Admiral, 755
Bosnia and Herzegovina, 964, 965, 967, 990, 1001, 1002
Boston (Lincolnshire), its foundation, 33
Boston (Massachusetts) occupied by British troops, 776
  tea-riots, 777
  port closed, *ib.*
  siege of, 779, 780
Bosworth, battle of, 301
Botha, Louis, 985
Bothwell, Earl of, 386–388
Botulf founds Boston, 33
Boulogne, Napoleon's camp at, 820
Boulogne, Eustace, Count of, 69, 82
Bouvines, battle of, 126
Bowring, Sir John, 942
Boxer risings, 978
Boyle, chemist, 611
Boyne, battle of, 693
"Boys," the, 732
Braddock, General, 747
Bradford, battle of, 34
Bradshaw, John, 571, 581, 586, 620
Brandywine, battle of, 780
Breauté, Faukes de, 142
Breda, Peace of, 635
Bremen, dispute about, 727
Breslau, Peace of, 741
Brétigny, treaty of, 231
Brigham, treaty of, 188
Bright, John, 860, 861, 864, 866, 867, 873, 874, 880, 884, 927, 930, 931, 935, 949, 970, 1000
Brindley, engineer, 792
Bristol, slave-trade at, 59, 88
  siege of, 549
  surrender, 550
  West Indian trade, 730
Bristol, Earl of, 635
Britain under the Romans, 5, 6
  attacked by Picts and Scots, 6
  English conquest of, 7–13
Britain, Great, 714
Britons, extermination of, 9, 10
  defeat at Dægsastan, 19
  end of their dominion, 43
Brooklyn, battle of, 780
Brougham, Lord, 851, 914, 918
Browne, Archbishop of Dublin, 452, 453
Browne's Pastorals, 526
Brownists, 472, 473, 507, 559, 560
Bruce, David, 215, 216, 224, 228
Bruce, Edward, 447
Bruce, Robert, the elder, 188, 192
Bruce, Robert, the younger, murders Comyn, 211, 212
  crowned, 212
  his successes, 213, 214
  truce with England, 214
  acknowledged king, 215
  dies, *ib.*
Brunanburh, battle of, 55

Brunswick, Ferdinand, Prince of, 754, 755, 763
Brunswick, Duke of, 805
Bucharest, treaty of, 1005
Buckingham, Duke of, beheaded, 324
Buckingham, George Villiers, Duke of, 487, 488
  his policy, 494, 495, 497
  impeached, 498
  expedition to Rochelle, 500, 501
  slain, 503
Buckingham, second Duke of, 607, 610, 639
  negotiates with Holland, 640
  dismissed, 646
  imprisoned, 648
Bulgarian atrocities, 965
Buller, Charles, 952, 953
Buller, Sir Redvers, 984, 985
Bulmer, Lady, burnt, 346
Bunker's Hill, battle of, 779
Bunyan, John, 467, 625–627
  his "Pilgrim's Progress," 627, 628
  released, 640
  refuses Indulgence, 670
Buonaparte, Joseph, King of Naples and Spain 824, 831
Buonaparte, Napoleon, 808
  successes in Italy, 809, 810
  in Egypt, 810
  designs on Syria, 811
  First Consul, *ib.*
  victory at Marengo, *ib.*
  Continental System, 818
  schemes of conquest, 819, 820
  France under him, 820
  war declared against, *ib.*
  threatens invasion of England, 821; *see* Napoleon
Burdett, Sir Francis, 829
Burford, battle of, 38
Burgh, Hubert de, 131, 141, 143, 144
Burgos, siege of, 831
Burgoyne, General, 780, 781
Burgundy, Charles the Bold, Duke of, 287
Burgundy, John, Duke of, 267, 270
Burgundy, Philip, Duke of, 270, 275, 278, 280
Burke, Edmund, 770–772
  supports American demands, 778
  his Bill of Economical Reform, 788
  moves impeachment of Hastings, 796
  hostility to the Revolution, 800–803, 805
  quarrel with Fox, 802
  "Letters on Regicide Peace," 809
  death, 810
Burke, Thomas Henry, 886
Burleigh, Lord, 417; *see* Cecil
Burmah, Upper, annexation of, 978
Burnet, Bishop of Salisbury, 614, 691
Busaco, battle of, 827
Bute, Earl of, 763, 766, 767
  his policy in America, 768, 769
Butler, Bishop, 614
Butler, Sir William, 984
Butler's "Hudibras," 607
Butt, Isaac, 884
Byng, Admiral, 748

"CABAL," the, 653, 654
Cabinet, the, 654, 847, 864, 874, 886, 897, 898, 971, 973
Cabot, Sebastian, 303, 506

Cade, John, 281, 282
Cadiz, English descent on, 443
    blockaded, 741
Cadwallon, king of the Welsh, 22, 23
Cædmon, 27–29
Caen, university founded at, 280
Calais, siege of, by Edward the Third, 228, 229
    ceded to him, 231
    lost, 369
Calcutta, its origin, 745
    Black Hole of, 753
Calne, council of, 61
Cambray, league of, 311
    treaty of, 330
Cambridge, the New Learning at, 309
    Erasmus at, ib., 313
    Protestants at, 352
Cambridge, George, Duke of, 720; see George
    the Second
Camden, 399
Campbell, Sir Colin, 940
Campeggio, Cardinal, 329
Camperdown, battle of, 810
Campian, Jesuit, 409, 410
Campo Formio, Treaty of, 809
Canada, conquest of, 755–757
    ceded by France, 764
    Constitution granted to, 802
    American invasions of, 833
    history after 1814, 952–956, 961, 980, 981,
      983, 985, 988–992
Canals, 792
Canning, Earl, 938, 941
Canning, George, Foreign Secretary, 823
    his policy, 824, 825
    retires, 826
    supports Catholic emancipation, 829
    after 1914, 847, 857, 871, 912–916
Canning, Sir Stratford (see Stratford de Red-
    cliffe, Lord)
Canningites, 851, 867
Canons of 1604, 482
    of 1636, 525
Canterbury, royal city of Kent, 17
    Augustine at, 18
    becomes ecclesiastical centre of England,
      32
    Theodore's school at, 39
    sacked by Danes, 62
    historians of, 118
Cape of Good Hope won by England, 809
Cardigan, conquest of, 165
Carlisle conquered by Ecgfrith, 34
    Cuthbert at, 35
    Mary Stuart at, 389
Carlos, Don, Spanish pretender, 922
Carlyle, Thomas, 952, 954, 965
Carolinas, their settlement, 758
Caroline of Anspach, wife of George the
    Second, 730, 733
Carteret, Lord, 741, 742
Carthusians, victims of T. Cromwell, 344, 345
Cartwright, Major John, 844, 896
Cartwright, Thomas, 468–471, 473, 474
Carucage, 129
Cassel, battle of, 648
Castlebar, battle of, 815
Castlemaine, Countess of, 640; see Cleveland
Castlereagh, Lord, 817, 826, 830, 846, 847, 907,
    908, 910–912, 915, 943, 947

Catesby, Robert, 483
Catharine of Aragon, wife of Henry the Eighth,
    311, 328, 329, 337
Catharine of Braganza, wife of Charles the
    Second, 634
Catharine of France, wife of Henry the Fifth,
    270
Catharine the Second, Empress of Russia, 799,
    803
Catholics, Roman, their position under Eliza-
    beth, 384, 385, 391
    revolt, 390
    revival, 408, 410, 475
    laws against them relaxed, 481
    priests banished, 624
    prospects under Charles the Second, 634
    excluded from Indulgence, 639, 640
    their hopes, 649, 650
    excluded from Parliament, 651
    admitted to office, etc., by James the
      Second, 667
    Confederate, 541, 551
    condition in Ireland, 811, 812
    struggles for emancipation, 813, 817, 818,
      823, 848, 849, 881, 902
"Caucus," the, 877
Cavagnari, Sir Lewis, 979
"Cavaliers," 544
Cavendish, Lord, 641, 652, 657; see Devon-
    shire
Cavendish, Lord Frederic, 886
Cavour, Camillo, Count di, 866, 943–946
Cawnpore, siege of, 939
Caxton, William, 295–298
Ceadda, Bishop of Mercia, 25, 26
Ceadwalla, King of Wessex, 37
Ceawlin, King of Wessex, 12
Cecil, Robert, see Salisbury
Cecil, William, 381, 390, 391; see Burleigh
Centwine, King of Wessex, 37
Cenwealh, King of Wessex, 34
Cenwulf, King of Mercia, 43, 44
Ceolfrid, founder of Jarrow, 39
Ceolred, King of Mercia, 37, 38
Ceorls, 4
Cerdic, first King of West Saxons, 11, 12
Cetewayo, King of the Zulus, 972
Ceylon won by England, 809
Chad, see Ceadda
Chadwick, Sir Edwin, 855, 857, 864
Chalgrove Field, battle of, 550
Châlus, siege of, 115
Chamberlain, Joseph, 877, 879, 886, 887, 977,
    982, 983, 986, 990, 997
Chambers, Alderman, 517
Chancellor, Richard, 395
Chancellor, the, his office, 96, 171
Chancery, Court of, 171
Chantries suppressed, 357
Charford, battle of, 11
Charles Albert, King of Sardinia, 920
Charles (the First), Prince, negotiations for his
    marriage, 488, 492
    goes to Madrid, 494
    his character, 495
    marriage, ib.
    King, 496
    policy, ib.
    protects Buckingham, 498, 499, 503
    levies forced loan, 500

Charles (the First) — *Continued.*
  consents to Petition of Right, 502
  his personal government, 514–517
  dealings with Scotland, 524, 530–534, 540,
      541
  tries to arrest five members, 544, 545
  attempt on Hull, 546, 547
  raises standard at Nottingham, 547, 548
  campaign of 1642, 548, 549
  besieges Gloucester, 550
  negotiates with Confederate Catholics, 551
  movements in 1644, 553
  negotiates at Uxbridge, 557
  defeated at Naseby, 557, 558
  treaty with the Irish, 558
  goes to Scotch camp, 563
  sold to Parliament, 564
  seized by army, 566
  flies, 568
  prisoner, *ib.*
  seized again, 570
  trial, 571
  death, 572
Charles the Second proclaimed King in Scot-
      land, 572
  negotiates with the Scots, 576
  crowned at Scone, 578
  defeated at Worcester, *ib.*
  restored, 600
  character, 629–631
  policy, 631, 632
  army, 633
  plans of Catholic toleration, 633, 634
  conversion, 638
  negotiates with Lewis, 638, 639
  relations with Parliament, 641, 645, 646,
      648
  relations with Lewis, 647, 649, 652
  plan for James's succession, 654
  change in his temper, 656
  treaty with France, 659
  triumph over Country party, 660, 661
  rule, 661–663
  death, 663, 664
Charles the Great, 43
Charles the Simple grants Normandy to Hrolf,
      71
Charles the Fifth, King of Spain, etc., 322
  Emperor, 324
  alliance with Henry the Eighth, *ib.*
  breaks his pledges, 327, 328
  treaty with France, 330
Charles the Sixth, Emperor, 729, 734
Charles the Seventh, Emperor, 741, 742
Charles the Fifth, King of France, 233
Charles the Sixth of France, 261, 267, 270, 275
Charles the Seventh of France, 275, 276, 278,
      280, 281
Charles the Eighth, King of France, his Italian
      campaign, 311
Charles the Second, King of Spain, 701, 703
Charles the Third, King of Spain, 713, 715
Charles the Fourth, King of Spain, 824
Charles the Twelfth, King of Sweden, 727
Charlestown, capture of, 782
Charmouth, battle of, 46
Charter of Henry the First, 91
  produced by Langton, 127
  the Great, 128, 129
  re-issued, 131

Charter of Henry the First — *Continued.*
  confirmed by Henry the Third, 142, 146
  confirmed by Edward the First, 207
  of towns, cancelled by Charles the Second,
      663
Chartered Company of South Africa, 975
Chartism, 859, 860, 863, 873, 928
Château-Gaillard, 114, 116
Chatham, Earl of (*see* Pitt), 772–774, 778, 781,
      782, 904
Chaucer, 219–222
  Caxton's edition of, 296
Chelmsford, Lord, 972, 973
Cherbourg surrendered to Charles the Seventh,
      281
Chester conquered by Æthelfrith, 19, 20
  Danes at, 53
  conquered by William, 83
Chesterfield, Earl of, 732, 742
Chichester, Sir Arthur, 457
Chilienwalah, battle of, 938
Chillingworth, William, theologian, 612, 613
Chinese wars, 941–942
Chippewa, battle of, 833
Chivalry, 182, 183
Chotusitz, battle of, 741
Christ Church, Oxford, 323
"Christian Brethren," the, 352
Chronicle, English, 52
  its end, 121
Church, English, its foundation, 18, 19
  in Northumbria, 23–27, 29, 30
  organized by Theodore, 30–32
  condition under William the First, 86
  under Rufus, 89, 90
  under Henry the First, 95, 96
  action during the anarchy, 103
  Henry the Second and, 106, 107, 109
  John and, 123, 124
  condition under John and Henry the Third,
      148
  under Edward the First, 172
  in fourteenth century, 236–238
  plans of reform in, 238–240
  political decline in fifteenth century, 273
  condition after Wars of the Roses, 291
  its reform undertaken by Parliament, 334
  Henry the Eighth Head of, 335–338
  its independent jurisdiction abolished, 336
  T. Cromwell's dealings with, 338–340
  spoliation of, 150, 351
  changes under Edward the Sixth, 358–360
  submission to Rome, 363, 364
  Elizabeth and, 376–379
  proposals for reform in Parliament, 405
  condition under Elizabeth, 406
  parties in, 476
  demand for its reform, 477
  the Long Parliament and, 543
  Cromwell's dealings with, 590
  condition under Charles the Second, 621,
      622
  bill for its security, 648
  James the Second's dealings with, 668
  temper after the Revolution, 690
  condition under the Georges, 735, 736
  influence of Methodists on, 739
  Irish, its mission work, 23, 24
  condition under Henry the Eighth, 451–453
  Scottish Presbyterian, 522–525, 686

Churchill, John, 666, 705, 706. *See* Marlborough
Churchill, Lord Randolph, 877
Cintra, Convention of, 825
Circuit, the Bloody, 666
Cistercians, 95
Ciudad Rodrigo stormed, 831
Civil Service, 869, 875, 896
Clair-sur-Epte, treaty of, 71
Clare, Earl of, settles in Pembroke, 164, 165
Clarence, George, Duke of, 287, 288
Clarendon, Assize of, 110, 111
    Constitutions of, 107
Clarendon, Edward Hyde, Earl of (*see* Hyde), Lord Chancellor, 617
    his policy, 621
    fall, 635, 636
Clarendon, Henry Hyde, Earl of, 669, 695
Claverhouse, 685
Clement the Seventh, Pope, 328, 329, 337
Clergy, representation of, in Parliament, 179, 180
    condition in fourteenth century, 237, 238
    submission to Henry the Eighth, 335, 336
    their enslavement, 340
    position under Elizabeth, 378, 406, 470, 471
    Puritan, expelled, 482
    Laud's dealings with, 510, 511
    condition under the Georges, 735–736
    effect of Methodist revival on, 739
Cleveland, Barbara Palmer, Duchess of, 630; *see* Castlemaine
Cleves, Anne of, 348, 356
Clifford, Lord, 284
Clifford, Sir Thomas, 638–641
Clive, Robert, 745, 746, 753, 782, 783
Closter-Seven, Convention of, 748
Cloth of Gold, Field of, 324
Cnichtenagild, in London, 95, 197
Cnut, King of Denmark and England, 64–67
Cnut the Fourth, King of Denmark, 88
Coal, discovery of its uses, 792
Coalition Ministry, 713, 788, 789
Cobbett, William, 842, 845, 847, 850, 857, 873, 909, 918, 1000
Cobden, Richard, 860, 861, 864, 866, 929–931, 935, 942, 947, 949, 1000
Cobham, Eleanor, 274
Cobham, Lord (Sir John Oldcastle), 259, 266, 267
Coercion Acts, Ireland, 876, 884–886, 888, 903
Coke, Sir Edward, 486, 502
Colchester, siege of, 569, 570
Coleman, secretary of Mary of Modena, 649, 651
Colenso, battle of, 985
Colet, John, 304, 305
    dean of St. Paul's, 308
    founds St. Paul's School, *ib.*
    his address to Convocation, 310
    charged with heresy, *ib.*
    denounces war, 312
Colley, Sir George, 973
Colman, Bishop of Lindisfarne, 30
Colonial Conferences, 982, 983, 986, 990, 991, 1002
Columba, S., 23
Commerce, Bolingbroke's proposed treaty of, 719
    Pitt's Treaty with France, 795

Commission, Ecclesiastical, under Elizabeth, 470, 471
    abolished, 540
    restored, 668
Commons summoned to Parliament, 158
    House of, 232
    its struggle with Wolsey, 325
    Petition to Henry the Eighth, 333, 334
    advance under Elizabeth, 403–405
    under James the First, 492, 493
    struggle with Charles the First, 498, 499, 501, 502, 505, 537–540, 542–547
    place in the constitution, 536
    proceedings in 1674, 645, 646
    temper after the Revolution, 691
    becomes supreme in the State, 696, 697
    its relation to the Crown and the Ministry, 697
    Whig ascendency in, 723
    character under George the Third, 764, 765
    struggle with Wilkes, 767, 773, 774
    with the Press, 775
    adopts Catholic emancipation, 829; *see* Parliament
    after 1814, 843, 847, 853, 859, 869, 874, 875, 877, 880–882, 884, 886, 889, 897, 899, 919, 925, 942, 945, 954, 980
Commons of Kent, their Complaint, 282
Commonwealth established, 573
    proclaimed, 574
"Communes," 156, 201
Communism (*see* Socialism)
Compact, the Family, 733
Compiègne, its defence by Jeanne d'Arc, 278
Comprehension Bill, 690
Compton, Bishop of London, 668, 678, 679
Compurgation abolished, 111
Comyn, regent of Scotland, 192
Comyn, the Red, slain, 211, 212
Confederation, German, 907, 911, 949
    North German, 949
Congested Districts Board, 890
Congregation, Lords of the, 381
Congregationalists, their rise, 560
Connecticut, origin of the settlement, 529
Conservatives, 844, 847, 857, 866, 886, 887, 894, 928, 930, 932, 941, 944, 961; *see* Tories
Conservators of the Peace, 173
Constable, Sir Robert, 346
Constance of Britanny, 119
Constantine, King of Scots, 55
Constantinople, Conquests at, 965
Constitution, the, 838, 853, 859, 872, 874, 896, 901
Constitutional Clubs, 803, 804
Continental system, Napoleon's, 818, 822
Contract, the Great, 484
Convention of 1660, 600
    declares itself a Parliament, 617
    of 1688, 682
    Constituent, 583, 584
    Scottish, 685
Convocation, Colet's address to, 310
    submits to Henry the Eighth, 336
    upholds Divine Right of Kings, 478
    its canons of 1604, 482
    suspended, 735
Cook, Captain, 758
Cooper, Sir Ashley, 599, 600
    Chancellor of the Exchequer, 617
    See Ashley, Shaftesbury

Co-operative societies, 863, 868, 894
Coote, Eyre, 782, 784, 785
Cope, Sir John, 743
Copenhagen, battle of, 819
    bombardment of, 824
Copy-holders, 246
Corn Laws, 848, 860, 862, 874
Cornwall conquered by Ecgberht, 43
    revolts, 46
    royalist rising in, 549
Cornwall, Richard, Earl of, 152, 157
Cornwallis, Lord, 782, 785, 815
Coroners, 176
Corporation Act, 848
Corresponding Society, 807
Corunna, battle of, 825
Council, the Continual, 155, 203
    Great, 111, 129, 173, 174
    of Officers, 574
    Royal, its criminal jurisdiction, 302
    reorganized by Temple, 653, 654
    Privy, 111
    of State, 573
County Court, the, 176
Country party, 641, 645, 647
Courcy, John de, 446
Courtenay, Bishop of London, 239
    Archbishop of Canterbury, 242, 259
Courtenay, see Exeter
Covenant, the Scottish, 531, 532
    signed in London, 551
    burnt there, 621
    abolished in Scotland, 632
Coventry, Sir William, 641
Coverdale, Miles, 341
Cowell, his theory of absolutism, 478
Cowper, William, Lord Keeper, 713
Craft-gilds, 198, 199, 201
Craggs, Secretary of State, 728
Cranfield, Treasurer, 494; see Middlesex
Cranmer, Thomas, his advice on Henry the
        Eighth's divorce, 334
    Archbishop of Canterbury, 337
    divorces Henry and Catharine, ib.
    crowns Anne Boleyn, ib.
    his Protestantism, 358
    imprisoned, 362
    his life and death, 367, 368
Crécy, battle of, 226, 227
Crew, Chief Justice, 500
Crimean war, 934-937, 942
Crompton invents the "mule," 792
Cromwell, Henry, 589
Cromwell, Oliver, his youth, 466, 467, 554
    at Marston Moor, 552, 553
    quarrel with Manchester, 553
    his regiment, 554, 555
    scheme of New Model, 556, 557
    victory at Naseby, 557, 558
    advocates toleration, 562
    defeats Scots, 570
    conquest of Ireland, 574-576
    victory at Dunbar, 576, 577
    at Worcester, 578
    drives out the Rump, 581
    his policy, 584
    named Protector, 585
    his rule, 586-591
    foreign policy, 592, 593, 596
    settlement of Ireland, 589

Cromwell, Oliver — Continued.
    refuses title of king, 594, 595
    inaugurated as Protector, 595
    death, 598
    his corpse outraged, 620
Cromwell, Richard, 598
Cromwell, Thomas, 332
    fidelity to Wolsey, 333
    counsel on the divorce, ib., 334
    policy, 335
    Vicar-General, 338
    dealings with the Church, 338-341, 354,
        356
    his rule, 341-343
    dealings with the nobles, 346, 347
    administrative activity, 347
    fall, 348
    success of his policy, 349, 350
    his revival of Parliaments, 350
Crowland Abbey, 33
    burnt by Danes, 46
Cuba, English conquest of, 764
Culloden Moor, battle of, 744
Cumberland granted to Constantine of Scot-
        land, 55
Cumberland, William, Duke of, 742, 744, 748
Cumbria, kingdom of, 19, 184, 185
    southern, conquered by Ecgfrith, 34
Cuthbert, S., 26, 27, 34, 35
Cuthwulf, King of the West Saxons, 12
Cynric, 11, 12

Dacre, Lord, 345, 346
Dacres, Leonard, 390
Dægsastan, battle of, 19
Dalhousie, Marquis of, 938
Dalton, John, 844
Danby, Thomas Osborne, Earl of, Lord Treas-
        urer, 646
    his policy, ib., 647, 648
    fall, 652
    correspondence with William, 678, 679
    prepares for a rising, 680, 681
    Lord President, 691
Danegeld, 97
Danelaw, the, 48
    conquest of, 54
    revolts, 55, 57
    submits to Swein, 62
Danes attack Britain, 45, 46
    conquer East Anglia and attack Wessex,
        47
    struggle with Ælfred, 48, 50, 53
    treaties with him, 48, 50
    routed by Edward and Æthelred, 53
    defeated at Brunanburh, 55
    massacre of, 62
    conquer England, 62-64
    their settlements in Ireland, 444
Daniel, poet and historian, 399
Danish war, 948
Darcy, Lord, 346
Dardanelles, the, 924, 925, 936
Darnley, Henry Stuart, Lord, 361, 385, 386,
        387
David, King of Scots, 187
David Bruce; see Bruce
David, Prince of Wales, 168
Davies, Sir John, 526
Davis, Thomas Osborne, 884

Deane, General, 589
"Defenders," Irish, 814
Deira, kingdom of, 13, 17
Delcassé, Théophile, 998
Delhi, siege of, 939
Deorham, battle of, 12
Derby, Edward Stanley, fourteenth Earl of, 872, 930, 944, 945
   Edward Henry Stanley, fifteenth Earl of, 964–966
Derby, Ferrars, Earl of, 109
Derby, Henry of Lancaster, Earl of, 261, 262, 263; see Henry the Fourth.
Dermod, King of Leinster, 445, 446
Desmond, Earl of, 456
Despensers, the, 209, 210
Dettingen, battle of, 741
Devonshire, Earl of (see Cavendish), 679, 680, 681
Digby, Lord, 537
Digges, Sir Dudley, 498, 499
Dilke, Sir Charles, 960, 961
Directory, the French, 809
Disraeli, Benjamin, Earl of Beaconsfield, 871–873, 876, 877, 892, 925–927, 930, 945, 947, 948, 958, 961, 962, 964–968, 970, 972, 978, 979, 982, 990
Dissidence, its growth, 561, 562
Doherty, John, 850, 858
Domesday Book, 85
Dominic, S., 148
Dominicans, see Friars
Donne, 526
Dorchester, first West-Saxon see, 24
Dorset, Sackville, Earl of, 427
Dost Mohammed, Amir of Afghanistan, 937, 938
Douglas, James, 213
Dover besieged by Lewis of France, 131
   treaty of, 63, 639
Dowdall Archbishop of Armagh, 453
Drake, Francis, 415–419, 421, 443
Drama, see Literature
Dreux, battle of, 383
Drogheda, storm of, 575
Dryden, 610, 637, 642
Dual Control, the, 970
Dublin, besieged by Ormond, 575
Dudley, minister of Henry the Seventh, 308
Dudley, Guildford, 361, 363
Duffy, Sir Charles Gavan, 958
Dumbarton taken by Eadberht, 41
Dunbar, battle of, 576, 577
Duncan, Admiral, 810
Dundas, Henry, 821
Dundee, John Graham of Claverhouse, Viscount, 685
Dunedin, 185
Dunes, battle of the, 596
Dunkirk ceded to England, 596
   sold to France, 635
Duns Scotus, 151
Dunstan, S., 55, 56
   his administration, 56–58
   death, 61
Dupleix, his designs in India, 745, 746
Duquesne, Fort, 747, 756
Durham, Earl of, 953
Durham, historians of, 117
Dyvnaint, 42

Eadberht, King of Northumbria, 41
Eadgar, King of England, 57, 58, 61
   his Law, 58, 65
Eadgar, the Ætheling, 80, 83, 90
Eadgar, King of Scots, 90
Eadmer, 118
Eadmund, S., of East Anglia, 46
Eadmund, King of Wessex, 55, 56
   grants Strathclyde to Malcolm, 186
Eadmund Ironside, 65
Eadred, King of Wessex, 56, 57
Eadric of Mercia, 65
Eadward the Elder, King of Wessex, 53, 54
Eadward the Confessor, 68–70
   his Laws, 68
   his promise to William, 78
Eadward the Martyr, 61
Eadwig, King of Wessex, 57
Eadwig, brother of Eadmund Ironside, 65
Eadwine, King of Northumbria, 20–22
Eadwine, Earl of Mercia, 70, 80–83
Ealdhelm, Bishop of Sherborne, 37
Ealdormen, 15
Ealdred, Archbishop of York, 81
Ealhstan, Bishop of Sherborne, 46
Earldoms created by Cnut, 65
East India Company, 940, 941
Eastern question, 926, 932, 963–968
Ebbsfleet, 7, 8, 18
Ecgberht of Wessex, 42–44
   death, 46
Ecgberht, Archbishop of York, 41
Ecgfrith, King of Northumbria, 33–35, 185
Ecgwine, Bishop of Worcester, 33
Economic theories, 839, 865
Edgehill, battle of, 548
Edinburgh, its origin, 21, 185
   capital of Scot Kings, 187
   French troops at, 260
Edinburgh Review, 829
Edington, battle of, 48
Edith, see Matilda
Edmund, son of Henry the Third, 154
Edmund Rich, 135
   reads Aristotle at Oxford, 138
   Archbishop of Canterbury, 145
   exile, 146
Education, 843, 854, 875, 888, 893; see Literature, Schools
Edward the First, his motto, 153
   defeated by Llewelyn, 154
   faithful to the Provisions of Oxford, 155
   captured at Lewes, 157
   escapes, 159
   takes Gloucester, ib.
   victory at Evesham, 159, 160
   character, 167, 181–184
   crusade, 168
   conquers Wales, 168, 169
   his policy, 169
   judicial reforms, 170, 171
   legislation, 172
   social changes under, 173, 175, 177, 202
   first conquest of Scotland, 188–190
   second, 191–193
   struggle with barons, 203, 204, 206, 207
   expels Jews, 205
   dealings with clergy, 206
   war with France, ib.

Edward the First — *Continued.*
confirms Charters, 207
death, 212
Edward the Second, King, 207
struggle with Lords Ordainers, 208, 209
defeated at Bannockburn, 213, 214
truce with Scotland, 214
deposed, 210
murdered, 211
Edward the Third proclaimed King, 210
arrests Mortimer, 215
struggle with Scotland, 216
quarrel with France, 223, 224
alliance with Flanders and Germany, 224
war with France, 225-231
loses Aquitaine, 233, 234
death, 251
Edward the Fourth, *see* March
King, 285
victor at Towton, *ib.*
marriage, 286, 287
struggle with Warwick, flight and return, 287
final success, 288
character, 292
policy, 293
patron of Caxton, 293, 294, 298
death, 299
Edward the Fifth, 299
More's Life of, 315
Edward the Sixth, King, 357
proposal for his marriage, 380
his Grammar Schools, 360
his "plan" for the succession, 361
death, *ib.*
Edward the Seventh, 962, 997, 1001, 1002
Edward the Black Prince at Crécy, 226, 227
plunders Gascony, 230
victory at Poitiers, *ib.*
expedition to Spain, 233
sacks Limoges, 233
death, 235
Egypt, conquered by Buonaparte, 810
French withdraw from, 819
history after 1814, 922-924, 969-972
"Eikon Basilike," 573
Eleanor of Poitou, wife of Henry the Second, 104, 106, 115, 116
Eleanor of Provence, wife of Henry the Third, 144, 156, 158, 159
Eleanor, sister of Henry the Third, marries Simon de Montfort, 152
Elgin, Earl of, 942, 954
Eliot, Sir John, 485, 497, 498
attacks Buckingham, 499
arrested, *ib.*
moves Remonstrance, 502
speeches in Parliament, 504, 505
death, 515
Elizabeth, daughter of Henry the Eighth, 357
her Greek scholarship, 312
accession, 369
character, 370-376
Church policy, 376-379, 468
dealings with Scotland, 381
with Huguenots, 384
with Roman Catholics, 384, 385, 408-410, 416
troubles with Mary Stuart and the Parliament, 386, 387

Elizabeth, daughter of Henry the Eighth — *Continued.*
troubles with Mary and Alva, 389
Catholic revolt and Bull of Deposition against her, 390, 391
relations with Parliament, 402-405, 481
plans for her marriage, 414
policy in Ireland, 455-457
death, 459
Elizabeth, daughter of Edward the Fourth, 300
marries Henry the Seventh, 301
Elizabeth, daughter of James the First, 488
Elizabeth, Empress of Russia, 747, 764
Ellandun, battle of, 44
Elliott, General, 782, 786
Ely, foundation of, 33
burnt by Danes, 46
surrendered to William, 83
Emma, wife of Æthelred the Second, 62
Empson, minister of Henry the Seventh, 308
Enclosures, riots against, 292
Engineers, Amalgamated Society of, 863
England, the making of, 7-44
intercourse with the Franks, 43
Danish conquest of, 62-64
condition under Cnut, 64-67
relations with Normandy, 77, 78
conquered by William, 80-83
immigration from the Continent into, 92
condition under Stephen, 103
under Interdict, 124
agrarian discontent in, 248, 250, 326, 327
Commines' account of, 288, 289
New Learning in, 304-314
effects of Wolsey's administration in, 322-324
change in attitude towards Rome, 336
industrial progress under Edward the First, 202
social condition in the sixth century, 14-16
in tenth and eleventh centuries, 59, 60
under the Edwards, 173, 175, 202, 217-219, 222, 223, 238
in fourteenth century, 245-250, 257-259
in fifteenth century, 272-274
during Wars of the Roses, 289
after, 290-292
under Elizabeth, 392-397
in Puritan time, 462-464, 466
modern, its beginning, 605
joins Triple Alliance, 637
position in Grand Alliance, 684
new position under House of Hanover, 721
growth of trade and wealth, 730
society in, under the Georges, 736
philanthropic revival in, 740
alliance with Prussia, 748
its place in the world, 758, 787
relations with America, 760, 777-781, 785, 786, 827, 828, 832-834
industrial progress in eighteenth century, 791, 792
condition compared with the Continent, 797
attitude towards French revolution, 803
efforts of revolutionists in, 804
panic in, 806, 807
colonial gains, 809
successes at sea, 809, 810

England — *Continued.*
  northern league against, 818, 819
  declares war with Buonaparte, 820
  condition during French war, 828, 829
England, New, 505–509, 513, 514
  return of Independents from, 560
  its four States, 758
  its schools, 759
England, Old, 1
Engle, their Sleswick home, 1, 2
  settle in East Anglia, 11
  conquer Mid-Britain and the North, 12, 13
English people, their life in the older England, 2–4
  their religion, 4, 5
  conquer Britain, 7–13
  their settlement, 14, 15
  significance of their history, 787; *see* England
English, Middle, 13
Entente, Triple, 1005
Eorls, 4
Episcopacy abolished in Scotland, 524
  restored, *ib.*
  demand for its abolition in England, 543
Erasmus, 305, 306
  his edition of S. Jerome, 307, 313
  "Praise of Folly," 308, 316
  denounces the war, 312
  his Greek Testament, 313
  his theology, 313, 314
Essex, Countess of, 487
Essex, Earl of, Elizabeth's favourite, 434, 457, 458
Essex, Earl of, commander of Parliamentary army, 547, 549
  relieves Gloucester, 550
  defeated in Cornwall, 553
  resigns his command, 556
Essex, Earl of, minister of Charles the Second, 652, 655, 657
  suicide, 661
Essex, Henry of, 165
Euphuism, 399, 400
Eustace the Monk, 131
Evesham, its origin, 33
  battle of, 160
Exchange, the Royal, 394
Exchequer, Court of, 97, 112
  Richard Fitz-Neal's treatise on, 118
  closed, 639
Excise Bill, Walpole's, 731
  Pitt's, 794
Exclusion Bill, 654, 658
Exeter, Danes in, 48
  revolts against the Conqueror, 82
Exeter, Courtenay, Marquis of, 347
Eylau, battle of, 823

Factory Acts, 840, 855, 863, 865, 876
Faddiley, battle of, 17
Fairfax, Lord, 548
Fairfax, Sir Thomas, 552, 556–558, 569, 570, 600
Falkirk, battles of, 192, 744
Falkland, Viscount, 542
  his demands of Church reform, 543
  leaves Parliament and joins Charles, 547
  death, 550
  his philosophy, 609, 611, 612

Famine, the Great, 883, 885, 955
Farmers, their rise, 246
Fashoda dispute, 976, 997
Fastolfe, Sir John, 276, 298
Fawkes, Guido, 483
Felton, John, 503
Fenians, 884, 885, 956, 961
Ferdinand the Catholic, King of Aragon, 311, 312
Ferdinand the First, Emperor of Austria, 927
Ferdinand the First, Tsar of Bulgaria, 995, 996, 1001, 1005
Ferdinand the Seventh, King of Spain, 824, 913
Ferrar, Bishop of St. David's, 366
Ferozeshah, battle of, 938
Feudalism, its growth under the Conqueror, 83, 84
  its ruin, 227
Fielden, John, 864
Fifth-Monarchy men, 633
Finch, Chief Justice, 531, 538
First of June, battle of, 809
Fisher, Bishop of Rochester, supports the New Learning, 309
  patron of Erasmus, 314
  his reply to Luther, 322
  opposes Henry the Eighth's divorce, 328
  imprisoned, 344
  death, 345
Fitzgerald, Lord Thomas, 449
Fitzgerald, Maurice, 445
Fitz-Hamo, Robert, 164
Fitzharris, his impeachment, 659
Fitz-Neal, Richard, his dialogue on the Exchequer, 118
Fitz-Osbern, William, 81, 82
Fitz-Peter, Geoffrey, Justiciar, 127
Fitz-Stephen, Robert, 445
Fitz-Thomas, Thomas, mayor of London, 201
Fitz-Urse, Reginald, 108, 109
Fitz-Walter, Robert, 127, 131
Fitz-Warenne, Fulk, 146
Five Boroughs, 49, 54
Flamsteed, astronomer, 611
Flanders, its relations with England, 224, 225, 394
  English Gild of Merchant Adventurers in, 295
  occupied by the French, 636
  delivered by Marlborough, 714
Flemings in Pembroke, 164, 165
  under Edward the Third, 224
Fletcher, Phineas and Giles, 526
Fleurus, battles of, 694, 808
Flodden, battle of, 380
Flood, Irish leader, 785
Florida ceded to England, 764
  restored to Spain, 786
Fontenoy, battle of, 742
Foreign Enlistment Act, 922
Fortescue, Sir John, his definition of English kingship, 289
Fort William (Calcutta), its origin, 745
Fourmigny, battle of, 281
Fox, Bishop of Winchester, 309, 314, 322
Fox, Charles, 787, 789
  his India Bill, 789
  supports Regency of Prince of Wales, 799
  attitude towards Revolution, *ib.*, 800
  his Libel Act, 802

Fox, Charles — *Continued*.
  Burke's quarrel with, *ib.*
  forsaken by the Whigs, 807
  returns to office, 822
  death, *ib.*
Foxe, John, his "Book of Martyrs," 407
France, William the First and, 89
  Edward the Third and, 223–231
  alliance with the Scots, 260
  truce with Richard the Second, 261
  Henry the Fifth and, 267–279
  Bedford's campaigns in, 275–280
  English expelled from, 281
  relations with Italy, 311
  with Henry the Eighth, Spain, and the
    Empire, *ib.*, 312, 322, 325, 327, 330
  civil wars in, 384, 388, 412, 443
  relations with England and Holland, 634,
    635
  Family Compact with Spain, 733
  alliance with Prussia, 742
  designs in America, 747
  withdraws thence, 764
  alliance with United States, 781, 798
  Pitt's treaty of commerce with, 795
  condition in eighteenth century, 797, 978
  revolution in, 798, 800, 803–806
  declares war on the Emperor, 804
  on Holland, 805
  on England, 806
  insurrections in, 808
  struggle against Europe, *ib.*
  conquers Holland, *ib.*
  Directory in, 809
  conquests in Italy, 809, 810
  Consulate, 811
  Buonaparte's rule in, 820
Franchise, Parliamentary, restricted under
  Henry the Sixth, 271, 272
  the forty shilling, 273
Franchise, the, 849, 851, 853, 863, 896
Francis, S., of Assisi, 149
Francis the First, King of France, conquers
  Lombardy, 322
  meeting with Henry the Eighth, 324
  prisoner, 327
  released, 328
Francis Ferdinand, Archduke, assassination
  of, 1006
Francis Joseph, Emperor of Austria, 927, 944,
  945, 965, 968, 1001, 1005, 1006
Franciscans, *see* Friars
Francis the Second, King of France, 380, 382
Franco-German war, 949–950
Frankfort, Diet of, 908, 949
  treaty of, 951
Franklin, Benjamin, 769
Frank-pledge, 197
Franks, their intercourse with England, 43
Frederick the Second, King of Prussia, 734
  victory at Chotusitz, 741
  alliance with France, 742
  seizes Prague, *ib.*
  drives Austrians from Silesia, 743
  treaty with England, 748
  seizes Dresden, *ib.*
  victory at Prague and defeat at Kolin, *ib.*
  victories at Rossbach, Leuthen, and Zorn-
    dorf, 754
  defeats in 1759, *ib.*

Frederick the Second, King of Prussia — *Con-
  tinued*.
  successes in 1760, 763
  share in partition of Poland, 799
  death, *ib.*
Frederick, Prince of Wales, 733
Frederick, Elector Palatine, 489, 494
Free Trade, 848, 860–863, 894, 900, 929, 943,
  950, 954, 981, 999
French Revolution, 838, 847
Frere, Sir Bartle, 972
Friars, the, 148–151
Frideswide, S., Priory of, at Oxford, 133
Friedland, battle of, 823
Frith-Gilds, 196, 197
Frobisher, Martin, 419, 506
Fuentes d'Onore, battle of, 827
Fulk the Black, Count of Anjou, 99, 100
Fulk the Good, Count of Anjou, 99
Fulk of Jerusalem, Count of Anjou, 100
Fulk the Red, Count of Anjou, 99

GAGE, General, 778
Gaimar, 119
Galen, Linacre's translation of, 304
Gardiner, Bishop of Winchester, 348, 358, 362,
  363
Garibaldi, Giuseppe, 927, 945, 946
Garnet, Jesuit, 483
Gauden, Dr., 573
Gaunt, Elizabeth, 666
Gaunt, John of, Duke of Lancaster, invades
  France, 233
  struggle with Parliament, 234–235
  supports Wyclif, 239, 240
  turns against him, 241, 243
  driven from power, 261
  expedition to Spain, *ib.*
Gavel-kind, 247
Gaveston, Piers, 207–208
Geoffry Grey-gown, Count of Anjou, 99
Geoffry Martel, Count of Anjou, 76, 99, 100
Geoffry Plantagenet, Count of Anjou, 101, 104
Geoffry, son of Henry the Second, 109, 112, 119
George, David Lloyd, 1004
George, Henry, 878
George the First, King, 720, 721, 727
George the Second, King (*see* Cambridge), 721,
  730, 741, 761
George the Third, King, 761
  his "friends," 762
  supports Whigs against Pitt, 762, 763
  his home policy, 764
  dealings with the Commons, 765, 766
  with the Whigs, 766
  with Pitt, 767
  his personal administration, 777
  dealings with America, 776–778
  madness, 799, 830
  refuses Catholic emancipation, 818
George the Fourth, 799, 830, 911
Georgia colonized, 759
Gerald de Barri, 118, 119, 134
Geraldines, the, 449
Gewissas, 11
Gibraltar, sieges of, 729, 782, 786
Gifford, William, 844
Gilbert, Sir Humphrey, 506
Gilbert discovers terrestrial magnetism, 609
Gildas, 14

Gilds, 93, 196–199
Ginkell, General, 604
Giraldus Cambrensis, see Gerald
Gladstone, William Ewart, 853, 864, 866–873, 875, 877, 878, 881, 885, 886, 900, 928, 942, 943, 950, 955, 962, 965, 966, 970–974, 977, 979, 980, 995
Glamorgan, conquest of, 164
Glanvill, Ralph, 110
   his treatise on law, 118
Glastonbury, 37
   Arthur's tomb at, 119
Glencoe, massacre of, 686
Glendower, see Glyndwr
Gloucester, siege of, 550
Gloucester, Eleanor Cobham, Duchess of, 274
Gloucester, Duke of, son of Edward the Third, 261, 262
Gloucester, Humphry, Duke of, 275, 280
   his library, 298
Gloucester, Richard, Duke of, see Richard the Third
Gloucester, Gilbert, Earl of, 157, 159
Gloucester, Richard, Earl of, 155, 156
Gloucester, Robert, Earl of, 101, 102
Glyndwr, Owen, 266
Godfrey, Sir Edmondsbury, 650
Godolphin, Earl of, 702, 708, 718
Godwine, Earl of Wessex, 67, 68
   exiled, 69
   returns and dies, 70
"Goliath, Bishop," 120
Gondomar, Count of, 492, 493
Goodrich, Bishop of Ely, 354
Goojerat, battle of, 938
Gordon, General, 885, 942, 971, 972
Goschen, Viscount, 881, 903
Government, Act of, 595
   Instrument of, 585, 586, 588
Gower, poet, 294
   Caxton's edition of, 296
Grafton, Duke of, 772, 776, 777
Granville, Earl, 742; see Carteret
Granville, Earl of, 950, 962, 971, 974, 975, 979
Grattan, 785, 813
Great Exhibition, 930, 943
Greco-Turkish war, 996
Greek, revived study of, 304
Greene, Robert, 401, 428, 429, 431
Greenvil, Sir Bevil, 549
Greenway, Jesuit, 483
Greenwich Observatory founded, 610
Gregory the Great, Pope, 18
   Ælfred's translation of his Pastoral, 52
Grenville, George, his ministry, 766–769
Grenville, Lord, 821–823
Gresham, Sir Thomas, 394
Grew, vegetable physiologist, 611
Grey, Earl, 850–852, 874, 921
Grey, Elizabeth, wife of Edward the Fourth, 287
Grey, Lady Jane, 361, 363
Grey, John de, Bishop of Norwich, 123
Grey, Lord, Deputy in Ireland, 422, 456
Grey, Lord Leonard, 449
Grey, Sir Edward, 990, 999, 1000, 1002, 1005
Grey, Sir George, 960, 987, 991
Grey, Sir Richard, 299
Grindecobbe, William, 252, 254
Grocyn, 304, 306, 307

Grosseteste, Robert, Bishop of Lincoln, 139, 145, 148, 151, 153
Gruffydd, prince of Wales, 164
Guienne, struggle of Edward the First and Philip the Sixth for, 223
   lost to England, 281
Guiscard, Robert, 74
Guise, Mary of, Regent of Scotland, 380, 381
Guises, the, 382, 384, 385, 412
Guisnes lost to England, 369
Guizot, François, 917, 927
Gunhild, sister of Swein, 62
Gunpowder, effect of its introduction, 301
Gunpowder Plot, 483
Gustavus Adolphus, 515
Guthlac, S., 33
Guthrum, King of East Anglia, 47
   treaties with Ælfred, 48, 50
Gwynn, Nell, 630
Gyrth, son of Godwine, 80
Gyrwas, 13

Habeas Corpus Act, 846, 847, 884, 885
Hadrian the Fourth, Pope, 445
Hague Conferences, 1000
Hainault, Jacqueline, Countess of, 275
Hale, Sir Matthew, 579, 584, 616, 620
Hales, Sir Edward, 667
Hales, John, theologian, 612, 613
Hales, John, leader of Peasant Revolt, 252
Halidon Hill, battle of, 216
Halifax, Viscount, 652, 655, 658, 659, 667
   share in the Revolution, 683
   Privy Seal, 691
Halifax (Nova Scotia) founded, 747
Hall, Bishop and satirist, 526
Halley, astronomer, 611
Halsbury, Earl of, 887
Hamilton, General, 687
Hamilton, Marquis and Duke of, 532, 569, 573
Hamilton, second Duke of, 577, 578
Hampden, John, resists a forced loan, 500
   refuses ship-money, 529
   trial, 530, 531
   judgment annulled, 538
   charged with treason, 544
   death, 550
Hampton Court Conference, 480
Hanover, Convention of, 744
   House of, 705, 721, 722
Harald, King of England, 67
Harald Hardrada, King of Norway, 78, 79
Harcourt, Sir William, 890
Hardwicke, Lord Chancellor, 732
Harfleur taken by Henry the Fifth, 268
Hargreaves, inventor of spinning-jenny, 792
Harlaw, battle of, 380
Harley, Robert, 713
   intrigues against Marlborough, 716, 718
   rivalry with Bolingbroke, 719
   countenances South Sea Company, 728; see Oxford
Harold, son of Godwine, 69
   his administration, 70
   Welsh campaign, 164
   King, 70
   his oath to William, 78
   struggle with Harald Hardrada and William, 78, 79
   death, 80

Hart, Sir Robert, 942
Harthacnut, King of England, 67
Hartington, Marquis of, 886, 887
Harvey discovers circulation of the blood, 609
Haselrig, one of the five members, 544, 580, 586, 597, 599
Hasting, 53
Hastings, battle of, 79, 80
Hastings, John, claims Scottish throne, 188
Hastings, Lord, minister of Edward the Fourth, 299
Hastings, Warren, 783, 785, 796
Hatfield, battle of, 22
Havelock, Sir Henry, 939
Hawke, Admiral, 755
Hawkins, John, 395, 419
Hawley, General, 744
Heaven's Field, battle of, 23
Hengest, 7, 8
Hengest-dun, battle of, 46
Henrietta Maria, wife of Charles the First, 495
Henry the First, his accession, charter, and marriage, 91
    suppresses revolt, 96
    conquers Normandy, ib.
    his administration, 96, 97
    struggle with Anjou, 100
    death, 101
    palace of Beaumont, 133
    dealings with Wales, 164
Henry the Second, his marriage and accession, 104
    person and character, 104, 105
    policy, 105, 106
    relations with France, 106
    Church policy, 106, 107
    quarrel with Becket, 108, 109
    war of Toulouse, 106, 109
    crowning of his eldest son, 108
    revolt against, 109, 110
    penance, 110
    legal reforms, 109, 110, 111
    death, 112
    visit to Glastonbury, 119
    dealings with Wales, 165
    with Scotland, 187, 188
    with Ireland, 445, 446
Henry the Third, crowned, 131
    confirms charter, 142, 145
    quarrel with Hubert de Burgh, 143
    character and policy, 144
    marriage, ib.
    misrule, 145, 146
    expedition to Poitou, 146
    quarrel with Simon de Montfort, 152, 153
    with the barons, 154, 155
    his English proclamation, 155
    treaties with France and Wales, ib.
    war with the barons, 156–160
    death, 168
Henry the Fourth, see Derby
    king, 264
    relations with Parliament, 265
    suppresses Lollardry, ib.
    revolts against him, 266
    death, ib.
Henry the Fifth, King, 266
    war with France, 267–269
    conquers Normandy, 269, 270
    marriage, 270.

Henry the Fifth — Continued.
    treaty with France, 270
    death, ib.
    Regency nominated by him, 275
Henry the Sixth, his minority, 271–274
    crowned at Paris, 279
    marriage, 280
    loses Normandy and Guienne, 281
    birth of his son, 282
    idiocy, ib., 283
    prisoner, 283
    deposed, 285
    flies to Scotland, ib.
    prisoner, 286
    restored, 287
    dies, 288
    his library, 298
Henry the Seventh, see Richmond
    king, 301
    marriage, ib.
    revolts against him, ib.
    his policy, 302
    title to the throne, ib.
    character, 303
    patron of Caxton, 298
    dealings with Ireland, 448
Henry the Eighth, his accession, 308
    person, ib.
    marries Catharine of Aragon, 311
    war with France, 311, 312
    education of his children, 312
    his "Assertion of the Seven Sacraments," 321
    treaty with France, 322
    seeks Imperial crown, 324
    meets Francis, ib.
    alliance with Charles the Fifth, ib., 325
    withdraws from the war, 328
    proceedings for divorce, ib., 329, 334, 337
    promises a translation of the Bible, 334
    "Head of the Church," 335, 336, 338
    marries Anne Boleyn, 337
    Jane Seymour, 348
    Anne of Cleves, ib.
    Catharine Howard, 356
    death, 357
    his will, ib., 361
    dealings with Ireland, 449–451
Henry, son of Henry the Second, 108, 109, 112
Henry of Blois, Bishop of Winchester, 103
Henry, King of Navarre (Henry the Fourth of France), 416, 443, 475
Herbert, Admiral, 679. See Torrington
Herbert, George, 526
Hereward, 83
Herford, Nicholas, 240, 242, 244
Herlouin of Brionne, 72
Herrick, 526
Herrings, battle of the, 276, 277
Hertford, Earl of, 357, 358. See Somerset
Hexham, battle of, 286
    historians of, 118
Highlands subdued by Monk, 589
    conquest of, 744
Hild, abbess of Whitby, 27
Hilsey, Bishop of Rochester, 354
History, English, its beginning, 40
    under Ælfred, 52
    its significance, 787
Hobbes, Thomas, 609, 614, 615

Hochkirch, battle of, 754
Hodgskin, Thomas, 844
Hohenfriedburg, battle of, 743
Hohenlinden, battle of, 811
Holland, its relations with England and France, 576, 579, 628, 629, 637–640, 646, 675, 808
Holland, Jacqueline, Countess of, 275
Holles, one of the five members, 544, 564, 566
Home Rule, 878, 884–887, 889, 890, 894, 902, 903
Homilies, Book of, 359
Hooke, microscopist, 611
Hooker, Richard, 469, 470
Hooper, Bishop of Gloucester, 360, 366
Hopton, Sir Ralph, 549
Horsa, 7, 9
Horsted, 9
Hotham, Sir John, 547
Hotspur, 266
Hough, President of Magdalen College, 671
Hounslow, camp at, 668
Howard, Catharine, 356, 357
Howard, John, 740, 741
Howard of Effingham, Lord, 418
Howden, Roger of, 118
Howel Dda, Laws of, 164
Howe, General, 780
Howe, Lord, 809
Hrolf the Ganger, 71
Hubert Walter, Archbishop of Canterbury, 113, 123, 200, 201
Hubert de Burgh, see Burgh
Hubertsberg, Treaty of, 764
Huddleston, Catholic priest, 663
Hudson, Sir James, 943, 945, 949
Huguenots, 382, 384, 412
  in England, 667
Humbert, General, 810, 815
Hume, Joseph, 918
Hundred Years' War, its origin, 223, 224
  change in its character, 267
  its effect on England, 273, 274
  its end, 281
Hunt, Henry, 847
Huntingdon, Henry of, 118
Huskisson, William, 838, 848
Hussey, Lord, 345, 346
Hutchinson, Colonel, 462–464
Hyde, Anne, 635, 669
Hyde, Edward, 542, 546, 547. See Clarendon.
Hyder Ali, 784, 785

IBRAHIM PASHA, 916, 922, 923
Ida founds kingdom of Bernicia, 13
Imperialism, 963, 968, 976, 982, 986, 990, 1003
Impositions of James the First, 483, 484
Indemnity, Bill of, 691, 692
Independence, Declaration of, 780
Independents, 559–563
India, English and Portuguese in, 745
  French in, ib., 746
  Clive's victories in, 746, 753, 754
  French withdraw from, 764
  Clive's rule in, 782, 783
  Regulating Act, 783
  condition under Hastings, 783–785
  Fox's India Bill, 789
  Pitt's, 795
  history after 1814, 937–941, 993

India Company, East, 396, 745, 783, 843
Indian Mutiny, 939–941
Indies, West, acquired by England, 809
Indulgence, Declarations of, 624, 639–641, 670–672
Industrial classes, 838–840, 857–865
Ine, king of Wessex, 37, 38
Ingelger, 98
Inkerman, battle of, 934
Innocent III., Pope, 123, 124, 130
Instrument of Government, 585, 586, 588, 595
Insurance, State, 895
Interdict in England, 124
Inverlochy, battle of, 557
Iona, 23
Ipswich, Wolsey's school at, 323
Ireland attacked by Ecgfrith, 35
  condition in twelfth century, 444, 445
  its conquest, 445, 446
  John in, 447
  Richard the Second in, 261, 263, 447
  Henry the Seventh's policy in, 448
  Henry the Eighth's, 450, 451
  English colonization under Mary, 454
  revolts against Elizabeth, 455–457
  colonization of Ulster, 458
  Wentworth in, 520, 521
  revolt, 541
  Cromwell's conquest of, 574, 576
  settlement, 589, 590
  James the Second's dealings with, 668, 686, 687
  rising in, 687, 688
  William's campaign in, 693
  Marlborough's, ib., 694
  first union with England, 579, 590
  dissolved, 632
  demands of the volunteers, 785
  made independent, 786, 813
  condition under the Georges, 795, 811, 812
  Pitt's dealings with, 795, 814
  efforts of French revolutionists in, 804
  revolt of 1798, 810, 815
  union with England, 815
Ireton, General, 565, 566, 567, 589, 620
Irish Church, disestablishment of, 875, 902
  emigration, 883
  Land Act, 875, 885, 903
  Land League, 885
Irishmen, United, 804, 814
Iron-trade, 792
Isabella of Angoulême, wife of King John, 145
Isabella of France, wife of Edward the Second, 210, 225
Isabella of France, wife of Richard the Second, 261
Isandhlwana, battle of, 973
Ismail Pasha, Khedive of Egypt, 970
Italy, its influence on English literature, 398–401

JACOBITES, 692, 695
  revolt, 725, 743, 744
  decline, 761
Jamaica, English conquest of, 593
James the First, King of Scotland, 380
James the Fourth, King of Scotland, 361, 380
James the Fifth, King of Scotland, 380

James the Sixth of Scotland (First of England)
       his birth, 386
       crowned, 388
       struggles with Presbyterianism, 523, 524
       person and character, 477
       theory of monarchy, 478
       of ecclesiastical supremacy, 479
       at Hampton Court Conference, 480
       relaxes penal laws, 481
       proposes union with Scotland, 482
       his impositions, 483, 484
       despotism, 485, 486
       Court and favourites, 487
       foreign policy, 481, 488, 489
       tears out Protestation of Parliament, 493
       death, 495, 496
James the Second, see York
       King, 664
       revolts against, ib., 665
       his vengeance, 665, 666
       increases the army, 666
       alliance with France, ib.
       dispenses with Test Act, 667
       dealings with Scotland, 668
       struggle with English Churchmen, 669
       tries to win Nonconformists, 670
       attacks Universities, 671
       struggle with clergy and Bishops, 671, 672
       birth of his son, 679
       deserted, 679–681
       flight, 682
       goes to St. Germain, 684
       dealings with Ireland, 668, 686–688, 693
       death, 704
Jameson Raid, 984, 986
Jarrow, 39
Java won by England, 809
Jeanne d'Arc, 274–279
Jeffreys, Chief-Justice, 665, 666
       Chancellor, 672
Jemappes, battle of, 805
Jena, battle of, 822
Jenkins' ear, 733
Jersey, New, 759
Jervis, Admiral, 810
Jesuits in England, 409, 410
Jews settle in England, 86, 87
       expelled, 205
       return, 591
Joan of Arc, see Jeanne
Johanna, daughter of King John, 165
John, son of Henry the Second, 112, 113
       King, 115
       loses Normandy, etc., 115, 116
       his character, 122
       quarrel with the Church, 123, 124
       with the barons, 124, 125
       Welsh wars, 124, 125, 165
       homage to the Pope, 125
       war with France, 125, 126
       with the barons, 127
       signs Charter, 128
       subdues Rochester and the North, 130
       dealings with Ireland, 446, 447
       death, 131
John, King of Bohemia, 227
John, King of France, 230
John the Old-Saxon, 51
John the Litster, 254
Jonson, Ben, 437

Joseph the Second, Emperor, 799
Judicature Act, 875
Junius, 768, 774
Junto, the, 698, 699, 702
Jurors in the shire-court, 176
Jury, the grand, 111
       petty, ib.
       trial by, 110
Justiciar, the, 96
Justices of the Peace, 173
Jutes, their country, 1
       land at Ebbsfleet, 7, 8
       found kingdom of Kent, 15
Juxon, Bishop of London and Treasurer, 512

KANT, Immanuel, 907
Kars, defence of, 935
Kenneth MacAlpin, King of Picts and Scots,
       185
Kent, English conquest of, 8–10
       kingdom of, 15
       greatness under Æthelberht, 17
       conversion, 18
       fall, 19
       subject to Mercia, 36, 41
       John Ball in, 250
       revolts in, 252, 281
       Complaint of Commons of, 282
Kent, Earl of, beheaded, 215
Ketel of S. Edmundsbury, 94
Kildare, Earl of, Lord Deputy of Ireland, 448,
       449
Kilkenny, Statute of, 447
Killiecrankie, battle of, 685
Kilmarnock, Earl of, 744
Kilsyth, battle of, 558
Kimberley, relief of, 985
King, growth of his dignity, 59
       the King in council, 171
       Divine right of, 478
       his feudal rights abolished, 619
King's Bench, Court of, 112
King's Court, the, 97, 111, 171
Kingdoms, the Three, 19
Kingship, English, its origin, 15
       theory of, in thirteenth century, 183, 184
       Sir John Fortescue's definition of, 289;
       see Monarchy
Kitchener, Earl, 985
Kit's Coty House, 9
Knights of the shire, 158, 176, 177
Knolles' "History of the Turks," 399
Knox, John, 383
Knox's Liturgy, 525
Kolin, battle of, 748
Kossuth, Louis, 927, 928, 931
Kruger, President, 959, 983–985
Kunersdorf, battle of, 754

LABOURERS, their rise, 246, 247
       condition after Black Death, 248, 249
       as painted by Longland, 257, 258
       their enfranchisement refused, 255
       Statute of, 249
       its failure, 257
       demand for its repeal, 282
       influence of labour question on the mon-
       archy, 292
Labour Party, 895, 896
Ladysmith, relief of, 985

La Hogue, battle of, 696
Laing's Nek, battle of, 973
Lambert, General, 569, 595, 599, 618, 621
Lambeth, treaty of, 131
Lancaster, John, Duke of, see Gaunt
Lancaster, Joseph, 843
Lancaster, Thomas, Earl of, 208, 209
Lancaster, House of, its claims to the Crown,
    264, 283
    its fall, 288
Land Acts, 876, 903
    Purchase Act, 891
    system, 841, 842, 888
    Transfer Bill, 887
Land-tenure, changes in, 84, 85, 173, 326, 327
Lanfranc at Bec, 72, 77
    Archbishop of Canterbury, 85
    secures the Crown for Rufus, 89
    death, ib.
Langport, battle of, 558
Langside, battle of, 389
Langton, Simon, 130
Langton, Stephen, Archbishop of Canterbury,
    123
    heads opposition to John, 126
    produces Charter of Henry the First, 127
    suspended, 130
    his care for the Charter, 142
    death, 143
Langton, Bishop of Winchester, 307
Language, English, under the Normans, 120,
    121
    Henry the Third's proclamation in, 155
    growing use of, 217, 218
    changes in Caxton's time, 297
    used in law courts, 217, 731
Lansdowne Hill, battle of, 549
Lansdowne, Marquis of, 850, 997
Latimer, Hugh, 352, 353
    Bishop of Worcester, 354
    imprisoned, 356, 362
    burned, 367
Latitudinarians, 476, 609, 611–613
Laud, Bishop, 496, 504
    character and policy, 509, 510
    Archbishop of Canterbury, 510
    plans of Church restoration, 511–514
    first minister, 522
    dealings with Scotch Church, 524, 525
    sent to the Tower, 538
Lauderdale, Earl of, 632
Lauffeld, battle of, 744
Lauzun, Count of, 693
Law, Andrew Bonar, 899
Law, national, its development under Ælfred, 50
    Roman, in England, 132, 133
    of Eadgar, 58, 65
    of Eadward, 68
    of Howel Dda, 164
Law Courts, Common, 170, 171
    English language adopted in, 731
Lawrence, Sir Henry, 940
Layamon, 121
League, the Holy, 311, 312
Learning, the New, 303, 304
    its educational reforms, 308, 309
    plans of Church reform, 310
    theology, 313, 314
    antagonism to Luther, 321, 322
Leases, their introduction, 246

Leicester, town of, 194, 195
Leicester, Earl of, revolts against Henry the
    Second, 109
Leicester, Earl of, Elizabeth's favourite, 375,
    416, 418
Leicester, Earl of, see Montfort
Leipzig, battle of, 832
Leith, siege of, 381
Leland, 399
Lenthall, Speaker, 545
Leopold the Second, King of the Belgians, 969,
    975
Leo the Tenth, Pope, 313, 320, 321
Leofric, Earl of Mercia, 68
Leslie, Alexander, 532; see Leven
Leslie, David, 576–578
Leuthen, battle of, 754
Levant Company, 484
Leven, Alexander Leslie, Earl of, 552, 563
Lewes, battle of, 157
    Mise of, 158
Lewis the Seventh, King of France, 106, 109
Lewis (the Eighth) of France, in England, 130,
    131
Lewis the Ninth, King of France, 156
Lewis the Eleventh, King of France, 311
Lewis the Twelfth, King of France, 311, 322
Lewis the Fourteenth, 634
    relations with England and Holland, 635
    claims Low Countries, 636
    makes peace at Aix-la-Chapelle, 637
    treaties with Charles the Second, 638, 639,
        647, 659
    revokes Edict of Nantes, 666, 667
    his power, 673
    character and policy, 674, 675
    attacks Flanders, 675
    Holland, ib.
    Italy, 676
    Germany, 677, 680, 684
    Netherlands, 696
    designs on Spain, 701, 702
    acknowledges the Pretender, 705
    campaign of 1703, 710
    offers terms, 717
    death, 725, 726
Lewis the Fifteenth, 726, 742
Lewis the Sixteenth, 798, 800, 803, 805, 806
Lewis the Eighteenth, 834, 836
Lexington, battle of, 779
Liberalism, 908, 911, 912, 927, 928, 934, 947,
    967
Liberals, 914–917, 926, 930, 943, 961–963, 973,
    985, 987, 988, 999; see also Whigs
Lichfield, seat of Mercian bishopric, 25, 26
    archbishop of, 42
    suppressed, 43
Liegnitz, battle of, 763
Ligny, battle of, 835
Lilburne, John, 560, 574, 575
Lille taken by Marlborough, 717
"Lillibullero," 680
Lilly, head of St. Paul's School, 309
Limerick, siege of, 693, 694
Limitation Bill, 659
Limited liability companies, 868
Limoges, sack of, 233
Linacre, 304
Lincoln, battle of, 102
    Fair of, 131

Lincoln, John de la Pole, Earl of, 301
Lincoln, President, 955, 956
Lindisfarne, See of, 24
  Irish monks of, withdraw to Iona, 30
  Cuthbert at, 34, 35
Lindiswara, 13
  submit to Penda, 22
  to Oswald, 24
  ceded to Ecgfrith, 34
  seized by Æthelred, 35
Lisle, Alice, 666
Litany, the English, 356
Literature, in Northumbria, 38–41
  under Ælfred, 51, 52
  under Dunstan, 58
  under Normans and Angevins, 117–121
  in fourteenth century, 218–222, 241
  literature of Peasant Revolt, 251, 252, 255–257
  decline in fifteenth century, 274, 294
  Caxton's translations, 296, 297
  New Learning, 303–309
  under Elizabeth, 398–401, 421–425
  Elizabethan drama, 426–437
  drama of the Restoration, 607
  beginnings of journalism, 775
  literature of Wales, 161–163
Lithsmen of London, 198
Liturgy, the Scottish, 525, 529
Liverpool, its rise, 730
Liverpool, Earl of, 829, 830, 846
Livery Companies of London, 201
Livingstone, David, 969
Llewelyn ap Gruffydd, 154, 167, 168
Llewelyn ap Jorwerth, 142, 165–167
Loan, forced, 500
Local Government Board, 875, 897
Locke, John, 615, 616
Lollardry, its origin, 242
  suppressed at Oxford, 243
  character after Wyclif's death, 259
  progress, 260
  suppressed, 265, 267
  under Henry the Sixth, 273
London, its position, 12
  submits to Wulfhere, 32
  to Ine, 37
  to Offa, 41
  plundered by northmen, 45
  subject to Ælfred, 50
  submits to William, 81
  Normans in, 92
  Henry the First's charter to, 93
  religious revival in, 95
  S. Paul's cathedral, ib.
  election of Stephen, 101
  defies Innocent the Third, 130
  Friars in, 149
  supports Earl Simon, 156, 157
  its cnihtengild, 95, 197
  lithsmen, 198
  rising of craftsmen in, 200, 201
  attacked by Peasants, 252
  supports Lollardry, 259
  Lollard rising in, 267
  supports Richard of York, 283
  declares for Edward the Fourth, 285
  its trade, 58, 395
  Merchant Adventurers of, 396
  its extension forbidden, 516

London — Continued.
  supports Shaftesbury, 654, 660
  Plague of, 629
  Fire of, ib.
  sympathy with America, 778
  Convention of (1841), 924, 933; (1884), 973
  Declaration of 1002
  Protocol of (1852), 948; (1877), 966
  treaty of (1827), 916; (1839), 919; (1913), 1005
Londonderry, Marquis of (see Castlereagh)
Londonderry, siege of, 687, 688
Longchamp, William of, 112, 113
Longland, William, 255–257
Lords, House of, Harley's dealings with, 719
  scheme for limiting its numbers, 727
  Pitt's dealings with, 816
  rejects Catholic emancipation, 829
  after 1814, 867, 869, 874, 875, 880–882, 887, 898, 899, 901, 928, 977
Lothian granted to the Scots, 186
Loughborough, Lord Chancellor, 817
Louisburg, capture of, 756
Louis Napoleon (see Napoleon the Third)
Louis Philippe, 917, 918, 920, 922, 924, 926, 927
Louis the Eighteenth, 908, 913
Lovat, Lord, 744
Lovett, William, 844
Lowestoft, battle of, 628
Lowlands, the, 184
Lucknow, relief of, 843, 940
Luddite riots, 829
Ludlow, General, 589
Luneville, Peace of, 811
Luther, 320, 321
  More's and Fisher's replies to, 322
Luttrell, Colonel, 774
Lutzen, battle of, 832
Lydgate, 294
  Caxton's edition of, 296
Lyly, John, 399
Lyttelton, Lord Keeper, 547
Lytton, Earl, 979

"MABINOGION," 162
Macaulay, Thomas Babington, Lord, 851
Macaulay, Zachary, 838
MacDonnell, Sir Antony, 891
Mackintosh, Sir James, 838
Mackay, General, 685
Madras, its origin, 745
Mafeking, relief of, 985
Magellan, Straits of, English explorers in, 758
Magenta, battle of, 945
Magersfontein, battle of, 985
Mahdi, the, 971, 972
Mahmoud the Second, Sultan of Turkey, 922, 923
Mahrattas, 746, 784
Maine, county of, 77, 115, 280
Maiwand, battle of, 979
Major-Generals, Cromwell's, 588, 594
Majuba Hill, battle of, 973
Malaccas won by England, 809
Malcolm the First, King of Scots, 186
Malcolm the Third, King of Scots, 83, 90, 187
Maldon, battle of, 61
Malmesbury, Earl of, 944, 947
Malmesbury, William of, 118

Malplaquet, battle of, 717
Malta, dispute for possession of, 818
Man, Isle of, conquered by Eadwine, 21
Manchester, Earl of, 550, 552, 553, 556
Manchester School, 929, 930
Manor, the English, 245, 246
Manufactures, English, 224, 394, 791, 792, 828
Map, Walter de, 120
Mar, Earl of, 720, 725
March, Edward, Earl of, 284; see Edward the Fourth
Mare, Peter de la, 235
Marengo, battle of, 811
Margaret, sister of Eadgar the Ætheling, 83, 187
Margaret, daughter of Henry the Seventh, 361, 380, 385
Margaret of Anjou, wife of Henry the Sixth, 280, 283, 285, 287, 288
Margaret, the Maid of Norway, 188
Margaret of York, Duchess of Burgundy, 287, 301
Maria Theresa of Austria, 729, 734, 741, 747
Marignano, battle of, 322
Marlborough, Earl of, see Churchill
  campaign in Ireland, 693, 694
  intrigues against William, 695, 707
  power over Anne, 707
  character and statesmanship, 708, 709
  campaign in Netherlands, 710
  victory at Blenheim, 711, 712
  Duke, 712
  relations with the Tories, 712, 713
  with the Whigs, 713, 715, 716
  victory at Ramillies, 713, 714
  successes in Flanders, 717
  fall, 718, 719
Marlborough, Sarah Jennings, Duchess of, 707, 716
Marlowe, Christopher, 429
Marsh, or de Marisco, Adam, 151, 152, 154
Marshal, Richard, Earl, 145
Marshal, William, Earl of Pembroke, 123, 131, 141
Marston Moor, battle of, 552, 553
Marten, Henry, 539, 574
Martinico, English conquest of, 764
"Martin Marprelate," 473
Marx, Karl, 860, 865, 866, 879
Mary, daughter of Henry the Eighth, betrothed to Charles the Fifth, 324
  Queen, 361
  her policy, 362
  marriage, ib., 363
  revolt against her, 363
  her persecutions, 364, 366, 368
  war with France, 369
  death, ib.
  Ireland under her, 453, 454
Mary, daughter of James, Duke of York, 646
  marriage, 647, 649
  Queen, 683
  death, 699
Mary Stuart, Queen of Scots, 361, 362
  claims to English throne, 362, 369, 370, 379, 380, 383
  proposed as wife for Edward the Sixth, 380
  marries the Dauphin, ib.
  returns to Scotland, 382
  character and policy, 382, 383

Mary Stuart — Continued.
  marries Darnley, 385
  her plans, 386, 387
  vengeance on Darnley, 387
  marries Bothwell, 388
  imprisonment and abdication, ib.
  escapes to England, 389
  plots against Elizabeth, 391
  death, 417
Mary, daughter of Henry the Seventh, 361
Mary of Modena, wife of James the Second, 645
Maryland, colonized, 507
Maserfeld, battle of, 24
Masham, Mrs., 716
Massachusetts, its settlement and charter, 508, 509
  Puritan emigration to, 513, 514
  charter, altered, 777
Massena, General, 811, 826, 827
Massey, dean of Christ Church, Oxford, 671
Matilda (Edith), wife of Henry the First, 91
Matilda, the Empress, daughter of Henry the First, 97, 98, 101, 102
Matilda of Flanders, wife of William the Conqueror, 77
Maunay, Sir Walter, 248
Maurice, Prince, 550
May, Sir Thomas Erskine, 870
Mayflower, the, 507
Mayne, Cuthbert, 408
Mazzini, Giuseppe, 920, 927, 943
Meaux, siege of, by Henry the Fifth, 270
Medeshamstead, 33
Medicis, Catharine of, 385, 388, 412
Medina Sidonia, Duke of, 419, 420
Mehemet Ali, 921–925
Melbourne, Viscount, 858, 953
Mellitus, Bishop of London, 22
Melrose, 26
Melville, Andrew, 523, 524
Menschikoff, Alexander Sergeievitch, 933, 934
Meon-wara, 32
Merchadé, 114
Merchant Adventurers, 396
Merchant-gilds, 197
Mercia, its origin, 13
  under Penda, 22
  its conversion, 25
  three provinces, ib.
  under Wulfhere, 32, 33
  struggle with Wessex, 38, 41–44
  pays tribute to Danes, 47
  extent after Peace of Wedmore, 49
  annexed to Wessex, 54
  earldom of, 65
Merlin, prophecies of, 166, 168
Methodists, 737–739
Metternich, Prince, 908, 910–912, 915, 919, 920, 924, 926, 927
Middlesex, electors of, their struggle with the Commons, 773, 774
Middlesex, Cranfield, Earl of, 495
"Midlothian Campaign," 878
Miguel, Dom, Portuguese pretender, 913, 922
Militia Bill, 931
Mill, John Stuart, 865, 870, 871, 873, 879, 896, 1000
Millenary Petition, 477
Milner, Sir Alfred, 984, 986

Milton, John, 464-466
 early poems, 526, 527
 "Lycidas," 531
 ecclesiastical views, 543, 544
 later years, 601
 "Paradise Lost," 602-604
Minden, battle of, 755
Minimum wage, 845, 894, 895
Ministry, Sunderland's organization of, 697, 698
Minorca ceded to England, 764
 restored to Spain, 786
Mirebeau, siege of, 115
Mise of Amiens, 156
 of Lewes, 158
Model, New, of the army, 556, 557
 its struggle with Parliament, 564-571, 599
 disbanded, 604
Molesworth, Sir William, 954
Moltke, Count von, 920, 923, 995
Monarchy, the new, its character and causes, 290-292
 its military power, 301
 growth under Wolsey, 322, 323
 height of its power, 349, 350
 under Elizabeth, 401
 abolished, 573
 effect of the Revolution on, 688
 decline of its influence, 721, 722
Monasteries, dissolution of, 339, 340, 356, 357
Monasticism, its reform under Eadgar, 58
Monk, General, 589, 599, 600, 617
Monmouth, Duke of, 630
 scheme for his succession, 655, 657
 flight, 661
 rebellion and death, 664, 665
Monmouth, Geoffry of, 119
Monopolies, 405, 490, 517
Monroe Doctrine, 913, 947, 958, 974, 977, 982, 987
Mons, siege of, 695
Montacute, Lord, 347
Montagu, Lord, brother of Warwick, 286-288
Montagu, Ralph, 652
Montague, Dr., 496, 497
Montague, his finance, 699, 700
 impeached, 704
Montcalm, Marquis of, 747, 748, 756, 757
Montfort, Eleanor de, 168
Montfort, Simon de, Earl of Leicester, 152
 Governor of Gascony, 153
 character, 153, 154
 heads the barons, 155
 negotiates with France, 155
 struggle with Henry the Third, 156, 157
 his rule, 157, 158
 summons Commons to Parliament, 158
 last struggle and death, 159, 160
Montfort, Simon de, the younger, 159
Montreal, capture of, 757
Montrose, Earl and Marquis of, 532
 joins the King's party, 541
 victory at Tippermuir, 553
 Inverlochy, 557
 Kilsyth, 558
 defeat at Philiphaugh, *ib.*
 death, 576
Moodke, battle of, 938
Moore, Sir John, 825
More, Hannah, 740, 844

More, Sir Thomas, 315, 316
 his "Utopia," 316-320
 reply to Luther, 321, 322
 Speaker, 325
 Chancellor, 333
 resigns, 336
 summoned to Lambeth, 343
 imprisoned, 344
 death, 345
Moreau, General, 809, 811
Morier, Sir Robert, 947, 950
Morkere, Earl of Northumbria, 70, 80, 83
Morley, Viscount, 875, 951
Moroccan question, 998, 1003
Morrison, Robert, botanist, 611
Mortemer, battle of, 76
Mortimer, Edmund, 264
Mortimer, House of, its claims to the Crown, 264, 283
Mortimer, Roger, 215
Mortimer's Cross, battle of, 284
Morton, Bishop of Ely, 299, 300
 his "fork," 302
Morton, Earl of, Regent of Scotland, 522
Moscow, Napoleon's retreat from, 831
Mountjoy, Lord, 457
Mowbray, Roger, 109
Murray, James Stuart, Earl of, 385
 Regent of Scotland, 388, 389
 murdered, 391, 522

Namur taken by Lewis the Fourteenth, 696
 by the Allies, 700
Nana Sahib, Rajah of Bithoor, 939
Nanking, treaty of, 941
Nantes, Edict of, 666
 revoked, 667
Napier, Sir Charles, 938
Napoleon the First, Emperor of the French
 (*see* Buonaparte), 821
 his victories over Austria and Germany, 821, 822
 Continental system, 822, 823
 alliance with Russia, 823
 mastery of Europe, 824
 dealings with Spain, *ib.*
 with America, 828
 with Northern Europe, 830, 831
 Russian campaign, 831
 fall, 832
 return, 834
 last struggle, 835, 836
Napoleon the Third, 924, 927, 930-933, 935, 937, 943-945, 948-950, 955, 978
Naseby, battle of, 557, 558
Nash, pamphleteer, 401
Navarino, battle of, 916
Nectansmere, battle of, 35, 185
Neerwinden, battle of, 696
Nelson, Admiral, 810, 821
Netherlands revolt against Philip the Second, 388, 412-413
 English volunteers in, 414
 claimed by Lewis the Fourteenth, 636
 invaded, 675, 696
 Marlborough's campaigns in, 710, 717
 invaded again, 742, 808
Neville, Anne, 287
Neville, George, Archbishop of York and Chancellor, 286, 288

Neville's Cross, battle of, 228
Newburgh, William of, 118
Newbury, battles of, 550, 553
Newcastle-on-Tyne founded, 89
Newcastle, Duke of, 742, 748, 749, 763, 850, 934
Newcastle, Earl of, Cavalier general, 546, 548, 552, 553
Newspapers, 858
Newton, Isaac, 611
Newtown Butler, battle of, 688
New Zealand, 958–959, 980, 982, 983, 985, 987, 990, 991
Niagara, Fort, 747, 756
Nicholas, Secretary of State, 617, 636
Nicholas the First, Tsar of Russia, 915, 920, 921, 923, 924, 932
Nicholas the Second, Tsar of Russia, 1000–1002
Nigeria, northern, protectorate of, 993
Nightingale, Florence, 935
Nile, battle of, 810
Nimeguen, Peace of, 649
Nonconformists, expulsion of ministers, 622, 623
  persecution of, 624, 660
  after 1814, 843, 854, 860, 861, 864, 866, 874, 875
Non-jurors, 691
Nootka Sound, 800
Norfolk, Duke of, his quarrel with Henry of Lancaster, 263
Norfolk, Duke of, uncle of Anne Boleyn, 328
  his policy, 333, 356
  dealings with insurgents, 346
  imprisoned, 357
Norfolk, Duke of, under Elizabeth, 390, 391
Norfolk, Duke of, under James the Second, 669, 681
Norfolk, Ralph of Guader, Earl of, 88
Norfolk, Earl of, see Bigod
Norham, Parliament at, 188
Normandy, 71, 72
  its relations with England, 61, 62, 77, 78
  with the Angevins, 113, 114
  conquered by Philip, 115, 116
  reconquered by Henry the Fifth, 269, 270
  Bedford's rule in, 280
  lost again, 281
Normandy, Richard the Fearless, Duke of, 72
Normandy, Robert, Duke of, 75
Normandy, Robert Curthose, Duke of, 89, 90, 96
Normandy, William Longsword, Duke of, 72
Normandy, William the Conqueror, Duke of, see William
Normans, their settlement in Gaul, 71, 72
  conquests, 74
North, Lord Keeper, 665
North, Lord, minister of George the Third, 777, 781, 785, 814
Northampton, Assize of, 111
  battle of, 283
  Council of, 108
  treaty of, 215
Northampton, John of, mayor of London, 259
North Briton, the, 767
North-folk, 11
Northmen, 45, 46; *see* Danes, Ostmen

Northumberland, Duke of (*see* Warwick), 361, 362
Northumberland, Robert Mowbray, Earl of, 89
Northumberland, Percy, Earl of, under Henry the Fourth, 266
Northumberland, Earl of, under Elizabeth, 390, 391
Northumbria, kingdom of, 13, 17
  its extent, 19
  greatness, 20, 21
  conversion, 21
  Irish missionaries in, 24
  Cuthbert in, 26, 27
  ecclesiastical strife in, 29, 30
  extent under Ecgfrith, 34
  its fall, 35, 36
  literary greatness, 38–41
  submits to Ecgberht, 44
  to the Danes, 46
  to Eadward, 54
  to Æthelstan, 55
  earldom of, 57, 65
  its northern part granted to the Scots, 186
Norwich, rising of John the Litster at, 254
Nottingham, peace of, 46
Novara, battle of, 927
Nova Scotia conquered, 747
  ceded by France, 764
Noy invents ship-money, 528

Oastler, Richard, 864
Oates, Titus, 650, 651, 691
O'Brien, William Smith, 884
Occleve, 294
Ockham, 151, 236
O'Connell, Daniel, 849, 859, 883, 918, 920
O'Connor, Feargus, 859
Odo, Archbishop of Canterbury, 55, 57
Odo, Bishop of Bayeux, 81, 88, 89
Offa, King of Mercia, 41–43
Oglethorpe, General, 759
Ohio Company, 747
Oldcastle, Sir John, 259. See Cobham.
Omdurman, battle of, 976
O'Neil, Hugh, 576
O'Neil, Owen Roe, 572
O'Neill, Hugh, 457
O'Neill, Shane, 455
Orange, William the First, Prince of, 412, 413, 416
Orange, William the Second, Prince of, 572
Orange, William the Third, Prince of, see William
Orangemen, 814
Ordainers, the Lords, 208
Ordeal, 111
Orders in Council, Canning's, 824, 827, 830
Ordinance, Self-denying, 556
  for Suppression of Blasphemies, 569
Orleans, Duke of, Regent of France, 726
Orleans, Henrietta, Duchess of, 639
Orleans, siege of, 275–278
Ormond, Earl of, general in Ireland, 551
  invites Charles the Second thither, 573
  besieges Dublin, 575
  Duke and Lord Steward, 617
  Governor in Ireland, 633
  retires, 636
  returns to the Council, 644, 645
Ormond, second Duke of, 720, 722, 725, 726

Orsini conspiracy, 944
Orthes, battle of, 832
Osbern's lives of English saints, 118
Osney Abbey, 133
Ostmen, 55
Oswald, Bishop of Worcester, 58
Oswald, King of Northumbria, 22–24
Oswiu, King of Northumbria, 25, 30, 33
Otford, battle of, 41
Othere's voyage, 50
Otto of Saxony, Emperor, 113, 125, 126
Otto the First, King of Greece, 916, 928
Oudenarde, battle of, 717
Outram, Sir James, 939
Overbury, Sir Thomas, 487
Owen, Robert, 845, 858, 879
Oxford besieged by Stephen, 102
    town, 133
    Vacarius at, *ib.*
    friars in, 149, 150
    Provisions of, 155, 156
    Charles the First at, 548, 549
    siege of, 552
    Parliament at, 659
    University, 133, 134, 136
    drives out a Papal Legate, 146
    Lollards at, 242, 243
    decline in fifteenth century, 294
    Duke Humphry gives his library to, 298
    the New Learning at, 304, 306, 309, 310
    Cardinal College at, 310, 323
    Protestants at, 352
    religious changes in, 407
    decrees passive obedience, 478
    struggle with James the Second, 671
    Jacobites in, 725
Oxford, Earl of, under Henry the Seventh, 302
Oxford, Earl of, son-in-law of Cecil, 409
Oxford, Harley, Earl of (*see* Harley), 720, 722

PAARDEBERG, battle of, 985
Pacifico, Don, debate on, 928
Packenham, General, 833
Palatinate ravaged by Lewis the Fourteenth, 684
Pale, the English, in Ireland, 446, 447
Palmerston, Viscount, 850, 851, 867, 872, 873, 875, 880, 881, 912, 918, 919, 921–932, 934, 935, 941–950, 955, 970
Pampeluna, siege of, 832
Pandulf, Cardinal, 125, 141, 142
Panther incident, 1003
Papacy, its claims on the English Church, 143, 236, 237
    its jurisdiction rejected, 336, 337
    Mary's submission to, 363
    rejected again, 377
Paris, English students at, 134–136
    Henry the Sixth crowned at, 279
    declares for Charles the Seventh, 280
    surrenders to the allies, 832, 836
    Peace of, 764
    Congress of, 937, 944
    Declaration of, 936
    treaty of, 936, 942, 950
Paris, Matthew, 146, 147
Parker, Matthew, Archbishop of Canterbury, 377, 399
Parkes, Sir Henry, 957, 958

Parliament, Commons summoned to, 158
    growth in thirteenth century, 173–181
    changes in its composition, 231
    two Houses, 232
    superseded by permanent committee, 262
    deposes Richard the Second and elects Henry the Fourth, 264
    position under House of Lancaster, 265
    importance during Wars of the Roses, 289, 293
    decline under Edward the Fourth, 293
    revival under Richard the Third, 300
    Henry the Seventh's dealings with, 302
    struggle with Wolsey, 325
    revival after his fall, 333
    undertakes Church reform, 334
    revival under Cromwell, 350
    opposes Mary's Church policy, 364
    position under Elizabeth, 402–405
    relations with the Crown, 480, 481
    suspension under Charles the First, 514
    struggle with Charles the Second, 641, 645, 646
    Danby's dealings with, 648
    Roman Catholics excluded from, 651
    James the Second's attempt to "regulate," 670
    position after the Revolution, 689
    composition after union with Scotland, 714, 715
    after union with Ireland, 815
    relations with the Press, 775
    Admonition to, 470
    Acts of, *see* Statutes
    reform of, 774, 788, 793, 794, 829
    Barebones' Parliament, 583, 584
    the Cavalier, 620–624, 652
    Club, 274
    Convention, 617–620
    Good, 234
    Long, its proceedings in 1640, 537, 538
    in 1641, 540
    Grand Remonstrance, 543
    schemes of Church Reform, 543, 544
    five members, 544, 545
    prepares for war, 546, 547
    dealings with religion, 561, 562, 564, 569
    with the army, 564–567
    Oxford, 659, 660
    Rump, 571, 573, 574; 577–581
    Short, 533
    of 1604, 481, 482, 586, 587; of 1606, 483; of 1610, 484; of 1614, 485; of 1621, 490–493; of 1624, 495; of 1625, 496; of 1628, 501–505; of 1654, 586, 587; of 1655, 593–595; of 1658, 597; of 1659, 599; of 1679, 652, 655; of 1680, 656, 658; of 1681, 659, 660; of 1686, 667; of 1690, 692; of 1696, 700; of 1698, 702; of 1701, 704; of 1702, 705; of 1784, 789, 791
    Irish, under Wentworth, 521, 522
    under James the Second, 688
    under the Georges, 812
    its independence restored, 785, 795, **813**
    rejects free trade, 795, 814
    action as to Regency, 815
    Scottish, the "Drunken," 632
Parliament Act, 901

Parliamentary reform, 845, 849, 852, 854, 873, 874, 879, 881
Parma, Duke of, 416, 418
Parnell, Charles Stewart, 884–886, 889, 964
Parr, Catherine, 357
Parry's Plot, 416
Parsons, Jesuit, 409, 410
Partition, Treaties of, 702
Paston Letters, 294
Paterson, William, financier, 699
"Patriots," 732, 733
Paul, Czar of Russia, 818, 819
Paulinus, 21, 23
Pavia, battle of, 327
Peace, effects of, 839, 866
Peasant revolt, 250–255
Peel, Sir Robert, 847, 857, 861, 864, 866, 869, 871, 872, 883, 919, 926, 928, 952
"Peep-o'-Day Boys," 814
Peerage Bill, 727–728
Pelham, Henry, 742, 748
Pembroke, Earls of, see Marshal, Striguil
Pembroke, settlement of, 164, 165
Penda, King of Mercia, 22, 24, 25
Pendjeh incident, 980
Pengwyrn becomes Shrewsbury, 42
Peninsular war, 824–827, 831
Penn, William, 660, 759
Pennsylvania founded, 660, 759
Penry, author of Marprelate tracts, 473
Pensions, old-age, 895
Perceval, Spencer, 826, 830
Percy, see Hotspur, Northumberland
Perrers, Alice, 235
Perth, Convocation of, 193
Peterborough, Earl of, 713, 716
Peterborough founded, 33
    burnt by Danes, 46
    Benedict of, 118
Peterloo, 847
Peters, Hugh, 560
Petition of Grievances, 484, 485
    Millenary, 477
    of Right, 501, 502
"Petitioners" and "Abhorrers," 657
Petitions changed into Statutes, 233
Petre, Father, 669
Petty, Sir William, 610
Pevensey, 11
    William lands at, 79
Phelips, Sir Robert, 497
Philadelphia, Congress at, 778–780
Philip Augustus, King of France, 112
    war with Richard the First, 113, 114
    conquers Normandy, etc., 115, 116
    charged to depose John, 124
    victory at Bouvines, 126
Philip of Valois, King of France, his war with Edward the Third, 225–227
Philip (the Second of Spain) son of Charles the Fifth, marries Mary Tudor, 362, 363
    supports Elizabeth, 381
    turns to Mary Stuart, 385
    position and character, 411, 412
    conquers Portugal, 415
    defeat of his Armada, 418–420
    designs on France, 443
Philip, Duke of Anjou, King of Spain, 703, 726
Philiphaugh, battle of, 558

Philippines, English conquest of, 764
Pict-land, 185
Picts attack Britain, 6
    defeated, 8
    subdued by Ecgfrith, 34, 185
    rise against him, 35, 185
Piers the Ploughman, 255–257
Pigott, Richard, 889
Pilgrim Fathers, 507, 508
Pilgrimage of Grace, 345, 346
Pillnitz, Conference of, 804
Pinkie Cleugh, battle of, 380
Pitt, William, 732
    enters office, 742
    character, 749–753
    supports Frederick the Second, 754
    policy towards America, 755, 756
    opposed by the Whigs, 762
    fall, 763
    recalled, 767, 769
    denounces Stamp Act, 770
    returns to office, 722; see Chatham
Pitt, William, the younger, 787, 788
    his plan of reform, 788
    Chancellor of the Exchequer, ib.
    first minister, 789
    his character, 790, 791
    policy, 793
    bill for Parliamentary reform, 794
    his finance, ib.
    treaty of commerce with France, 795
    dealings with Ireland, ib., 815, 817
    with foreign politics, 800, 801, 804–806
    supports Libel Act, 802
    gives Constitution to Canada, ib.
    financial difficulties, 809, 810
    dealings with the peerage, 816
    resigns, 818
    returns to office, 820
    death, 822
Pittsburg, 756
Place, Francis, 845, 852, 854, 866
Place Bill, 689
Plassey, battle of, 753, 754
Plattsburg, English attack on, 833
Plauen, battle of, 754
Pleas, Court of Common, 112
Plevna, defence of, 966
Poitiers, battle of, 230
Poland, disputed election in, 732
    partition of, 799
Pole, Reginald, 346, 347, 364
Poll-tax, 251
Poor Laws, 855, 856, 859, 861, 872, 875, 895–897
"Popish Plot," 650, 651
Portland, Duke of, 807, 823, 826
Port Mahon taken by the French, 748
Porto Bello captured by Vernon, 734
Portreeves of London, 92, 93
Portsmouth, Louise de Quérouaille, Duchess of, 630, 659, 664
Portugal, conquered by Spain, 415
    Wellington's campaigns in, 825–827
Post Office savings banks, 868
Poynings, Sir Edward, 448
Pragmatic Sanction, 729, 730
Prague, battles of, 489, 748
Prayer, Book of Common, 358
    Scottish, 525, 529

Presbyterianism in England, 468, 470, 472, 543
  in Ireland, 812, 813
  in Scotland, 523, 686
Press, regulated by Star-Chamber, 473
  censorship of, abolished, 662
  proposal to revive, 700
  growth of its influence, 767
  Grenville's struggle with, *ib.*, 768
  influence on Parliament, 775
  beginnings of journalism, *ib.*
Preston, battle of, 569, 570
Preston Pans, battle of, 743
Pride's Purge, 571
Primogeniture, 838, 841, 887, 901
Printing, invention of, 295
Protectorate, the, 585
Protestants, their triumph under T. Cromwell, 354, 355
  under Hertford, 358
  persecuted under Mary, 364-366, 368
  growth under Elizabeth, 406, 407
  fortunes on the Continent, 474, 475
  attitude at Elizabeth's death, 476, 477
  French, *see* Huguenots
Prussia rises against Napoleon, 831
Prynne, John, 527, 528
Pulteney, head of the "Patriots," 732
Puritanism, its rise, 462
  temper, 463, 464, 479
  growth, 471-472
  Laud's struggle with, 510
  its attitude towards the stage, 527
  fall, 604
  work, *ib.*
  ideal, 606
  revolt against, 607, 608
  Puritan clergy expelled, 482
  emigration to America, 513, 514
Pym, John, 502, 535-537
  his Grand Remonstrance, 542
  plans for Church reform, 543, 544
  charged with treason, 544
  proposes terms with Scotland, 550
  death, 552
  his corpse outraged, 620

Quakers, persecution of, 625
  released, 640
Quarles, 526
Quatre Bras, battle of, 835
Quebec, capture of, 756, 757
Quiberon, battle of, 755
  Quo Warranto," 203, 204

Radicals, the, 925, 930, 931, 943, 954
Rædwald, King of East-Anglia, 19, 20, 22
Raglan, Lord, 934
Rahere founds S. Bartholomew's, Smithfield, 95
Railways, 840
Raikes, founder of Sunday Schools, 740
Ralegh, his "History of the World," 399
  discovers Virginia, 506
  friendship with Spenser, 423
  last expedition and death, 488, 489
Ramillies, battle of, 713, 714
Ray, John, zoologist, 611
Red River Rebellion, 961
Reform, Economical, 788
  Parliamentary, *see* Parliament

Reform Act, First, 851, 852, 874, 880, 901, 918, 919
  Second, 872, 873, 874
  Third, 878, 886, 977
Reformation, the, its beginning, 320
  antagonism to the Renascence, 321
Regicides, their fate, 617, 618
Reginald, sub-prior of Canterbury, elected Archbishop, 123
Remonstrance, the Grand, 542
Renascence, *see* Learning, New
Restoration, its social effects, 607, 608
Revolution, the English, 682, 683
  results, 688-690
  the French, 798, 800, 803-806
  of 1830, 917
  of 1848, 927
Rhodes, Cecil John, 972, 975, 984
Rhys ap Tewdor, Prince of South Wales, 164
Rich, Edmund, *see* Edmund
Richard the First, son of Henry the Second, his rebellions, 109, 112
  Crusade, 112
  wars with France and alliance with Germany, 113
  builds Château-Gaillard, 114
  releases Scotland from homage, 188
  death, 115
Richard the Second, son of the Black Prince acknowledged heir to the Crown, 235
  King, 251
  dealings with Peasant Revolt, 252, 254
  takes government in his own hands, 261
  truce with France, *ib.*
  marriage, 261
  character, *ib.*
  rule, 262
  banishes Henry of Lancaster, 263
  expeditions to Ireland, 261, 263, 447
  prisoner, 263
  deposed, 264
Richard the Third, patron of Caxton, 298
  King, 299-301
Richmond, Edmund Tudor, Earl of, 299
Richmond, Henry Tudor, Earl of, 299
  claim to the Crown, 300
  plan for his marriage, *ib.*
  victory at Bosworth, 301; *see* Henry the Seventh
Richmond, Margaret Beaufort, Countess of, 299
Ridley, Bishop of London, 362, 367
Right, Claim of, 685
  Petition of, 501, 502
Rights, Bill of, 688
  Declaration of, 683
Rivers, Earl, father of Elizabeth Woodville, 287
Rivers, Earl, brother of Elizabeth Woodville, his "Sayings of the Philosophers," 298
  executed, 299
Rizzio, 386
Roberts, Earl, 979, 985, 1003
Robinson, John, Brownist minister, 473, 507
"Rochdale Pioneers," 863
Rochelle, Buckingham's expedition to, 500, 501
  its fall, 504
Roches, Peter des, 142, 145
Rochester, siege of, by William the Second, 89
Rochester, Carr, Viscount, 487

Rochester, Laurence Hyde, Earl of, 663, 669, 702
Rochester, Wilmot, Earl of, 607
Rochford, Lord, 328
Rockingham, Marquis of, 770, 772, 785, 788
Rodney, Admiral, 786
Roger, Bishop of Salisbury and Justiciar, 102
Roger, son of William Fitz-Osbern, 88
Rohese, wife of Gilbert Beket, 103
Rome, Cnut at, 66
    Church of, its revival in sixteenth century, 475
Romilly, Sir Samuel, 838, 843
Rorke's Drift, defence of, 973
Rosebery, Earl of, 977, 998
Roses, Wars of the, their beginning, 283
    results, 289, 290
Ross, General, 833
Rossbach, battle of, 754
Roucoux, battle of, 744
Rouen, siege of, by Henry the Fifth, 269, 270
    Henry the Sixth at, 280
    submits to Charles the Seventh, 281
"Roundheads," 544
Roundway Down, battle of, 549
Royal Society, the, 609, 610
Runnymede, 128
Rupert, Prince, at Edgehill, Reading, and Brentford, 548
    at Chalgrove, 550
    enters York, 552
    defeated at Marston Moor, 552, 553
    at Naseby, 558
    commands a fleet for Charles the Second, 572, 575, 576, 628
    returns to the Council, 645
    his "drops," 610
Russell, William, Lord, leader of Country party, 641
    enters the Council, 652
    resigns, 657
    beheaded, 661
Russell, Admiral, 695, 696
    enters the Ministry, 699
    resigns, 702
    impeached, 704
Russell, Lord John, 850, 853, 859, 866, 872, 913, 928, 930–933, 943, 945–948, 952, 953, 965
Russia, its policy in eighteenth century, 747, 799, 801, 811, 818, 819, 821, 823
    quarrel with Napoleon, 830, 831
    Company, 789
Russo-Japanese war, 998
Rutland, Earl of, 284
Ruyter, Admiral, 580, 592, 628, 640
Rye-house Plot, 661
Ryswick, Peace of, 700

Sabraon, battle of, 938
Sacheverell, Dr., 717
Sadler, Michael Thomas, 855, 864
Sadowa, battle of, 949
St. Albans, its historical school, 146
    revolt of its burghers, 253, 254
    battles at, 284, 285
St. Edmundsbury, its origin, 47
    history, 93–95
    confirmation of its privileges, 254
St. John, Henry, 713, 716, 718; see Bolingbroke

St. Paul's School, 308, 309
St. Ruth, General, 694
St. Vincent, Cape, battles of, 786, 810
Salamanca, battle of, 831
Salisbury, Margaret, Countess of, 346, 347
Salisbury, Earl of, adherent of Richard the Second, 263, 266
Salisbury, Earl of, partisan of York, 283
    beheaded, 284
Salisbury, Marquis of, 878, 881, 882, 887, 888, 893, 897, 965–968, 976, 977, 979, 982, 985, 997
Salisbury, Robert Cecil, Earl of, 484, 487, 488
Sancroft, Archbishop of Canterbury, 672, 682, 690, 691
Sand River Convention, 960, 973
Sandwich, Montagu, Earl of, 617
San Sebastian, siege of, 832
San Stefano, treaty of, 966, 979
Saratoga, Burgoyne's surrender at, 781
Sarsfield, General, 693, 694
Sautre, William, 265
Savoy, the, 144
    sacked, 252
    conference at, 621
Savoy, Boniface of, Archbishop of Canterbury, 144
Savoy, Prince Eugene of, 710, 711, 715, 716
Savoy, Peter of, 144
Saxe, Marshal, 742, 744
Saxons, their home-land, 2
    East, their settlements, 11, 12
    West, conquer Southern Britain, ib.
    defeated at Faddiley, 17
    conquer Somerset, 34, 37
    conquer Dyvnaint, 42
    South, kingdom of, 11
"Saxony," 184, 185
Say, Lord, 282
Scholasticism, 151
Schomberg, Duke of, 692, 693
Schools founded under Henry the Eighth, 308, 309
    under Edward the Sixth, 360
    "Circulating," 736
    Sunday, 740
Science, English, its beginnings, 609–611
Scotland, condition in thirteenth century, 184
    kingdom of, its origin, 185, 186
    relations with England, 186–188
    first conquest of, 188–190
    second, 191–193
    revolt under Bruce, 211–214
    its independence recognized, 215
    alliance with France, 260
    history after Bruce, 379, 380
    Elizabeth's dealings with, 381
    union with England proposed, 482
    relations with the Stuarts, 522, 523
    revolts against Charles the First, 532
    reaction in, 568
    condition under Cromwell, 589
    under Charles the Second, 632
    acknowledges William and Mary, 685
    first union with England, 579, 589
    dissolved, 632
    second union, 714, 715
    Jacobite risings in, 725, 743, 744
Scots attack Britain, 6
    their origin, 185

Scots—*Continued.*
    submit to Eadward the Elder, 54, 186
    league with the Percies, 266
    in service of France, 275
Scrope, Archbishop of York, 266
Scutage, 109, 129
Sea-Dogs, the, 414
Sebastopol, siege of, 934, 935
Securities Bill, 646, 654, 658
Sedan, battle of, 950
Sedgemoor, battle of, 665
Sedley, Sir Charles, 607
Seminary Priests, 408
Seneff, battle of, 676
Separatists, 472
Seven Years' War, its beginning, 748
    its effects, 757
    end, 764
Seville, treaty of, 730
Seymour, Jane, 348
Shaftesbury, Earl of (*see* Ashley, Cooper), 640
    character and career, 642, 643
    policy, 643, 644
    dismissed, 645
    new policy, *ib.*, 646
    demands a dissolution, 648
    imprisoned, *ib.*
    dealings with Popish Plot, 650, 651, 656,
      657-659
    President of Council, 652
    plans for Monmouth's succession, 655
    dismissed, 656
    recalls Monmouth, 657
    fall and death, 660
Shaftesbury, Earl of, 850, 855, 857, 859, 862,
    864, 866, 874, 880, 941, 943
Shakspere, 429-436
Shaxton, Bishop of Salisbury, 354
Shelburne, Earl of, 766, 773, 787
Sherborne, see of, 37
Shere Ali, Amir of Afghanistan, 979
Sheriff, his function in the shire-court, 176
Sheriffmuir, battle of, 725
Ship-money, 528, 529
    declared illegal, 538
Shire, Knights of the, 158, 176, 177
Shire-court, 175, 176
Shrewsbury (Scrobsbyryg), 42
    battle of, 266
Shrewsbury, Duke of, 720
Shrewsbury, Talbot, Earl of, 280, 281
Shrewsbury, Earl of, Secretary of State, 691, 699
Sidmouth, Lord, 822
Sidney, Algernon, 661
Sidney, Sir Henry, 455
Sidney, Sir Philip, 400, 416, 422
Sigeberht, king of East Anglia, 22
Sikhs, 746, 938
Simnel, Lambert, 301
Siward, Earl of Northumbria, 68
Six Acts, the, 847
Skeffington, Deputy in Ireland, 449
Slanning, Sir Nicholas, 549
Slavery in early England, 15, 16
    its decline, 58, 59
    disappearance, 245
Slave-trade in early England, 59, 88
    African, 395
    movement for its abolition, 796, 797
    abolished, 823

Sleswick, its people in the fifth century, 1
Sluys, battle of, 225
Smerwick, massacre at, 456
Smith, Adam, 793
Smith, John, settles in Virginia, 507
Smith, Sir Sidney, 811
Smithfield, St. Bartholomew's Priory at, 95
Snowdon, Lords of, 165
Socialism, 859, 865, 866, 870, 877-879, 887,
    927, 999
Solferino, battle of, 945
Solway Moss, battle of, 380
Somers, John, 683
    Lord Keeper, 699
    dismissed, 702
    impeached, 704
    effects union with Scotland, 714
    President of Council, 716
Somerset conquered by West-Saxons, 34, 37
Somerset, Beaufort, Duke of, 282, 283
Somerset, Margaret, Duchess of, patron of
    Caxton, 298
Somerset, Protector, *see* Hertford
    invades Scotland, 380
Somerset, Duke of, and James the Second, 669
Somerset, Carr, Viscount Rochester and Earl
    of, 487
Somerton taken by Æthelbald of Mercia, 38
Somerville's plot, 416
Sophia, Electress of Hanover, 705
Soult, Marshal, 825, 831, 832
South Africa, 959-960, 972-974, 980, 987,
    989, 992
Southampton, Earl of, friend of Shakspere,
    433, 434
Southampton, Earl of, Lord Treasurer, 617, 636
Southey, Robert, 864
South-folk, 11
South Sea Bubble, 728
Southumbrians, 13
Spain, growth of its power, 311
    alliance with Henry the Seventh, *ib.*
    under Philip the Second, 411
    relations with James the First, 488, 489,
      492, 494, 495
    its decline, 674
    disputed succession in, 701-703
    war in, 713
    alliance with Charles the Sixth, 729
    Family Compact with France, 733
    war with England, 634, 763, 764
    league with France and America, 782
    mastered by Napoleon, 824
    rises, 825
    Wellington's campaign in, 831, 832
Speed, chronicler, 399
Spence, Thomas, 844
Spencer, Earl, 807
Spenser, Edmund, 422-426
    influence on Milton, 526
Sports, Book of, 511
Spurs, battle of the, 311, 312
Stafford, Lord, 658, 659
Stair, Dalrymple, Master of, 686
Stamford Bridge, battle of, 79
Standard, battle of the, 102
Stanhope, Lord, Secretary of State, 725
    his Ministry, 727
    death, 728
Stanley, Sir Henry, 969

Star Chamber, Court of, established, 302
  regulates the Press, 473
  employment by Charles the First, 516, 517
  abolished, 540
Stationers, Company of, 473
Statutes, change in mode of passing them, 293
  of Apparel, 282
  Appeals, 337
  Conventicle, 624
  Corporation Act, 621
  Five Mile, 624, 635
  of Grace, 692
  of Government, 595
  Habeas Corpus, 662
  suspended, 725
  Statute of Heresy, 265
  repealed, 358, 360
  re-enacted, 364
  India, 795
  of Indemnity and Oblivion, 617, 618
  of Kilkenny, 447
  of Labourers, 249
  Libel, 802
  of Liveries, 302
  of Merchants, 172
  of Mortmain, ib.
  Mutiny, 689
  Navigation, 579, 768, 769
  Occasional Conformity, 712
  repealed, 725
  Poor Laws, 392, 393
  Poynings', 448
  repealed, 786
  of Præmunire, 237
  used by Henry the Eighth against Wolsey, 330
  against the clergy, 335
  of Provisors, 237
  "Quia Emptores," 173
  Regulating, 783
  of Rights, 688
  Schism, 719
  repealed, 725
  of Security, 715
  Sentennial, 726
  of Settlement, 705
  Six Articles, 355
  repealed, 358
  Stamp Act, 769
  resisted in America, 770
  repealed, 772
  of Succession, 343
  of Supremacy, 337
  Test, 384, 641
  set aside, 667
  Triennial, 538, 689, 699
  Toleration, 690
  of Uniformity, 377, 621
  of Union with Ireland, 815
  with Scotland, 714, 715
  of Wales, 169
  of Winchester, 172
Steam-engine, 792
Steinkirk, battle of, 696
Stephen, King, 101, 102, 104, 133
Stewart, Sir Donald, 979
Stigand, Archbishop of Canterbury, 70, 85
Stillingfleet, 636, 668
Stirling, battle of, 191
Stormberg, battle of, 985

Stowe, chronicler, 399
Strafford, Earl of (see Wentworth), 533, 534
  impeached, 537
  trial, 538
  death, 539, 540
Stratford de Redcliffe, Lord, 923, 933, 947
Strathclyde, 19
  submits to Oswald, 24
  to Eadberht, 41
  to Eadward, 54
  granted to Malcolm, 186
Stratton Hill, battle of, 549
Streoneshealh, see Whitby
Striguil, Richard of Clare, Earl of Pembroke and, 445, 446
Strikes, 892
Strode, one of the Five Members, 544
Strongbow, 446
Stuart, Charles Edward, 743, 744
Stuart, James Francis, son of James the Second, 679, 725
Stukely, 456
Sudanese wars, 971, 976
Sudbury, Archbishop, 252, 253
Suffolk, Michael de la Pole, Earl of, 261
Suffolk, Earl of, minister of Henry the Sixth, 280, 281
Suffolk, Grey, Duke of (Lord Dorset), 361, 363
Suffrage (see Parliamentary reform)
Sunderland, Robert, Earl of, 652, 655, 659, 680, 681
  his ministerial system, 697
Sunderland, Charles, Earl of, 713, 715, 716, 727
Supplies, grant of, made annual, 689
Surajah Dowlah, 753, 754
Surrey, John de Warrenne, Earl of, 191
Surrey, Henry Howard, Earl of, 357
Sussex submits to Wulfhere, 32
  to Ceadwalla, 37
  to Offa, 41
Sussex, Earl of, Deputy in Ireland, 454, 455
Swein Estrithson, King of Denmark, 82
Swein Forkbeard, King of Denmark, 62, 65
Swein, son of Godwine, 69
Swithun, bishop of Winchester, 46
Sydenham, medical writer, 611

" TABLES," the, 530
Taillebourg, battle of, 145
Talavera, battle of, 826
Talleyrand, Prince, 907, 917, 919, 922, 946
Tariff reform, 876, 894, 900, 981
Taunton founded, 37
Taxation regulated by Great Charter, 129
  how levied, 175, 177
  under Elizabeth, 402
  arbitrary, see Benevolence, Impositions, Loan
  regulated by Long Parliament, 538
  Parliament regains control over, 689
  reduced by Walpole, 730
  during French war, 809
  of America, 760, 769, 770, 776
  Papal, on the English clergy, 146, 237
Taylor, Jeremy, 612, 613
Taylor, Rowland, 364-366
Tel-el-Kebir, battle of, 970
Temple, Earl, 769, 772
Temple, Sir William, 637
  Secretary of State, 652

Temple, Sir William — *Continued.*
  his Council, 653, 654
  agrees to the Exclusion, 658
Tenchebray, battle of, 96
Test Act, 848
Testament, New, Erasmus's edition of, 313
Tewfik Pasha, Khedive of Egypt, 970
Tewkesbury, battle of, 288
Thanet, English land in, 7, 8
  Augustine lands in, 18
Theatre, first erected in London, 427
Thegn, the, 60
Theobald, Archbishop of Canterbury, 103
  his court, 133
Theodore, Archbishop of Canterbury, 30–32
  his school at Canterbury, 39
Thiers, Adolphe, 924, 950
Thirty Years' War, 489
Thompson, William, 844
"Thorough," Wentworth's, 528
Thurstan, Archbishop of York, 102
Ticonderoga, Fort, 747, 756
Tientsin, treaty of, 942
Tillotson, theologian, 614, 630, 668
  Archbishop of Canterbury, 691
Tilsit, Peace of, 823
Tippermuir, battle of, 553
Tippoo Sahib, 810
Tithes, 31
Tone, Wolfe, 814
Torgau, battle of, 763
"Tories," their origin, 657
  attitude towards Grand Alliance, 699
  relations with Marlborough, 712, 713
  withdraw from politics, 722
  return, 733, 762
  govern during French war, 823
  after 1814, 839, 847, 849, 851, 852, 857,
    867, 871–874, 876–878, 898, 901, 913–
    918, 926, 944, 949, 952, 953, 979, 981;
    see also Conservatives
Torres Vedras, Wellington's defence of, 827
Torrington, Herbert, Earl of, 692, 695
Tortulf the Forester, 98
Tostig, son of Godwine, 70, 78
Toulon, revolt of, 808
Toulouse, siege of, 106
  battle of, 832
Tourville, Admiral, 694, 695
Tower of London founded, 81
Towns, 840–841, 851, 853, 856–857, 873
  early English, 92–95
  their privileges confirmed by Great Char-
    ter, 129
  share in the Barons' War, 156
  taxation of, 177
  struggle for freedom, 194–196
  social life, 196–199
  strife of classes in, 199–201
  charters cancelled by Charles the Second,
    663
Townshend, Charles, 766
Townshend, Viscount, 725, 727, 728, 732
Township, the old English, 3, 4
Towton, battle of, 285
Trade, English, under Eadgar, 58
  under Cnut, 66, 67
  under Edward the First, 202
  Edward the Third, 224, 225
  Elizabeth, 394–396

Trade, English — *Continued.*
  with the colonies, 730, 758, 768–769
  with Spanish America, 733
  in coal and iron, 792
  Buonaparte's efforts to check, 818, 822, 823
  Board of, 700, 879, 897
  Irish, 795, 812, 814, 815. *See* Slave-trade
Trades Disputes Act, 895
Trade unions, 862, 863, 865, 866, 874, 876, 877,
    879, 892
Trafalgar, battle of, 821
Treaties, secret, 967, 975
Trek, the Great, 959
Trent affair, 955
Trent, Council of, 357
Tresham, Francis, 483
Trevanion, Sir John, 549
Trevelyan, Mr., 878
Trichinopoly relieved by Clive, 746
Tromp, Admiral, 579, 580, 592
Troyes, Treaty of, 270
Trumwine, Bishop of Abercorn, 34, 36
Tudor, House of, its claim to the Crown, 299,
    300. *See* Richmond
Turgot, annalist of Durham, 117
Twysden, 399
Tyler, Wat, 252, 253
Tyndale, William, 351
Tyrconnell, Earl of, 668, 687

Udall, author of Marprelate tracts, 473
Ulm, capitulation of, 821
Ulster, Plantation of, 457
Ulundi, battle of, 973
Union, the, 882, 883, 886, 887, 890, 902
Unionists, 985; *see also* Conservatives *and* Tories
Universities, 854, 875
  their rise, 132
  relation to feudalism, 136
  to the Church, 136, 137
  influence of New Learning on, 309, 310
  consulted on Henry the Eighth's divorce,
    334
  struggle with James the Second, 671
Unkiar Skelessi, treaty of, 923
Uriconium, 12
Usher, Archbishop, 543
Utrecht, Treaty of, 719
Uxbridge, Treaty of, 557

Vacarius, 133
Val-ès-Dunes, battle of, 75
Valley Forge, battle of, 780
Vane, Sir Harry, the elder, 585
Vane, Sir Harry, the younger, supports Inde-
    pendents, 543, 563
  negotiates at Edinburgh, 550
  organizes navy, 576
  his policy, 579
  quarrel with Cromwell, 581
  offered seat in Council, 582
  share in union with Scotland, 589
  excluded from pardon, 618
  executed, 621
Varangians, 82
Varaville, battle of, 76
Vaudois, massacre of, 596
Venezuelan dispute, 977
Verden, dispute about, 727
Vere, Sir Horace, 489

Vereeniging, Peace of, 986
Verneuil, battle of, 275
Verney, Sir Edmund, 542
Vernon, Admiral, 734
Vervins, Treaty of, 443
Vespucci, Amerigo, his travels, 303, 316
Victor Emmanuel the Second, 943, 945, 946
Victoria Cross, 935
Victoria, Queen, 871, 874, 876–878, 883, 926, 930, 931, 935, 941, 944, 948, 951, 964, 965, 979, 982, 983
Vienna, Congress of, 907, 908, 910, 914, 916–919, 926, 942, 946, 947
Villafranca, truce of, 945
Villeins 247
  become copy-holders, 246
  revolt, 249, 250
  excluded from school and college, 258
  extinction, 257
Vimiera, battle of, 825
Vinegar Hill, battle of, 810, 815
Virginia discovered, 506
  settled, 507
Vitoria, battle of, 832
  Irish, 785, 813
Volunteer movement, 937

Wace, 119
Wagram, battle of, 826
Wakefield, battle of, 284
Wakefield, Edward Gibbon, 952, 953, 957, 959
Walcheren expedition, 826
Walcourt, battle of, 685
Wales, William the First's dealings with, 89
  its literature, 161–163
  relations with England, 163, 164
  revival in twelfth century, 165–167
  conquest of, 168
  statute of, 169
  revolt in, 266
Wallace, William, 191–193
Waller, Sir William, 549, 556
Wallingford, Treaty of, 104
Wallington, Nehemiah, 464
Wallis, Captain, 758
Wallis, Dr., 610
Walpole, Sir Robert, 723, 724
  his offices in Townshend ministry, 725
  resigns, 727
  opposes Peerage Bill, ib.
  returns to office, 728
  his peace policy, 729
  finance, 730, 731
  greed of power, 732
  attitude in Polish war, ib.
  towards Spain, 733
  fall, 734
Walter, Hubert, see Hubert
Walters, Lucy, 630
Walworth, William, 253
Wanborough, battle of, 37
Wandewash, battle of, 782
Warbeck, Perkin, 301
Ward, Dr., mathematician, 610
Warham, Archbishop of Canterbury, friend of the New Learning, 307
  protects Church reformers, 310
  supports Erasmus, 313
  his share in submission of the clergy, 336
  death, 337

Warwick, Neville, Earl of (the King-maker), 283, 285
  his character and position, 286
  policy, 287
  death, 288
Warwick, Earl of, son of Clarence, 301
Warwick, Earl of, Protector, 359. See Northumberland
Warwick, Earl of, buys Connecticut valley, 529
  commander of the fleet, 547
Washington, George, 747, 756, 779, 780, 785
Washington, English capture of, 833
Washington, treaty of, 962
Waterloo, battle of, 835, 836
Watling Street, 49
Watt, James, 792
Wearmouth, monastery at, 29
Wedmore, peace of, 48, 49
Wellesley, Sir Arthur, 825, 826. See Wellington
Wellesley, Marquis, 826
Wellington, Lord (see Wellesley), campaign in Portugal, 826, 827
  in Spain, 831, 832
  in France, 832
  in Belgium, 834–836
Welsh, their alliance with Penda, 22
  submit to Offa, 42
  to Ecgberht, 43, 46
  to Æthelstan, 55
Welsh Church, disestablishment of, 889
Wentworth, Peter, 404
Wentworth, Thomas, 485, 501
  his policy, 519, 520, 528
  Deputy in Ireland, 520, 521; see Strafford
Wesley, Charles, 737, 738
Wesley, John, 738, 739
Wessex, kingdom of, 11, 12
  its extent, 19
  submits to Oswald's overlordship, 24
  becomes Christian, ib.
  ravaged by Wulfhere, 32
  revival under Centwine, Ceadwalla, and Ine, 37
  struggle with Mercia, 37, 38, 42–44
  attacked by northmen, 45, 46
  by Danes, 47
  revival under Ælfred, 49–52
  fall, 61, 62
  earldom of, 65
Westminster Abbey, 144, 202
  Assembly and Confession, 561
  Parliament settled at, 180
  Provisions of, 155
Weston, Lord Treasurer, 503, 516, 522
Wharton, Lord-Lieutenant of Ireland, 716
Whiggamore raid, 570
"Whigs," their origin, 570, 657
  support war against France, 699
  relations with Marlborough, 713, 715, 716
  their long rule, 722, 723
  factions under Walpole, 732
  reunited under Pelham, 742
  oppose Pitt, 762, 763
  divisions under Rockingham, 787
  the "Old," 807
Whigs, 847, 848, 850, 854, 857, 861, 867, 869, 871, 873, 874, 887, 911, 913, 914, 918, 932, 943, 944, 949, 952, 954

Whitby, abbey of, 27
  synod of, 29, 30
Whitefield, 737, 738
White Ship, wreck of the, 97
Whitgift, Archbishop, 471, 473, 474
Wiglaf, King of Mercia, 44
Wilberforce, William, 797
Wilfrid of York, 29, 30
Wilkes, John, 767, 768, 773, 774
Wilkins, Dr., 610, 611
William the Conqueror, Duke of Normandy, 74, 76
  war with France, 76
  subdues Maine and Brittany, 77
  his rule in Normandy, ib.
  marriage, ib.
  relations with Lanfranc, ib.
  visits England, 78
  his claims, ib.
  lands at Pevensey, 79
  victory at Hastings, 79, 80
  crowned, 81
  his conquest of England, 81-83
  dealings with feudalism, 83-85
  administration, 85
  Church policy, 85-86
  revolts against him, 82, 88
  his rule, 88
  bridles Scotland and Wales, 88, 89
  death, 89
William Rufus, King, 89
  revolts against him, ib.
  struggle with the Church, 89, 90
  Continental wars, 90
  dealings with Scotland, ib.
  with Wales, ib., 164
  death, 90, 91
William the Third, Prince of Orange, 640, 644, 675, 676
  proposed marriage, 647
  defeat at Cassel, 648
  marriage, 649
  policy in England, 658, 660, 677, 678
  on the Continent, 676, 677
  invited to England, 679
  lands, 681
  King, 683
  forms Grand Alliance, 684
  dealings with Scotland, 685, 686
  with the Church, 690, 691
  campaign in Ireland, 693
  in Flanders, 695
  motives for peace of Ryswick, 701, 702
  last struggle with Lewis, 703, 704
  death, 707
William the Fourth, 917, 919, 947
William the Ætheling, 97
William the Lion, King of Scots, invades England, 109
  prisoner, 110
  homage to Henry the Second, 187, 188
  release from it by Richard, 188
William, son of Robert of Normandy, 96, 97, 101
William of the Long Beard, 200, 201
William the First, German Emperor, 949, 951
William the Second, German Emperor, 978, 986, 994-996, 998, 1001, 1002, 1005
Williams, Bishop of Lincoln, 543, 544
Williams, Roger, 514

Willis, physiologist, 611
Wiltshire, Earl of, 328
Winchelsey, Archbishop of Canterbury, 207
Winchester, Marquis of, 558
Winchester surrendered to the Conqueror, 80
  Statute of, 172
Windebank, Secretary of State, 538
Windham, leader of "Old Whigs," 807
Winfrith, see Boniface
Winthrop, John, 508
Winwæd, battle of, 25
Wippedsfleet, battle of, 10
Witenagemot, the, 60, 61
Wither, George, 526
Witt, John de, 675
Wolfe, General, 756, 757
Wolseley, Sir Garnet, 970, 971, 973
Wolsey, Thomas, 322
  his foreign policy, ib.
  his offices, 323
  educational foundations, 310, 323
  administration, 323, 324
  financial measures, 325, 326
  struggle with Parliament, ib.
  conduct in the king's divorce case, 328, 329
  fall, 330
  results of his career, 331
Women, 895-896
Woodville, Elizabeth, see Grey
Woodward, mineralogist, 611
Worcester, battle of, 578
Worcester, Tiptoft, Earl of, 274, 298, 299
Workmen's Compensation Act, 892
Wulfhere, King of Mercia, 32-34
Wulfstan, Archbishop of York, 55, 57
Wulfstan, Bishop of Worcester, 89
Wulfstan's voyage, 50
Wyatt, Sir Thomas, 363
Wycherly, 607
Wyclif, John, 235, 236
  his plans of reform, 239
  charged with heresy, ib., 240
  his "poor preachers," 240, 242
  denies Transubstantiation, 241
  his writings, ib.
  condemned, 242
  death, 244
  translation of the Bible, ib.
  its effects, 259
  influence in Bohemia, 263
Wykeham, William of, Bishop of Winchester, 234
Wyndham, Sir William, 722, 725

York, conquered by the Deiri, 13
  by Cadwallon, 22
  revolts against William the First, 82
  massacre of Jews at, 205
  Parliament at, 210
  siege of, 552
York, New, its origin, 758
York Town, surrender of Cornwallis at, 785
York, Duke of, joins Henry the Fourth, 263
York, Frederick, Duke of, 808
York, James, Duke of, Lord Admiral, 617
  marries Anne Hyde, 635, 669
  conversion, 638
  fight with De Ruyter, 640
  resigns office, 641
  second marriage, 645

York, James, Duke of — *Continued.*
  plans for his succession, 654, 658, 659
  see James the Second
York, Richard, Duke of, Regent in France for
  Henry the Sixth, 280
  rivalry with Henry, 282, 284
  death, 284

York, Richard, Duke of, son of Edward the
  Fourth, 299

ZARAGOZA, sieges of, 825
Zollverein, the, 919, 946
Zorndorf, battle of, 754
Zutphen, battle of, 410

171

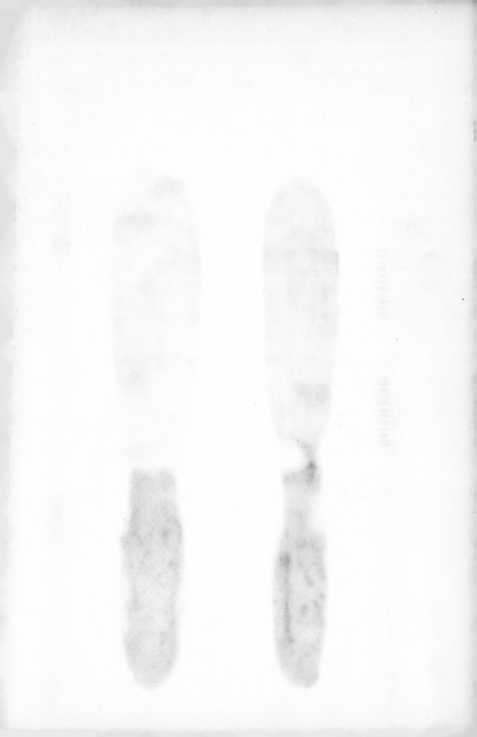

DATE DUE	